The
Shelly
Cashman
Series®

AF901336

Microsoft® Office 365®
Word® 2021

Comprehensive

Cengage

Australia • Brazil • Canada • Mexico • Singapore • United Kingdom • United States

Cengage

Shelly Cashman Series® Microsoft® Office 365® & Word 2021 Comprehensive
Misty Vermaat

SVP, Product: Erin Joyner

VP, Product: Thais Alencar

Product Director: Mark Santee

Senior Product Manager: Amy Savino

Product Assistant: Ciara Horne

Learning Designer: Zenya Molnar

Senior Content Manager: Anne Orgren

Digital Delivery Quality Partner: Jim Vaughey

Developmental Editor: Lyn Markowicz

VP, Product Marketing: Jason Sakos

Director, Product Marketing: Danaë April

Executive Product Marketing Manager: Jill Staut

IP Analyst: Ann Hoffman

IP Project Manager: Ilakkiya Jayagopi

Production Service: Lumina Datamatics, Inc.

Designer: Erin Griffin

Cover Image Source: MirageC/Getty Images

Mac Users: If you're working through this product using a Mac, some of the steps may vary. Additional information for Mac users is included with the Data files for this product.

Disclaimer: This text is intended for instructional purposes only; data is fictional and does not belong to any real persons or companies.

Disclaimer: The material in this text was written using Microsoft Windows 10 and Office 365 Professional Plus and was Quality Assurance tested before the publication date. As Microsoft continually updates the Windows 10 operating system and Office 365, your software experience may vary slightly from what is presented in the printed text.

Library of Congress Control Number: 2022905500

Student Edition ISBN: 978-0-357-67709-4
Looseleaf available as part of a digital bundle

Cengage
200 Pier 4 Boulevard
Boston, MA 02210
USA

Cengage is a leading provider of customized learning solutions with employees residing in nearly 40 different countries and sales in more than 125 countries around the world. Find your local representative at **www.cengage.com.**

To learn more about Cengage platforms and services, register or access your online learning solution, or purchase materials for your course, visit **www.cengage.com.**

Notice to the Reader

Printed at CLDPC, USA, 07-22

Brief Contents

Getting to Know Microsoft Office Versions OFF-1
Using SAM Projects and Textbook Projects SAM-2

Word 2019

MODULE 1: Creating and Modifying a Flyer .... WD 1-1
MODULE 2: Creating a Research Paper .... WD 2-1
MODULE 3: Creating a Business Letter .... WD 3-1
MODULE 4: Creating a Multipage Document .... WD 4-1
MODULE 5: Creating a Resume and Sharing Documents .... WD 5-1
MODULE 6: Using Mail Merge .... WD 6-1
MODULE 7: Creating a Newsletter .... WD 7-1
MODULE 8: Using Collaboration, Integration, and Charts .... WD 8-1
MODULE 9: Creating a Reference Document .... WD 9-1
MODULE 10: Creating an Online Form .... WD 10-1
MODULE 11: Enhancing an Online Form and Using Macros .... WD 11-1

Index IND-1

Contents

Getting to Know Microsoft Office Versions **OFF-1**
Using SAM Projects and Textbook Projects **SAM-2**

Microsoft **WORD 2021**

MODULE ONE
Creating and Modifying a Flyer

What Is Word? **WD 1-1**
Introduction **WD 1-2**
Project: Flyer with a Picture **WD 1-2**
Starting and Using Word **WD 1-3**
- To Start Word and Create a Blank Document WD 1-3
- The Word Window WD 1-5
- To Display a Different Tab on the Ribbon WD 1-10
- To Adjust the Margins WD 1-11

Entering Text in a Document **WD 1-12**
- To Type Text WD 1-12
- To Change the Zoom to Page Width WD 1-13
- To Display Formatting Marks WD 1-14
- Wordwrap WD 1-14
- To Wordwrap Text as You Type WD 1-15
- Spelling and Grammar Check WD 1-15
- To Enter More Text with Spelling and Grammar Errors WD 1-16
- To Check Spelling and Grammar as You Work in a Document WD 1-16
- To Insert a Blank Line WD 1-18
- To Enter More Text WD 1-19
- Navigating a Document WD 1-20
- To Save a Document for the First Time WD 1-21

Formatting Paragraphs and Characters **WD 1-23**
- Font, Font Sizes, and Themes WD 1-24
- To Change the Document Theme WD 1-25
- To Center a Paragraph WD 1-27
- To Center Another Paragraph WD 1-28
- Formatting Single versus Multiple Paragraphs and Characters WD 1-28
- To Select a Line WD 1-28
- To Change the Font Size of Selected Text WD 1-29
- To Change the Font of Selected Text WD 1-30
- To Change the Case of Selected Text WD 1-31
- To Apply a Preset Text Effect to Selected Text WD 1-32
- To Shade a Paragraph WD 1-33
- To Select a Paragraph WD 1-34
- To Change the Font Color of Selected Text WD 1-35
- To Change the Font Size of Selected Text WD 1-35
- To Change the Zoom Percentage WD 1-36
- To Select Multiple Lines WD 1-37
- To Change the Font Size of Selected Text WD 1-38
- To Number a List of Paragraphs WD 1-38
- To Undo and Redo an Action WD 1-40
- To Bullet a List of Paragraphs WD 1-40
- AutoFormat As You Type WD 1-42
- To Remove a Hyperlink WD 1-42
- To Center Another Paragraph WD 1-43
- To Use the Mini Toolbar to Format Text WD 1-43
- To Select a Group of Words WD 1-45
- To Underline Text WD 1-45
- To Italicize Text WD 1-46
- To Select Nonadjacent Text WD 1-47
- To Bold Text WD 1-48
- Selecting Text WD 1-48
- To Save an Existing Document with a Different File Name WD 1-49

Inserting and Formatting a Picture in a Word Document **WD 1-50**
- To Center a Paragraph WD 1-51
- To Insert a Picture from a File WD 1-51
- To Change the Zoom to One Page WD 1-53
- To Resize an Object Proportionally WD 1-53
- To Apply a Picture Style WD 1-55
- To Apply a Picture Effect WD 1-56

Enhancing the Page **WD 1-57**
- To Change Theme Colors WD 1-58
- To Add a Page Border WD 1-59
- To Change Spacing before and after Paragraphs WD 1-60
- To Change the Document Properties WD 1-61
- To Save an Existing Document with the Same File Name WD 1-62
- To Close a Document WD 1-63

Correcting Errors and Revising a Document **WD 1-64**
- Types of Changes Made to Documents WD 1-64
- To Open a Document WD 1-64
- To Change the Zoom to Page Width WD 1-65

To Insert Text in an Existing Document WD 1-65
Cutting, Copying, and Pasting WD 1-66
To Delete or Cut Text WD 1-66
To Copy and Paste WD 1-67
To Display the Paste Options Menu WD 1-68
To Move Text WD 1-69
To Switch to Read Mode WD 1-70
To Switch to Print Layout View WD 1-71
To Save a Document with the Same File Name WD 1-71
To Print a Document WD 1-71
Using Word Help WD 1-72
To Use the Search Box WD 1-73
To Use the Help Pane WD 1-74
Obtaining Help while Working in Word WD 1-75
To Sign Out of a Microsoft Account WD 1-75
To Exit Word WD 1-76
Summary WD 1-77
Apply Your Knowledge WD 1-78
Extend Your Knowledge WD 1-80
Expand Your World WD 1-82
In the Lab WD 1-84

MODULE TWO
Creating a Research Paper

Introduction WD 2-1
Project: Research Paper WD 2-1
MLA Documentation Style WD 2-2
Changing Document Settings WD 2-4
To Start Word and Specify Settings WD 2-4
Styles WD 2-4
To Modify a Style WD 2-5
Adjusting Line and Paragraph Spacing WD 2-6
To Change Line Spacing WD 2-6
To Remove Space after a Paragraph WD 2-7
To Update a Style to Match a Selection WD 2-8
Creating a Header WD 2-8
To Insert a Header WD 2-9
To Right-Align a Paragraph WD 2-10
To Enter Text in a Header WD 2-10
To Insert Page Numbers WD 2-10
To Close the Header WD 2-12
Typing the Research Paper Text WD 2-12
To Enter Name and Course Information WD 2-13
To Click and Type WD 2-14
Keyboard Shortcuts for Formatting Text WD 2-15
To Format Text Using a Keyboard Shortcut WD 2-15
To Display the Rulers WD 2-16
To First-Line Indent Paragraphs WD 2-16
To AutoCorrect as You Type WD 2-18
To Use the AutoCorrect Options Button WD 2-18
To Create an AutoCorrect Entry WD 2-19
The AutoCorrect Dialog Box WD 2-20
To Enter More Text WD 2-21
Citations WD 2-22
To Change the Bibliography Style WD 2-22
To Insert a Citation for a New Source WD 2-23
To Enter More Text WD 2-25
Footnotes WD 2-25
To Insert a Footnote WD 2-26
To Insert a Citation Placeholder WD 2-27
Footnote Text Style WD 2-28
To Modify a Style Using a Shortcut Menu WD 2-28
To Edit a Source WD 2-30
To Edit a Citation WD 2-32
Working with Footnotes and Endnotes WD 2-33
To Enter More Text WD 2-34
To Count Words WD 2-34
Automatic Page Breaks WD 2-35
To Enter More Text and Insert a Citation Placeholder WD 2-35
To Hide and Show White Space WD 2-35
To Edit a Source WD 2-37
To Enter More Text WD 2-38
Creating an Alphabetical Works Cited Page WD 2-38
To Insert a Page Break WD 2-39
To Apply a Style WD 2-39
To Center Text WD 2-40
To Create a Bibliographical Reference List WD 2-40
Proofreading and Revising the Research Paper WD 2-42
To Edit a Source Using the Source Manager Dialog Box WD 2-43
To Update a Field (the Bibliography) WD 2-43
To Open the Navigation Pane WD 2-45
To Go to a Page WD 2-45
To Insert a Citation Using an Existing Source WD 2-46
To Move a Citation WD 2-47
To Find Text WD 2-47
To Replace Text WD 2-48
Find and Replace Dialog Box WD 2-49
To Use the Thesaurus WD 2-49
To Check Spelling and Grammar at Once WD 2-50
The Main and Custom Dictionaries WD 2-52
To Save and Print the Document WD 2-53
To Look Up Information WD 2-54
To Use Researcher WD 2-54
To Change the Zoom to Multiple Pages WD 2-55
To Change Read Mode Color WD 2-56
Working with Comments in a Document WD 2-57
To Insert a Comment WD 2-57
To Insert Another Comment WD 2-59
To Go To a Comment WD 2-59
To Edit a Comment in a Comment Box WD 2-60
To Go to a Comment WD 2-60
To Reply to a Comment WD 2-61
To Hide and Show Comments WD 2-61
To Delete a Comment WD 2-62
To Delete All Comments WD 2-62
To Exit Word WD 2-63
Summary WD 2-63
Apply Your Knowledge WD 2-64
Extend Your Knowledge WD 2-65
Expand Your World WD 2-68
In the Lab WD 2-69

MODULE THREE
Creating a Business Letter

Introduction WD 3-1
Project: Business Letter WD 3-1
To Start Word and Change Word Settings WD 3-3
Creating a Letterhead WD 3-4
To Insert a Shape WD 3-5
Floating versus Inline Objects WD 3-6
To Change an Object's Position WD 3-7
To Change an Object's Text Wrapping WD 3-8

To Apply a Shape Style WD 3-8
To Change the Shape Outline WD 3-9
To Apply a Shape Effect WD 3-10
To Add Text to a Shape WD 3-10
To Use the 'Increase Font Size' Button WD 3-11
To Bold Selected Text and Save the Letterhead Document WD 3-12
To Insert an Online Picture WD 3-12
To Resize a Picture to a Percent of the Original Size WD 3-14
To Change the Color of a Picture WD 3-15
To Adjust the Brightness and Contrast of a Picture WD 3-16
To Add a Picture Border WD 3-16
To Change an Object's Text Wrapping WD 3-17
To Move an Object WD 3-18
To Copy an Object WD 3-18
To Use Paste Options to Paste an Object WD 3-18
To Move an Object WD 3-19
To Flip an Object WD 3-19
To Format and Enter Text WD 3-20
To Insert a Symbol from the Symbol Gallery WD 3-20
To Enter Text WD 3-21
To Add a Paragraph Border WD 3-21
To Clear Formatting WD 3-22
Creating a Business Letter WD 3-23
To Save a Document with a New File Name WD 3-24
To Apply a Style WD 3-24
Using Tab Stops to Align Text WD 3-25
To Display the Ruler WD 3-26
To Set Custom Tab Stops WD 3-26
To Insert the Current Date in a Document WD 3-27
To Enter the Inside Address and Salutation WD 3-28
Tables WD 3-29
To Insert an Empty Table WD 3-30
To Enter Data in a Table WD 3-31
To Enter More Data in a Table WD 3-32
To Apply a Table Style WD 3-32
To Select a Column WD 3-34
Selecting Table Contents WD 3-35
To Insert a Row in a Table WD 3-35
Deleting Table Data WD 3-37
To Add More Text WD 3-37
To Bullet a List as You Type WD 3-38
To Enter More Text and then Save the Letter WD 3-39
Working with SmartArt Graphics WD 3-39
To Insert a Page Break WD 3-39
To Enter and Format Text WD 3-40
To Add and Format a Paragraph Border WD 3-41
To Clear Formatting WD 3-43
To Apply a Style and Enter More Text WD 3-43
To Change the Underline Style WD 3-44
To Use the Format Painter Button WD 3-45
SmartArt Graphics WD 3-46
To Insert a SmartArt Graphic WD 3-47
To Delete Shapes from a SmartArt Graphic WD 3-49
To Add Text to Shapes in a SmartArt Graphic WD 3-50
To Add a Shape to a SmartArt Graphic WD 3-51
To Add More Shapes and Text to a SmartArt Graphic WD 3-52
To Change Colors of a SmartArt Graphic WD 3-54
To Apply a SmartArt Style WD 3-55
To Resize the SmartArt Graphic WD 3-55
To Save and Print the Letter WD 3-56
Enhancing a Document's Accessibility WD 3-56
Addressing and Printing Envelopes and Mailing Labels WD 3-57
To Address and Print an Envelope WD 3-57
Envelopes and Labels WD 3-58
Summary WD 3-59
Apply Your Knowledge WD 3-60
Extend Your Knowledge WD 3-62
Expand Your World WD 3-64
In the Lab WD 3-65

MODULE FOUR
Creating a Multipage Document

Objectives WD 4-1
Introduction WD 4-1
Project: Sales Proposal WD 4-1
To Start Word, Open the Proposal Draft File, Save It with a New File Name, and Specify Word Settings WD 4-2
Creating a Cover Page WD 4-4
To Insert a Cover Page WD 4-5
To Enter Text in Content Controls WD 4-6
To Format Characters in Small Caps and Modify Character Spacing WD 4-7
Modifying Page Formatting WD 4-9
To Print Specific Pages in a Document WD 4-9
To Delete a Page Break WD 4-12
To Apply Heading Styles WD 4-12
To Change Left Paragraph Indent WD 4-13
To Insert a Different First Page Formatted Header WD 4-14
To Remove a Content Control WD 4-15
To Insert a Different First Page Formatted Footer WD 4-16
To Format Page Numbers WD 4-18
To Format Text Using the Font Dialog Box WD 4-19
Editing and Formatting Lists WD 4-19
To Select a Predefined Bullet Character for a List WD 4-20
To Change Bullet Color WD 4-20
To Change Left Paragraph Indent WD 4-22
To Change Right Paragraph Indent WD 4-22
To Insert a Page Break WD 4-23
To Create a Multilevel List WD 4-23
To Change the Bullet Character to Picture Bullets WD 4-26
To Change the Bullet Character to a Predefined Bullet Character WD 4-28
To Sort Paragraphs WD 4-29
Editing and Formatting Tables WD 4-30
To Change Column Width WD 4-30
To Change Row Height WD 4-32
To Apply a Table Style WD 4-33
To Align Data in Cells WD 4-34
To Center a Table WD 4-35
To Sort a Table WD 4-36
To Add a Row to a Table WD 4-37
To Insert a Formula in a Table WD 4-38
To Change Cell Spacing WD 4-40
To Change Margins in Table Cells WD 4-41
To Distribute Columns WD 4-41
To Delete a Blank Paragraph WD 4-42

To Show Gridlines WD 4-42
To Split a Table Cell WD 4-43
To Move a Cell Boundary WD 4-44
To Enter Text in Cells WD 4-45
To Distribute Rows WD 4-45
To Insert a Column WD 4-46
To Merge Table Cells WD 4-47
To Change the Direction of Text in a Table Cell WD 4-48
To Resize Table Columns Using AutoFit WD 4-50
To Change Column Width WD 4-51
To Insert a Row and Merge Cells WD 4-51
To Shade a Table Cell WD 4-52
To Change Row Height WD 4-53
To Hide Gridlines WD 4-53
To Add a Table Border WD 4-53
Creating a Watermark WD 4-55
To Change the Zoom to Multiple Pages WD 4-55
To Create a Watermark WD 4-55
To Check Spelling, Save, Print, and Exit Word WD 4-57
Summary WD 4-57
Apply Your Knowledge WD 4-58
Extend Your Knowledge WD 4-61
Expand Your World WD 4-63
In the Lab WD 4-65

MODULE FIVE
Creating a Resume and Sharing Documents

Objectives WD 5-1
Introduction WD 5-1
Project: Resume WD 5-1
To Start Word and Specify Settings WD 5-3
Using a Template to Create a Resume WD 5-3
To Create a New Document from an Online Template WD 5-3
Resume Template WD 5-6
To Change Theme Colors WD 5-6
To Set Custom Margins WD 5-7
To View Gridlines WD 5-8
To Change Theme Fonts WD 5-8
To Enter Text in a Content Control WD 5-9
To Enter Text in More Content Controls WD 5-10
To Create Custom Theme Fonts WD 5-11
To Create Custom Theme Colors WD 5-12
To Enter Text in a Content Control WD 5-14
To Use Cut and Paste to Move Table Rows and Paragraphs with Source Formatting WD 5-14
To Copy and Paste a Table Row WD 5-16
To Delete a Row and Paragraph WD 5-17
To Create a Building Block WD 5-17
To Modify a Building Block WD 5-18
To Use AutoComplete WD 5-19
To Insert a Building Block WD 5-20
Building Blocks versus AutoCorrect WD 5-21
To Enter Text in Content Controls WD 5-21
To Delete a Row WD 5-22
To Enter Text in Content Controls WD 5-22
To Remove Bullets from a Paragraph WD 5-23
To Resize Table Columns WD 5-24
To Enter Text in a Content Control WD 5-24
To Enter a Line Break WD 5-25
To Enter Text in Content Controls WD 5-25
To Decrease Indent of a Paragraph WD 5-26
To Change a Bullet to a Predefined Symbol WD 5-27
To Create a Paragraph Style WD 5-28
To Apply a Style WD 5-29
To Reveal Formatting WD 5-29
To Modify a Style Using the Styles Dialog Box WD 5-30
To Center Page Contents Vertically WD 5-31
Sharing a Document with Others WD 5-31
To Insert a Quick Part WD 5-32
To Export a Word Document to a PDF File and View the PDF File in Adobe Reader WD 5-34
To Open a PDF File from Word to Edit It WD 5-36
To Check Document Compatibility WD 5-38
To Save a Word 365 Document in an Earlier Word Format WD 5-39
File Types WD 5-40
To Share a Document on OneDrive WD 5-42
To Get a Sharing Link WD 5-43
To Remove a Watermark WD 5-44
To Send a Document Using Email WD 5-45
Creating a Webpage from a Word Document WD 5-46
To Save a Word Document as a Webpage WD 5-47
To Format Text as a Hyperlink WD 5-49
To Change the Style Set WD 5-50
To Highlight Text WD 5-51
To Test a Webpage in a Browser WD 5-53
Summary WD 5-54
Apply Your Knowledge WD 5-55
Extend Your Knowledge WD 5-57
Expand Your World WD 5-59
In the Lab WD 5-61

MODULE SIX
Using Mail Merge

Objectives WD 6-1
Introduction WD 6-1
Project: Form Letters, Mailing Labels, and a Directory WD 6-1
To Start Word and Specify Settings WD 6-2
Identifying the Main Document for Form Letters WD 6-4
To Start the Mail Merge Wizard WD 6-4
To Change Theme Colors WD 6-7
To Enter and Format the Sender Information WD 6-7
To Change a Picture and Format It WD 6-7
To Shade Cells and a Shape WD 6-8
To Change Margin Settings WD 6-9
To Specify the Position of a Graphic WD 6-10
To Create a Folder while Saving WD 6-11
Creating a Data Source WD 6-12
To Type a New Recipient List for a Data Source WD 6-13
To Enter More Recipients WD 6-18
To Save a Data Source when Prompted by Word WD 6-18
Editing Data Records (Recipients) in the Data Source WD 6-20
Using an Existing Data Source WD 6-20
Composing the Main Document for the Form Letters WD 6-20
To Display the Next Step in the Mail Merge Wizard WD 6-21
To Enter the Date from a Content Control WD 6-21
Merge Fields WD 6-22

To Insert the AddressBlock Merge Field WD 6-23
To Preview Results in the Main Document WD 6-24
To Insert the GreetingLine Merge Field WD 6-25
To View Merge Fields in the Main Document WD 6-26
To Begin Typing the Body of the Form Letter WD 6-26
To Insert a Merge Field in the Main Document WD 6-27
To Enter More Text and Merge Fields in the Main Document WD 6-28
IF Fields WD 6-28
To Insert an IF Field in the Main Document WD 6-29
To Enter the Remaining Text in the Main Document WD 6-30
To Toggle Field Codes WD 6-31
Opening a Main Document WD 6-33
Merging the Recipient List in the Data Source with the Main Document to Generate Form Letters WD 6-33
To Preview a Mail Merge Using the Mail Merge Wizard WD 6-33
To Merge the Form Letters to a New Document Using the Mail Merge Wizard WD 6-34
Correcting Merge Field Errors in Merged Documents WD 6-36
To Select Mail Merge Recipients WD 6-36
To Merge the Form Letters to a New Document Using the Ribbon WD 6-37
To Remove a Merge Condition WD 6-39
To Sort a Recipient List WD 6-39
To Find Mail Merge Recipients WD 6-40
Displaying Mail Merge Recipients in the Main Document WD 6-41
Addressing Mailing Labels and Envelopes WD 6-41
To Address and Print Mailing Labels Using an Existing Data Source WD 6-42
Merging All Data Records to a Directory WD 6-48
To Change Page Orientation WD 6-49
To Merge to a Directory WD 6-50
To Merge to a New Document WD 6-52
To Convert Text to a Table WD 6-52
To Modify and Format a Table WD 6-54
To Sort a Table by Multiple Columns WD 6-54
Summary WD 6-56
Apply Your Knowledge WD 6-57
Extend Your Knowledge WD 6-59
Expand Your World WD 6-61
In the Lab WD 6-63

MODULE SEVEN
Creating a Newsletter

Objectives WD 7-1
Introduction WD 7-1
Project: Newsletter WD 7-2
Desktop Publishing Terminology WD 7-2
To Start Word and Specify Settings WD 7-4
To Change Spacing above and below Paragraphs and Adjust Margins WD 7-4
To Change Theme Colors and Fonts WD 7-5
Creating the Nameplate WD 7-5
To Convert Text to WordArt WD 7-6
To Resize WordArt WD 7-7
To Change the Font and Font Size of WordArt Text WD 7-7
To Change an Object's Text Wrapping WD 7-7
To Change the Text Fill Color of WordArt WD 7-8
To Change the WordArt Shape Using the Transform Effect WD 7-11
To Set Custom Tab Stops Using the Tabs Dialog Box WD 7-12
To Enter Text WD 7-13
To Border One Edge of a Paragraph WD 7-13
To Insert a Picture WD 7-14
To Change the Color of a Graphic WD 7-15
To Crop a Graphic WD 7-16
To Change an Object's Text Wrapping and Size WD 7-17
To Move a Graphic WD 7-17
To Use the Selection Pane WD 7-18
To Rotate a Graphic WD 7-18
Formatting the First Page of the Body of the Newsletter WD 7-19
To Clear Formatting WD 7-20
To Format Text as a Heading Style, Modify a Heading Style, and Adjust Spacing before and after the Paragraph WD 7-20
Columns WD 7-21
Sections WD 7-21
To Insert a Continuous Section Break WD 7-21
To Format Text in Columns WD 7-22
To Justify a Paragraph WD 7-23
To Insert Text from a File into a Document WD 7-24
To Adjust the Width of Columns and Place a Vertical Line between Columns WD 7-25
To Hyphenate a Document WD 7-26
To Format a Character as a Drop Cap WD 7-27
To Format the Drop Cap WD 7-28
To Insert a Next Page Section Break WD 7-29
To Enter Text WD 7-30
To Insert a Column Break WD 7-30
To Insert Text from a File in to a Document WD 7-31
Creating a Pull-Quote WD 7-32
To Insert a Preformatted Text Box WD 7-32
To Split the Word Window WD 7-33
To Copy and Paste Using Split Windows WD 7-34
To Remove a Split Window WD 7-36
To Edit and Format Text in the Text Box WD 7-36
To Resize a Text Box WD 7-36
To Apply a Shape Style to a Text Box WD 7-37
To Position a Text Box WD 7-37
Formatting the Second Page of the Newsletter WD 7-38
To Change Column Formatting WD 7-39
To Set Custom Tab Stops Using the Tabs Dialog Box WD 7-41
To Format and Enter Text and Add a Border WD 7-42
To Enter Text WD 7-42
To Balance Columns WD 7-43
Modifying and Formatting a SmartArt Graphic WD 7-43
To Open a Document from Word WD 7-44
To Change the Layout of a SmartArt Graphic WD 7-45
To Add a Shape to a SmartArt Graphic WD 7-45
To Use the Text Pane to Add Text to a SmartArt Graphic WD 7-46
To Format SmartArt Graphic Text WD 7-47
Copying and Pasting WD 7-47
To Copy a SmartArt Graphic Using the Office Clipboard WD 7-48

To Switch from One Open Document Window to Another WD 7-48
To Paste from the Office Clipboard WD 7-49
To Format a Graphic as Floating WD 7-50
To Format, Resize, and Position the SmartArt Graphic WD 7-50
To Edit Wrap Points in an Object WD 7-50
Finishing the Newsletter WD 7-52
To Turn Off Formatting Marks and Zoom Multiple Pages WD 7-52
To Add an Art Page Border WD 7-52
To Save and Print the Newsletter and then Exit Word WD 7-54
Summary WD 7-54
Apply Your Knowledge WD 7-55
Extend Your Knowledge WD 7-57
Expand Your World WD 7-59
In the Lab WD 7-61

MODULE EIGHT
Using Collaboration, Integration, and Charts

Objectives WD 8-1
Introduction WD 8-1
Project: Memo with Chart WD 8-1
To Start Word and Specify Settings WD 8-3
Reviewing a Document WD 8-3
To Open a Document and Save It with a New File Name WD 8-4
To Customize the Status Bar WD 8-5
To Enable Tracked Changes WD 8-5
To Track Changes WD 8-6
To Disable Tracked Changes WD 8-8
To Use the Reviewing Pane or the Markup Area WD 8-9
To Display Tracked Changes as Simple Markup WD 8-11
To Show All Markup WD 8-12
Reviewing Tracked Changes WD 8-12
To Review Tracked Changes WD 8-13
Changing Tracking Options WD 8-15
To Compare Documents WD 8-15
To Combine Revisions from Multiple Authors WD 8-18
To Show Tracked Changes and Comments by a Single Reviewer WD 8-21
To Customize the Status Bar and Close the Document WD 8-22
Linking an Excel Worksheet to a Word Document WD 8-22
To Open a Word Document, Start Excel, and Open an Excel Workbook WD 8-24
Excel Basics WD 8-24
To Link an Excel Worksheet to a Word Document WD 8-25
To Break a Link WD 8-27
Charting a Word Table WD 8-29
To Open and Save a Document WD 8-29
To Insert a Chart WD 8-29
To Remove a Data Series from the Chart WD 8-32
To Apply a Chart Style WD 8-33
To Change Colors of a Chart WD 8-34
To Add a Chart Element WD 8-35
To Select a Chart Element and Edit It WD 8-36
To Format Chart Elements WD 8-37
To Add an Outline to a Chart WD 8-39
To Change a Chart Type WD 8-41
To View and Scroll through Documents Side by Side WD 8-42
Creating a Blog Post WD 8-44
To Create a Blank Document for a Blog Post WD 8-46
To Enter Text WD 8-47
To Insert a Quick Table WD 8-47
To Edit and Format a Table WD 8-48
To Publish a Blog Post WD 8-49
To Display a Blog Webpage in a Browser Window WD 8-49
Summary WD 8-50
Apply Your Knowledge WD 8-51
Extend Your Knowledge WD 8-53
Expand Your World WD 8-55
In the Lab WD 8-56

MODULE NINE
Creating a Reference Document

Objectives WD 9-1
Introduction WD 9-1
Project: Reference Document WD 9-1
To Start Word and Specify Settings WD 9-2
Preparing a Document to Be Included in a Reference Document WD 9-4
To Open a Document and Save It with a New File Name WD 9-4
To Insert a Screenshot WD 9-5
To Insert a Caption WD 9-8
Caption Numbers WD 9-9
To Hide White Space WD 9-9
To Insert a Cross-Reference WD 9-9
To Go to an Object WD 9-11
To Insert Captions and Cross-References WD 9-12
To Mark an Index Entry WD 9-13
To Hide Formatting Marks WD 9-15
To Show White Space WD 9-15
To Insert a Sidebar Text Box WD 9-15
To Enter and Format Text in the Sidebar Text Box WD 9-16
To Use the Navigation Pane to Go to a Page WD 9-17
To Insert Another Sidebar Text Box WD 9-18
To Link Text Boxes WD 9-19
To Compress Pictures WD 9-21
To Close Open Panes, Documents, and Windows WD 9-22
Working with a Master Document WD 9-22
To Change the Document Theme WD 9-22
Outlines WD 9-23
To Switch to Outline View WD 9-23
To Enter Text in Outline View WD 9-24
To Show Only the First Line of Each Paragraph in Outline View WD 9-25
To Insert a Subdocument in a Master Document WD 9-26
Master Documents and Subdocuments WD 9-27
To Hide Formatting Marks WD 9-27
To Close Outline View WD 9-27
Organizing a Reference Document WD 9-28
To Insert a Cover Page WD 9-29
To Enter Text in Content Controls WD 9-29
To Center Text WD 9-30

To Insert a Continuous Section Break and Change the Margins in the Section WD 9-30
To Insert a Symbol from the Symbol Dialog Box WD 9-31
To Adjust Vertical Alignment on a Page WD 9-32
To Insert a Blank Page WD 9-33
To Insert a Table of Contents WD 9-33
To Insert a Continuous Section Break and Change the Starting Page Number in a Section WD 9-34
To Update Page Numbers in a Table of Contents WD 9-35
To Find a Format WD 9-36
To Format Text as a Heading WD 9-38
To Update the Entire Table of Contents WD 9-39
To Change the Format of a Table of Contents WD 9-40
To Use the Navigation Pane to Go to a Heading in a Document WD 9-41
To Insert a Table of Figures WD 9-42
To Edit a Caption and Update the Table of Figures WD 9-43
To Insert an Index WD 9-44
To Mark Another Index Entry WD 9-45
To Update an Index WD 9-46
Table of Authorities WD 9-47
To Specify Different Odd and Even Page Footers Using a Footer Building Block WD 9-50
To Set a Gutter Margin WD 9-52
To Check the Layout of the Printed Pages WD 9-53
To Switch to Draft View WD 9-54
To Insert an Odd Page Section Break WD 9-54
To Insert a Bookmark WD 9-55
To Save and Print a Document and Then Exit Word WD 9-57
Summary WD 9-57
Apply Your Knowledge WD 9-58
Extend Your Knowledge WD 9-59
Expand Your World WD 9-62
In the Lab WD 9-64

MODULE TEN
Creating an Online Form

Objectives WD 10-1
Introduction WD 10-1
Project: Online Form WD 10-1
To Start Word and Specify Settings WD 10-3
Saving a Document as a Template WD 10-4
To Save a Document as a Template WD 10-4
Changing Document Settings WD 10-5
To Change Paper Size WD 10-6
To Collapse the Ribbon WD 10-7
To Expand the Ribbon WD 10-7
To Set Custom Margins WD 10-8
To Change the Theme Colors and Theme Fonts WD 10-9
To Add a Page Color WD 10-9
To Apply a Pattern Fill Effect to a Page Color WD 10-10
Enter Content in the Online Form WD 10-11
To Enter and Format Text WD 10-11
To Insert an Icon WD 10-12
To Apply a Graphics Style WD 10-13
To Format a Graphic's Text Wrapping WD 10-14
To Move a Graphic WD 10-15
To Use a Table to Control Layout WD 10-16
To Show Table Gridlines WD 10-17
Content Controls WD 10-18
To Show the Developer Tab WD 10-19
To Insert a Plain Text Content Control WD 10-20
To Use Design Mode to Edit Placeholder Text WD 10-21
To Change the Properties of a Plain Text Content Control WD 10-23
To Format Placeholder Text WD 10-24
To Insert Another Plain Text Content Control and Use Design Mode to Edit Its Placeholder Text WD 10-25
To Change the Properties of a Plain Text Content Control WD 10-26
To Format Placeholder Text WD 10-27
To Increase Space before a Paragraph WD 10-27
To Insert a Drop-Down List Content Control WD 10-27
To Use Design Mode to Edit Placeholder Text WD 10-28
To Change the Properties of a Drop-Down List Content Control WD 10-28
To Format Placeholder Text WD 10-30
To Enter Text and Use a Table to Control Layout WD 10-30
To Insert a Check Box Content Control WD 10-31
To Change the Properties of a Check Box Content Control WD 10-31
To Add a Label to a Check Box Content Control WD 10-32
To Insert Additional Check Box Content Controls WD 10-33
To Insert a Rich Text Content Control WD 10-34
To Use Design Mode to Edit Placeholder Text WD 10-34
To Change the Properties of a Rich Text Content Control WD 10-35
To Format Placeholder Text and Add Space before a Paragraph WD 10-36
To Insert a Combo Box Content Control WD 10-36
To Use Design Mode to Edit Placeholder Text WD 10-37
To Change the Properties of a Combo Box Content Control WD 10-38
To Format Placeholder Text WD 10-39
To Insert a Date Picker Content Control WD 10-39
To Use Design Mode to Edit Placeholder Text WD 10-40
To Change the Properties of a Date Picker Content Control WD 10-40
To Format Placeholder Text WD 10-41
To Enter and Format Text WD 10-41
To Hide Gridlines and Formatting Marks WD 10-42
To Draw a Rectangle WD 10-42
To Send a Graphic behind Text WD 10-44
To Apply a Shape Style with an Outline WD 10-45
To Add a Shadow to a Shape WD 10-46
To Protect a Form WD 10-46
Protecting Documents WD 10-48
To Hide the Developer Tab WD 10-48
To Hide the Ruler, Collapse the Ribbon, Save the Template, and Exit Word WD 10-49
Working with an Online Form WD 10-49
To Use File Explorer to Create a New Document That Is Based on a Template WD 10-49
To Fill In a Form and Save It WD 10-50
Working with Templates WD 10-52

Summary **WD 10-53**
Apply Your Knowledge **WD 10-54**
Extend Your Knowledge **WD 10-57**
Expand Your World **WD 10-60**
In the Lab **WD 10-61**

MODULE ELEVEN
Enhancing an Online Form and Using Macros

Objectives **WD 11-1**
Introduction **WD 11-1**
Project: Online Form Revised **WD 11-1**
To Start Word and Specify Settings WD 11-3
To Save a Macro-Enabled Template WD 11-4
To Show the Developer Tab WD 11-4
To Unprotect a Document WD 11-5
To Specify Macro Settings in Word WD 11-6
Modifying Text and Form Content Controls **WD 11-6**
To Delete a Graphic, Format Text, and Change Paragraph Alignment WD 11-7
To Change the Properties of a Plain Text Content Control WD 11-8
To Convert a Table to Text WD 11-8
To Change the Properties of a Plain Text Content Control WD 11-9
To Adjust Paragraph Spacing and Resize the Rectangle Shape WD 11-10
To Change the Properties of a Date Picker Content Control WD 11-11
To Insert a Date Field WD 11-12
To Edit a Field WD 11-13
To Modify a Style Using the Styles Pane WD 11-14
To Modify a Style WD 11-15
To Create a Character Style WD 11-17
To Apply a Style WD 11-18
Enhancing with Color, Shapes, Effects, and Graphics **WD 11-19**
To Use a Fill Effect for the Page Color WD 11-20
To Change a Shape WD 11-21
To Apply a Glow Shape Effect WD 11-22
To Apply a Shadow Shape Effect WD 11-23
To Fill a Shape with a Picture WD 11-24
To Change the Color of a Picture WD 11-24
To Insert, Change Wrapping Style, and Resize a Picture WD 11-25
To Remove a Background WD 11-26
To Apply an Artistic Effect WD 11-27
To Move the Graphic WD 11-28
To Draw a Text Box WD 11-28
To Add Text to a Text Box and Format the Text WD 11-29
To Change Text Direction in a Text Box WD 11-29
To Apply a Shadow Shape Effect to a Text Box WD 11-30
To Change a Shape Outline of a Text Box WD 11-30
To Apply a 3-D Effect to a Text Box WD 11-31
To Move the Text Box WD 11-32
To Group Objects WD 11-32
Using a Macro to Automate a Task **WD 11-33**
To Record a Macro and Assign It a Shortcut Key WD 11-34
To Run a Macro WD 11-36
To Add a Command and a Macro as Buttons on the Quick Access Toolbar WD 11-37
To Use the New Buttons on the Quick Access Toolbar WD 11-39
To Delete Buttons from the Quick Access Toolbar WD 11-39
Automatic Macros WD 11-40
To Create an Automatic Macro WD 11-40
To Run the AutoNew Macro WD 11-42
To Edit a Macro's VBA Code WD 11-42
To Run the AutoNew Macro WD 11-44
VBA WD 11-44
To Protect a Form Using Backstage View and Exit Word WD 11-45
Working with 3-D Models **WD 11-45**
To Save the Template with a New File Name and Unprotect It WD 11-45
To Delete a Graphic WD 11-46
To Insert a 3-D Model WD 11-46
To Resize a 3-D Model WD 11-48
To Tilt and Rotate a 3-D Model WD 11-48
To Apply a 3-D Model View WD 11-49
To Reset a 3-D Model WD 11-50
To Save the Template, Protect It, and Exit Word WD 11-51
Supplementary Word Tasks **WD 11-51**
Adding a Digital Signature to a Document WD 11-51
Copying and Renaming Styles and Macros WD 11-52
Preparing a Document for Internationalization WD 11-54
Working with XML WD 11-55
Summary **WD 11-57**
Apply Your Knowledge **WD 11-58**
Extend Your Knowledge **WD 11-60**
Expand Your World **WD 11-62**
In the Lab **WD 11-64**

Index **IND-1**

The
Shelly
Cashman
Series®

Microsoft® Office 365®

Word® 2021

Comprehensive

Getting to Know Microsoft Office Versions

Cengage is proud to bring you the next edition of Microsoft Office. This edition was designed to provide a robust learning experience that is not dependent upon a specific version of Office.

Microsoft supports several versions of Office:

- **Office 365:** A cloud-based subscription service that delivers Microsoft's most up-to-date, feature-rich, modern productivity tools direct to your device. There are variations of Office 365 for business, educational, and personal use. Office 365 offers extra online storage and cloud-connected features, as well as updates with the latest features, fixes, and security updates.
- **Office 2021:** Microsoft's "on-premises" version of the Office apps, available for both PCs and Macs, offered as a static, one-time purchase and outside of the subscription model.
- **Office Online:** A free, simplified version of Office web applications (Word, Excel, PowerPoint, and OneNote) that facilitates creating and editing files collaboratively.

Office 365 (the subscription model) and Office 2021 (the one-time purchase model) had only slight differences between them at the time this content was developed. Over time, Office 365's cloud interface will continuously update, offering new application features and functions, while Office 2021 will remain static. Therefore, your onscreen experience may differ from what you see in this product. For example, the more advanced features and functionalities covered in this product may not be available in Office Online or may have updated from what you see in Office 2021.

For more information on the differences between Office 365, Office 2021, and Office Online, please visit the Microsoft Support site.

Cengage is committed to providing high-quality learning solutions for you to gain the knowledge and skills that will empower you throughout your educational and professional careers.

Thank you for using our product, and we look forward to exploring the future of Microsoft Office with you!

Using SAM Projects and Textbook Projects

SAM Projects allow you to actively apply the skills you learned live in Microsoft Word, Excel, PowerPoint, or Access. Become a more productive student and use these skills throughout your career.

To complete SAM Textbook Projects, please follow these steps:

SAM Textbook Projects allow you to complete a project as you follow along with the steps in the textbook. As you read the module, look for icons that indicate when you should download **sam**↓ your SAM Start file(s) and when to upload **sam**↑ the final project file to SAM for grading.

Everything you need to complete this project is provided within SAM. You can launch the eBook directly from SAM, which will allow you to take notes, highlight, and create a custom study guide, or you can use a print textbook or your mobile app. Download IOS or Download Android.

To get started, launch your SAM Project assignment from SAM, MindTap, or a link within your LMS.

Step 1: Download Files

- Click the "Download All" button or the individual links to download your **Start File** and **Support File(s)** (when available). You must use the SAM Start file.
- Click the Instructions link to launch the eBook (or use the print textbook or mobile app).
- Disregard any steps in the textbook that ask you to create a new file or to use a file from a location outside of SAM.
- Look for the SAM Download icon **sam**↓ to begin working with your start file.
- Follow the module's step-by-step instructions until you reach the SAM Upload icon **sam**↑.
- Save and close the file.

Step 2: Save Work to SAM

- Ensure you rename your project file to match the Expected File Name.
- Upload your in-progress or completed file to SAM. You can download the file to continue working or submit it for grading in the next step.

Step 3: Submit for Grading

- Upload the completed file to SAM for immediate feedback and to view the available Reports.
  - The **Graded Summary Report** provides a detailed list of project steps, your score, and feedback to aid you in revising and resubmitting the project.
  - The **Study Guide Report** provides your score for each project step and links to the associated training and textbook pages.
- If additional attempts are allowed, use your reports to assist with revising and resubmitting your project.
- To re-submit the project, download the file saved in step 2.
- Edit, save, and close the file, then re-upload and submit it again.

<u>**For all other SAM Projects, please follow these steps:**</u>

To get started, launch your SAM Project assignment from SAM, MindTap, or a link within your LMS.

Step 1: Download Files

- Click the "Download All" button or the individual links to download your **Instruction File**, **Start File**, and **Support File(s)** (when available). You <u>must</u> use the SAM Start file.
- Open the Instruction file and follow the step-by-step instructions. Ensure you rename your project file to match the Expected File Name (change _1 to _2 at the end of the file name).

Step 2: Save Work to SAM

- Upload your in-progress or completed file to SAM. You can download the file to continue working or submit it for grading in the next step.

Step 3: Submit for Grading

- Upload the completed file to SAM for immediate feedback and to view available Reports.
  - The **Graded Summary Report** provides a detailed list of project steps, your score, and feedback to aid you in revising and resubmitting the project.
  - The **Study Guide Report** provides your score for each project step and links to the associated training and textbook pages.
- If additional attempts are allowed, use your reports to assist with revising and resubmitting your project.
- To re-submit the project, download the file saved in step 2.
- Edit, save, and close the file, then re-upload and submit it again.

For additional tips to successfully complete your SAM Projects, please view our Common Student Errors Infographic.

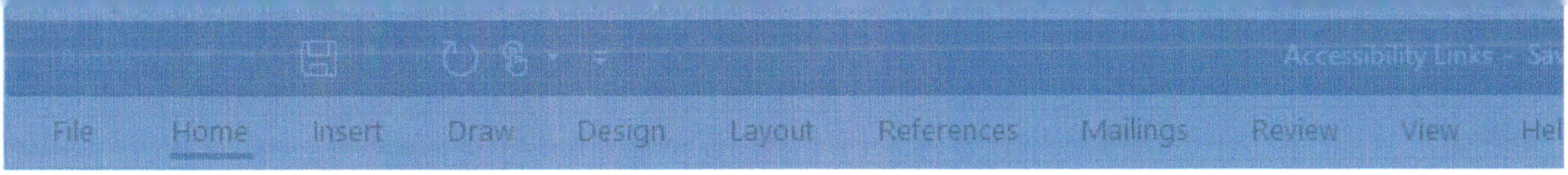

1 Creating and Modifying a Flyer

Objectives

After completing this module, you will be able to:

- Start and exit Word
- Enter text in a Word document
- Adjust margins
- Check spelling and grammar as you work in a document
- Save a document
- Format text, paragraphs, and document elements
- Undo and redo commands or actions
- Insert and format a picture
- Add a page border
- Change document properties
- Open and close a document
- Correct errors and revise a document
- Cut, copy, and paste text
- Print a document
- Use Word Help

What Is Word?

Microsoft Word, or Word, is a full-featured word processing app that allows you to create professional-looking documents and revise them easily. With Word, you can create business, academic, and personal documents, including flyers, research papers, letters, memos, resumes, reports, mailing labels, and newsletters.

Word has many features designed to simplify the production of documents and add visual appeal. Using Word, you easily can change the shape, size, and color of text. You also can include borders, shading, tables, pictures, charts, and other objects in documents. While you are typing, Word performs many tasks automatically. For example, Word detects and corrects spelling and grammar errors in several languages. Word's thesaurus allows you to add variety and precision to your writing. In addition to formatting text as you type, such as headings, lists, fractions, borders, and web addresses, Word includes a great deal of predefined text and many predefined objects and document types. Word also provides tools that enable you to create webpages and save the webpages directly on a web server.

To illustrate the features of Word, this book presents a series of projects that use Word to create documents similar to those you will encounter in business and academic environments.

Introduction

To convey a message or announcement to employees or staff members, campus or school students, or the community or public, you may want to create a flyer. You then can post the flyer in a location targeted to your intended audience, such as on an employee bulletin board or in an office cubicle, at a kiosk, or on a hallway wall. You may also see flyers on webpages, on social media, or in email messages.

Project: Flyer with a Picture

Businesses create flyers to gain attention for a message or an announcement. Flyers, which usually are a single page in length, are an inexpensive means of reaching an audience. Many flyers, however, go unnoticed because they are designed poorly.

The project in this module follows generally accepted design guidelines and uses Microsoft Word to create the flyer shown in Figure 1–1. This colorful, eye-catching flyer is intended to convey proper handwashing techniques to food service employees at a campus or school cafeteria. The flyer, which will be hung above every sink in the kitchen and restroom areas, contains a digital picture of an employee washing his hands. The headline on the flyer is large and colorful to draw attention into the text. The body copy

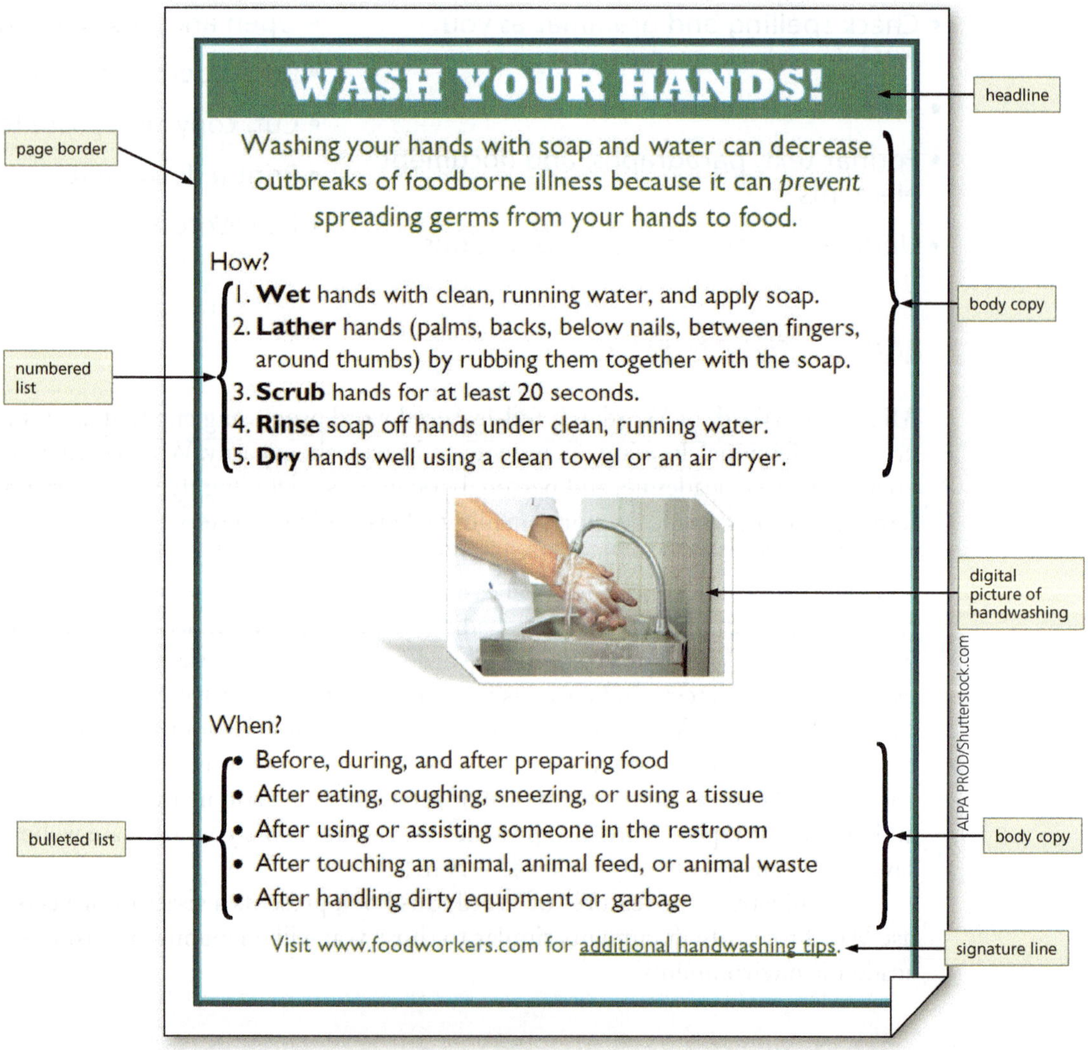

Figure 1–1

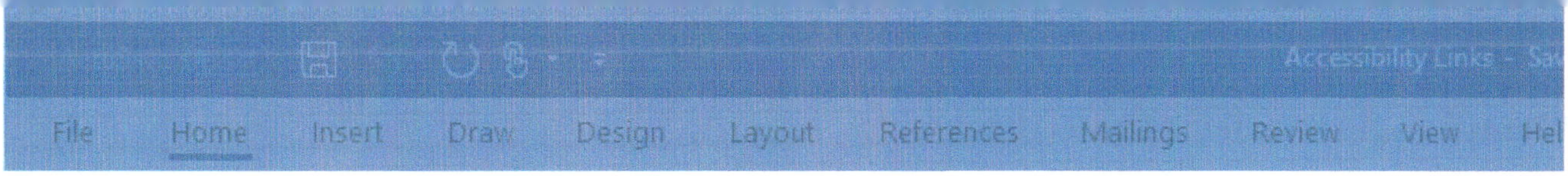

below the headline briefly describes the purpose of handwashing, along with a numbered list that highlights how to wash hands and a bulleted list that concisely describes when to wash hands. The signature line of the flyer identifies a website that employees can visit for additional handwashing tips. Some words in the flyer are in a different color or further emphasized so that they stand apart from the rest of the text on the flyer. Finally, the page border nicely frames and complements the contents of the flyer.

In this module, you will learn how to create the flyer shown in Figure 1–1. You will perform the following general tasks as you progress through this module:

1. Start and use Word.
2. Enter text in a document.
3. Format the text in the flyer.
4. Insert and format a picture in the flyer.
5. Enhance the layout of the flyer on the page.
6. Correct errors and revise text in the flyer.

Starting and Using Word

To use Word, you must instruct the operating system (i.e., Windows) to start the app. The following sections start Word, discuss some elements of the Word window, and perform tasks to specify Word settings.

If you are using a computer or device to step through the project in this module and you want your screen to match the figures in this book, you should change your screen's resolution to 1366 × 768.

BTW
Resolution
For information about how to change a computer's resolution, search for 'change resolution' in your operating system's help files.

To Start Word and Create a Blank Document

The following steps, which assume Windows is running, start Word and create a blank document based on a typical installation. **Why?** You will use Word to create the flyer in this module. You may need to ask your instructor how to start Word on your computer or device.

1

- **sam** Click the Start button on the Windows taskbar to display the Start menu.

Q&A **What is a menu?**
A **menu** contains a list of related items, including commands, apps, programs, and folders. Each **command** is a menu item that performs a specific action, such as saving a file or obtaining help. A **folder** is a named location on a storage medium that usually contains related documents.

- If necessary, scroll through the list of apps on the Start menu until the Word app name appears (Figure 1–2).

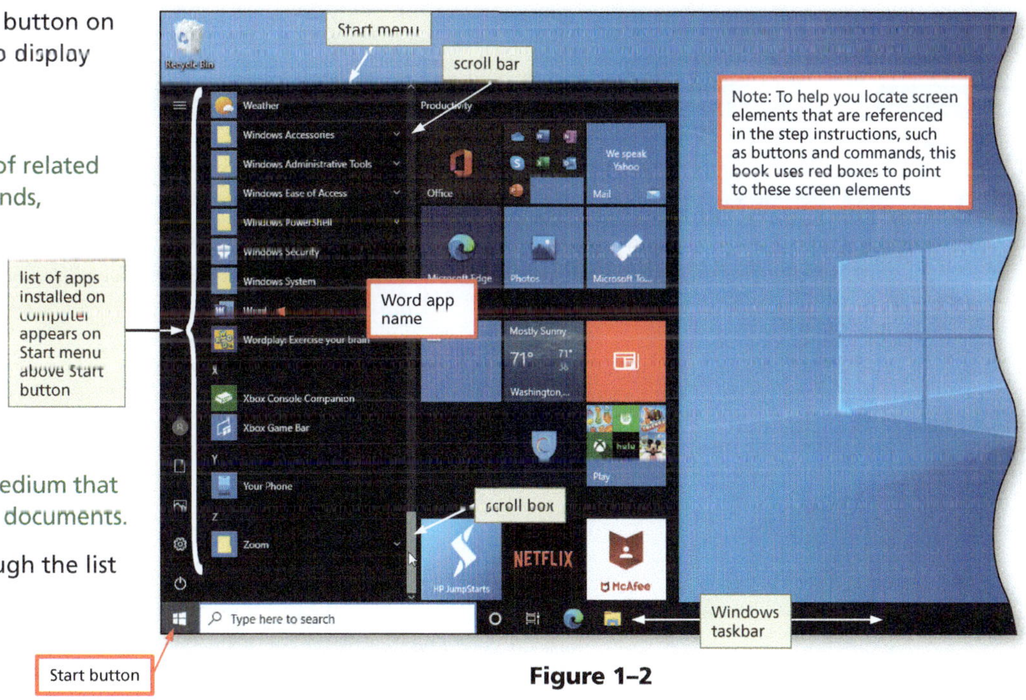

Figure 1–2

Q&A **What if my Word app is in a folder?**
Click the appropriate folder name to display the contents of the folder.

2

- Click Word on the Start menu to start Word and display the Word start screen (Figure 1–3).

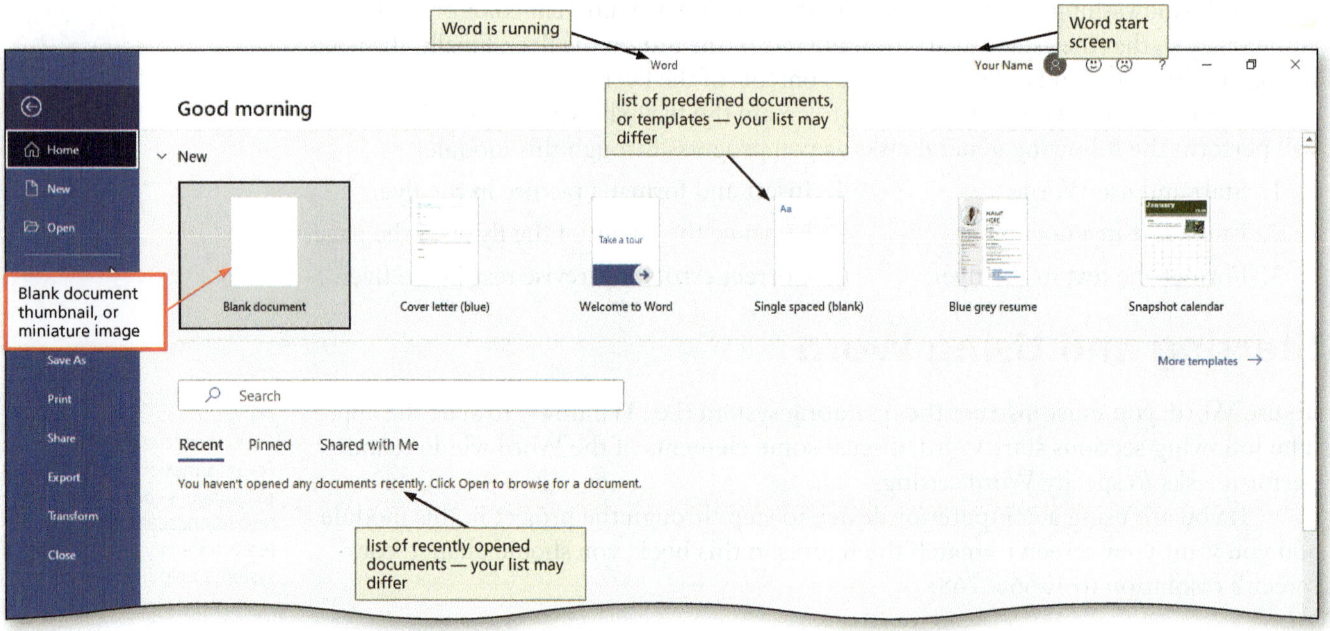

Figure 1–3

3

- Click the Blank document thumbnail on the Word start screen to create a blank document in the Word window (Figure 1–4).
- If the Word window is not maximized, click the Maximize button next to the Close button on the title bar to maximize the window.

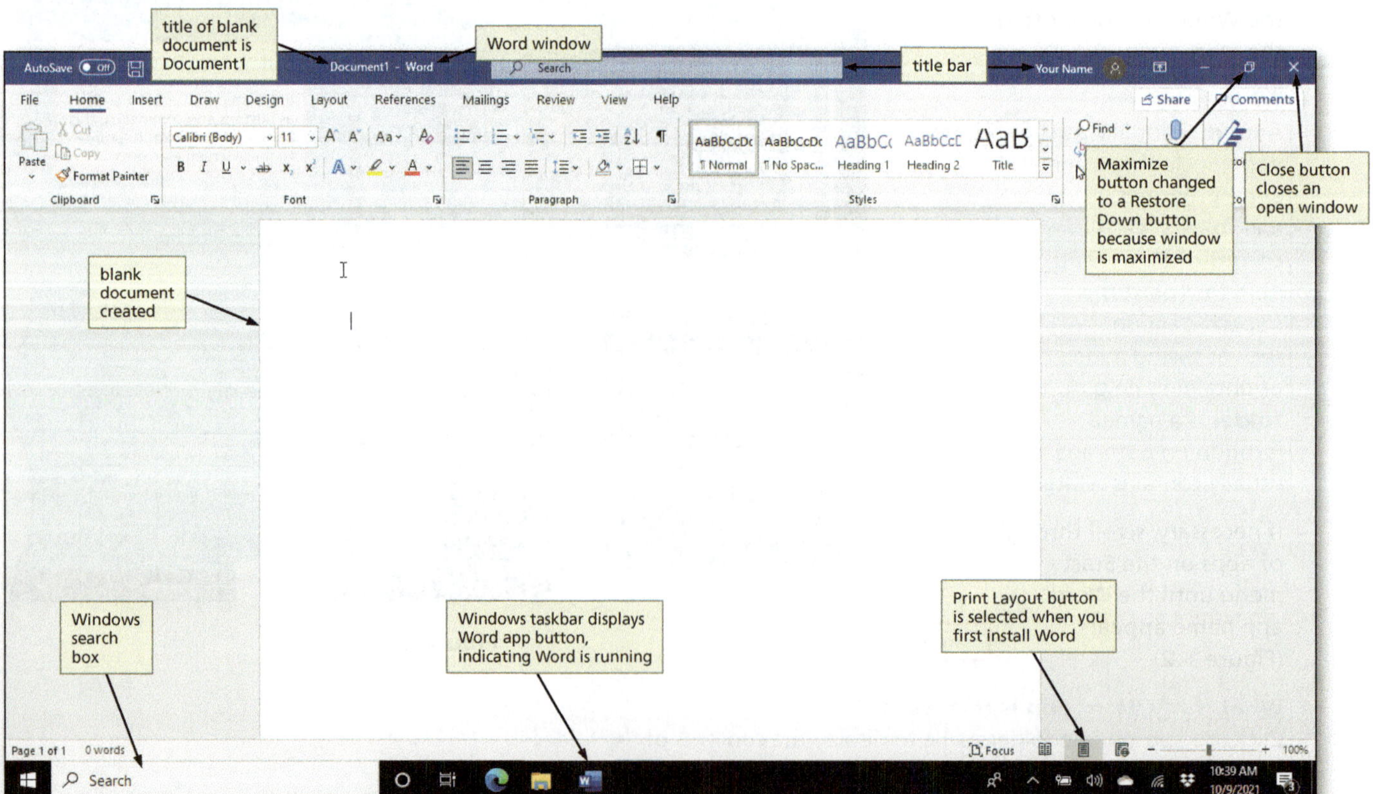

Figure 1–4

Q&A **What is a maximized window?**
A maximized window fills the entire screen. When you maximize a window, the Maximize button changes to a Restore Down button.

4

- If the Print Layout button is not selected, click it so that your screen layout matches Figure 1–4.

Q&A **What is Print Layout view?**
The default (preset) view in Word is **Print Layout view**, which shows the document on an image of a sheet of paper in the document window.

Other Ways

1. Type app name in Windows search box, click app name in results list
2. Double-click Word icon on desktop, if one is present

The Word Window

The Word window consists of a variety of components to make your work more efficient and documents more professional. These include the document window and several other elements, depending on the task you are performing: scroll bar(s), status bar, ribbon, Search box, Quick Access Toolbar, Mini toolbar, shortcut menus, KeyTips, and Microsoft Account area. Most of these are common to other Microsoft 365 apps; others are unique to Word. The following sections briefly describe these elements; others are discussed as they appear in the Word window.

You view or work with a document on the screen through a **document window**, which is a window within Word that displays all or part of an open document (Figure 1–5). In the document, the **insertion point** is a blinking vertical line that appears when you click in the document and indicates where new text, pictures, and other objects will be inserted. As you type, the insertion point moves to the right, and when you reach the end of a line, it moves down to the beginning of the next line. The **pointer** is a small symbol on the screen that becomes different shapes depending on the task you are performing in Word and the pointer's location on the screen. You move the pointer with a pointing device, such as a mouse or touchpad. The pointer in Figure 1–5 is the shape of an I-beam.

BTW
The Word Window
The modules in this book begin with the Word window appearing as it did at the initial installation of the software. Your Word window may look different depending on your screen resolution and other Word settings.

Scroll Bar You use **scroll bars**, which appear at the right and bottom edges of the document window, to view documents that are too large to fit on the screen at once. At the right edge of the document window is a vertical scroll bar. If a document is too wide to fit in the document window, a horizontal scroll bar also appears at the bottom of the document window. On a scroll bar, the position of the **scroll box** reflects the location of the portion of the document that is displayed in the document window; you can drag the scroll box, or click above or below it, to scroll through or display different parts of the document in the document window. A **scroll arrow** is a small triangular up or down arrow that is located at each end of a scroll bar; you can click the scroll arrows to scroll through the document in small increments.

Status Bar The **status bar**, located at the bottom of the document window above the Windows taskbar, presents information about the document, the progress of current tasks, and the status of certain commands and keys; it also provides controls for viewing the document, such as zoom controls. As you type text or perform certain commands, various indicators and buttons may appear on the status bar.

The left side of the status bar in Figure 1–5 shows the current page followed by the total number of pages in the document, the number of words in the document, and an icon to check spelling and grammar. The right side of the status bar includes buttons and controls you can use to change the view of a document and adjust the size of the displayed document.

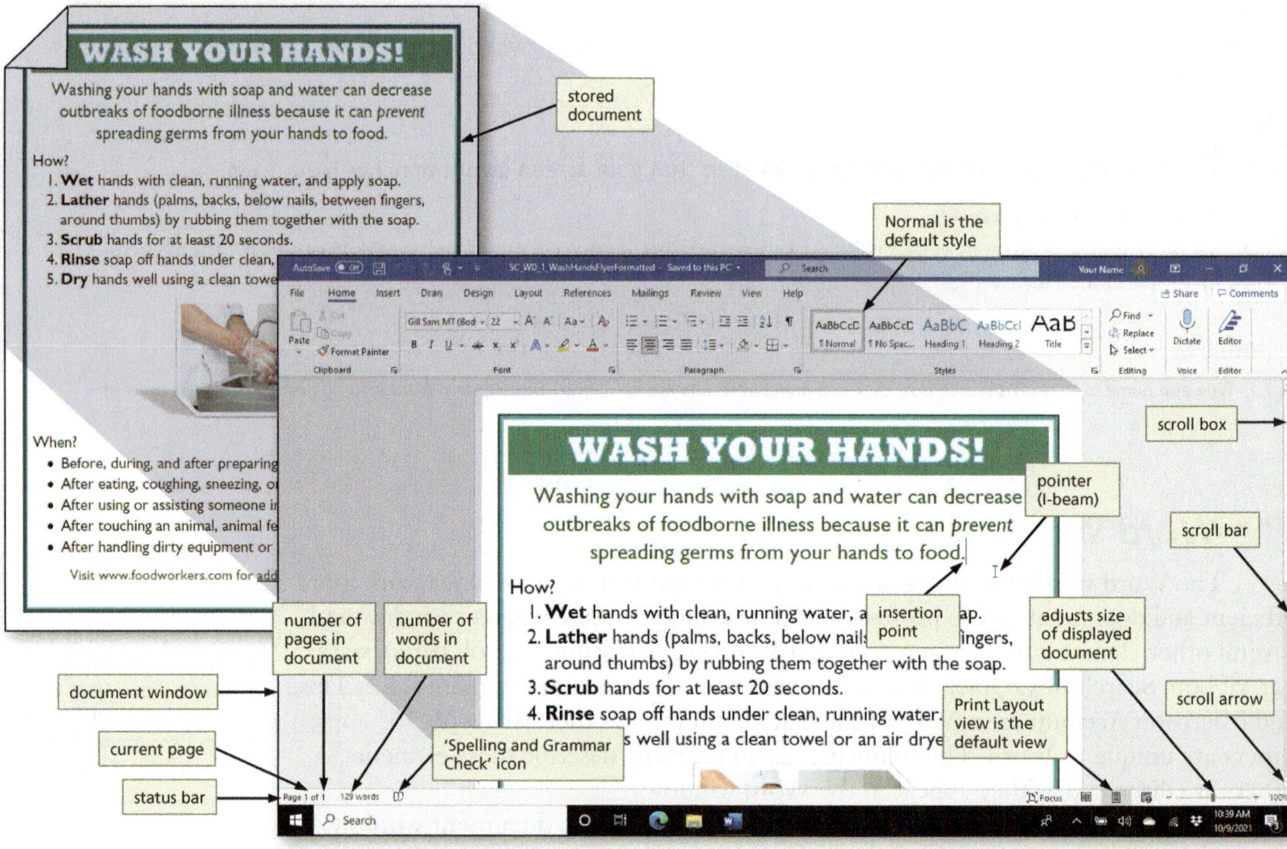

Figure 1–5

Ribbon The **ribbon**, which is a horizontal strip located near the top of the Word window below the title bar, is the control center in Word that contains tabs of grouped commands that you click to interact with Word (Figure 1–6a). Each **tab** contains a collection of groups, and each **group** contains related commands. The ribbon provides easy, central access to the tasks you perform while creating a document.

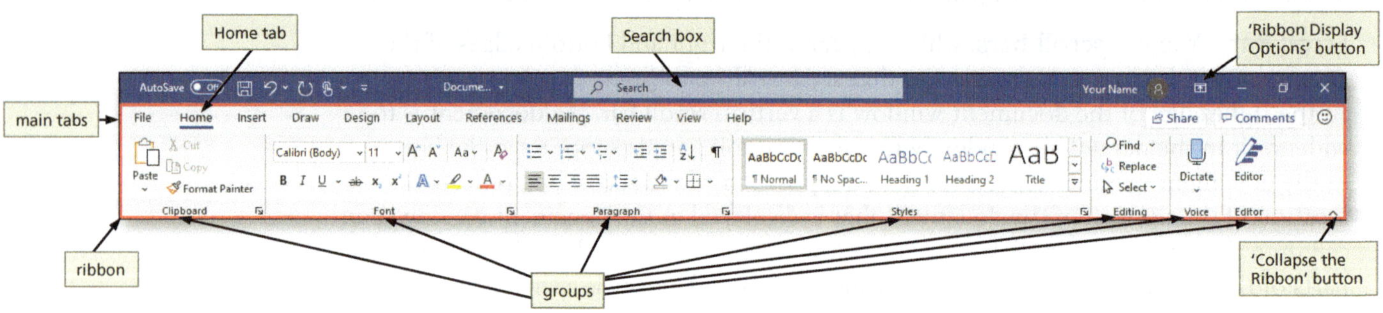

Figure 1–6a

BTW

Pointer

If you are using a touch screen, the pointer may not appear on the screen as you perform touch gestures. The pointer will reappear when you begin using the mouse.

When you start Word, the ribbon displays several main tabs, also called default or top-level tabs (i.e., File, Home, Insert, Draw, Design, Layout, References, Mailings, Review, View, and Help). (Note that depending on the type of computer or device you are using, the Draw tab may not appear.) The **Home tab**, also called the primary tab, contains the more frequently used commands. The tab currently displayed is called the **active tab**.

To display more of the document in the document window, some users prefer to minimize the ribbon, which hides the groups on the ribbon and displays only the main tabs (Figure 1–6b). To minimize the ribbon, click the 'Collapse the Ribbon' button or click the 'Ribbon Display Options' button on the title bar and then click Show Tabs on the menu. To use commands on a minimized ribbon, sometimes called a simplified ribbon, click the tab that you wish to expand. To expand the ribbon, double-click a tab, click the 'Pin the ribbon' button on an expanded tab, or click the 'Ribbon Display Options' button on the title bar and then click 'Show Tabs and Commands' on the menu.

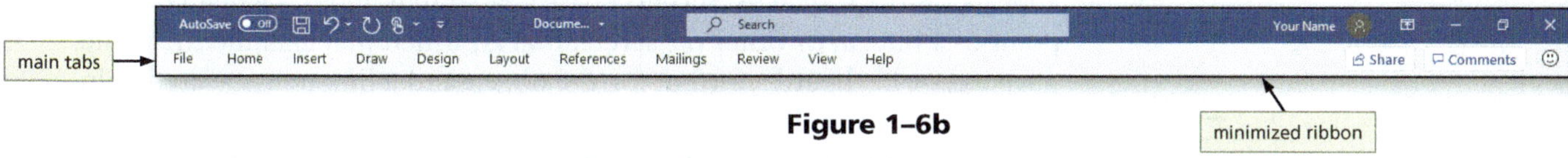

Figure 1–6b

Each time you start Word, the ribbon appears the same way it did the last time you used Word. The modules in this book, however, begin with the ribbon appearing as it did at the initial installation of the software.

In addition to the main tabs, Word displays other tabs, called **contextual tabs**, when you perform certain tasks or work with objects such as pictures or tables. If you insert a picture in the document, for example, the Picture Format tab appears (Figure 1–7). When you are finished working with the picture, the Picture Format tab disappears from the ribbon. Word determines when contextual tabs should appear and disappear based on tasks you perform. Some tasks involve more than one contextual tab. For example, when you work with tables, the Table Design tab and the Layout tab appear.

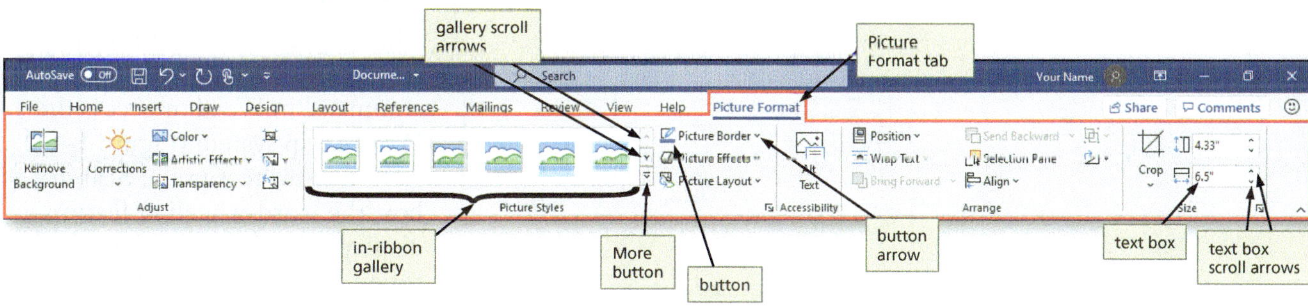

Figure 1–7

Items on the ribbon include buttons, boxes (text boxes, check boxes, etc.), and galleries (shown in Figure 1–7). A **gallery** is a set of choices, often graphical, arranged in a grid or in a list that you can browse through before making a selection. You can scroll through choices in an in-ribbon gallery by clicking the gallery's scroll arrows. Or, you can click a gallery's More button to view more gallery options on the screen at a time.

Some buttons and boxes have arrows that, when clicked, also display a gallery; others always cause a gallery to be displayed when clicked. Most galleries support **Live Preview**, which is a feature that allows you to point to a gallery choice and see its effect in the document — without actually selecting the choice (Figure 1–8).

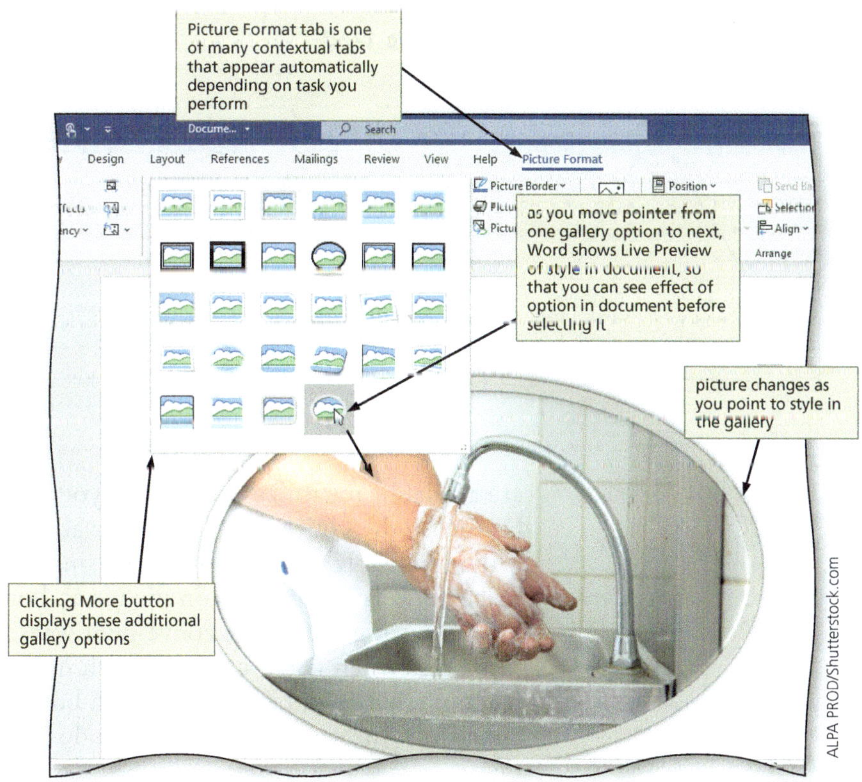

ALPA PROD/Shutterstock.com

Figure 1–8

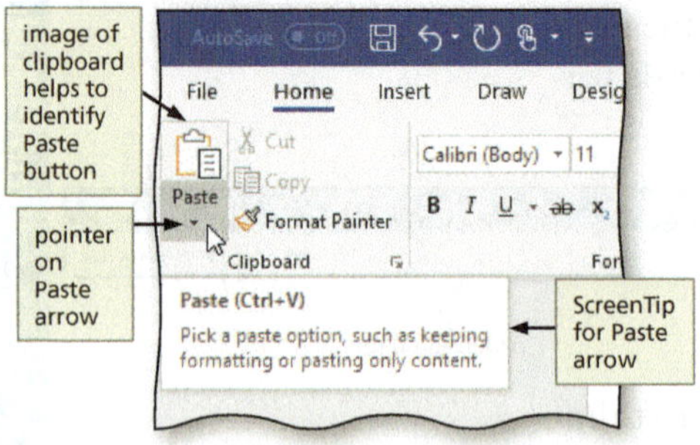

Figure 1–9

Some commands on the ribbon display an image to help you remember their function. When you point to a command on the ribbon, all or part of the command glows in shades of gray, and a ScreenTip appears on the screen. A **ScreenTip** is a label that appears when you point to a button or other on-screen object, which may include the name, purpose, or keyboard shortcut for the object and a link to associated help topics, if any exist (Figure 1–9).

Some groups on the ribbon have a small arrow in the lower-right corner, called a **Dialog Box Launcher**, that when clicked, displays a dialog box or opens a pane with additional options for the group (Figure 1–10). When presented with a dialog box, you make selections and must close the dialog box before returning to the document. A **pane**, in contrast to a dialog box, is a window that can remain open and visible while you work in the document and provides additional options.

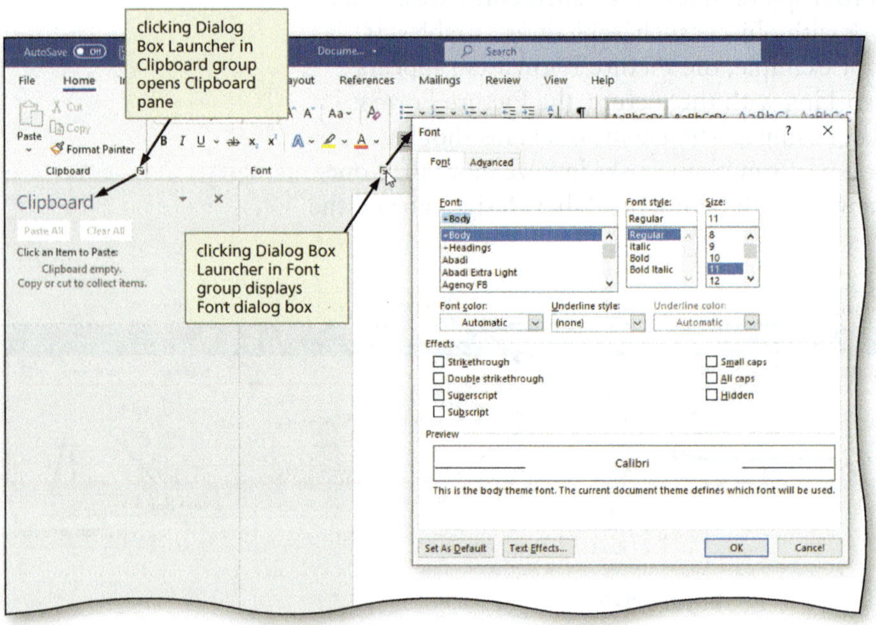

Figure 1–10

Search Box The **Search box**, which appears on the title bar, is a text box that helps you to find a command in Word or access the Word Help system (Figure 1–11). As you enter text in the Search box, the word-wheeling feature displays search results that are refined as you type. For example, if you want to insert a picture in a document, you can type the text "insert picture" in the Search box and then select the appropriate command.

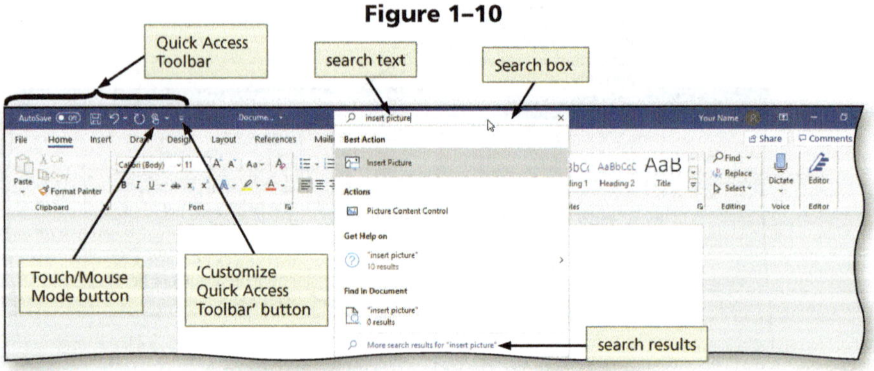

Figure 1–11

Quick Access Toolbar The **Quick Access Toolbar**, located initially (by default) above the ribbon at the left edge of the title bar, is a customizable toolbar that contains buttons you can click to perform frequently used commands (shown in Figure 1–11). The commands on the Quick Access Toolbar always are available, regardless of the task you are performing. The Touch/Mouse Mode button on the Quick Access Toolbar allows you to switch between Touch mode and Mouse mode. If you primarily are using touch gestures, Touch mode will add more space between commands on menus and on the ribbon so that they are easier to tap. While touch gestures are convenient ways to interact with Word, not all features are supported when you are using Touch mode. If you are using a mouse, Mouse mode will not add the extra space between buttons and commands. The modules in this book show the screens in Mouse mode.

BTW

Mouse Mode

The figures in this book use Mouse mode. To switch to Mouse mode, click the 'Touch/Mouse Mode' button on the Quick Access Toolbar and then click Mouse on the Touch/Mouse Mode menu. If you are using Touch mode, you might notice that the function or appearance of your touch screen in Word differs slightly from this module's presentation.

You can add other commands to or delete commands from the Quick Access Toolbar so that it contains the commands you use most often. To do this, click the 'Customize Quick Access Toolbar' button on the Quick Access Toolbar and then select the commands you want to add or remove. As you add commands to the Quick Access Toolbar, its length may interfere with the document title on the title bar. For this reason, Word provides an option of displaying the Quick Access Toolbar below the ribbon on the Quick Access Toolbar menu.

Each time you start Word, the Quick Access Toolbar appears the same way it did the last time you used Word. The modules in this book, however, begin with the Quick Access Toolbar appearing as it did at the initial installation of the software.

BTW
Turning Off the Mini Toolbar
If you do not want the Mini toolbar to appear, click File on the ribbon to open Backstage view, click Options in Backstage view, if necessary, click General (Options dialog box), remove the check mark from the 'Show Mini Toolbar on selection' check box, and then click OK.

Mini Toolbar and Shortcut Menus The **Mini toolbar**, which appears next to selected text, contains the most frequently used text formatting commands (which are those commands related to changing the appearance of text in a document). If you do not use the Mini toolbar, it disappears from the screen. The buttons, arrows, and boxes on the Mini toolbar vary, depending on whether you are using Touch mode or Mouse mode. To use the Mini toolbar, move the pointer into the Mini toolbar.

All commands on the Mini toolbar also exist on the ribbon. The purpose of the Mini toolbar is to minimize hand or mouse movement. For example, if you want to use a command that currently is not displayed on the active tab, you can use the command on the Mini toolbar — instead of switching to a different tab to use the command.

A **shortcut menu**, which appears when you right-click an object, is a list of frequently used commands that relate to the right-clicked object. When you right-click selected text, for example, a shortcut menu appears with commands related to text. If you right-click an item in the document window, Word displays both the Mini toolbar and a shortcut menu (Figure 1–12).

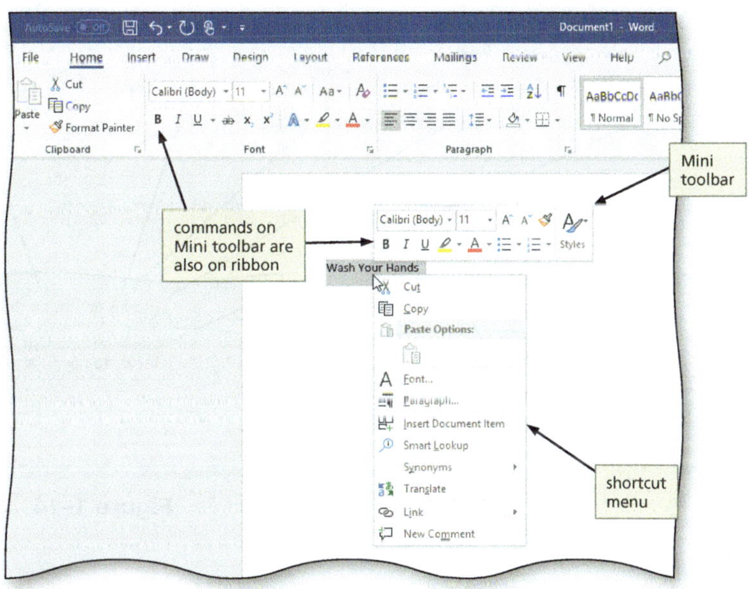

Figure 1–12

KeyTips If you prefer using the keyboard instead of the mouse, you can press ALT on the keyboard to display **KeyTips**, which are labels that appear over each tab and command on the ribbon (Figure 1–13). To select a tab or command using the keyboard, press the letter or number displayed in the KeyTip, which may cause additional KeyTips related to the selected command to appear. For example, to select the Bold button on the Home tab, press ALT, then press H, and then press 1. To remove the KeyTips from the screen, press ALT or ESC until all KeyTips disappear, or click anywhere in the Word window.

Microsoft Account Area In the Microsoft Account Area (shown in Figure 1–13), you can use the Sign in link to sign in to your Microsoft account. Once signed in, you will see your account information.

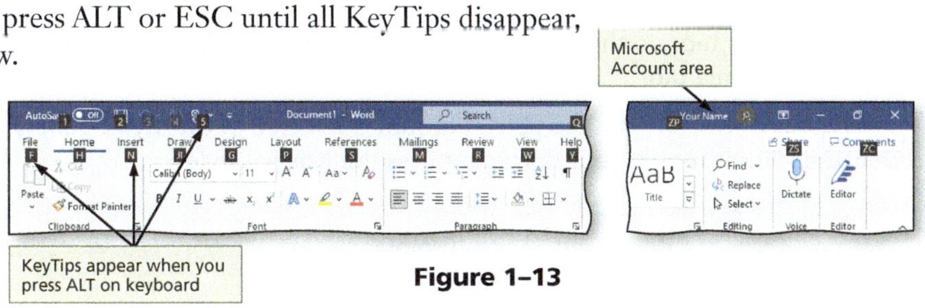

Figure 1–13

To Display a Different Tab on the Ribbon

When you start Word, the ribbon displays 11 main tabs: File, Home, Insert, Draw, Design, Layout, References, Mailings, Review, View, and Help. (Note that depending on the type of computer or device you are using, the Draw tab may not appear.) The tab currently displayed is called the active tab. To display a different tab on the ribbon, you click the tab. The following step displays the View tab, that is, makes it the active tab. **Why?** When working with Word, you may need to switch tabs to access other options for working with a document or to verify settings.

1

- Click View on the ribbon to display the View tab (Figure 1–14).

Q&A **Why did the groups on the ribbon change?**
When you switch from one tab to another on the ribbon, the groups on the ribbon change to show commands related to the selected tab.

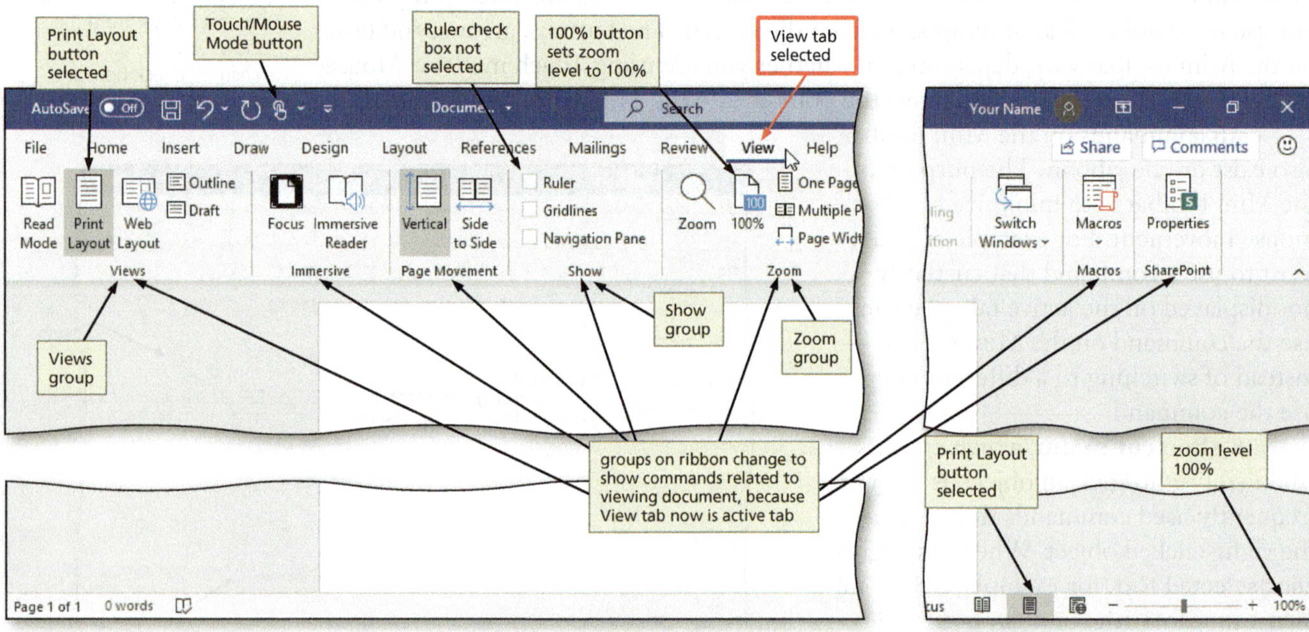

Figure 1–14

2

- Verify that the Print Layout button (View tab | Views group) is selected. (If it is not selected, click it to ensure the screen is in Print Layout view.)
- Verify that the zoom level is 100% on the status bar. (If it is not, click the 100% button (View tab | Zoom group) to set the zoom level to 100%.)
- Verify that the Ruler check box (View tab | Show group) is not selected. (If it is selected, click it to remove the selection because you do not want the rulers to appear on the screen.)

Experiment

- Click the other tabs on the ribbon to view their contents. When you are finished, click Home on the ribbon to display the Home tab.
- Verify that Normal (Home tab | Styles group) is selected in the Styles gallery (shown in Figure 1–5). (If it is not selected, click it so that your document uses the Normal style.)

Q&A **What is the Normal style?**
When you create a document, Word formats the text using a particular style. The **Normal style** is the default style that is applied to all text when you start Word.

- If you are using a mouse, verify that you are using Mouse mode so that your screens match the figures in this book by clicking the Touch/Mouse Mode button on the Quick Access Toolbar (shown in Figure 1–5) and then, if necessary, clicking Mouse on the menu (if your Quick Access Toolbar does not display the Touch/Mouse Mode button, click the Customize Quick Access Toolbar button on the Quick Access Toolbar and then click Touch/Mouse Mode on the menu to add the button to the Quick Access Toolbar).

To Adjust the Margins

Word is preset to use standard 8.5-by-11-inch paper, with 1-inch top, bottom, left, and right margins. The flyer in this module uses .5-inch top, bottom, left, and right margins. **Why?** You would like more text to fit from left to right and top to bottom on the page.

When you change the default (preset) margin settings, the new margin settings affect every page in the document. If you wanted the margins to affect just a portion of the document, you would divide the document into sections (discussed in a later module), which enables you to specify different margin settings for each section. The following steps change margin settings.

1

- Click Layout on the ribbon to display the Layout tab.
- Click the Margins button (Layout tab | Page Setup group) to display the Margins gallery (Figure 1–15).

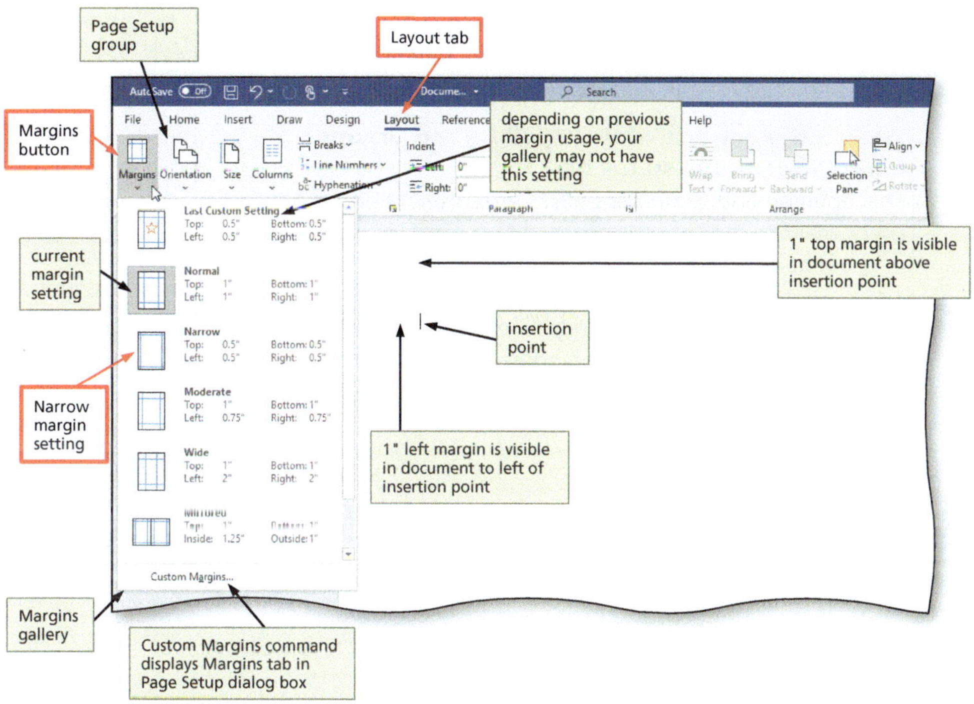

Figure 1–15

2

- Click Narrow in the Margins gallery to change the margins to the specified settings (Figure 1–16).

Q&A **What if the margin settings I want are not in the Margins gallery?**
You can click Custom Margins in the Margins gallery and then enter your desired margin values in the top, bottom, left, and right boxes in the Page Setup dialog box.

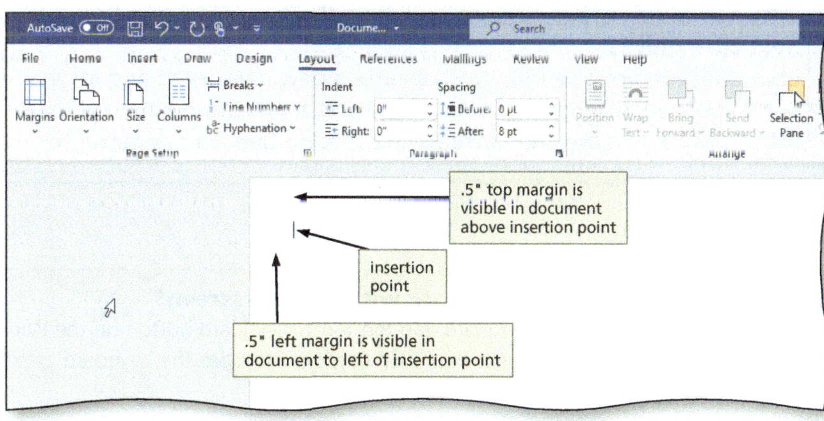

Figure 1–16

Other Ways

1. Position pointer on margin boundary on ruler; when pointer changes to two-headed arrow, drag margin boundary on ruler

BTW

Character Widths

Many word processing documents use variable character fonts, where some characters are wider than others; for example, the letter w is wider than the letter i.

Entering Text in a Document

The first step in creating a document is to enter its text. With the projects in this book, you enter text by typing on the keyboard. By default, Word positions text you type at the left margin. In a later section of this module, you will learn how to format, or change the appearance of, the entered text.

To Type Text

To begin creating the flyer in this module, type the headline in the document window. **Why?** The headline is the first line of text in the flyer. The following steps type the first line of text in the document.

1

- Type **Wash Your Hands!** as the headline (Figure 1–17).

Q&A **What if I make an error while typing?**
You can press BACKSPACE until you have deleted the text in error and then retype the text correctly.

What is the purpose of the 'Spelling and Grammar Check' icon on the status bar?
The 'Spelling and Grammar Check' icon displays either a check mark to indicate the entered text contains no spelling or grammar errors, or an X to indicate that it found potential errors. Word flags potential errors in the document with squiggly, dotted, or double underlines that appear in a variety of colors. Later in this module, you will learn how to fix or ignore flagged errors.

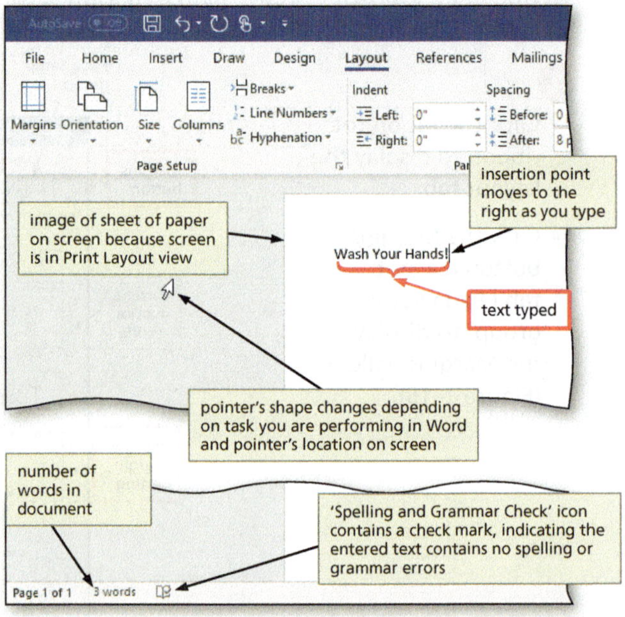

Figure 1–17

2

- Press ENTER to move the insertion point to the beginning of the next line (Figure 1–18).

Q&A **Why did blank space appear between the headline and the insertion point?**
Each time you press ENTER, Word creates a new paragraph and inserts blank space between the two paragraphs. Later in this module, you will learn how to increase and decrease the spacing between paragraphs.

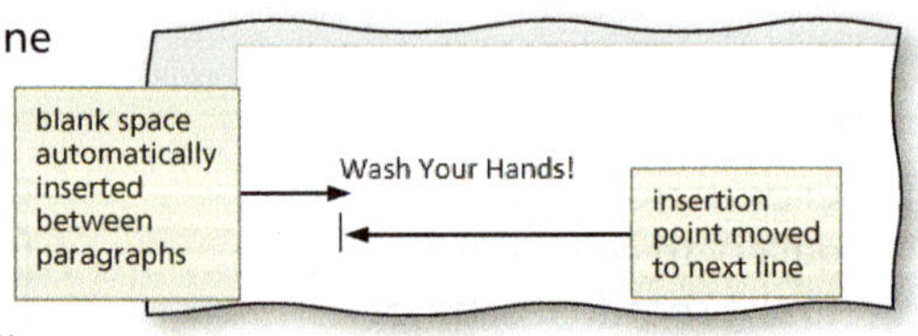

Figure 1–18

Consider This

How do you use the touch keyboard with a touch screen?
To display the on-screen touch keyboard, tap the Touch Keyboard button on the Windows taskbar. When finished using the touch keyboard, tap the X button on the touch keyboard to close the keyboard.

To Change the Zoom to Page Width

The next step in creating this flyer is to enlarge the contents that appear on the screen. **Why?** You would like the text on the screen to be larger so that it is easier to read. The document currently displays at a zoom level of 100% (shown in Figure 1–14). With Word, you can change the zoom to page width, which zooms (enlarges or shrinks) the image of the sheet of paper on the screen so that it is the width of the Word window. The following step changes the zoom to page width.

1

- Click View on the ribbon to display the View tab.
- Click the Page Width button (View tab | Zoom group) to display the page the same width as the document window (Figure 1–19).

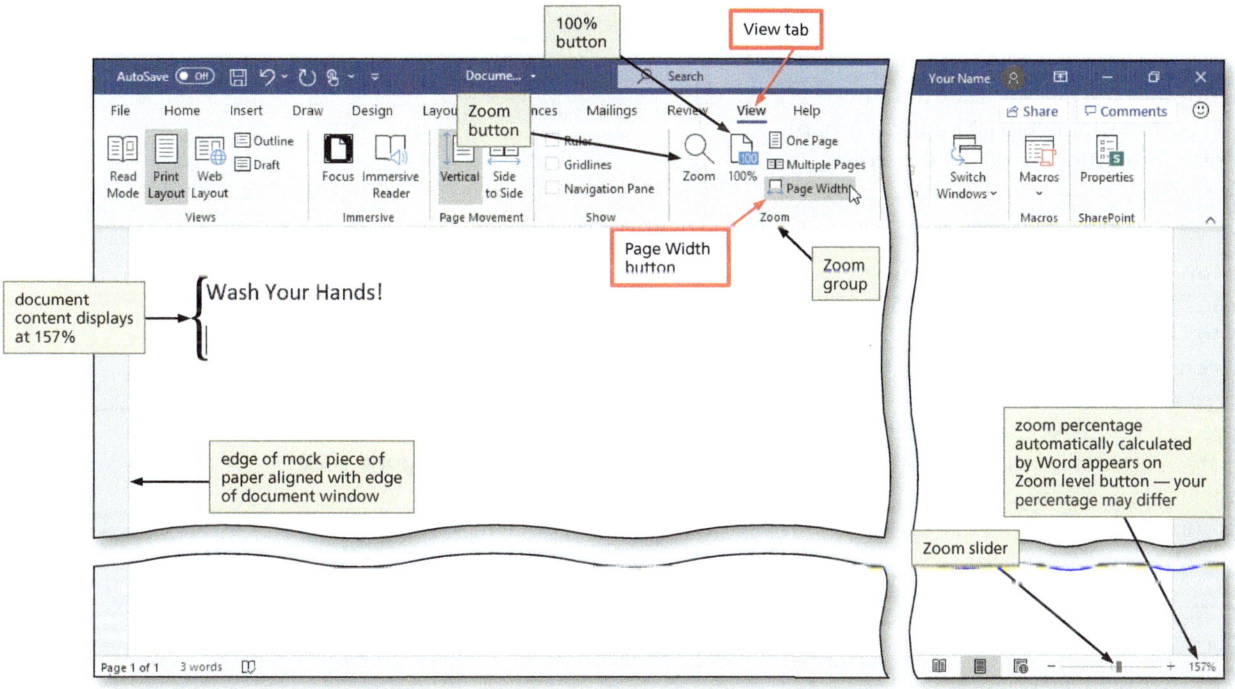

Figure 1–19

Q&A

If I change the zoom, will the document print differently?
Changing the zoom has no effect on the printed document.

What are the other predefined zoom options?
Through the View tab | Zoom group or the Zoom dialog box (Zoom button in Zoom group), you can zoom to one page (an entire single page appears in the document window), many pages (multiple pages appear at once in the document window), page width, text width, and a variety of set percentages. Whereas changing the zoom to page width places the edges of the page at the edges of the document window, changing the zoom to text width places the document contents at the edges of the document window.

What if I wanted to change the Zoom back to 100%?
You could click the 100% button (View tab | Zoom group) or drag the zoom slider until 100% appears on Zoom level button.

Other Ways

1. Click Zoom button (View tab | Zoom group), click Page width (Zoom dialog box), click OK

To Display Formatting Marks

You may find it helpful to display formatting marks while working in a document. **Why?** Formatting marks indicate where in a document you pressed ENTER, SPACEBAR, and other nonprinting characters. A **formatting mark** is a nonprinting character that appears on the screen to indicate the ends of paragraphs, tabs, and other formatting elements. For example, the paragraph mark (¶) is a formatting mark that indicates where you pressed ENTER. A raised dot (·) shows where you pressed SPACEBAR. Formatting marks are discussed as they appear on the screen.

Depending on settings made during previous Word sessions, your Word screen already may display formatting marks (shown in Figure 1–20). The following step displays formatting marks, if they do not show already on the screen.

1

- Click Home on the ribbon to display the Home tab.
- If it is not selected already, click the 'Show/Hide ¶' button (Home tab | Paragraph group) to display formatting marks on the screen (Figure 1–20).

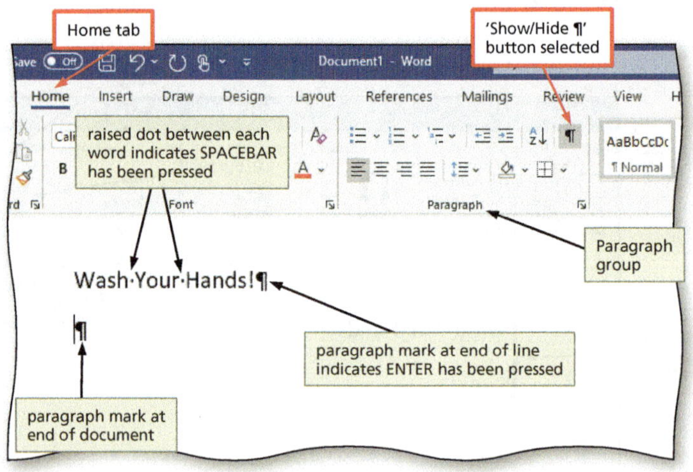

Figure 1–20

Q&A **What if I do not want formatting marks to show on the screen?**
You can hide them by clicking the 'Show/Hide ¶' button (Home tab | Paragraph group) again. It is recommended that you display formatting marks so that you visually can identify when you press ENTER, SPACEBAR, and other keys associated with nonprinting characters. Most of the document windows presented in this book, therefore, show formatting marks.

Other Ways

1. Press CTRL+SHIFT+*

BTW
Formatting Marks
With some fonts, the formatting marks will not be displayed properly on the screen. For example, the raised dot that signifies a blank space between words may be displayed behind a character instead of in the blank space, causing the characters to look incorrect.

Wordwrap

Wordwrap allows you to type words in a paragraph continually without pressing ENTER at the end of each line. As you type, if a word extends beyond the right margin, Word also automatically positions that word on the next line along with the insertion point.

Word creates a new paragraph each time you press ENTER. Thus, as you type text in the document window, do not press ENTER when the insertion point reaches the right margin. Instead, press ENTER only in these circumstances:

1. To insert a blank line(s) in a document (as shown in a later set of steps)
2. To begin a new paragraph
3. To terminate a short line of text and advance to the next line
4. To respond to questions or prompts in Word dialog boxes, panes, and other on-screen objects

To Wordwrap Text as You Type

The next step in creating the flyer is to type the body copy. **Why?** In many flyers, the body copy text appears below the headline. The following steps illustrate how the body copy text wordwraps as you enter it in the document, which means you will not have to press ENTER at the end of the line.

1

- Type the first sentence of the body copy: **`Washing your hands with soap and water can decrease outbreaks of foodborne illness because it can prevent spreading germs from your hands to food.`**

Q&A **Why does my document wrap on different words?**
The printer connected to a computer or device is one factor that can control where wordwrap occurs for each line in a document. Thus, it is possible that the same document could wordwrap differently if printed on different printers.

2

- Press ENTER to position the insertion point on the next line in the document (Figure 1–21).

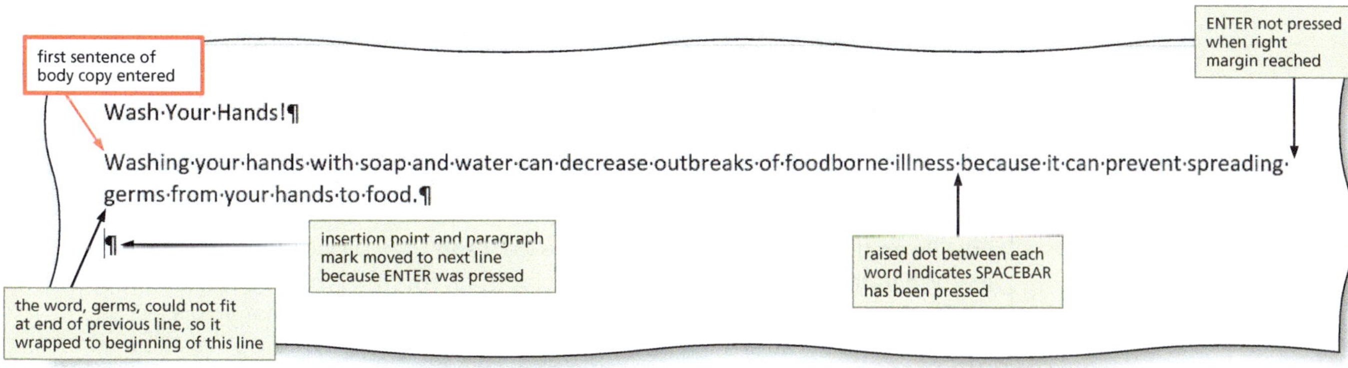

Figure 1–21

Spelling and Grammar Check

As you type text in a document, Word checks your typing for possible spelling and grammar errors. If all the words you have typed are in Word's dictionary and your grammar is correct, as mentioned earlier, the Spelling and Grammar Check icon on the status bar displays a check mark. Otherwise, the icon shows an X. In this case, Word flags the potential error(s) in the document window with a red, green, or blue underline.

- A red wavy underline means the flagged text is not in Word's dictionary (because it is a proper name or misspelled).
- A blue double underline indicates the text may be incorrect grammatically, such as a misuse of homophones (words that are pronounced the same but that have different spellings or meanings, such as one and won).
- A purple dotted underline indicates that Word can present a suggestion for more concise writing or different word usage.

A flagged word is not necessarily misspelled or grammatically incorrect. For example, many names, abbreviations, and specialized terms are not in Word's main dictionary. In these cases, you can instruct Word to ignore the flagged word. As you type, Word also detects duplicate words while checking for spelling errors. For example, if your document contains the phrase, to the the store, Word places a red wavy underline below the second occurrence of the word, the.

BTW

Automatic Spelling Correction

As you type, Word automatically corrects some misspelled words. For example, if you type recieve, Word automatically corrects the misspelling and displays the word, receive, when you press the SPACEBAR or type a punctuation mark. To see a complete list of automatically corrected words, click File on the ribbon to open Backstage view, click Options in Backstage view, click Proofing in the left pane (Word Options dialog box), click the AutoCorrect Options button, and then scroll through the list near the bottom of the dialog box.

To Enter More Text with Spelling and Grammar Errors

BTW
Zooming
If text is too small for you to read on the screen, you can zoom the document by dragging the Zoom slider on the status bar or by clicking the Zoom Out or Zoom In buttons on the status bar. Changing the zoom has no effect on the printed document.

When entering the following text in the flyer, you will intentionally make some spelling and grammar errors, because the next set of steps illustrates checking spelling and grammar as you work in a document. The following steps enter text in the flyer that contains spelling and grammar errors. Later in this module, the text you enter here will be formatted as a numbered list.

1. With the insertion point positioned as shown in Figure 1–21, type **`How?`**
2. Press ENTER and then type **`Wet hands with cleane, running water, and apply soap.`**
3. Press ENTER and then type **`Lather hands (palms, backs, below nails, between fingers, around thumbs) by rubbing them together with the soap.`**
4. Press ENTER and then type **`Scrub hands fore at least 20 seconds.`**
5. Press ENTER and then type **`Rinse soap off of hands under clean, running water.`**
6. Press ENTER and then type **`Dry hands well using a towel or or an air dryer.`** (as shown in Figure 1–22).

Q&A

What if Word does not flag my spelling and grammar errors with wavy, dotted, or double underlines?
To verify that the features to check spelling and grammar as you type are enabled, click File on the ribbon to open Backstage view and then click Options in Backstage view. When the Word Options dialog box is displayed, click Proofing in the left pane and then ensure the 'Check spelling as you type' and 'Mark grammar errors as you type' check boxes contain check marks. Click OK to close the Word Options dialog box.

What if Word flags different errors on my screen?
Don't be concerned if the errors flagged on your screen differ from the errors flagged in Figure 1-22. Simply continue with the steps to correct any errors.

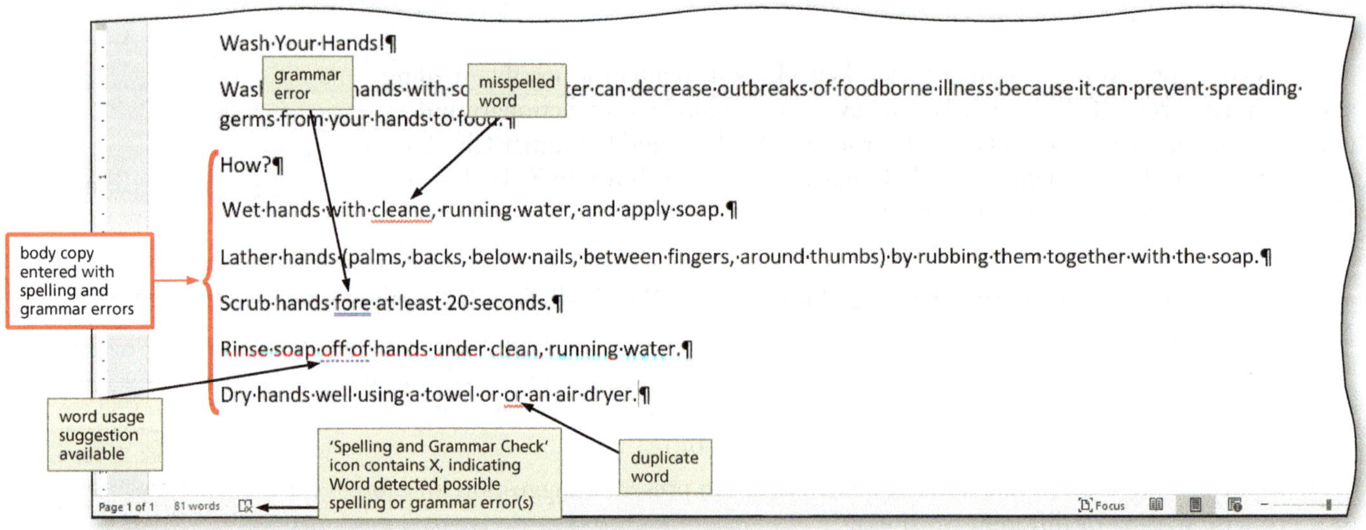

Figure 1–22

To Check Spelling and Grammar as You Work in a Document

Although you can check an entire document for spelling and grammar errors at once, you also can check flagged errors as they appear on the screen while you work in a document. The following steps correct the spelling and grammar errors entered in the previous steps. **Why?** These steps illustrate Word's features that check spelling and grammar as you type. If you are completing this project on a computer or device, your flyer may contain additional or different flagged words, depending on the accuracy of your typing. If your screen does not flag the text shown here, correct the errors without performing these steps.

1

- Right-click the word flagged with a red wavy underline (cleane, in this case) to display a shortcut menu that presents a list of suggested spelling corrections for the flagged word (Figure 1–23).

Q&A **What if, when I right-click the misspelled word, my desired correction is not in the list on the shortcut menu?**
You can click outside the shortcut menu to close the shortcut menu and then retype the correct word.

What if a flagged word actually is, for example, a proper name and spelled correctly?
Click Ignore All on the shortcut menu to instruct Word not to flag future occurrences of the same word in this document. Or, click 'Add to Dictionary' to add it to Word's dictionary so that it is not flagged in the future.

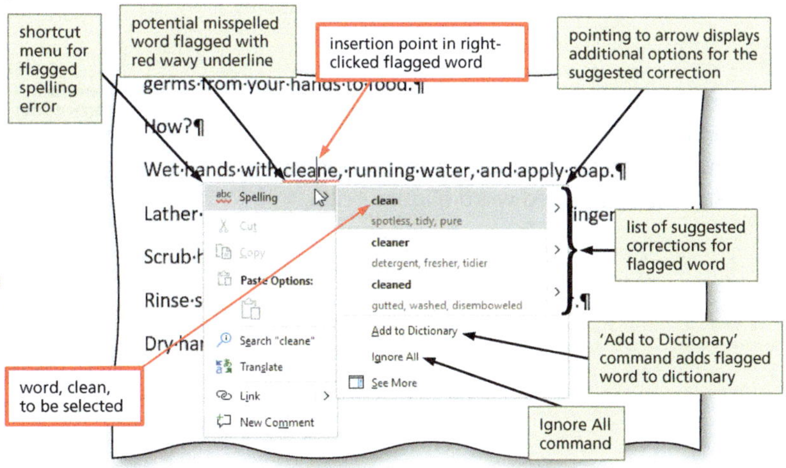

Figure 1–23

2

- Click the desired correction (clean, in this case) on the shortcut menu to replace the flagged misspelled word in the document with a correctly spelled word.

3

- Right-click the text flagged with a blue double underline (fore, in this case) to display a shortcut menu that presents a suggested grammar correction for the flagged word (Figure 1–24).

Q&A **What if flagged text is not a grammar error?**
Click Ignore Once on the shortcut menu to instruct Word to ignore flagged text.

What if a true error is not flagged?
Simply correct the error yourself by adding or deleting the appropriate text.

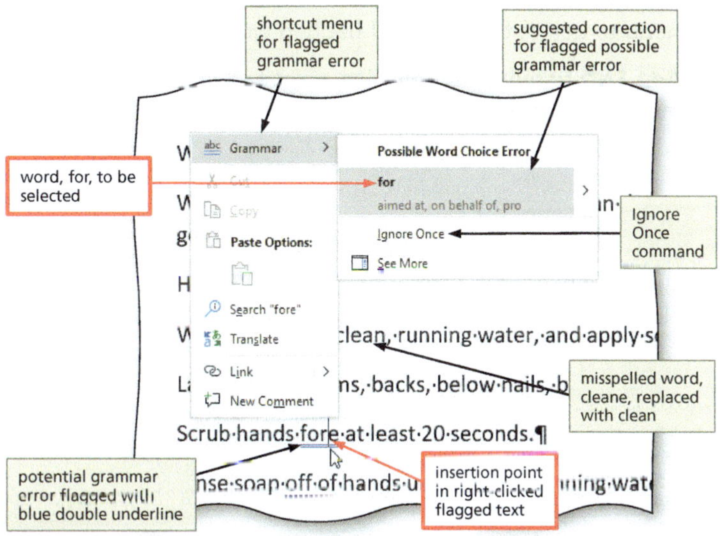

Figure 1–24

4

- Click the desired correction (for, in this case) on the shortcut menu to replace the flagged grammar error in the document with the selected suggestion (shown in Figure 1–27).

5

- Right-click the text flagged with a purple dotted underline (off of, in this case) to display a shortcut menu that presents suggested wording options for the flagged text (Figure 1–25).

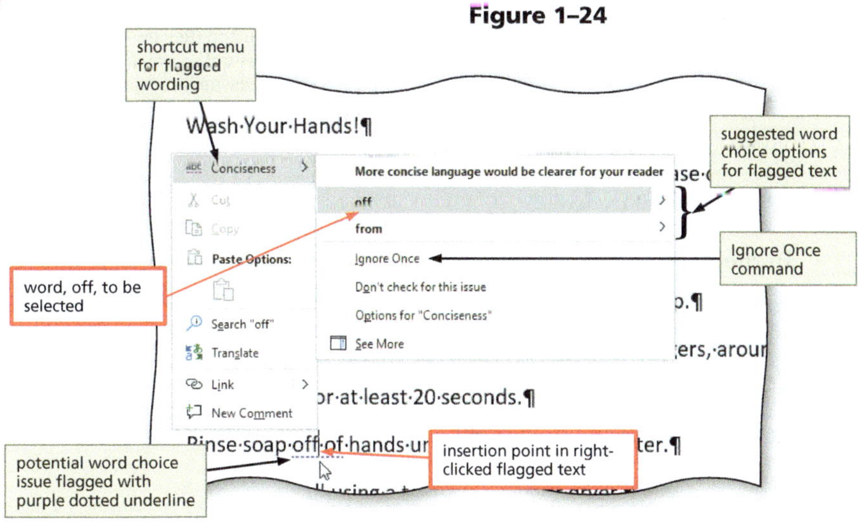

Figure 1–25

6

- Click the desired word choice (off, in this case) on the shortcut menu to replace the flagged wording issue in the document with the selected suggestion.

7

- Right-click the duplicate word flagged with a red wavy underline (or, in this case) to display a shortcut menu that presents a menu option for deleting the repeated word (Figure 1–26).

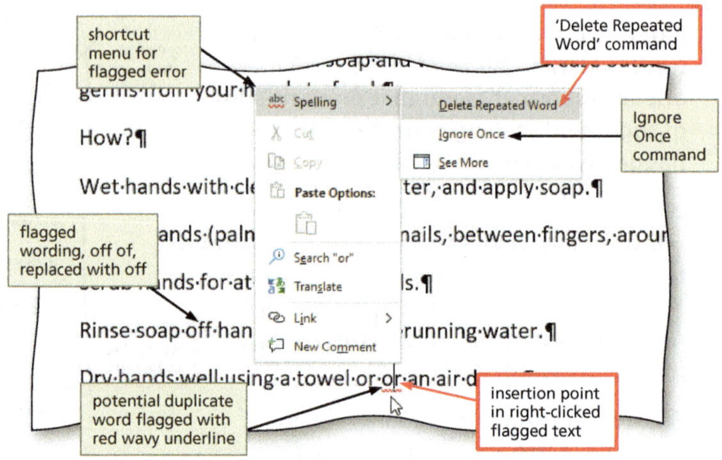

Figure 1–26

8

- Click 'Delete Repeated Word' on the shortcut menu to delete the repeated flagged wording.
- Press END to move the insertion point to the end of the current line (Figure 1–27).

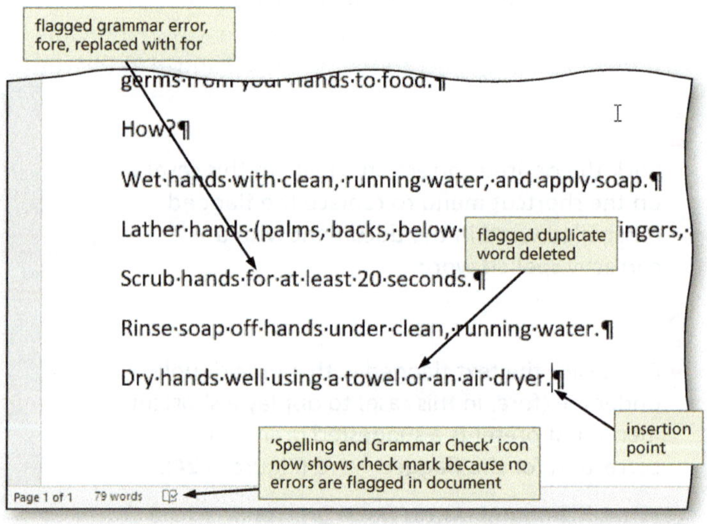

Figure 1–27

Other Ways

1. Click 'Spelling and Grammar Check' icon on status bar, click desired commands in Editor pane, close Editor pane
2. Click 'Editor' button (Review tab | Proofing group), click desired commands in Editor pane, close Editor pane
3. Press F7, click desired commands in Editor pane, close Editor pane

To Insert a Blank Line

In the flyer, the digital picture showing handwashing appears between the two lists in the body copy. You will not insert this picture, however, until after you enter and format all text. **Why?** Although you can format text and insert pictures in any order, for illustration purposes, this module formats all text first before inserting the picture. Thus, you leave a blank line in the document as a placeholder for the picture.

To enter a blank line in a document, press ENTER without typing any text on the line. The following step inserts a blank line in the document.

1

- With the insertion point at the end of the last line of text on the page (shown in Figure 1–27), press ENTER to position the insertion point on a blank line below the last line of text on the page.
- With the insertion point on a blank line, press ENTER to insert a blank line in the document above the insertion point; if necessary, scroll to see the insertion point (Figure 1–28).

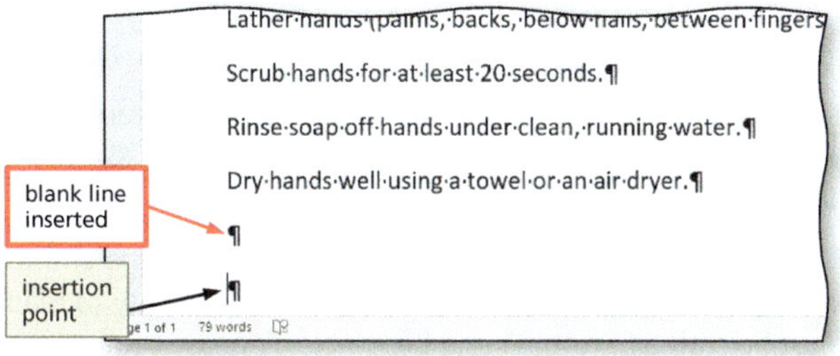

Figure 1–28

To Enter More Text

In the flyer, the text yet to be entered includes the remainder of the body copy, some of which will be formatted as a bulleted list, and the signature line. The following steps enter the remainder of text in the flyer.

1. With the insertion point positioned as shown in Figure 1–28, type `When?` and then press ENTER.
2. Type `After eating, coughing, sneezing, or using a tissue` and then press ENTER.
3. Type `Before, during, and after preparing food` and then press ENTER.
4. Type `After using or assisting someone in the restroom` and then press ENTER.
5. Type `After touching an animal, animal feed, or animal waste` and then press ENTER.
6. Type `After handling dirty equipment or garbage` and then press ENTER.
7. Type the signature line in the flyer (Figure 1–29): `Visit www.foodworkers.com for additional handwashing tips.`

Q&A **Why is the text www.foodworkers.com the color blue and underlined?**
Word recognized the text as a web address and automatically changed its appearance to look and function like a web link. Later in this project, you will change its appearance and function back to regular text.

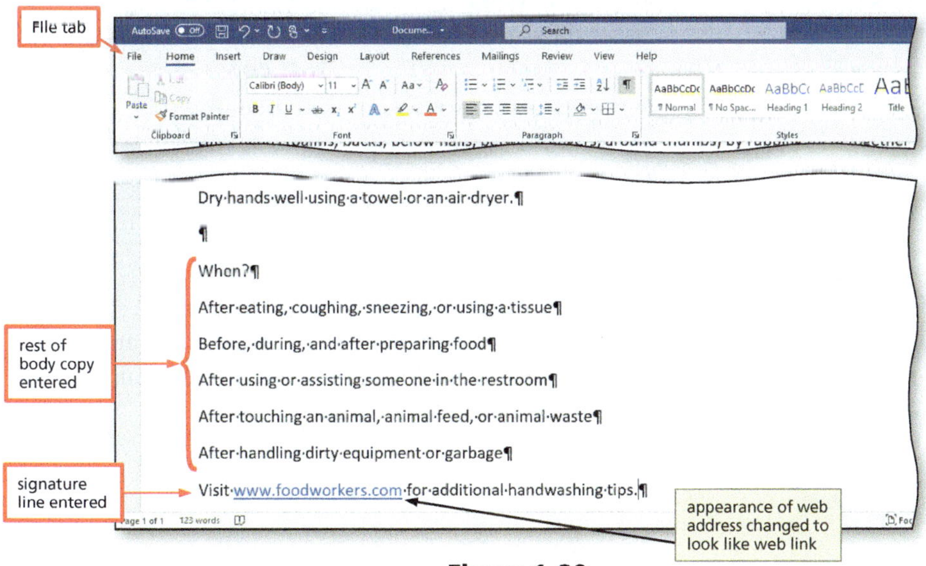

Figure 1–29

BTW
The Ribbon and Screen Resolution
Word may change how the groups and buttons within the groups appear on the ribbon, depending on the computer or mobile device's screen resolution. Thus, your ribbon may look different from the ones in this book if you are using a screen resolution other than 1366 × 768.

Consider This

How should you organize text in a flyer?

The text in a flyer typically is organized into three areas: headline, body copy, and signature line.

- The **headline** is the first line of text on the flyer. It can contain a message (i.e., wash your hands), name the product or service being offered (i.e., blood drive or job fair), or identify the benefit that will be gained (such as a convenience, better performance, greater security, or higher earnings).
- The **body copy** consists of text between the headline and the signature line. This text highlights the key points of the message in as few words as possible. It should be easy to read and follow. While emphasizing the positive, the body copy must be realistic, truthful, and believable. For ease of reading, the body copy often contains a numbered list and/or a bulleted list and a picture or other graphical object.
- The **signature line**, which is the last line of text on the flyer, may contain contact information, reference additional information, or identify a call to action.

BTW

Minimize Wrist Injury

Computer users frequently switch among the keyboard, the mouse, and touch gestures during a word processing session; such switching strains the wrist. To help prevent wrist injury, minimize switching. For instance, if your fingers already are on the keyboard, use keyboard keys to scroll. If your hand already is on the mouse, use the mouse to scroll. If your fingertips already are on the touch screen, use your finger to slide the document to a new location (or use touch gestures to scroll).

Navigating a Document

You view only a portion of a document on the screen through the document window. At some point when you type text or insert objects (such as pictures), Word probably will scroll the top or bottom portion of the document off the screen. Although you cannot see the text and objects once they scroll off the screen, they remain in the document.

You can use touch gestures, the keyboard, or a mouse to scroll to a different location in a document and/or move the insertion point around a document. If you are using a touch screen, simply use your finger to slide the document up or down to display a different location in the document and then tap to move the insertion point to a new location. When you use the keyboard, the insertion point automatically moves when you press the desired keys. Table 1–1 outlines various techniques to navigate a document using the keyboard.

Table 1–1 Moving the Insertion Point with the Keyboard

Insertion Point Direction	Key(s) to Press	Insertion Point Direction	Key(s) to Press
Left one character	LEFT ARROW	Up one paragraph	CTRL+UP ARROW
Right one character	RIGHT ARROW	Down one paragraph	CTRL+DOWN ARROW
Left one word	CTRL+LEFT ARROW	Up one screen	PAGE UP
Right one word	CTRL+RIGHT ARROW	Down one screen	PAGE DOWN
Up one line	UP ARROW	To top of document window	ALT+CTRL+PAGE UP
Down one line	DOWN ARROW	To bottom of document window	ALT+CTRL+PAGE DOWN
To end of line	END	To beginning of document	CTRL+HOME
To beginning of line	HOME	To end of document	CTRL+END

With the mouse, you can use the scroll arrows or the scroll box on the scroll bar to display a different portion of the document in the document window and then click the mouse to move the insertion point to that location. Table 1–2 explains various techniques for using the scroll bar to scroll vertically with the mouse.

Table 1–2 Using the Scroll Bar to Scroll Vertically with the Mouse

Scroll Direction	Mouse Action	Scroll Direction	Mouse Action
Up	Drag the scroll box upward.	Down one screen	Click anywhere below the scroll box on the vertical scroll bar.
Down	Drag the scroll box downward.	Up one line	Click the scroll arrow at the top of the vertical scroll bar.
Up one screen	Click anywhere above the scroll box on the vertical scroll bar.	Down one line	Click the scroll arrow at the bottom of the vertical scroll bar.

To Save a Document for the First Time

While you are creating a document, the computer or mobile device stores it in memory. When you **save** a document, the computer or mobile device places it on a storage medium such as a hard drive, USB flash drive, or online using a cloud storage service such as OneDrive, so that you can retrieve it later. A saved document is referred to as a **file**, which contains a collection of information stored on a computer, such as a document, photo, or song. A **file name** is a unique, descriptive name that identifies the file's content and is assigned to a file when it is saved.

When saving a document, you must decide which storage medium to use:

- If you always work on the same computer and have no need to transport your projects to a different location, then your computer's hard drive will suffice as a storage location. It is a good idea, however, to save a backup copy of your projects on a separate medium in case the file becomes corrupted or the computer's hard drive fails. The documents created in this book are saved to the computer's hard drive.
- If you plan to work on your documents in various locations or on multiple computers or mobile devices, then you should save your documents on a portable medium, such as a USB flash drive. Alternatively, you can save your documents to an online cloud storage service, such as OneDrive.

The following steps save a document in the Documents library on your computer's hard drive. **Why?** You have performed many tasks while creating this project and do not want to risk losing the work completed thus far. Accordingly, you should save the file.

1

- Click File on the ribbon (shown in Figure 1–29) to open Backstage view (Figure 1–30).

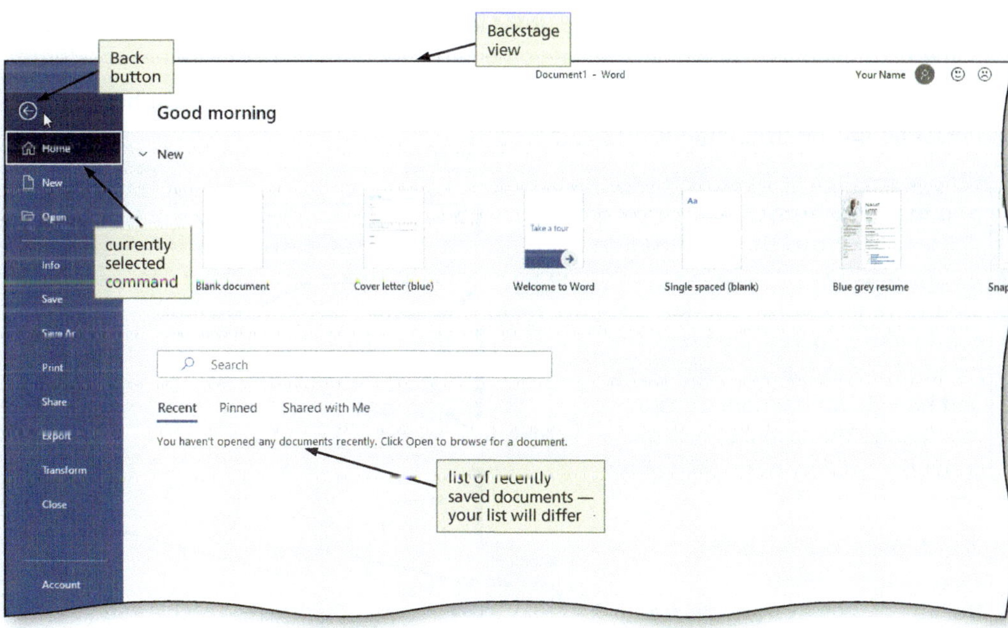

Figure 1–30

Q&A **What is the purpose of the File tab on the ribbon, and what is Backstage view?**
The File tab opens **Backstage view**, which contains a set of commands that enable you to manage documents and options for Word. As you click different commands along the left side of Backstage view, the associated screen is displayed on the right side of Backstage view.

What if I accidentally click the File tab on the ribbon?
Click the Back button in Backstage view to return to the document window.

2

- Click Save As in Backstage view to display the Save As screen.
- Click This PC in the Save As screen to display the default save location on the computer or mobile device (Figure 1–31).

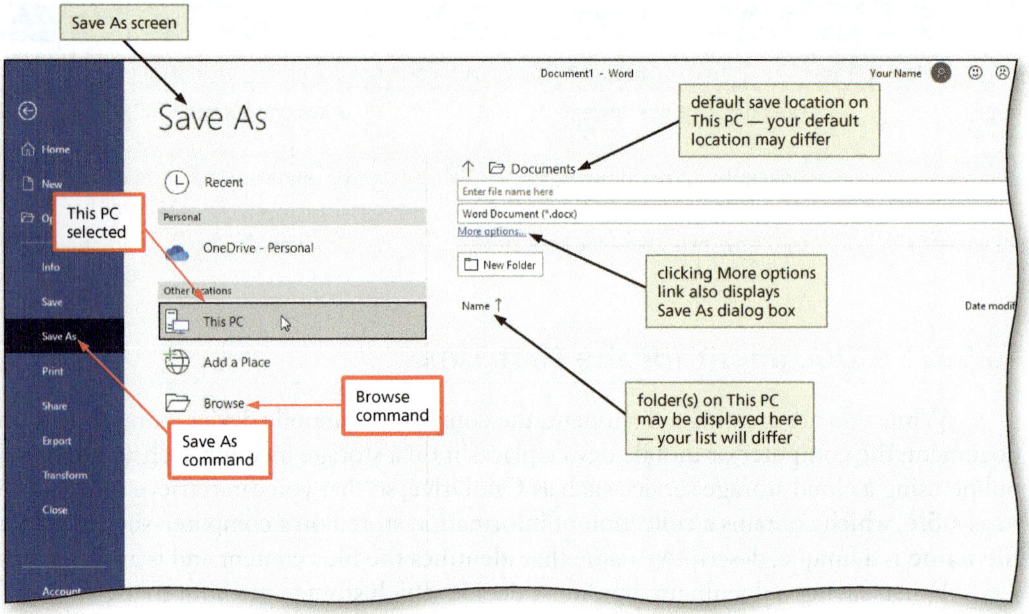

Figure 1–31

Q&A **Can I type the file name below the default save location that displays in the Save As screen?**
If you want to save the file in the default location, you can type the file name in the text box below the default save location and then click the Save button to the right of the default save location. These steps show how to display the Browse dialog box, in case you wanted to change the save location.

What if I wanted to save to OneDrive instead?
You would click OneDrive in the Save As screen.

3

- Click Browse in the Save As screen to display the Save As dialog box.

Q&A **Why does a file name already appear in the File name box in the Save As dialog box?**
Word automatically suggests a file name the first time you save a document. The suggested name usually consists of the first few words contained in the document. Because the suggested file name is selected in the File Name box, you do not need to delete it; as soon as you begin typing, the new file name replaces the selected text.

- Type `SC_WD_1_WashHandsFlyerUnformatted` in the File name text box (Save As dialog box) to specify the file name for the flyer (Figure 1–32).

Q&A **Why is my list of files, folders, and drives arranged and named differently from those shown in the figure?**
Your computer or mobile device's configuration determines how the list of files and folders is displayed and how drives are named. You can change the save location by clicking locations in the Navigation pane.

Do I have to save to the Documents library?
No. You can save to any device or folder. You also can create your own folders by clicking the New folder button shown in Figure 1–32.

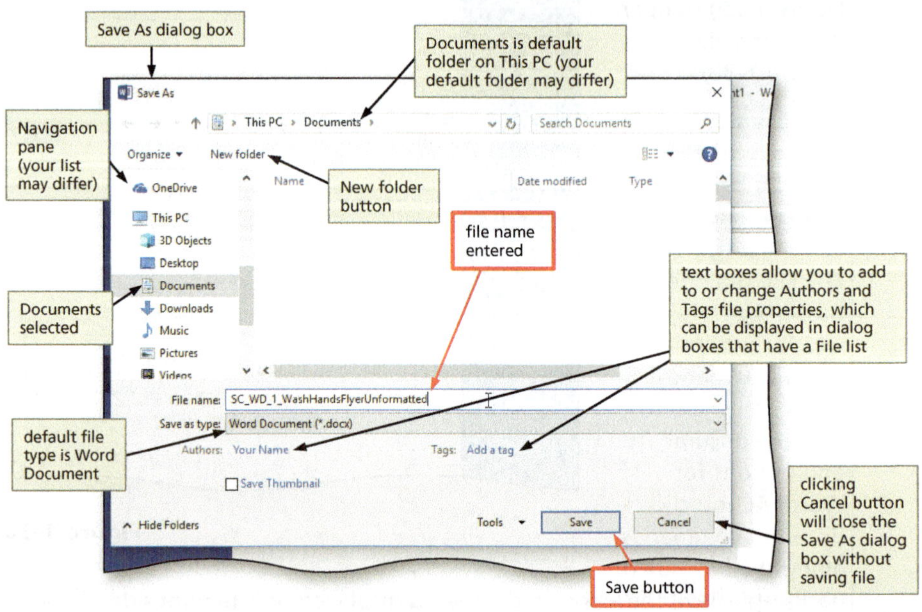

Figure 1–32

Q&A **What characters can I use in a file name?**
The only invalid characters are the backslash (\), slash (/), colon (:), asterisk (*), question mark (?), quotation mark ("), less than symbol (<), greater than symbol (>), and vertical bar (|).

What are all those characters in the file name in this project?
Some companies require certain rules be followed when creating file names; others allow you to choose your own. While you could have used the file name 'Wash Hands Flyer Unformatted' with spaces inserted for readability, the file names in this book do not use spaces and all begin with SC (for Shelly Cashman) and WD (for Word) followed by the module number and then a descriptor of the file contents, so that they work with SAM, if you are using that platform as well.

4

- Click Save to save the flyer with the file name, SC_WD_1_WashHandsFlyerUnformatted, to the default save location (Figure 1–33).

Q&A **How do I know that Word saved the document?**
While Word is saving your file, it briefly displays a message on the status bar indicating the amount of the file saved. When the document appears after saving, the new file name will be displayed in the title bar.

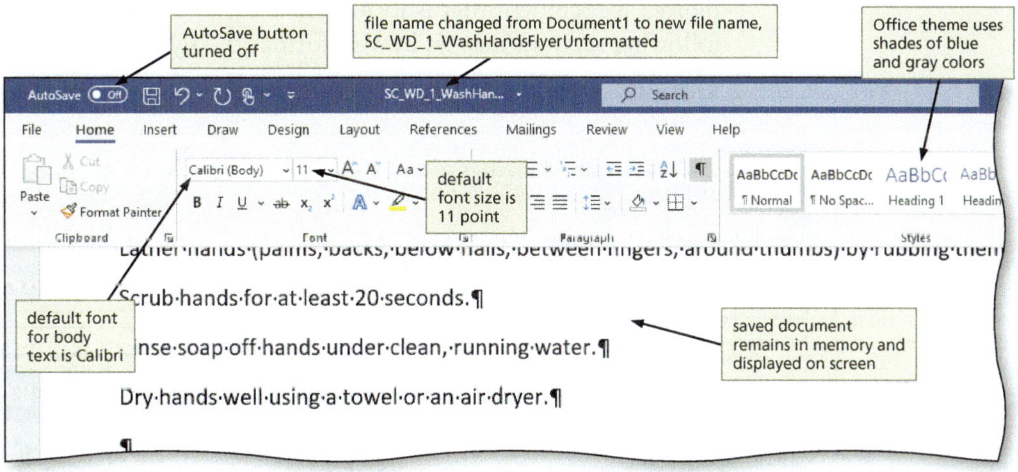

Figure 1–33

Why is the AutoSave button turned off on the title bar?
If you are saving the file on a computer or mobile device, the AutoSave button on the title bar is turned off. If you are saving the file on OneDrive, the AutoSave button is turned on, allowing Word to save the document as you make changes to it. If AutoSave is turned off, you will need to continue saving changes manually.

Other Ways

1. Press F12, type file name (Save As dialog box), navigate to desired save location, click Save

Consider This

How often should you save a document?
It is important to save a document frequently for the following reasons:

- The document in memory might be lost if the computer or mobile device is turned off or you lose electrical power while Word is running.
- If you run out of time before completing a project, you may finish it at a future time without starting over.

BTW
File Type
Depending on your Windows settings, the file type .docx may be displayed on the title bar immediately to the right of the file name after you save the file. The file type .docx identifies the most recent type of Word document.

Formatting Paragraphs and Characters

With the text for the flyer entered, the next step is to **format**, which is the process of changing the appearance of text and objects. A paragraph encompasses the text from the first character in the paragraph up to and including its paragraph mark (¶). **Paragraph formatting** is the process of changing the appearance of a paragraph on-screen and in print. For example, you can center or add bullets to a paragraph. Characters include letters, numbers, punctuation marks, and symbols. **Character formatting** is the process of changing the way characters appear on the screen and in print. You use character formatting to emphasize certain words and improve readability of a document. For example, you can color, italicize, or underline characters. Often, you apply both paragraph and character formatting to the same text. For example, you may center a paragraph (paragraph formatting) and underline some of the characters in the same paragraph (character formatting).

Although you can format paragraphs and characters before you type, many Word users enter text first and then format the existing text. Figure 1–34a shows the flyer in this module before formatting its paragraphs and characters. Figure 1–34b shows the flyer after formatting its paragraphs and characters. As you can see from the two figures, a document that is formatted is easier to read and looks more professional. The following sections discuss how to format the flyer so that it looks like Figure 1–34b.

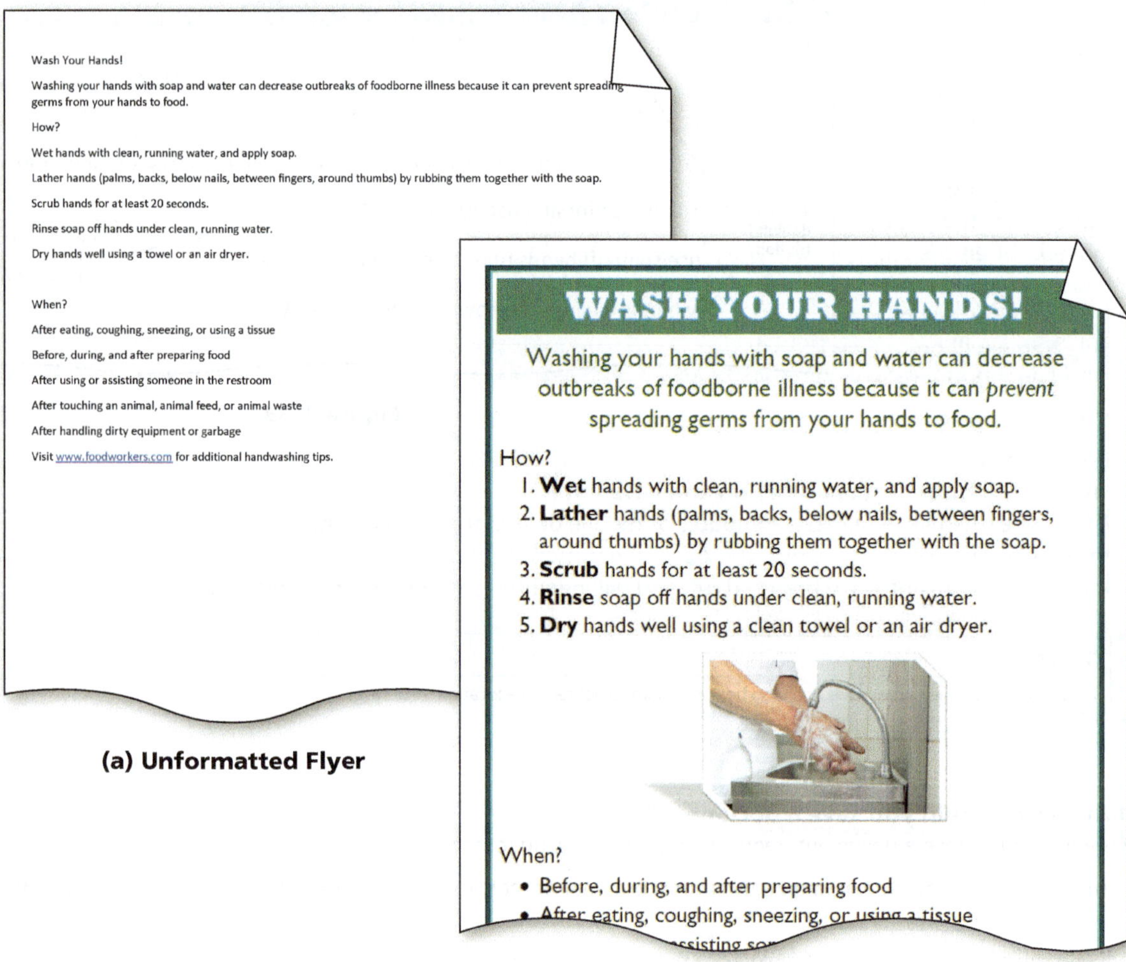

Wash Your Hands!

Washing your hands with soap and water can decrease outbreaks of foodborne illness because it can prevent spreading germs from your hands to food.

How?

Wet hands with clean, running water, and apply soap.

Lather hands (palms, backs, below nails, between fingers, around thumbs) by rubbing them together with the soap.

Scrub hands for at least 20 seconds.

Rinse soap off hands under clean, running water.

Dry hands well using a towel or an air dryer.

When?

After eating, coughing, sneezing, or using a tissue

Before, during, and after preparing food

After using or assisting someone in the restroom

After touching an animal, animal feed, or animal waste

After handling dirty equipment or garbage

Visit www.foodworkers.com for additional handwashing tips.

(a) Unformatted Flyer

WASH YOUR HANDS!

Washing your hands with soap and water can decrease outbreaks of foodborne illness because it can *prevent* spreading germs from your hands to food.

How?

1. **Wet** hands with clean, running water, and apply soap.
2. **Lather** hands (palms, backs, below nails, between fingers, around thumbs) by rubbing them together with the soap.
3. **Scrub** hands for at least 20 seconds.
4. **Rinse** soap off hands under clean, running water.
5. **Dry** hands well using a clean towel or an air dryer.

When?

- Before, during, and after preparing food
- After eating, coughing, sneezing, or using a tissue

ALPA PROD/Shutterstock.com

(b) Formatted Flyer

Figure 1–34

BTW

Microsoft Updates

The material in this book was written using Microsoft 365 and was quality assurance tested before the publication date. As Microsoft continually updates Microsoft 365, your software experience may vary slightly from what is seen in the printed text.

Font, Font Sizes, and Themes

Characters that appear on the screen are a specific shape and size. The **font**, or typeface, defines the appearance and shape of the letters, numbers, and special characters. In Word, the default font usually is Calibri (shown in Figure 1–33). You can leave characters in the default font or change them to a different font. **Font size** specifies the size of the characters, measured in units called points. A single **point**, which is a unit of measure for font size, is about 1/72 of one inch in height. The default font size in Word typically is 11 (shown in Figure 1–33). Thus, a character with a font size of 11 is about 11/72 or a little less than 1/6 of one inch in height. You can increase or decrease the font size of characters in a document. A **style** is a named collection of character and paragraph formats, including font, font size, font styles, font color, and alignment, that are stored together and can be applied to text to format it quickly, such as Heading 1 or Title.

A **document theme** is a coordinated combination of formats for fonts, colors, pictures, and other objects. Word includes a variety of document themes to assist you with coordinating these visual elements in a document. The default theme fonts are Calibri Light for headings and Calibri for body text. By changing the document theme, you quickly can give your document a new look. You also can define your own document themes.

Consider This

How do you know which formats to use in a flyer?

In a flyer, consider the following formatting suggestions.

- **Increase the font size of characters.** Flyers usually are posted on a bulletin board, on a wall, or in a window. Thus, the font size should be as large as possible so that your audience easily can read the flyer. To give the headline more impact, its font size should be larger than the font size of the text in the body copy.
- **Change the font of characters.** Use fonts that are easy to read. Try to use only two different fonts in a flyer; for example, use one for the headline and the other for all other text. Too many fonts can make the flyer visually confusing.
- **Change the paragraph alignment.** The default alignment for paragraphs in a document is **left-aligned**, that is, flush at the left margin of the document with uneven right edges. Consider changing the alignment of some of the paragraphs to add interest and variety to the flyer.
- **Highlight key paragraphs with numbers or bullets.** A numbered paragraph is a paragraph that begins with a number. Use numbered paragraphs (lists) to organize a sequence. A bulleted paragraph is a paragraph that begins with a dot or other symbol. Use bulleted paragraphs to highlight important points in a flyer.
- **Emphasize important words.** To call attention to certain words or lines, you can underline them, italicize them, or bold them. Use these formats sparingly, however, because overuse will minimize their effect and make the flyer look too busy.
- **Use color.** Use colors that complement each other and convey the meaning of the flyer. Vary colors in terms of hue and brightness. Headline colors, for example, can be bold and bright. Signature lines should stand out but less than headlines. Keep in mind that too many colors can detract from the flyer and make it difficult to read.

To Change the Document Theme

The current default document theme is Office, which uses Calibri and Calibri Light as its fonts and shades of grays and blues primarily (shown in the Styles group in Figure 1–33). Calibri and Calibri Light are **sans serif fonts**, which are fonts that do not include short decorative lines at the upper and lower ends of their characters. Other fonts such as Calisto MT are **serif fonts**, which are fonts that have short decorative lines at the upper and lower ends of their characters. The following steps change the document theme to Gallery for the flyer in this module, which uses the Gill Sans MT sans serif font and shades of red, blue, and purple primarily. **Why?** Some organizations specify document themes that all employees should use when creating printed and online documents. The Gallery theme provides colors and fonts appropriate for a flyer.

1

- Press CTRL+HOME to display the top of the flyer in the document window.
- Click Design on the ribbon to display the Design tab.
- Click the Themes button (Design tab | Document Formatting group) to display the Themes gallery (Figure 1–35).

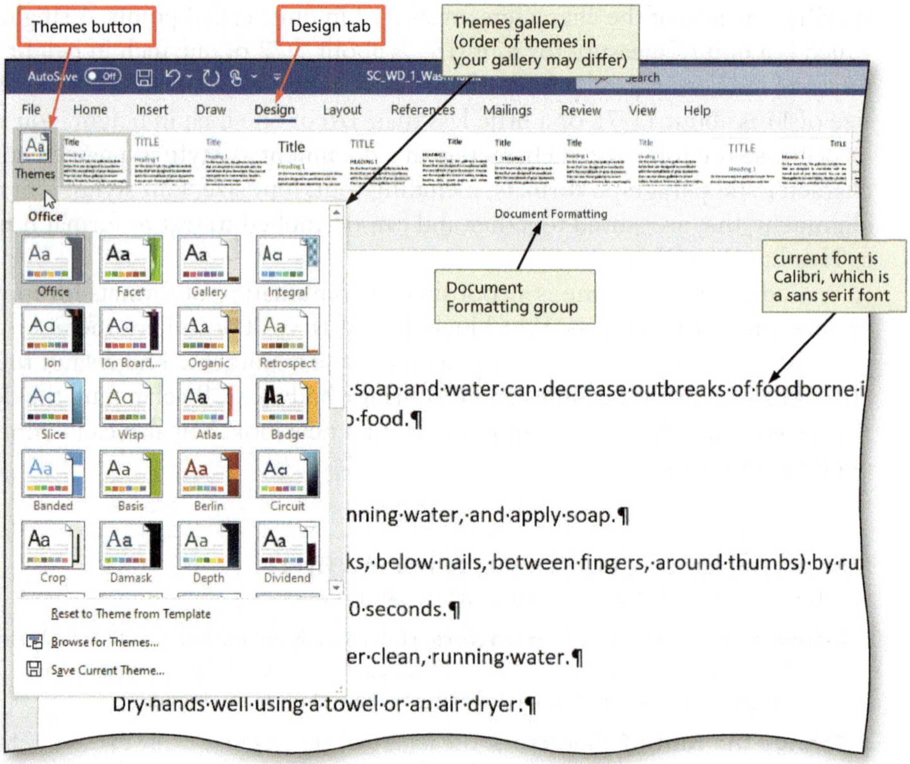

Figure 1–35

2

- Point to Gallery in the Themes gallery to display a Live Preview of that theme applied to the document (Figure 1–36).

Experiment

- Point to various themes in the Themes gallery to display a Live Preview of the various themes applied to the document in the document window.

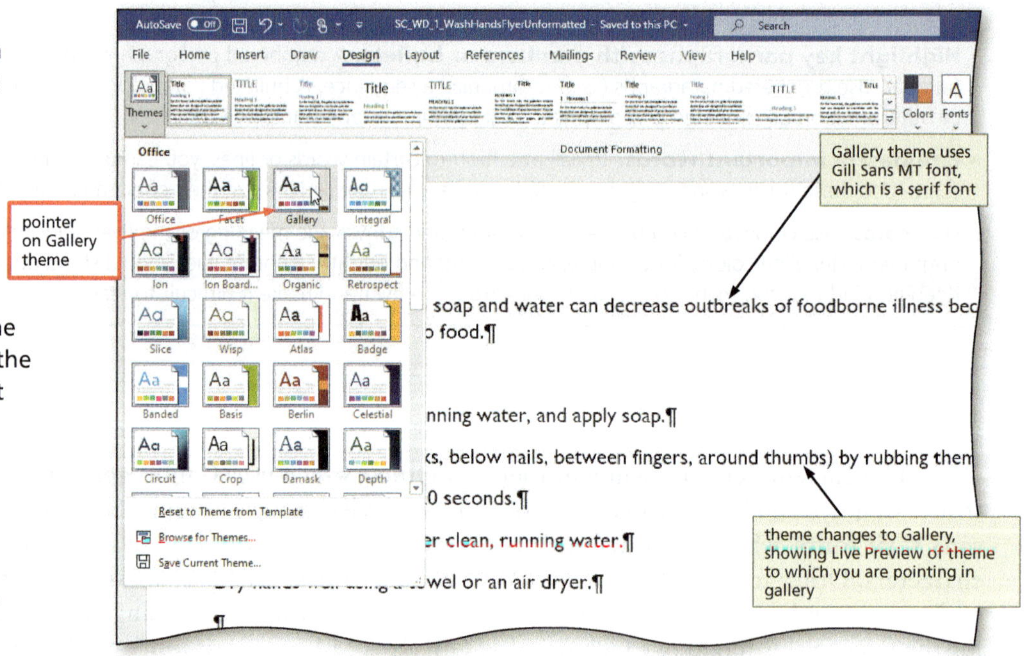

Figure 1–36

Q&A

What is Live Preview?
Recall from the discussion earlier in this module that Live Preview is a feature that allows you to point to a gallery choice and see its effect in the document — without actually selecting the choice.

Can I use Live Preview on a touch screen?
Live Preview may not be available on all touch screens.

3

- Click Gallery in the Themes gallery to change the document theme.

To Center a Paragraph

The headline in the flyer currently is left-aligned. **Why?** Word, by default, left-aligns text, unless you specifically change the alignment. You want the headline to be **centered**, that is, positioned evenly between the left and right margins, or placeholder edges, on the page. Recall that Word considers a single short line of text, such as the one-word headline, a paragraph. Thus, you will center the paragraph containing the headline. The following steps center a paragraph.

1

- Click Home on the ribbon to display the Home tab.
- Click somewhere in the paragraph to be centered (in this case, the headline) to position the insertion point in the paragraph to be centered (Figure 1–37).

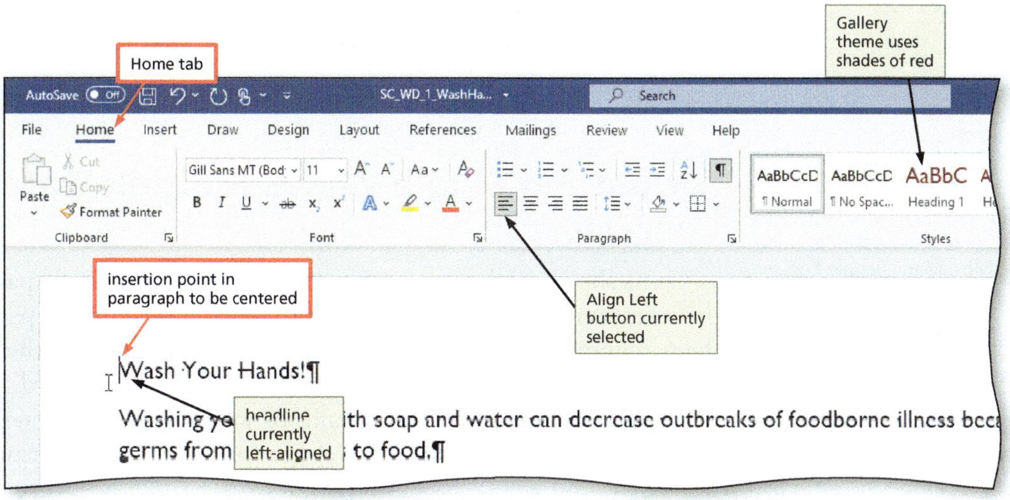

Figure 1–37

2

- Click the Center button (Home tab | Paragraph group) to center the paragraph containing the insertion point (Figure 1–38).

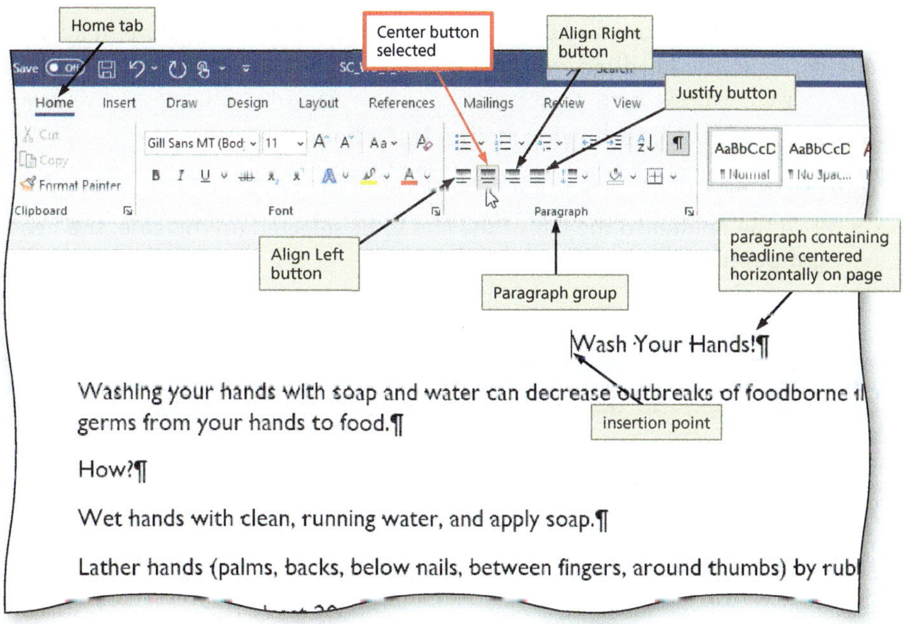

Figure 1–38

Q&A

What if I want to return the paragraph to left-aligned?
You would click the Center button again or click the Align Left button (Home tab | Paragraph group).

What are other ways to align a paragraph?
A **right-aligned** paragraph appears flush at the right margin of the document with uneven left edges. You right-align a paragraph by clicking the Align Right button (Home tab | Paragraph group). A **justified** paragraph means that full lines of text are evenly spaced between both the left and right margins, like the edges of newspaper columns, with extra space placed between words. You justify a paragraph by clicking the Justify button (Home tab | Paragraph group).

Other Ways

1. Right-click paragraph (or if using touch, tap 'Show Context Menu' button on Mini toolbar), click Paragraph on shortcut menu, click Indents and Spacing tab (Paragraph dialog box), click Alignment arrow, click Centered, click OK
2. Click Paragraph Dialog Box Launcher (Home tab or Layout tab | Paragraph group), click Indents and Spacing tab (Paragraph dialog box), click Alignment arrow, click Centered, click OK
3. Press CTRL+E

To Center Another Paragraph

The second paragraph in the flyer (the first paragraph of body copy) also is centered. The following steps center the first paragraph of body copy.

1. Click somewhere in the paragraph to be centered (in this case, the second paragraph on the flyer) to position the insertion point in the paragraph to be formatted.

2. Click the Center button (Home tab | Paragraph group) to center the paragraph containing the insertion point (shown in Figure 1–39).

BTW

Touch Screen
If you are using your finger on a touch screen and are having difficulty completing the steps in this module, consider using a stylus. Many people find it easier to be precise with a stylus than with a finger. In addition, with a stylus you see the pointer. If you still are having trouble completing the steps with a stylus, try using a mouse.

Formatting Single versus Multiple Paragraphs and Characters

As shown in the previous sections, to format a single paragraph, simply position the insertion point in the paragraph to make it the current paragraph and then format the paragraph. Similarly, to format a single word, position the insertion point in the word to make it the current word, and then format the word.

To format multiple paragraphs or words, however, you first must select the paragraphs, lines, or words you want to format and then format the selection.

To Select a Line

The default font size of 11 point is too small for a headline in a flyer. To increase the font size of the characters in the headline, you first must select the line of text containing the headline. **Why?** If you increase the font size of text without selecting any text, Word will increase the font size only of the word containing the insertion point. The following steps select a line.

1

- Move the pointer to the left of the line to be selected (in this case, the headline) until the pointer changes to a right-pointing block arrow (Figure 1–39).

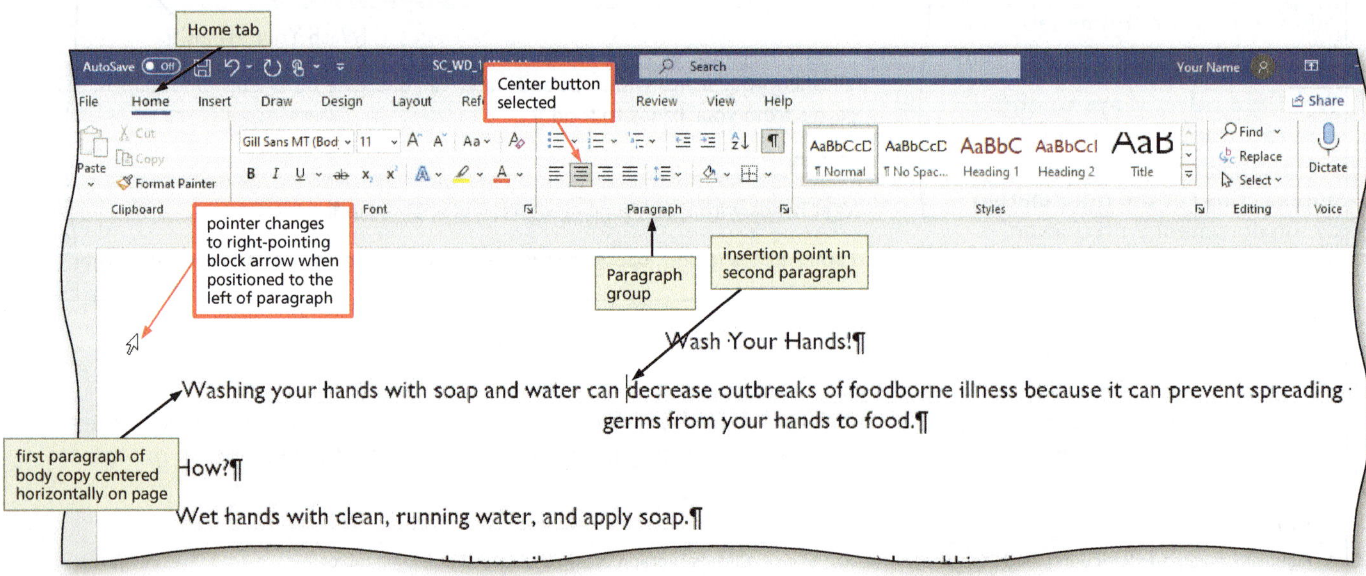

Figure 1–39

2

- While the pointer is a right-pointing block arrow, click the mouse button to select the entire line to the right of the pointer (Figure 1–40).

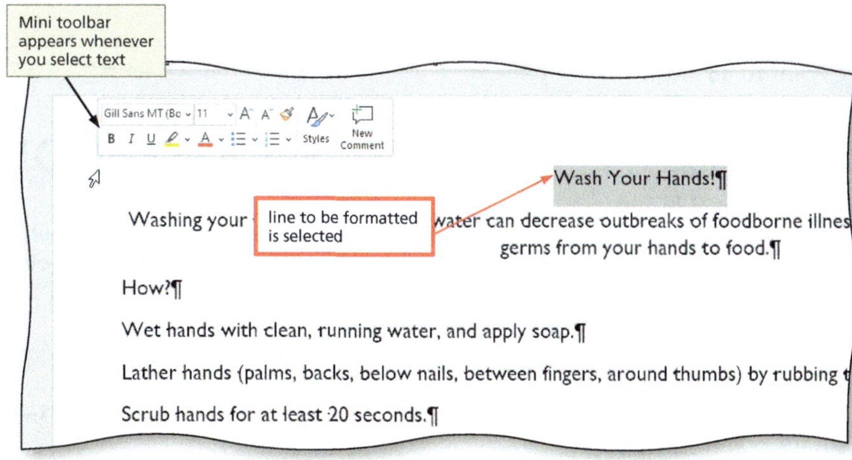

Figure 1–40

Q&A

What if I am using a touch screen?
You would double-tap to the left of the line to be selected to select the line.

Why is the selected text shaded gray?
If your screen normally displays dark letters on a light background, which is the default setting in Word, then selected text is displayed with a light shading color, such as gray, on the dark letters. Note that the selection that appears on the text does not print.

Other Ways

1. Drag pointer through line
2. With insertion point at beginning of desired line, press CTRL+SHIFT+DOWN ARROW

To Change the Font Size of Selected Text

The next step is to increase the font size of the characters in the selected headline. **Why?** You would like the headline to be as large as possible and still fit on a single line, which in this case is 36 point. The following steps increase the font size of the headline from 11 to 36 point.

1

- With the text selected, click the Font Size arrow (Home tab | Font group) to display the Font Size gallery (Figure 1–41).

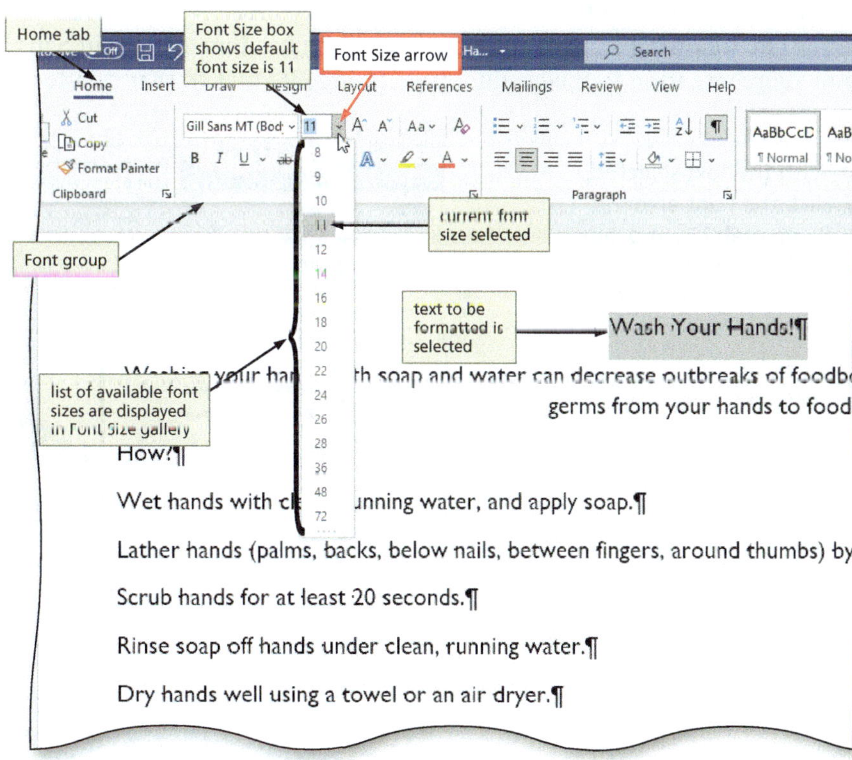

Figure 1–41

Q&A

What is the Font Size arrow?
The Font Size arrow is the arrow to the right of the Font Size box, which is the text box that displays the current font size.

Why are the font sizes in my Font Size gallery different from those in Figure 1–41?
Font sizes may vary depending on the current font and your printer driver.

What happened to the Mini toolbar?
Recall that the Mini toolbar disappears if you do not use it. These steps use the Font Size arrow on the Home tab instead of the Font Size arrow on the Mini toolbar.

2

- Point to 36 in the Font Size gallery to display a Live Preview of the selected text at the selected point size (Figure 1–42).

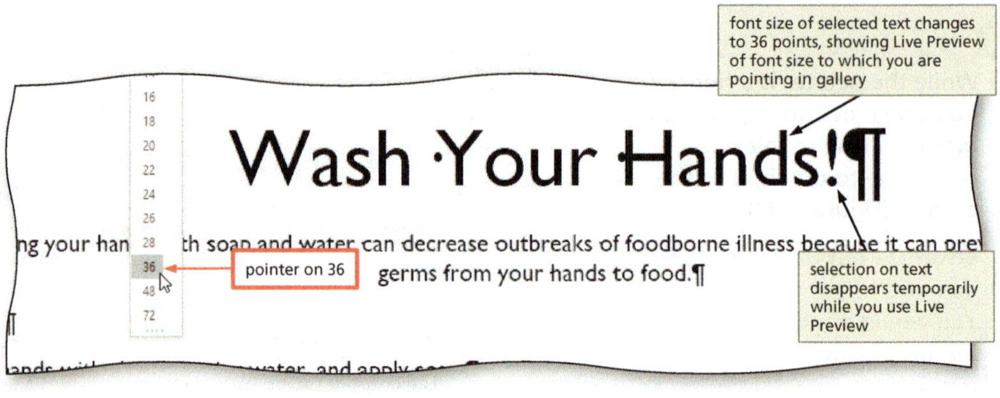

Figure 1–42

Experiment

- Point to various font sizes in the Font Size gallery and watch the font size of the selected text change in the document window.

3

- Click 36 in the Font Size gallery to increase the font size of the selected text.

Other Ways

1. Click Font Size arrow on Mini toolbar, click desired font size in Font Size gallery
2. Right-click selected text (or, if using touch, tap 'Show Context Menu' button on Mini toolbar), click Font on shortcut menu, click Font tab (Font dialog box), select desired font size in Size list, click OK
3. Click Font Dialog Box Launcher (Home tab | Font group), click Font tab (Font dialog box), select desired font size in Size list, click OK
4. Press CTRL+D, click Font tab (Font dialog box), select desired font size in Size list, click OK

To Change the Font of Selected Text

The default font when you install Word is Calibri. The font for characters in this document is Gill Sans MT because earlier you changed the theme to Gallery. Many other fonts are available, however, so that you can add variety to documents.

The following steps change the font of the headline from Gill Sans MT to Rockwell Extra Bold. **Why?** To draw more attention to the headline, you change its font so that it differs from the font of other text in the flyer.

1

- With the text selected, click the Font arrow (Home tab | Font group) to display the Font gallery (Figure 1–43).

Q&A

Will the fonts in my Font gallery be the same as those in Figure 1–43?
Your list of available fonts may differ, depending on the type of printer you are using and other settings.

What if the text no longer is selected?
Follow the steps described earlier to select a line and then perform Step 1.

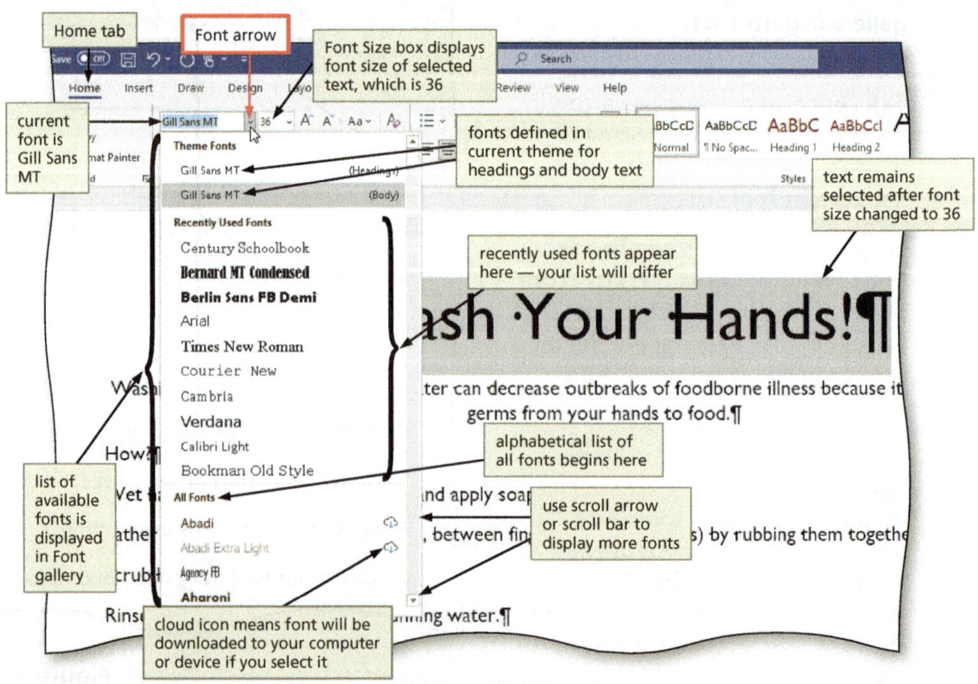

Figure 1–43

2

- If necessary, scroll through the Font gallery to display 'Rockwell Extra Bold' (or a similar font).
- Point to 'Rockwell Extra Bold' (or a similar font) to display a Live Preview of the selected text in the selected font (Figure 1–44).

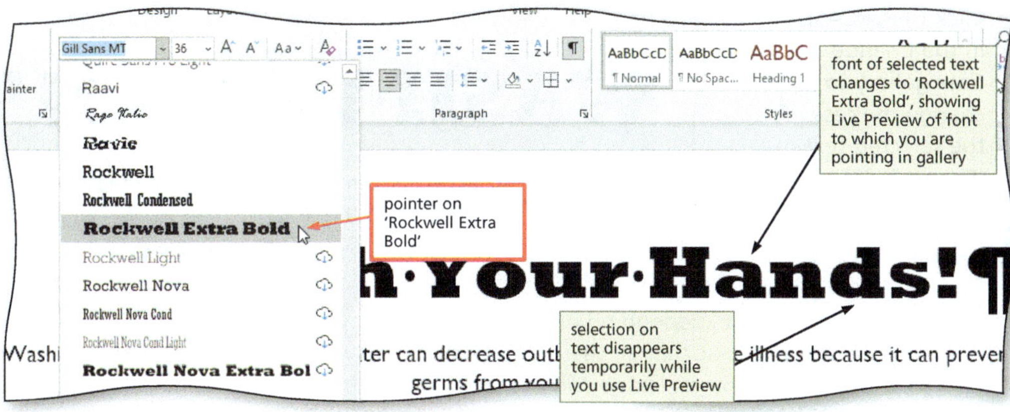

Figure 1–44

Experiment

- Point to various fonts in the Font gallery and watch the font of the selected text change in the document window.

3

- Click 'Rockwell Extra Bold' (or a similar font) in the Font gallery to change the font of the selected text.

Q&A **If the font I want to use appears in the Recently Used Fonts list at the top of the Font gallery, could I click it there instead?**
Yes.

Other Ways

1. Click Font arrow on Mini toolbar, click desired font in Font gallery
2. Right-click selected text (or, if using touch, tap 'Show Context Menu' button on Mini toolbar), click Font on shortcut menu, click Font tab (Font dialog box), select desired font in Font list, click OK
3. Click Font Dialog Box Launcher (Home tab | Font group), click Font tab (Font dialog box), select desired font in Font list, click OK
4. Press CTRL+D, click Font tab (Font dialog box), select desired font in Font list, click OK

To Change the Case of Selected Text

The headline currently shows the first letter in each word capitalized, which sometimes is referred to as initial cap. The following steps change the headline to uppercase. **Why?** To draw more attention to the headline, you would like the entire line of text to be capitalized, or in uppercase letters.

1

- With the text selected, click the Change Case button (Home tab | Font group) to display the Change Case gallery (Figure 1–45).

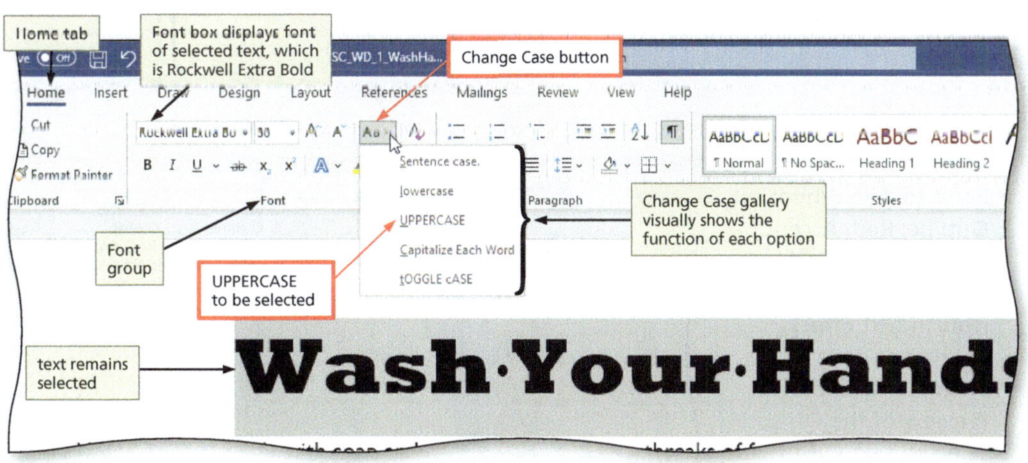

Figure 1–45

2

- Click UPPERCASE in the Change Case gallery to change the case of the selected text (Figure 1–46).

Figure 1–46

Q&A **What if a ruler appears on the screen or the pointer shape changes?**
If you are using a mouse, depending on the position of your pointer and locations you click on the screen, a ruler may appear automatically or the pointer's shape may change. Simply move the mouse and the ruler should disappear and/or the pointer shape will change. If you wanted to show the rulers, you would select the Ruler check box (View tab | Show group). To hide the rulers, deselect the Ruler check box (View tab | Show group).

Other Ways

1. Right-click selected text (or, if using touch, tap 'Show Context Menu' button on Mini toolbar), click Font on shortcut menu, click Font tab (Font dialog box), select All caps in Effects area, click OK
2. Click Font Dialog Box Launcher (Home tab | Font group), click Font tab (Font dialog box), select All caps in Effects area, click OK
3. Press SHIFT+F3 repeatedly until text is desired case

To Apply a Preset Text Effect to Selected Text

Word provides many text effects to add interest and variety to text. The following steps apply a preset text effect to the headline. **Why?** You would like the text in the headline to be even more noticeable.

1

- With the text selected, click the 'Text Effects and Typography' button (Home tab | Font group) to display the Text Effects and Typography gallery (Figure 1–47).

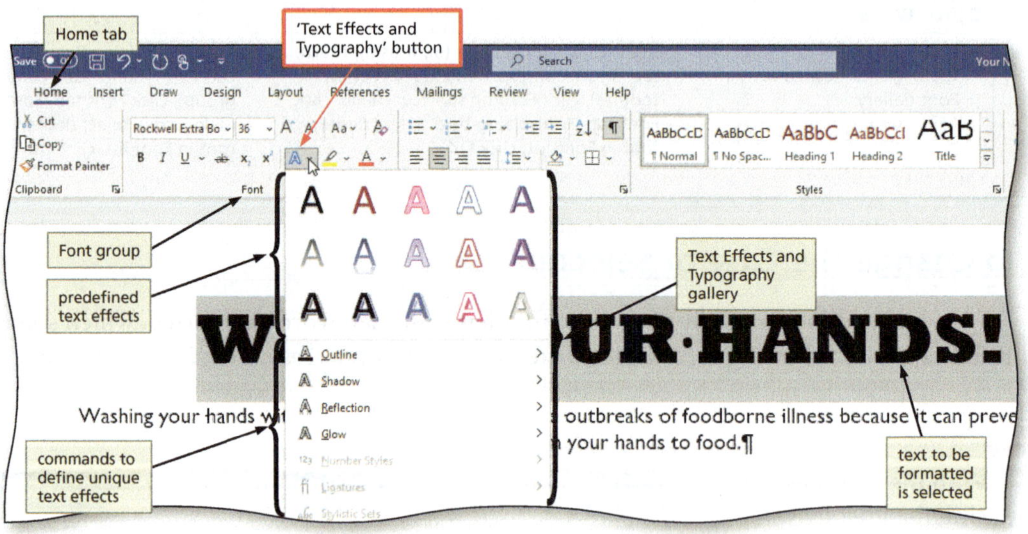

Figure 1–47

2

- Point to 'Fill: White; Outline: Red, Accent color 1; Glow: Red, Accent color 1' (fourth text effect in second row) to display a Live Preview of the selected text with the selected text effect (Figure 1–48).

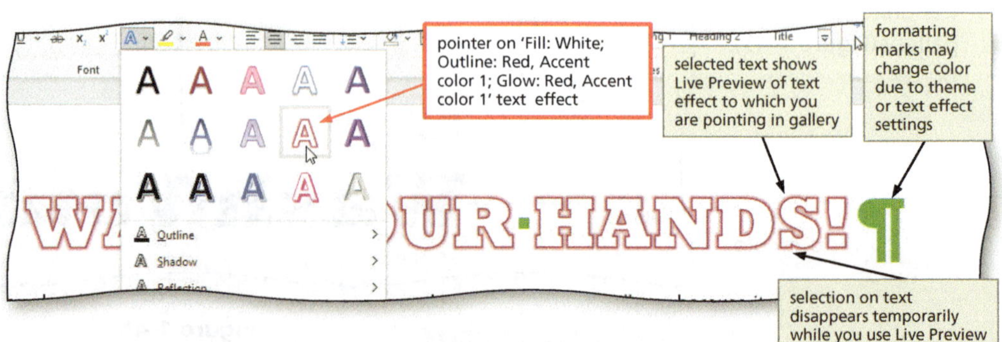

Figure 1–48

Experiment

- Point to various text effects in the Text Effects and Typography gallery and watch the text effects of the selected text change in the document window.

3

- Click 'Fill: White; Outline: Red, Accent color 1; Glow: Red, Accent color 1' to change the text effect of the selected text.

4

- Click anywhere in the document window to remove the selection from the selected text.

Other Ways

1. Right-click selected text (or, if using touch, tap 'Show Context Menu' button on Mini toolbar), click Font on shortcut menu, click Font tab (Font dialog box), click Text Effects button, expand Text Fill or Text Outline section and then select the desired text effect(s) (Format Text Effects dialog box), click OK, click OK
2. Click Font Dialog Box Launcher (Home tab | Font group), click Font tab (Font dialog box), click Text Effects button, expand Text Fill or Text Outline section and then select desired text effect (Format Text Effects dialog box), click OK, click OK

To Shade a Paragraph

Shading is the process of applying a background color or pattern to a page, text, table, or other object. When you shade a paragraph, Word shades the area from the left margin to the right margin of the current paragraph. To shade a paragraph, place the insertion point in the paragraph. To shade any other text, you must first select the text to be shaded. For example, to shade a word, you would select the word before performing these steps.

This flyer uses a shading color for the headline. **Why?** To make the headline of the flyer more eye-catching, you shade it. The following steps shade a paragraph.

1

- Click somewhere in the paragraph to be shaded (in this case, the headline) to position the insertion point in the paragraph to be formatted.
- Click the Shading arrow (Home tab | Paragraph group) to display the Shading gallery (Figure 1–49).

Q&A

What if I click the Shading button by mistake?
Click the Shading arrow and proceed with Step 2. Note that if you are using a touch screen, you may not have a separate Shading button.

Why does my Shading gallery display different colors?
Your theme colors setting may display colors in a different order.

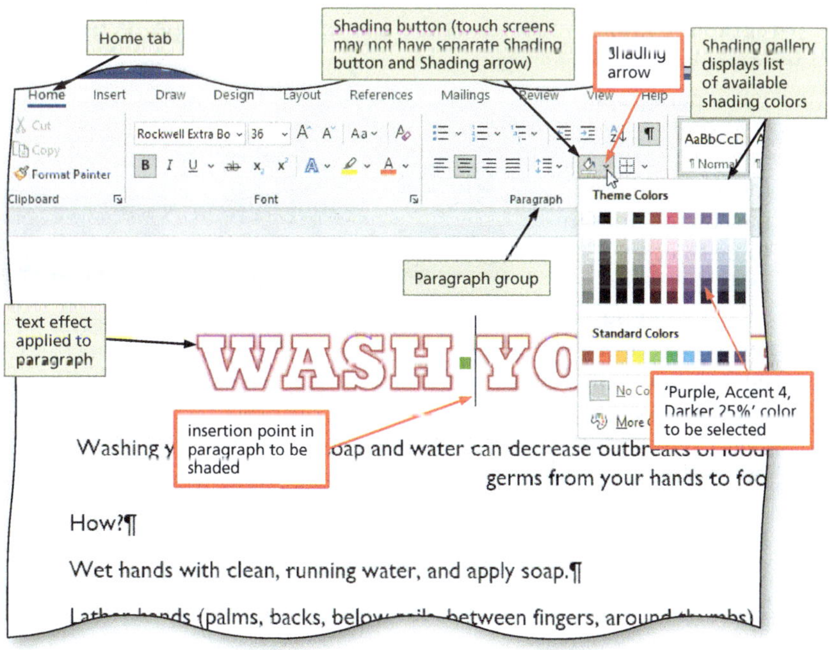

Figure 1–49

Experiment

- Point to various colors in the Shading gallery and watch the shading color of the current paragraph change.

2

- Click 'Purple, Accent 4, Darker 25%' (eighth color in fifth row) to shade the current paragraph (Figure 1–50).

Q&A **What if I apply a dark shading color to dark text?**
When the font color of text is Automatic, the color usually is black. If you select a dark shading color, Word automatically may change the text color to white so that the shaded text is easier to read.

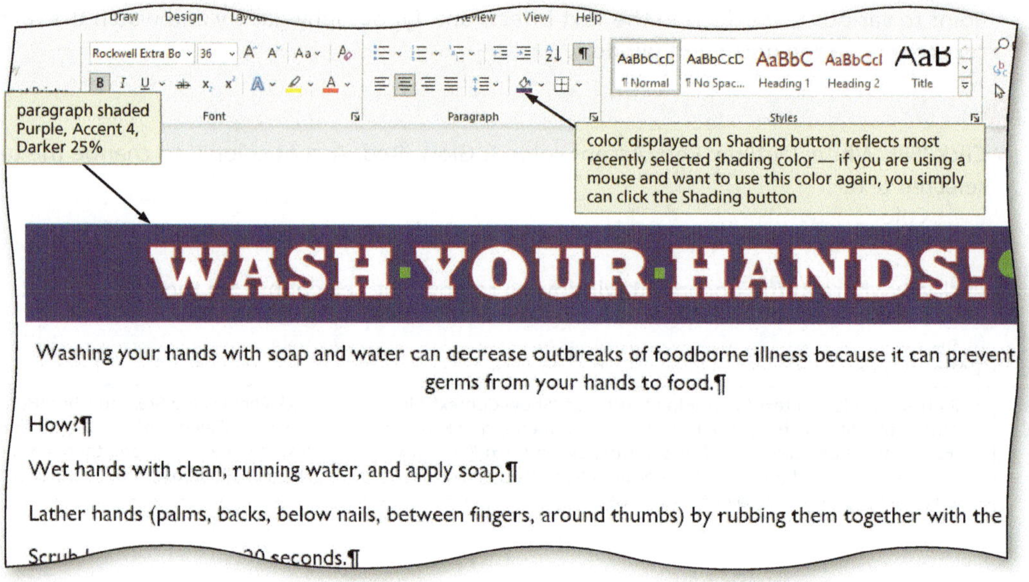

Figure 1–50

Other Ways

1. Click Borders arrow (Home tab | Paragraph group), click 'Borders and Shading', click Shading tab (Borders and Shading dialog box), click Fill arrow, select desired color, click OK

To Select a Paragraph

The next step is to change the color of the paragraph below the headline. To format all the characters in a paragraph, you first must select the text in the paragraph. **Why?** If you change the font color without selecting any text, Word will change the font color only of the word containing the insertion point. The following step selects a paragraph.

1

- Move the pointer into the paragraph to be selected and then triple-click the mouse button to select the entire paragraph (Figure 1–51).

Q&A **What if I am using a touch screen?**
You would triple-tap the paragraph to be selected to select the line.

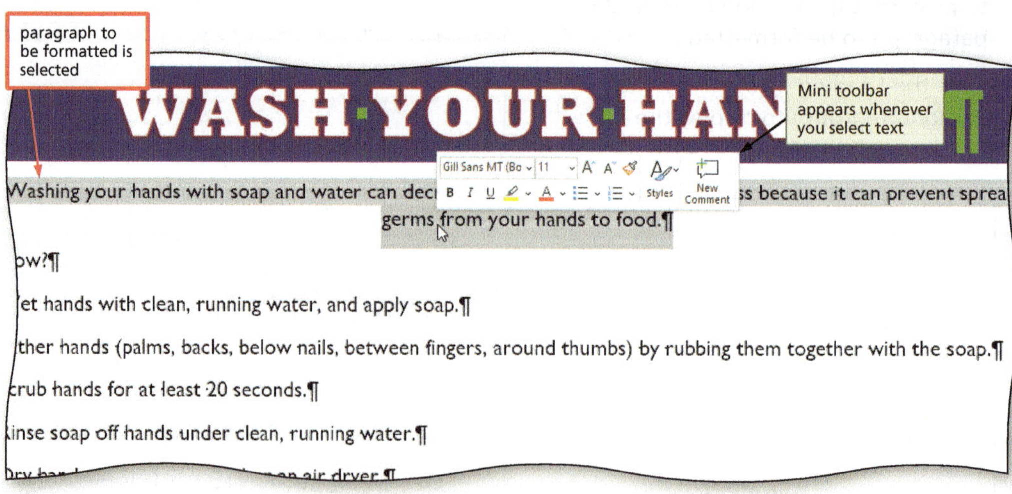

Figure 1–51

Other Ways

1. Move pointer to left of paragraph until pointer changes to right-pointing arrow and then double-click
2. With insertion point at beginning of first character in paragraph, press CTRL+SHIFT+DOWN ARROW until paragraph is selected

To Change the Font Color of Selected Text

The following steps change the color of the selected paragraph. **Why?** To emphasize the paragraph, you change its color.

1

- With the paragraph selected, click the Font Color arrow (Home tab | Font group) to display the Font Color gallery (Figure 1–52).

Q&A **What if I click the Font Color button by mistake?**
Click the Font Color arrow and then proceed with Step 2. Note that you may not have a separate Font Color button if you are using a touch screen.

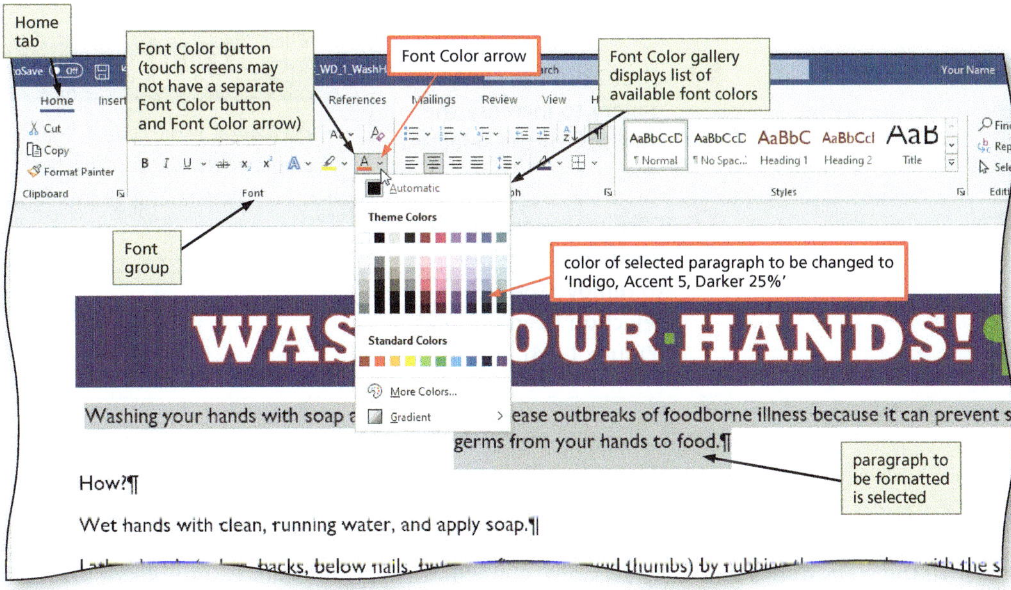

Figure 1–52

Experiment

- If you are using a mouse, point to various colors in the Font Color gallery and watch the color of the current word change.

2

- Click 'Indigo, Accent 5, Darker 25%' (ninth color in fifth row) to change the color of the selected text (Figure 1–53).

Figure 1–53

Q&A **How would I change the text color back to black?**
You would select the text or position the insertion point in the word to format, click the Font Color arrow (Home tab | Font group) again, and then click Automatic in the Font Color gallery.

Other Ways

1. Click Font Color arrow on Mini toolbar, click desired color
2. Right-click selected text (or, if using touch, tap 'Show Context Menu' button on Mini toolbar), click Font on shortcut menu, click Font tab (Font dialog box), click Font color arrow, click desired color, click OK
3. Click Font Dialog Box Launcher (Home tab | Font group), click Font tab (Font dialog box), click Font color arrow, click desired color, click OK

To Change the Font Size of Selected Text

The font size of characters in the currently selected paragraph is 11 point. To make them easier to read from a distance, this flyer uses a 22-point font size for these characters. The following steps change the font size of the selected text.

1. With the text selected, click the Font Size arrow (Home tab | Font group) to display the Font Size gallery.
2. Click 22 in the Font Size gallery to increase the font size of the selected text.
3. Click anywhere in the document window to remove the selection from the text (Figure 1–54).

Figure 1–54

To Change the Zoom Percentage

In the steps in the following sections, you will format multiple paragraphs of text at once that currently cannot all be displayed in the document window at the same time. The next task is to adjust the zoom percentage. **Why?** You want to be able to see all the text to be formatted in the document window. The following step zooms the document.

1.

Experiment

- Repeatedly click the Zoom Out and Zoom In buttons on the status bar and watch the size of the document change in the document window.

Q&A **What if I am using a touch screen?**
Repeatedly pinch (move two fingers together on the screen) and stretch (move two fingers apart on the screen) and watch the size of the document change in the document window.

- Click the Zoom Out or Zoom In button as many times as necessary until the Zoom level button on the status bar displays 120% on its face.
- Scroll if necessary to display all text beginning with the word, How?, to the signature line (Figure 1–55).

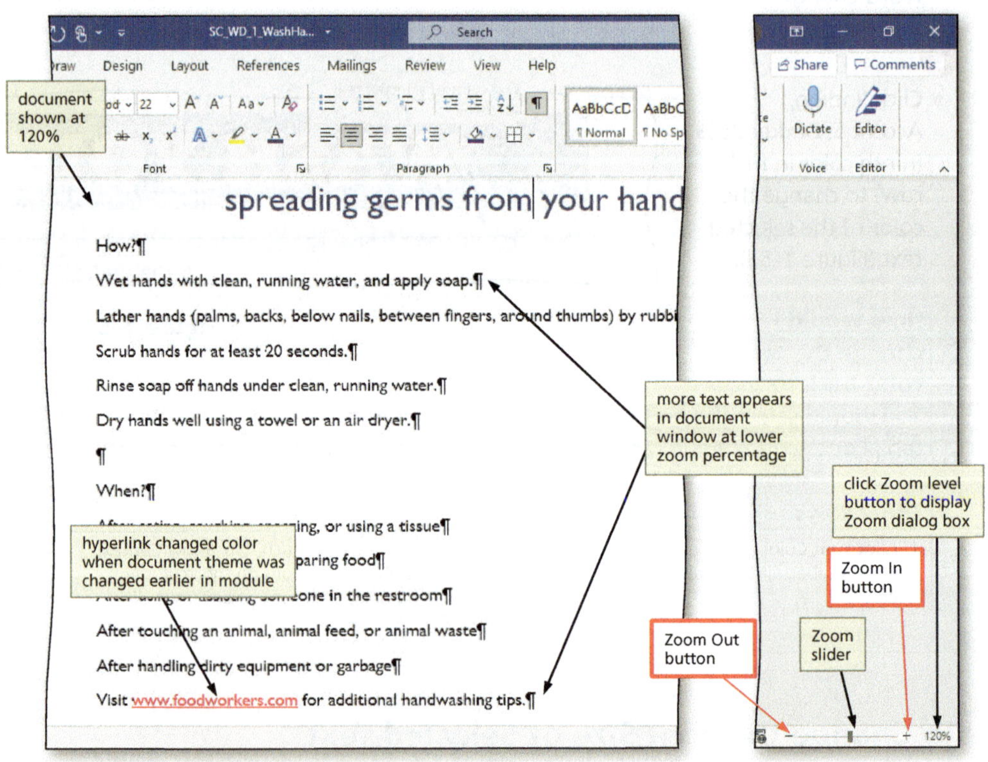

Figure 1–55

Other Ways

1. Drag Zoom slider on status bar
2. Click Zoom level button on status bar, select desired zoom percent or zoom type (Zoom dialog box), click OK
3. Click Zoom button (View tab | Zoom group), select desired zoom percent or zoom type (Zoom dialog box), click OK

To Select Multiple Lines

The next formatting step for the flyer is to increase the font size of the characters from the word, How?, to the last line of body copy above the signature line. **Why?** You want this text to be easier to read from a distance.

To change the font size of the characters in multiple lines, you first must select all the lines to be formatted. The following steps select multiple lines.

1

- Scroll, if necessary, so that all text to be formatted is displayed on the screen.
- Move the pointer to the left of the first paragraph to be selected until the pointer changes to a right-pointing block arrow (Figure 1–56).

Q&A **What if I am using a touch screen?**
You would tap to position the insertion point in the text to select.

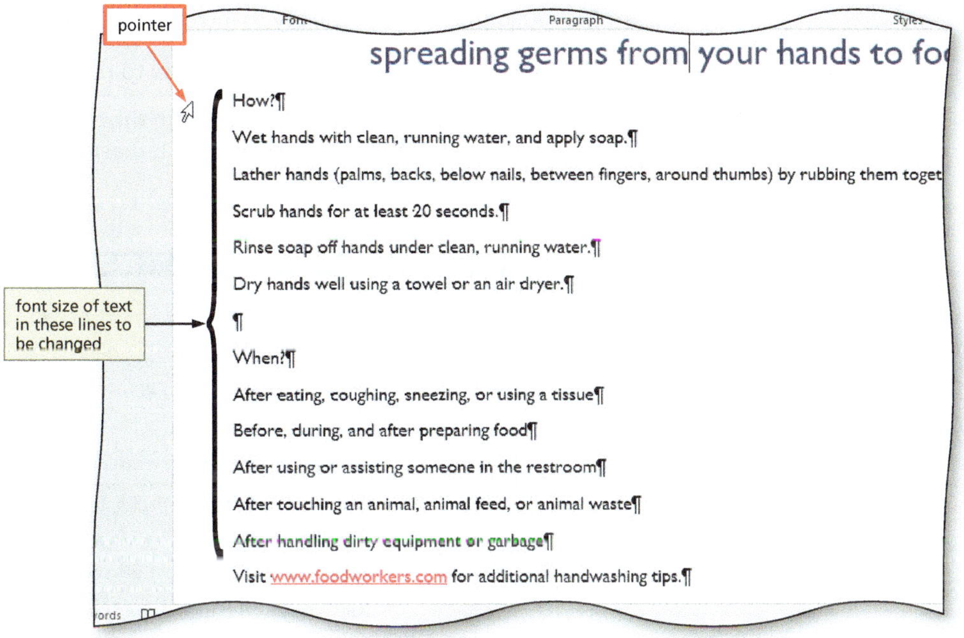

Figure 1–56

2

- While the pointer is a right-pointing block arrow, drag downward to select all lines that will be formatted (Figure 1–57).

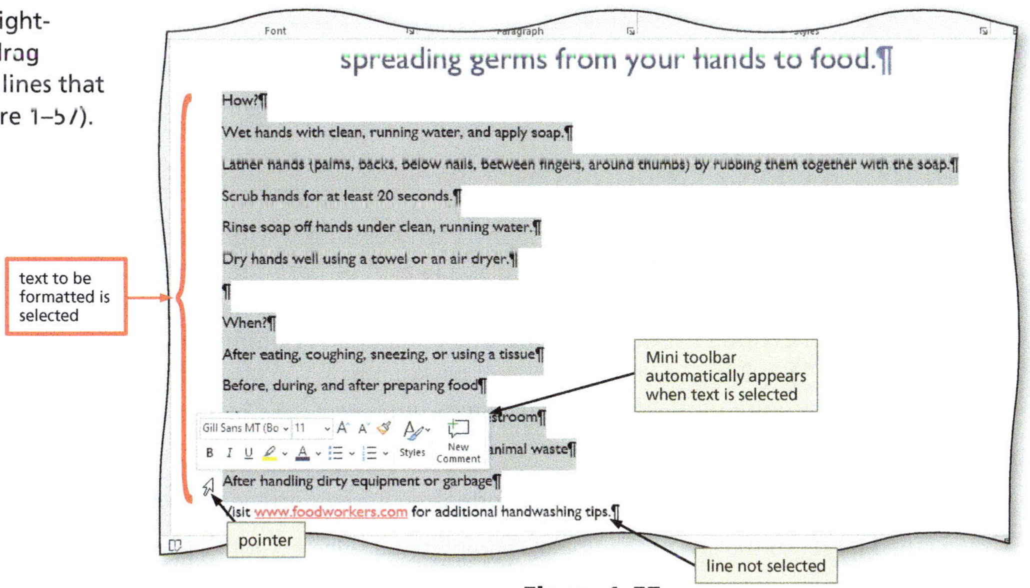

Figure 1–57

Other Ways

1. With insertion point at beginning of desired line, press SHIFT+DOWN ARROW repeatedly until all lines are selected
2. Click first character to be selected and then SHIFT+click last character to be selected.

To Change the Font Size of Selected Text

The characters in the selected text currently are 11 point. To make them easier to read from a distance, this flyer uses a 20-point font size for these characters. The following steps change the font size of the selected text.

1 With the text selected, click the Font Size arrow (Home tab | Font group) to display the Font Size gallery.

2 Click 20 in the Font Size gallery to increase the font size of the selected text (Figure 1–58).

3 Click anywhere in the document window to remove the selection from the text.

Q&A **How do I see the format for the text that scrolled off the screen?**
Use one of the techniques described in Table 1–1 or Table 1–2 earlier in this module to scroll through the document.

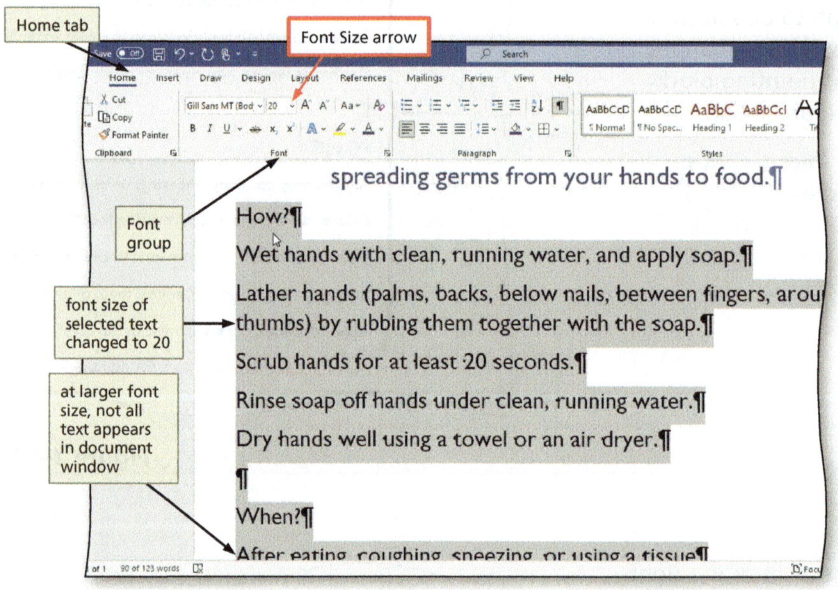

Figure 1–58

To Number a List of Paragraphs

A **numbered list** is a series of paragraphs, each beginning with a sequential number that may or may not be followed by a separator character, such as a period or parenthesis. The next step is to format the five paragraphs that describe the procedure of how to wash your hands as a numbered list.

To format an existing list of paragraphs in a document as a numbered list, you first must select all the lines in the paragraphs. **Why?** If you do not select all paragraphs, Word will place a number only in the paragraph containing the insertion point. The following steps number a list of paragraphs.

1

- If necessary, scroll to position the text to be formatted in the document window.
- Move the pointer to the left of the first paragraph to be selected until the pointer changes to a right-pointing block arrow.

- Drag downward until all paragraphs that will be formatted as a numbered list are selected (Figure 1–59).

Q&A **What if I am using a touch screen?**
Tap to position the insertion point in the text to select and then drag the selection handle(s) as necessary to select the text that will be formatted. When working on a touch screen, a **selection handle** is a small circle that appears below the insertion point as you drag with a fingertip to select text.

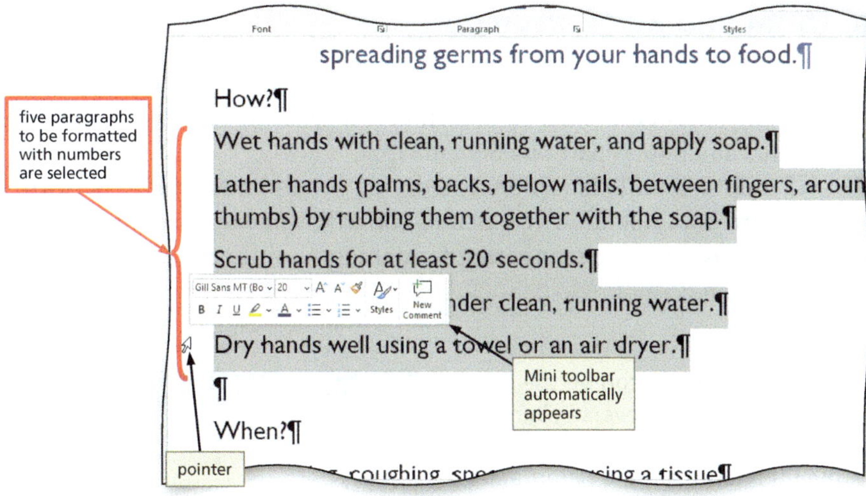

Figure 1–59

2

- Click the Numbering button (Home tab | Paragraph group) to place a number followed by a period at the beginning of each selected paragraph (Figure 1–60).

Q&A **Why does my screen display a Numbering gallery?**
If you are using a touch screen, you may not have a separate Numbering button and Numbering arrow. In this case, select the desired numbering style in the Numbering gallery.

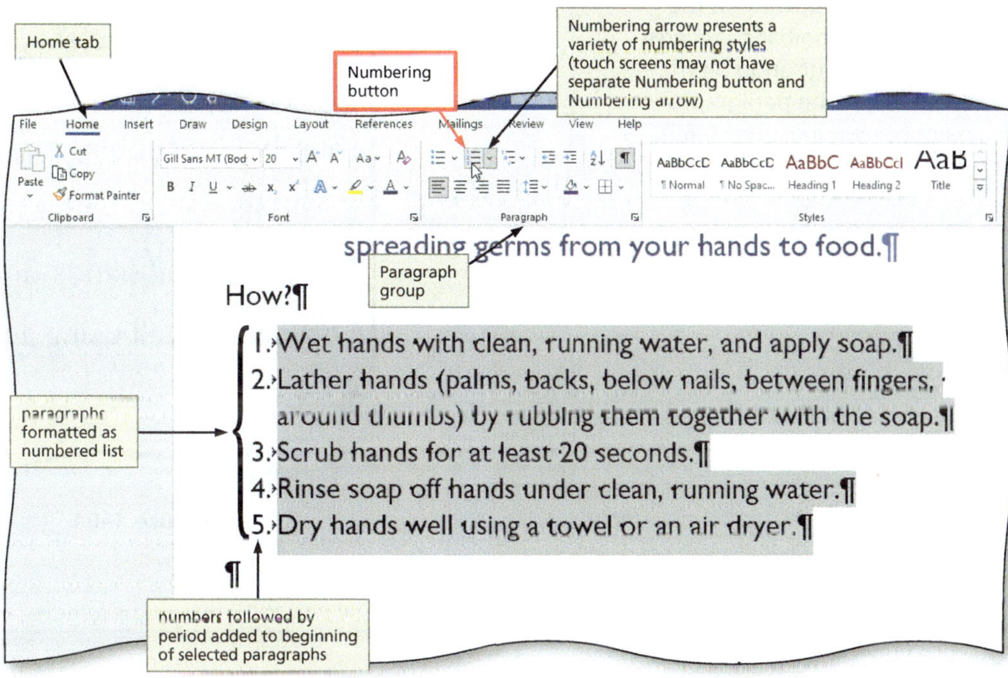

Figure 1–60

What if I accidentally click the Numbering arrow?
Press ESC to remove the Numbering gallery from the screen and then repeat Step 2.

How do I remove numbering from a list or paragraph?
Select the list or paragraph and then click the Numbering button again, or click the Numbering arrow and then click None in the Numbering Library.

Other Ways

1. Click Numbering button on Mini toolbar

To Undo and Redo an Action

Word provides a means of canceling your recent command(s) or action(s). For example, if you format text incorrectly, you can undo the format and try it again. When you point to the Undo button, Word displays the action you can undo as part of a ScreenTip.

If, after you undo an action, you decide you did not want to perform the undo, you can redo the undone action. Word does not allow you to undo or redo some actions, such as saving or printing a document. The following steps undo the numbering format just applied and then redo the numbering format. **Why?** These steps illustrate the undo and redo actions.

1

- Click the Undo button on the Quick Access Toolbar to reverse your most recent action (in this case, remove the numbers from the paragraphs) (Figure 1–61).

2

- Click the Redo button on the Quick Access Toolbar to reverse your most recent undo (in this case, number the paragraphs again) (shown in Figure 1–60).

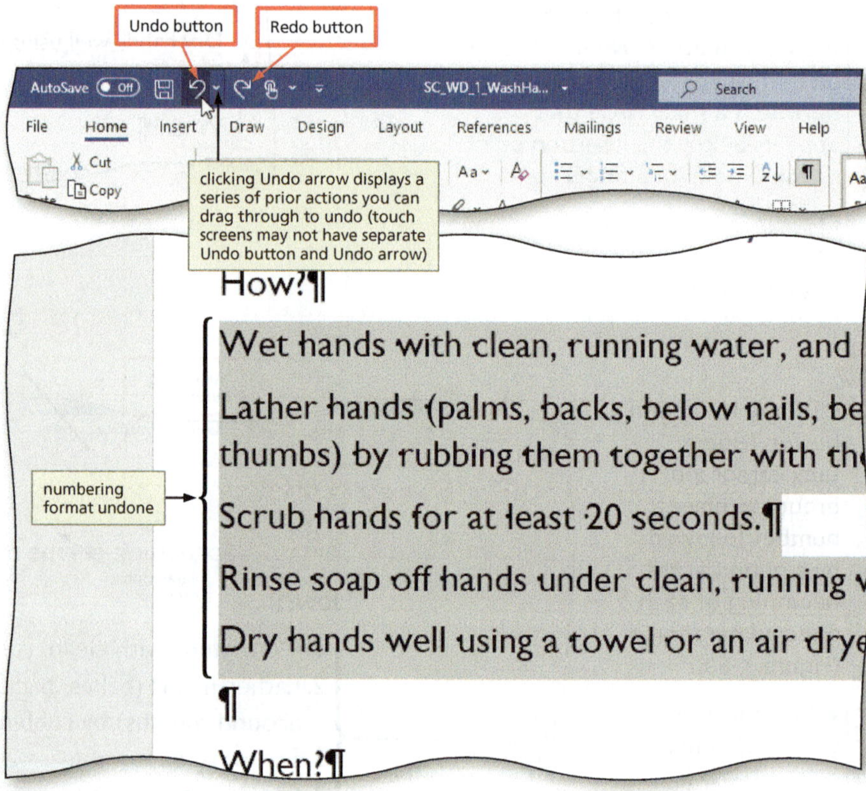

Figure 1–61

Other Ways

1. Press CTRL+Z to undo; press CTRL+Y to redo

To Bullet a List of Paragraphs

A **bulleted list** is a series of paragraphs, each beginning with a bullet character, such as a dot or check mark. The next step is to format the five paragraphs that describe when to wash your hands as a bulleted list.

To format a list of paragraphs as a bulleted list, you first must select all the lines in the paragraphs. **Why?** If you do not select all paragraphs, Word will place a bullet only in the paragraph containing the insertion point. The following steps bullet a list of paragraphs.

1

- If necessary, scroll to position the text to be formatted in the document window.
- Move the pointer to the left of the first paragraph to be selected until the pointer changes to a right-pointing block arrow.

- Drag downward until all paragraphs that will be formatted with a bullet character are selected (Figure 1–62).

Q&A **What if I am using a touch screen?**
Tap to position the insertion point in the text to select and then drag the selection handle(s) as necessary to select the text that will be formatted.

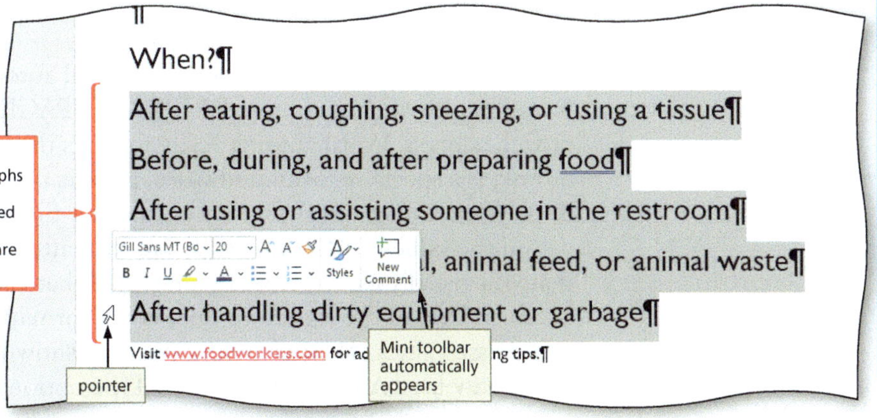

Figure 1–62

2

- Click the Bullets button (Home tab | Paragraph group) to place a bullet character at the beginning of each selected paragraph.
- Click anywhere in the document window to remove the selection from the text (Figure 1–63).

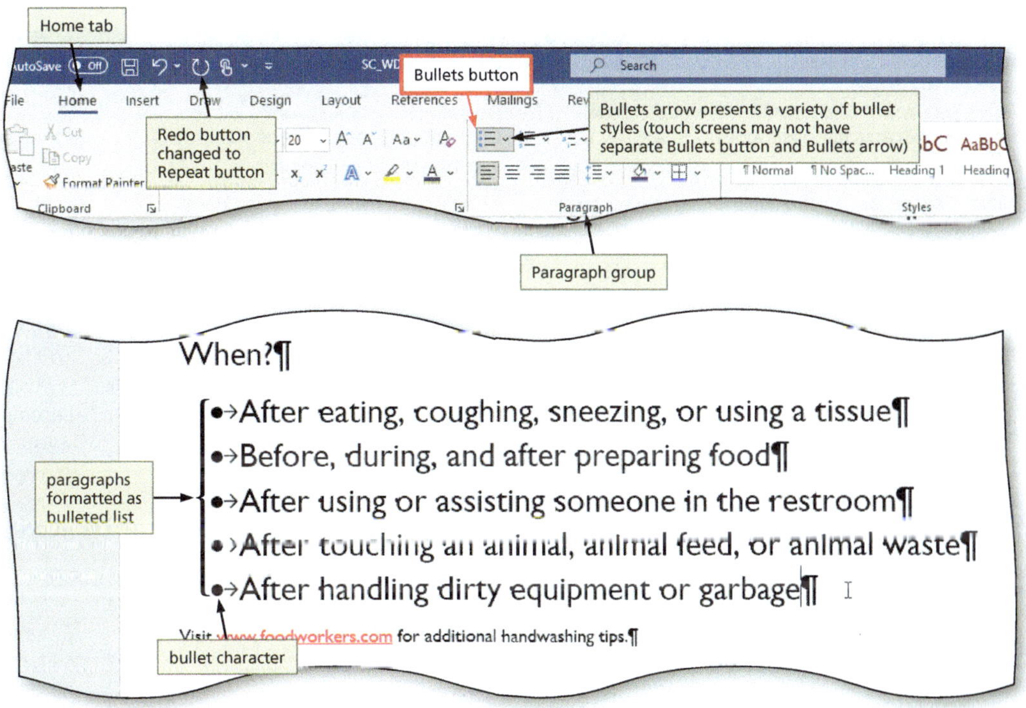

Figure 1–63

Q&A **Why does my screen display a Bullets gallery?**
If you are using a touch screen, you may not have a separate Bullets button and Bullets arrow. In this case, select the desired bullet style in the Bullets gallery.

What if I accidentally click the Bullets arrow?
Press ESC to remove the Bullets gallery from the screen and then repeat Step 2.

How do I remove bullets from a list or paragraph?
Select the list or paragraph and then click the Bullets button again, or click the Bullets arrow and then click None in the Bullets Library.

Why did the appearance of the Redo button change?
It changed to a Repeat button. When it is a Repeat button, you can click it to repeat your last action. For example, you can select different text and then click the Repeat button to apply (repeat) the bullet format to the selected text.

Other Ways

1. Click Bullets button on Mini toolbar

AutoFormat As You Type

As you type text in a document, Word automatically formats some of it for you. For example, when you press ENTER or SPACEBAR after typing an email address or web address, Word automatically formats the address as a hyperlink. A **hyperlink**, or link, is a specially formatted word, phrase, or object, which, when clicked or tapped, displays a webpage on the Internet, another file, an email window, or another location within the same file. Links usually are formatted in a different color and underlined so that you visually can identify them. Recall that earlier in this module, when you typed a web address in the signature line, Word formatted the text as a hyperlink because you pressed SPACEBAR after typing the text (shown in Figure 1–64). Table 1–3 outlines commonly used AutoFormat As You Type options and their results.

Table 1–3 Commonly Used AutoFormat As You Type Options

Typed Text	AutoFormat As You Type Feature	Example
Quotation marks or apostrophes	Changes straight quotation marks or apostrophes to curly ones	"the" becomes “the”
Text, a space, one hyphen, one or no spaces, text, space	Changes the hyphen to an en dash	ages 20-45 becomes ages 20–45
Text, two hyphens, text, space	Changes the two hyphens to an em dash	Two types--yellow and red becomes Two types—yellow and red
Web or email address followed by SPACEBAR or ENTER	Formats web or email address as a hyperlink	www.cengage.com becomes www.cengage.com
Number followed by a period, hyphen, right parenthesis, or greater than sign and then a space or tab followed by text	Creates a numbered list	1. Word 2. PowerPoint becomes 1. Word 2. PowerPoint
Asterisk, hyphen, or greater than sign and then a space or tab followed by text	Creates a bulleted list	* Home tab * Insert tab becomes • Home tab • Insert tab
Fraction and then a space or hyphen	Condenses the fraction entry so that it consumes one space instead of three	1/2 becomes ½
Ordinal and then a space or hyphen	Makes part of the ordinal a superscript	3rd becomes 3rd

To Remove a Hyperlink

The web address in the signature line of the flyer should be formatted as regular text; that is, it should not be a different color or underlined. **Why?** Hyperlinks are useful only in online documents, and this flyer will be printed instead of distributed electronically. The following steps remove a hyperlink format.

1

- Right-click the hyperlink (in this case, the web address) to display a shortcut menu (or, if using a touch screen, press and hold the hyperlink and then tap the 'Show Context Menu' button on the Mini toolbar) (Figure 1–64).

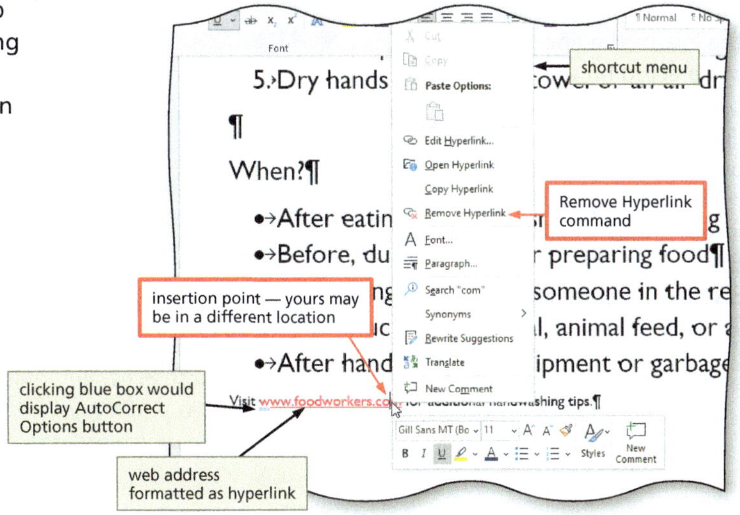

Figure 1–64

2

- Click Remove Hyperlink on the shortcut menu to remove the hyperlink format from the text; if the text remains colored and underlined, change the color to Automatic and remove the underline (Figure 1–65).

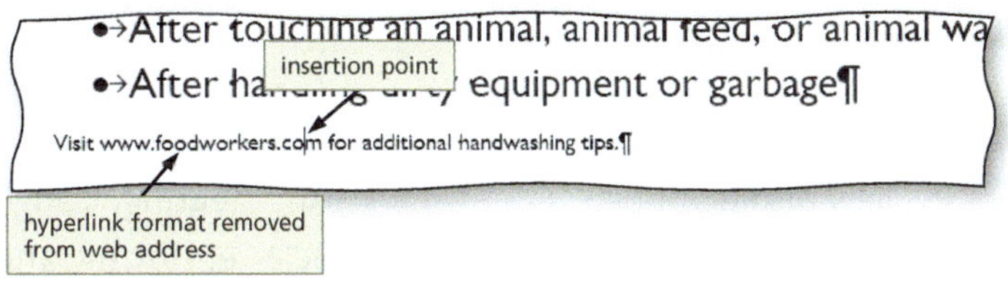

Figure 1–65

Q&A

Could I have used the AutoCorrect Options button instead of the Remove Hyperlink command?

Yes. Alternatively, you could have pointed to the small blue box at the beginning of the hyperlink (if it is visible), clicked the AutoCorrect Options button, and then clicked Undo Hyperlink on the AutoCorrect Options menu.

Other Ways

1. With insertion point in hyperlink, click Link button (Insert tab | Links group), click Remove Link button (Edit Hyperlink dialog box)

To Center Another Paragraph

In the flyer, the signature line is to be centered to match the paragraph alignment of the headline. The following steps center the signature line.

1 Click somewhere in the paragraph to be centered (in this case, the signature line) to position the insertion point in the paragraph to be formatted.

2 Click the Center button (Home tab | Paragraph group) to center the paragraph containing the insertion point (shown in Figure 1–66).

To Use the Mini Toolbar to Format Text

Recall that the Mini toolbar automatically appears based on certain tasks you perform. **Why?** Word places commonly used buttons and boxes on the Mini toolbar for your convenience. If you do not use the Mini toolbar, it disappears from the screen. All commands on the Mini toolbar also exist on the ribbon.

The following steps use the Mini toolbar to change the font size and color of text in the signature line of the flyer.

1

- Move the pointer to the left of the line to be selected (in this case, the signature line) until the pointer changes to a right-pointing block arrow and then click to select the line and display the Mini toolbar (Figure 1–66).

Figure 1–66

Q&A **What if I am using a touch screen?**
Double-tap to the left of the line to be selected to select the line and then tap the selection to display the Mini toolbar. If you are using a touch screen, the buttons and boxes on the Mini toolbar differ. For example, it contains a 'Show Context Menu' button at the far-right edge, which you tap to display a shortcut menu.

2

- Click the Font Size arrow on the Mini toolbar to display the Font Size gallery.
- Point to 18 in the Font Size gallery to display a Live Preview of the selected font size (Figure 1–67).

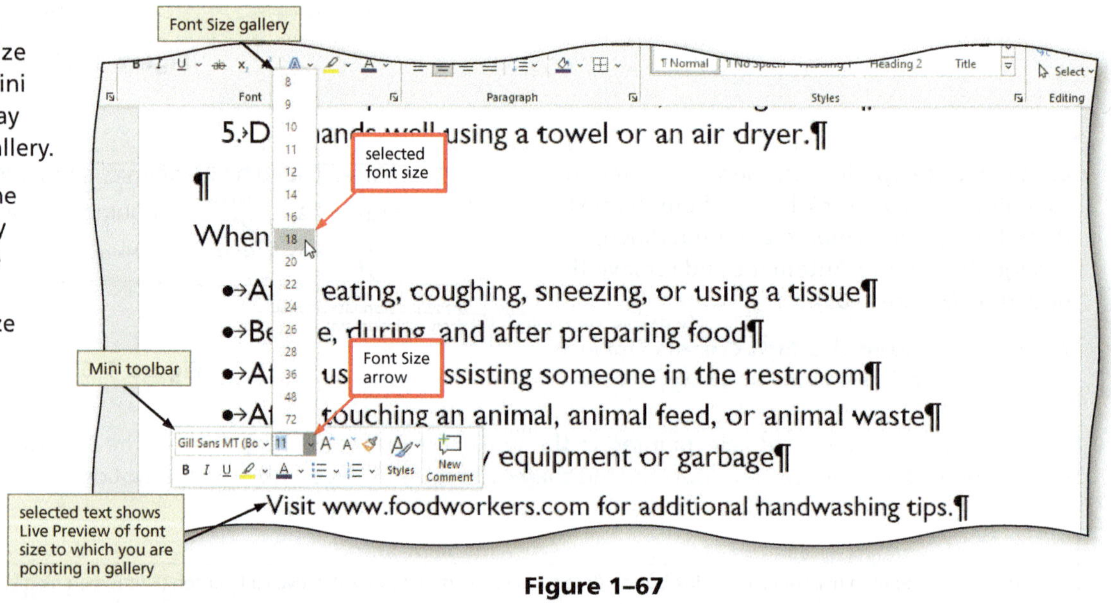

Figure 1–67

3

- Click 18 in the Font Size gallery to increase the font size of the selected text.

4

- With the text still selected and the Mini toolbar still displayed, click the Font Color arrow on the Mini toolbar to display the Font Color gallery.
- Point to 'Indigo, Accent 5, Darker 25%' (ninth color in the fifth row) to display a Live Preview of the selected font color (Figure 1–68).

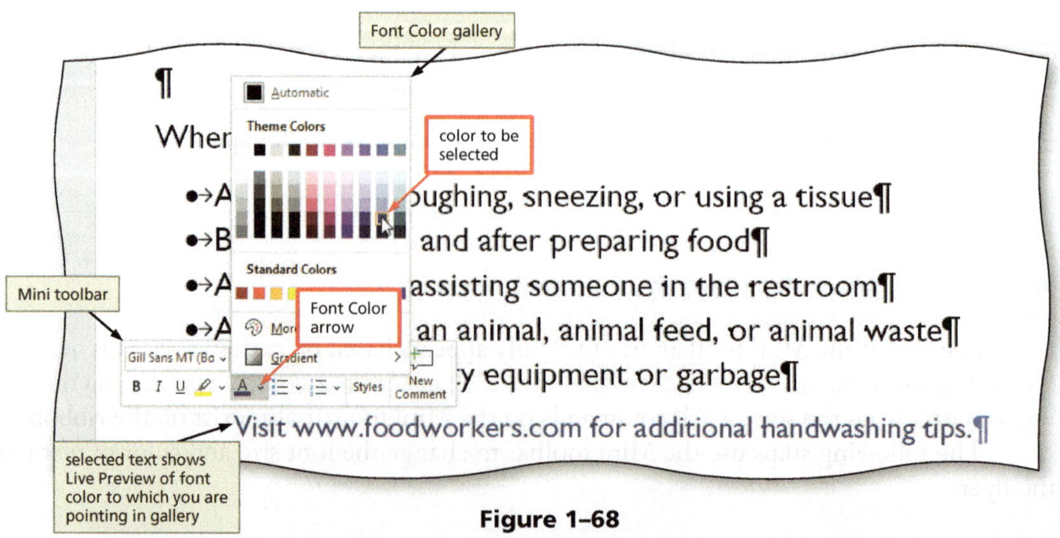

Figure 1–68

5

- Click 'Indigo, Accent 5, Darker 25%' to change the color of the selected text (shown in Figure 1–69).
- Click anywhere in the document window to remove the selection from the text.

To Select a Group of Words

The words, additional handwashing tips, in the signature line of the flyer, are underlined to further emphasize them. To format a group of words, you first must select them. **Why?** If you underline text without selecting any text first, Word will underline only the word containing the insertion point. The following steps select a group of words.

1

- Position the pointer immediately to the left of the first character of the text to be selected, in this case, the a in the word, additional (Figure 1–69).

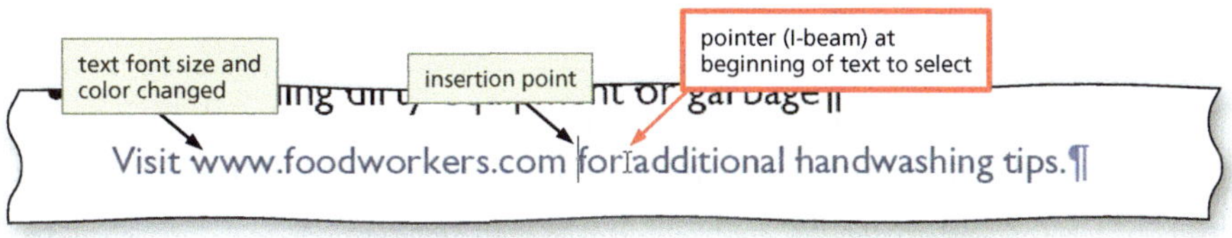

Figure 1–69

Q&A **Why did the shape of the pointer change?**
The pointer's shape is an I-beam when positioned in unselected text in the document window.

2

- Drag the pointer through the last character of the text to be selected, in this case, the s in the word, tips (Figure 1–70).

Q&A **Why did the pointer shape change again?**
When the pointer is positioned in selected text, its shape is a left-pointing block arrow.

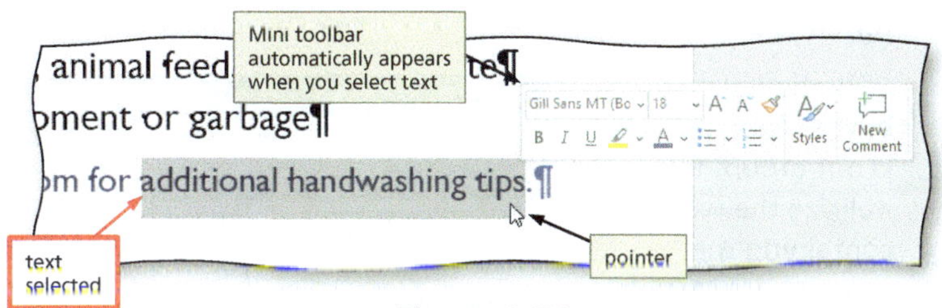

Figure 1–70

Other Ways

1. With insertion point at beginning of first word in group, press CTRL+SHIFT+RIGHT ARROW repeatedly until all words are selected

To Underline Text

Underlined text prints with an underscore (_) below each character, including spaces. In the flyer, the text, additional handwashing tips, in the signature line is underlined. **Why?** Underlines are used to emphasize or draw attention to specific text. The following step formats selected text with an underline.

1

- With the text selected, click the Underline button (Home tab | Font group) to underline the selected text (Figure 1–71).

Q&A **What if my screen displays an Underline gallery?**
If you are using a touch screen, you may not have a separate Underline button and Underline arrow. In this case, select the desired underline style in the Underline gallery.

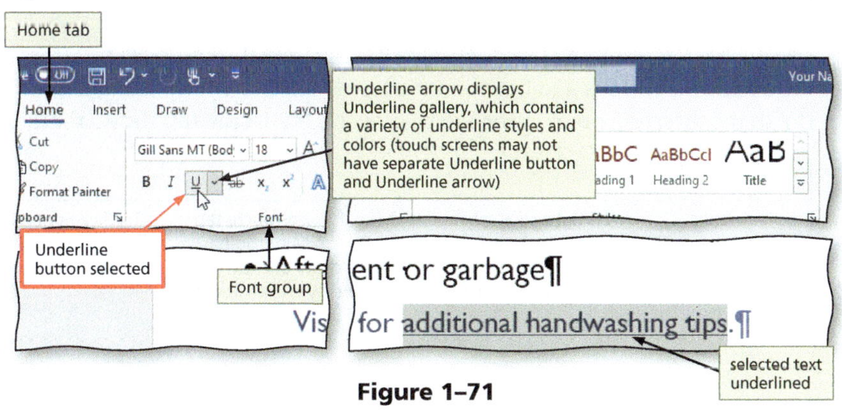

Figure 1–71

Q&A

If a button exists on the Mini toolbar, can I click that instead of using the ribbon?
Yes.

How would I remove an underline?
You would click the Underline button a second time, or you immediately could click the Undo button on the Quick Access Toolbar or press CTRL+Z.

Other Ways

1. Click Underline button on Mini toolbar
2. Right-click text (or, if using touch, tap 'Show Context Menu' button on Mini toolbar), click Font on shortcut menu, click Font tab (Font dialog box), click Underline style box arrow, click desired underline style, click OK
3. Click Font Dialog Box Launcher (Home tab | Font group), click Font tab (Font dialog box), click Underline style arrow, click desired underline style, click OK
4. Press CTRL+U

To Italicize Text

Italic is a type of format applied to text that makes the characters slant to the right. The next step is to italicize the word, prevent, near the top of the flyer to further emphasize it. If you want to format the characters in a single word, you do not need to select the word. **Why?** To format a single word, you simply position the insertion point somewhere in the word and apply the desired format. The following step italicizes a word.

1

- If necessary, scroll to the top of the document in the document window.
- Click somewhere in the word to be italicized (prevent, in this case) to position the insertion point in the word to be formatted.
- Click the Italic button (Home tab | Font group) to italicize the word containing the insertion point (Figure 1–72).

Figure 1–72

Q&A

How would I remove an italic format?
You would click the Italic button a second time, or you immediately could click the Undo button on the Quick Access Toolbar or press CTRL+Z.

How can I tell what formatting has been applied to text?
The selected buttons and boxes on the Home tab show formatting characteristics of the location of the insertion point. With the insertion point in the word, prevent, the Home tab shows these formats: 22-point Gill Sans MT italic font.

Other Ways

1. Click Italic button on Mini toolbar
2. Right-click selected text (or, if using touch, tap 'Show Context Menu' button on Mini toolbar), click Font on shortcut menu, click Font tab (Font dialog box), click Italic in Font style list, click OK
3. Click Font Dialog Box Launcher (Home tab | Font group), click Font tab (Font dialog box), click Italic in Font style list, click OK
4. Press CTRL+I

To Select Nonadjacent Text

The next step is to select the first word in every paragraph in the numbered list (Wet, Lather, Scrub, Rinse, Dry) and bold them. **Why?** You want to emphasize these words further. Word provides a method of selecting nonadjacent items, which are items such as text, pictures, or other objects that are not immediately beside one another. When you select nonadjacent items, you can format all occurrences of the selected items at once. The following steps select nonadjacent text.

1

- If necessary, scroll to display the entire numbered list in the document window.
- Select the first word to format (in this case, double-click the word, Wet) (Figure 1–73).

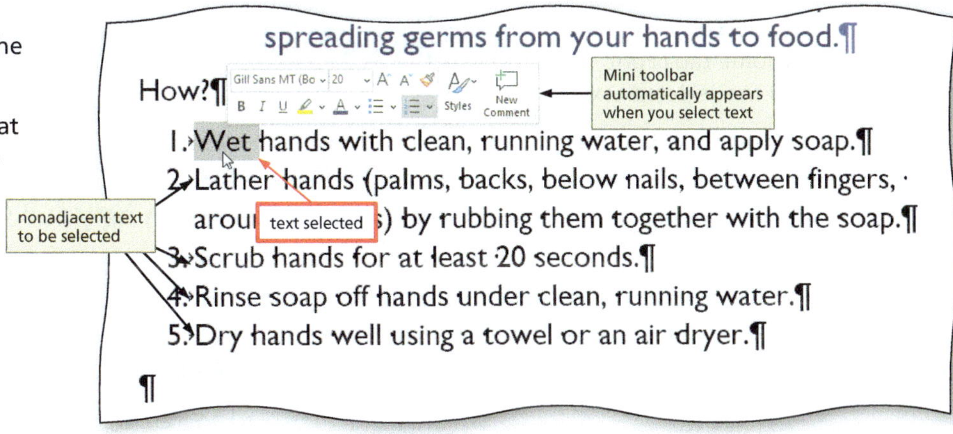

Figure 1–73

2

- While holding down CTRL, select the next word to format (in this case, double-click the word, Lather), which selects the nonadjacent text (Figure 1–74).

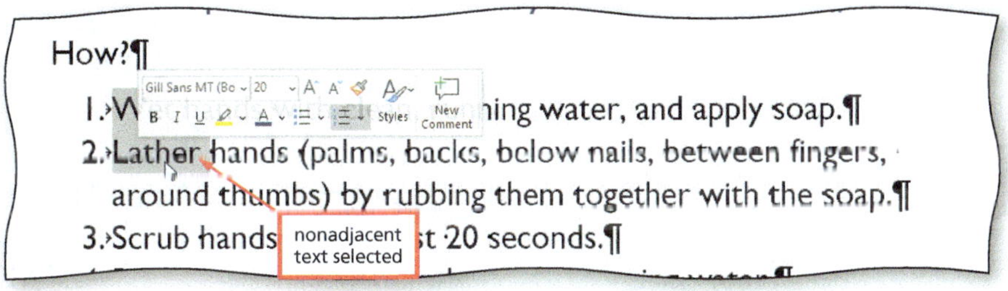

Figure 1–74

3

- While holding down CTRL, select the remaining nonadjacent text (that is, the words, Scrub, Rinse, Dry), as shown in Figure 1–75.

Q&A **Do I follow the same procedure to select any nonadjacent item?**
Yes. Select the first item and then hold down CTRL while selecting the remaining items.

What if my keyboard does not have a key labelled CTRL?
You will need to format each item individually, one at a time.

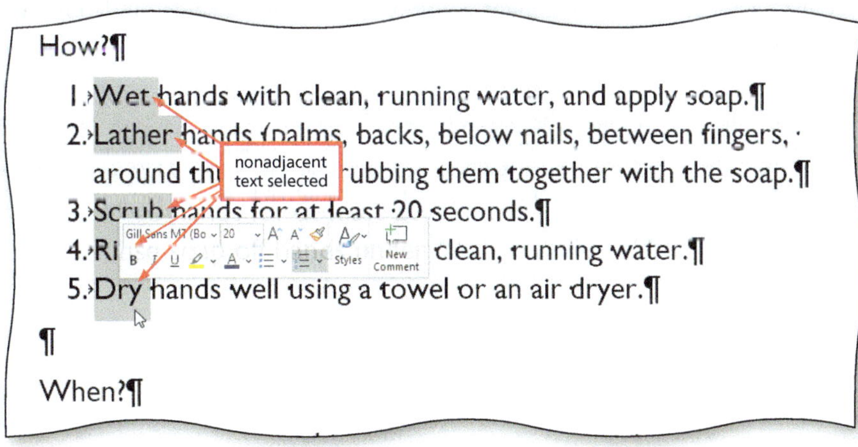

Figure 1–75

To Bold Text

Bold is a type of format applied to text that makes the characters appear somewhat thicker and darker than those that are not bold. The following steps format the selected text in bold characters. **Why?** To further emphasize this text, it is bold in the flyer. Recall that if you want to format a single word, you simply position the insertion point in the word and then format the word. To format text that consists of more than one word, as you have learned previously, you select the text first.

1

- With the text selected, click the Bold button (Home tab | Font group) to bold the selected text (Figure 1–76).

Q&A **How would I remove a bold format?**
You would click the Bold button a second time, or you immediately could click the Undo button on the Quick Access Toolbar or press CTRL+Z.

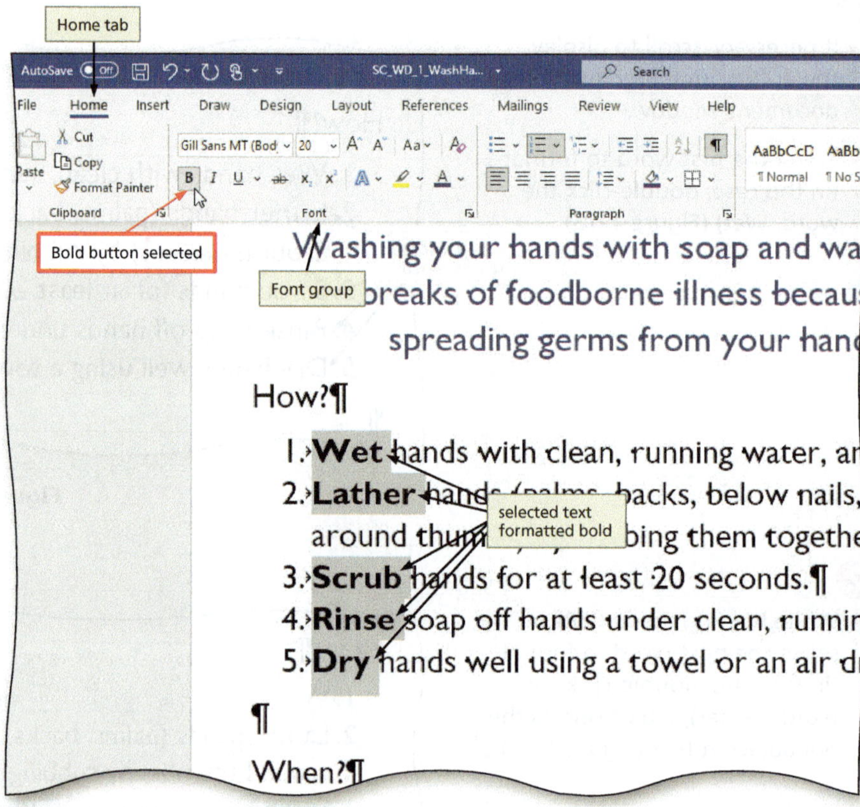

Figure 1–76

2

- Click anywhere in the document window to remove the selection from the screen.

Other Ways

1. Click Bold button on Mini toolbar
2. Right-click selected text (or, if using touch, tap 'Show Context Menu' button on Mini toolbar), click Font on shortcut menu, click Font tab (Font dialog box), click Bold in Font style list, click OK
3. Click Font Dialog Box Launcher (Home tab | Font group), click Font tab (Font dialog box), click Bold in Font style list, click OK
4. Press CTRL+B

Selecting Text

In many of the previous steps, you have selected text. Table 1–4 summarizes the techniques you can use to select various items.

Table 1–4 Techniques for Selecting Text

Item to Select	Touch	Mouse	Keyboard (where applicable)
Block of text	Tap to position insertion point in text to select and then drag selection handle(s) to select text.	Click at beginning of selection, scroll to end of selection, position pointer at end of selection, hold down SHIFT, and then click; or drag through the text.	
Character(s)	Tap to position insertion point in text to select and then drag selection handle(s) to select text.	Drag through character(s).	SHIFT+RIGHT ARROW or SHIFT+LEFT ARROW
Entire Document		Move pointer to left of text until pointer changes to right-pointing block arrow and then triple-click.	CTRL+A
Line	Double-tap to left of line to be selected.	Move pointer to left of line until pointer changes to right-pointing block arrow and then click.	HOME, then SHIFT+END or END, then SHIFT+HOME
Lines	Tap to position insertion point in text to select and then drag selection handle(s) to select text.	Move pointer to left of first line until pointer changes to right-pointing block arrow and then drag up or down.	HOME, then SHIFT+DOWN ARROW or END, then SHIFT+UP ARROW
Paragraph	Tap to position insertion point in text to select and then drag selection handle(s) to select text.	Triple-click paragraph; or move pointer to left of paragraph until pointer changes to right-pointing block arrow and then double-click.	CTRL+SHIFT+DOWN ARROW or CTRL+SHIFT+UP ARROW
Paragraphs	Tap to position insertion point in text to select and then drag selection handle(s) to select text.	Move pointer to left of paragraph until pointer changes to right-pointing block arrow, double-click, and then drag up or down.	CTRL+SHIFT+DOWN ARROW or CTRL+SHIFT+UP ARROW repeatedly
Picture or other object	Tap the graphic.	Click the object.	
Sentence	Tap to position insertion point in text to select and then drag selection handle(s) to select text.	Press and hold down CTRL and then click sentence.	
Word	Double-tap word.	Double-click word.	CTRL+SHIFT+RIGHT ARROW or CTRL+SHIFT+LEFT ARROW
Words	Tap to position insertion point in text to select and then drag selection handle(s) to select text.	Drag through words.	CTRL+SHIFT+RIGHT ARROW or CTRL+SHIFT+LEFT ARROW repeatedly

To Save an Existing Document with a Different File Name

You might want to save a file with a different file name. For example, you might start a homework assignment with a data file and then save it with a final file name for submission to your instructor, saving it to a location designated by your instructor.

The following steps save the SC_WD_1_WashHandsFlyerUnformatted file with a different file name.

1. Click File on the ribbon to open Backstage view.
2. Click Save As in Backstage view to display the Save As screen.
3. Type **SC_WD_1_WashHandsFlyerFormatted** in the File name box, replacing the existing file name (Figure 1–77).
4. Click the Save button in the Save As screen to save the flyer with the new name in the same save location.

BTW

Organizing Files and Folders

You should organize and store files in folders so that you easily can find the files later. For example, if you are taking an introductory technology class called CIS 101, a good practice would be to save all Word files in a Word folder in a CIS 101 folder.

Q&A

What if I wanted to save the file to a different location?
You would click Browse or click the More options link in the Save As screen to display the Save As dialog box, navigate to the desired save location, and then click Save in the dialog box.

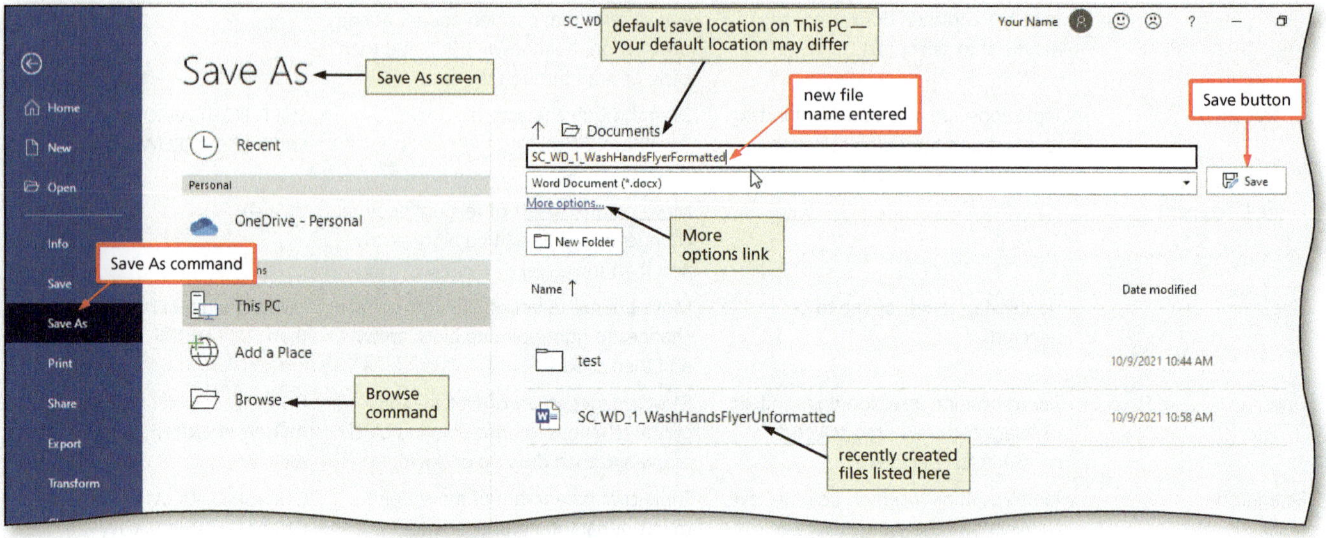

Figure 1–77

Break Point: If you want to take a break, this is a good place to do so. You can exit Word now. To resume later, start Word, open the file called SC_WD_1_WashHandsFlyerFormatted.docx, and continue following the steps from this location forward.

Inserting and Formatting a Picture in a Word Document

With the text formatted in the flyer, the next step is to insert a digital picture in the flyer and format the picture. Flyers usually contain a picture or other object to attract the attention of passersby. In the following sections, you will perform these tasks:

1. Insert a digital picture into the flyer.
2. Reduce the size of the picture.
3. Change the look of the picture.

Consider This

How do you locate a picture to use in a document?
To use a picture in a Word document, the image must be stored digitally in a file. Files containing pictures are available from a variety of sources:

- The web has pictures available, some of which are free, while others require a fee.
- You can take a picture with a digital camera or smartphone and **download** it, which is the process of transferring (copying) a file (such as a picture) from a server, computer, or device (such as a camera or phone) to another computer or device.
- With a scanner, you can convert a printed picture, drawing, diagram, or other object to a digital file.

If you receive a picture from a source other than yourself, do not use the file until you are certain it does not contain a virus. A **virus** is a computer program designed to copy itself into other programs with the intention of causing mischief, harm, or damage to files, programs, and apps on your computer, usually without the user's knowledge or permission. Use an antivirus program or app to verify that any files you use are virus free.

To Center a Paragraph

In the flyer, the digital picture showing handwashing should be centered on the blank line between the numbered list and the bulleted list. The blank paragraph below the numbered list currently is left-aligned. The following steps center this paragraph.

1. Click somewhere in the paragraph to be centered (in this case, the blank line below the numbered list) to position the insertion point in the paragraph to be formatted.
2. Click the Center button (Home tab | Paragraph group) to center the paragraph containing the insertion point (shown in Figure 1–78).

To Insert a Picture from a File

The next step in creating the flyer is to insert a digital picture showing handwashing in the flyer on the blank line below the numbered list. The picture, which was taken with a digital camera, is available in the Data Files. Please contact your instructor for information about accessing Data Files.

The following steps insert a picture, which, in this example, is located in a folder in the Data Files folder. **Why?** It is good practice to organize and store files in folders so that you easily can find the files at a later date.

1

- If necessary, position the insertion point at the location where you want to insert the picture (in this case, on the centered blank paragraph below the numbered list).
- Click Insert on the ribbon to display the Insert tab (Figure 1–78).

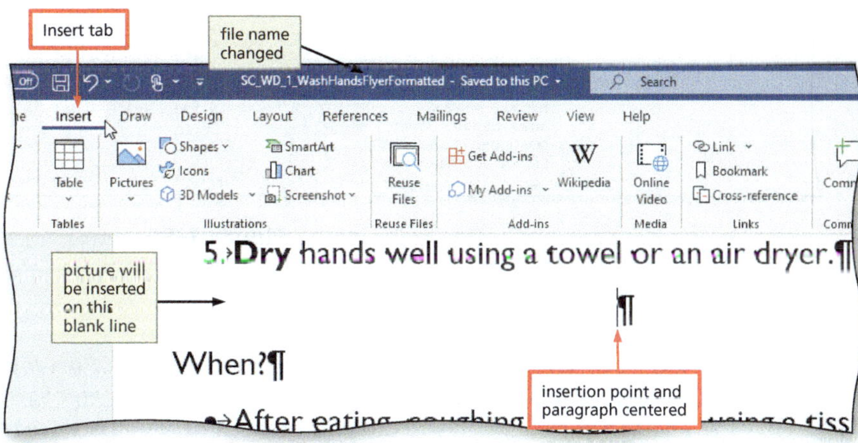

Figure 1–78

2

- Click the Pictures button (Insert tab | Illustrations group) to display the Insert Picture From menu.
- Click This Device on the Insert Picture From menu to display the Insert Picture dialog box.

3

- In the Insert Picture dialog box, navigate to the location of the digital picture (in this case, the Module folder in the Data Files folder).
- Click Support_WD_1_WashingHands to select the file (Figure 1–79).

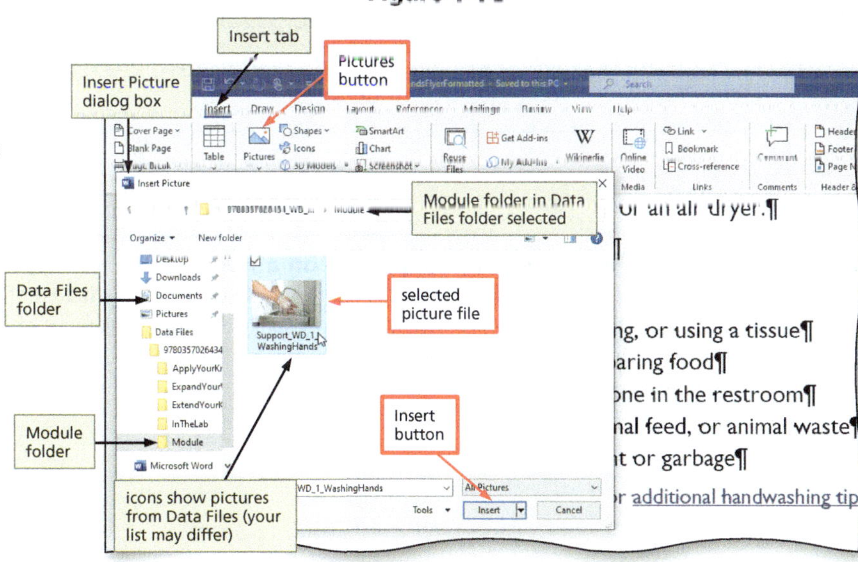

Figure 1–79

4

- Click the Insert button (Insert Picture dialog box) to insert the picture at the location of the insertion point in the document (Figure 1–80).

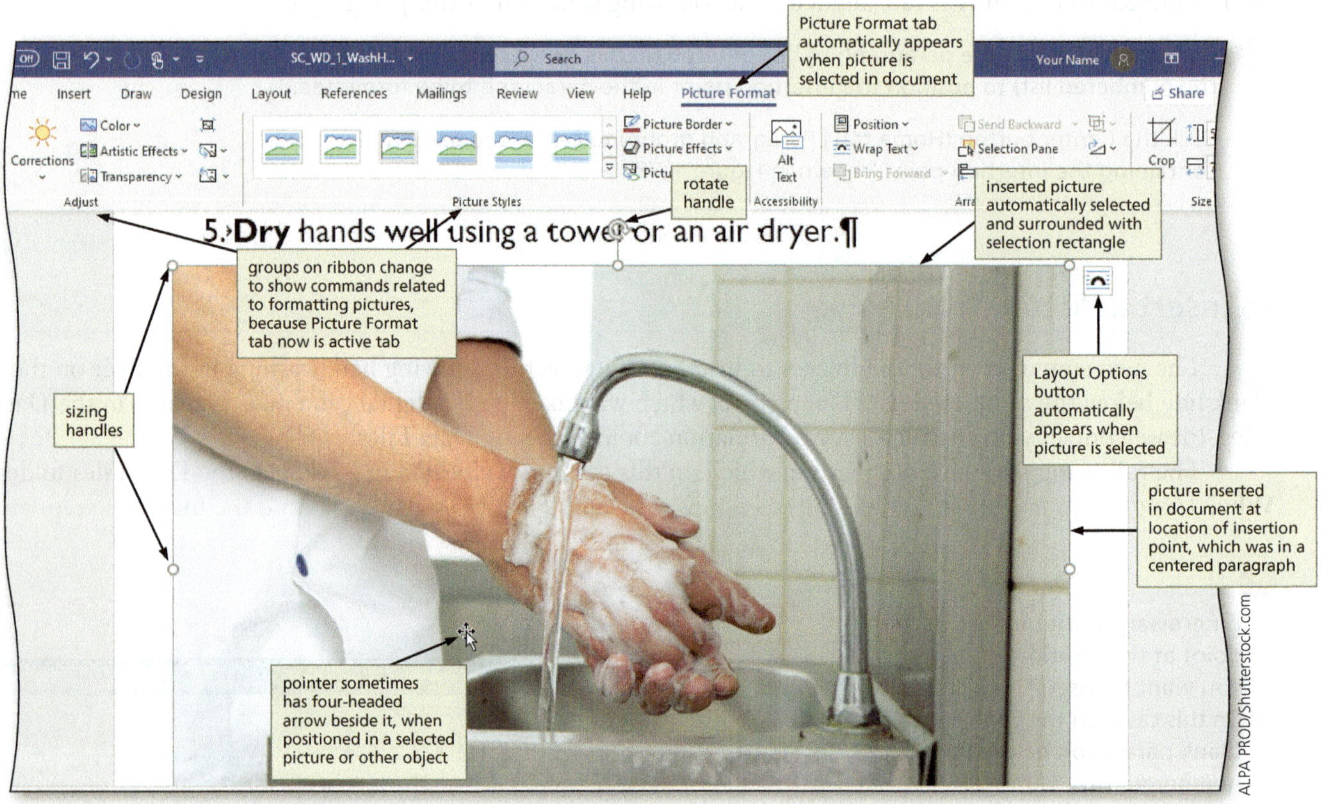

Figure 1–80

Q&A

What are the symbols around the picture?
A selected object, such as a picture, appears surrounded by a **selection rectangle**, which is a box that has small circles, called **sizing handles**, at each corner and middle location, and a rotate handle; you drag the sizing handles to resize the selected object. When you drag a picture or other object's **rotate handle**, which is the small circular arrow at the top of the selected object, the object moves in either a clockwise or counterclockwise direction.

What is the purpose of the Layout Options button?
When you click the Layout Options button, Word provides options for changing how the selected picture or other object is positioned with text in the document.

Consider This

How do you know where to position a picture on a flyer?
The content, size, shape, position, and format of a picture should capture the interest of your audience, enticing them to read the flyer. Often, the picture is the center of attention and visually the largest element on a flyer. If you use colors in the picture, be sure they are part of the document's theme colors.

To Change the Zoom to One Page

Earlier in this module, you changed the zoom to page width so that the text on the screen was larger and easier to read. In the next set of steps, you want to see the entire page (as an image of a sheet of paper) on the screen at once. **Why?** The large size of the picture caused the flyer contents to spill to a second page. You want to resize the picture enough so that the entire flyer fits on a single page. The following step changes the zoom to one page so that an entire page can be displayed in the document window at once.

1

- Click View on the ribbon to display the View tab.
- Click the One Page button (View tab | Zoom group) to change the zoom to one page (Figure 1–81).

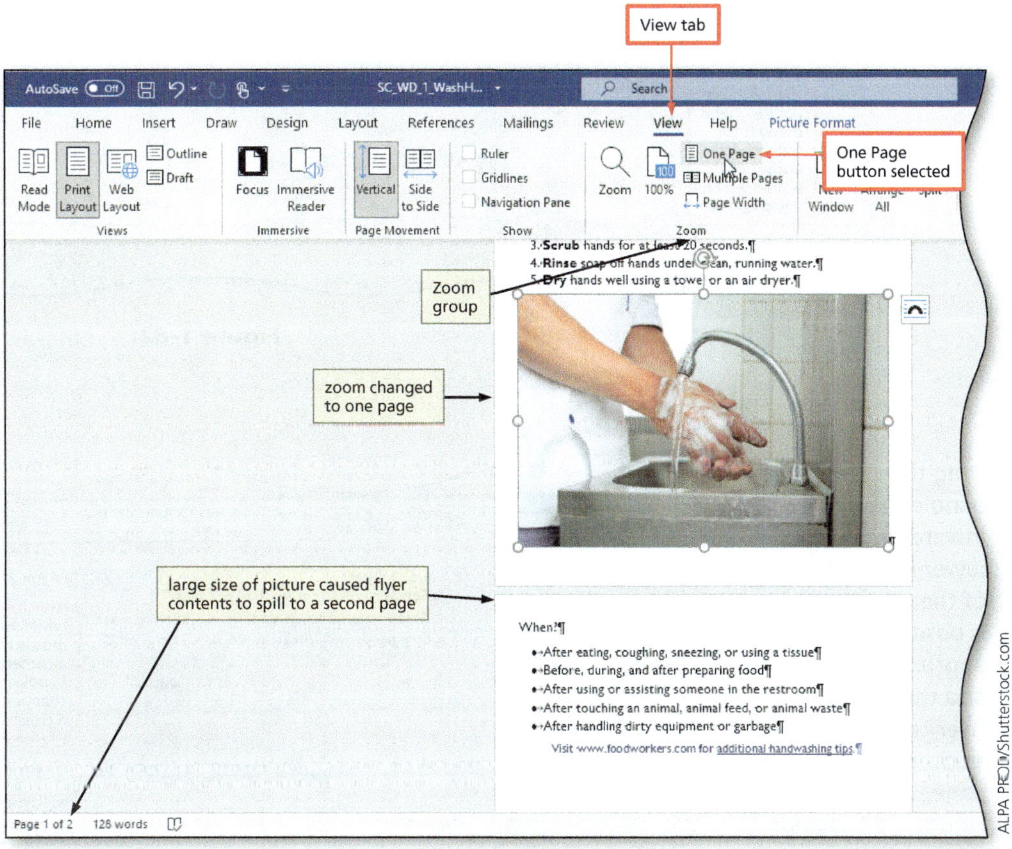

Figure 1–81

Other Ways

1. Click Zoom button (View tab | Zoom group), click Whole page (Zoom dialog box), click OK

To Resize an Object Proportionally

When you **resize** an object, such as a picture, you increase or decrease its size. The next step is to resize the picture so that it is smaller in the flyer. **Why?** You want the picture and all the text on the flyer to fit on a single sheet of paper. The following steps resize a selected object (picture).

1

- Be sure the picture still is selected.

Q&A **What if the object (picture) is not selected?**
To select a picture, click it.

- If necessary, click Picture Format on the ribbon to display the Picture Format tab.

- Point to the lower-left corner sizing handle on the picture so that the pointer shape changes to a two-headed arrow (Figure 1–82).

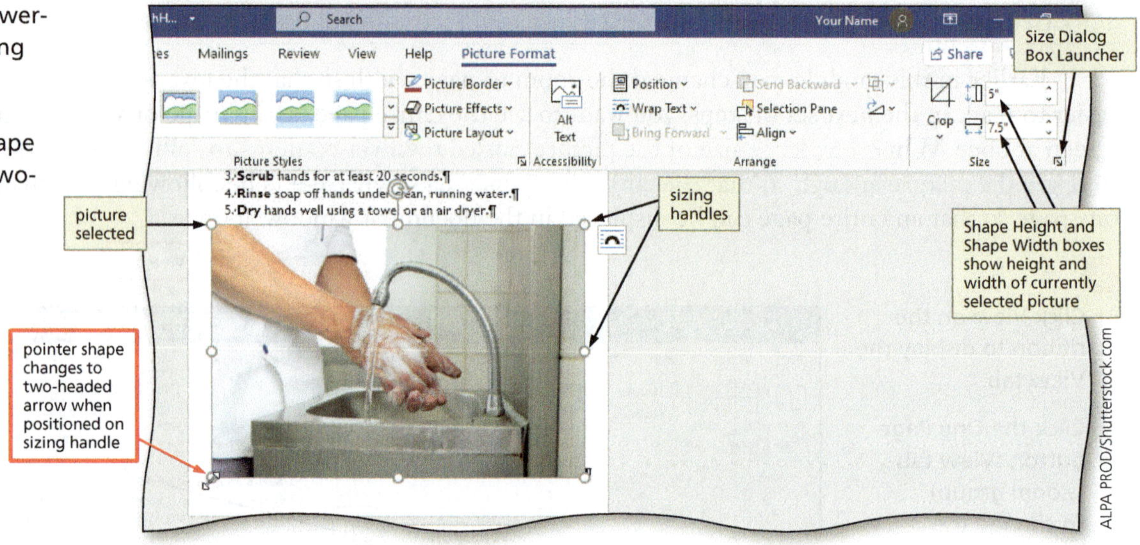

Figure 1–82

2

- Drag the sizing handle diagonally inward until the lower-left corner of the picture is positioned approximately, and the entire flyer contents fit on a single page, as shown in Figure 1–83. Do not release the mouse button at this point.

Q&A **What if I am using a touch screen?**
Drag a corner of the picture, without lifting your finger, until the picture is the desired size.

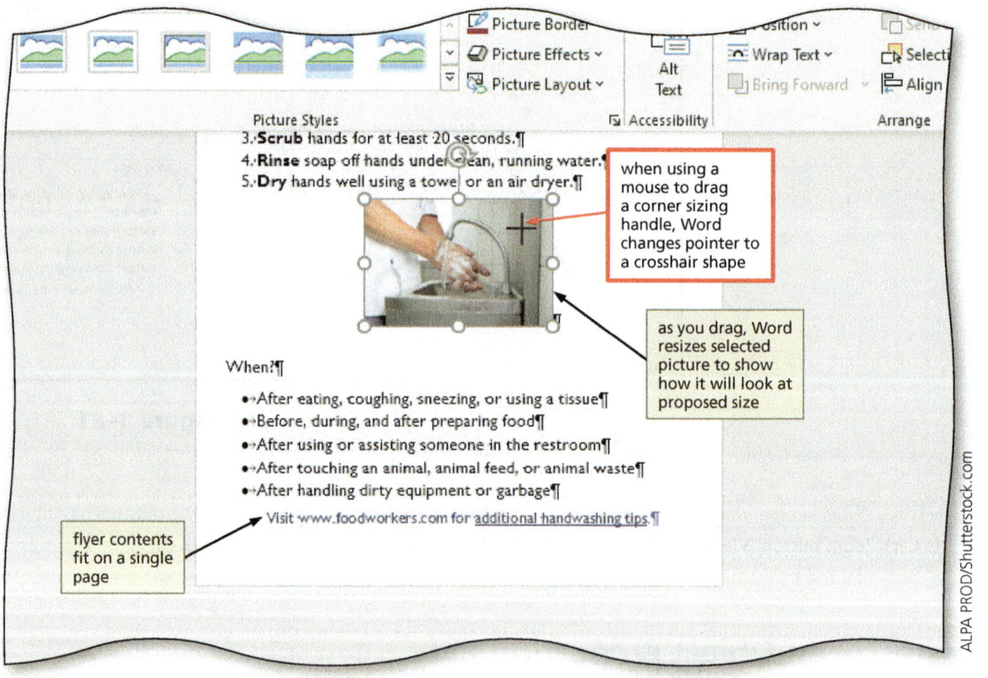

Figure 1–83

3

- Release the mouse button to resize the picture, which, in this case, should have a height of about 2" and a width of about 3" (shown in Figure 1–84).

Q&A **How can I see the height and width measurements?**
Look in the Size group on the Picture Format tab to see the height and width measurements of a currently selected graphic (shown in Figure 1–84). If necessary, click the Picture Format tab on the ribbon to display the tab.

What if the object (picture) is the wrong size?
Repeat Steps 1, 2, and 3, or enter the desired height and width values in the Shape Height and Shape Width boxes (Picture Format tab | Size group).

Q&A **What if I want to return an object (picture) to its original size and start again?**
With the object (picture) selected, click the Size Dialog Box Launcher (Picture Format tab | Size group), click the Size tab (Layout dialog box), click the Reset button, and then click OK.

Other Ways

1. Enter height and width of selected object in Shape Height and Shape Width boxes (Picture Format tab | Size group)
2. Click Size Dialog Box Launcher (Picture Format tab | Size group), click Size tab (Layout dialog box), enter desired height and width values in boxes, click OK

To Apply a Picture Style

Word provides more than 25 picture styles. **Why?** Picture styles enable you easily to change a picture's look to a more visually appealing style, including a variety of shapes, angles, borders, and reflections. The flyer in this module uses a style that applies a snip corner shape to the picture. The following steps apply a picture style to a picture.

1

- Ensure the picture still is selected and that the Picture Format tab is displayed on the ribbon (Figure 1–84).

Q&A **What if the picture is not selected?**
To select a picture or other object, click it.

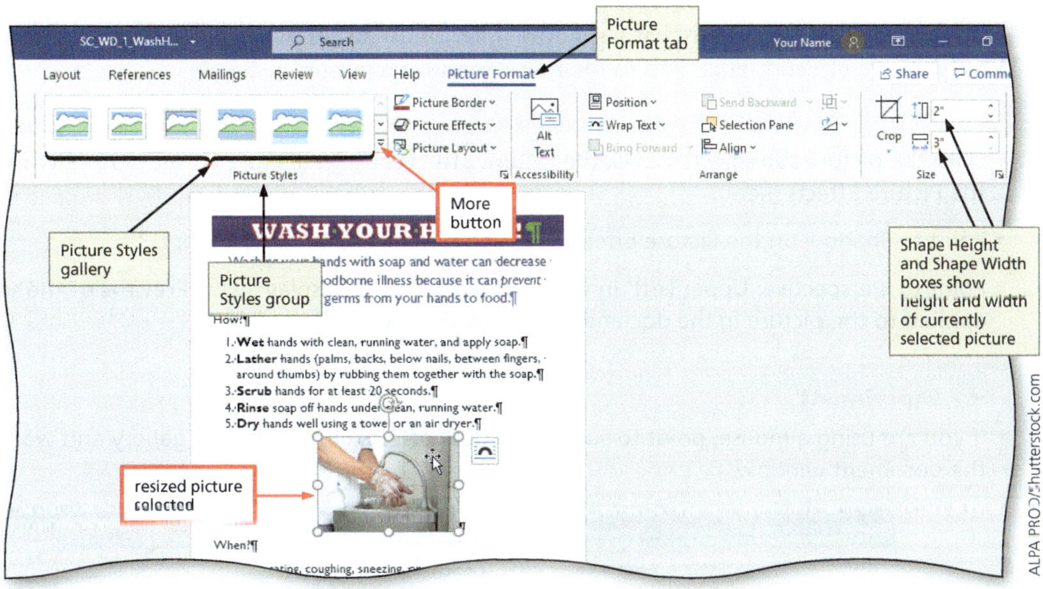

ALPA PROD/Shutterstock.com

Figure 1–84

2

- Click the More button in the Picture Styles gallery (Picture Format tab | Picture Styles group) to expand the gallery.
- Point to 'Snip Diagonal Corner, White' in the Picture Styles gallery to display a Live Preview of that style applied to the picture in the document (Figure 1–85).

Experiment

- Point to various picture styles in the Picture Styles gallery and watch the style of the picture change in the document window.

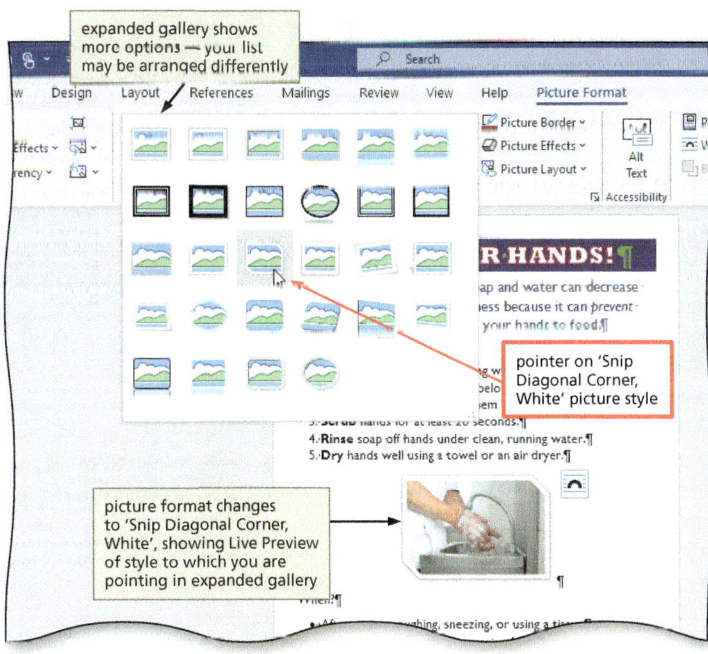

ALPA PROD/Shutterstock.com

Figure 1–85

3

- Click 'Snip Diagonal Corner, White' in the Picture Styles gallery (third style in third row) to apply the style to the selected picture.

Q&A **What if the flyer contents spill to a second page?**
Reduce the size of the picture.

Other Ways

1. Right-click picture, click Style button on Mini toolbar, select desired style

To Apply a Picture Effect

Word provides a variety of picture effects, such as shadows, reflections, glows, soft edges, bevels, and 3-D rotations. The difference between the effects and the styles is that each effect has several options, providing you with more control over the exact look of the image.

In this flyer, the picture has a shadow. The following steps apply a picture effect to the selected picture. **Why?** Picture effects enable you to further customize a picture.

1

- With the picture still selected, click the Picture Effects button (Picture Format tab | Picture Styles group) to display the Picture Effects menu.
- Point to Shadow on the Picture Effects menu to display the Shadow gallery.
- Point to 'Perspective: Upper Left' in the Shadow gallery to display a Live Preview of the selected shadow effect applied to the picture in the document window (Figure 1–86).

Experiment

- If you are using a mouse, point to various shadow effects in the Shadow gallery and watch the picture change in the document window.

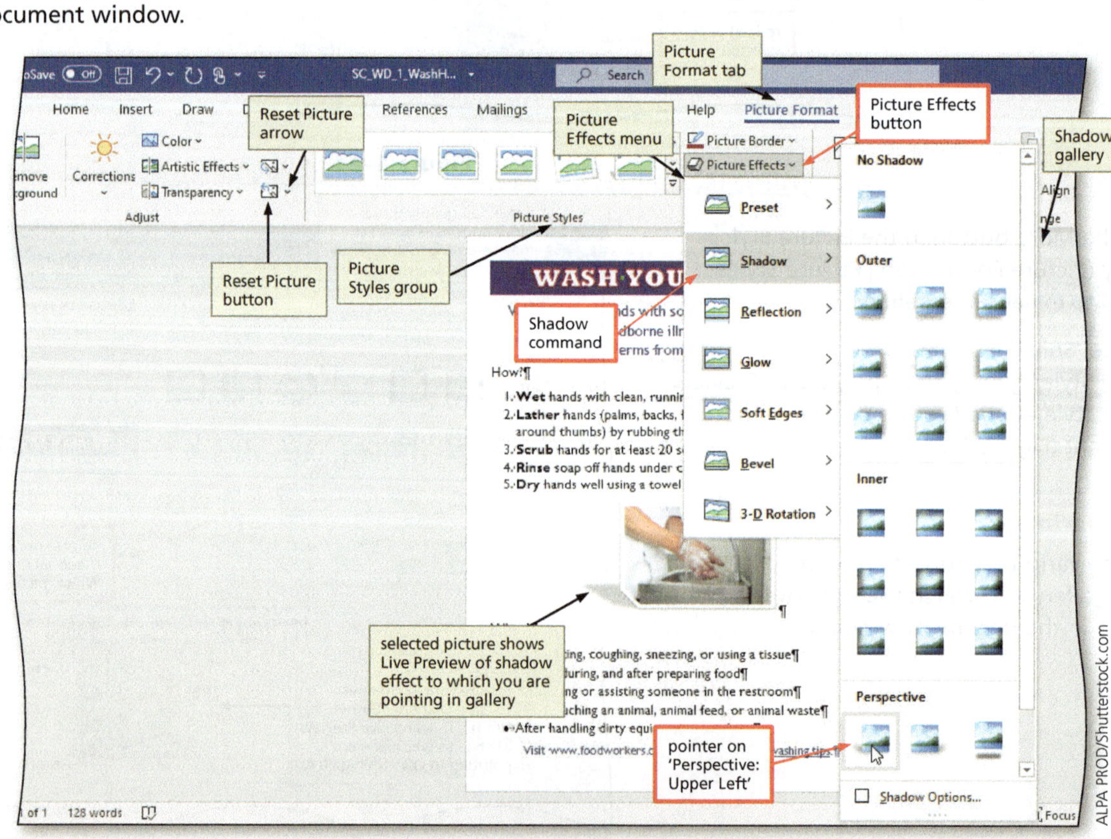

Figure 1–86

2

- Click 'Perspective: Upper Left' in the Shadow gallery to apply the selected picture effect.
- Click somewhere in the document other than the picture and notice the Picture Format tab disappears from the screen when the picture is not selected (shown in Figure 1–87).

Q&A

How would I redisplay the Picture Format tab?
Click the picture to select it and the Picture Format tab will reappear.

What if I wanted to discard formatting applied to a picture?
You would click the Reset Picture button (Picture Format tab | Adjust group). To reset formatting and size, you would click the Reset Picture arrow (Picture Format tab | Adjust group) and then click 'Reset Picture & Size' on the Reset Picture menu.

Other Ways

1. Right-click picture (or, if using touch, tap 'Show Context Menu' button on Mini toolbar), click Format Picture on shortcut menu, click Effects button (Format Picture pane), select desired options, click Close button
2. Click Picture Styles Dialog Box Launcher (Picture Format tab | Picture Styles group), click Effects button (Format Picture pane), select desired options, click Close button

Enhancing the Page

With the text and picture entered and formatted, the next step is to look at the page as a whole and determine if it looks finished in its current state. As you review the page, answer these questions:

- Are the colors appropriate for the message?
- Does it need a page border to frame its contents, or would a page border make it look too busy?
- Is the spacing between paragraphs and the picture on the page adequate? Do any sections look as if they are positioned too closely to the items above or below them?

You determine that you would like to change the text and shading colors and that a graphical, color-coordinated border would enhance the flyer. You also notice that the flyer would look better proportioned if it had a little more space above and below the picture. The following sections make these enhancements to the flyer.

Consider This

What colors should you choose when creating documents?
When choosing color, associate the meaning of the color with your message. For example, in Western culture:

- Red expresses danger, power, or energy and often is associated with sports or physical exertion.
- Brown represents simplicity, honesty, and dependability.
- Orange denotes success, victory, creativity, and enthusiasm.
- Yellow suggests sunshine, happiness, hope, liveliness, and intelligence.
- Green symbolizes growth, healthiness, harmony, and healing and often is associated with safety or money.
- Blue indicates integrity, trust, importance, confidence, and stability.
- Purple represents wealth, power, comfort, extravagance, magic, mystery, and spirituality.
- White stands for purity, goodness, cleanliness, precision, and perfection.
- Black suggests authority, strength, elegance, power, and prestige.
- Gray conveys neutrality and, thus, often is found in backgrounds and other effects.

To Change Theme Colors

A **theme color** in Word is a named set of complementary colors for text, background, accents, and links in a document. With more than 20 predefined theme colors, Word provides a simple way to coordinate colors in a document.

In the flyer, you will change the theme colors. **Why?** You want the colors in the flyer to represent healthiness, healing, integrity, and trust, which are conveyed by shades of greens and blues. In Word, the Blue II theme color uses these colors. The following steps change theme colors.

1

- Click Design on the ribbon to display the Design tab.
- Click the Colors button (Design tab | Document Formatting group) to display the Colors gallery.
- Point to Blue II in the Colors gallery to display a Live Preview of the selected theme color (Figure 1–87).

Experiment

- Point to various theme colors in the Colors gallery and watch the colors change in the document.

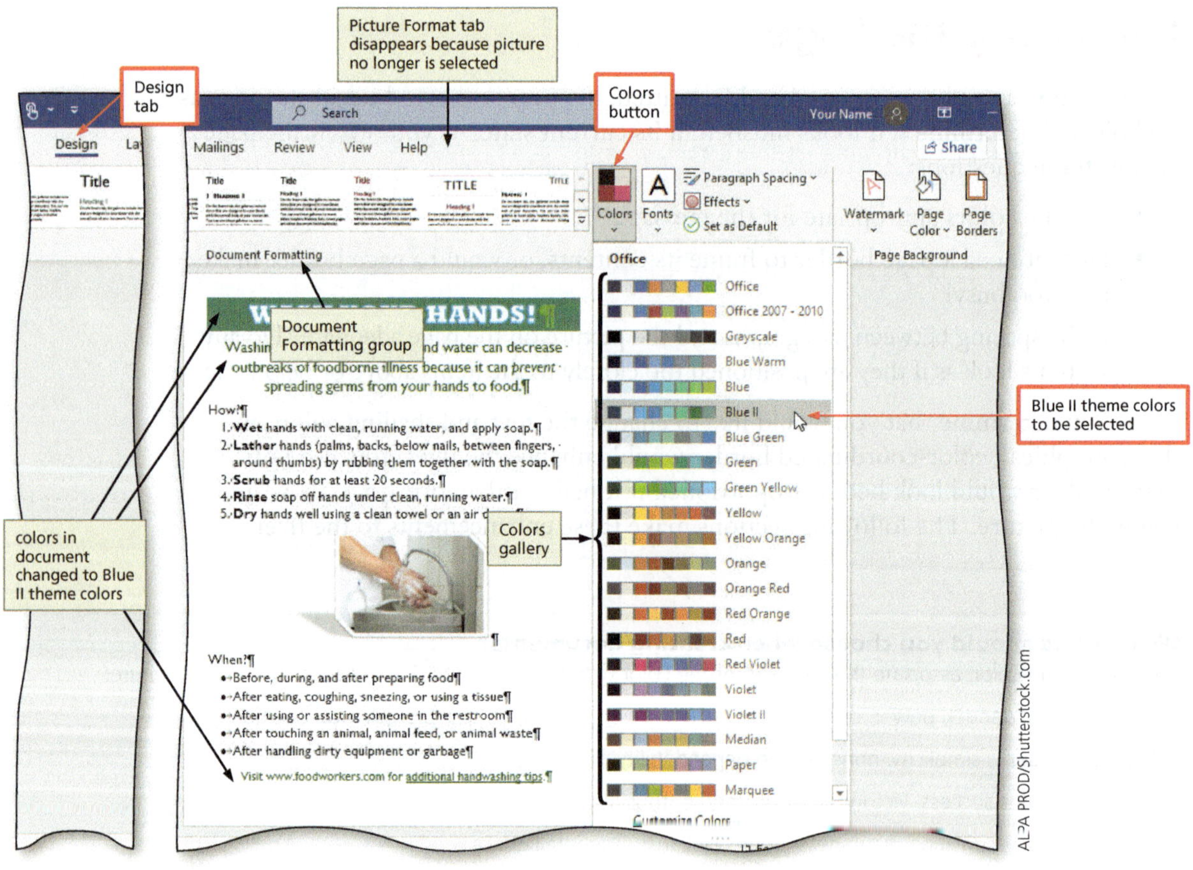

Figure 1–87

2

- Click Blue II in the Colors gallery to change the document theme colors.

Q&A **What if I want to return to the default theme colors?**
You would click the Colors button again and then click Office in the Colors gallery.

To Add a Page Border

In Word, you can add a border around the perimeter of an entire page. The flyer in this module has a blue-green border. **Why?** This border color complements the color of the flyer contents. The following steps add a page border.

1

- Click the Page Borders button (Design tab | Page Background group) to display the Borders and Shading dialog box (Figure 1–88).

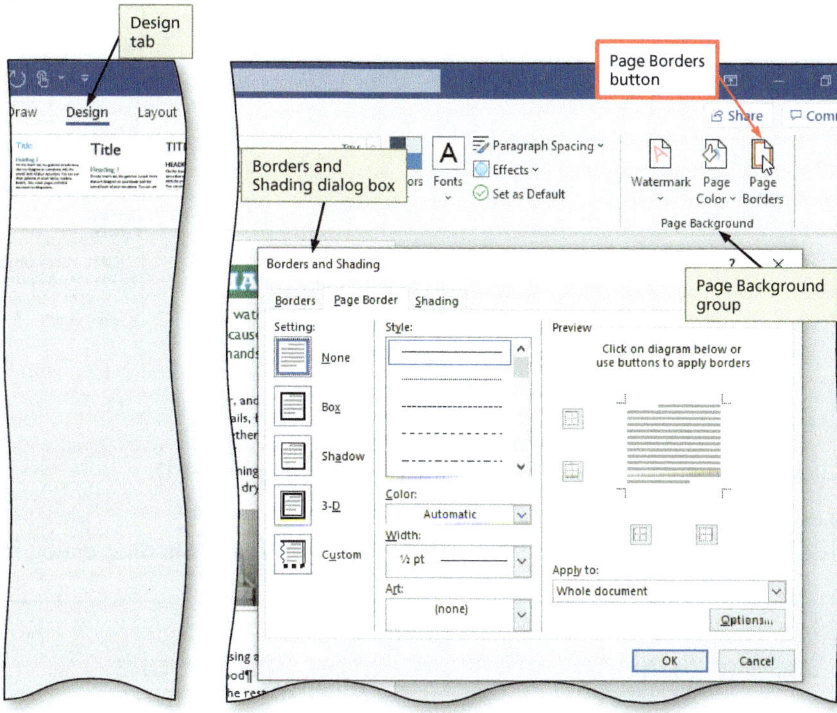

Figure 1–88

2

- Click Box in the Setting list to select the border setting.
- Scroll to, if necessary, and then click the third border style from the bottom of the Style list (Borders and Shading dialog box) to select the border style.
- Click the Color arrow to display a color palette (Figure 1–89).

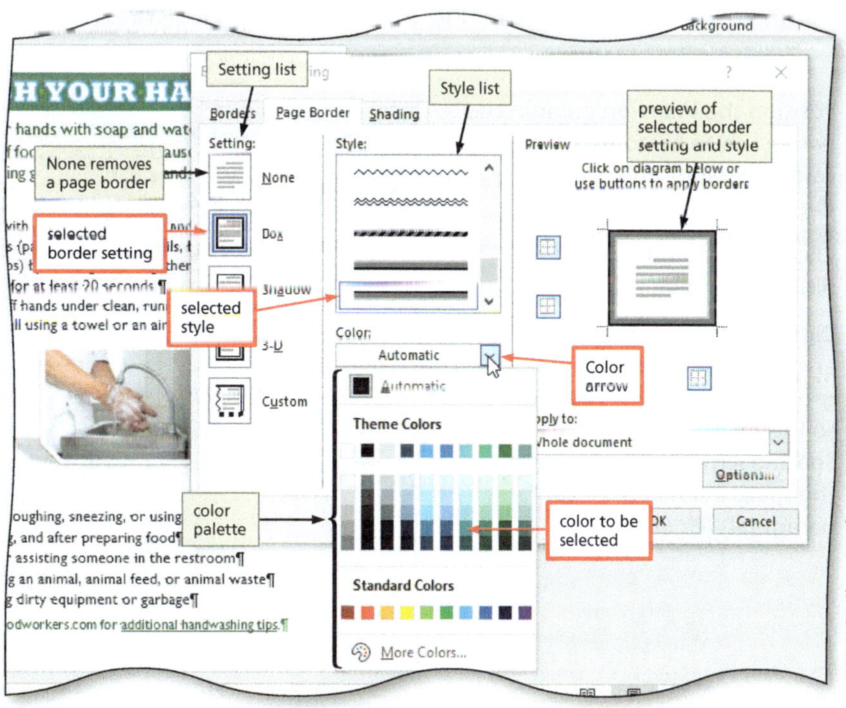

Figure 1–89

3

- Click 'Turquoise, Accent 3, Darker 25%' (seventh color in fifth row) in the color palette to select the color for the page border (Figure 1–90).

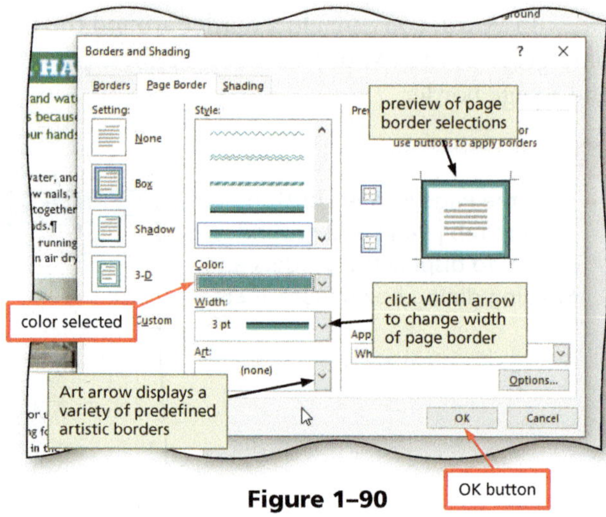

Figure 1–90

ALPA PROD/Shutterstock.com

4

- Click OK to add the border to the page (shown in Figure 1–91).

Q&A **What if I wanted to remove the border?**
You would click None in the Setting list in the Borders and Shading dialog box.

To Change Spacing before and after Paragraphs

The default spacing above (before) a paragraph in Word is 0 points and below (after) is 8 points. In the flyer, you want to decrease the spacing below (after) the paragraphs containing the words, How? and When?, and increase the spacing above (before) the signature line. **Why?** The flyer spacing will look more balanced with spacing adjusted above and below these paragraphs. The following steps change the spacing before and after paragraphs.

1

- Position the insertion point in the paragraph to be adjusted, in this case, the paragraph containing the word, How?.
- Click Layout on the ribbon to display the Layout tab.
- Click the Spacing After down arrow (Layout tab | Paragraph group) as many times as necessary so that 0 pt is displayed in the Spacing After box to decrease the space below the current paragraph (Figure 1–91).

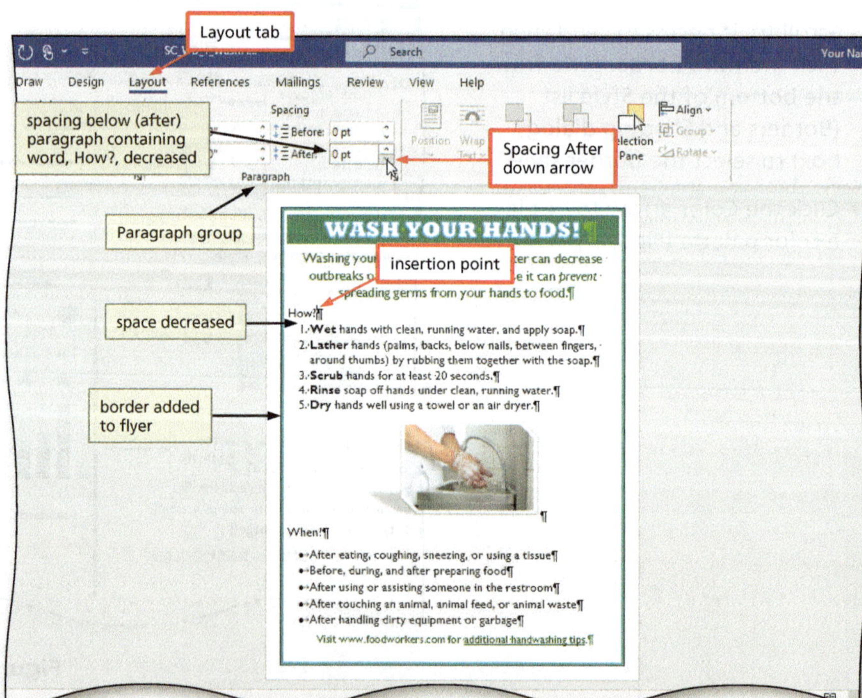

Figure 1–91

ALPA PROD/Shutterstock.com

2

- Position the insertion point in the next paragraph to be adjusted, in this case, the paragraph containing the word, When?.
- Click the Spacing After down arrow (Layout tab | Paragraph group) as many times as necessary so that 0 pt is displayed in the Spacing After box to decrease the space below the current paragraph.
- Position the insertion point in the paragraph to be adjusted, in this case, the paragraph containing the signature line.
- Click the Spacing Before up arrow (Layout tab | Paragraph group) as many times as necessary so that 12 pt is displayed in the Spacing Before box to increase the space above the current paragraph (Figure 1–92).
- If the text flows to two pages, reduce the spacing above and below paragraphs as necessary so that the entire flyer fits on a single page.

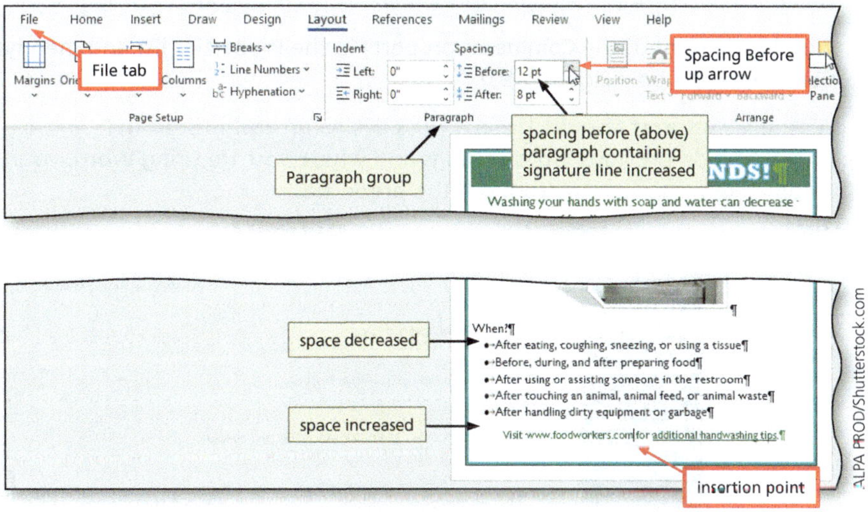

Figure 1–92

Other Ways

1. Right-click paragraph (or, if using touch, tap 'Show Context Menu' button on Mini toolbar), click Paragraph on shortcut menu, click Indents and Spacing tab (Paragraph dialog box), enter spacing before and after values, click OK
2. Click Paragraph Dialog Box Launcher (Home tab or Layout tab | Paragraph group), click Indents and Spacing tab (Paragraph dialog box), enter spacing before and after values, click OK

To Change the Document Properties

Word helps you organize and identify your files by using **document properties**, which are the details about a file, such as the project author, title, and subject. For example, a class name or document topic can describe the file's purpose or content.

Document properties are valuable for a variety of reasons:

- You can save time locating a particular file because you can view a document's properties without opening the document.
- By creating consistent properties for files having similar content, you can better organize your documents.
- Some organizations require Word users to add document properties so that other employees can view details about these files.

The more common document properties are standard and automatically updated properties. **Standard properties** are associated with all Microsoft Office files and include author, title, and subject. **Automatically updated properties** include file system properties, such as the date you create or change a file, and statistics, such as the file size.

You can change the document properties while working with the file in Word. When you save the file, Word will save the document properties with the file. The following steps change the comment document property. **Why?** Adding document properties will help you identify characteristics of the file without opening it.

1

- Click File on the ribbon (shown in Figure 1–92) to open Backstage view and then, if necessary, click Info in Backstage view to display the Info screen.

Q&A **What is the purpose of the Info screen in Backstage view?**
The Info screen contains commands that enable you to protect a document, inspect a document, and manage versions of a document, as well as view and change document properties.

- Click to the right of the Comments property in the Properties list and then type `CIS 101 Assignment` in the Comments text box (Figure 1–93).

Q&A **Why are some of the document properties already filled in?**
Depending on previous Word settings and where you are using Word, your school, university, or place of employment may have customized the properties.

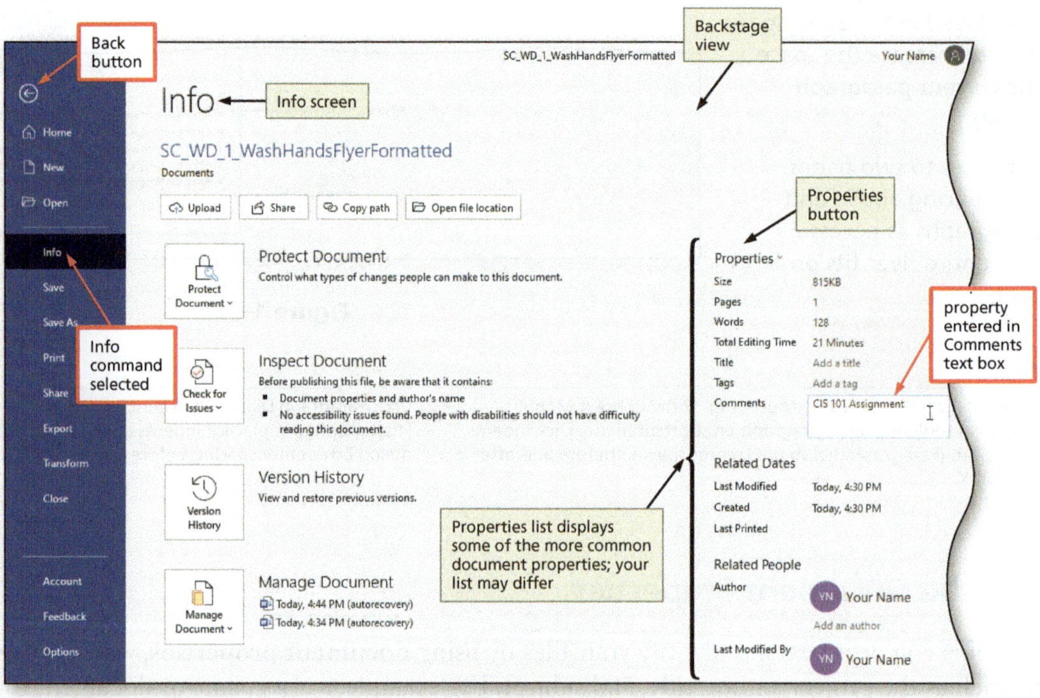

Figure 1–93

2

- Click the Back button in the upper-left corner of Backstage view to return to the document window.

Q&A **What if the property I want to change is not displayed in the Properties list?**
Scroll to the bottom of the Info screen and then click the 'Show All Properties' link to display more properties in the Properties list, or click the Properties button to display the Properties menu, and then click Advanced Properties on the Properties menu to display the Summary tab in the Properties dialog box. Type your desired text in the appropriate property text boxes. Click OK (Properties dialog box) to close the dialog box and then click the Back button in the upper-left corner of Backstage view to return to the document window.

To Save an Existing Document with the Same File Name

Saving frequently cannot be overemphasized. **Why?** You have made modifications to the document since you last saved it. Thus, you should save it again. Similarly, you should continue saving files frequently so that you do not lose the changes you have made since the time you last saved the file. You can use the same file name, such as SC_WD_1_WashHandsFlyerFormatted, to save the changes made to the document. The following step saves a file again with the same file name in the same save location.

1

- Click the Save button on the Quick Access Toolbar to overwrite the previously saved file (SC_WD_1_WashHandsFlyerFormatted, in this case) in the same location it was saved previously (Documents library) (Figure 1–94).

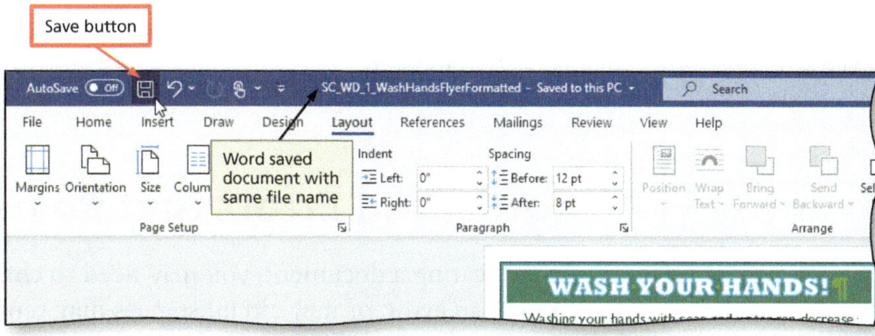

Figure 1–94

Other Ways

1. Press CTRL+S
2. Press SHIFT+F12

To Close a Document

Although you still need to make some edits to this document, you want to close the document at this time. **Why?** You should close a file when you are done working with it or wish to take a break so that you do not make inadvertent changes to it. The following steps close the current active Word document, SC_WD_1_WashHandsFlyerFormatted.docx, without exiting Word.

1

- Click File on the ribbon to open Backstage view (Figure 1–95).

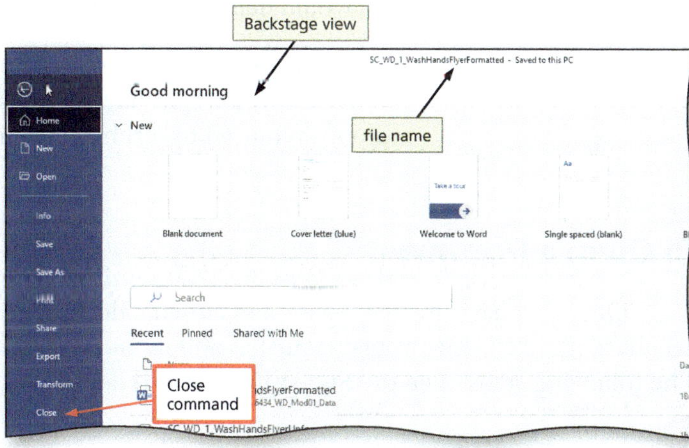

Figure 1–95

2

- Click Close in Backstage view to close the currently open document (SC_WD_1_WashHandsFlyerFormatted.docx, in this case) without exiting Word (Figure 1–96).

Q&A

What if Word displays a dialog box about saving?

Click Save if you want to save the changes, click Don't Save if you want to ignore the changes since the last time you saved, and click Cancel if you do not want to close the document.

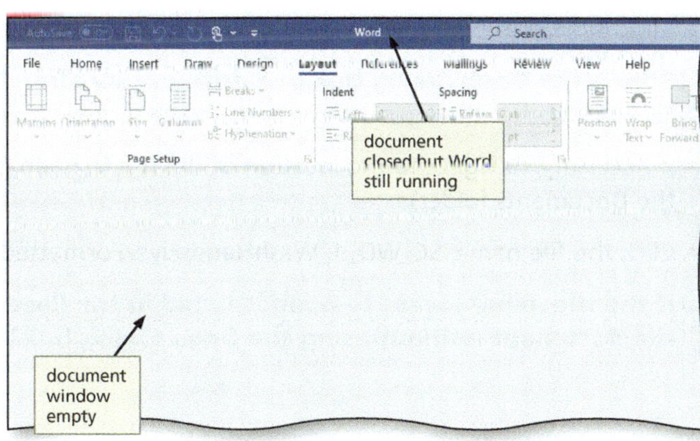

Figure 1–96

Other Ways

1. Press CTRL+F4

Break Point: If you want to take a break, this is a good place to do so. To resume later, start Word and continue following the steps from this location forward.

Correcting Errors and Revising a Document

After creating a document, you may need to change it. For example, the document may contain an error, or new circumstances may require you to add text to the document.

Types of Changes Made to Documents

The types of changes made to documents normally fall into one of the three following categories: additions, deletions, or modifications.

Additions Additional words, sentences, or paragraphs may be required in a document. Additions occur when you omit text from a document and want to insert it later. For example, you may want to add an email address to the flyer.

Deletions Sometimes, text in a document is incorrect or no longer is needed. For example, you may discover that air dryers are no longer used to dry hands. In this case, you would delete the words, or air dryer, from the flyer.

Modifications If an error is made in a document or changes take place that affect the document, you might have to revise a word(s) in the text. For example, the number of seconds required to scrub hands may change.

To Open a Document

Once you have created, saved, and closed a document, you may need to retrieve it from storage. **Why?** You may have more changes to make, such as adding more content or correcting errors, or you may want to print it. The following steps open the SC_WD_1_WashHandsFlyerFormatted.docx file.

1

- Click File on the ribbon to open Backstage view.
- If necessary, click Open in Backstage view to display the Open screen.
- Click Browse to display the Open dialog box.

Q&A **Why is the Open dialog box in a different location from my screen?**
You can move a dialog box anywhere on the screen by dragging its title bar.

- If necessary, navigate to the location of the file to open (in this case, SC_WD_1_WashHandsFlyerFormatted.docx in the Documents folder).
- Click the file name, SC_WD_1_WashHandsFlyerFormatted, to select the file (Figure 1–97).

Q&A **If the file name I want to open is listed in the Recent Documents list, can I click the file name to open the document without using the Open dialog box?**
Yes.

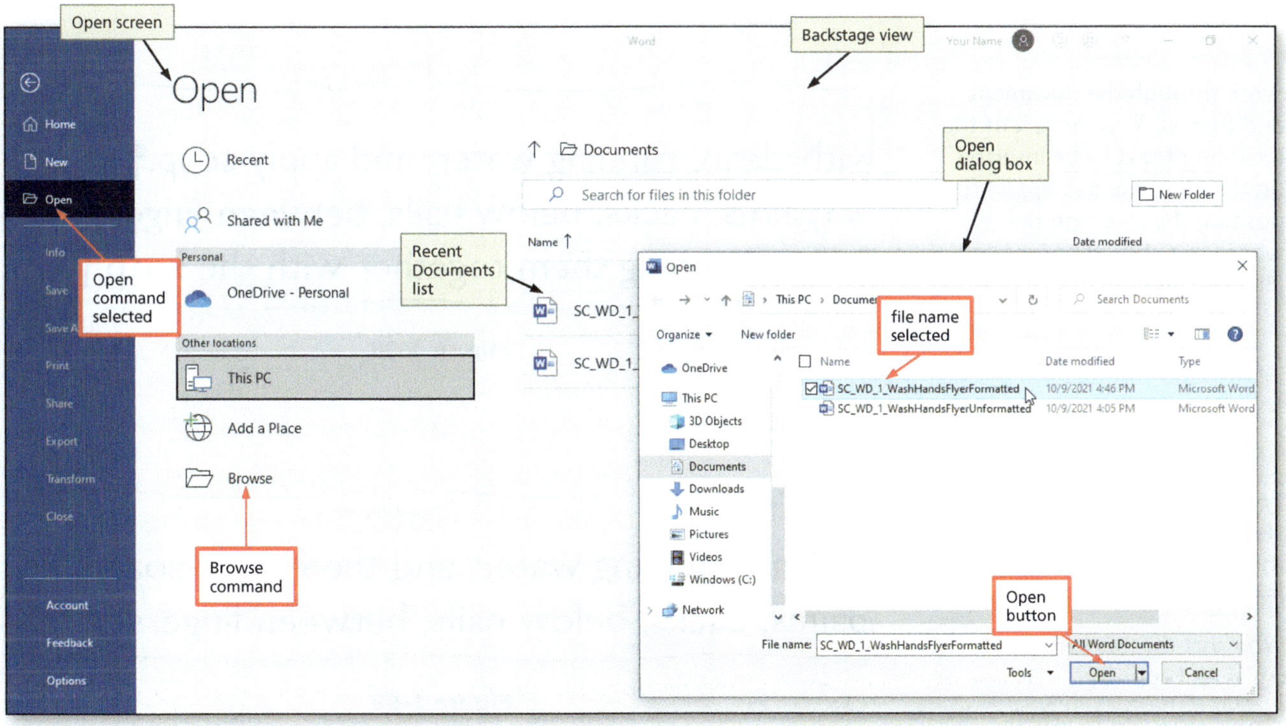

Figure 1–97

2

- Click the Open button (Open dialog box) to open the selected file and display its contents in the document window (shown in Figure 1–98). If necessary, click the Enable Content button.

Other Ways

1. If file appears in Recent Documents list, click file name
2. Press CTRL+O
3. Navigate to file in File Explorer window, double-click file name

To Change the Zoom to Page Width

Because the document contents are small when displayed on one page, the following steps zoom page width again.

1. Click View on the ribbon to display the View tab.
2. Click the Page Width button (View tab | Zoom group) to display the page the same width as the document window.

To Insert Text in an Existing Document

Word inserts text to the left of the insertion point. The text to the right of the insertion point moves to the right and downward to fit the new text. The following steps insert the word, then, to the left of the word, apply, in the numbered list in the flyer. **Why?** These steps illustrate the process of inserting text.

1

- Scroll through the document and then click to the left of the location of text to be inserted (in this case, the a in apply) to position the insertion point where text should be inserted (Figure 1–98).

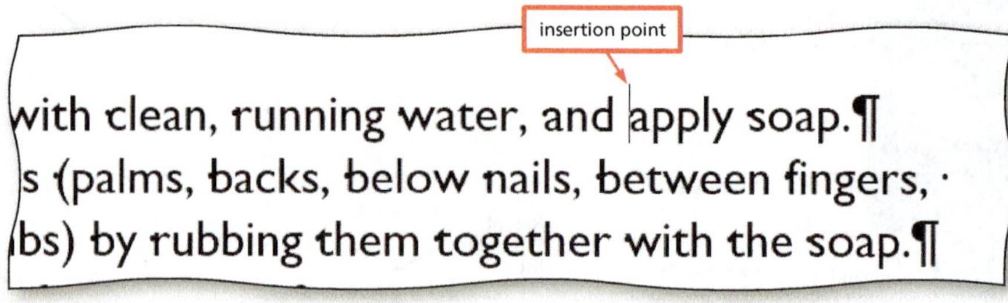

Figure 1–98

2

- Type **then** and then press SPACEBAR to insert the word to the left of the insertion point (Figure 1–99).

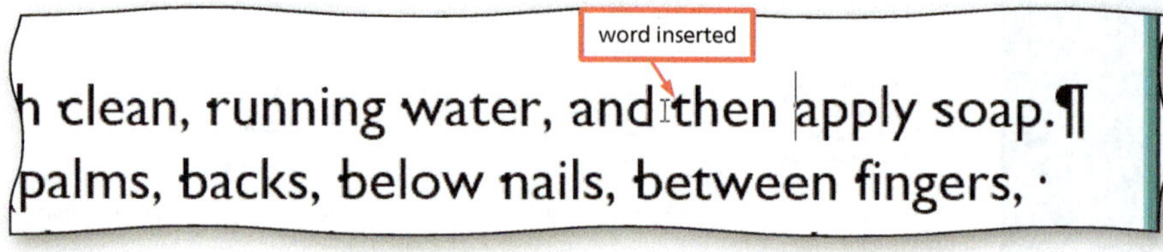

Figure 1–99

Q&A **Why did the text move to the right as I typed?**
In Word, the default typing mode is **insert mode**, which means as you type a character, Word moves all the characters to the right of the typed character one position to the right.

BTW
Delete versus Cut
When you press DELETE, the deleted text is not placed on the Office Clipboard. If you want deleted text to be placed on the Office Clipboard, use the Cut button (Home tab | Clipboard group).

Cutting, Copying, and Pasting

The **Office Clipboard** is a temporary storage area in a computer's memory that lets you collect up to 24 items (text or objects) from any Office document and then paste these items into almost any other type of document. The Office Clipboard works with the copy, cut, and paste commands:

- To **copy** is the process of selecting text or an object and placing a copy of the selected items on the Office Clipboard, leaving the item in its original location in the document.
- To **cut** is the process of removing text or an object from a document and placing it on the Office Clipboard.
- To **paste** is the process of placing an item stored on the Office Clipboard in the document at the location of the insertion point.

To Delete or Cut Text

It is not unusual to type incorrect characters or words in a document. As discussed earlier in this module, you can click the Undo button on the Quick Access Toolbar or press CTRL+Z to undo a command or action immediately — this includes typing. Word also provides other methods of correcting typing errors.

To delete an incorrect character in a document, simply click next to the incorrect character and then press BACKSPACE to erase to the left of the insertion point, or press DELETE to erase to the right of the insertion point.

To cut a word or phrase, you first must select the word or phrase. The following steps select the word, then, which was just added in the previous steps, and then cuts the selection. **Why?** These steps illustrate the process of selecting a word and then cutting selected text.

1

- Click Home on the ribbon to display the Home tab.
- Double-click the word to be selected (in this case, then) to select the word (Figure 1–100).

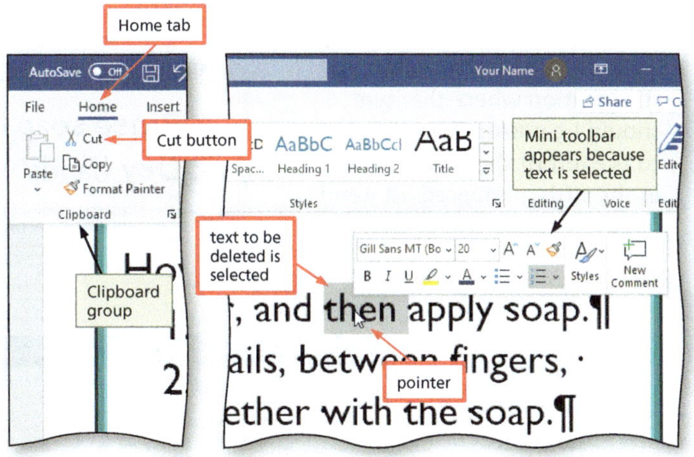

Figure 1–100

2

- Click the Cut button (Home tab | Clipboard group) to cut the selected text (shown in Figure 1–98).

Q&A **What if I am using a touch screen?**
Tap the selected text to display the Mini toolbar and then tap the Cut button on the Mini toolbar to delete the selected text.

Other Ways

1. Right-click selected item, click Cut on shortcut menu
2. Select item, press BACKSPACE to delete to left of insertion point or press DELETE to delete to right of insertion point
3. Select item, press CTRL+X or DELETE

To Copy and Paste

In the flyer, you copy a word from one location (the first numbered list item) to another location (the fifth numbered list item). **Why?** The fifth numbered item is clearer with the word, clean, inserted before the word, towel. The following steps copy and paste a word.

1

- If necessary, scroll so that all the numbered list items appear in the document window.
- Select the item to be copied (the word, clean, in this case).
- Click the Copy button (Home tab | Clipboard group) to copy the selected item in the document to the Office Clipboard (Figure 1–101).

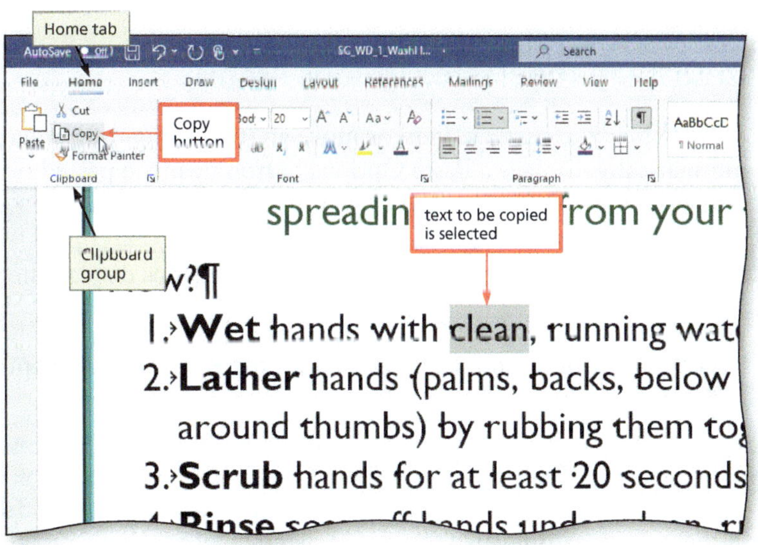

Figure 1–101

2

- Position the insertion point at the location where the item should be pasted (immediately to the left of the word, towel, in the fifth numbered list item) (Figure 1–102).

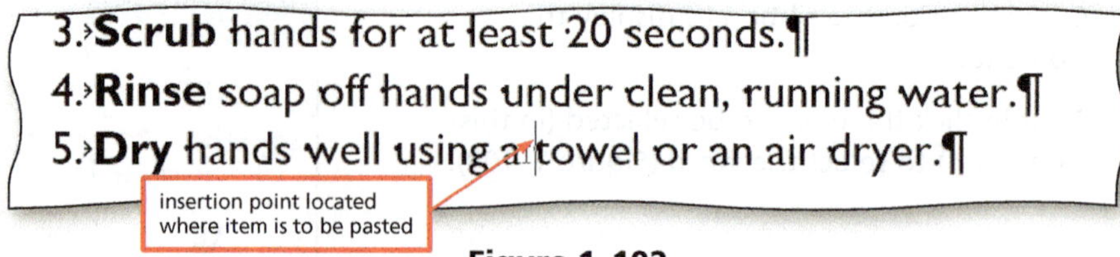

Figure 1–102

3

- Click the Paste button (Home tab | Clipboard group) to paste the copied item in the document at the location of the insertion point (Figure 1–103).

Q&A **What if I click the Paste arrow by mistake?**
Click the Paste arrow again to remove the Paste menu and repeat Step 3.

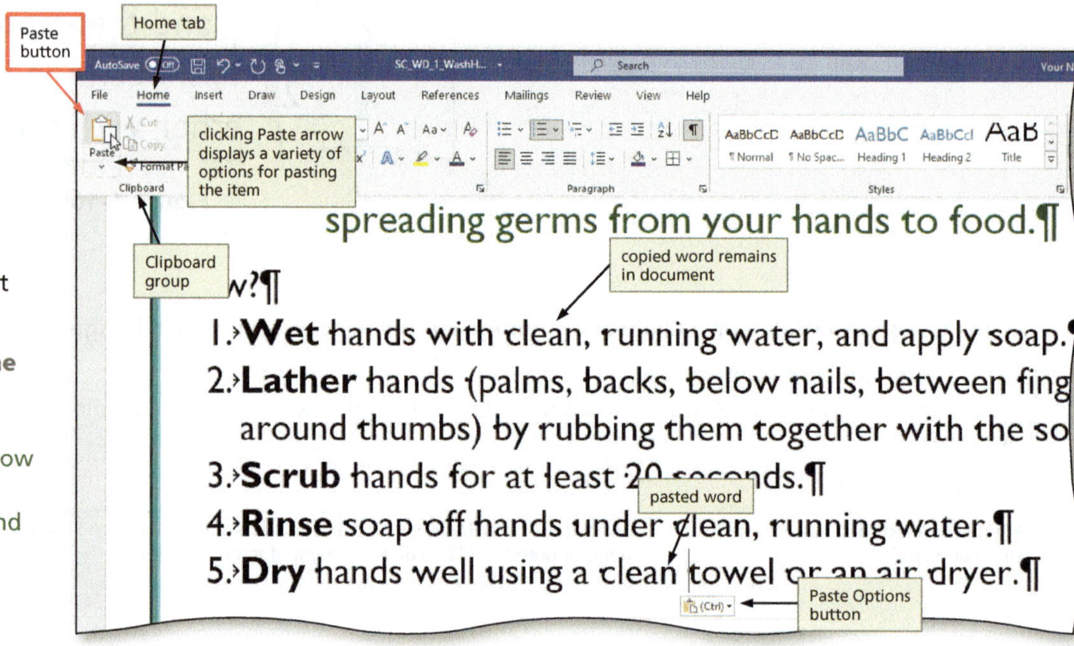

Figure 1–103

Other Ways

1. Right-click selected text (or, if using touch, tap 'Show Context Menu' button on Mini toolbar), click Copy on shortcut menu (or, if using touch, tap Copy on Mini toolbar), right-click where item is to be pasted, click 'Keep Source Formatting' in Paste Options area on shortcut menu (or, if using touch, tap Paste on Mini toolbar)
2. Select item, press CTRL+C, position insertion point at paste location, press CTRL+V

To Display the Paste Options Menu

When you paste an item or move an item using drag and drop (discussed in the next section), Word automatically displays a Paste Options button near the pasted or moved text (shown in Figure 1–103). **Why?** The Paste Options button allows you to change the format of a pasted item. For example, you can instruct Word to format the pasted item the same way as where it was copied (the source) or format it the same way as where it is being pasted (the destination). The following steps display the Paste Options menu.

1

- Click the Paste Options button to display the Paste Options menu (Figure 1–104).

Q&A **What are the functions of the buttons on the Paste Options menu?**
In general, the left button indicates the pasted item should look the same as it did in its original location (the source). The second button formats the pasted text to match the rest of the item where it was pasted (the destination). The third button pastes the item and a picture, and the fourth button removes all formatting from the pasted item. The 'Set Default Paste' command displays the Word Options dialog box. Keep in mind that the buttons shown on a Paste Options menu will vary, depending on the item being pasted.

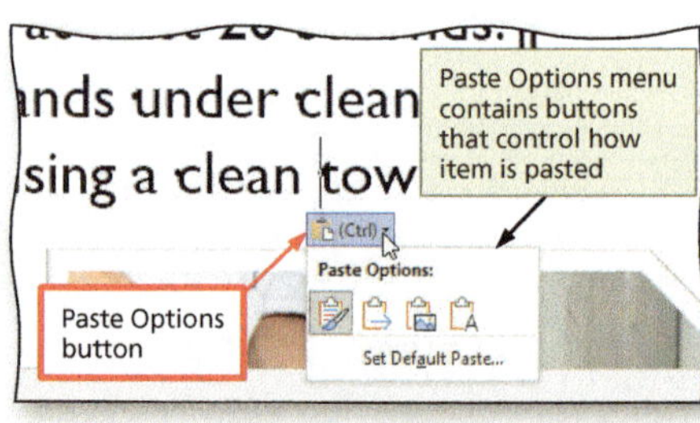

ALPA PROD/Shutterstock.com

Figure 1–104

2

- Click anywhere to remove the Paste Options menu from the window.

Other Ways

1. Press CTRL or ESC (to remove the Paste Options menu)

To Move Text

If you are moving text a short distance, instead of using cut and paste, you could use drag and drop. With **drag and drop**, you move an item by selecting it, dragging the selected item to a new location, and then dropping, or inserting, it in the new location.

The following steps use drag and drop to move text. **Why?** While proofreading the flyer, you realize that the body copy would read better if the first two bulleted paragraphs were reversed.

1

- Scroll to, if necessary, and then select the text to be moved (in this case, the second bulleted item).
- With the pointer in the selected text, press and hold down the mouse button, which displays a small dotted box with the pointer (Figure 1–105).

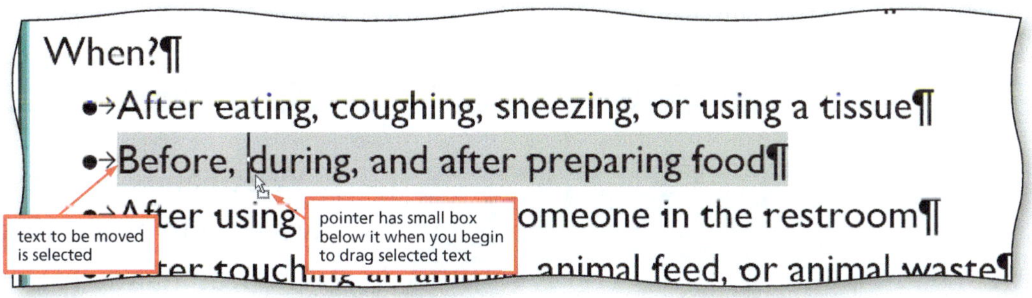

Figure 1–105

2

- Drag the insertion point to the location where the selected text is to be moved, as shown in Figure 1–106.

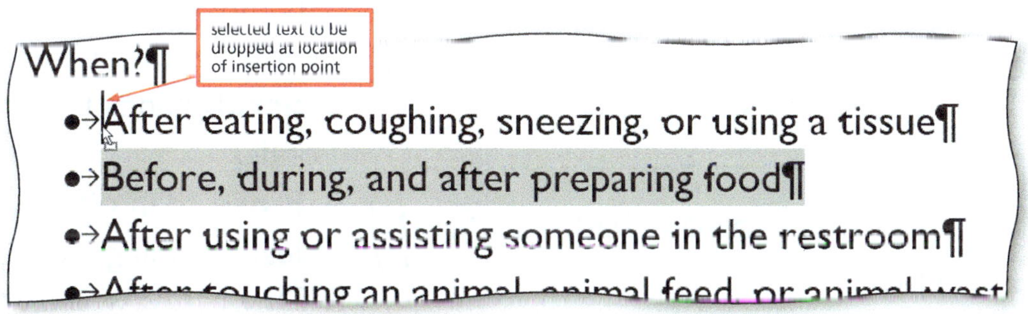

Figure 1–106

3

- Release the mouse button to move the selected text to the location of the dotted insertion point (Figure 1–107).

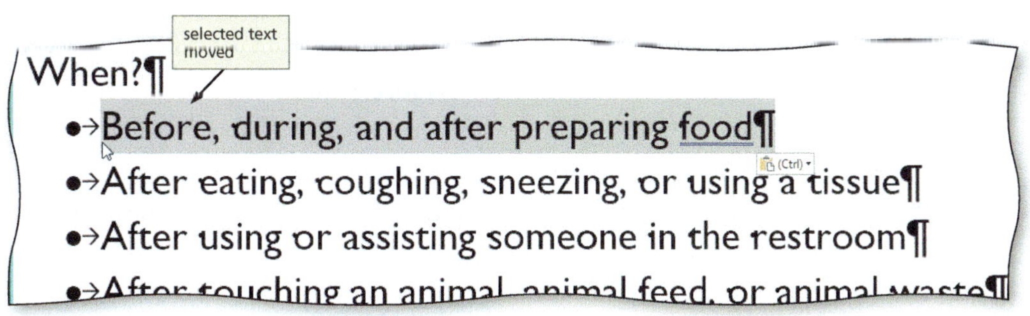

Figure 1–107

Q&A **What if I accidentally drag text to the wrong location?**
Click the Undo button on the Quick Access Toolbar or press CTRL+Z and try again.

Q&A **Can I use drag and drop to move any selected item?**
Yes, you can select words, sentences, phrases, pictures, or any object and then use drag and drop to move them.

- Click anywhere in the document window to remove the selection from the bulleted item.

Q&A **What if I am using a touch screen?**
If you have a stylus, you can follow Steps 1 through 3 using the stylus. If you are using your finger, you will need to use cut and paste, which was described earlier in this section.

To Switch to Read Mode

Some users prefer reading a document on-screen instead of on paper. **Why?** If you are not composing a document, you can switch to Read mode, which is a document view that makes the document easier to read by hiding the ribbon and other writing tools so that more content fits on the screen. The following step switches from Print Layout view to Read mode.

1

- Press CTRL+HOME to position the insertion point at the top of the document.
- Click the Read Mode button on the status bar to switch to Read mode (Figure 1–108).

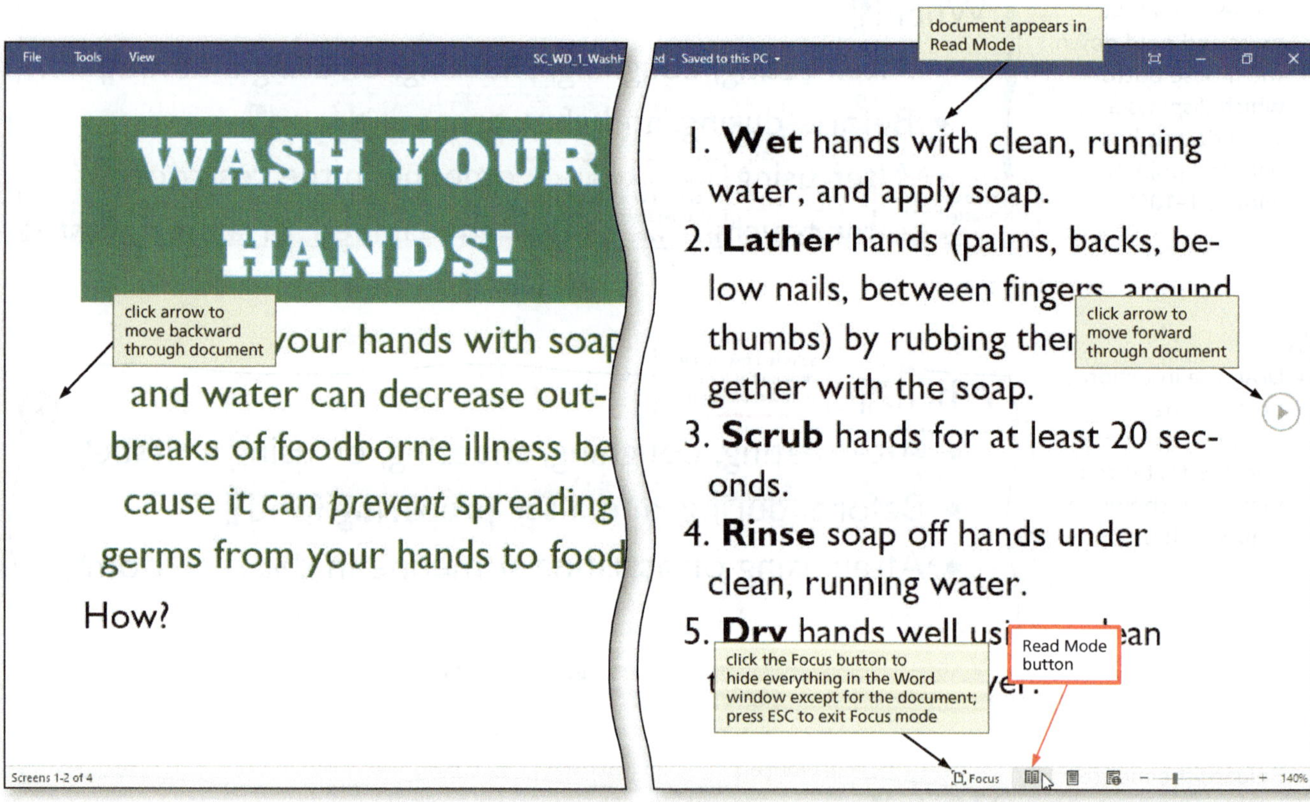

Figure 1–108

Experiment

- Click the arrows to advance forward and then move backward through the document.

Q&A **Besides reading, what can I do in Read mode?**
You can zoom, copy text, highlight text, search, add comments, and more.

Other Ways

1. Click Read Mode button (View tab | Views group)

To Switch to Print Layout View

The next step switches back to Print Layout view. **Why?** If you want to show the document on an image of a sheet of paper in the document window, along with the ribbon and other writing tools, you should switch to Print Layout view. The following step switches to Print Layout view.

1

- Click the Print Layout button on the status bar to switch to Print Layout view (Figure 1–109).

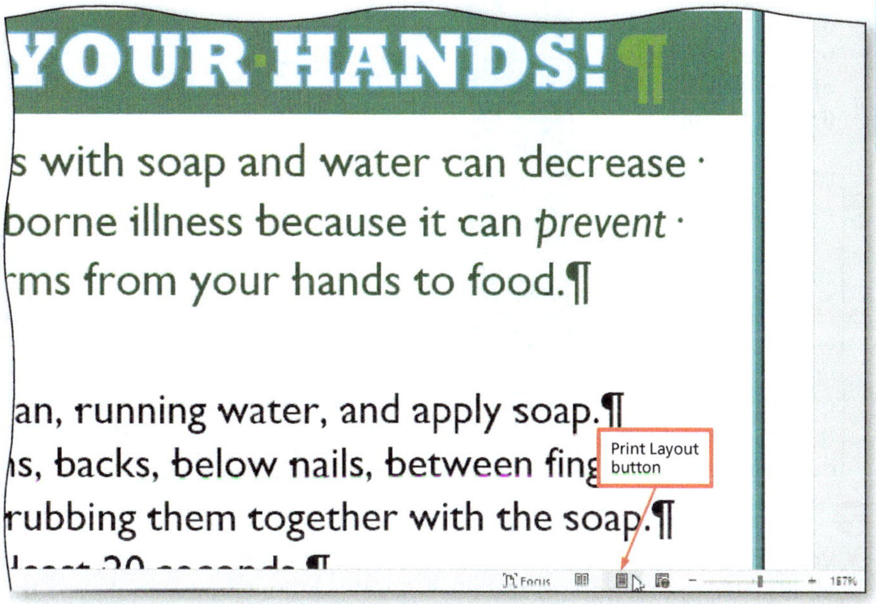

Figure 1–109

Other Ways

1. Click Print Layout button (View tab | Views group)
2. In Read Mode, click View on the ribbon, click Edit Document

To Save a Document with the Same File Name

It is a good practice to save a document before printing it, in the event you experience difficulties printing. The following step saves the document again on the same storage location with the same file name.

1 Click the Save button on the Quick Access Toolbar to overwrite the previously saved file (SC_WD_1_WashHandsFlyerFormatted, in this case) in the same location it was saved previously (Documents library).

Q&A **Why should I save the flyer again?**
You have made several modifications to the flyer since you last saved it; thus, you should save it again.

BTW

Conserving Ink and Toner

If you want to conserve ink or toner, you can instruct Word to print draft quality documents by clicking File on the ribbon to open Backstage view, clicking Options in Backstage view to display the Word Options dialog box, clicking Advanced in the left pane (Word Options dialog box), scrolling to the Print area in the right pane, placing a check mark in the 'Use draft quality' check box, and then clicking OK. Then, use Backstage view to print the document as usual.

To Print a Document

After creating a document, you may want to print it. **Why?** You want to see how the flyer will appear on a printed piece of paper. The following steps print the contents of the document on a printer.

1

- Click File on the ribbon to open Backstage view.
- Click Print in Backstage view to display the Print screen and a preview of the document (Figure 1–110).

Q&A **What if I decide not to print the document at this time?**
Click the Back button in the upper-left corner of Backstage view to return to the document window.

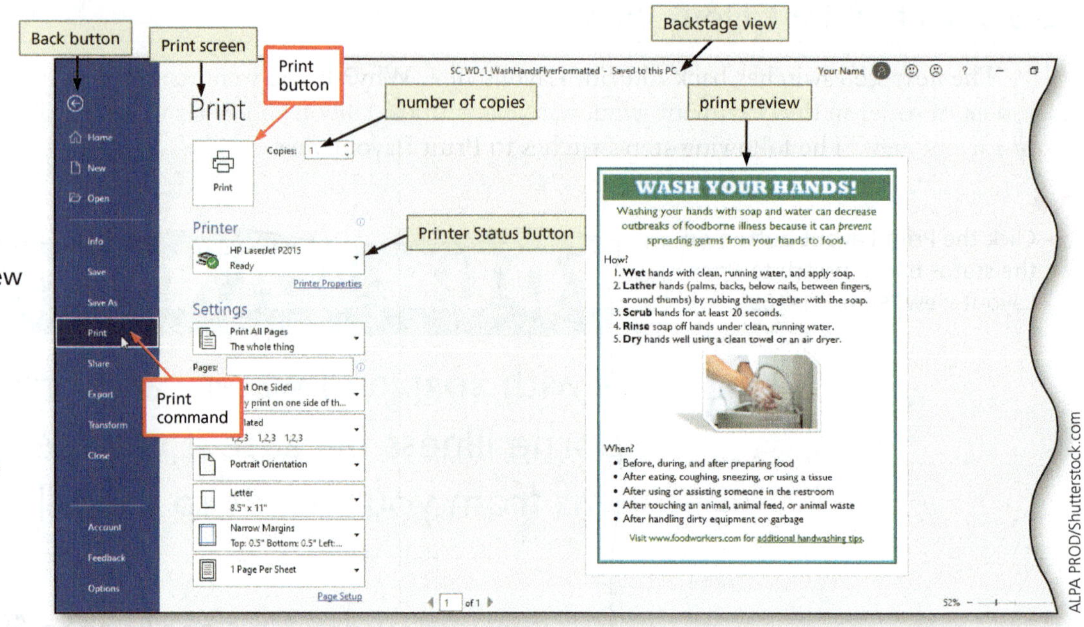

Figure 1–110

2

- Verify that the selected printer will print the document. If necessary, click the Printer Status button to display a list of available printer options and then click the desired printer to change the currently selected printer.

Q&A **How can I print multiple copies of my document?**
Increase the number in the Copies box in the Print screen.

3

- Click the Print button in the Print screen to print the document on the currently selected printer.
- When the printer stops, retrieve the printed document (shown in Figure 1–1).

Q&A **What if one or more of my borders do not print?**
Click the Page Borders button (Design tab | Page Background group), click the Options button (Borders and Shading dialog box), click the Measure from arrow and click Text, change the four text boxes to 15 pt, and then click OK in each dialog box. Try printing the document again. If the borders still do not print, adjust the boxes in the dialog box to a number smaller than 15 point.

Do I have to wait until my document is complete to print it?
No, you can print a document at any time while you are creating it.

Other Ways

1. Press CTRL+P

BTW
Printing Document Properties
To print document properties, click File on the ribbon to open Backstage view, click Print in Backstage view to display the Print screen, click the first button in the Settings area to display a list of options specifying what you can print, click Document Info in the list to specify you want to print the document properties instead of the actual document, and then click the Print button in the Print screen to print the document properties on the currently selected printer.

Using Word Help

At any time while you are using Word, you can use Word Help to display information about all topics associated with Word. You can search for help by using the Search box or the Help pane.

To Use the Search Box

If you are having trouble finding a button, box, or other command in Word, you can use the Search box to search for the task you are trying to perform. As you type, the Search box will suggest commands that match the search text you are entering. **Why?** You can use the Search box to access commands quickly that you otherwise may be unable to find on the ribbon or to display help about a command in the Help pane. The following steps find information about margins.

1

- Type **margins** in the Search box and watch the search results appear.
- Point to (or click, if necessary) Adjust Margins on the Search menu to display the Margins gallery (Figure 1–111).

Q&A **Does this Margins gallery work the same as the one I used earlier in this module to change the margins?**
Yes, it is the exact same Margins gallery. You can select an option in the gallery to apply that command to the document.

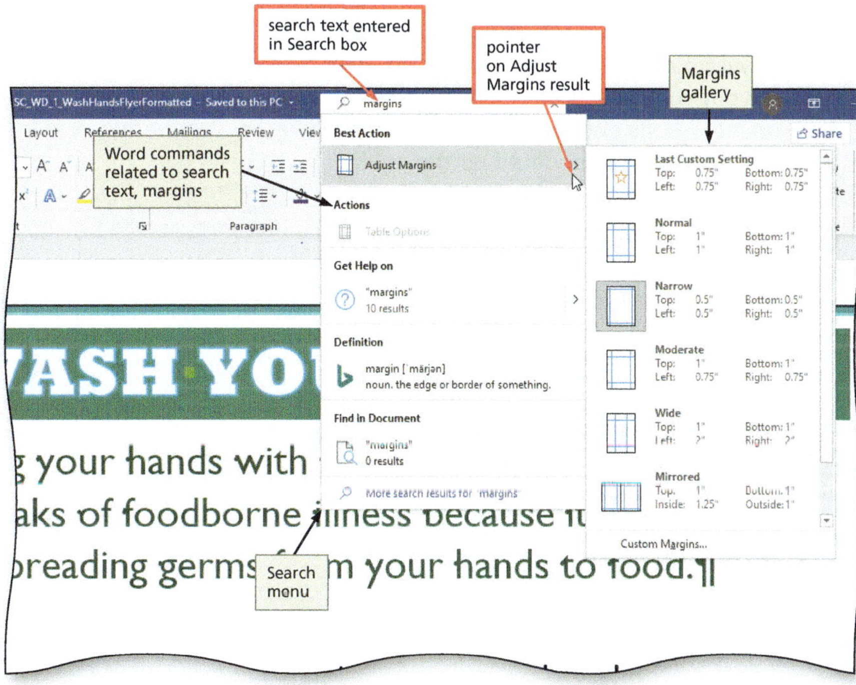

Figure 1–111

2

- Point to the 'Get Help on "margins" arrow' on the Search menu to display a submenu displaying the various help topics about the entered search text, margins (Figure 1–112).

Q&A **What is a submenu?**
A **submenu** is a list of additional commands associated with the selected command on a menu. If you point to an arrow on a menu, Word displays submenu.

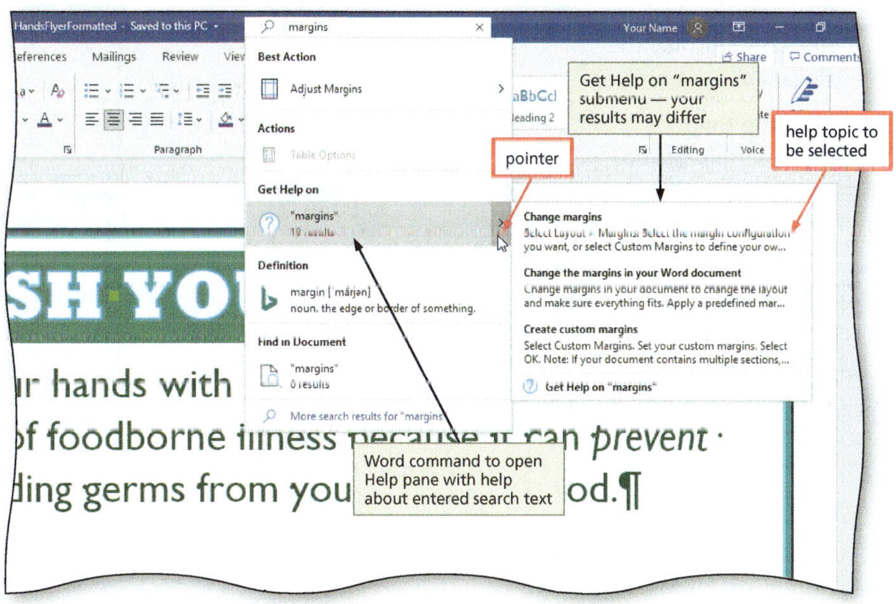

Figure 1–112

3

- Click the first help topic displayed on the submenu to open the Help pane, which displays a help topic about the selected command (Figure 1–113).

Q&A

Why do my search results differ?
If you do not have an Internet connection, your results will reflect only the content of the Help files on your computer. When searching for help online, results also can change as content is added, deleted, and updated on the online Help webpages maintained by Microsoft.

Can I search for additional help topics by entering search text in the search box in the Help pane?
Yes.

4

- After you have finished reading the help information, click the Close button in the Help pane to close the pane.

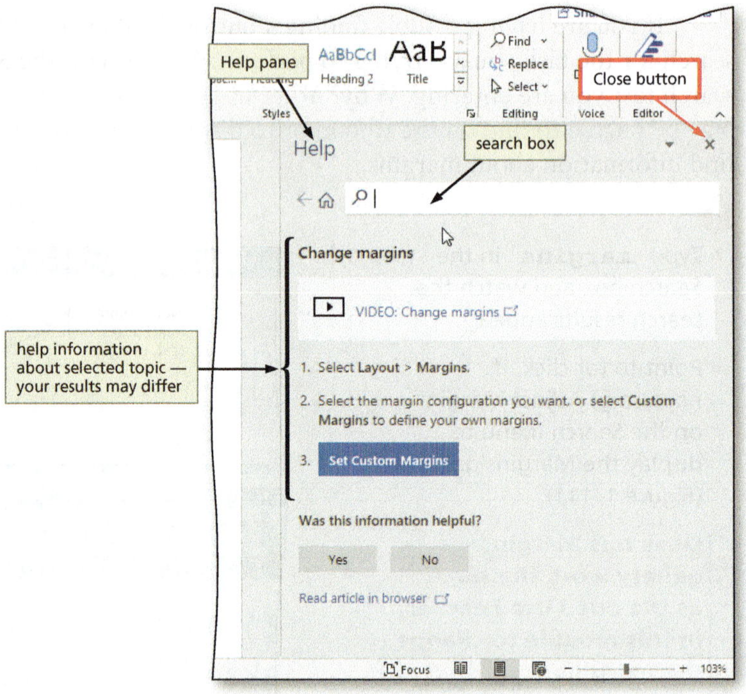

Figure 1–113

To Use the Help Pane

The following steps open the Help pane. **Why?** You may not know the exact help topic you are looking to find, so you want to navigate the Help pane.

1

- Click Help on the ribbon to display the Help tab.
- Click the Help button (Help group) to open the Help pane (Figure 1–114).

Q&A

How do I navigate the Help pane?
You can scroll through the displayed information in the Help pane, click any of the links to additional help, click the Back button on the Help pane to return to a previously displayed screen, or enter search text in the search box.

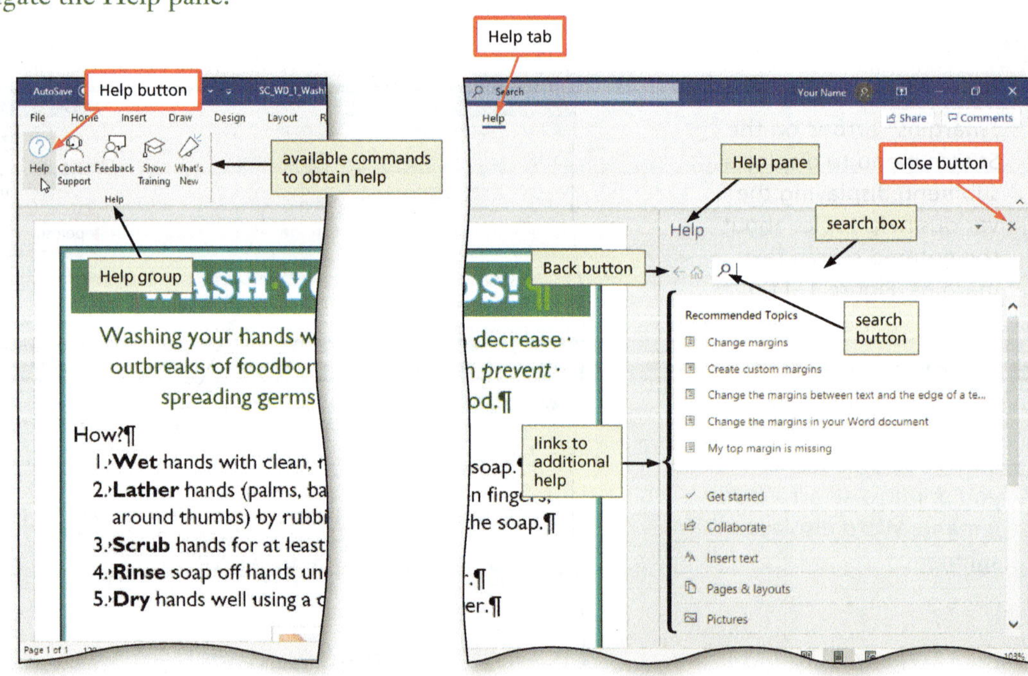

Figure 1–114

Q&A **Does the search box in the Help pane work the same as the Search box?**
Yes. In the same way that you entered search text in the Search box, you would enter search text in the search box in the Help pane and then press ENTER or click the search button to display a list of Help topics that match the entered search text.

2

- When you are finished with the Help pane, click its Close button to close the pane.

Other Ways

1. Press F1

Obtaining Help while Working in Word

You also can access Help without first using the Search box or opening the Help pane and initiating a search. For example, you may be unsure about how a particular command works, or you may be presented with a dialog box that you are not sure how to use.

If you want to learn more about a command, point to its button and wait for the ScreenTip to appear, as shown in Figure 1–115. If the Help icon and 'Tell me more' link appear in the ScreenTip, click the 'Tell me more' link (or press F1 while pointing to the button) to open the Help pane and display a help topic associated with that command.

Dialog boxes also contain Help buttons, as shown in Figure 1–116. Clicking the Help button or pressing F1 while the dialog box is displayed opens a help window in your browser, which will display help contents specific to that dialog box, if available.

BTW
Word Help
At any time while using Word, you can find answers to questions and display information about various topics through Word Help. Used properly, this form of assistance can increase your productivity and reduce your frustrations by minimizing the time you spend learning how to use Word.

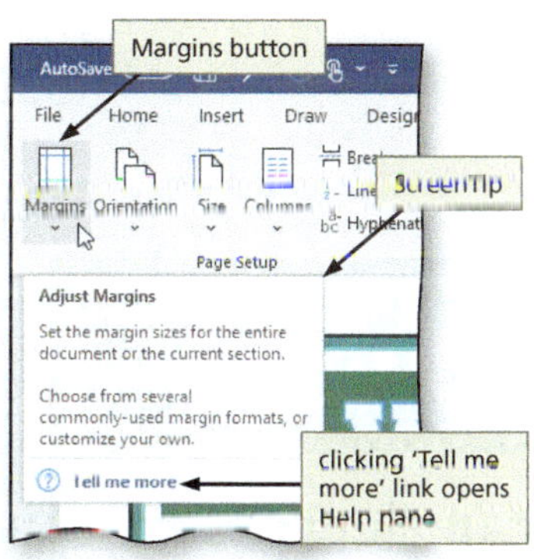

Figure 1–115

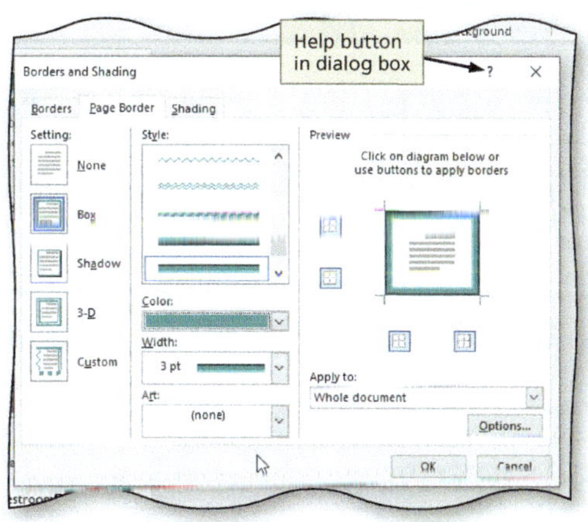

Figure 1–116

To Sign Out of a Microsoft Account

If you are using a public computer or otherwise wish to sign out of your Microsoft account, you should sign out of the account from the Accounts screen in Backstage view. Signing out of the account is the safest way to ensure that no one else can access online files or settings stored in your Microsoft account. If you wanted to sign out of a Microsoft account from Word, you would perform the following steps.

1. Click File on the ribbon to open Backstage view and then click Account to display the Account screen.

2. Click the Sign out link, which displays the Remove Account dialog box. If a Can't remove Windows accounts dialog box appears instead of the Remove Account dialog box, click OK and skip the remaining steps.

Q&A **Why does a Can't remove Windows accounts dialog box appear?**
If you signed in to Windows using your Microsoft account, then you also must sign out from Windows, rather than signing out from within Word. When you are finished using Windows, be sure to sign out at that time.

3. Click the Yes button (Remove Account dialog box) to sign out of your Microsoft account on this computer.

Q&A **Should I sign out of Windows after removing my Microsoft account?**
When you are finished using the computer, you should sign out of Windows for maximum security.

4. Click the Back button in the upper-left corner of Backstage view to return to the document window.

BTW
Office 365 Apps
Word is part of Microsoft 365 apps; other Premium Office apps include Microsoft PowerPoint, Microsoft Excel, Microsoft Access, and Microsoft Outlook. The Microsoft 365 apps typically use a similar interface and share features.

To Exit Word

You saved the document prior to printing and did not make any changes to the project. The following step exits Word. **Why?** The SC_WD_1_WashHandsFlyerFormatted.docx project now is complete, and you are ready to exit Word.

1.
- Click the Close button in the upper-right corner of the Word window to Exit Word.
- **sam** If a Microsoft Word dialog box is displayed (Figure 1–117), click Save to save changes before exiting.

Q&A **When I exited Word, a dialog box did not display. Why not?**
If you made changes to your document since you last saved it, the dialog box shown in Figure 1–117 will appear when you exit Word. If you want to save changes before exiting, click Save; if you do not want to save changes, click Don't Save; if you change your mind and do not want to exit Word, click Cancel to return to the document in the document window.

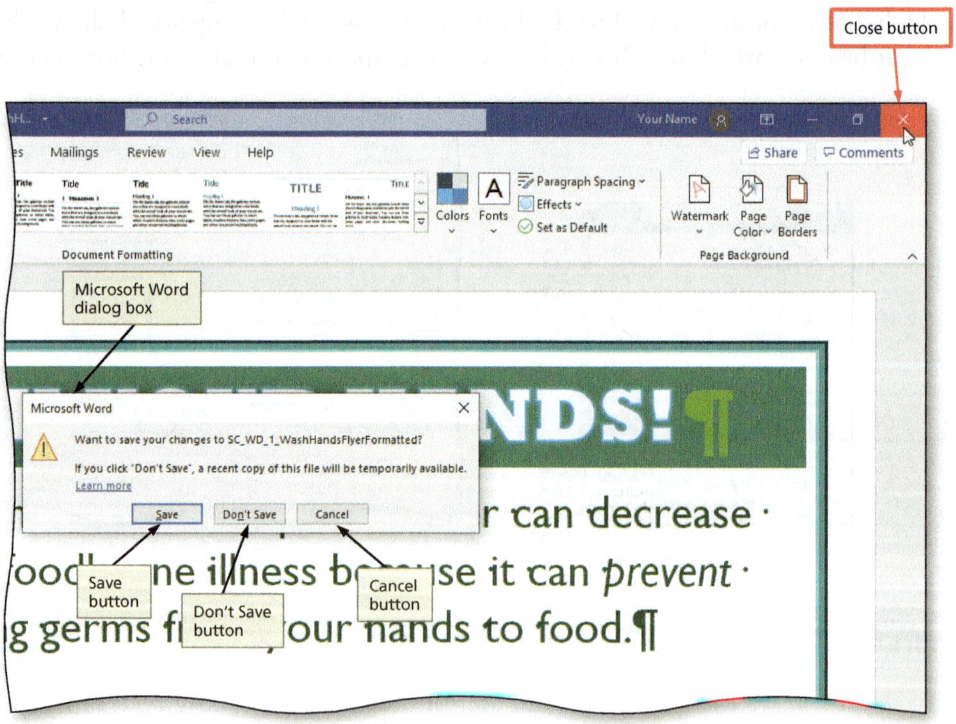

Figure 1–117

Other Ways
1. Right-click Microsoft Word button on Windows taskbar, click Close Window on shortcut menu

Summary

In this module, you learned how to start and use Word, enter text in a document, correct spelling and grammar errors as you work in a document, format paragraphs and characters, insert and format a picture, add a page border, adjust paragraph and page spacing, revise a document, print a document, and use Word Help.

Consider This

What decisions will you need to make when creating your next flyer?

Use these guidelines as you complete the assignments in this module and create your own flyers outside of this class.

1. Choose the text for the headline, body copy, and signature line, using as few words as possible to make a point.
2. Format various elements of the text.
   a) Select appropriate font sizes for text in the headline, body copy, and signature line.
   b) Select appropriate fonts for text in the headline, body copy, and signature line.
   c) Adjust paragraph alignment, as appropriate.
   d) Highlight key paragraphs with bullets or numbers.
   e) Emphasize important words.
   f) Use color to convey meaning and add appeal.
3. Find an eye-catching picture(s) that conveys the overall message and meaning of the flyer.
4. Establish where to position and how to format the picture(s) so that it grabs the attention of passersby and draws them into reading the flyer.
5. Determine whether the flyer needs enhancements, such as a graphical, color-coordinated border, or spacing adjustments to improve readability or overall appearance.
6. Correct errors and revise the document as necessary.
   a) Post the flyer on a wall and make sure all text and images are legible from a distance.
   b) Ask someone else to read the flyer and give you suggestions for improvements.
7. Determine the best method for distributing the document, such as printing, sending via email, or posting on the web or social media.

BTW

Distributing a Document

Instead of printing and distributing a hard copy of a document, you can distribute the document electronically. Options include sending the document via email; posting it on cloud storage (such as OneDrive) and sharing the file with others; posting it on social media, a blog, or other website; and sharing a link associated with an online location of the document. You also can create and share a PDF or XPS image of the document, so that users can view the file in Acrobat Reader or XPS Viewer instead of in Word.

Apply Your Knowledge

Reinforce the skills and apply the concepts you learned in this module.

Modifying Text and Formatting a Document

Note: To complete this assignment, you will be required to use the Data Files. Please contact your instructor for information about accessing the Data Files.

Instructions: Start Word. Open the document, SC_WD_1-1.docx, which is located in the Data Files. The file you open contains an unformatted flyer that announces a blood drive for Lightwing Center for Outpatient Care. The manager of medical services, who created the text in the unformatted flyer, has asked you to modify the text in the flyer, format its paragraphs and characters, and insert a picture to create the formatted flyer shown in Figure 1–118.

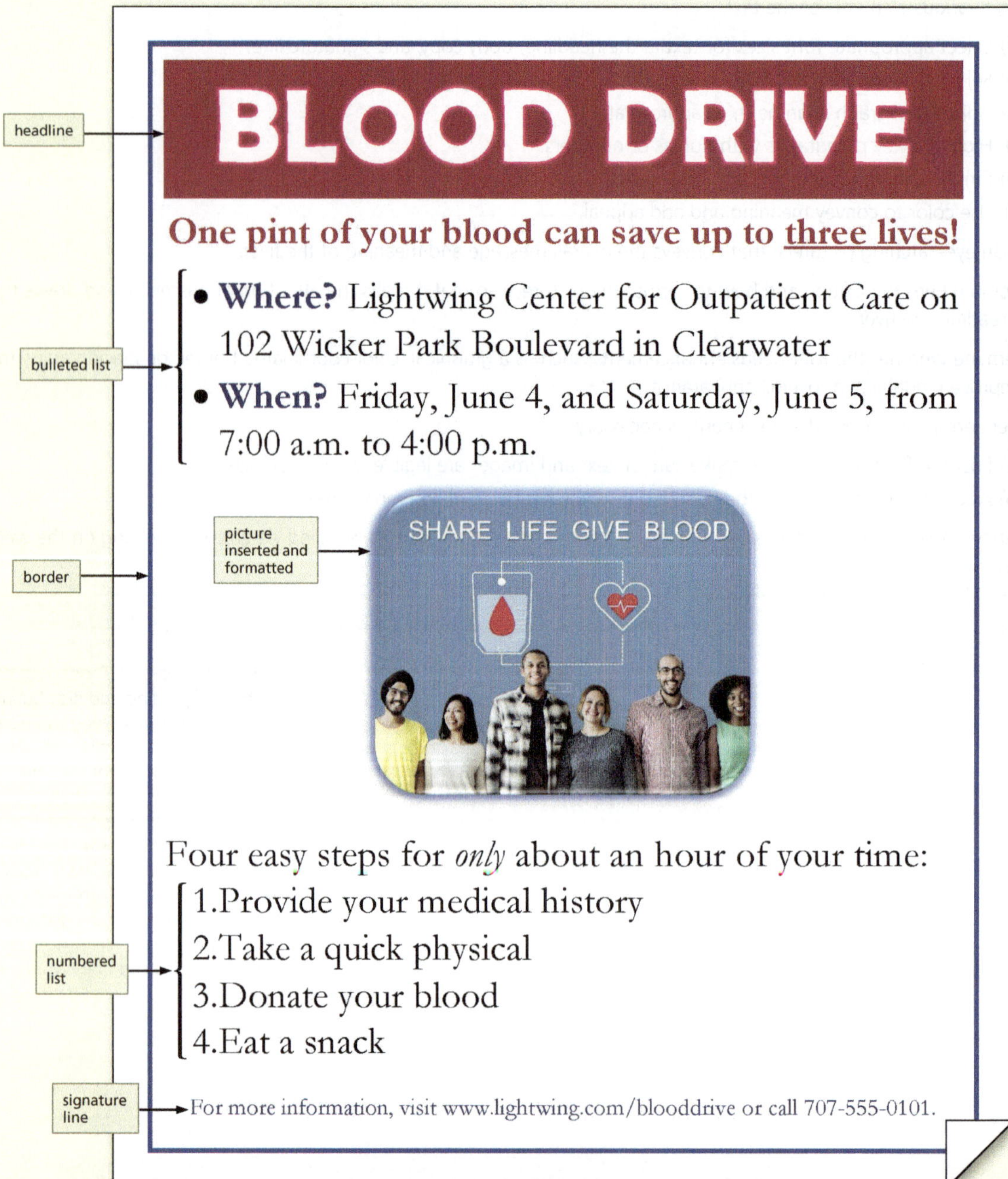

Rawpixel.com/Shutterstock.com

Figure 1–118

Perform the following tasks:

1. Display formatting marks on the screen.
2. Click File on the ribbon, click Save As, and then save the document using the new file name, SC_WD_1_BloodDriveFlyer.
3. Review each spelling (red wavy underline), grammar (blue double underline), and word choice (purple dotted underline) suggestion in the document by right-clicking the flagged text and then clicking the appropriate correction on the shortcut menu. Use the Ignore All command if the name of the medical center, Lightwing, is flagged because it is a proper name and spelled correctly. Use the Ignore Once command to ignore each suggestion to add punctuation at the end of the sixth through eighth lines.
4. Delete the second question mark after the text, When??, so that only one question mark follows the word.
5. Delete the word, single, in the line of text below the headline.
6. Insert the word, call, to the left of the phone number in the signature line (so that it reads: ...or call 707-555-0101).
7. Change the word, Sunday, to the word, Saturday, in the fourth line.
8. If requested by your instructor, change the phone number in the flyer to your phone number.
9. Change the document theme to Organic.
10. Change the margins to Narrow (that is, .5" top, bottom, left, and right margins).
11. Center the headline, the first paragraph of body copy below the headline, and the signature line in the flyer.
12. Change the font size of all the body copy text between the headline and signature line to 26 point.
13. Select the second and third paragraphs of body copy in the flyer and format the selected paragraphs as a bulleted list (that is, the paragraphs that begin with the words, Where? and When?).
14. Select the four paragraphs immediately above the signature line and format the selected paragraphs as a numbered list.
15. Change the font and font size of the headline to 72-point Berlin Sans FB Demi, or a similar font. Change the case of the text in the headline to uppercase letters. Apply the preset text effect called 'Fill: White; Outline: Green, Accent color 1; Glow: Green, Accent color 1' to the entire headline. Shade the text in the headline Gold, Accent 6, Darker 25%.
16. Change the theme colors to Red Violet.
17. Change the font color of the first line (paragraph) of body copy below the headline to Red, Accent 6, Darker 25%. Bold the text in this line.
18. Cut the word, Park, in the first bulleted paragraph. Paste the cut word in the same paragraph before the word, Boulevard, so the address reads: 102 Wicker Park Boulevard.
19. Copy the word, your, before the word, time, in the line above the numbered list. Paste the copied word before the word, blood, in the first paragraph of body copy below the headline, so that it reads: One pint of your blood can save up to three lives! Click the Paste Options button that appears before the pasted text and then click Merge Formatting on the Paste Options menu so that the pasted text has the same formats as the location of the insertion point.
20. Remove the hyperlink format from the web address in the signature line. If the text is still colored and underlined, change the color to Automatic and remove the underline.
21. Select the last paragraph on the page (the signature line) and then use the Mini toolbar to change the font size of the text in this paragraph to 16 point and its font color to Blue, Accent 4, Darker 50%.

Continued >

Apply Your Knowledge *continued*

22. Switch the second and third paragraphs in the numbered list. That is, select the 'Take a quick physical' numbered paragraph and use drag and drop to move it so that it is the second numbered paragraph (and then the 'Donate your blood' numbered paragraph will be the third numbered paragraph).
23. Select the words, three lives, in the first paragraph of body copy below the headline and underline these words. Undo this change and then redo the change.
24. Select the text, Where?, in the first bulleted paragraph and then select the nonadjacent text, When?, in the second bulleted paragraph. Bold the selected text. Change the font color of this same selected text to Blue, Accent 4, Darker 50%.
25. Italicize the word, only, in the paragraph above the numbered list.
26. Change the zoom to One Page, so that the entire page is visible in the document window.
27. Insert the blood drive picture so that it is centered on the blank line below the bulleted list. The picture is called Support_WD_1_GiveBlood.jpg and is available in the Data Files. Resize the picture proportionally so that it is approximately 2.8" × 3.53". Apply the Bevel Rectangle picture style to the inserted picture. Add the 'Glow: 8 point; Blue, Accent color 4' picture effect to the inserted picture.
28. Add a page border to the flyer using these formats: Setting: Box; Style: first style in list; Color: Blue, Accent 4, Darker 25% (eighth color in fifth row); Width 3 pt.
29. Change the spacing after the paragraph above the numbered list to 0 points. Change the spacing before the signature line to 18 points.
30. The entire flyer should fit on a single page. If it flows to two pages, resize the picture or decrease spacing before and after paragraphs until the entire flyer text fits on a single page.
31. Change the zoom to text width, then page width, then 25%, then 100% and notice the differences.
32. If requested by your instructor, enter the text, Blood Drive Flyer, as the comments in the document properties. Change the other document properties, as specified by your instructor.
33. Proofread your flyer, compare it to Figure 1-118, and correct any spelling, grammar, or punctuation errors. Save the document again with the same file name.
34. Print the document. Switch to Read Mode and browse pages through the document. Switch to Print Layout view.
35. Close the document. Exit Word.
36. Submit the revised document, shown in Figure 1–118, in the format specified by your instructor.
37. If this flyer were announcing a company picnic instead of a blood drive, which theme colors would you apply and why?

Extend Your Knowledge

Extend the skills you learned in this module and experiment with new skills. You may need to use Help to complete the assignment.

Modifying Text, Lists, and Picture Formats and Adding Page Borders

Note: To complete this assignment, you will be required to use the Data Files. Please contact your instructor for information about accessing the Data Files.

Instructions: Start Word. Open the document called SC_WD_1-2.docx, which is located in the Data Files. The document contains a flyer that communicates phone tips for customer service representatives at Trustland Insurance. You will enhance the look of the flyer shown in Figure 1–119.

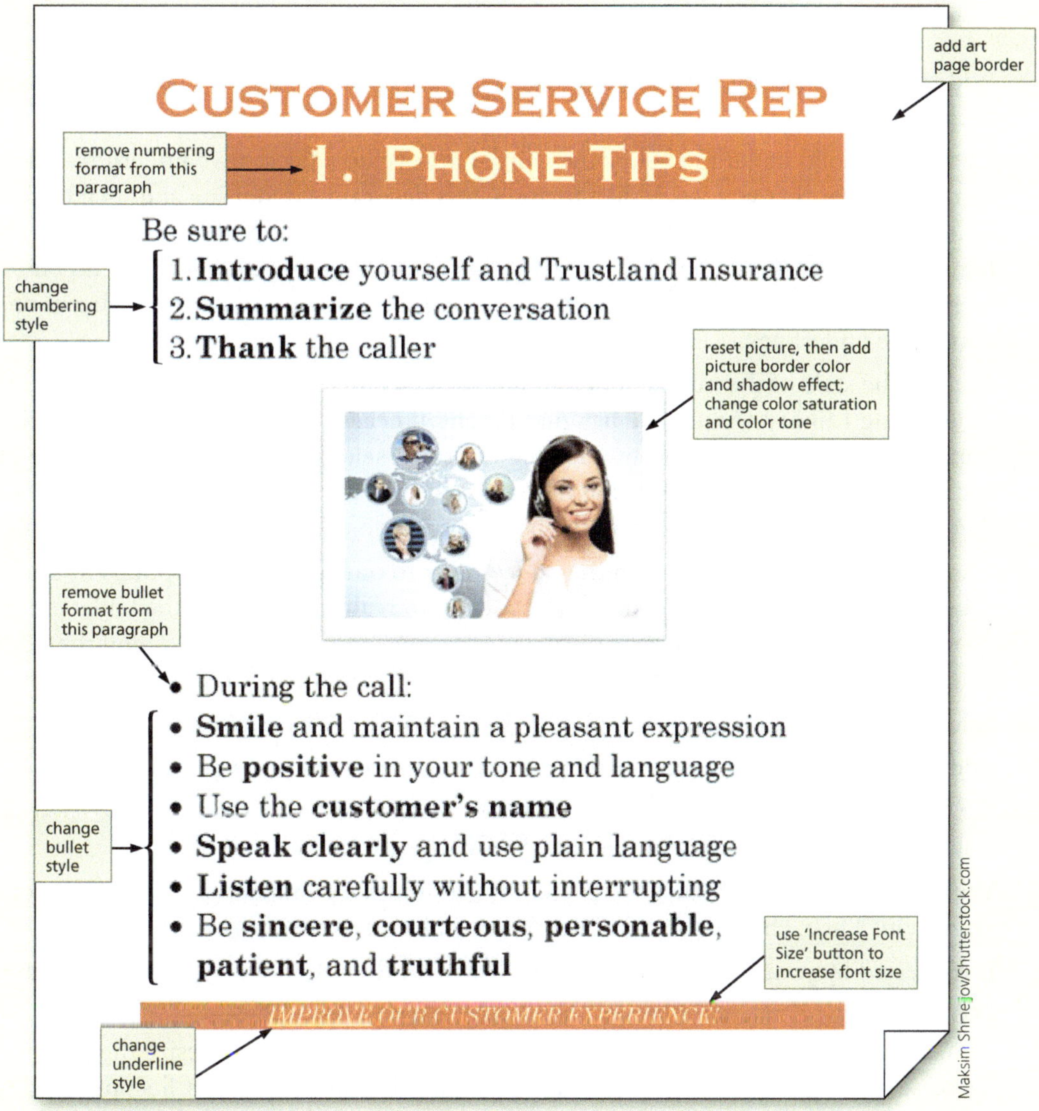

Maksim Shmeljov/Shutterstock.com

Figure 1–119

Perform the following tasks:

1. Use Help and the Search box to learn about the following: remove bullets from a paragraph, remove numbers from a paragraph, grow font, shrink font, art page borders, decorative underlines, bulleted list formats, numbering formats, hanging indents, picture border shading, picture border color, shadow picture effects, increase and decrease indents, and color saturation and tone.
2. Click File on the ribbon, click Save As, and then save the document using the new file name, SC_WD_1_PhoneTipsFlyer.
3. Remove the numbering format from the second line of the headline, so that it reads: Phone Tips. Use the Decrease Indent button (Home tab | Paragraph group) to remove the indent from the paragraph.
4. Remove the bullet format from the paragraph immediately below the picture, so that it reads: During the call:. Use the Decrease Indent button (Home tab | Paragraph group) to remove the indent from the paragraph.
5. Select the paragraph containing the signature line, IMPROVE OUR CUSTOMER EXPERIENCE!, and use the 'Increase Font Size' button (Home tab | Font group) to increase its font size.

Continued >

Extend Your Knowledge *continued*

6. Add an art page border to the flyer. If the border is not in color, add color to it if the border supports color.
7. Change the solid underline below the word, improve, to a decorative underline. Select more text in the flyer that you would like to apply this decorative underline and then click the Repeat Underline Style button on the Quick Access Toolbar (which appears to the right of the Undo button) to repeat the action of formatting the selected text (recall that the Redo button changes to a Repeat button when you perform certain tasks in Word). Change the color of one of the decorative underlines.
8. Change the style of the numbers in the numbered list to one of the other options in the Numbering Library. (Adjust the hanging indent, if necessary, to realign the text in the numbered list. You can do this by showing the ruler, selecting the paragraphs in the numbered list, and then dragging the Hanging Indent marker on the ruler to the desired location (note that the Hanging Indent marker is the bottom triangle). When finished, hide the ruler.)
9. Change the style of the bullets in the bulleted list to one of the other options in the Bullet Library. (Adjust the hanging indent, if necessary, to realign the text in the bulleted list. You can do this by showing the ruler, selecting the paragraphs in the bulleted list, and then dragging the Hanging Indent marker on the ruler to the desired location. When finished, hide the ruler.)
10. Select the picture and then reset the picture to remove all formatting applied to it.
11. Add a border to the picture in a color that complements the other colors on the flyer. Change the weight of the picture border.
12. Add a shadow picture effect to the picture. Change the color of the shadow.
13. With the picture selected, use the Search box to find the command to change the color saturation. Then, change the color saturation and color tone of the picture.
14. If requested by your instructor, change the name of the insurance company (Trustland) to your last name.
15. The entire flyer should fit on a single page. If it flows to two pages, resize the picture or decrease spacing before and after paragraphs until the entire flyer text fits on a single page.
16. Save the revised flyer again with the same name and then submit it in the format specified by your instructor.
17. In this assignment, you changed the numbering and bullet formats on the numbered and bulleted lists. Which numbering style and bullet character did you select and why?

Expand Your World

Create a solution that uses cloud or web technologies by learning and investigating on your own from general guidance.

Using Word Online to Create a Flyer with a Picture

Note: To complete this assignment, you will be required to use the Data Files. Please contact your instructor for information about accessing the Data Files.

Instructions: You will use Word Online to prepare a flyer. As a career services specialist at Cengage College, you will create a flyer announcing an upcoming job fair to be held on campus. Figure 1–120 shows the unformatted flyer. You will enter the text and insert the picture in Word Online and then use its tools to enhance the look of the flyer.

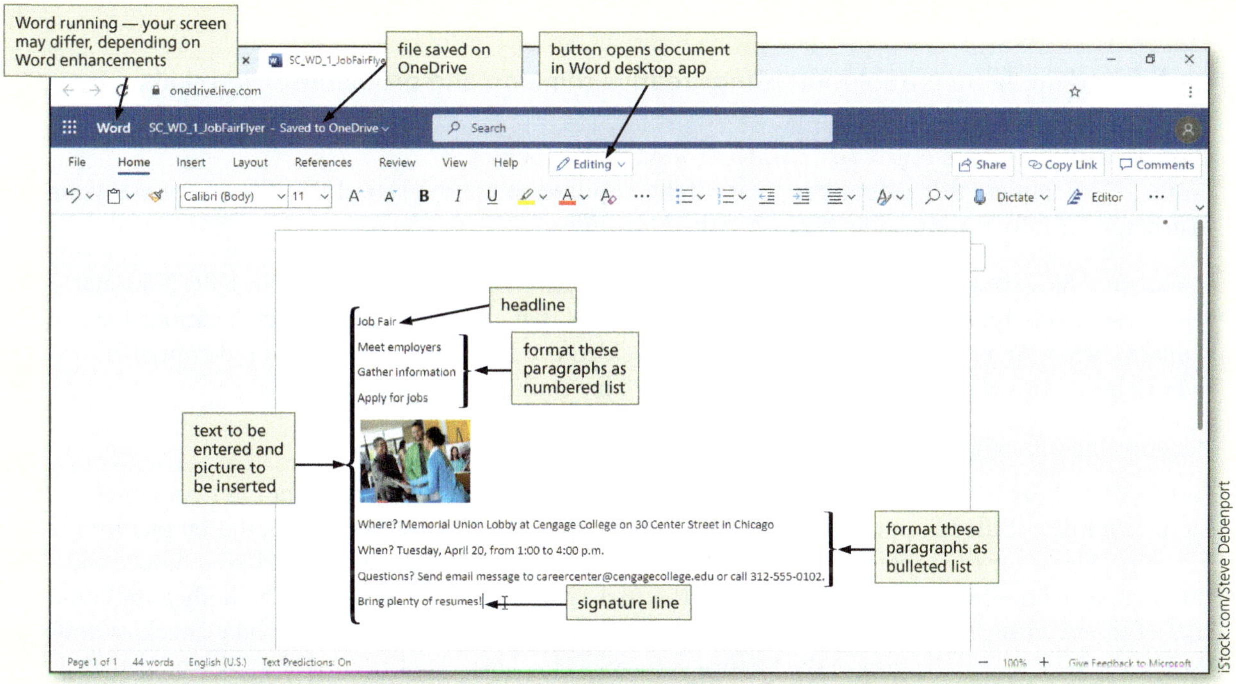

Figure 1–120

Perform the following tasks:

1. Start a browser. Search for the text, Word Online, using a search engine. Visit several websites to learn about Word Online. Navigate to the Word Online website. You will need to sign in to your OneDrive account.
2. Create a new blank Word document using Word Online. Name the document SC_WD_1_JobFairFlyer.
3. Notice the differences between Word Online and the Word desktop app you used to create the project in this module.
4. Enter the text in the flyer, shown in Figure 1–120, checking spelling and grammar as you work in the document.
5. Insert the picture called Support_WD_1_JobFair.jpg, which is located in the Data Files, below the numbered list.
6. Use the features available in Word Online, along with the concepts and techniques presented in this module, to format this flyer. Be sure to change the document margins, font and font size of text, center a paragraph(s), bold text, italicize text, color text, and underline text. Apply bullets and numbering to paragraphs as indicated in the figure. Resize the picture and apply a picture style. Adjust spacing above and below paragraphs as necessary. The flyer should fit on a single page.
7. If requested by your instructor, replace the email address in the flyer with your email address.
8. Save the document again. Click the button to open the document in the Word desktop app. If necessary, sign in to your Microsoft account when prompted. Notice how the document appears in the Word desktop app.
9. Using either Word Online or the Word desktop app, submit the document in the format requested by your instructor.
10. Exit Word and Word Online. If necessary, sign out of your OneDrive account and your Microsoft account in Word.
11. What is Word Online? Which features that are covered in this module are not available in Word Online? Do you prefer using Word Online or the Word desktop app? Why?

In the Lab

Design and implement a solution using creative thinking and problem-solving skills.

Design and Create a Flyer for the National Park Service

Note: To complete this assignment, you will be required to use the Data Files. Please contact your instructor for information about accessing the Data Files.

Problem: As assistant director for the parks and recreation department of Rolling Falls National Park, you create flyers for the park's information boards that are placed in key park locations for public viewing. At a recent staff meeting, it was decided the information board should contain a flyer that lists tips about how the public can safely hike trails in the park.

Perform the following tasks:

Part 1: The flyer should contain a digital picture appropriately resized; the Data Files contain a picture of hikers called Support_WD_1_ParkHikers.jpg, or you can use your own digital picture if it is appropriate for the topic of the flyer. The flyer should contain the headline, Hiking Safely, and this signature line: In case of emergency, call the park ranger at 214-555-0105. The body copy consists of the two lists, the contents of which can appear in any order: a before your hike checklist and during the hike tips. Following is the 'before your hike checklist': Pack plenty of food, water, and supplies. Bring a fully charged cell phone with backup battery, a battery-powered GPS, and two-way radios for all members of the hiking party. Bring binoculars or a telephoto camera lens to view wildlife from a safe distance. Check weather conditions and dress appropriately. Tell others when you plan to leave and which trail(s) at Rolling Falls National Park that you will be hiking. Following is the 'during the hike tips': Do not litter. Stay on official park trails and follow all park signs. Make noise while hiking. Do not approach, feed, or touch wildlife. Keep a distance of 100 feet between you and larger wildlife and a distance of 50 feet from smaller wildlife. Stay alert and watch your surroundings.

Use the concepts and techniques presented in this module to create a new blank document and format this flyer. Be sure to check spelling and grammar, accepting and ignoring suggested spelling and grammar changes as appropriate. When finished, save the flyer with the file name SC_WD_1_SafeHikingFlyer. Submit your assignment and answers to the Part 2 critical thinking questions in the format specified by your instructor.

Part 2: You made several decisions while creating the flyer in this assignment: where to place text, which margin settings and document themes to use, how to format the text (i.e., font, font size, paragraph alignment, bulleted paragraphs, numbered paragraphs, underlines, italics, bold, color, etc.), which picture to use, where to position the picture, how to format the picture, and which page enhancements to add (i.e., theme colors, borders, and spacing before/after paragraphs, etc.). What was the rationale behind each of these decisions? When you proofread the document, what further revisions did you make and why?

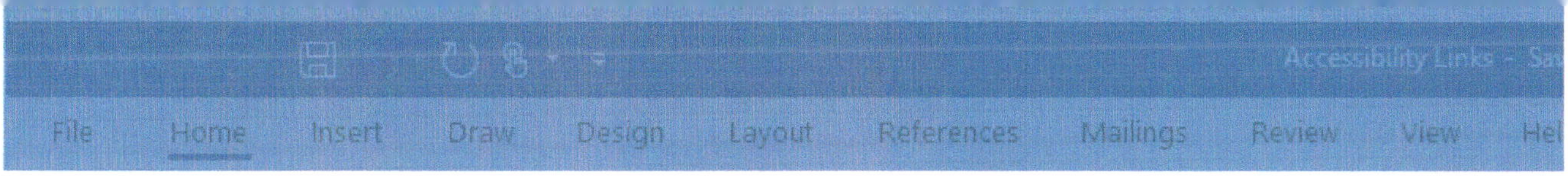

2 Creating a Research Paper

Objectives

After completing this module, you will be able to:

- Describe the MLA documentation style for research papers
- Modify a style
- Change line and paragraph spacing in a document
- Use a header to number pages of a document
- Apply formatting using keyboard shortcuts
- Modify paragraph indentation
- Insert and edit citations and their sources
- Add a footnote to a document
- Insert a page break
- Create a bibliographical list of sources
- Find text and replace text
- Use the thesaurus
- Check spelling and grammar at once
- Look up and research information
- Work with comments in a document

Introduction

In both business and academic environments, you will be asked to write reports. Business reports range from proposals to cost justifications to five-year plans to research findings. Academic reports focus mostly on research findings.

A **research paper** is a document you can use to communicate the results of research findings. To write a research paper, you learn about a particular topic from a variety of sources (research), organize your ideas from the research results, and then present relevant facts and/or opinions that support the topic. Your final research paper combines properly credited outside information along with personal insights. Thus, no two research papers — even if they are about the same topic — will or should be the same.

Project: Research Paper

When preparing a research paper, you should follow a standard documentation style that defines the rules for creating the paper and crediting sources. A variety of documentation styles exists, depending on the nature of the research paper. Each style requires the same basic information; the differences in styles relate to requirements for presenting the information. For example, one documentation style uses the term, bibliography, for the list of sources, whereas another uses the term, references, and yet a third prefers the term, works cited. Two popular documentation styles for research papers are the

BTW

APA Documentation Style

In the APA style, a separate title page is required instead of placing the name and course information on the paper's first page. Double-space all pages of the paper with one-inch top, bottom, left, and right margins. Indent the first word of each paragraph one-half inch from the left margin. In the upper-right margin of each page, including the title page, place a running head that consists of the page number preceded by a brief summary of the paper title.

MLA and APA styles. The **MLA (Modern Language Association of America)** style defines a set of formatting and content guidelines for publications and student research papers in the humanities and other fields, whereas the **APA (American Psychological Association)** style defines a set of formatting and content guidelines for publications and student research papers in the social and behavioral sciences. This module uses the MLA documentation style because it is used in a wider range of disciplines.

The project in this module follows research paper guidelines and uses Word to create the short research paper shown in Figure 2–1. As communications associate at a local outpatient care center, you communicate with and educate patients about a variety of health issues. You also are a part-time student who has been assigned a research paper. You decide to combine your work and school interests and compose a short research paper about health concerns of using technology. Your supervisor has expressed interest in incorporating the information in your paper for use in a patient brochure.

This paper, which discusses repetitive strain injuries and hearing loss, follows the MLA documentation style. Each page contains a page number. The first two pages present the name and course information (student name, instructor name, course name, and paper due date), paper title, an introduction with a thesis statement, details that support the thesis, and a conclusion. This section of the paper also includes references to research sources and a footnote. The third page contains a detailed, alphabetical list of the sources referenced in the research paper. All pages include a header at the upper-right edge of the page.

In this module, you will learn how to create the research paper shown in Figure 2–1. You will perform the following general tasks as you progress through this module:

1. Change the document settings.
2. Create the header, which will appear on each page of the research paper.
3. Type the research paper text with citations.
4. Create an alphabetical works cited page.
5. Proofread and revise the research paper.
6. Work with comments in the research paper.

MLA Documentation Style

The research paper in this project follows the guidelines presented by the MLA. To follow the MLA documentation style, use a 12-point Times New Roman or similar font. Double-space text on all pages of the paper using one-inch top, bottom, left, and right margins. Indent the first word of each paragraph one-half inch from the left margin. At the right margin of each page, place a page number one-half inch from the top margin. On each page, precede the page number with your last name.

The MLA documentation style does not require a title page. Instead, place your name and course information in a block at the left margin beginning one inch from the top of the page. Center the title one double-spaced line below your name and course information.

In the text of the paper, place author references in parentheses with the page number(s) of the referenced information. The MLA documentation style uses in-text **parenthetical references** to reference sources used in a research paper instead of noting each source at the bottom of the page or at the end of the paper. In the MLA documentation style, notes are used only for optional content or bibliographic notes.

If used, content notes elaborate on points discussed in the paper, and bibliographic notes direct the reader to evaluations of statements in a source or provide a means for

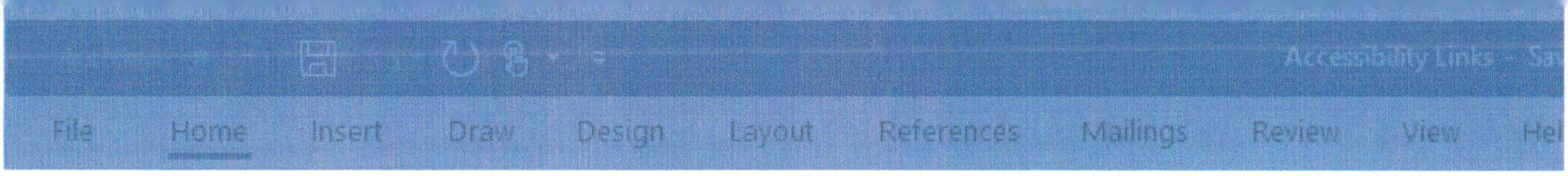

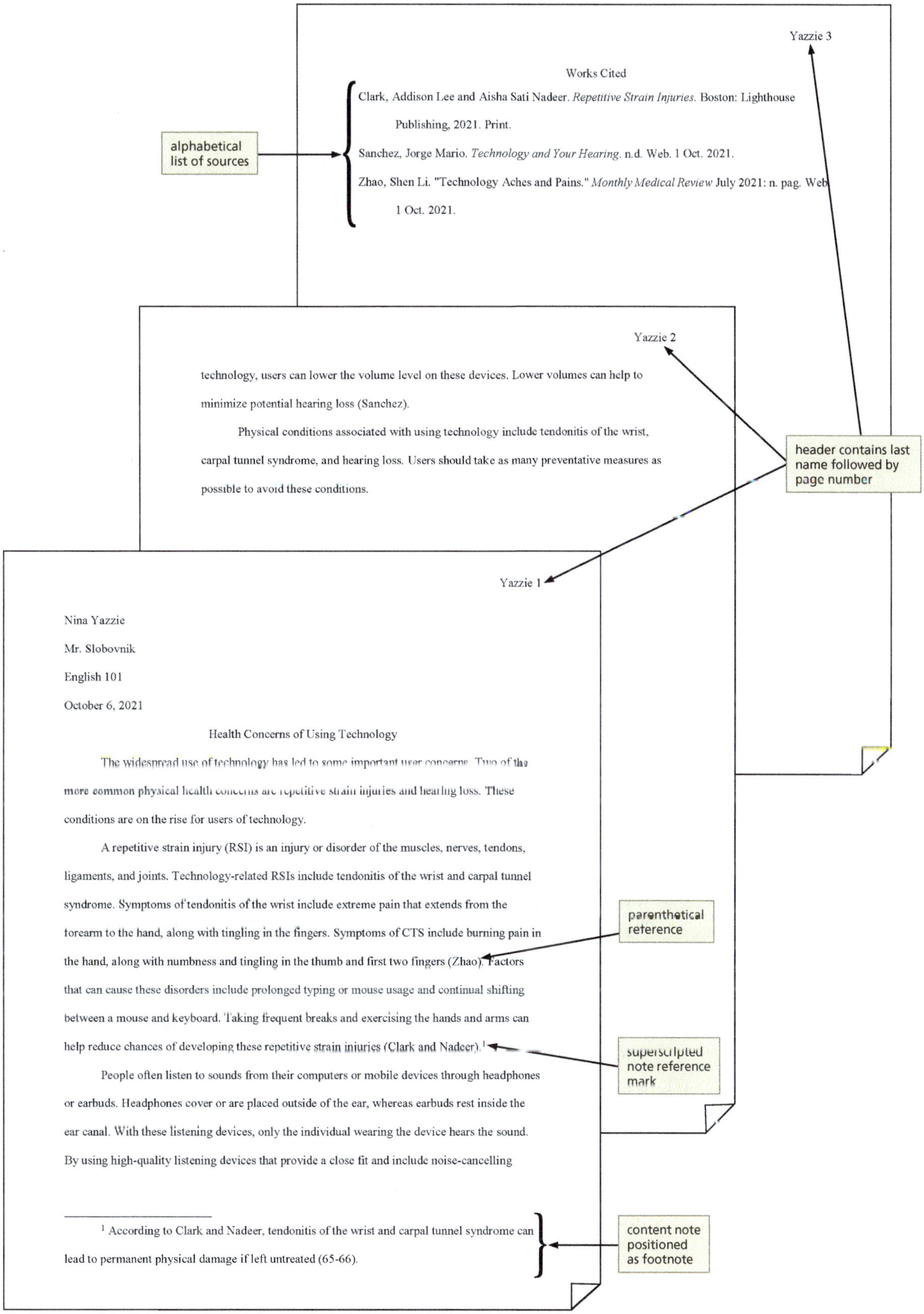

Yazzie 3

Works Cited

Clark, Addison Lee and Aisha Sati Nadeer. *Repetitive Strain Injuries.* Boston: Lighthouse Publishing, 2021. Print.

Sanchez, Jorge Mario. *Technology and Your Hearing.* n.d. Web. 1 Oct. 2021.

Zhao, Shen Li. "Technology Aches and Pains." *Monthly Medical Review* July 2021: n. pag. Web. 1 Oct. 2021.

Yazzie 2

technology, users can lower the volume level on these devices. Lower volumes can help to minimize potential hearing loss (Sanchez).

Physical conditions associated with using technology include tendonitis of the wrist, carpal tunnel syndrome, and hearing loss. Users should take as many preventative measures as possible to avoid these conditions.

Yazzie 1

Nina Yazzie

Mr. Slobovnik

English 101

October 6, 2021

Health Concerns of Using Technology

The widespread use of technology has led to some important user concerns. Two of the more common physical health concerns are repetitive strain injuries and hearing loss. These conditions are on the rise for users of technology.

A repetitive strain injury (RSI) is an injury or disorder of the muscles, nerves, tendons, ligaments, and joints. Technology-related RSIs include tendonitis of the wrist and carpal tunnel syndrome. Symptoms of tendonitis of the wrist include extreme pain that extends from the forearm to the hand, along with tingling in the fingers. Symptoms of CTS include burning pain in the hand, along with numbness and tingling in the thumb and first two fingers (Zhao). Factors that can cause these disorders include prolonged typing or mouse usage and continual shifting between a mouse and keyboard. Taking frequent breaks and exercising the hands and arms can help reduce chances of developing these repetitive strain injuries (Clark and Nadeer).[1]

People often listen to sounds from their computers or mobile devices through headphones or earbuds. Headphones cover or are placed outside of the ear, whereas earbuds rest inside the ear canal. With these listening devices, only the individual wearing the device hears the sound. By using high-quality listening devices that provide a close fit and include noise-cancelling

[1] According to Clark and Nadeer, tendonitis of the wrist and carpal tunnel syndrome can lead to permanent physical damage if left untreated (65-66).

Figure 2–1

identifying multiple sources. Use a superscript (raised number) both to signal that a note exists and to sequence the notes (shown in Figure 2–1). Position notes at the bottom of the page as footnotes or at the end of the paper as endnotes. Indent the first line of each note one-half inch from the left margin. Place one space following the superscripted number before beginning the note text. Double-space the note text (shown in Figure 2–1).

The MLA documentation style uses the term, works cited, to refer to the bibliographic list of sources at the end of the paper. The **works cited page** is a page in the research paper that alphabetically lists sources that are referenced directly in the paper. Place this list of sources on a separate numbered page. Center the title, Works Cited, one inch from the top margin. Double-space all lines. Begin the first line of each source at the left margin, indenting subsequent lines of the same source one-half inch from the left margin. List each source by the author's last name or, if the author's name is not available, by the title of the source.

Changing Document Settings

The MLA documentation style defines some global formats that apply to the entire research paper. Some of these formats are the default in Word. For example, the default left, right, top, and bottom margin settings in Word are one inch, which meets the MLA documentation style. You will modify, however, the font, font size, and line and paragraph spacing.

To Start Word and Specify Settings

BTW
Resolution
For information about how to change a computer's resolution, search for 'change resolution' in your operating system's help files.

If you are using a computer to step through the project in this module and you want your screens to match the figures in this book, you should change your screen's resolution to 1366 × 768. The following steps start Word and specify settings.

1. sam Start Word and create a blank document in the Word window.
2. If the Word window is not maximized, click the Maximize button on its title bar to maximize the window.
3. If the Print Layout button on the status bar is not selected (shown in Figure 2–2), click it so that your screen is in Print Layout view.
4. If Normal (Home tab | Styles group) is not selected in the Styles gallery (shown in Figure 2–2), click it so that your document uses the Normal style.
5. Display the View tab. To display the page the same width as the document window, if necessary, click the Page Width button (View tab | Zoom group).
6. Display the Home tab. If the 'Show/Hide ¶' button (Home tab | Paragraph group) is not selected already, click it to display formatting marks on the screen.
7. If you are using a mouse and you want your screens to match the figures in the book, verify that you are using Mouse mode by clicking the Touch/Mouse Mode button on the Quick Access Toolbar and then, if necessary, clicking Mouse on the menu. (If your Quick Access Toolbar does not display the Touch/Mouse Mode button, click the 'Customize Quick Access Toolbar' button on the Quick Access Toolbar and then click Touch/Mouse Mode on the menu to add the button to the Quick Access Toolbar.)

Styles

When you create a document, Word formats the text using a particular style. A **style** is a named collection of character and paragraph formats, including font, font size, font styles, font color, and alignment, that are stored together and can be applied to text or objects to format them quickly. The default style that is applied to all text in Word is called the **Normal style**, which most likely uses an 11-point Calibri font. If you do not specify a style for text you type, Word applies the Normal style to the text. In addition to the Normal style, Word has many other built-in, or predefined, styles that you can use to format text. Styles make it easy to apply many formats at once to text. You can modify existing styles and create your own styles. Styles are discussed as they are used in this book.

To Modify a Style

The MLA documentation style requires that all text in the research paper use a 12-point Times New Roman or similar font. If you change the font and font size using buttons on the ribbon, you will need to make the change many times during the course of creating the paper. **Why?** Word formats various areas of a document based on the Normal style, which uses an 11-point Calibri font. For example, body text, headers, and bibliographies all display text based on the Normal style.

Thus, instead of changing the font and font size for various document elements, a more efficient technique is to change the Normal style for this document to use a 12-point Times New Roman font. **Why?** By changing the Normal style, you ensure that all text in the document will use the format required by the MLA. The following steps change the Normal style.

1

- Right-click Normal in the Styles gallery (Home tab | Styles group) to display a shortcut menu related to styles (Figure 2–2).

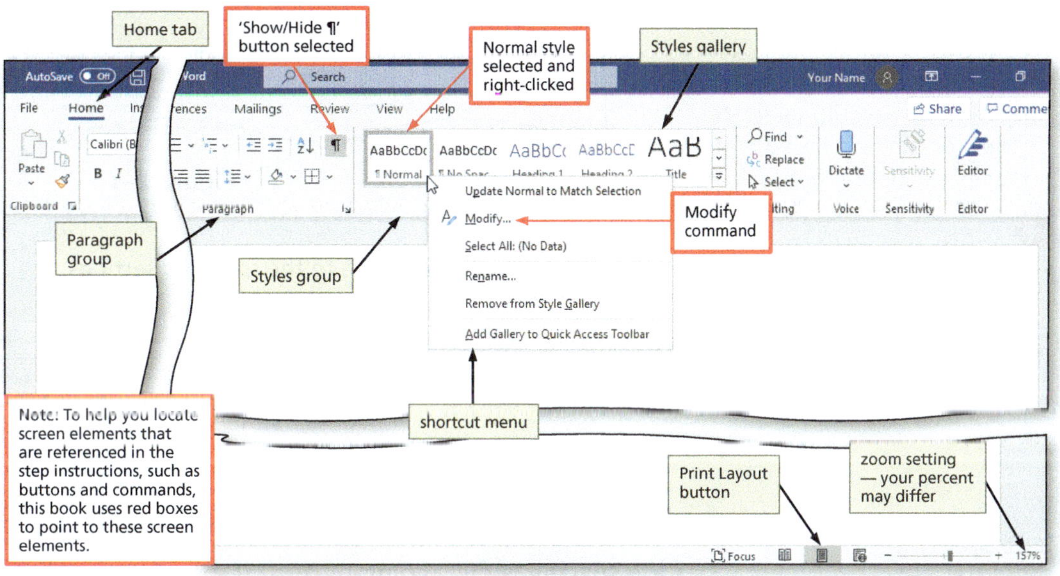

Figure 2–2

2

- Click Modify on the shortcut menu to display the Modify Style dialog box (Figure 2–3).

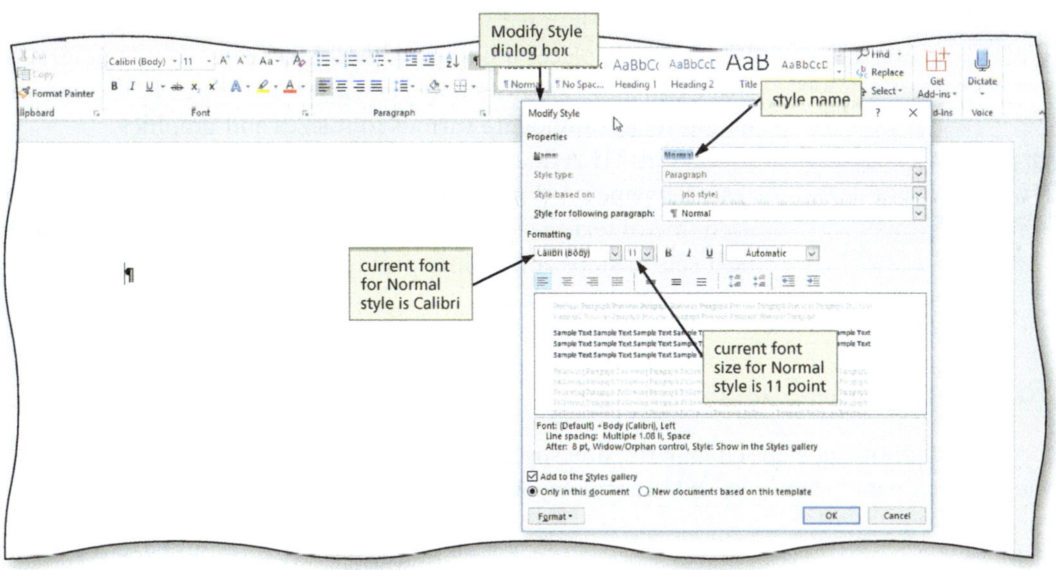

Figure 2–3

3

- Click the Font arrow (Modify Style dialog box) to display the Font list. Scroll to and then click Times New Roman in the list to change the font for the style being modified.
- Click the Font Size arrow (Modify Style dialog box) and then click 12 in the Font Size list to change the font size for the style being modified.
- Ensure that the 'Only in this document' option button is selected (Figure 2–4).

Q&A **Will all future documents use the new font and font size?**
No, because the 'Only in this document' option button is selected. If you wanted all future documents to use a new setting, you would select the 'New documents based on this template' option button.

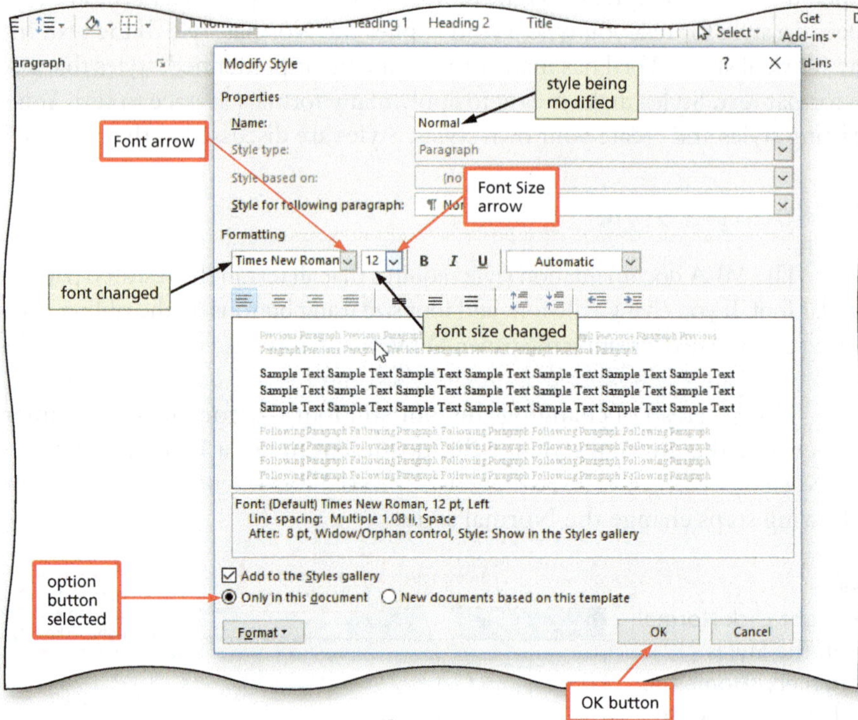

Figure 2–4

4

- Click OK (Modify Style dialog box) to update the Normal style to the specified settings.

Other Ways

1. Click Styles Dialog Box Launcher, click arrow next to style name, click Modify on menu, change settings (Modify Style dialog box), click OK
2. Press ALT+CTRL+SHIFT+S, click arrow next to style name, click Modify on menu, change settings (Modify Style dialog box), click OK

BTW
Line Spacing
If the top of a set of characters or a graphical image is chopped off, then line spacing may be set to Exactly. To remedy the problem, change line spacing to 1.0, 1.15, 1.5, 2.0, 2.5, 3.0, or At least (in the Paragraph dialog box), all of which accommodate the largest font or image.

Adjusting Line and Paragraph Spacing

Line spacing is the amount of vertical space between lines of text in a paragraph. **Paragraph spacing** is the space, measured in points, that appears directly above and below a paragraph, or between lines of paragraph text. By default, the Normal style places 8 points of blank space after each paragraph and inserts a vertical space equal to 1.08 lines between each line of text. It also automatically adjusts line height to accommodate various font sizes and graphics.

The MLA documentation style requires that you double-space the entire research paper. A **double-spaced** paragraph format places one blank line between each line of text in a paragraph and one blank line above and below a paragraph. The next sets of steps adjust line spacing and paragraph spacing according to the MLA documentation style.

To Change Line Spacing

The following steps change the line spacing to 2.0 to double-space lines in a paragraph. **Why?** The lines of the research paper should be double-spaced, according to the MLA documentation style.

1

- Click the 'Line and Paragraph Spacing' button (Home tab | Paragraph group) to display the Line and Paragraph Spacing gallery (Figure 2–5).

Q&A **What do the numbers in the Line and Paragraph Spacing gallery represent?**
The options 1.0, 2.0, and 3.0 set line spacing to single, double, and triple, respectively. Similarly, the 1.15, 1.5, and 2.5 options set line spacing to 1.15, 1.5, and 2.5 lines. All of these options adjust line spacing automatically to accommodate the largest font or graphic on a line.

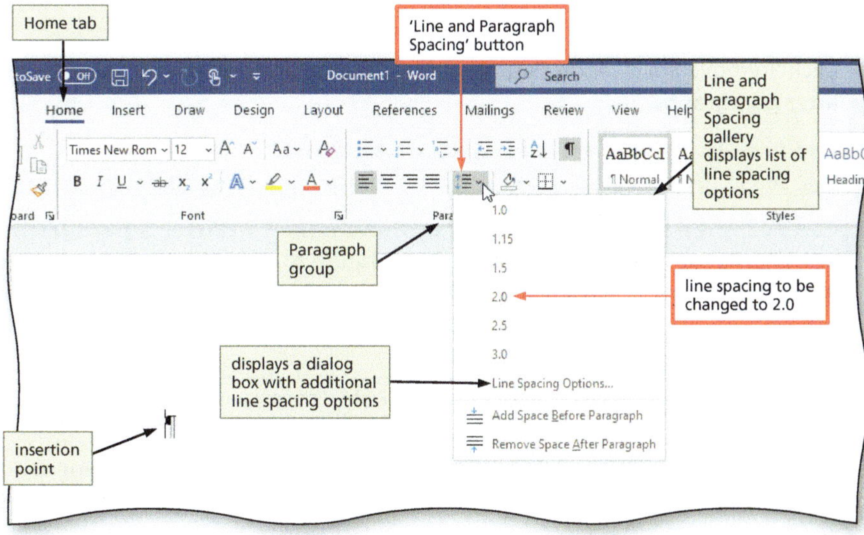

Figure 2–5

2

- Click 2.0 in the Line and Paragraph Spacing gallery to change the line spacing at the location of the insertion point.

Q&A **Can I change the line spacing of existing text or the entire document?**
Yes. Select the text first or select the entire document, and then change the line spacing as described in these steps. To select the entire document, click the Select button (Home tab | Editing group) and then click Select All on the Select menu or press CTRL+A.

Other Ways

1. Right-click paragraph (or, if using touch, tap 'Show Context Menu' on Mini toolbar), click Paragraph on shortcut menu, or click Indents and Spacing tab (Paragraph dialog box), click Line spacing arrow, select desired spacing, click OK
2. Click Paragraph Dialog Box Launcher (Home tab or Layout tab | Paragraph group), click Indents and Spacing tab (Paragraph dialog box), click Line spacing arrow, select desired spacing, click OK
3. Press CTRL+2 for double-spacing

To Remove Space after a Paragraph

The following steps remove space after a paragraph. **Why?** The research paper should not have additional blank space after each paragraph, according to the MLA documentation style.

1

- Click the 'Line and Paragraph Spacing' button (Home tab | Paragraph group) to display the Line and Paragraph Spacing gallery (Figure 2–6).

Q&A **Why does a check mark appear to the left of 2.0 in the gallery?**
The check mark indicates the currently selected line spacing.

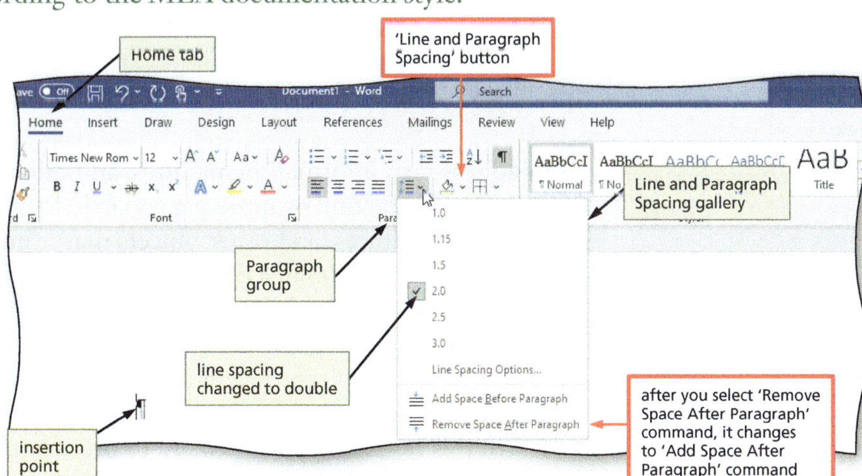

Figure 2–6

2

- Click 'Remove Space After Paragraph' in the Line and Paragraph Spacing gallery so that no blank space appears after paragraphs.

Q&A

Can I remove space after existing paragraphs?
Yes. Select the paragraphs first and then remove the space as described in these steps.

Can I remove space before a paragraph instead of after a paragraph?
Yes. If space exists before the paragraph, position the insertion point in the paragraph to adjust, click the 'Line and Paragraph Spacing' button, and then click 'Remove Space Before Paragraph' in the Line and Paragraph Spacing gallery.

Other Ways

1. Adjust Spacing After arrows (Layout tab | Paragraph group) until 0 pt is displayed
2. Right-click paragraph (or, if using touch, tap 'Show Context Menu' on Mini toolbar), click Paragraph on shortcut menu, click Indents and Spacing tab (Paragraph dialog box), adjust After arrows until 0 pt is displayed, click OK
3. Click Paragraph Dialog Box Launcher (Home tab or Layout tab | Paragraph group), click Indents and Spacing tab (Paragraph dialog box), adjust After arrows until 0 pt is displayed, click OK

To Update a Style to Match a Selection

To ensure that all paragraphs in the paper will be double-spaced and do not have space after the paragraphs, you want the Normal style to include the line and paragraph spacing changes made in the previous two sets of steps. The following steps update the Normal style. **Why?** You can update a style to reflect the settings of the location of the insertion point or selected text. Because no text has been typed in the research paper yet, you do not need to select text prior to updating the Normal style.

1

- Right-click Normal in the Styles gallery (Home tab | Styles group) to display a shortcut menu (Figure 2–7).

2

- Click 'Update Normal to Match Selection' on the shortcut menu to update the selected (or current) style to reflect the settings at the location of the insertion point.

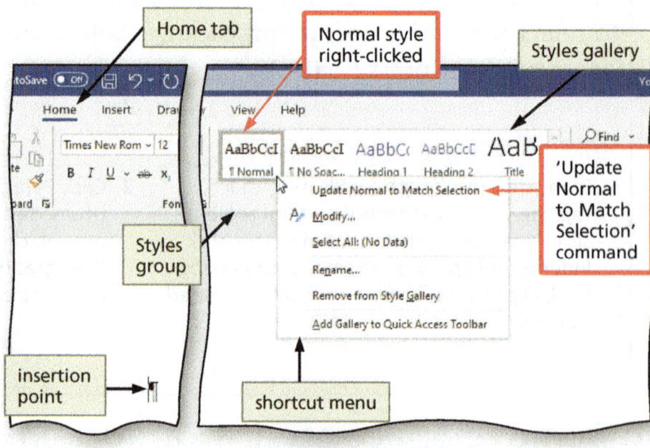

Figure 2–7

Other Ways

1. Click Styles Dialog Box Launcher, click arrow next to style name, click 'Update Normal to Match Selection'
2. Press ALT+CTRL+SHIFT+S, click arrow next to style name in Styles pane, click 'Update Normal to Match Selection'

BTW

Footers

If you wanted to create a footer, you would click the Footer button (Insert tab | Header & Footer group) and then select the desired built-in footer. If you wanted to edit a footer, you would click the Footer button (Insert tab | Header & Footer group) and then click Edit Footer in the Footer gallery, or you could double-click the dimmed footer.

Creating a Header

A **header** is text, information, pictures, and other objects that print in an area above the top margin on one or more page(s) in a document. Similarly, a **footer** is text, information, pictures, and other objects that print in an area below the bottom margin on one or more page(s) in a document. Unless otherwise specified in Word, headers print one-half inch from the top of every page, and footers print one-half inch from the bottom of each page, which meets the MLA documentation style. In addition to text, pictures, and objects, headers and footers can include document information, such as the page number, current date, current time, and author's name.

In this research paper, you are to precede the page number with your last name placed one-half inch from the upper-right edge of each page. The procedures in the following sections enter your name and the page number in the header, as specified by the MLA documentation style.

To Insert a Header

The following steps insert a blank built-in header. **Why?** To enter text in the header, you instruct Word to insert a header, which you will edit.

1

- Click Insert on the ribbon to display the Insert tab.
- Click the Header button (Insert tab | Header & Footer group) to display the Header gallery (Figure 2–8).

Experiment

- Click the down scroll arrow in the Header gallery to see the available built-in headers.

Q&A

How would I enter a footer in a document?
You would click the Footer button (Insert tab | Header & Footer group) and select the desired footer in the list. To edit a footer, you would click the Footer button (Insert tab | Header & Footer group) and the click Edit Footer in the Footer gallery.

How would I remove a header from a document?
You would click Remove Header in the Header gallery. Similarly, to remove a footer, you would click Remove Footer in the Footer gallery.

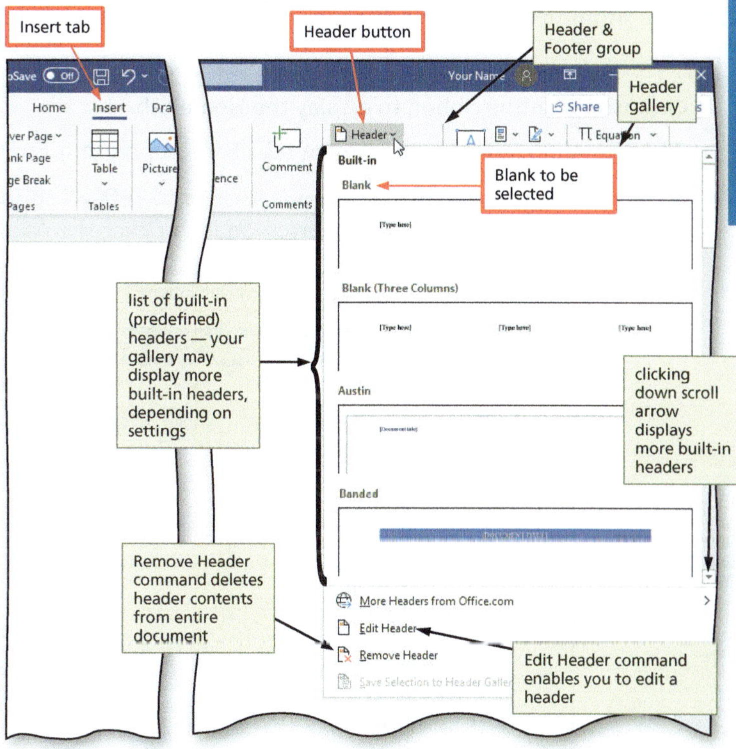

Figure 2–8

2

- Click Blank in the Header gallery to switch from the document text to the header and insert placeholder text in the header (Figure 2–9).

Q&A

What is placeholder text?
Placeholder text is default text that indicates where text can be typed.

How do I remove the Header & Footer tab from the ribbon?
When you are finished editing the header, you will close it, which removes the Header & Footer tab.

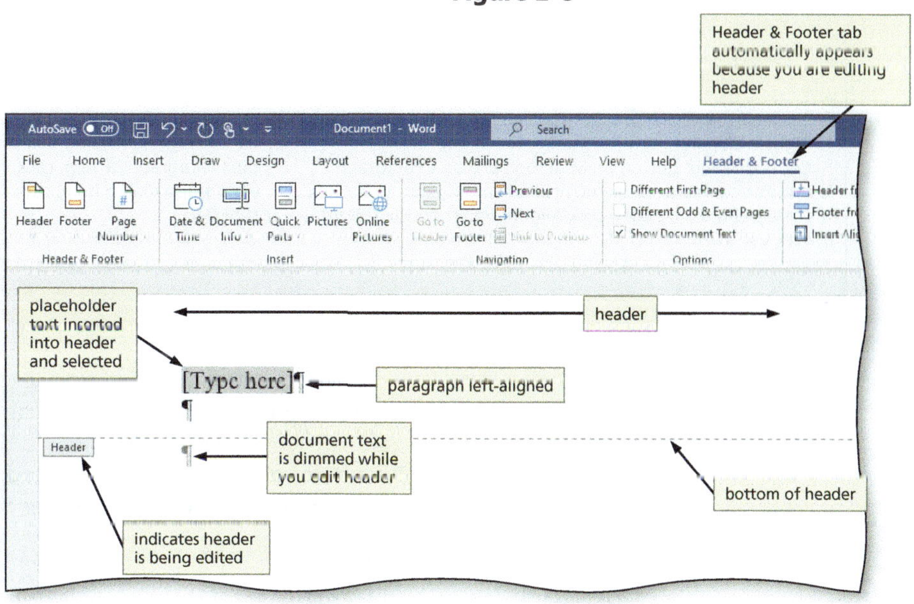

Figure 2–9

Other Ways

1. Double-click dimmed header
2. Right-click header in document, click Edit Header button that appears

To Right-Align a Paragraph

The paragraph in the header currently is left-aligned (shown in Figure 2–9). The following step right-aligns this paragraph. **Why?** Your last name and the page number in the header should print **right-aligned**; that is, they should print at the right margin, according to the MLA documentation style.

1

- Click Home on the ribbon to display the Home tab.
- Click the Align Right button (Home tab | Paragraph group) to right-align the current paragraph (Figure 2–10).

Q&A **What if I wanted to return the paragraph to left-aligned?**
You would click the Align Right button again, or click the Align Left button (Home tab | Paragraph group).

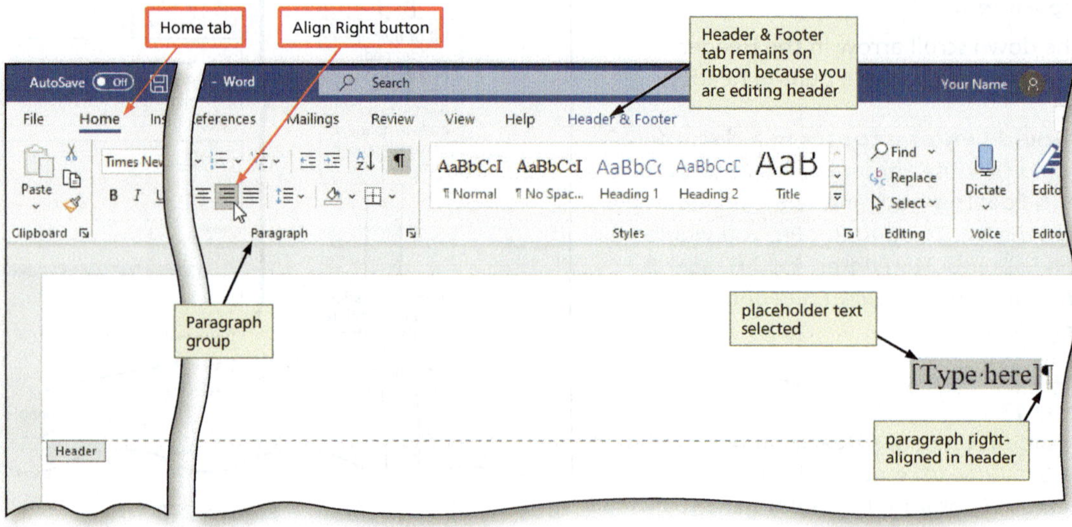

Figure 2–10

Other Ways

1. Right-click paragraph (or, if using touch, tap 'Show Context Menu' button on Mini toolbar), click Paragraph on shortcut menu, click Indents and Spacing tab (Paragraph dialog box), click Alignment arrow, click Right, click OK
2. Click Paragraph Dialog Box Launcher (Home tab or Layout tab | Paragraph group), click Indents and Spacing tab (Paragraph dialog box), click Alignment arrow, click Right, click OK
3. Press CTRL+R

To Enter Text in a Header

The following step enters the last name right-aligned in the header area.

1 With the [Type here] placeholder text selected (as shown in Figure 2–10), type **`Yazzie`** and then press SPACEBAR to enter the last name in the header.

Q&A **What if my placeholder text is not selected?**
Drag through the placeholder text to select it and then perform Step 1.

To Insert Page Numbers

The following steps insert a page number at the location of the insertion point and in the same location on all subsequent pages in the document. **Why?** The MLA documentation style requires a page number following the last name in the header.

1

- Click Header & Footer on the ribbon to display the Header & Footer tab.
- Click the Page Number button (Header & Footer tab | Header & Footer group) to display the Page Number menu.

Q&A **Why does my button name differ from the name on the face of the button in the figure?**
The text that appears on the face of the button may vary, depending on screen resolution.

- Point to Current Position on the Page Number menu to display the Current Position gallery (Figure 2–11).

Experiment

- Click the down scroll arrow in the Current Position gallery to see the available page number formats.

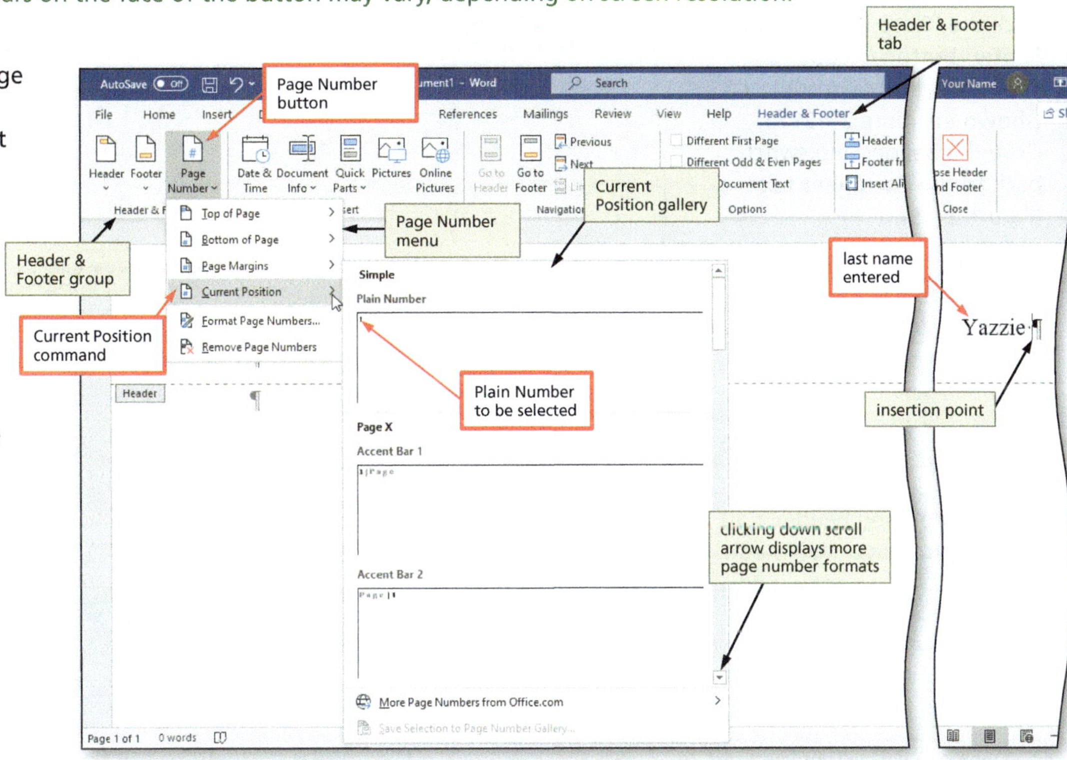

Figure 2–11

2

- If necessary, scroll to the top of the Current Position gallery.
- Click Plain Number in the Current Position gallery to insert an unformatted page number at the location of the insertion point (Figure 2–12).

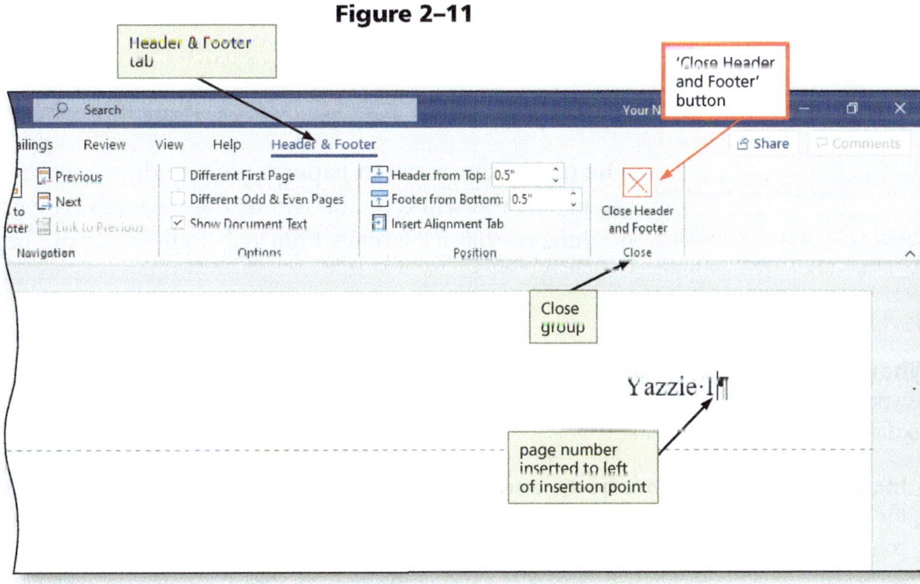

Figure 2–12

Other Ways

1. Click Page Number button (Insert tab | Header & Footer group)
2. Click Quick Parts button (Insert tab | Text group or Header & Footer tab | Insert group), click Field on Quick Parts menu, select Page in Field names list (Field dialog box), select desired format in Format list, click OK

To Close the Header

The next task is to close the header and switch back to the document text. **Why?** You are finished entering text in the header. The following step closes the header.

1

- Click the 'Close Header and Footer' button (Header & Footer tab | Close group) (shown in Figure 2–12) to close the header and switch back to the document text (Figure 2–13).

Q&A **How do I make changes to existing header text?**
If you wanted to edit a header, you would click the Header button (Insert tab | Header & Footer group) and then click Edit Header in the Header gallery, or you could double-click the dimmed header, edit the header as you would edit text in the document window, and then close the header as shown here.

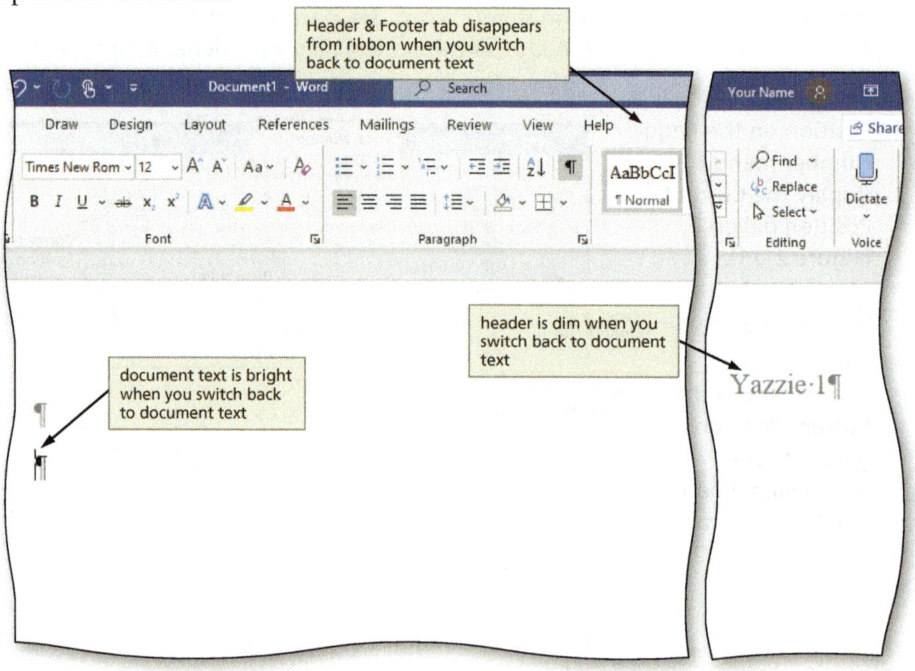

Figure 2–13

Other Ways

1. Double-click dimmed document text

Typing the Research Paper Text

The text of the research paper in this module encompasses the first two pages of the paper. You will type the text of the research paper and then modify it later in the module, so that it matches Figure 2–1 shown at the beginning of this module.

Consider This

What should you consider when writing the first draft of a research paper?
As you write the first draft of a research paper, be sure it includes the proper components, uses credible sources, and does not contain any plagiarized material.

- **Include an introduction, body, and conclusion.** The first paragraph of the paper introduces the topic and captures the reader's attention. The body, which follows the introduction, consists of several paragraphs that support the topic. The conclusion summarizes the main points in the body and restates the topic.
- **Evaluate sources for authority, currency, and accuracy.** Be especially wary of information obtained on the web. Any person, company, or organization can publish a webpage on the Internet. When evaluating the source, consider the following:
  - Authority: Does a reputable institution or group support the source? Is the information presented without bias? Are the author's credentials listed and verifiable?
  - Currency: Is the information up to date? Are dates of sources listed? What is the last date revised or updated?
  - Accuracy: Is the information free of errors? Is it verifiable? Are the sources clearly identified?

- **Acknowledge all sources of information; do not plagiarize.** Sources of research include books, magazines, newspapers, the Internet, and more. As you record facts and ideas, list details about the source: title, author, place of publication, publisher, date of publication, etc. When taking notes, be careful not to **plagiarize**, that is, do not copy or use someone else's work and claim it to be your own. If you copy information directly, place it in quotation marks and identify its source. Not only is plagiarism unethical, but it is considered an academic crime that can have severe punishments, such as failing a course or being expelled from school.

  When you summarize, paraphrase (rewrite information in your own words), present facts, give statistics, quote exact words, or show a map, chart, or other object, you must acknowledge the source. Information that commonly is known or accessible to the audience constitutes common knowledge and does not need to be acknowledged. If, however, you question whether certain information is common knowledge, you should acknowledge it — just to be safe.

To Enter Name and Course Information

As discussed earlier in this module, the MLA documentation style does not require a separate title page for research papers. Instead, place your name and course information in a block at the top of the page, below the header, at the left margin. The following steps enter the name and course information in the research paper.

1. With the insertion point positioned as shown in Figure 2–13, type **`Nina Yazzie`** as the student name and then press ENTER.
2. Type **`Mr. Slobovnik`** as the instructor name and then press ENTER.
3. Type **`English 101`** as the course name and then press ENTER.
4. Type **`October 6, 2021`** as the paper's due date and then press ENTER (Figure 2–14).

Q&A

Why did the word, October, appear on the screen as I began typing the month name?

Word has an AutoComplete feature, where it predicts some words or phrases as you are typing and displays its prediction in a ScreenTip. If the AutoComplete prediction is correct, you can press ENTER (or, if using touch, tap the ScreenTip) to instruct Word to finish your typing with the word or phrase that appears in the ScreenTip.

BTW

Date Formats

The MLA style prefers the day-month-year (6 October 2021) or month-day-year (October 6, 2021) format.

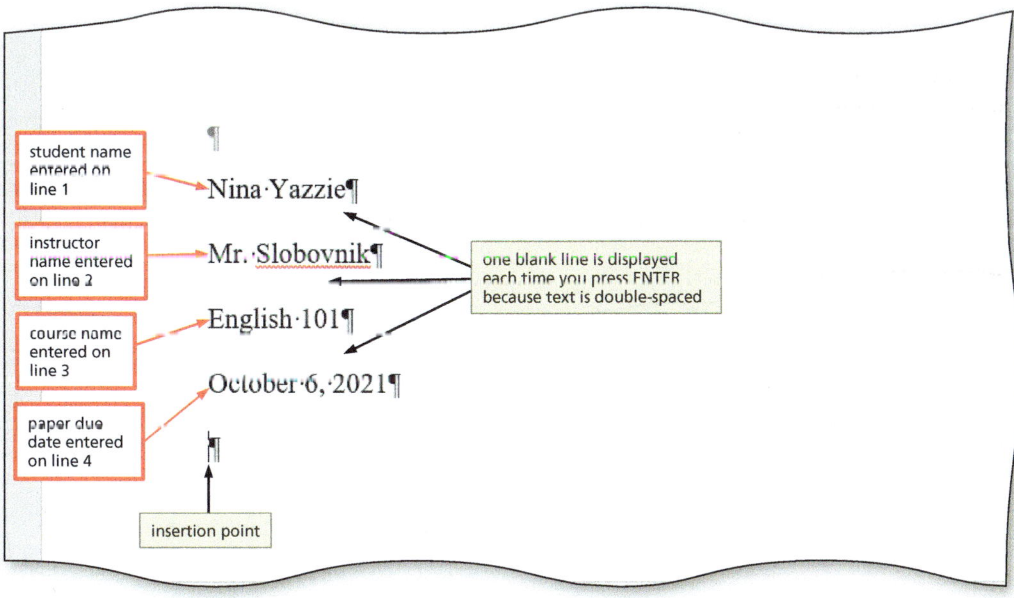

Figure 2–14

To Click and Type

The next task is to enter the title of the research paper centered between the page margins. In Module 1, you used the Center button (Home tab | Paragraph group) to center text and pictures. As an alternative, if you are using a mouse, you can use Word's Click and Type feature to format and enter text, pictures, and other objects. **Why?** With **Click and Type**, you can double-click a blank area of the document and Word automatically formats the item you type or insert based on the location where you double-clicked. The following steps use Click and Type to center and then type the title of the research paper.

1

Experiment

- Move the pointer around the document below the entered name and course information and observe the various icons that appear with the I-beam.
- Position the pointer in the center of the document at the approximate location for the research paper title until a center icon appears below the I-beam (Figure 2–15).

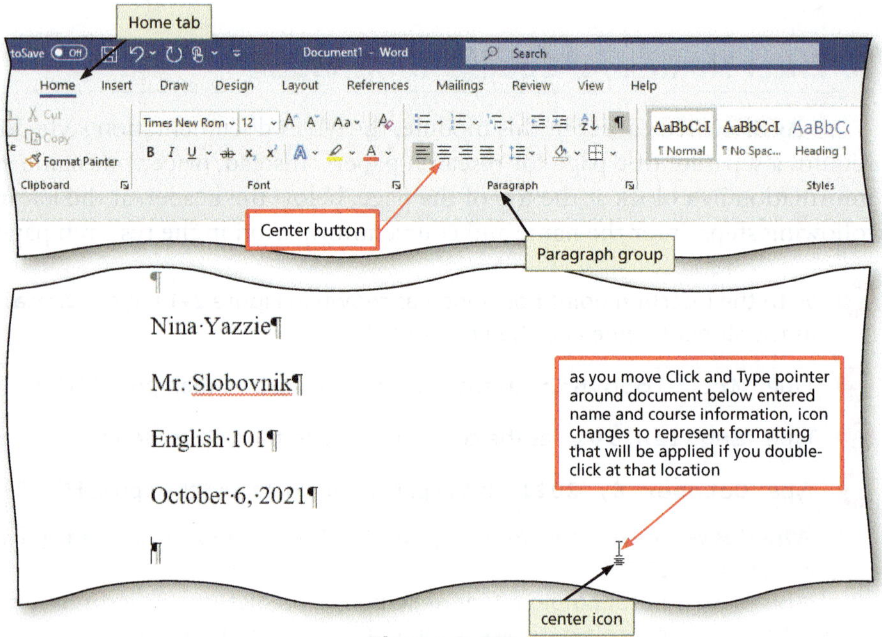

Figure 2–15

Q&A **What are the other icons that appear in the Click and Type pointer?**
A left-align icon appears to the right of the I-beam when the Click and Type pointer is in certain locations on the left side of the document window. A right-align icon appears to the left of the I-beam when the Click and Type pointer is in certain locations on the right side of the document window.

What if I am using a touch screen?
Tap the Center button (Home tab | Paragraph group) and then proceed to Step 3 because the Click and Type feature does not work with a touch screen.

2

- Double-click to center the paragraph mark and insertion point between the left and right margins.

3

- Type `Health Concerns of Using Technology` as the paper title and then press ENTER to position the insertion point on the next line (Figure 2–16).

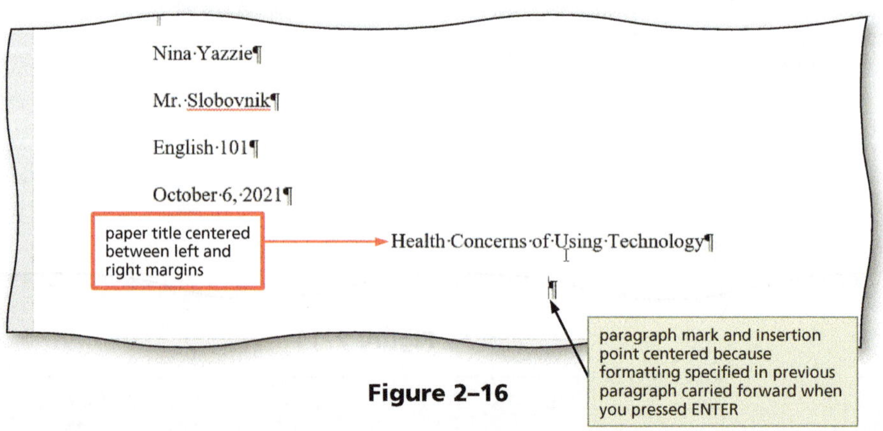

Figure 2–16

Keyboard Shortcuts for Formatting Text

Word has many **keyboard shortcuts**, sometimes called shortcut keys or keyboard key combinations, which are a key or combination of keys you press to access a feature or perform a command, instead of using a mouse or touch gestures. Many users find keyboard shortcuts a convenience while typing. Table 2–1 lists the common keyboard shortcuts for formatting characters. Table 2–2 lists common keyboard shortcuts for formatting paragraphs.

Table 2–1 Keyboard Shortcuts for Formatting Characters

Character Formatting Task	Keyboard Shortcut	Character Formatting Task	Keyboard Shortcut
All capital letters	CTRL+SHIFT+A	Italic	CTRL+I
Bold	CTRL+B	Remove character formatting (plain text)	CTRL+SPACEBAR
Case of letters	SHIFT+F3	Small uppercase letters	CTRL+SHIFT+K
Decrease font size	CTRL+SHIFT+<	Subscript	CTRL+EQUAL SIGN
Decrease font size 1 point	CTRL+[	Superscript	CTRL+SHIFT+PLUS SIGN
Double-underline	CTRL+SHIFT+D	Underline	CTRL+U
Increase font size	CTRL+SHIFT+>	Underline words, not spaces	CTRL+SHIFT+W
Increase font size 1 point	CTRL+]		

Table 2–2 Keyboard Shortcuts for Formatting Paragraphs

Paragraph Formatting	Keyboard Shortcut	Paragraph Formatting	Keyboard Shortcut
1.5 line spacing	CTRL+5	Justify paragraph	CTRL+J
Add/remove one line above paragraph	CTRL+0 (ZERO)	Left-align paragraph	CTRL+L
Center paragraph	CTRL+E	Remove hanging indent	CTRL+SHIFT+T
Decrease paragraph indent	CTRL+SHIFT+M	Remove paragraph formatting	CTRL+Q
Double-space lines	CTRL+2	Right-align paragraph	CTRL+R
Hanging indent	CTRL+T	Single-space lines	CTRL+1
Increase paragraph indent	CTRL+M		

To Format Text Using a Keyboard Shortcut

The paragraphs below the paper title should be left-aligned, instead of centered. Thus, the next step is to left-align the paragraph below the paper title. When your fingers already are on the keyboard, you may prefer using keyboard shortcuts to format text as you type it.

The following step left-aligns a paragraph using the keyboard shortcut CTRL+L. (A notation such as CTRL+L means to press the letter L on the keyboard while holding down CTRL.)

1. Press CTRL+L to left-align the current paragraph, that is, the paragraph containing the insertion point (shown in Figure 2–17).

Q&A **Why would I use a keyboard shortcut instead of the ribbon to format text?**
Switching between the mouse and the keyboard takes time. If your hands are already on the keyboard, use a keyboard shortcut. If your hand is on the mouse, use the ribbon.

BTW

Keyboard Shortcuts
To see a complete list of keyboard shortcuts in Word, press F1 to open the Help pane, type `keyboard shortcuts` in the Search box in the Word Help pane, press ENTER, and then click the 'Keyboard shortcuts in Word link. To create a Word document with all keyboard shortcuts, click the 'Word 2016 for Windows keyboard shortcuts' link in the Help pane to open a Downloads window. Click the link in the Downloads window to open a Word document with all keyboard shortcuts, and then, if necessary, click the Enable Editing button. You can print or save the Word document. When finished, exit Word and then close the Help pane.

2 Save the research paper on your hard drive, OneDrive, or other storage location using the file name, SC_WD_2_TechnologyHealthConcernsPaper.

Q&A **Why should I save the research paper at this time?**
You have performed many tasks while creating this research paper and do not want to risk losing work completed thus far.

To Display the Rulers

According to the MLA documentation style, the first line of each paragraph in the research paper is to be indented one-half inch from the left margin. Although you can use a dialog box to indent paragraphs, Word provides a quicker way through the **horizontal ruler**, which is a ruler that appears below the ribbon in the document window in Print Layout and other views. Word also provides a **vertical ruler** that appears along the left edge of the document window in Print Layout view. The following step displays the rulers. **Why?** You want to use the horizontal ruler to indent paragraphs.

1

- If necessary, scroll the document so that the research paper title is at the top of the document window.
- Click View on the ribbon to display the View tab.
- If the rulers are not displayed, click the Ruler check box (View tab | Show group) to place a check mark in the check box and display the horizontal and vertical rulers on the screen (Figure 2–17).

Q&A **What tasks can I accomplish using the rulers?**
You can use the horizontal and vertical rulers, usually simply called **rulers**, to indent paragraphs, set tab stops, change page margins, adjust column widths, and measure or place objects.

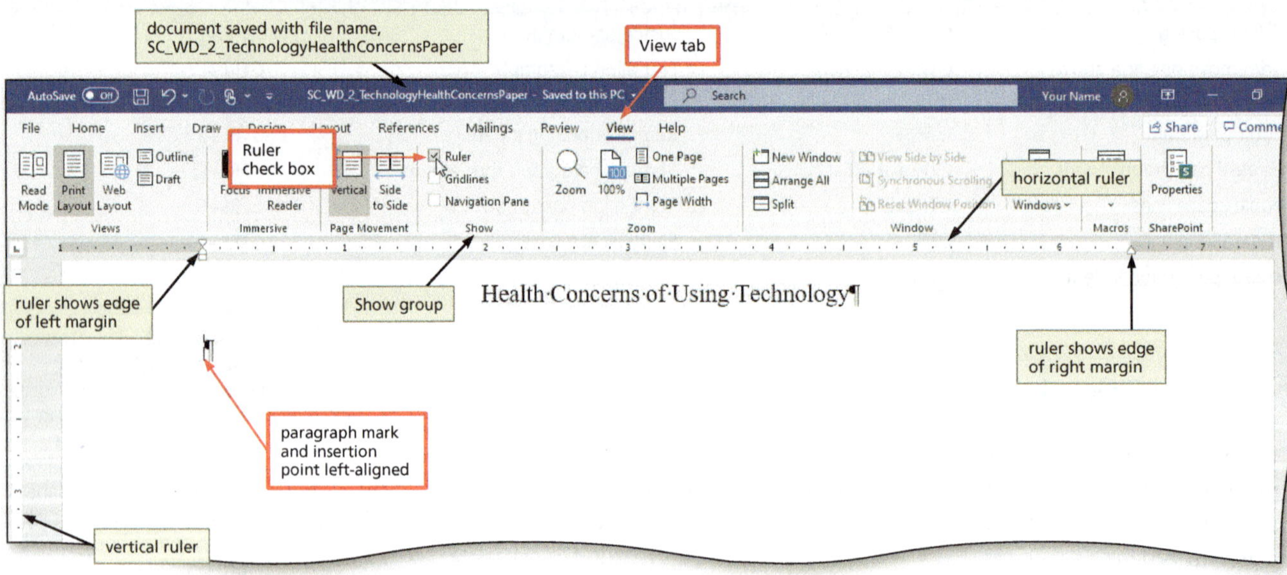

Figure 2–17

To First-Line Indent Paragraphs

If you are using a mouse, you can use the horizontal ruler to indent just the first line of a paragraph, which is called a **first-line indent**. The left margin on the ruler contains two triangles above a square. The 'First Line Indent' marker is the top triangle at the 0" mark on the ruler (shown in Figure 2–18). The bottom triangle, which is the Hanging Indent marker, is discussed later in this module. The small square at the 0" mark is the Left Indent marker. The Left Indent marker allows you to change the entire left margin, whereas the 'First Line Indent' marker indents only the first line of the paragraph.

The following steps first-line indent paragraphs in the research paper. **Why?** The first line of each paragraph in the research paper is to be indented one-half inch from the left margin, according to the MLA documentation style.

1

- With the insertion point on the paragraph mark below the research paper title, point to the 'First Line Indent' marker on the ruler (Figure 2–18).

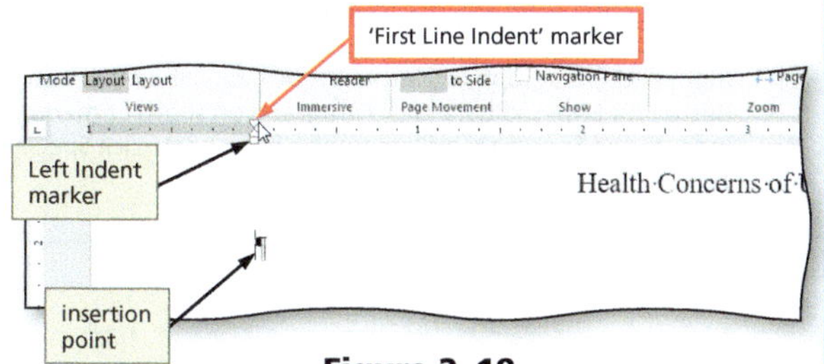

Figure 2–18

2

- Drag the 'First Line Indent' marker to the .5" mark on the ruler to display a vertical dotted line in the document window, which indicates the proposed indent location of the first line of the paragraph (Figure 2–19).

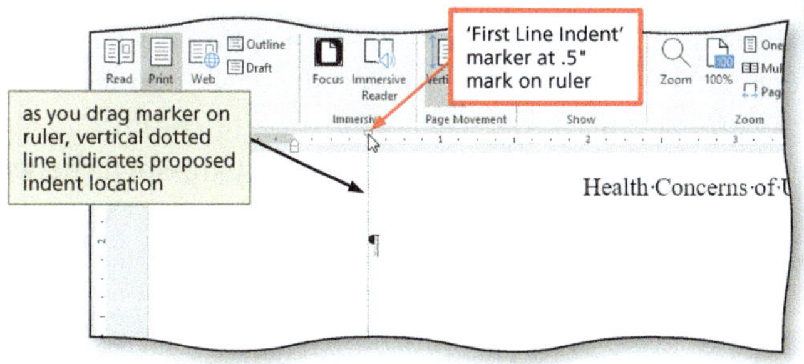

Figure 2–19

3

- Release the mouse button to place the 'First Line Indent' marker at the .5" mark on the ruler, or one-half inch from the left margin (Figure 2–20).

Q&A **What if I am using a touch screen?**
If you are using a touch screen, you cannot drag the 'First Line Indent' marker and must follow these steps instead: tap the Paragraph Dialog Box Launcher (Home tab or Layout tab | Paragraph group) to display the Paragraph dialog box, tap the Indents and Spacing tab (Paragraph dialog box), tap the Special arrow, tap First line, and then tap OK.

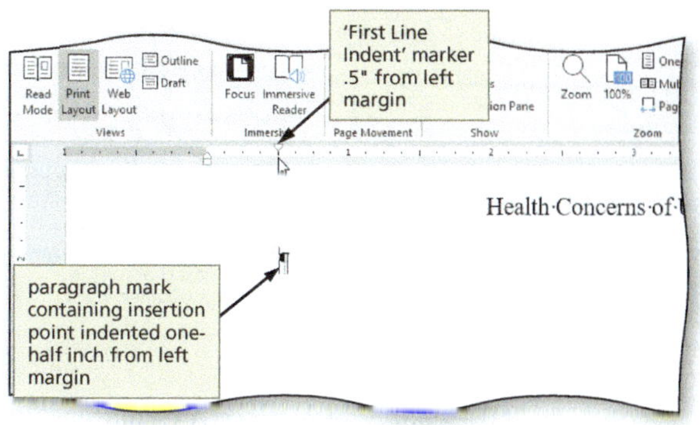

Figure 2–20

4

- Type `The widespread use of technology has led to some important user concerns. Two of the more common physical health concerns are repetitive strain injuries and hearing loss.` and notice that Word automatically indents the first line of the paragraph by one-half inch (Figure 2–21).

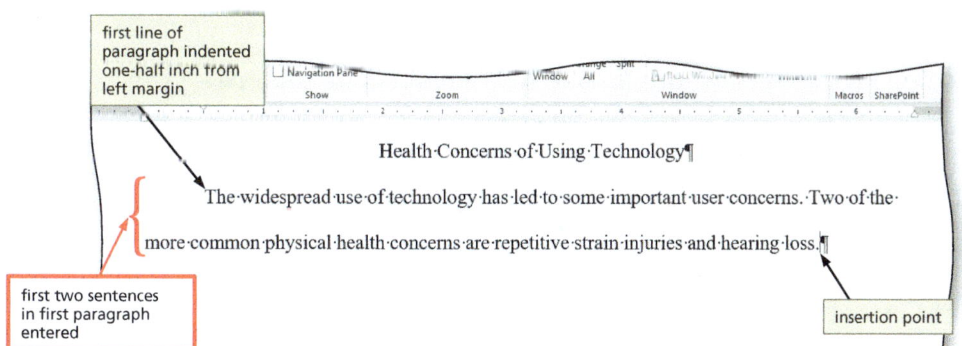

Figure 2–21

Q&A **Will I have to set a first-line indent for each paragraph in the paper?**
No. Each time you press ENTER, paragraph formatting in the previous paragraph carries forward to the next paragraph. Thus, once you set the first-line indent, its format carries forward automatically to each subsequent paragraph you type.

Other Ways

1. Right-click paragraph (or, if using touch, tap 'Show Context Menu' button on Mini toolbar), click Paragraph on shortcut menu, click Indents and Spacing tab (Paragraph dialog box), click Special arrow, click First line, click OK
2. Click Paragraph Dialog Box Launcher (Home tab or Layout tab | Paragraph group), click Indents and Spacing tab (Paragraph dialog box), click Special arrow, click First line, click OK

To AutoCorrect as You Type

Word has predefined many commonly misspelled words, which it automatically corrects for you. **Why?** As you type, you may make typing, spelling, capitalization, or grammar errors. Word's AutoCorrect feature automatically corrects these kinds of errors as you type them in the document. For example, if you type the characters, ahve, Word automatically changes it to the correct spelling, have, when you press SPACEBAR or a punctuation mark key, such as a period or comma.

The following steps intentionally misspell the word, the, as teh to illustrate the AutoCorrect feature.

1

- Press SPACEBAR.
- Type the beginning of the next sentence, misspelling the word, the, as follows: **`These conditions are on teh`** (Figure 2–22).

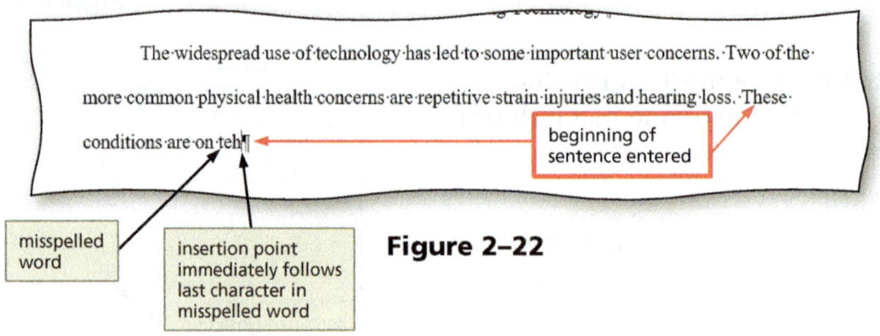

Figure 2–22

2

- Press SPACEBAR and watch Word automatically correct the misspelled word.
- Type the rest of the sentence (Figure 2–23): **`rise for users of technology.`**

Q&A **What if I do not want to keep a change made automatically by Word?**
If you notice the automatically corrected text immediately, you can press CTRL+Z or click the Undo button on the Quick Access Toolbar to undo the automatic correction. If you do not notice it immediately, you can undo a correction through the AutoCorrect Options button shown in the next set of steps.

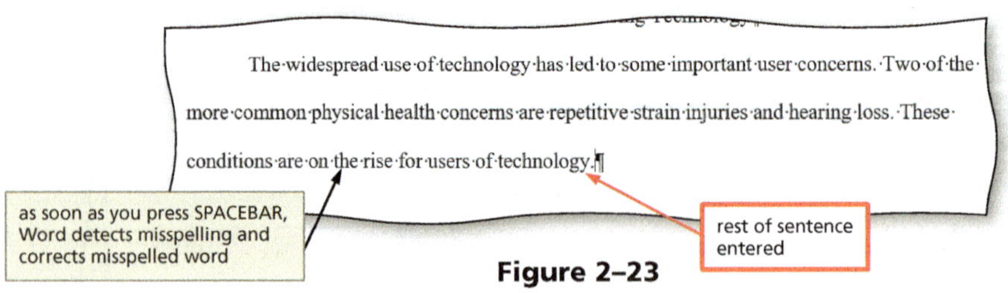

Figure 2–23

To Use the AutoCorrect Options Button

The following steps illustrate the AutoCorrect Options button and menu. **Why?** If you are using a mouse, when you position the pointer on text that Word automatically corrected, a small blue box appears below the text. If you point to the small blue box, Word displays the AutoCorrect Options button. When you click the **AutoCorrect Options button**, which appears below the automatically corrected text, Word displays a menu that allows you to undo a correction or change how Word handles future automatic corrections of this type.

1

- Position the pointer in the text automatically corrected by Word (the word, the, in this case) to display a small blue box below the automatically corrected word (Figure 2–24).

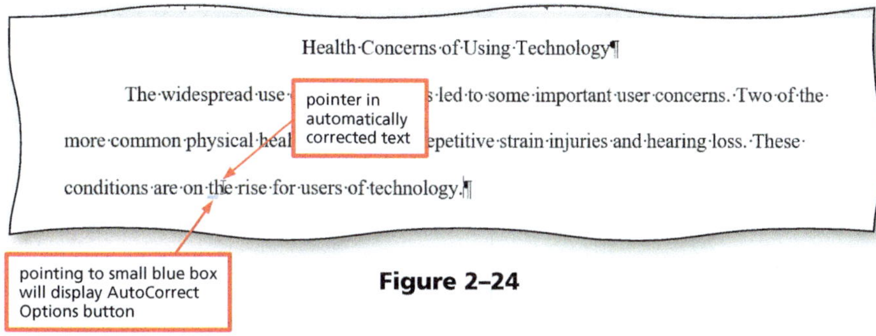

Figure 2–24

2

- Point to the small blue box to display the AutoCorrect Options button.
- Click the AutoCorrect Options button to display the AutoCorrect Options menu (Figure 2–25).
- Press ESC to remove the AutoCorrect Options menu from the screen.

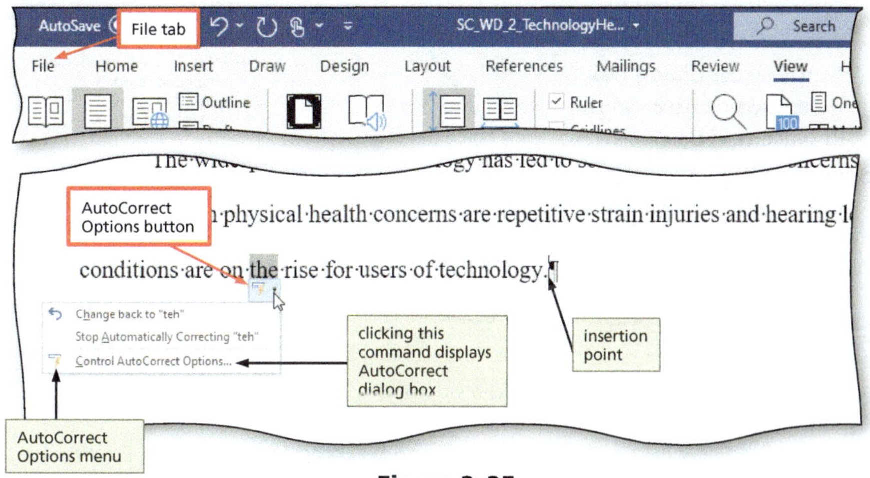

Figure 2–25

Q&A **Do I need to remove the AutoCorrect Options button from the screen?**
No. When you move the pointer, the AutoCorrect Options button will disappear from the screen. If, for some reason, you wanted to remove the AutoCorrect Options button from the screen, you could press ESC a second time.

To Create an AutoCorrect Entry

The next steps create an AutoCorrect entry. **Why?** In addition to the predefined list of AutoCorrect spelling, capitalization, and grammar errors, you can create your own AutoCorrect entries to add to the list. For example, if you tend to mistype the word computer as comptuer, you should create an AutoCorrect entry for it.

1

- Click File on the ribbon (shown in Figure 2–25) to open Backstage view (Figure 2–26).

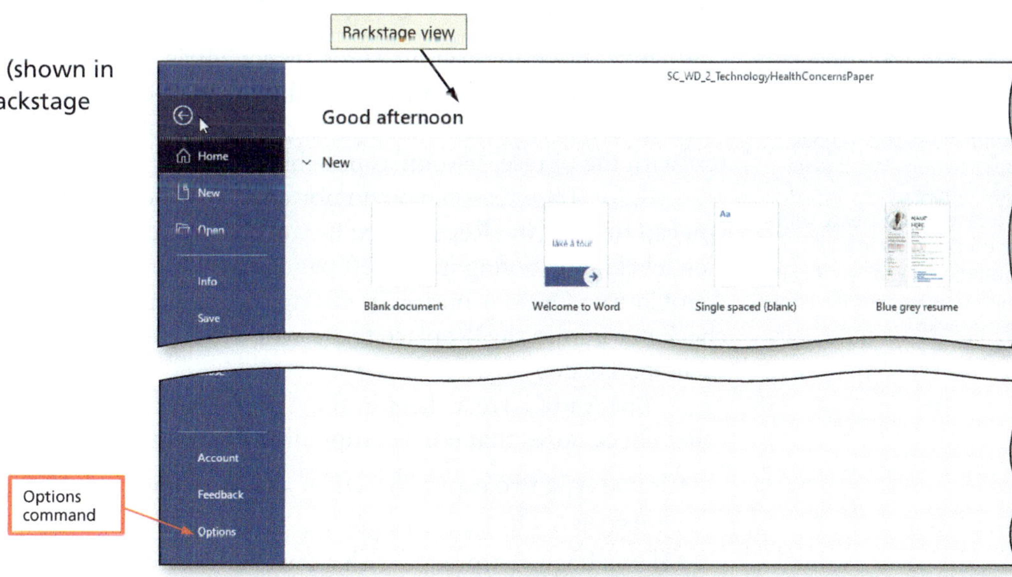

Figure 2–26

2

- Click Options in Backstage view to display the Word Options dialog box.
- Click Proofing in the left pane (Word Options dialog box) to display proofing options in the right pane.
- Click the AutoCorrect Options button in the right pane to display the AutoCorrect dialog box.
- When Word displays the AutoCorrect dialog box, type `comptuer` in the Replace text box.
- Press TAB and then type `computer` in the With text box (Figure 2–27).

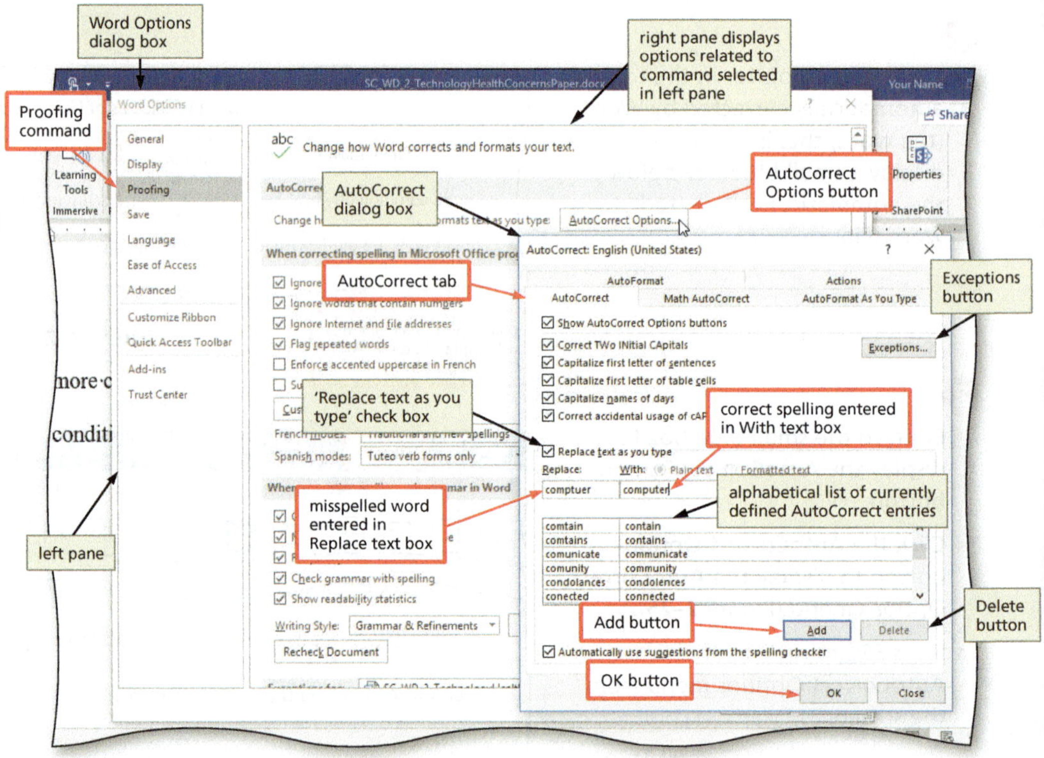

Figure 2–27

Q&A **How would I delete an existing AutoCorrect entry?**
You would select the entry to be deleted in the list of defined entries in the AutoCorrect dialog box and then click the Delete button (AutoCorrect dialog box).

3

- Click the Add button (AutoCorrect dialog box) to add the entry alphabetically to the list of words to correct automatically as you type. (If your dialog box displays a Replace button instead, click it and then click the Yes button in the Microsoft Word dialog box to replace the previously defined entry.)
- Click OK (AutoCorrect dialog box) to close the dialog box.
- Click OK (Word Options dialog box) to close the dialog box.

BTW
Word Help
At any time while using Word, you can find answers to questions and display information about various topics through Word Help. Used properly, this form of assistance can increase your productivity and reduce your frustrations by minimizing the time you spend learning how to use Word.

The AutoCorrect Dialog Box

In addition to creating AutoCorrect entries for words you commonly misspell or mistype, you can create entries for abbreviations, codes, and so on. For example, you could create an AutoCorrect entry for asap, indicating that Word should replace this text with the phrase, as soon as possible.

If, for some reason, you do not want Word to correct automatically as you type, you can turn off the Replace text as you type feature by clicking Options in Backstage view, clicking Proofing in the left pane (Word Options dialog box), clicking the AutoCorrect Options button in the right pane (shown in Figure 2–27), removing the check mark from the 'Replace text as you type' check box, and then clicking OK in each open dialog box.

The AutoCorrect sheet in the AutoCorrect dialog box (Figure 2–27) contains other check boxes that correct capitalization errors if the check boxes are selected:

- If you type two capital letters in a row, such as TH, Word makes the second letter lowercase, Th.
- If you begin a sentence with a lowercase letter, Word capitalizes the first letter of the sentence.

- If you type the name of a day in lowercase letters, such as tuesday, Word capitalizes the first letter in the name of the day, Tuesday.
- If you leave CAPS LOCK on and begin a new sentence, Word corrects the typing and turns off CAPS LOCK.

If you do not want Word to perform any of these corrections automatically, simply remove the check mark from the appropriate check box in the AutoCorrect dialog box.

Sometimes, you do not want Word to AutoCorrect a particular word or phrase. For example, you may use WD. as a code in your documents. Because Word automatically capitalizes the first letter of a sentence, the character you enter following the period will be capitalized (in the previous sentence, it would capitalize the letter a in the word, as). To allow the code, WD., to be entered into a document and still leave the AutoCorrect feature turned on, you would set an exception. To set an exception to an AutoCorrect rule, click Options in Backstage view, click Proofing in the left pane (Word Options dialog box), click the AutoCorrect Options button in the right pane, click the Exceptions button (Figure 2–27), click the appropriate tab in the AutoCorrect Exceptions dialog box, type the exception entry in the text box, click the Add button, click the Close button (AutoCorrect Exceptions dialog box), and then click OK in each of the remaining dialog boxes.

To Enter More Text

The next task is to continue typing text in the research paper up to the location of the in-text parenthetical reference. The following steps enter this text.

1 With the insertion point positioned at the end of the first paragraph in the paper, as shown in Figure 2–25, press ENTER to start a new paragraph and then type the following text: **A repetitive strain injury (RSI) is an injury or disorder of the muscles, nerves, tendons, ligaments, and joints. Technology-related RSIs include tendonitis of the wrist and carpal tunnel syndrome. Symptoms of tendonitis of the wrist include extreme pain that extends from the forearm to the hand, along with tingling in the fingers. Symptoms of CTS include burning pain in the hand, along with numbness and tingling in the thumb and first two fingers**

2 Press SPACEBAR (Figure 2–28).

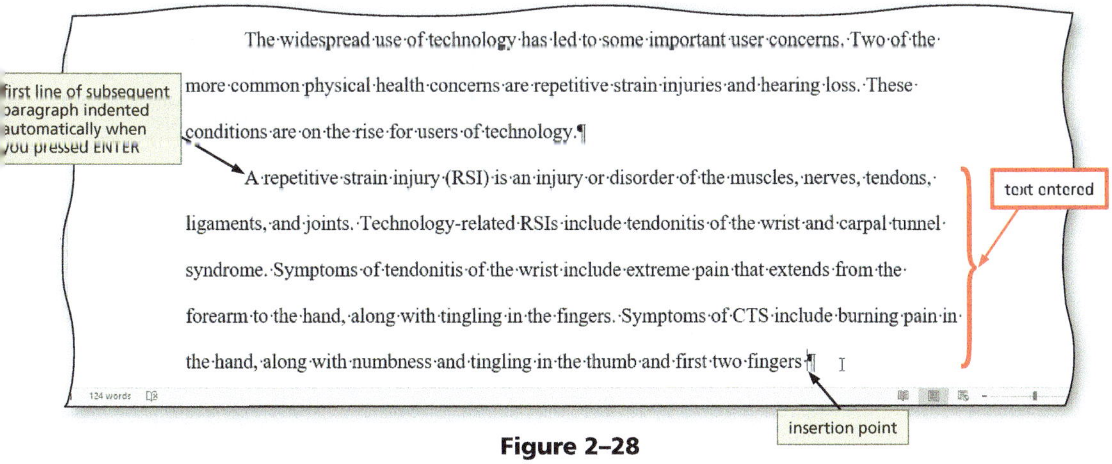

Figure 2–28

BTW

Spacing after Punctuation

Because word processing documents use variable character fonts, it often is difficult to determine in a printed document how many times someone has pressed the SPACEBAR between sentences. Thus, the rule is to press the SPACEBAR only once after periods, colons, and other punctuation marks.

Citations

Both the MLA and APA guidelines suggest the use of in-text parenthetical references (placed at the end of a sentence), instead of footnoting each source of material in a paper. These parenthetical references, called citations in Word, guide the reader to the end of the paper for complete information about the source.

Word provides tools to assist you with inserting citations in a paper and later generating a list of sources from the citations. With a documentation style selected, Word automatically formats the citations and list of sources according to that style. The process for adding citations in Word is as follows:

1. Change the documentation style, if necessary.
2. Insert a citation placeholder.
3. Enter the source information for the citation.

You can combine Steps 2 and 3, where you insert the citation placeholder and enter the source information at once. Or, you can insert the citation placeholder as you write and then enter the source information for the citation at a later time. While creating the research paper in this module, you will use both methods.

BTW
The Ribbon and Screen Resolution
Word may change how the groups and buttons within the groups appear on the ribbon, depending on the computer or mobile device's screen resolution. Thus, your ribbon may look different from the ones in this book if you are using a screen resolution other than 1366 × 768.

To Change the Bibliography Style

The first step in inserting a citation is to be sure the citations and sources will be formatted using the correct documentation style, called the bibliography style in Word. **Why?** You want to ensure that Word is using the MLA documentation style for this paper. The following steps change the specified documentation style.

1

- Click References on the ribbon to display the References tab.
- Click the Style arrow (References tab | Citations & Bibliography group) to display the Style gallery, which lists predefined documentation styles (Figure 2–29).

2

- Click 'MLA Seventh Edition' in the Style gallery to change the documentation style to MLA.

Q&A **What if I am using a different edition of a documentation style shown in the Bibliography Style gallery?**
Select the closest one and then, if necessary, perform necessary edits before submitting the paper.

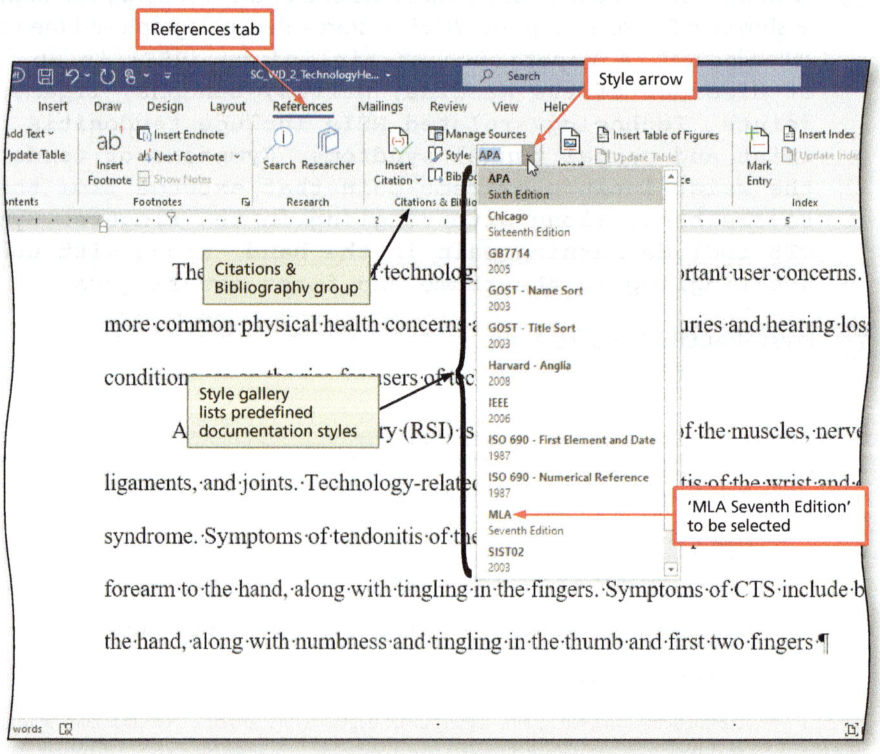

Figure 2–29

Consider This

What details are required for sources?

During your research, be sure to record essential publication information about each of your sources. Following is a sample list of types of required information for the MLA documentation style.

- Book: full name of author(s), complete title of book, edition (if available), volume (if available), publication city, publisher name, publication year, and publication medium
- Magazine: full name of author(s), complete title of article, magazine title, issue number (if available), date of magazine, page numbers of article, publication medium, and date viewed (if medium is a website)
- Website: full name of author(s), title of website, publication date (if none, write n.d.), publication medium, and date viewed

To Insert a Citation for a New Source

With the documentation style selected, the next task is to insert a citation at the location of the insertion point and enter the source information for the citation. You can accomplish these steps at once by instructing Word to add a new source. The following steps add a new source for a magazine (periodical) article on the web. **Why?** The material preceding the insertion point was summarized from an online magazine article.

1

- With the insertion point at the location for the citation (as shown in Figure 2–28), click the Insert Citation button (References tab | Citations & Bibliography group) to display the Insert Citation menu (Figure 2–30).

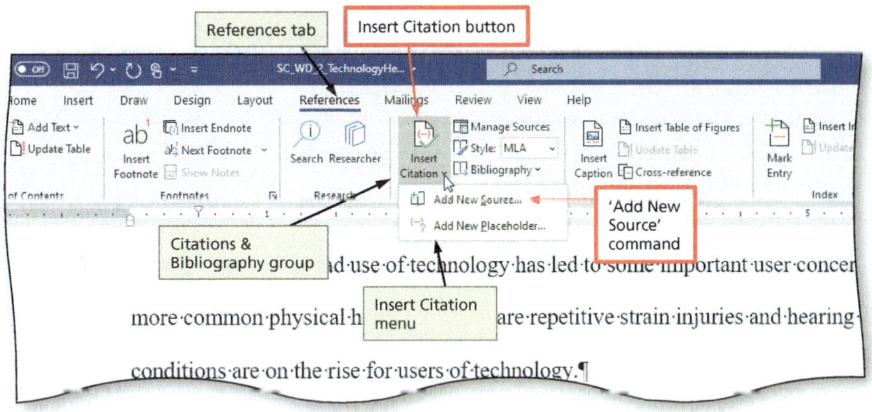

Figure 2–30

2

- Click 'Add New Source' on the Insert Citation menu to display the Create Source dialog box (Figure 2–31).

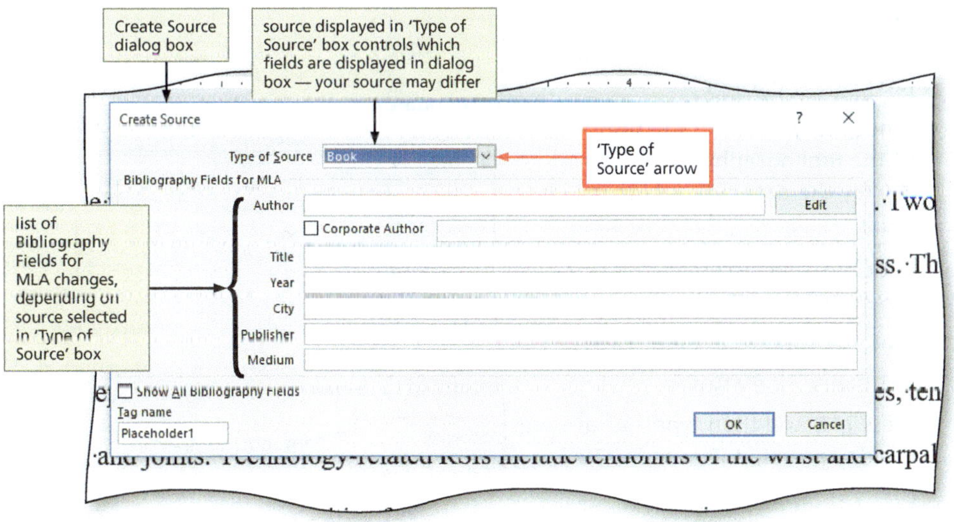

Figure 2–31

Q&A

What are the Bibliography Fields in the Create Source dialog box?

A **field** is a code that serves as a placeholder for data whose contents can change. You enter data in some fields; Word supplies data for others. In this case, you enter the contents of the fields for a particular source, for example, the author name in the Author field.

Experiment

- Click the 'Type of Source' arrow and then click one of the source types in the list, so that you can see how the list of fields changes to reflect the type of source you selected.

3

- If necessary, click the 'Type of Source' arrow (Create Source dialog box) and then click 'Article in a Periodical', so that the list shows fields required for a magazine (periodical).
- Click the Author text box. Type **`Zhao, Shen Li`** as the author.
- Click the Title text box. Type **`Technology Aches and Pains`** as the article title.
- Press TAB and then type **`Monthly Medical and Review`** as the periodical title.
- Press TAB and then type **`2021`** as the year.
- Press TAB and then type **`July`** as the month.
- Press TAB twice and then type **`n. pag.`** as the number of pages.
- Press TAB and then type **`Web`** as the medium (Figure 2–32).

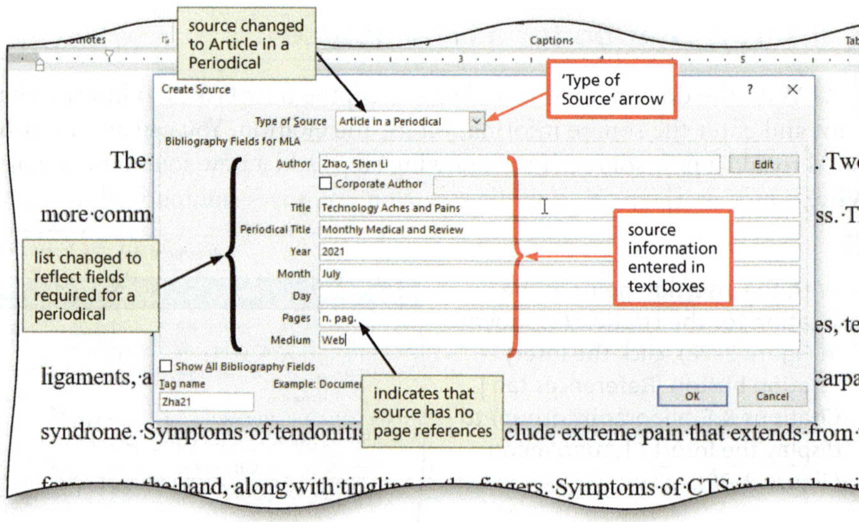

Figure 2–32

Q&A **Should the month names ever be abbreviated?**
The MLA documentation style abbreviates all months, except May, June, and July, when they appear in a source.

What does the n. pag. entry mean in the Pages text box?
The MLA documentation style uses the abbreviation n. pag. for no pagination, which indicates the source has no page references. This is common for web sources.

4

- Place a check mark in the 'Show All Bibliography Fields' check box so that Word displays all fields available for the selected source, including the date viewed (accessed) fields.
- If necessary, scroll to the bottom of the Bibliography Fields list to display the date viewed (accessed) fields.
- Click the Year Accessed text box. Type **`2021`** as the year.
- Press TAB and then type **`Oct.`** as the month accessed.
- Press TAB and then type **`1`** as the day accessed (Figure 2–33).

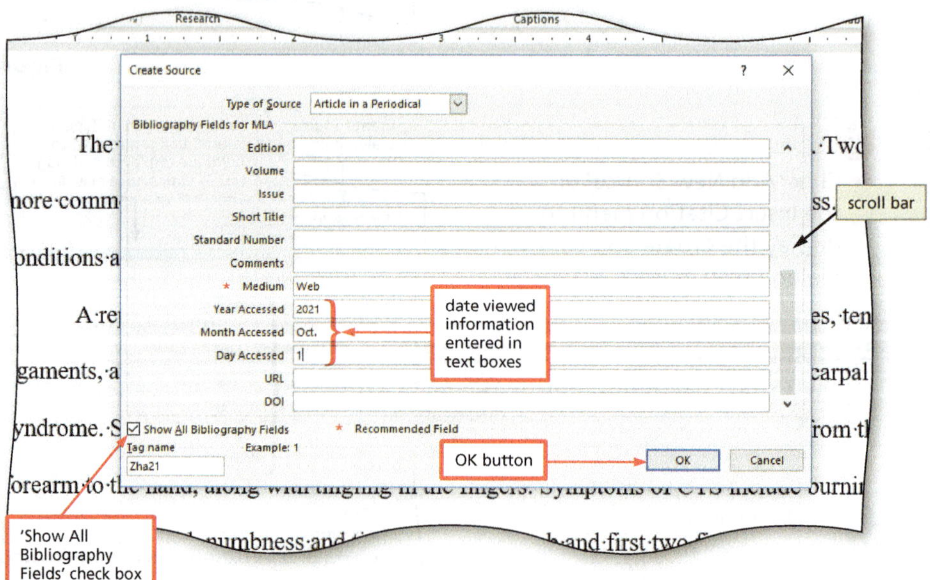

Figure 2–33

Q&A **What if some of the text boxes disappear as I enter the fields?**
With the 'Show All Bibliography Fields' check box selected, the dialog box may not be able to display all fields at the same time. In this case, some may scroll up off the screen.

5

- Click OK to close the dialog box, create the source, and insert the citation in the document at the location of the insertion point.
- Press END to move the insertion point to the end of the line, if necessary, which also deselects the citation.
- Press the PERIOD key to end the sentence (Figure 2–34).

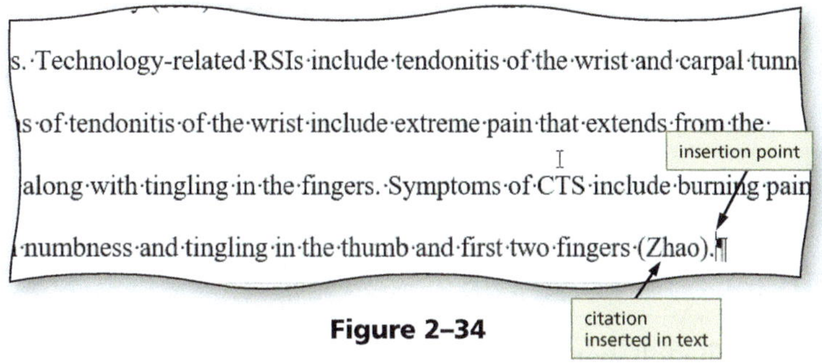

Figure 2–34

To Enter More Text

The next task is to continue typing text in the research paper up to the location of the footnote. The following steps enter this text.

1 Press SPACEBAR.

2 Type the next sentences (Figure 2–35): **`Factors that can cause these disorders include prolonged typing or mouse usage and continual shifting between a mouse and keyboard. Taking continual breaks and exercising the hands and arms can help reduce chances of developing these repetitive strain injuries.`**

3 Save the research paper again on the same storage location with the same file name.

Q&A **Why should I save the research paper again?**
You have made several modifications to the research paper since you last saved it; thus, you should save it again.

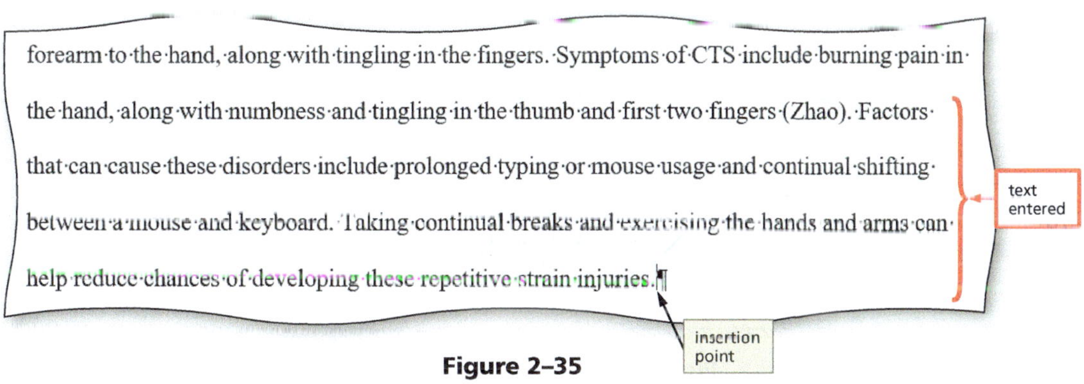

Figure 2–35

BTW
Organizing Files and Folders
You should organize and store files in folders so that you easily can find the files later. For example, if you are taking an introductory technology class called CIS 101, a good practice would be to save all Word files in a Word folder in a CIS 101 folder.

Footnotes

As discussed earlier in this module, notes are optional in the MLA documentation style. If used, content notes elaborate on points discussed in the paper, and bibliographic notes direct the reader to evaluations of statements in a source or provide a means for identifying multiple sources. The MLA documentation style specifies that a superscript (raised number or letter) be used for a **note reference mark** to signal that additional information is offered in a note that exists either as a footnote or endnote. A **footnote**, which is located at the bottom of the page on which the note reference mark appears, is text that provides additional information or acknowledges sources for text in a document. Similarly, an **endnote** is text that provides additional information or acknowledges sources for text in a document but is located at the end of a document (or section) and uses the same note reference mark that appears in the main text.

In Word, **note text**, which is the content of footnotes or endnotes, can be any length and format. Word automatically numbers notes sequentially by placing a note reference mark both in the body of the document and to the left of the note text. If you insert, rearrange, or remove notes, Word renumbers any subsequent note reference marks according to their new sequence in the document.

To Insert a Footnote

The following steps insert a note reference mark in the document at the location of the insertion point and at the location where the footnote text will be typed. **Why?** You will insert a content note elaborating on the seriousness of tendonitis and carpal tunnel syndrome, which you want to position as a footnote.

1

- With the insertion point positioned as shown in Figure 2–35, click the Insert Footnote button (References tab | Footnotes group) to display a note reference mark (a superscripted 1) in two places: (1) in the document window at the location of the insertion point and (2) at the bottom of the page where the footnote text will be positioned, just below a separator line (Figure 2–36).

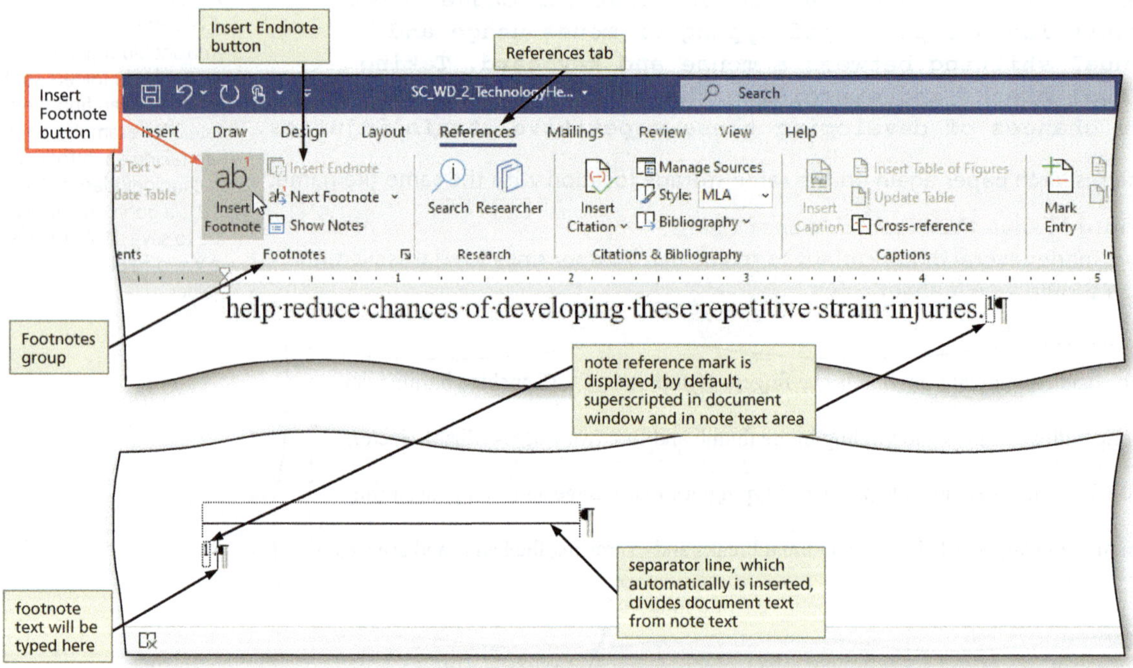

Figure 2–36

Q&A **What if I wanted notes to be positioned as endnotes instead of as footnotes?**
You would click the Insert Endnote button (References tab | Footnotes group), which places the separator line and the endnote text at the end of the document, instead of the bottom of the page containing the reference.

2

- Type the footnote text up to the citation (shown in Figure 2–37): `According to Clark and Nadeer, tendonitis of the wrist and carpal tunnel syndrome can lead to permanent physical damage if left untreated` and then press SPACEBAR.

Other Ways

1. Press ALT+CTRL+F

To Insert a Citation Placeholder

Earlier in this module, you inserted a citation and its source at once. In Word, you also can insert a citation without entering the source information. **Why?** Sometimes, you may not have the source information readily available and would prefer to enter it at a later time.

The following steps insert a citation placeholder in the footnote, so that you can enter the source information later.

1

- With the insertion point positioned as shown in Figure 2–37, click the Insert Citation button (References tab | Citations & Bibliography group) to display the Insert Citation menu (Figure 2–37).

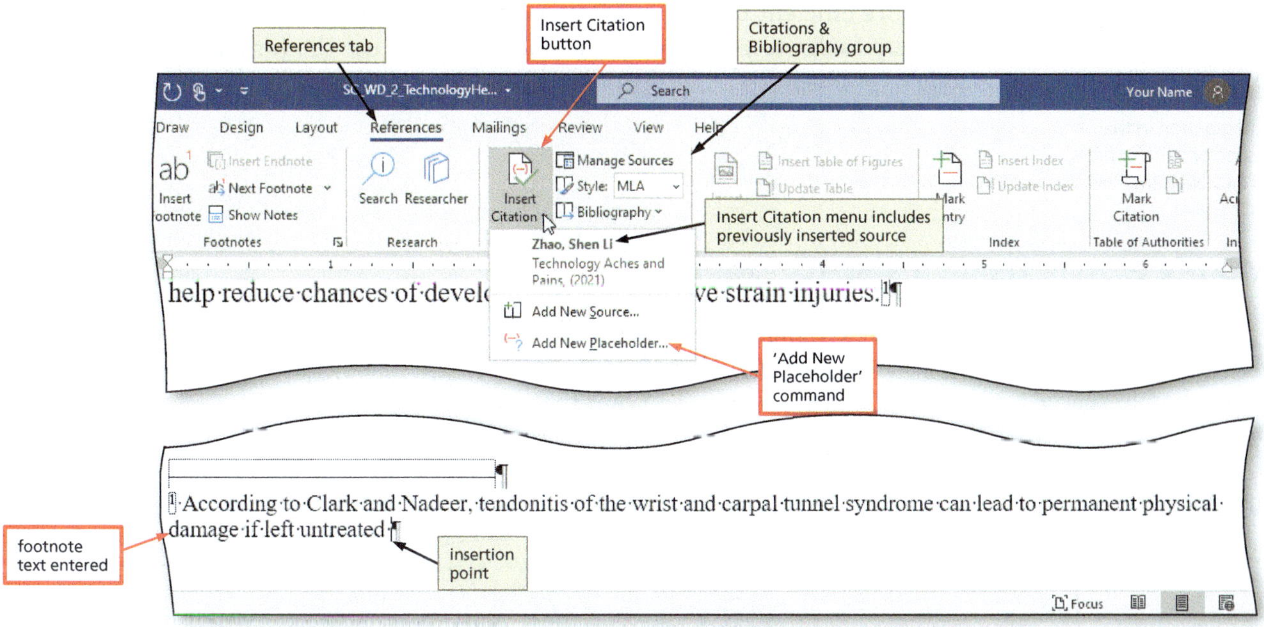

Figure 2–37

2

- Click 'Add New Placeholder' on the Insert Citation menu to display the Placeholder Name dialog box.
- Type `Clark` as the tag name for the source (Figure 2–38).

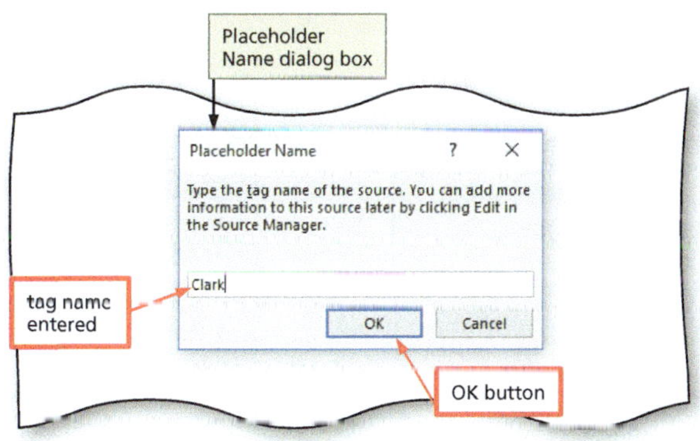

Figure 2–38

Q&A **What is a tag name?**
A tag name is an identifier that links a citation to a source. Word automatically creates a tag name when you enter a source. When you create a citation placeholder, enter a meaningful tag name, which will appear in the citation placeholder until you edit the source.

3

- Click OK (Placeholder Name dialog box) to close the dialog box and insert the entered tag name in the citation placeholder in the document (shown in Figure 2–39).
- Press the PERIOD key to end the sentence.

Q&A **What if the citation is in the wrong location?**
Click the citation to select it and then drag the citation tab (on the upper-left corner of the selected citation) to any location in the document.

BTW
Style Formats
To see the formats assigned to a particular style in a document, click the Styles Dialog Box Launcher (Home tab | Styles group) and then click the Style Inspector button in the Styles pane. Position the insertion point in the style in the document and then point to the Paragraph formatting or Text level formatting areas in the Style Inspector pane to display a ScreenTip describing formats assigned to the location of the insertion point. You also can click the Reveal Formatting button in the Style Inspector pane or press SHIFT+F1 to open the Reveal Formatting pane.

Footnote Text Style

When you insert a footnote, Word formats it using the Footnote Text style, which does not adhere to the MLA documentation style. For example, notice in Figure 2–37 that the footnote text is single-spaced, left-aligned, and a smaller font size than the text in the research paper. According to the MLA documentation style, notes should be formatted like all other paragraphs in the paper.

You could change the paragraph formatting of the footnote text to first-line indent and double-spaced and then change the font size from 10 to 12 point. If you use this technique, however, you will need to change the format of the footnote text for each footnote you enter into the document.

A more efficient technique is to modify the format of the Footnote Text style so that every footnote you enter in the document will use the formats defined in this style.

To Modify a Style Using a Shortcut Menu

The Footnote Text style specifies left-aligned single-spaced paragraphs with a 10-point font size for text. The following steps modify the Footnote Text style. **Why?** To meet MLA documentation style, the footnotes should be double-spaced with a first-line indent and a 12-point font size for text.

1

- Right-click the note text in the footnote to display a shortcut menu related to footnotes (Figure 2–39).

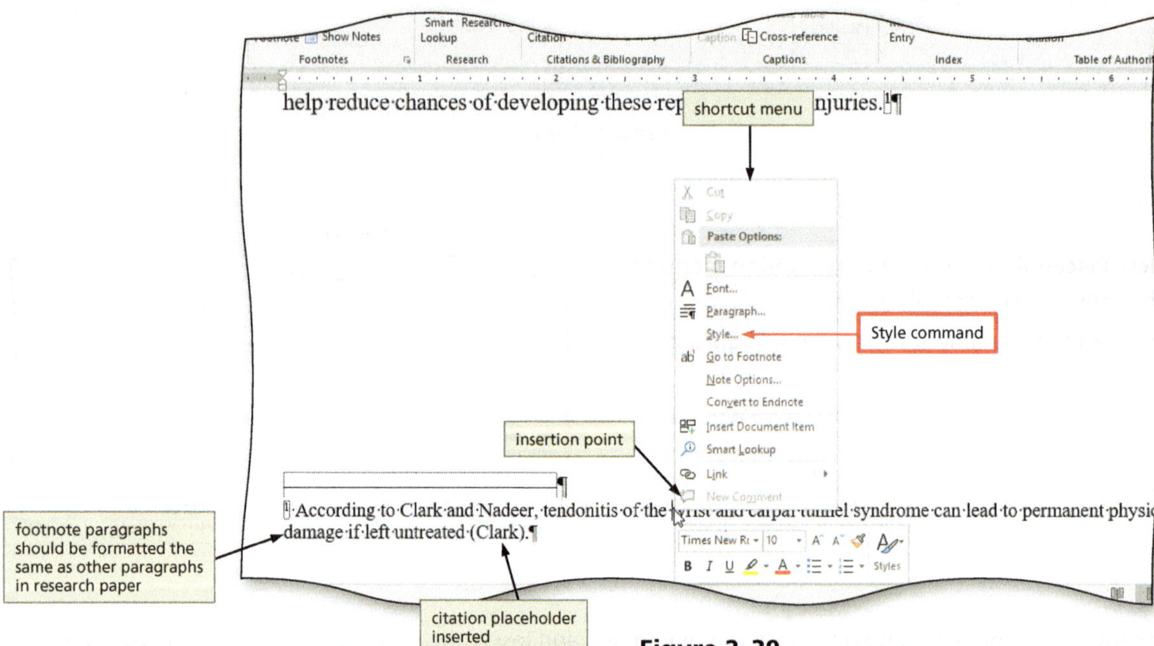

Figure 2–39

2

- Click Style on the shortcut menu to display the Style dialog box. If necessary, click the Category arrow, click All styles in the Category list, and then click Footnote Text in the Styles list to select the style to modify.
- Click the Modify button (Style dialog box) to display the Modify Style dialog box.
- Click the Font Size arrow (Modify Style dialog box) to display the Font Size list and then click 12 in the Font Size list to change the font size.
- Click the Double Space button to change the line spacing.

- Click the Format button to display the Format menu (Figure 2–40).

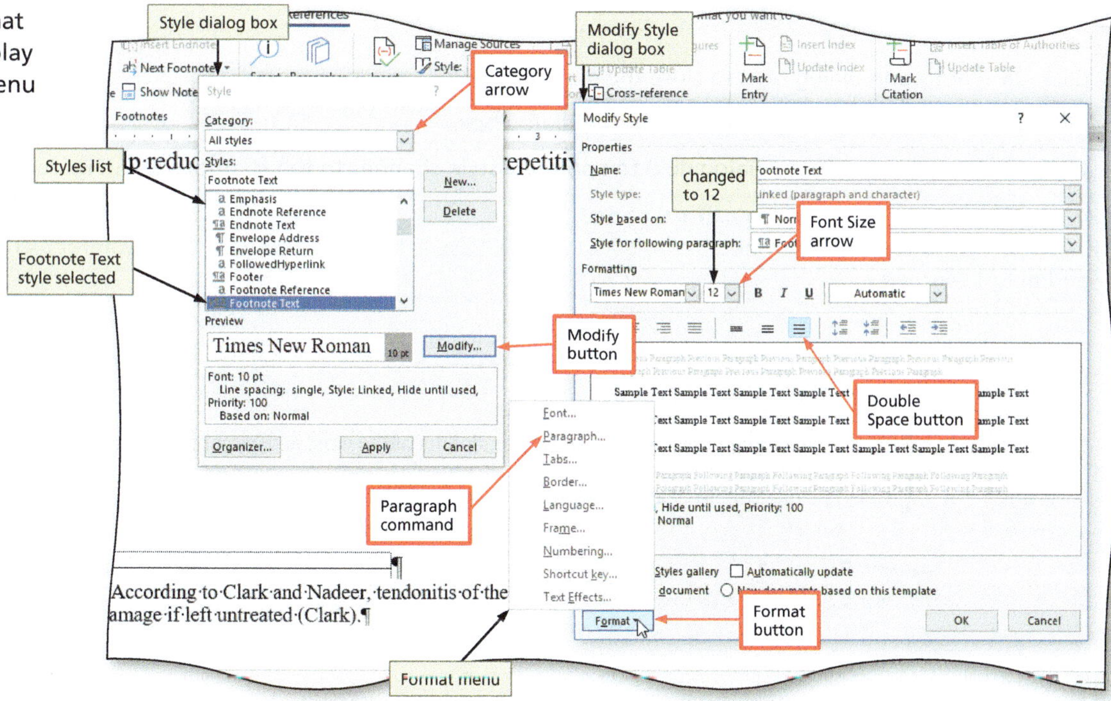

Figure 2–40

3

- Click Paragraph on the Format menu (Modify Style dialog box) to display the Paragraph dialog box.
- Click the Special arrow in the Indentation area (Paragraph dialog box) and then click First line (Figure 2–41).

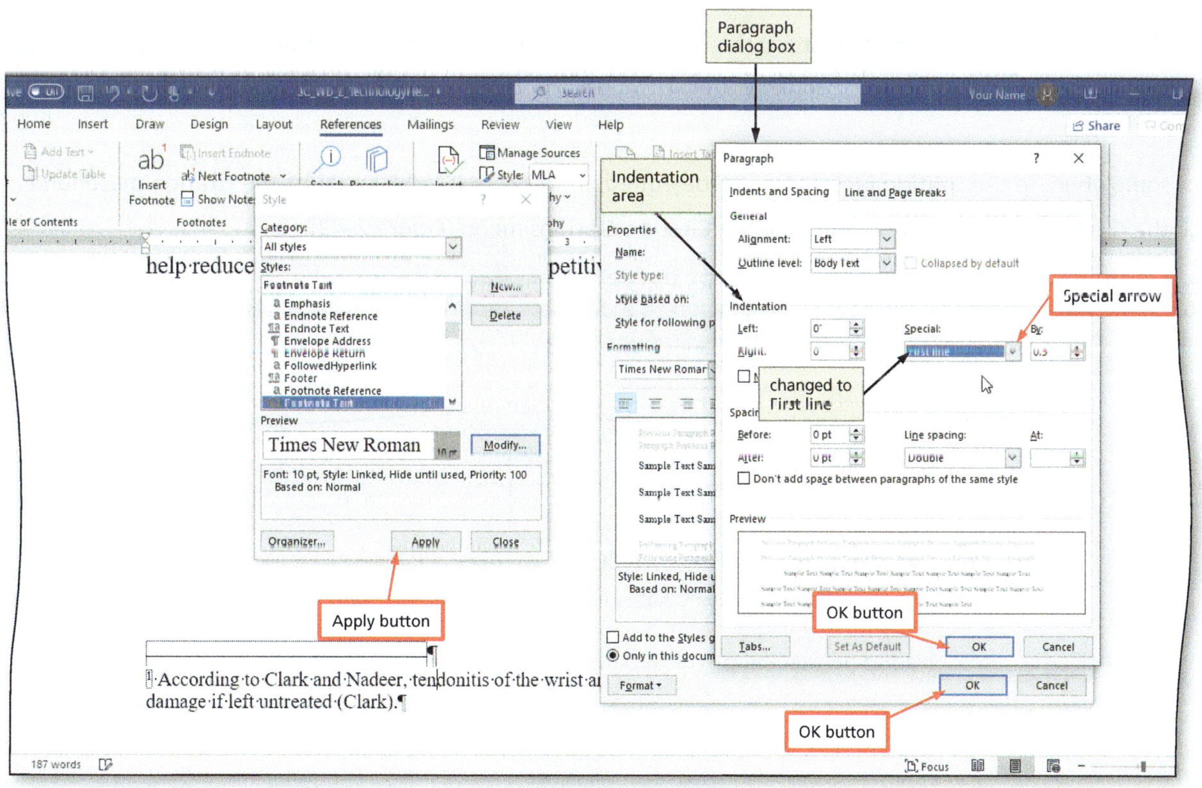

Figure 2–41

4

- Click OK (Paragraph dialog box) to close the dialog box.
- Click OK (Modify Style dialog box) to close the dialog box.
- Click the Apply button (Style dialog box) to apply the style changes to the footnote text (Figure 2–42).

Q&A **Will all footnotes use this modified style?**
Yes. Any future footnotes entered in the document will use a 12-point font with the paragraphs first-line indented and double-spaced.

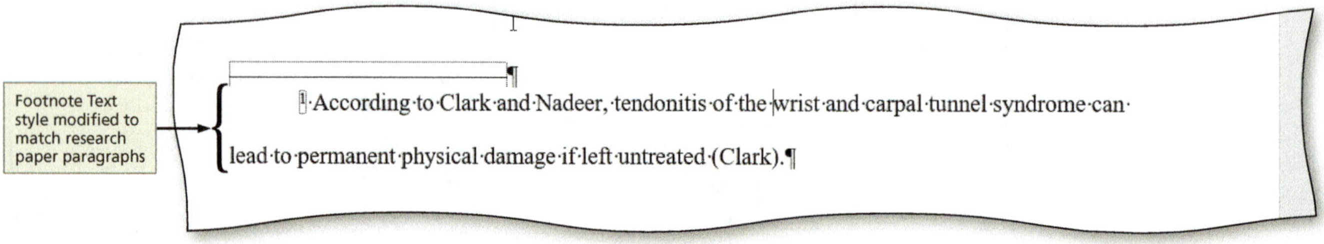

Figure 2–42

Other Ways

1. Click Styles Dialog Box Launcher (Home tab | Styles group), point to style name in list, click style name arrow, click Modify, change settings (Modify Style dialog box), click OK
2. Click Styles Dialog Box Launcher (Home tab | Styles group), click Manage Styles button in pane, select style name in list, click Modify button (Manage Styles dialog box), change settings (Modify Style dialog box), click OK in each dialog box

To Edit a Source

When you typed the footnote text for this research paper, you inserted a citation placeholder for the source. The following steps edit a source. **Why?** Assume you now have the source information and are ready to enter it.

1

- Click somewhere in the citation placeholder to be edited, in this case (Clark), to select the citation placeholder.
- Click the Citation Options arrow to display the Citation Options menu (Figure 2–43).

Q&A **What is the purpose of the tab to the left of the selected citation?**
If, for some reason, you wanted to move a citation to a different location in the document, you would select the citation and then drag the citation tab to the desired location.

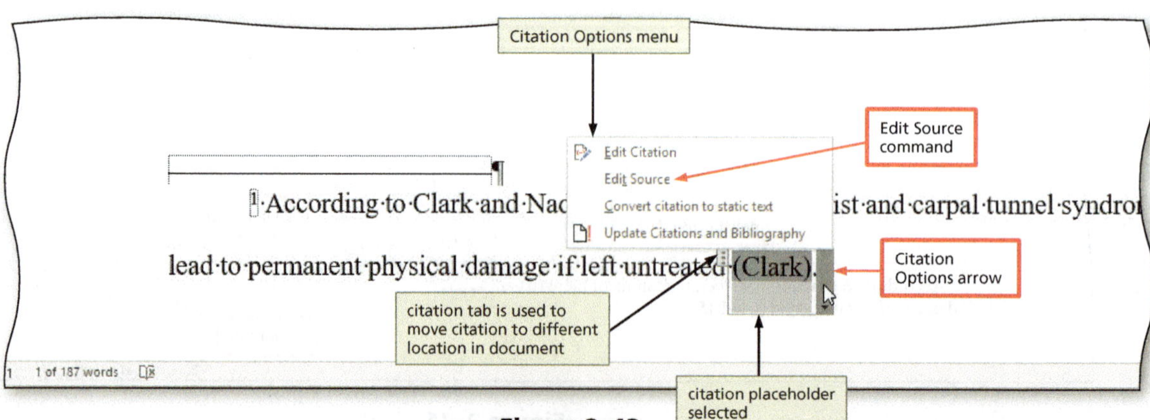

Figure 2–43

2

- Click Edit Source on the Citation Options menu to display the Edit Source dialog box.
- If necessary, click the 'Type of Source' arrow (Edit Source dialog box) and then click Book, so that the list shows fields required for a book.
- Because this source has two authors, click the Edit button to display the Edit Name dialog box, which assists you with entering multiple author names.
- Type **Clark** as the first author's last name; press TAB and then type **Addison** as the first name; press TAB and then type **Lee** as the middle name (Figure 2–44).

Q&A **What if I already know how to punctuate the author entry properly?**
You can enter the name directly in the Author box.

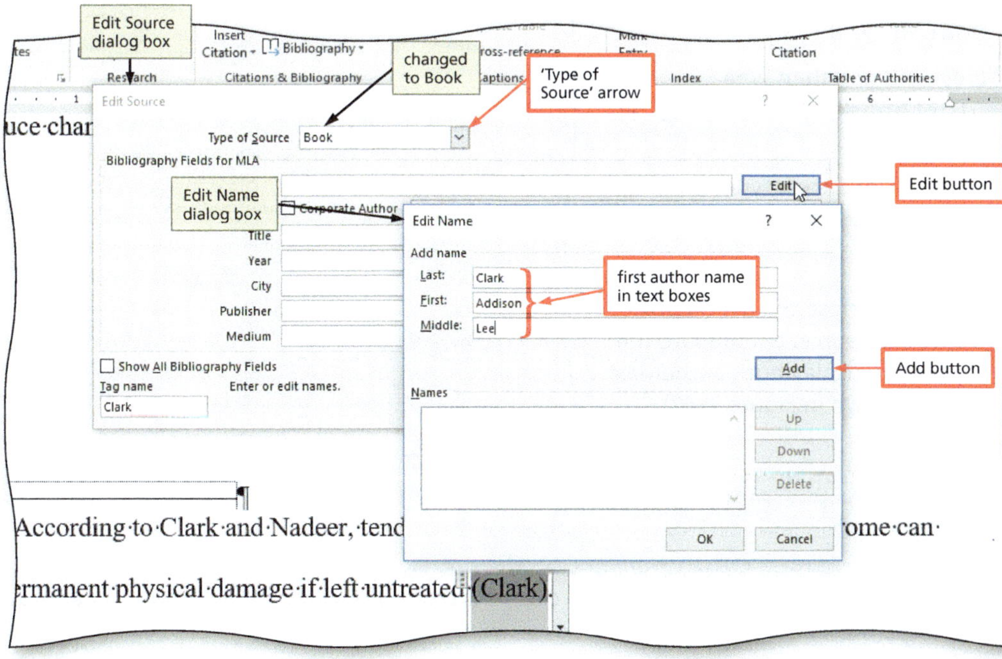

Figure 2–44

3

- Click the Add button (Edit Name dialog box) to add the first author name to the Names list.
- Type **Nadeer** as the second author's last name; press TAB and then type **Aisha** as the first name; press TAB and then type **Sati** as the middle name.
- Click the Add button (Edit Name dialog box) to add the second author name to the Names list (Figure 2–45).

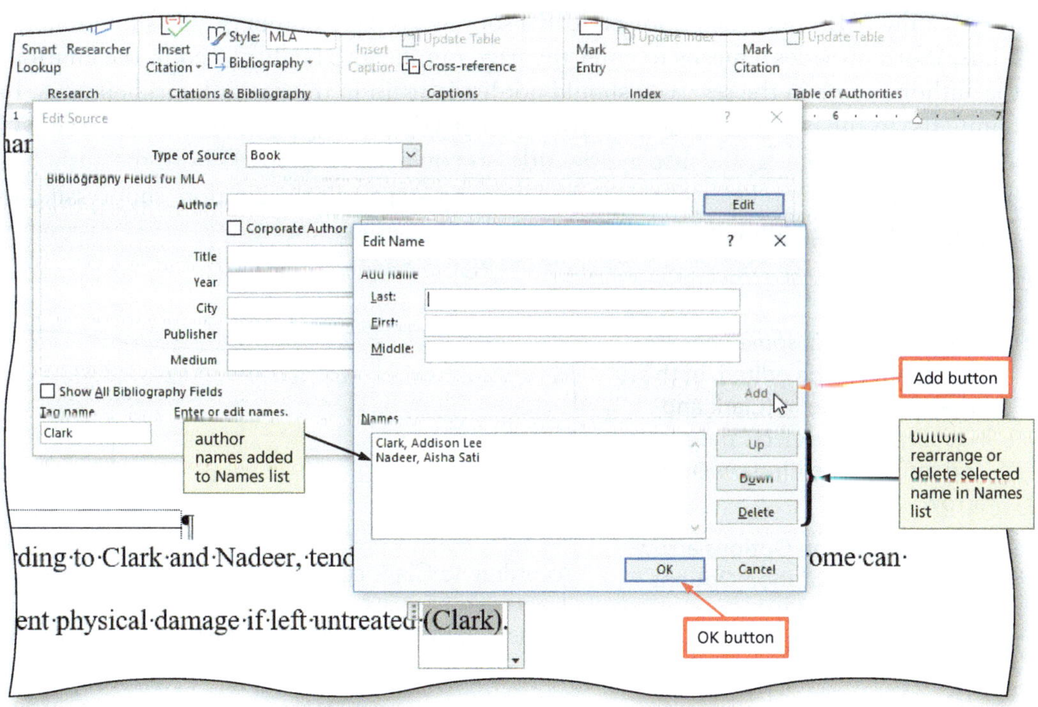

Figure 2–45

4

- Click OK (Edit Name dialog box) to add the author names that appear in the Names list to the Author box in the Edit Source dialog box.
- Click the Title text box (Edit Source dialog box). Type **Repetitive Strain Injuries** as the book title.
- Press TAB and then type **2021** as the year.
- Press TAB and then type **Boston** as the city.
- Press TAB and then type **Lighthouse Publishing** as the publisher.
- Press TAB and then type **Print** as the medium (Figure 2–46).

5

- Click OK to close the dialog box, create the source, and update the citation to display both author last names (shown in Figure 2–47).

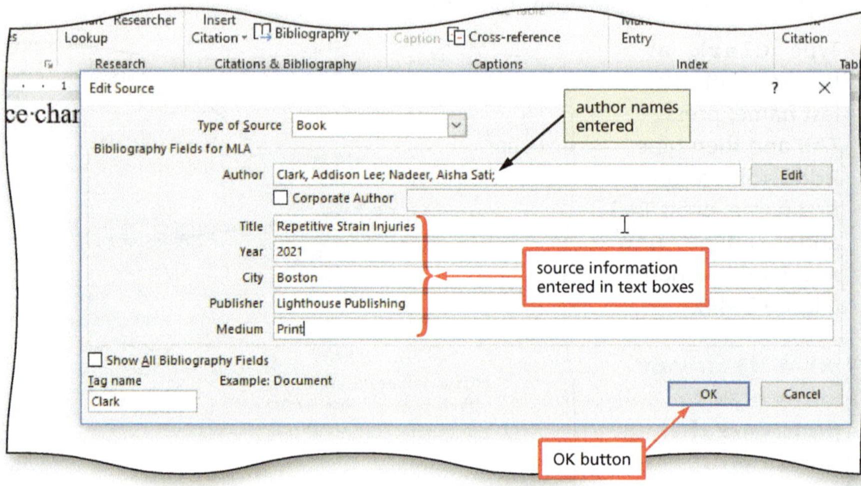

Figure 2–46

Other Ways

1. Click Manage Sources button (References tab | Citations & Bibliography group), click placeholder source in Current List, click Edit button (Source Manager dialog box)

To Edit a Citation

In the MLA documentation style, if a source has page numbers, you should include them in the citation. Thus, Word provides a means to enter the page numbers to be displayed in the citation. Also, if you reference the author's name in the text, you should not list it again in the parenthetical citation. Instead, just list the page number(s) in the citation. To do this, you instruct Word to suppress author and title. **Why?** If you suppress the author, Word automatically displays the title, so you need to suppress both the author and title if you want just the page number(s) to be displayed. The following steps edit the citation, suppressing the author and title but displaying the page numbers.

1

- If necessary, click somewhere in the citation to be edited, in this case somewhere in (Clark and Nadeer), which selects the citation and displays the Citation Options arrow.
- Click the Citation Options arrow to display the Citation Options menu (Figure 2–47).

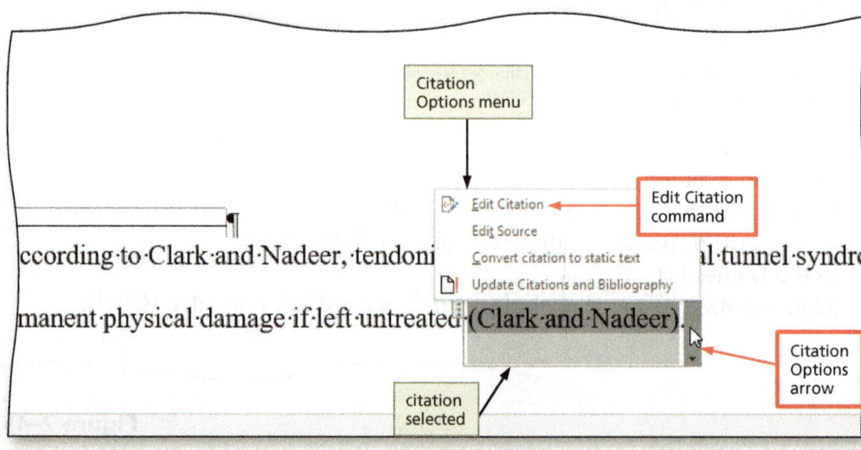

Figure 2–47

2

- Click Edit Citation on the Citation Options menu to display the Edit Citation dialog box.
- Type `65-66` in the Pages text box (Edit Citation dialog box).
- Click the Author check box to place a check mark in it.
- Click the Title check box to place a check mark in it (Figure 2–48).

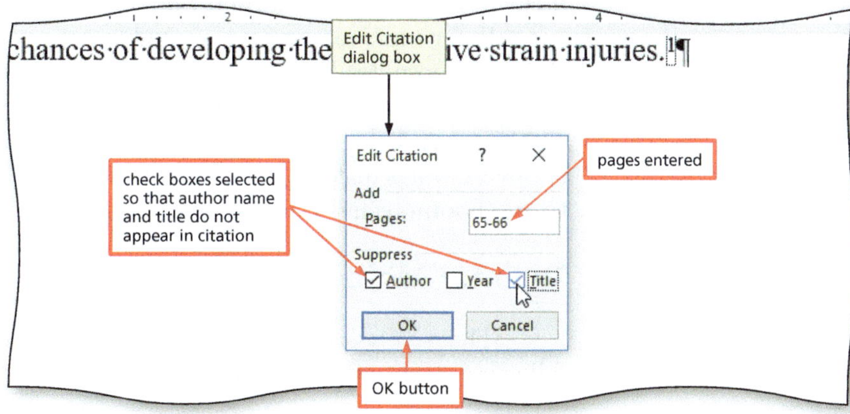

Figure 2–48

3

- Click OK to close the dialog box, remove the author names from the citation in the footnote, suppress the title from showing, and add page numbers to the citation.
- Press END to move the insertion point to the end of the line, which also deselects the citation (Figure 2–49).

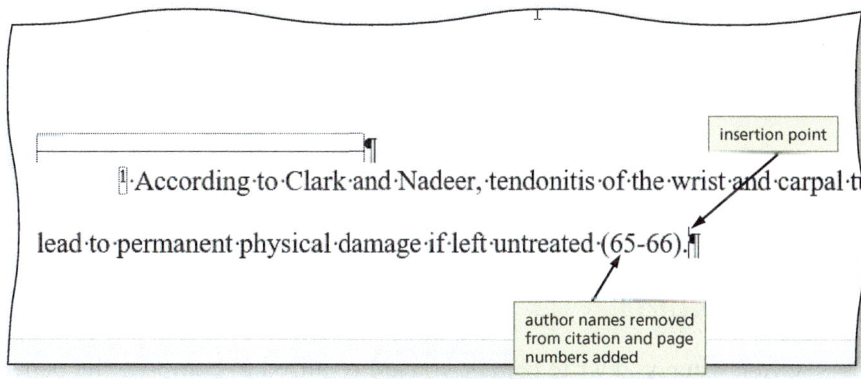

Figure 2–49

Working with Footnotes and Endnotes

You edit footnote text just as you edit any other text in the document. To delete or move a note reference mark, however, the insertion point must be in the document text (not in the footnote text).

To delete a note, select the note reference mark in the document text (not in the footnote text) by dragging through the note reference mark and then click the Cut button (Home tab | Clipboard group). Or, click immediately to the right of the note reference mark in the document text and then press BACKSPACE twice, or click immediately to the left of the note reference mark in the document text and then press DELETE twice.

To move a note to a different location in a document, select the note reference mark in the document text (not in the footnote text), click the Cut button (Home tab | Clipboard group), click the location where you want to move the note, and then click the Paste button (Home tab | Clipboard group). When you move or delete notes, Word automatically renumbers any remaining notes in the correct sequence.

If you are using a mouse and position the pointer on the note reference mark in the document text, the note text is displayed above the note reference mark as a ScreenTip. To remove the ScreenTip, move the pointer.

If, for some reason, you wanted to change the format of note reference marks in footnotes or endnotes (i.e., from 1, 2, 3 to A, B, C), you would click the Footnotes Dialog Box Launcher (References tab | Footnotes group) to display the Footnote and Endnote dialog box, click the Number format arrow (Footnote and Endnote dialog box), click the desired number format in the list, and then click Apply button.

If, for some reason, you wanted to change a footnote number, you would click the Footnotes Dialog Box Launcher (References tab | Footnotes group) to display the

BTW

Footnote and Endnote Location

You can change the location of footnotes from the bottom of the page to the end of the text by clicking the Footnotes Dialog Box Launcher (References tab | Footnotes group), clicking the Footnotes arrow (Footnote and Endnote dialog box), and then clicking Below text. Similarly, clicking the Endnotes arrow (Footnote and Endnote dialog box) enables you to change the location of endnotes from the end of the document to the end of a section.

Footnote and Endnote dialog box, enter the desired number in the Start at box, and then click Apply (Footnote and Endnote dialog box).

If, for some reason, you wanted to convert footnotes to endnotes, you would click the Footnotes Dialog Box Launcher (References tab | Footnotes group) to display the Footnote and Endnote dialog box, click the Convert button (Footnote and Endnote dialog box), select the 'Convert all footnotes to endnotes' option button (Convert Notes dialog box), click OK (Convert Notes dialog box), and then click Close (Footnote and Endnote dialog box).

To Enter More Text

The next task is to continue typing text in the body of the research paper. The following steps enter this text.

1. Position the insertion point after the note reference mark in the document and then press ENTER.

2. Type the first three sentences in the third paragraph of the research paper (shown in Figure 2–50): **People often listen to sounds from their computers or mobile devices through headphones or earbuds. Headphones cover or are placed outside of the ear, whereas earbuds rest inside the ear canal. With these auditory devices, only the individual wearing the device hears the sound.**

To Count Words

Often when you write papers, you are required to compose the papers with a minimum number of words. The minimum requirement for the research paper in this module is 275 words. You can look on the status bar and see the total number of words thus far in a document. For example, Figure 2–50 shows the research paper has 231 words, but you are not sure if that count includes the words in your footnote. The following steps display the Word Count dialog box. **Why?** You want to verify that the footnote text is included in the count.

1

- Click the Word Count indicator on the status bar to display the Word Count dialog box.
- If necessary, place a check mark in the 'Include textboxes, footnotes and endnotes' check box (Word Count dialog box) (Figure 2–50).

Q&A **Why do the statistics in my Word Count dialog box differ from those in Figure 2–50?**
Depending on the accuracy of your typing, your statistics may differ.

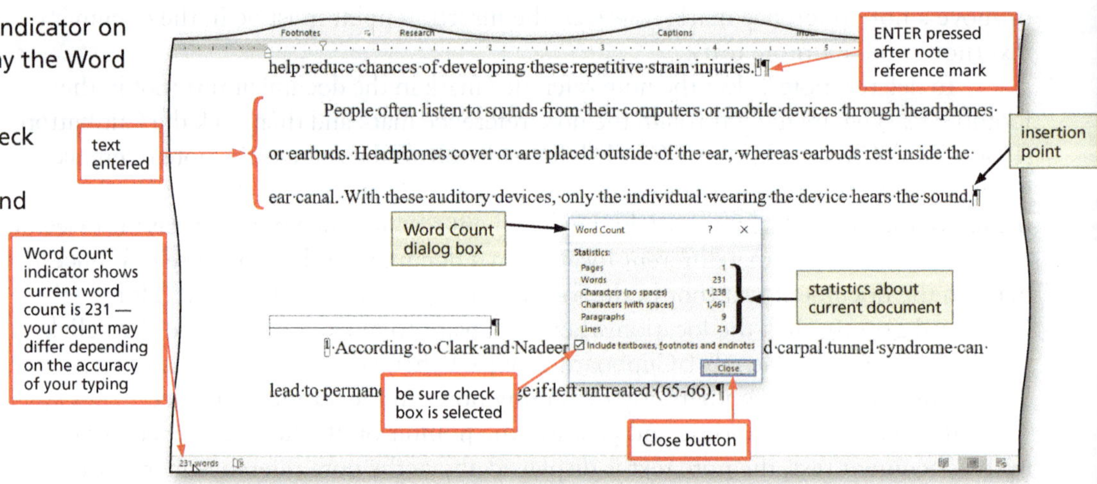

Figure 2–50

2

- Click the Close button (Word Count dialog box) to close the dialog box.

Q&A **Can I display statistics for just a section of the document?**
Yes. Select the section and then click the Word Count indicator on the status bar to display statistics about the selected text.

Other Ways

1. Click Word Count button (Review tab | Proofing group)
2. Press CTRL+SHIFT+G

Automatic Page Breaks

As you type documents that exceed one page, Word automatically inserts page breaks at the bottom of a page, called **automatic page breaks** or **soft page breaks**, when it determines the text has filled one page according to paper size, margin settings, line spacing, and other settings. If you add text, delete text, or modify text on a page, Word recalculates the location of automatic page breaks and adjusts them accordingly.

Word performs page recalculation between the keystrokes, that is, in between the pauses in your typing. Thus, Word refers to the automatic page break task as **background repagination**. An automatic page break will occur in the next set of steps.

BTW

Page Break Locations

As you type, your page break may occur at different locations depending on Word settings and the type of printer connected to the computer.

To Enter More Text and Insert a Citation Placeholder

The next task is to type the remainder of the third paragraph in the body of the research paper. The following steps enter this text and a citation placeholder at the end of the paragraph.

1. With the insertion point positioned at the end of the third sentence in the third paragraph, as shown in Figure 2–50, press SPACEBAR.

2. Type the rest of the third paragraph: `By using high-quality auditory devices that provide a close fit and include noise-cancelling technology, users can lower the volume level on these devices. Lower volumes can help to minimize potential hering loss` and then press SPACEBAR.

   Q&A

   Why does the text move from the second page to the first page as I am typing?
   Word, by default, will not allow the first line of a paragraph to appear by itself at the bottom of a page (an **orphan**) or the last line of a paragraph to appear by itself at the top of a page (a **widow**). As you type, Word adjusts the placement of the paragraph to avoid orphans and widows.

   Why is the word, hering, misspelled?
   Later in this module, you will use Word's check spelling and grammar at once feature to check the entire document for errors.

3. Click the Insert Citation button (References tab | Citations & Bibliography group) to display the Insert Citation menu. Click 'Add New Placeholder' on the Insert Citation menu to display the Placeholder Name dialog box.

4. Type `Sanchez` as the tag name for the source.

5. Click OK (Placeholder Name dialog box) to close the dialog box and insert the tag name in the citation placeholder.

6. Press the PERIOD key to end the sentence (shown in Figure 2–51).

To Hide and Show White Space

With the page break and header, it is difficult to see the entire third paragraph at once on the screen. With the screen in Print Layout view, you can hide white space, which is the space that is displayed at the top and bottom of pages (including headers and footers) and also the space between pages. The following steps hide white space, if your screen displays it, and then shows white space. **Why?** You want to see as much of the third paragraph as possible at once, which spans the bottom of the first page and the top of the second page.

1

- Position the pointer in the document window in the space between pages so that the pointer changes to a 'Hide White Space' button (Figure 2–51).

Q&A **What if I am using a touch screen?**
Proceed to step 2.

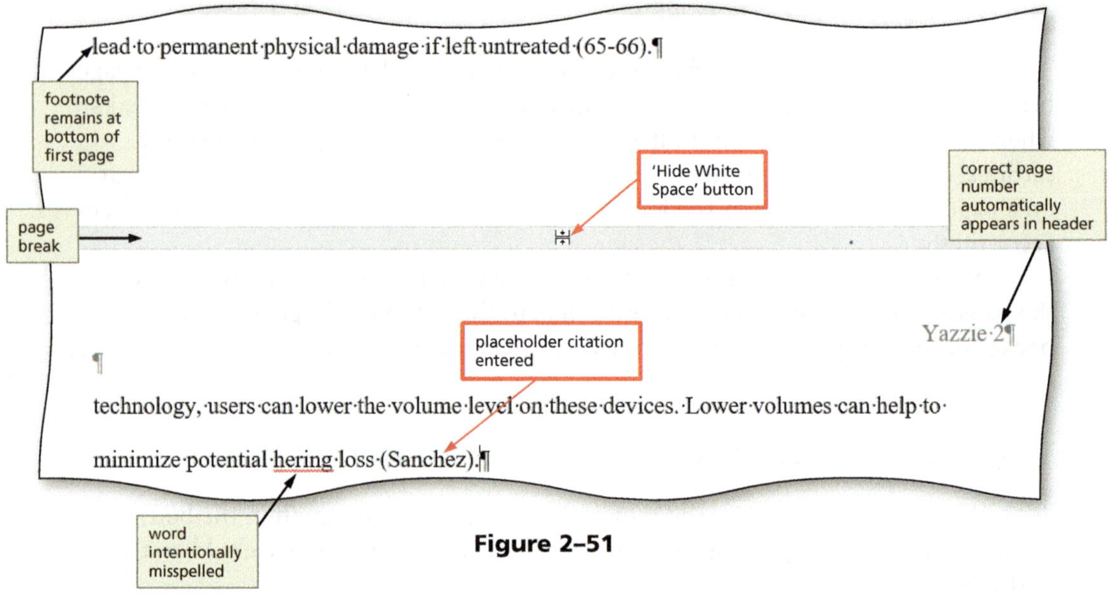

Figure 2–51

2

- Double-click while the pointer is a 'Hide White Space' button to hide white space.
- If necessary, scroll so that both pages appear in the document window at once.

Q&A **What if I am using a touch screen?**
Double-tap in the space between pages.

Does hiding white space have any effect on the printed document?
No.

3

- Position the pointer in the document window on the page break between pages so that the pointer changes to a 'Show White Space' button (Figure 2–52).

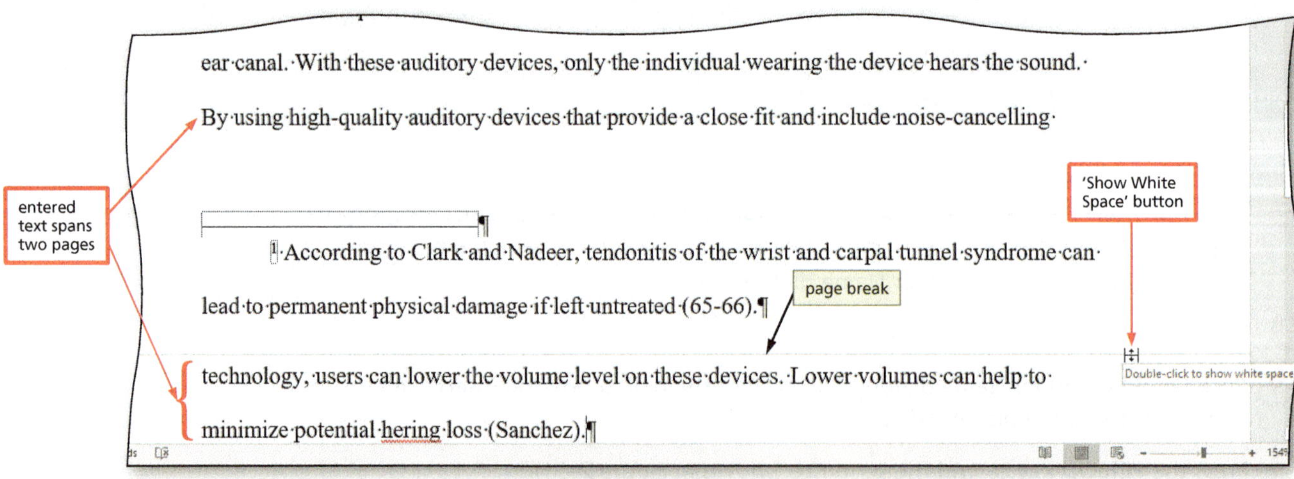

Figure 2–52

4

- Double-click while the pointer is a 'Show White Space' button to show white space.

Q&A **What if I am using a touch screen?**
Double-tap the page break.

Other Ways

1. Click File on ribbon, click Options in Backstage view, click Display in left pane (Word Options dialog box), remove or select check mark from 'Show white space between pages in Print Layout view' check box, click OK

To Edit a Source

When you typed the third paragraph of the research paper, you inserted a citation placeholder, Sanchez, for the source. You now have the source information, which is for a website, and are ready to enter it. The following steps edit the source for the Sanchez citation placeholder.

1. Click somewhere in the citation placeholder to be edited, in this case (Sanchez), to select the citation placeholder.
2. Click the Citation Options arrow to display the Citation Options menu.
3. Click Edit Source on the Citation Options menu to display the Edit Source dialog box.
4. If necessary, click the 'Type of Source' arrow (Edit Source dialog box); scroll to and then click Web site, so that the list shows fields required for a Web site.
5. Click the Author text box. Type `Sanchez, Jorge Mario` as the author.
6. Click the 'Name of Web Page' text box. Type `Technology and Your Hearing` as the webpage name.
7. Click the Year Accessed text box. Type `2021` as the year accessed.
8. Press TAB and then type `Oct.` as the month accessed.
9. Press TAB and then type `1` as the day accessed.
10. Press TAB and then type `Web` as the Medium (Figure 2–53).

Q&A **Do I need to enter a web address (URL)?**
The latest MLA documentation style update does not require the web address in the source.

11. Click OK to close the dialog box and create the source.

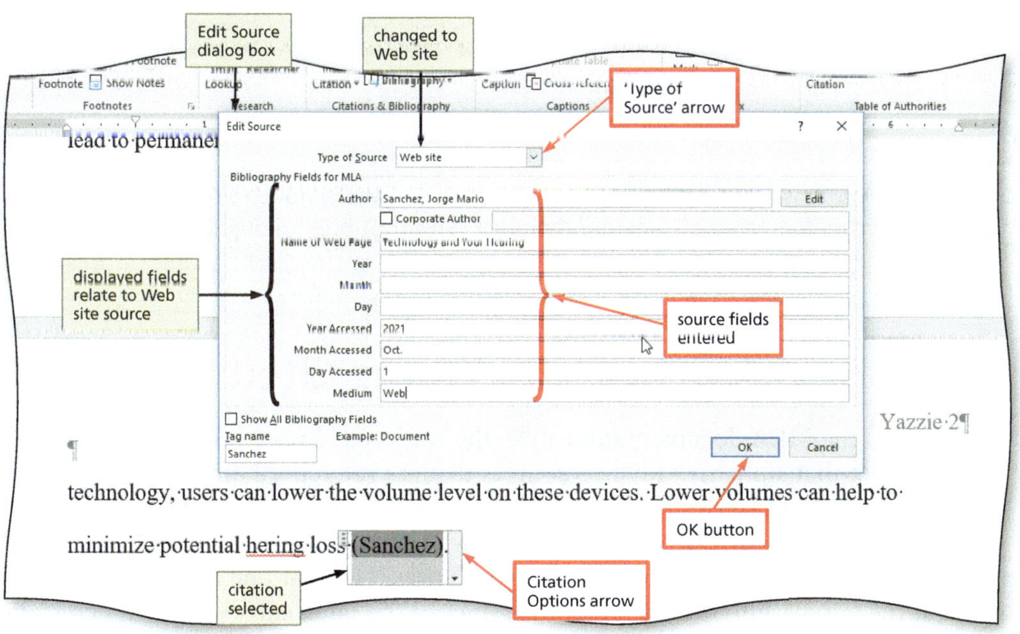

Figure 2–53

BTW
Touch Screen Differences
The Office and Windows interfaces may vary if you are using a touch screen. For this reason, you might notice that the function or appearance of your touch screen differs slightly from this module's presentation.

To Enter More Text

The next task is to type the last paragraph of text in the research paper. The following steps enter this text.

1. Press END to position the insertion point at the end of the third paragraph and then press ENTER.

2. Type the last paragraph of the research paper (Figure 2–54): **Physical conditions associated with using technology include tendonitis of the wrist, carpal tunnel syndrome, and also hearing loss. Users should take as many preventative measures as possible to avoid these conditions.**

Q&A **Why do the words, and also, have a purple dotted underline below them?**
The purple dotted underline indicates that Word can present a suggestion for more concise writing or different word usage. Later in this module, you will use Word's check spelling and grammar at once feature to check the entire document for flagged text.

3. Save the research paper again on the same storage location with the same file name.

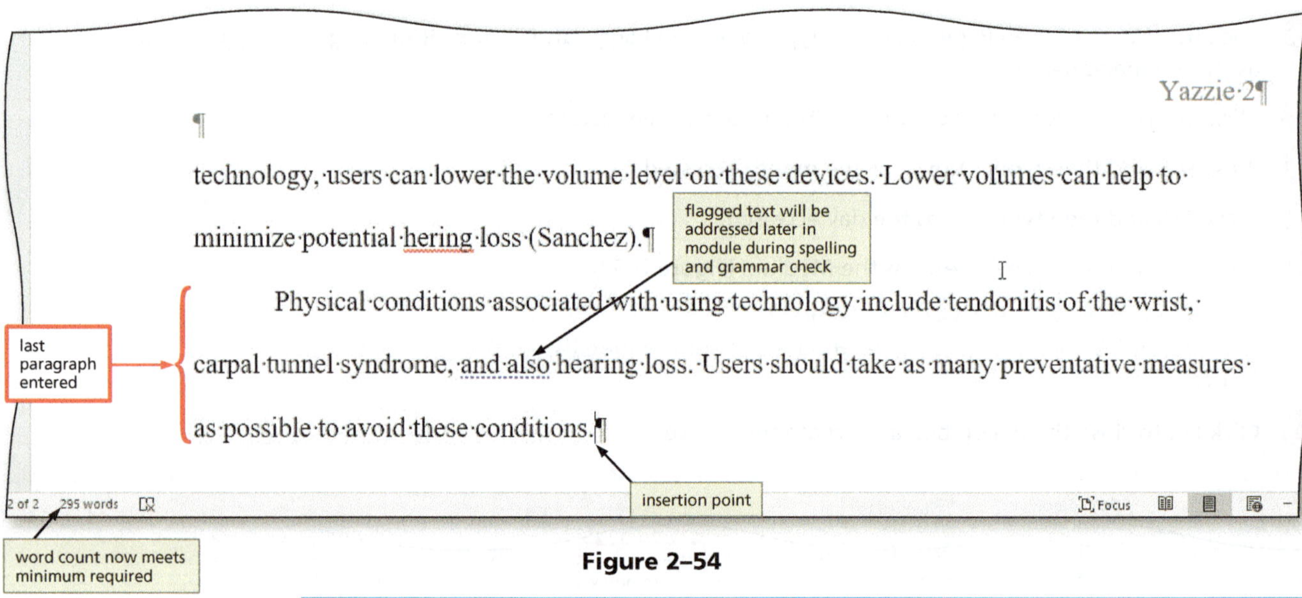

Figure 2–54

Break Point: If you want to take a break, this is a good place to do so. You can exit Word now. To resume later, start Word, open the file called SC_WD_2_TechnologyHealthConcernsPaper.docx, and continue following the steps from this location forward.

Creating an Alphabetical Works Cited Page

According to the MLA documentation style, the works cited page is a page in a research paper that alphabetically lists sources that are referenced directly in the paper. You place the list on a separate numbered page with the title, Works Cited, centered one inch from the top margin. The works are to be alphabetized by the author's last name or, if the work has no author, by the work's title. The first line of each entry begins at the left margin. Indent subsequent lines of the same entry one-half inch from the left margin.

Consider This

What is a bibliography?

A **bibliography**, also called a bibliographical list, is an alphabetical list of sources referenced in a paper. Whereas the text of the research paper contains brief references to the source (the citations), the bibliography lists all publication information about the source. Documentation styles differ significantly in their guidelines for preparing a bibliography. Each style identifies formats for various sources, including books, magazines, pamphlets, newspapers, websites, television programs, paintings, maps, advertisements, letters, memos, and much more. You can find information about various styles and their guidelines in printed style guides and on the web.

To Insert a Page Break

The next step is to insert a manual page break following the body of the research paper. **Why?** According to the MLA documentation style, the works cited are to be displayed on a separate numbered page.

A **manual page break**, or **hard page break**, is a page break that you force into the document at a specific location so that the text following the break begins at the top of the next page, whether or not the previous page is full. Word never moves or adjusts manual page breaks. Word, however, does adjust any automatic page breaks that follow a manual page break. Word inserts manual page breaks immediately above or to the left of the location of the insertion point. The following step inserts a manual page break after the text of the research paper.

1

- Verify that the insertion point is positioned at the end of the text of the research paper, as shown in Figure 2–54.
- Click Insert on the ribbon to display the Insert tab.
- Click the Page Break button (Insert tab | Pages group) to insert a manual page break immediately to the left of the insertion point and position the insertion point immediately below the manual page break (Figure 2–55).

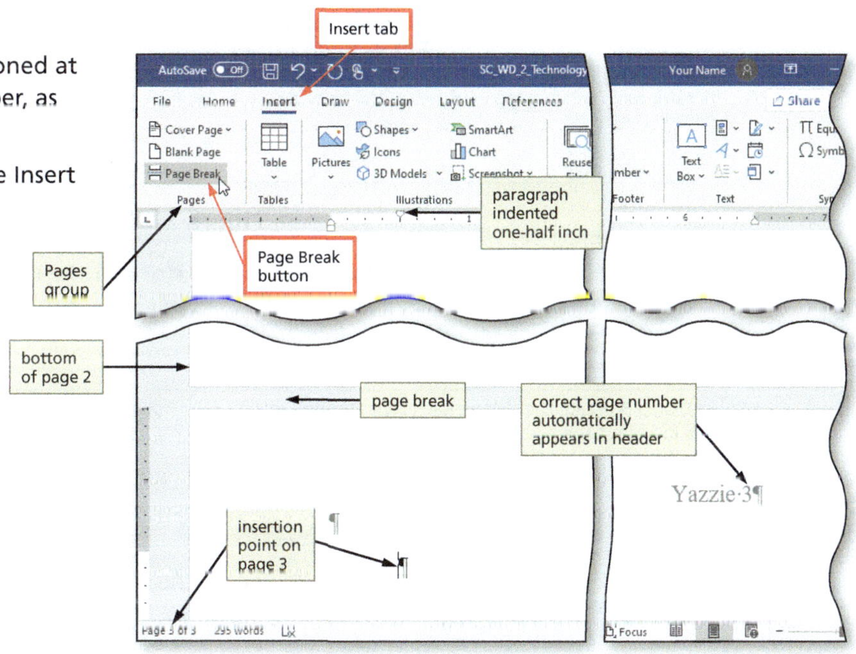

Figure 2–55

Other Ways

1. Press CTRL+ENTER

To Apply a Style

The works cited title is to be centered between the margins of the paper. If you simply issue the Center command, the title will not be centered properly. **Why?** It will be to the right of the center point because earlier you set the first-line indent for paragraphs to one-half inch.

To properly center the title of the works cited page, you could drag the 'First Line Indent' marker back to the left margin before centering the paragraph, or you could apply the Normal style to the location of the insertion point. Recall that you modified the Normal style for this document to 12-point Times New Roman with double-spaced, left-aligned paragraphs that have no space after the paragraphs.

To apply a style to a paragraph, first position the insertion point in the paragraph and then apply the style. The following step applies the modified Normal style to the location of the insertion point.

1

- Click Home on the ribbon to display the Home tab.
- With the insertion point on the paragraph mark at the top of page 3 (as shown in Figure 2–55) even if Normal is selected, click Normal in the Styles gallery (Home tab | Styles group) to apply the Normal style to the paragraph containing the insertion point (Figure 2–56).

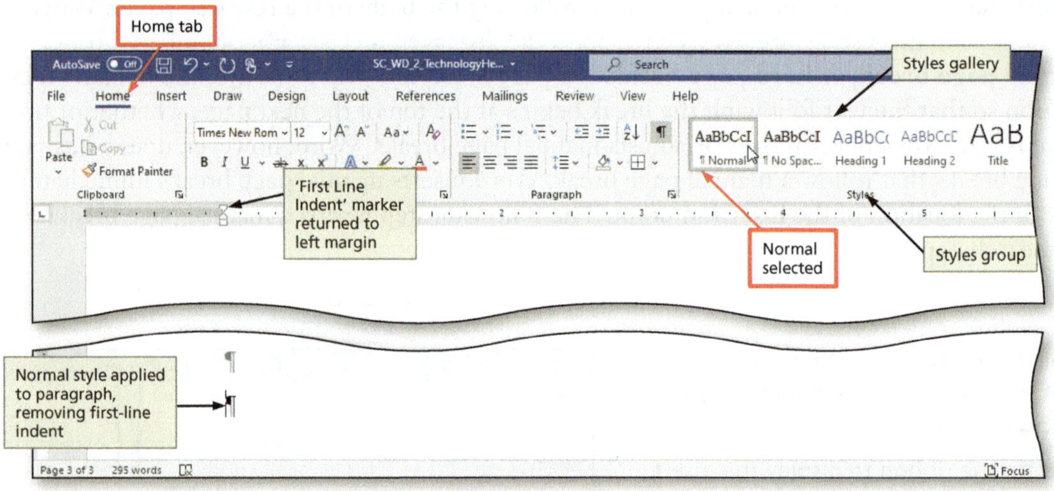

Figure 2–56

Q&A **What if I wanted to apply a different style (besides Normal) to the paragraph?**
You would click desired style in the Styles gallery (Home tab | Styles group) to apply a style to the current paragraph.

Other Ways

1. Click Styles Dialog Box Launcher (Home tab | Styles group), select desired style in Styles pane
2. Press CTRL+SHIFT+S, click Style Name arrow in Apply Styles pane, select desired style in list

To Center Text

The next task is to enter the title, Works Cited, centered between the margins of the paper. The following steps use a keyboard shortcut to format the title.

1. Press CTRL+E to center the paragraph mark.
2. Type `Works Cited` as the title.
3. Press ENTER.
4. Press CTRL+L to left-align the paragraph mark (shown in Figure 2–57).

To Create a Bibliographical Reference List

While typing the research paper, you created several citations and their sources. The next task is to use Word to format the list of sources and alphabetize them in a bibliographical list. **Why?** Word can create a bibliographical list with each element of the source placed in its correct position with proper punctuation, according to the specified style, saving you time looking up style guidelines. For example, in this research paper, the book source will list, in this order, the author name(s), book title, publisher city, publishing company name, and publication year with the correct punctuation between each element according to the MLA documentation style. The following steps create an MLA-styled bibliographical list from the sources previously entered.

1

- Click References on the ribbon to display the References tab.
- With the insertion point positioned as shown in Figure 2–57, click the Bibliography button (References tab | Citations & Bibliography group) to display the Bibliography gallery (Figure 2–57).

Q&A **Will I select the Works Cited option from the Bibliography gallery?**
No. The title it inserts is not formatted according to the MLA documentation style. Thus, you will use the Insert Bibliography command instead.

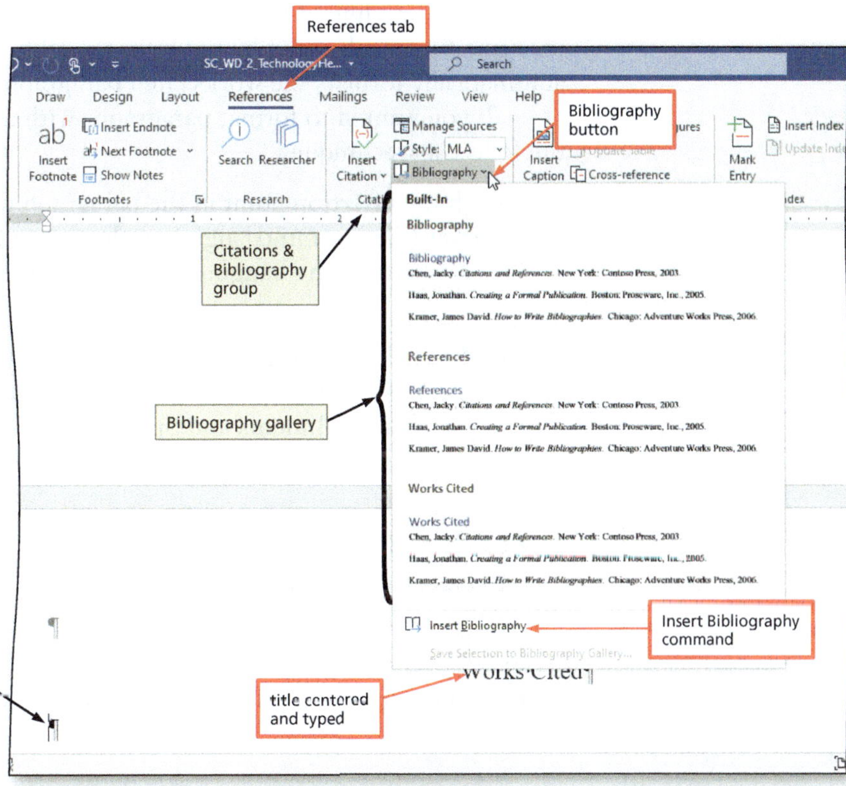

Figure 2–57

2

- Click Insert Bibliography in the Bibliography gallery to insert a list of sources at the location of the insertion point.
- If necessary, scroll to display the entire list of sources in the document window (Figure 2–58).

Q&A **What is the n.d. in the second work?**
The MLA documentation style uses the abbreviation n.d. for no date (for example, no date appears on the webpage).

What if my list is not double-spaced and has extra spacing after each paragraph?
You skipped a step earlier in this module. Select the entire bibliography, change line spacing to double, and remove space after the paragraph.

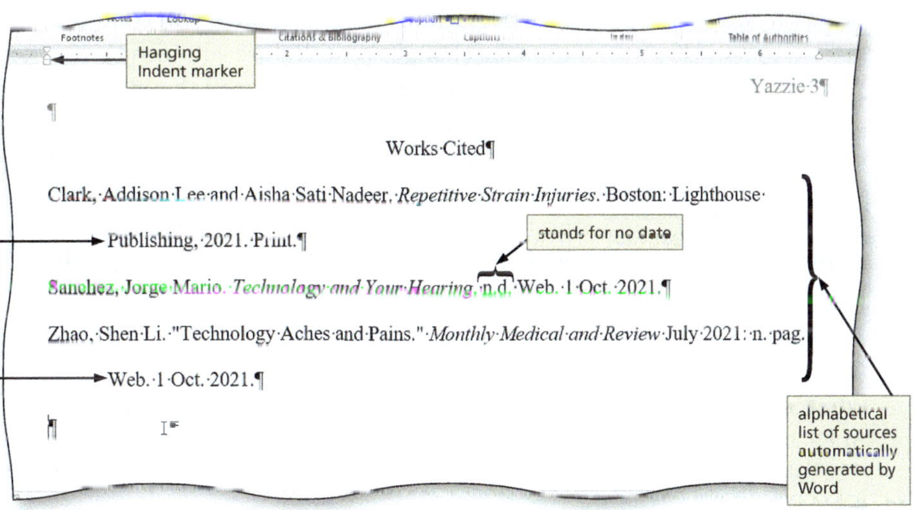

Figure 2–58

- Save the research paper again on the same storage location with the same file name.

To Format Paragraphs with a Hanging Indent

Notice in Figure 2–58 that the first line of each source entry hangs to the left of the rest of the paragraph; this type of paragraph formatting is called a **hanging indent** because the first line of the paragraph begins at the left margin and subsequent lines in the same paragraph are indented from the left margin. The Bibliography style in Word automatically formats the works cited paragraphs with a hanging indent.

If you wanted to format paragraphs with a hanging indent, you would use one of the following techniques.

- With the insertion point in the paragraph to format, drag the Hanging Indent marker (the bottom triangle) on the ruler to the desired mark on the ruler (i.e., .5") to set the hanging indent at that location from the left margin.

  or

- Right-click the paragraph to format (or, if using a touch screen, tap the 'Show Context Menu' button on the Mini toolbar), click Paragraph on the shortcut menu, click the Indents and Spacing tab (Paragraph dialog box), click the Special arrow, click Hanging, and then click OK.

  or

- Click the Paragraph Dialog Box Launcher (Home tab or Layout tab | Paragraph group), click the Indents and Spacing tab (Paragraph dialog box), click the Special arrow, click Hanging, and then click OK.

  or

- With the insertion point in the paragraph to format, press CTRL+T.

BTW
Rewrite Suggestions Feature
To find suggestions for revising text, use the Rewrite Suggestions feature. Select a phrase, right-click the selection, and then click Rewrite Suggestions on the shortcut menu. The Editor pane opens, listing suggestions for improving the text. Click a suggestion to replace the selected text with the revision.

Proofreading and Revising the Research Paper

As discussed in Module 1, once you complete a document, you might find it necessary to make changes to it. Before submitting a paper to be graded, you should proofread it. While **proofreading**, ensure all the information is correct and look for grammatical, typographical, and spelling errors. Also ensure that transitions between sentences flow smoothly and the sentences themselves make sense.

To assist you with the proofreading effort, Word provides several tools. You can go to a page, find text, replace text, insert a synonym, check spelling and grammar, and look up information. The following pages discuss these tools.

Consider This

What should you consider when proofreading and revising a paper?

As you proofread the paper, look for ways to improve it. Check all grammar, spelling, and punctuation. Be sure the text is logical and transitions are smooth. Where necessary, add text, delete text, reword text, and move text to different locations. Ask yourself these questions:

- Does the title suggest the topic?
- Is the thesis clear?
- Is the purpose of the paper clear?
- Does the paper have an introduction, body, and conclusion?
- Does each paragraph in the body relate to the thesis?
- Is the conclusion effective?
- Are sources acknowledged correctly?

To Edit a Source Using the Source Manager Dialog Box

While proofreading the paper, you notice an error in the magazine title; specifically, the word, and, should be removed. If you modify the contents of any source, the list of sources automatically updates. **Why?** Word automatically updates the contents of fields, and the bibliography is a field. The following steps delete a word from the title of the magazine article.

1

- Click the Manage Sources button (References tab | Citations & Bibliography group) to display the Source Manager dialog box.
- Click the source you wish to edit in the Current List, in this case the article by Zhao, to select the source.
- Click the Edit button (Source Manager dialog box) to display the Edit Source dialog box.
- In the Periodical Title text box, delete the word, and, from the title (Figure 2–59).

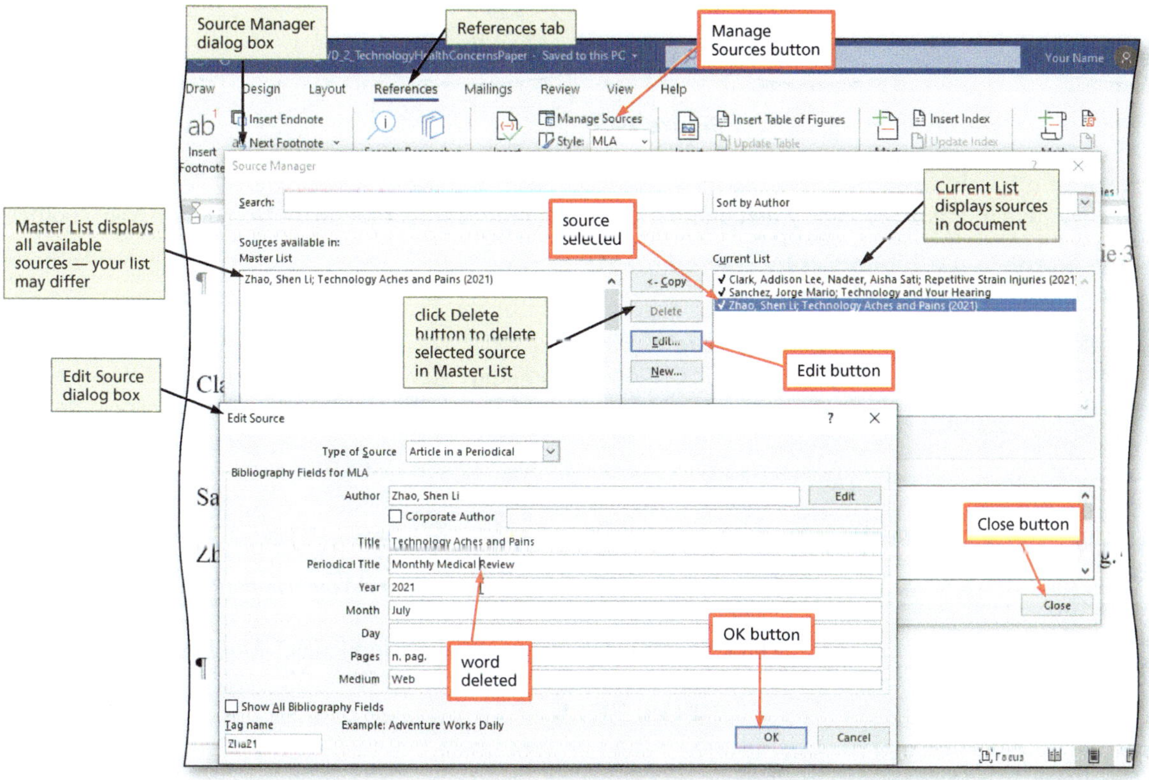

Figure 2–59

2

- Click OK (Edit Source dialog box) to close the dialog box.
- If a Microsoft Word dialog box appears, click Yes to update all occurrences of the source.
- Click the Close button (Source Manager dialog box) to update the list of sources and close the dialog box.

Q&A **How would I delete an existing source?**
You would select the source in the Master List and then click Delete (Source Manager dialog box). If the source is not listed in the Master List, click the source in the Current List and then click Copy (Source Manager dialog box) to copy the source from the Current List to the Master List.

To Update a Field (the Bibliography)

Depending on settings, the bibliography field may not automatically reflect the edited magazine title. Thus, the following steps update the bibliography field. **Why?** Because the bibliography is a field, you may need to instruct Word to update its contents.

1

- Right-click anywhere in the bibliography text to display a shortcut menu related to fields (Figure 2–60).

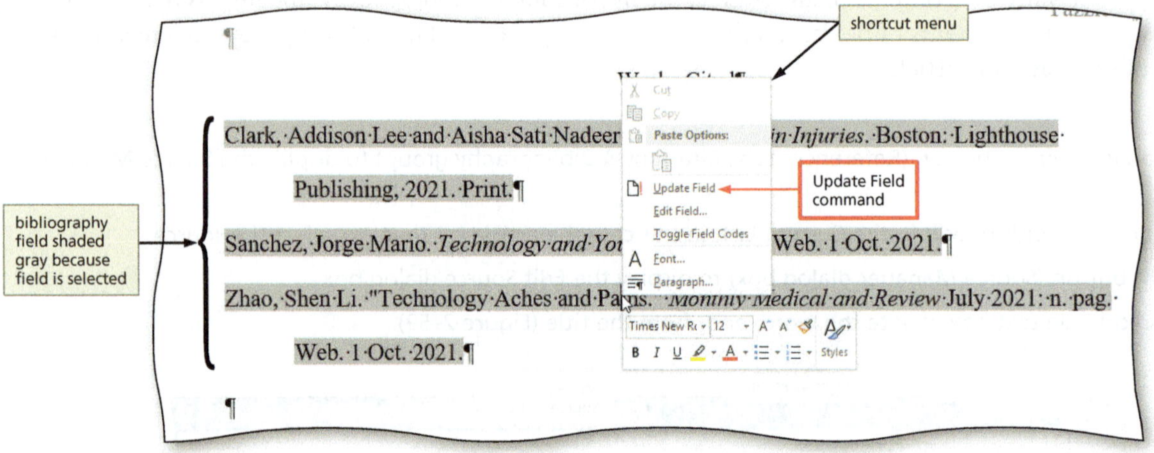

Figure 2–60

> **Q&A**
>
> **What if I am using a touch screen?**
> Press and hold anywhere in the bibliography text and then tap the 'Show Context Menu' button on the Mini toolbar.
>
> **Why are all the words in the bibliography shaded gray?**
> By default, Word shades selected fields gray.
>
> **What if the bibliography field is not shaded gray?**
> Click File on the ribbon to open Backstage view, click Options in Backstage view, click Advanced in the left pane (Word Options dialog box), scroll to the 'Show document content' area, click the Field shading arrow, click When selected, and then click OK.

2

- Click Update Field on the shortcut menu to update the selected field (Figure 2–61).

> **Q&A**
>
> **Can I update all fields in a document at once?**
> Yes. Select the entire document and then follow these steps.

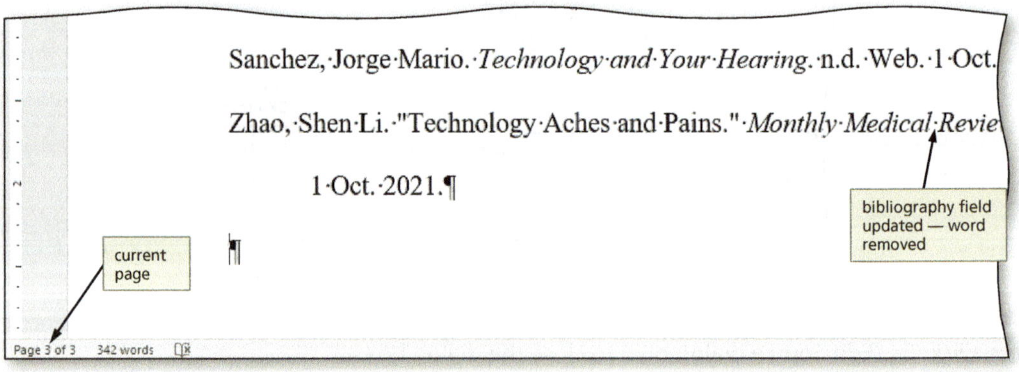

Figure 2–61

Other Ways

1. Select the field, press F9

To Convert a Field to Regular Text

If, for some reason, you wanted to convert a field, such as the bibliography field, to regular text, you would perform the following steps. Keep in mind, though, once you convert the field to regular text, it no longer is a field that can be updated.

1. Click somewhere in the field to select it, in this case, somewhere in the bibliography.
2. Press CTRL+SHIFT+F9 to convert the selected field to regular text.

To Open the Navigation Pane

The next task in revising the paper is to modify text on the first page of the document. **Why?** You want to insert another citation on the first page. You could scroll to the desired location in the document or you can use the Navigation Pane to browse through pages in a document. The following step opens the Navigation Pane.

1

- Click View on the ribbon to display the View tab.
- Place a checkmark in the Navigation Pane check box (View tab | Show group) to open the Navigation Pane on the left side of the Word window.
- If necessary, click the Pages tab in the Navigation Pane to display thumbnails of the pages in the document (Figure 2–62).

Q&A

What is the Navigation Pane?
The Navigation Pane is a window that enables you to browse through headings in a document, browse through pages in a document, or search for text in a document.

How do I close the Navigation Pane?
You click the Close button in the upper-right corner of the Navigation Pane, or remove the checkmark from the Navigation Pane check box (View tab | Show group).

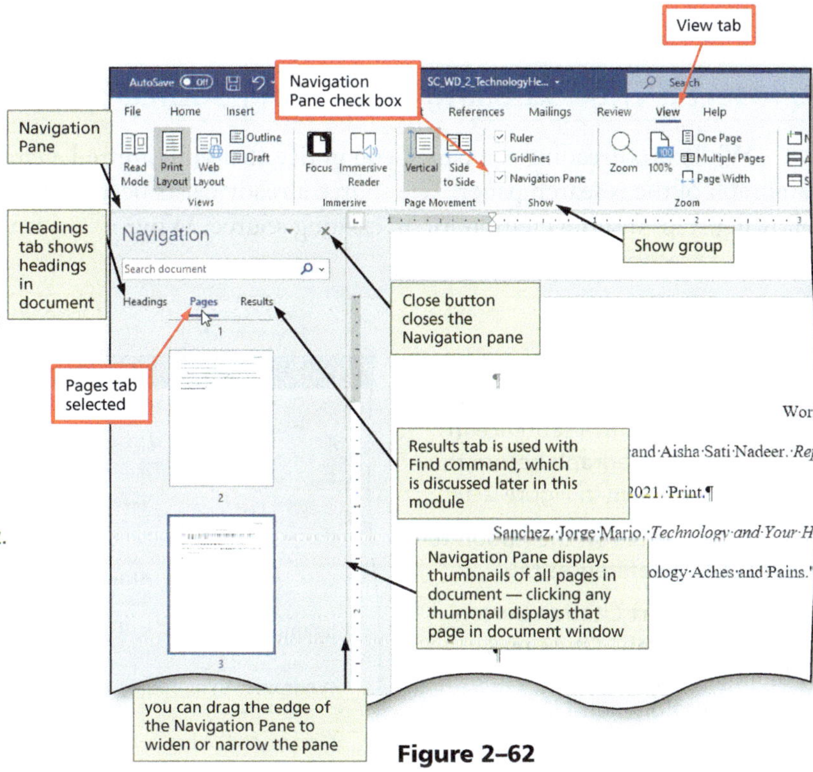

Figure 2–62

To Go to a Page

The next task in revising the paper is to insert a citation on the first page of the document. **Why?** You overlooked a citation when you created the paper. The following steps display the top of the first page in the document window using the Navigation Pane.

1

- With the Navigation Pane open in the document window, if the Pages tab is not selected, click it to select it.

Q&A

What if the Navigation Pane is not open?
Repeat the previous set of steps.

- Scroll to, if necessary, and then click the thumbnail of the first page in the Navigation Pane to display the top of the selected page in the top of the document window (Figure 2–63).

2

- Click the Close button in the Navigation Pane to close the pane.

Q&A

What if I wanted to use the Go To dialog box instead of the Navigation Pane to go to a page?
You would click the Find arrow (Home tab | Editing group) to display the Find menu, click Go To on the Find menu to display the Go To dialog box, click the Go To tab (Find and Replace dialog box), enter the desired page number in the text box, and then click the Go To button to display the desired page in the document window.

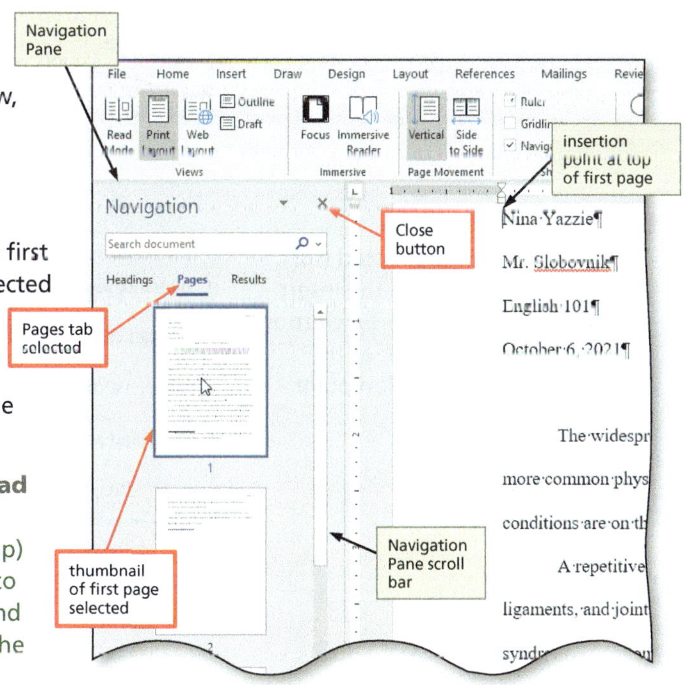

Figure 2–63

Other Ways

1. Click Find arrow (Home tab | Editing group), click Go To on Find menu, click Go To tab (Find and Replace dialog box), enter page number, click Go To button
2. Click Page Number indicator on status bar, click Pages tab in Navigation Pane, click thumbnail of desired page (Navigation Pane)
3. Press CTRL+G, enter page number (Find and Replace dialog box), click Go To button

To Insert a Citation Using an Existing Source

While proofreading the paper, you notice that you omitted a citation that should appear in the second paragraph of the research paper. The source already exists because you referenced it in the footnote. The following steps insert a citation for an existing source. **Why?** You want to insert a citation for an existing source in a second location in the document.

1

- Position the insertion point at the location for the citation (at the end of the fifth sentence in the second paragraph before the period, as shown in Figure 2–64).
- Click References on the ribbon to display the References tab.
- Click the Insert Citation button (References tab | Citations & Bibliography group) to display the Insert Citation menu (Figure 2–64).

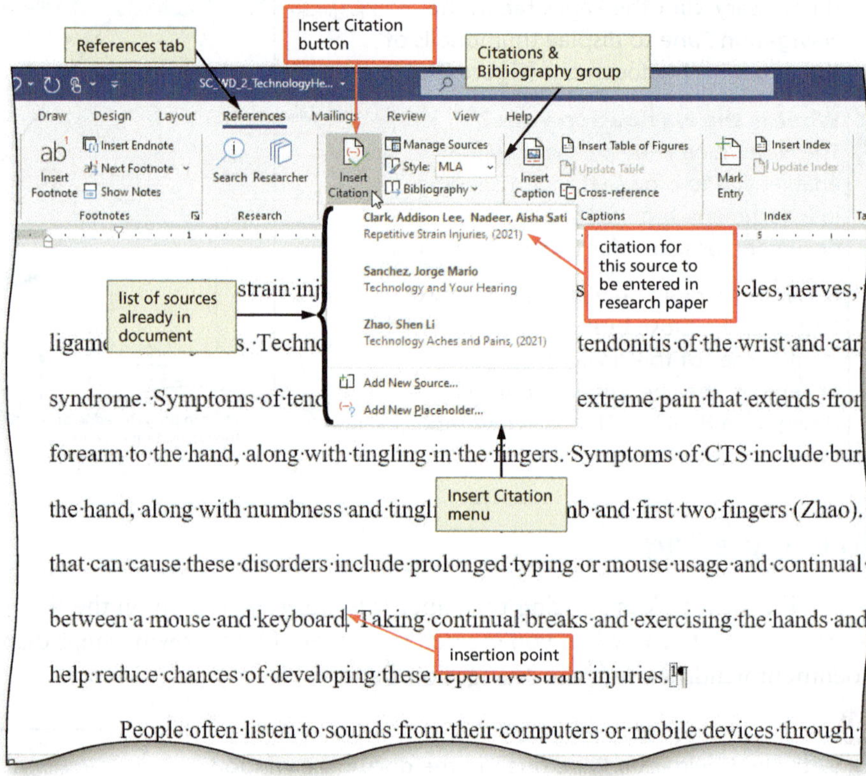

Figure 2–64

2

- Click the first source listed (for Clark and Nadeer) on the Insert Citation menu to insert a citation for the existing source at the location of the insertion point (Figure 2–65).

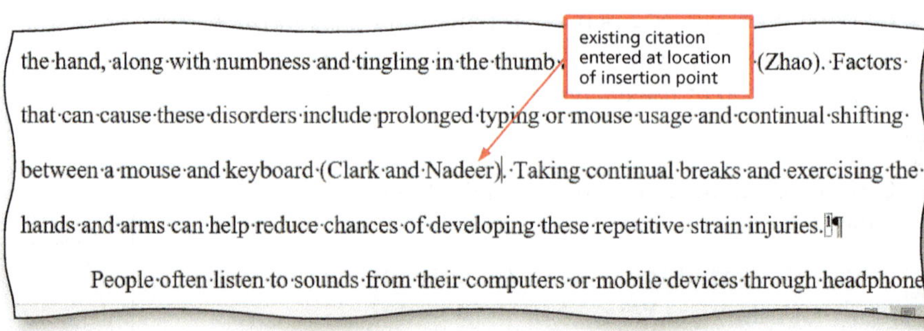

Figure 2–65

To Move a Citation

The citation just entered is not in the correct location. The following steps move a citation in a document. **Why?** You want to move the citation to the end of the next sentence.

1

- Click somewhere in the citation to be moved to select it.
- Position the pointer on the citation tab until the pointer changes to a left-pointing block arrow (Figure 2–66).

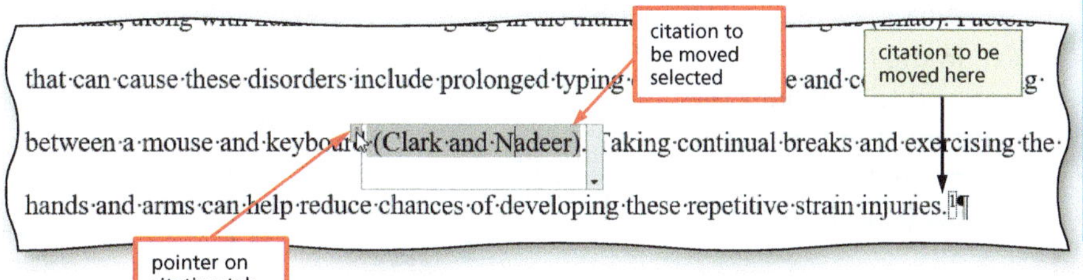

Figure 2–66

2

- Drag the citation tab, which changes to an insertion point as you drag, to the location where the selected citation is to be moved (Figure 2–67).

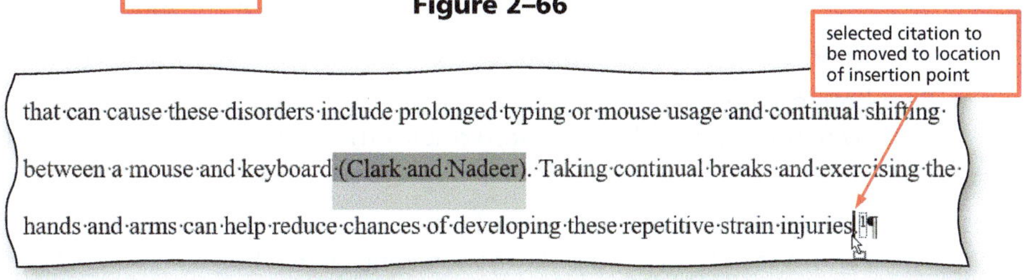

Figure 2–67

3

- When you release the mouse button, the citation moves to the location of the dragged insertion point.
- Click outside the citation to deselect it. If necessary, delete the extra space to the left of the moved citation (Figure 2–68).

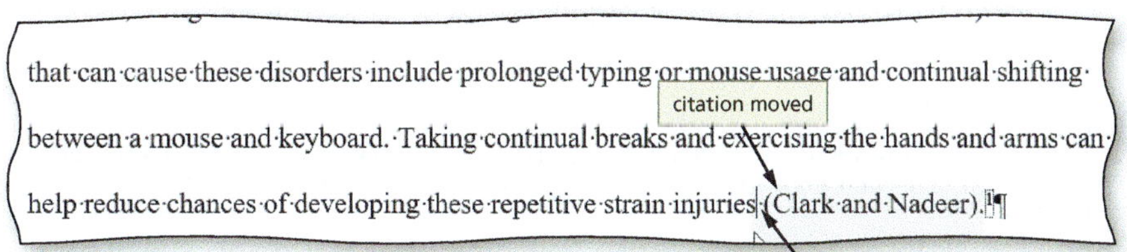

Figure 2–68

To Find Text

While proofreading the paper, you would like to locate all occurrences of the word, auditory. **Why?** You are contemplating changing occurrences of this word to the word, listening. The following steps find all occurrences of specific text in a document.

1

- Click Home on the ribbon to display the Home tab.
- Click the Find button (Home tab | Editing group) to open the Navigation Pane.

Q&A

Why did the Find menu appear?
You clicked the Find arrow. Press ESC and repeat Step 1.

What if I am using a touch screen?
Tap the Find button (Home tab | Editing group) and then tap Find on the menu.

- If necessary, click the Results tab in the Navigation Pane, which displays a Search box where you can type text for which you want to search (Figure 2–69).

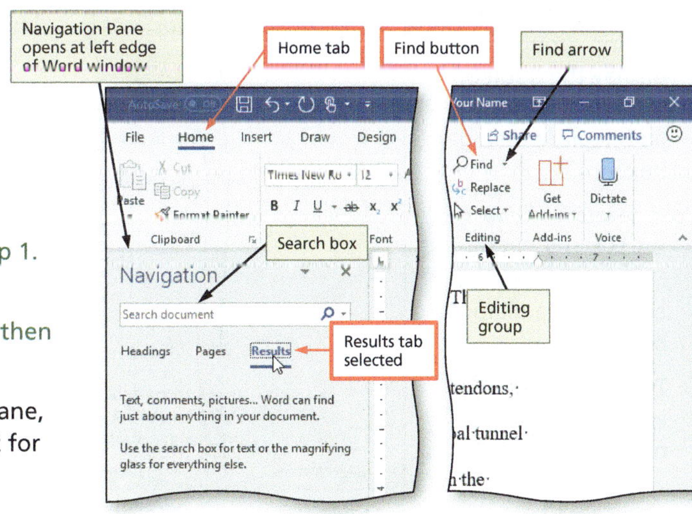

Figure 2–69

2

- Type **`auditory`** in the Navigation Pane Search box to display all occurrences of the typed text, called the search text, in the Navigation Pane and to highlight the occurrences of the search text in the document window (Figure 2–70).

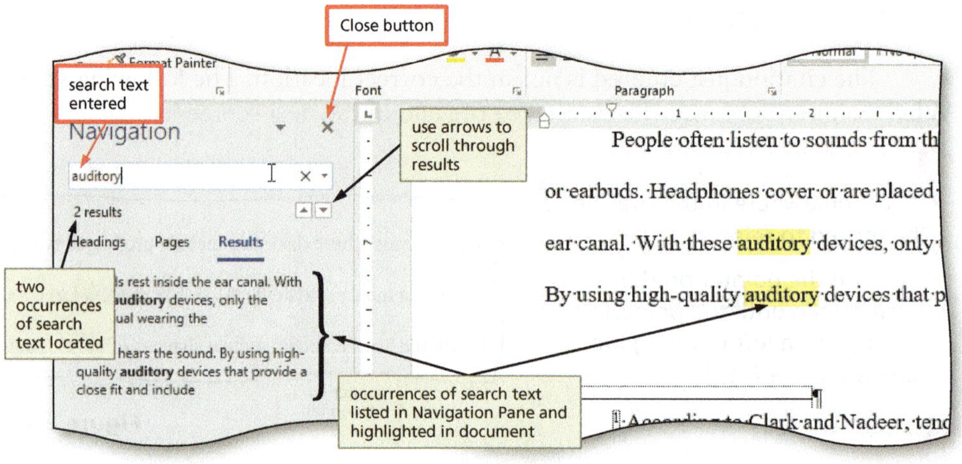

Figure 2–70

3

Experiment

- Click both occurrences in the Navigation Pane and watch Word display the associated text in the document window.

Experiment

- Type various search text in the Navigation Pane Search box, and watch Word list matches in the Navigation Pane and highlight matches in the document window.

- Click the Close button in the Navigation Pane to close the pane.

Other Ways

1. Click Find arrow (Home tab | Editing group), click Find on Find menu, enter search text in Navigation Pane
2. Click Page Number indicator on status bar, enter search text in Navigation Pane
3. Press CTRL+F, enter search text in Navigation Pane

To Replace Text

You decide to change all occurrences of the word, auditory, to the word, listening. **Why?** The term, listening devices, is more commonly used than auditory devices. Word's find and replace feature locates each occurrence of a word or phrase and then replaces it with text you specify. The following steps find and replace text.

1

- Click the Replace button (Home tab | Editing group) to display the Replace sheet in the Find and Replace dialog box.
- If necessary, type **`auditory`** in the Find what box (Find and Replace dialog box).
- Type **`listening`** in the Replace with box (Figure 2–71).

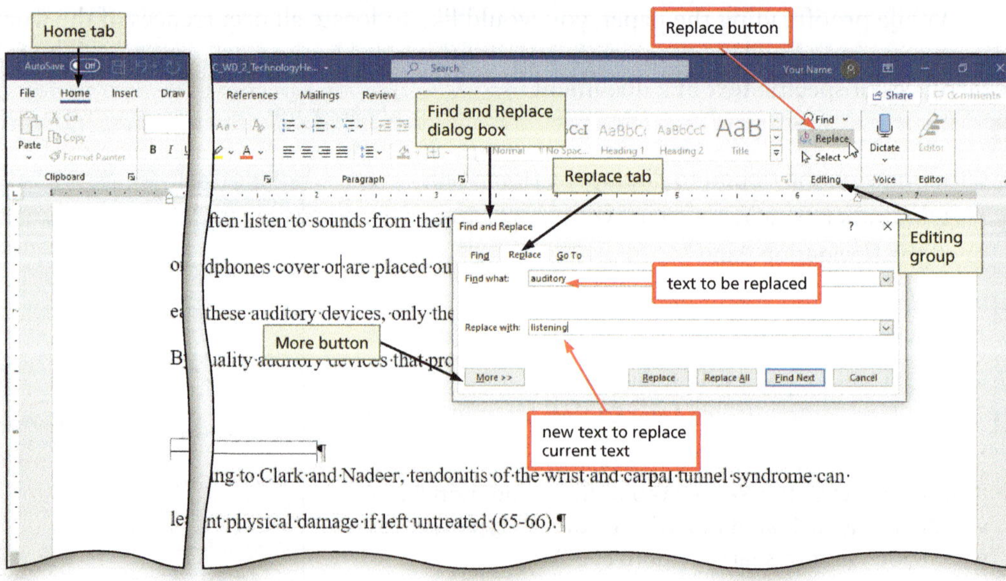

Figure 2–71

2

- Click the Replace All button to instruct Word to replace all occurrences of the Find what text with the Replace with text (Figure 2–72). If Word displays a dialog box asking if you want to continue searching from the beginning of the document, click Yes.

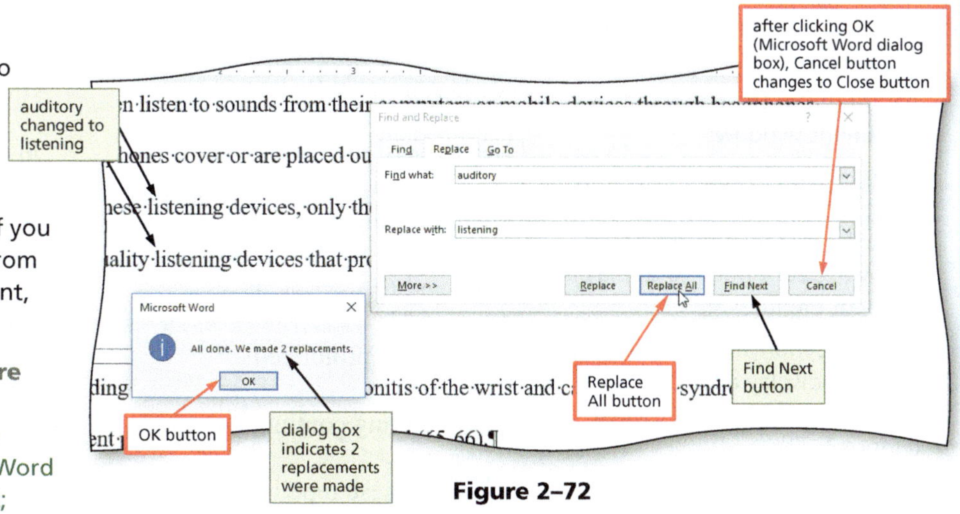

Figure 2–72

Q&A **Does Word search the entire document?**
If the insertion point is at the beginning of the document, Word searches the entire document; otherwise, Word may search from the location of the insertion point to the end of the document and then display a dialog box asking if you want to continue searching from the beginning. You also can search a section of text by selecting the text before clicking the Replace or Replace All button.

3

- Click OK (Microsoft Word dialog box) to close the dialog box.
- Click the Close button (Find and Replace dialog box) to close the dialog box.

Other Ways

1. Press CTRL+H

Find and Replace Dialog Box

The Replace All button (Find and Replace dialog box) replaces all occurrences of the Find what text with the Replace with text. In some cases, you may want to replace only certain occurrences of a word or phrase, not all of them. To instruct Word to confirm each change, click the Find Next button (Find and Replace dialog box) (shown in Figure 2–72), instead of the Replace All button. When Word locates an occurrence of the text, it pauses and waits for you to click either the Replace button or the Find Next button. Clicking the Replace button changes the text; clicking the Find Next button instructs Word to disregard the replacement and look for the next occurrence of the Find what text.

If you accidentally replace the wrong text, you can undo a replacement by clicking the Undo button on the Quick Access Toolbar or by pressing CTRL+Z. If you used the Replace All button, Word undoes all replacements. If you used the Replace button, Word undoes only the most recent replacement.

BTW
Finding Formatting and Special Characters
To search for formatting or a special character, click the Find tab or Replace tab in the Find and Replace dialog box and then click the More button (Find and Replace dialog box) (shown in Figure 2–71). To find formatting, use the Format button in the Find dialog box. To find a special character, use the Special button. To specify search options, place a check mark in the desired option in the Search Options area.

To Use the Thesaurus

In this project, you would like a synonym for the word, continual, in the second paragraph of the research paper. **Why?** When writing, you may discover that you used the same word in multiple locations or that a word you used was not quite appropriate, the former of which is the case here. In these instances, you will want to look up a **synonym**, or a word similar in meaning, to the duplicate or inappropriate word. A **thesaurus** is list of alternate word choices. Word provides synonyms and a thesaurus pane for your convenience. The following steps find a suitable synonym.

1

- Scroll to display the second paragraph of the paper in the document window.
- Right-click the word for which you want to find a synonym (in this case, the second occurrence of the word, continual) to display a shortcut menu.
- Point to Synonyms on the shortcut menu to display a list of synonyms for the word you right-clicked (Figure 2–73).

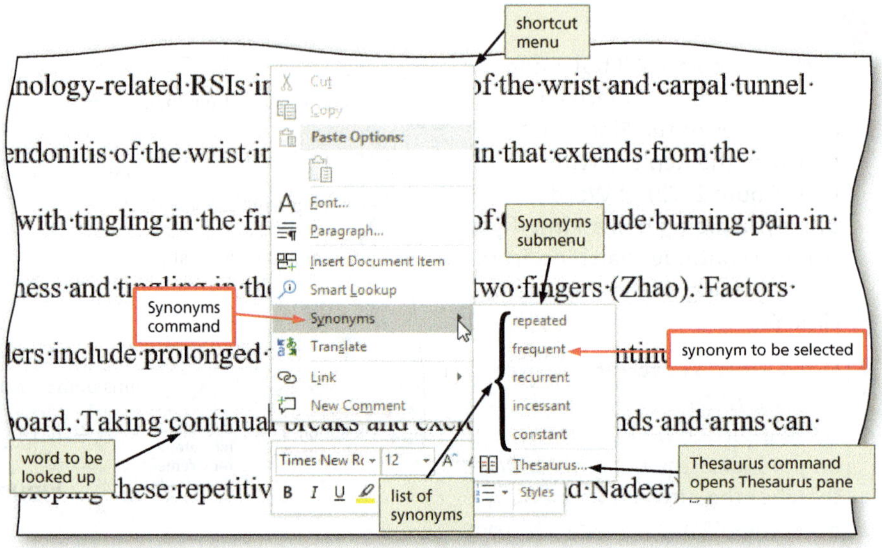

Figure 2–73

Q&A **What if I am using a touch screen?**
Press and hold the word for which you want a synonym, tap the 'Show Context Menu' button on the Mini toolbar, and then tap Synonyms on the shortcut menu.

2

- Click the synonym you want (in this case, frequent) on the Synonyms submenu to replace the selected word in the document with the selected synonym (Figure 2–74).

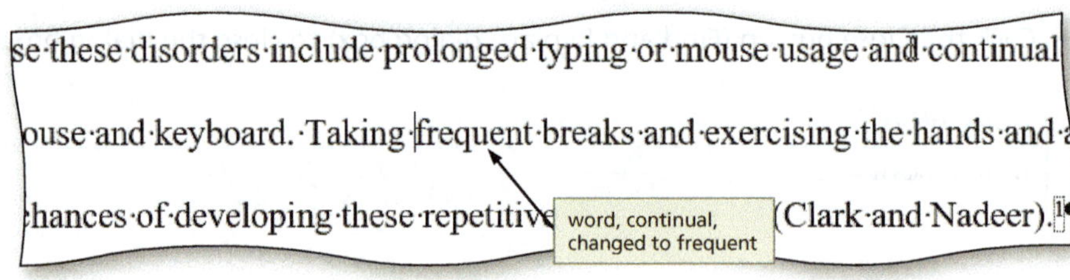

Figure 2–74

Q&A **What if the synonyms list on the shortcut menu does not display a suitable word?**
You can display the thesaurus in the Thesaurus pane by clicking Thesaurus on the Synonyms submenu. The Thesaurus pane displays a complete thesaurus, in which you can look up synonyms for various meanings of a word.

Other Ways

1. Click Thesaurus button (Review tab | Proofing group)
2. Press SHIFT+F7

To Check Spelling and Grammar at Once

As discussed previously, Word checks spelling and grammar as you type and flags possible spelling or grammar errors with different types of underlines, depending on the potential error type. The following steps check spelling and grammar in the entire document at once. **Why?** Some users prefer to wait and check their entire document for spelling and grammar errors at once rather than checking as they type.

Previously in this module, you entered the word, hearing, misspelled intentionally as hering and entered the words, and also, to illustrate the use of Word's check spelling and grammar at once feature. If you are completing this project on a computer or mobile device, your research paper may contain different misspelled words, depending on the accuracy of your typing.

1

- Press CTRL+HOME because you want the spelling and grammar check to begin from the top of the document.
- Click Review on the ribbon to display the Review tab.
- Click the Editor button (Review tab | Proofing group) to begin the spelling and grammar check at the location of the insertion point, which, in this case, is at the beginning of the document; when Word identifies a potential spelling error, it opens the Editor pane with categories of suggestions.
- Click Spelling in the Corrections list to display suggestions for the flagged text (Figure 2–75).

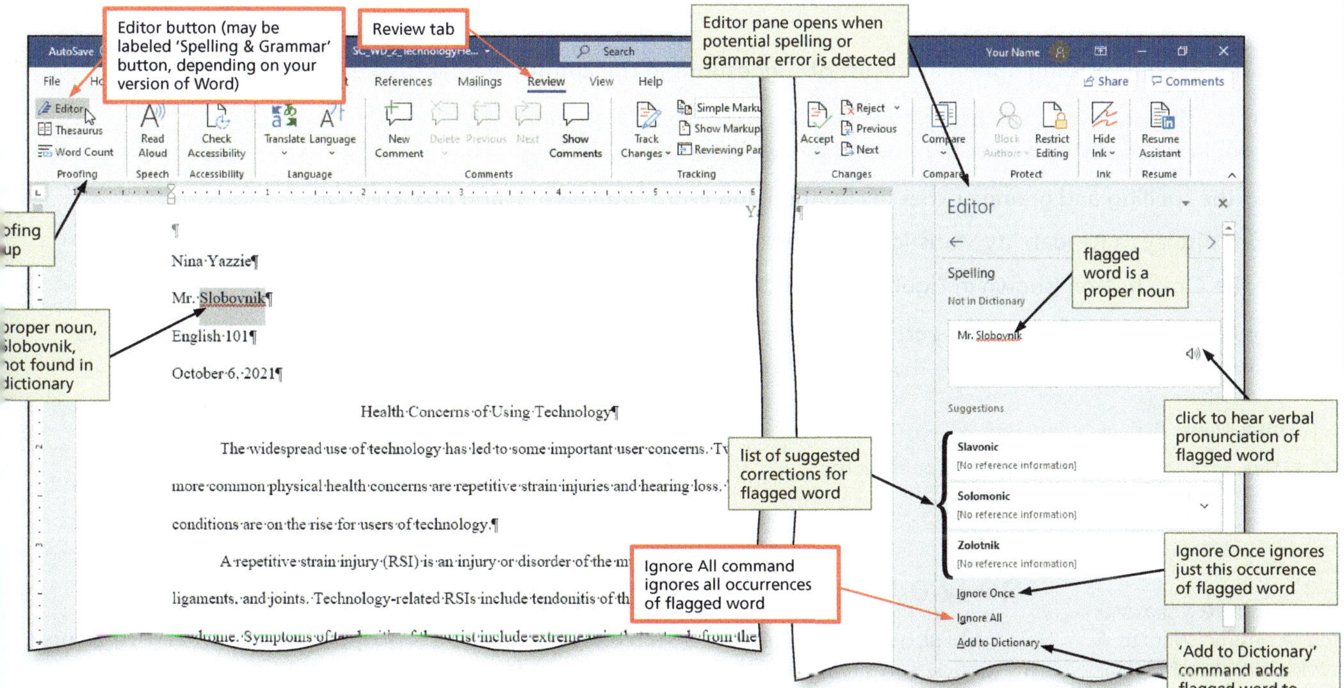

Figure 2–75

2

- Because the first occurrence of flagged text is a proper noun and spelled correctly (Slobovnik), click Ignore All in the Editor pane to ignore this and future occurrences of the flagged proper noun and then continue the spelling and grammar check until the next potential error is identified or the end of the document is reached; In this case, it identifies the potential misspelled word, hering.

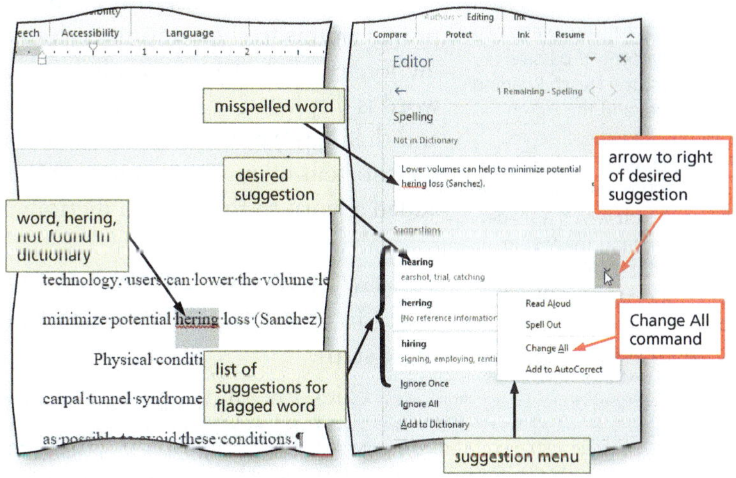

Figure 2–76

3

- Click the arrow to the right of the desired suggestion (hearing) to display a suggestion menu for the desired suggestion (Figure 2–76).

4

- Click Change All on the suggestion menu to change the flagged word, and any other exact misspellings of this word, to the selected suggestion and then continue the spelling and grammar check until the next error is identified or the end of the document is reached, which in this case is a suggestion in the Conciseness category.
- Click Conciseness to display a suggestion for the flagged text (Figure 2–77).

Q&A **How would I change just the flagged text (and not all occurrences of the misspelled word)?**
You would click the desired suggestion instead of the arrow to the right of the suggestion.

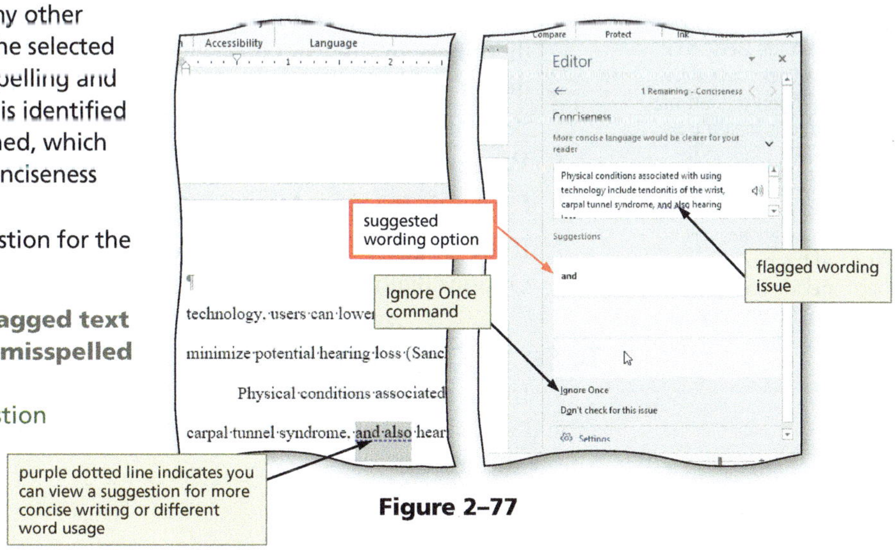

Figure 2–77

5

- Click the desired wording option in the list of suggestions in the Editor pane (and, in this case).

Q&A **What if I did not want to change the flagged text to any of the suggestions?**
You would click Ignore Once at the bottom of the Editor pane.

- When the spelling and grammar check is finished and Word displays a dialog box, click OK.
- If Word displays a Readability Statistics dialog box, click OK.
- Click the Close button (shown in Figure 2-77) to close the Editor pane.

Q&A **Can I check spelling of just a section of a document?**
Yes, select the text before starting the spelling and grammar check.

Other Ways

1. Click 'Spelling and Grammar Check' icon on status bar
2. Press F7

BTW
Readability Statistics
You can instruct Word to display readability statistics when it has finished a spelling and grammar check on a document. Three readability statistics presented are the percent of passive sentences, the Flesch Reading Ease score, and the Flesch-Kincaid Grade Level score. The Flesch Reading Ease score uses a 100-point scale to rate the ease with which a reader can understand the text in a document. A higher score means the document is easier to understand. The Flesch-Kincaid Grade Level score rates the text in a document on a U.S. school grade level. For example, a score of 10.0 indicates a student in the tenth grade can understand the material. To show readability statistics when the spelling check is complete, open Backstage view, click Options in Backstage view, click Proofing in the left pane (Word Options dialog box), place a check mark in the 'Show readability statistics' check box, and then click OK. Readability statistics will be displayed the next time you check spelling and grammar at once in the document.

The Main and Custom Dictionaries

As shown in the previous steps, Word may flag a proper noun as an error because the proper noun is not in its main dictionary. You may want to add some proper nouns that you use repeatedly, such as a company name or employee names, to Word's dictionary. To prevent Word from flagging proper nouns as errors, you can add the proper nouns to the custom dictionary. To add a correctly spelled word to the custom dictionary, click 'Add to Dictionary' at the bottom of the Editor pane when the flagged word is displayed or right-click the flagged word (or, if using touch, press and hold and then tap 'Show Context Menu' button on the mini toolbar), point to Spelling on the shortcut menu, and then click 'Add to Dictionary' on the submenu. Once you have added a word to the custom dictionary, Word no longer will flag it as an error.

To View or Modify Entries in a Custom Dictionary

To view or modify the list of words in a custom dictionary, you would follow these steps.

1. Click File on the ribbon and then click Options in Backstage view.
2. Click Proofing in the left pane (Word Options dialog box).
3. Click the Custom Dictionaries button.
4. When Word displays the Custom Dictionaries dialog box, if necessary, place a checkmark next to the dictionary name to view or modify and then select the dictionary in the list. Click the 'Edit Word List' button (Custom Dictionaries dialog box). (In this dialog box, you can add or delete entries to and from the selected custom dictionary.)
5. When finished viewing and/or modifying the list, click OK in the dialog box.
6. Click OK (Custom Dictionaries dialog box).
7. If the 'Suggest from main dictionary only' check box is selected in the Word Options dialog box, remove the checkmark. Click OK (Word Options dialog box).

To Set the Default Custom Dictionary

If you have multiple custom dictionaries, you can specify which one Word should use when checking spelling. To set the default custom dictionary, you would follow these steps.

1. Click File on the ribbon and then click Options in Backstage view.
2. Click Proofing in the left pane (Word Options dialog box).
3. Click the Custom Dictionaries button.
4. When the Custom Dictionaries dialog box is displayed, place a checkmark next to the desired dictionary name and then select the dictionary name in the list. Click the Change Default button (Custom Dictionaries dialog box).
5. Click OK (Custom Dictionaries dialog box).
6. If the 'Suggest from main dictionary only' check box is selected in the Word Options dialog box, remove the checkmark. Click OK (Word Options dialog box).

To Save and Print the Document

The following steps save and print the document.

1. **sam ↑** Save the research paper again on the same storage location with the same file name.
2. If requested by your instructor, print the research paper.

BTW

Conserving Ink and Toner

If you want to conserve ink or toner, you can instruct Word to print draft quality documents by clicking File on the ribbon to open Backstage view, clicking Options in Backstage view to display the Word Options dialog box, clicking Advanced in the left pane (Word Options dialog box), scrolling to the Print area in the right pane, placing a check mark in the 'Use draft quality' check box, and then clicking OK. Then, use Backstage view to print the document as usual.

To Recover Unsaved Documents (Draft Versions)

If you accidently exit Word without saving a document, you may be able to recover the unsaved document, called a draft version, in Word. If you wanted to recover an unsaved document, you would perform these steps.

1. Start Word and create a blank document in the Word window.
2. Open Backstage view and then, if necessary, click Info to display the Info screen. If the autorecovery file name appears below the Manage Document list, click the file name to display the unsaved file in the Word window.

   or

   Open Backstage view and then, if necessary, click Open to display the Open screen. Scroll to the bottom of the Recent Documents list and then click the 'Recover Unsaved Documents' button to display an Open dialog box that lists unsaved files retained by Word. Select the file to recover and then click Open to display the unsaved file in the Word window.

   or

   Open Backstage view and then, if necessary, click Info to display the Info screen. Click the Manage Document button to display the Manage Document menu. Click 'Recover Unsaved Documents' on the Manage Document menu to display an Open dialog box that lists unsaved files retained by Word. Select the file to recover and then click Open to display the unsaved file in the Word window.
3. To save the document, click the Save As button on the Message Bar.

To Delete All Unsaved Documents (Draft Versions)

If you wanted to delete all unsaved documents, you would perform these steps.

1. Start Word and create a blank document in the Word window.
2. Open Backstage view and then, if necessary, click Info to display the Info screen.
3. Click the Manage Document button to display the Manage Document menu.
4. If available, click 'Delete All Unsaved Documents' on the Manage Document menu.
5. When Word displays a dialog box asking if you are sure you want to delete all copies of unsaved files, click Yes to delete all unsaved documents.

To Look Up Information

If you are connected to the Internet, you can use the Search pane to search through various forms of reference information, including images, on the web and/or look up a definition of a word. The following steps use the Search pane to look up information about a series of words. **Why?** Assume you want to see some images and know more about the words, headphones or earbuds.

1

- Select the words you want to look up (in this case, headphones or earbuds).

Q&A **What if I wanted to look up a single word?**
You would position the insertion point in the word you want to look up.

- Click References on the ribbon to display the References tab.
- Click the Search button (References tab | Research group) to open the Search pane (Figure 2–78).

Q&A **What if Word asks if I want to turn on intelligent services?**
Select the option to turn on intelligent services.

Why does my Search pane look different?
Depending on your settings, your Search pane may appear different from the figure shown here.

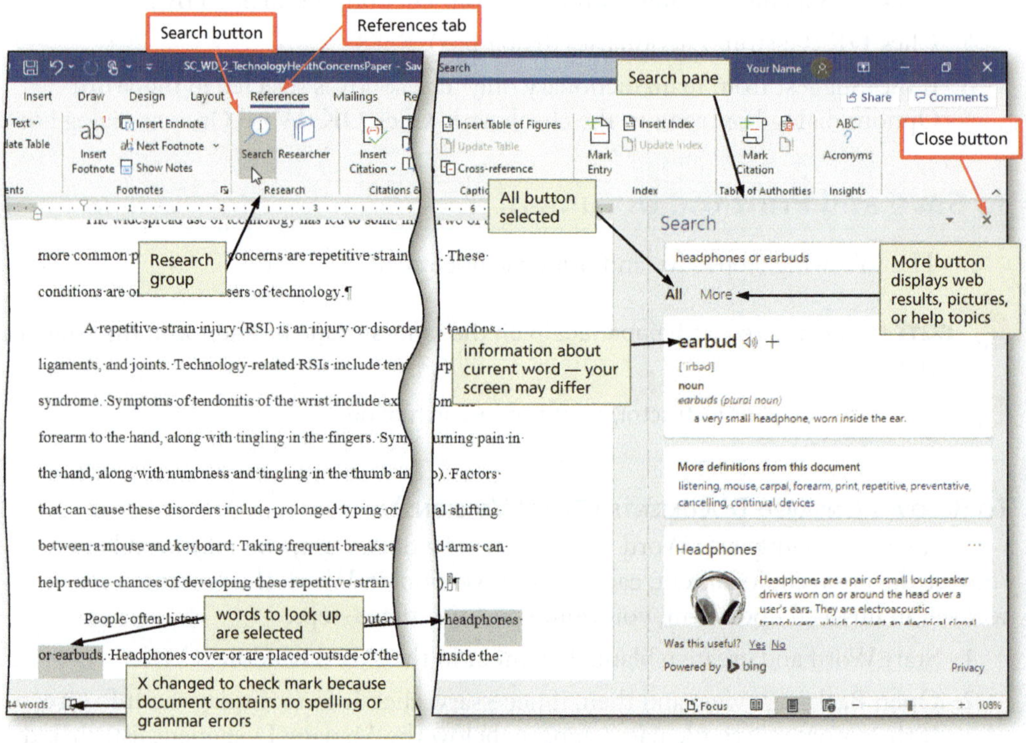

Figure 2–78

Experiment

- With the All button selected in the Search pane, scroll through the information that appears in the Search pane. Click the More button in the Search pane and then click an option to see other types of information. Click the All button to redisplay information from the web about the selected text. Click a Show more link in the Search pane to view additional information. If a Back button appears at the top of the Search pane, click it to return to the previous display.

2

- Click the Close button in the Search pane to close the pane.
- Click anywhere in the document window to deselect the text.

Other Ways

1. Right-click selected text and then click Search "headphones or..." on shortcut menu
2. Press F7

To Use Researcher

If you are connected to the Internet, you can use the Researcher pane to search through various forms of reference information on the web and locate sources for research papers from within Word. The following steps use the Researcher pane to look up information about carpal tunnel syndrome. **Why?** Assume you want to see additional sources for this topic. Note that the Researcher is only available to Microsoft 365 installations. If you do not have Microsoft 365, read these steps without performing them.

1

- Click the Researcher button (References tab | Research group) to open the Researcher pane (Figure 2–79).

Q&A **Why does my Researcher pane look different?** Depending on your settings, your Researcher pane may appear different from the figure shown here.

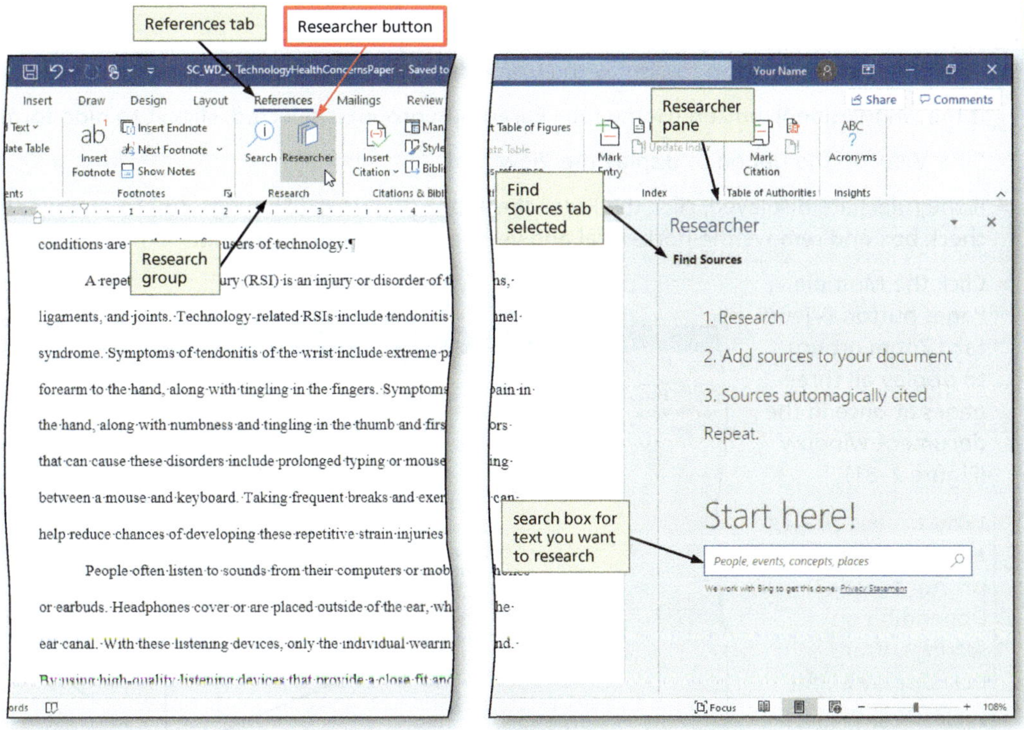

Figure 2–79

2

- Type `carpal tunnel syndrome` in the search box in the Researcher pane and then press ENTER to display topics and sources related to the search text (Figure 2–80).

Experiment

- Scroll through the topics and sources that appear in the Researcher pane. Point to the + symbols on the right edge of the topics and sources and read their function. Click one of the topics and read its information. Drag through text in the topic and notice the submenu with the 'Add and Cite' command, which allows you to add the text in your document at the location of the insertion point and cite its source. Click the Back button at the top of the Researcher pane to return to the previous display. Click one of the sources and read its information. Click the Back button to return to the previous display.

- Click the Close button in the Researcher pane to close the pane.

Q&A **Can I use the information in my paper that I add from the Researcher pane?** When using Word to insert material from the Researcher pane or any other online reference, be careful not to plagiarize.

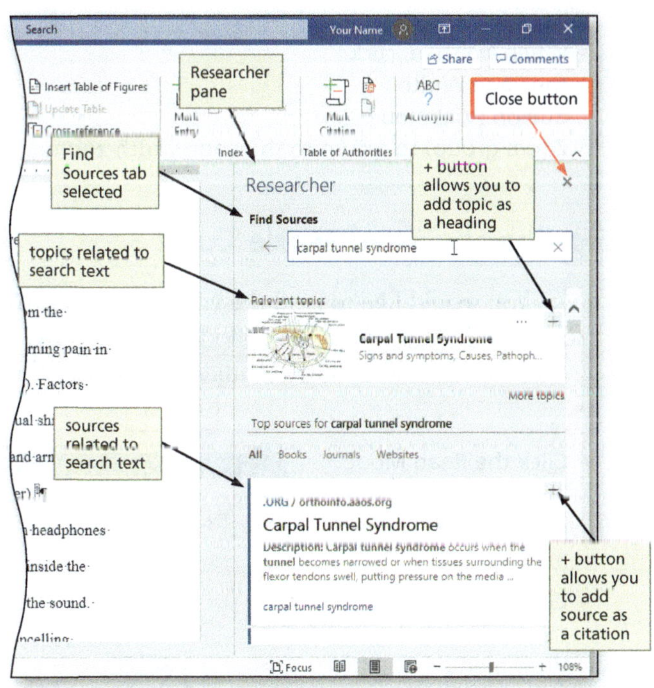

Figure 2–80

To Change the Zoom to Multiple Pages

The following steps display multiple pages in the document window at once. **Why?** You want to be able to see all pages in the research paper on the screen at the same time. You also hide formatting marks and the rulers so that the display is easier to view.

1

- Click Home on the ribbon to display the Home tab.
- If the 'Show/Hide ¶' button (Home tab | Paragraph group) is selected, click it to hide formatting marks.
- Click View on the ribbon to display the View tab.
- If the rulers are displayed, click the Ruler check box (View tab | Show group) to remove the checkmark from the check box and remove the horizontal and vertical rulers from the screen.
- Click the Multiple Pages button (View tab | Zoom group) to display all three pages at once in the document window (Figure 2–81).

Q&A **Why do the pages appear differently on my screen?** Depending on settings, Word may display all the pages as shown in Figure 2–81 or may show the pages differently.

2

- When finished, click the Page Width button (View tab | Zoom group) to return to the page width zoom.

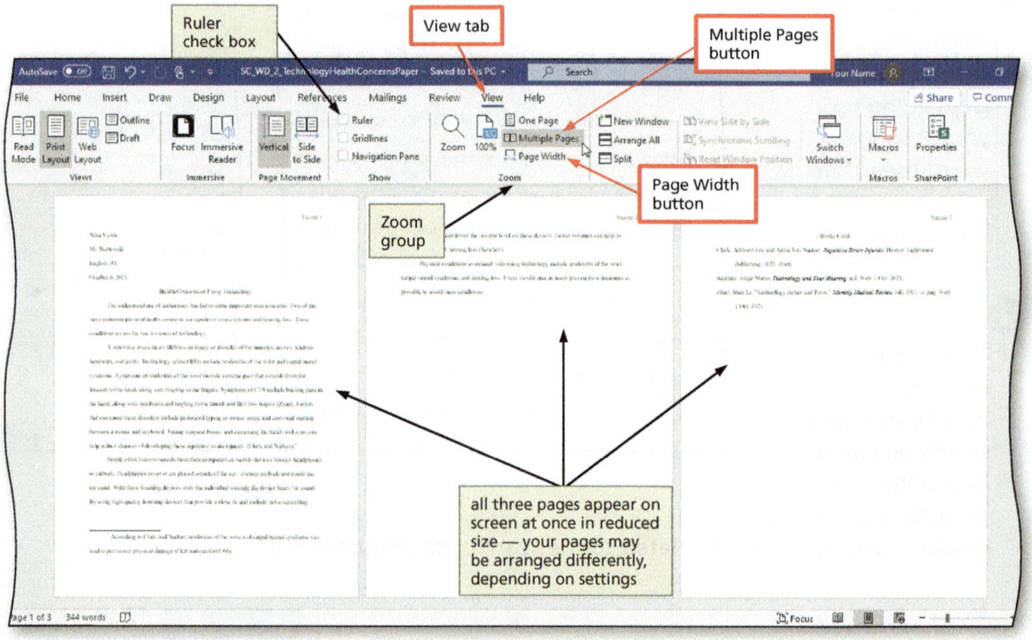

Figure 2–81

To Change Read Mode Color

You would like to read the entire research paper using Read mode but would like to change the background color of the Read mode screen. **Why?** You prefer a softer background color for reading on the screen. The following steps change the color of the screen in Read mode.

1

- Click the Read Mode button on the status bar to switch to Read mode.
- Click the View tab to display the View menu.
- Point to Page Color on the View menu to display the Page Color submenu (Figure 2–82).

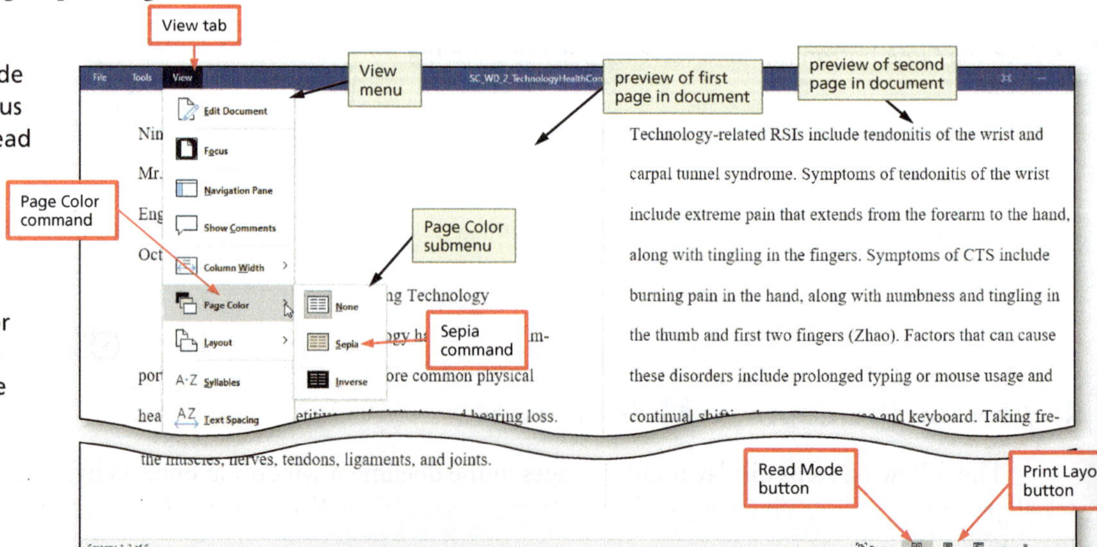

Figure 2–82

2

- Click Sepia on the Page Color submenu to change the color of the Read mode screen to sepia (Figure 2–83).

3

- When finished, click the Print Layout button (shown in Figure 2–82) on the status bar to return to Print Layout view.

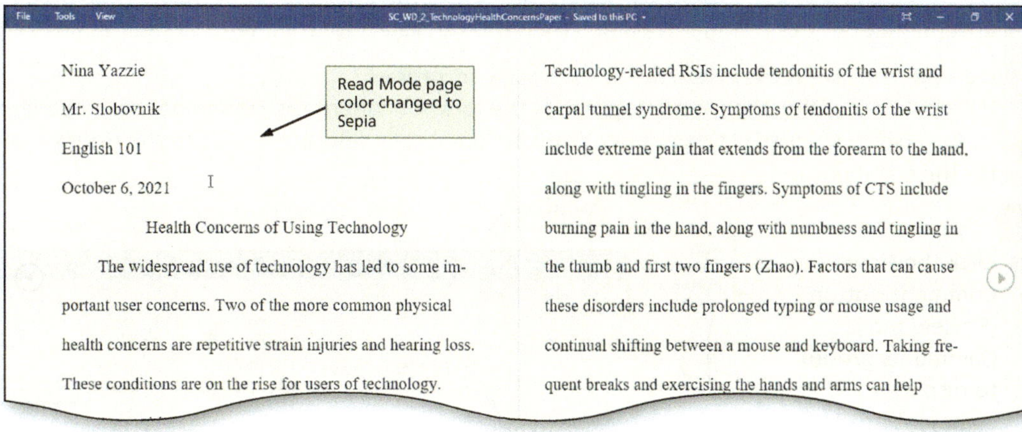

Figure 2–83

Working with Comments in a Document

Word provides tools, such as comments, that allow users to collaborate on a document. A **comment** is a note that an author or reviewer adds to a document. Reviewers often use comments to communicate suggestions, tips, and other messages to the author of a document. Comments do not affect the text of the document.

To Insert a Comment

After reading through the paper, you have two comments for the originator (author) of the document related to the patient brochure that will be created from content in the research paper. The following steps insert a comment in the document. **Why?** You insert a comment, which creates a note for the author of the document. Because you want the comment associated with several words, you select the text before inserting the comment.

1

- Select the text to which the comment applies (in this case, in the last sentence of the second paragraph).
- Click Review on the ribbon to display the Review tab.
- If the 'Display for Review' box (Review tab | Tracking group) does not show Simple Markup, click the 'Display for Review' arrow (Review tab | Tracking group) and then click Simple Markup on the Display for Review menu to instruct Word to display a simple markup.

Q&A **What is Simple Markup?**
Simple Markup is a less cluttered view of comments and other collaboration elements than All Markup.

- If the Show Comments button (Review tab | Comments group) is not selected, click it to select it (Figure 2–84).

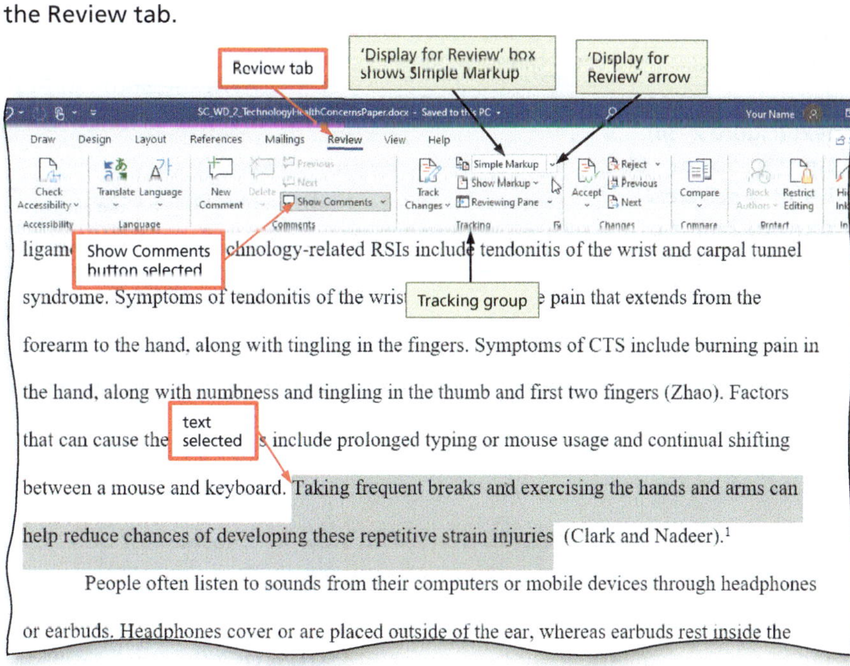

Figure 2–84

Q&A

What is the purpose of the Show Comments button?
When the Show Comments button is selected, the comments appear in the markup area to the right of the document, or in the Comments pane. When it is not selected, comments appear as icons in the document.

Do I have to select text before inserting a comment?
No, you can position the insertion point at the location where the comment should be located. If you do not select text on which you wish to comment, Word automatically selects the text to the right or left of the insertion point for the comment.

2

- Click the New Comment button (Review tab | Comments group) to display a comment box in the markup area in the document window.
- If necessary, change the zoom so that the entire document and markup area are visible in the document window (Figure 2–85).

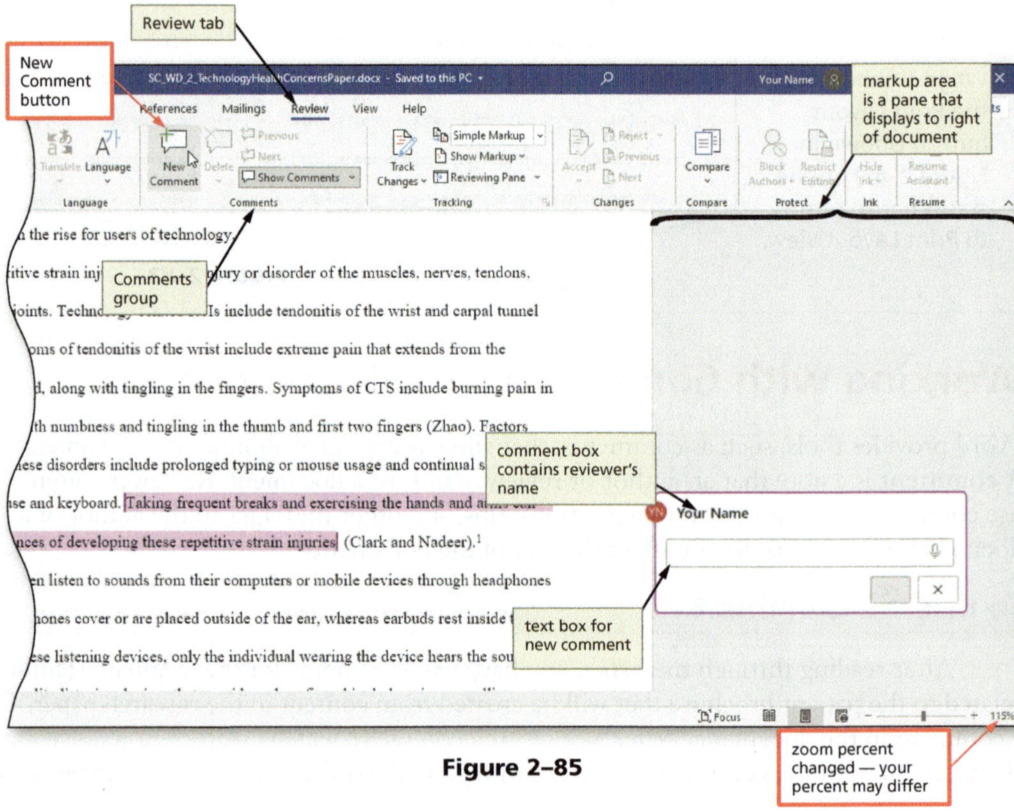

Figure 2–85

Q&A

What should I do if the comment box appears in the Comments pane?
Click the Show Comments arrow (Review tab | Comments group) and then click Contextual to display the comment box in the markup area next to the page content.

3

- In the comment box, type the following comment text (Figure 2–86): `Let's cover the hand and arm exercises in our brochure for patients.`

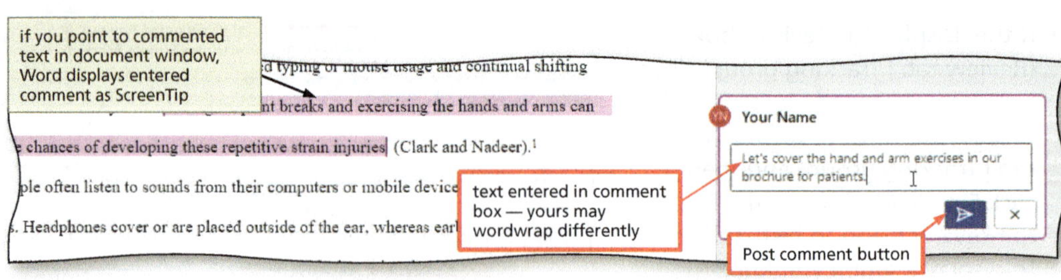

Figure 2–86

4

- Click the Post comment button (shown in Figure 2-86) to post the comment.

Q&A

What does it mean to post a comment?
Posting a new comment creates a **thread**, or a collection of related comments. Replies appear with the original comment to help you follow the discussion.

What if I don't have a Post comment button in a comment box?
Click outside a comment box to post a comment.

Other Ways

1. Click Comment button (Insert tab | Comments group)
2. Click Comments button on title bar, click New button in Comments pane
3. Press CTRL+ALT+M

To Insert Another Comment

The second comment you want to insert in the document refers to a topic for the brochure. The following steps insert another comment in the document.

1. Select the text to which the comment applies (in this case, the last sentence of the fourth paragraph).
2. Click the New Comment button (Review tab | Comments group) to display another comment box in the markup area in the document window.
3. In the new comment box, type the following comment text: **`Let's stress this point in our brochure for patients.`**
4. Click the Post comment button to post the comment (Figure 2-87).

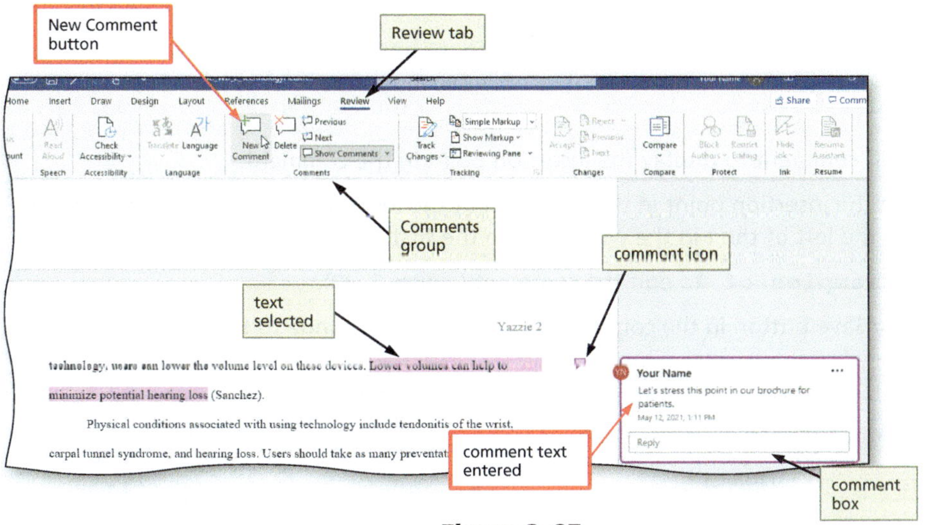

Figure 2–87

To Go To a Comment

The next step is to display the previous comment. **Why?** You could scroll through the document to locate a comment by reading them as they appear in the markup area, but it is more efficient to use the Review tab. The following step displays the previous comment in the document.

1

- Click the Previous button (Review tab | Comments group), which causes Word to locate and select the previous comment in the document (Figure 2–88).

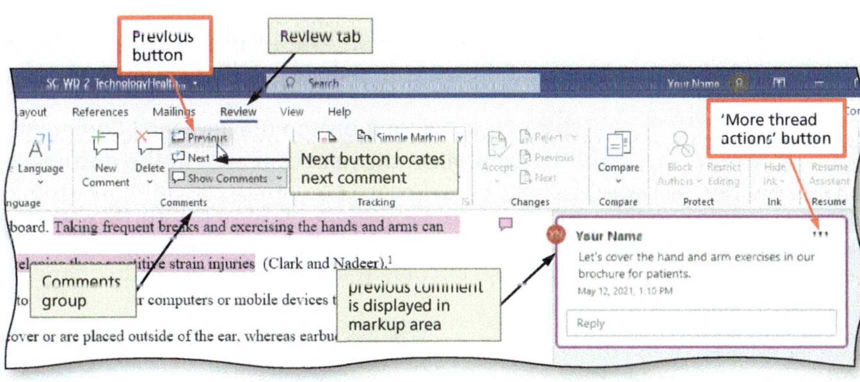

Figure 2–88

Q&A

What if I wanted to see the next comment, instead of the previous comment, in a document?
You would click the Next button (Review tab | Comments group) instead of the Previous button.

What if I wanted to move from one comment to the next in a document from the beginning of the document?
You would position the insertion point at the top of the document, and then click the Next button (Review tab | Comments group) repeatedly until you have seen all comments in the document.

Other Ways

1. Click Find arrow (Home tab | Editing group), click Go To, click Comment in Go to what area (Find and Replace dialog box), click Next button
2. Press CTRL+G, click Comment in Go to what area (Find and Replace dialog box), click Next button

To Edit a Comment in a Comment Box

You modify a comment in a comment box by clicking the 'More thread actions' button in the comment box and then clicking Edit comment. You can then edit the comment text the same way you edit text in the document window. In this project, you insert the words, examples of, in the first comment. The following steps edit a comment.

1. If necessary, click the comment box to select it.
2. Click the 'More thread actions' button (shown in Figure 2-88) to display the More thread actions menu.

   Q&A **How can I tell if a comment is selected?**
   A selected comment appears with a colored border and the text associated with the comment is highlighted in the document.

   What if I don't have a 'More thread actions' button in a comment box?
   Click inside the comment box and edit the same way you edit text in the document window.

3. Click Edit comment to display the insertion point in the comment.
4. Position the insertion point in the comment at the location of the text to edit (in this case, to the left of the t in the word, the, in the first comment).
5. Type **`examples of`** to edit the comment (Figure 2–89).
6. Click the Save button in the comment box to save the change to the comment.

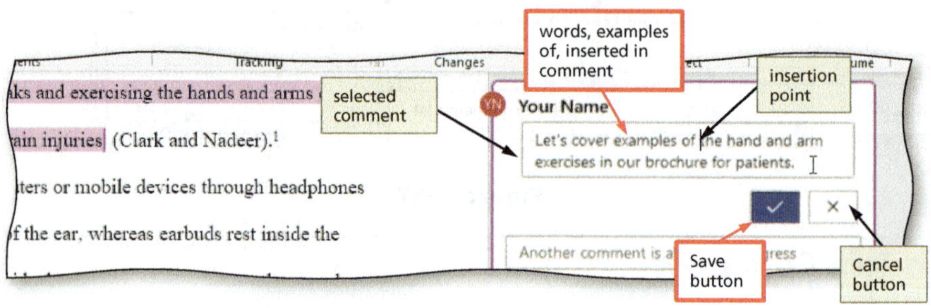

Figure 2–89

BTW
Locating Comments by Reviewer
You can find a comment from a specific reviewer through the Go To dialog box. Click the Find arrow (Home tab | Editing group) and then click Go To or press CTRL+G to display the Go To sheet in the Find and Replace dialog box. Click Comment in the Go to what list (Find and Replace dialog box). Select the reviewer whose comments you wish to find and then click the Next button.

To Go to a Comment

The next step is to display the next comment because you want to reply to it. The following step displays the next comment in the document.

1. Click the Next button (Review tab | Comments group), which causes Word to locate and select the next comment in the document (Figure 2–90).

   Q&A **What if I reach the last comment in a document?**
   When you click the Next button (Review tab | Comments group), Word moves to the top of the document and displays the first comment in the document.

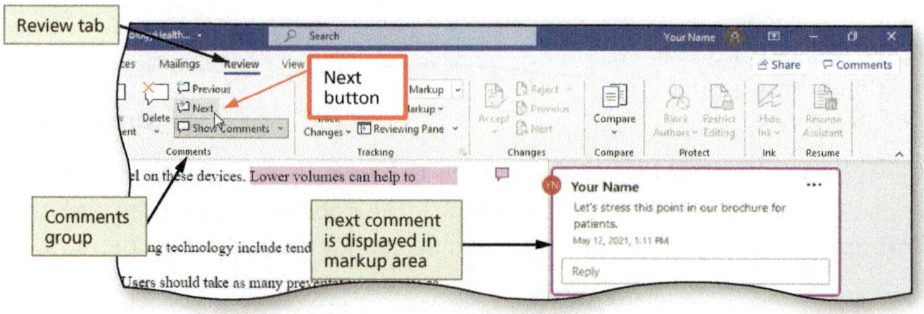

Figure 2–90

To Reply to a Comment

Sometimes, you want to reply to an existing comment. **Why?** You may want to respond to a question by another reviewer or provide additional information to a previous comment you inserted. The following steps reply to the comment you inserted on the second page of the document.

1

- If necessary, click the comment to which you wish to reply so that the comment is selected (in this case, the second comment).

2

- Click the Reply box in the selected comment to position the insertion point.

3

- Type the following comment text: **`Excellent idea!`** (Figure 2–91).

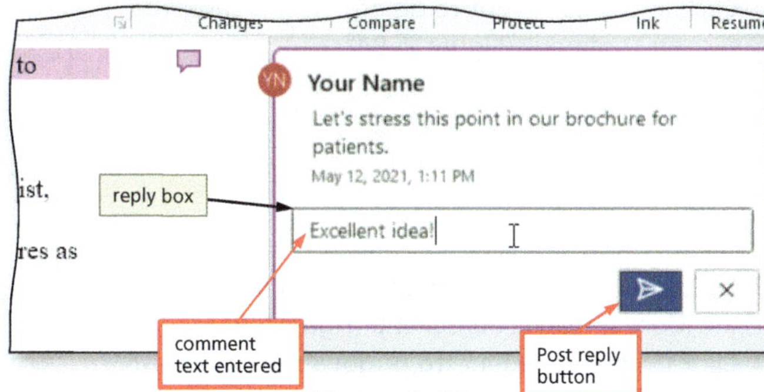

Figure 2–91

4

- Click the Post reply button to add the reply to the thread.

Other Ways

1. Right-click commented text (or, if using touch, tap 'Show Context Menu' button on Mini toolbar), click 'Reply To Comment' on shortcut menu

To Hide and Show Comments

The next step is to hide all comments in the document. **Why?** You would like to view the document without the markup area on the screen but do not want to delete the comments at this time. The following steps hide comments and then show them.

1

- If the Show Comments button (Review tab | Comments group) is selected, click it to deselect it, which hides comments in the document (Figure 2–92).

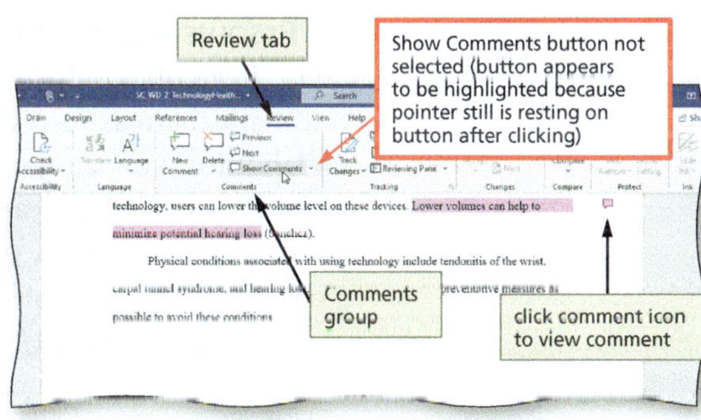

Figure 2–92

Q&A

What happened to the markup area?
When the Show Comments button is not selected, the markup area is hidden and comments appear as icons in the document.

Are the hidden comments deleted from the document?
No.

What happens when I open a document containing comments?
The comments appear in the markup area by default.

2

- Click the comment icon to display the associated comment (Figure 2–93).

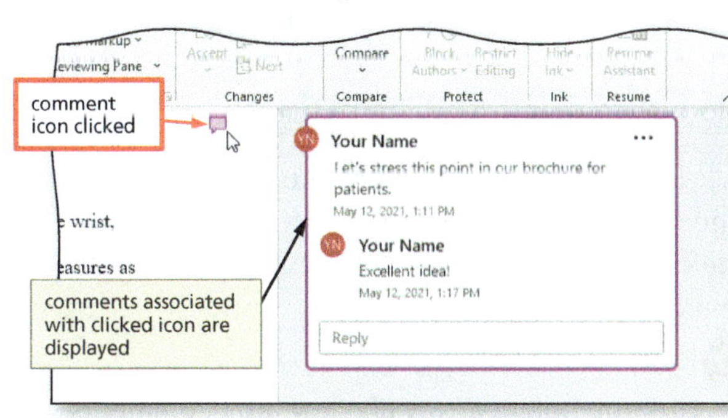

Figure 2–93

3

- Click the Show Comments button (Review tab | Comments group) to hide the comment.
- Click the Show Comments button (Review tab | Comments group) to show comments again, which redisplays the comments in the markup area (as shown in Figure 2–91).

Other Ways

1. Click the comment icon again to hide comment
2. Click Close button in comment box to hide comment

To Delete a Comment

The following steps delete a comment. **Why?** You have read the comment and want to remove it from the document.

1

- Click in the comment to delete, in this case, the second comment (Figure 2–94).

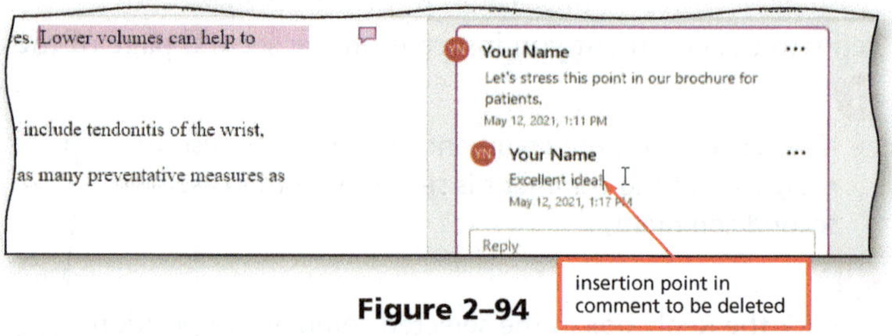

Figure 2–94

2

- Click the 'More thread actions' button to display the More thread actions menu (Figure 2-95).
- Click Delete comment to remove the comment containing the insertion point from the markup area (Figure 2–95).

Q&A **What if I accidentally click the Delete arrow?**
Click Delete on the Delete menu.

If the insertion point was in a comment that contained a reply, would the reply also be deleted?
Yes.

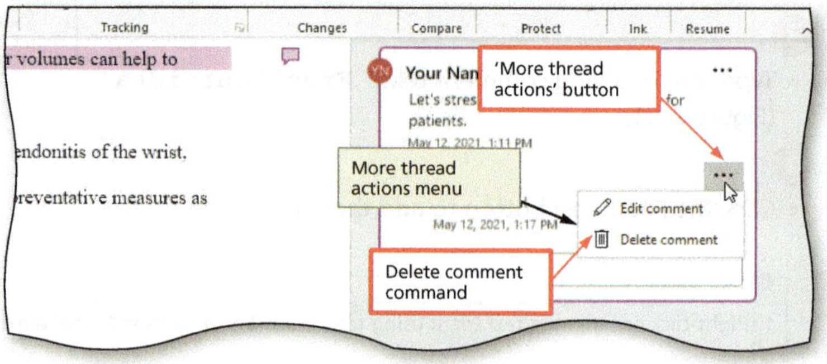

Figure 2–95

Other Ways

1. Right-click commented text (or, if using touch, tap 'Show Context Menu' button on Mini toolbar), click Delete Comment on shortcut menu
2. Click Delete button (Review tab | Comments group) to remove comment containing insertion point

To Resolve a Comment

Instead of deleting comments, some users prefer to leave them in the document but mark them as resolved. This is especially useful when multiple users are collaborating on the same document. When you resolve a comment, Word removes it from the markup area and displays a check mark in the comment icon. If you wanted to resolve a comment, you would perform one of the following steps.

1. Click the 'More thread actions' button in the comment box and then click Resolve Thread.

or

1. Right-click the commented text to display a shortcut menu and then click Resolve Comment on the shortcut menu.

To Delete All Comments

The following steps delete all comments at once. **Why?** Assume you now want to delete all the comments in the document at once because you have addressed them all.

1

- Click the Delete arrow (Review tab | Comments group) to display the Delete menu (Figure 2–96).

2

- Click 'Delete All Comments in Document' on the Delete menu to remove all comments from the document, which also closes the markup area.

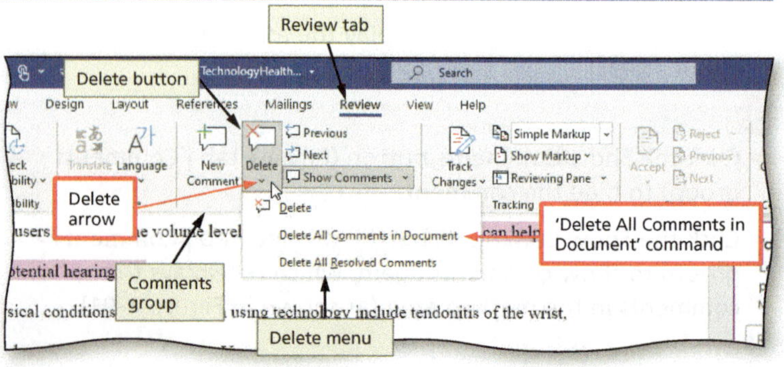

Figure 2–96

To Use the Document Inspector

Word includes a Document Inspector that checks a document for content you might not want to share with others, such as comments or personal information. Before sharing a document with others, you may want to check for this type of content. If you wanted to use the Document Inspector, you would do the following:

1. Open Backstage view and, if necessary, click Info in Backstage view to display the Info screen.
2. Click the 'Check for Issues' button in the Info screen to display the Check for Issues menu.
3. Click Inspect Document on the Check for Issues menu to display the Document Inspector dialog box. Select the check boxes for which you would like to check the document.
4. Click the Inspect button (Document Inspector dialog box) to instruct Word to inspect the document.
5. Review the results (Document Inspector dialog box) and then click the Remove All button(s) for any item that you do not want to be saved with the document.
6. When finished removing information, click the Close button to close the dialog box.

To Exit Word

You are finished with this project. The following step exits Word.

1 Exit Word.

Summary

In this module, you learned how to modify styles, adjust line and paragraph spacing, use headers to number pages, insert and edit citations and their sources, add footnotes, create a bibliographical list of sources, update a field, go to a page, find and replace text, check spelling and grammar, look up information, and work with comments.

Consider This: Plan Ahead

What decisions will you need to make when creating your next research paper?

Use these guidelines as you complete the assignments in this module and create your own research papers outside of this class.

1. Select a topic.
   a) Spend time brainstorming ideas for a topic.
   b) Choose a topic you find interesting.
   c) For shorter papers, narrow the scope of the topic; for longer papers, broaden the scope.
   d) Identify a tentative thesis statement, which is a sentence describing the paper's subject matter.
2. Research the topic and take notes, being careful not to plagiarize.
3. Organize your notes into related concepts, identifying all main ideas and supporting details in an outline.
4. Write the first draft from the outline, referencing all sources of information and following the guidelines identified in the required documentation style.
5. Create the list of sources, using the formats specified in the required documentation style.
6. Proofread and revise the paper.

Apply Your Knowledge

Reinforce the skills and apply the concepts you learned in this module.

Revising Content and Working with Citations and Sources in a Document

Note: To complete this assignment, you will be required to use the Data Files. Please contact your instructor for information about accessing the Data Files.

Instructions: Start Word. Open the document, SC_WD_2-1.docx, which is located in the Data Files. The document you open contains two paragraphs of text that are notes about shopping safely online with respect to passwords and credit cards. The manager of Brayden Department Stores, who created the shopping safely online notes, has asked you to revise the document as follows: check spelling and grammar, change paragraph indentation, change line spacing, remove space before and after paragraphs, find all occurrences of a word, replace all occurrences of a word with another series of words, locate a synonym, edit the header, add a sentence, insert and edit citations and sources, delete a source, and insert a reference list. The modified document is shown in Figure 2–97.

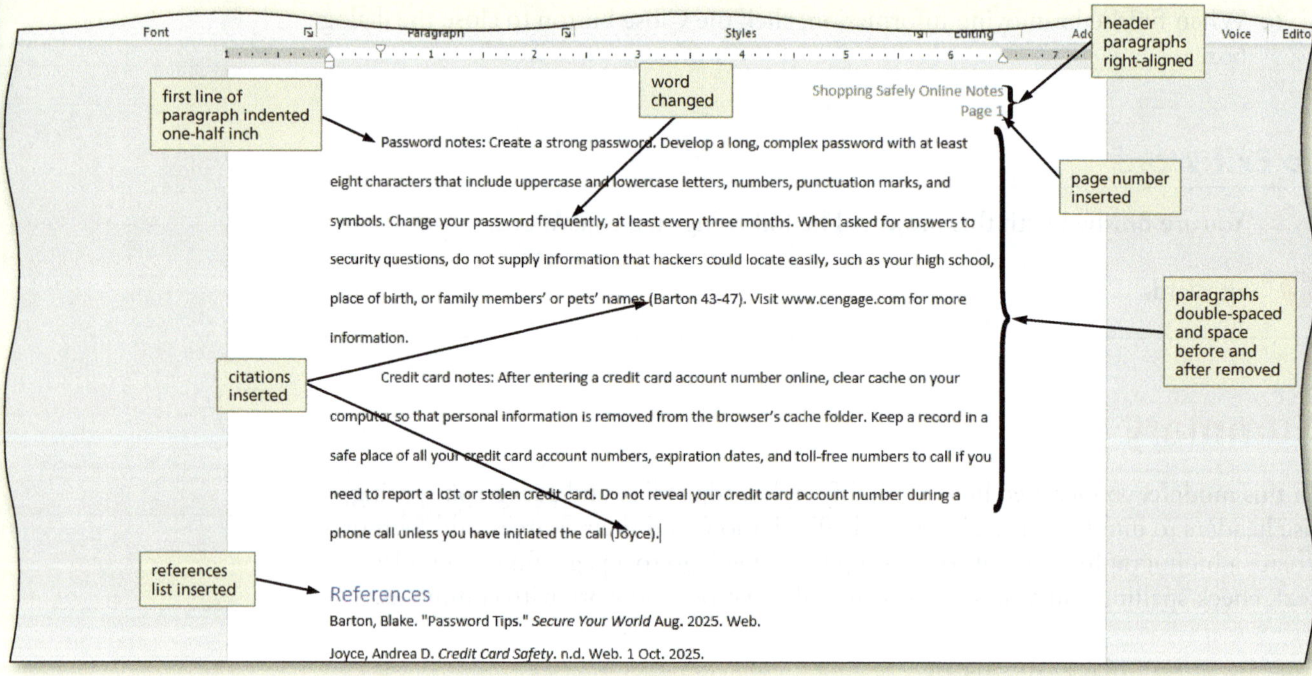

Figure 2–97

Perform the following tasks:

1. Click File on the ribbon, click Save As, and then save the document using the new file name, SC_WD_2_ShoppingSafelyOnlineNotes.
2. Check spelling and grammar at once. Correct the spelling and grammar mistakes in the document. Change all instances of the suggested spelling change, account, for the misspelled word, accounte.
3. Display the ruler, if necessary. Use the ruler to indent the first line of the first paragraph one-half inch. (If you are using a touch screen, use the Paragraph dialog box.) Hide the ruler.
4. Select the entire document and change the line spacing to double. With the entire document selected, remove space before and after paragraphs. (Hint: Use the 'Line and Paragraph Spacing' button for each command.)
5. Find all occurrences of the word, password. How many are there?

6. Use the Find and Replace dialog box to replace all occurrences of the word, card, with the words, credit card. How many replacements were made?
7. Show the Navigation Pane. Use the Navigation Pane to find the word, often. Close the Navigation Pane. Use Word's thesaurus to change the word, often, to the word, frequently. What other words are in the list of synonyms?
8. Switch to the header so that you can edit it. In the first line of the header, insert the word, Online, after the word, Safely, so that it reads: Shopping Safely Online Notes.
9. In the second line of the header, insert a page number (a plain number with no formatting) one space after the word, Page.
10. If requested by your instructor, enter your first and last name on a separate line below the page number in the header.
11. Change the alignment of all lines of text in the header from left-aligned to right-aligned. Close the header and footer.
12. At the end of the Password notes paragraph, type **`Visit www.cengage.com for more information.`** After you type the web address, continue typing to accept the automatic correction of the web address to a hyperlink format. Use the AutoCorrect Options button (point to the web address to display the small blue underline and then point to the blue underline to display the AutoCorrect Options button) and then undo the automatic hyperlink correction using the AutoCorrect Options button.
13. Verify that the Citations and Bibliography style is set to MLA Seventh Edition. At the end of the fourth sentence in the Password notes paragraph (before the period), insert a citation using the existing source in the document for the article by Blake Barton. Edit this citation to include the page numbers 43–47.
14. At the end of the last sentence in the Credit card notes paragraph (before the period), insert a citation placeholder called Joyce. Edit the source for the placeholder, Joyce, as follows: Type of source is Web site, author is Andrea D. Joyce, name of webpage is Credit Card Safety, year accessed is 2021, month accessed is Oct., day accessed is 1, and medium is Web.
15. Delete the source for the author named Anastasia Maria Pappas. (Hint: Use the Manage Sources button.)
16. Press ENTER at the end of the document. Apply the Normal style to the blank line at the end of the document. Insert a bibliography using the References format in the Bibliography gallery.
17. Save the document again with the same file name.
18. Submit the modified document, shown in Figure 2–97, in the format specified by your instructor.
19. Use the Search pane to look up the word, cache. If necessary, click the All button in the Search pane. Which web articles appeared? Show all the definitions. How many definitions are displayed?
20. Exit Word.
21. Answer the questions posed in #5, #6, #7, and #19. How would you find and replace a special character, such as a paragraph mark?

Extend Your Knowledge

Extend the skills you learned in this module and experiment with new skills. You may need to use Help to complete the assignment.

Working with References and Proofing Tools

Note: To complete this assignment, you will be required to use the Data Files. Please contact your instructor for information about accessing the Data Files.

Continued >

STUDENT ASSIGNMENTS

Extend Your Knowledge *continued*

Instructions: As a customer relationship coordinator at Windermere Bank and Trust, you communicate banking tips to customers. You also are a part-time student who has been assigned a research paper. You decide to combine your work and school interests and compose a short research paper about ATM safety. You will communicate your findings with bank customers.

Start Word. Open the document, SC_WD_2-2.docx, which is located in the Data Files. The document is your draft research paper. You will do the following to finish the paper: find formats and special characters, delete a footer, add another footnote to the paper, change the format of the note reference marks, convert the footnotes to endnotes, modify a style, use Word's readability statistics, work with comments, and translate the document to another language (Figure 2–98).

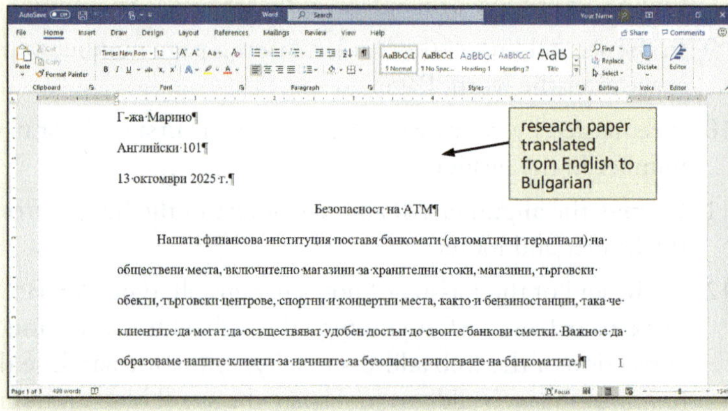

Figure 2–98

Perform the following tasks:

1. Use Help to learn more about finding formats and special characters, footers, footnotes and endnotes, readability statistics, bibliography styles, AutoCorrect, and Word's translation features.
2. Click File on the ribbon, click Save As, and then save the revised document using the new file name, SC_WD_2_SafelyUsingATMs. Verify that the Citations and Bibliography style is set to MLA Seventh Edition.
3. Use the Advanced Find command on the Find menu and the Replace tab in the Find and Replace dialog box to find the italic format in the body of the research paper and then remove the italic format. Click the No Formatting button in the Find and Replace dialog box to clear the format from the next search.
4. Use the Advanced Find command on the Find menu to find a footnote mark in the paper (which is a special character). What characters did Word place in the Find what box to search for the footnote mark? What number in the research paper is the footnote reference mark?
5. Edit the footer so that it reads: Delete this footer from the research paper. Delete the footer from the document.
6. Insert a second footnote at an appropriate place in the research paper. Use the following footnote text: `If you suspect someone is following you, immediately walk to a populated area or business, or drive to a police or fire station.`
7. Change the location of the footnotes from bottom of page to below text. How did the placement of the footnotes change?
8. Change the format of the note reference marks to capital letters (A, B, etc.). (Hint: Change the footnote number format using the Footnote and Endnote dialog box.)
9. Convert the footnotes to endnotes. Use the Navigation Pane to display each page in the document. Where are the endnotes positioned? What is the format of the note reference marks when they are endnotes?
10. Modify the Endnote Text style to 12-point Times New Roman font, double-spaced text with a hanging indent by clicking Style on the shortcut menu, clicking Endnote Text (Style dialog box), clicking the Modify button, and then selecting appropriate options in the Modify Style dialog box.

11. Insert this endnote for the first paragraph in the paper: **`Our ATMs enable customers to withdraw and deposit money, transfer funds, or inquire about an account balance.`**
12. Add an AutoCorrect entry that replaces the word, costomers, with the word, customers. Type the following sentence as the last sentence in the last paragraph of the paper, misspelling the word, customers, as costomers to test the AutoCorrect entry: **`Taking precautions when using our ATMs can help costomers avoid becoming a target of criminal activity.`** Delete the AutoCorrect entry that replaces costomers with the word, customers.
13. Display the Word Count dialog box. How many words, characters without spaces, characters with spaces, paragraphs, and lines are in the document? Be sure to include footnote and endnote text in the statistics.
14. Check spelling of the document, displaying readability statistics. What are the Flesch-Kincaid Grade Level and the Flesch Reading Ease score? How could you modify the paper to increase the reading ease score and lower the grade level?
15. If requested by your instructor, change the student name at the top of the paper to your name, including the last name in the header.
16. Change the zoom to multiple pages. How many pages are in the document?
17. Save the revised document paper again with the same name and then submit it in the format specified by your instructor.
18. Display the Info screen in Backstage view. How many draft versions of the document have been saved? How would you recover unsaved changes? If you have unsaved changes, recover them.
19. If it is not dimmed, test the Read Aloud button (Review tab | Speech group). What is the purpose of the Read Aloud button?
20. If requested by your instructor, perform these tasks:
    a. Insert this comment in the third paragraph: **`Add a discussion about skimmers after this paragraph.`**
    b. Insert another comment in the fourth paragraph: **`Add a paragraph about reviewing bank statements after this paragraph.`**
    c. Go to the first comment. Change the word, discussion, to the word, paragraph, in the first comment.
    d. Go to the second comment. Reply to the second comment with this comment text: **`Also discuss reviewing transactions online.`**
    e. Submit the document with comments in the format specified by your instructor.
    f. Inspect the document and review the results.
    g. Hide comments and then show comments.
    h. Delete the first comment. Resolve the second comment.
    i. Delete all comments.
21. If you have an Internet connection, translate the research paper into a language of your choice using the Translate button (Review tab | Language group), as shown in Figure 2–98. If requested by your instructor, submit the translated document in the format specified by your instructor.
22. Answer the questions posed in #4, #7, #9, #13, #14, #16, #18, and #19. Where did you insert the second footnote and why?

Expand Your World

Create a solution that uses cloud or web technologies by learning and investigating on your own from general guidance.

Using an Online Bibliography Tool to Create a List of Sources

Instructions: Assume you are attending a conference about workplace diversity and the computer or mobile device you have available at the conference does not have Word but has Internet access. As a human resources generalist at Whole Health Foods, you decide while attending this conference that you would like to educate employees about workplace diversity. You decide to use an online bibliography tool to create a list of sources that you can copy and paste into the Works Cited pages of a research paper you will create when you return to the office.

Perform the following tasks:

1. Start a browser. Search for the text, online bibliography tool, using a search engine. Visit several of the online bibliography tools and determine which you would like to use to create a list of sources. Navigate to the desired online bibliography tool.
2. Use the online bibliography tool to enter list of sources shown below (Figure 2–99):

   Chung, Kim Li, and Jordan Taylor Green. Managing Diversity in the Workplace. Chicago: Windy City Press, 2025. Print.

   Delhi, Rajesh. "Workplace Monthly Review." Your Workplace. Sept. 2025. Web. 1 Oct. 2025.

   Garlapati, Vidya. "Creating an Inclusive Workplace." *Diversity Learning*. July 2025. Web. 9 Oct. 2025.

   Hidalgo, Ronald P. The Workplace Diversity Handbook. Dallas: Lone Star Publishing, 2025. Print.

   Samaras, Alexander Lee. Workplace Diversity. Los Angeles: Sunshine Publications, 2025. Print.

   VanWijk, Fred J., and John L. Walker. "Work Team Diversity." The Successful Workplace. June 2025. Web. 8 Oct. 2025.

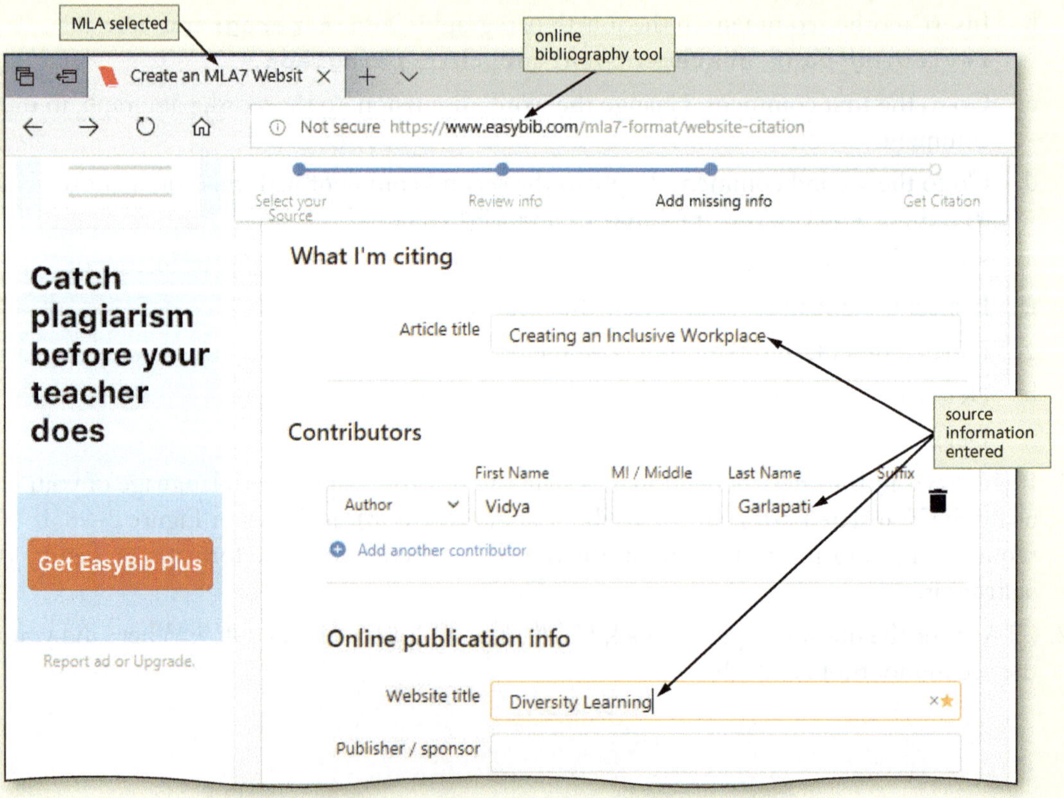

Figure 2–99

3. If requested by your instructor, replace the name in one of the sources above with your name.
4. Search for another source that discusses workplace diversity. Add that source.
5. Use the Export option in the online bibliography tool or copy and paste the list of sources into a Word document.
6. Save the document with the file name, SC_WD_2_WorkplaceDiversitySources. Submit the document in the format specified by your instructor.
7. Which online bibliography tools did you evaluate? Which one did you select to use and why? Do you prefer using the online bibliography tool or Word to create sources? Why? What differences, if any, did you notice between the list of sources created with the online bibliography tool and the lists created when you use Word?

In the Lab

Design and implement a solution using creative thinking and problem-solving skills.

Create a Research Paper about Drones

Note: To complete this assignment, you will be required to use the Data Files. Please contact your instructor for information about accessing the Data Files.

Problem: As the marketing communications coordinator for Darden Aircraft, you create a research paper about drones because you want to educate the public about them.

Perform the following tasks:

Part 1: The source for the text in your research paper is in a file named SC_WD_2-3.docx, which is located in the Data Files. Organize the notes in the text in the file in the Data Files, rewording as necessary so that you can create a research paper. Using the concepts and techniques presented in this module, along with your organized notes from the Data File, create and format a research paper according to the MLA documentation style (be sure to write an appropriate conclusion). While creating the paper, be sure to do the following:

1. Modify the Normal style to the 12-point Times New Roman font.
2. Adjust line spacing to double.
3. Remove space below (after) paragraphs.
4. Update the Normal style to reflect the adjusted line and paragraph spacing.
5. Insert an MLA-style header, and insert page numbers in the header.
6. Type the name and course information at the left margin. Use your name and course information. Center and type the title.
7. Set a first-line indent to one-half inch for paragraphs in the body of the research paper.
8. Add an AutoCorrect entry to correct a word you commonly mistype.
9. Type the body of the research paper from the notes. Change the bibliography style to MLA. As you insert citations, enter their source information. Edit the citations so that they are displayed according to the MLA documentation style.
10. At the end of the research paper text, press ENTER and then insert a page break so that the Works Cited page begins on a new page. Enter and format the works cited title and then use Word to insert the bibliographical list (bibliography).

Continued >

In the Lab *continued*

11. If your instructor requests, use the Researcher pane to obtain information from another source and include that information as a note positioned as a footnote in the paper, and enter its corresponding source information as appropriate. Update the bibliography.
12. Check the spelling and grammar of the paper at once. Add one of the source last names to the dictionary. Ignore all instances of one of the source last names. If necessary, set the default dictionary.

When you are finished with the research paper, save it with the file name, SC_WD_2_DronesPaper. Submit your assignment and answers to the Part 2 critical thinking questions in the format specified by your instructor.

Part 2: You made several decisions while creating the research paper in this assignment: how to organize the notes, what text to use for the conclusion, where to place citations, how to format sources, and which source on the web to use for the footnote text (if requested by your instructor). What was the rationale behind each of these decisions? When you proofread the document, what further revisions did you make and why?

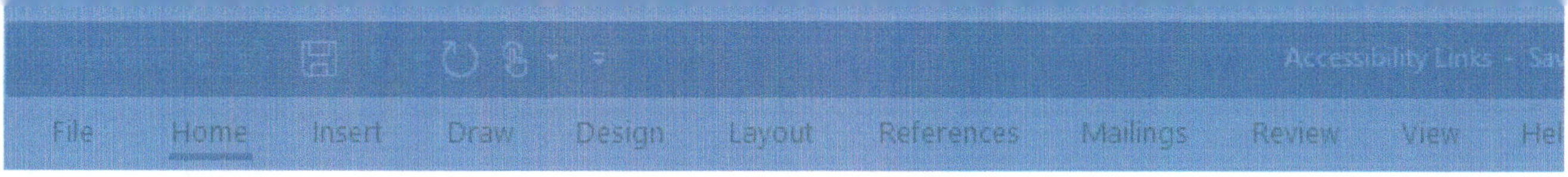

3 Creating a Business Letter

Objectives

After completing this module, you will be able to:

- Insert and format a shape
- Change text wrapping
- Insert an online picture and format it
- Insert a symbol
- Add a border to a paragraph
- Clear formatting
- Apply a style
- Set and use tab stops
- Insert the current date
- Insert a Word table, enter data in the table, and format the table
- Format a paragraph border
- Use the format painter
- Insert and format a SmartArt graphic
- Address and print an envelope

Introduction

In a business environment, people use documents to communicate with others. Business documents can include letters, memos, newsletters, proposals, and resumes. An effective business document clearly and concisely conveys its message and has a professional, organized appearance. You can use your own creative skills to design and compose business documents. Using Word, for example, you can develop the content and decide on the location of each item in a business document.

Project: Business Letter

At some time, you more than likely will prepare a business letter. Contents of business letters include requests, inquiries, confirmations, acceptances, applications, acknowledgements, recommendations, notifications, responses, thank you letters, invitations, offers, referrals, references, complaints, and more.

The project in this module follows generally accepted guidelines for writing letters and uses Word to create the business letter shown in Figure 3–1. This letter, written by the services coordinator for the director of admissions at Sunset State College, is an acceptance

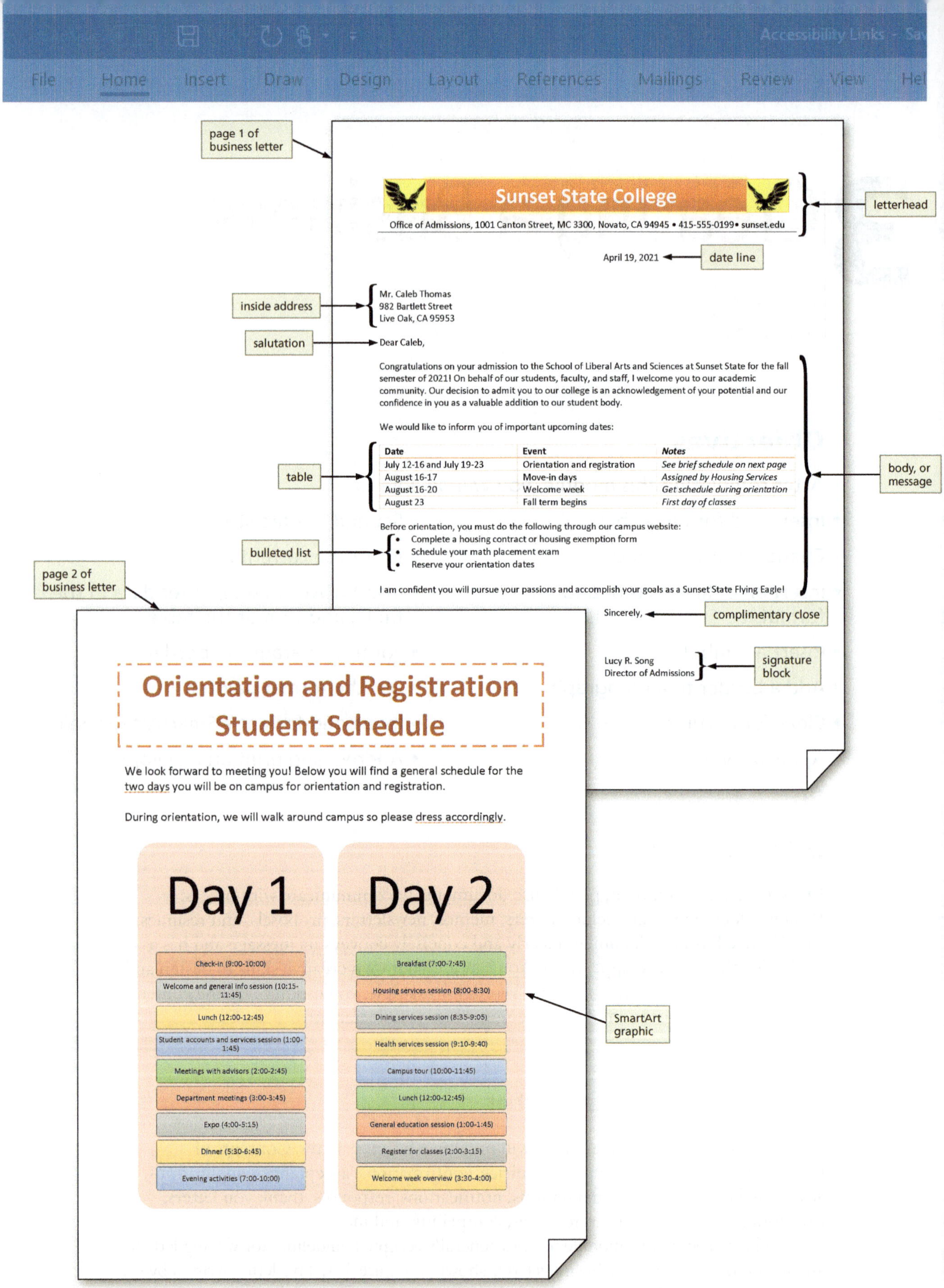
File
Home
Insert
Draw
Design
Layout
References
Mailings
Review
View
page 1 of business letter
Sunset State College
Office of Admissions, 1001 Canton Street, MC 3300, Novato, CA 94945 • 415-555-0199• sunset.edu
letterhead
April 19, 2021
date line
inside address
Mr. Caleb Thomas
982 Bartlett Street
Live Oak, CA 95953
salutation
Dear Caleb,
Congratulations on your admission to the School of Liberal Arts and Sciences at Sunset State for the fall semester of 2021! On behalf of our students, faculty, and staff, I welcome you to our academic community. Our decision to admit you to our college is an acknowledgement of your potential and our confidence in you as a valuable addition to our student body.
We would like to inform you of important upcoming dates:
table
Date | Event | Notes
July 12-16 and July 19-23 | Orientation and registration | See brief schedule on next page
August 16-17 | Move-in days | Assigned by Housing Services
August 16-20 | Welcome week | Get schedule during orientation
August 23 | Fall term begins | First day of classes
body, or message
Before orientation, you must do the following through our campus website:
bulleted list
• Complete a housing contract or housing exemption form
• Schedule your math placement exam
• Reserve your orientation dates
I am confident you will pursue your passions and accomplish your goals as a Sunset State Flying Eagle!
page 2 of business letter
Sincerely,
complimentary close
Lucy R. Song
Director of Admissions
signature block
Orientation and Registration Student Schedule
We look forward to meeting you! Below you will find a general schedule for the two days you will be on campus for orientation and registration.
During orientation, we will walk around campus so please dress accordingly.
Day 1
Check-in (9:00-10:00)
Welcome and general info session (10:15-11:45)
Lunch (12:00-12:45)
Student accounts and services session (1:00-1:45)
Meetings with advisors (2:00-2:45)
Department meetings (3:00-3:45)
Expo (4:00-5:15)
Dinner (5:30-6:45)
Evening activities (7:00-10:00)
Day 2
Breakfast (7:00-7:45)
Housing services session (8:00-8:30)
Dining services session (8:35-9:05)
Health services session (9:10-9:40)
Campus tour (10:00-11:45)
Lunch (12:00-12:45)
General education session (1:00-1:45)
Register for classes (2:00-3:15)
Welcome week overview (3:30-4:00)
SmartArt graphic

Figure 3–1

letter that welcomes the student to the campus and presents important information related to upcoming deadlines and events. The letter includes a custom letterhead, as well as all essential business letter components: date line, inside address, salutation, body, complimentary close, and signature block. To easily present the important upcoming dates for the student, the letter shows this information in a table. The immediate requirements appear in a bulleted list. The second page contains a visual of the schedule for orientation and registration.

In this module, you will learn how to create the letter shown in Figure 3–1. You will perform the following general tasks as you progress through this module:

1. Create and format a letterhead with graphics.
2. Specify the letter formats according to business letter guidelines.
3. Insert a table in the letter.
4. Format the table in the letter.
5. Insert a bulleted list in the letter.
6. On a second page, insert and format a SmartArt graphic.
7. Address an envelope for the letter.

To Start Word and Change Word Settings

If you are using a computer to step through the project in this module and you want your screens to match the figures in this book, you should change your screen's resolution to 1366 × 768.

The following steps start Word, display formatting marks, and change the zoom to page width.

1. Start Word and create a blank document in the Word window. If necessary, maximize the Word window.
2. If the Print Layout button on the status bar is not selected (shown in Figure 3–2), click it so that your screen is in Print Layout view.
3. If the 'Show/Hide ¶' button (Home tab | Paragraph group) is not selected already, click it to display formatting marks on the screen.
4. To display the page the same width as the document window, if necessary, click the Page Width button (View tab | Zoom group).
5. If you are using a mouse and you want your screens to match the figures in the book, verify that you are using Mouse mode by clicking the Touch/Mouse Mode button on the Quick Access Toolbar and then, if necessary, clicking Mouse on the menu. (If your Quick Access Toolbar does not display the Touch/Mouse Mode button, click the 'Customize Quick Access Toolbar' button on the Quick Access Toolbar and then click Touch/Mouse Mode on the menu to add the button to the Quick Access Toolbar.)

BTW

Touch Mode Differences

The Microsoft 365 and Windows interfaces may vary if you are using Touch mode. For this reason, you might notice that the function or appearance of your touch screen differs slightly from this module's presentation.

Creating a Letterhead

The cost of preprinted letterhead can be high; thus, some organizations and individuals create their own letterhead and save it in a file. Then, when you want to create a letter at a later time, you can start by using the letterhead file. The following sections create a letterhead and then save it in a file for future use.

Consider This

What is a letterhead?

A **letterhead**, which often appears at the top of a letter, is the section of a letter that identifies an organization or individual. Although you can design and print a letterhead yourself, many businesses pay an outside firm to design and print their letterhead, usually on higher-quality paper. They then use the professionally preprinted paper for external business communications.

If you do not have preprinted letterhead paper, you can design a creative letterhead. It is important the letterhead appropriately represent the essence of the organization or individual (i.e., formal, technical, creative, etc.). That is, it should use text, graphics, formats, and colors that reflect the organization or individual. The letterhead should leave ample room for the contents of the letter.

When designing a letterhead, consider its contents, placement, and appearance.

- **Contents of letterhead.** A letterhead should contain these elements:
  - Complete name of the individual, group, or company
  - Complete mailing address: street address including building, room, suite number, or post office box, along with city, state, and postal code
  - Phone number(s) and fax number, if applicable
  - Email address, if applicable
  - Web address, if applicable
  - Many letterheads also include a logo or other image; if an image is used, it should express the organization or individual's personality or goals
- **Placement of elements in the letterhead.** Many letterheads center their elements across the top of the page. Others align some or all of the elements with the left or right margins. Sometimes, the elements are split between the top and bottom of the page. For example, a name and logo may be at the top of the page with the address at the bottom of the page.
- **Appearance of letterhead elements.** Use fonts that are easy to read. Give the organization or individual name impact by making its font size larger than the rest of the text in the letterhead. For additional emphasis, consider formatting the name in bold, italic, or a different color. Choose colors that complement each other and convey the goals of the organization or individual.

When finished designing the letterhead, determine if a divider line would help to visually separate the letterhead from the remainder of the letter.

The letterhead for the letter in this module consists of the school name, postal address, phone number, web address, and images of an eagle (the school's mascot). The name and images are enclosed in a rectangular shape (shown in Figure 3–1), and the contact information is below the shape. You will follow these general steps to create the letterhead in this module:

1. Insert and format a shape.
2. Enter and format the school name in the shape.
3. Insert, format, and position the images in the shape.
4. Enter the contact information below the shape.
5. Add a border below the contact information.

To Insert a Shape

Word has a variety of predefined shapes, which are a type of drawing object, that you can insert in documents. A **drawing object** is a graphic that you create using Word. Examples of shape drawing objects include rectangles, circles, triangles, arrows, flowcharting symbols, stars, banners, and callouts. The following steps insert a rectangle shape in the letterhead. **Why?** The school name is placed in a rectangle for emphasis and visual appeal.

1

- Display the Insert tab.
- Click the Shapes button (Insert tab | Illustrations group) to display the Shapes gallery (Figure 3–2).

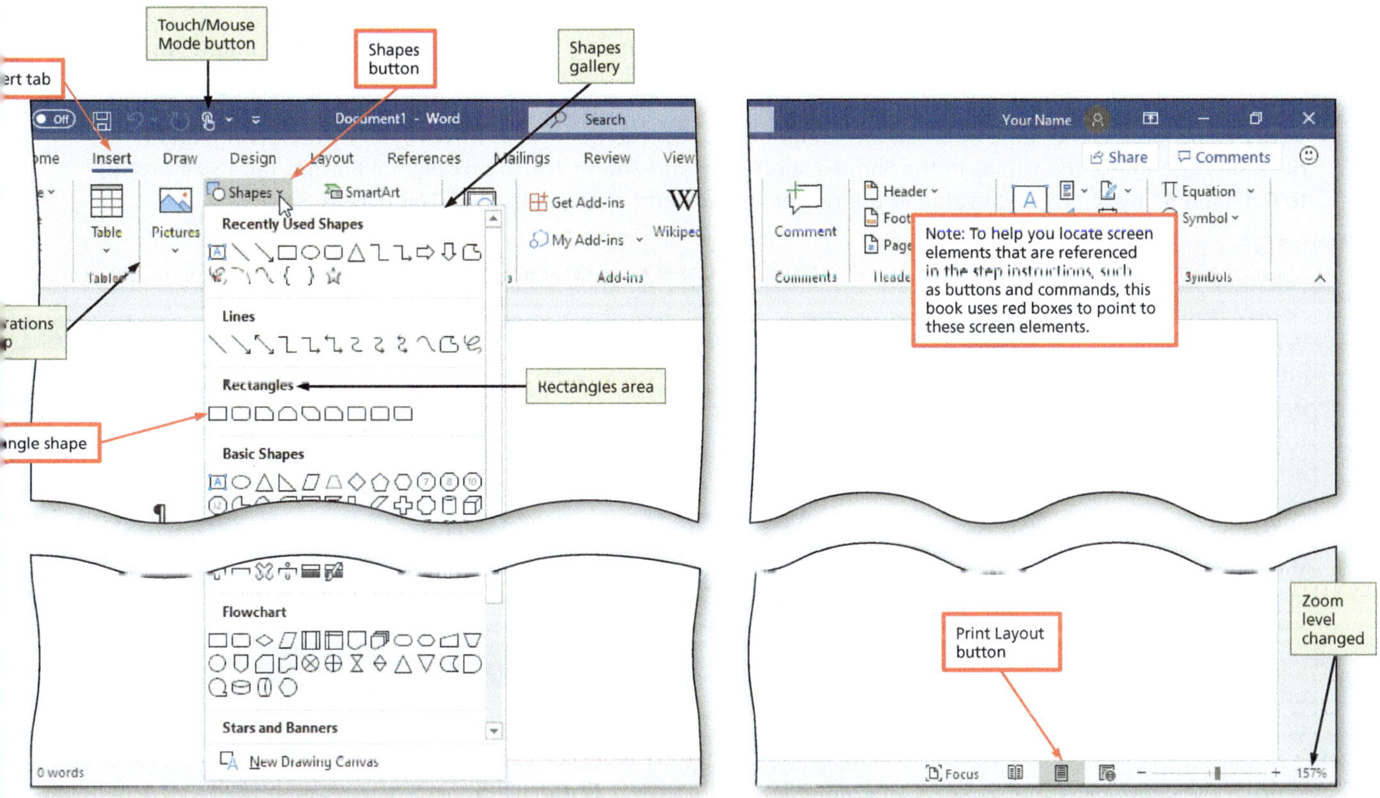

Figure 3–2

2

- Click the Rectangle shape in the Rectangles area in the Shapes gallery, which removes the gallery.

Q&A **What if I am using a touch screen?**
The shape is inserted in the document window. Skip Steps 3 and 4, and proceed to Step 5.

- Position the pointer (a crosshair) in the approximate location for the upper-left corner of the desired shape (Figure 3–3).

Q&A **What is the purpose of the crosshair pointer?**
You drag the crosshair pointer from the upper-left corner to the lower-right corner to form the desired location and size of the shape.

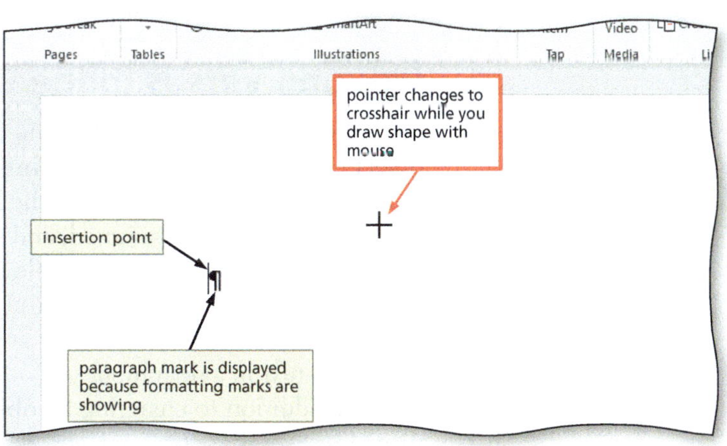

Figure 3–3

3

- Drag the mouse to the right and downward to form the boundaries of the shape, as shown in Figure 3–4. Do not release the mouse button.

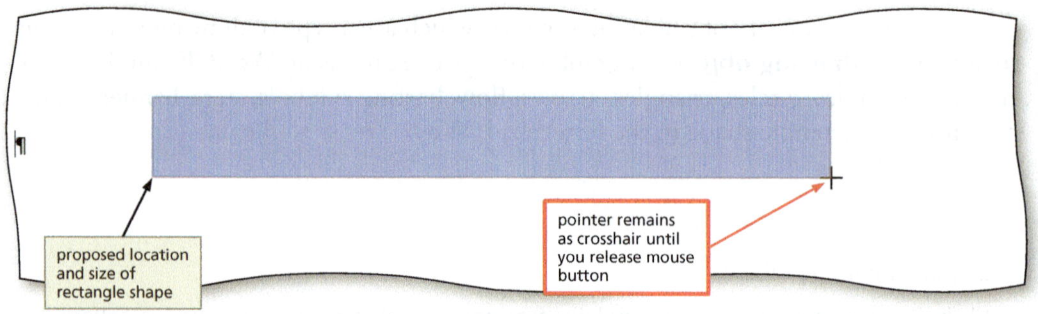

Figure 3–4

4

- Release the mouse button so that Word draws the shape according to your drawing in the document window.

5

- Verify your shape is the same approximate height and width as the one in this project by reviewing, and if necessary changing, the values in the Shape Height box and Shape Width box (Shape Format tab | Size group) to 0.5" and 5" by typing each value in the respective box and then pressing ENTER (Figure 3–5).

Q&A

What is the purpose of the rotate handle?
When you drag an object's **rotate handle**, which is the small circular arrow at the top of the selected object, Word turns the selected object in a clockwise or counterclockwise direction, depending on the direction you drag the mouse.

What if I wanted to delete a shape and start over?
With the shape selected, you would press DELETE.

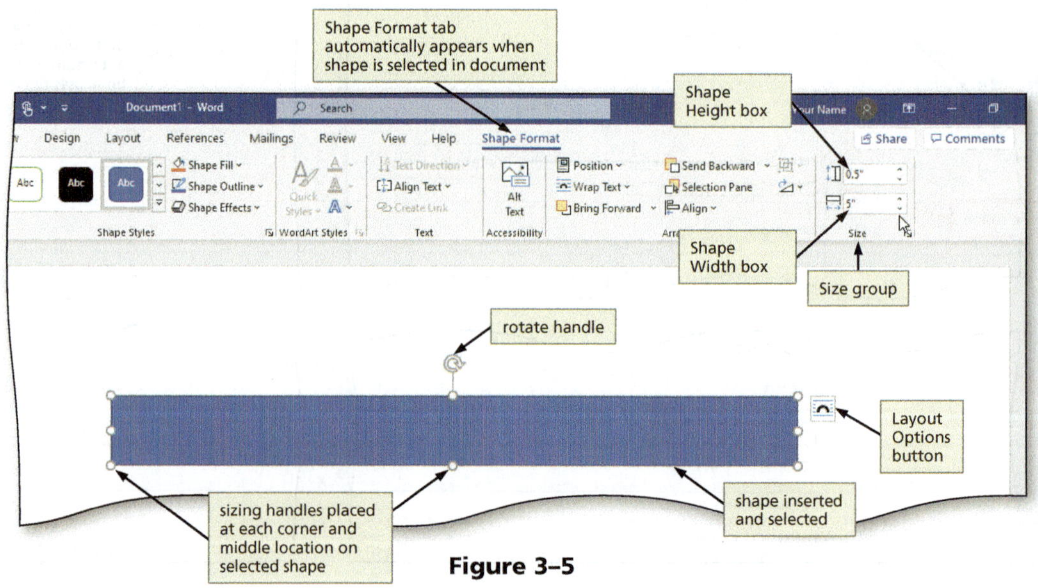

Figure 3–5

BTW

Resizing Shapes

In the above steps, you resized the shape nonproportionally, that is, with different height and width values. To maintain size proportions when resizing a shape, click the Size Dialog Box Launcher (Shape Format tab | Size group) and then place a check mark in the 'Lock aspect ratio' check box (Layout dialog box).

Floating versus Inline Objects

When you insert an object in a document, Word inserts it as either an inline object or a floating object. An **inline object** is an object that is part of a paragraph. With inline objects, you change the location of the object by setting paragraph options, such as centered, right-aligned, and so on. A **floating object**, by contrast, is an object that is independent of text and able to be moved anywhere on a page. The shape you just inserted is a floating object. You have more flexibility with floating objects because you can position a floating object at a specific location in a document or in a layer over or behind text in a document.

In addition to changing an object from inline to floating and vice versa, Word provides several floating options, which (along with inline) are called text wrapping options because they affect how text wraps with or around the object. Table 3–1 presents the various text wrapping options.

Table 3–1 Text Wrapping Options

Text Wrapping Option	Object Type	How It Works
In Line with Text	Inline	Object positioned according to paragraph formatting; for example, if the paragraph is centered, the object will be centered with any text in the paragraph.
Square	Floating	Text wraps around the object, with the text forming a box around the object.
Tight	Floating	Text wraps around the object, with the text forming to the shape of the object.
Through	Floating	Object appears at the beginning, middle, or end of text. Moving the object changes location of the text.
Top and Bottom	Floating	Object appears above or below text. Moving the object changes location of the text.
Behind Text	Floating	Object appears behind the text.
In Front of Text	Floating	Object appears in front of the text and may cover the text.

To Change an Object's Position

You can specify an object's vertical position within the margins on a page (top, middle, bottom) and its horizontal position (left, center, right). The following steps change the position of an object, specifically, the rectangle shape. **Why?** You want the shape to be centered at the top of the page in the letterhead.

1

- With the shape still selected, click the Position button (Shape Format tab | Arrange group) to display the Position gallery (Figure 3–6).

Q&A **What if the shape is not still selected?**
Click the shape to select it.

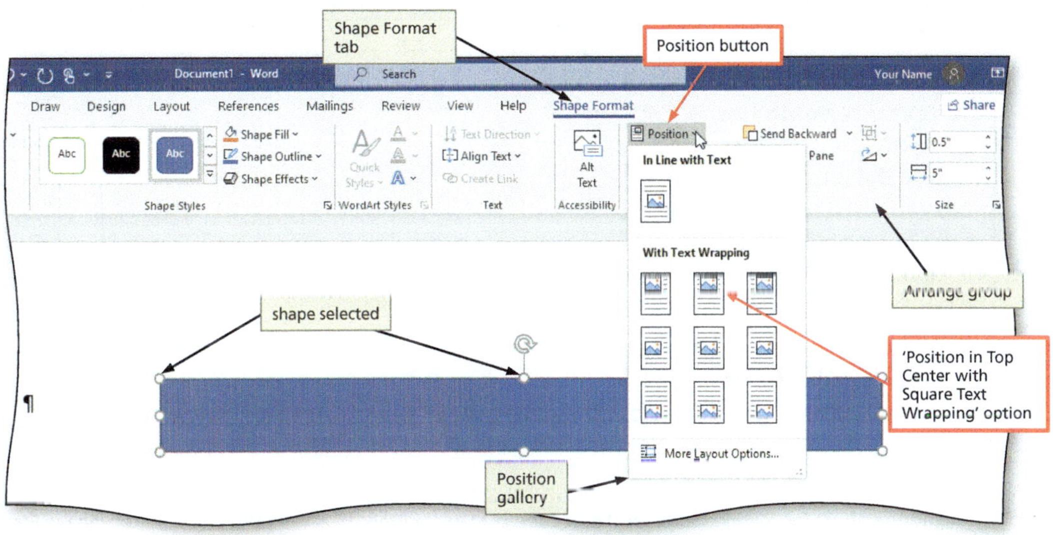

Figure 3–6

Experiment

- Point to various options in the Position gallery and watch the shape move to the selected position option.

2

- Click 'Position in Top Center with Square Text Wrapping' in the Position gallery so that the object does not cover the document and is centered at the top margin of the document.

Q&A **What if I wanted to center the object in its current vertical location (and not at the top, center, or bottom of the page)?**
You would click the Align button (Shape Format tab | Arrange group) (shown in Figure 3–7) and then click the desired alignment in the list.

Other Ways

1. Click Layout Options button attached to object (shown in Figure 3–5), click See more link in Layout Options gallery, click Horizontal Alignment arrow and select alignment (Layout dialog box), click Vertical Alignment arrow and select alignment, click OK
2. Click a Size Dialog Box Launcher (Shape Format tab | Size group), click Position tab (Layout dialog box), click Horizontal Alignment arrow and select alignment, click Vertical Alignment arrow and select alignment, click OK

To Change an Object's Text Wrapping

When you insert a shape in a Word document, the default text wrapping is In Front of Text, which means the object will cover any text behind it. The previous steps, which changed the shape's position, changed the text wrapping to Square. In the letterhead, you want the shape's text wrapping to be Top and Bottom. **Why?** You want the letterhead above the contents of the letter when you type it, instead of covering the contents of the letter. The following steps change an object's text wrapping, specifically, the shape.

1

- With the shape still selected, click the Layout Options button attached to the object to display the Layout Options gallery (Figure 3–7).

2

- Click 'Top and Bottom' in the Layout Options gallery so that the object does not cover the document text.

Q&A **How can I tell that the text wrapping has changed?**
Because the letter has no text, you need to look at the paragraph mark, which now is positioned below the shape instead of to its left.

- Click the Close button in the Layout Options gallery to close the gallery.

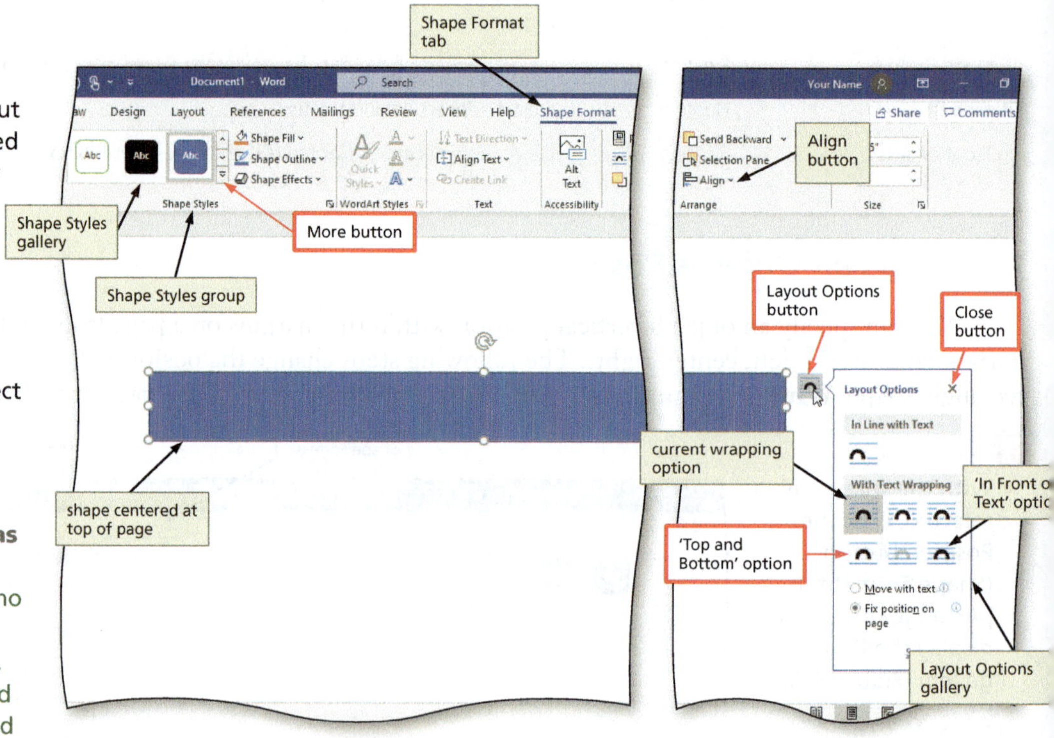

Figure 3–7

Other Ways

1. Right-click object (or, if using touch, tap 'Show Context Menu' button on Mini toolbar), point to Wrap Text on shortcut menu, click desired wrapping option
2. Click Wrap Text button (Shape Format tab | Arrange group), select desired wrapping option

To Apply a Shape Style

Why apply a shape style? Word provides a Shape Styles gallery so that you easily can change the appearance of the shape. The following steps apply a shape style to the rectangle shape.

1

- With the shape still selected, click the More button (shown in Figure 3–7) in the Shape Styles gallery (Shape Format tab | Shape Styles group) to expand the gallery.

Q&A **What if the shape no longer is selected?**
Click the shape to select it.

- Point to 'Moderate Effect - Orange, Accent 2' (third style in fifth row) in the Shape Styles gallery to display a Live Preview of that style applied to the shape in the document (Figure 3–8).

Experiment

- Point to various styles in the Shape Styles gallery and watch the style of the shape change in the document.

2

- Click 'Moderate Effect - Orange, Accent 2' in the Shape Styles gallery to apply the selected style to the shape.

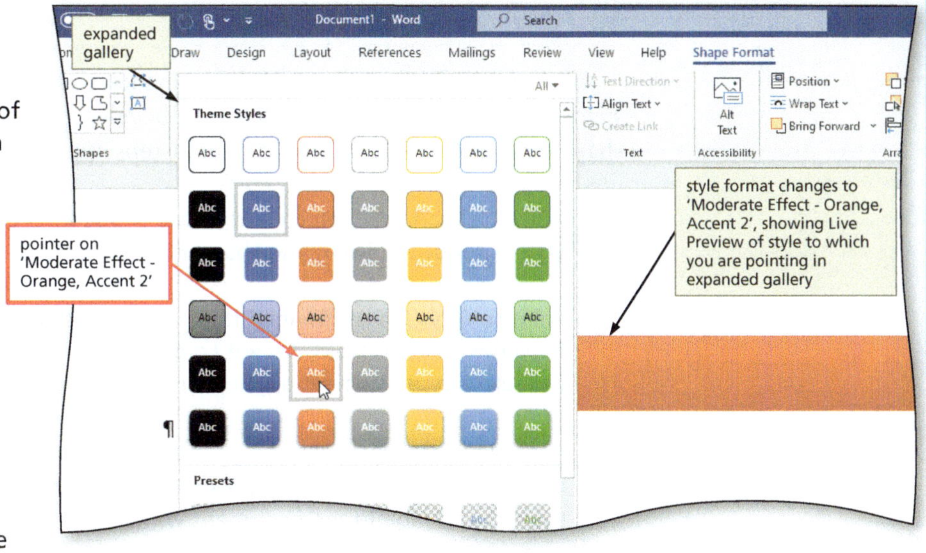

Figure 3–8

Other Ways

1. Right-click shape, click Style button on Mini toolbar, select desired style
2. Click Shape Styles Dialog Box Launcher (Shape Format tab | Shape Styles group), click 'Fill & Line' button (Format Shape pane), expand Fill section, select desired colors, click Close button

To Change the Shape Outline

The rectangle shape currently has an orange outline that matches the fill color inside the shape. The following steps change the outline color on the shape. **Why?** You would like to differentiate the outline from the fill color on the shape.

1

- Click the Shape Outline arrow (Shape Format tab | Shape Styles group) to display the Shape Outline gallery.
- Point to 'Gold, Accent 4' (eighth color in first row) in the Shape Outline gallery to display a Live Preview of that outline color around the shape (Figure 3–9).

Experiment

- Point to various colors in the Shape Outline gallery and watch the outline color on the shape change in the document window.

2

- Click 'Gold, Accent 4' in the Shape Outline gallery to change the shape outline color.

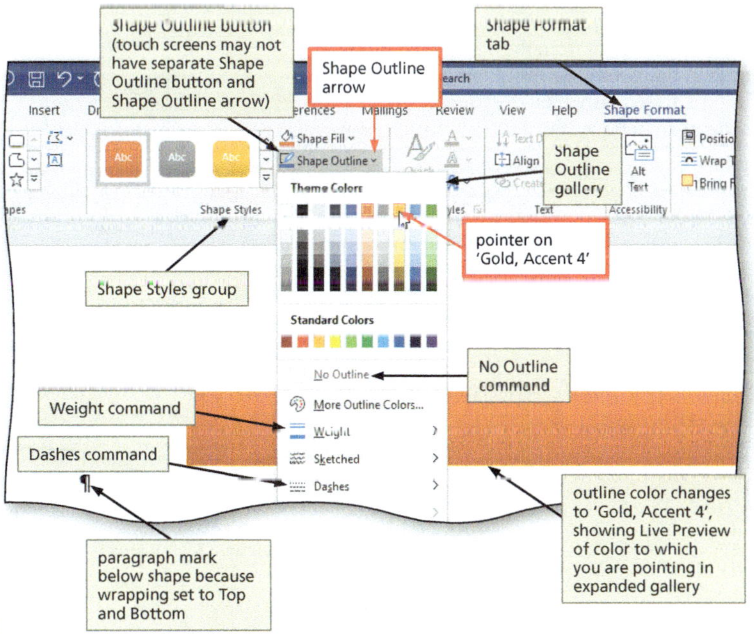

Figure 3–9

Q&A

How would I remove an outline color from a shape?
With the graphic selected, you would click No Outline in the Shape Outline gallery.

When would I use the Weight and Dashes commands in the Shape Outline gallery?
The Weight command enables you to change the thickness of the outline, and the Dashes command provides a variety of dashed outline options.

To Apply a Shape Effect

As with picture effects, Word provides a variety of shape effects, including shadows, reflections, glows, soft edges, bevels, and 3-D rotations. In this letterhead, the shape has a glow effect. The following steps apply a shape effect to the selected shape.

1. With the shape still selected, click the Shape Effects button (Shape Format tab | Shape Styles group) to display the Shape Effects menu.

2. Point to Glow on the Shape Effects menu to display the Glow gallery and then point to 'Glow: 5 point; Gold, Accent color 4' in the Glow gallery to display a Live Preview of the selected glow effect applied to the picture in the document window (Figure 3–10).

   Experiment

   If you are using a mouse, point to various glow effects in the Glow gallery and watch the glow change in the document window.

3. Click 'Glow: 5 point; Gold, Accent color 4' in the Glow gallery to apply the selected glow effect.

BTW

The Ribbon and Screen Resolution

Word may change how the groups and buttons within the groups appear on the ribbon, depending on the screen resolution of your computer. Thus, your ribbon may look different from the ones in this book if you are using a screen resolution other than 1366 × 768.

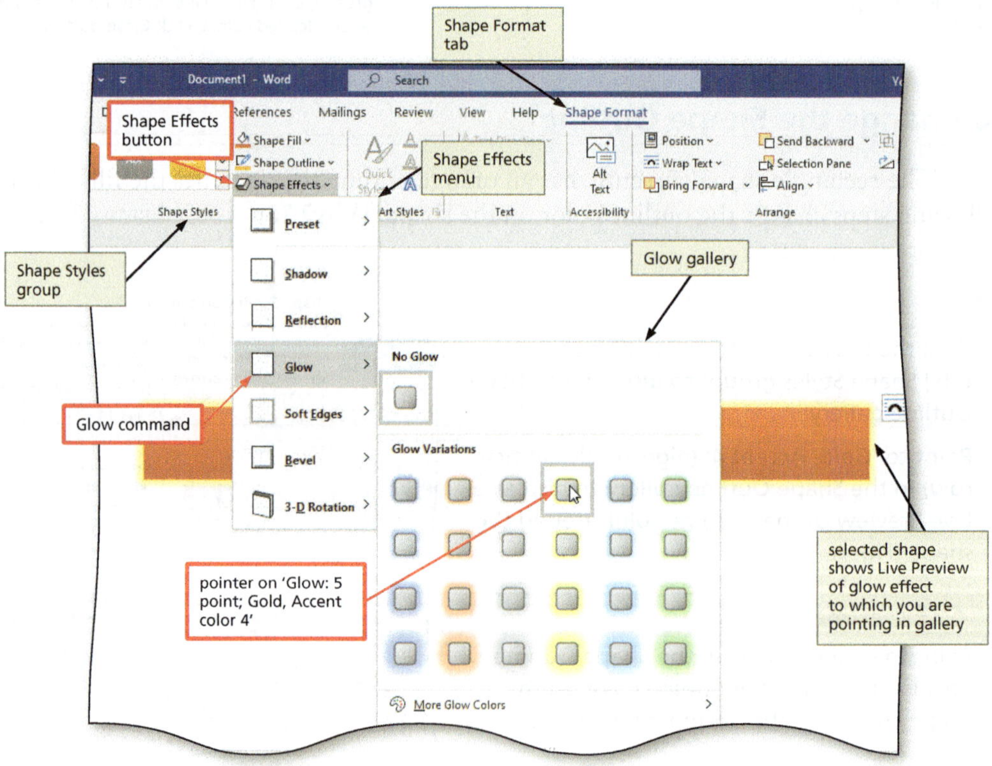

Figure 3–10

To Add Text to a Shape

The following steps add text (the school name) to a shape. **Why?** In the letterhead for this module, the name is in the shape. Similarly, an individual could put his or her name in a shape on a letterhead in order to create personalized letterhead.

1

- Right-click the shape to display a Mini toolbar and/or shortcut menu (Figure 3–11).

2

- Click Add Text on the shortcut menu to place an insertion point in the shape.

Q&A **What if I am using a touch screen?**
Tap the Edit Text button on the Mini toolbar.

Why do the buttons on my Mini toolbar differ?
If you are using a mouse in Mouse mode, the buttons on your Mini toolbar will differ from those that appear when you use a touch screen in Touch mode.

- If the insertion point and paragraph mark are not centered in the shape, click the Center button (Home tab | Paragraph group) to center them.
- Type `Sunset State College` as the name in the shape (Figure 3–12).

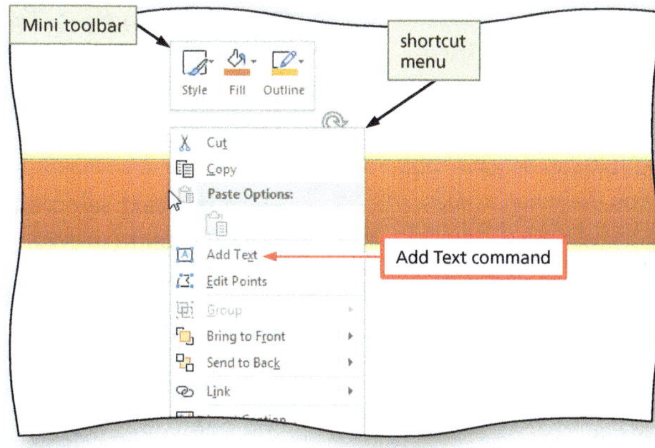

Figure 3–11

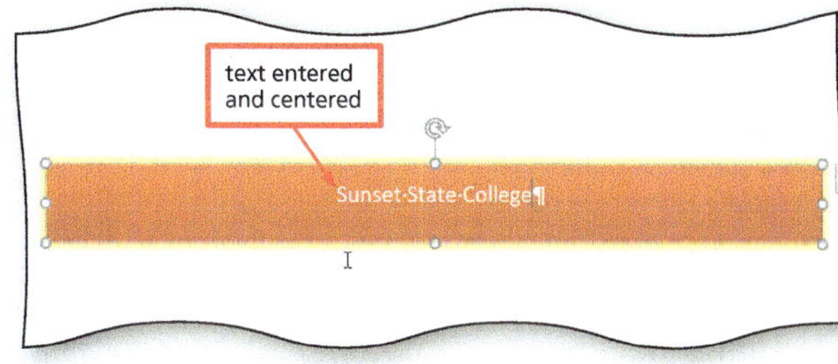

Figure 3–12

To Use the 'Increase Font Size' Button

While you can use the Font Size arrow (Home tab | Font group) to change the font size of text, Word also provides an 'Increase Font Size' button (Home tab | Font group) that increases the font size of selected text each time you click the button. The following steps use the 'Increase Font Size' button to increase the font size of the name in the shape to 24 point. **Why?** You want the name to be larger in the shape.

1

- Drag through the text to be formatted (in this case, the name in the shape).

2

- If necessary, display the Home tab.
- Repeatedly click the 'Increase Font Size' button (Home tab | Font group) until the Font Size box displays 24 to increase the font size of the selected text (Figure 3–13).

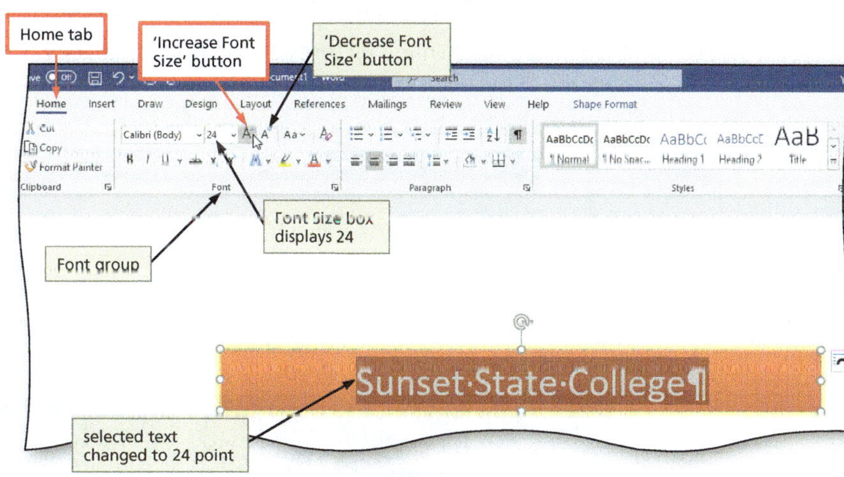

Figure 3–13

Q&A **What if I click the 'Increase Font Size' button (Home tab | Font group) too many times, causing the font size to be too big?**
Click the 'Decrease Font Size' button (Home tab | Font group) until the desired font size is displayed.

Experiment

- Repeatedly click the 'Increase Font Size' and 'Decrease Font Size' buttons (Home tab | Font group) and watch the font size of the selected text change in the document window. When you are finished experimenting with these two buttons, set the font size to 24.

Other Ways

1. Press CTRL+SHIFT+>

BTW

Saving a Template

As an alternative to saving the letterhead as a Word document, you could save it as a template. To do so, click File on the ribbon to open Backstage view, click Export to display the Export screen, click 'Change File Type', click Template in the right pane, click the Save As button, enter the template file name (Save As dialog box), if necessary select the Templates folder, and then click the Save button in the dialog box. To use the template, click File on the ribbon to open Backstage view, click New to display the New gallery, click the Personal tab in the New screen, and then click the template icon or file name.

To Bold Selected Text and Save the Letterhead Document

To make the name stand out even more, bold it. The following steps bold the selected text.

1. With the text selected, click the Bold button (Home tab | Font group) to bold the selected text (shown in Figure 3–16).
2. Click anywhere in the text in the shape to remove the selection and place the insertion point in the shape.
3. Save the letterhead on your hard drive, OneDrive, or other storage location using the file name, SC_WD_3_SunsetStateLetterhead.

Q&A **Why should I save the letterhead at this time?**
You have performed many tasks while creating this letterhead and do not want to risk losing work completed thus far.

To Insert an Online Picture

Files containing pictures and other images are available from a variety of sources. In this project, you insert a picture from the web. Microsoft 365 applications can access a collection of royalty-free photos and animations.

The letterhead in this project contains a picture of a flying eagle (shown in Figure 3–1). **Why?** The school mascot is a flying eagle. The following steps insert an online picture in the document.

1

- If necessary, click the paragraph mark below the shape to position the insertion point where you want to insert the picture.
- Display the Insert tab.
- Click the Pictures button (Insert tab | Illustrations group) to display the Insert Picture From menu.
- Click Online Pictures on the Insert Picture From menu to display the Online Pictures dialog box.
- Type `eagle` in the Search box (Online Pictures dialog box) to specify the search text, which indicates the type of image you want to locate (Figure 3–14).

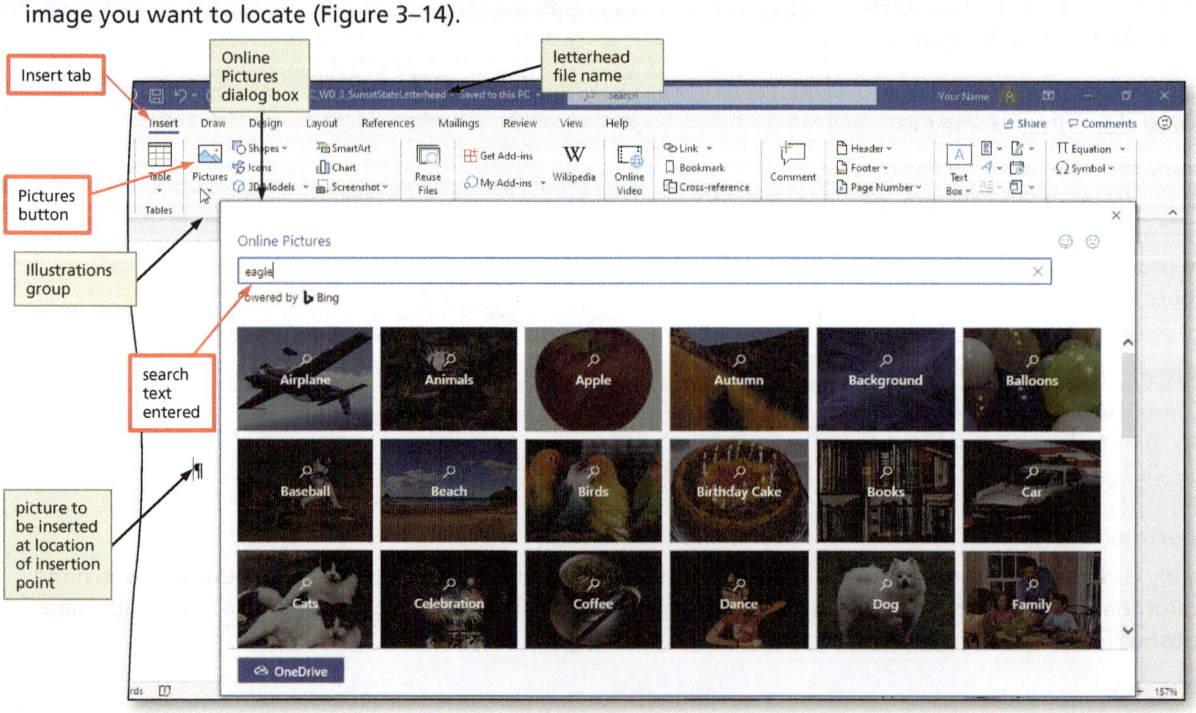

Figure 3–14

2

- Press ENTER to display a list of online pictures that matches the entered search text.
- Scroll through the list of pictures to locate the one shown in Figure 3–15, or a similar rectangular image.

Q&A

Why is my list of pictures different from Figure 3–15?
The online images are continually updated.

What is Creative Commons?
Creative Commons is a nonprofit organization that makes it easy for content creators to license and share their work by supplying easy-to-understand copyright licenses; the creator chooses the conditions under which the work can be used. Be sure to follow an image's guidelines when using it in a document.

Can I access other types of online pictures from within Word?
Yes. If you use Word 365, you can access a library of stock photos by clicking the Pictures button (Insert tab | Illustrations group) and then clicking Stock Images.

What if I cannot locate the image in Figure 3–15, and I would like to use that exact image?
The image is located in the Data Files. You can click the Cancel button (Online Pictures dialog box) and then click the Pictures button (Insert tab | Illustrations group), click This Device, navigate to the file called Support_WD_3_FlamingEagle.png in the Data Files, and then click the Insert button (Insert Picture dialog box).

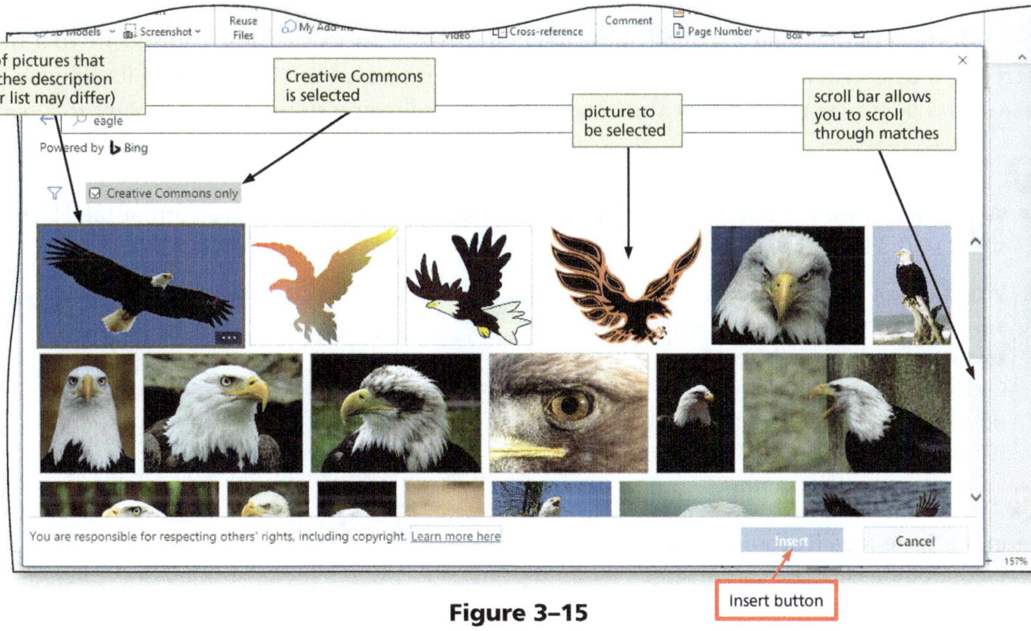

Figure 3–15

3

- Click the desired picture to select it.
- Click the Insert button to insert the selected image in the document at the location of the insertion point. If necessary, scroll to display the image (picture) in the document window (Figure 3–16).

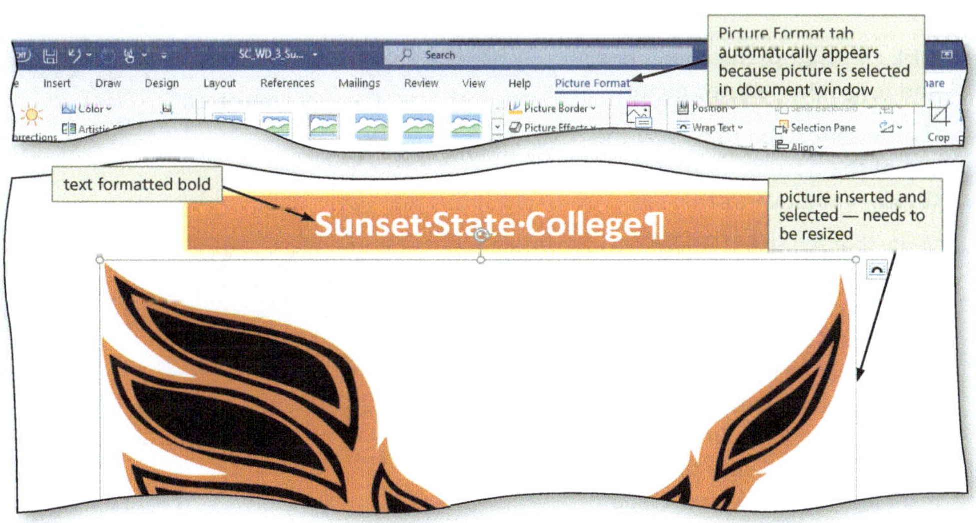

Figure 3–16

To Resize a Picture to a Percent of the Original Size

Instead of dragging a sizing handle to change the picture's size, you can specify that the picture be resized to a percent of its original size. In this module, the picture is resized to 10 percent of its original size. **Why?** The original size of the picture is too large for the letterhead. The following steps resize a picture to a percent of the original.

1

- With the picture still selected, click the Size Dialog Box Launcher (Picture Format tab | Size group) to display the Size sheet in the Layout dialog box.

Q&A

What if the picture is not selected or the Picture Format tab is not on the ribbon?
Click the picture to select it or double-click the picture to make the Picture Format tab the active tab.

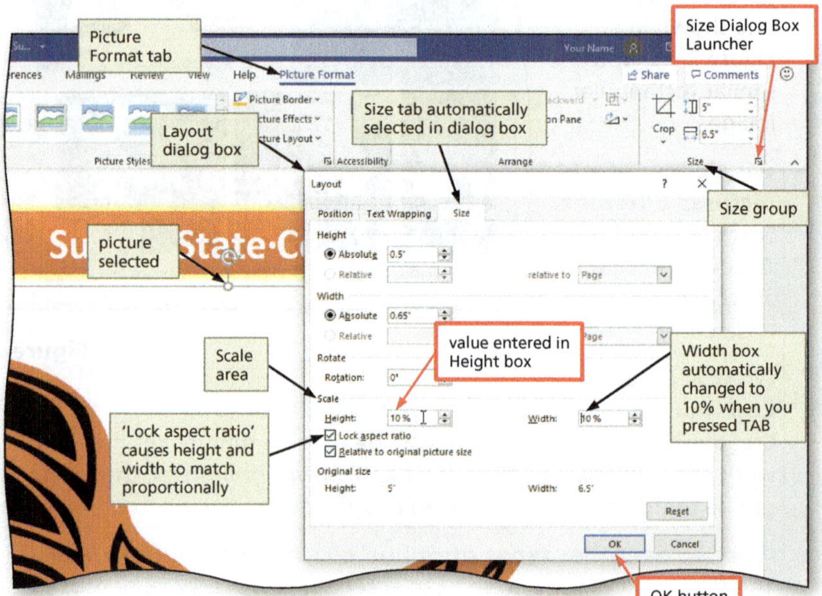

Figure 3–17

2

- In the Scale area (Layout dialog box), double-click the current value in the Height box to select it.
- Type `10` in the Height box and then press TAB to display the same percent value in the Width box (Figure 3–17).

Q&A

Why did Word automatically fill in the value in the Width box?
When the 'Lock aspect ratio' check box (Layout dialog box) is selected, Word automatically maintains the size proportions of the selected picture. If you wanted to resize the picture nonproportionally, you would remove the check mark from this check box.

How do I know to use 10 percent for the resized picture?
The larger picture consumed too much room on the page. Try various percentages to determine the size that works best in the letterhead design.

3

- Click OK to close the dialog box and resize the selected picture.
- If necessary, scroll to display the top of the document in the document window.
- Verify that the Shape Height and Shape Width boxes (Picture Format tab | Size group) display 0.5" and 0.65", respectively. If they do not, change their values to these measurements (Figure 3–18). If you are not able to resize the picture exactly, remove the check mark from the 'Lock aspect ratio' check box (Layout dialog box) and then try again.

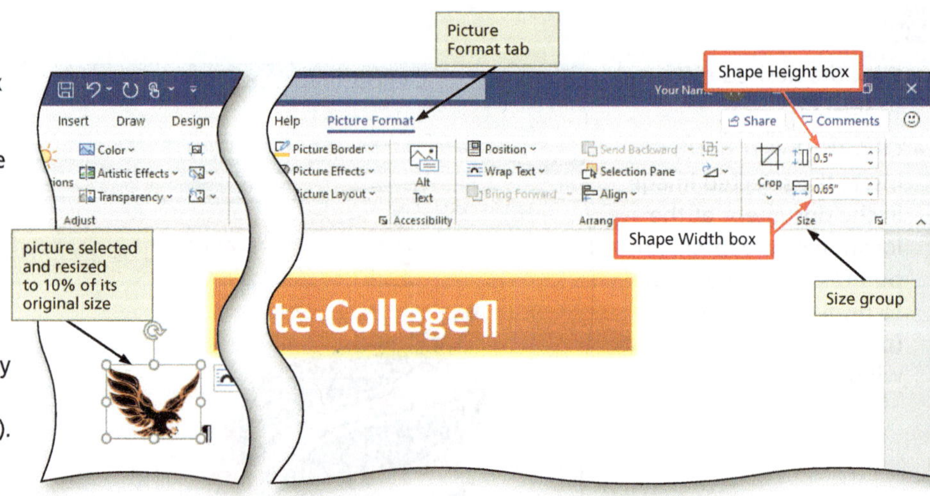

Figure 3–18

Other Ways

1. Click Layout Options button attached to picture, click See more link in the Layout Options gallery, click Size tab (Layout dialog box), enter height and width values, click OK
2. Right-click picture, click 'Size and Position' on shortcut menu, enter height and width values (Layout dialog box), click OK

To Change the Color of a Picture

In Word, you can change the color of a picture. The flying eagle picture currently is bright orange and black colors. The following steps change the color of the picture. **Why?** Because the image in this project will be placed beside the rectangle shape, you prefer to use lighter colors.

1

- With the picture still selected (shown in Figure 3–18), click the Color button (Picture Format tab | Adjust group) to display the Color gallery.
- Point to 'Gold, Accent color 4 Dark' in the Recolor area in the Color gallery (fifth color in second row), which would display a Live Preview of that color applied to the selected picture in the document if the picture was not hidden by the Color gallery (Figure 3–19).

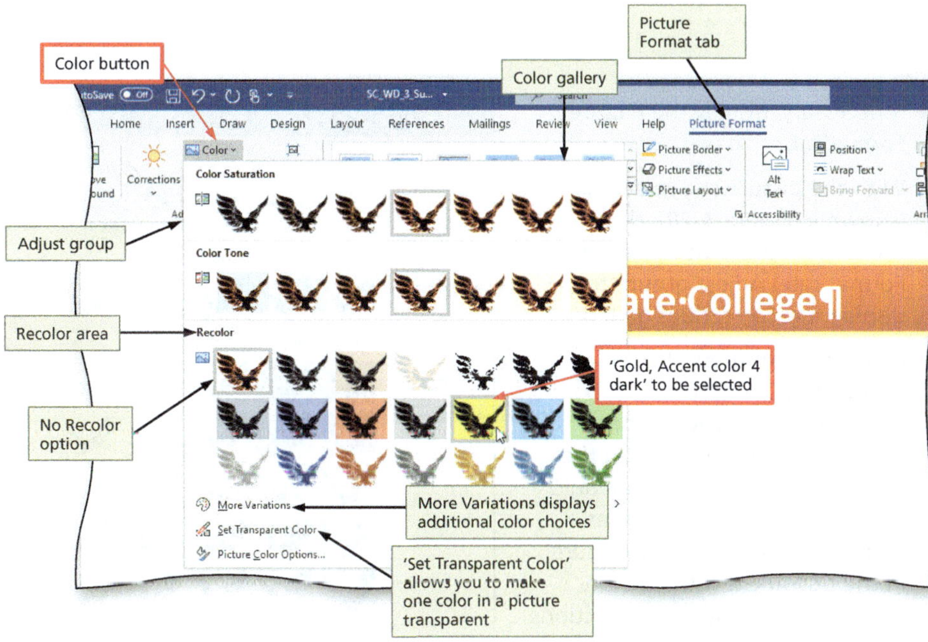

Figure 3–19

2

- Click 'Gold, Accent color 4 Dark' in the Color gallery to change the color of the selected picture (Figure 3–20).

Q&A **How would I change a picture back to its original colors?**
With the picture selected, you would click No Recolor, which is the upper-left color in the Color gallery.

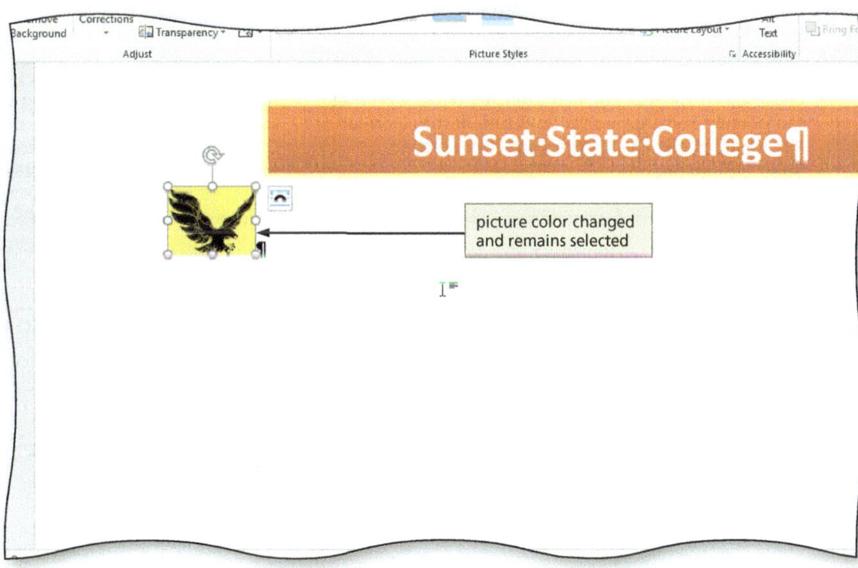

Figure 3–20

Other Ways

1. Click Picture Styles Dialog Box Launcher (Picture Format tab | Picture Styles group), click Picture button (Format Picture pane), expand Picture Color section, select desired options
2. Right-click picture (or, if using touch, tap 'Show Context Menu' button on Mini toolbar), click Format Picture on shortcut menu (or, if using touch, tap Format Object), click Picture button (Format Picture pane), expand Picture Color section, select desired options

To Adjust the Brightness and Contrast of a Picture

In Word, you can adjust the brightness, or lightness, of a picture and also the **contrast**, or the difference between the lightest and darkest areas of the picture. The following steps increase the brightness of the flying eagle picture by 20% and decrease contrast by 20%. **Why?** You want to lighten the picture slightly and, at the same time, decrease the difference between the light and dark areas of the picture.

1

- If necessary, display the Picture Format tab.
- With the picture still selected (shown in Figure 3–20), click the Corrections button (Picture Format tab | Adjust group) to display the Corrections gallery.
- Point to 'Brightness: +20% Contrast: -20%' (fourth image in second row in the Brightness/Contrast area) in the Corrections gallery, which would display a Live Preview of that correction applied to the picture in the document if the picture was not hidden by the Corrections gallery (Figure 3–21).

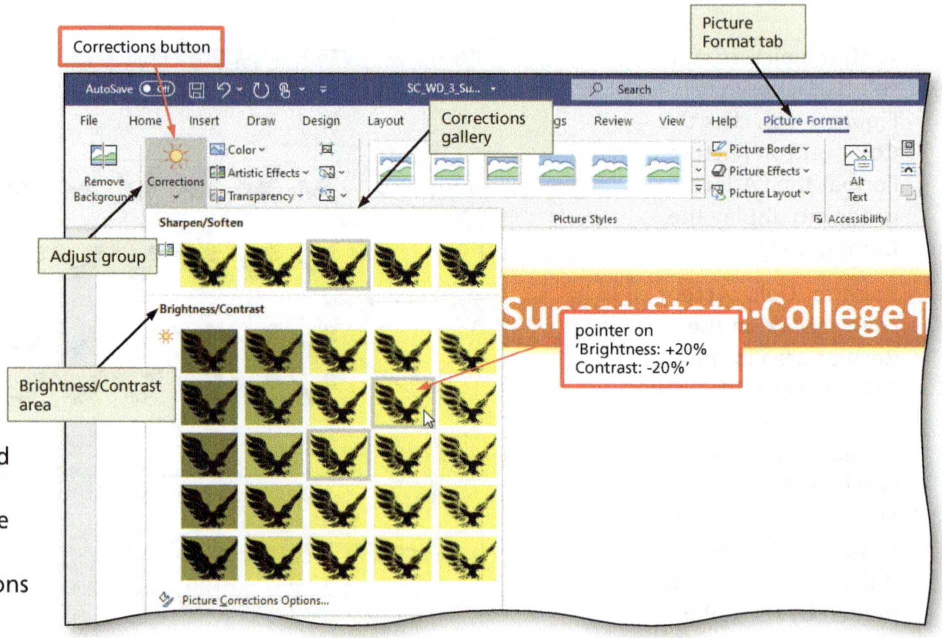

Figure 3–21

2

- Click 'Brightness: +20% Contrast: -20%' in the Corrections gallery to change the brightness and contrast of the selected picture (shown in Figure 3–22).

Other Ways

1. Click Picture Styles Dialog Box Launcher (Picture Format tab | Picture Styles group), click Picture button (Format Picture pane), expand Picture Corrections section, select desired options
2. Right-click picture (or, if using touch, tap 'Show Context Menu' button on Mini toolbar), click Format Picture on shortcut menu (or, if using touch, tap Format Object on shortcut menu), click Picture button (Format Picture pane), expand Picture Corrections section, select desired options

To Add a Picture Border

The flying eagle picture currently has no border (outline). The following steps add a border to the picture. **Why?** You would like the picture to have a gold border so that it matches the rectangle shape outline.

1

- Click the Picture Border arrow (Picture Format tab | Picture Styles group) to display the Picture Border gallery.

Q&A

What if I click the Picture Border button by mistake?
Click the Picture Border arrow and proceed with Step 2.

- Point to 'Gold, Accent 4' (eighth theme color in first row) in the Picture Border gallery to display a Live Preview of that border color around the picture (Figure 3–22).

Experiment

- Point to various colors in the Picture Border gallery and watch the border color on the picture change in the document window.

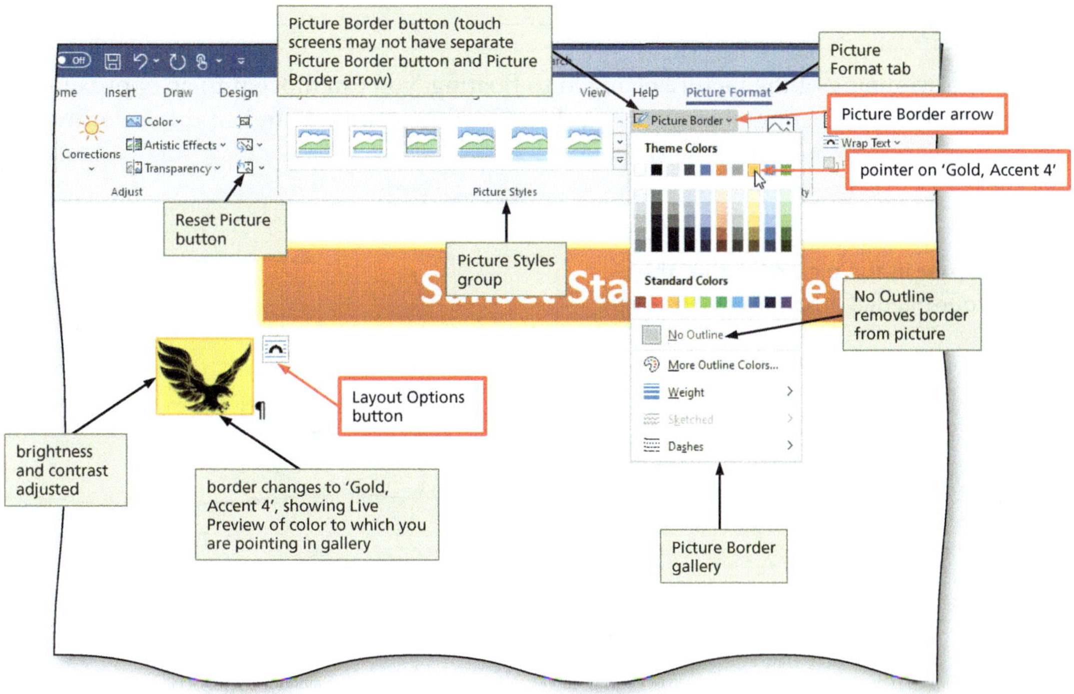

Figure 3–22

2

- Click 'Gold, Accent 4' in the Picture Border gallery to change the picture border color.

Q&A

How would I remove a border from a picture?
With the picture selected, you would click No Outline in the Picture Border gallery.

Can I remove all formatting applied to a picture and start over?
Yes. With the picture selected, you would click the Reset Picture button (Picture Format tab | Adjust group).

To Change an Object's Text Wrapping

The flying eagle picture is to be positioned to the left of the shape. By default, when you insert a picture, it is formatted as an inline graphic. Inline graphics cannot be moved to a precise location on a page. Recall that inline graphics are part of a paragraph and, thus, can be positioned according to paragraph formatting, such as centered or left-aligned. To move the picture to the left of the shape, you format it as a floating object with In Front of Text wrapping. The following steps change a picture's text wrapping.

1. If necessary, click the picture to select it.
2. Click the Layout Options button attached to the picture (shown in Figure 3–22) to display the Layout Options gallery.
3. Click 'In Front of Text' in the Layout Options gallery (shown in Figure 3–7) so that you can position the object on top of any item in the document, in this case, on top of the rectangular shape.
4. Click the Close button to close the Layout Options gallery.

To Move an Object

With the text wrapping of the picture changed to floating, you can move it to an approximate position. The following steps move a floating object, specifically a floating picture. **Why?** In this letterhead, the first flying eagle picture is positioned to the left of the shape.

1

- Position the pointer in the picture so that the pointer has a four-headed arrow attached to it (Figure 3–23).

Figure 3–23

2

- Drag the picture to the left of the shape, as shown in Figure 3–24.

Q&A **What if I moved the picture to the wrong location?** Repeat these steps. You can drag a floating picture to any location in a document.

Why do green lines appear on my screen as I drag a picture? You have alignment guides set, which help you line up objects. To set alignment guides, click the Align button (Picture Format tab | Arrange group) and then click 'Use Alignment Guides'.

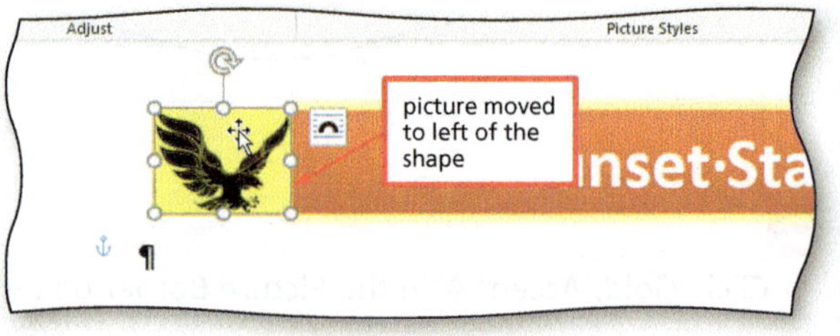

Figure 3–24

To Copy an Object

In this project, the same flying eagle picture is to be placed to the right of the shape. Instead of performing the same steps to insert and format a second identical flying eagle picture, you can copy the picture to the Office Clipboard, paste it from the Office Clipboard, and then move it to the desired location.

You use the same steps to copy a picture as to copy text. The following steps copy a picture.

1. If necessary, click the picture to select it.
2. Display the Home tab and then click the Copy button, shown in Figure 3–25 (Home tab | Clipboard group), or press CTRL+C to copy the selected item to the Office Clipboard.

To Use Paste Options to Paste an Object

The following steps paste a picture using the Paste Options gallery. **Why?** You can specify the format of a pasted item using Paste Options.

1

- If necessary, display the Home tab.
- Click the Paste arrow (Home tab | Clipboard group) to display the Paste gallery.

Q&A **What if I accidentally click the Paste button?**
Click the Paste Options button below the picture pasted in the document to display a Paste Options gallery.

- Point to the 'Keep Source Formatting' button in the Paste gallery to display a Live Preview of that paste option (Figure 3–25).

Experiment

- Point to the two buttons in the Paste gallery and watch the appearance of the pasted picture change.

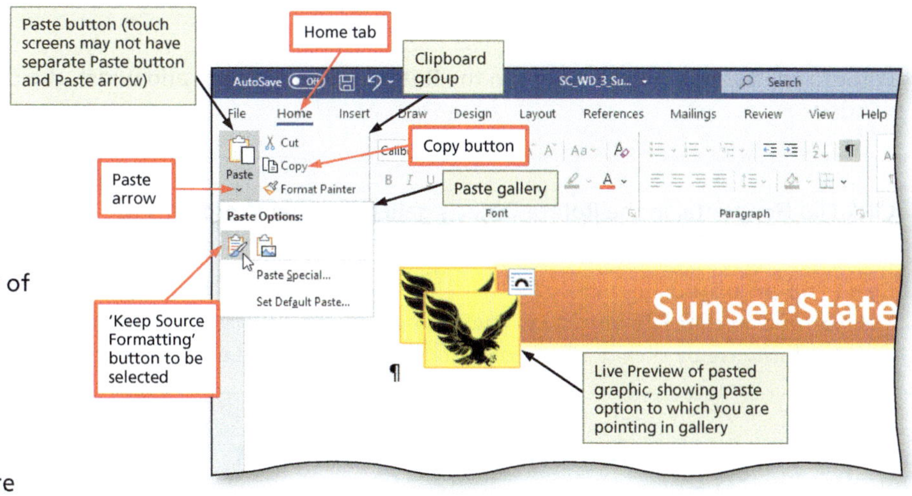

Figure 3–25

Q&A **What do the buttons in the Paste gallery mean?**
The 'Keep Source Formatting' button indicates the pasted object should have the same formats as it did in its original location. The Picture button removes some formatting from the object.

Why are these paste buttons different from when you paste text?
The buttons that appear in the Paste gallery differ depending on the item you are pasting. Use Live Preview to see how the pasted object will look in the document.

2

- Click the 'Keep Source Formatting' button in the Paste gallery to paste the picture using the same formatting as the original.

To Move an Object

The next step is to move the second flying eagle picture so that it is positioned to the right of the rectangle shape. The following steps move an object.

1 If you are using a mouse, position the pointer in the picture so that the pointer has a four-headed arrow attached to it.

2 Drag the picture to the location shown in Figure 3–26.

To Flip an Object

The following steps flip a selected object horizontally. **Why?** In this letterhead, you want the flying eagle pictures to face each other.

1

- If necessary, display the Picture Format tab.
- With the picture still selected, click the Rotate Objects button (Picture Format tab | Arrange group) to display the Rotate Objects gallery (Figure 3–26).

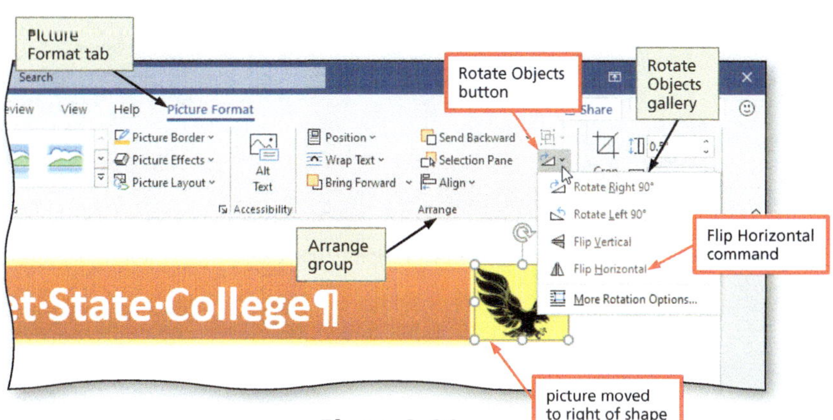

Figure 3–26

Experiment

- Point to the various rotate options in the Rotate Objects gallery and watch the picture rotate in the document window.

2

- Click Flip Horizontal in the Rotate Objects gallery, so that Word flips the picture to display its mirror image (shown in Figure 3–27).

Q&A

Can I flip an object vertically?
Yes, you would click Flip Vertical in the Rotate Objects gallery. You also can rotate an object clockwise or counterclockwise by clicking 'Rotate Right 90°' and 'Rotate Left 90°', respectively, in the Rotate Objects gallery.

BTW

Grouping Objects
You can group objects together if you want to move or format them together as a group. To group multiple objects, you select the first object and then SHIFT+click each additional object until all objects are selected. Then click the Group button (Shape Format tab | Arrange group) and click Group on the Group menu to group the selected objects into a single selected object.

To Format and Enter Text

The contact information for the letterhead in this project is located on the line below the shape containing the name. The following steps enter the mailing address in the letterhead.

1. Position the insertion point on the line below the shape containing the name.
2. If necessary, display the Home tab. Click the Center button (Home tab | Paragraph group) or press CTRL+E to center the paragraph.
3. Type **`Office of Admissions, 1001 Canton Street, MC 3300, Novato, CA 94945`** and then press SPACEBAR (shown in Figure 3–27).

To Insert a Symbol from the Symbol Gallery

Word provides a method of inserting dots and other symbols, such as letters in the Greek alphabet and mathematical characters, that are not on the keyboard. In the letterhead, a dot symbol separates the phone number from the email address. The following steps use the Symbol gallery to insert a dot symbol in the letterhead. **Why?** You want a visual separator between the mailing address and the phone number.

1

- Display the Insert tab.

2

- Click the Symbol button (Insert tab | Symbols group) to display the Symbol gallery (Figure 3–27).

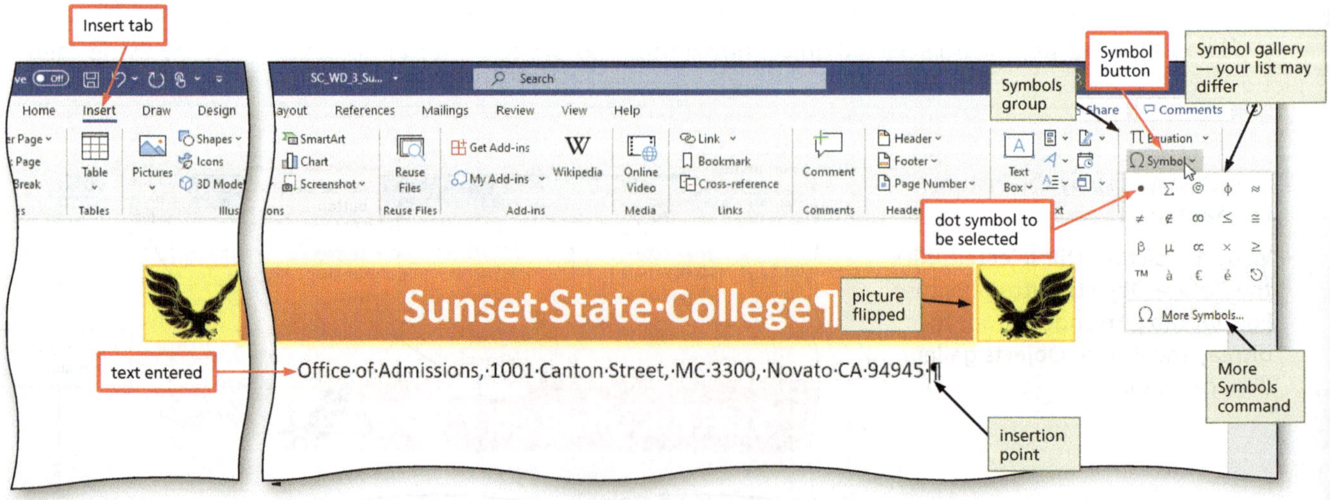

Figure 3–27

3

- Click the dot symbol in the Symbol gallery to insert the symbol at the location of the insertion point (shown in Figure 3–28).

Q&A **What if the dot symbol is not in the Symbol gallery?**
Click the More Symbols command in the Symbol gallery to display the Symbol dialog box, scroll through the symbols in the dialog box to locate the desired symbol, click the desired symbol to select it, and then click the Insert button in the dialog box to insert the symbol in the document.

To Enter Text

The following steps finish the text in the letterhead.

1. Press SPACEBAR. Type **`415-555-0199`** and then press SPACEBAR.
2. Click the Symbol button (Insert tab | Symbols group) to display the Symbol gallery and then click the dot symbol to insert another dot symbol in the letterhead at the location of the insertion point.
3. Press SPACEBAR and then type **`sunset.edu`** to finish the text in the letterhead (Figure 3–28).

Figure 3–28

BTW
Inserting Special Characters
In addition to symbols, you can insert a variety of special characters, including dashes, hyphens, spaces, apostrophes, and quotation marks. Click More Symbols in the Symbol gallery (shown in Figure 3–27), click the Special Characters tab in the Symbol dialog box, click the desired character in the Character list, click the Insert button, and then click the Close button (Symbol dialog box).

To Add a Paragraph Border

In Word, you can draw a solid line, called a **border**, at any edge of a paragraph. That is, borders may be added above or below a paragraph, to the left or right of a paragraph, or in any combination of these sides.

The letterhead in this project has a border that extends from the left margin to the right margin immediately below the mailing address, phone, and web address information. **Why?** The horizontal line separates the letterhead from the rest of the letter. The following steps add a border to the bottom of a paragraph.

1

- Display the Home tab.
- With the insertion point in the paragraph to border, click the Borders arrow (Home tab | Paragraph group) to display the Borders gallery (Figure 3–29).

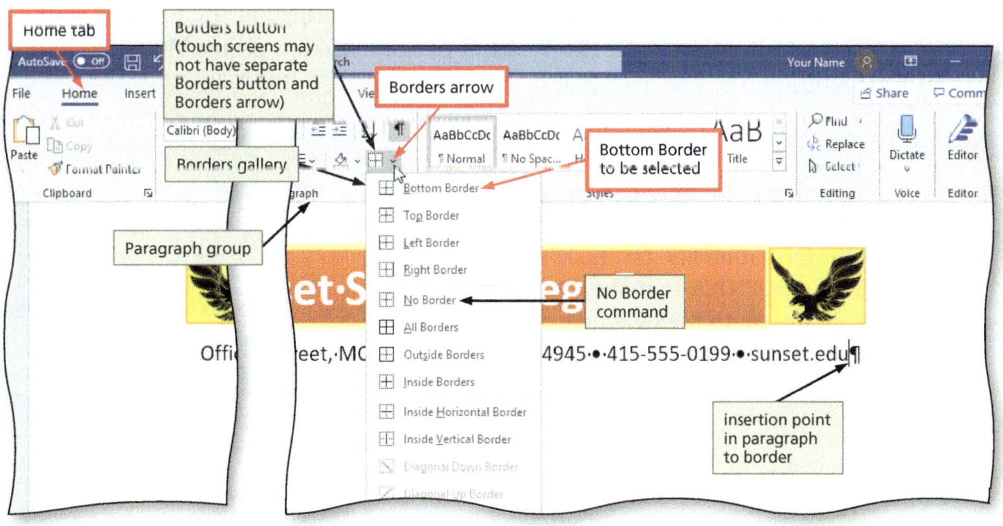

Figure 3–29

2

- Click Bottom Border in the Borders gallery to place a border below the paragraph containing the insertion point (Figure 3–30).

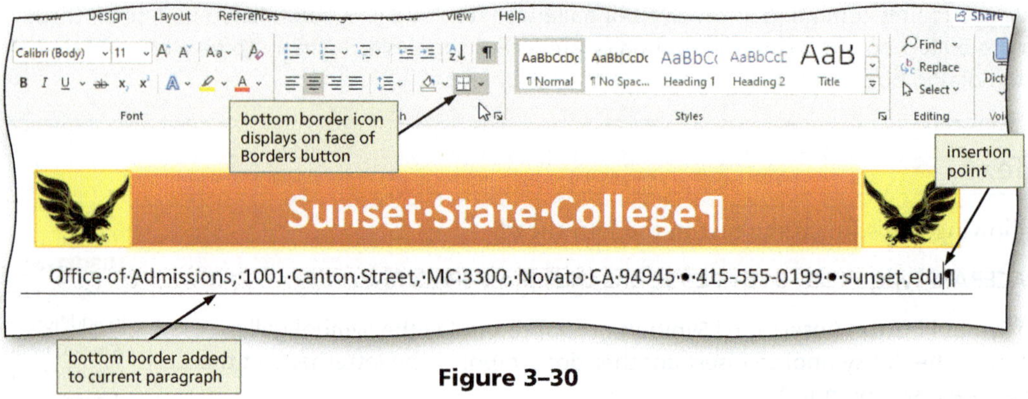

Figure 3–30

Q&A

If the face of the Borders button displays the border icon I want to use, can I click the Borders button instead of using the Borders arrow?
Yes.

How would I remove an existing border from a paragraph?
If, for some reason, you wanted to remove a border from a paragraph, you would position the insertion point in the paragraph, click the Borders arrow (Home tab | Paragraph group), and then click No Border in the Borders gallery.

Other Ways

1. Click Page Borders button (Design tab | Page Background group), click Borders tab (Borders and Shading dialog box), select desired border options, click OK

To Clear Formatting

The next step is to position the insertion point below the letterhead, so that you can type the contents of the letter. When you press ENTER at the end of a paragraph containing a border, Word moves the border forward to the next paragraph. The paragraph also retains all current settings, such as the center format. Instead, you want the paragraph and characters on the new line to use the Normal style: black font with no border.

Word uses the term, **clear formatting**, to refer to returning the formats to the Normal style. The following steps clear formatting at the location of the insertion point. **Why?** You do not want to retain the current formatting in the new paragraph.

1

- With the insertion point between the web address and paragraph mark at the end of the contact information line (as shown in Figure 3–30), press ENTER to move the insertion point and paragraph to the next line (Figure 3–31).

Figure 3–31

2

- Click the 'Clear All Formatting' button (Home tab | Font group) to apply the Normal style to the location of the insertion point (Figure 3–32).

3

- Save the letterhead again on the same storage location with the same file name.

Q&A **Why should I save the letterhead at this time?**
You are finished editing the letterhead.

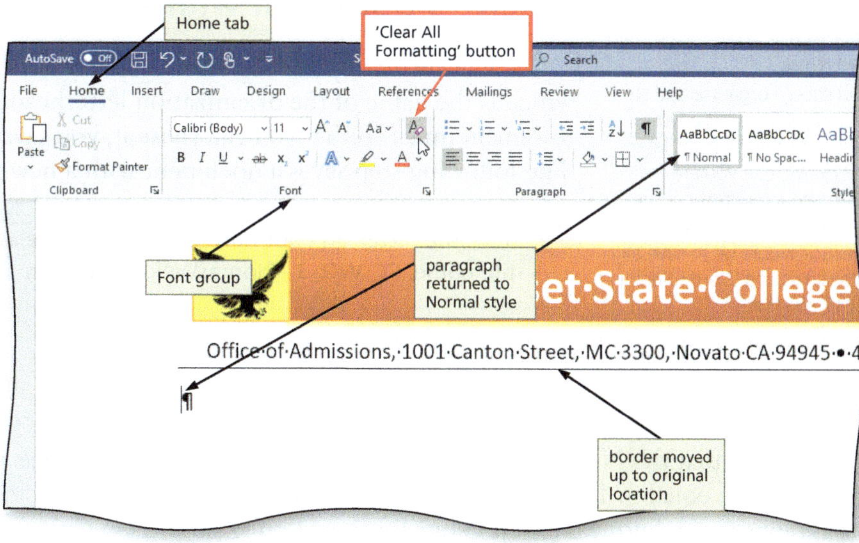

Figure 3–32

Other Ways

1. Click More button in Styles gallery (Home tab | Styles group), click Clear Formatting
2. Click Styles Dialog Box Launcher (Home tab | Styles group), click Clear All in Styles pane
3. Select text, press CTRL+SPACEBAR, press CTRL+Q

Break Point: If you want to take a break, this is a good place to do so. You can exit Word now. To resume later, start Word, open the file called SC_WD_3_SunsetStateLetterhead.docx, and continue following the steps from this location forward.

Creating a Business Letter

With the letterhead for the business letter complete, the next task is to create the remainder of the content in the letter. The following sections use Word to create a business letter that contains a table and a bulleted list.

Consider This

What should you consider when writing a business letter?

A finished business letter should look like a symmetrically framed picture with evenly spaced margins, all balanced below an attractive letterhead. The letter should be well written, properly formatted, logically organized, and use visuals where appropriate. The content of a letter should contain proper grammar, correct spelling, logically constructed sentences, flowing paragraphs, and sound ideas.

Be sure to include all essential elements, use proper spacing and formats, and determine which letter style to use.

- **Include all essential letter elements.** All business letters contain the same basic elements, including the date line, inside address, message, and signature block (shown in Figure 3–1 at the beginning of this module). If a business letter does not use a letterhead, then the top of the letter should include return address information in a heading.
- **Use proper spacing and formats for the contents of the letter below the letterhead.** Use a font that is easy to read, in a size between 8 and 12 point. Add emphasis with bold, italic, and lists where appropriate, and use tables to present numeric information. Paragraphs should be single-spaced, with double-spacing between paragraphs.
- **Determine which letter style to use.** You can follow many different styles when creating business letters. A letter style specifies guidelines for the alignment and spacing of elements in the business letter.

If possible, keep the length of a business letter to one page. Be sure to proofread the finished letter carefully.

BTW
Organizing Files and Folders
You should organize and store files in folders so that you easily can find the files later. For example, if you are taking an introductory technology class called CIS 101, a good practice would be to save all Word files in a Word folder in a CIS 101 folder.

To Save a Document with a New File Name

The current open file has the name SC_WD_3_SunsetStateLetterhead.docx, which is the name of the organization letterhead. Because you want the letterhead file to remain intact so that you can reuse it, you save the document with a new file name. The following step saves a document with a new file name.

1 Save the letter on your hard drive, OneDrive, or other storage location using a new file name, SC_WD_3_ThomasWelcomeLetter.

To Apply a Style

Recall that the Normal style in Word places 8 points of blank space after each paragraph and inserts a vertical space equal to 1.08 lines between each line of text. You will need to modify the spacing used for the paragraphs in the business letter. **Why?** Business letters should use single spacing for paragraphs and double spacing between paragraphs.

Word has many built-in, or predefined, styles that you can use to format text. The No Spacing style, for example, defines line spacing as single and does not insert any additional blank space between lines when you press ENTER. To apply a style to a paragraph, you first position the insertion point in the paragraph. The following step applies the No Spacing style to a paragraph.

1
- With the insertion point positioned in the paragraph to be formatted, click No Spacing in the Styles gallery (Home tab | Styles group) to apply the selected style to the current paragraph (Figure 3–33).

Q&A **Will this style be used in the rest of the document?**
Yes. The paragraph formatting, which includes the style, will carry forward to subsequent paragraphs each time you press ENTER.

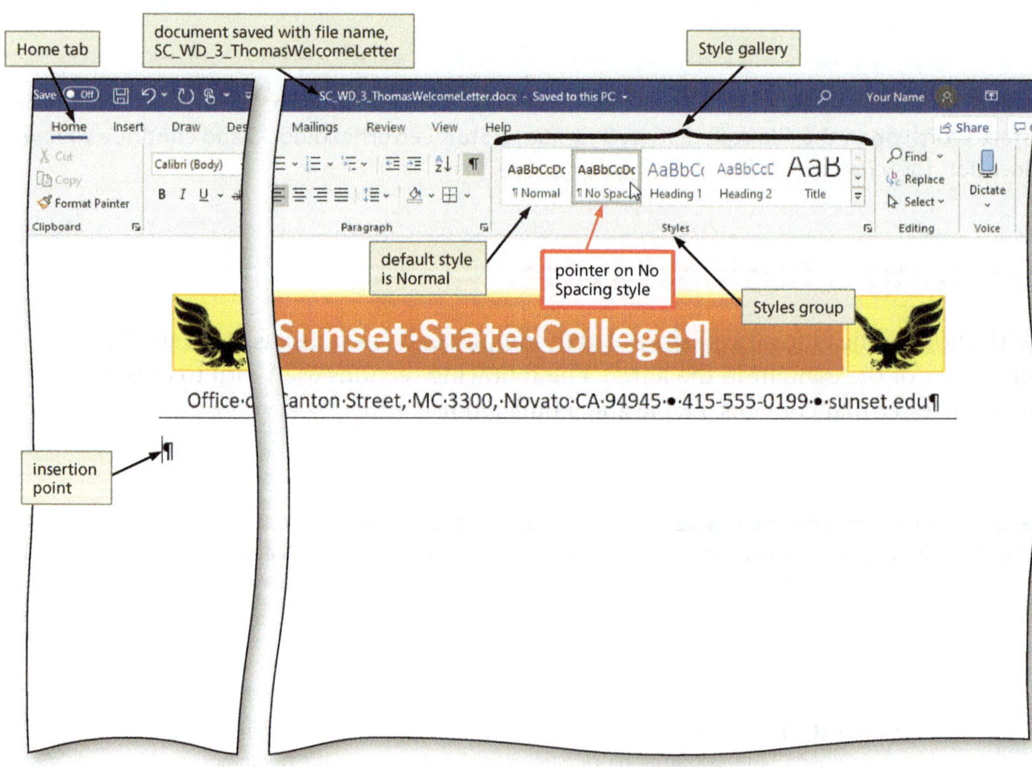

Figure 3–33

Other Ways

1. Click Styles Dialog Box Launcher (Home tab | Styles group), click desired style in Styles pane
2. Press CTRL+SHIFT+S, click Style Name arrow in Apply Styles pane, click desired style in list

Consider This

What elements should a business letter contain?

Be sure to include all essential business letter elements, properly spaced, in your letter:

- The **date line**, which consists of the month, day, and year, is positioned two to six lines below the letterhead.
- The **inside address**, placed three to eight lines below the date line, usually contains the addressee's courtesy title plus full name, job title, business affiliation, and full geographical address.
- The **salutation**, if present, is the greeting in the letter that begins two lines below the last line of the inside address. If you do not know the recipient's name, avoid using the salutation "To whom it may concern" — it is impersonal. Instead, use the recipient's title in the salutation, e.g., Dear Personnel Director. In a formal business letter, use a colon (:) at the end of the salutation; in a casual business letter or personal letter, use a comma.
- The body of the letter, the **message**, begins two lines below the salutation. Within the message, paragraphs are single-spaced with one blank line between paragraphs.
- Two lines below the last line of the message, the closing line or **complimentary close** is displayed. Capitalize only the first word in a complimentary close.
- Type the **signature block** at least four blank lines below the complimentary close, allowing room for the author to sign his or her name.

Consider This

What are the common styles of business letters?

Three common business letter styles are the block, the modified block, and the modified semi-block. Each style specifies different alignments and indentations.

- In the block letter style, all components of the letter begin flush with the left margin.
- In the modified block letter style, the date, complimentary close, and signature block are positioned approximately one-half inch to the right of center or at the right margin. All other components of the letter begin flush with the left margin.
- In the modified semi-block letter style, the date, complimentary close, and signature block are centered, positioned approximately one-half inch to the right of center or at the right margin. The first line of each paragraph in the body of the letter is indented one-half to one inch from the left margin. All other components of the letter begin flush with the left margin.

The business letter in this project follows the modified block style.

Using Tab Stops to Align Text

A **tab stop** is a location on the horizontal ruler that tells Word where to position the insertion point when you press TAB on the keyboard. Word, by default, places a tab stop at every one-half inch mark on the ruler. You also can set your own custom tab stops. Tab settings are a paragraph format. Thus, each time you press ENTER, any custom tab stops are carried forward to the next paragraph.

To move the insertion point from one tab stop to another, press TAB on the keyboard. When you press TAB, a **tab character** formatting mark appears in the empty space between the tab stops.

When you set a custom tab stop, you specify how the text will align at a tab stop. The tab marker on the ruler reflects the alignment of the characters at the location of the tab stop. Table 3–2 shows types of tab stop alignments in Word and their corresponding tab markers.

BTW

Tabs Dialog Box

You can use the Tabs dialog box to set, change the alignment of, and remove custom tab stops. To display the Tabs dialog box, click the Paragraph Dialog Box Launcher (Home tab or Layout tab | Paragraph group) and then click the Tabs button (Paragraph dialog box). To set a custom tab stop, enter the desired tab position (Tabs dialog box) and then click the Set button. To change the alignment of a custom tab stop, click the tab stop position to be changed, click the new alignment, and then click the Set button. To remove an existing tab stop, click the tab stop position to be removed and then click the Clear button. To remove all tab stops, click the Clear All button in the Tabs dialog box.

Table 3–2 Types of Tab Stop Alignments

Tab Stop Alignment	Tab Marker	Result of Pressing TAB	Example
Left Tab	L	Left-aligns text at the location of the tab stop	toolbar ruler
Center Tab	⊥	Centers text at the location of the tab stop	toolbar ruler
Right Tab	┘	Right-aligns text at the location of the tab stop	toolbar ruler
Decimal Tab	⊥.	Aligns text on decimal point at the location of the tab stop	45.72 223.75
Bar Tab	I	Aligns text at a bar character at the location of the tab stop	| toolbar | ruler

To Display the Ruler

One way to set custom tab stops is by using the horizontal ruler. Thus, the following steps display the ruler in the document window.

1. If the rulers are not showing, display the View tab.
2. Click the Ruler check box (View tab | Show group) to place a check mark in the check box and display the horizontal and vertical rulers on the screen (shown in Figure 3–34).

To Set Custom Tab Stops

The first required element of the business letter is the date line, which in this letter is positioned two lines below the letterhead. The date line contains the month, day, and year, and begins 3½ inches from the left margin. **Why?** Business letter guidelines specify to begin the date line approximately one-half inch to the right of center. Thus, you should set a custom tab stop at the 3.5" mark on the ruler. The following steps set a left-aligned tab stop.

1

- With the insertion point on the paragraph mark below the border (shown in Figure 3–33), press ENTER so that a blank line appears above the insertion point.
- If necessary, click the tab selector at the left edge of the horizontal ruler until it displays the type of tab you wish to use, which is the Left Tab icon in this case.
- Position the pointer on the 3.5" mark on the ruler, which is the location of the desired custom tab stop (Figure 3–34).

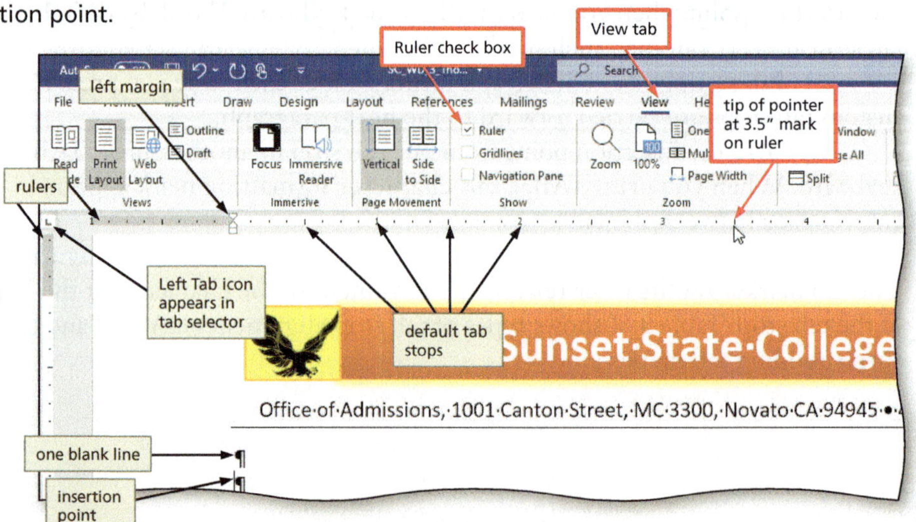

Figure 3–34

Q&A **What is the purpose of the tab selector?**
Before using the ruler to set a tab stop, ensure the correct tab stop icon appears in the tab selector. Each time you click the tab selector, its icon changes. The Left Tab icon is the default. For a list of the types of tab stops, see Table 3–2.

2

- Click the 3.5" mark on the ruler to place a tab marker at that location (Figure 3–35).

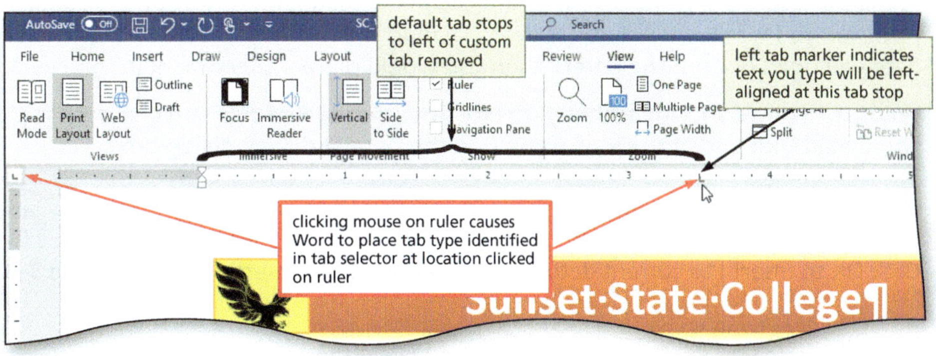

Figure 3–35

Q&A

What if I click the wrong location on the ruler?
You can move a custom tab stop by dragging the tab marker to the desired location on the ruler. Or, you can remove an existing custom tab stop by pointing to the tab marker on the ruler and then dragging the tab marker down and out of the ruler.

What if I am using a touch screen?
Display the Home tab, tap the Paragraph Dialog Box Launcher (Home tab | Paragraph group), tap the Tabs button (Paragraph dialog box), type `3.5` in the Tab stop position box (Tabs dialog box), tap the Set button, and then tap OK to set a custom tab stop and place a corresponding tab marker on the ruler.

Other Ways

1. Click Paragraph Dialog Box Launcher (Home tab or Layout tab | Paragraph group), click Tabs button (Paragraph dialog box), type tab stop position (Tabs dialog box), click Set button, click OK

To Insert the Current Date in a Document

The next step is to enter the current date at the 3.5" tab stop in the document. **Why?** The date in this letter will be positioned according to the guidelines for a modified block style letter. In Word, you can insert a computer's system date in a document. The following steps insert the current date in the letter.

1

- Press TAB to position the insertion point at the location of the tab stop in the current paragraph.
- Display the Insert tab.
- Click the 'Date and Time' button (Insert tab | Text group) to display the Date and Time dialog box.
- Select the desired format (Date and Time dialog box), in this case April 19, 2021.
- If the Update automatically check box is selected, click the check box to remove the check mark (Figure 3–36).

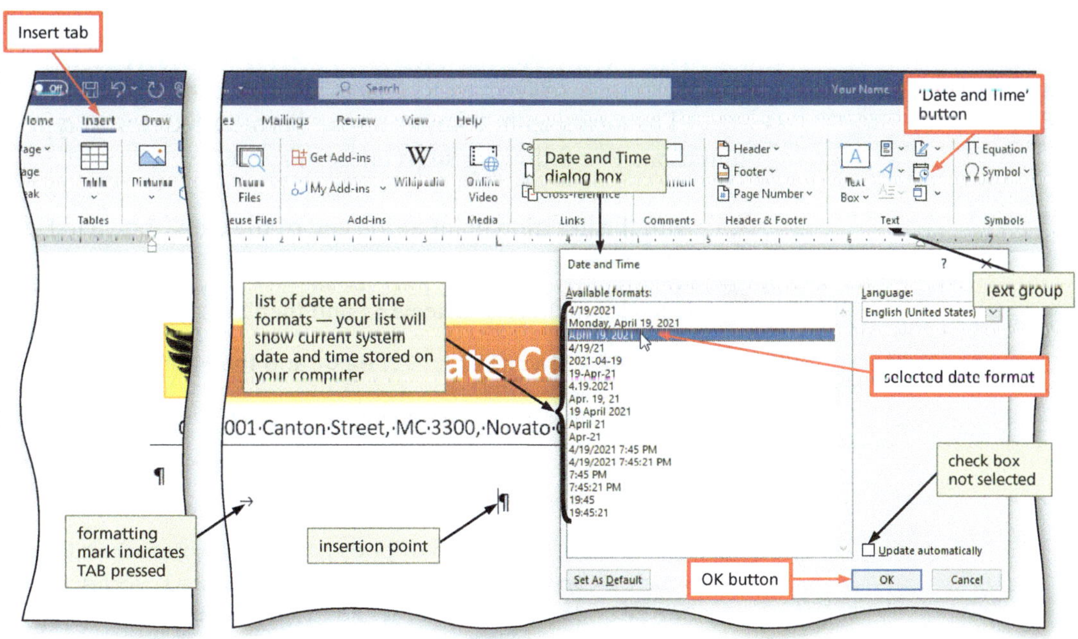

Figure 3–36

Q&A

Why should the Update automatically check box not be selected?
In this project, the date at the top of the letter always should show today's date (for example, April 19, 2021). If, however, you wanted the date always to change to reflect the current computer date (for example, showing the date you open or print the letter), then you would place a check mark in this check box.

What if I wanted to insert the current time instead of the current date?
You would click one of the time formats in the Date and Time dialog box.

2

- Click OK to insert the current date at the location of the insertion point (Figure 3–37).

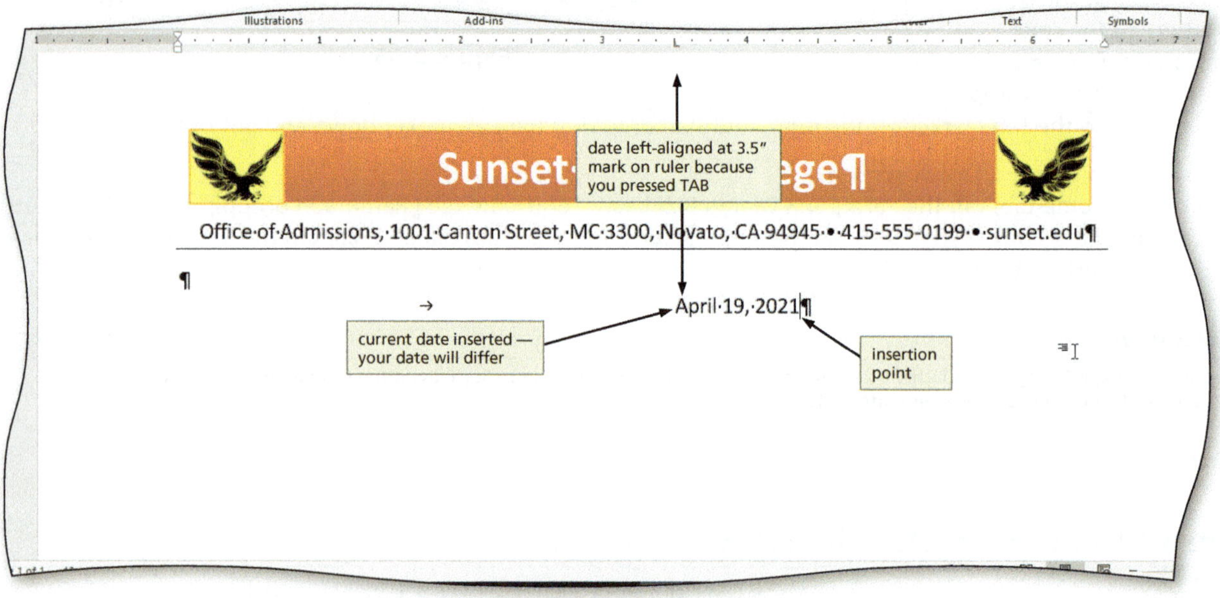

Figure 3–37

To Enter the Inside Address and Salutation

The next step in composing the business letter is to type the inside address and salutation. The following steps enter this text.

1. With the insertion point at the end of the date (shown in Figure 3–37), press ENTER three times.
2. Type `Mr. Caleb Thomas` and then press ENTER.
3. Type `982 Bartlett Street` and then press ENTER.
4. Type `Live Oak, CA 95953` and then press ENTER twice.
5. Type `Dear Caleb,` and then press ENTER twice to complete the inside address and salutation entries.
6. Type the first paragraph of body copy: `Congratulations on your admission to the School of Liberal Arts and Sciences at Sunset State for the fall semester of 2021! On behalf of our students, faculty, and staff, I welcome you to our academic`

`community. Our decision to admit you to our college is an acknowledgement of your potential and our confidence in you as a valuable addition to our student body.`

7. Press ENTER twice.

8. Type **`We would like to inform you of important upcoming dates:`** and then press ENTER twice (Figure 3–38).

Q&A **Why does my document wrap on different words?**
Differences in wordwrap may relate to the printer connected to your computer. Thus, it is possible that the same document could wordwrap differently if associated with a different printer.

9. Save the letter again on the same storage location with the same file name.

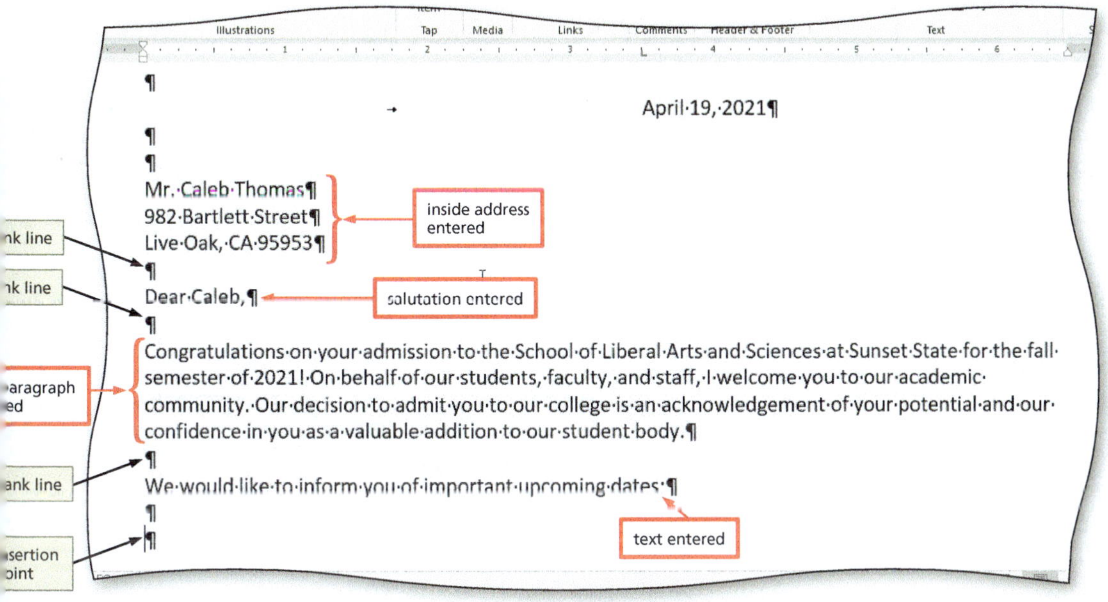

Figure 3–38

Tables

The next step in composing the business letter is to place a table listing the important upcoming dates (shown in Figure 3–1). A Word **table** is a grid of rows and columns that can contain text and graphics. The intersection of a row and a column is called a **cell** (which looks like a box), and cells are filled with data.

The first step in creating a table is to insert an empty table in the document. When inserting a table, you must specify the total number of rows and columns required, which is called the **dimension** of the table. The table in this project has three columns. You often do not know the total number of rows in a table. Thus, many Word users create one row initially and then add more rows as needed. In Word, the first number in a dimension is the number of columns, and the second is the number of rows. For example, in Word, a 3 × 1 (pronounced "three by one") table consists of three columns and one row.

BTW
Word Help
At any time while using Word, you can find answers to questions and display information about various topics through Word Help. Used properly, this form of assistance can increase your productivity and reduce your frustrations by minimizing the time you spend learning how to use Word.

To Insert an Empty Table

The next step is to insert an empty table in the letter. The following steps insert a table with three columns and one row at the location of the insertion point. **Why?** The first column will identify the date(s), the second will identify the event, and the third will identify notes. You will start with one row and add more rows as needed.

1

- Scroll the document so that you will be able to see the table in the document window.
- If necessary, display the Insert tab.
- With the insertion point positioned as shown in Figure 3–39, click the Table button (Insert tab | Tables group) to display the Table gallery (Figure 3–39).

Experiment

- Point to various cells on the grid to see a preview of various table dimensions in the document window.

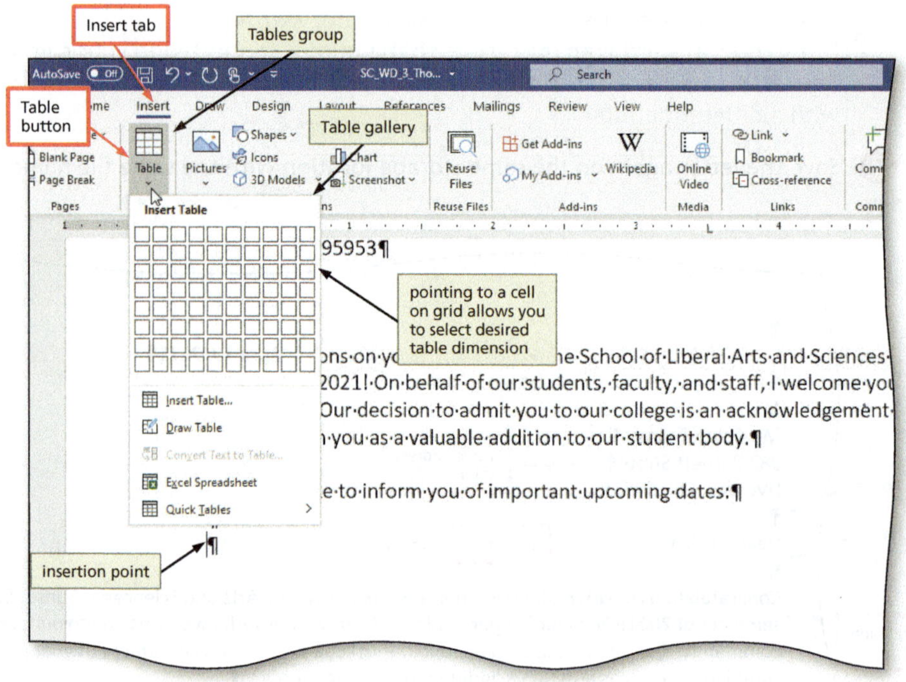

Figure 3–39

2

- Position the pointer on the cell in the first row and third column of the grid to preview the desired table dimension in the document (Figure 3–40).

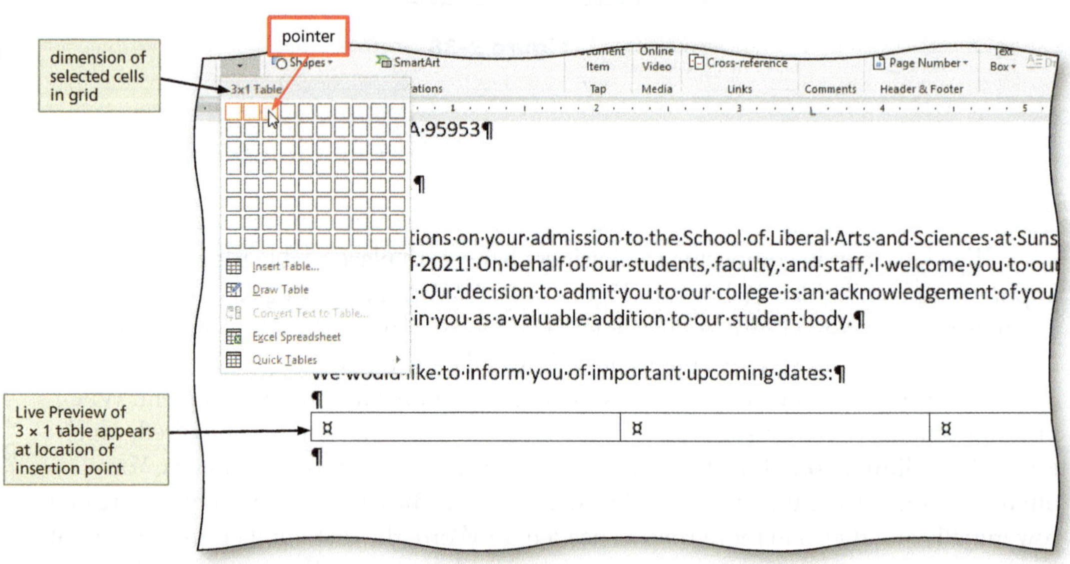

Figure 3–40

3

- Click the cell in the first row and third column of the grid to insert an empty table with one row and three columns in the document.
- If necessary, scroll the document so that the table is visible (Figure 3–41).

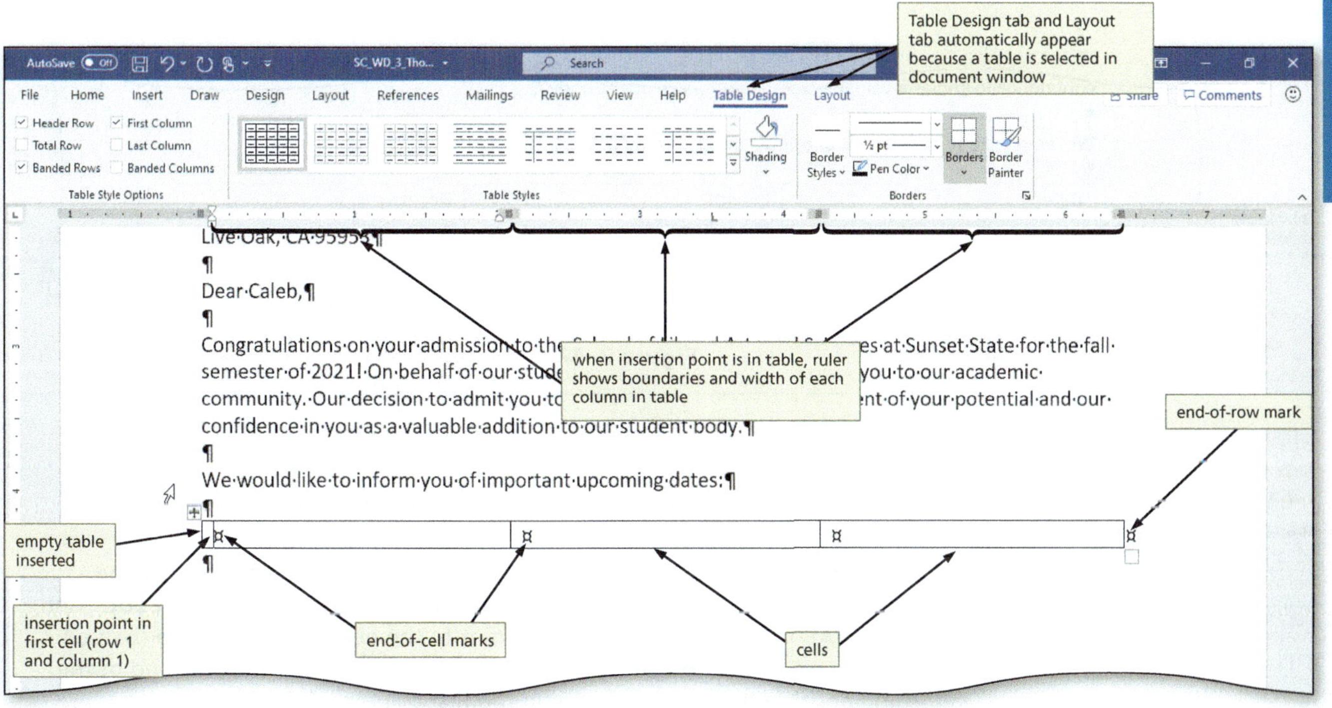

Figure 3–41

Q&A **What are the small circles in the table cells?**
Each table cell has an **end-of-cell mark**, which is a formatting mark that assists you with selecting and formatting cells. Similarly, each row has an **end-of-row mark**, which is a formatting mark that you can use to add columns to the right of a table. Recall that formatting marks do not print on a hard copy. The end-of-cell marks currently are left-aligned, that is, positioned at the left edge of each cell.

Other Ways

1. Click Table button (Insert tab | Tables group), click Insert Table in Table gallery, enter number of columns and rows (Insert Table dialog box), click OK

To Enter Data in a Table

The next step is to enter data in the cells of the empty table. The data you enter in a cell wordwraps just as text wordwraps between the margins of a document. To place data in a cell, you click the cell and then type.

To advance rightward from one cell to the next, press TAB. When you are at the rightmost cell in a row, press TAB to move to the first cell in the next row; do not press ENTER. **Why?** You press ENTER when you want to begin a new paragraph within a cell. One way to add new rows to a table is to press TAB when the insertion point is positioned in the bottom-right corner cell of the table. The following step enters data in the first row of the table and then inserts a blank second row.

1

- With the insertion point in the left cell of the table, type `Date` and then press TAB to advance the insertion point to the next cell.

- Type **`Event`** and then press TAB to advance the insertion point to the next cell.
- Type **`Notes`** and then press TAB to add a second row at the end of the table and position the insertion point in the first column of the new row (Figure 3–42).

Q&A
How do I edit cell contents if I make a mistake?
Click in the cell and then correct the entry.

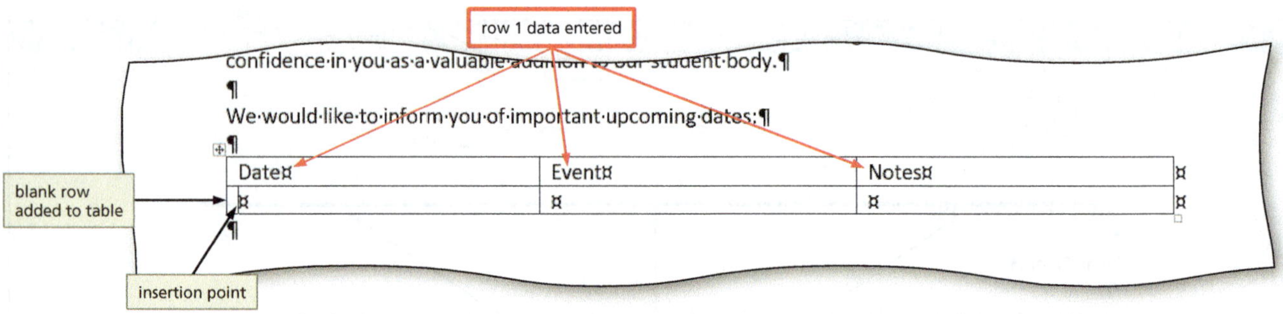

Figure 3–42

BTW
Tab Character in Tables
In a table, pressing TAB advances the insertion point from one cell to the next. To insert a tab character in a cell, you must press CTRL+TAB.

To Enter More Data in a Table

The following steps enter the remaining data in the table.

1 Type **`July 12-16 and July 19-23`** and then press TAB to advance the insertion point to the next cell. Type **`Orientation and registration`** and then press TAB to advance the insertion point to the next cell. Type **`See brief schedule on next page`** and then press TAB to add a row at the end of the table and position the insertion point in the first column of the new row.

2 In the third row, type **`August 16-17`** in the first column, **`Move-in days`** in the second column, and **`Assigned by Housing Services`** in the third column. Press TAB to position the insertion point in the first column of a new row.

3 In the fourth row, type **`August 23`** in the first column, **`Fall term begins`** in the second column, and **`First day of classes`** in the third column (Figure 3–43).

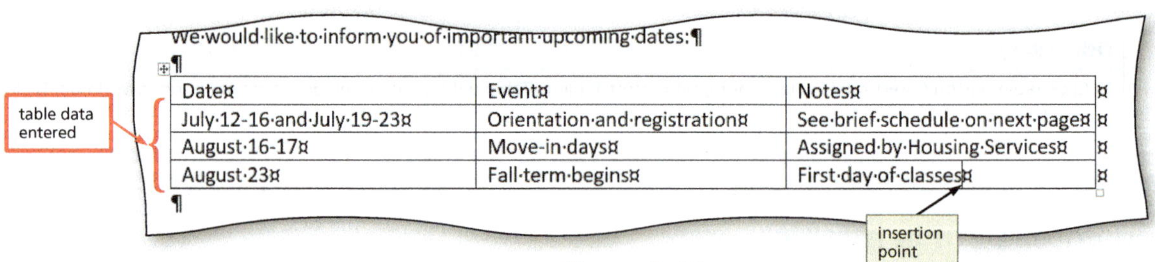

Figure 3–43

To Apply a Table Style

Word provides a gallery of more than 90 table styles, which include a variety of colors and shading. **Why?** Table styles allow you to change the basic table format to a more visually appealing style. The following steps apply a table style to the table in the letter.

1

- If the First Column check box in the Table Style Options group (Table Design tab) contains a check mark, click the check box to remove the check mark because you do not want the first column in the table formatted differently from the rest of the table. Be sure the remaining check marks match those in the Table Style Options group (Table Design tab) (Figure 3–44).

Q&A

What if the Table Design tab no longer is the active tab?
Click in the table and then display the Table Design tab.

What do the options in the Table Style Options group mean?
When you apply table styles, if you want the top row of the table (header row), a row containing totals (total row), first column, or last column to be formatted differently, select those check boxes. If you want the rows or columns to alternate with colors, select Banded Rows or Banded Columns, respectively.

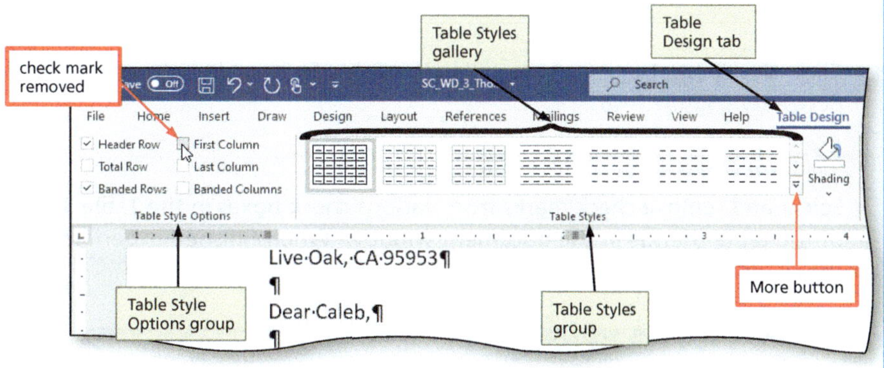

Figure 3–44

2

- With the insertion point in the table, click the More button in the Table Styles gallery (Table Design tab | Table Styles group), shown in Figure 3–44, to expand the gallery.
- Scroll and then point to 'Grid Table 1 Light - Accent 2' in the Table Styles gallery to display a Live Preview of that style applied to the table in the document (Figure 3–45).

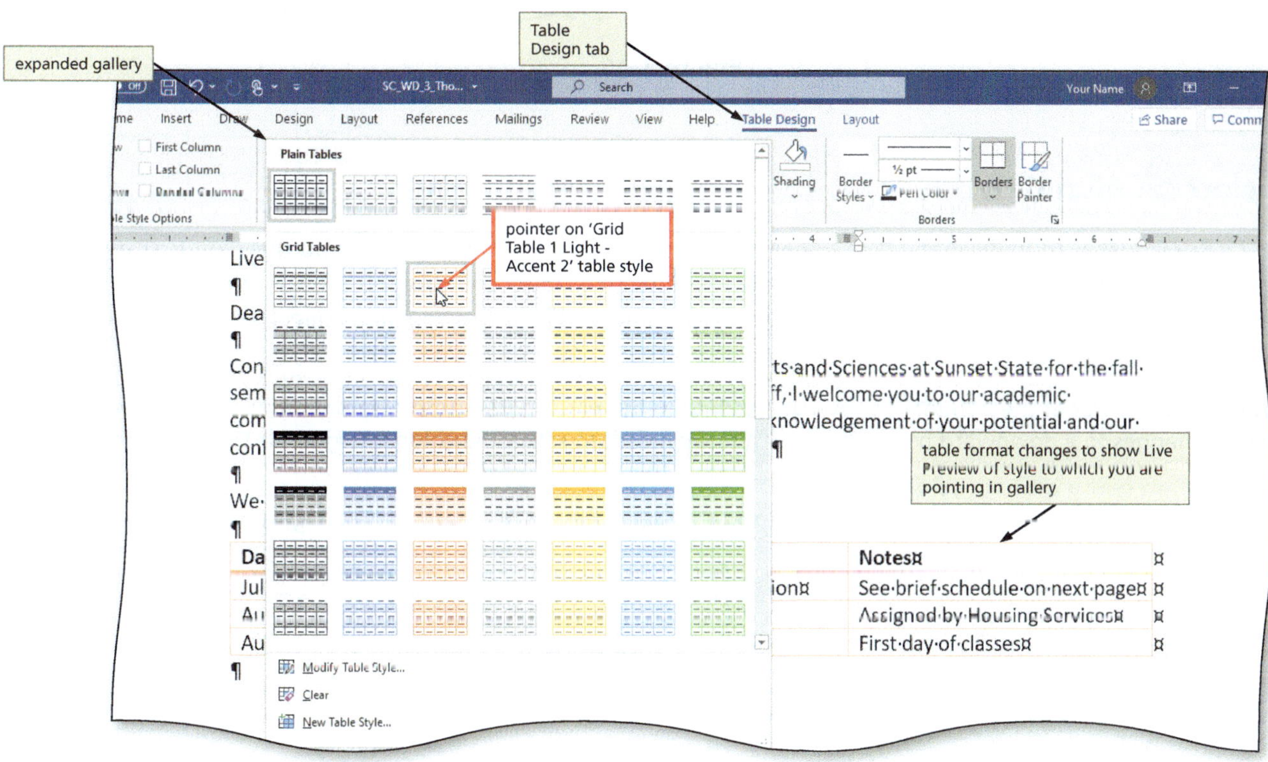

Figure 3–45

Experiment

- Point to various styles in the Table Styles gallery and watch the format of the table change in the document window.

3

- Click 'Grid Table 1 Light - Accent 2' in the Table Styles gallery to apply the selected style to the table. Scroll up, if necessary (Figure 3–46).

Experiment

- Select and remove check marks from various check boxes in the Table Style Options group and watch the format of the table change in the document window. When finished experimenting, be sure the check marks match those shown in Figure 3–46.

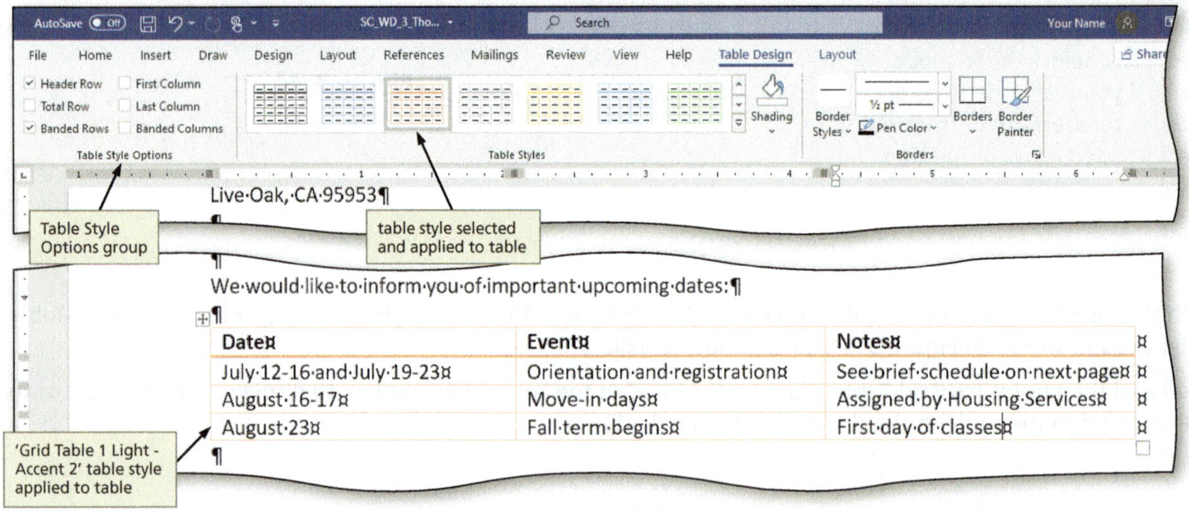

Figure 3–46

To Select a Column

The next task is to italicize the data in cells in the third column of the table. To do this, you first must select the column. **Why?** If you want to format the contents of a single cell, simply position the insertion point in the cell. To format a series of cells, you first must select them. The following steps select a column.

1

- Position the pointer at the boundary above the column to be selected, the third column in this case, so that the pointer changes to a downward pointing arrow and then click to select the column (Figure 3–47).

Q&A **What if I am using a touch screen?**
Position the insertion point in the third column, tap the Select button (Layout tab | Table group), and then tap Select Column on the Select menu.

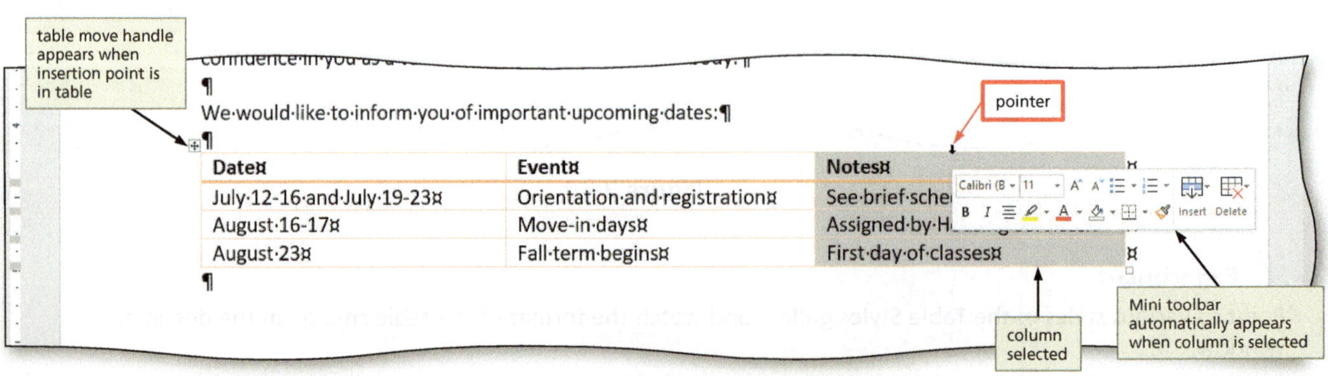

Figure 3–47

2

- Press CTRL+I to italicize the selected text.
- Click anywhere to remove the selection from the table.

Other Ways

1. Click Select button (Layout tab | Table group), click Select Column on Select menu

Selecting Table Contents

When working with tables, you may need to select the contents of cells, rows, columns, or the entire table. Table 3–3 identifies ways to select various items in a table.

Table 3–3 Selecting Items in a Table

Item to Select	Action
Cell	Point to left edge of cell and then click when the pointer changes to a small solid upward angled pointing arrow. Or Position insertion point in cell, click Select button (Layout tab | Table group), and then click Select Cell on the Select menu.
Column	Point to border at top of column and then click when the pointer changes to a small solid downward-pointing arrow. Or Position insertion point in column, click Select button (Layout tab | Table group), and then click Select Column on the Select menu.
Row	Point to the left of the row and then click when pointer changes to a right-pointing block arrow. Or Position insertion point in row, click Select button (Layout tab | Table group), and then click Select Row on the Select menu.
Multiple cells, rows, or columns adjacent to one another	Drag through cells, rows, or columns.
Multiple cells, rows, or columns not adjacent to one another	Select first cell, row, or column (as described above) and then hold down CTRL while selecting next cell, row, or column.
Next cell	Press TAB.
Previous cell	Press SHIFT+TAB.
Table	Point somewhere in table and then click table move handle that appears in upper-left corner of table (shown in Figure 3–47). Or Position insertion point in table, click Select button (Layout tab | Table group), and then click Select Table on the Select menu.

BTW

Moving Tables

If you wanted to move a table to a new location, you would point to the upper-left corner of the table until the table move handle appears (shown in Figure 3–47), point to the table move handle, and then drag it to move the entire table to a new location.

BTW

Tables

For simple tables, such as the one just created, Word users often select the table dimension in the Table gallery to create the table. For a more complex table, such as one with a varying number of columns per row, Word has a Draw Table feature that allows users to draw a table in the document using a pencil pointer. To use this feature, click the Table button (Insert tab | Tables group) and then click Draw Table on the Table menu.

To Insert a Row in a Table

The next step is to insert a row in the table. **Why?** You want to add a row about welcome week. As discussed earlier, you can insert a row at the end of a table by positioning the insertion point in the bottom-right corner cell and then pressing TAB. You cannot use TAB to insert a row at the beginning or middle of a table. Instead, you use the Insert Above or Insert Below command (Layout tab | Rows & Columns group) or the Insert Control. The **Insert Control**, which allows you to insert rows or columns in a table, is a circle containing a plus sign that appears when you use a mouse to point immediately above or to the left of columns or rows in a table. The following steps insert a row in the middle of a table.

1

- Position the pointer to the left of the table between the rows where you want the row to be inserted to display the Insert Control (Figure 3–48).

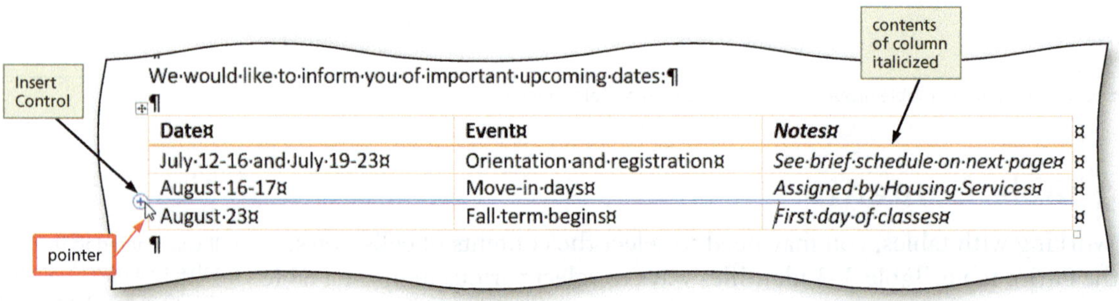

Figure 3–48

2

- Click the Insert Control to insert a row at the location of the pointer and then select the newly inserted row (Figure 3–49).

Experiment

- Click the Layout tab to see the options available on this tab (shown in Figure 3–49).

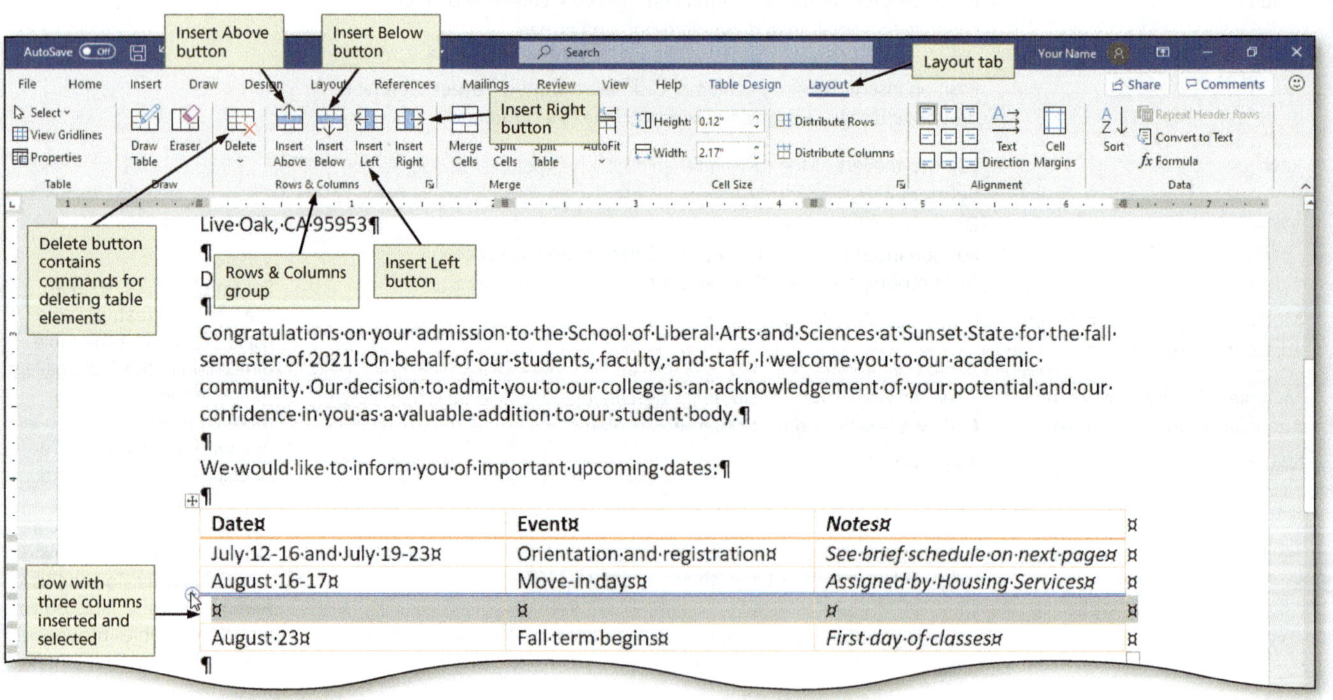

Figure 3–49

3

- Type **`August 16-20`** and then press TAB.
- Type **`Welcome week`** and then press TAB.
- Type **`Get schedule during orientation`** (Figure 3–50).

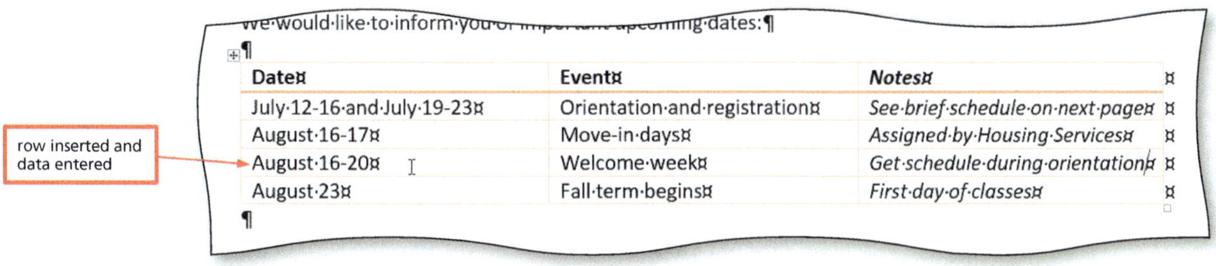

Figure 3–50

Other Ways

1. Click Insert Above or Insert Below button (Layout tab | Rows & Columns group)
2. Right-click row, point to Insert on shortcut menu (or, if using touch, tap Insert button on Mini toolbar), click desired option on Insert submenu

To Insert a Column in a Table

If you wanted to insert a column in a table, instead of inserting rows, you would perform the following steps.

1. Point above the table and then click the desired Insert Control.

or

1. Position the insertion point in the column to the left or right of where you want to insert the column.
2. Click the Insert Left button (Layout tab | Rows & Columns group) to insert a column to the left of the current column, or click the Insert Right button (Layout tab | Rows & Columns group) to insert a column to the right of the current column.

or

1. Right-click the table, point to Insert on the shortcut menu (or, if using touch, tap Insert button on the Mini toolbar), and then click Insert Left or Insert Right on the Insert submenu (or, if using touch, tap Insert Left or Insert Right).

BTW

Resizing Table Columns and Rows

To change the width of a column or height of a row to an exact measurement, hold down ALT while dragging markers on the ruler. Or, enter values in the Width or Height boxes (Layout tab | Cell Size group).

Deleting Table Data

If you want to delete row(s) or delete column(s) from a table, position the insertion point in the row(s) or column(s) to delete, click the Delete button (Layout tab | Rows & Columns group) (shown in Figure 3–49), and then click Delete Rows or Delete Columns on the Delete menu. Or, select the row or column to delete, right-click the selection, and then click Delete Rows or Delete Columns on the Mini toolbar or shortcut menu.

To delete the contents of a cell, select the cell contents and then press DELETE or BACKSPACE. You also can drag and drop or cut and paste the contents of cells. To delete an entire table, select the table, click the Delete button (Layout tab | Rows & Columns group), and then click Delete Table on the Delete menu. To delete the contents of a table and leave an empty table, you would select the table and then press DELETE.

BTW

Aligning Tables

To align an entire table, such as centering it between the margins on the page, select the table and then press CTRL+E or click the Center button (Home tab | Paragraph group). To align contents of cells, select the cells and then click the desired alignment button in the Alignment group on the Layout tab.

To Add More Text

The table now is complete. The next step is to enter text below the table. The following steps enter text.

1. Scroll up, if necessary, to see the space below the table on the letter.
2. Position the insertion point on the paragraph mark below the table and then press ENTER.
3. Type `Before orientation, you must do the following through our campus website:` and then press ENTER (shown in Figure 3–51).

To Bullet a List as You Type

If you know before you type that a list should be bulleted, you can use Word's AutoFormat As You Type feature to bullet the paragraphs as you type them instead of formatting the paragraphs with bullets after you enter them. **Why?** The AutoFormat As You Type feature saves you time because it applies formats automatically. The following steps add bullets to a list as you type.

1

- Press the ASTERISK key (*) as the first character on the line (Figure 3–51).

2

- Press SPACEBAR to convert the asterisk to a bullet character.

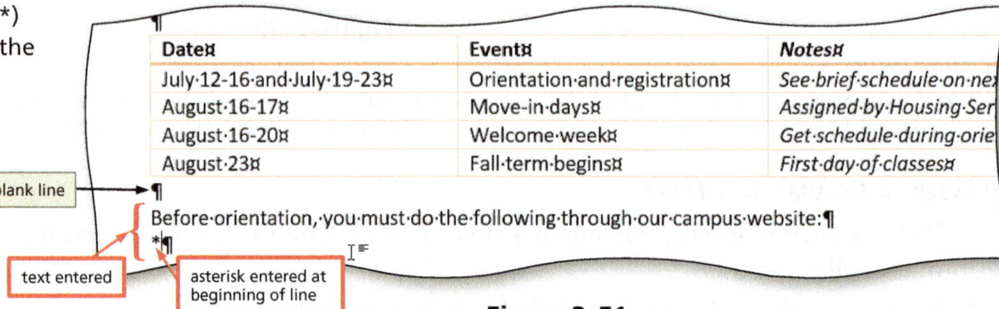

Figure 3–51

Q&A **What if I did not want the asterisk converted to a bullet character?**
You could undo the AutoFormat by clicking the Undo button; pressing CTRL+Z; clicking the AutoCorrect Options button that appears to the left of the bullet character as soon as you press SPACEBAR and then clicking 'Undo Automatic Bullets' on the AutoCorrect Options menu; or clicking the Bullets button (Home tab | Paragraph group).

3

- Type `Complete a housing contract or housing exemption form` as the first bulleted item.
- Press ENTER to place another bullet character at the beginning of the next line (Figure 3–52).

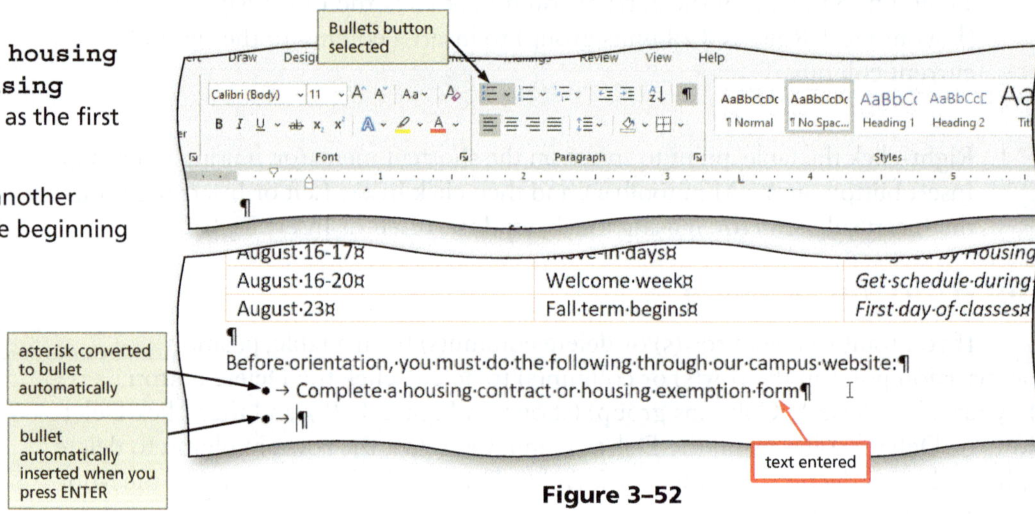

Figure 3–52

4

- Type `Schedule your math placement exam` and then press ENTER.
- Type `Reserve your orientation dates` and then press ENTER.
- Press ENTER again to turn off automatic bullets as you type (Figure 3–53).

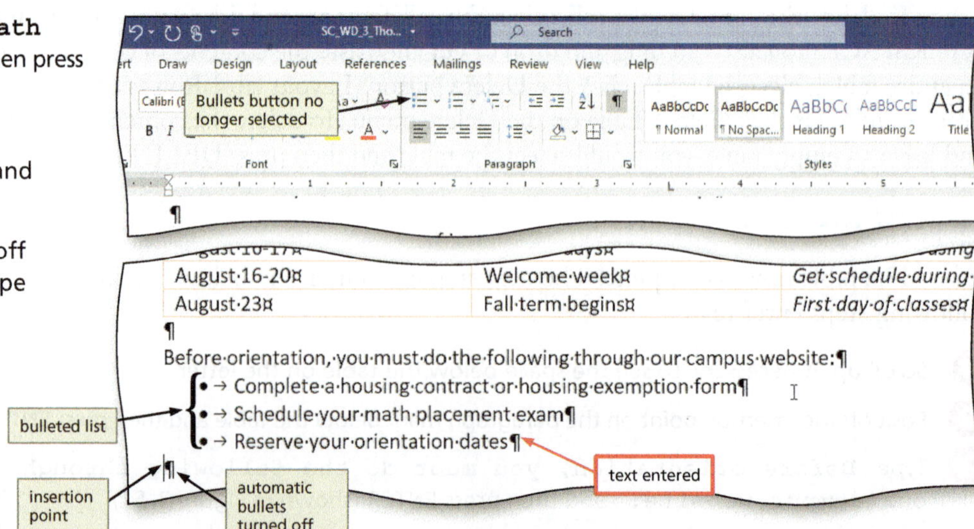

Figure 3–53

Q&A

Why did automatic bullets stop?

When you press ENTER without entering any text after the automatic bullet character, Word turns off the automatic bullets feature.

Other Ways

1. Click Bullets arrow (Home tab | Paragraph group), click desired bullet style
2. Right-click paragraph to be bulleted, click Bullets button on Mini toolbar, click desired bullet style, if necessary

To Enter More Text and then Save the Letter

The following steps enter the remainder of text in the letter.

1. With the insertion point positioned on the paragraph below the bulleted list, press ENTER and then type the sentence: `I am confident you will pursue your passions and accomplish your goals as a Sunset State Flying Eagle!`
2. Press ENTER twice. Press TAB to position the insertion point at the tab stop set at the 3.5" mark on the ruler. Type `Sincerely,` and then press ENTER four times.
3. Press TAB to position the insertion point at the tab stop set at the 3.5" mark on the ruler. Type `Lucy R. Song` and then press ENTER.
4. Press TAB to position the insertion point at the tab stop set at the 3.5" mark on the ruler. Type `Director of Admissions` to finish the letter. Scroll up, if necessary (Figure 3–54).
5. Save the letter again on the same storage location with the same file name.

BTW

Nonbreaking Spaces and Hyphens

If you do not want a compound word, such as a proper noun, date, unit of time and measure, abbreviations, and geographic destinations, to be split, where part of the compound word appears at the end of one line and the other part appears at the beginning of the next line, you can insert a nonbreaking space or a nonbreaking hyphen. To insert a nonbreaking space, you would press CTRL+SHIFT+SPACEBAR instead of SPACEBAR in the middle of the compound word. To insert a nonbreaking hyphen, you would press CTRL+SHIFT+HYPHEN instead of a hyphen in the middle of the compound word.

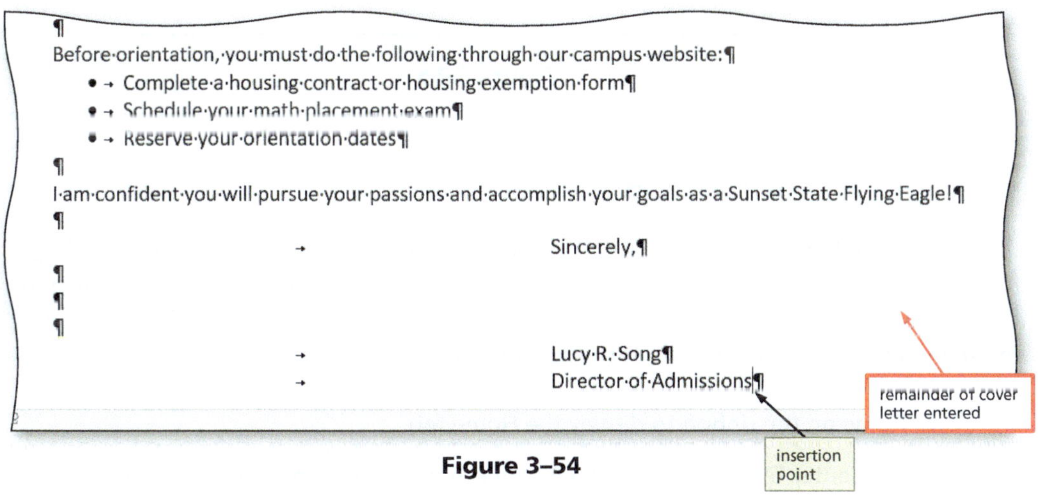

Figure 3–54

Working with SmartArt Graphics

The acceptance letter to the student referenced a brief schedule for the orientation and registration. This schedule is to appear on a separate page after the content of the letter. The following sections insert a page break and then create the content for the orientation and registration student schedule.

To Insert a Page Break

The first step in creating the page that will contain the student schedule for orientation and registration is to insert a page break at the end of the acceptance letter. The following steps insert a page break.

BTW
Sections and Section Breaks
Every document has at least one section. You can create multiple sections if you need to change page formatting in a portion of a document. A section break divides one section from another. To insert a next page section break, click the Breaks button (Layout tab | Page Setup group) and then click Next Page in the Section Breaks area of the Breaks gallery. Other section break options are in the Breaks gallery, as well.

1. Verify that the insertion point is positioned at the end of text in the letter, as shown in Figure 3–54.
2. Click Insert on the ribbon to display the Insert tab.
3. Click the Page Break button (Insert tab | Pages group) to insert a page break immediately to the left of the insertion point and position the insertion point at the beginning of a new blank page (Figure 3–55).

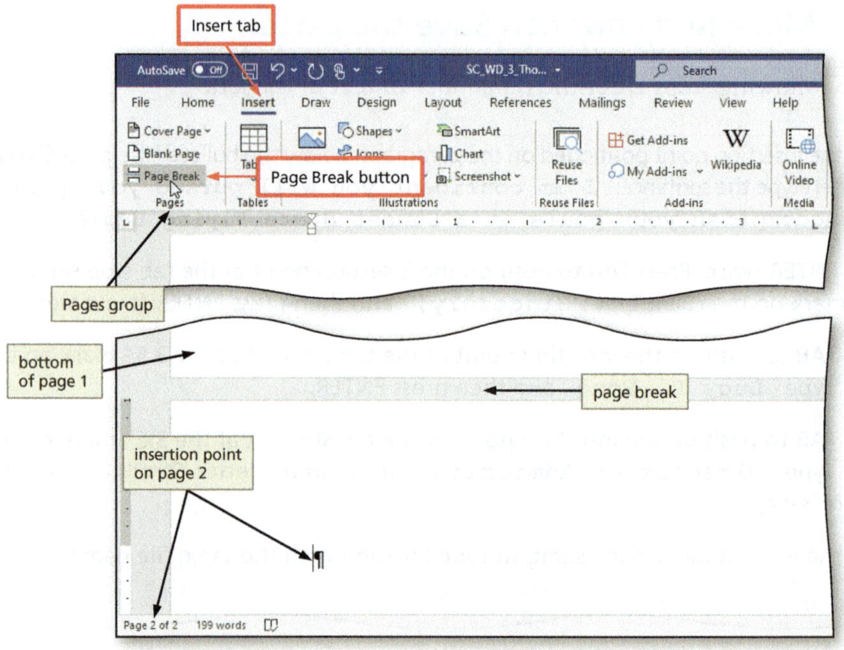

Figure 3–55

To Enter and Format Text

The title for the orientation and registration student schedule should use a large font size and an easy-to-read font. The following steps enter the title, Orientation and Registration Student Schedule, with the first three words centered on the first line and the second two words centered on the second line.

1. Click Home on the ribbon to display the Home tab.
2. Click the Center button (Home tab | Paragraph group) to center the paragraph that will contain the title.
3. Click the Bold button (Home tab | Font group), so that the text you type will be formatted with bold characters.
4. Click the Font Size arrow (Home tab | Font group) and then click 36 in the Font Size gallery, so that the text you type will use the selected font size.
5. Click the Font Color arrow (Home tab | Font group) and then click 'Orange, Accent 2, Darker 25%' (sixth color, fifth row) in the Font Color gallery, so that the text you type will use the selected font color.
6. Scroll, if necessary, to see the insertion point and paragraph mark. Type `Orientation and Registration` and then press ENTER to enter the first line of the title.
7. Type `Student Schedule` as the second line of the title (Figure 3–56).

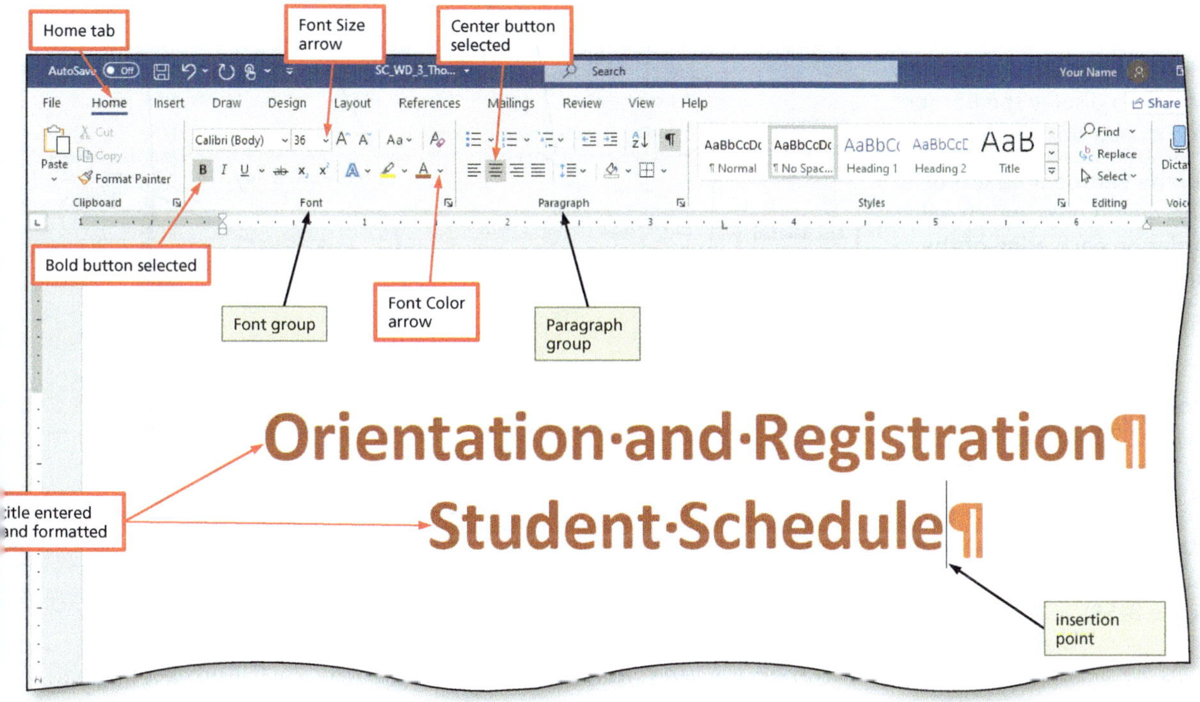

Figure 3–56

To Add and Format a Paragraph Border

If you click the Borders button (Home tab | Paragraph group), Word applies the most recently defined border, or, if one has not been defined, it applies the default border to the current paragraph. To specify a border different from the most recently defined border, you click the Borders arrow (Home tab | Paragraph group).

In this project, the title in the orientation schedule has a 2¼-point orange border around it. **Why?** You want the title to stand out on the page. The following steps add a border to all edges of the selected paragraphs.

1

- Select the paragraphs to border, in this case, the first two lines of the page.
- Click the Borders arrow (Home tab | Paragraph group) to display the Borders gallery (Figure 3–57).

Q&A **What if I wanted to border just a single paragraph?**
You would position the insertion point in the paragraph before clicking the Borders arrow.

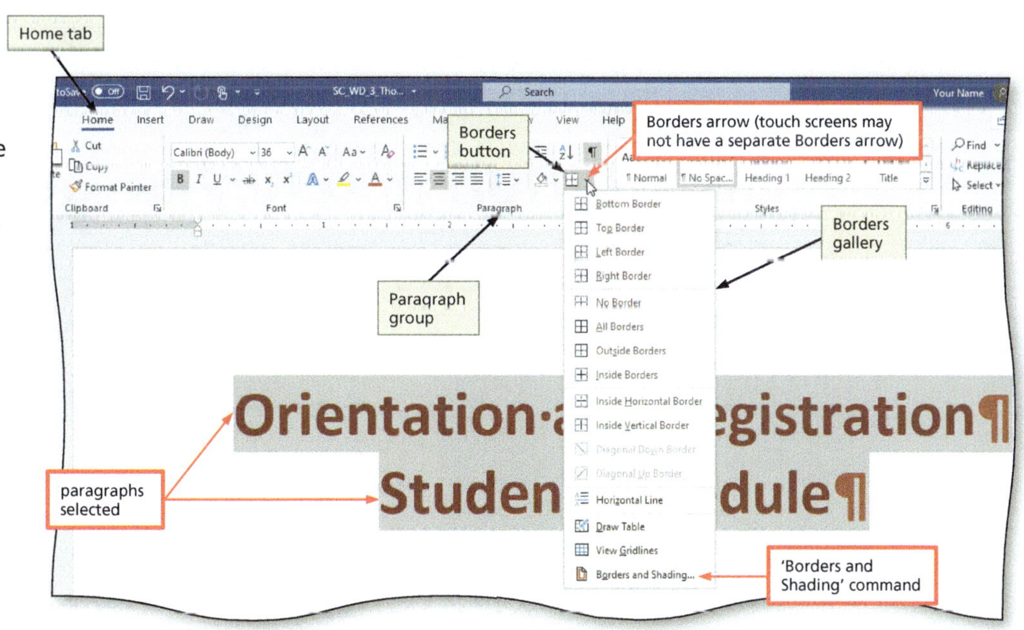

Figure 3–57

2

- Click 'Borders and Shading' in the Borders gallery to display the Borders and Shading dialog box.
- Click Box in the Setting area (Borders and Shading dialog box), which will place a border on each edge of the selected paragraphs.
- Click the fifth style in the Style list to specify the border style.
- Click the Color arrow and then click 'Orange, Accent 2' (sixth color, first row) in the color palette to specify the border color.
- Click the Width arrow and then click 2 ¼ pt to specify the thickness of the border (Figure 3–58).

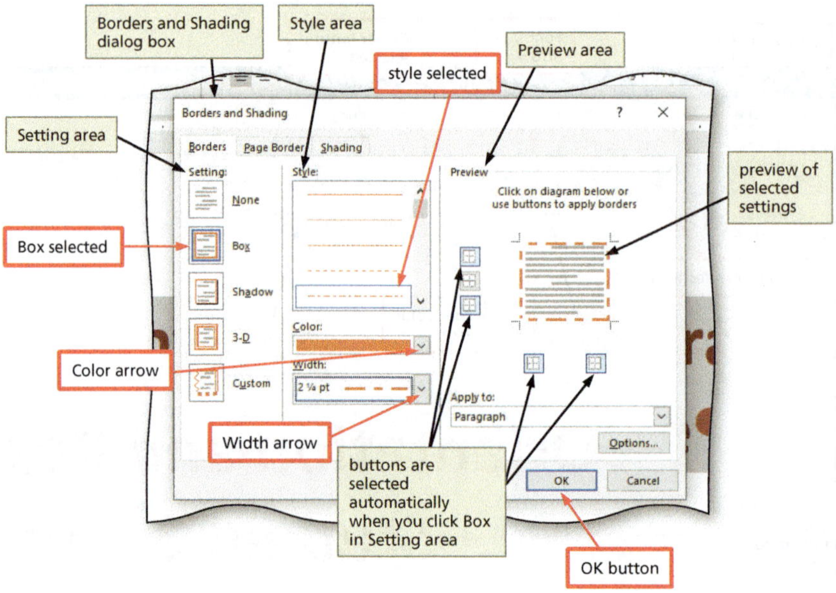

Figure 3–58

Q&A **For what purpose are the buttons in the Preview area used?**
They are toggles that display and remove the top, bottom, left, and right borders from the diagram in the Preview area.

3

- Click OK (Borders and Shading dialog box) to place the border shown in the preview area of the dialog box around the selected paragraphs in the document.
- Click anywhere in the title to remove the selection (Figure 3–59).

Q&A **How would I remove an existing border from a paragraph?**
Click the Borders arrow (Home tab | Paragraph group) and then click the border in the Borders gallery that identifies the border you wish to remove, or click No Border to remove all borders.

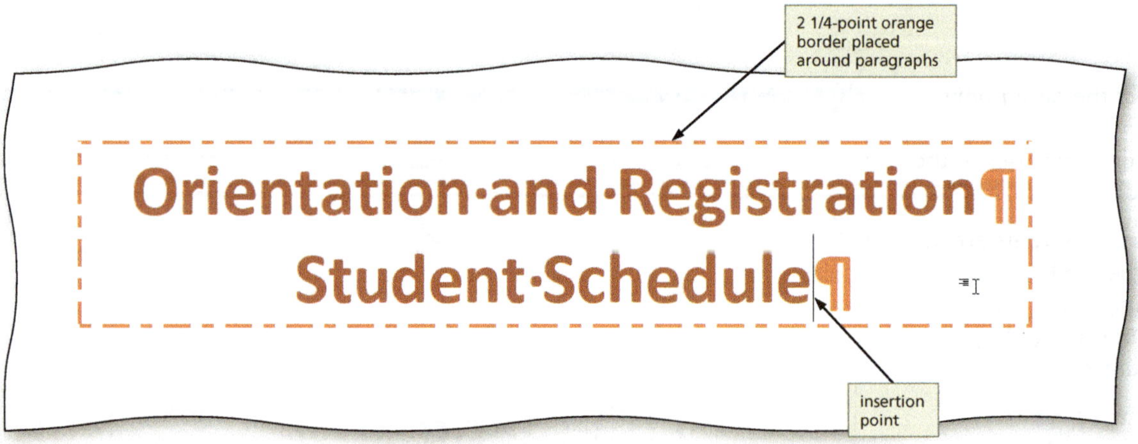

Figure 3–59

Other Ways

1. Click Page Borders button (Design tab | Page Background group), click Borders tab (Borders and Shading dialog box), select desired border options, click OK

To Clear Formatting

When you press ENTER, Word carries forward any formatting at the location of the insertion point to the next line. You want the text you type below the title to be returned to the Normal style. Thus, the following steps clear formatting.

1. Position the insertion point at the end of the second line of the title, as shown in Figure 3–59, and then press ENTER.
2. Click the 'Clear All Formatting' button (Home tab | Font group) to apply the Normal style to the location of the insertion point (Figure 3–60).

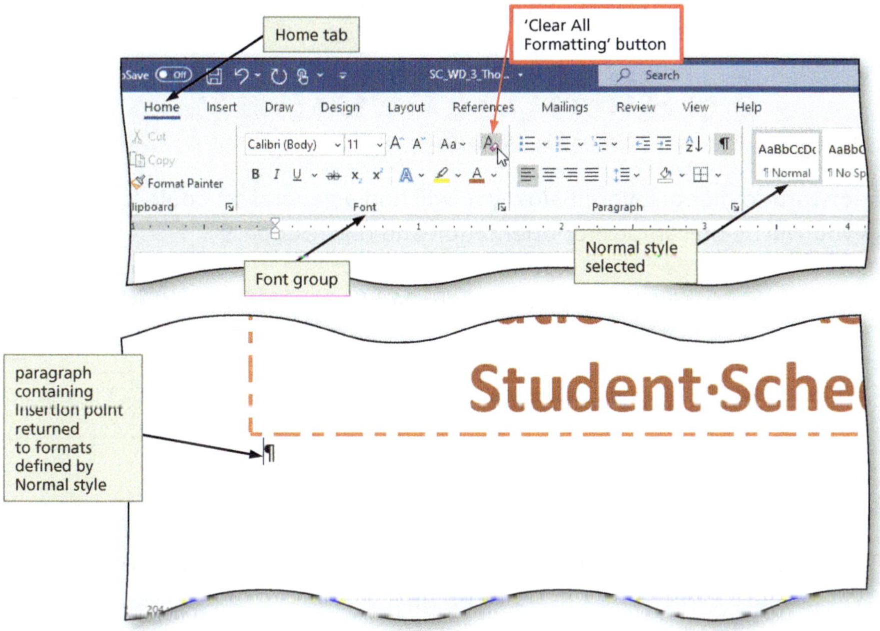

Figure 3–60

To Apply a Style and Enter More Text

The text below the title should use single spacing with double spacing between paragraphs. Thus, the following steps apply the No Spacing style and then enter two paragraphs of text.

1. With the insertion point positioned below the title, click No Spacing in the Styles gallery (Home tab | Styles group) to apply the selected style to the current paragraph.
2. Click the Font Size arrow (Home tab | Font group) and then click 14 in the Font Size gallery, so that the text you type will use the selected font size.
3. Press ENTER and then type `We look forward to meeting you! Below you will find a general schedule for the two days you will be on campus for orientation and registration.`
4. Press ENTER twice and then type `During orientation, we will walk around campus so please dress accordingly.` (Figure 3–61).

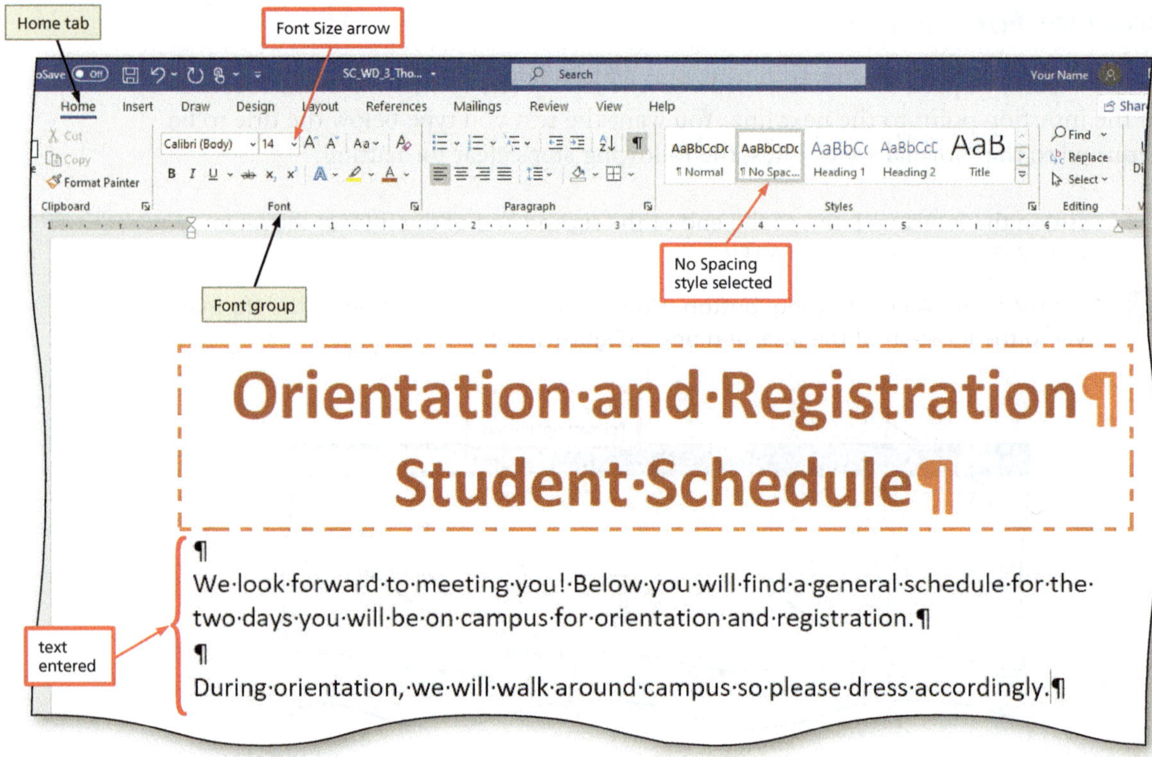

Figure 3–61

To Change the Underline Style

The following steps place a decorative underline below text in the text below the title. **Why?** You would like to emphasize text and use a line style similar to the border around the title.

1

- Select the text to format (the words, two days, in this case).
- Click the Underline arrow (Home tab | Font group) to display the Underline gallery (Figure 3–62).

Experiment

- Point to various underline styles in the Underline gallery and watch the underline style on the selected text change in the document window.

2

- Click the sixth underline style in the Underline gallery to apply the selected underline style to the selected text.

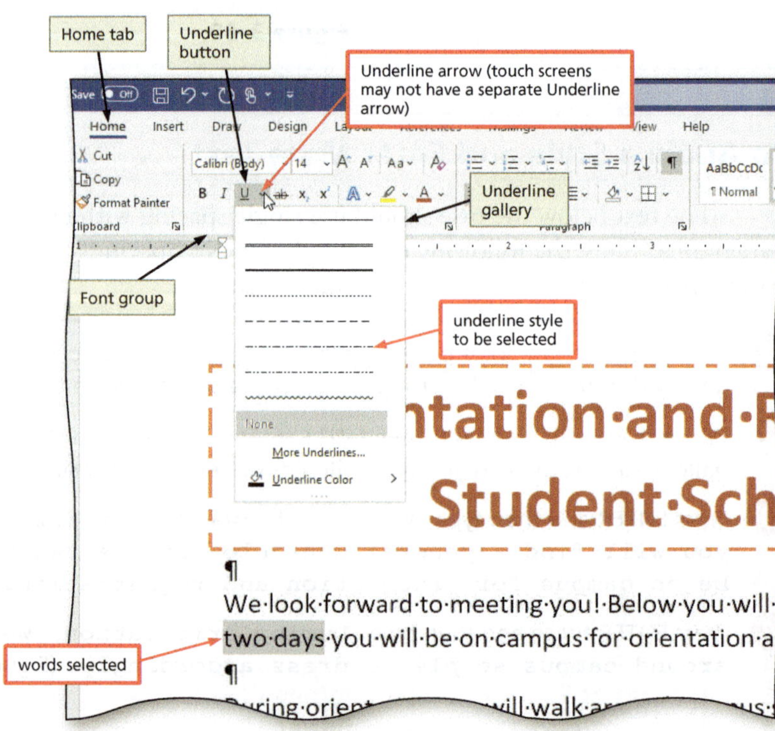

Figure 3–62

- Click the Underline arrow (Home tab | Font group) to display the Underline gallery again.
- Point to Underline Color in the Underline gallery to display a color palette.
- Point to 'Orange, Accent 2' (sixth color in first row) in the color palette to display a Live Preview of that underline color on the selected text (Figure 3–63).

Experiment

- Point to various underline colors in the color palette and watch the underline color on the selected text change in the document window.

Q&A **How would I remove underline from text?**
With the text selected, you would click the Underline button (Home tab | Font group).

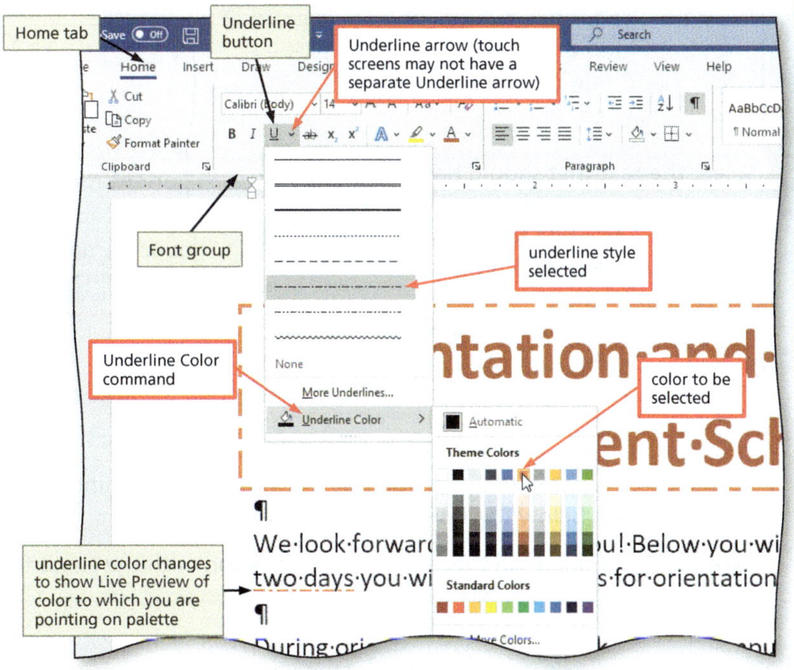

Figure 3–63

3

- Click 'Orange, Accent 2' in the color palette to apply the selected color to the underline.

Other Ways

1. Click Font Dialog Box Launcher (Home tab | Font group), click Underline style arrow (Font dialog box), select desired underline style, click Underline color arrow, select desired underline color, click OK

To Use the Format Painter Button

The last two words in the next sentence, dress accordingly, are to use the same decorative underline as the words, two days, that you just formatted. **Why?** You would like the underline format to be consistent. Instead of selecting the words, dress accordingly, and following the steps to apply the same underline format, you will copy the format from the currently selected text. The following steps copy formatting using the Format Painter button.

1

- With the text selected that contains the formatting you wish to copy (the text, two days, in this case), click the Format Painter button (Home tab | Clipboard group) to turn on the format painter.

Q&A **What if I wanted to copy a format to multiple locations?**
To copy formats to only one other location, click the Format Painter button (Home tab | Clipboard group) once. If you want to copy formatting to multiple locations, double-click the Format Painter button so that the format painter remains active until you turn it off, or click it again.

- Move the pointer to where you want to copy the formatting (the text, dress accordingly, in this case) and notice that the format painter is active (Figure 3–64).

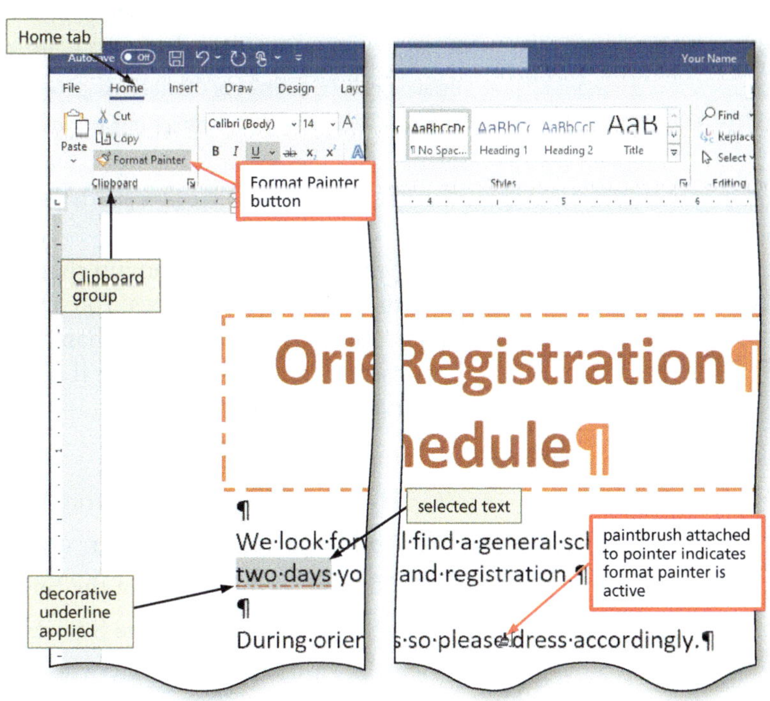

Figure 3–64

Q&A **How can I tell if the format painter is active?**
The pointer has a paintbrush attached to it when the format painter is active.

2

- Select the text that should have the same underline format (the text, dress accordingly, in this case) to paste the copied format to the selected text (Figure 3–65).

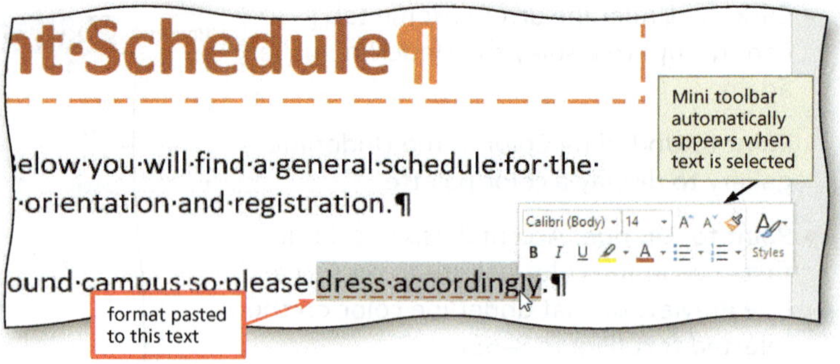

Figure 3–65

Q&A **What if I wanted to copy formats from one object to another, such as a picture or table cell?**
You would follow these same steps, except select object instead of text.

3

- Press END to position the insertion point at the end of the line and then press ENTER twice to position the insertion point two lines below the last line of text on the page.
- Save the letter again on the same storage location with the same file name.

BTW

Format Painter

If you also want to copy paragraph formatting, such as alignment and line spacing, select the paragraph mark at the end of the paragraph prior to clicking the Format Painter button (Home tab | Clipboard group). If you want to copy only character formatting, such as fonts and font sizes, do not include the paragraph mark in your selected text.

SmartArt Graphics

Microsoft Office includes **SmartArt graphics**, which are customizable diagrams that you use to pictorially present lists, processes, and relationships. Many different types of SmartArt graphics are available, allowing you to choose one that illustrates your message best. Table 3–4 identifies the purpose of some of the more popular types of SmartArt graphics. Within each type, Office provides numerous layouts. For example, you can select from 40 different layouts of the list type.

Table 3–4 SmartArt Graphic Types

Type	Purpose
List	Shows nonsequential or grouped blocks of information.
Process	Shows progression, timeline, or sequential steps in a process or workflow.
Cycle	Shows a continuous sequence of steps or events.
Hierarchy	Illustrates organization charts, decision trees, and hierarchical relationships.
Relationship	Compares or contrasts connections between concepts.
Matrix	Shows relationships of parts to a whole.
Picture	Uses images to present a message.
Pyramid	Shows proportional or interconnected relationships with the largest component at the top or bottom.

SmartArt graphics contain shapes. You can add text or pictures to shapes, add more shapes, or delete shapes. You also can modify the appearance of a SmartArt graphic by applying styles and changing its colors. The next several sections demonstrate the following general tasks to create the SmartArt graphic on the title page in this project:

1. Insert a SmartArt graphic.
2. Delete unneeded shapes from the SmartArt graphic.
3. Add shapes to the SmartArt graphic.
4. Add text to the shapes in the SmartArt graphic.
5. Change the colors of the SmartArt graphic.
6. Apply a style to the SmartArt graphic.

To Insert a SmartArt Graphic

Below the paragraphs of text you wish to add a Grouped List SmartArt graphic. **Why?** The Grouped List SmartArt graphic allows you to place multiple lists side by side on the document, which works well for the student schedule for the two days of orientation and registration. The following steps insert a SmartArt graphic centered at the location of the insertion point.

1

- With the insertion point on the blank paragraph, click the Center button (Home tab | Paragraph group) so that the inserted SmartArt graphic will be centered at the location of the insertion point.
- Display the Insert tab.
- Click the SmartArt button (Insert tab | Illustrations group) to display the Choose a SmartArt Graphic dialog box (Figure 3–66).

Experiment

- Click various SmartArt graphic types in the left pane of the dialog box and watch the related layout choices appear in the middle pane.
- Click various layouts in the list of layouts in the middle pane to see the preview and description of the layout appear in the right pane of the dialog box.

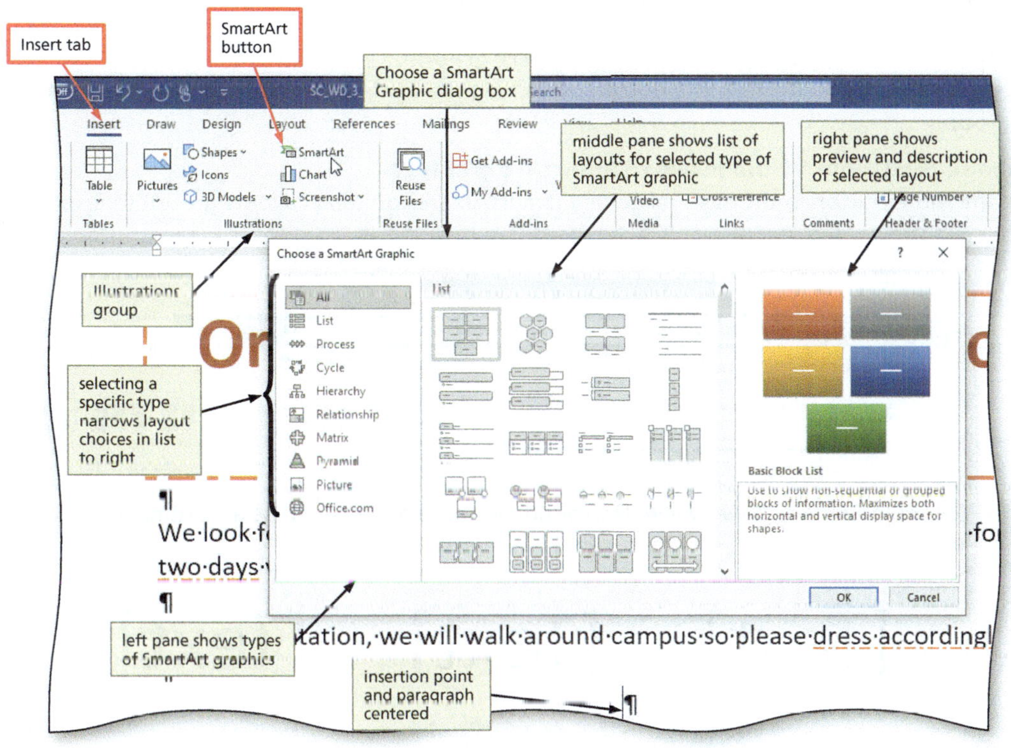

Figure 3–66

2

- Click List in the left pane (Choose a SmartArt Graphic dialog box) to display the layout choices related to the selected SmartArt graphic type.
- Click Grouped List in the middle pane, which displays a preview and description of the selected layout in the right pane (Figure 3–67).

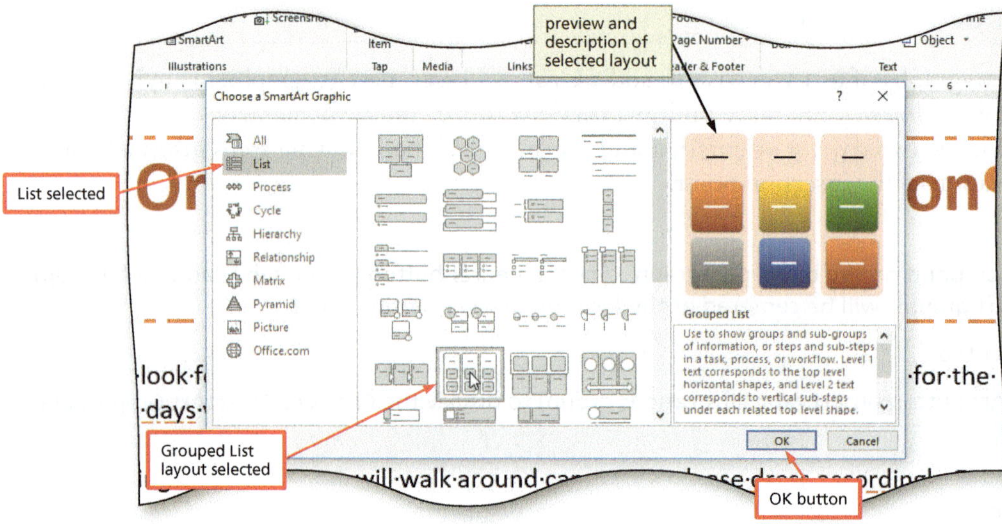

Figure 3–67

3

- Click OK to insert the selected SmartArt graphic in the document at the location of the insertion point (Figure 3–68). Scroll up, if necessary, to see the SmartArt graphic.

Q&A

What if the Text Pane opens next to the SmartArt graphic?
Close the Text Pane by clicking its Close button or clicking the Text Pane button (SmartArt Design tab | Create Graphic group).

Can I change the layout of the inserted SmartArt graphic?
Yes. Click the More button in the Layouts gallery (SmartArt Design tab | Layouts group) to display the list of layouts and then select the desired layout.

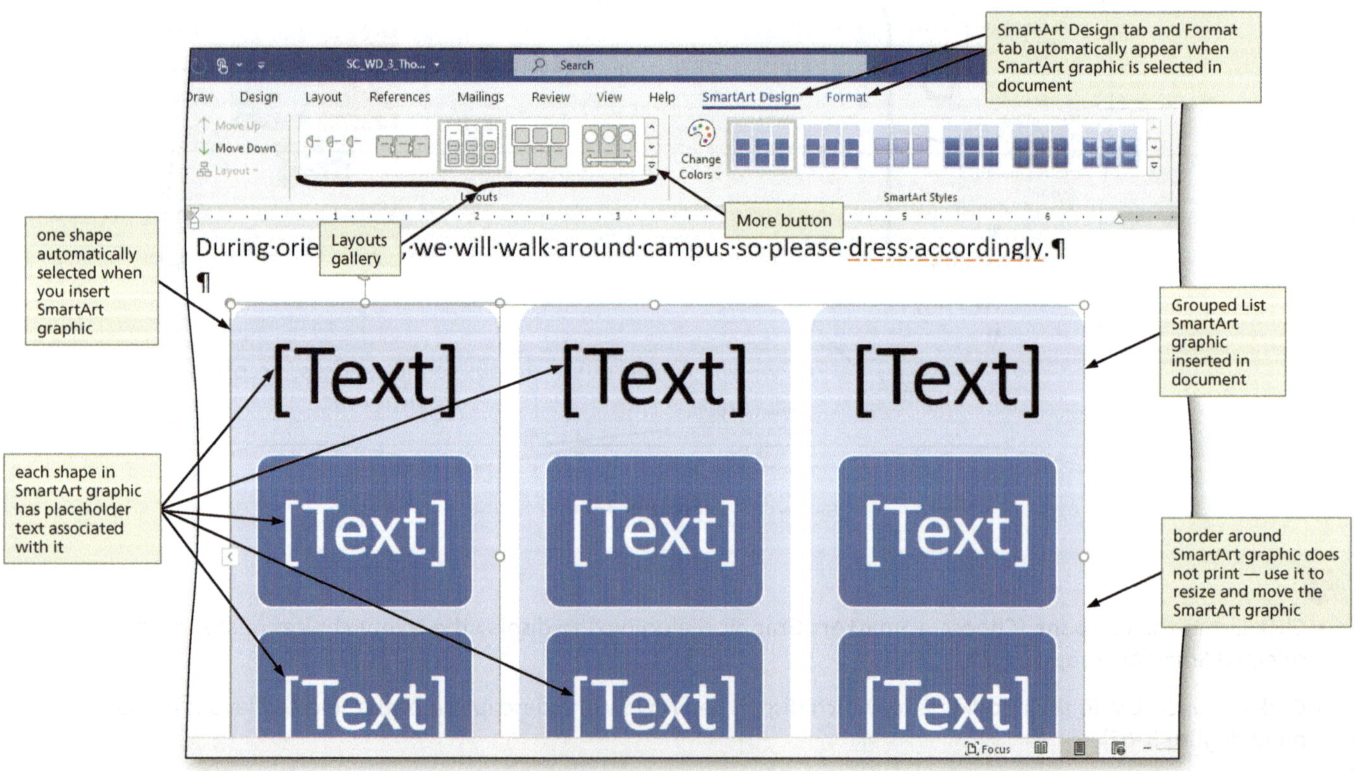

Figure 3–68

To Delete Shapes from a SmartArt Graphic

The Grouped List SmartArt graphic initially has three outer groups that consist of nine different shapes (shown in Figure 3–68). Notice that each shape in the SmartArt graphic initially shows **placeholder text**, which indicates where text can be typed. The next step in this project is to delete one entire group. **Why?** The SmartArt graphic in this project consists of only two major groups (Day 1 and Day 2). The following steps delete one entire group, or three shapes, in the SmartArt graphic.

1

- Click one of the edges of the shapes that says the word, [Text], in the rightmost group in the SmartArt graphic to select it (Figure 3–69).

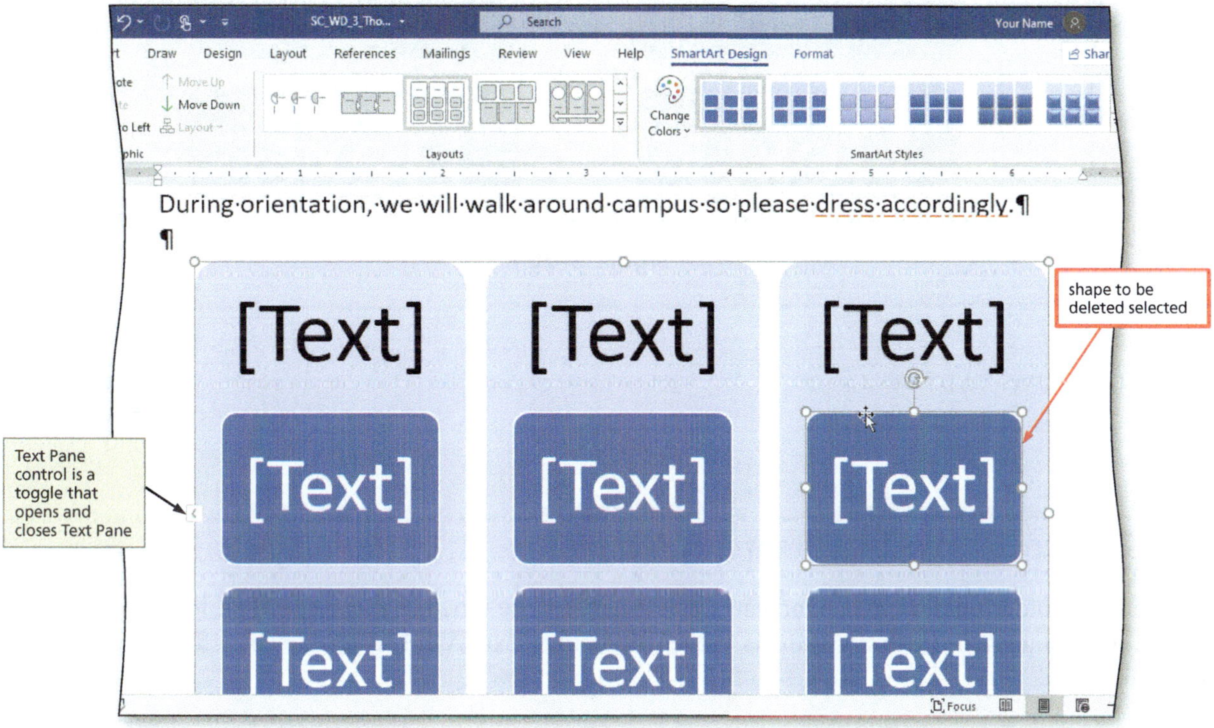

Figure 3–69

2

- Press DELETE to delete the selected shape from the SmartArt graphic (or, if using touch, tap the Cut button (Home tab | Clipboard group)).

Q&A **What if the text inside the shape is selected instead the shape itself?**
Click the shape again, ensuring you click the edge of the shape.

3

- Repeat Steps 1 and 2 to delete the next shape in the rightmost group.

4

- Repeat Steps 1 and 2 to delete the rightmost group and notice the other shapes resize and relocate in the graphic (Figure 3–70).

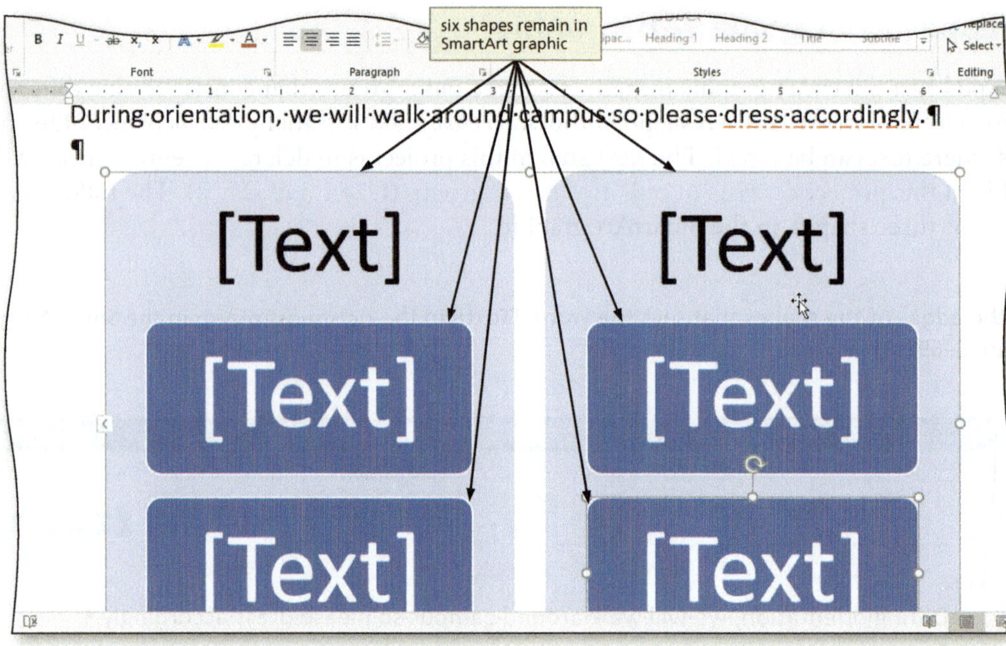

Figure 3–70

Other Ways

1. Click Cut button (Home tab | Clipboard group)
2. Right-click selected shape, click Cut on shortcut menu
3. Press BACKSPACE with shape selected

To Add Text to Shapes in a SmartArt Graphic

The placeholder text in a shape indicates where text can be typed in the shape. The following steps add text to the three shapes in the first group via their placeholder text. **Why?** After entering the text in these three shapes, you will need to add more shapes to finish the content in the group.

1

- Click the top-left shape to select it and then type `Day 1` to replace the placeholder text, [Text], with the entered text (Figure 3–71).

Q&A

How do I edit placeholder text if I make a mistake?
Click the placeholder text to select it and then correct the entry.

What if my typed text is longer than the shape?
The font size of the text in the shape may be adjusted or the text may wordwrap within the shape.

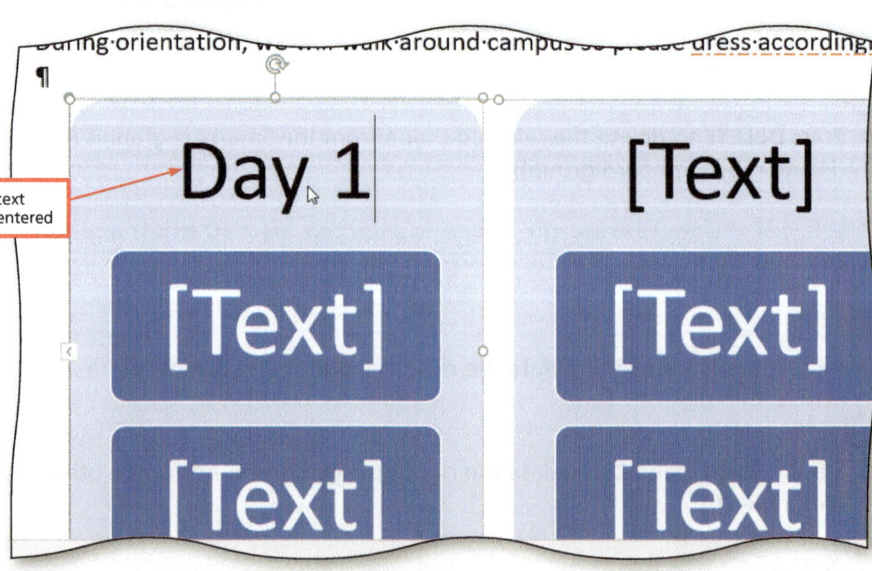

Figure 3–71

2

- Click the middle-left shape to select it and then type `Check-in (9:00-10:00)` as the new text.
- Click the lower-left shape to select it and then type `Welcome and general info session (10:15-11:45)` as the new text (Figure 3–72). Scroll up, if necessary, to see the entered text.

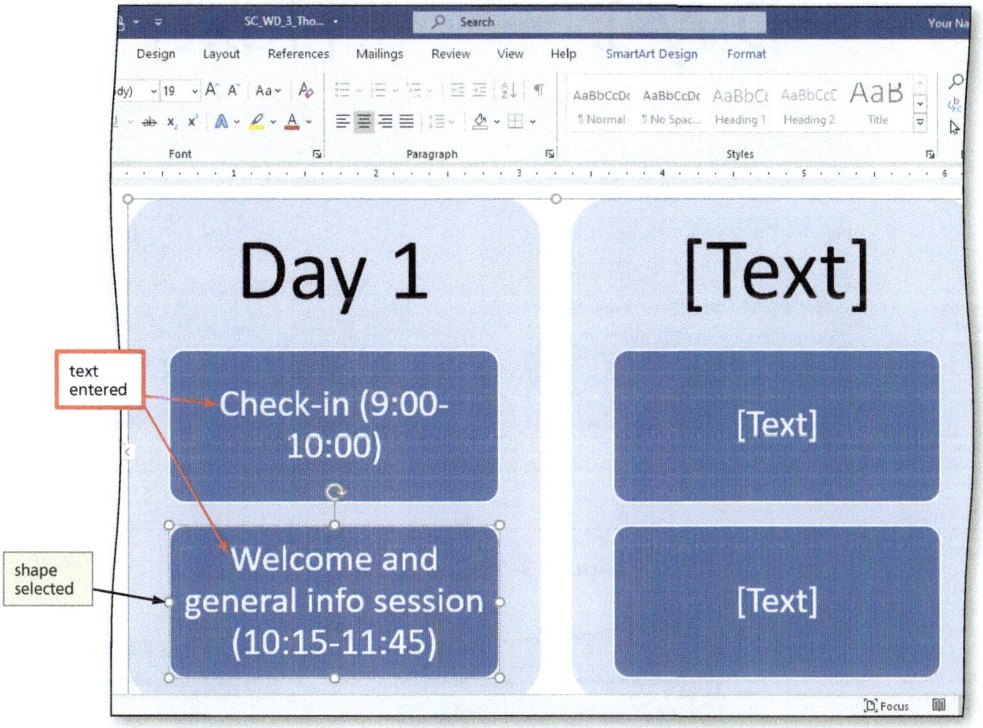

Figure 3–72

Other Ways

1. Click Text Pane control, enter text in Text Pane, close Text Pane
2. Click Text Pane button (SmartArt Design tab | Create Graphic group), enter text in Text Pane, click Text Pane button again
3. Right-click shape (or, if using touch, tap Edit Text button on Mini toolbar), click 'Exit Edit Text' on shortcut menu, enter text

To Add a Shape to a SmartArt Graphic

The following steps add shapes to the SmartArt graphic. **Why?** *Each group in this project has nine subordinate items, which means seven shapes need to be added to each group.*

1

- Click SmartArt Design on the ribbon to display the SmartArt Design tab.
- With a shape in the left group selected (as shown in Figure 3–72), click the Add Shape button (SmartArt Design tab | Create Graphic group) to add a shape to the SmartArt graphic (or, if using touch, tap the Add Shape button (SmartArt Design tab | Create Graphic group) and then tap 'Add Shape After') (Figure 3–73).

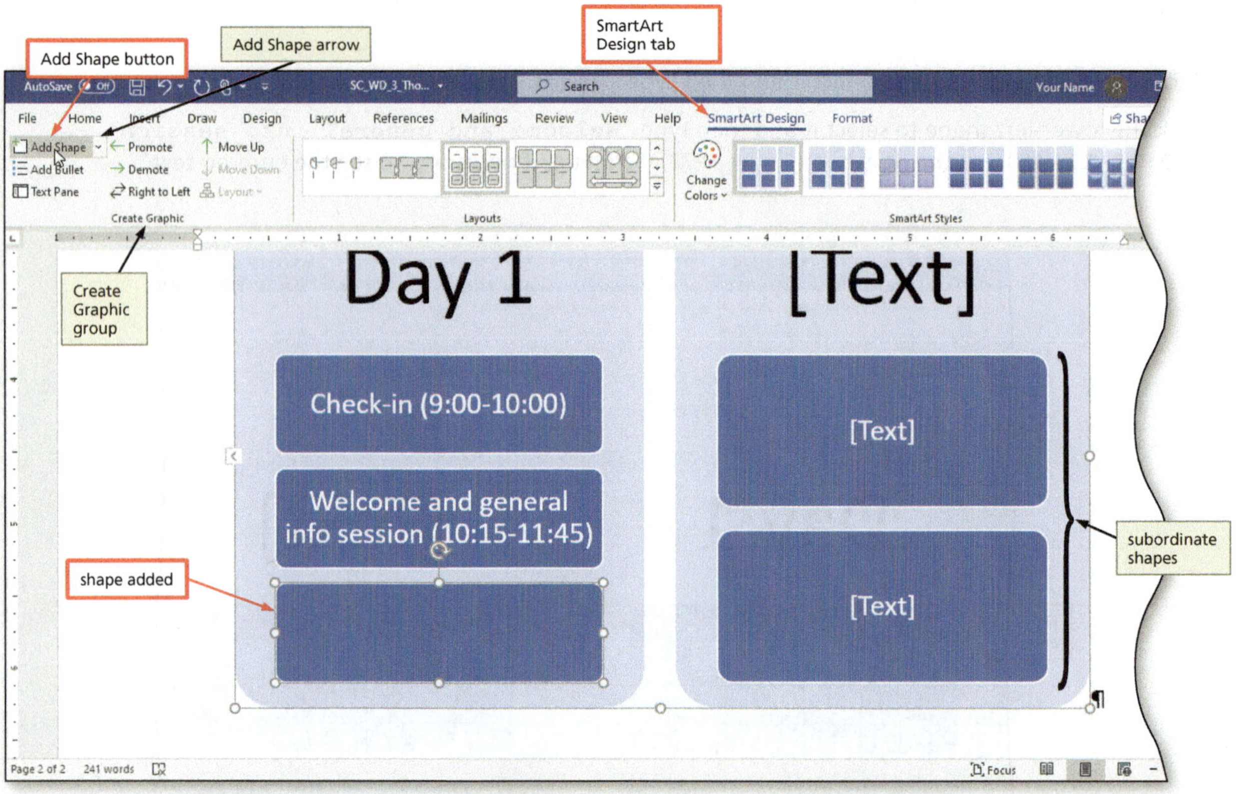

Figure 3–73

2

- Type **`Lunch (12:00-12:45)`** as the text for the added shape (Figure 3–74).

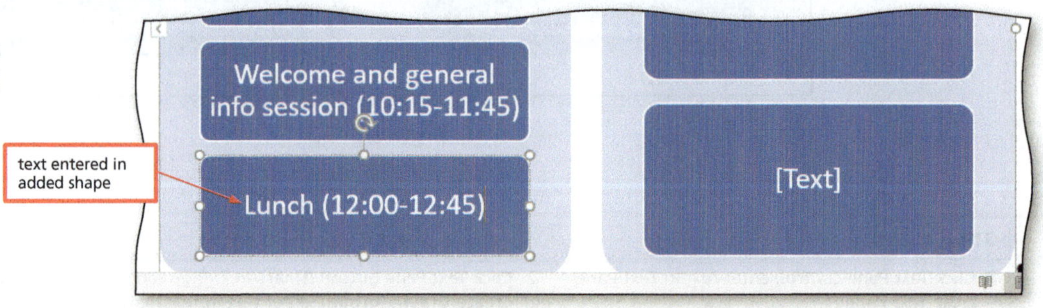

Figure 3–74

Other Ways

1. Click Add Shape arrow (SmartArt Design tab), click desired shape position
2. Right-click paragraph (or, if using touch, tap 'Show Context Menu' button on Mini toolbar), point to Add Shape on shortcut menu, click desired shape position

To Add More Shapes and Text to a SmartArt Graphic

The following steps add the remaining shapes and text in the SmartArt graphic.

1 With a shape in the left group selected, click the Add Shape button (SmartArt Design tab | Create Graphic group) to add a shape to the SmartArt graphic (or, if using touch, tap the Add Shape button (SmartArt Design tab | Create Graphic group) and then tap 'Add Shape After') and then type **`Student accounts and services session (1:00-1:45)`** as the text for the shape.

2 Add another shape to the left group and then type **`Meetings with advisors (2:00-2:45)`** as the text for the shape.

3 Add another shape to the left group and then type **`Department meetings (3:00-3:45)`** as the text for the shape.

4. Add another shape to the left group and then type **`Expo (4:00-5:15)`** as the text for the shape.

5. Add another shape to the left group and then type **`Dinner (5:30-6:45)`** as the text for the shape.

6. Add another shape to the left group and then type **`Evening activities (7:00-10:00)`** as the text for the shape.

7. In the top of the right group, type **`Day 2`** in the placeholder text.

8. In the first shape below Day 2 in the right group, type **`Breakfast (7:00-7:45)`** as the text.

9. In the second shape below Day 2 in the right group, type **`Housing services session (8:00-8:30)`** as the text.

10. With a shape in the right group selected, click the Add Shape button (SmartArt Design tab | Create Graphic group) to add a shape to the SmartArt graphic (or, if using touch, tap the Add Shape button (SmartArt Design tab | Create Graphic group) and then tap 'Add Shape After') and then type **`Dining services session (8:35-9:05)`** as the text for the shape.

11. Add another shape to the right group and then type **`Health services session (9:10-9:40)`** as the text for the shape.

12. Add another shape to the right group and then type **`Campus tour (10:00-11:45)`** as the text for the shape.

13. Add another shape to the right group and then type **`Lunch (12:00-12:45)`** as the text for the shape.

14. Add another shape to the right group and then type **`General education session (1:00-1:45)`** as the text for the shape.

15. Add another shape to the right group and then type **`Register for classes (2:00-3:15)`** as the text for the shape.

16. Add another shape to the right group and then type **`Welcome week overview (3:30-4:00)`** as the text for the shape (Figure 3–75).

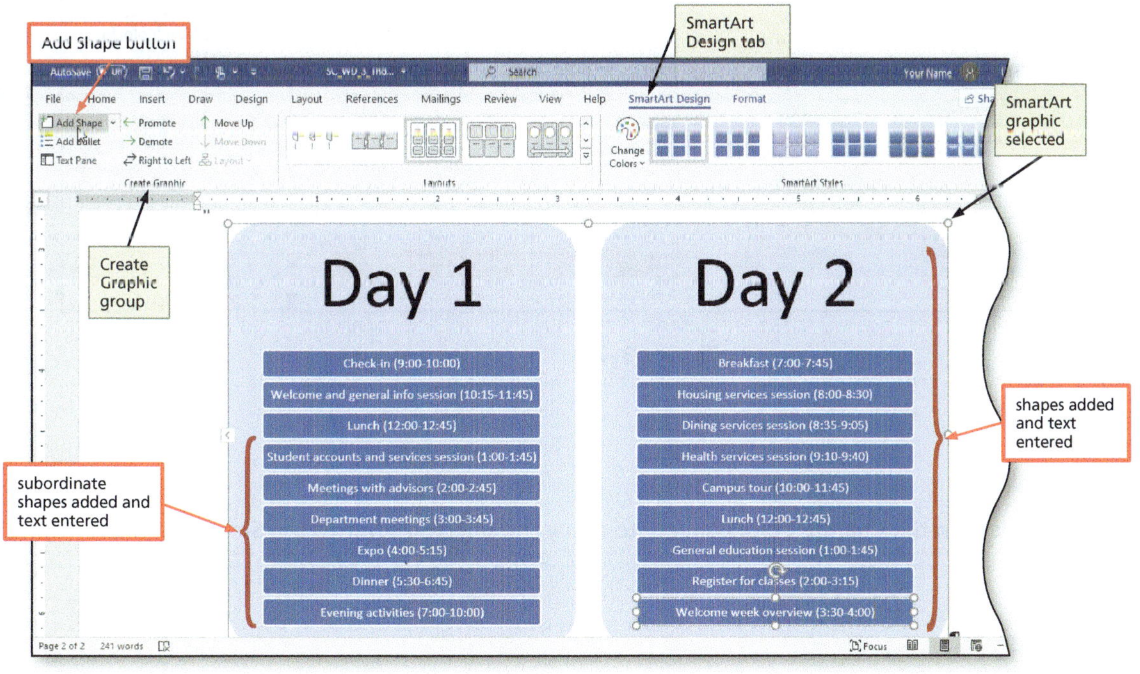

Figure 3–75

To Change Colors of a SmartArt Graphic

Word provides a variety of colors for a SmartArt graphic and the shapes in the graphic. In this project, the inside shapes are multicolor, instead of blue. **Why?** You want more vibrant colors for the shapes. The following steps change the colors of a SmartArt graphic.

1

- With the SmartArt graphic selected (shown in Figure 3–75), click the Change Colors button (SmartArt Design tab | SmartArt Styles group) to display the Change Colors gallery.

Q&A

What if the SmartArt graphic is not selected?
Click the SmartArt graphic to select it.

- Point to 'Colorful - Accent Colors' in the Change Colors gallery to display a Live Preview of the selected color applied to the SmartArt graphic in the document (Figure 3–76).

Experiment

- Point to various colors in the Change Colors gallery and watch the colors of the graphic change in the document window.

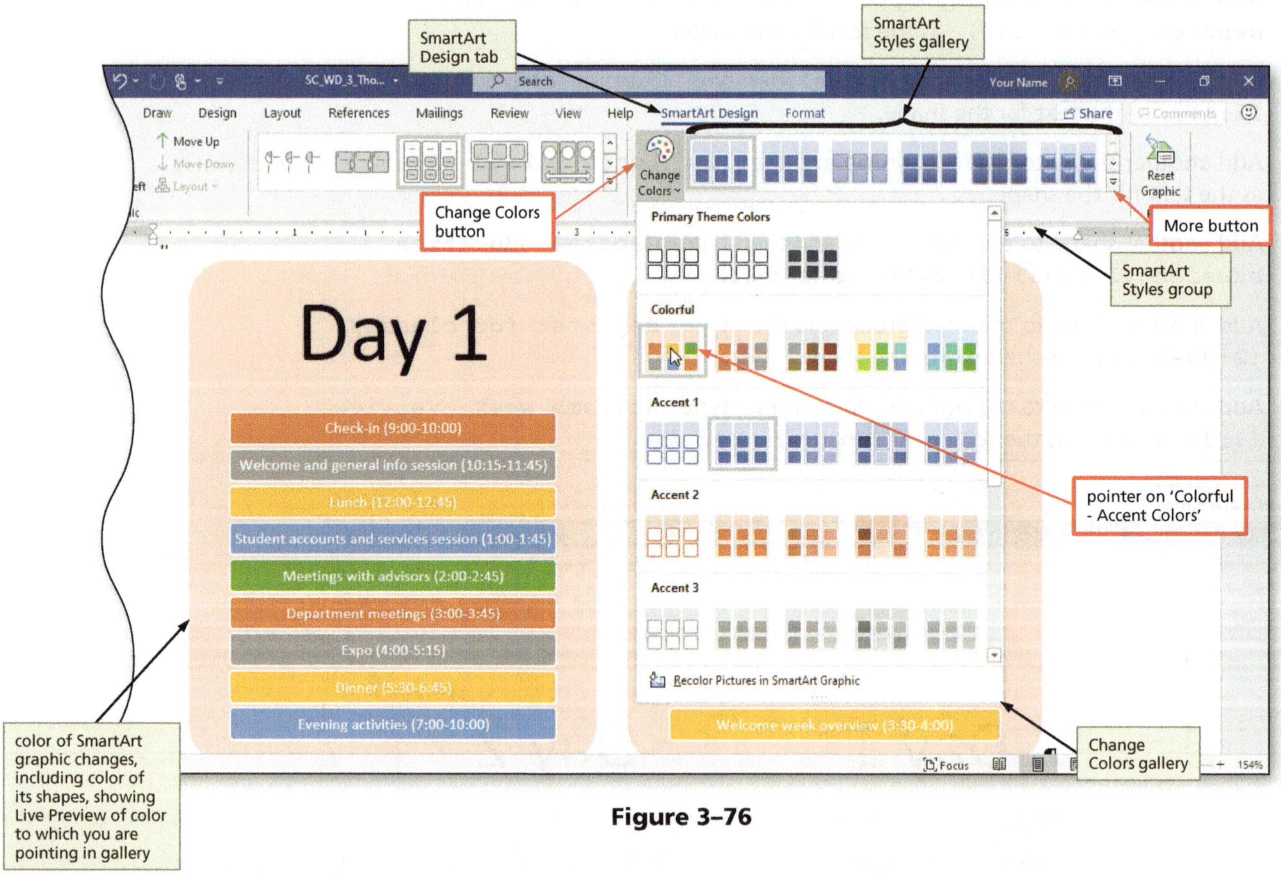

Figure 3–76

2

- Click 'Colorful - Accent Colors' in the Change Colors gallery to apply the selected color to the SmartArt graphic.

To Apply a SmartArt Style

The next step is to apply a SmartArt style to the SmartArt graphic. **Why?** Word provides a SmartArt Styles gallery, allowing you to change the SmartArt graphic's format to a more visually appealing style. The following steps apply a SmartArt style to a SmartArt graphic.

1

- With the SmartArt graphic still selected, click the More button in the SmartArt Styles gallery (shown in Figure 3–76) to expand the SmartArt Styles gallery.
- Point to Subtle Effect in the SmartArt Styles gallery to display a Live Preview of that style applied to the graphic in the document (Figure 3–77).

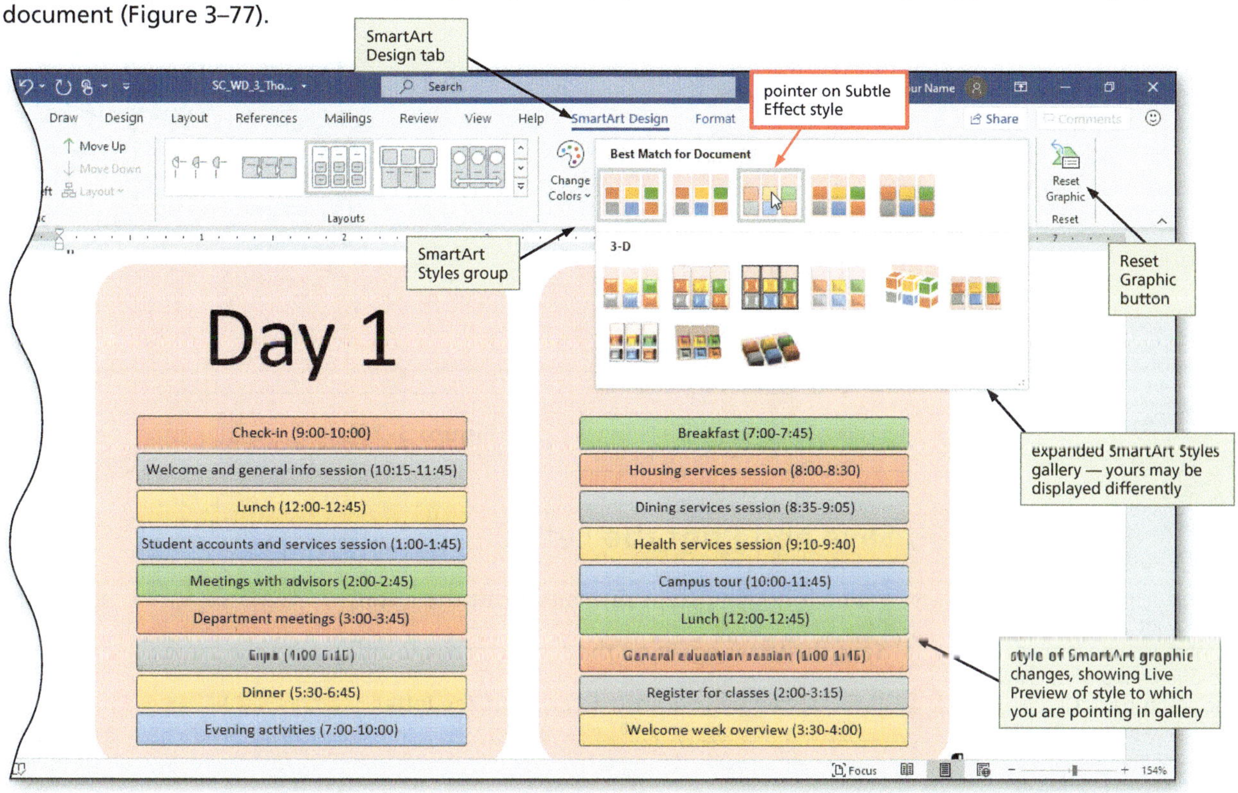

Figure 3–77

Experiment

- Point to various SmartArt styles in the SmartArt Styles gallery and watch the style of the graphic change in the document window.

2

- Click Subtle Effect in the SmartArt Styles gallery to apply the selected style to the SmartArt graphic.

To Resize the SmartArt Graphic

The following steps resize the SmartArt graphic.

1. Display both pages on the screen at once by displaying the View tab and then clicking the Multiple Pages button (View tab | Zoom group).
2. Click the outer edge of the SmartArt graphic to select the entire graphic.
3. Drag the lower-right sizing handle on the SmartArt graphic until it is the same approximate size as in Figure 3–78.
4. Change the zoom to page width by clicking the Page Width button (View tab | Zoom group).

BTW

Resetting Graphics

If you want to remove all formats from a SmartArt graphic and start over, you would click the Reset Graphic button (SmartArt Design tab | Reset group), which is shown in Figure 3–77.

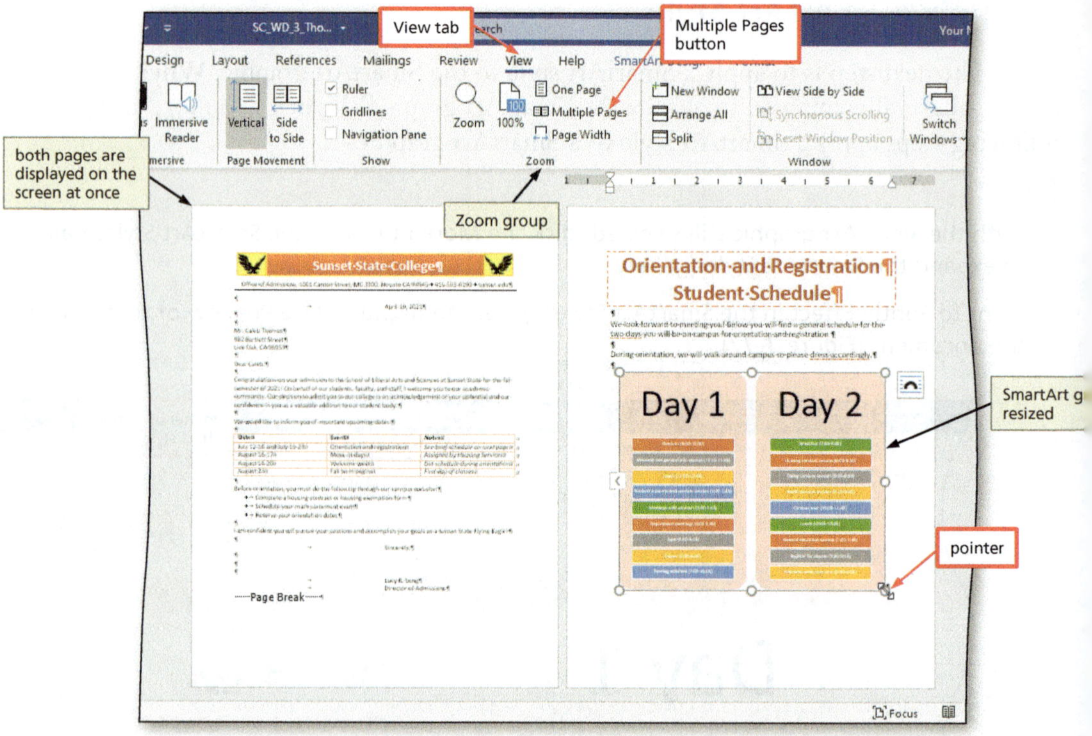

Figure 3–78

BTW

Conserving Ink and Toner

If you want to conserve ink or toner, you can instruct Word to print draft quality documents by clicking File on the ribbon to open Backstage view, clicking Options in Backstage view to display the Word Options dialog box, clicking Advanced in the left pane (Word Options dialog box), scrolling to the Print area in the right pane, placing a check mark in the 'Use draft quality' check box, and then clicking OK. Then, use Backstage view to print the document as usual.

To Save and Print the Letter

The following steps save and print the letter.

1. Save the letter again on the same storage location with the same file name.
2. If requested by your instructor, print the letter.

Enhancing a Document's Accessibility

Word provides several options for enhancing the accessibility of documents for individuals who are vision impaired. Some tasks you can perform to assist users include increasing zoom and font size, ensuring tab/reading order in tables is logical, and using Read mode. You also can use the accessibility checker to locate and address problematic issues, and you can add alternative text to graphics and tables.

To Use the Accessibility Checker

The accessibility checker scans a document and identifies issues that could affect a person's ability to read the content. Once identified, you can address each individual issue in the document. If you wanted to check accessibility of a document, you would perform the following steps.

1. Click the Check Accessibility button (Review tab | Accessibility group) to display the Check Accessibility menu.
2. Click Check Accessibility on the Check Accessibility menu, which scans the document and then displays accessibility issues in the Accessibility pane.
3. Address the errors and warnings in the Accessibility pane and then close the pane.

To Add Alternative Text to Graphics

For users who have difficulty seeing images on the screen, you can include **alternative text**, also called **alt text**, to your graphics so that these users can see or hear the alternative text when working with your document. Graphics you can add alt text to include pictures, shapes, text boxes, SmartArt graphics, and charts. If you wanted to add alternative text to graphics, you would perform the following steps.

1. Click the Alt Text button (Picture Format tab or Shape Format tab | Accessibility group), or right-click the object and then click Edit Alt Text on the shortcut menu to display the Alt Text pane.
2. Type a narrative description of the graphic in the text box.
3. Close the pane.

To Add Alternative Text to Tables

For visually impaired persons, you can include alternative text to your tables so that these users can see or hear the alternative text when working with your document. If you wanted to add alternative text to a table, sometimes called a table title, you would perform the following steps.

1. Click the Properties button (Layout tab | Table group), or right-click the table and then click Table Properties on the shortcut menu to display the Table Properties dialog box.
2. Click the Alt Text tab (Table Properties dialog box) to display the Alt Text sheet.
3. Type a brief title and then type a narrative description of the table in the respective text boxes.
4. Click OK to close the dialog box.

Addressing and Printing Envelopes and Mailing Labels

With Word, you can print mailing address information on an envelope or on a mailing label. Computer-printed addresses look more professional than handwritten ones.

To Address and Print an Envelope

The following steps address and print an envelope. If you are in a lab environment, check with your instructor before performing these steps. **Why?** Some printers may not accommodate printing envelopes; others may stop printing until an envelope is inserted.

1

- Scroll through the letter to display the inside address in the document window.
- Drag through the inside address to select it (Figure 3–79).

2

- Display the Mailings tab.
- Click the Envelopes button (Mailings tab | Create group) to display the Envelopes and Labels dialog box.

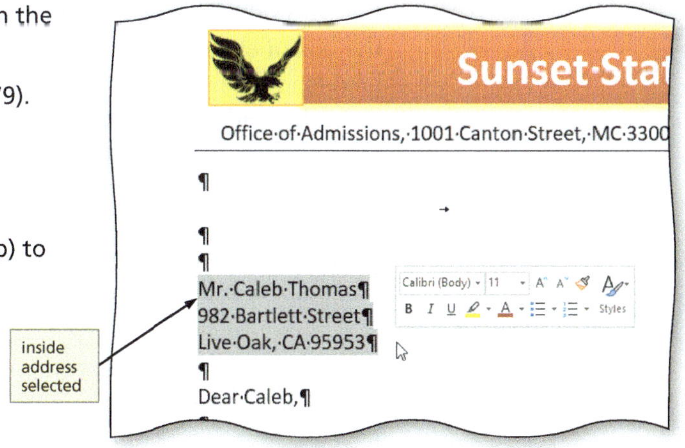

Figure 3–79

- If necessary, click the Envelopes tab (Envelopes and Labels dialog box), which automatically displays the selected delivery address in the dialog box.
- Type the return address as shown in Figure 3–80.

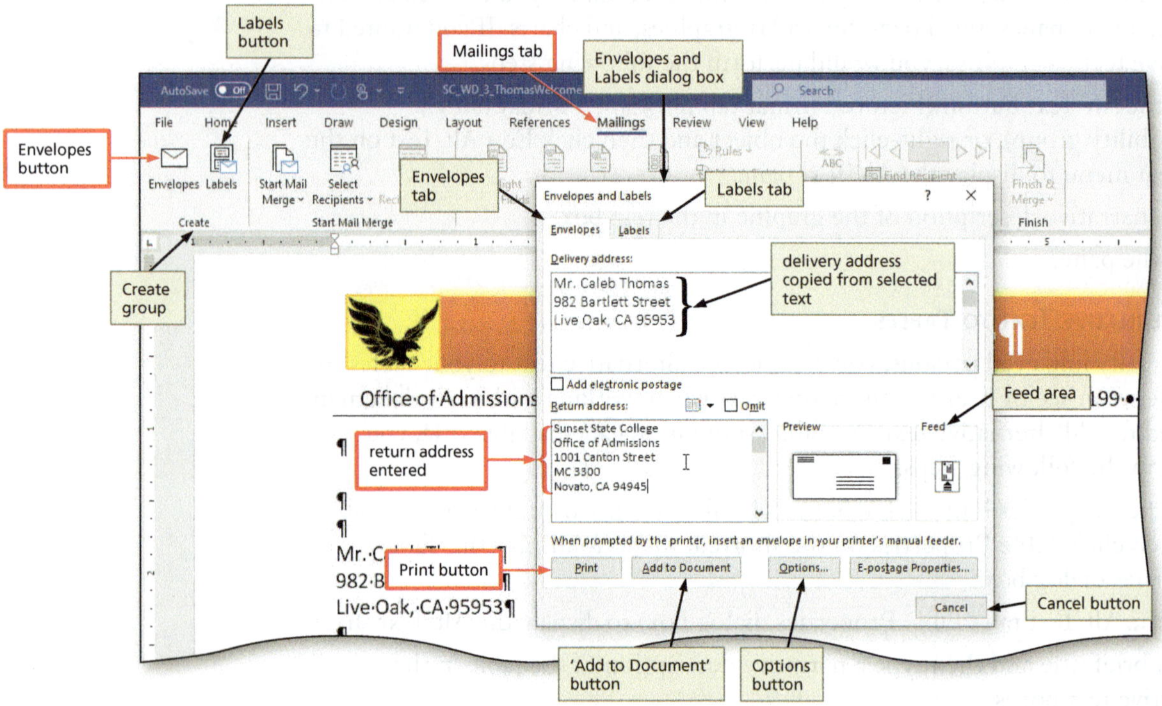

Figure 3–80

3

- Insert an envelope in your printer, as shown in the Feed area of the dialog box (your Feed area may be different depending on your printer).
- If your printer can print envelopes, click Print (Envelopes and Labels dialog box) to print the envelope; otherwise, click Cancel to close the dialog box.
- **sam** Because the project now is complete, you can exit Word.

Envelopes and Labels

Instead of printing the envelope immediately, you can add it to the document by clicking the 'Add to Document' button (Envelopes and Labels dialog box) (shown in Figure 3–80). To specify a different envelope or label type (identified by a number on the box of envelopes or labels), click the Options button (Envelopes and Labels dialog box) (shown in Figure 3–80).

Instead of printing an envelope, you can print a mailing label. To do this, click the Labels button (Mailings tab | Create group) (shown in Figure 3–80) and then type the delivery address in the Address box. To print the same address on all labels on the page, select the 'Full page of the same label' option button in the Print area. Click the Print button (Envelopes and Labels dialog box) to print the label(s).

Summary

In this module, you have learned how to use Word to insert and format a shape, change text wrapping, insert and format a picture, move and copy objects, insert symbols, add a border, clear formatting, set and use tab stops, insert the current date, insert and format tables, use the format painter, insert and format a SmartArt graphic, and address and print envelopes and mailing labels.

Consider This: Plan Ahead

What decisions will you need to make when creating your next business letter?

Use these guidelines as you complete the assignments in this module and create your own business letters outside of this class.

1. Create a letterhead.
   a) Ensure that the letterhead contains a complete name, mailing address, phone number, and if applicable, fax number, email address, web address, logo, or other image.
   b) Place elements in the letterhead in a visually appealing location.
   c) Format the letterhead with appropriate fonts, font sizes, font styles, and color.
2. Compose an effective business letter.
   a) Include a date line, inside address, message, and signature block.
   b) Use proper spacing and formats for letter contents.
   c) Follow the alignment and spacing guidelines based on the letter style used (i.e., block, modified block, or modified semi-block).
   d) Ensure the message is well written, properly formatted, and logically organized.

BTW

Distributing a Document

Instead of printing and distributing a hard copy of a document, you can distribute the document electronically. Options include sending the document via email; posting it on cloud storage (such as OneDrive) and sharing the file with others; posting it on social media, a blog, or other website; and sharing a link associated with an online location of the document. You also can create and share a PDF or XPS image of the document, so that users can view the file in Acrobat Reader or XPS Viewer instead of in Word.

Apply Your Knowledge

Reinforce the skills and apply the concepts you learned in this module.

Working with Tabs, Tables, and SmartArt Graphics

Note: To complete this assignment, you will be required to use the Data Files. Please contact your instructor for information about accessing the Data Files.

Instructions: Start Word. Open the document called SC_WD_3-1.docx, which is located in the Data Files. The document you open contains a Word table. As relationship coordinator for Pine River Wildlife Refuge, you reach out to previous donors each year and ask if they would consider donating again. Although letters will not go out for several weeks, you want to create some of the letter components at this time. You began composing a Word table of donor categories that you need to edit and format. You also want to create a SmartArt graphic for the letter that identifies how donations are used at the refuge. The revised table, along with the SmartArt graphic you create, is shown in Figure 3–81.

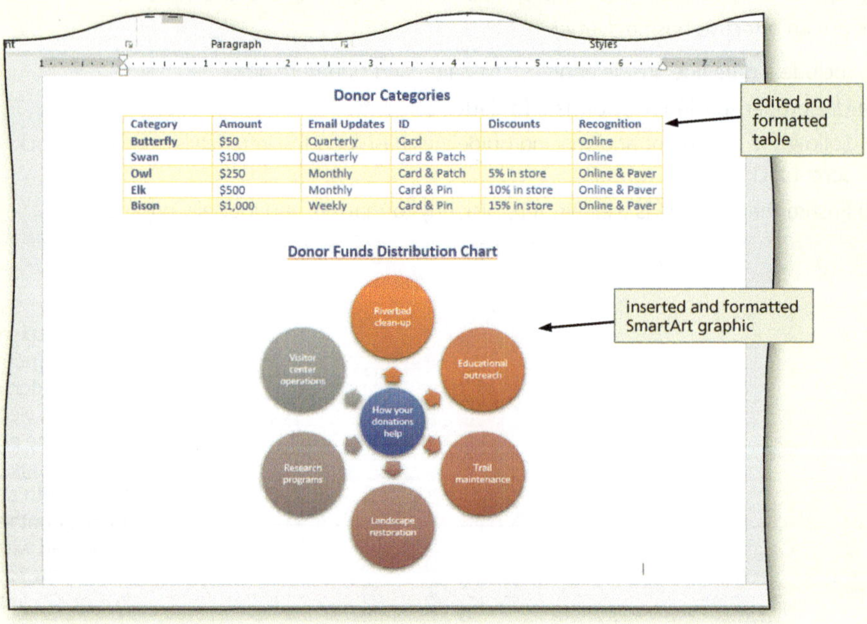

Figure 3–81

Perform the following tasks:

1. Click File on the ribbon, click Save As, and then save the document using the new file name, SC_WD_3_DonorTableAndSmartArt.
2. In the line containing the table title, Donor Categories, remove the tab stop at the 1" mark on the ruler.
3. Set a centered tab at the 3" mark on the ruler. Move the centered tab stop to the 3.25" mark on the ruler.
4. In the line containing the SmartArt graphic title, Donor Funds Distribution Chart, remove (clear) all tab stops.
5. Bold the characters in the Donor Categories title. Use the 'Increase Font Size' button to increase their font size to 16. Use the 'Decrease Font Size' button to decrease their font size to 14. Change their color to Blue, Accent 1, Darker 25%.

6. Use the format painter to copy the formatting from the table title paragraph to the SmartArt graphic title paragraph (so that the SmartArt graphic title has a centered tab stop at the 3.25" mark on the ruler and has the same text formats).
7. Apply the underline style called Thick underline below the characters in the Donor Funds Distribution Chart title. Change the underline color to Orange, Accent 2, Lighter 40% (sixth color in the fourth row).
8. In the table, select one of the duplicate rows containing the Butterfly category and delete the row.
9. In the table, select one of the duplicate columns containing the Recognitions and delete the column.
10. Insert a column between the Amount and ID columns. Fill in the column as follows:

    Column Title – Email Updates

    Butterfly – Quarterly

    Swan – Quarterly

    Owl – Monthly

    Bison – Weekly
11. Insert a new row above the bison row. In the first cell of the new row, enter the word, Elk, in the cell. Fill in the cells in the remainder of the row as follows:

    Amount – $500

    Email Updates – Monthly

    ID – Card & Pin

    Discounts – 10% in store

    Recognition – Online & Paver
12. In the Table Style Options group (Table Design tab), ensure that these check boxes have check marks: Header Row, Banded Rows, and First Column. The Total Row, Last Column, and Banded Columns check boxes should not have check marks.
13. Apply the Grid Table 6 Colorful - Accent 4 style to the table.
14. Select the entire table. Change the font color of all text in the selected table to Blue, Accent 1, Darker 25%.
15. Position the insertion point at the end of the Donor Funds Distribution Chart title and then press ENTER. Clear formatting on this new line and then center the insertion point on the line.
16. On the blank line below the title Donor Funds Distribution Chart, insert a Diverging Radial SmartArt graphic (in the Cycle category). Add two shapes to the inserted SmartArt graphic.
17. In the SmartArt graphic, enter the text, How your donations help, in the center shape. In the exterior shapes, starting with the top and moving clockwise, enter this text: Riverbed clean-up, Educational outreach, Trail maintenance, Landscape restoration, Research programs, and Visitor center operations. (Note: if the placeholder text does not appear, open the Text Pane to add the text.)
18. Change the SmartArt colors to Colorful Range - Accent Colors 2 to 3, and apply the SmartArt Style called Intense Effect.
19. If requested by your instructor, enter your name on the line below the table.
20. Save the document again with the same file name.
21. Submit the modified document, shown in Figure 3–81, in the format specified by your instructor.
22. Exit Word.
23. If you wanted to add a row to the end of the table, how would you add the row?

Extend Your Knowledge

Extend the skills you learned in this module and experiment with new skills. You may need to use Help to complete the assignment.

Working with Shapes and Pictures

Note: To complete this assignment, you will be required to use the Data Files. Please contact your instructor for information about accessing the Data Files.

Instructions: Start Word. Open the document, SC_WD_3-2.docx, which is located in the Data Files. The document is a draft of a letter you began earlier this week. As community education coordinator for Midland Medical Center, you are responsible for sending confirmation letters to those who have signed up for education workshops offered by the center. You will work with shapes and pictures to design the letterhead in the letter and will complete the table so that the letter is ready to send.

Perform the following tasks:

1. Use Help to learn about grouping objects and the formatting pictures and shapes.
2. Click File on the ribbon, click Save As, and then save the document using the new file name, SC_WD_3_ConfirmationLetter.
3. Select the arrow shape at the top of the letter. Drag the rotate handle on top of the selected shape clockwise and watch the shape rotate. Delete the selected shape.
4. Insert a Rectangle: Rounded Corners shape at the top of the letter, sizing it across the top of the page. Drag the edges to form a rectangle. After drawing the shape, specify the exact dimensions of a height of 0.7" and a width of 6.5".
5. Position the shape in the 'Position in Top Center with Square Text Wrapping' using the Position button (Shape Format tab | Arrange group). Then, change the text wrapping to 'Top and Bottom'.
6. Apply a shape style of your choosing to the shape. Enter the text, Midland Medical Center, in the shape. Format the text as you deem appropriate. Apply an appropriate shape outline to the shape. Apply a shape effect of your choosing to the shape.
7. Resize the caduceus picture to 50 percent of its original size. With the picture inline, click the paragraph mark to the right of the picture and then click the Center button (Home tab | Paragraph group). Then, click the Align Right button (Home tab | Paragraph group). How do you move inline pictures?
8. Resize the picture so its height is exactly 0.6" and its width is 0.48". Change the text wrapping of the picture to 'In Front of Text'. Click the Position button (Picture Format tab | Arrange group) and select different options. Click the Align button (Picture Format tab | Arrange group) and select different alignments. Drag the picture into the shape (Figure 3–82). How do you move floating pictures?
9. Change the brightness and contrast of the picture as you deem appropriate. Copy the picture. Use Paste Options arrow to paste as a Picture. Is the pasted picture an inline or floating object? Delete the pasted picture. Use the Paste Options arrow to paste with source formatting. Why did it paste the picture as a floating object this time? Drag the picture into the shape.
10. Rotate one of the pictures 90 degrees to the right. Rotate the same picture 90 degrees to the right again. Flip the same picture vertically. Flip the same picture horizontally.
11. Recolor one of the pictures to a color of your choice. Add a border color of your choice to the same picture. Use the Reset Picture button (Picture Format tab | Adjust group) to clear the formatting of this picture. How would you reset the formatting and the size of the picture?

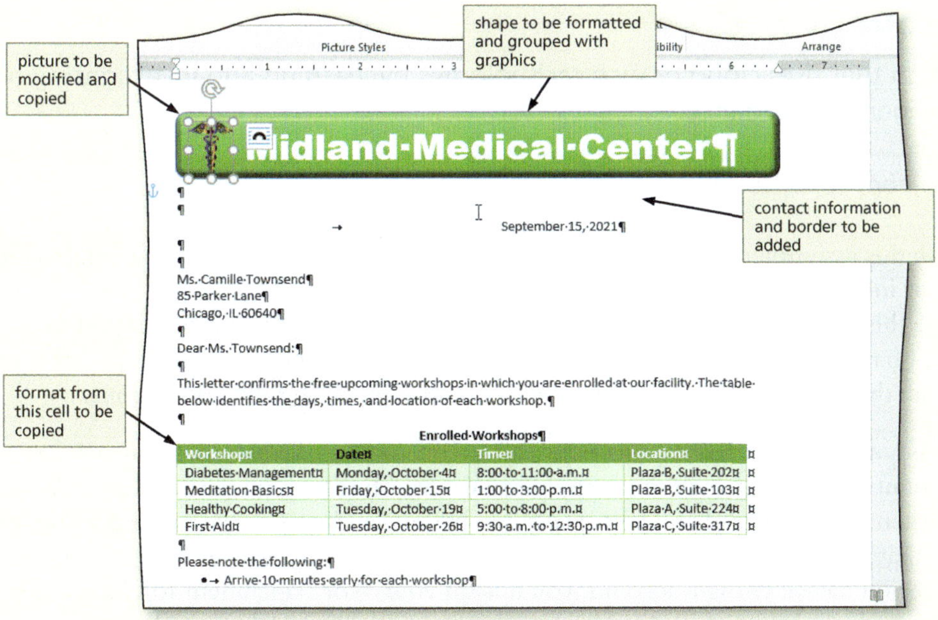

Figure 3–82

12. Select the shape around the Midland Medical Center title and then use the Edit Shape button (Shape Format tab | Insert Shapes group) to change the shape to a shape of your preference.
13. Group the two caduceus pictures with the shape. Change the text wrapping of the grouped shape to Top and Bottom.
14. Add the contact information below the shape, using a symbol of your choice from the Symbol gallery between the mailing address (101 Carrington Road, Chicago, IL 60640), phone number (312-555-0198), web address (midlandmc.net), and email address (info@midlandmc.net).
15. Add a bottom border to the paragraph containing the contact information.
16. Select the table in the letter and center it between the margins.
17. Select the upper-left cell in the table that contains the text, Workshop. Use the format painter to copy the formats of the selected cell to the cell immediately to the right with the text, Date.
18. Position the insertion point in the table and one at a time, select and deselect each check box in the Table Style Options group. What are the functions of each check box: Header Row, Total Row, Banded Rows, First Column, Last Column, and Banded Columns? Select the check boxes you prefer for the table.
19. If requested by your instructor, change the name in the signature block to your name.
20. Save the document again with the same file name.
21. Submit the modified document in the format specified by your instructor.
22. If requested by your instructor, create an envelope for the letter.
23. If requested by your instructor, print a single mailing label for the letter and then a full page of mailing labels, each containing the address shown in Figure 3–82.
24. Answer the questions posed in #7, #8, #9, #11, and #18. Why would you group objects? (If requested by your instructor, insert a next page section break at the end of the letter and write your responses on the inserted blank page and insert the current time.)

Expand Your World

Create a solution that uses cloud or web technologies by learning and investigating on your own from general guidance.

Using Google Docs to Upload and Edit Files

Notes:

- To complete this assignment, you will be required to use the Data Files. Please contact your instructor for information about accessing the Data Files.
- To complete this assignment, you will use a Google account, which you can create at no cost. If you do not have a Google account and do not want to create one, perform Steps 1 through 3 and then read the remainder of his assignment without performing the instructions.

Instructions: Assume you are a faculty member and a student has asked you to write a reference letter for an accounting job for which she is applying. You will finish creating the letter in Word at your office and then will proofread and edit it at home before sending it to the potential employer. The problem is that you do not have Word at home. You do, however, have an Internet connection at home. Because you have a Google account, you upload your Word document to Google Drive so that you can view and edit it later from a computer that does not have Word installed.

Perform the following tasks:

1. In Word, open the document, SC_WD_3-3.docx, from the Data Files. Click File on the ribbon, click Save As, and then save the document using the new file name, SC_WD_3_ReferenceLetter.
2. Add a box border around the two paragraphs containing the name, Prof. Kim Chung, and the contact information in the letterhead. Select style, width, and color for the box border other than the default. Apply a shading color to the paragraph containing the name.
3. Look through the letter so that you are familiar with its contents and formats. If desired, print the letter so that you easily can compare it to the Google Docs converted file. Close the document.
4. Start a browser. Search for the text, google docs, using a search engine. Visit several websites to learn about Google Docs and Google Drive. Navigate to the Google website. Read about how to create files in Google Docs and upload files to Google Drive. If you do not have a Google account and you want to create one, follow the instructions to create an account. If you do not have a Google account and you do not want to create one, read the remaining instructions without performing them. If you have a Google account, sign in to your account.
5. If necessary, display Google Drive. Upload the file, SC_WD_3_ReferenceLetter.docx, to Google Drive.
6. Rename the file on Google Drive to SC_WD_3_ReferenceLetter_inGoogle. Open the file in Google Docs (Figure 3–83). What differences do you see between the Word document and the Google Docs converted document?
7. Modify the document in Google Docs as follows: change the font and font size of the name in the letterhead, bold the name in the letterhead, change the font color of the name in the letterhead, change the background color for the paragraph containing the name, change the border color around the letterhead, change the name of the insurance company to Wide Country Insurance, and then display the document at various zoom levels.
8. If requested by your instructor, change the name in the letterhead and signature block to your name.

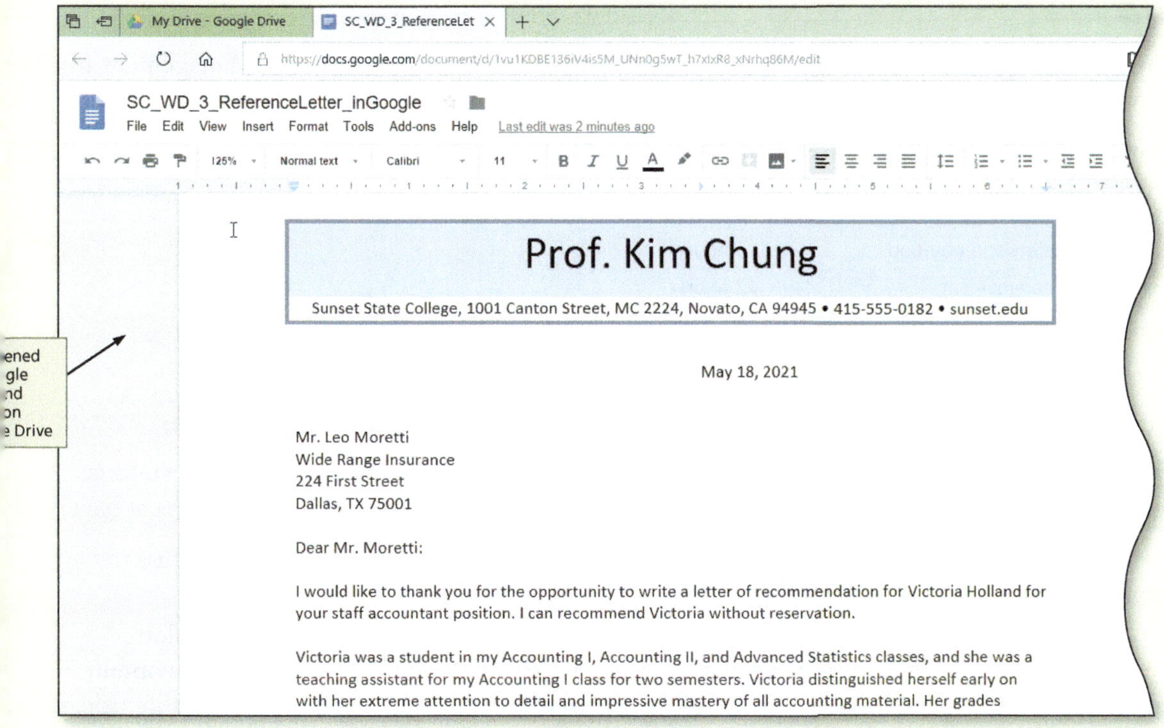

Figure 3–83

9. Download the revised document to your local storage media, changing its format to Microsoft Word. Submit the document in the format requested by your instructor.
10. What is Google Drive? What is Google Docs? Answer the question posed in #6. Do you prefer using Google Docs or Word? Why?

In the Lab

Design and implement a solution using creative thinking and problem-solving skills.

Create a Letter to a Potential Employer

Problem: As an extern in the career development office at your school, your boss has asked you to prepare a sample letter to a potential employer in the hospitality industry. Students on campus seeking employment will use this letter as a reference document when creating their own letters.

Perform the following tasks:

Part 1: Using your name, mailing address, phone number, and email address, create a letterhead for the letter. Be sure to include an image in the letterhead and appropriate separator lines and marks. Once the letterhead is designed, write the letter to this potential employer: Ms. Lynette Galens, Human Resources Director, Mountain Top Hotels, 125 Cedar Road, P.O. Box 1250, Denver, CO 80230.

The draft wording for the letter is as follows:

First paragraph: I am responding to your online advertisement for the assistant manager position. I have the credentials you are seeking and believe I can be a valuable asset to Mountain Top Hotels.

Continued >

In the Lab *continued*

Second paragraph: In May, I will be earning my bachelor's degree in Hospitality Management from Parkview College. My relevant coursework includes the following:

Below the second paragraph, insert the following table:

Event management	12 hours
Food safety and nutrition	15 hours
Hotel management	12 hours
Restaurant management	18 hours
Tourism management	12 hours

Third paragraph: In addition to my college coursework, I have the following experience:

Below the third paragraph, insert the following items as a bulleted list: Assisted school cafeteria director; Volunteered in Cedar Mission kitchen; Developed social media platforms for local bakery.

Last paragraph: I look forward to hearing from you to schedule an interview and to discuss my career opportunities at Mountain Top Hotels.

Use the concepts and techniques presented in this module to create and format a letter according to a letter style and creating appropriate paragraph breaks. The letter should contain a letterhead that includes a shape and an online picture(s); a table with an appropriate table title, column headings, and table style applied (unformatted table contents listed above); and a bulleted list (unformatted experience list items above). If requested by your instructor, insert nonbreaking spaces in the company name, Mountain Top Hotels. If requested by your instructor, set a transparent color in the picture.

While creating the letter, be sure to do the following:

1. Create a letterhead: insert and format a shape, insert and format at least one online picture, insert symbols from the Symbol gallery in the contact line, and add a paragraph border.
2. Create the letter contents: apply the No Spacing style, set left-aligned tab stops where appropriate, insert the current date, insert the table and format it, center the table, bullet the list as you type it, and use your name in the signature line in the letter.
3. Be sure to check the spelling and grammar of the finished letter.
4. Add alt text to the table and to the picture(s) in the document. Check the document accessibility of the finished letter.

When you are finished with the letter, save it with the file name, SC_WD_3_LetterToEmployer. Submit your assignment and answers to the Part 2 critical thinking questions in the format specified by your instructor.

Part 2: You made several decisions while creating the letter in this assignment: where to position elements in the letterhead, how to format elements in the letterhead, which shape and picture(s) to use in the letterhead, which font size to use for the letter text, which table style to use, and which letter style to use. What was the rationale behind each of these decisions?

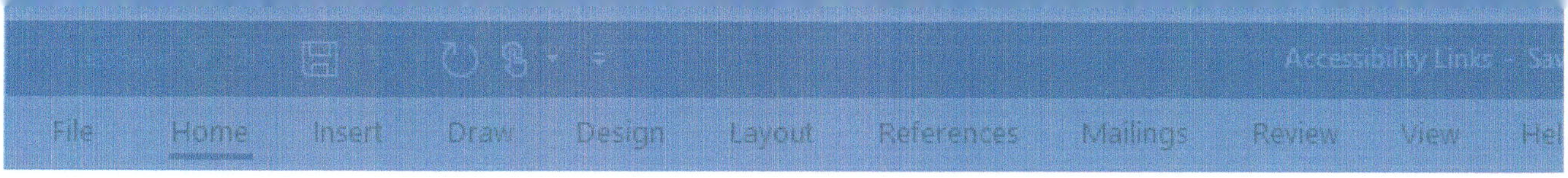

4 Creating a Multipage Document

Objectives

After completing this module, you will be able to:

- Insert a cover page
- Insert text in content controls
- Apply character effects
- Change paragraph indentation
- Insert formatted headers and footers
- Remove a content control
- Format page numbers
- Sort paragraphs and tables
- Change the color of bullets in a list
- Add picture bullets to a list
- Create a multilevel list
- Edit and format Word tables
- Insert a formula in a table
- Create a watermark

Introduction

During your business and personal endeavors, you may want or need to provide a recommendation to a person or group of people for their consideration. You might suggest they purchase a product, such as a vehicle or food, or contract a service, such as veterinary services or website design services. Or, you might try to convince an audience to take an action, such as visiting an establishment or donating to a cause. You may be asked to request funds for a new program or to promote an idea, such as a benefits package to company employees or a budget plan to upper management. To present these types of recommendations, you may find yourself writing a proposal.

A proposal generally is one of three types: sales, research, or planning. A **sales proposal** sells an idea, a product, or a service. A **research proposal** usually requests funding for a research project. A **planning proposal** offers solutions to a problem or improvement to a situation.

Project: Sales Proposal

Sales proposals describe the features and value of products and services being offered, with the intent of eliciting a positive response from the reader. Desired outcomes include the reader accepting ideas, purchasing products, contracting services, volunteering time, contributing to a cause, or taking an action. A well-written proposal can be the key to obtaining the desired results.

The project in this module follows generally accepted guidelines for writing short sales proposals and uses Word to create the sales proposal shown in Figure 4–1. The sales proposal in this module, written by the event coordinator at Awakenings Lodge and Conference Center, is designed to persuade employers to use the facility for their employee retreats. The proposal has a pleasing cover page to attract readers' attention. To add impact, the sales proposal has a watermark consisting of the word, TEAM, positioned behind the content on each page. The proposal also uses lists and tables to summarize and highlight important data.

In this module, you will learn how to create the sales proposal shown in Figure 4–1. You will perform the following general tasks as you progress through this module:

1. Create a cover page for the proposal.
2. Modify page formatting in the proposal.
3. Edit and format lists in the proposal.
4. Edit and format tables in the proposal.
5. Create a watermark in the proposal.

To Start Word, Open the Proposal Draft File, Save It with a New File Name, and Specify Word Settings

Assume you already have prepared a draft of the body of the proposal, which is located in the Data Files. Please see your instructor for information about accessing the Data Files. To convert the draft into a final document, you will fix formatting issues, modify page formatting, format an existing list, create a new list, edit and format existing tables, and add a watermark.

The following steps start Word, open the proposal draft file, save it with a new file name, display formatting marks, change the zoom to page width, and display rulers on the screen. If you are using a computer to step through the project in this module and you want your screens to match the figures in this book, you should change your screen's resolution to 1366 × 768.

If your instructor wants you to submit your work as a SAM Project for automatic grading, you must download the Data Files from the assignment launch page.

1. Start Word and open the file called SC_WD_4-1.docx from the Data Files. If necessary, maximize the Word window.
2. Save the file on your hard drive, OneDrive, or other storage location using the file name, SC_WD_4_Employee_Retreat_Sales_Proposal.
3. If the Print Layout button on the status bar is not selected, click it so that your screen is in Print Layout view.
4. If the 'Show/Hide ¶' button (Home tab | Paragraph group) is not selected already, click it to display formatting marks on the screen.
5. To display the page the same width as the document window, if necessary, click the Page Width button (View tab | Zoom group).
6. To display rulers on the screen, if necessary, click the Ruler check box (View tab | Show group).

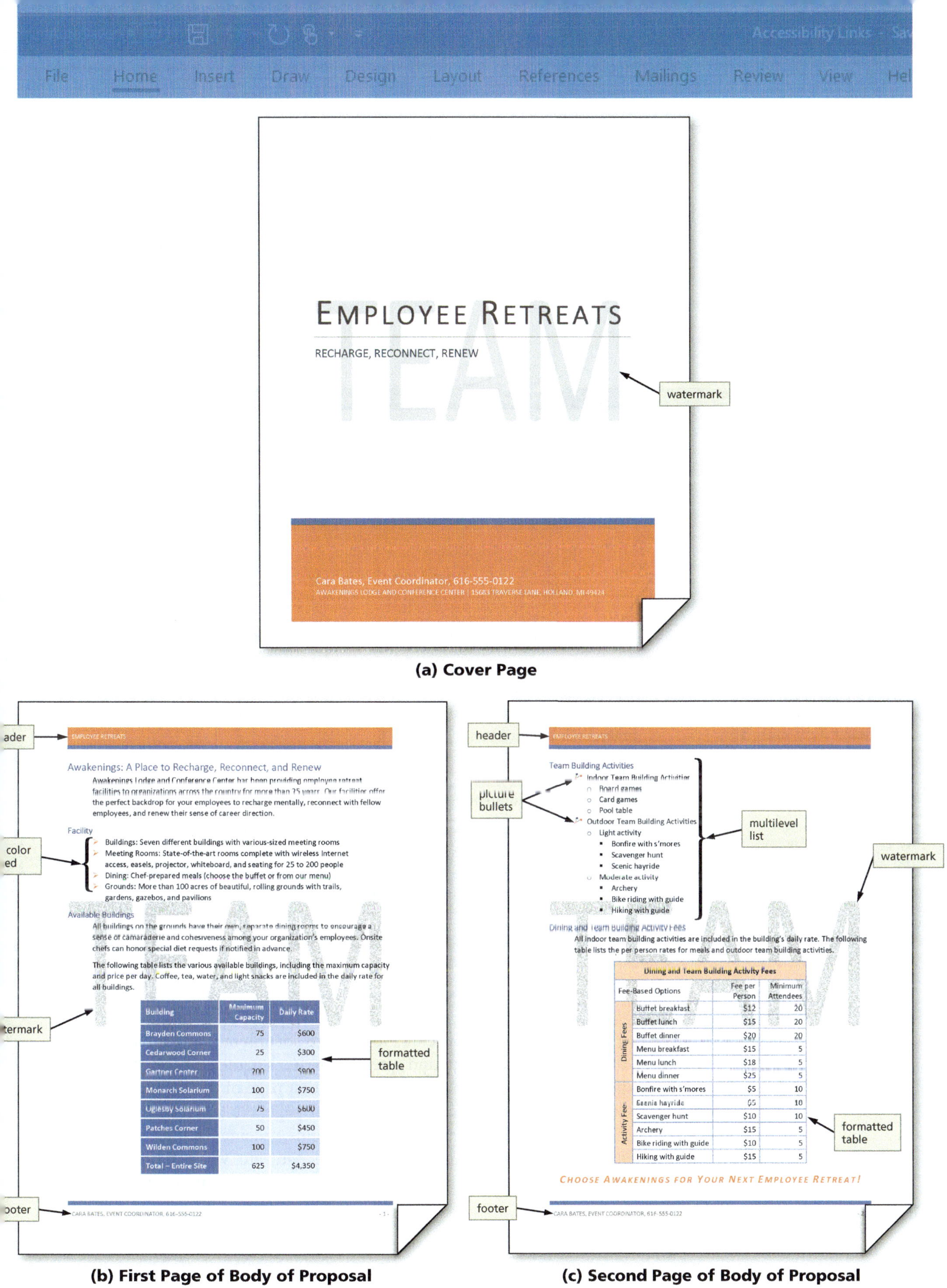

File
Home
Insert
Draw
Design
Layout
References
Mailings
Review
View
EMPLOYEE RETREATS
RECHARGE, RECONNECT, RENEW
TEAM
watermark
Cara Bates, Event Coordinator, 616-555-0122
(a) Cover Page
header
Awakenings: A Place to Recharge, Reconnect, and Renew
the perfect backdrop for your employees to recharge mentally, reconnect with fellow
employees, and renew their sense of career direction.
Facility
Buildings: Seven different buildings with various-sized meeting rooms
Meeting Rooms: State-of-the-art rooms complete with wireless Internet
access, easels, projector, whiteboard, and seating for 25 to 200 people
Dining: Chef-prepared meals (choose the buffet or from our menu)
Grounds: More than 100 acres of beautiful, rolling grounds with trails,
gardens, gazebos, and pavilions
Available Buildings
chefs can honor special diet requests if notified in advance.
The following table lists the various available buildings, including the maximum capacity
and price per day. Coffee, tea, water, and light snacks are included in the daily rate for
all buildings.
Building
Maximum Capacity
Daily Rate
Brayden Commons 75 $600
Cedarwood Corner 25 $300
Monarch Solarium 100 $750
Patches Corner 50 $450
Wilden Commons 100 $750
Total – Entire Site 625 $4,350
formatted table
footer
(b) First Page of Body of Proposal
header
Team Building Activities
picture bullets
Card games
Pool table
Outdoor Team Building Activities
Light activity
Bonfire with s'mores
Scavenger hunt
Scenic hayride
Archery
Bike riding with guide
Hiking with guide
multilevel list
watermark
All indoor team building activities are included in the building's daily rate. The following
table lists the per person rates for meals and outdoor team building activities.
Dining and Team Building Activity Fees
Fee-Based Options
Fee per Person
Minimum Attendees
Dining Fees
Buffet breakfast $12 20
Buffet lunch $15 20
Buffet dinner $20 20
Menu breakfast $15 5
Menu lunch $18 5
Menu dinner $25 5
Activity Fees
Bonfire with s'mores $5 10
Scavenger hunt $10 10
Archery $15 5
Bike riding with guide $10 5
Hiking with guide $15 5
formatted table
CHOOSE AWAKENINGS FOR YOUR NEXT EMPLOYEE RETREAT!
footer
(c) Second Page of Body of Proposal

Figure 4–1

7 If you are using a mouse and you want your screens to match the figures in the book, verify that you are using Mouse mode by clicking the Touch/Mouse Mode button on the Quick Access Toolbar and then, if necessary, clicking Mouse on the menu (Figure 4–2). (If your Quick Access Toolbar does not display the Touch/Mouse Mode button, click the 'Customize Quick Access Toolbar' button on the Quick Access Toolbar and then click Touch/Mouse Mode on the menu to add the button to the Quick Access Toolbar.)

BTW

Normal Style

If your screen settings differ from Figure 4–2, it is possible the default settings in your Normal style have been changed. Normal style settings are saved in a file called normal.dotm. To restore the original Normal style settings, exit Word and use File Explorer to locate the normal.dotm file (be sure that hidden files and folders are displayed, and include system and hidden files in your search — you may need to use Help to assist you with these tasks). Rename the normal.dotm file as oldnormal.dotm. After renaming the normal .dotm file, it no longer will exist as normal.dotm. The next time you run Word, it will recreate a normal.dotm file using the original default settings.

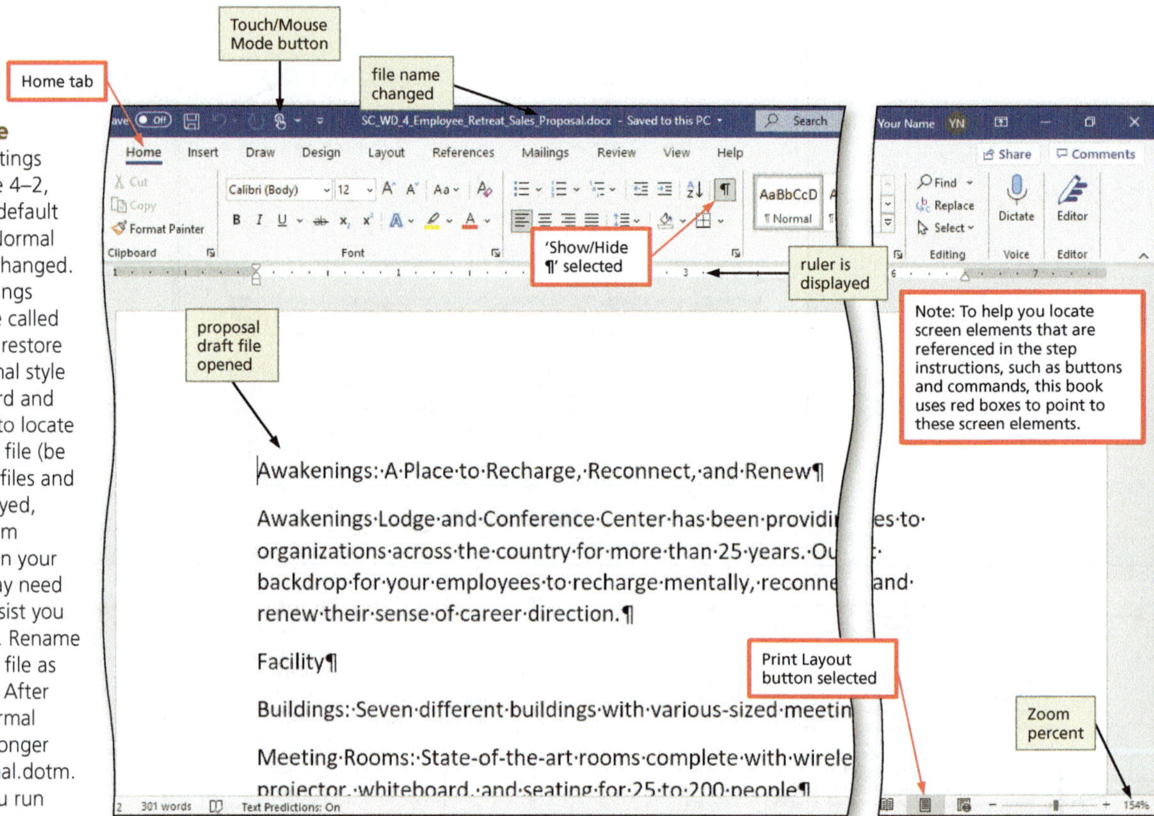

Figure 4–2

Creating a Cover Page

A **cover page** is a separate title page in a multipage document that contains, at a minimum, the title of a document, and often the writer's name and sometimes the date. For a sales proposal, the cover page usually is the first page of the document. Solicited proposals often have a specific format for the cover page. Guidelines for the cover page of a solicited proposal may stipulate the margins, spacing, layout, and required contents, such as title, sponsor name, author name, date, etc. With an unsolicited proposal, by contrast, you can design the cover page in a way that best presents its message.

Consider This

How do you design an effective cover page?

The cover page is the first section a reader sees on a sales proposal. Thus, it is important that the cover page appropriately reflects the goal of the sales proposal. When designing the cover page, consider its content.

- **Use concise, descriptive text.** The cover page should contain a short, descriptive title that accurately reflects the message of the sales proposal. The cover page also may include a theme or slogan. Do not place a page number on the cover page.
- **Identify appropriate fonts, font sizes, and colors for the text.** Use fonts that are easy to read. Avoid using more than three different fonts because too many fonts can make the cover page visually confusing. Use larger font sizes to add impact to the cover page. To give the title more emphasis, its font size should be larger than any other text on the cover page. Use colors that complement one another and convey the meaning of the proposal.
- **Use graphics, if desired, to reinforce the goal.** Select simple graphics that clearly communicate the fundamental nature of the proposal. Possible graphics include shapes, pictures, and logos.
- **Use colors that complement text colors.** Be aware that too many graphics and colors can be distracting. Arrange graphics with the text so that the cover page is attractive and uncluttered.

The cover page of the sales proposal in this module (shown in Figure 4–1a) contains text, colors, and the faded word, TEAM, in the background. The steps in the next section create the cover page. The faded word, TEAM, is added to all pages at the end of this module.

To Insert a Cover Page

Word has many predefined cover page formats that you can use for the cover page in a document. When you insert a predefined cover page, Word inserts it at the top of the document by default. The following steps insert a cover page. **Why?** The predefined cover pages use complementary colors and fonts for a document's cover page.

1

- Display the Insert tab.
- Click the Cover Page button (Insert tab | Pages group) to display the Cover Page gallery.

Experiment

- Scroll through the Cover Page gallery to see the variety of available predefined cover pages. When finished, display the Retrospect cover page in the Cover Page gallery, as shown in Figure 4–3.

Q&A **Does it matter where I position the insertion point before inserting a cover page?**
No. By default, Word inserts the cover page as the first page in a document.

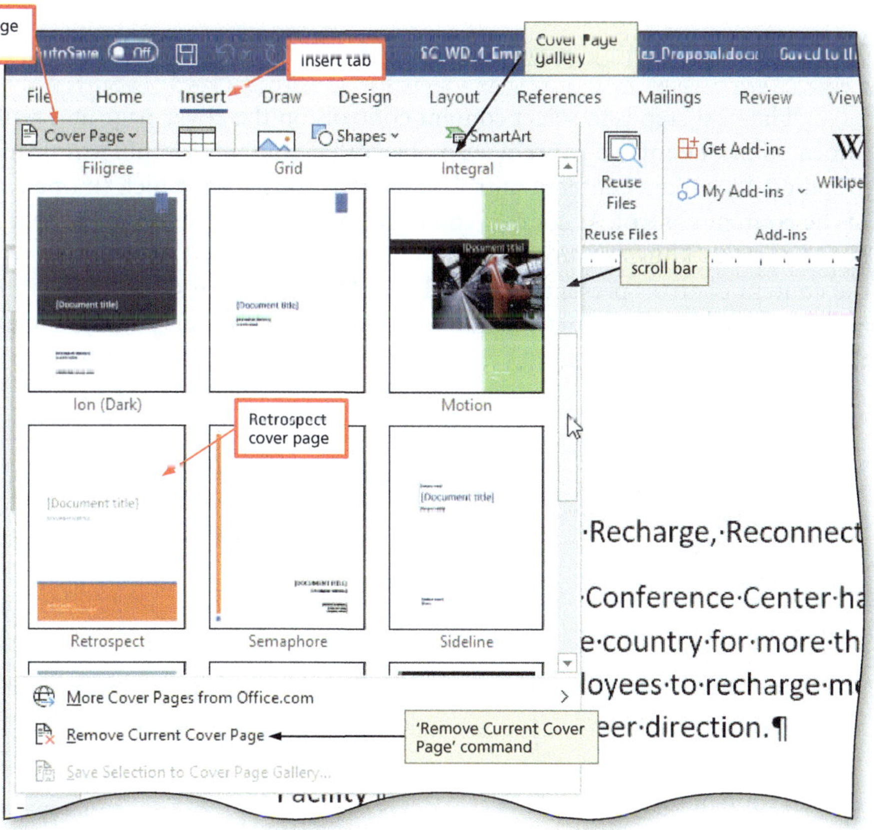

Figure 4–3

2

- If necessary, scroll to and then click Retrospect in the Cover Page gallery to insert the selected cover page as the first page in the current document.
- Display the View tab. Click the One Page button (View tab | Zoom group) to display the entire cover page in the document window (Figure 4–4).

Q&A

Does the cover page have to be the first page?
No. You can right-click the desired cover page in the Cover Page gallery and then click the desired location on the submenu.

How would I delete a cover page?
You would click the Cover Page button (Insert tab | Pages group) and then click 'Remove Current Cover Page' in the Cover Page gallery (shown in Figure 4–3).

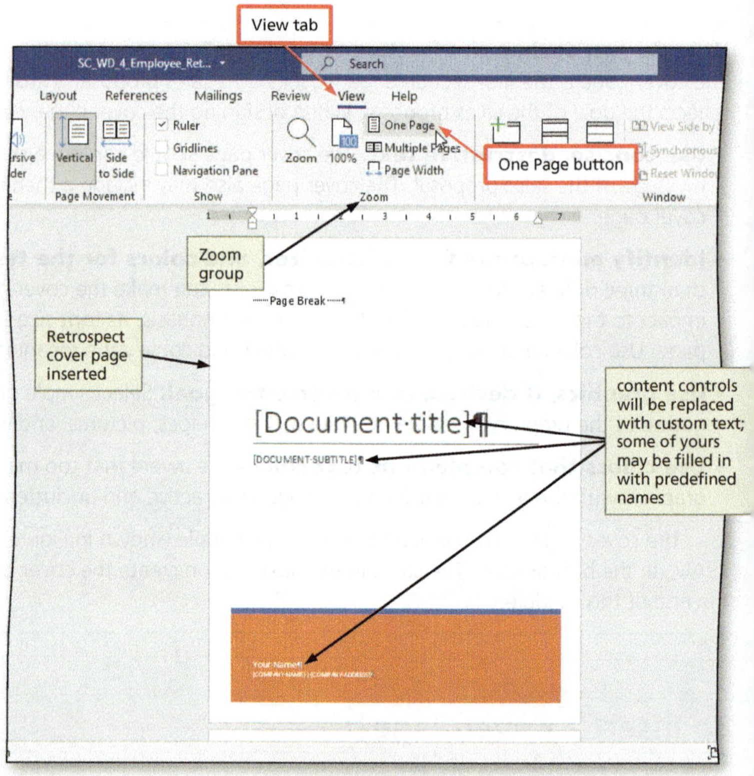

Figure 4–4

Other Ways

1. Click Quick Parts button (Insert tab | Text group), click 'Building Blocks Organizer' on Quick Parts menu, select desired cover page building block (Building Blocks Organizer dialog box), click Insert button, click Close

To Enter Text in Content Controls

The next step is to select content controls on the cover page and replace their text with the cover page information. A **content control** is an object that contains sample text or instructions for filling in text and graphics. To select a content control, you click it or its tag, which (if one exists) is located in the upper-left corner of the content control. As soon as you begin typing in the selected content control, your typing replaces the text in the control. Thus, you do not need to delete the selected text before you begin typing. Keep in mind that the content controls present suggested text. Depending on settings on your computer or mobile device, some content controls already may contain customized text, which you will change. The following steps enter text on the cover page. **Why?** You want to replace the content controls with customized text.

1

- Click the Page Width button (View tab | Zoom group) to display the page as wide as the document window.
- If necessary, scroll to display the [Document title] content control in the document window.
- Click the [Document title] content control or its tag to select the content control (Figure 4–5).

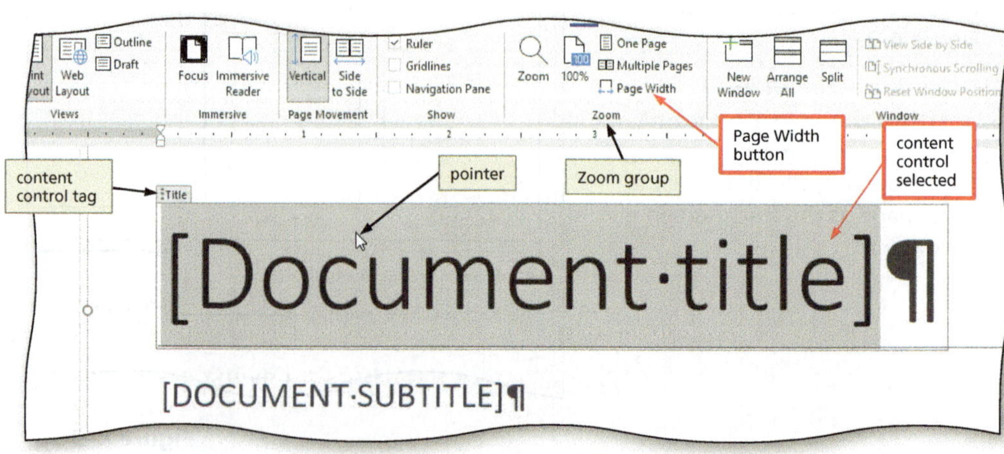

Figure 4–5

2

- Type **`Employee Retreats`** as the document title.
- Click the [DOCUMENT SUBTITLE] content control or its tag to select the content control (Figure 4–6).

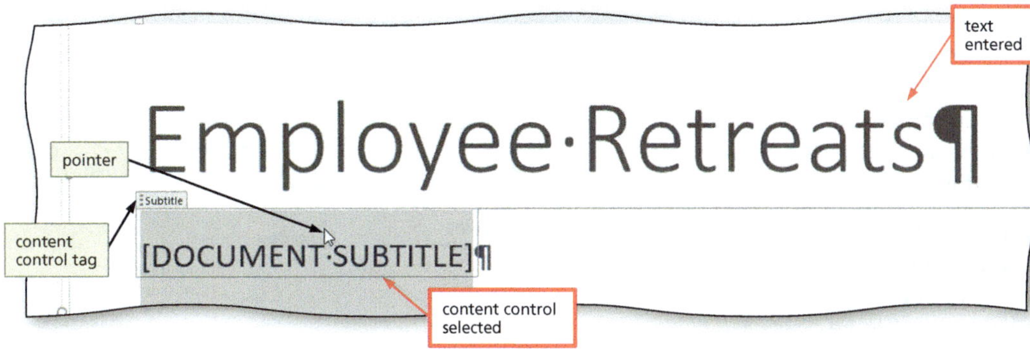

Figure 4–6

3

- Type **`Recharge, Reconnect, Renew`** as the document subtitle.

Q&A **Why is my document subtitle text capitalized?**
Word automatically changes the text to uppercase letters.

- Scroll to display the author content control in the document window.
- Select the author content control and then type **`Cara Bates, Event Coordinator, 616-555-0122`** as the text.

Q&A **Why is my author content control filled in?**
Depending on settings, your content control already may display an author name.

- Select the company control and then type **`Awakenings Lodge and Conference Center`** as the text.
- Select the address content control and then type **`15683 Traverse Lane, Holland, MI 49424`** as the text.
- Press END to deselect the content control (Figure 4–7).

Figure 4–7

To Format Characters in Small Caps and Modify Character Spacing

The next step in this project is to enter and format the document title text in the middle of the cover page. Its characters are to be bold, and each letter in this text is formatted in **small caps**, which are letters that look like uppercase letters but are smaller than other uppercase letters in the document. Also, you want extra space between each character so that the text spans the width of the page.

Thus, the next steps apply the formats mentioned above using the Font dialog box. **Why?** Although you could use buttons on the Home tab to apply some of these formats, the small caps effect and expanded spacing are applied using the Font dialog box. Thus, you apply all the formats using the Font dialog box.

1

- Scroll up, if necessary, and select the text to be formatted, Employee Retreats, in this case.
- Display the Home tab and then click the Font Dialog Box Launcher (Home tab | Font group) to display the Font dialog box. If necessary, click the Font tab in the dialog box to display the Font sheet.
- Click Bold in the Font style list to bold the selected text.
- Click the Small caps check box in the Effects area so that each character is displayed as a small uppercase letter (Figure 4–8).

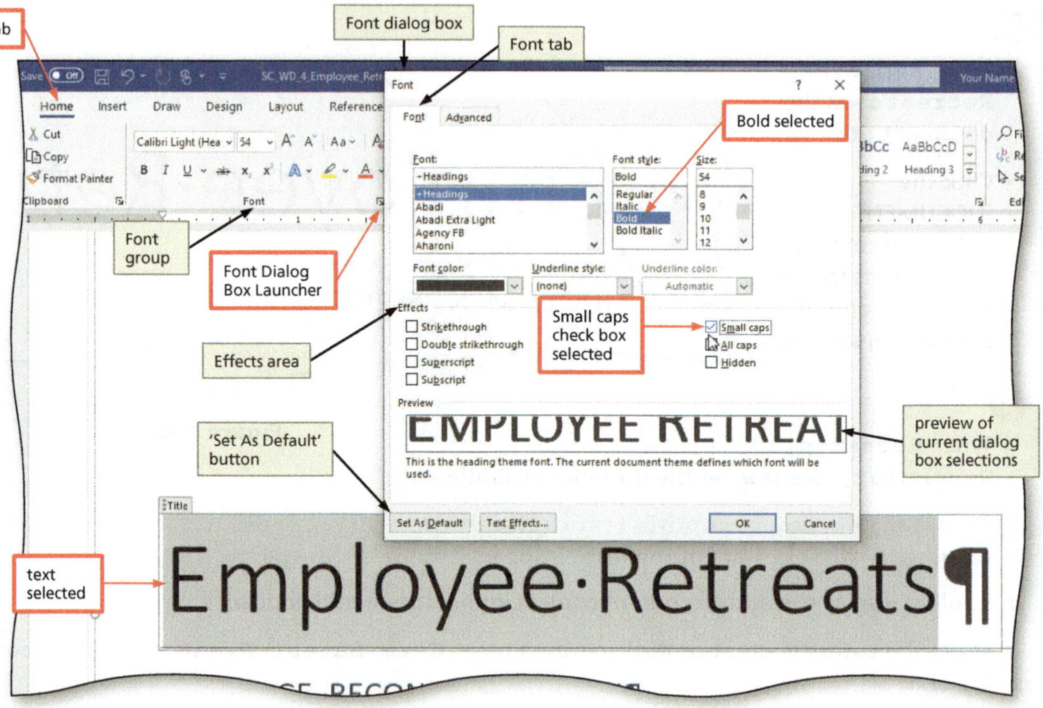

Figure 4–8

2

- Click the Advanced tab (Font dialog box) to display the Advanced sheet in the Font dialog box.
- Click the Spacing arrow in the Character Spacing area and then click Expanded to increase the amount of space between characters by 1 pt, which is the default.
- Double-click the value in the Spacing By box to select it and then type 5 because you want this amount of blank space to be displayed between each character.
- Click in any box in the dialog box for the change to take effect and display a preview of the entered value in the Preview area (Figure 4–9).

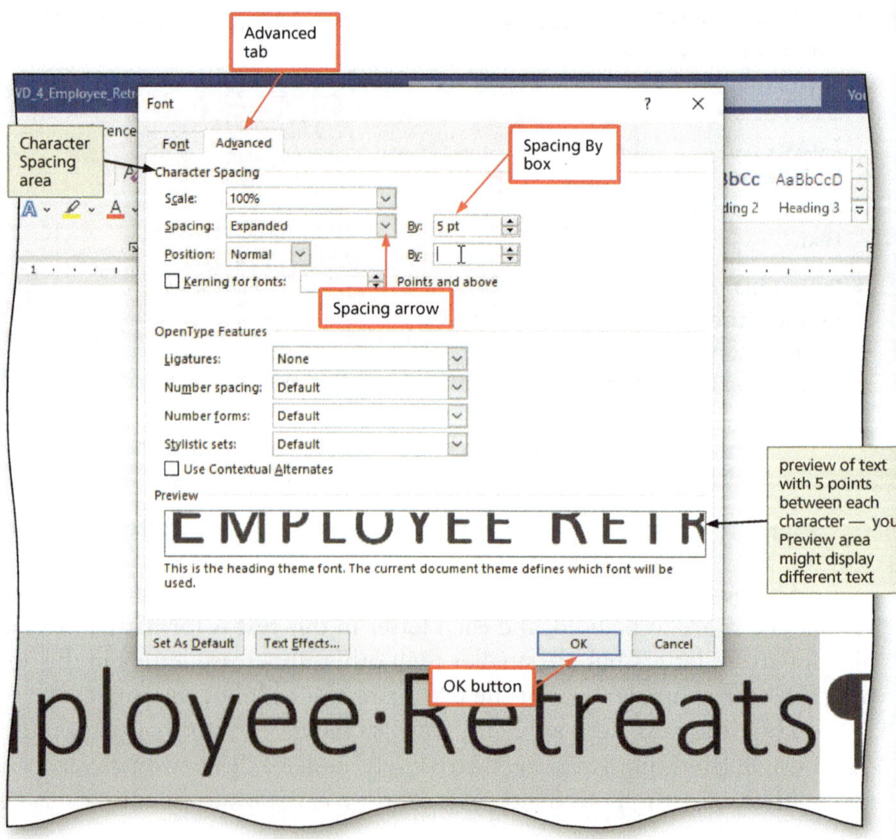

Figure 4–9

Q&A **Can I click the Spacing By arrows instead of typing a value in the box?**
Yes.

3

- Click OK to apply font changes to the selected text.
- Click anywhere to remove the selection from the text (Figure 4–10).

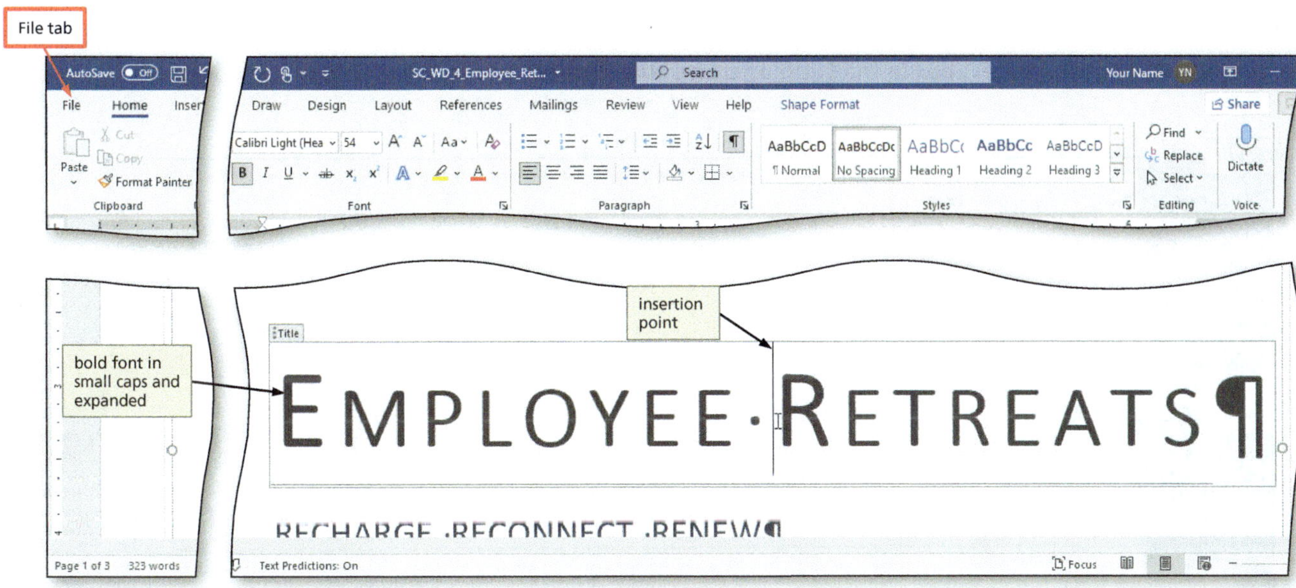

Figure 4–10

Other Ways

1. Right-click selected text (or, if using touch, tap 'Show Context Menu' button on Mini toolbar), click Font on shortcut menu, select formats (Font dialog box), click OK
2. Press CTRL+D, select formats (Font dialog box), click OK

Modifying Page Formatting

In the following sections, you edit and format the draft of the proposal that is below the cover page by deleting a page break, applying styles, changing paragraph indentation, inserting a header and a footer, and formatting page numbers.

BTW

Conserving Ink and Toner

If you want to conserve ink or toner, you can instruct Word to print draft quality documents by clicking File on the ribbon to open Backstage view, clicking Options in Backstage view to display the Word Options dialog box, clicking Advanced in the left pane (Word Options dialog box), scrolling to the Print area in the right pane, placing a check mark in the 'Use draft quality' check box, and then clicking OK. Then, use Backstage view to print the document as usual.

To Print Specific Pages in a Document

The cover page is the first page of the proposal. The body of the proposal spans the second and third pages, but when you inserted the cover page, Word formatted the page numbers so that numbering begins on the page that follows the cover page. **Why?** Cover pages typically do not have a page number on them. You would like to review a printout of the draft of the proposal, that is, the pages that follow the cover page. The following steps print only the body of the proposal, that is, the pages that follow the cover page.

BTW

Headers and Footers

If a portion of a header or footer does not print, it may be in a nonprintable area. Check the printer user instructions to see how close the printer can print to the edge of the paper. Then, click the Page Setup Dialog Box Launcher (Layout tab | Page Setup group), click the Layout tab (Page Setup dialog box), adjust the From edge text box to a value that is larger than the printer's minimum margin setting, click OK, and then print the document again.

1

- Click File on the ribbon to open Backstage view and then click Print in Backstage view to display the Print screen.
- Verify that the printer listed on the Printer Status button will print a hard copy of the document. If necessary, click the Printer Status button to display a list of available printer options and then click the desired printer to change the selected printer.
- Type **1–2** in the Pages text box in the Settings area of the Print screen (Figure 4–11).

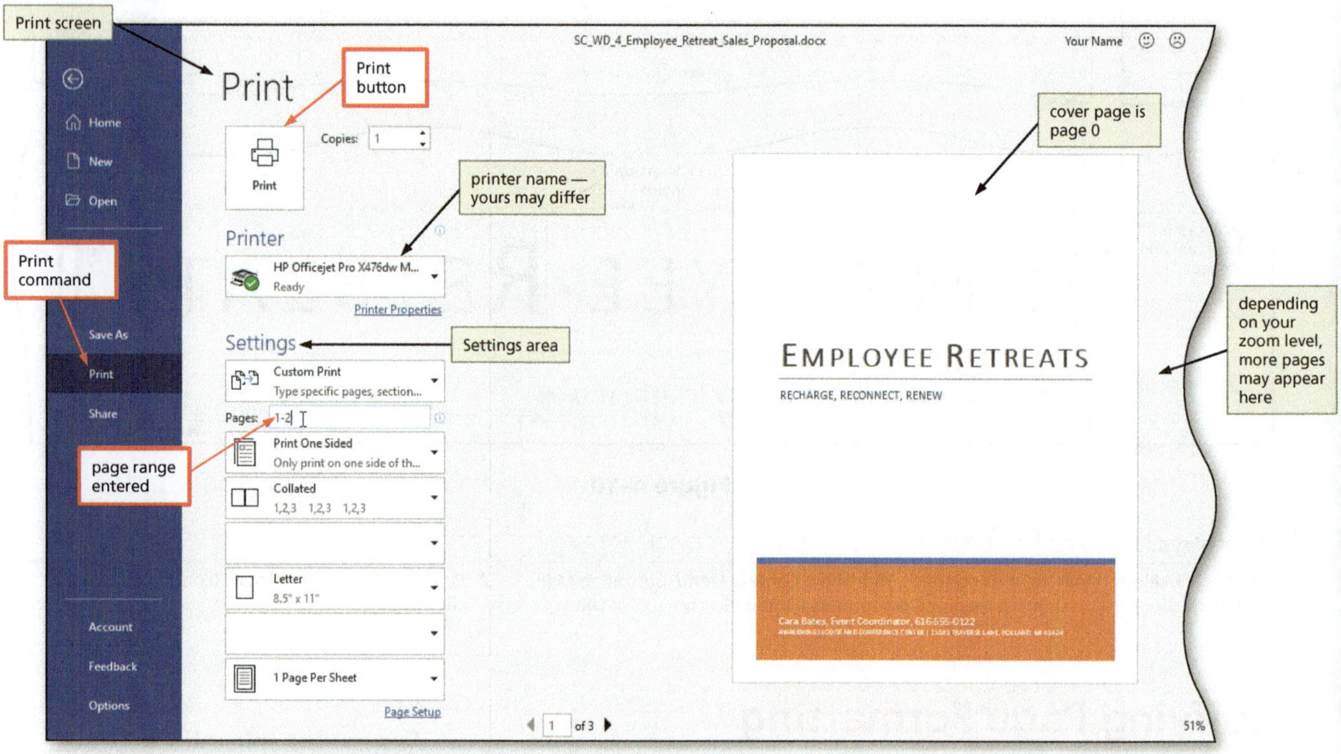

Figure 4–11

2

- Click the Print button to print the specified pages of the sales proposal (Figure 4–12).

Q&A

How would I print pages from a certain point to the end of a document or just selected text?
You would enter the page number followed by a dash in the Pages text box. For example, 5- will print from page 5 to the end of the document. To print up to a certain page, put the dash first (e.g., -5 will print pages 1 through 5). To print part of a document, select the text or objects to be printed before opening Backstage view, click the first button in the Settings area, and then click Print Selection in the list.

Why does my document wrap on different words than Figure 4–12?
Differences in wordwrap may be related to the printer used by your computer.

BTW

Page Numbers

If Word displays {PAGE} instead of the actual page number, press ALT+F9 to turn off field codes. If Word prints {PAGE} instead of the page number, open Backstage view, click Options to display the Word Options dialog box, click Advanced in the left pane (Word Options dialog box), scroll to the Print area, remove the check mark from the 'Print field codes instead of their values' check box, and then click OK.

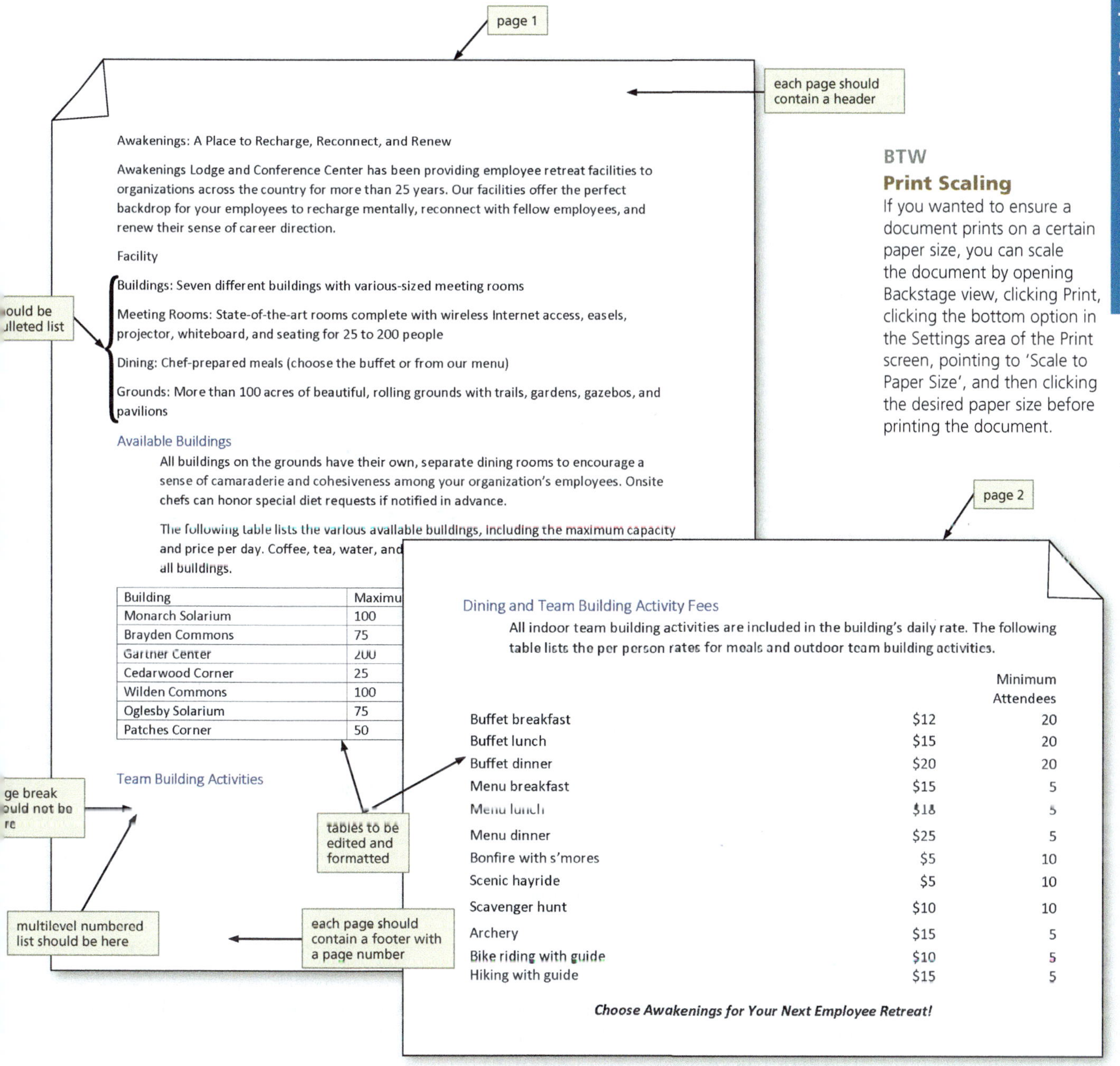

Building	Maximu
Monarch Solarium	100
Brayden Commons	75
Gartner Center	200
Cedarwood Corner	25
Wilden Commons	100
Oglesby Solarium	75
Patches Corner	50

		Minimum Attendees
Buffet breakfast	$12	20
Buffet lunch	$15	20
Buffet dinner	$20	20
Menu breakfast	$15	5
Menu lunch	$18	5
Menu dinner	$25	5
Bonfire with s'mores	$5	10
Scenic hayride	$5	10
Scavenger hunt	$10	10
Archery	$15	5
Bike riding with guide	$10	5
Hiking with guide	$15	5

Figure 4–12

BTW

Print Scaling

If you wanted to ensure a document prints on a certain paper size, you can scale the document by opening Backstage view, clicking Print, clicking the bottom option in the Settings area of the Print screen, pointing to 'Scale to Paper Size', and then clicking the desired paper size before printing the document.

Other Ways

1. Press CTRL+P; press ENTER

Consider This

What elements should the body of a sales proposal contain?

Be sure to include basic elements in your sales proposals:

- **Include an introduction, body, and conclusion.** The introduction could contain the subject, purpose, statement of problem, need, background, or scope. The body may include costs, benefits, supporting documentation, available or required facilities, feasibility, methods, timetable, materials, or equipment. The conclusion summarizes key points or requests an action.
- **Use headers and footers.** Headers and footers help to identify every page. A page number should be in either the header or footer. If the sales proposal should become disassembled, the reader can use the page numbers in the headers or footers to determine the order and pieces of your proposal.

To Delete a Page Break

After reviewing the draft in Figure 4–12, you notice it contains a page break below the Team Building Activities heading. The following steps delete a page break. **Why?** This page break should not be in the proposal.

1

- Scroll to display the page break notation in the document.
- To select the page break notation, double-click it (Figure 4–13).

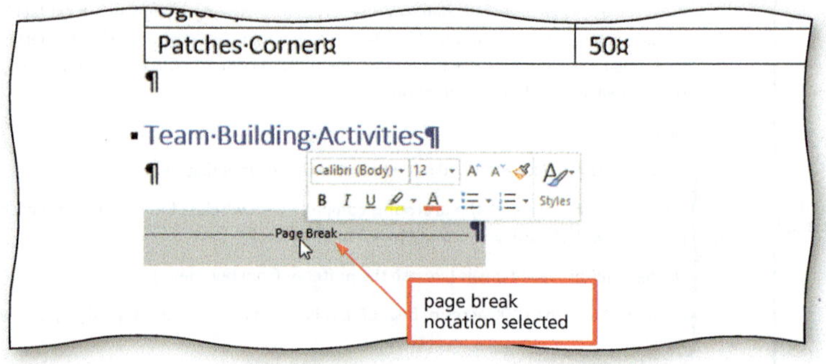

Figure 4–13

2

- Press DELETE to remove the page break from the document (Figure 4–14).

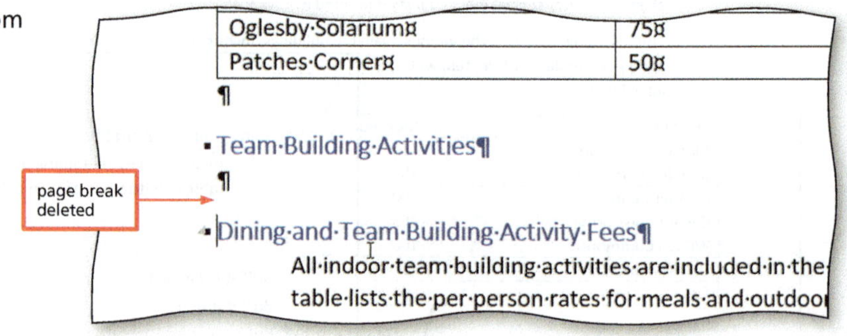

Figure 4–14

Other Ways

1. With page break notation selected, click Cut button (Home tab | Clipboard group)
2. With page break notation selected, right-click selection and then click Cut on Mini toolbar or shortcut menu
3. With the insertion point to the left or right of the page break notation, press DELETE or BACKSPACE, respectively

BTW

Page Breaks and Tables

If you do not want a page break to occur in the middle of a table, position the insertion point in the table, click the Properties button (Layout tab | Table group), click the Row tab (Table Properties dialog box), remove the check mark from the 'Allow row to break across pages' check box, and then click OK. To force a table to break across pages at a particular row, click in the row that you want to appear on the next page and then press CTRL+ENTER.

To Apply Heading Styles

Word has many built-in, or predefined, styles that you can use to format text. Three of the styles shown in the Styles gallery in Figure 4–15 are for headings: Heading 1 for the major headings and Heading 2 and Heading 3 for minor headings. In the draft document, all headings except for the first two were formatted using heading styles.

The following steps apply the Heading 1 style to the paragraph containing the text, Awakenings: A Place to Recharge, Reconnect, and Renew, and the Heading 2 style to the paragraph containing the text, Facility.

1 Position the insertion point in the paragraph to be formatted to the Heading 1 style, in this case, the first line on the page below the cover page with the text, Awakenings: A Place to Recharge, Reconnect, and Renew.

2 Click Heading 1 in the Styles gallery (Home tab | Styles group) to apply the selected style to the paragraph containing the insertion point.

Q&A

Why did a square appear on the screen near the left edge of the paragraph formatted with the Heading 1 style?

The square is a nonprinting character, like the paragraph mark, that indicates text to its right has a special paragraph format applied to it.

3. Position the insertion point in the paragraph to be formatted to the Heading 2 style, in this case, the line containing the text, Facility.

4. Click Heading 2 in the Styles gallery (Home tab | Styles group) to apply the selected style to the paragraph containing the insertion point (Figure 4–15).

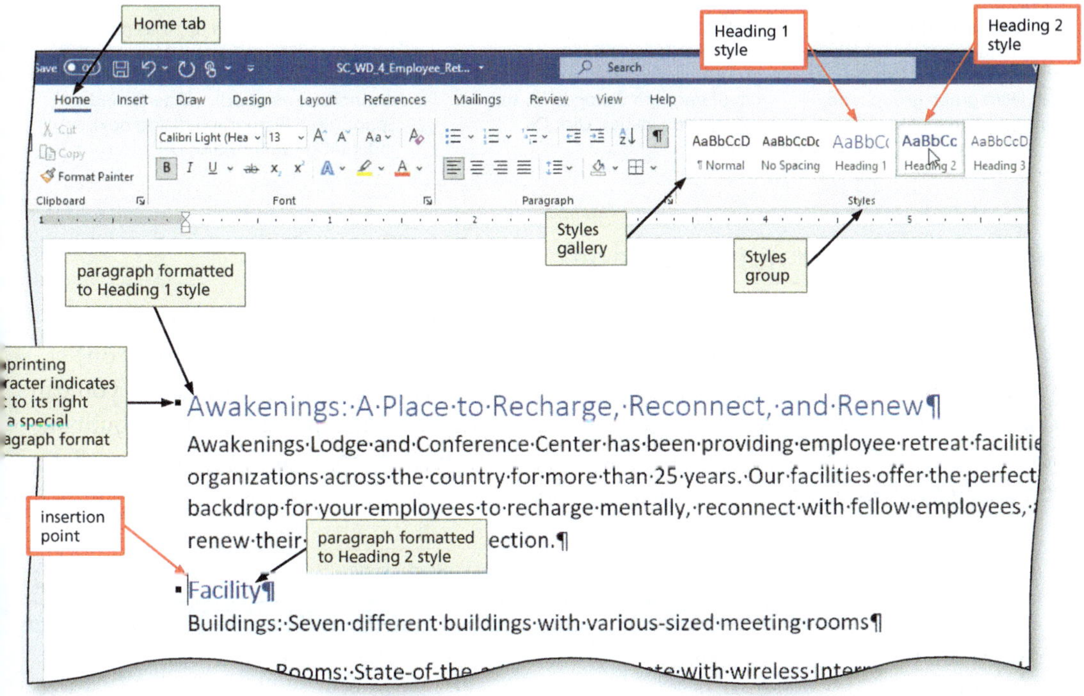

Figure 4–15

To Change Left Paragraph Indent

The paragraphs in the proposal are indented from the left margin by one-half inch. **Why?** You want the headings to begin at the left margin and the paragraphs to be indented from the left margin. The Increase Indent and Decrease Indent buttons (Home tab | Paragraph group) change the left indent by one-half inch, respectively. The following step changes the left paragraph indent of the first paragraph in the proposal.

1.
- Position the insertion point in the paragraph to indent, in this case, the paragraph that begins "Awakenings Lodge and Conference Center has been…"
- Click the Increase Indent button (Home tab | Paragraph group) to indent the paragraph one-half inch from the left margin (Figure 4–16).

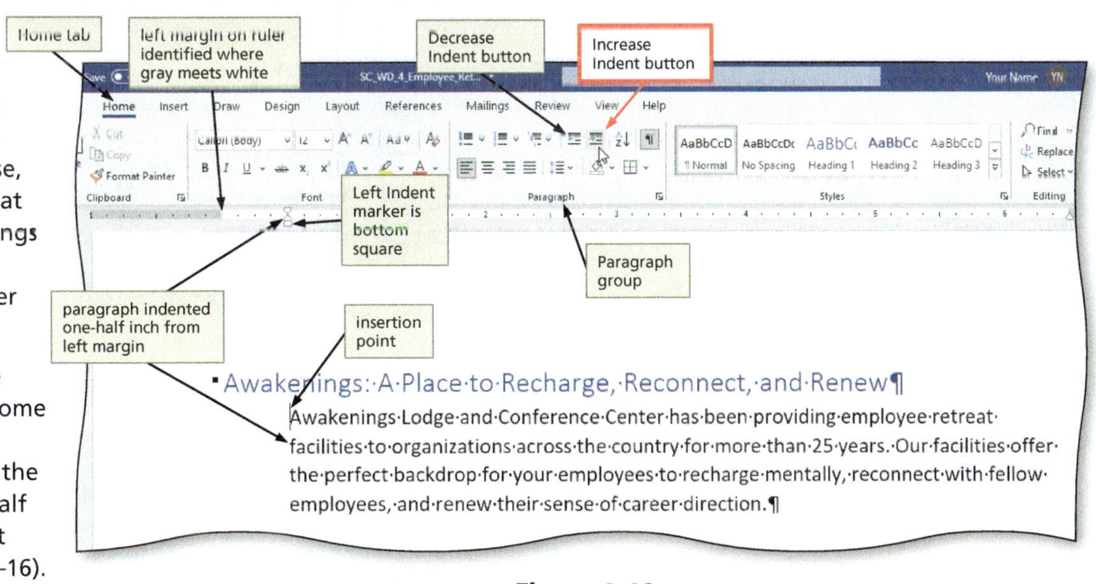

Figure 4–16

Experiment

- Repeatedly click the Increase Indent and Decrease Indent buttons (Home tab | Paragraph group) and watch the left edge of the current paragraph move in the document window. When you have finished experimenting, set the left indent so that it is one-half inch from the left margin as shown in Figure 4–16.

Other Ways

1. Drag Left Indent marker on ruler	2. Click Indent Left up or down arrows (Layout tab | Paragraph group) (or, if using touch, tap Indent Left box (Layout tab | Paragraph group) and then enter desired indent value)	3. Click Paragraph Settings Dialog Box Launcher (Home tab | Paragraph group), click Indents and Spacing tab (Paragraph dialog box), set indentation values, click OK	4. Right-click paragraph (or, if using touch, tap 'Show Context Menu' button on Mini toolbar), click Paragraph on shortcut menu, click Indents and Spacing tab (Paragraph dialog box), set indentation values, click OK

To Insert a Different First Page Formatted Header

A header is information that appears at the top of each page in the document. A footer is information that appears at the bottom of each page. In this proposal, you want the header and footer you insert to appear on each page after the cover page. **Why?** You do not want the header to appear on the cover page. In Word, you can instruct the header and footer not to appear on the first page in a document. Word also provides several built-in preformatted header designs for you to insert in documents. The following steps insert a formatted header that does not appear on the first page of a document.

1

- Display the Insert tab.
- Click the Header button (Insert tab | Header & Footer group) to display the Header gallery.

Experiment

- Scroll through the list of built-in headers to see the variety of available formatted header designs (Figure 4–17).

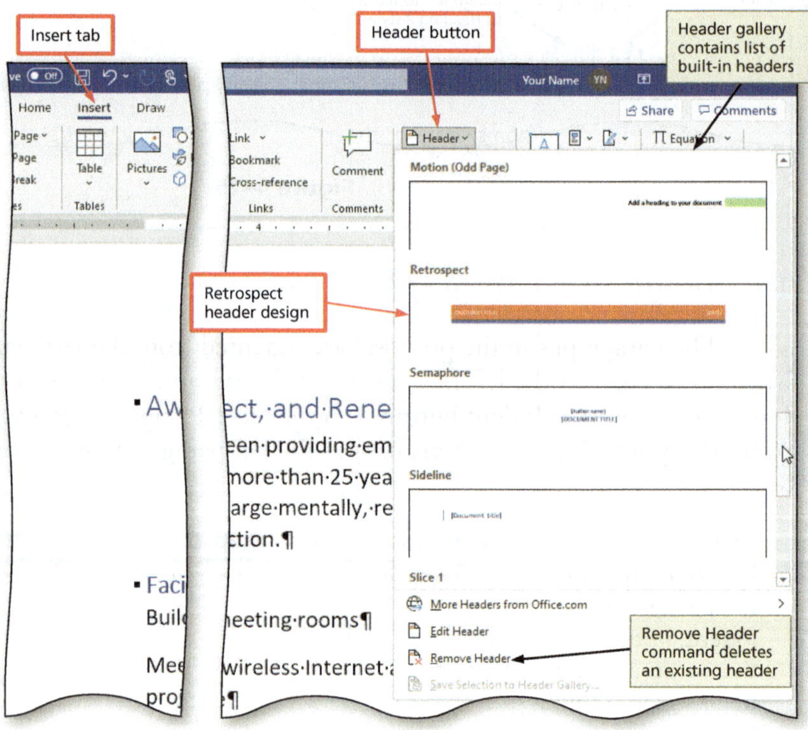

Figure 4–17

2

- If necessary, scroll to and then click the Retrospect header design in the Header gallery to insert the formatted header, which contains two content controls, at the top of the page.

Q&A **Why choose the Retrospect header design?**
You want to use the same theme throughout the document and the cover page used the Retrospect design.

- If the 'Different First Page' check box (Header & Footer tab | Options group) is not selected, click it to select it so that this header does not appear on the cover page (Figure 4–18).

Q&A **How would I delete a header?**
You would click Remove Header in the Header gallery (shown in Figure 4–17).

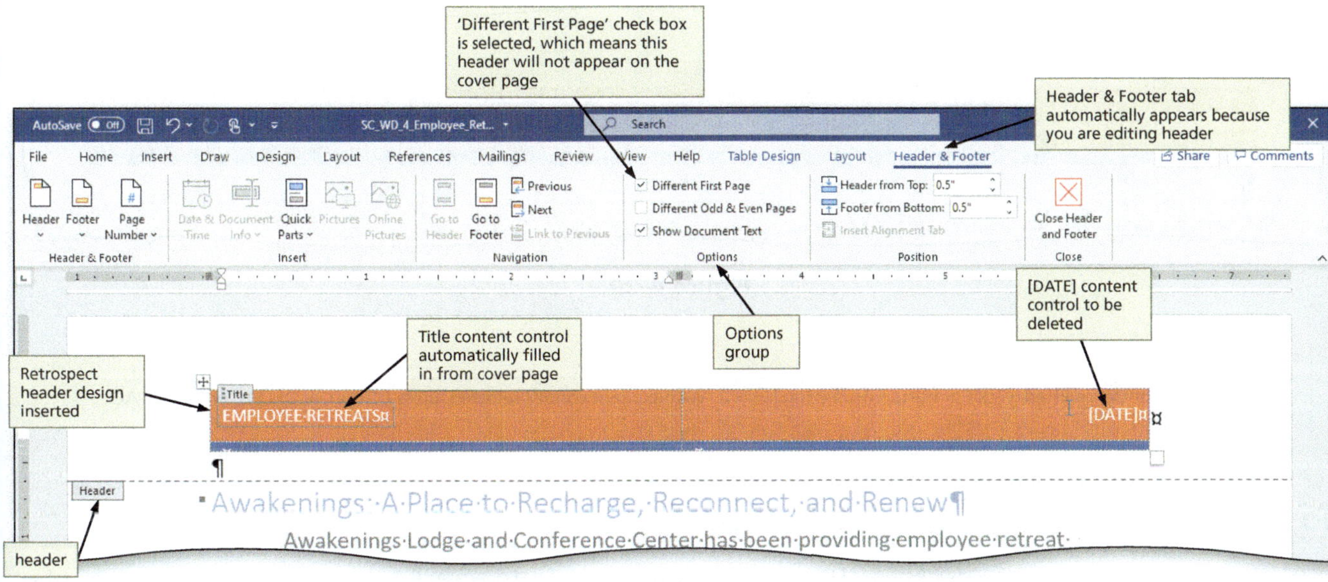

Figure 4–18

Other Ways

1. Click Quick Parts button (Insert tab | Text group), click 'Building Blocks Organizer' on Quick Parts menu, select desired header (Building Blocks Organizer dialog box), click Insert button, click Close

To Remove a Content Control

The following steps delete the [DATE] content control. **Why?** You do not want the date to appear in the header.

1

- Right-click the [DATE] content control to display a shortcut menu (Figure 4–19).

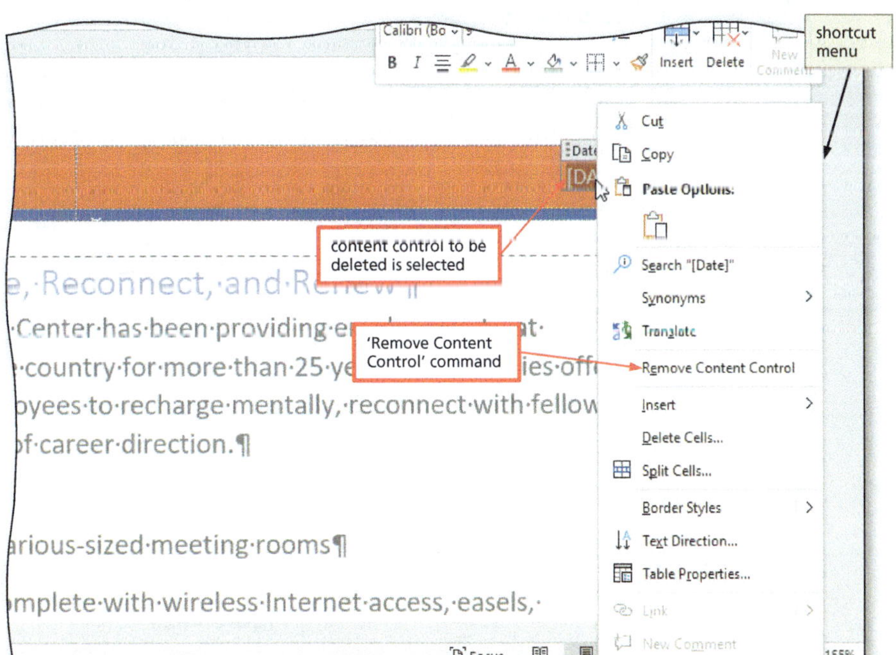

Figure 4–19

2

- Click 'Remove Content Control' on the shortcut menu to delete the selected content control, which also deletes the placeholder text contained in the content control (Figure 4–20).

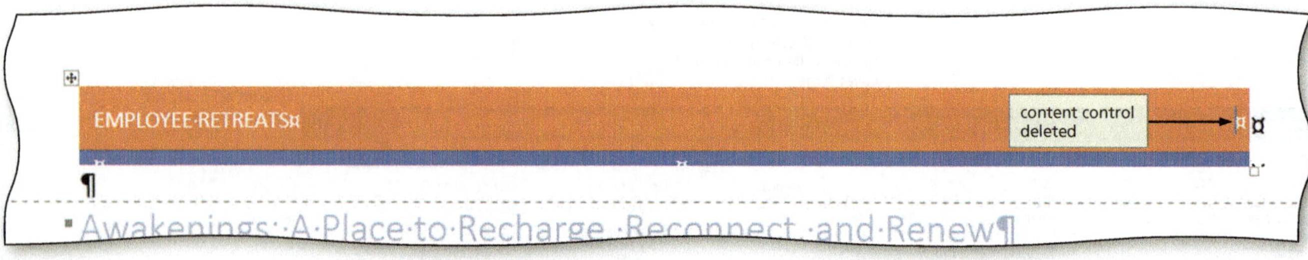

Figure 4–20

Other Ways

1. With content control selected, click Cut button (Home tab | Clipboard group)
2. With content control selected, press CTRL+X or DELETE or BACKSPACE

To Insert a Different First Page Formatted Footer

The next step is to insert the footer. Word provides the same built-in preformatted footer designs as header designs. The footer design that corresponds to the header just inserted contains a content control and a page number. The following steps insert a formatted footer that corresponds to the header just inserted. **Why?** You do not want the footer to appear on the cover page, and you want the footer design to complement the header.

1

- Click the 'Go to Footer' button (Header & Footer tab | Navigation group) to display the footer in the document window (Figure 4–21).

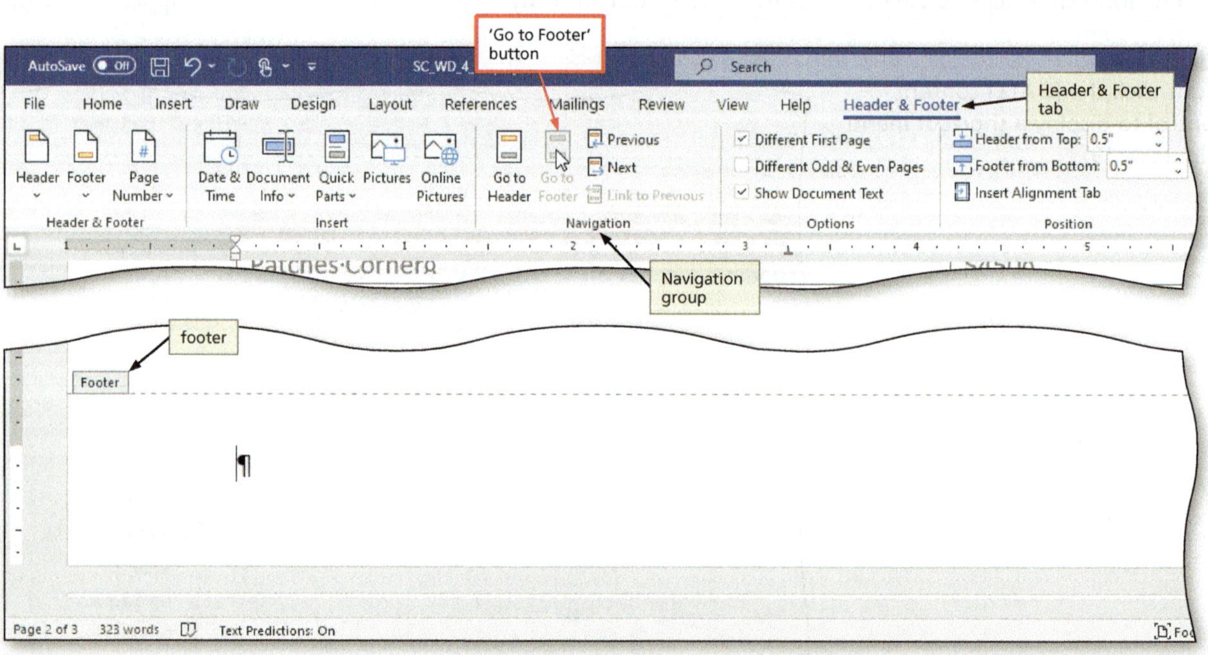

Figure 4–21

2

- Click the Footer button (Header & Footer tab | Header & Footer group) to display the Footer gallery.

Experiment

- Scroll through the list of built-in footers to see the variety of available formatted footer designs (Figure 4–22).

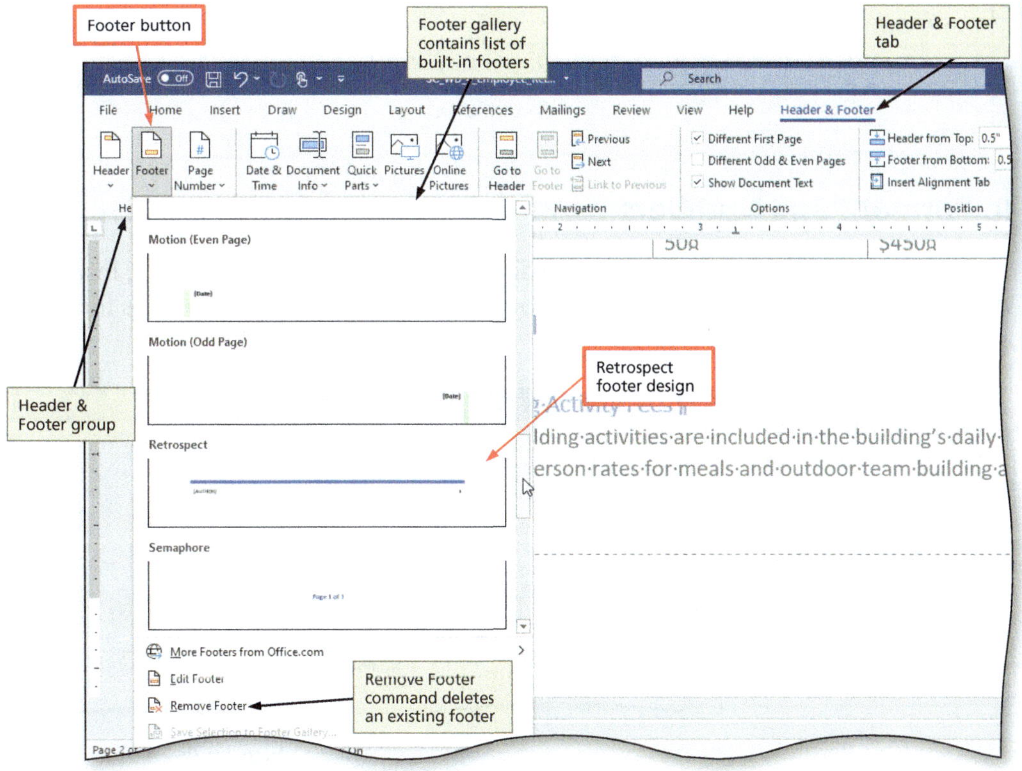

Figure 4–22

3

- Scroll to and then click the Retrospect footer design to insert the formatted footer in the document.
- If the 'Different First Page' check box (Header & Footer tab | Options group) is not selected, click it to select the button so that this footer does not appear on the cover page (Figure 4–23).

Q&A

Why is the page number a 1?

When you inserted the cover page, Word automatically removed the page number from the first page because numbering typically begins on the page after the cover page.

How would I delete a footer?

You would click Remove Footer in the Footer gallery (shown in Figure 4–22).

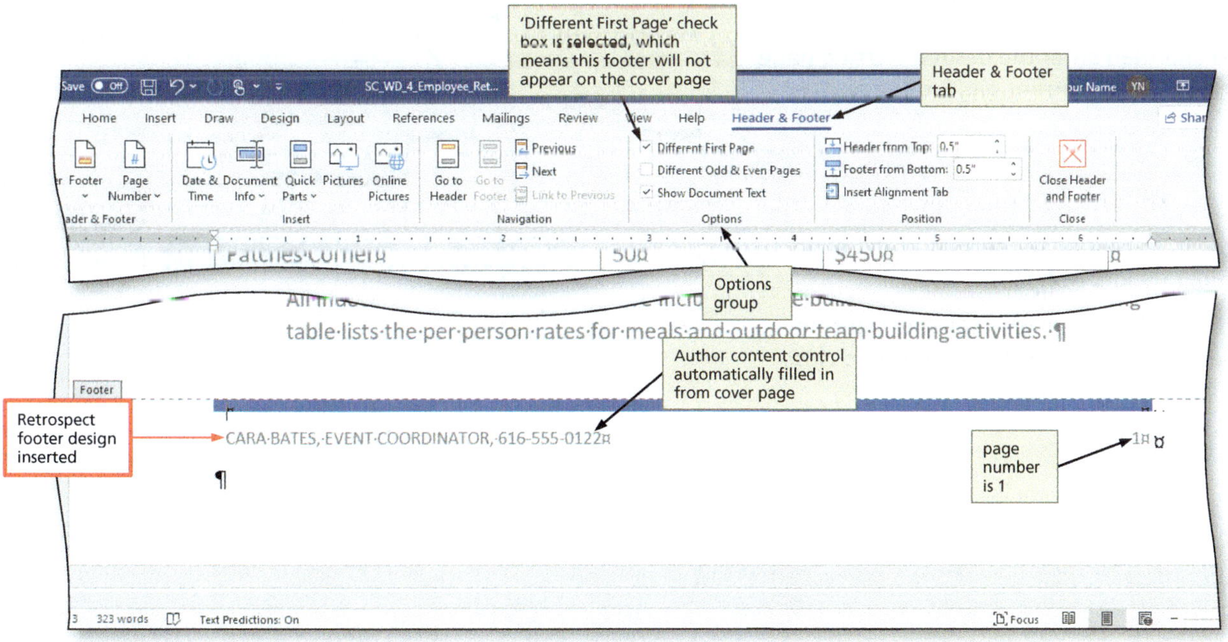

Figure 4–23

Other Ways

1. Click Footer button (Insert tab | Header & Footer group), select desired header in list
2. Click Quick Parts button (Insert tab | Text group), click 'Building Blocks Organizer' on Quick Parts menu, select desired footer (Building Blocks Organizer dialog box), click Insert button, click Close

To Format Page Numbers

You would like the page number to display with dashes around it, - 1 -, instead of just the single number, 1. **Why?** You want the page number to be more noticeable. The following steps format the page numbers.

1

- Click the Page Number button (Header & Footer tab | Header & Footer group) to display the Page Number menu (Figure 4–24).

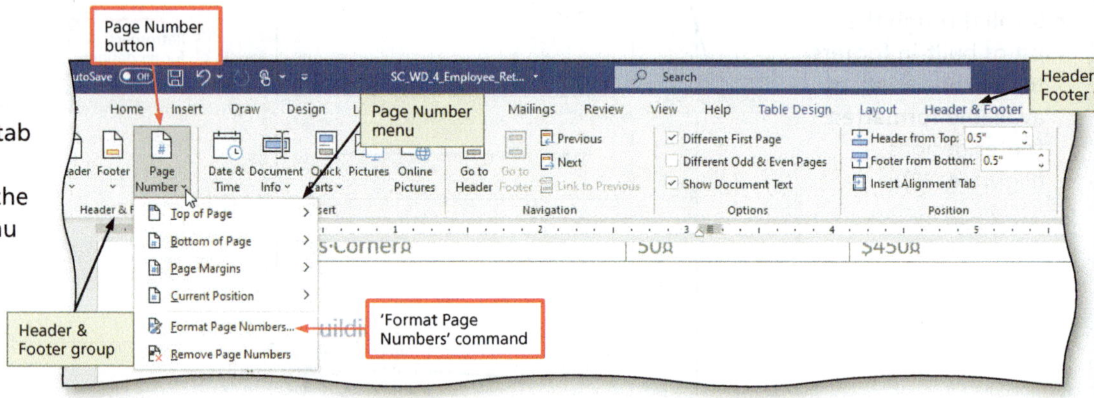

Figure 4–24

2

- Click 'Format Page Numbers' on the Page Number menu to display the Page Number Format dialog box.
- Click the Number format arrow (Page Number Format dialog box) and then click the second format in the list, - 1 -, - 2 -, - 3 -, ... (Figure 4–25).

Q&A **Can I also change the starting page number?**
Yes. Click the Start at option button in the Page numbering area (Page Number Format dialog box) and then enter the desired starting page number for the current page in the document.

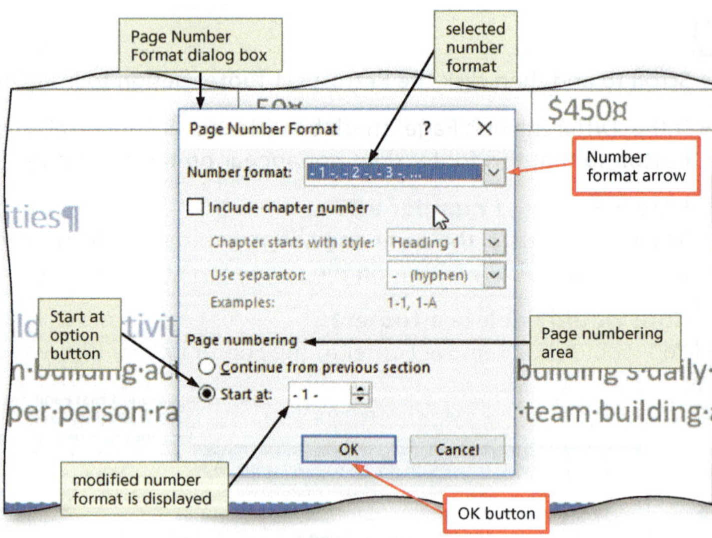

Figure 4–25

3

- Click OK to change the format of the page number (Figure 4–26).
- Click the 'Close Header and Footer' button (Header & Footer tab | Close group) to close the header and footer.

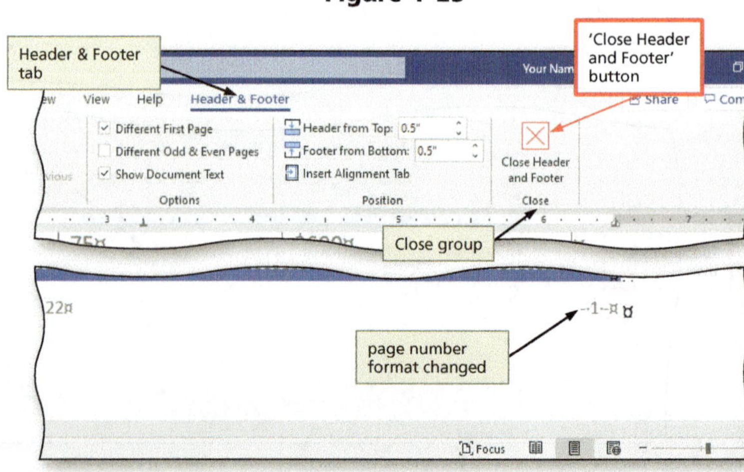

Figure 4–26

Other Ways

1. Click Page Number button (Insert tab | Header & Footer group), click 'Format Page Numbers' on Page Number menu, set page formats (Page Number Format dialog box), click OK

To Format Text Using the Font Dialog Box

The following steps format the conclusion (the last line of text in the body of the proposal) so that it is colored, uses small caps, and has expanded spacing.

1. Select the text to be formatted (in this case, the sentence that begins 'Choose Awakenings for Your...').
2. Click the Font Dialog Box Launcher (Home tab | Font group) to display the Font dialog box. If necessary, click the Font tab in the dialog box to display the Font sheet.
3. Click the Font color arrow (Font dialog box) and then click 'Orange, Accent 2' (sixth color in first row) in the Font color gallery to change the color.
4. Click 16 in the Size list to increase the font size.
5. Click the Small caps check box in the Effects area so that each character is displayed as a small uppercase letter.
6. Click the Advanced tab (Font dialog box) to display the Advanced sheet in the Font dialog box.
7. Click the Spacing arrow in the Character Spacing area and then click Expanded to increase the amount of space between characters by 1 pt, which is the default.
8. Double-click the value in the Spacing By box to select it and then type 2 because you want this amount of blank space to be displayed between each character.
9. Click OK to apply font changes to the selected text.
10. Click anywhere to remove the selection from the text (Figure 4–27).
11. Save the sales proposal again with the same file name in the same storage location.

BTW

Touch Mode Differences

The Microsoft 365 and Windows interfaces may vary if you are using Touch mode. For this reason, you might notice that the function or appearance of your touch screen differs slightly from this module's presentation.

Figure 4–27

Editing and Formatting Lists

The finished sales proposal in this module has two lists: a bulleted list and a multilevel list (shown in Figures 4–1b and 4–1c at the beginning of this module). The bulleted list uses a predefined bullet character instead of simple round dots, and the color of the bullet character is changed from the default. The multilevel list has multiple levels for each item and also uses a picture for one of the bullet characters. The following sections illustrate steps used to edit and format the lists in the proposal:

1. Select a predefined bullet character and change its color.
2. Change the left and right indent of bulleted paragraphs.
3. Create a multilevel list.
4. Change the bullet character of list items to picture bullets.
5. Sort a list of paragraphs.

To Select a Predefined Bullet Character for a List

The paragraphs below the heading, Facility, should be a bulleted list. Instead of simply clicking the Bullets button to apply the default bullet character, you will select a predefined character for the bulleted list. **Why?** You want to use a more visually appealing bullet for this list. The following steps format the bullets in a list from the default round dot to a predefined bullet character.

1

- Select the paragraphs to be formatted as a bulleted list, in this case, the paragraphs below the Facility heading.
- Click the Bullets arrow (Home tab | Paragraph group) to display the Bullets gallery (Figure 4–28).

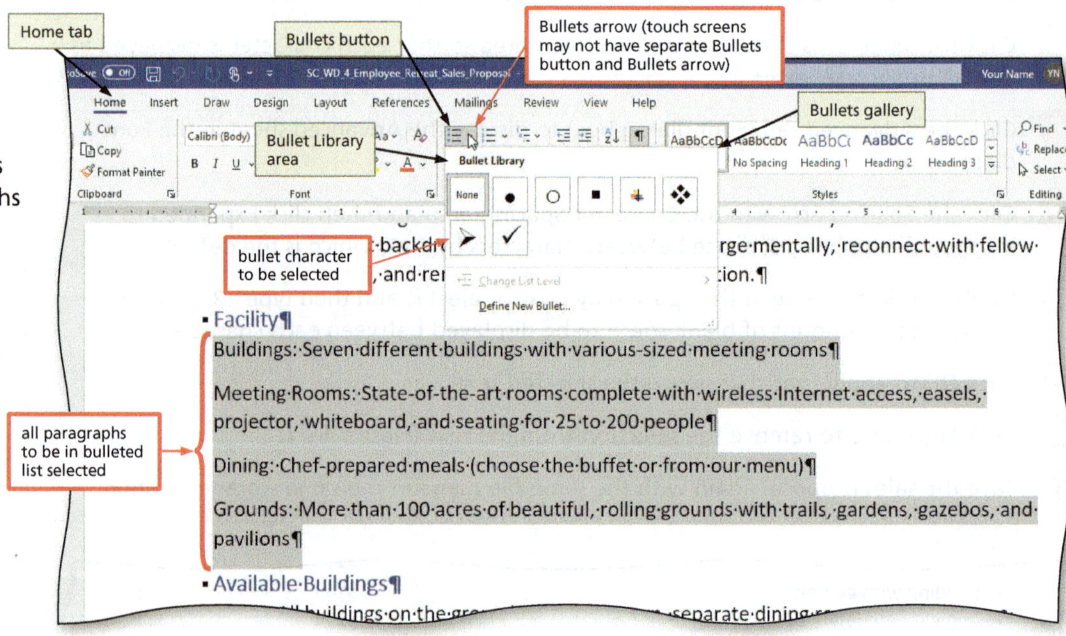

Figure 4–28

2

- Click the desired predefined bullet character in the Bullet Library area, in this case, the right-pointing chevron symbol, to format the selected paragraphs with the selected bullet character (shown in Figure 4–29).

To Change Bullet Color

The predefined bullet character is colored orange in the proposal. **Why?** You want the bullet character color to complement the cover page and header and footer colors. The following steps change the color of bullet characters in a list.

1

- With the bulleted list selected, click the Bullets arrow (Home tab | Paragraph group) to display the Bullets gallery again (Figure 4–29).

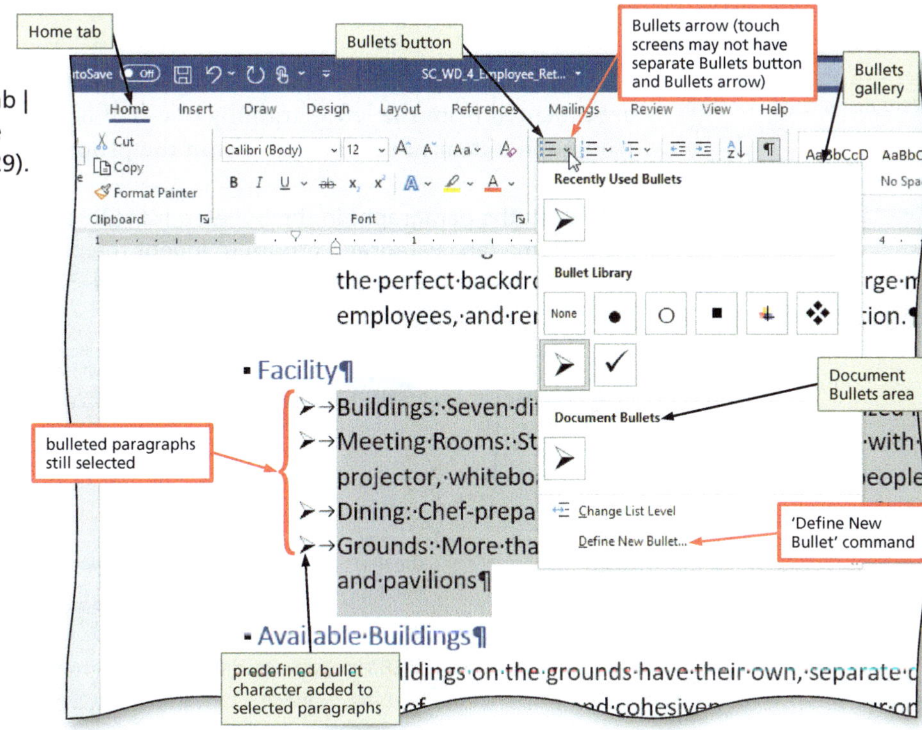

Figure 4–29

2

- Click 'Define New Bullet' in the Bullets gallery to display the Define New Bullet dialog box.
- Click the Font button (Define New Bullet dialog box) to display the Font dialog box.
- Click the Font color arrow (Font dialog box) and then click 'Orange, Accent 2' (sixth color in first row) in the color gallery (Figure 4–30).

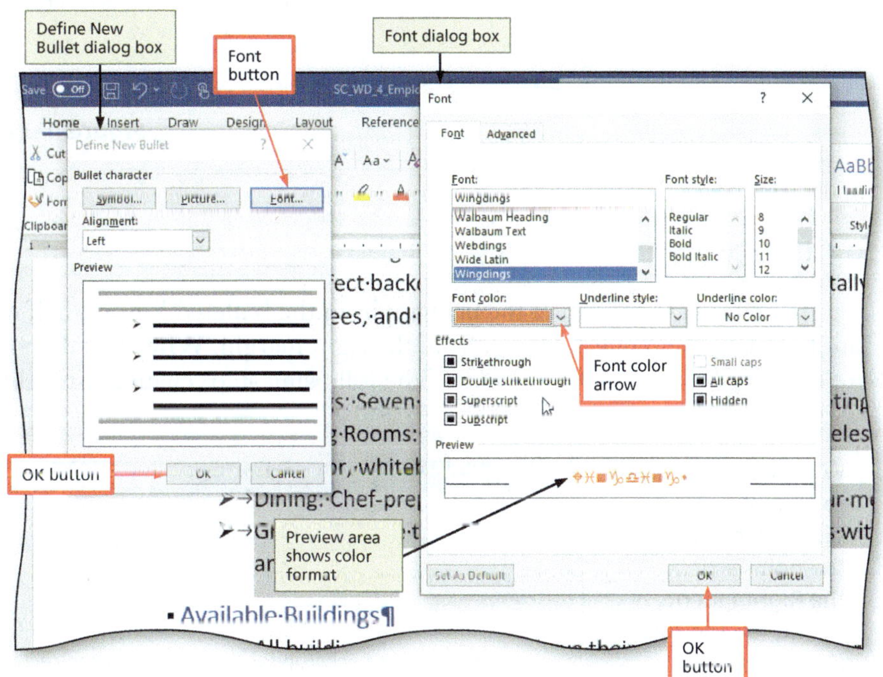

Figure 4–30

3

- Click OK (Font dialog box) to change the color of the bullet character to the selected color.
- Click OK (Define New Bullet dialog box) to change the color of the bullet character in the selected list in the document (Figure 4–31).

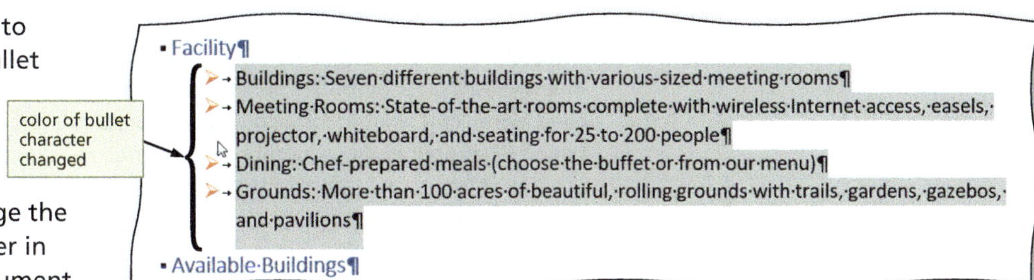

Figure 4–31

BTW
The Ribbon and Screen Resolution
Word may change how the groups and buttons within the groups appear on the ribbon, depending on the screen resolution of your computer. Thus, your ribbon may look different from the ones in this book if you are using a screen resolution other than 1366 × 768.

To Change Left Paragraph Indent

As with other paragraphs in the proposal, the paragraphs in the bulleted list also are indented from the left margin by one-half inch. The following step changes the left paragraph indent of the bulleted list in the proposal.

1 With the paragraphs in the bulleted list still selected, click the Increase Indent button (Home tab | Paragraph group) to indent the paragraphs in the selected bulleted list one-half inch from the left margin (Figure 4–32).

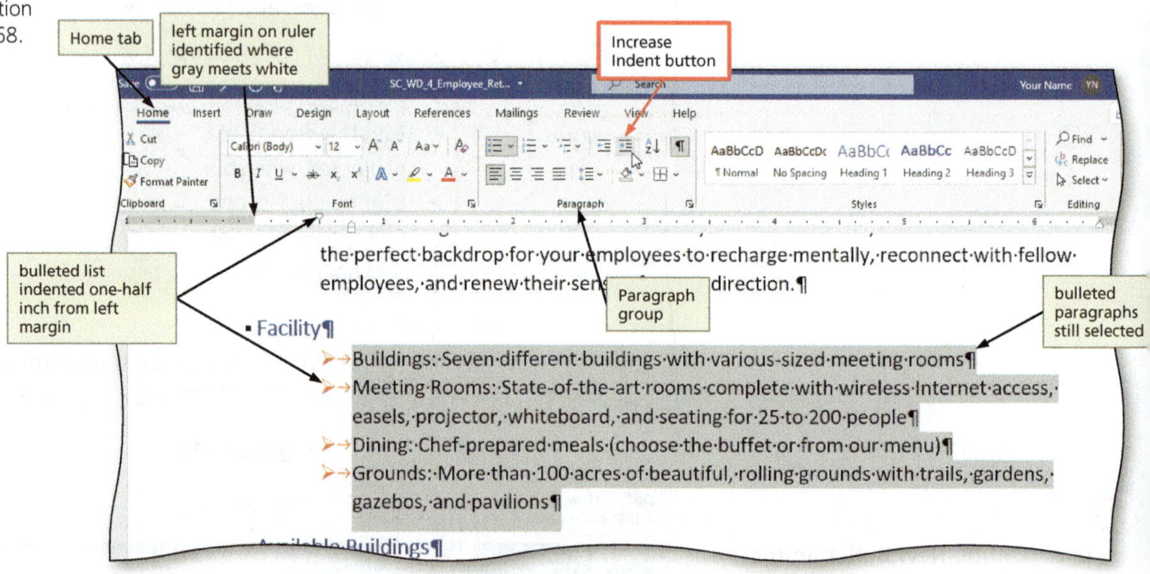

Figure 4–32

To Change Right Paragraph Indent

In addition to indenting the paragraphs in the bulleted list one-half inch from the left margin, you also want to indent them one-half inch from the right margin. **Why?** You do not want the bulleted list paragraphs to extend as far as the paragraphs of text. The following steps change the right paragraph indent.

1

- With the paragraphs to format still selected, position the pointer on the Right Indent marker on the ruler (Figure 4–33).

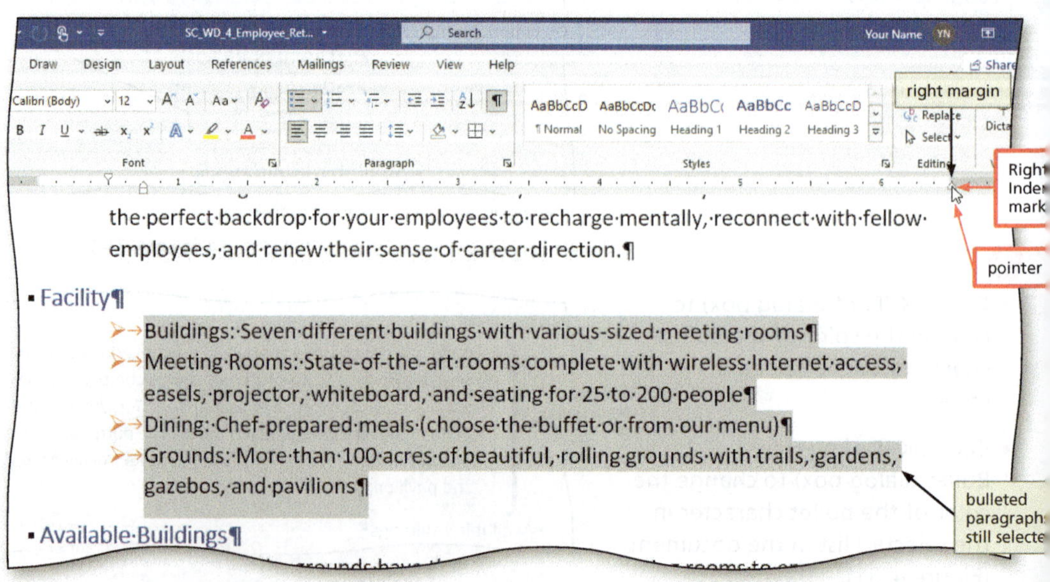

Figure 4–33

2

- Drag the Right Indent marker inward to the 6" mark on the ruler (Figure 4–34).

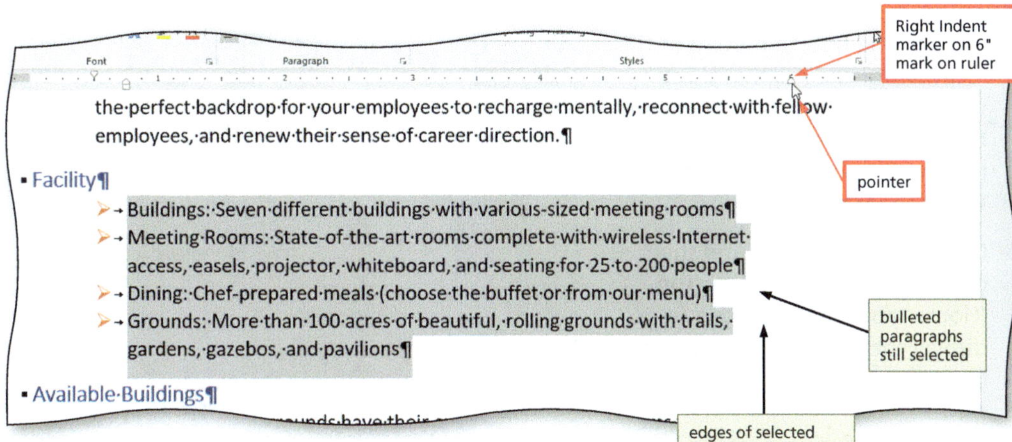

Figure 4–34

Other Ways

1. Click Indent Right up or down arrows (Layout tab | Paragraph group) (or, if using touch, tap Indent Right box (Layout tab | Paragraph group) and then enter desired indent value)
2. Click Paragraph Settings Dialog Box Launcher (Home tab | Paragraph group), click Indents and Spacing tab (Paragraph dialog box), set indentation values, click OK
3. Right click paragraph (or, if using touch, tap 'Show Context Menu' button on Mini toolbar), click Paragraph on shortcut menu, click Indents and Spacing tab (Paragraph dialog box), set indentation values, click OK

To Insert a Page Break

The Team Building Activities heading should appear at the beginning of the next page. The following steps insert a page break.

1. Scroll to the heading, Team Building Activities, and position the insertion point immediately to the left of the T in Team.
2. Display the Insert tab.
3. Click the Page Break button (Insert tab | Pages group) to insert a page break at the location of the insertion point, which will move the Team Building Activities heading to the last page of the proposal (shown in Figure 4–35).

BTW

Word Help

At any time while using Word, you can find answers to questions and display information about various topics through Word Help. Used properly, this form of assistance can increase your productivity and reduce your frustrations by minimizing the time you spend learning how to use Word.

To Create a Multilevel List

The next step is to create a multilevel list below the Team Building Activities heading on the last page of the sales proposal in this module (shown in Figure 4–1c at the beginning of this module). **Why?** You would like to list the indoor and outdoor team building activities available during employee retreats.

A **multilevel list** is a list that contains several levels of list items, with each lower level displaying a different numeric, alphabetic, or bullet character. In a multilevel list, the first level is displayed at the left edge of the list and subsequent levels are indented; that is, the second level is indented below the first, the third level is indented below the second level, and so on. The list is referred to as a numbered list if the first level contains numbers or letters and is referred to as a bulleted list if the first level contains a character other than a number or letter. The multilevel list in this project uses bullet characters. The following steps create a multilevel list.

1

- Position the insertion point at the location for the multilevel list, which in this case is the blank line below the Team Building Activities heading on the last page of the sales proposal.
- Display the Home tab and then click the Multilevel List button (Home tab | Paragraph group) to display the Multilevel List gallery (Figure 4–35).

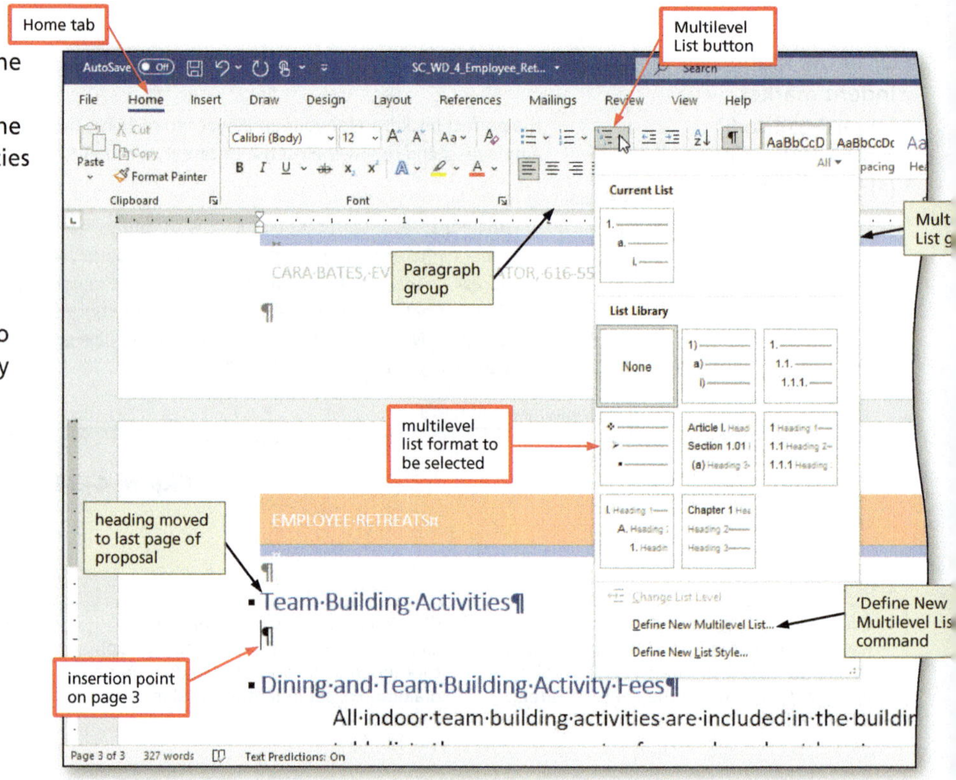

Figure 4–35

2

- Click the character format in the Multilevel List gallery (shown in Figure 4–35) to display the current paragraph as a multilevel list item using the selected multilevel list format.
- Click the Increase Indent button (Home tab | Paragraph group) to indent the list one-half inch from the left margin.

Q&A **What if I wanted a different number format?**

You would click the Multilevel List button (Home tab | Paragraph group) and then select the desired format in the Multilevel List gallery, or click 'Define New Multilevel List' in the Multilevel List gallery (shown in Figure 4–35) to define your own format.

- Type **Indoor Team Building Activities** as a first-level list item and then press ENTER, which automatically places the next bullet for the current level at the beginning of the next line (Figure 4–36).

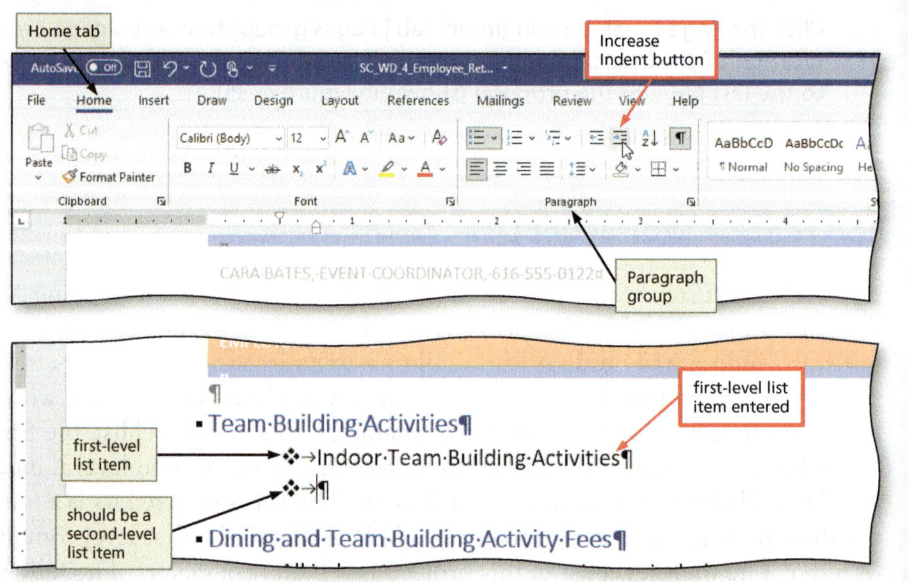

Figure 4–36

3

- Press TAB to demote the current list item to the next lower level, which is indented below the higher-level list item.

4

- Type **Board games** as a second-level list item and then press ENTER, which automatically places the next sequential list item for the current level on the next line.
- Type **Card games** as a second-level list item and then press ENTER.
- Type **Pool table** as a second-level list item and then press ENTER (Figure 4–37).

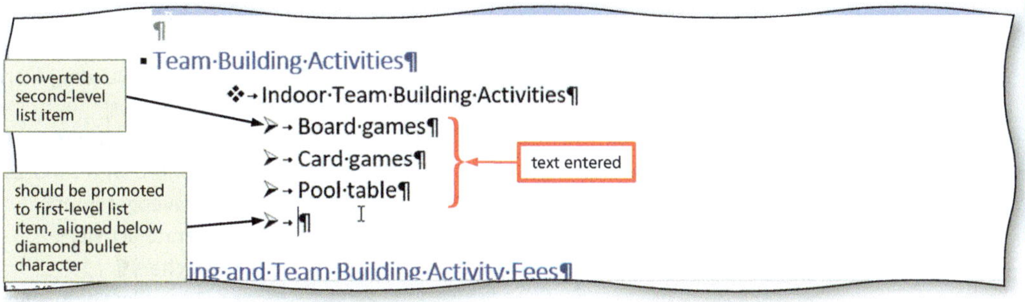

Figure 4–37

5

- Press SHIFT+TAB to promote the current-level list item to a higher-level list item.

Q&A **Can I use buttons on the ribbon instead of pressing TAB or SHIFT+TAB to promote and demote list items?**
Yes. With the insertion point in the item to adjust, you can click the Increase Indent or Decrease Indent button (Home tab | Paragraph group) or right-click the list item, click 'Adjust List Indents' on the shortcut menu, and select the desired options in the dialog box.

6

- Type **Outdoor Team Building Activities** as a first-level list item and then press ENTER.
- Press TAB to demote the current level list item to a lower-level list item.
- Type **Light activity** as a second-level list item and then press ENTER (Figure 4–38).

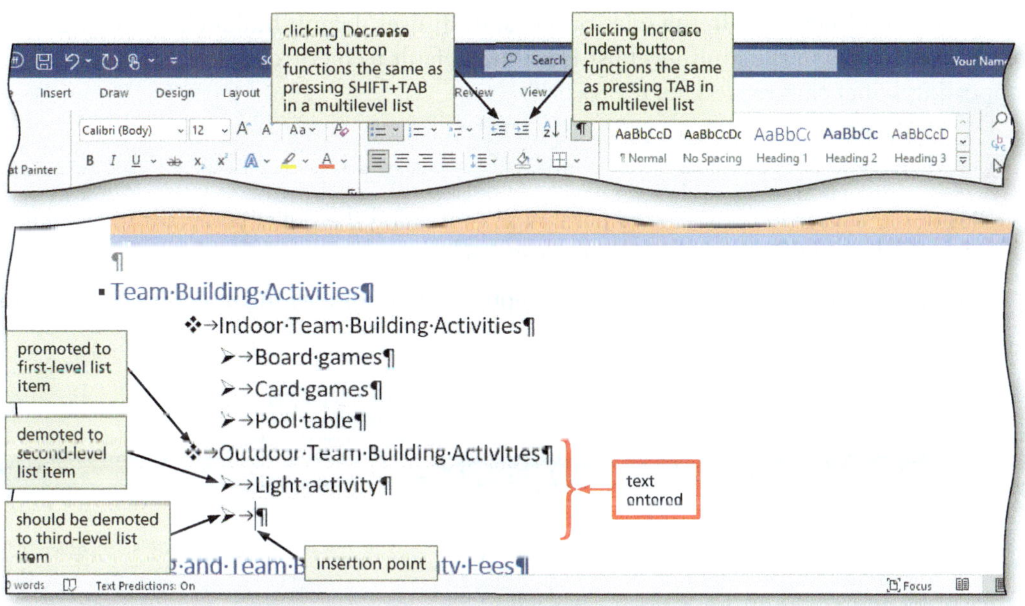

Figure 4–38

7

- Press TAB to demote the current-level list item to a lower-level list item.
- Type **Scenic hayride** as a third-level list item and then press ENTER.
- Type **Bonfire with s'mores** as a third-level list item and then press ENTER.
- Type **Scavenger hunt** as a third-level list item and then press ENTER.
- Press SHIFT+TAB to promote the current-level list item to a higher-level list item.
- Type **Moderate activity** as a second-level list item and then press ENTER.
- Press TAB to demote the current-level list item to a lower-level list item.
- Type **Archery** as a third-level list item and then press ENTER.

- Type **Bike riding with guide** as a third-level list item and then press ENTER.
- Type **Hiking with guide** as a third-level list item (Figure 4–39).

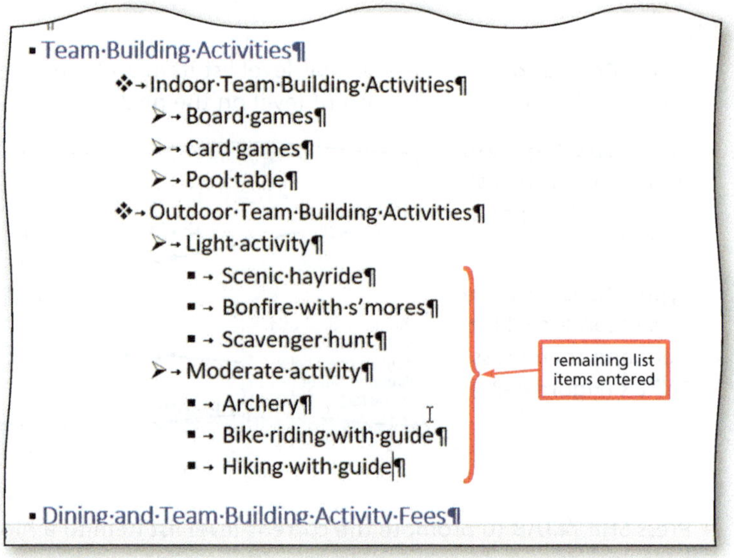

Figure 4–39

To Change the Bullet Character to Picture Bullets

The multilevel list in the sales proposal draft uses default bullet characters. The following steps change the first-level bullets in the multilevel list from the default to picture bullets. **Why?** You want to use a more visually appealing bullet that represents teamwork.

1

- Position the insertion point in the paragraph containing the bullet you want to change to a picture bullet, in this case, the first bulleted item in the multilevel list.
- Click the Bullets arrow (Home tab | Paragraph group) to display the Bullets gallery (Figure 4–40).

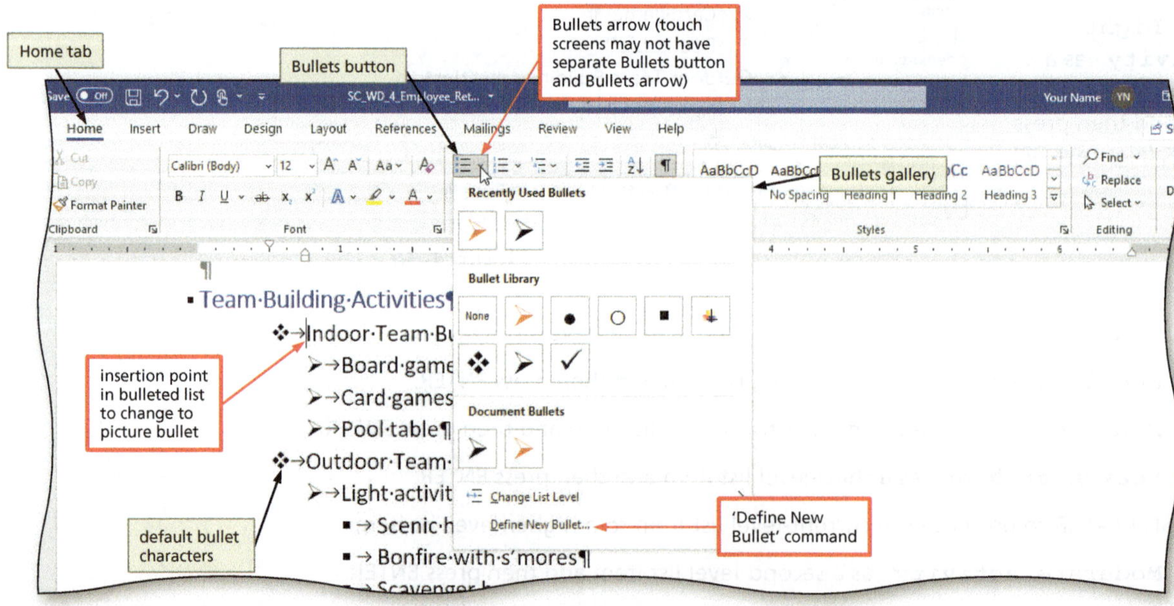

Figure 4–40

2

- Click 'Define New Bullet' in the Bullets gallery to display the Define New Bullet dialog box.
- Click the Picture button (Define New Bullet dialog box) to display the Insert Pictures dialog box.
- Type **abstract group interaction** in the Bing Image Search box (Insert Pictures dialog box) (Figure 4–41).

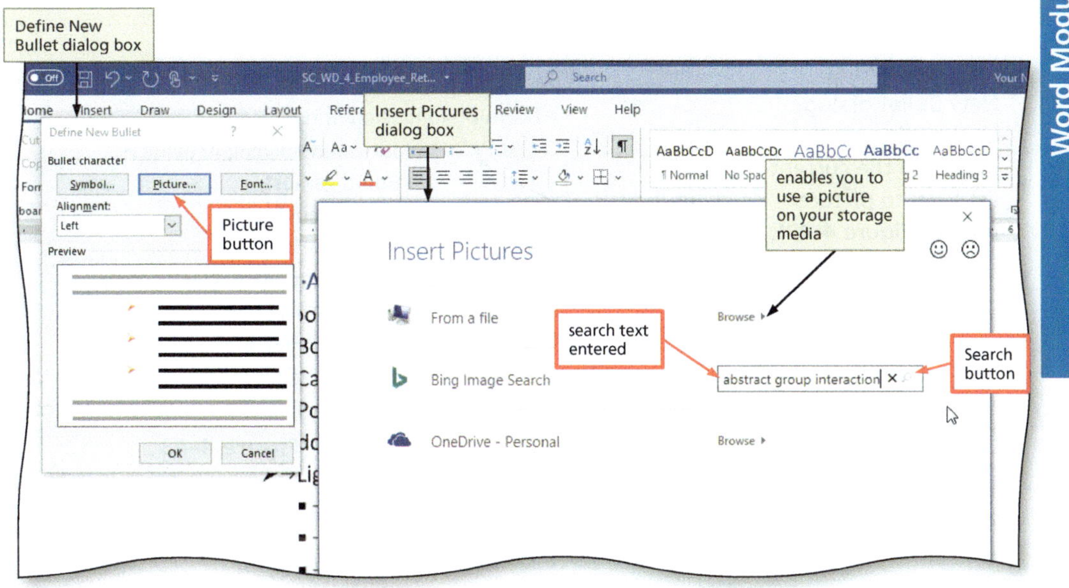

Figure 4–41

3

- Click the Search button to display a list of pictures (Online Pictures dialog box) that matches the entered search text.
- Scroll through the list of pictures to locate the one shown in Figure 4–42, or a similar image.

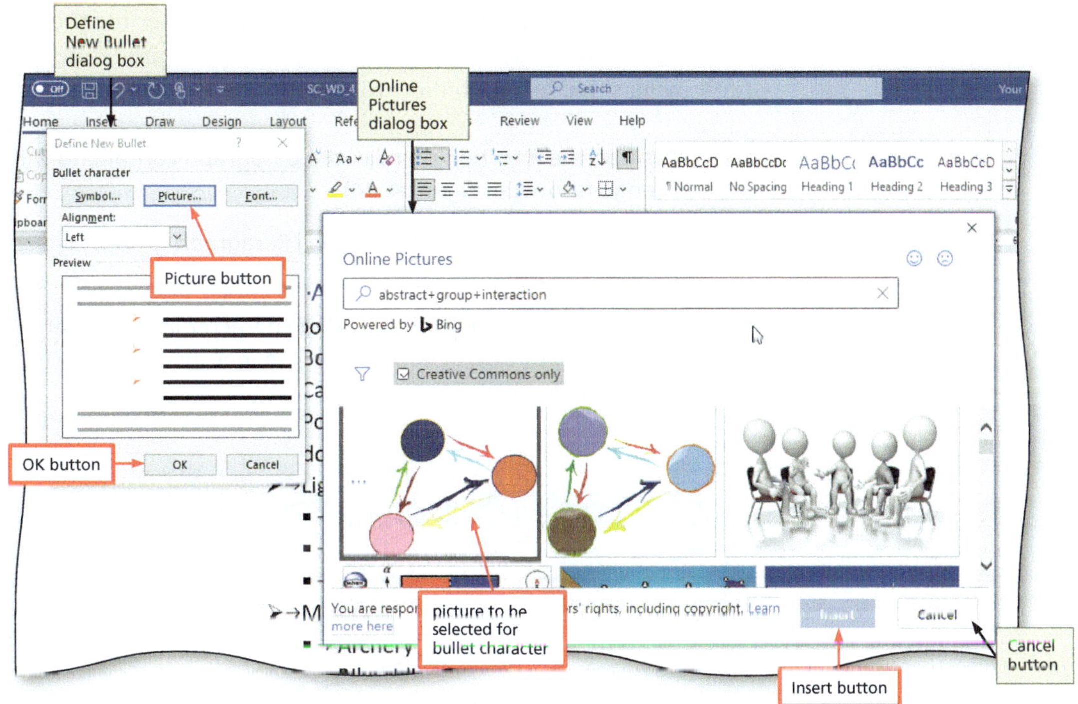

Figure 4–42

Q&A **What if I cannot locate the image in Figure 4–42, and I would like to use that exact image?**
The image is located in the Data Files. You can click Cancel (Online Pictures dialog box), click the Picture button (Define New Bullet dialog box) to display the Insert Pictures dialog box again, click Browse in the Insert Pictures dialog box, navigate to the file called Support_WD_4_AbstractGroupInteraction.png in the Data Files, select the file, and then click the Insert button (Insert Picture dialog box) to show a preview of the selected picture bullet in the Define New Bullet dialog box. Proceed to Step 5.

4

- Click the desired picture to select it.
- Click the Insert button (Online Pictures dialog box) to download the image, close the dialog box, and show a preview of the selected picture bullet in the Define New Bullet dialog box.

5

- Click OK (Define New Bullet dialog box) to change the bullets in the current list level to picture bullets (Figure 4–43).

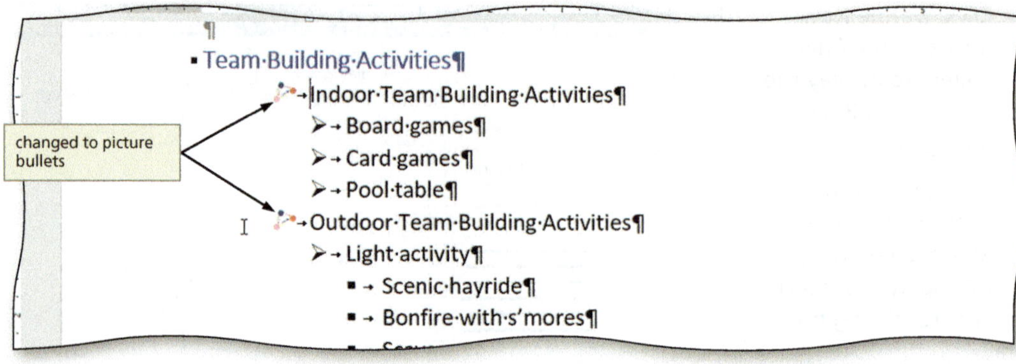

Figure 4–43

To Change the Bullet Character to a Predefined Bullet Character

You would like to change the bullet character for the second-level list items in the multilevel list to an open circle, which is a predefined bullet character. The following steps format bullets to a predefined bullet character.

1. Position the insertion point in the paragraph containing the bullet you want to change (shown in Figure 4–44).
2. Click the Bullets arrow (Home tab | Paragraph group) to display the Bullets gallery (Figure 4–44).
3. Click the desired predefined bullet character in the Bullet Library area, in this case, the open circle, to format current list level paragraphs with the selected bullet character (shown in Figure 4–45).

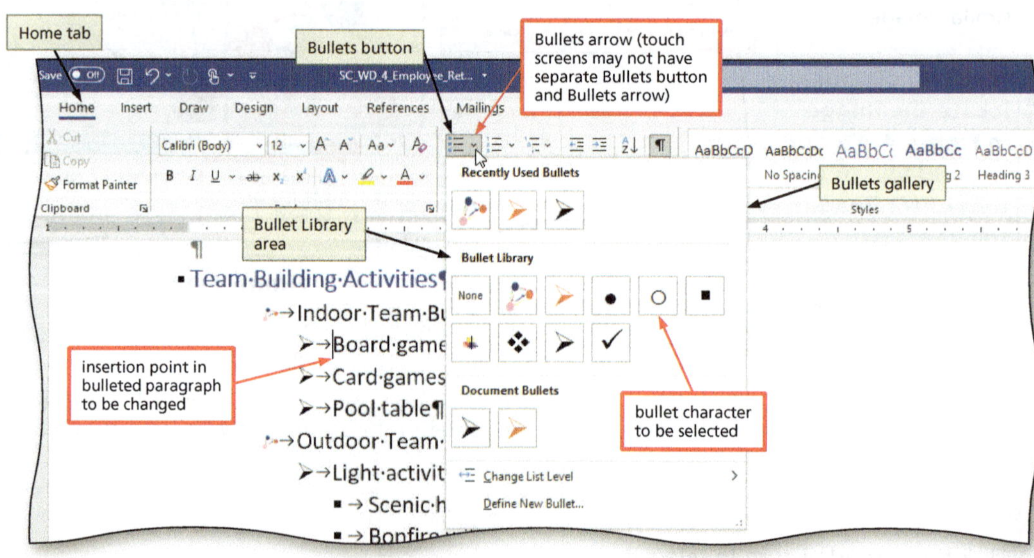

Figure 4–44

BTW

Bullets

In addition to selecting from a variety of bullet symbols and changing font attributes of a bullet by clicking 'Define New Bullet' in the Bullets gallery and then clicking the desired button in the Define New Bullet dialog box, you also can change the level of a bullet by pointing to 'Change List Level' in the Bullets gallery and then clicking the desired level.

To Sort Paragraphs

The next step is to alphabetize the paragraphs below Light activity in the bulleted list. **Why?** It is easier for readers to locate information in lists that are in alphabetical order. In Word, you can **sort** paragraphs, which is the process of arranging them in ascending or descending alphabetic, numeric, or date order based on the first character in each paragraph. Ascending means to sort in alphabetic, numeric, or earliest-to-latest date order. Descending means to sort in reverse alphabetic, numeric, or latest-to-earliest date order. The following steps sort paragraphs in ascending order.

1

- Select the paragraphs to be sorted.
- Click the Sort button (Home tab | Paragraph group) to display the Sort Text dialog box (Figure 4–45).

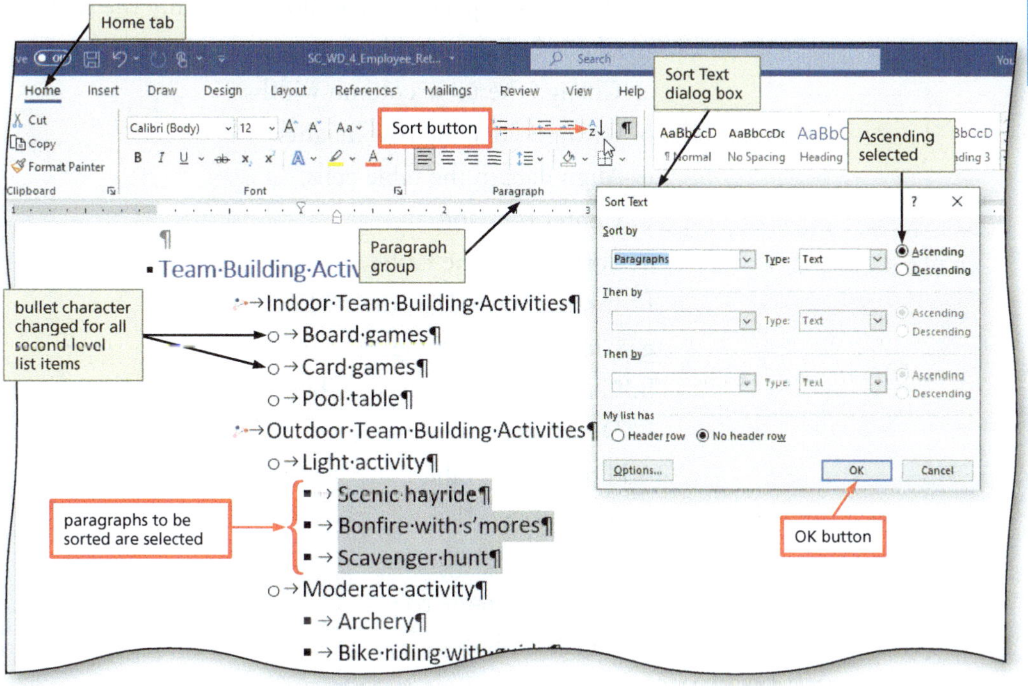

Figure 4–45

2

- Click OK (Sort Text dialog box) to instruct Word to alphabetize the selected paragraphs.
- Click anywhere to remove the selection from the text (Figure 4–46).
- Save the sales proposal again with the same file name in the same storage location.

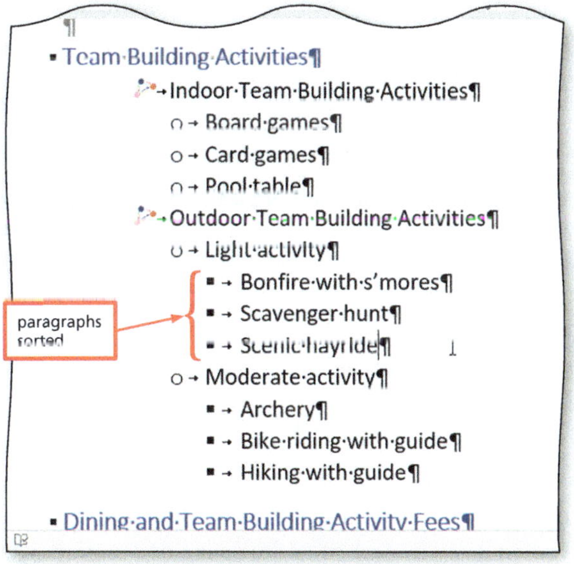

Figure 4–46

Break Point: If you want to take a break, this is a good place to do so. You can exit Word now. To resume later, start Word, open the file called SC_WD_4_Employee_Retreat_Sales_Proposal.docx, and continue following the steps from this location forward.

Editing and Formatting Tables

The sales proposal draft contains two Word tables: the available buildings table and the additional fees table (shown earlier in the module in Figure 4–12). The available buildings table shows the maximum capacity and daily rate for various buildings on site, and the additional fees table shows costs and minimum attendees for dining and team building activities. In this section, you will make several modifications to these two tables so that they appear as shown in Figure 4–1 at the beginning of this module.

The following pages explain how to modify the tables in the sales proposal draft:

1. Available buildings table
   a. Change the table column widths.
   b. Change the table row heights.
   c. Align data in the table cells.
   d. Center the table.
   e. Sort data in the table.
   f. Insert a formula in the table.
   g. Change cell spacing.
   h. Change margins in the table cells.
   i. Distribute table columns.
2. Additional fees table
   a. Split table cells.
   b. Move a cell boundary.
   c. Distribute table rows.
   d. Merge table cells.
   e. Change the direction of text in table cells.
   f. Resize table columns using AutoFit.
   g. Shade table cells.
   h. Add a table border.

BTW

Moving Tables

If you wanted to move a table to a new location, you would click in the table to display the table move handle in the upper-left corner of the table (shown in Figure 4–47) and then drag the table move handle to move the entire table to a new location.

Consider This

Why should you include visuals in a sales proposal?

Studies have shown that most people are visually oriented, preferring images to text. Use tables to clarify ideas and illustrate points. Be aware, however, that too many visuals can clutter a document.

To Change Column Width

Notice in Figure 4–47 that the columns in the available buildings table are much wider than their contents. Thus, you will change the widths of the columns. **Why?** You want the columns to be narrower to reduce the amount of white space between the end of the text in the columns and the column boundaries. The following steps change column widths.

1

- Position the insertion point somewhere in the table to be formatted.
- Position the pointer on the column boundary to the right of the column to adjust (in this case, to the right of the first column) so that the pointer changes to a double-headed arrow split by two vertical bars (Figure 4–47).

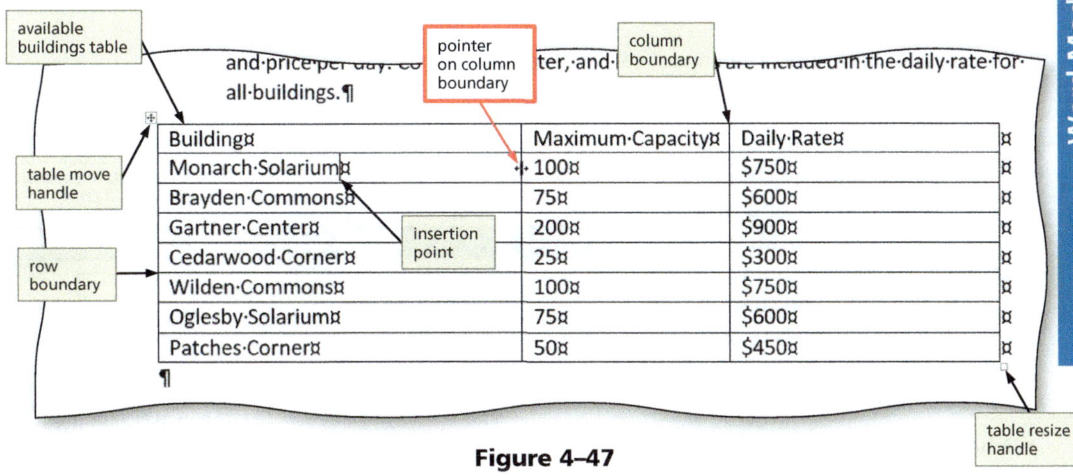

Building	Maximum Capacity	Daily Rate
Monarch Solarium	100	$750
Brayden Commons	75	$600
Gartner Center	200	$900
Cedarwood Corner	25	$300
Wilden Commons	100	$750
Oglesby Solarium	75	$600
Patches Corner	50	$450

Figure 4–47

Q&A

What is the column boundary?
You can drag a **column boundary**, the border to the right of a column, until the column is the desired width. Similarly, you can resize a row by dragging the **row boundary**, the border at the bottom of a row, until the row is the desired height. You also can resize the entire table by dragging the **table resize handle**, which is a small square that appears when you point to a corner of the table.

What causes the table move handle and table resize handle to appear and disappear from the table?
They appear whenever you position the pointer in the table.

2

- Double-click the column boundary so that Word adjusts the column width to the width of the column's contents.
- Position the pointer on the column boundary to the right of the next column to adjust (in this case, to the right of the second column) so that the pointer changes to a double-headed arrow split by two vertical bars (Figure 4–48).

Q&A

What if I am using a touch screen?
Position the insertion point in the column to adjust, tap the AutoFit button (Layout tab | Cell Size group), and then tap AutoFit Contents on the AutoFit menu.

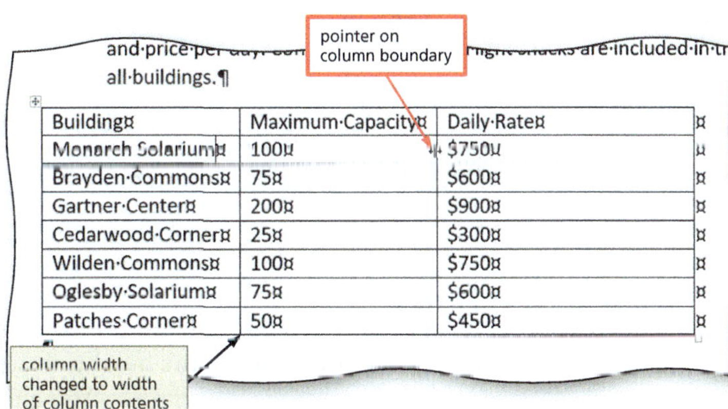

Building	Maximum Capacity	Daily Rate
Monarch Solarium	100	$750
Brayden Commons	75	$600
Gartner Center	200	$900
Cedarwood Corner	25	$300
Wilden Commons	100	$750
Oglesby Solarium	75	$600
Patches Corner	50	$450

Figure 4–48

3

- Drag the column boundary so that Word adjusts the column width so that the column heading wraps to two lines (Figure 4–49).

Q&A

Why drag the column boundary instead of double-clicking it?
When you double-click the column boundary, Word adjusts the width of the column to the column contents, usually adjusting the width to the widest item in the column, which, in this case, is the text, Maximum Capacity. To make the column even narrower and cause the text, Maximum Capacity, to wrap to two lines, you drag the column to make it narrower than the column heading.

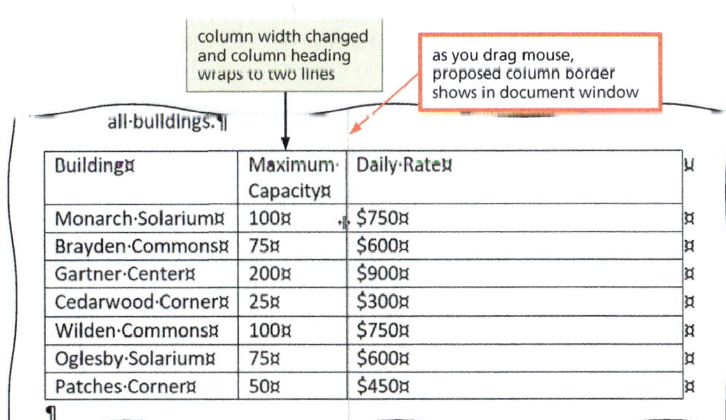

Building	Maximum Capacity	Daily Rate
Monarch Solarium	100	$750
Brayden Commons	75	$600
Gartner Center	200	$900
Cedarwood Corner	25	$300
Wilden Commons	100	$750
Oglesby Solarium	75	$600
Patches Corner	50	$450

Figure 4–49

4

- Click Layout to display the Layout tab on the ribbon.

Experiment

- Practice changing the column widths in the table using other techniques: drag the 'Move Table Column' marker on the horizontal ruler to the right and then to the left. Click the Width box up and down arrows (Table Design tab | Cell Size group).
- When you have finished experimenting, position the insertion point in the first column and then type `1.6` in the Width box (Layout tab | Cell Size group) to specify the column width, position the insertion point in the second column and then type `.98` in the Width box (Layout tab | Cell Size group) to specify the column width, and position the insertion point in the third column and then type `1.06` to specify the column width (Figure 4–50).

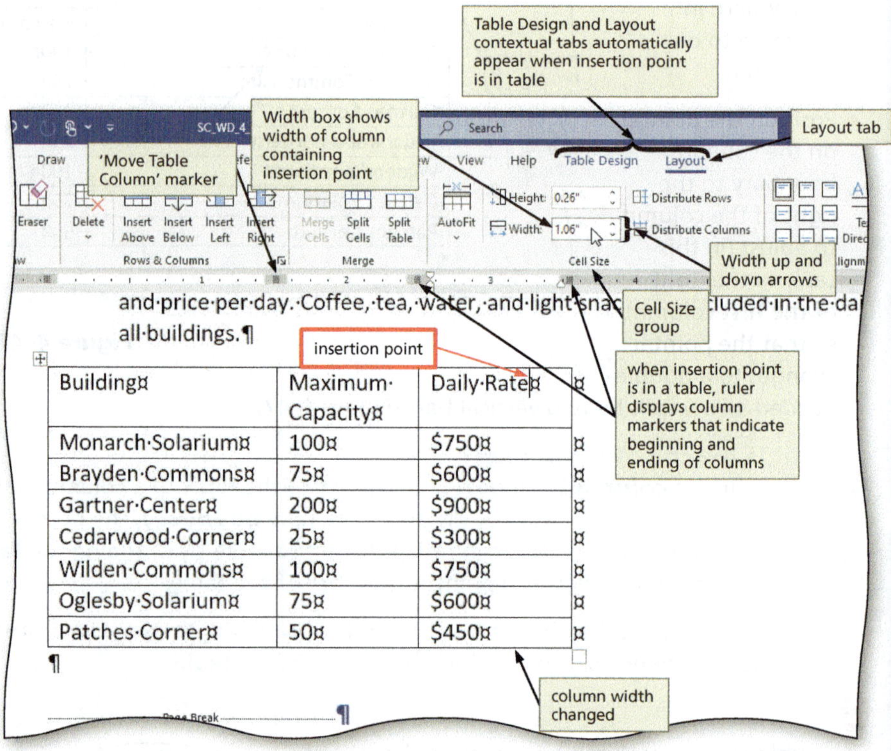

Figure 4–50

Other Ways

1. Drag 'Move Table Column' marker on horizontal ruler to desired width
2. Enter desired value in Width box (Layout tab | Cell Size group)
3. Click Properties button (Layout tab | Table group), click Column tab (Table Properties dialog box), enter width, click OK

To Change Row Height

The next step in this project is to make the height of the rows containing the building names taller. **Why?** For ease of reading, you want more space in the rows. You change row height in the same ways you change column width. That is, you can change row height by entering a specific value on the ribbon or in a dialog box, or by using a marker on the ruler or the row boundary. The latter two methods, however, work only for a single or for selected rows. The following steps change row height.

1

- Select the rows to format (in this case, all the rows below the first row).

Q&A **How do I select rows?**
Point to the left of the first row and then drag downward when the pointer changes to a right-pointing arrow (or, if using touch, drag through the rows).

2

- Click the Height box up or down arrows (Layout tab | Cell Size group) as many times as necessary until the box displays 0.3" to change the row height to this value (or, if using touch, enter `0.3` in the Height box (Layout tab | Cell Size group) (Figure 4–51).
- Click anywhere in the table to remove the selection from the table.

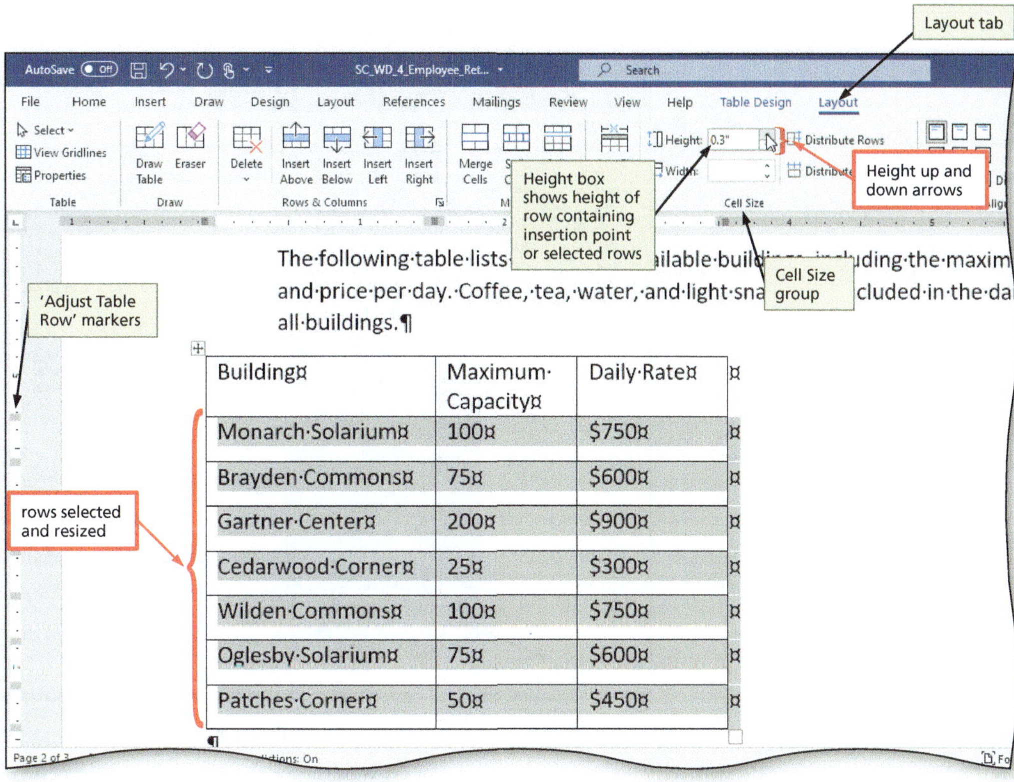

Figure 4–51

Other Ways

1. Click Properties button (Layout tab | Table group), click Row tab (Table Properties dialog box), enter row height, click OK
2. Right-click selected row (or, if using touch, tap 'Show Context Menu' button on Mini toolbar), click Table Properties on shortcut menu, click Row tab, enter row height (Table Properties dialog box), click OK
3. For a single row or selected rows, drag row boundary (horizontal gridline at bottom of row in table) to desired height
4. Drag 'Adjust Table Row' marker on vertical ruler to desired height

To Apply a Table Style

The following steps apply a table style to the table so that the table is more visually appealing.

1 Display the Table Design tab.

Q&A **What if the Table Design tab no longer is the active tab?**
Click in the table and then display the Table Design tab.

2 With the insertion point in the table, click the More button in the Table Styles gallery (Table Design tab | Table Styles group) to expand the gallery and then click 'Grid Table 5 Dark - Accent 1' in the Table Styles gallery to apply the selected style to the table in the document (Figure 4–52).

3 If the First Column check box in the Table Style Options group (Table Design tab) does not contain a check mark, click the check box to add a check mark because you do want the first column in the table formatted differently from the rest of the table. Be sure the remaining check marks match those in the Table Style Options group (Table Design tab) as shown in Figure 4–52.

BTW

Table Wrapping

If you want text to wrap around a table, instead of displaying above and below the table, do the following: either right-click the table and then click Table Properties on the shortcut menu, or click the Properties button (Layout tab | Table group), click the Table tab (Table Properties dialog box), click Around in the Text wrapping area, and then click OK.

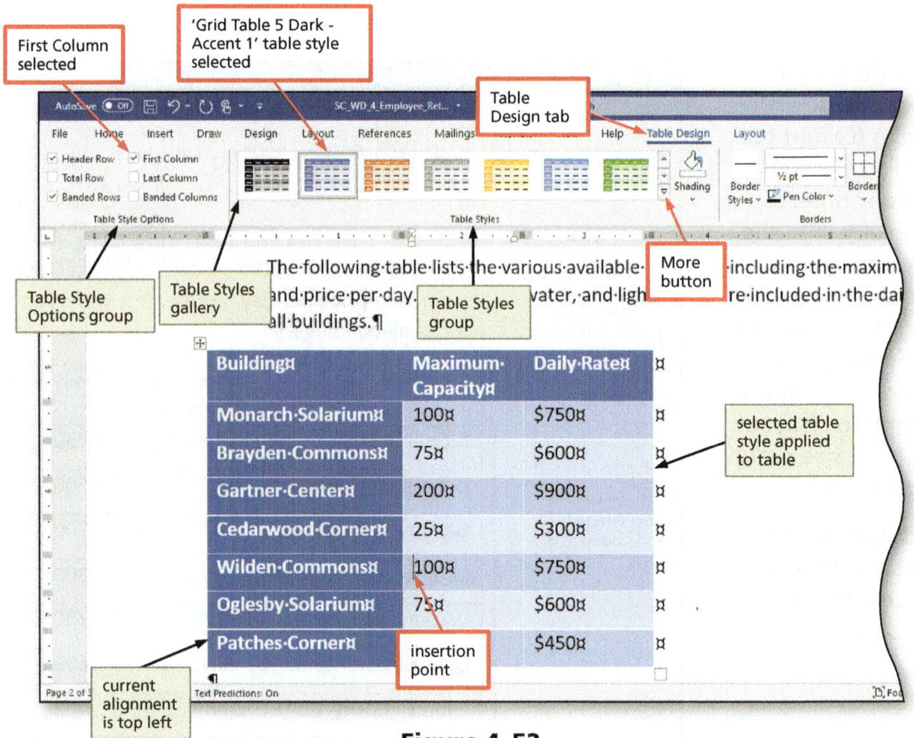

Figure 4–52

To Align Data in Cells

The next step is to change the alignment of the data in cells in the table. In addition to aligning text horizontally in a cell (left, center, or right), you can align it vertically within a cell (top, center, bottom). When the height of the cell is close to the same height as the text, however, differences in vertical alignment are not readily apparent. Because the rows are taller in this table, you will vertically center the data in the cells. The following step aligns data in cells. **Why?** In tables, textual data often is left-aligned and numeric data often is right-aligned.

1

- Display the Layout tab.
- Select the leftmost column, as shown in Figure 4–53, and then click the desired alignment, in this case the 'Align Center Left' button (Layout tab | Alignment group) to align the contents of the selected cells (Figure 4–53).

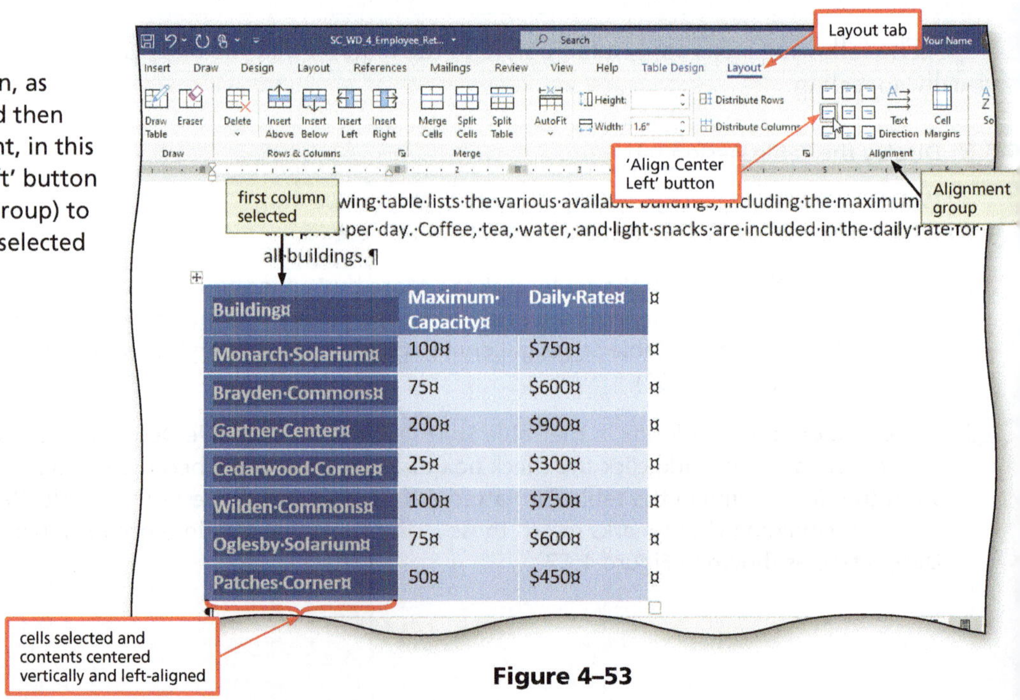

Figure 4–53

2

- Select the second and third columns, as shown in Figure 4–54, and then click the desired alignment, in this case the 'Align Center Right' button (Layout tab | Alignment group) to align the contents of the selected cells (Figure 4–54).

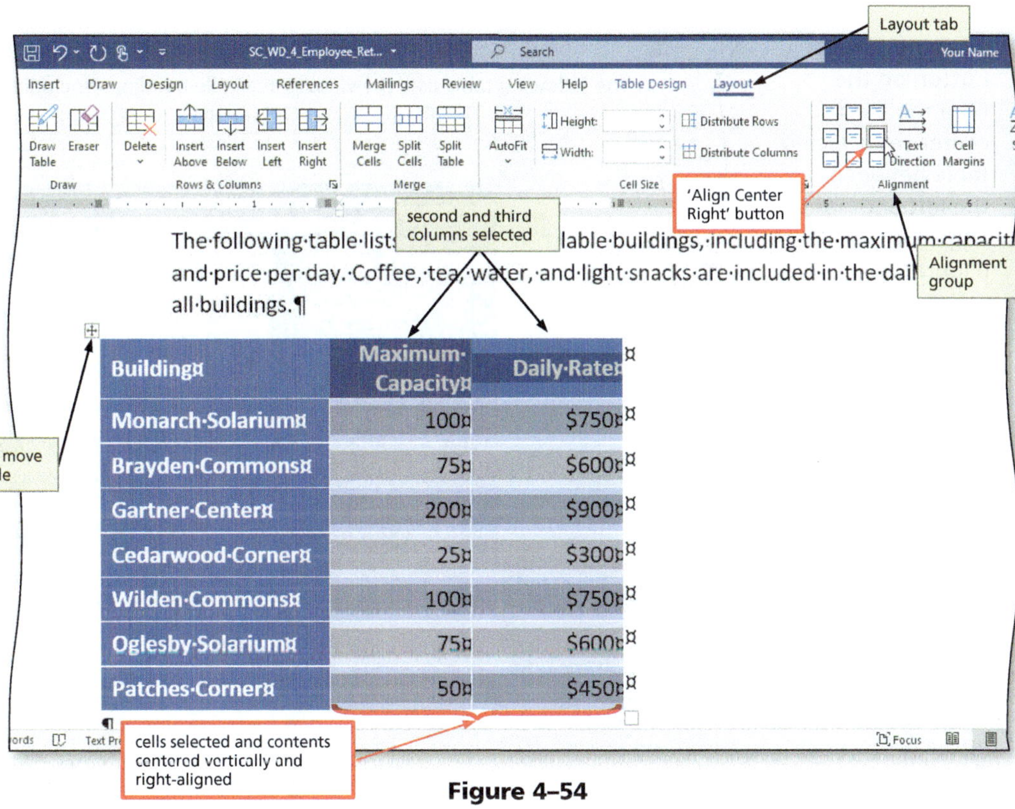

Figure 4–54

To Center a Table

The entire table in this document should be centered between the margins of the page. To center a table, you first select the entire table. The following steps select and center a table using the Mini toolbar. **Why?** You can use buttons and boxes on the Mini toolbar instead of those on the ribbon.

1

- Position the pointer in the table so that the table move handle appears (shown in Figure 4–54) and then click the table move handle to select the entire table (Figure 4–55).

Q&A

What if the table move handle does not appear?
You also can select a table by clicking the Select button (Layout tab | Table group) and then clicking Select Table on the menu.

What if I am using a touch screen?
Tap the Select button (Layout tab | Table group) and then tap Select Table on the Select menu to select the table.

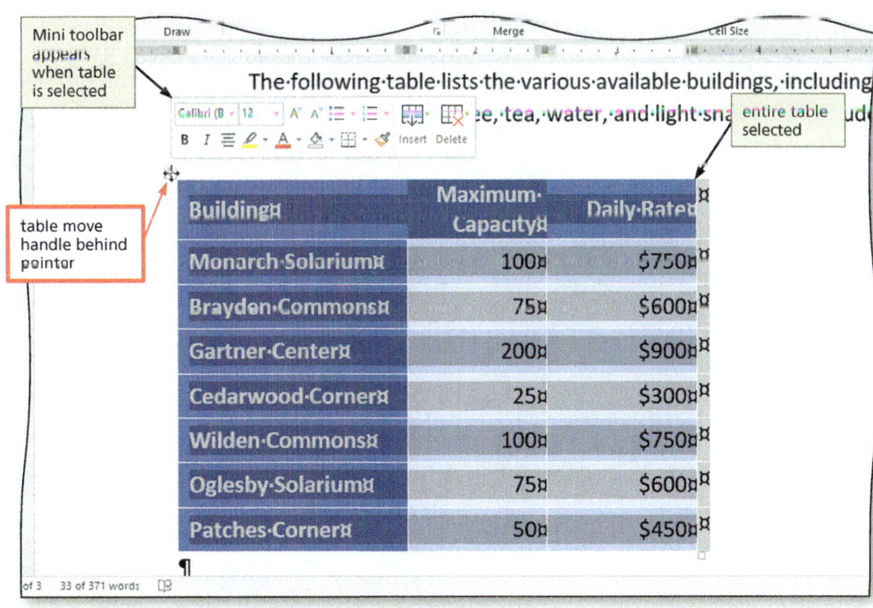

Figure 4–55

2

- Click the Center button on the Mini toolbar to center the selected table between the left and right page margins (Figure 4–56).

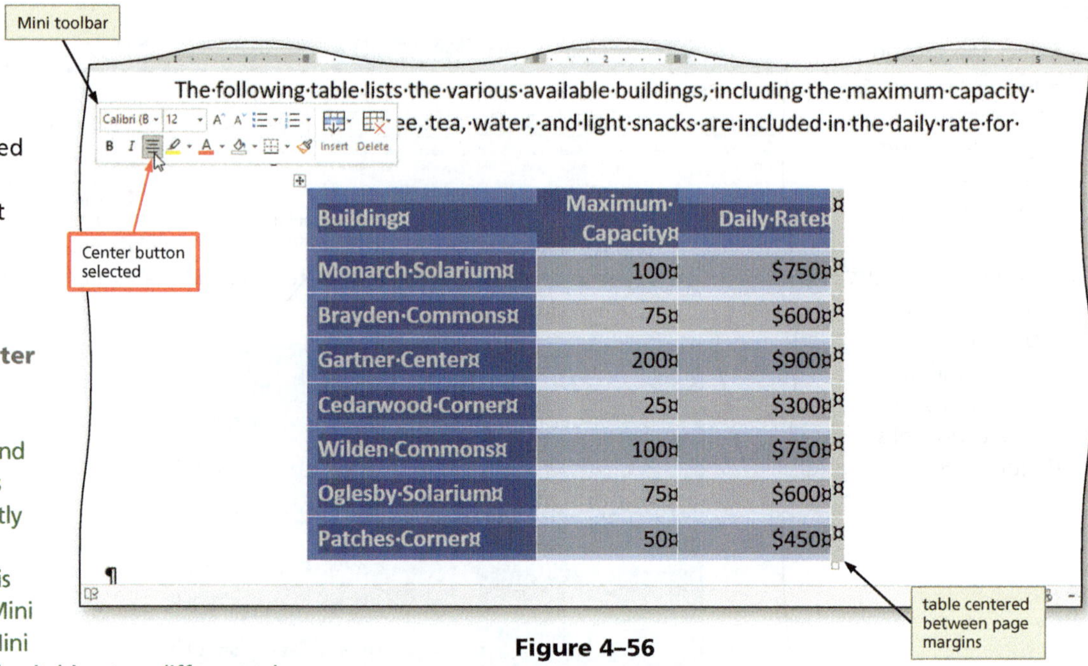

Figure 4–56

Q&A

Could I have clicked the Center button on the Home tab?
Yes. If the command you want to use is not on the currently displayed tab on the ribbon and it is available on the Mini toolbar, use the Mini toolbar instead of switching to a different tab. This technique minimizes mouse movement.

What if I am using a touch screen?
Display the Home tab and then tap the Center button (Home tab | Paragraph group) to center the table.

To Sort a Table

The next task is to sort rows in the table on one column. **Why?** The building names should be listed in alphabetical order. The following steps sort rows in a table on the Building column.

1

- With the table selected, click the Sort button (Layout tab | Data group) to display the Sort dialog box (Figure 4–57).

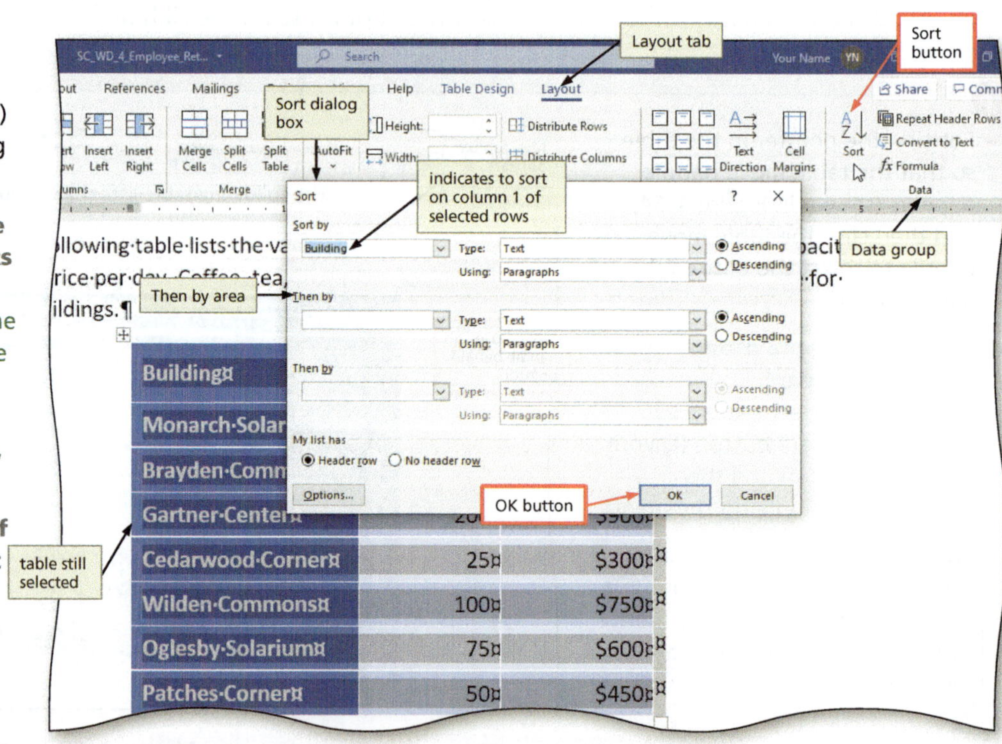

Figure 4–57

Q&A

Do I need to select the table before sorting its contents?
No, you can also place the insertion point anywhere in the table instead of selecting it. If you want to sort only certain rows, select those rows first.

What is the purpose of the Then by area (Sort dialog box)?
If you have multiple values for a particular column, you can sort on multiple columns by sorting on columns within columns. For example, if the table had a city column and a last name column, you could sort by last names within cities.

2

- Click OK (Sort dialog box) to instruct Word to alphabetize the selected rows.
- Click anywhere in the table to remove the selection from the table (Figure 4–58).

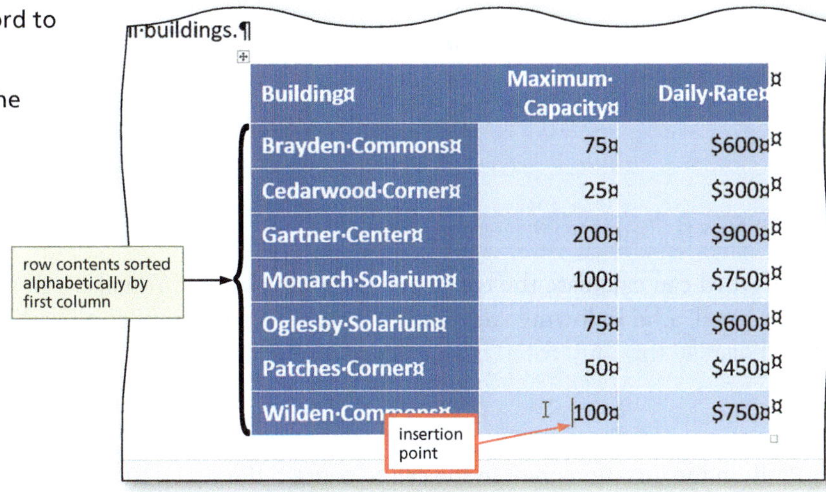

Figure 4–58

To Add a Row to a Table

The next step is to insert a row at the bottom of the table because you want to add totals to the bottom of the two right columns. You can add a row at the end of a table by positioning the insertion point in the bottom-right corner cell and then pressing TAB. Or, you use the Insert Below command (Layout tab | Rows & Columns group) or the Insert Control. The following steps insert a row at the bottom of a table.

1 Position the insertion point somewhere in the last row of the table because you want to insert a row below this row (shown in Figure 4–58).

2 Click the Insert Below button (Layout tab | Rows & Columns group) to insert a row below the row containing the insertion point and then select the newly inserted row.

3 Click in the leftmost column of the added row and then type `Total - Entire Site` (shown in Figure 4–59).

Q&A

Why did the hyphen I entered in Step 3 change to an en dash?
As you type text in a document, Word automatically formats some of it for you. If your entered hyphen did not automatically change to an en dash, you can enter an en dash by clicking the Symbol button (Insert tab | Symbols group), clicking More Symbols in the Symbol gallery, clicking the Special Characters tab (Symbol dialog box), clicking En Dash in the Character list, clicking the Insert button, and then closing the dialog box.

To Delete a Row

If you wanted to delete a row, you would perform the following tasks.

1. Position the insertion point in the row to be deleted; click the Delete button (Layout tab | Rows & Columns group) and then click Delete Rows on the Delete menu.

   or

2. If using touch, press and hold row to delete, tap Delete button on Mini toolbar, and then tap Delete Rows.

   or

BTW

Table Headings
If a table continues on the next page, you can instruct Word to repeat the table headings at the top of the subsequent page(s) containing the table. To do this, select the first row in the table and then click the 'Repeat Header Rows' button (Layout tab | Data group).

3. Right-click the row to delete, click Delete Cells on the shortcut menu, click 'Delete entire row' (Delete Cells dialog box), and then click OK.

   or

4. Select the row to be deleted, right-click the selected row, and then click Delete Rows on the shortcut menu.

To Insert a Formula in a Table

Word can calculate the totals of rows and columns. You also can specify the format for how the totals will be displayed. The following steps sum the right two columns in the table. **Why?** In this project, the last row should display the sum (total) of the values in the Maximum Capacity and Daily Rate columns.

1

- Position the insertion point in the cell to contain the sum (last row, Maximum Capacity column).

2

- Click the Formula button (Layout tab | Data group) to display the Formula dialog box (Figure 4–59).

Q&A **What is the formula that shows in the Formula box, and can I change it?** Word places a default formula in the Formula box, depending on the location of the numbers in surrounding cells. In this case, because numbers are above the current cell, Word displays a formula that will add the numbers above the current cell. You can change the formula that Word proposes, or you can type a different formula. For example, instead of summing numbers you can multiply them.

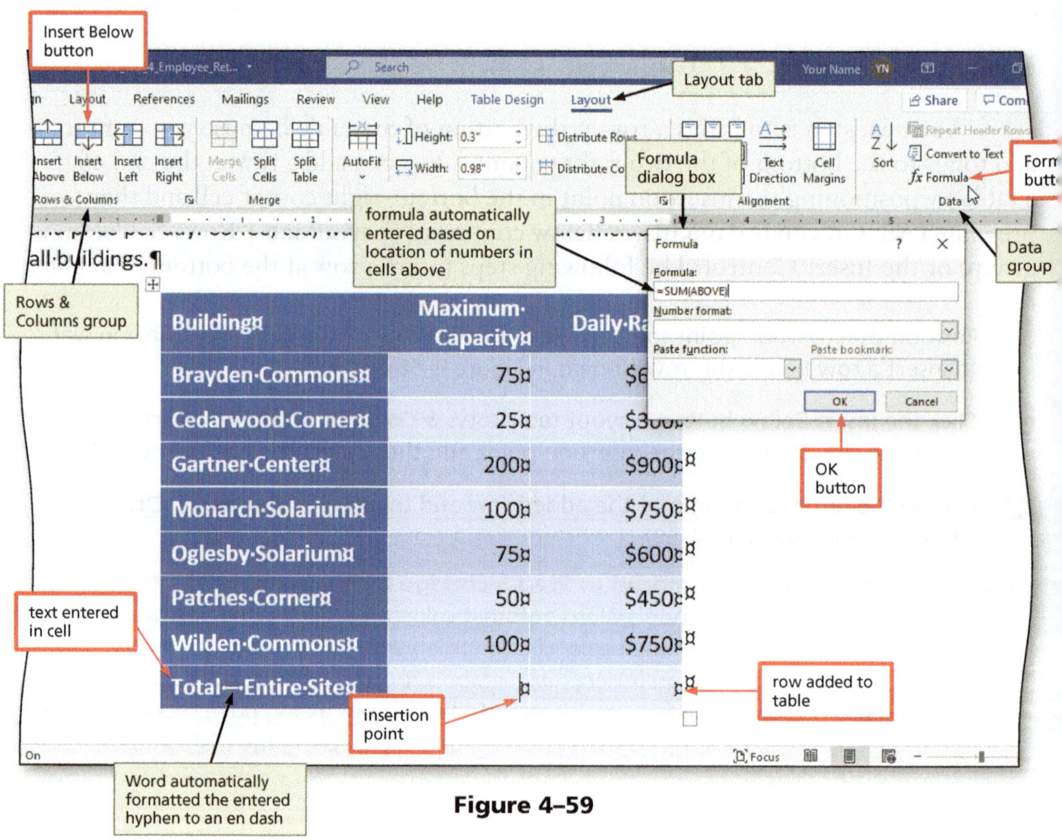

Figure 4–59

3

- Click OK (Formula dialog box) to place the sum of the numbers in the current cell.

4

- Position the insertion point in the cell to contain the sum (last row, Daily Rate column).
- Click the Formula button (Layout tab | Data group) to display the Formula dialog box.

- Click the Number format arrow (Formula dialog box) to display a list of formats for numbers (Figure 4–60).

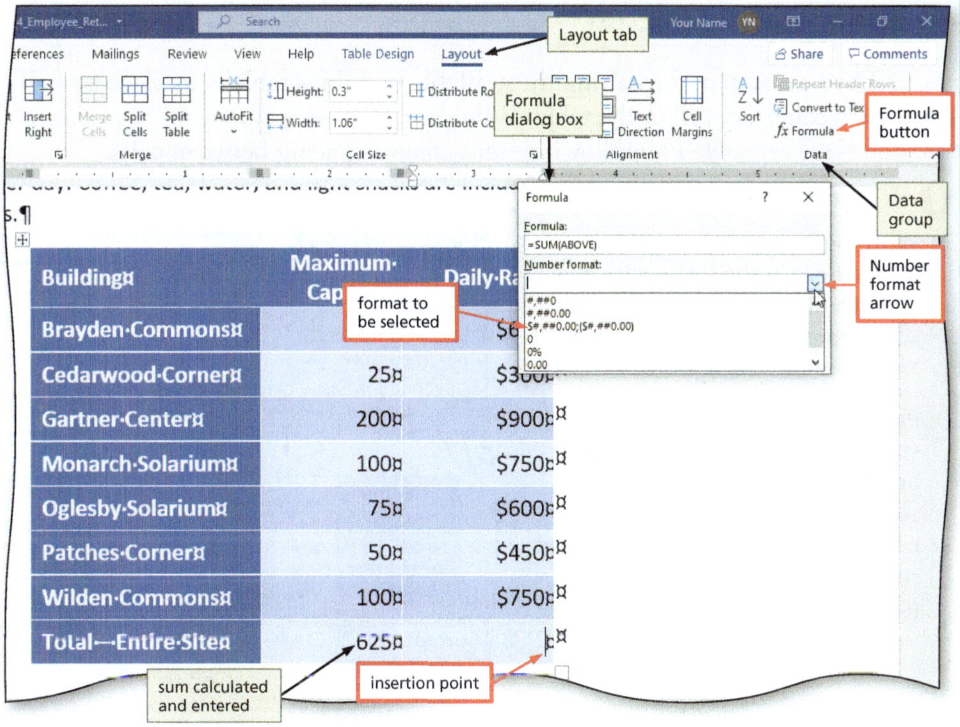

Figure 4–60

5

- Select the desired format for the result of the computation, in this case, the format $#,##0.00;($#,##0.00).

Q&A **What do # symbols mean in the format?**
The # symbol means to display a blank if the number has a value of zero. The format in the parentheses is for negative numbers.

- Click the Number format box (Formula dialog box) and then delete the .00 from the format in two places because you want the number to display as a whole number without cents (Figure 4–61).

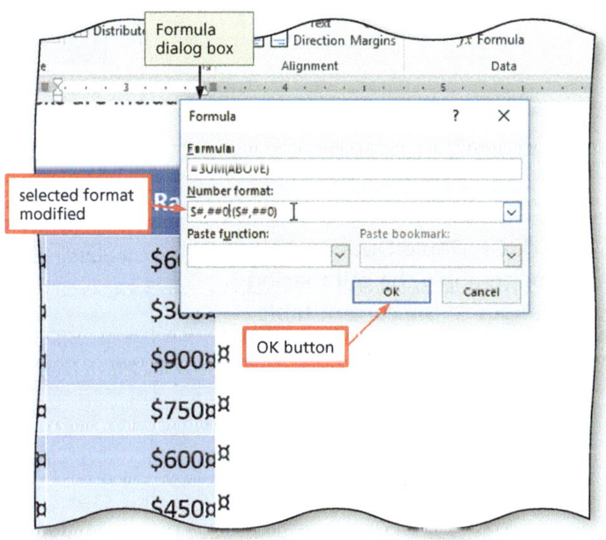

Figure 4–61

6

- Click OK (Formula dialog box) to place the sum of the numbers using the specified format in the current cell (shown in Figure 4–62).

Q&A **Can I sum a row instead of a column?**
Yes. You would position the insertion point in an empty cell at the right edge of the row before clicking the Formula button.

If I make a change to a number in a table, does Word automatically recalculate the sum?
No. You will need to update the field by right-clicking it and then clicking Update Field on the shortcut menu or by selecting the field and then pressing F9.

To Change Cell Spacing

The next step in formatting the available buildings table is to place a small amount of additional white space between every cell in the table. **Why?** You feel the table would be easier to read with more white space surrounding each cell. The following steps change spacing between cells.

1

- With the insertion point somewhere in the table, click the Cell Margins button (Layout tab | Alignment group) to display the Table Options dialog box.
- Place a check mark in the 'Allow spacing between cells' check box and then click the up arrow once so that 0.02" is displayed in this box, because you want to increase space between cells by this value (Figure 4–62).

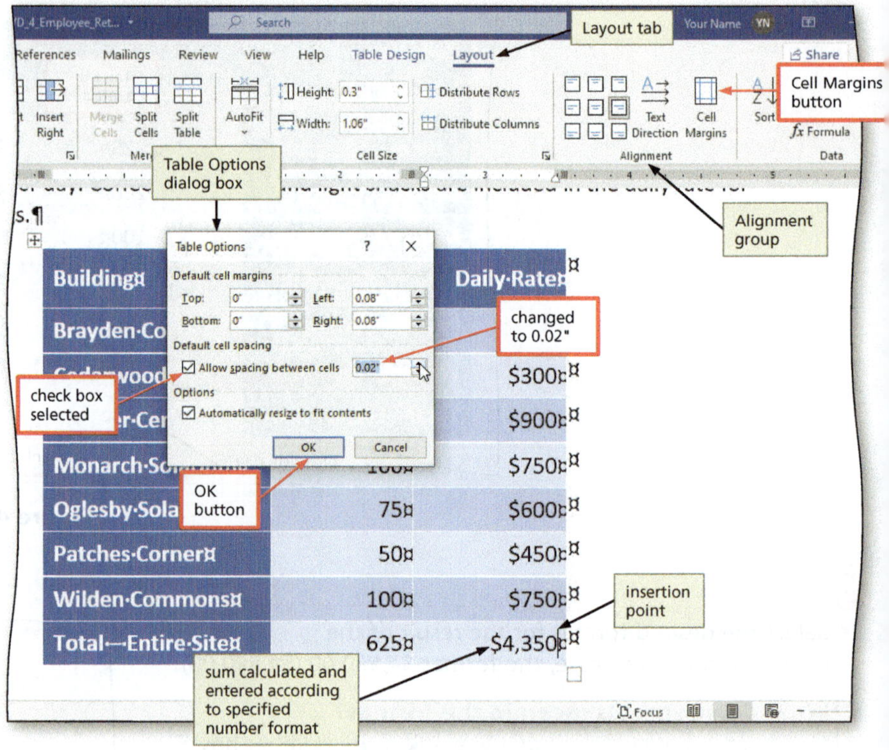

Figure 4–62

2

- Click OK (Table Options dialog box) to apply the cell spacing changes to the current table (Figure 4–63).

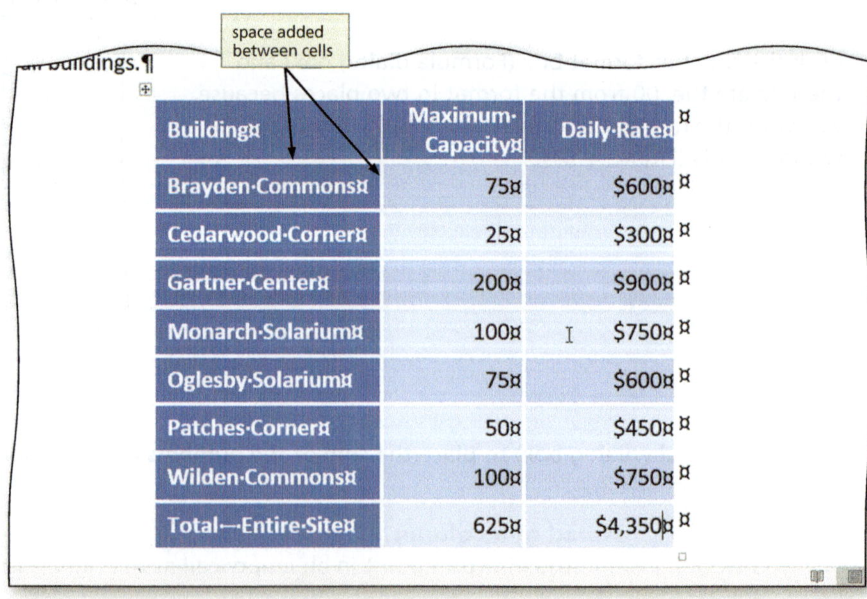

Figure 4–63

Other Ways

1. Click Properties button (Layout tab | Table group), click Table tab (Table Properties dialog box), click Options button, select desired options (Table Options dialog box), click OK in each dialog box
2. Right-click table (or, if using touch, tap 'Show Context Menu' button on Mini toolbar), click Table Properties on shortcut menu, click Table tab (Table Properties dialog box), click Options button, select desired options (Table Options dialog box), click OK in each dialog box

To Change Margins in Table Cells

The next step in formatting the available buildings table is to adjust the cell margins, that is, the space at the top, bottom, left, and right edge of the cells. **Why?** You feel the table would be easier to read with bigger margins in the cells. The following steps change margins in table cells.

1

- Position the insertion point somewhere in the table and then click the Cell Margins button (Layout tab | Alignment group) to display the Table Options dialog box.
- Use the up arrows in the Top and Bottom boxes to change values to 0.02", and use the up arrows in the Left and Right boxes to change their values to 0.1", because you want to increase cell margins to these measurements (Figure 4–64).

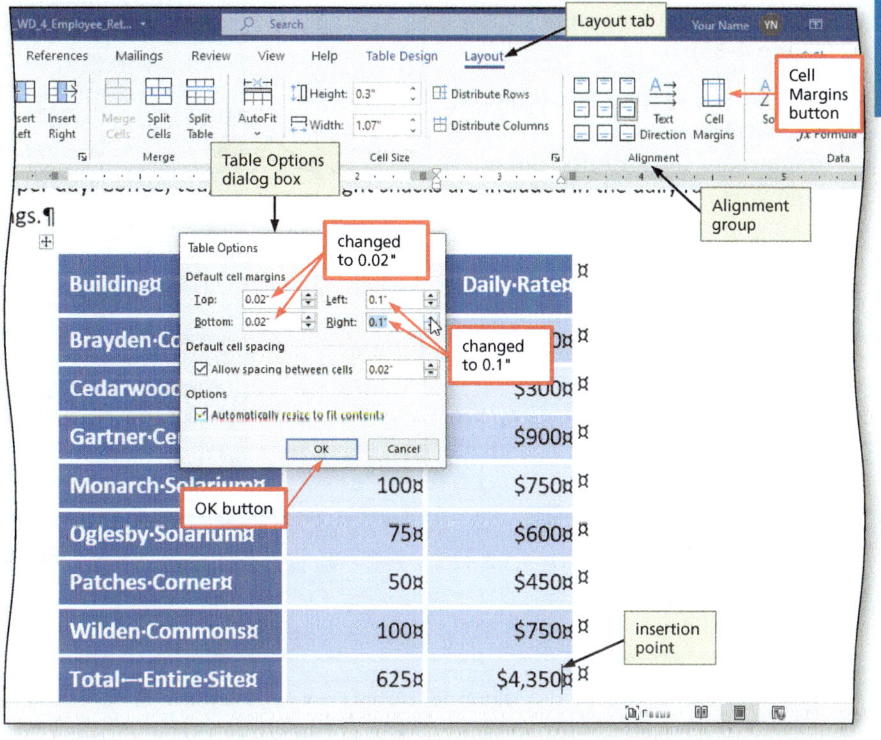

Figure 4–64

2

- Click OK (Table Options dialog box) to apply the cell margin changes to the current table (shown in Figure 4–65).

Q&A **Why is there an extra page in my document?**
The increased table margins may have added an extra page in the document. If this occurred, the blank page will be deleted after the next steps.

Other Ways

1. Click Properties button (Layout tab | Table group), click Table tab (Table Properties dialog box), click Options button, select desired options (Table Options dialog box), click OK in each dialog box
2. Right-click table (or, if using touch, tap 'Show Context Menu' button on Mini toolbar), click Table Properties on shortcut menu, click Table tab (Table Properties dialog box), click Options button, select desired options (Table Options dialog box), click OK in each dialog box

To Distribute Columns

The last step in formatting the available buildings table is to make the width of the second and third columns uniform, that is, the same width. The following step distributes selected columns. **Why?** Instead of checking and adjusting the width of each column individually, you can format multiple columns uniform at the same time.

1

- Select the columns to format, in this case, the second and third columns.
- Click the Distribute Columns button (Layout tab | Cell Size group) to make the width of the selected columns uniform (Figure 4–65).

Q&A **How would I make all columns in the table uniform?**
Simply place the insertion point somewhere in the table before clicking the Distribute Columns button.

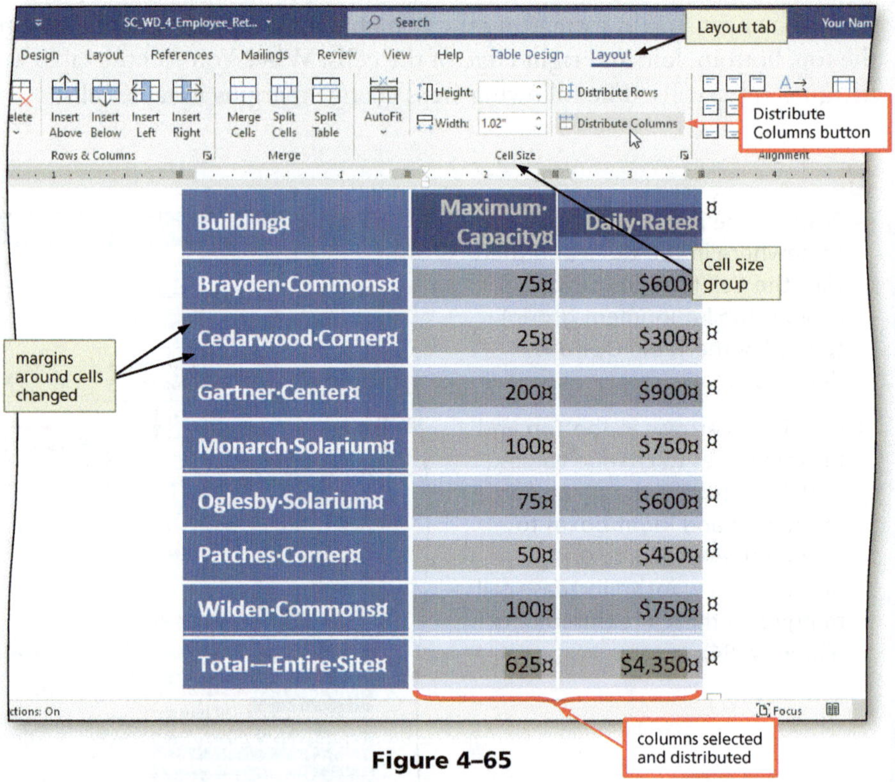

Figure 4–65

Other Ways

1. Right-click selected columns, click 'Distribute Columns Evenly' on shortcut menu (or, if using touch, tap 'Show Context Menu' button on Mini toolbar)

To Delete a Blank Paragraph

If you notice an extra paragraph mark below the available buildings table that is causing an extra blank page in the document, you should delete the blank paragraph. If necessary, the following steps delete a blank paragraph.

1. Position the insertion point on the blank paragraph mark below the available buildings table.
2. If necessary, press DELETE to remove the extra blank paragraph and delete the blank page.
3. If a blank page still exists or if one or more rows in the table spill onto the next page, remove space above and below paragraphs in the sales proposal until the entire proposal fits on three pages, as shown in Figure 4–1 at the beginning of this module.

To Show Gridlines

When a table contains no borders or light borders, it may be difficult to see the individual cells in the table. Thus, the following step shows gridlines. **Why?** To help identify the location of cells in the additional fees table, you can display gridlines, which show cell outlines on the screen. **Gridlines** are formatting marks that show cell boundaries but do not print.

1

- Display the table to be edited in the document window (in this case, the additional fees table).
- Position the insertion point in any cell in the table.
- Display the Layout tab.
- If gridlines are not displayed on the screen, click the View Gridlines button (Layout tab | Table group) to show gridlines in the table (Figure 4–66).

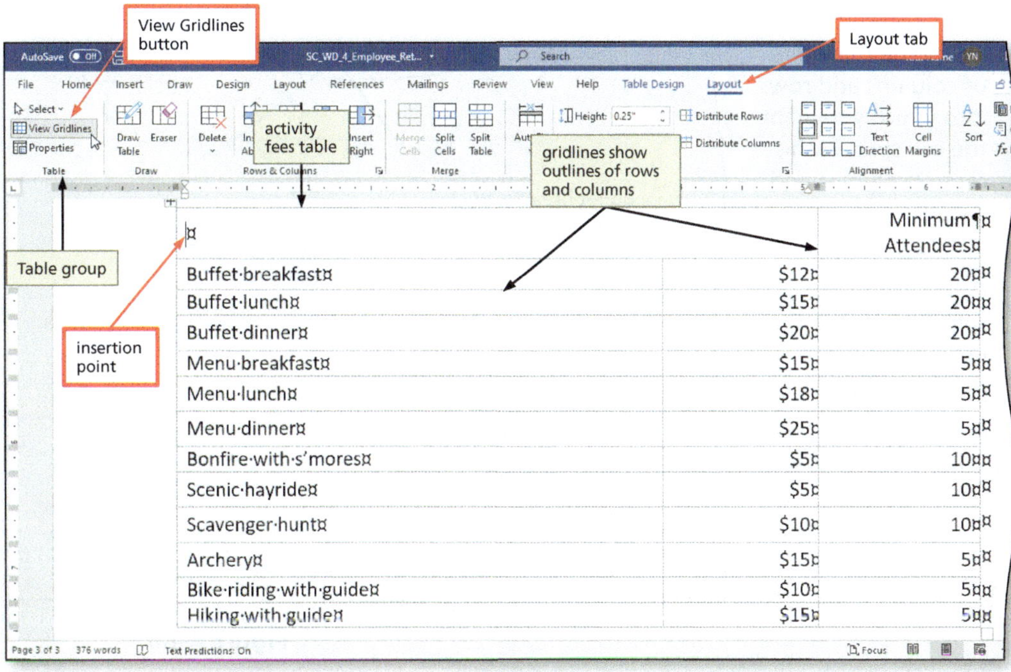

Figure 4–66

Q&A **How do I turn off table gridlines?**
Click the View Gridlines button again.

To Split a Table Cell

The top, left cell of the table contains one long cell that appears above two columns (the options and fees columns). The heading, Fee-Based Options, should be above the first column, and the heading, Fee per Person, should be above the second column. Thus, you will split the cell into two cells. **Why?** With the cell split, you can enter a heading above each of the first two columns. The following steps split a single cell into two separate cells.

1

- Position the insertion point in the cell to split, in this case the top left cell as shown in Figure 4–67.
- Click the Split Cells button (Layout tab | Merge group) to display the Split Cells dialog box (Figure 4–67).

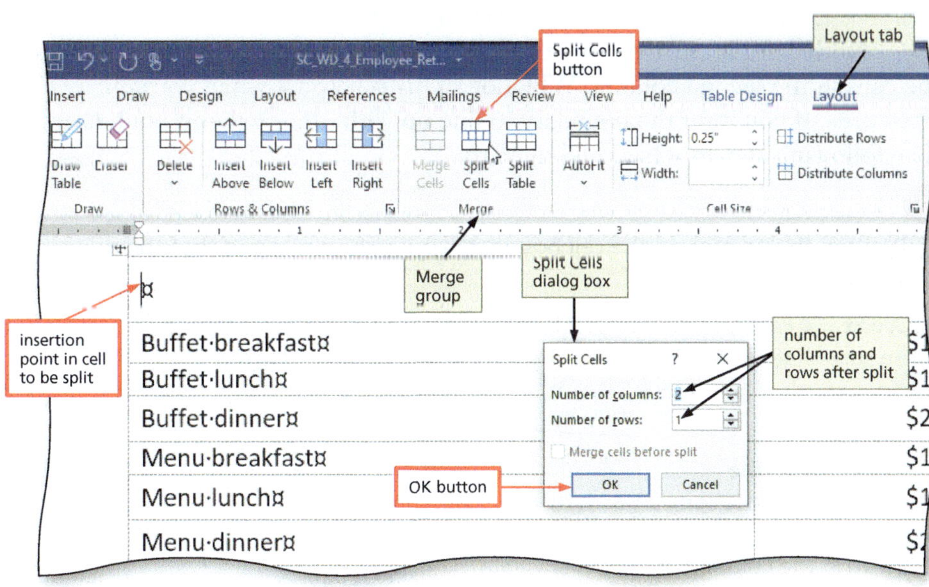

Figure 4–67

2

- Verify the number of columns and rows into which you want the cell split, in this case, 2 columns and 1 row.
- Click OK (Split Cells dialog box) to split the one cell into two columns (Figure 4–68).
- Click in the table to remove the selection from the cells.

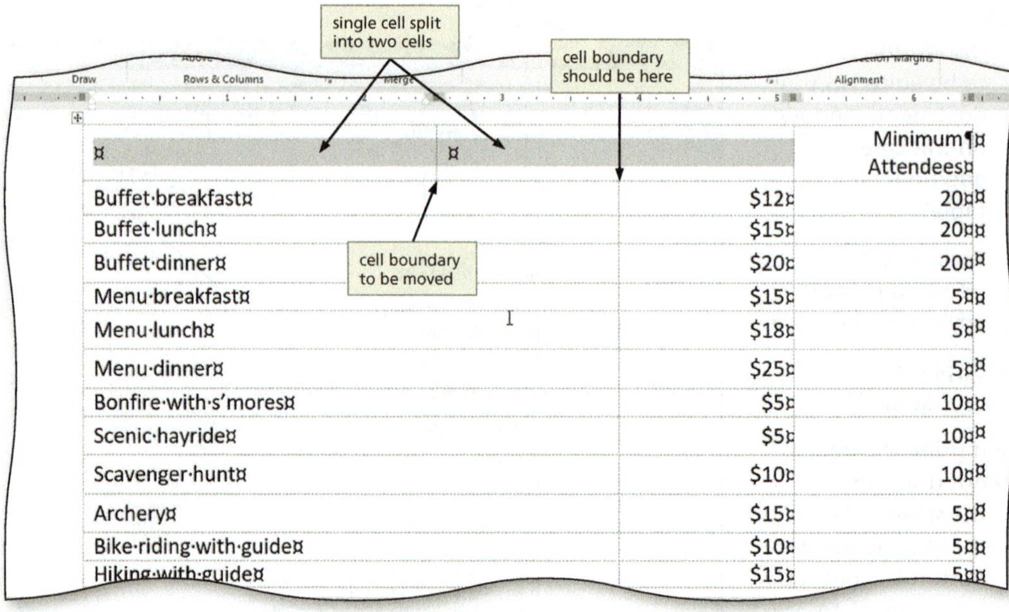

Figure 4–68

Other Ways

1. Right-click cell, click Split Cells on shortcut menu (or, if using touch, tap 'Show Context Menu' button on Mini toolbar)

To Split a Table

Instead of splitting table cells into multiple cells, sometimes you want to split a single table into multiple tables. If you wanted to split a table, you would perform the following steps.

1. Position the insertion point in the cell where you want the table to be split.
2. Click the Split Table button (Layout tab | Merge group) to split the table into two tables at the location of the insertion point.

To Move a Cell Boundary

Notice in Figure 4–68 that the cell boundary above the second column does not line up with the rest of the cells in the second column. **Why not?** This is because when you split a cell, Word divides the cell into evenly sized cells. If you want the boundary to line up with other column boundaries, drag it to the desired location. The following step moves a cell boundary.

1

- Position the pointer on the cell boundary you wish to move so that the pointer changes to a double-headed arrow split by two vertical bars.

Q&A **What if I cannot see the cell boundary?**
Be sure that table gridlines are showing: View Gridlines button (Layout tab | Table group).

- Drag the cell boundary to the desired new location, in this case, to line up with the column boundary to its right, as shown in Figure 4–69.

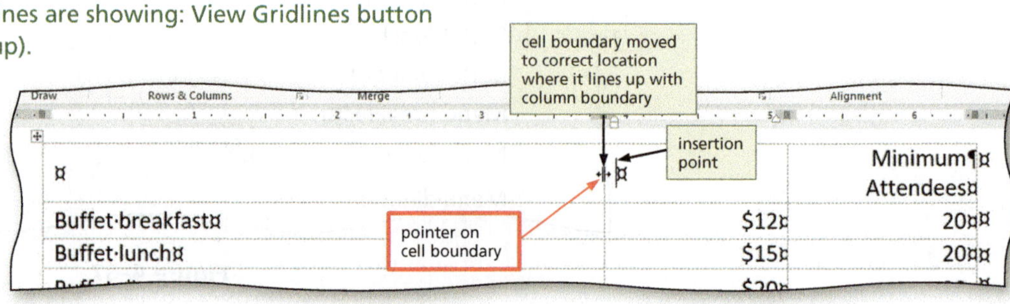

Figure 4–69

Q&A **What if I am using a touch screen?**
Position the insertion point in the upper-left cell and then type `1.28` in the Width box (Layout tab | Table group).

Other Ways

1. Drag 'Move Table Column' marker on horizontal ruler to desired width

To Enter Text in Cells

With the cells split, you can enter the column headings for the first and second column in the table. The following steps enter text in cells.

1. Position the insertion point in the upper-left table cell and then type **`Fee-Based Options`** as the column heading.
2. If necessary, click the 'Align Center Left' button (Layout tab | Alignment group) to align the contents of the cell.
3. Press TAB and then click the 'Align Center Right' button (Layout tab | Alignment group) to align the contents of the cell. Type **`Fee per`** as the first line of the heading, press ENTER, type **`Person`** as the heading (shown in Figure 4–70).

To Distribute Rows

The next step in formatting the additional fees table is to make the height of the rows below the column headings uniform, that is, the same height. The following step distributes selected rows. **Why?** Instead of checking and adjusting the width of each row individually, you can format multiple rows uniform at the same time.

1.
- Select the rows to format, in this case, all rows below the column headings.
- Click the Distribute Rows button (Layout tab | Cell Size group) to make the height of the selected rows uniform (Figure 4–70).

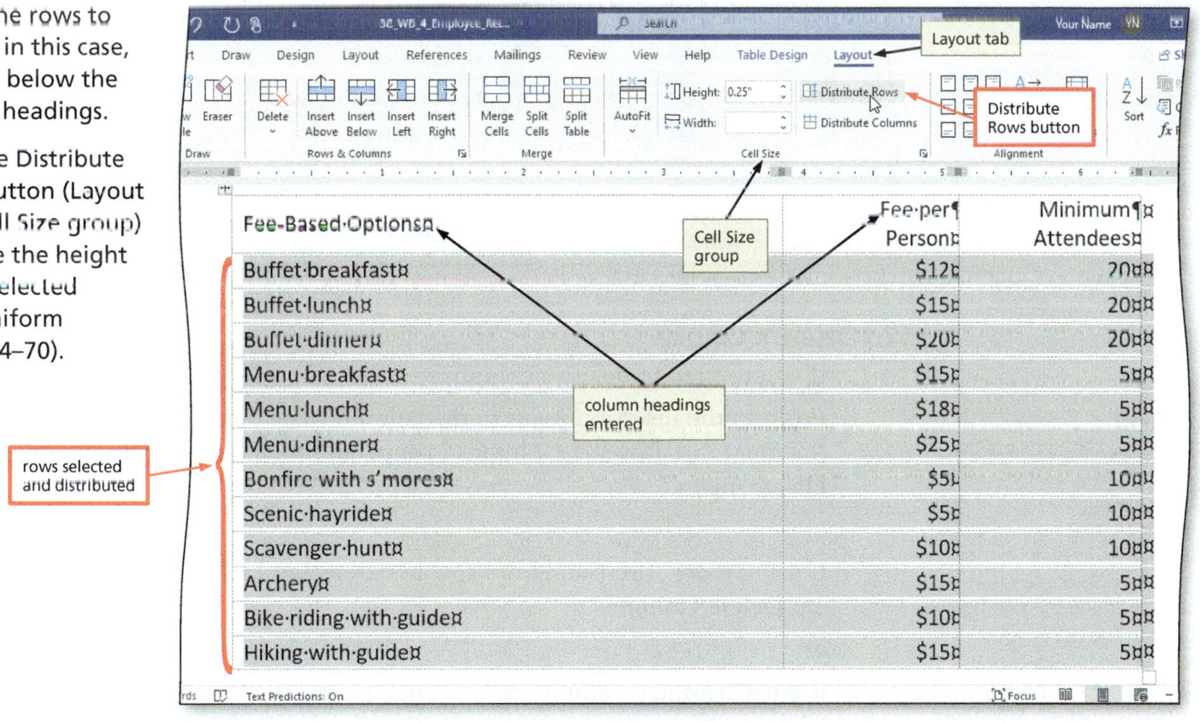

Figure 4–70

Other Ways

1. Right-click selected rows, click 'Distribute Rows Evenly' on shortcut menu (or, if using touch, tap 'Show Context Menu' button on Mini toolbar)

To Insert a Column

In this project, the left edge of the additional fees table has a column that displays the labels, Dining Fees and Activity Fees. Thus, the following steps insert a column at the left edge of the table.

1. Position the insertion point somewhere in the first column of the table.
2. Click the Insert Left button (Layout tab | Rows & Columns group) to insert a column to the left of the column containing the insertion point (Figure 4–71).
3. Click anywhere in the table to remove the selection.

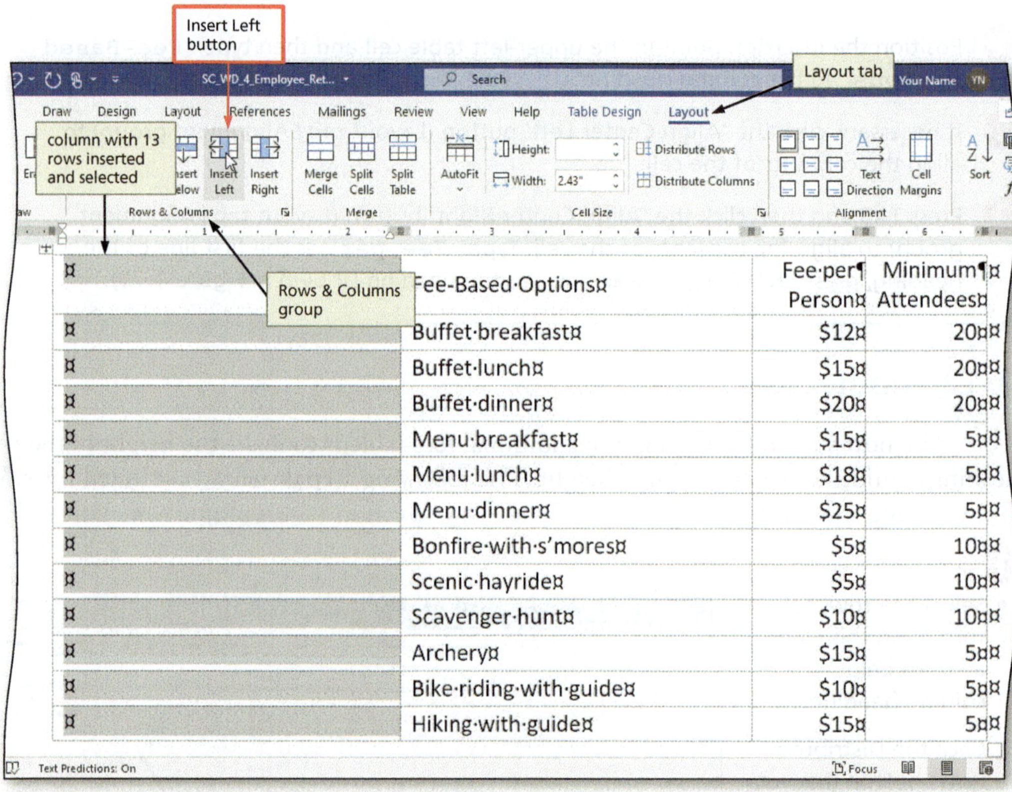

Figure 4–71

To Delete a Column

If you wanted to delete a column, you would perform the following tasks.

1. Position the insertion point in the column to be deleted, click the Delete button (Layout tab | Rows & Columns group), and then click Delete Columns on the Delete menu.

   or

2. If using touch, press and hold row to delete, tap Delete button on Mini toolbar, tap Delete Columns.

   or

3. Right-click the column to delete, click Delete Cells on the shortcut menu, click 'Delete entire column' (Delete Cells dialog box), and then click OK.

   or

4. Select the column to be deleted, right-click the selected column, and then click Delete Columns on the shortcut menu.

BTW

Deleting Table Cells
If you wanted to delete the contents of a table cell, you would select the cell contents and then press DELETE or BACKSPACE. To delete one or more cells entirely from a table, position the insertion point in the cell or select the cells to delete, click the Delete button (Layout tab | Rows & Columns group), click Delete Cells on the Delete menu, select the desired option in the Delete Cells dialog box, and then click OK.

To Merge Table Cells

The column just inserted has one cell for each row, in this case, 13 cells (shown in Figure 4–71). The top row of the first and second columns of the table are to be a single cell that spans above both columns. **Why?** The column heading, Fee-Based Options, should span above both columns. Also, the next two groups of six rows should be a single cell, each with the label, Dining Fees and Activity Fees, respectively. Thus, the following steps merge cells.

1

- Select the cells to merge, in this case, the cells in the first and second column of the first row of the table (Figure 4–72).

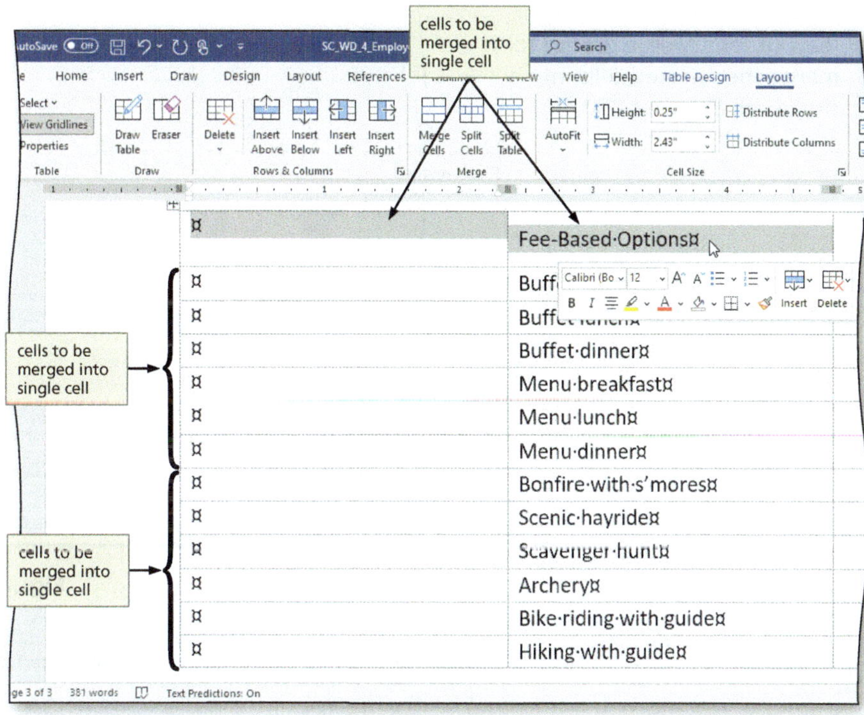

Figure 4–72

2

- With the cells to merge selected, click the Merge Cells button (Layout tab | Merge group) to merge the selected cells into a single cell (shown in Figure 4–73).
- If necessary, click the 'Align Center Left' button (Layout tab | Alignment group) to realign the cell contents.

3

- Select the cells to merge, in this case, the six cells in the first column to the left of the dining options (Figure 4–73).

4

- With the cells to merge selected, click the Merge Cells button (Layout tab | Merge group) to merge the selected cells into a single cell.

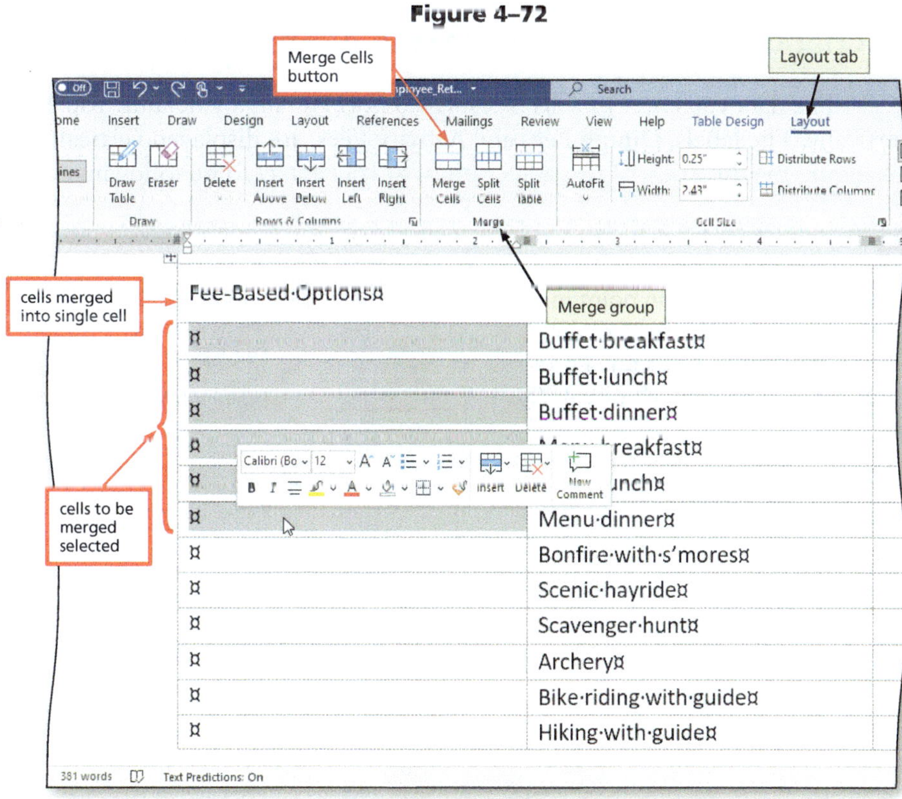

Figure 4–73

5

- Select the cells to merge, in this case, the bottom six cells in the first column to the left of the activity options.
- With the cells to merge selected, click the Merge Cells button (Layout tab | Merge group) to merge the selected cells into a single cell (Figure 4–74).

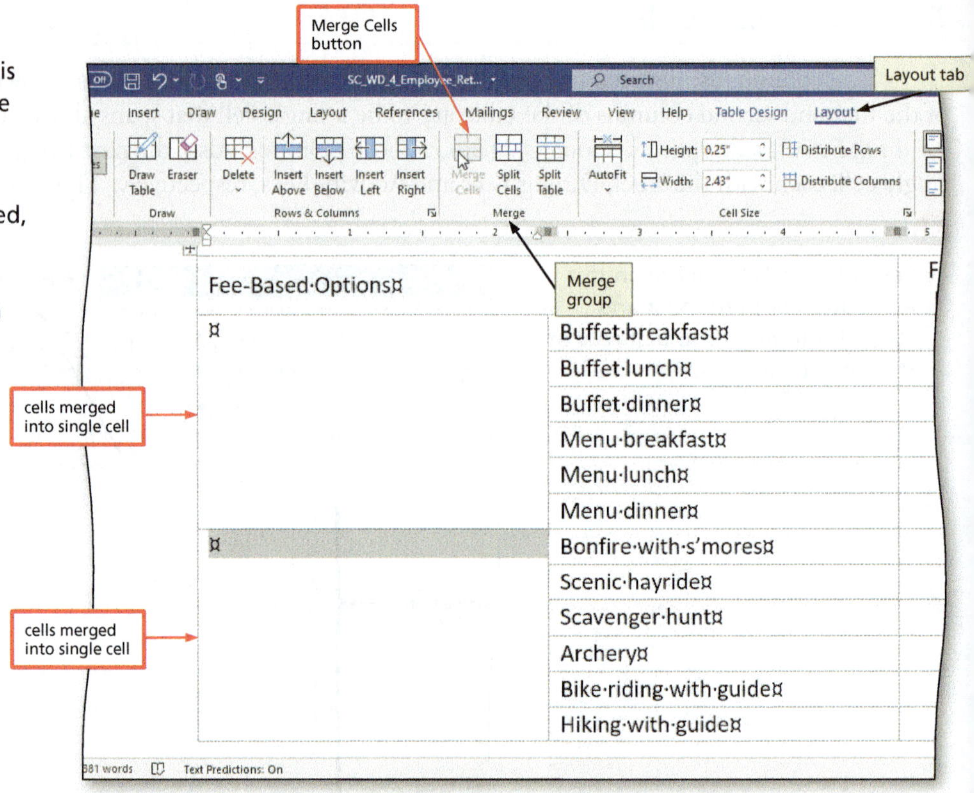

Figure 4–74

Other Ways

1. Right-click selected cells (or, if using touch, tap 'Show Context Menu' button on Mini toolbar), click Merge Cells on shortcut menu

To Change the Direction of Text in a Table Cell

The data you enter in cells is displayed horizontally by default. You can rotate the text so that it is displayed vertically. The labels, Dining Fees and Activity Fees, are displayed vertically at the left edge of the table. **Why?** Changing the direction of text adds variety to your tables. The following steps display text vertically in cells.

1

- Position the insertion point in the second row of the first column and then type **`Dining Fees`** as the row heading (Figure 4–75).

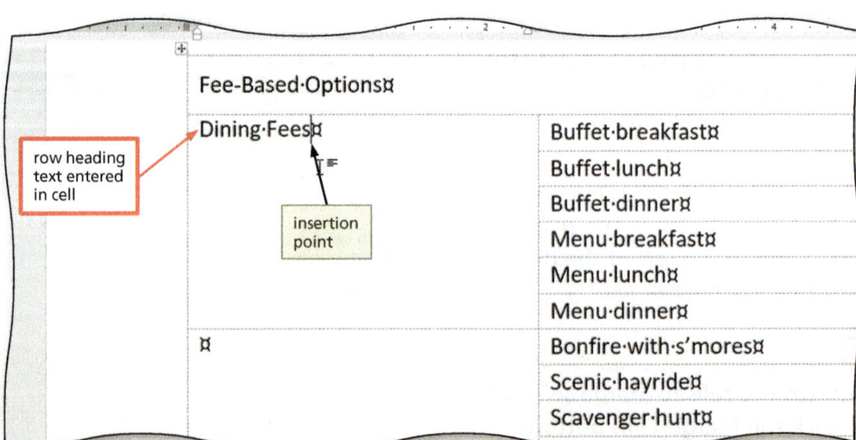

Figure 4–75

2

- With the insertion point in the cell that contains the text to rotate (in this case, Dining Fees), click the Text Direction button twice (Layout tab | Alignment group) so that the text reads from bottom to top in the cell (Figure 4–76).

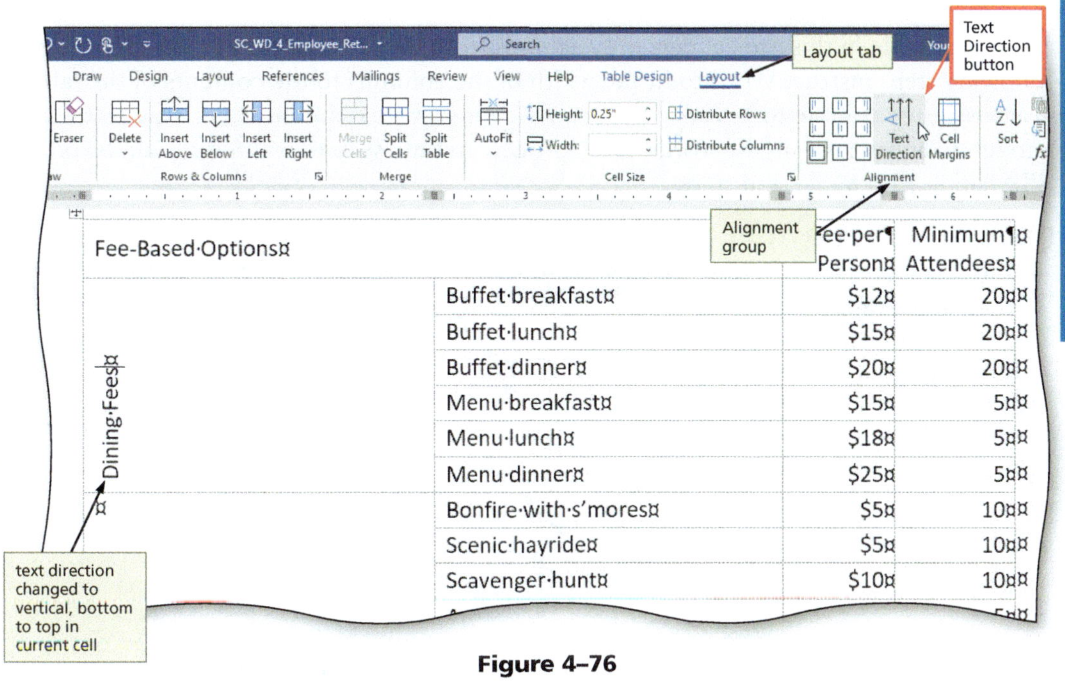

Figure 4–76

Q&A **Why click the Text Direction button twice?**
The first time you click the Text Direction button (Layout tab | Alignment group), the text in the cell reads from top to bottom. The second time you click it, the text is displayed so that it reads from bottom to top (as shown in Figure 4–76). If you were to click the button a third time, the text would be displayed horizontally again.

3

- Click the Align Center button (Layout tab | Alignment group) to center the row heading in the cell.
- Position the insertion point in the third row of the first column and then type **Activity Fees** as the row heading.
- With the insertion point in the cell that contains the text to rotate (in this case, Activity Fees), click the Text Direction button twice (Layout tab | Alignment group) so that the text reads from bottom to top in the cell.
- Click the Align Center button (Layout tab | Alignment group) to center the row heading in the cell (Figure 4–77).
- Click in the table to remove the selected cell.

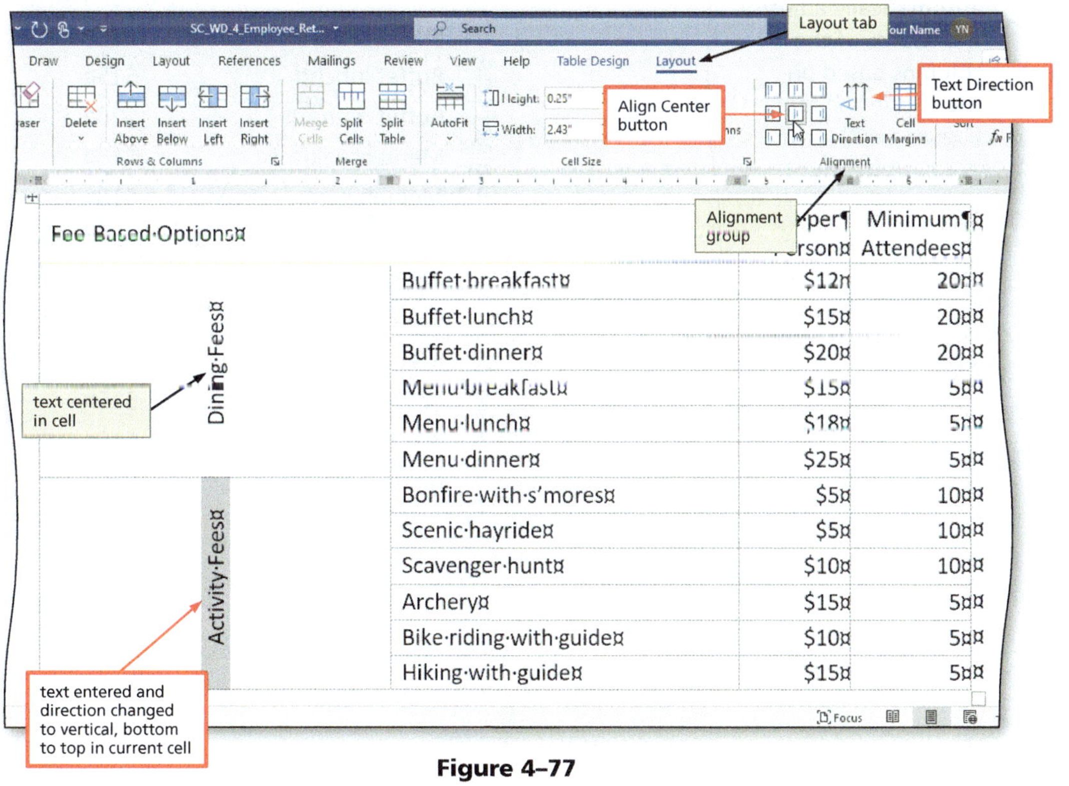

Figure 4–77

To Resize Table Columns Using AutoFit

The table in this project currently extends from the left margin to the right margin of the document. The following steps instruct Word to fit the width of the columns to the contents of the table automatically. **Why?** You want each column to be only as wide as the longest entry in the table. That is, the first column must be wide enough to accommodate the words, Dining Fees, and the second column should be only as wide as the words, Bike riding with guide, and so on.

1

- With the insertion point in the table, click the AutoFit button (Layout tab | Cell Size group) to display the AutoFit menu (Figure 4–78).

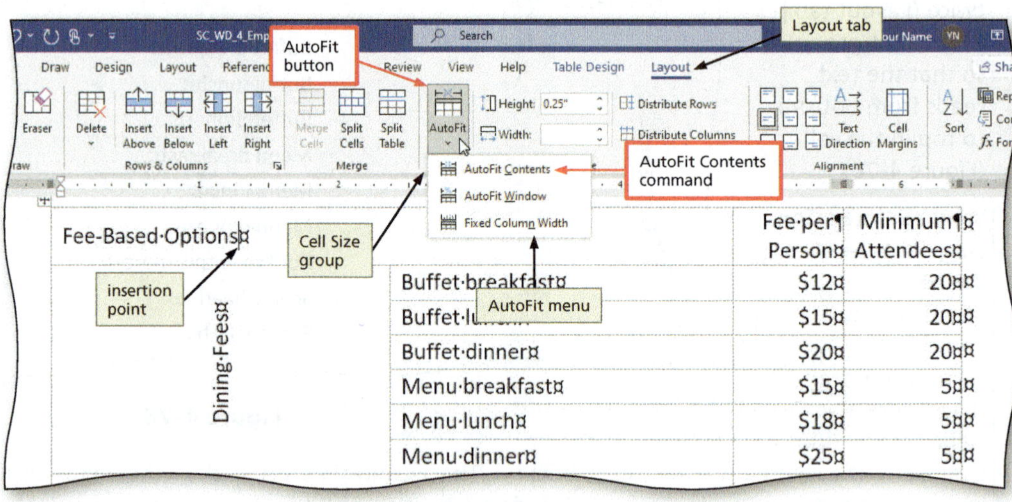

Figure 4–78

2

- Click AutoFit Contents on the AutoFit menu, so that Word automatically adjusts the widths of the columns based on the text in the table (Figure 4–79).

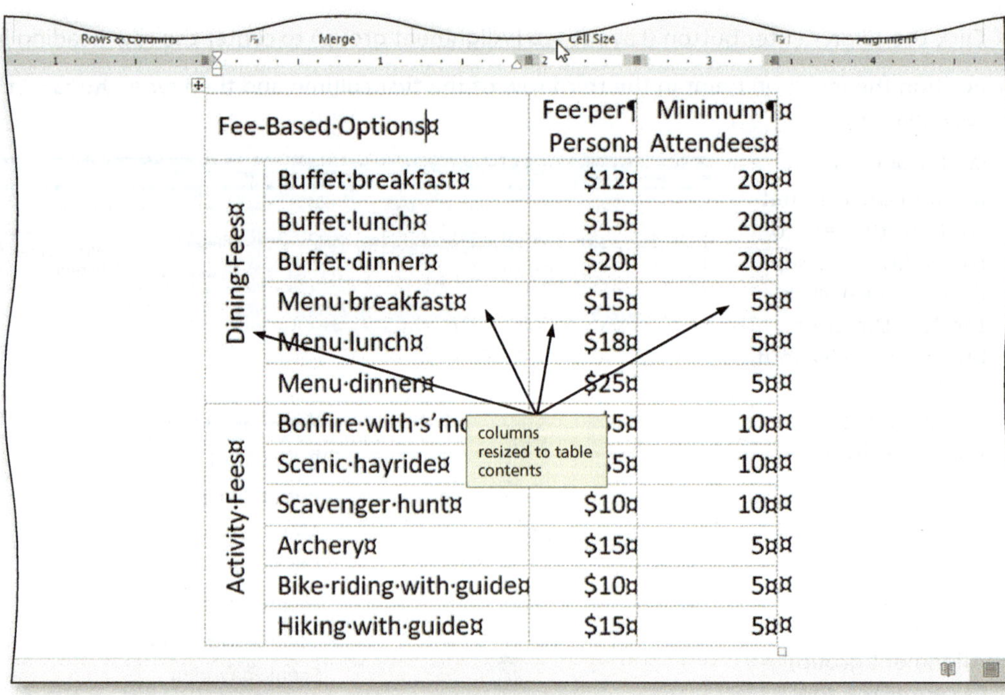

Figure 4–79

Other Ways

1. Double-click column boundary

To Change Column Width

You would like the Minimum Attendees column slightly wider. Thus, the next step is to change the width of that column. The following step changes column width.

1. Position the insertion point in the column to format, in this case, the Minimum Attendees column.
2. Type `.95` in the Width box (Layout tab | Cell Size group) and then press ENTER to change the width of the column containing the insertion point (Figure 4–80).

Q&A **What if I am using a touch screen?**
Position the insertion point in the column to adjust. Tap the Width box (Layout tab | Cell Size group), type `.95` as the column width, and then press ENTER.

BTW
Table Columns
If you hold down ALT while dragging a column marker on the ruler or a column boundary in the table, the width measurements of all columns appear on the ruler as you drag the column marker or boundary.

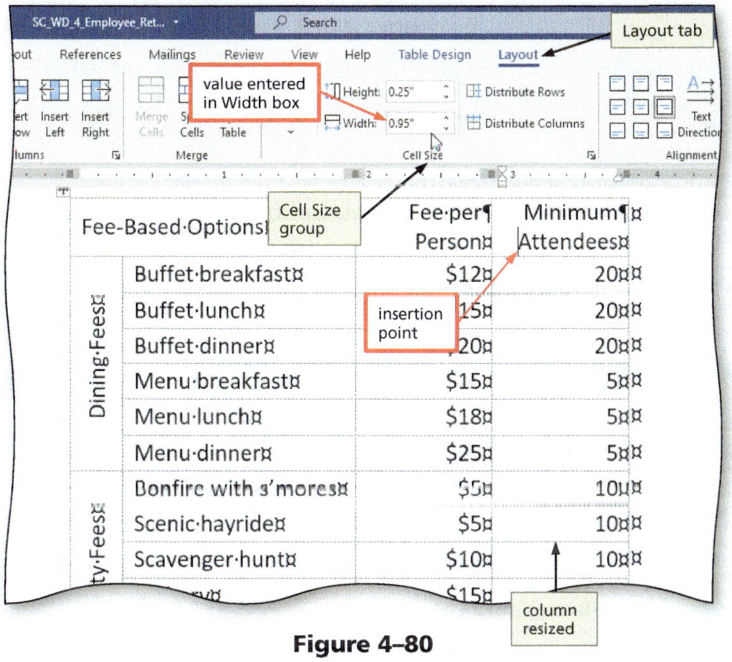

Figure 4–80

To Insert a Row and Merge Cells

The title, Dining and Team Building Activity Fees, is to be displayed in a row across the top of the table. To display this title as part of the table, you insert a row at the top of the table and then merge the three cells in the inserted row into a single cell. The following steps insert a row, merge cells, and then enter text in the merged cell.

1. Insert a row at the top of the table.
2. Select the cells to merge, in this case, the cells in the row added to the top of the table.
3. Click the Merge Cells button (Layout tab | Merge group) to merge the three selected cells into one cell. Click in the merged cell to remove the selection.
4. Click the Align Center button (Layout tab | Alignment group) to align the insertion point in the merged cell.
5. Type **`Dining and Team Building Activity Fees`** in the merged cell.
6. Bold the entered text (Figure 4–81).

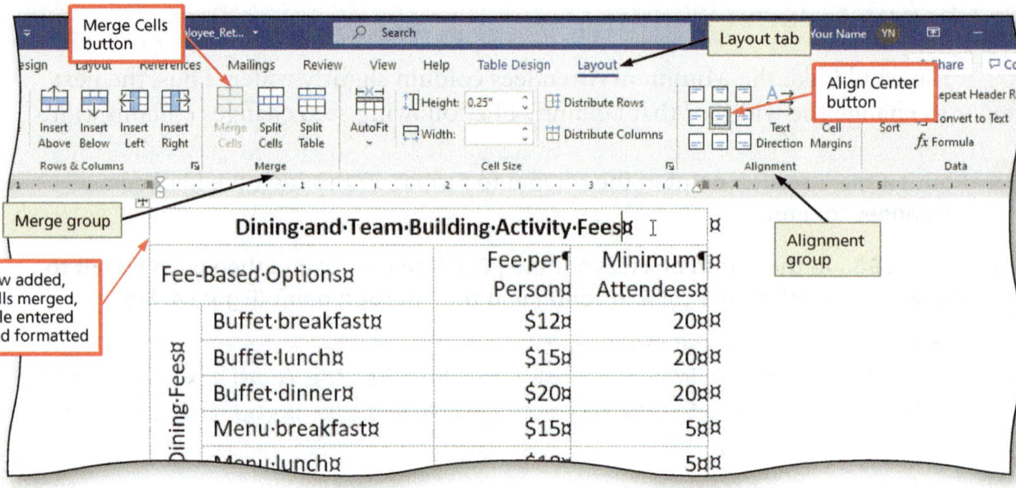

Figure 4–81

To Shade a Table Cell

In this table, the cell containing the table title and the cells containing the row headers, Dining Fees and Activity Fees, are to be shaded orange. **Why?** You want the cell shading color to complement the colors on the cover page and headers and footers. The following steps shade cells.

1

- Position the insertion point in the cell to shade (in this case, the cell containing the title).
- Display the Table Design tab.
- Click the Shading arrow (Table Design tab | Table Styles group) to display the Shading gallery (Figure 4–82).

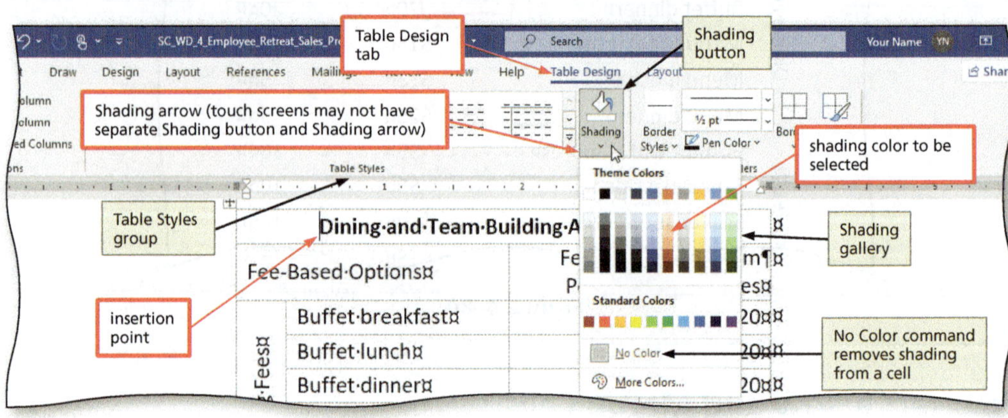

Figure 4–82

Experiment

- Point to various colors in the Shading gallery and watch the shading color of the current cell change.

2

- Click 'Orange, Accent 2, Lighter 60%' (sixth color, third row) in the Shading gallery to apply the selected shading color to the current cell.

3

- Position the insertion point in the cell to shade (in this case, the cell containing the row header, Dining Fees).
- Click the Shading button (Table Design tab | Table Styles group) to apply the most recently selected shading color to the current cell.

Q&A **Can I select the Shading arrow (Table Design tab | Table Styles group) instead?**
Yes, you would click the desired color from the Shading gallery.

4

- Position the insertion point in the cell to shade (in this case, the cell containing the row header, Activity Fees).
- Click Shading button (Table Design tab | Table Styles group) to apply the most recently selected shading color to the current cell (Figure 4–83).

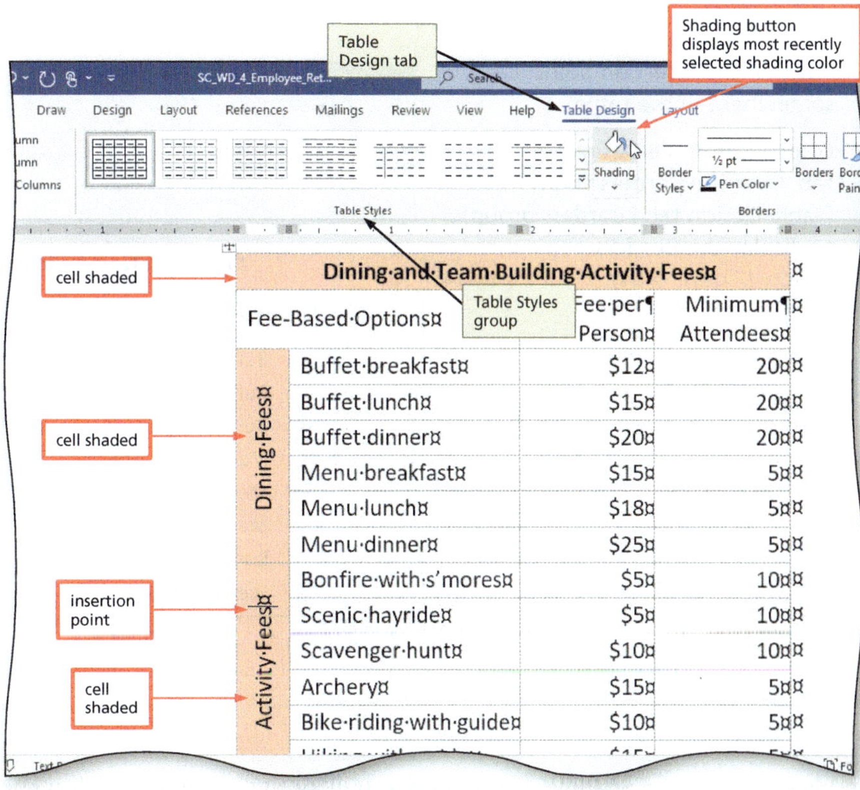

Figure 4–83

To Change Row Height

The next step in this project is to increase the height of the row containing the title. The following steps change row height.

1 Position the insertion point in the row to format (in this case, the row containing the title).

2 Display the Layout tab. Type **.34** in the Height box (Layout tab | Cell Size group) and then press ENTER to change the row height to this value.

To Hide Gridlines

You no longer need to see the gridlines in the table. Thus, you can hide the gridlines. The following steps hide gridlines.

1 If necessary, position the insertion point in a table cell.

2 Click the View Gridlines button (Layout tab | Table group) to hide gridlines in the table on the screen.

BTW

Draw Table

If you want to draw the boundary, rows, and columns of a table, click the Table button (Insert tab | Tables group) and then click Draw Table in the Table gallery. Use the pencil-shaped pointer to draw the perimeter of the table and the inside rows and columns. Use the Eraser button (Layout tab | Draw group) to erase lines in the table. To continue drawing, click the Draw Table button (Table Design tab | Draw group).

To Add a Table Border

The table in this project has a ½-point, blue double line border around all cells. The following steps change the border color in a table using the Borders and Shading dialog box. **Why?** Because the table border should be a double line with a blue color, you will use the Borders and Shading dialog box to specify the border settings for the table.

1

- Position the insertion point somewhere in the table.
- Display the Table Design tab. Click the Borders arrow (Table Design tab | Borders group) to display the Borders gallery (Figure 4–84).

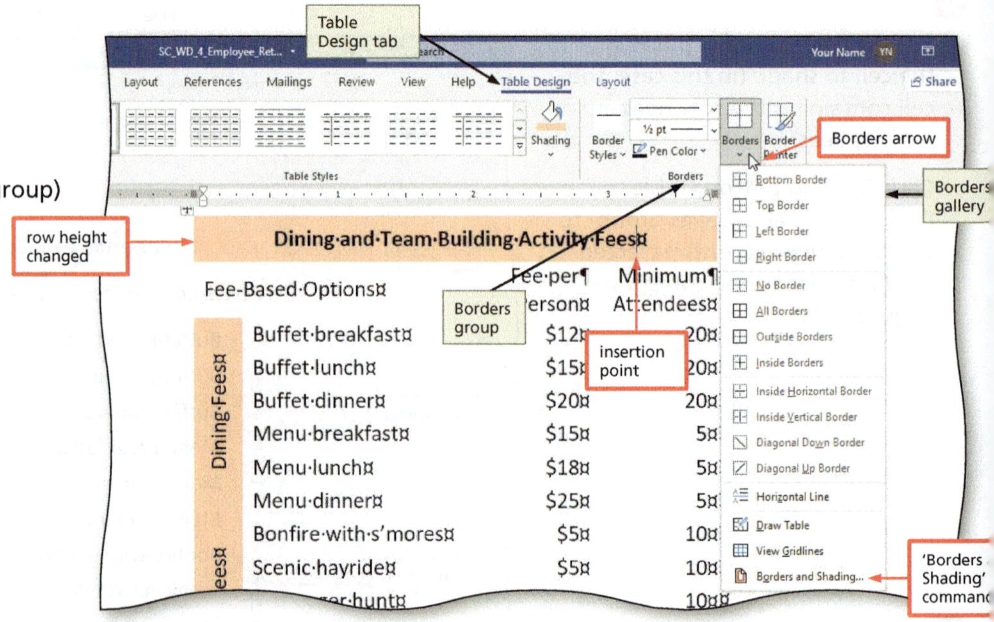

Figure 4–84

2

- Click 'Borders and Shading' in the Borders gallery to display the Borders and Shading dialog box.
- Click All in the Setting area (Borders and Shading dialog box), which will place a border on every cell in the table.
- Click the double line in the Style list.
- Click the Color arrow and then click 'Blue, Accent 1' (fifth color, first row) in the Color palette to specify the border color (Figure 4–85).

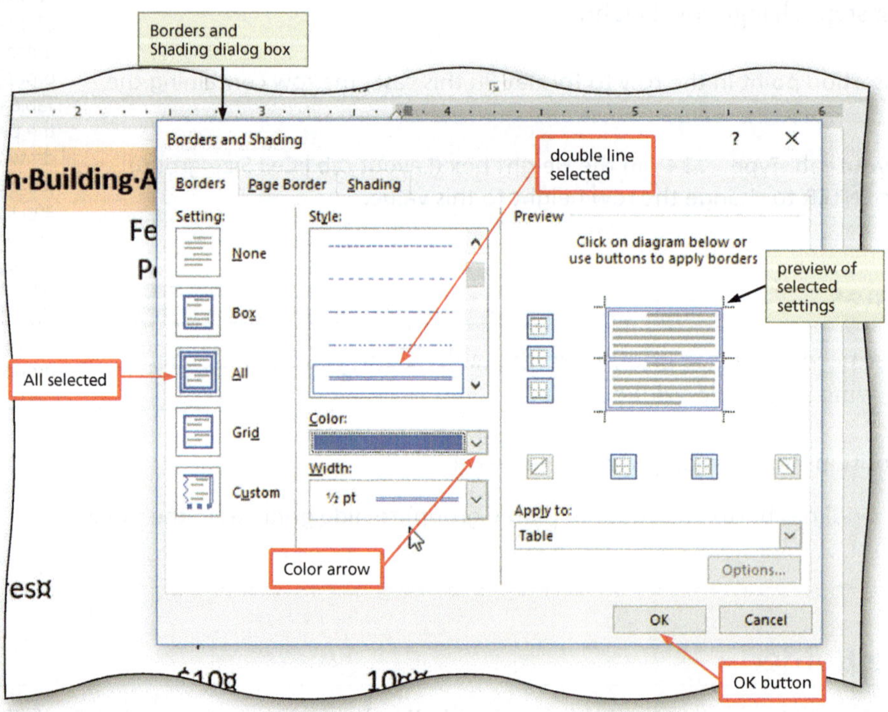

Figure 4–85

3

- Click OK to place the border shown in the preview area of the dialog box around the table cells in the document (Figure 4–86).

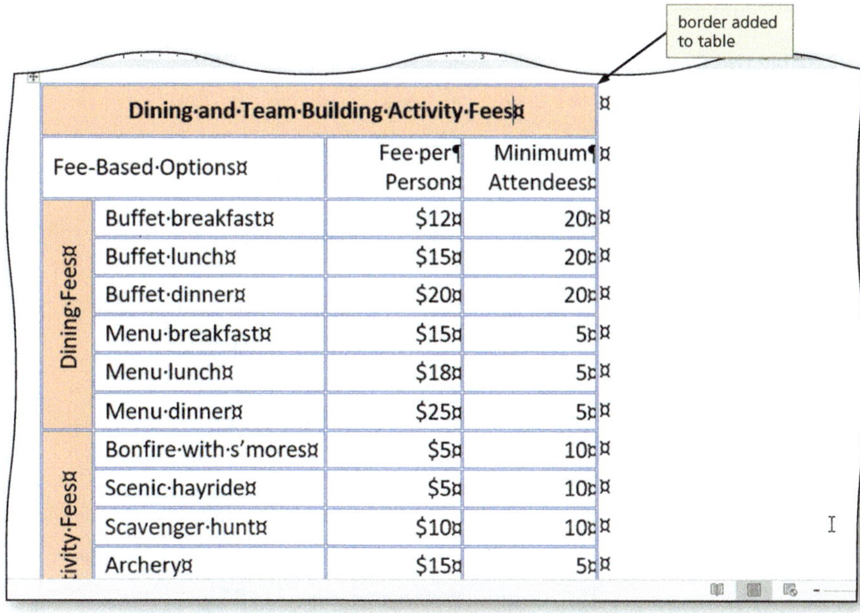

Dining and Team Building Activity Fees			
Fee-Based Options		Fee per Person	Minimum Attendees
Dining Fees	Buffet breakfast	$12	20
	Buffet lunch	$15	20
	Buffet dinner	$20	20
	Menu breakfast	$15	5
	Menu lunch	$18	5
	Menu dinner	$25	5
tivity Fees	Bonfire with s'mores	$5	10
	Scenic hayride	$5	10
	Scavenger hunt	$10	10
	Archery	$15	5

Figure 4–86

Creating a Watermark

The final task in this project is to create a watermark for the pages of the sales proposal. A **watermark** is text or a graphic, often semi-transparent, that is displayed on top of or behind the text in a document. For example, a catalog may print the words, Sold Out, on top of sold-out items. The first draft of a five-year-plan may have the word, Draft, printed behind the text of the document. Some companies use their logos or other graphics as watermarks to add visual appeal to their documents.

To Change the Zoom to Multiple Pages

The following steps display multiple pages in their entirety in the document window as large as possible, so that you can see the position of the watermark as you create it.

1 Display the View tab.

2 Click the Multiple Pages button (View tab | Zoom group) to display all three pages in the document window as large as possible (shown in Figure 4–87).

To Create a Watermark

In this project, the text, TEAM, is displayed behind all content in the proposal as a watermark. **Why?** The text adds visual appeal to the document, enticing readers to look at its contents. The following steps create a watermark.

1

- Display the Design tab.
- Click the Watermark button (Design tab | Page Background group) to display the Watermark gallery (Figure 4–87).

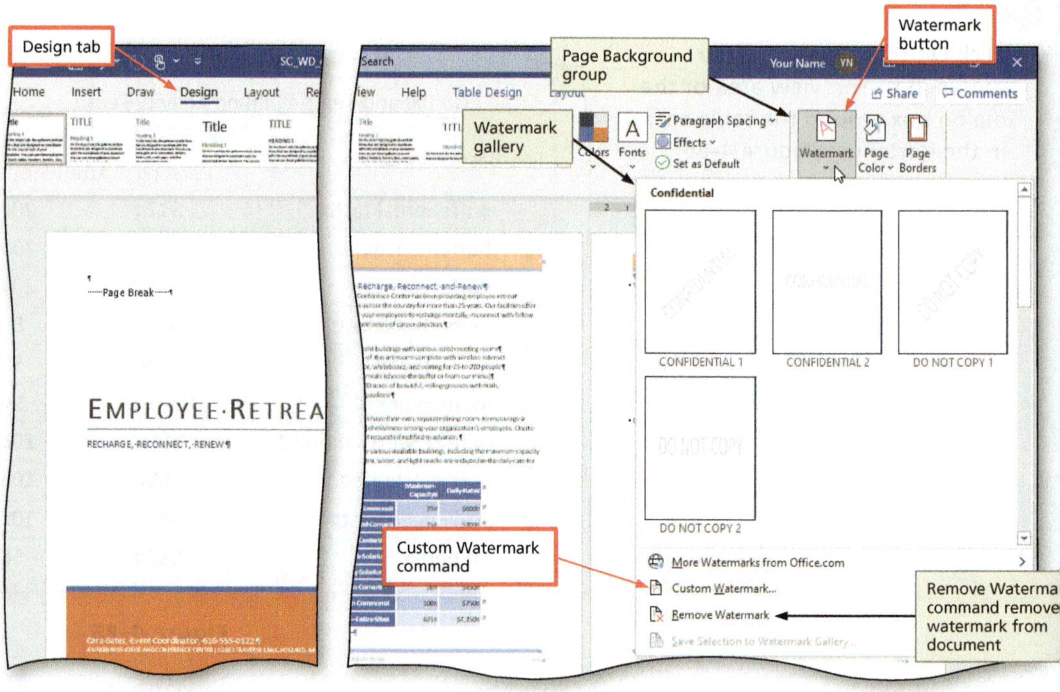

Figure 4–87

2

- Click Custom Watermark in the Watermark gallery to display the Printed Watermark dialog box.
- Click the Text watermark option button to select it (Printed Watermark dialog box), which enables you to enter or select text for the watermark.
- Select the text in the Text box and type **TEAM** in the Text box to replace the text.
- Click Horizontal to specify the direction for the text watermark.
- Click the Apply button to show a preview of the watermark on the pages in the document window (Figure 4–88).

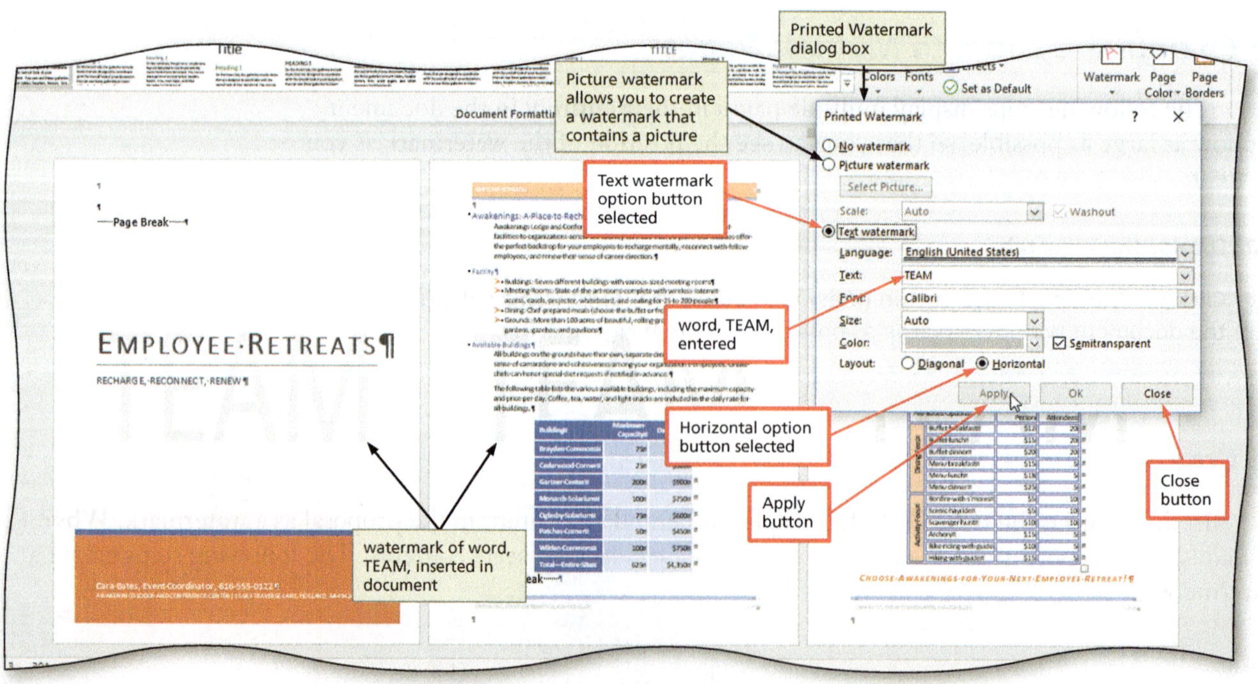

Figure 4–88

3

- Click Close to close the dialog box.

Q&A

How do I remove a watermark from a document?
Click the Watermark button (Design tab | Page Background group) and then click Remove Watermark in the Watermark gallery (shown in Figure 4–87).

How do I create a picture watermark?
Click Picture watermark in the Printed Watermark dialog box (shown in Figure 4–88), click the Select Picture button to display the Insert Pictures dialog box, locate the desired picture, click the Insert button, click the Apply button, and then click Close.

Other Ways

1. Click Quick Parts button (Insert tab | Text group), click 'Building Blocks Organizer' on Quick Parts menu, select desired watermark (Building Blocks Organizer dialog box), click Insert button

To Check Spelling, Save, Print, and Exit Word

The following steps check the spelling of the document, save and print the document, and then exit Word.

1. Display the Review tab. Click the Editor button (Review tab | Proofing group) to begin the spelling and grammar check. Correct any misspelled words.
2. sam Save the sales proposal again with the same file name.
3. If requested by your instructor, print the sales proposal (shown in Figure 4–1 at the beginning of this module).
4. Exit Word.

BTW

Distributing a Document

Instead of printing and distributing a hard copy of a document, you can distribute the document electronically. Options include sending the document via email; posting it on cloud storage (such as OneDrive) and sharing the file with others; posting it on social media, a blog, or other website; and sharing a link associated with an online location of the document. You also can create and share a PDF or XPS image of the document, so that users can view the file in Acrobat Reader or XPS Viewer instead of in Word.

Summary

In this module, you learned how to insert a cover page, insert text in content controls, apply character effects, change paragraph indentation, insert formatted headers and footers, format page numbers, sort lists and tables, format bullet characters, create a multilevel list, edit and format Word tables, insert a formula in a table, and insert a watermark.

Consider This

What decisions will you need to make when creating your next proposal?

Use these guidelines as you complete the assignments in this module and create your own proposals outside of this class.

1. Identify the nature of the proposal.

a) If someone else requests that you develop the proposal, it is a **solicited proposal**. Be sure to include all requested information in a solicited proposal.

b) When you write a proposal because you recognize a need, it is considered an **unsolicited proposal**. With an unsolicited proposal, you must gather information you believe will be relevant and of interest to the intended audience.

2. Design an eye-catching cover page.

a) The cover page should convey the overall message of the sales proposal.

b) Use text, graphics, formats, and colors that reflect the goals of the sales proposal.

c) Be sure to include a title.

3. Compose the text of the sales proposal.

a) Sales proposals vary in length, style, and formality, but all should be designed to elicit acceptance from the reader.

b) The sales proposal should have a neat, organized appearance.

c) A successful sales proposal uses succinct wording and includes lists for textual messages.

d) Write text using active voice, instead of passive voice.

e) Assume that readers of unsolicited sales proposals have no previous knowledge about the topic.

f) Be sure the goal of the proposal is clear.

g) Establish a theme and carry it throughout the proposal.

4. Enhance the sales proposal with appropriate visuals.

a) Use visuals to add interest, clarify ideas, and illustrate points.

b) Visuals include tables, charts, and graphical images (i.e., photos, etc.).

5. Proofread and edit the proposal.

a) Carefully review the sales proposal to be sure it contains no spelling, grammar, mathematical, or other errors.

b) Check that transitions between sentences and paragraphs are smooth. Ensure that the purpose of the proposal is stated clearly.

c) Ask others to review the proposal and give you suggestions for improvements.

Apply Your Knowledge

Reinforce the skills and apply the concepts you learned in this module.

Working with Headers, Multilevel Lists, Tables, and Footers

Note: To complete this assignment, you will be required to use the Data Files. Please contact your instructor for information about accessing the Data Files.

Instructions: Start Word. Open the document, SC_WD_4-2.docx, which is located in the Data Files. The document is a draft for a proposal that presents the menu and other information for Healthy Bites, a food chain that prides itself on fresh and nutritious fast food. The office manager, who created the draft, has asked you to delete its watermark; modify the header, footer, and table; and insert a multilevel list to create the finished document shown in Figure 4–89.

Perform the following tasks:

1. Click File on the ribbon and then click Save As and save the document using the new file name, SC_WD_4_FoodChainProposal.
2. Remove the watermark. (Hint: Use the Watermark button (Design tab | Page Background group).)
3. Apply the Heading 1 style to the first line of text that reads: Our Menu: Nutritional and Delicious.
4. Remove the current header from the document. (Hint: Use the Header button (Insert tab | Header & Footer group).)
5. Add the predefined header called Banded to the document. Insert the text, Healthy Bites, in the Title content control in the header.
6. Format the text, Healthy Bites, in the header as small caps, bold the text, change its font size to 18 point, and expand its character spacing by 5 points. (Hint: Use the Font dialog box.)

header inserted

HEALTHY BITES

Our Menu: Nutritional and Delicious

paragraph indented

Each store bakes all its bread daily, slices meats and veggies fresh every day, and purchases produce locally.

multilevel list

1) Sandwiches
    a) Bread
        i) 6-inch and 12-inch
        ii) Wheat, white, multigrain, flatbread, gluten-free white
    b) Fresh ingredients
        i) Meat and poultry: chicken, ham, salami, roast beef, turkey
        ii) Seafood: tuna, crab salad
        iii) Cheese: American, mozzarella, provolone, Swiss
        iv) Veggies: cucumber, green pepper, lettuce, onion, pickle, spinach, tomato
        v) Condiments: buffalo sauce, honey mustard, mayonnaise, yellow mustard
2) Salads
    a) Full or half-size: Caesar, classic vegetable, turkey chef
    b) Dressings
        i) Regular: Caesar, chipotle, French, ranch
        ii) Light: honey mustard, ranch, raspberry vinaigrette

Every store also makes its soup fresh daily. Soups are available in cup, bowl, and gallon sizes. The table below shows the days that each type of soup is available.

table formats changed

Daily Soup Selection					
	Broccoli Cheddar	Chicken Noodle	Corn Chowder	Tomato Basil	Vegetable Medley
Monday					
Tuesday					
Wednesday					
Thursday					
Friday					
Saturday					
Sunday					

Happy to Serve You!

bullets changed to picture bullets

- Free delivery on all orders within a 10 mile radius.
- Catering available.
- More than 50,000 locations worldwide
- All locations open seven days a week from 11:00 a.m. until 9:00 p.m.

footer inserted

ORDER ONLINE STOP IN CALL AHEAD

Figure 4–89

Continued >

Apply Your Knowledge *continued*

7. Increase by one-half inch the left indent of the first paragraph of text that begins, Each store bakes.... (Hint: Use the Increase Indent button, the Left Indent marker on the ruler, the Layout tab on the ribbon, or the Paragraph dialog box.)
8. Increase by one-half inch the right indent of the first paragraph of text that begins, Each store bakes.... (Hint: Use the Right Indent marker on the ruler, the Layout tab on the ribbon, or the Paragraph dialog box.)
9. On the blank line below the paragraph that begins, Each store bakes..., create the following multilevel list using the number style shown. Increase the indent of the multilevel list so the 1. in the first list item is lined up with the left indent of the paragraphs above and below it. (That is, the 1 should be at the .5" mark on the ribbon.) Be sure to promote and demote the list items as shown below.

    1) Sandwiches
        a) Bread
            i) 6-inch and 12-inch
            ii) Wheat, white, multigrain, flatbread, gluten-free white
        b) Fresh ingredients
            i) Meat and poultry: chicken, ham, salami, roast beef, turkey
            ii) Seafood: tuna, crab salad
            iii) Cheese: American, mozzarella, provolone, Swiss
            iv) Veggies: cucumber, green pepper, lettuce, onion, pickle, spinach, tomato
            v) Condiments: buffalo sauce, honey mustard, mayonnaise, yellow mustard
    2) Salads
        a) Full or half-size: Caesar, classic vegetable, turkey chef
        b) Dressings
            i) Regular: Caesar, chipotle, French, ranch
            ii) Light: honey mustard, ranch, raspberry vinaigrette

10. Delete the page break below the table. This entire assignment should fit on a single page.
11. Use the Distribute Rows command to evenly space the rows containing the days of the week in the table. (Hint: Select the rows first.)
12. Use the Distribute Columns command to evenly space the columns containing the soup names in the table. (Hint: Select the columns first.)
13. Use the AutoFit Contents command to change the cell widths so they are as wide as the longest content of each column in the table.
14. Change the width of the column containing the days of the week to 1".
15. Select the rows containing the days of the week and change the row height to .23".
16. Change the alignment of the cells that contain the soup names to Align Center.
17. Change the alignment of the cells containing days of the week to Align Center Left.
18. Center the entire table across the width of the page.
19. Shade the cell intersecting the Broccoli Cheddar column and the Saturday row so that it is Teal, Accent 2.

20. Shade the cell intersecting the Corn Chowder column and the Tuesday row so that it is Orange, Accent 5.
21. Add a row to the top of the table. Merge all cells in the first row into a single cell. Enter the title, Daily Soup Selection, formatted in bold as the table title. Change the alignment of the entered text to Align Center. Make sure the row height is .19".
22. Change the cell spacing for the table to allow 0.01" spacing between cells.
23. Change the cell margins so that the top and bottom cell margins are 0.01" and the left and right cell margins are 0.09".
24. Change the bullets in the bulleted list at the bottom of the page to picture bullets using a smiley face picture (or use the image in the file called Support_WD_4_HappyFace.png in the Data Files).
25. Delete the current footer from the document. (Hint: Use the Footer button (Insert tab | Header & Footer group).)
26. Insert the Blank (Three Columns) footer in the document. Enter the text, ORDER ONLINE, in the left placeholder text; the text, STOP IN, in the middle placeholder text; and the text, CALL AHEAD, in the right placeholder text.
27. If requested by your instructor, change the title of the business in the header from Healthy Bites to a name that contains your last name.
28. Save the document again with the same file name.
29. Submit the modified document, shown in Figure 4–89, in the format specified by your instructor.
30. Exit Word.
31. This proposal contains a multilevel numbered list. How would you change the font size and font color of the numbers and letters at the beginning of each list item?

Extend Your Knowledge

Extend the skills you learned in this module and experiment with new skills. You may need to use Help to complete the assignment.

Working with Lists, Picture Watermarks, and Word's Draw Table Feature

Note: To complete this assignment, you will be required to use the Data Files. Please contact your instructor for information about accessing the Data Files.

Instructions: Start Word. Open the document, SC_WD_4-3.docx, which is located in the Data Files. The document is a draft for a proposal that presents information about Acorn Run State Park to the public. The marketing coordinator, who created the draft, has asked you to delete the cover page, format the lists, add a table using Word's Draw Table feature, and insert a picture watermark.

Perform the following tasks:

1. Use Help to learn about Draw Table and picture watermarks.
2. Click File on the ribbon and then click Save As and save the document using the new file name, SC_WD_4_StateParkFacilityProposal.
3. If requested by your instructor, use the Print command to print only the second page of this document. Then select just a bulleted list and use the Print command to print just the selected text.

Continued >

Extend Your Knowledge *continued*

4. Remove the cover page from the document. (Hint: Use the Cover Page button (Insert tab | Pages group).)
5. Sort the paragraphs in the bulleted list at the top of the document.
6. Change the color of the bullets in the bulleted list to a color of your choice.
7. Draw the table shown in Figure 4–90 below the paragraph in the Fees section (above the Lodging Options heading). (Hint: Click Table button (Insert tab | Tables group) and then click Draw Table and then draw the table.) If necessary, use the Eraser button (Layout tab | Draw group) to erase lines you do not need. Switch back to drawing the table anytime by clicking the Draw Table button (Layout tab | Draw group).

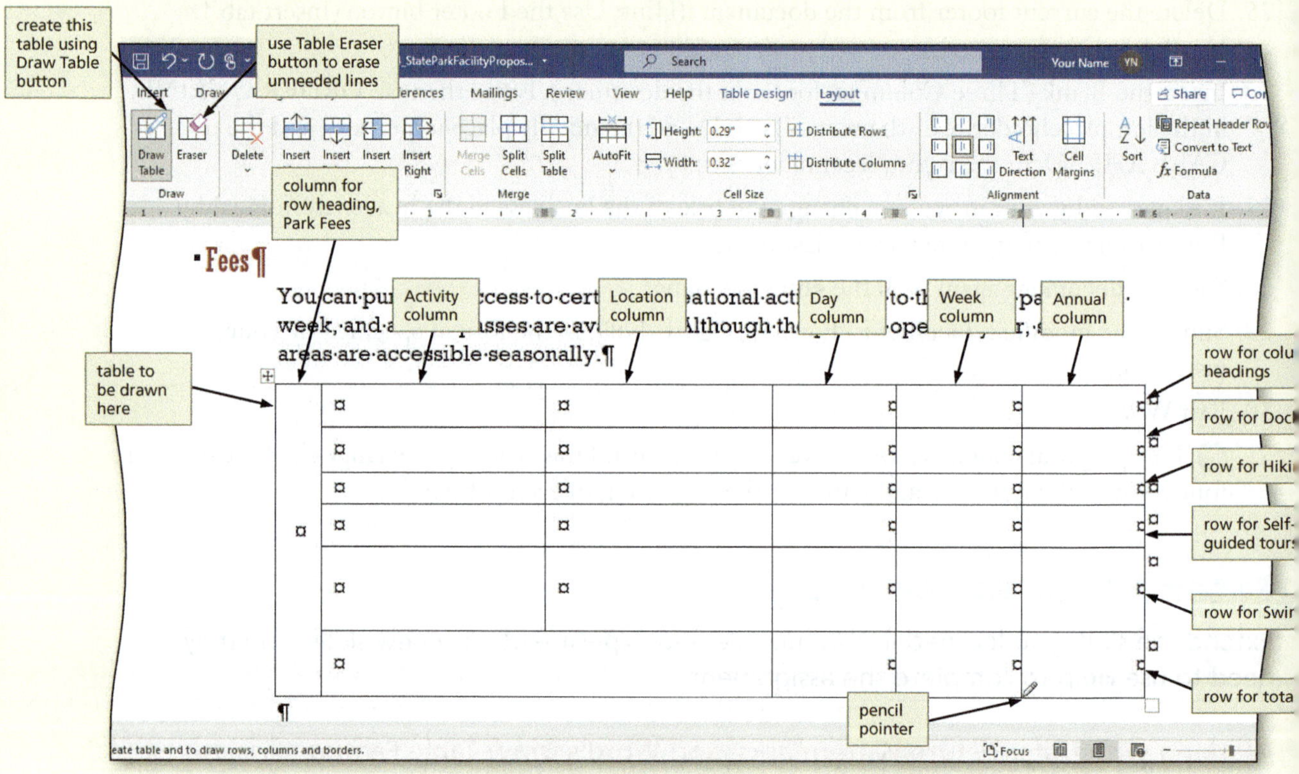

Figure 4–90

8. Show table gridlines, if they are not showing.
9. In the top row, enter these headings in the five rightmost columns: Activity, Location, Day, Week, Annual.
10. In the leftmost column of the table, enter the text, Park Fees, and then change its direction so that it displays vertically in the cell.
11. In the second column of the table titled Activity, enter these labels: Docks, Hiking, Self-guided tours, Swimming, Access to all park recreation.
12. In the third column of the table titled Location, enter this text: Boat and canoe docks, All trails, Nature center and historic sites, Public beach and outdoor pool.
13. In the fourth column of the table titled Day, enter these values: $3, $2, $3, $2.
14. In the fifth column of the table titled Week, enter these values: $8, $5, $8, $5.

15. In the last column of the table titled Annual, enter these values: $45, $25, $45, $25.
16. Resize table columns and rows by dragging to locations you deem appropriate.
17. Distribute the last three columns containing monetary amounts so that they are evenly spaced.
18. Use the Formula button (Layout tab | Data group) to place totals in the bottom row for the Day, Week, and Annual columns. The totals should be formatted to display dollar signs (no cents). (Hint: You will need to edit the formula number format and remove the .00 from the end of it.)
19. Change the values for Swimming to $1, $4, and $20 (for day, week, and annual).
20. Update the fields containing the formulas by selecting the cells containing the formulas and then pressing F9.
21. Select the table and change the spacing after each paragraph to 0 point. (Hint: Use the options in the Paragraph group in the Layout tab.)
22. Change the alignment of all cells containing numbers to Align Center Right. Align all other cells as you deem appropriate.
23. Shade the table cells, along with any other relevant enhancements, as you deem appropriate.
24. Set the column widths for the table to fixed column width. (Hint: Use the AutoFit button (Layout tab | Cell Size group).)
25. Position the insertion point in the bottom-right cell in the table. Practice deleting a cell by clicking the Delete button (Layout tab | Rows & Columns group), clicking Delete Cells on the Delete menu, clicking 'Shift cells left' (Delete Cells dialog box), and then clicking OK. Press CTRL+Z to undo the deletion. Hide gridlines.
26. Change the number style in the list at the bottom of the page to a style of your choice.
27. In the last line on the page, indent the left margin by one-half inch so that the paragraph shading starts one-half inch from the left margin.
28. Add an appropriate picture watermark to the document (or use the image in the file called Support_WD_4_AcornOakLeafPattern.png in the Data Files). Change the scale in the Printed Watermark dialog box as necessary so that the watermark fills the entire page.
29. If requested by your instructor, change the name of the park to include your last name.
30. Save the revised document again with the same name and then submit it in the format specified by your instructor.
31. Which alignment and shading for the table cells did you choose and why?

Expand Your World

Create a solution that uses cloud or web technologies by learning and investigating on your own from general guidance.

Using Word Online to Create a Table

Instructions: You will use Word Online to create a table and then you will download the table to your desktop version of Word to edit it further. As project coordinator for Bidwell Construction, while attending a conference, you will use Word Online to create a table for a proposal that you are developing. Then, when back at the office, you will download the table and edit it further in your desktop version of Word.

Continued >

Expand Your World *continued*

Perform the following tasks:

1. Start a browser. Search for the text, Word Online, using a search engine. Visit several websites to learn about Word Online. Navigate to the Office Online website. You will need to sign in to your OneDrive account.
2. Create a new blank Word document using Word Online. Name the document SC_WD_4_AvailableLots.
3. Create the table and enter the data shown in Figure 4–91.

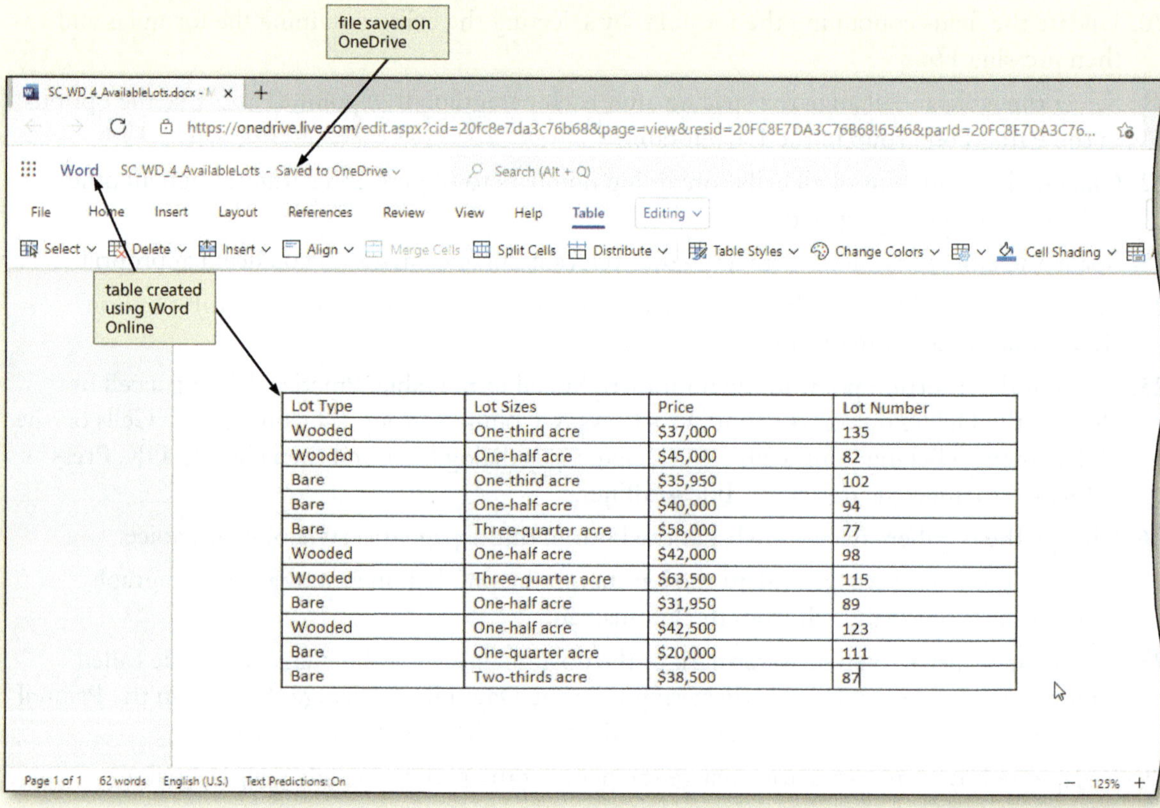

Lot Type	Lot Sizes	Price	Lot Number
Wooded	One-third acre	$37,000	135
Wooded	One-half acre	$45,000	82
Bare	One-third acre	$35,950	102
Bare	One-half acre	$40,000	94
Bare	Three-quarter acre	$58,000	77
Wooded	One-half acre	$42,000	98
Wooded	Three-quarter acre	$63,500	115
Bare	One-half acre	$31,950	89
Wooded	One-half acre	$42,500	123
Bare	One-quarter acre	$20,000	111
Bare	Two-thirds acre	$38,500	87

Figure 4–91

4. Apply the 'Grid Table 5 Dark - Accent 1' table style to the table.
5. Make sure Header Row and First Column are selected in the Style Options.
6. Change the colors of the table to a color of your choice.
7. Change the alignment of the prices column to Align Top Right.
8. Change the alignment of the lot number column to Align Top Center.
9. Adjust the column widths so that the contents better fit the columns. How did you adjust the column width?
10. Open the document in Word using the Editing button on the ribbon and then select 'Open in Desktop App'. (Note that the AutoSave button may become enabled if you are saving the file on OneDrive.)
11. Distribute the rows in the table so that they are evenly spaced.
12. Remove the first column shading. (Hint: Use the check boxes in the Table Style Options group in the Table Design tab.)
13. Split the cell in the Lot Number column with the number 82 into two columns and one row. Enter the value 83 in the empty cell.

14. Split the cell in the Lot Number column with the number 135 into two columns and one row. Enter the value 136 in the empty cell.
15. Position the insertion point in the column headings and then click the 'Repeat Header Rows' button (Layout tab | Data group) to repeat header rows if the table continues to a second page.
16. Sort the table on the Price column only with the highest price at the top. Did you use ascending or descending order?
17. Sort the table on the Lot Type column and then by the Lot Sizes column and then by Price so that the lot types and lot sizes are in alphabetical order and the highest price in each category is at the top.
18. Add a 1 pt, Blue, Accent 1 border to all cells in the table. In the Borders and Shading dialog box, select a border style of your choice. (Hint: Change the color first from white so that you easily can see the border styles.)
19. Split the table where the lot type changes from Bare to Wooded so that one table is the bare lots and the other table is the wooded lots.
20. Copy the row containing the column headings from the first table to the second table. If necessary, use the format painter to copy formats from the column headings in the first table to the column headings second table, or apply borders again so that the column headings in the two tables are the same.
21. If requested by your instructor, add your name on a line below the second table.
22. Save the document again and submit it in the format requested by your instructor. Sign out of your OneDrive account.
23. Which table features that are covered in the module are not available in Word Online? Answer the questions posed in #9 and #16.

In the Lab

Design and implement a solution using creative thinking and problem-solving skills.

Create a Proposal for an Animal Hospital

Note: To complete this assignment, you will be required to use the Data Files. Please contact your instructor for information about accessing the Data Files.

Problem: As administrative specialist for the Caring Companion Animal Hospital, you have been asked to design a multipage sales proposal that presents information about the hospital's facility and services to the public and potential clients.

Part 1: The source content for the proposal is in a file called SC_WD_4-4.docx, which is located in the Data Files. The proposal should contain a cover page, followed by two pages of information about the animal hospital. Using the concepts and techniques presented in this module, along with the source content in the Data Files, create and format the sales proposal. While creating the proposal, be sure to do the following:

1. Insert an appropriate cover page. If requested by your instructor, include your name on the cover page.
2. Insert a formatted header and footer. The header or footer should contain page numbers. Format the page number so that it is in the format of - 1 -, - 2 -, etc.
3. Arrange content in a meaningful order.

Continued >

In the Lab *continued*

4. Format headings and indent paragraphs appropriately.
5. Organize and format bulleted lists. Include a multilevel list. Sort paragraphs in lists as needed.
6. Format the table(s) as needed and sort table contents appropriately.
7. Include an appropriate text watermark.
8. Be sure to check the spelling and grammar of the finished document.

When you are finished with the proposal, save it with the file name, SC_WD_4_AnimalHospitalProposal. Submit your assignment and answers to the Part 2 critical thinking questions in the format specified by your instructor.

Part 2: You made several decisions while creating the sales proposal in this assignment: how to organize elements on the cover page and the body of the proposal, which cover page to use and how to format its text, how to organize and format the tables and lists, and what text watermark to use and how to format it. What was the rationale behind each of these decisions? When you proofread the document, what further revisions did you make and why?

5 Creating a Resume and Sharing Documents

Objectives

After completing this module, you will be able to:

- Use a template to create a document
- Change document margins
- Personalize a document template
- Customize theme fonts and theme colors
- Create and modify a style
- Create, modify, and insert a building block
- Export a Word document to a PDF file and edit a PDF file in Word
- Check document compatibility
- Share a document on OneDrive
- Get a sharing link
- Send a Word document using email
- Save a Word document as a webpage
- Format text as a hyperlink
- Change a style set
- Highlight text

Introduction

Some people prefer to use their own creative skills to design and compose Word documents. Using Word, for example, you can develop the content and decide the location of each item in a document. On occasion, however, you may have difficulty composing a particular type of document. To assist with the task of creating certain types of documents, such as resumes and letters, Word provides templates. A **template** is a file with a theme applied and that may contain formatted placeholder text in content controls, headers and footers, and graphics that you replace with your own information. After Word creates a document from a template, you fill in the blanks or replace placeholder text or content controls in the document.

Once you have created a document, such as a resume, you often share it with others electronically via email, webpages, or links.

Project: Resume

At some time, you will prepare a resume to send to prospective employers. In addition to some personal information, a **resume** usually contains the applicant's personal information, educational background, and job experience. Employers review many resumes for each vacant position. Thus, you should design your resume carefully so that it presents you as the best candidate for the job.

The project in this module follows generally accepted guidelines for creating resumes and uses Word to create the resume shown in Figure 5–1. The resume for Dwayne Jackman, an upcoming graduate of a public health program who is seeking employment as a sales representative with a pharmaceutical sales firm, uses a Word template to present relevant information to a potential employer.

DWAYNE JACKMAN

4413 Parker Road, New Orleans, LA 70116 | 504-555-0127 | dj97@cengage.net

OBJECTIVE

To obtain a sales representative position with a pharmaceutical sales firm that will allow me to grow professionally.

EDUCATION

September 2018-May 2020 B.S. Public Health, New Orleans, LA, *Gulf College*
- GPA 3.8/4.0

September 2016-May 2018 A.S. Nursing, New Orleans, LA, *Bridgeview College*
- GPA 3.9/4.0

EXPERIENCE

November 2018-Present Customer Service Agent, New Orleans, LA, *Harbor Nutrition*
Answer customer queries onsite, on the phone, and via online chat; set up rewards memberships; generate new customers by cold calling; meet with suppliers

CERTIFICATIONS

Certified Nursing Assistant (CNA)
Adult and Pediatric CPR
Red Cross Certified Lifeguard

COMMUNITY SERVICE

- Organize and implement public health awareness programs for New Orleans Medical Center, 2017-Present
- Volunteer at annual flu shot clinic, 2016-Present
- Volunteer at Lafayette Free Clinic, 2016-Present
- Participant at Gulf College's phone-a-thon fundraiser, 2018-Present

Figure 5–1

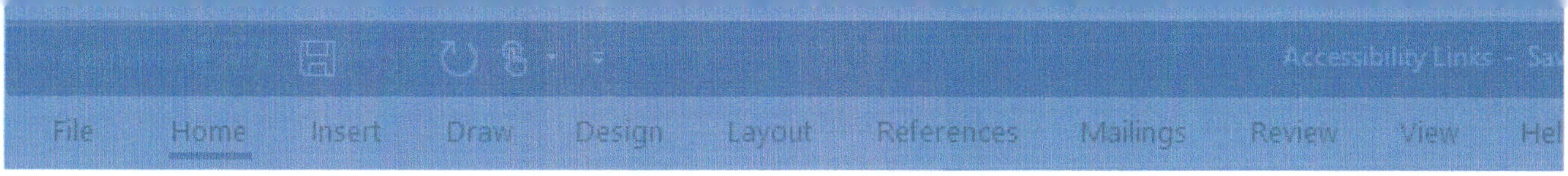

In this module, you will learn how to create the resume shown in Figure 5–1. You will perform the following general tasks as you progress through this module:

1. Create a new resume document from a Word template.
2. Modify and format the resume template.
3. Save the resume document in other formats so that you can share it with others.
4. Make the resume document available online so that others can access it.
5. Create a webpage from the resume Word document.
6. Format the resume webpage.

To Start Word and Specify Settings

If you are using a computer to step through the project in this module and you want your screens to match the figures in this book, you should change your screen's resolution to 1366 × 768. The following steps start Word, display formatting marks, change the zoom to page width, and verify ruler and Mouse mode settings.

1. Start Word and create a blank document in the Word window. If necessary, maximize the Word window.

2. If the Print Layout button on the status bar is not selected (shown in Figure 5–4), click it so that your screen is in Print Layout view.

3. If the 'Show/Hide ¶' button (Home tab | Paragraph group) is not selected already, click it to display formatting marks on the screen.

4. To display the page the same width as the document window, if necessary, click the Page Width button (View tab | Zoom group).

5. Verify that the Ruler check box (View tab | Show group) is not selected. (If it is selected, click it to remove the selection because you do not want the rulers to appear on the screen.)

6. If you are using a mouse and you want your screens to match the figures in the book, verify that you are using Mouse mode by clicking the Touch/Mouse Mode button on the Quick Access Toolbar and then, if necessary, clicking Mouse on the menu. (If your Quick Access Toolbar does not display the Touch/Mouse Mode button, click the 'Customize Quick Access Toolbar' button on the Quick Access Toolbar and then click Touch/Mouse Mode on the menu to add the button to the Quick Access Toolbar.)

Using a Template to Create a Resume

Although you could compose a resume in a blank document window, this module shows how to use a template instead, where Word formats the resume with appropriate headings and spacing. You then customize the resume that the template generated by filling in blanks and by selecting and replacing text.

To Create a New Document from an Online Template

Word has a variety of templates available online to assist you with creating documents. Available online templates include agendas, award certificates, calendars, expense reports, greeting cards, invitations, invoices, letters, meeting minutes, memos, resumes, statements, and more. When you select an online template, Word downloads (or copies) it from the Office.com website to your computer or mobile device. Many of the templates use the same design or style. **Why?** If you create related documents, such as a resume and a cover letter, you can use the same template design or style so that the documents complement one another. Because the Word window already is open, the following steps use Backstage view to create a resume using the Resume template.

1

- Click File on the ribbon to open Backstage view and then click New in Backstage view to display the New screen, which initially lists several featured templates.
- Type **resume** in the 'Search for online templates' box and then click the Start searching button to display a list of online resume templates.
- If necessary, scroll through the list of templates to display the Resume thumbnail (Figure 5–2).

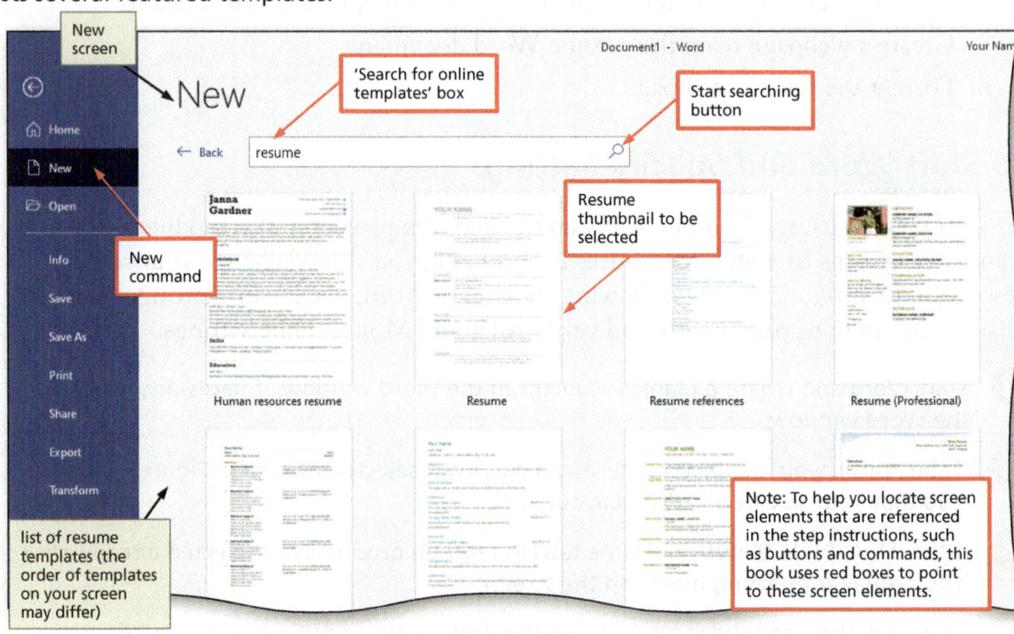

Figure 5–2

Q&A **Can I select a template from the Word start screen that appears when I initially start Word?**
Yes, instead of selecting Blank document from the Word start screen, you can select any of the available templates.

2

- Click the Resume thumbnail to select the template and display it in a preview window (Figure 5–3).

Experiment

- Click the Back and Forward buttons on the sides of the preview window to view previews of other templates. When finished, display the Resume thumbnail in the preview window.

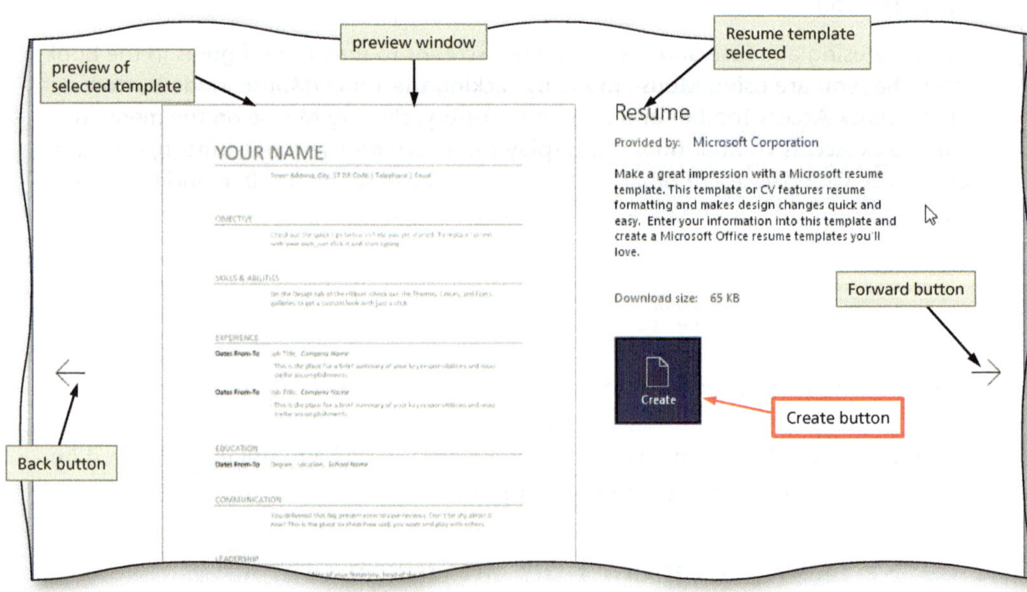

Figure 5–3

Q&A **What if I cannot locate the Resume template?**
Close Backstage view, open the document called Support_WD_5_ResumeTemplate from the Data Files (please contact your instructor for information about accessing the Data Files), and then skip Steps 2, 3, and 4.

3

- Click the Create button to create a new document based on the selected template (Figure 5–4).
- If the resume template displays your name instead of the text, YOUR NAME, as shown in Figure 5–4, click the Undo button on the Quick Access Toolbar to reset the content control.

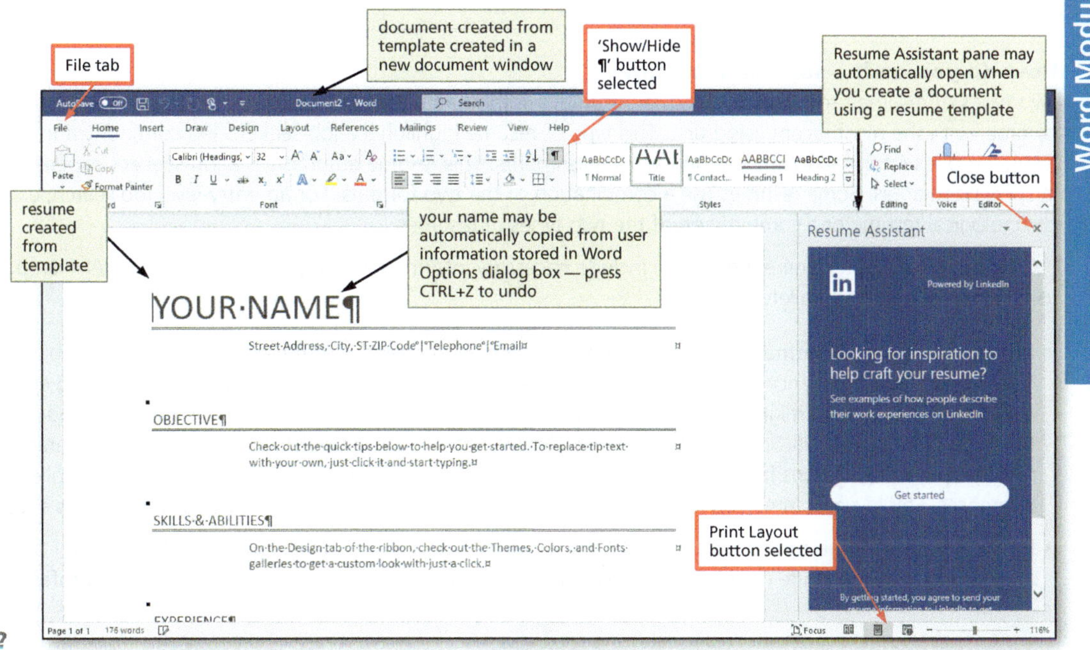

Figure 5–4

Q&A **What is the Resume Assistant?** The Resume Assistant pane, available to Office 365 subscribers, provides examples of wording you can use in your resume.

4

- If requested by your instructor, print the resume template so that you can see the entire resume created by the resume template using the Resume (Figure 5–5).

5

- If your screen opens the Resume Assistant pane, close the pane.

6

- Save the resume on your hard drive, OneDrive, or other storage location using the file name, SC_WD_5_JackmanResume.

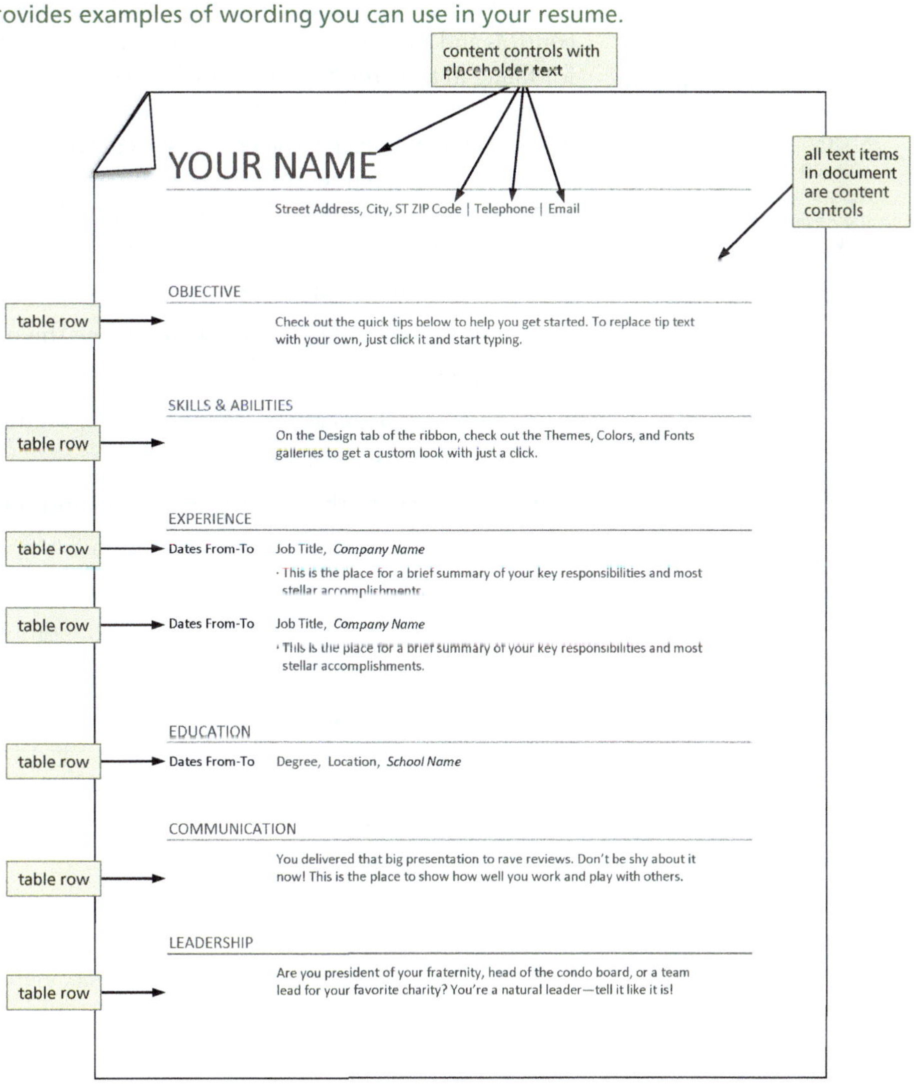

Figure 5–5

Consider This

How do you craft a successful resume?

Two types of resumes are the chronological resume and the functional resume. A chronological resume sequences information by time, with the most recent listed first. This type of resume highlights a job seeker's job continuity and growth. A functional resume groups information by skills and accomplishments. This resume emphasizes a job seeker's experience and qualifications in specialized areas. Some resumes use a combination of the two formats. For an entry-level job search, experts recommend a chronological resume or a combination of the two types of resumes.

When creating a resume, be sure to include necessary information and present it appropriately. Keep descriptions concise, using action words and bulleted lists.

- **Include necessary information.** Your resume should include contact information, a clearly written objective, educational background, and experience. Use your name and mailing address, along with your phone number and email address, if you have one. Other sections you might consider including are memberships, skills, recognitions and awards, and/or community service. Do not include your Social Security number, marital status, age, height, weight, gender, physical appearance, health, citizenship, previous pay rates, reasons for leaving a prior job, current date, high school information (if you are a college graduate), and references. Employers assume you will provide references, if asked, and this information simply clutters a resume.
- **Present your resume appropriately.** For printed resumes, use a high-quality ink-jet or laser printer to print your resume on standard letter-sized white or ivory paper. Consider using paper that contains cotton fibers for a professional look.

BTW

Resume Assistant

The Resume Assistant, which is powered by LinkedIn (a social network that connects career and business professionals), is available to Microsoft 365 subscribers. You can open the Resume Assistant pane by displaying the Review tab and then clicking the Resume Assistant button (Review tab | Resume group). If the Resume Assistant button is dim, you may need to enable LinkedIn integration by doing the following: open Backstage view, click Options to display the Word Options dialog box, click General in the left pane (Word Options dialog box), place a check mark in the 'Enable LinkedIn features in my Office applications' check box, and then click OK.

Resume Template

The resume created from the template, shown in Figure 5–5, contains several content controls and a table. A content control is an object that contains sample text or instructions for filling in text and graphics. To select a content control, you click it. As soon as you begin typing in the selected content control, your typing replaces the instructions in the control. Thus, you do not need to delete the selected instructions before you begin typing.

Below the name in the document are several individual one- or two-row tables, some with headings above the table rows. The following pages personalize the resume created by the resume template using these general steps:

1. Change the name at the top of the resume.
2. Fill in the contact information below the name.
3. Fill in the Objective section.
4. Move the Education and Experience sections above the Skills & Abilities section.
5. Fill in the Experience section.
6. Add a row to the Education section and fill in this section.
7. Delete the Skills & Abilities section.
8. Change the heading, Communication, to Certifications and fill in this section.
9. Change the heading, Leadership, to Community Service, and fill in this section.

To Change Theme Colors

Word provides document themes, which contain a variety of color schemes and other effects. This resume uses the Orange Red theme colors. The following steps change the theme colors.

1. Click Design on the ribbon to display the Design tab.
2. Click the Colors button (Design tab | Document Formatting group) to display the Colors gallery.
3. Scroll to and then click Orange Red in the Colors gallery to change the theme colors to the selected theme.

To Set Custom Margins

The resume template selected in this project uses .75-inch top and bottom margins and 1.1-inch left and right margins. You prefer 1-inch margins for the top, left, and right edges of the resume and a smaller bottom margin. **Why?** You want the margins to be even on the top edge and sides of the page and do not want the resume to spill to a second page. Because the margins you will use for the resume in this module are not predefined, you cannot use the predefined settings in the Margins gallery. Thus, the following steps set custom margins.

1

- Display the Layout tab.
- Click the Margins button (Layout tab | Page Setup group) to display the Margins gallery (Figure 5–6).

Q&A

What is the difference between the Custom Margins setting and the Custom Margins command?

The Custom Margins setting applies the most recent custom margins to the current document, whereas the Custom Margins command displays the Page Setup dialog box so that you can specify new margin settings.

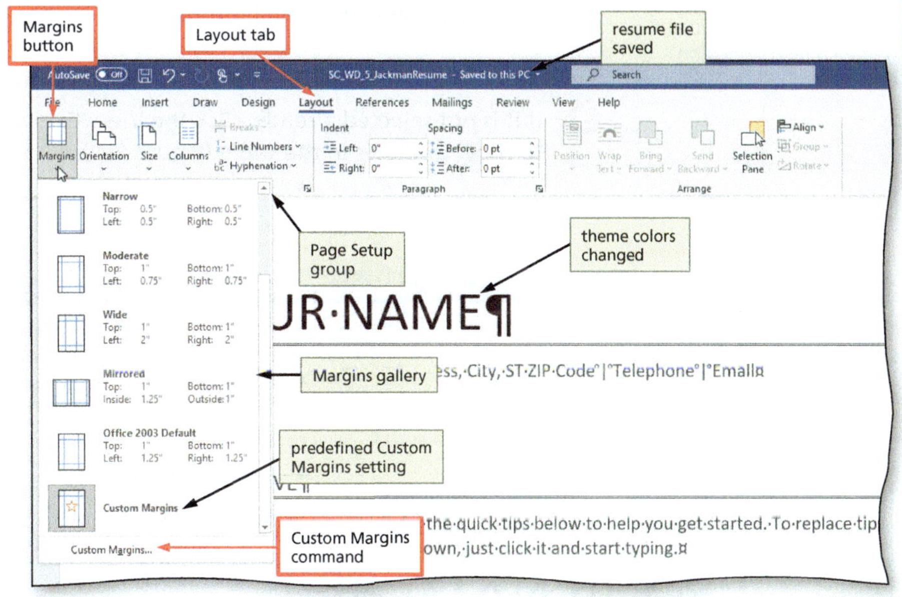

Figure 5–6

2

- Click Custom Margins at the bottom of the Margins gallery to display the Page Setup dialog box. If necessary, click the Margins tab (Page Setup dialog box) to display the Margins sheet.
- Type `1` in the Top box to change the top margin setting and then press TAB to position the insertion point in the Bottom box.
- Type `.5` in the Bottom box to change the bottom margin setting and then press TAB to position the insertion point in the Left box.
- Type `1` in the Left box to change the left margin setting and then press TAB to position the insertion point in the Right box.
- Type `1` in the Right box to change the right margin setting (Figure 5–7).

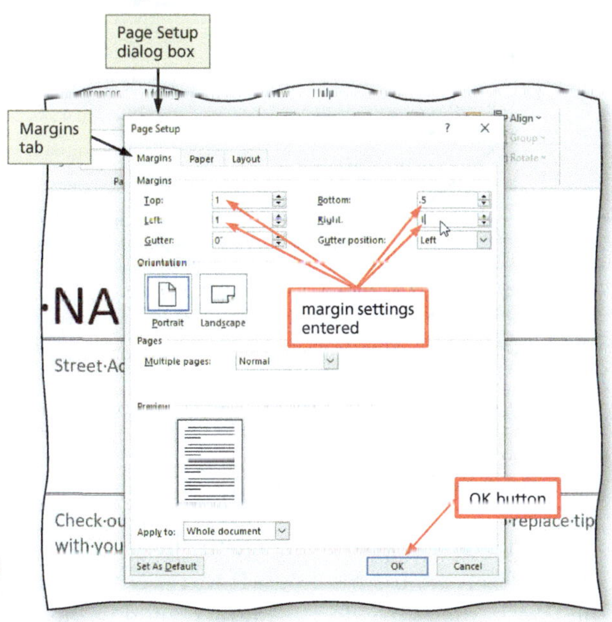

Figure 5–7

3

- Click OK to set the custom margins for this document.

Other Ways

1. Drag margin boundaries on ruler

BTW
The Ribbon and Screen Resolution
Word may change how the groups and buttons within the groups appear on the ribbon, depending on the screen resolution of your computer. Thus, your ribbon may look different from the ones in this book if you are using a screen resolution other than 1366 × 768.

To View Gridlines

When tables contain no borders, such as those in this resume, it can be difficult to see the individual cells in the table. To help identify the location of cells, you can display gridlines, which show cell outlines on the screen. The following steps show gridlines if they are not already displayed on your screen.

1. Position the insertion point in any table cell (in this case, the cell containing the address, phone, and email information).
2. Display the Layout tab.
3. If it is not selected already, click the View Gridlines button (Layout tab | Table group) to show gridlines in the table (Figure 5–8).

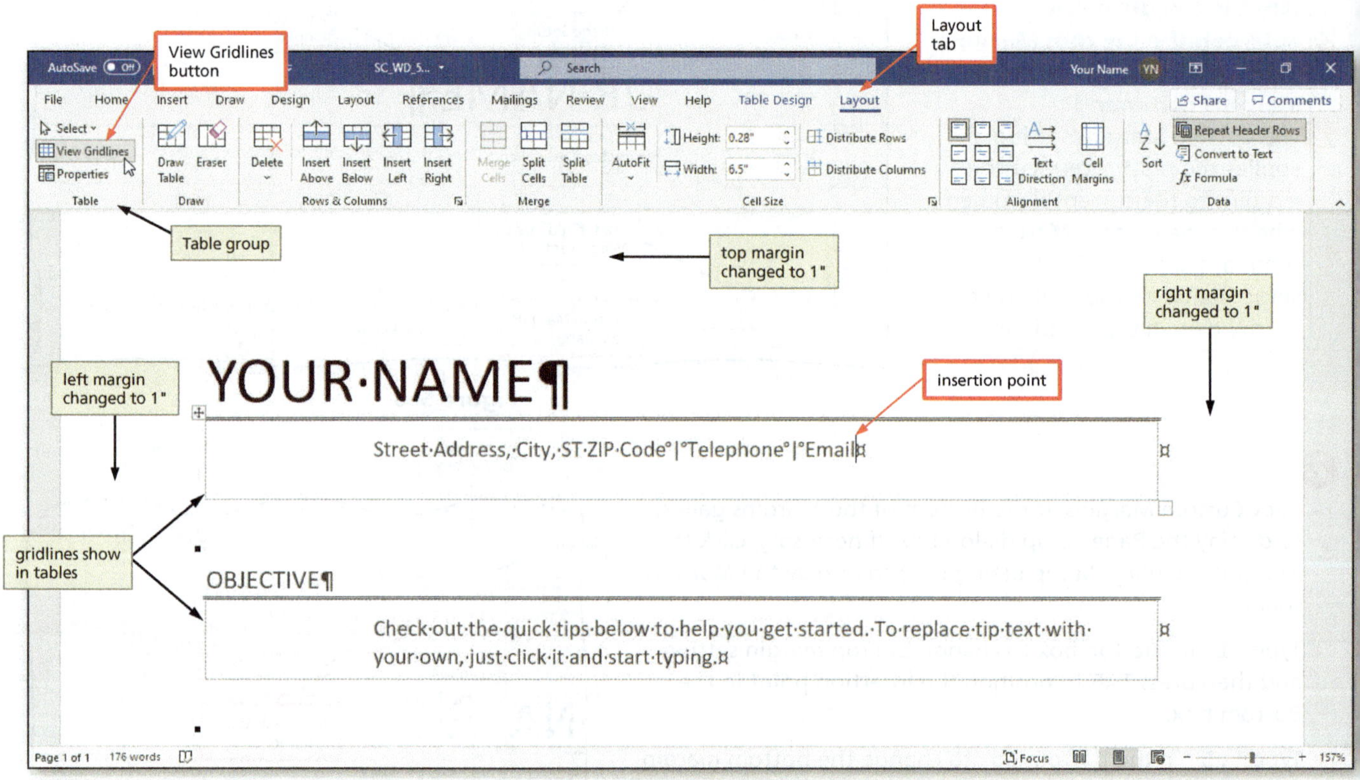

Figure 5–8

To Change Theme Fonts

The next step is to change the heading and body text fonts used in the resume. **Why?** You would prefer a bolder font for the headings. If text is entered using the headings and body text fonts, you easily can change the font in the entire document by changing the theme fonts, or font set. A **font set** is a format that defines one font for headings and another for body text. The default font set is Office, which uses the Calibri Light font for headings and the Calibri font for body text. In Word, you can select from more than 20 predefined, coordinated font sets to give the document's text a new look.

If you previously changed a font using buttons on the ribbon or Mini toolbar, Word will not alter those when you change the font set because changes to the font set are not applied to individually changed fonts. The following steps change the theme fonts to Arial Black for headings and Arial for body text.

1

- Display the Design tab.
- Click the Fonts button (Design tab | Document Formatting group) to display the Fonts gallery.
- Scroll to display the Arial Black-Arial theme font in the gallery (Figure 5–9).

Experiment

- Point to various theme fonts in the Fonts gallery and watch the fonts of text in the document change.

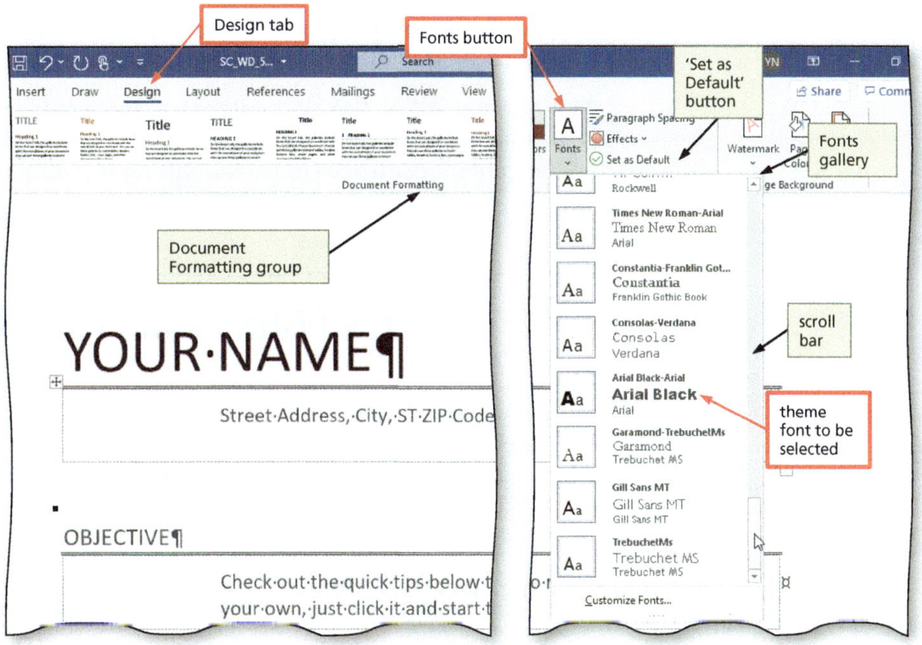

Figure 5–9

2

- Click Arial Black-Arial in the Fonts gallery to set the theme fonts to the selected font set (Figure 5–10).

Q&A **What if I want to return to the default theme fonts?**
You would click the Fonts button and then click Office in the Fonts gallery.

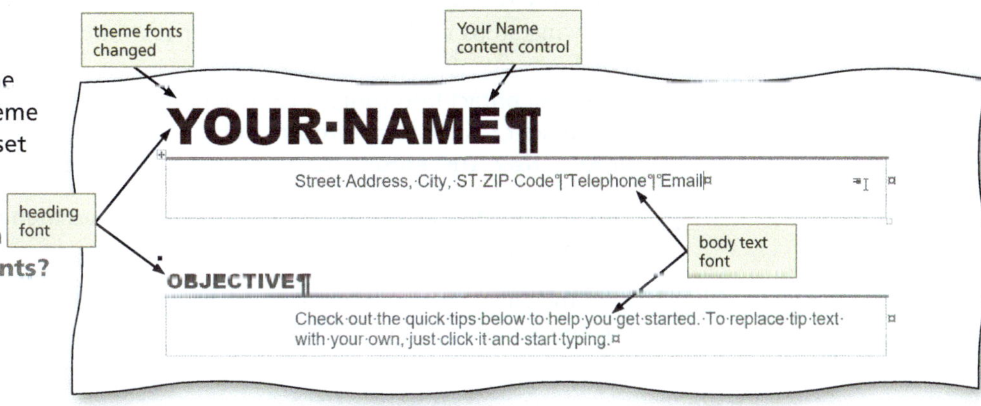

Figure 5–10

To Enter Text in a Content Control

The next step is to select the Your Name content control that the template inserted at the top of the resume and replace its placeholder text with the job seeker's name. Word uses **placeholder text** to indicate where text can be typed. To replace placeholder text in a content control, you select the content control and then type.

The Your Name content control on your resume may already contain your name because Word may copy the user name from the Word Options dialog box and place it in the Your Name content control. Note that if your name appears instead of the text, YOUR NAME, the following steps may execute differently. The following steps enter text in a content control.

1 Click the content control to be modified (in this case, the Your Name content control) to select it.

Q&A **How can I tell if a content control is selected?**
The appearance of selected content controls varies. When you select some content controls, they are surrounded by a rectangle; others appear selected. Selected content controls also may have a name that is attached to the top and/or a tag that is attached to its upper-left corner. You can drag a tag to move a content control from one location to another.

BTW

Touch Mode Differences

The Office and Windows interfaces may vary if you are using Touch mode. For this reason, you might notice that the function or appearance of your touch screen differs slightly from this module's presentation.

2. Type **`Dwayne Jackman`** to replace the content control with the job seeker's name (Figure 5–11).

Q&A **Why does all of the text appear in uppercase letters even though I type some letters in lowercase?**
This content control includes formatting that displays the text in uppercase letters.

Figure 5–11

To Enter Text in More Content Controls

The next step is to select the Contact Info, Telephone, and Email content controls in the resume and replace their placeholder text with personal information. The following steps replace the placeholder text in content controls.

1. Click the Contact Info content control to select it, that is, the content control with the placeholder text of Street Address, City, ST ZIP Code, and then type **`4413 Parker Road, New Orleans, LA 70116`** as the contact info.
2. Click the Telephone content control to select it and then type **`504-555-0127`** as the phone number.
3. Click the Email content control to select it and then type **`dj97@cengage.net`** as the email address (Figure 5–12).

Q&A **What are the small raised circles between content controls?**
They are nonbreaking spaces, which are formatting marks. A nonbreaking space is a special space character that prevents two words from splitting if the first word falls at the end of a line. Similarly, a nonbreaking hyphen is a special type of hyphen that prevents two words separated by a hyphen from splitting at the end of a line. To insert a nonbreaking space, press CTRL+SHIFT+SPACEBAR (instead of SPACEBAR), and to insert a nonbreaking hyphen, press CTRL+SHIFT+HYPHEN (instead of HYPHEN). Or, click the Symbol button (Insert tab | Symbols group), click More Symbols, click the Special Characters tab (Symbol dialog box), click Nonbreaking Space or Nonbreaking Hyphen in the Character list, click the Insert button, and then click Close.

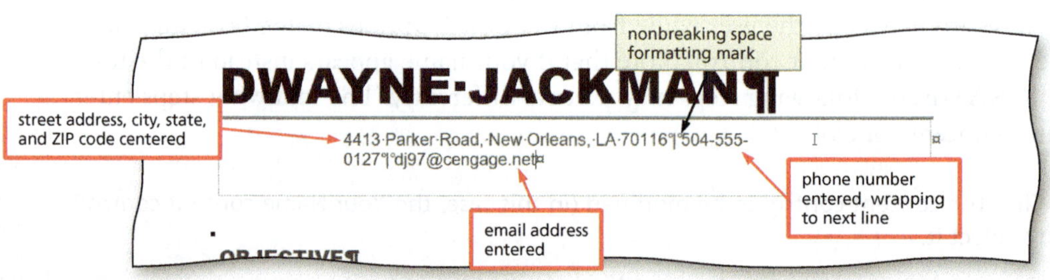

Figure 5–12

To Delete a Content Control

To delete a content control, you would follow these steps.

1. Right-click the selected content control to display a shortcut menu.
2. Click 'Remove Content Control' on the shortcut menu to delete the content control, which also deletes any placeholder text contained in the content control.

To Create Custom Theme Fonts

This resume currently uses the Arial Black-Arial theme fonts, which specifies the Arial Black font for the headings and the Arial font for body text. The resume in this module creates a custom theme font. **Why?** With the Arial font for body text, the contact info wraps to two lines, and you want it to fit on a single line. The following steps create a customized theme font set with the name, Resume Text, that changes the font for the body text in the resume to Times New Roman.

1

- Display the Design tab.
- Click the Fonts button (Design tab | Document Formatting group) to display the Fonts gallery (Figure 5–13).

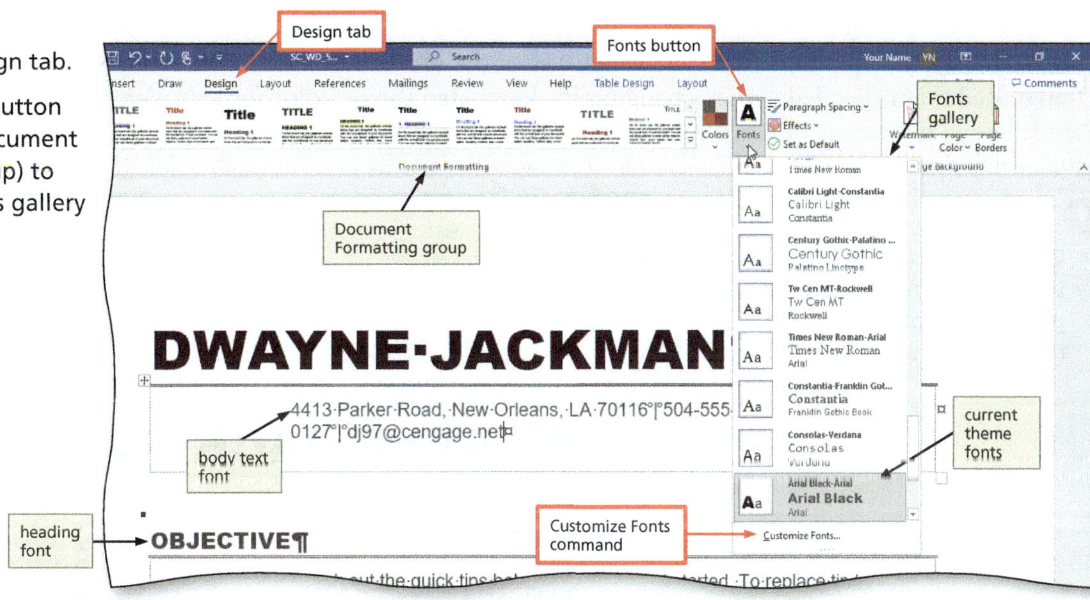

Figure 5–13

2

- Click Customize Fonts in the Fonts gallery to display the Create New Theme Fonts dialog box.
- Click the Body font arrow (Create New Theme Fonts dialog box); scroll to and then click 'Times New Roman' (or a similar font).
- If necessary, select any text in the Name text box and then type `Resume Text` as the name for the new theme font (Figure 5–14).

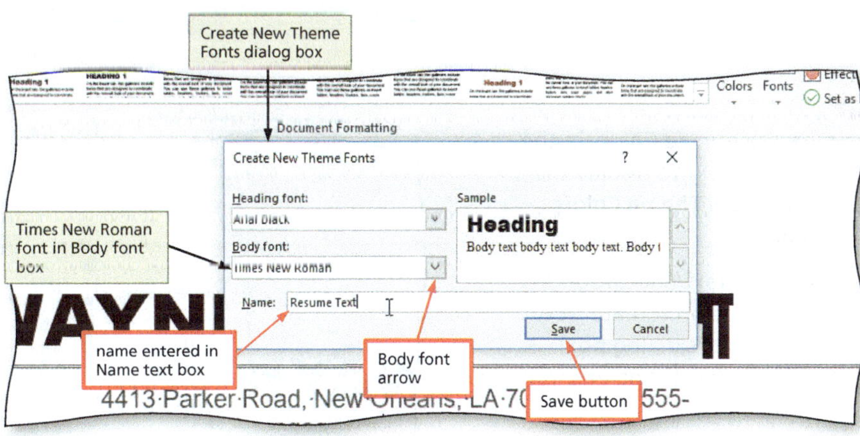

Figure 5–14

3

- Click the Save button (Create New Theme Fonts dialog box) to create the customized theme font with the entered name (Resume Text, in this case) and apply the new body text fonts to the current document (Figure 5–15). (If your contact info does not fit on a single line, adjust the font size so that it looks like Figure 5–15.)

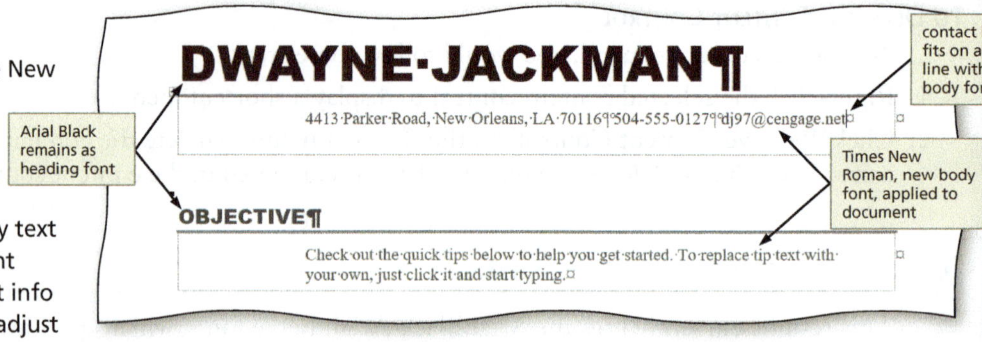

Figure 5–15

To Create Custom Theme Colors

The next step in formatting the online form in this module is to change the color of the text in the document. A document theme has 12 predefined colors for various on-screen objects, including text, backgrounds, and hyperlinks. You can change any of the theme colors. The following steps customize the Orange Red theme applied earlier, changing its designated theme color for text. **Why?** You would like the text in the resume to be a shade of tan, instead of a shade of black.

1

- Click the Colors button (Design tab | Document Formatting group) to display the Colors gallery (Figure 5–16).

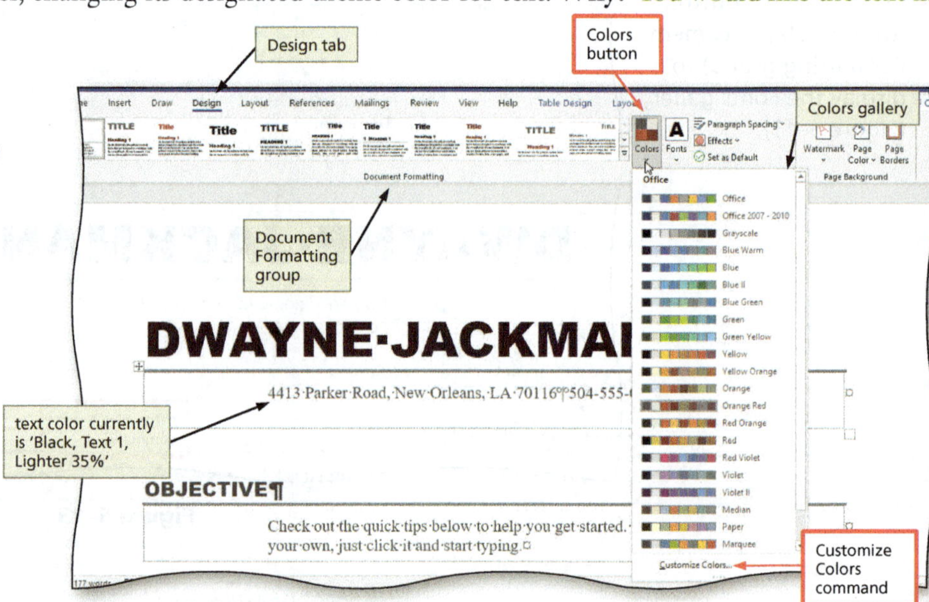

Figure 5–16

2

- Click Customize Colors in the Colors gallery to display the Create New Theme Colors dialog box.
- Click the 'Text/Background - Dark 1' button (Create New Theme Colors dialog box) to display a color palette (Figure 5–17).

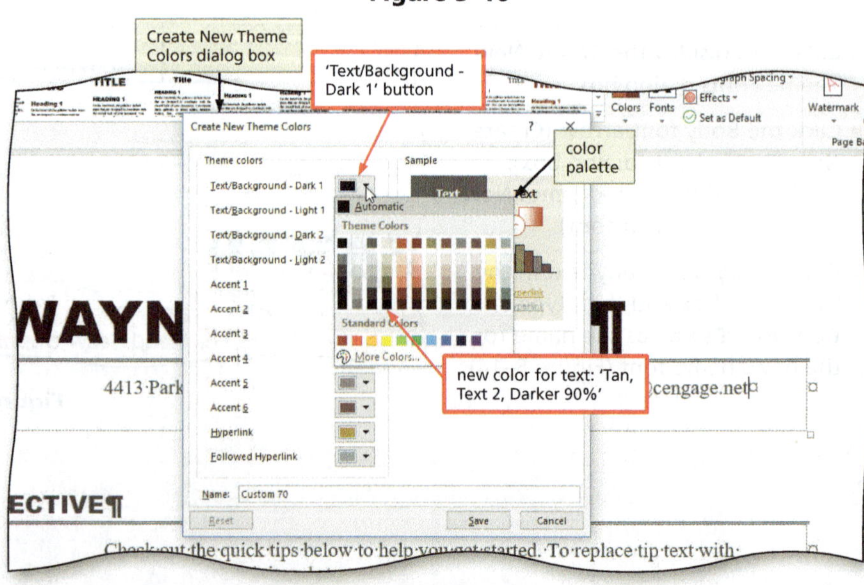

Figure 5–17

3

- Click 'Tan, Text 2, Darker 90%' (fourth color in sixth row) as the new text color.
- If necessary, select any text in the Name text box and then type **Resume Text** (Figure 5–18).

Q&A **What if I wanted to reset all the original theme colors?**
You would click the Reset button (Create New Theme Colors dialog box) before clicking the Save button.

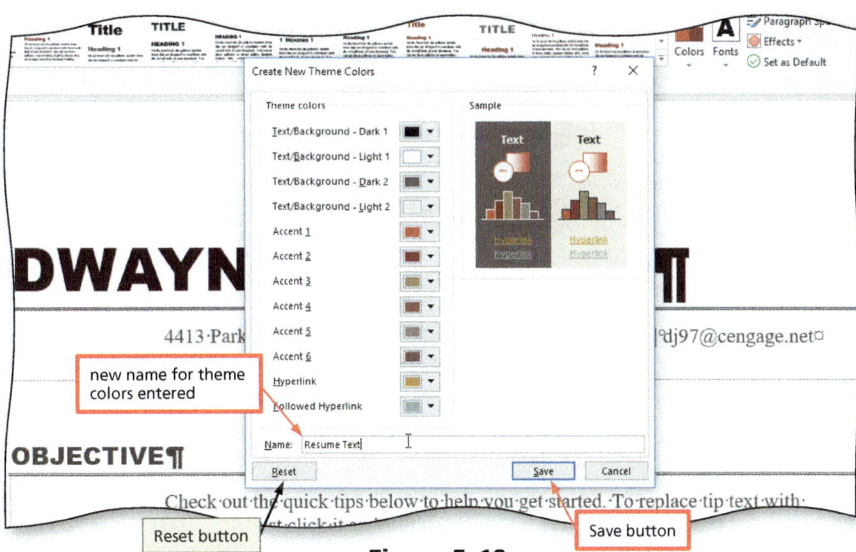

Figure 5–18

4

- Click the Save button (Create New Theme Colors dialog box) to save the modified color theme with the name, Resume Text, which will be positioned at the top of the Colors gallery for future access, and change the theme colors in the current document (Figure 5–19).

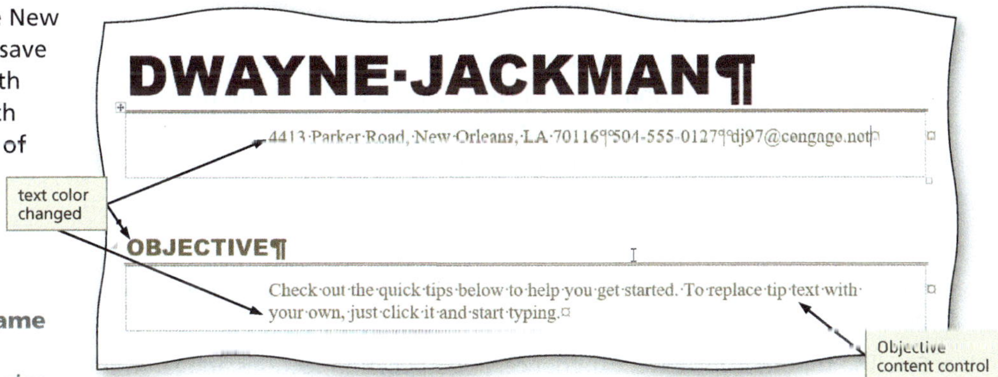

Figure 5–19

Q&A **What if I do not enter a name for the modified theme?**
Word assigns a name that begins with the letters, Custom, followed by a number (i.e., Custom8).

Other Ways

1. Make changes to theme colors, fonts, and/or effects; click Themes button (Design tab | Document Formatting group), click 'Save Current Theme' in Themes gallery

To Save Customized Themes

When you modify the theme colors, theme fonts, or theme effects, you can save the modified theme for future use. If you wanted to save a customized theme, you would perform the following steps.

1. Click the Themes button (Design tab | Document Formatting group) to display the Themes gallery.
2. Click 'Save Current Theme' in the Themes gallery.
3. Enter a theme name in the File name box (Save Current Theme dialog box).
4. Click the Save button to add the saved theme to the Themes gallery.

To Change Theme Effects

If you wanted to change the look of graphics, such as SmartArt graphics, you would perform the following steps to change the theme effects.

1. Click the Effects button (Design tab | Document Formatting group).
2. Click the desired effect in the Effects gallery.

BTW

Set Theme Settings as the Default

If you wanted to change the default theme, you would select the theme you want to be the default theme, or select the color scheme, font set, and theme effects you would like to use as the default. Then, click the 'Set as Default' button (Design tab | Document Formatting group) (shown in Figure 5-9), which uses the current settings as the new default.

To Enter Text in a Content Control

The following steps select the Objective content control in the resume and then replace its placeholder text with personal information.

BTW
Selecting Rows
To move table rows, you must select them first. To do this, point to the left of the first row to select and then drag downward or upward when the pointer changes to a right-pointing block arrow. If you are using a touch screen, drag the selection handles to select the rows.

1. If necessary, scroll to display the Objective section of the resume in the document window.
2. In the Objective section of the resume, click the placeholder text that begins, 'Check out the quick tips…', in the Objective content control (shown in Figure 5–19) to select it.
3. Type the objective (shown in Figure 5–20): `To obtain a sales representative position with a pharmaceutical sales firm that will allow me to grow professionally.`

To Use Cut and Paste to Move Table Rows and Paragraphs with Source Formatting

In the resume, you would like the Education and Experience sections immediately below the Objective section, in that order. **Why?** You want to emphasize your educational background and experience. Thus, the next step is to move the Education section in the resume below the Objective section by selecting the table row and associated heading paragraph for the Education section, cutting the selected items, and then pasting them from the Office Clipboard to the appropriate location. Then, you will use the same process to move the Experience section so that it appears below the moved Education section. The following steps use cut and paste to move table rows and paragraphs.

1

- Click the Zoom Out button on the status bar as many times as necessary so that the resume is displayed at 70 percent zoom in the document window.
- Scroll so that the Objective, Experience, and Education sections appear in the document window at the same time.

2

- Select the row and heading paragraph to be moved by dragging through it, in this case, the Education section (Figure 5–20).

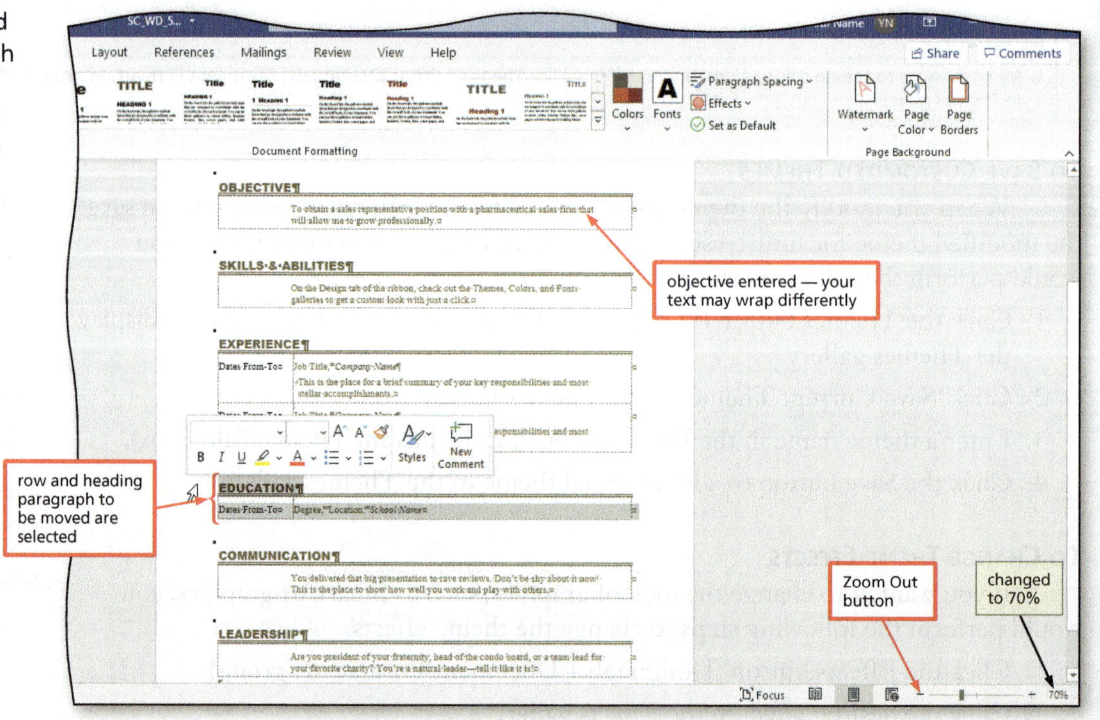

Figure 5–20

3

- Display the Home tab.
- Click the Cut button (Home tab | Clipboard group) to cut the selection and place it on the Office Clipboard.
- Position the insertion point at the location where the cut text is to be moved (pasted), in this case, to the left of the S in the Skills & Abilities heading (you may need to press the LEFT ARROW key after clicking Skills & Abilities to position the insertion point) (Figure 5–21).

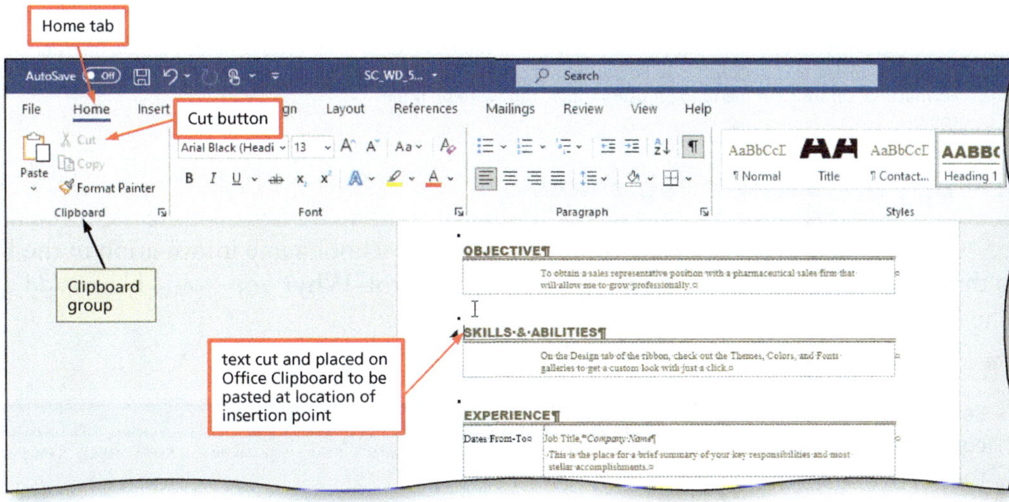

Figure 5–21

4

- Click the Paste arrow (Home tab | Clipboard group) to display the Paste menu.
- Point to the 'Keep Source Formatting' button on the Paste menu to display a Live Preview of that paste option applied to the selected content in the document (Figure 5–22).

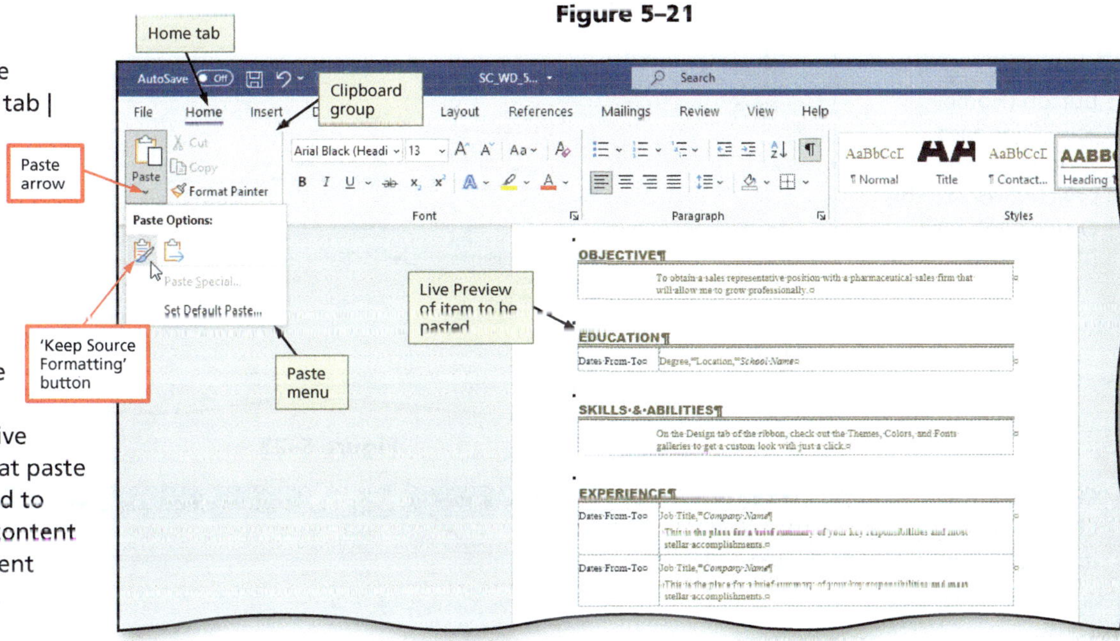

Figure 5–22

5

Experiment

- Point to each paste option button on the Paste menu and watch the Live Preview of the pasted item change.
- Click the 'Keep Source Formatting' button on the Paste menu to paste the content on the Office Clipboard using source formatting at the location of the insertion point.

Q&A

Can I use this procedure to copy and paste an entire table with source formatting?
Yes, you would select the table to be copied, position the insertion point at the location where you want to paste the table, click the Paste arrow, and then click the 'Keep Source Formatting' button on the Paste menu to paste the table with source formatting.

Can I use drag and drop instead of cut and paste to move the selected content?
Yes, but because the resume templates have many individual tables, it often is easier to use cut and paste.

6

- Repeat Steps 2 through 5 to move the rows and heading in the Experience section so that the Experience section is positioned below the Education section (shown in Figure 5–23).

Other Ways

1. Right-click selected text, click Cut on shortcut menu or Mini toolbar, right-click where text or object is to be pasted, click 'Keep Source Formatting' on shortcut menu (or, if using touch, tap Paste on Mini toolbar)
2. Press CTRL+X, position insertion point where text or object is to be pasted, press CTRL+V

To Copy and Paste a Table Row

In the resume, you copy the row containing the school name information in the Education section so that it appears twice in the Education content control. **Why?** You would like to add two degrees to the resume. The following steps copy and paste a table row.

1

- Select the row to be copied (in this case, the row containing the school information).
- Click the Copy button (Home tab | Clipboard group) to copy the selected row to the Office Clipboard (Figure 5–23).

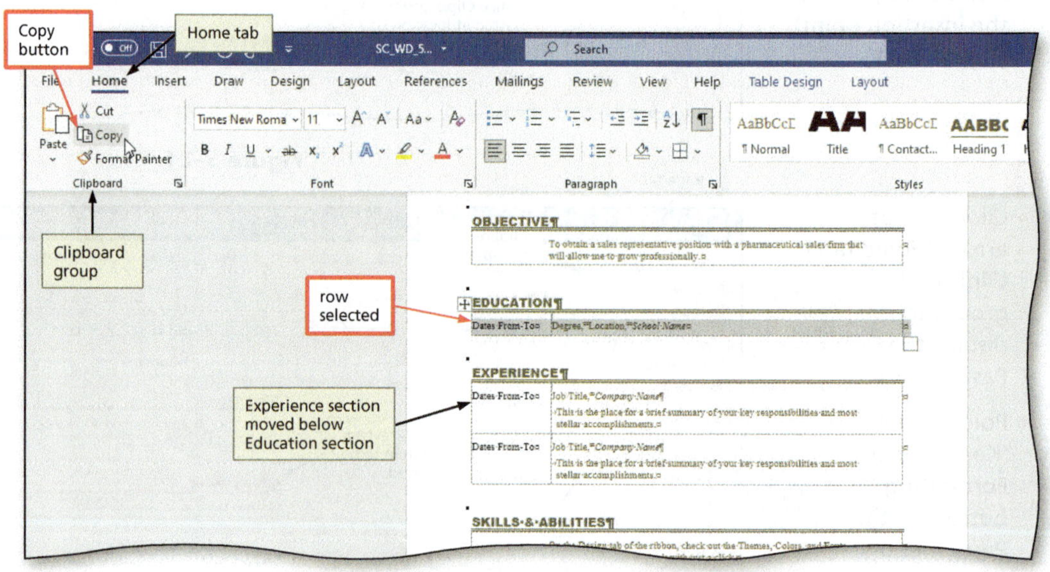

Figure 5–23

2

- Click the Paste button (Home tab | Clipboard group) to paste the copied item below the selection (Figure 5–24).

Q&A

What if I click the Paste arrow by mistake?
Click the Paste arrow again to remove the Paste menu and repeat Step 2.

What if I wanted to paste in a different location in the document?
You would position the insertion point at the location where the copied item should be pasted and then click the Paste button (Home tab | Clipboard group).

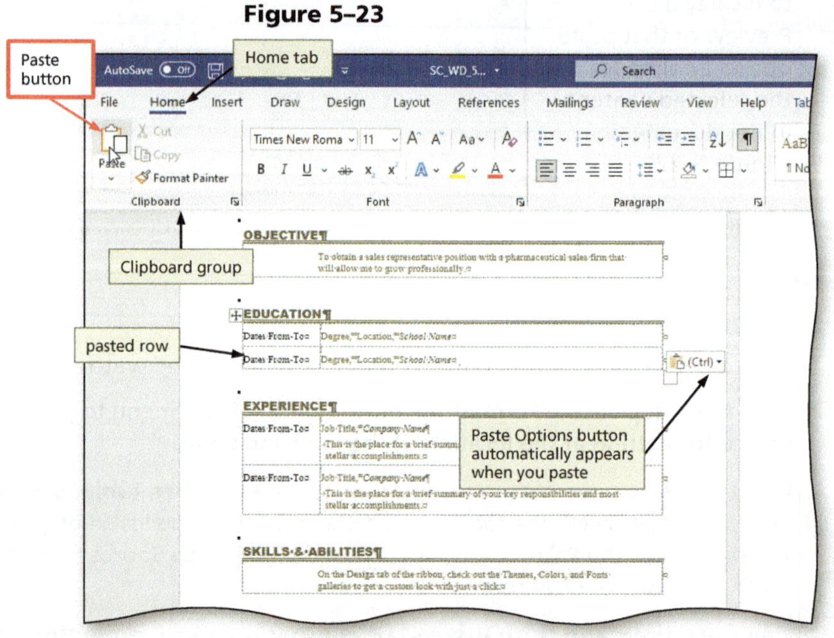

Figure 5–24

Other Ways

1. Click Copy on shortcut menu (or, if using touch, tap Copy on Mini toolbar), right-click where item is to be pasted, click 'Keep Source Formatting' in Paste Options area on shortcut menu (or, if using touch, tap Paste on Mini toolbar)
2. Select item, press CTRL+C, position insertion point at paste location, press CTRL+V

To Delete a Row and Paragraph

Because you will not be using the Skills & Abilities section of the resume template, the next task is to delete this section. The following steps delete a row and a paragraph.

1. Select the Skills & Abilities paragraph heading and associated table row (Figure 5–25).

2. Press DELETE to delete the selected text and ensure the document has one page only (shown in Figure 5–26).

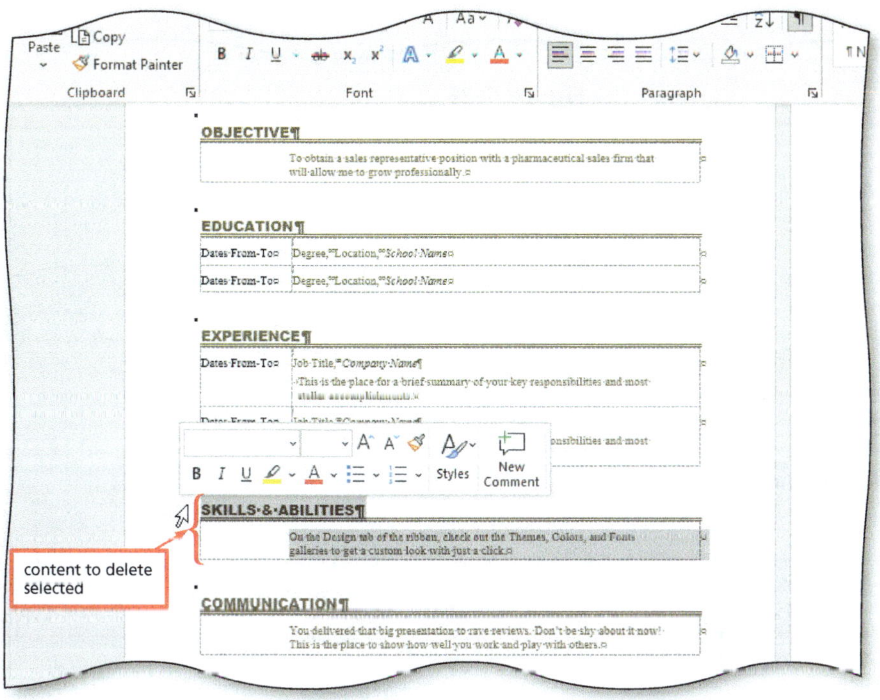

Figure 5 25

To Create a Building Block

If you use the same text or graphic frequently, you can store the text or graphic as a **building block**, which is a ready-made stored text element or graphic that you can insert in a document. That is, you can create the entry once as a building block and then insert the building block when you need it. In this way, you avoid entering text or graphics inconsistently or incorrectly in different locations throughout the same or multiple documents.

The following steps create a building block for the city name, New Orleans. **Why?** You use the city name multiple times throughout the resume and want to use a building block to insert it instead of typing the city name repeatedly.

1

- Select the text to be a building block, in this case, New Orleans, in the contact information at the top of the resume.
- Display the Insert tab.
- Click the 'Explore Quick Parts' button (Insert tab | Text group) to display the Explore Quick Parts gallery (Figure 5–26).

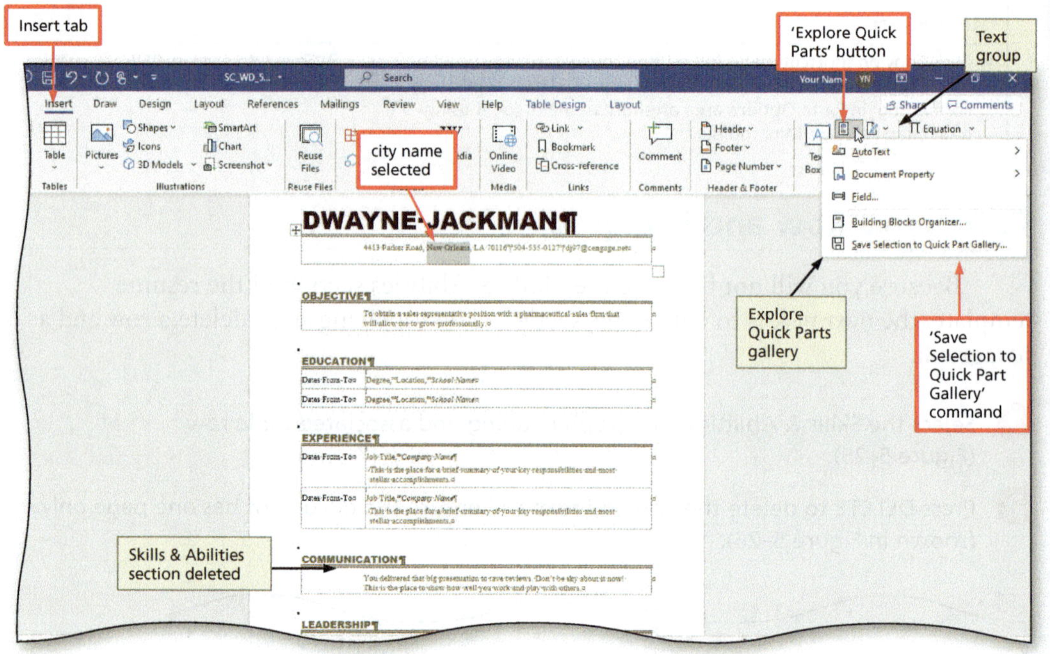

Figure 5–26

2

- Click 'Save Selection to Quick Part Gallery' in the Explore Quick Parts gallery to display the Create New Building Block dialog box.
- Type **no** in the Name text box (Create New Building Block dialog box) to replace the proposed building block name (New Orleans, in this case) with a shorter building block name (Figure 5–27).

3

- Click OK to store the building block entry and close the dialog box.
- If Word displays another dialog box, click Yes to save changes to the building blocks.

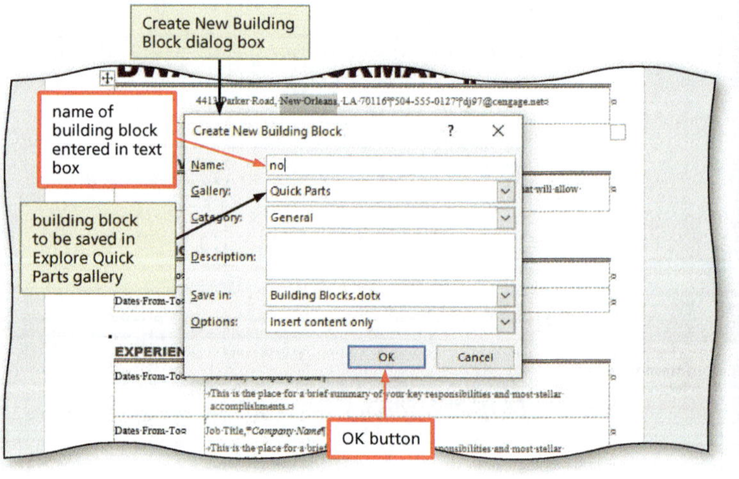

Figure 5–27

Q&A **Will this building block be available in future documents?**
When you exit Word, a dialog box may appear asking if you want to save changes to the building blocks. Click Save if you want to use the new building block in future documents.

To Modify a Building Block

When you save a building block in the Explore Quick Parts gallery, the building block is displayed at the top of the Explore Quick Parts gallery. When you point to the building block in the Explore Quick Parts gallery, a ScreenTip displays the building block name. If you want to display more information when the user points to the building block, you can include a description in the ScreenTip.

The following steps modify a building block to include a description and change its category to AutoText. **Why?** Because you want to reuse this text, you place it in the AutoText gallery, which also is accessible through the Explore Quick Parts gallery.

1

- Click the 'Explore Quick Parts' button (Insert tab | Text group) to display the Explore Quick Parts gallery.
- Right-click the New Orleans building block to display a shortcut menu (Figure 5–28).

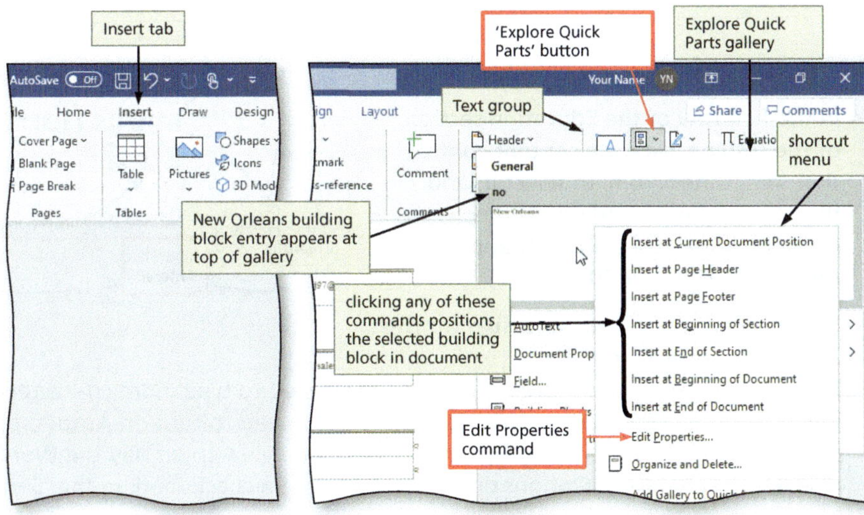

Figure 5–28

2

- Click Edit Properties on the shortcut menu to display the Modify Building Block dialog box, filled in with information related to the selected building block.
- Click the Gallery arrow (Modify Building Block dialog box) and then click AutoText to change the gallery in which the building block will be placed.
- Type **shortcut for entering the city name, New Orleans** in the Description text box (Figure 5–29). (Note that depending on settings, your dialog box may display the extension of .dotm after Normal in the Save in box.)

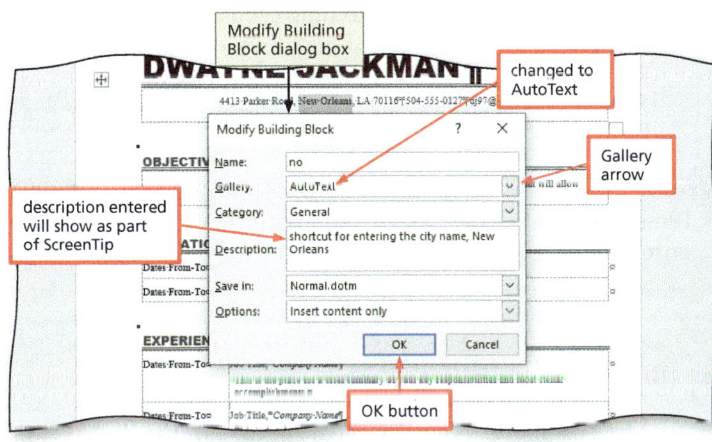

Figure 5–29

3

- Click OK to store the building block entry and close the dialog box.
- Click Yes when asked if you want to redefine the building block entry.

To Use AutoComplete

As you begin typing, Word may display a ScreenTip that presents a suggestion for the rest of the word or phrase you are typing. **Why?** With its AutoComplete feature, Word predicts the text, numbers, dates, or phrases you are typing and displays its prediction in a ScreenTip. If the AutoComplete prediction is correct, you can instruct Word to finish your typing with its prediction, or you can ignore Word's prediction. Word draws its AutoComplete suggestions from its dictionary and from AutoText entries you create and save in the Normal template.

The following steps use the AutoComplete feature as you type the graduation date in the Education section of the resume.

1

- Change the zoom to page width.
- In the first row of the Education section of the resume, click the content control that says, Dates From, to select it, and then type **Sept** and notice the AutoComplete ScreenTip that appears on the screen (Figure 5–30).

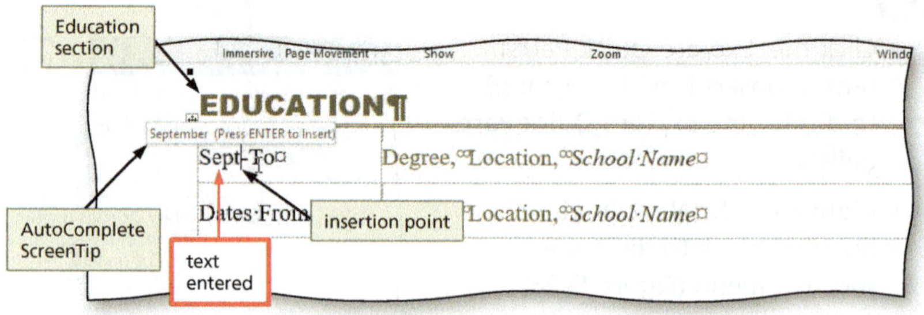

Figure 5–30

Q&A **Why would my screen not display the AutoComplete ScreenTip?**
Depending on previous Word entries, you may need to type more characters in order for Word to predict a particular word or phrase accurately. Or, you may need to turn on AutoComplete by clicking File on the ribbon to open Backstage view, clicking Options in Backstage view to display the Word Options dialog box, clicking Advanced in the left pane (Word Options dialog box), placing a check mark in the 'Show AutoComplete suggestions' check box, and then clicking OK.

2

- Press ENTER to instruct Word to finish your typing with the word or phrase that appeared in the AutoComplete ScreenTip.

Q&A **What if I do not want to use the text proposed in the AutoComplete ScreenTip?**
Simply continue typing and the AutoComplete ScreenTip will disappear from the screen.

3

- Press SPACEBAR. Type **2018** and then click the content control that says, To, to select it. Type **May 2020** to enter the date (shown in Figure 5–31).

To Insert a Building Block

The city name, New Orleans, appears in the degree in the Education section of the resume. You will type the building block name, no, and then instruct Word to replace this building block name with the stored building block entry, New Orleans. The following steps insert a building block. **Why?** Instead of typing the name, you will insert the stored building block.

1

- Click the content control that says, Degree, to select it, and then type **B.S. Public Health** as the degree name.
- Click the content control that says, Location, to select it, and then type the building block name, **no** (Figure 5–31).

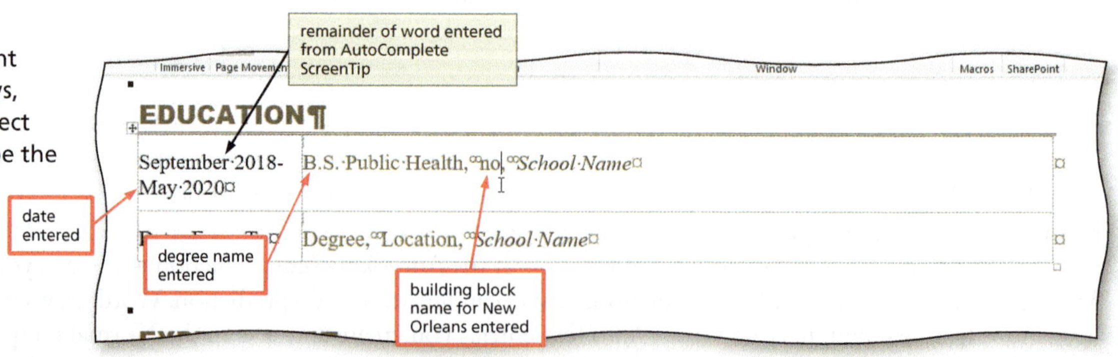

Figure 5–31

2

- Press F3 to instruct Word to replace the building block name (no) with the stored building block entry (New Orleans).
- Type **, LA** as the state.

- Click the content control that says, School Name, and then type **Gulf College** as the school name.
- Press ENTER and then type **- GPA 3.8/4.0** (Figure 5–32). (If your GPA is italicized, select the line containing the GPA and then press CTRL+I to remove the italic format.)

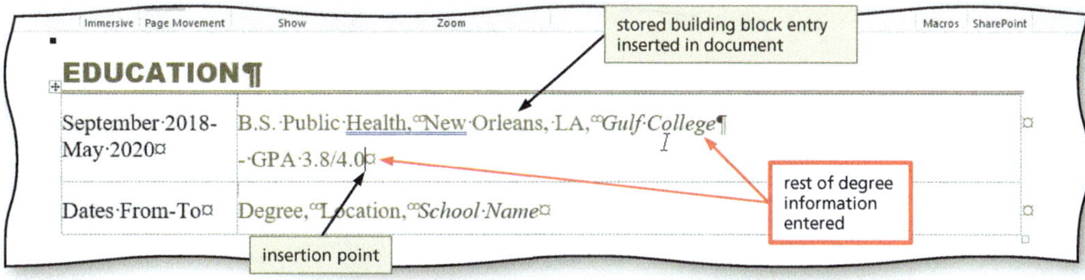

Figure 5–32

Other Ways

1. Click 'Explore Quick Parts' button (Insert tab | Text group), if necessary point to AutoText, select desired building block
2. Click 'Explore Quick Parts' button (Insert tab | Text group), click 'Building Blocks Organizer', select desired building block, click Insert button

Building Blocks versus AutoCorrect

The AutoCorrect feature enables you to insert and create AutoCorrect entries, similarly to how you created and inserted building blocks in this module. The difference between an AutoCorrect entry and a building block entry is that the AutoCorrect feature makes corrections for you automatically as soon as you press SPACEBAR or type a punctuation mark, whereas you must instruct Word to insert a building block. That is, you enter the building block name and then press F3, or click the Quick Parts button and then select the building block from one of the galleries or the Building Blocks Organizer.

BTW

Building Blocks

If you wanted to make building blocks available in other documents and templates, instead of just the current document or template, you would save them in the Normal .dotm file instead of the Building Blocks.dotx file. To do this, click the 'Explore Quick Parts' button (Insert tab | Text group), click 'Building Blocks Organizer' in the Explore Quick Parts gallery, click the building block for which you want to change the save location, click the Edit Properties button (Building Blocks Organizer dialog box), click the Save in arrow (Modify Building Block dialog box), select Normal in the list, click OK (Modify Building Block dialog box), and then close the Building Blocks Organizer dialog box.

To Enter Text in Content Controls

The next step is to enter the rest of the text in the Education section of the resume. The following steps enter text in content controls.

1. In the second row of the Education section of the resume, click the content control that says, Dates From, to select it, and then type **September 2016** as the from date.
2. Click the content control that says, To, to select it, and then type **May 2018** as the end date.
3. Click the content control that says, Degree, to select it, and then type **A.S. Nursing** as the degree name.
4. Click the content control that says, Location, to select it, and then type **no** as the building block name. Press F3 to instruct Word to replace the building block name (no) with the stored building block entry (New Orleans).
5. Type **, LA** as the state.
6. Click the content control that says, School Name, and then type **Bridgeview College** as the school name.
7. Press ENTER and then type **- GPA 3.9/4.0** (Figure 5–33). (If your GPA is italicized, select the line containing the GPA and then press CTRL+I to remove the italic format.)

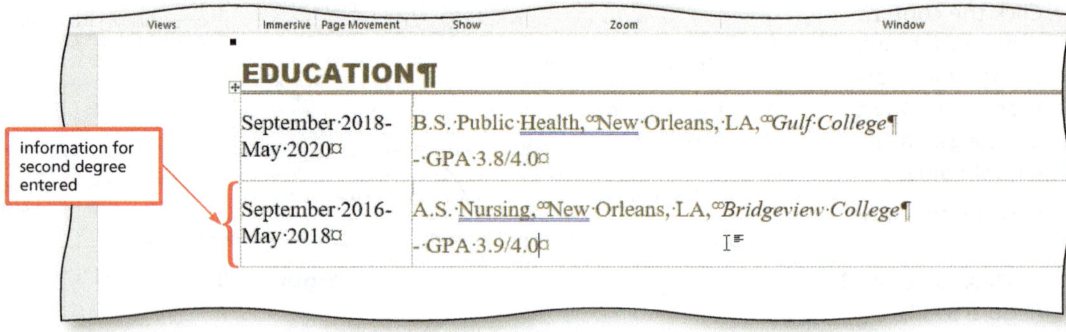

Figure 5–33

To Delete a Row

Because you have only one job to list in the Experience section, the next step is to delete the second row in the Experience section. The following steps delete a row.

1. Position the insertion point somewhere in the second row of the Experience section, as shown in Figure 5–34.
2. Display the Layout tab.
3. Click the Delete button (Layout tab | Rows & Columns group) to display the Delete menu (Figure 5–34).
4. Click Delete Rows on the Delete menu to delete the row containing the insertion point (in this case, the second row in the Experience section) (shown in Figure 5–35).

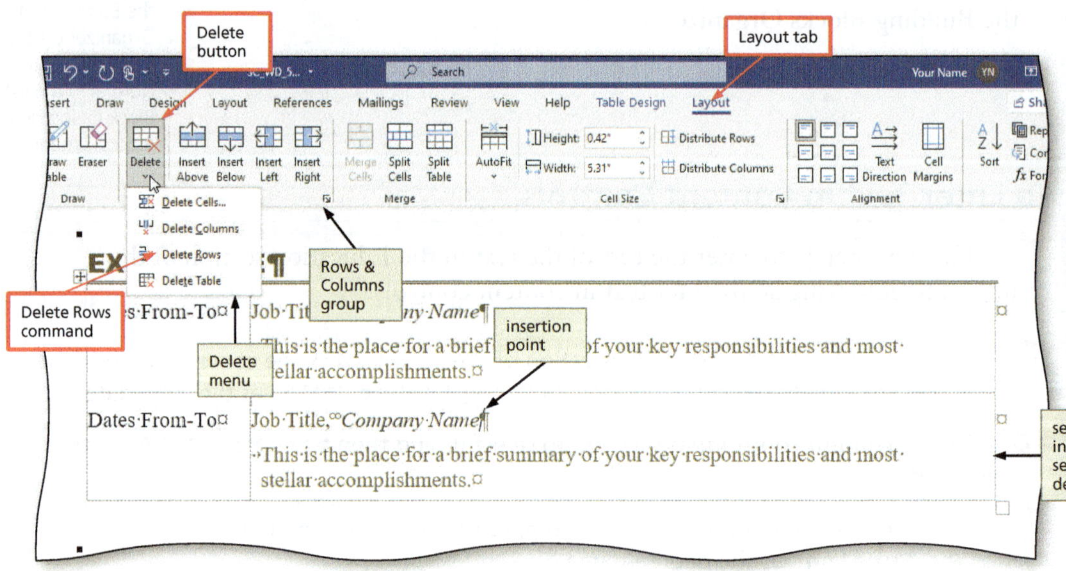

Figure 5–34

To Enter Text in Content Controls

The next step is to enter the job experience information in the Experience section of the resume. The following steps enter text in content controls.

1. In the row of the Experience section of the resume, click the content control that says, Dates From, to select it, and then type `November 2018` as the from date.
2. Click the content control that says, To, to select it, and then type `Present` as the end date.

3. Click the content control that says, Job Title, to select it, and then type **`Customer Service Agent, New Orleans, LA`** for the job title, city, and state (be sure to use the building block name for the city name, New Orleans).

4. Click the content control that says, Company Name, and then type **`Harbor Nutrition`** as the company name.

5. Click the content control that begins, 'This is the place for …', and then type **`Answer customer queries onsite, on the phone, and via online chat; set up rewards memberships; generate new customers by cold calling; meet with suppliers`** (Figure 5–35).

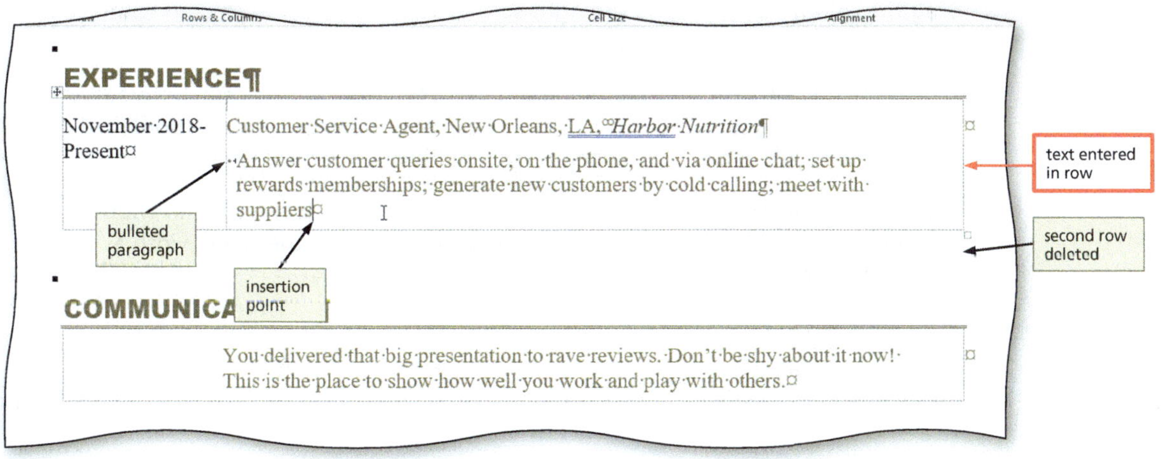

Figure 5–35

To Remove Bullets from a Paragraph

You do not want the experience entry to be a list. Thus, the following steps remove bullets from a list.

1. Display the Home tab.

2. With the insertion point in the bulleted paragraph, click the Bullets button (Home tab | Paragraph group) to remove the bullet from the paragraph (Figure 5–36).

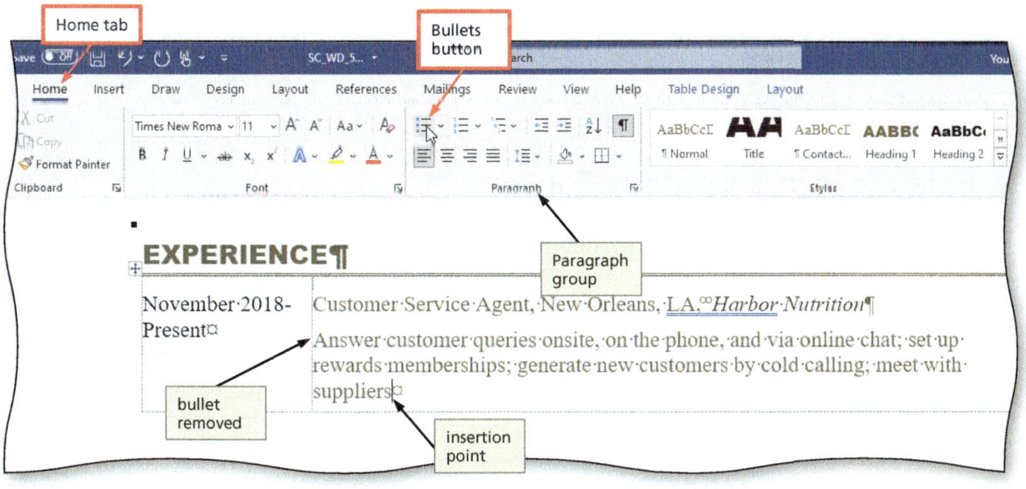

Figure 5–36

To Resize Table Columns

You do not want the dates to wrap in the Education and Experience sections of the resume. Thus, you will widen the columns containing these dates. The following steps resize table columns to make them wider.

1. Display the Education and Experience sections in the document window.
2. Position the pointer on the column boundary to the right of the column to adjust (in this case, to the right of the first column of dates in the Education section) so that the pointer changes to a double-headed arrow split by two vertical bars.
3. Drag the column boundary to the right so that Word adjusts the column width so that the from and to dates fit on a single line.
4. Position the pointer on the column boundary to the right of the column to adjust (in this case, to the right of the first column of dates in the Experience section) so that the pointer changes to a double-headed arrow split by two vertical bars.
5. Drag the column boundary to the right so that Word adjusts the column width so that the from and to dates fit on a single line and this column is the same width as the one containing dates in the Education section (Figure 5–37).

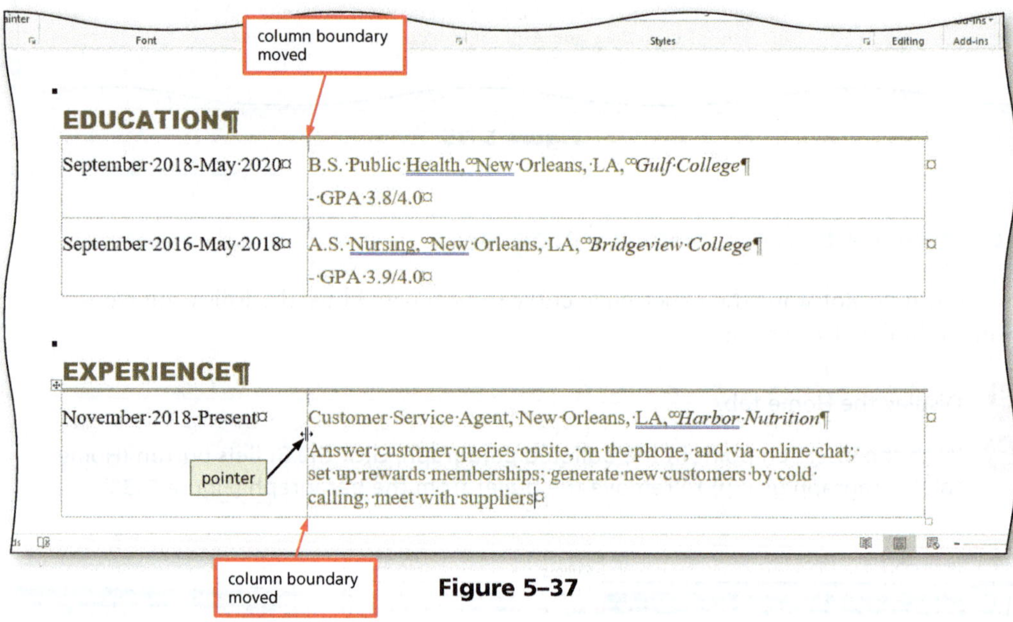

Figure 5–37

To Enter Text in a Content Control

The following step enters the heading in the Certifications section of the resume.

1. Click the Communication content control and then type `Certifications` as the heading (shown in Figure 5–38).

To Enter a Line Break

The next step in personalizing the resume is to enter content in the Certifications section. The default paragraph spacing in the resume placed 5 points after each line. For the list of certifications, you do not want this extra space after paragraphs. Thus, you will not press ENTER between each line. Instead, you will create a line break. **Why?** A line break, which is created by pressing SHIFT+ENTER, inserts a nonprinting character that advances the insertion point to the beginning of the next physical line, ignoring any paragraph formatting. The following steps enter the list of certifications using a line break, instead of a paragraph break, between each line.

1

- In the Certifications section of the resume, click the content control that begins, 'You delivered that ...', to select it.
- Type `Certified Nursing Assistant (CNA)` and then, if Word automatically changed (corrected) the letters CNA to CAN, press CTRL+Z to undo the autocorrection.
- Press SHIFT+ENTER to insert a line break character and move the insertion point to the beginning of the next physical line (Figure 5–38).

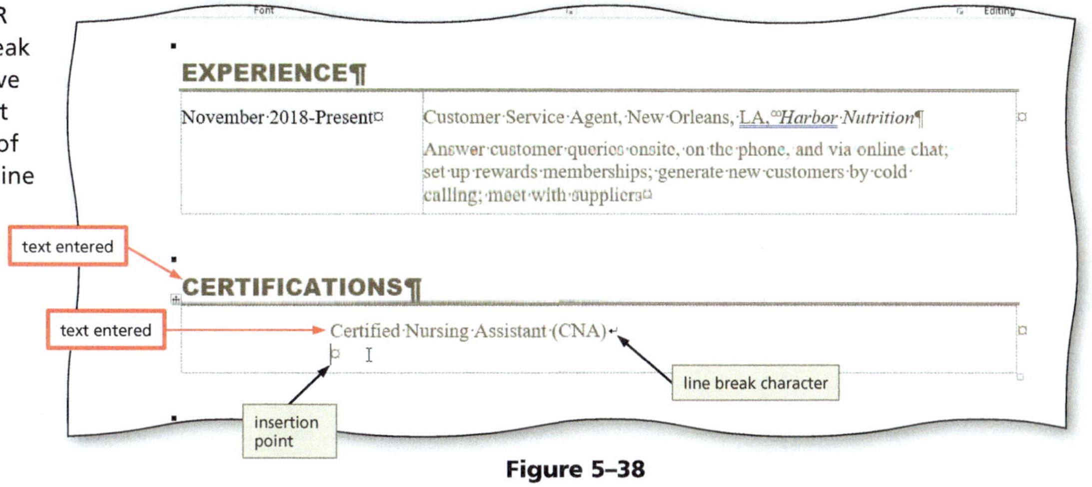

Figure 5–38

2

- Type `Adult and Pediatric CPR` and then press SHIFT+ENTER.
- Type `Red Cross Certified Lifeguard` as the last entry. Do not press SHIFT+ENTER at the end of this line (Figure 5–39).

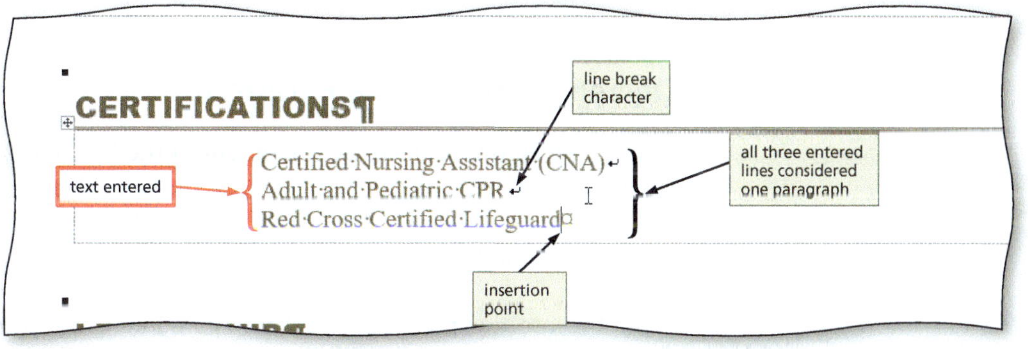

Figure 5–39

To Enter Text in Content Controls

The next step is to begin to enter content in the Community Service section of the resume. This should be a bulleted list. The following steps enter text in content controls.

BTW

Line Break Characters

A line break character is a formatting mark that indicates a line break at the end of the line. Like paragraph marks, tab characters, and other formatting marks, line break characters do not print.

1. Click the Leadership content control and then type **`Community Service`** as the heading (shown in Figure 5–40).

2. In the Community Service section of the resume, click the content control that begins, 'Are you president of ...', to select it.

3. Click the Bullets button (Home tab | Paragraph group) to format the current paragraph as a bulleted list item.

4. Type this text, making sure you use the building block for New Orleans: **`Organize and implement public health awareness programs for New Orleans Medical Center, 2017-Present`** (Figure 5–40).

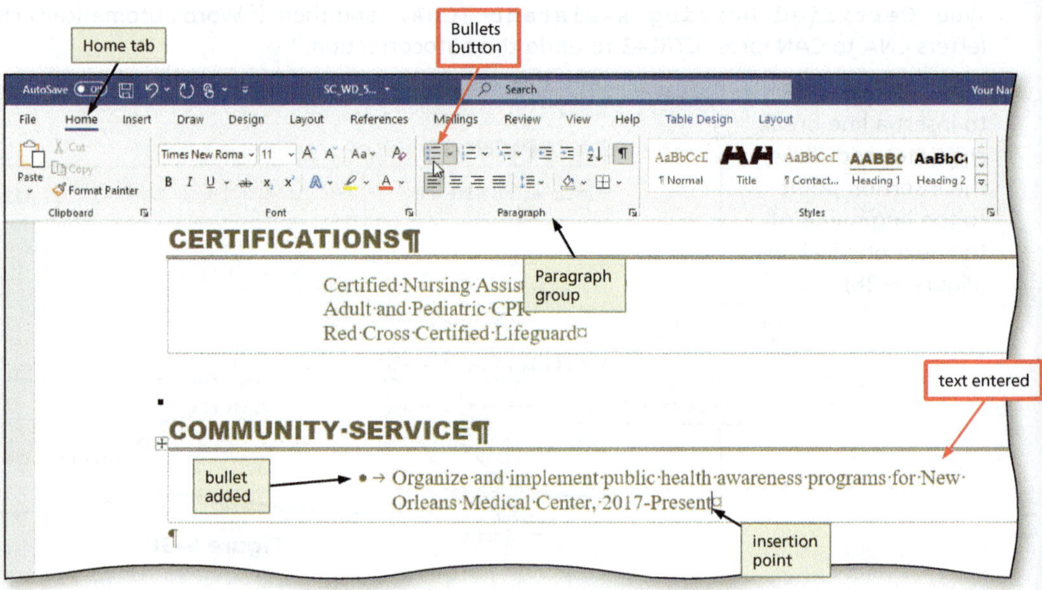

Figure 5–40

To Decrease Indent of a Paragraph

The next step is to decrease the indent of the bulleted paragraph because you want the bullet character to be aligned with the certifications listed in the Certification section. The following steps decrease the indent of a paragraph and enter the remainder of the bulleted list items.

1. With the insertion point in the bulleted paragraph, as shown in Figure 5–40, click the Decrease Indent button (Home tab | Paragraph group) to decrease the indent of the bulleted list item.

2. Press ENTER and then type **`Volunteer at annual flu shot clinic, 2016-Present`** to enter the second community service item.

3. Press ENTER and then type **`Volunteer at Lafayette Free Clinic, 2016-Present`** to enter the third community service item.

4. Press ENTER and then type **`Participant at Gulf College's phone-a-thon fundraiser, 2018-Present`** to complete the bulleted list (Figure 5–41).

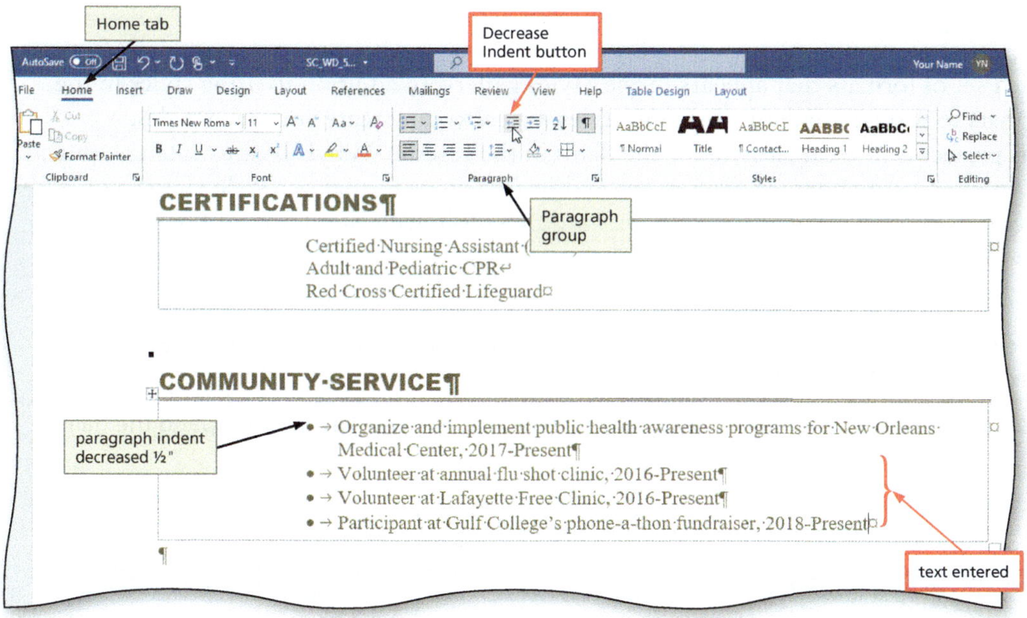

Figure 5–41

To Change a Bullet to a Predefined Symbol

The next step is to change the bullet character in the bulleted list in the Community Service section from a dot to a square. The following steps change a bullet character.

1. Select the bulleted list in the Community Service section.
2. Click the Bullets arrow (Home tab | Paragraph group) to display the Bullets gallery (Figure 5–42).
3. Click the desired bullet character in the Bullets gallery, in this case, the square, to change the bullet character in the selected bulleted list (shown in Figure 5–43).
4. Click anywhere to remove the selection from the text.
5. Save the resume again on the same storage location with the same file name.

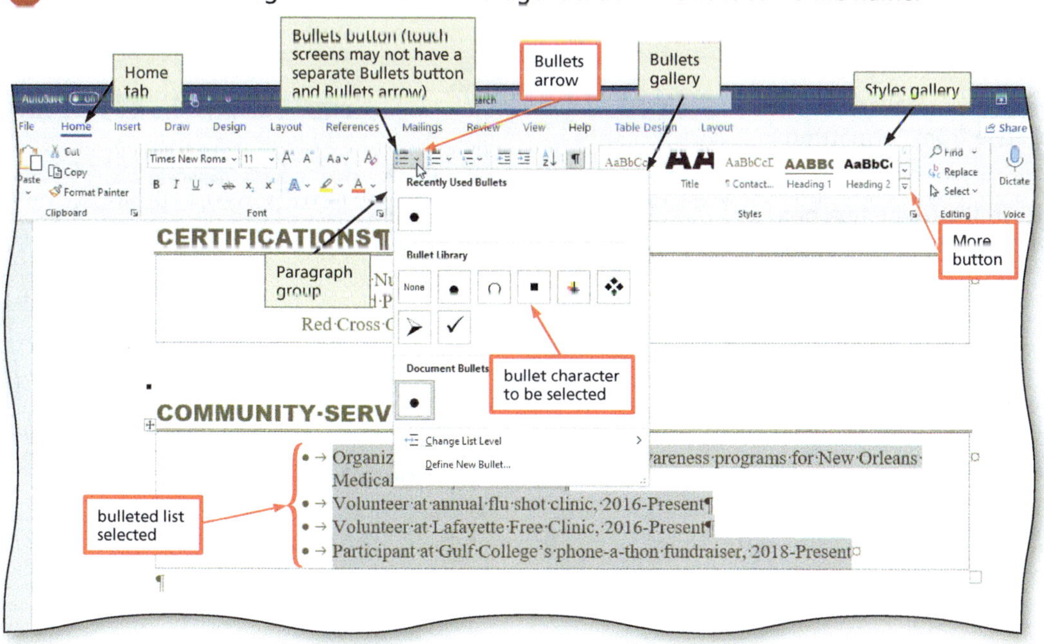

Figure 5–42

BTW

Working with Lists

In a numbered list, if you wanted to restart numbering, you would click the Numbering arrow, click 'Set Numbering Value' in the Numbering Library gallery to display the Set Numbering Value dialog box, if necessary, click to select the 'Start new list' option button (Set Numbering Value dialog box), and then click OK. To continue list numbering in a subsequent list, you would click the 'Continue from previous list' option button in the Set Numbering Value dialog box. You also can specify a starting number in a list by clicking the Numbering arrow, clicking 'Set Numbering Value' on the Numbering menu, and then entering the value in the 'Set value to' box (Set Numbering Value dialog box).

To Create a Paragraph Style

A style is a predefined set of formats that appears in the Styles gallery. In addition to using styles in the Styles gallery to apply formats to text and updating existing styles, you also can create your own styles.

The next task in this project is to create a style for the dates in the resume. **Why?** To illustrate creating a style, you will change the color of a date range in the resume and save the new format as a style. Then, you will apply the newly defined style to the remaining dates in the resume. The following steps format text and then create a style based on the formats in the selected text.

1

- Select the date range in the Experience section and then use the Font Color gallery to change the color of the selected text to 'Dark Red, Accent 2, Darker 50%'.
- Click the More button (shown in Figure 5–42) in the Styles gallery (Home tab | Styles group) to expand the gallery (Figure 5–43).

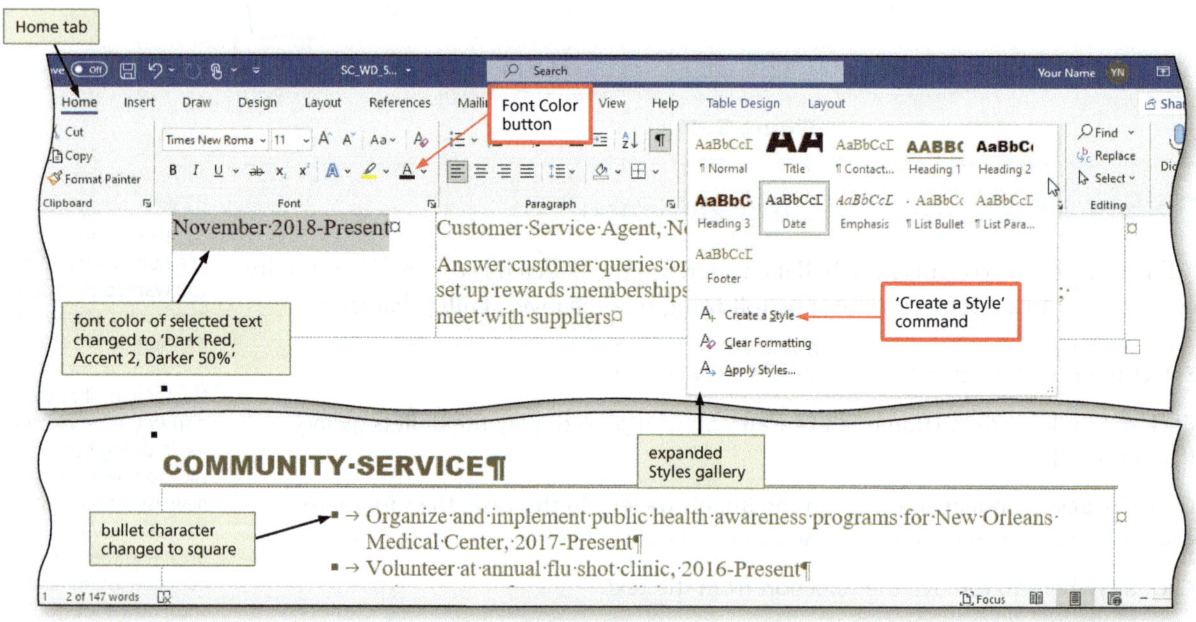

Figure 5–43

2

- Click 'Create a Style' in the Styles gallery to display the Create New Style from Formatting dialog box.
- Type `Resume Dates` in the Name text box (Create New Style from Formatting dialog box) (Figure 5–44).

3

- Click OK to create the new style and add it to the Styles gallery (shown in Figure 5–45).

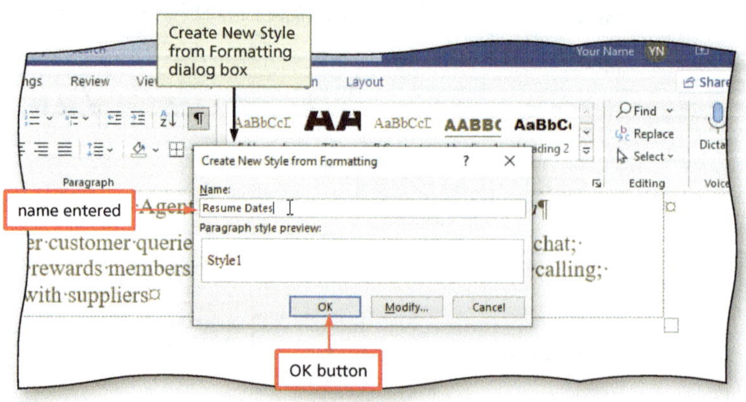

Figure 5–44

Q&A **How can I see the style just created?**
If the style name does not appear in the in-ribbon Styles gallery, click the More button in the Styles gallery (Home tab | Styles group) to display the expanded Styles gallery.

To Apply a Style

The next task is to apply the style just created to the other dates in the resume. The following step applies a style.

1 One at a time, position the insertion point in the remaining dates in the Education section of the resume and then click Resume Dates in the Styles gallery to apply the selected style to each heading (shown in Figure 5–45).

To Reveal Formatting

Sometimes, you want to know which formats were applied to certain text items in a document. **Why?** For example, you may wonder which font, font size, font color, and other effects were applied to the dates in the resume. To display formatting applied to text, use the Reveal Formatting pane. The following steps open and then close the Reveal Formatting pane.

1

- Position the insertion point in the text for which you want to reveal formatting (in this case, the dates in the Education section).
- Press SHIFT+F1 to open the Reveal Formatting pane, which shows formatting applied to the location of the insertion point (Figure 5–45). (If necessary, drag the edge of the pane to widen or narrow it.)

Experiment

- Click the Font collapse button to hide the Font formats. Click the Font expand button to redisplay the Font formats.

Q&A

Why do some of the formats in the Reveal Formatting pane appear as links?
Clicking a link in the Reveal Formatting pane displays an associated dialog box, allowing you to change the format of the current text. For example, clicking the Font link in the Reveal Formatting pane would display the Font dialog box. If you made changes in the Font dialog box and then clicked OK, Word would change the format of the current text.

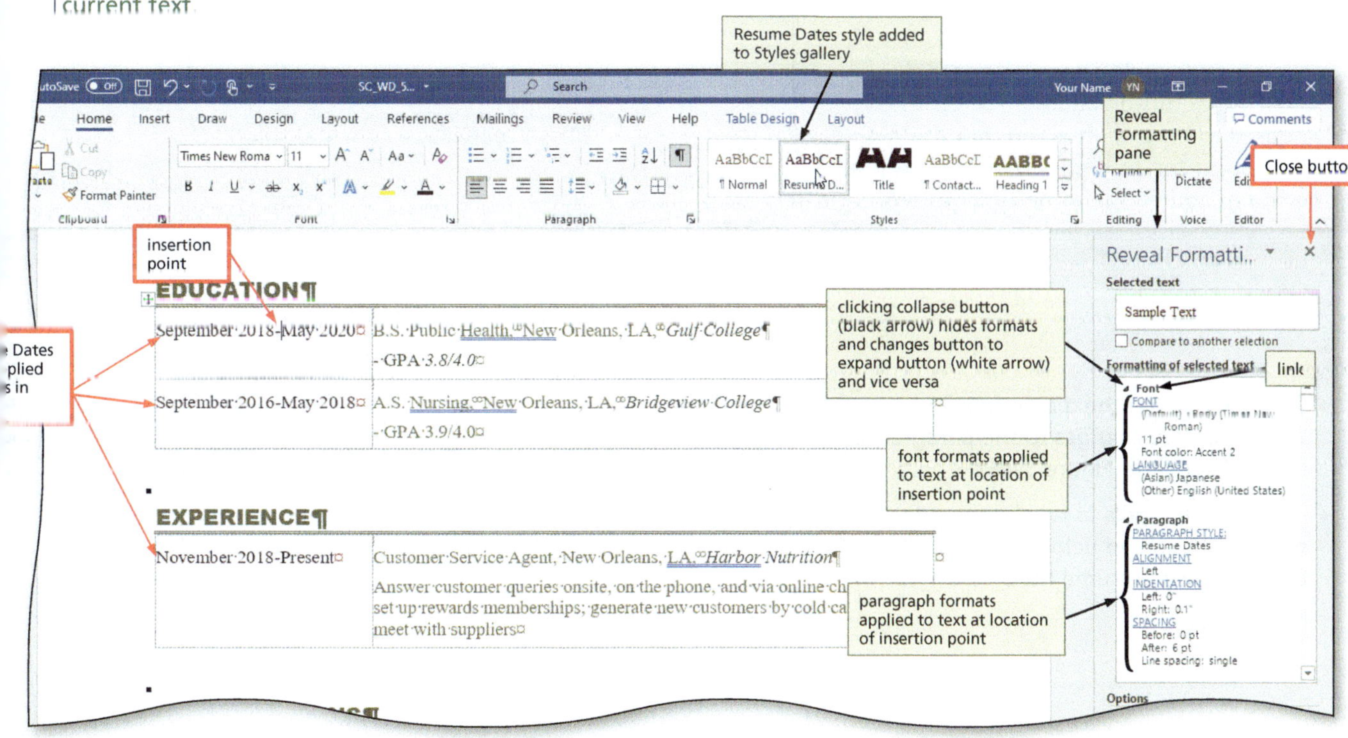

Figure 5–45

2

- Close the Reveal Formatting pane by clicking its Close button.

To Modify a Style Using the Styles Dialog Box

The next step is to modify the Normal style. **Why?** The tan text in the resume is a little light. You prefer that it be a bit darker. Thus, the following steps modify a style.

1

- Right-click the style name to modify in the Styles gallery (Normal in this case) (Home tab | Styles group) to display a shortcut menu (Figure 5–46).

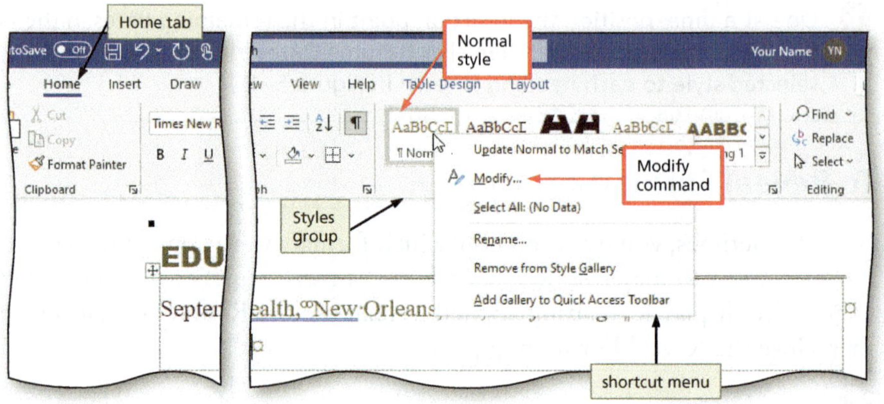

Figure 5–46

2

- Click Modify on the shortcut menu to display the Modify Style dialog box.
- Click the Font Color arrow (Modify Style dialog box) and then click 'Brown, Text 1, Lighter 25%' (second color, fifth row) in the Font Color gallery to change the font color of the current style (Figure 5–47).

Q&A **What is the purpose of the Format button in the Modify Style dialog box?**
If the formatting you wish to change for the style is not available in the Modify Style dialog box, you can click the Format button and then select the desired command after you click the Format button to display a dialog box that contains additional formatting options.

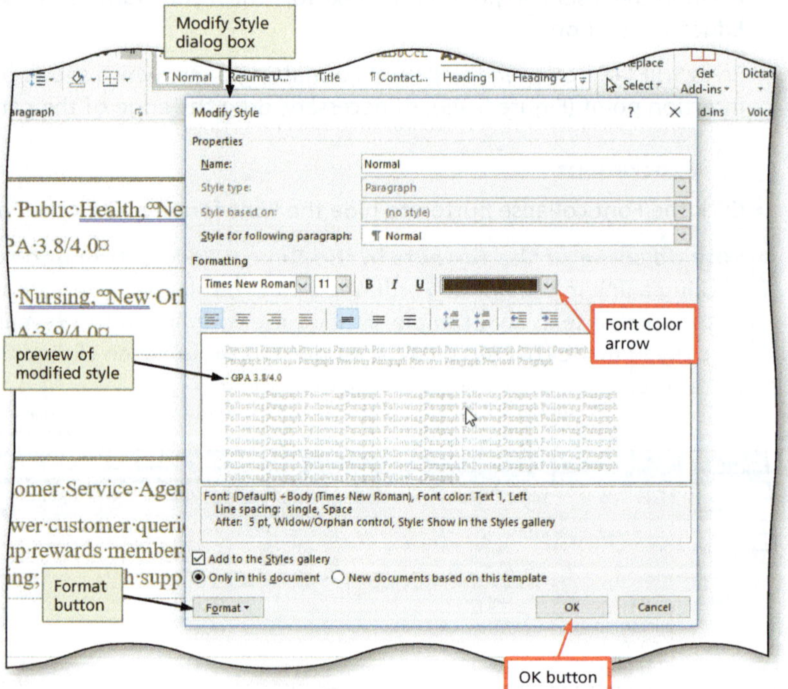

Figure 5–47

3

- Click OK to close the dialog box and apply the style changes to the paragraphs in the document (Figure 5–48).
- If the resume spills to two pages, adjust spacing above and below paragraphs so that the entire resume fits on a single page.

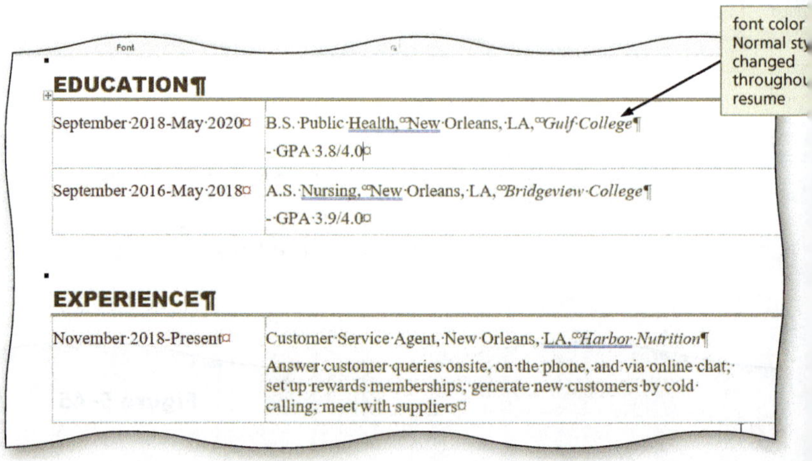

Figure 5–48

Other Ways

1. Click Styles Dialog Box Launcher (Home tab | Styles group), click arrow to right of style to modify, click Modify on menu, change settings (Modify Style dialog box), click OK
2. Click Styles Dialog Box Launcher, click Manage Styles button, scroll to style and then select it (Manage Styles dialog box), click Modify button, change settings (Modify Style dialog box), click OK in each dialog box

To Center Page Contents Vertically

In Word, you can center the page contents vertically. **Why?** This places the same amount of space at the top and bottom of the page. The following steps center resume page contents vertically.

1

- If necessary, click Layout on the ribbon to display the Layout tab.
- Click the Page Setup Dialog Box Launcher (Layout tab | Page Setup group) to display the Page Setup dialog box.
- Click the Layout tab (Page Setup dialog box) to display the Layout sheet.
- Click the Vertical alignment arrow (Page Setup dialog box) to display the list of alignment options and then click Center in the list (Figure 5–49).

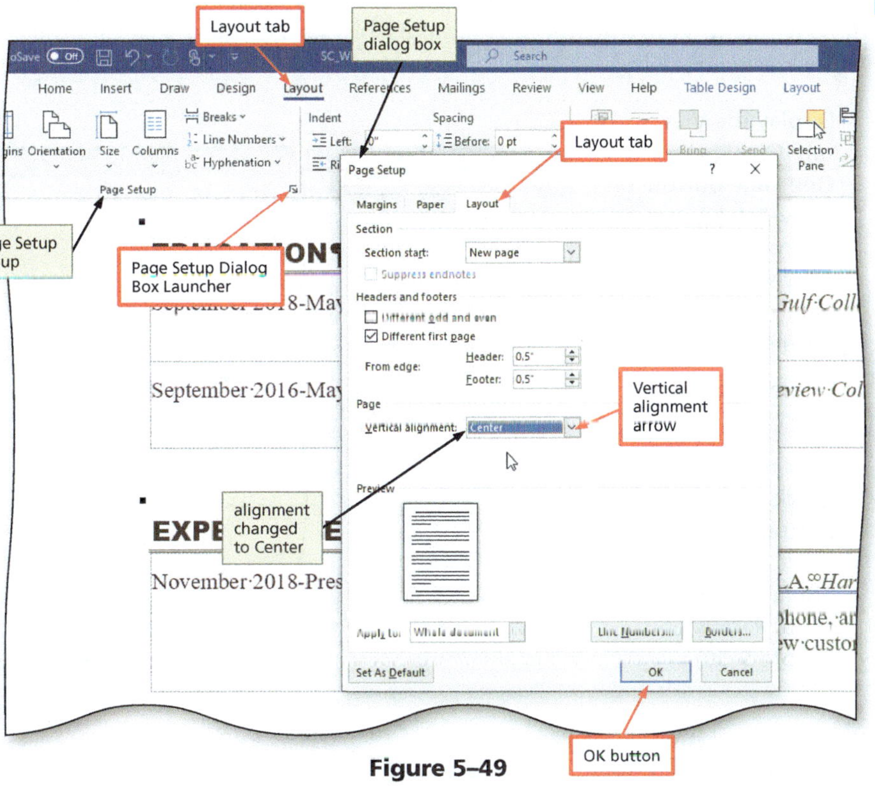

Figure 5–49

2

- Click OK to center the page contents vertically on the screen (shown in Figure 5–1 at the beginning of this module).

Q&A **What if I wanted to change the alignment back?**
You would select the Top vertical alignment from the Vertical alignment list in the Layout sheet (Page Setup dialog box).

- Save the resume again on the same storage location with the same file name.
- If requested by your instructor, print the finished resume (shown in Figure 5–1).

Break Point: If you want to take a break, this is a good place to do so. You can exit Word now. To resume later, start Word, open the file called SC_WD_5_JackmanResume.docx, and continue following the steps from this location forward.

Sharing a Document with Others

You may want to share Word documents with others electronically, such as via email, USB flash drive, or cloud storage. To ensure that others can read and/or open the files successfully, Word provides a variety of formats and tools to assist with sharing documents. This section uses the Jackman Resume created in this module to present a variety of these formats and tools.

To Insert a Quick Part

You would like to place the text, DRAFT, as a watermark on the resume before you share it, so that others are aware you might be making additional changes to the document. While you can insert a watermark using the ribbon, you also can use the Building Blocks Organizer to insert them because watermarks are a type of building block.

A building block, as described earlier in this module, is a reusable formatted ready-made graphic or text element that is stored in a gallery. Examples of building blocks include cover pages, headers, footers, page numbers, watermarks, and text boxes. You can see a list of every available building block in the **Building Blocks Organizer**. From the Building Blocks Organizer, you can sort building blocks, change their properties, or insert them in a document.

The next steps sort the Building Blocks Organizer by gallery and then insert the Draft 1 building block in the document. **Why?** Sorting the building blocks by gallery makes it easier to locate them.

1

- Display the View tab. Click the One Page button (View tab | Zoom group) to display the resume in its entirety in the document window.
- Display the Insert tab.
- Click the 'Explore Quick Parts' button (Insert tab | Text group) to display the Explore Quick Parts menu (Figure 5–50).

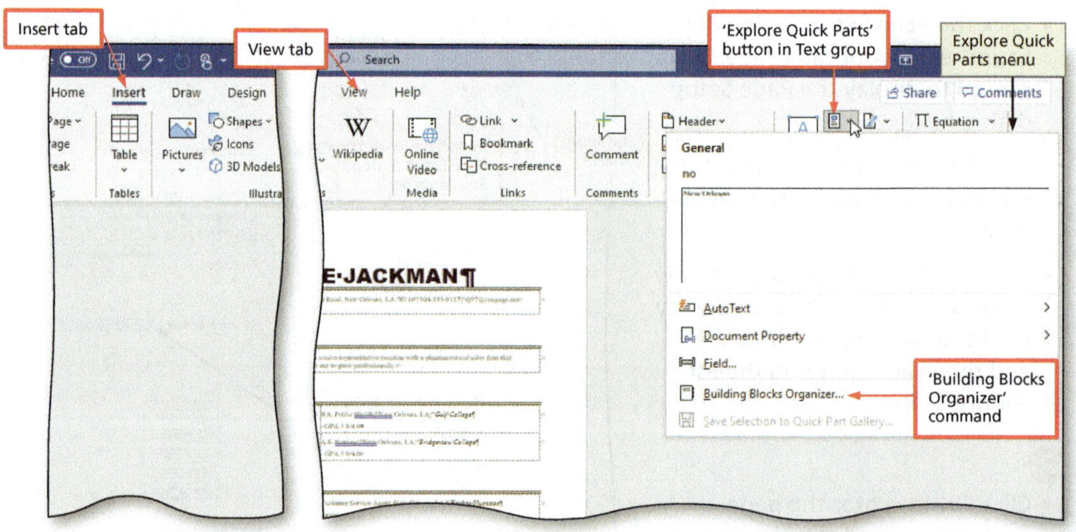

Figure 5–50

2

- Click 'Building Blocks Organizer' on the Explore Quick Parts menu to display the Building Blocks Organizer dialog box.

Experiment

- Drag the scroll bars in the Building Blocks Organizer so that you can look at all the columns and rows in the dialog box.
- Click the Gallery heading (Building Blocks Organizer dialog box) in the building blocks list to sort the building blocks by gallery (Figure 5–51).

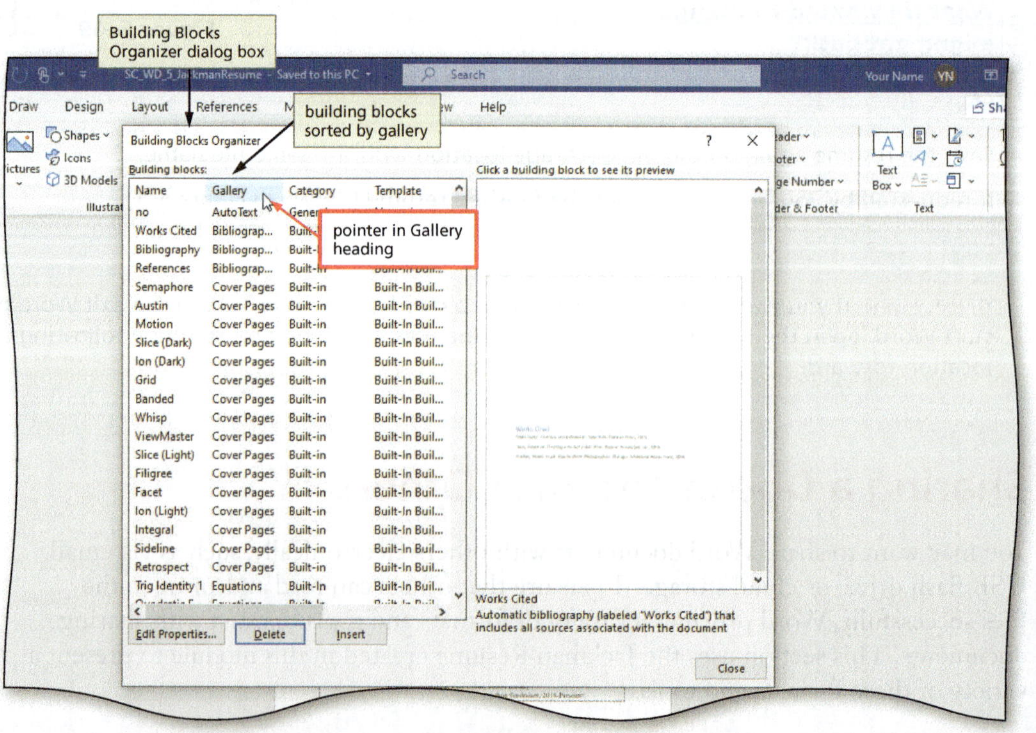

Figure 5–51

Experiment

- Click various names in the building blocks list and notice that a preview of the selected building block appears in the dialog box.

3

- Scroll through the building blocks list to the Watermarks group in the Gallery column and then click DRAFT 1 to select this building block (Figure 5–52).

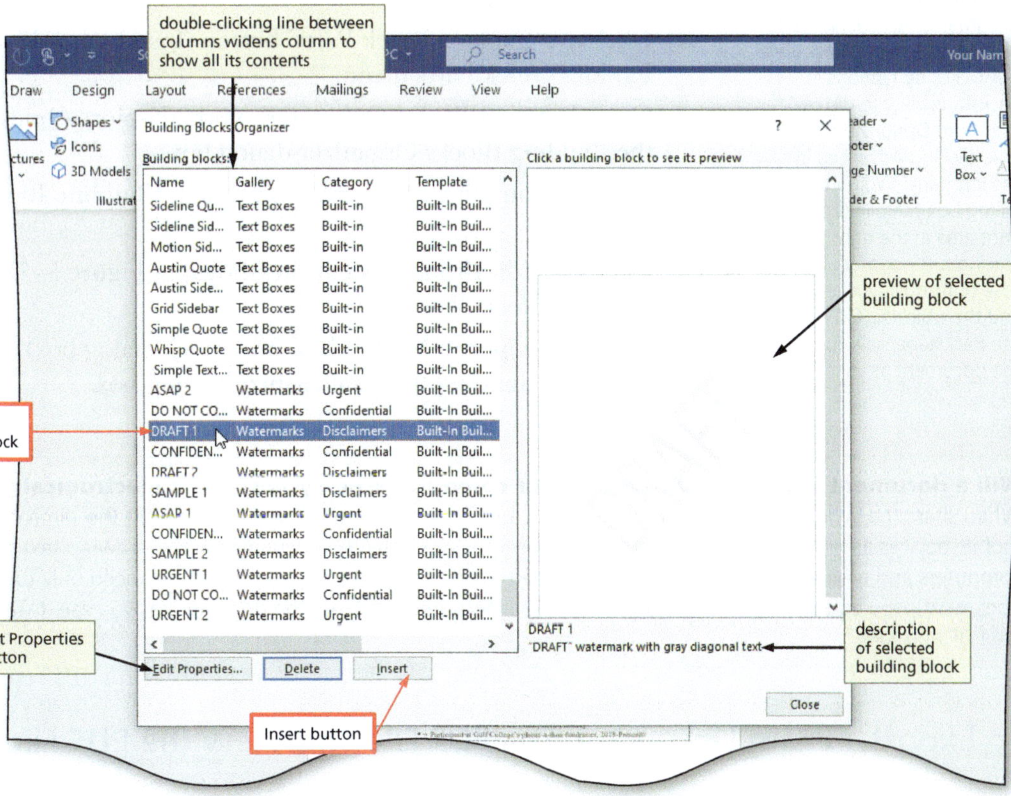

Figure 5–52

4

- Click the Insert button to insert the selected building block in the document (Figure 5–53).

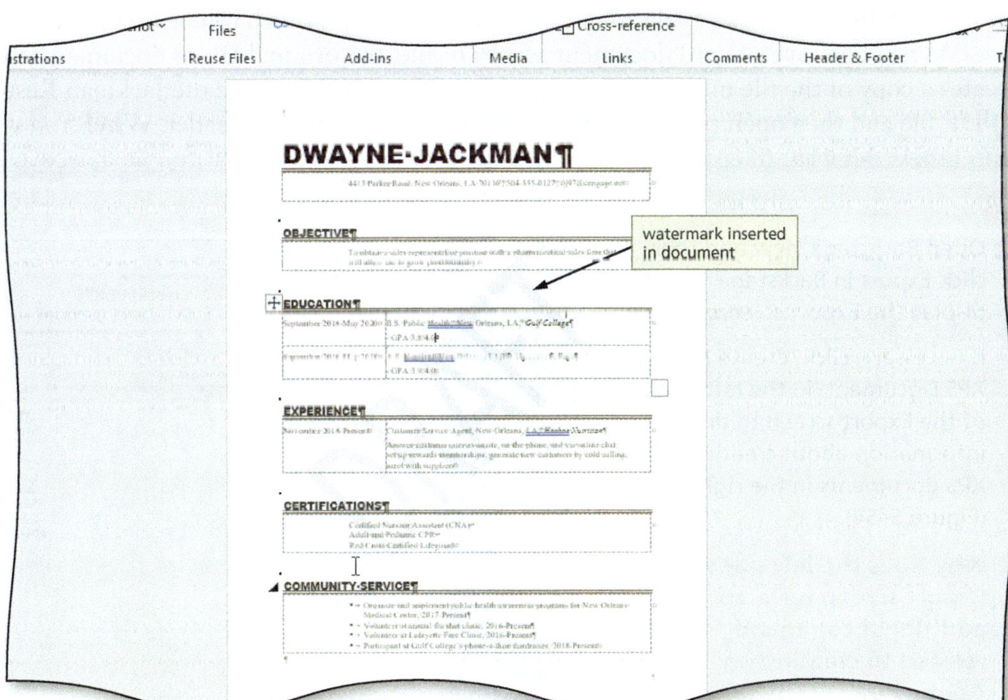

Figure 5–53

BTW
Conserving Ink and Toner
If you want to conserve ink or toner, you can instruct Word to print draft quality documents by clicking File on the ribbon to open Backstage view, clicking Options in Backstage view to display the Word Options dialog box, clicking Advanced in the left pane (Word Options dialog box), scrolling to the Print area in the right pane, placing a check mark in the 'Use draft quality' check box, and then clicking OK. Then, use Backstage view to print the document as usual.

To Edit Properties of Building Block Elements (Quick Parts)

Properties of a building block include its name, gallery, category, description, location where it is saved, and how it is inserted in the document. If you wanted to change any of these building block properties for a particular building block, you would perform these steps.

1. Click the 'Explore Quick Parts' button (Insert tab | Text group) to display the Explore Quick Parts menu.
2. Click 'Building Blocks Organizer' on the Explore Quick Parts menu to display the Building Blocks Organizer dialog box.
3. Select the building block you wish to edit (Building Blocks Organizer dialog box).
4. Click the Edit Properties button (shown in Figure 5–52) to display the Modify Building Block dialog box.
5. Edit any property (Modify Building Block dialog box) and then click OK. Close the Building Blocks Organizer dialog box.

Consider This

Will a document look the same on another computer when you share it electronically?
When sharing a Word document with others, you cannot be certain that it will look or print the same on their computers or mobile devices as on your computer or mobile device. For example, the document may wordwrap text differently on others' computers and mobile devices. If others do not need to edit the document (that is, if they need only to view and/or print the document), you could save the file in a format that allows others to view the document as you see it. Two popular such formats are PDF and XPS.

To Export a Word Document to a PDF File and View the PDF File in Adobe Reader

PDF, which stands for Portable Document Format, is a file format created by Adobe Systems. PDF is a standard format for exchanging documents and allows users to view a PDF file without the software that created the original document. Thus, the PDF format enables users to share documents with others easily. To view, navigate, and print a PDF file, you use an application called **Adobe Reader**, which can be downloaded free from Adobe's website.

When you save a Word document as a PDF file, the original Word document remains intact; that is, Word creates a copy of the file in the PDF format. The following steps save the Jackman Resume Word document as a PDF file and then open the Jackman Resume PDF file in Adobe Reader. **Why?** You want to share the resume with others but want to ensure it looks the same on their computer or mobile device as it does on yours.

1

- Open Backstage view and then click Export in Backstage view to display the Export screen.
- If necessary, click 'Create PDF/XPS Document' in the left pane of the Export screen to display information about creating PDF/XPS documents in the right pane (Figure 5–54).

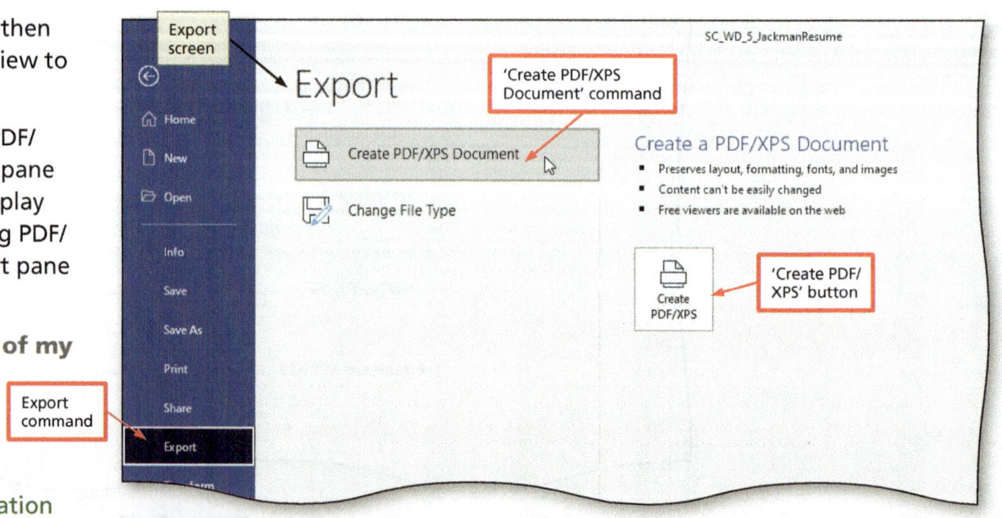

Figure 5–54

Q&A **Why does the left pane of my Export screen have an additional command related to creating an Adobe PDF?**
Depending on your installation settings in Adobe, you may have an additional tab on your ribbon and/or additional commands in screens, etc., related to Adobe functionality.

2

- Click the 'Create PDF/XPS' button in the right pane to display the Publish as PDF or XPS dialog box.
- Navigate to the desired save location (Publish as PDF or XPS dialog box).

Q&A **Can the file name be the same for the Word document and the PDF file?**
Yes. The file names can be the same because the file types (and the file extensions) are different: one is a Word document and the other is a PDF file.

- If necessary, click the 'Save as type' arrow and then click PDF.
- If necessary, place a check mark in the 'Open file after publishing' check box so that Word will display the resulting PDF file in Adobe Reader (Figure 5–55).

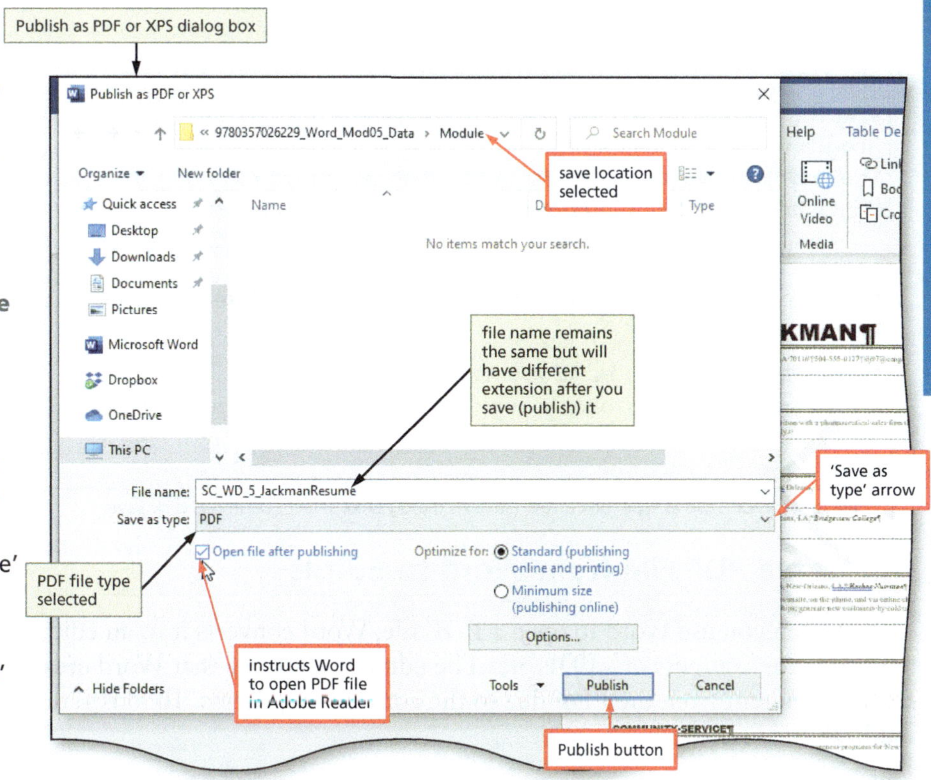

Figure 5–55

Q&A **Why is my 'Open file after publishing' check box dimmed?**
You do not have Adobe Reader installed on your computer. Use a search engine, such as Google, to search for the text, get adobe reader. Then, click the link in the search results to download Adobe Reader and follow the on-screen instructions to install the program. After installing Adobe Reader, repeat these steps.

3

- Click the Publish button to create the PDF file from the Word document and then, because the check box was selected, open the resulting PDF file in Adobe Reader.
- If necessary, click the Maximize button in the Adobe Reader window to maximize the window (Figure 5–56). Note that your screen may differ depending on your version of Adobe Reader.

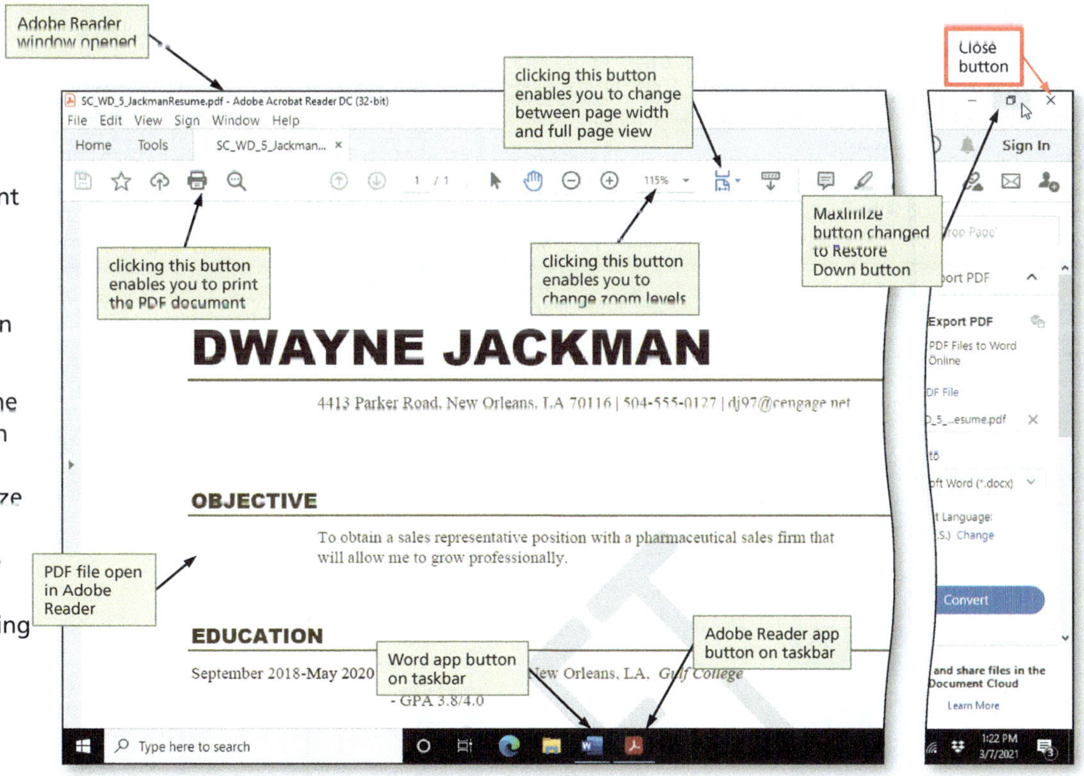

Figure 5–56

Q&A **Do I have to display the resulting PDF file in Adobe Reader?**
No. If you do not want to display the document in Adobe Reader, you would not place a check mark in the 'Open file after publishing' check box in the Publish as PDF or XPS dialog box (shown in Figure 5–55).

Q&A **Is the Jackman Resume Word document still open?**
Yes. Word still is running with the Jackman Resume document opened.

What if a blank screen appears instead of Adobe Reader or if the document appears in a different program?
You may not have Adobe Reader installed. Press the Start key on the keyboard to redisplay the Start screen and then navigate back to Word, or close the program in which the document opened.

4

- Click the Close button on the Adobe Reader title bar to close the SC_WD_5_JackmanResume.pdf file and exit Adobe Reader.

Q&A **Can I edit documents in Adobe Reader?**
No, you need Adobe Acrobat or some other program that enables editing of PDF files.

Other Ways

1. Press F12, click 'Save as type' box arrow (Save As dialog box), select PDF in list, click Save

To Open a PDF File from Word to Edit It

When you use Word to open a PDF file, Word converts it to an editable document. **Why?** You may want to change the contents of a PDF file. The editable PDF file that Word creates from the PDF file may appear slightly different from the PDF due to the conversion process. To illustrate this feature, the following steps open the PDF file just saved.

1

- Open Backstage view and then click Open in Backstage view to display the Open screen.
- Click OneDrive, This PC, or another location in the left pane that references the location of the saved PDF file, click Browse, and then navigate to the location of the PDF file to be opened.
- If necessary, click the File Type arrow (Open dialog box) to display a list of file types that can be opened by Word (Figure 5–57).

Q&A **Why does the PDF file already appear in my list?**
If the file type is All Word Documents, Word displays all file types that it can open in the file list.

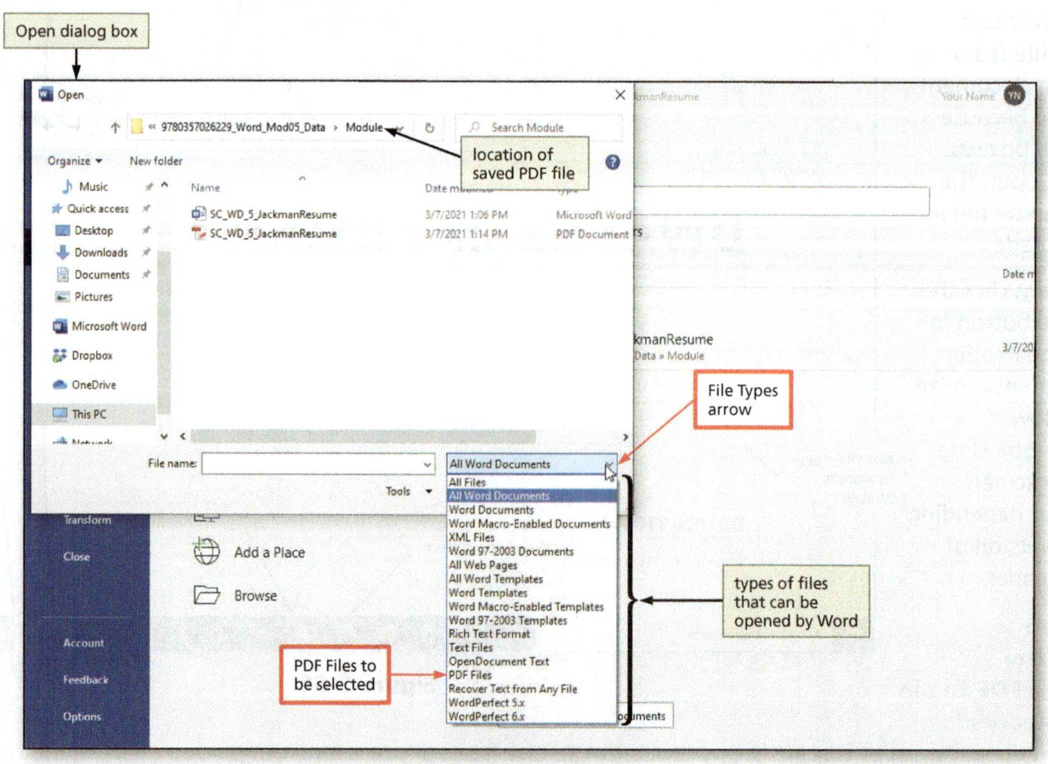

Figure 5–57

2

- Click PDF Files in the File Type list, so that Word displays PDF file names in the dialog box.
- Click SC_WD_5_JackmanResume to select the PDF file to be opened (Figure 5–58). (Depending on settings, the file name box may show the .pdf extension after the file name.)

3

- Click the Open button (Open dialog box) to open the selected file and display the opened document in the Word window.
- If Word displays a dialog box indicating it will begin converting the document, click OK.

4

- If necessary, click the Print Layout button on the status bar to switch to Print Layout view.

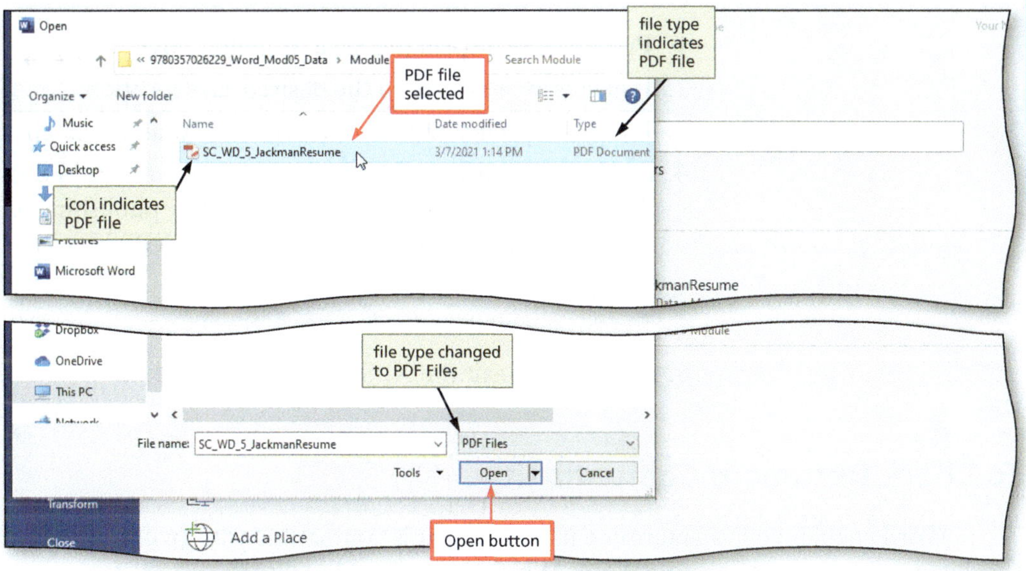

Figure 5–58

Experiment

- Scroll through the PDF that Word converted, noticing any differences between it and the original resume created in this module. Change a word in the document to practice editing it.
- Close the Word window and do not save this converted PDF file.

To Export a Word Document to an XPS Document

XPS, which stands for XML Paper Specification, is a file format created by Microsoft that shows all elements of a printed document as an electronic image. As with the PDF format, users can view an XPS document without the software that created the original document. Thus, the XPS format also enables users to share documents with others easily. Windows includes an XPS Viewer, which enables you to view, navigate, and print XPS files.

When you save a Word document as an XPS document, the original Word document remains intact; that is, Word creates a copy of the file in the XPS format. If you wanted to save a Word document as an XPS document, you would perform the following steps.

1. Open Backstage view and then click Export in Backstage view to display the Export screen.
2. Click 'Create PDF/XPS Document' in the left pane of the Export screen to display information about PDF/XPS documents in the right pane and then click the 'Create PDF/XPS' button to display the Publish as PDF or XPS dialog box.
3. If necessary, navigate to the desired save location.

BTW

Distributing a Document

Instead of printing and distributing a hard copy of a document, you can distribute the document electronically. Options include sending the document via email; posting it on cloud storage (such as OneDrive) and sharing the file with others, posting it on social media, a blog, or other website; and sharing a link associated with an online location of the document. You also can create and share a PDF or XPS image of the document, so that users can view the file in Acrobat Reader or XPS Viewer instead of in Word.

4. If necessary, click the 'Save as type' arrow and then click XPS Document.
5. Click the Publish or Save button to create the XPS document from the Word document and then, if the 'Open file after publishing' check box was selected, open the resulting XPS document in the XPS Viewer.

or

1. Press F12 to display the Save As dialog box.
2. If necessary, navigate to the desired save location.
3. If necessary, click the 'Save as type' arrow and then click XPS Document.
4. Click the Publish or Save button to create the XPS document from the Word document and then, if the 'Open file after publishing' check box was selected, open the resulting XPS document in the XPS Viewer.

Q&A **What if I do not have an XPS Viewer?**
The document will open in a browser window.

5. If necessary, exit the XPS Viewer.

To Check Document Compatibility

Word enables you to determine if a document is compatible with (will work with) versions earlier than the current version of Microsoft Word. **Why?** If you would like to save a document, such as your resume, in the Word 97-2003 format so that it can be opened by users with earlier versions of Microsoft Word, you want to ensure that all of its elements (such as building blocks, content controls, and graphics) are compatible with earlier versions of Word. The following steps run the compatibility checker.

1

- Open Backstage view and then, if necessary, click Info in Backstage view to display the Info screen.
- Click the 'Check for Issues' button in the Info screen to display the Check for Issues menu (Figure 5–59).

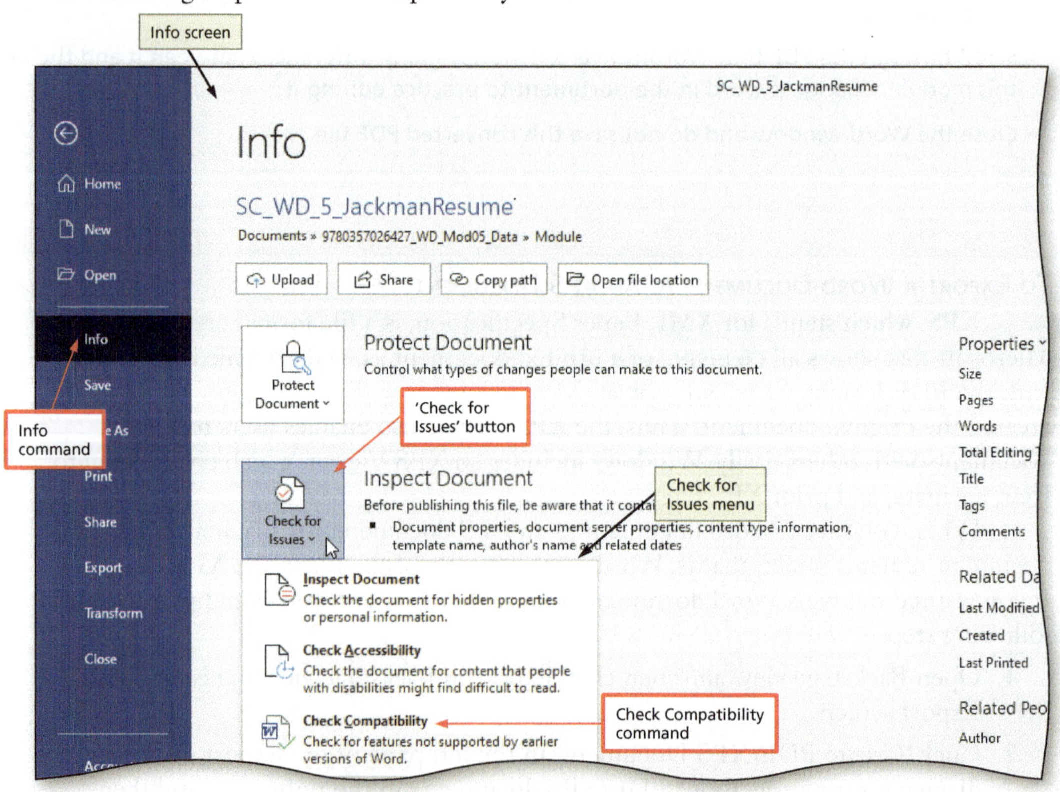

Figure 5–59

2

- Click Check Compatibility on the Check for Issues menu to display the Microsoft Word Compatibility Checker dialog box, which shows any content that may not be supported by earlier versions of Word (Figure 5–60).

3

- Click OK (Microsoft Word Compatibility Checker dialog box) to close the dialog box.

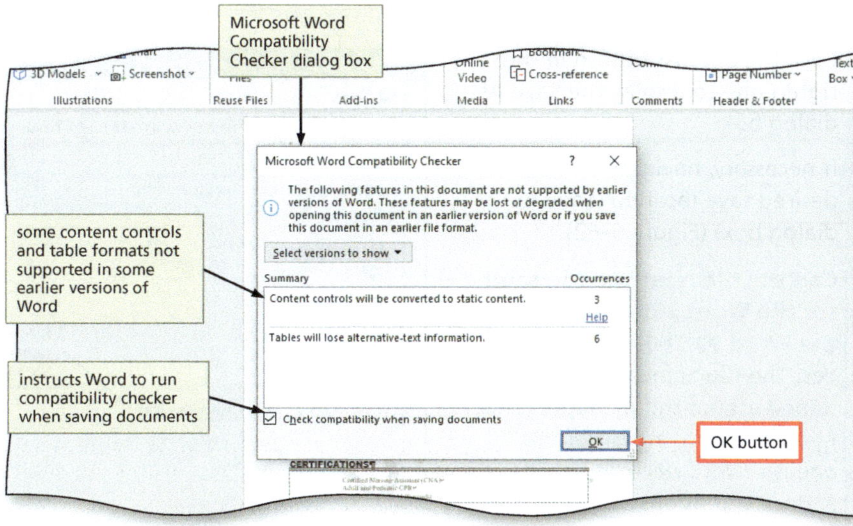

Figure 5–60

To Save a Word 365 Document in an Earlier Word Format

If you send a document created in Word 365 to users who have a version of Word earlier than Word 2007, they will not be able to open the Word 365 document. **Why?** Word 365 saves documents in a format that is not backward compatible with versions earlier than Word 2007. Word 365 documents have a file type of .docx, and versions prior to Word 2007 have a .doc file type. To ensure that all Word users can open your Word 365 document, you should save the document in a Word 97-2003 format. The following steps save the Word 365 format of the SC_WD_5_JackmanResume.docx document in the Word 97-2003 format.

1

- Open Backstage view and then click Export in Backstage view to display the Export screen.
- Click 'Change File Type' in the left pane of the Export screen to display information in the right pane about various Word file types.
- Click 'Word 97-2003 Document' in the right pane to specify the new file type (Figure 5–61).

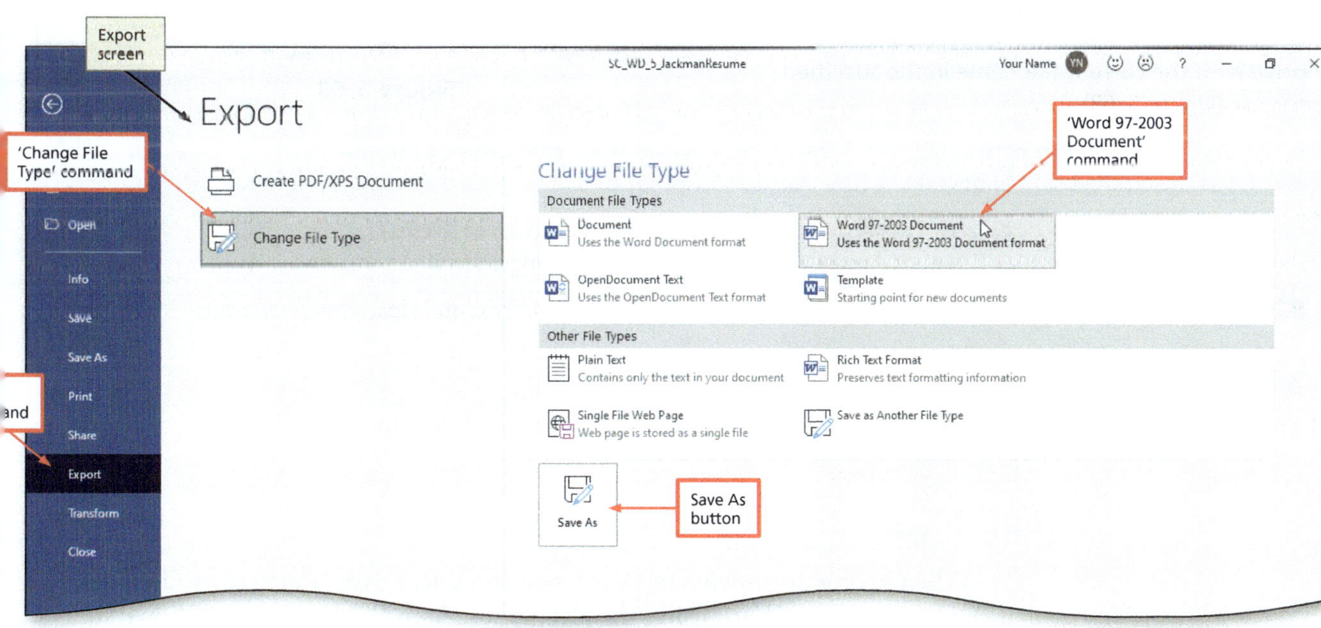

Figure 5–61

2

- Click the Save As button in the right pane to display the Save As dialog box.
- If necessary, navigate to the desired save location (Save As dialog box) (Figure 5–62).

Q&A **Can the file name be the same for the Word 365 document and the Word 97-2003 document?**
Yes. The file names can be the same because the file types (and file extensions) are different: one is a Word document with a .docx extension, and the other is a Word document with a .doc extension. The next section discusses file types and extensions.

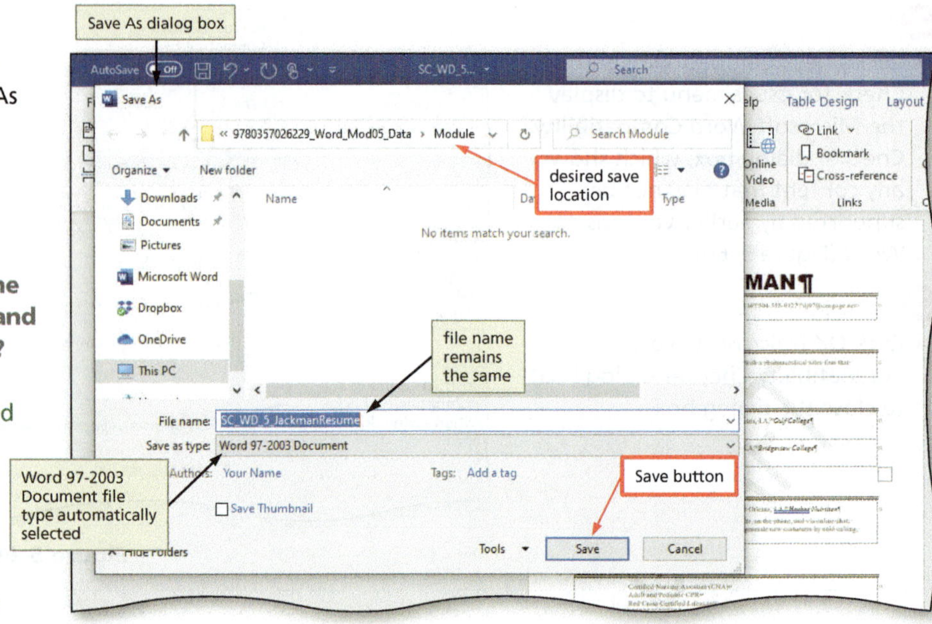

Figure 5–62

3

- Click Save, which may display the Microsoft Word Compatibility Checker dialog box before saving the document (shown in Figure 5–60).

Q&A **My screen did not display the Microsoft Word Compatibility Checker dialog box. Why not?**
If the 'Check compatibility when saving documents' check box is not selected (as shown in Figure 5–60), Word will not check compatibility when saving a document.

- If the Microsoft Word Compatibility Checker dialog box is displayed, click its Continue button to save the document on the selected drive with the current file name in the specified format (Figure 5–63).

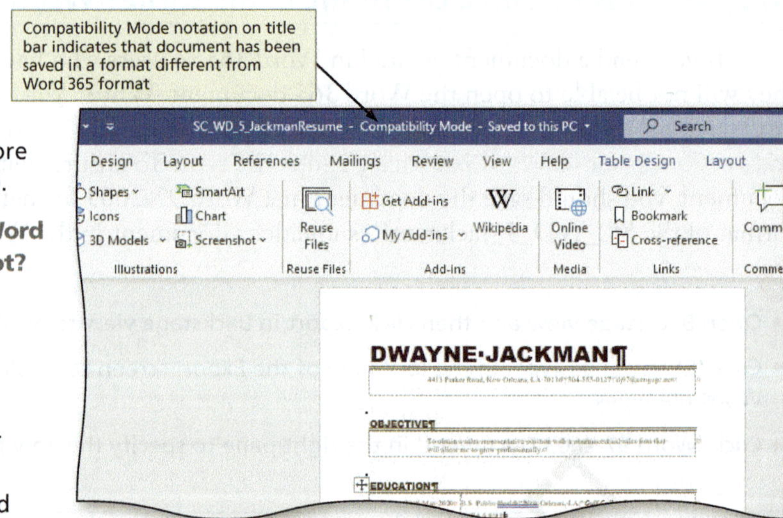

Figure 5–63

Q&A **Is the Word 365 format of the SC_WD_5_JackmanResume.docx document still open?**
No. Word closed the original document (the Word 365 format of the SC_WD_5_JackmanResume.docx).

Can I use Word 365 to open a document created in an earlier version of Word?
Yes, but you may notice that the appearance of the document differs when opened in Word 365.

- **sam** Because you are finished with the Word 97-2003 format of the resume, close the document.

Other Ways

1. Press F12, click 'Save as type' arrow (Save As dialog box), select 'Word 97-2003 Document' in list, click Save

File Types

When saving documents in Word, you can select from a variety of file types that can be opened in Word using the Export screen in Backstage view (shown in Figure 5–61) or by clicking the 'Save as type' arrow in the Save As dialog box. To save in these varied formats (Table 5–1), you follow the same basic steps as just illustrated.

Table 5–1 File Types

File Type	File Extension	File Explorer Image	Description
OpenDocument Text	.odt		Format used by other word processing programs, such as Google Docs and OpenOffice.org
PDF	.pdf		Portable Document Format, which can be opened in Adobe Reader
Plain Text	.txt		Format where all or most formatting is removed from the document
Rich Text Format	.rtf		Format designed to ensure file can be opened and read in many programs; some formatting may be lost to ensure compatibility
Single File Web Page	.mht		HTML (Hypertext Markup Language) format that can be opened in a browser; all elements of the webpage are saved in a single file
Web Page	.htm		HTML format that can be opened in a browser; various elements of the webpage, such as graphics, saved in separate files and folders
Word 97-2003 Document	.doc		Format used for documents created in versions of Word from Word 97 to Word 2003
Word 97-2003 Template	.dot		Format used for templates created in versions of Word from Word 97 and Word 2003
Word Document	.docx		Format used for Word 2019, Word 2016, Word 2013, Word 2010, or Word 2007 documents
Word Template	.dotx		Format used for Word 2019, Word 2016, Word 2013, Word 2010, or Word 2007 templates
XPS	.xps		XML (Extensible Markup Language) Paper Specification, which can be opened in the XPS Viewer

To Save a Word 365 Document as a Different File Type

To save a Word 365 document as a different file type, you would follow these steps.

1. Open Backstage view and then click Export in Backstage view to display the Export screen.
2. Click 'Change File Type' in the Export screen to display information in the right pane about various file types that can be opened in Word.
3. Click the desired file type in the right pane and then click the Save As button to display the Save As dialog box.
4. Navigate to the desired save location (Save As dialog box) and then click Save in the dialog box.
5. If the Microsoft Word Compatibility Checker dialog box appears and you agree with the changes that will be made to the document, click the Continue button (Microsoft Word Compatibility Checker dialog box) to save the document on the selected drive with the current file name in the specified format.

BTW

Word Help

At any time while using Word, you can find answers to questions and display information about various topics through Word Help. Used properly, this form of assistance can increase your productivity and reduce your frustrations by minimizing the time you spend learning how to use Word.

To Share a Document on OneDrive

If you have a OneDrive account, you can share a Word document saved on OneDrive with others through email message invitations. **Why?** Invited users can click a link in an email message that displays a webpage enabling them to view or edit the document on OneDrive. The following steps invite a user to view the resume. If you do not have a Microsoft account or an Internet connection, read these steps without performing them.

1

- If necessary, start Word. Open the Word 365 format of the SC_WD_5_JackmanResume.docx file and then save the resume document on OneDrive.
- Click the Share button in the upper-right corner of the ribbon to open the Share pane (Figure 5–64).

Q&A **Why does a Share dialog box appear instead of a Send link dialog box?**
The document has not been saved on OneDrive and/or you are not signed in to your Microsoft account.

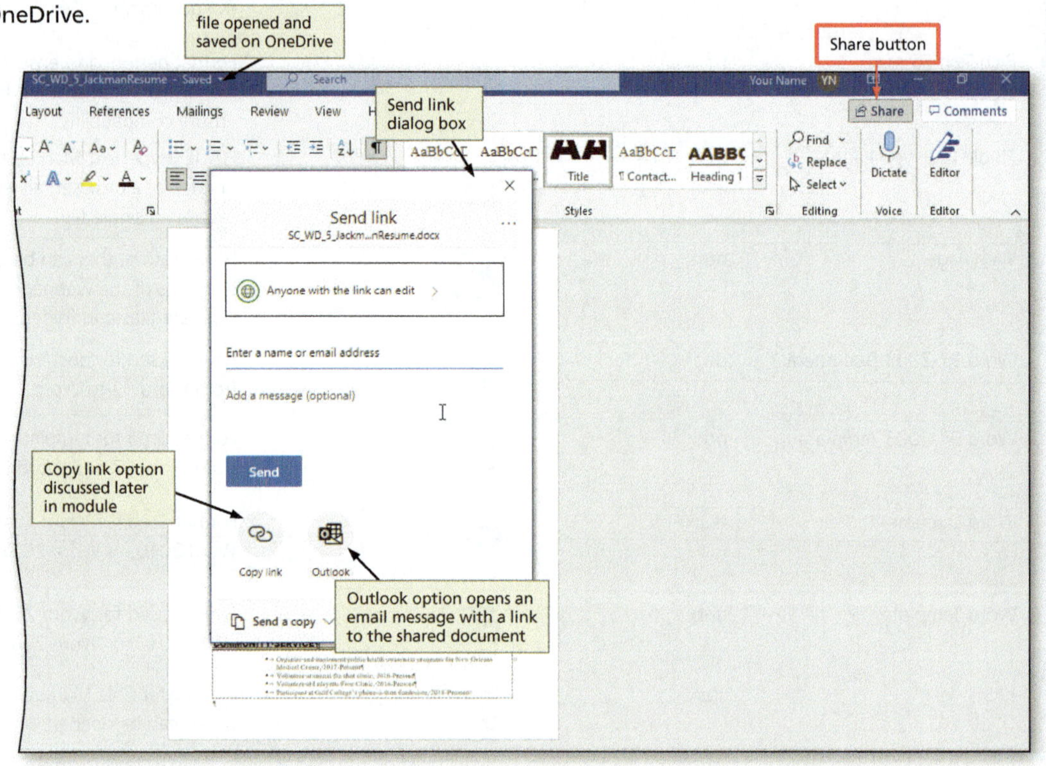

Figure 5–64

2

- In the Send link dialog box, type the email address(es) of the person(s) with whom you want to share the document, click the box arrow so that you can specify Can edit, if necessary, and then type a message to the recipient(s) (Figure 5–65).

3

- Click the Send button (Send link dialog box) to send the message along with a link to the document on OneDrive to the listed recipient(s) and then close the confirmation message.

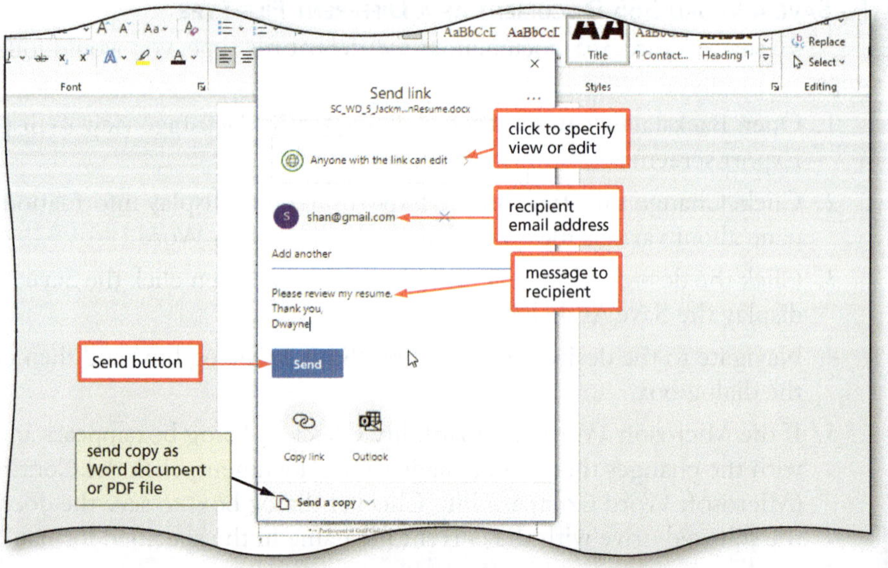

Figure 5–65

Other Ways

1. Open Backstage view, click Share, select desired sharing options

Consider This

How does a recipient access the shared document?

The recipient receives an email message that indicates it contains a link to a shared document (Figure 5–66). When the recipient clicks the link in the email message, the document opens in Word Online on OneDrive (Figure 5–67).

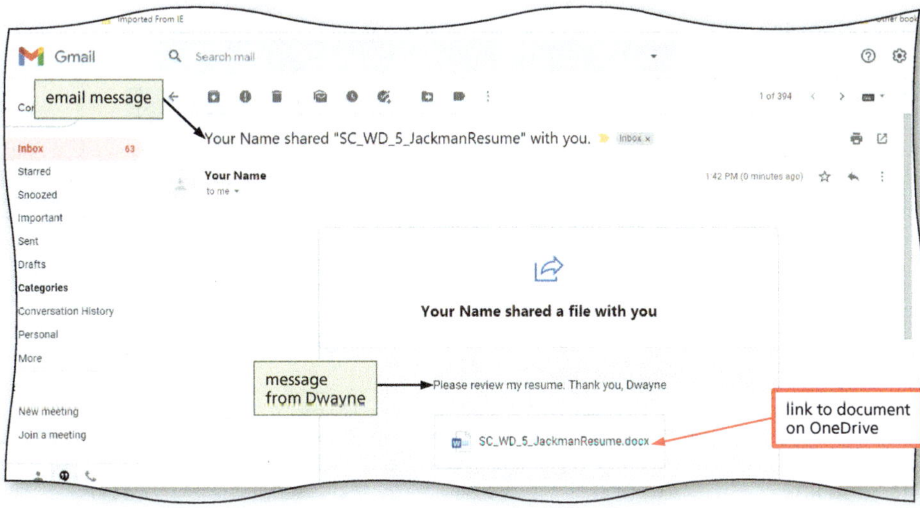

Figure 5–66

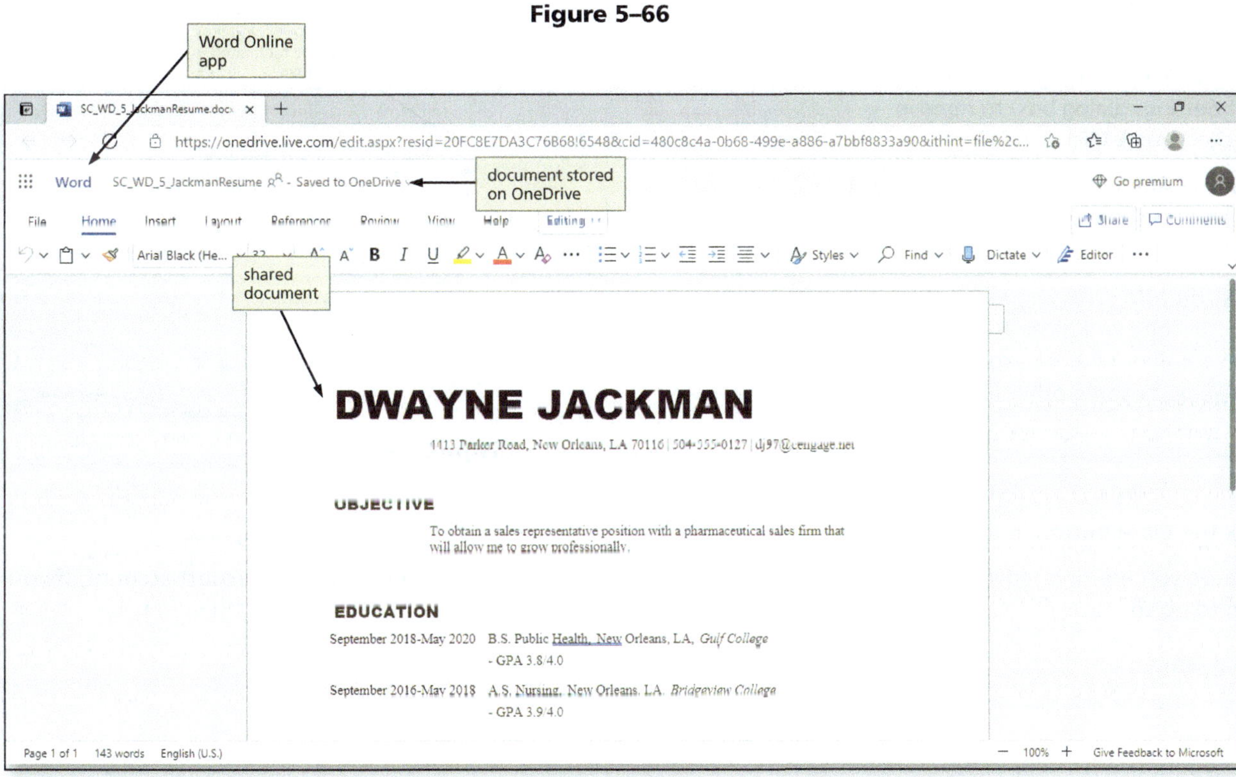

Figure 5–67

To Get a Sharing Link

Why share a link? Instead of inviting people to view or edit a document, you can create a link to the document's location on OneDrive and then send others the link via an email message or text message, post it on a website or online social network, or communicate it via some other means. The following steps get a sharing link. If you do not have a Microsoft account or an Internet connection, read these steps without performing them.

1

- If necessary, click the Share button in the upper-right corner of the ribbon to display the Send link dialog box and then click the Copy link at the bottom of the Send link dialog box (shown in Figure 5–64) to display options for obtaining a link to a document on OneDrive in the Send link dialog box (Figure 5–68).

Q&A **Why does a Share dialog box appear instead of a Send link dialog box?**
The document has not been saved on OneDrive and/or you are not signed in to your Microsoft account.

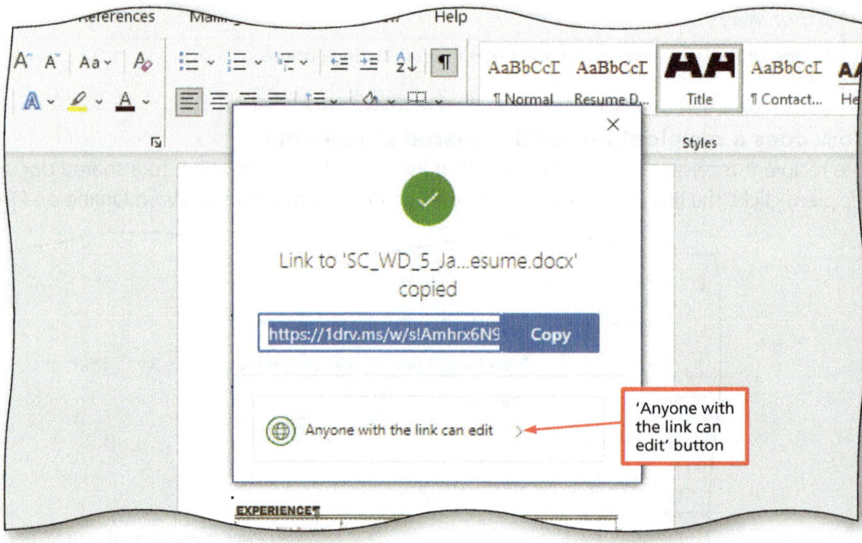

Figure 5–68

2

- Click the 'Anyone with a link can edit' button in the Send link dialog box to display the Link settings dialog box.
- Click the Allow editing check box (Link Settings dialog box) to remove the check mark (Figure 5-69).
- Click the Apply button to create the link associated with the file on OneDrive.

Q&A **What do I do with the link?**
You can copy and paste the link in an email or text message, on a webpage, or some other location.

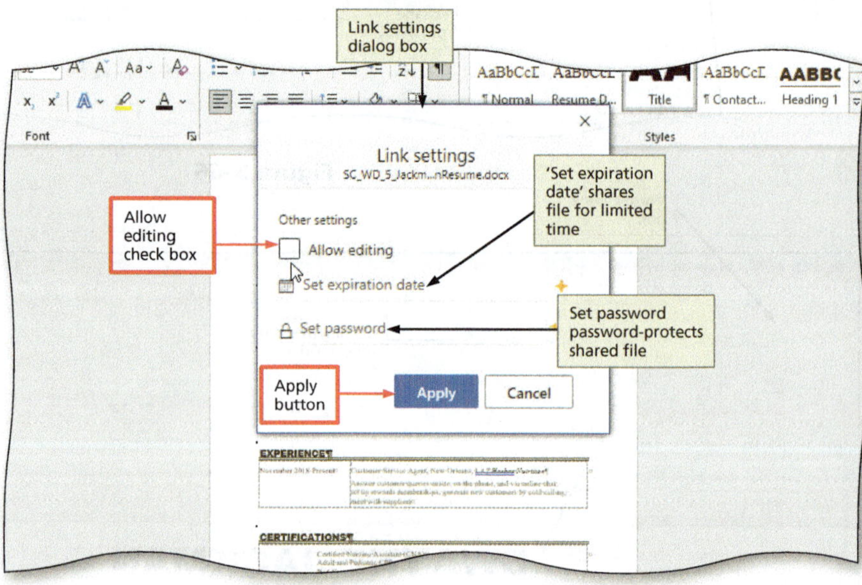

Figure 5–69

3

- Click the Close button in the upper-right corner of the Send link dialog box to close the dialog box.
- Because you are finished working with the resume on OneDrive, you can sign out of your Microsoft account, if you wish to do so.

Other Ways

1. Open Backstage view, click Share, select desired sharing options

To Remove a Watermark

The following steps remove the DRAFT watermark from the resume in the document window, if it was saved with the document, because you now consider the document final and would like to distribute it to potential employers.

1. If necessary, open the SC_WD_5_JackmanResume (Word 365 format).
2. Display the Design tab.

3 Click the Watermark button (Design tab | Page Background group) to display the Watermark gallery.

4 Click Remove Watermark in the Watermark gallery to remove the watermark.

5 Save the resume again with the same file name.

Consider This

What file type should you use when emailing documents?
If you email a document, such as your resume, consider that the recipient, such as a potential employer, may not have the same software you used to create the resume and, thus, may not be able to open the file. As an alternative, you could save the file in a format, such as a PDF or XPS, that can be viewed with a reader program. Many job seekers also post their resumes on the web.

To Send a Document Using Email

In Word, you can include the current document as an attachment to an email message. An attachment is a file included with an email message. The following steps send the resume as an email attachment, assuming you use Outlook as your default email program. **Why?** When you attach an email document from within Word, it automatically uses the default email program, which is Outlook in this case.

1

- Click Share in the upper-right corner of the ribbon to display a Share dialog box (if your document is saved on local media) or the Send link dialog box (if your document is saved on OneDrive) (Figure 5–70).

Q&A

What if the Send as link dialog box appears?
Click the 'Send a copy' button at the bottom of the dialog box and then click Word document.

What is the purpose of the PDF button?
Word converts the current document to the PDF format and then attaches the PDF to the email message.

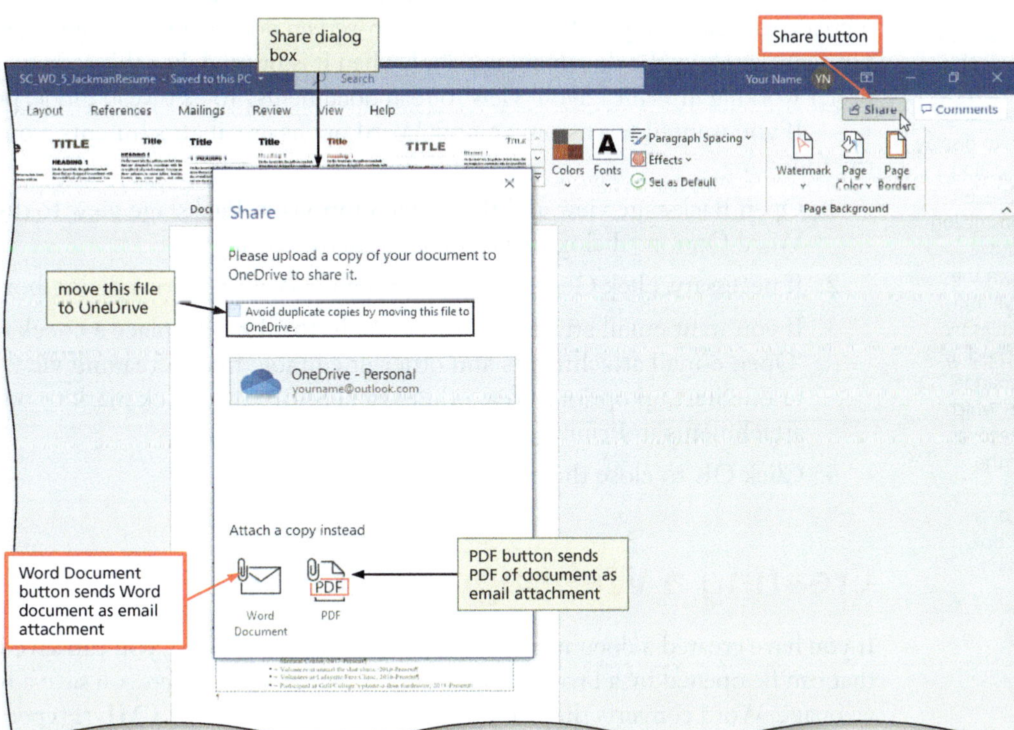

Figure 5–70

2

- Click the Word Document button (Share dialog box) to start your default email program (Outlook, in this case), which automatically attaches the active Word document to the email message (or click the 'Send a copy' link if your screen displays the Send link dialog box).
- Fill in the To text box with the recipient's email address.
- Fill in the message text (Figure 5–71).

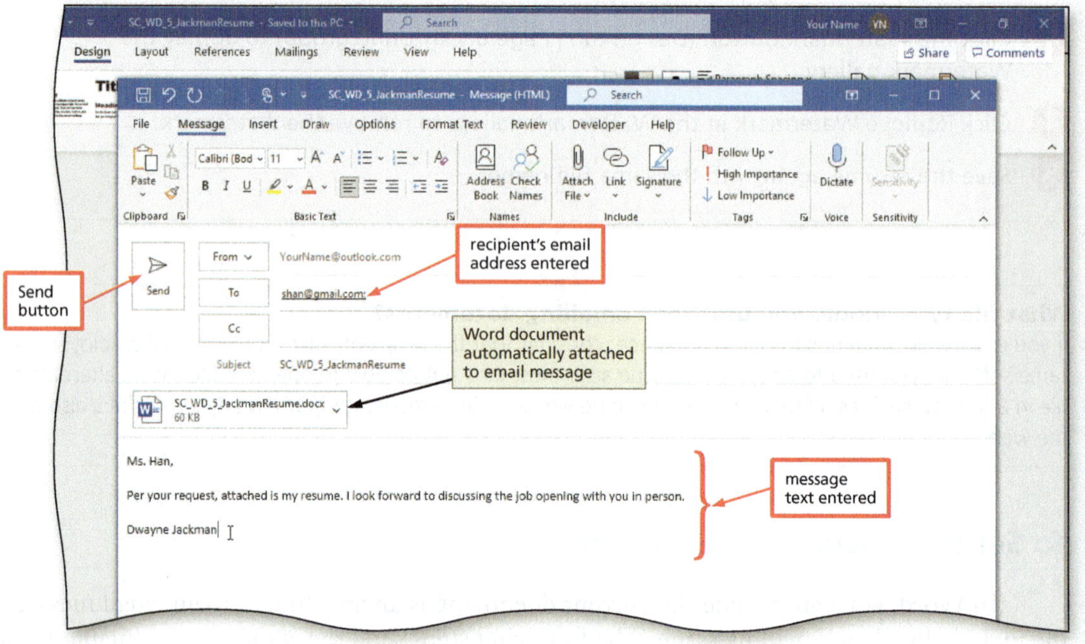

Figure 5–71

3

- Click the Send button to send the email message along with its attachment to the recipient named in the To text box and then close the email window.

BTW
AutoSave and AutoRecover
If you do not want Word to save files automatically on OneDrive, you can disable this option by doing the following: open Backstage view, click Options to display the Word Options dialog box, click Save in the left pane (Word Options dialog box), and then remove the check mark from the 'AutoSave OneDrive and SharePoint Online files by default on Word' check box. If you wanted to change the frequency with which Word saves AutoRecover information, enter the number of minutes in the 'Save AutoRecover information every' box.

To Customize How Word Opens Email Attachments

When a user sends you an email message that contains a Word document as an attachment, Word may display the document in Read mode. This view is designed to increase the readability and legibility of an on-screen document. Read mode, however, does not represent how the document will look when it is printed. For this reason, many users prefer working in Print Layout view to read documents. To exit Read mode, press ESC.

If you wanted to customize how Word opens email attachments, you would do the following.

1. Open Backstage view and then click Options in Backstage view to display the Word Options dialog box.
2. If necessary, click General in the left pane (Word Options dialog box).
3. If you want email attachments to open in Read mode, place a check mark in the 'Open e-mail attachments and other uneditable files in reading view' check box in the Start up options area; otherwise, remove the check mark to open email attachments in Print Layout view.
4. Click OK to close the dialog box.

Creating a Webpage from a Word Document

If you have created a document, such as a resume, using Word, you can save it in a format that can be opened by a browser, such as Microsoft Edge. When you save a file as a webpage, Word converts the contents of the document into **HTML** (Hypertext Markup Language), which is a special language that software developers use to create and format webpage elements. Some of Word's formatting features are not supported by webpages. Thus, your webpage may look slightly different from the original Word document.

When saving a document as a webpage, Word provides you with three choices:

- The **single file web page format** saves all of the components of the webpage in a single file that has a **.mht** extension. This format is particularly useful for sending documents via email in HTML format.
- The **web page format** saves some of the components of the webpage in a folder, separate from the webpage. This format is useful if you need access to the individual components, such as images, that make up the webpage.
- The **filtered web page format** saves the file in webpage format and then reduces the size of the file by removing specific Microsoft Office formats. This format is useful if you want to speed up the time it takes to download a webpage that contains graphics, video, audio, or animations.

The webpage created in this section uses the single file web page format.

To Save a Word Document as a Webpage

The following steps save the resume created earlier in this module as a webpage. **Why?** You intend to post your resume online.

1

- If necessary, open the Word 365 format of the resume file. Open Backstage view and then click Export in Backstage view to display the Export screen.
- Click 'Change File Type' in the left pane of the Export screen to display information in the right pane about various file types that are supported by Word.
- Click 'Single File Web Page' in the right pane to specify a new file type (Figure 5–72).

Q&A **What if I wanted to save the document as a web page instead of a single file web page?**
You would click 'Save as Another File Type' in the Change File Type area, click the Save As button, click the 'Save as type' arrow in the Save As dialog box, and then click Web Page in the Save as type list.

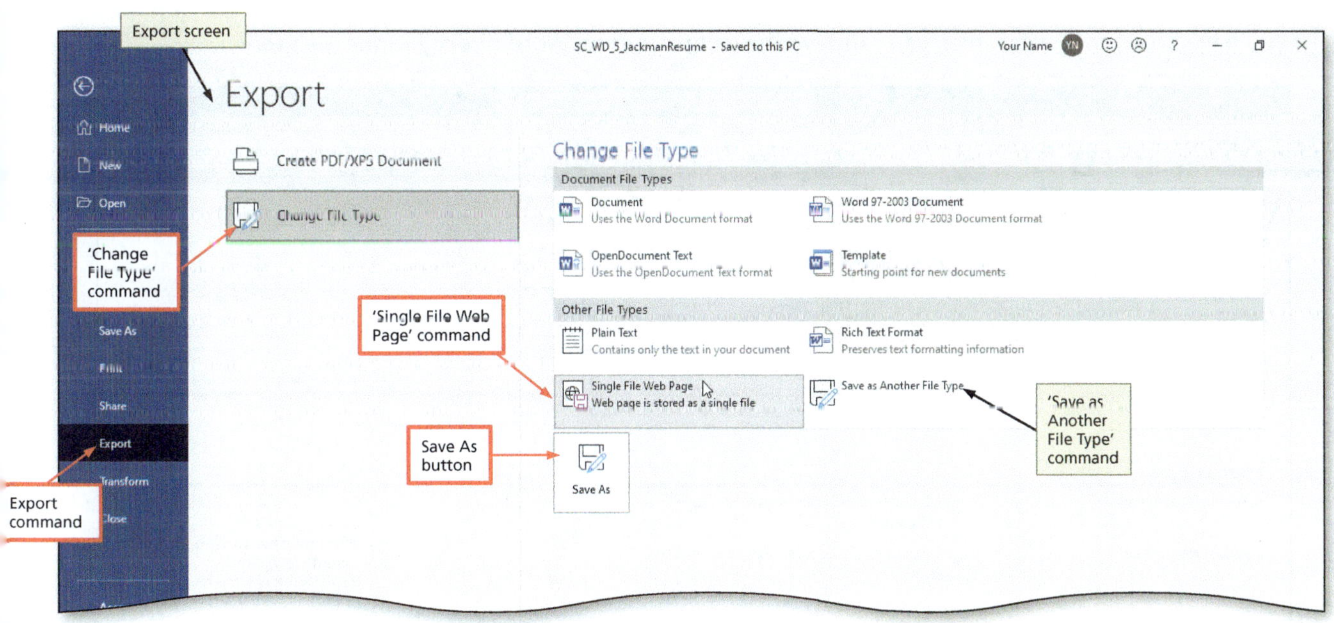

Figure 5–72

2

- Click the Save As button in the right pane to display the Save As dialog box.
- If necessary, navigate to the desired save location (Save As dialog box).
- If necessary, type `SC_WD_5_JackmanResume` in the File name box to change the file name.
- Click the Change Title button to display the Enter Text dialog box.
- Type `Jackman Resume` in the Page title text box (Enter Text dialog box) (Figure 5–73).

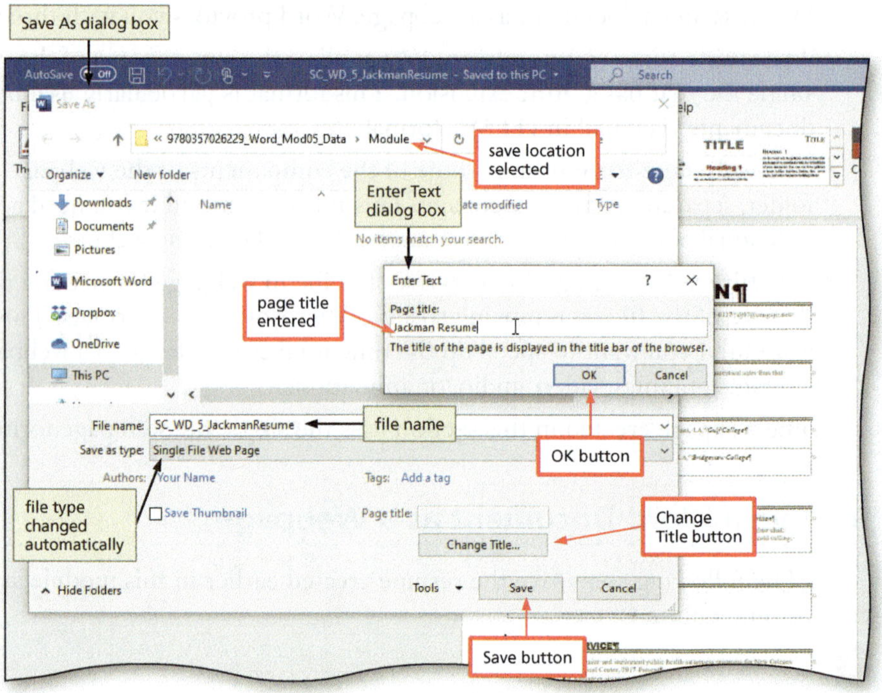

Figure 5–73

3

- Click OK (Enter Text dialog box) to close the dialog box.
- Click Save (Save As dialog box) to save the resume as a webpage and then display it in the document window in Web Layout view.
- If necessary, change the zoom to 100% (Figure 5–74).
- If the Microsoft Word Compatibility Checker dialog box appears, click its Continue button.

Q&A

Can I switch to Web Layout view at any time by clicking the Web Layout button on the taskbar?
Yes.

Can I save the webpage to a web server?
If you have access to a web server, you can save the webpage from Word directly to the web server.

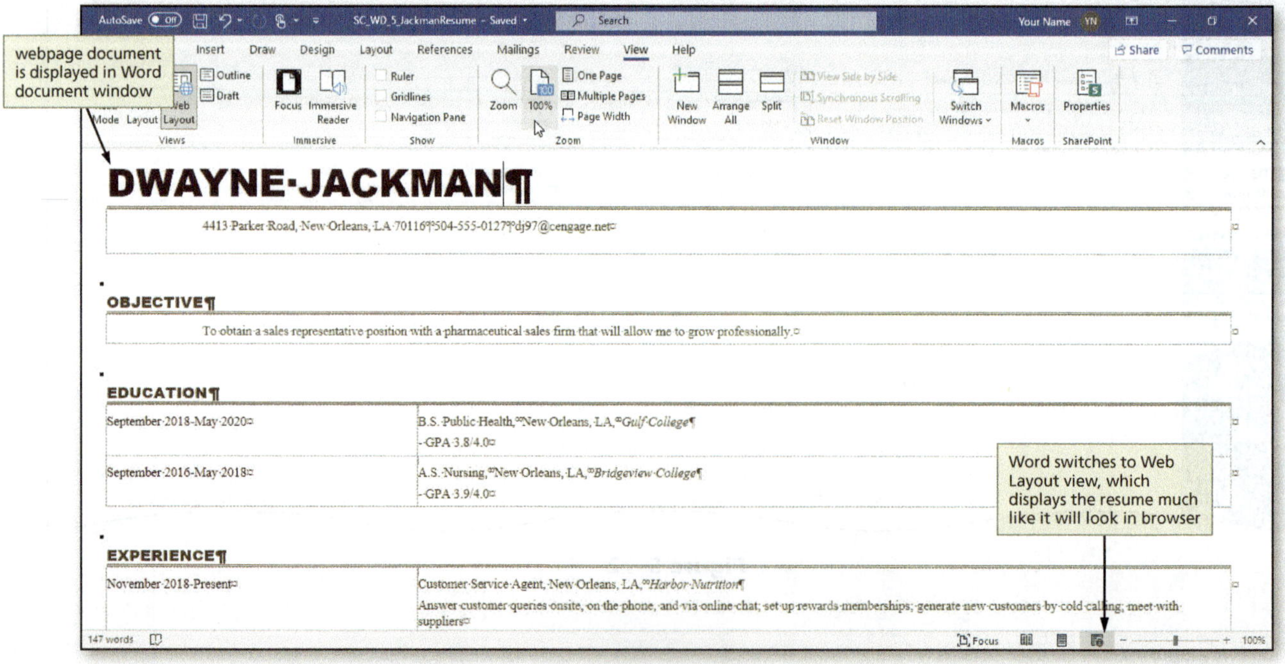

Figure 5–74

To Set a Default Save Location

If you wanted to change the default location that Word uses when it saves a document, you would do the following.

1. Open Backstage view and then click Options in Backstage view to display the Word Options dialog box.
2. Click Save in the left pane (Word Options dialog box) to display options for saving documents in the right pane.
3. In the 'Default local file location' text box, type the new desired save location.
4. Click OK to close the dialog box.

To Format Text as a Hyperlink

The email address in the resume webpage should be formatted as a hyperlink. **Why?** When webpage visitors click the hyperlink-formatted email address, you want their email program to run automatically and open an email window with the email address already filled in. The following steps format the email address as a hyperlink.

1

- Select the email address in the resume webpage (dj97@cengage.net, in this case).
- Display the Insert tab.
- Click the Link button (Insert tab | Links group) to display the Insert Hyperlink dialog box (Figure 5–75).

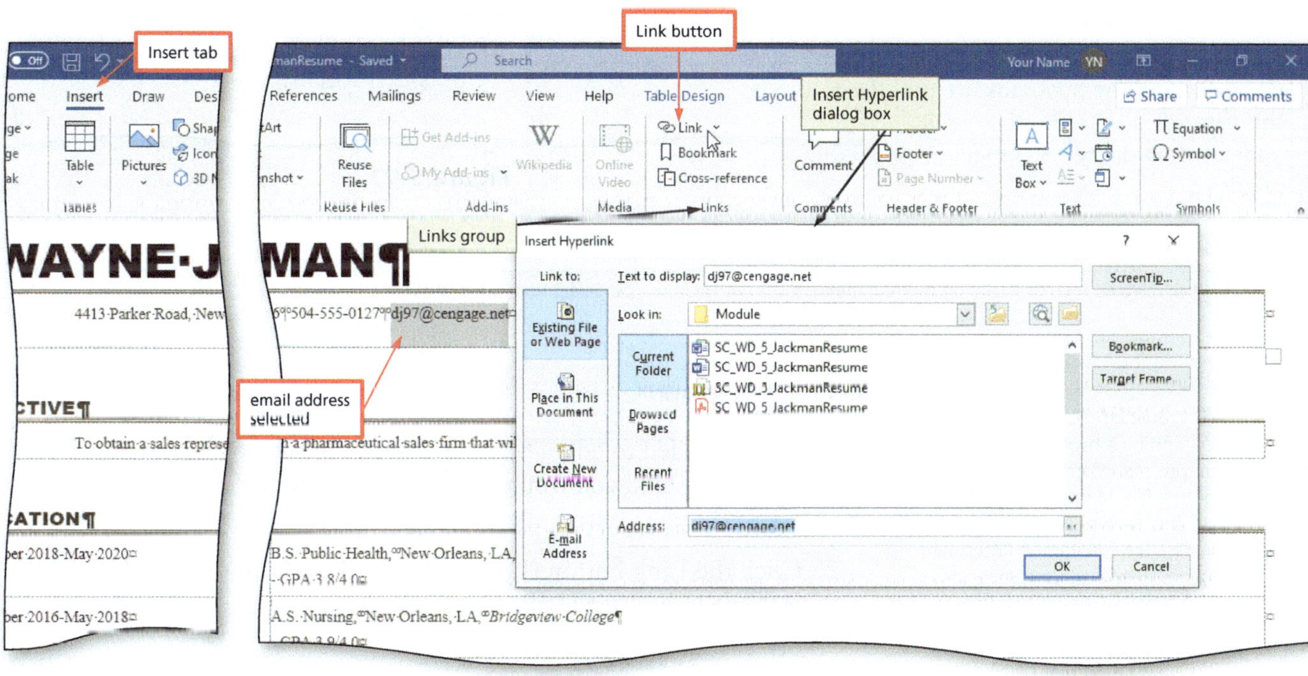

Figure 5–75

2

- Click E-mail Address in the Link to bar (Insert Hyperlink dialog box) so that the dialog box displays email address settings instead of webpage settings.
- In the E-mail address text box, type `dj97@cengage.net` to specify the email address that the browser uses when a user clicks the hyperlink.

Q&A **Can I change the text that automatically appeared in the 'Text to display' text box?**
Yes. Word assumes that the hyperlink text should be the same as the email address, so as soon as you enter the email address, the same text is entered in the 'Text to display' text box.

- If the email address in the 'Text to display' text box is preceded by the text, mailto:, delete this leading text because you want only the email address to appear in the document.
- Click the ScreenTip button to display the Set Hyperlink ScreenTip dialog box.
- Type **Send email message to Dwayne Jackman.** in the 'ScreenTip text' text box (Set Hyperlink ScreenTip dialog box) to specify the text that will be displayed when a user points to the hyperlink (Figure 5–76).

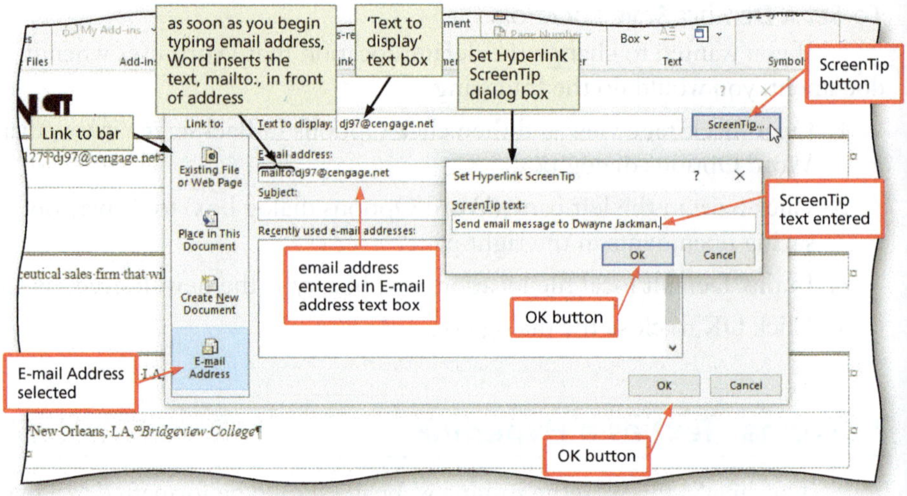

Figure 5–76

3

- Click OK in each dialog box to format the email address as a hyperlink (Figure 5–77).

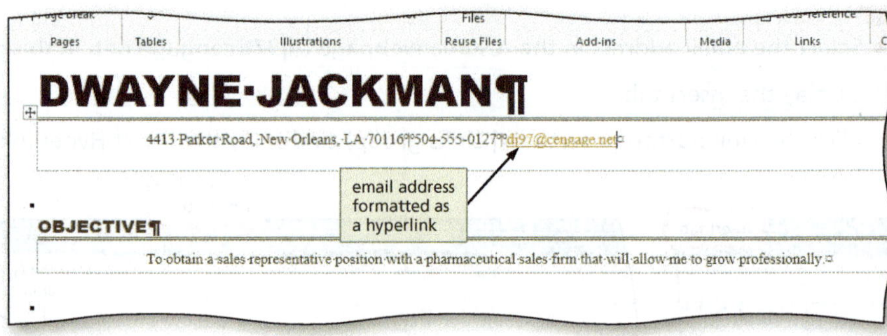

Figure 5–77

Q&A **How do I know if the hyperlink works?**
In Word, you can test the hyperlink by holding down CTRL while clicking the hyperlink. In this case, CTRL+clicking the email address should open an email window.

Other Ways

1. Right-click selected text, click Link on shortcut menu
2. Select text, press CTRL+K

BTW
Inserting Hyperlinks
In addition to inserting a hyperlink to an email address, you can insert a hyperlink to a webpage or to a file. To insert a hyperlink to a webpage, enter and select the text to be the hyperlink, click the Link button (Insert tab | Links group) to display the Insert Hyperlink dialog box, click 'Existing File or Web Page' in the Link to bar (Insert Hyperlink dialog box), be sure the web address is correct in the Address text box, and then click OK. To insert a hyperlink to a file, follow the same steps except select the location of the file instead of entering a web address in the Address text box.

To Edit a Hyperlink

If you needed to edit a hyperlink, for example, to change its ScreenTip or its link, you would follow these steps.

1. Position the insertion point in the hyperlink.
2. Click the Link button (Insert tab | Links group) or press CTRL+K to display the Edit Hyperlink dialog box.

or

1. Right-click the hyperlink to display a shortcut menu.
2. Click Edit Hyperlink on the shortcut menu to display the Edit Hyperlink dialog box.

To Change the Style Set

Word provides several built-in style sets to help you quickly change the look of an entire document. **Why?** A style set contains formats for fonts and paragraphs. The following steps change the style set to the Shaded style set.

1

- Display the Design tab (Figure 5–78).
- Click the More button (Design tab | Document Formatting group) to display the expanded Style Set gallery.

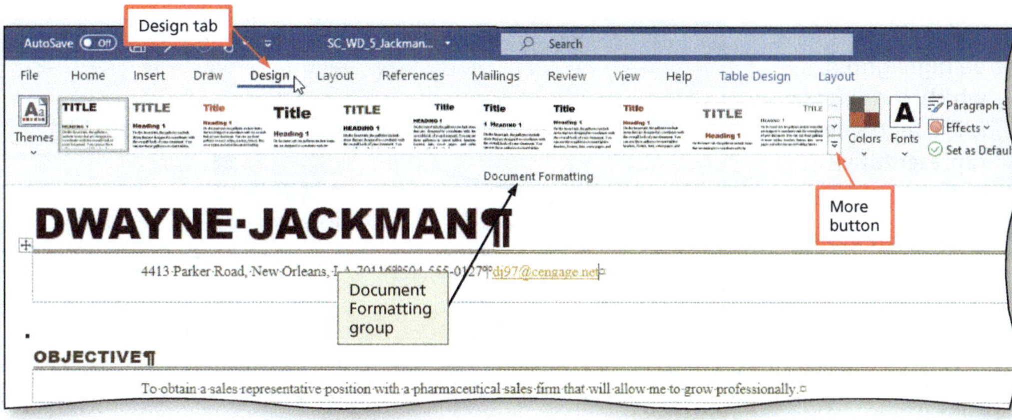

Figure 5–78

2

- Point to Shaded in the Style Set gallery to display a Live Preview of the style set applied to the document (Figure 5–79).

Experiment

- Point to various style sets in the Style Set gallery and watch the font and paragraph formatting change in the document window.

Figure 5–79

3

- Click Shaded to change the style set to the selected style set.

Q&A

Can I create my own style sets?

Yes. Modify the fonts and other formats as desired, click 'Save as a New Style Set' in the expanded Style Set gallery (shown in Figure 5–79), enter the name for the style set (Save as a New Style Set dialog box), and then click Save to create the custom style set. You then can access the custom style set through the Style Set gallery.

To Highlight Text

To emphasize text in an online document, you can highlight it. **Highlighting** alerts a reader to online text's importance, much like a highlighter pen does on a printed page. Word provides 15 colors you can use to highlight text, including the traditional yellow and green, as well as some nontraditional highlight colors, such as gray, dark blue, and dark red. The following steps highlight the job title being sought in the color yellow. **Why?** You want to emphasize this text on the resume.

1

- Select the text to be highlighted, which, in this case, is the text, sales representative position.
- Display the Home tab.
- Click the 'Text Highlight Color' arrow (Home tab | Font group) to display the Text Highlight Color gallery (Figure 5–80).

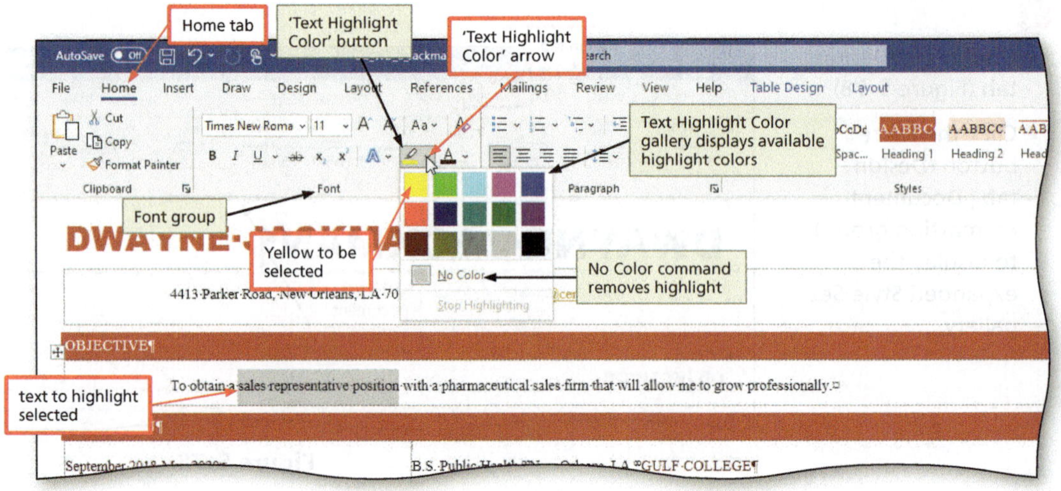

Figure 5–80

Q&A **The Text Highlight Color gallery did not appear. Why not?**
You clicked the 'Text Highlight Color' button instead of the 'Text Highlight Color' arrow. Click the Undo button on the Quick Access Toolbar and then repeat Step 1.

What if the icon on the 'Text Highlight Color' button already displays the color I want to use?
You can click the 'Text Highlight Color' button instead of the arrow.

2

Experiment

- Point to various colors in the Text Highlight Color gallery and watch the highlight color on the selected text change.
- Click Yellow in the Text Highlight Color gallery to highlight the selected text in the selected highlight color (Figure 5–81).

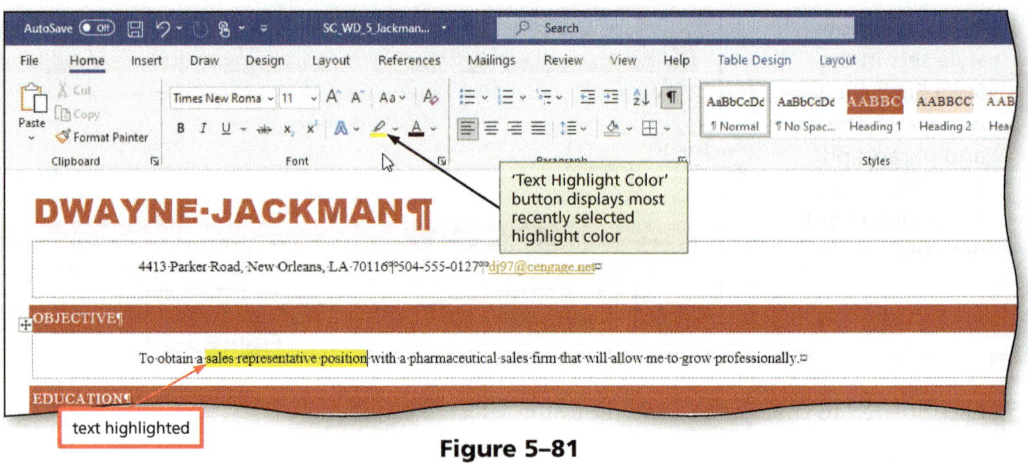

Figure 5–81

- Save the resume webpage again on the same storage location with the same file name and then exit Word.

Q&A **How would I remove a highlight from text?**
Select the highlighted text, click the 'Text Highlight Color' arrow, and then click No Color in the Text Highlight Color gallery.

Other Ways

1. Click 'Text Highlight Color' arrow (Home tab | Font group), select desired color, select text to be highlighted in document, select any additional text to be highlighted, click 'Text Highlight Color' button to turn off highlighting

To Test a Webpage in a Browser

After creating and saving a webpage, you should test it in at least one browser. **Why?** You want to be sure it looks and works the way you intended. The following steps use File Explorer to display the resume webpage in the Internet Explorer browser.

1

- Click the File Explorer button on the Windows taskbar to open the File Explorer window.
- Navigate to the location of the saved resume webpage file (Figure 5–82).

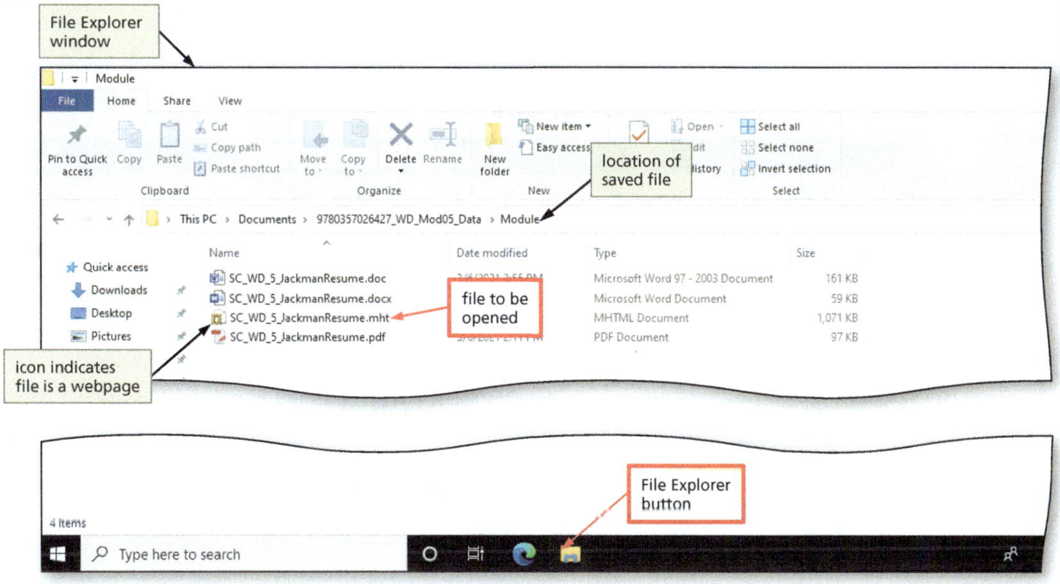

Figure 5–82

2

- Double-click the webpage file name, SC_WD_5_JackmanResume.mht, to start Internet Explorer and display the webpage file in the browser window (Figure 5–83).

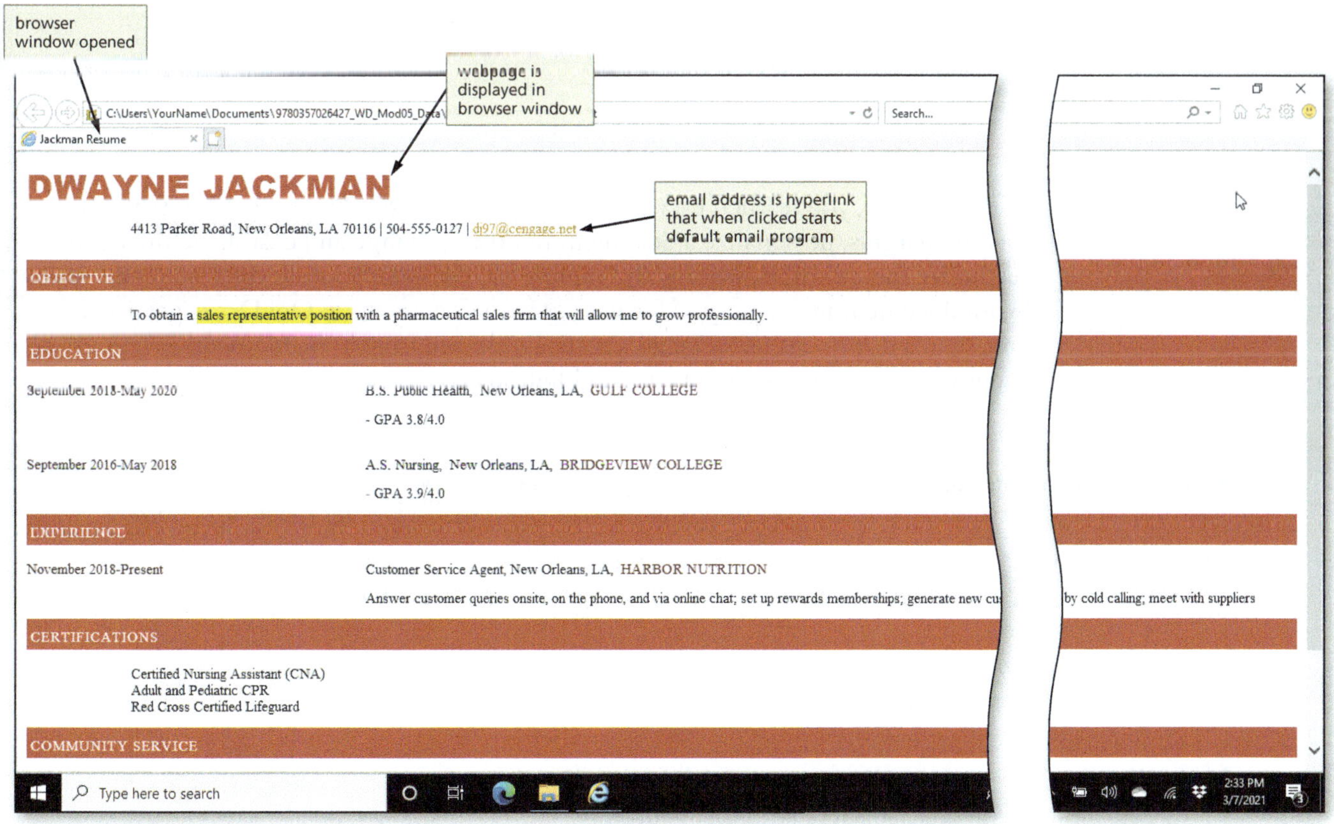

Figure 5–83

3

- With the webpage document displayed in the browser, click the email address link to start the email program with the email address displayed in the email window (Figure 5–84).
- If Internet Explorer displays a security dialog box, click its Allow button.

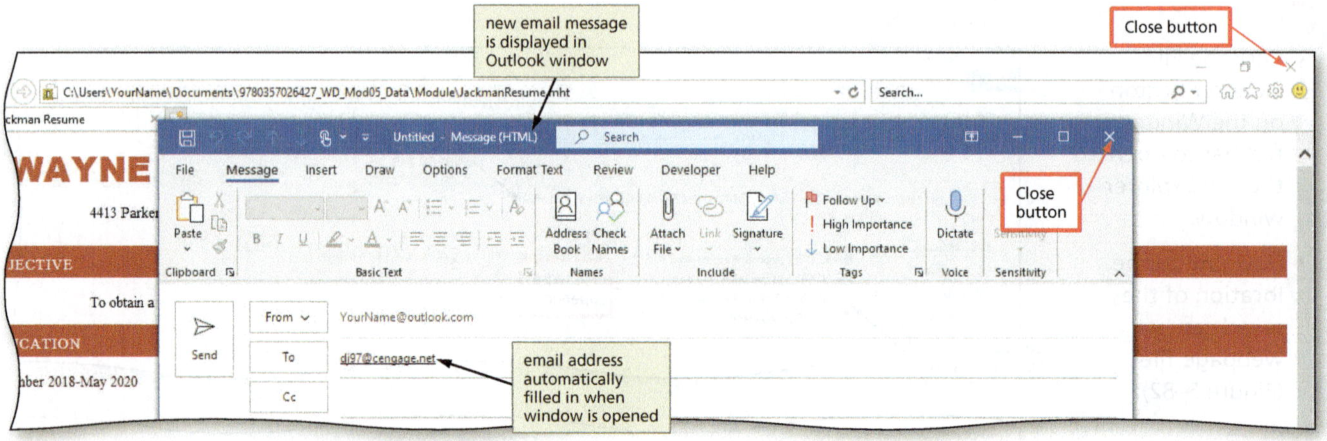

Figure 5–84

4

- Exit all running apps.

Consider This

How do you publish a webpage?
Once you have created a webpage, you can publish it. **Publishing** is the process of making a webpage available to others on a network, such as the Internet or a company's intranet. Many Internet service providers (ISPs) offer storage space on their web servers at no cost to their subscribers.

Summary

In this module, you learned how to use a Word template to create a document, set custom margins, personalize a document template, change and customize theme fonts, customize theme colors, work with building blocks, create a style, modify a style, save a Word document in a variety of formats, share a document on OneDrive, get a sharing link, send a document using email, create a webpage from a Word document, insert a hyperlink, change the style set, and highlight text.

Consider This: Plan Ahead

What decisions will you need to make when creating your next resume?
Use these guidelines as you complete the assignments in this module and create your own resumes outside of this class.

1. Craft a successful resume.
   a) Include necessary information (at a minimum, your contact information, objective, educational background, and work experience).
   b) Honestly present all your positive points.
   c) Organize information appropriately.
   d) Ensure the resume is error free.
2. For electronic distribution, ensure the document is in the proper format.
   a) Save the resume in a format that can be shared with others.
   b) Ensure that others will be able to open the resume using software on their computers or mobile devices and that the look of the resume will remain intact when recipients open the resume.

3. If desired, create a resume webpage from your resume Word document.
   a) Improve the usability of the resume webpage by making your email address a link to an email program.
   b) Enhance the look of the webpage by adding, for example, a background color.
   c) Test your finished webpage document in at least one browser to be sure it looks and works as intended.
   d) Publish your resume webpage.

Apply Your Knowledge

Reinforce the skills and apply the concepts you learned in this module.

Saving a Word Document in a Variety of Formats

Note: To complete this assignment, you will be required to use the Data Files. Please contact your instructor for information about accessing the Data Files.

Instructions: Start Word. Open the document, SC_WD_5-1.docx, which is located in the Data Files. You are to change the theme fonts, create custom theme fonts, change theme effects (Figure 5-85), and then save the revised document as a single file web page, a PDF document, an XPS document, and in the Word 97-2003 format.

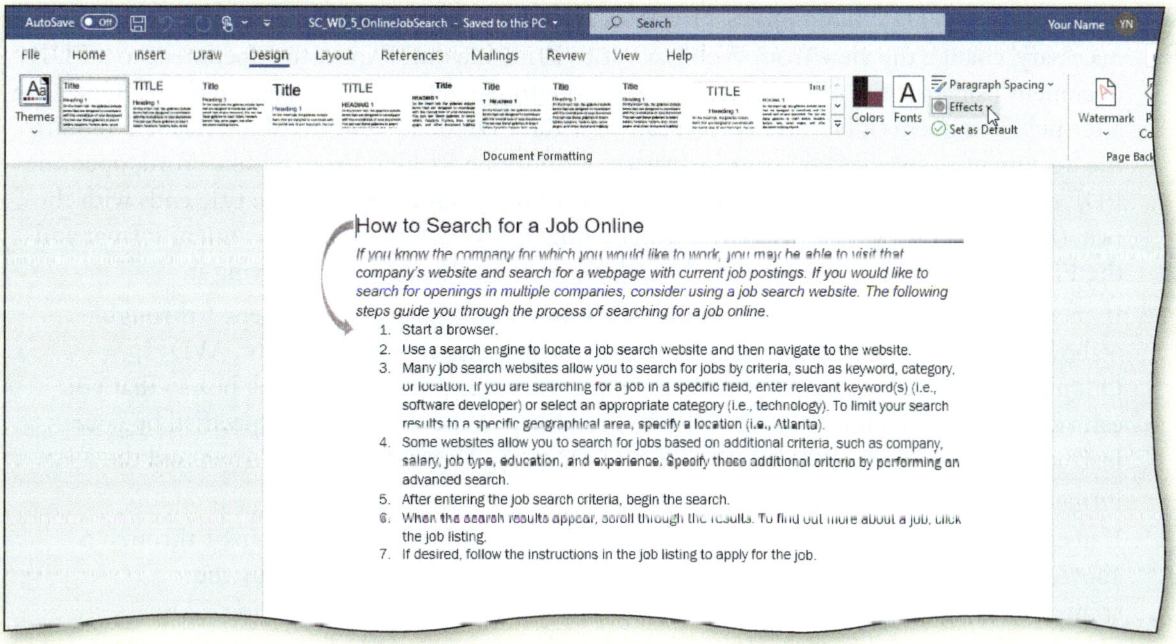

Figure 5–85

Perform the following tasks:

1. Click File on the ribbon and then click Save As and save the document using the new file name, SC_WD_5_OnlineJobSearch.
2. Change the theme fonts to Arial-Times New Roman.
3. Create custom theme fonts to change the body font from Times New Roman to Franklin Gothic Book. Save the custom theme with the name, Job Search Steps.

Continued >

Apply Your Knowledge *continued*

4. Change the theme effects to Grunge Texture. What did the theme effects change in the document?
5. If requested by your instructor, add your name in parentheses immediately after the title of this document (on the same line).
6. Save the document again with the same file name (Figure 5-85).
7. Save the document as a single file web page using the file name, SC_WD_5_OnlineJobSearch_Webpage. In the Save As dialog box, click the Change Title button and then change the webpage title to Online Job Search. If necessary, change the view from Print Layout to Web Layout. If necessary, increase the zoom percentage so that the document is readable on your screen.
8. Delete the arrow shape in the upper-left corner of the document.
9. Change the style set to Centered.
10. Highlight the title, How to Search for a Job Online, in the yellow highlight color.
11. Save the document again with the same file name.
12. Use Internet Explorer or another browser to view the webpage. If requested by your instructor, print the webpage. What differences do you notice between the Word document format and the single file web page format? Exit the browser and then close the webpage document in Word.
13. Open the SC_WD_5_OnlineJobSearch.docx file created in Steps 1 through 6 above. If necessary, change the view from Web Layout to Print Layout. Export the document to a PDF document using the file name, SC_WD_5_OnlineJobSearch, ensuring you check the 'Open file after publishing' check box so that you can view the PDF document in Adobe Reader. Submit the document as specified by your instructor. Exit Adobe Reader. From within Word, open the PDF document just created. Edit the converted PDF document so that the title ends with the text, (PDF Version). What differences do you notice between the Word document format and the PDF format? Close the converted PDF document in Word without saving it.
14. If necessary, open the SC_WD_5_OnlineJobSearch.docx file created in Steps 1 through 6 above. Export the document to an XPS Document using the file name, SC_WD_5_OnlineJobSearch, ensuring you check the 'Open file after publishing' check box so that you can view the XPS document in the XPS Viewer. Submit the document as specified by your instructor. What differences do you notice between the Word document format and the XPS format? Exit the XPS Viewer.
15. If necessary, open the SC_WD_5_OnlineJobSearch.docx file created in Steps 1 through 6 above. Check the document's compatibility. What issue(s) were identified by the compatibility checker? Save the document in the Word 97-2003 format using SC_WD_5_OnlineJobSearch_Word97-2003 as the file name. Submit the document as specified by your instructor. Close the document window.
16. Open the SC_WD_5_OnlineJobSearch.docx file created in Steps 1 through 6 above. If your instructor allows, use the Share button to send this Word document as an attachment to an email message to your instructor's email account. If your instructor allows, use the Share button again to send a PDF of this document to your instructor's email account.
17. Answer the questions posed in #4, #12, #13, #14, and #15. If you wanted to send this document in an email message to others, which format would you choose and why?

Extend Your Knowledge

Extend the skills you learned in this module and experiment with new skills. You may need to use Help to complete the assignment.

Modifying and Editing a Resume Template and Creating a Multi-File Webpage

Note: To complete this assignment, you will be required to use the Data Files. Please contact your instructor for information about accessing the Data Files.

Instructions: Start Word. Open the document, SC_WD_5-2.docx, which is located in the Data Files. You will modify and edit a resume template by working with content controls and table elements, hyperlinks, building blocks, and the Resume Assistant, and you will save a Word document as a multi-file webpage and format it by inserting links, adding a pattern fill effect as the background, and applying highlights to text.

Perform the following tasks:

1. Use Help to learn more about the Resume Assistant, saving as a webpage (not a single file web page), hyperlinks, and pattern fill effects.
2. Click File on the ribbon and then click Save As and save the document using the new file name, SC_WD_5_VetTechResume.
3. If requested by your instructor, change the name on the resume to your name.
4. Enter the text, 207-555-0154, in the Telephone content control.
5. Delete the Website content control.
6. Insert a hyperlink to the email address. Add the following ScreenTip for the hyperlink: Send me an email message.
7. Edit the hyperlink to change the 98 in the email address to 97.
8. The applicant would like to work at a veterinary hospital as a full-time veterinary technician. Click the text in the Objective section, use the Resume Assistant to research the role and job skills, and then write an objective for the resume. (*Hint:* Click the Resume Assistant button (Review tab | Resume group)) (Figure 5–86). Note that to use the Resume Assistant you may need to agree to send your resume information to LinkedIn for suggestions.

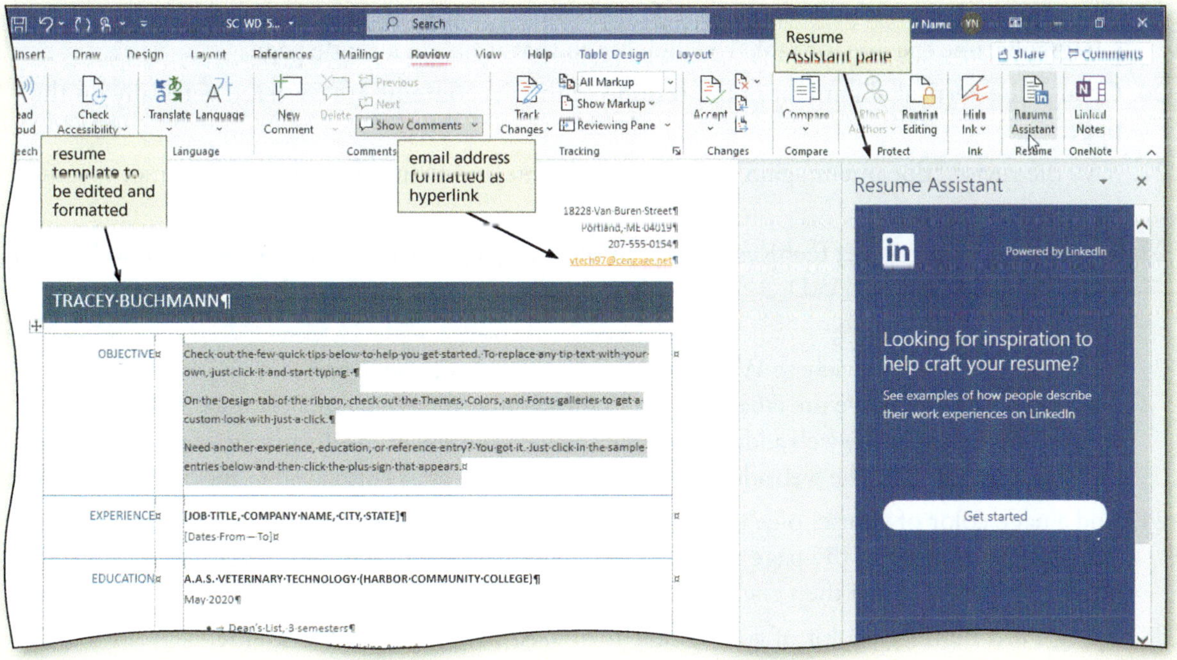

Figure 5–86

Continued >

Extend Your Knowledge *continued*

9. Create a building block (Quick Part) for the text, veterinary, and save the building block with the name vy. Insert the building block (Quick Part) whenever you have to enter the text, veterinary.
10. Use copy and paste or drag and drop to move the row containing the Education section so that it appears above the Experience row.
11. Copy the Memberships row and then paste the row (with source formatting) so that the pasted row appears immediately below the Education section. Change the heading of the pasted row from Memberships to Skills. Change the text in the right column of the pasted row to the following, with each item on a separate line: Anesthesia and surgery, Client education, Laboratory testing and procedures, Pharmacology, Recordkeeping.
12. In the Experience section of the resume, insert a content control so that you can enter two jobs. (Hint: Click the job experience content control to the right of the Experience heading and then click the Insert Control button at the right of the control, or right-click the job experience content control and then click the location to insert the content control on the shortcut menu.)
13. Enter this job information for two jobs in the Experience section: Veterinary Assistant, Harbor Animal Clinic, Portland, ME, May 2018-Present; Groomer, Delaney's Doggie Care, Portland, ME, September 2017-May 2018.
14. Below the dates in the Veterinary Assistant job, add this description on a separate paragraph, indented: Sterilized surgical kits, assisted during routine physical examinations, collected patient histories, walked dogs, communicated with clients, and booked appointments.
15. Copy and paste with source formatting the paragraph you entered in #14 on a blank paragraph below the dates in the Groomer job. Change the pasted text so that it reads: Bathed dogs; brushed, combed, clipped, and shaped dogs' coats; trimmed nails; and cleaned ears.
16. Change the format of the Objective heading in the resume to a format you feel is more noticeable. Create a paragraph style for the newly formatted Objective heading and name the format Resume Headings. Apply the Resume Headings style to the remaining headings in the resume.
17. Change the format of the bulleted lists in the resume to a bullet symbol of your choice.
18. Insert one of the SAMPLE watermarks using the Quick Part button and the Building Blocks Organizer dialog box.
19. The resume should fit on a single page. If it does not, adjust spacing above and below paragraphs, line spacing, or table row heights so that it fits on a single page.
20. Change the vertical alignment of the resume so that its contents are centered vertically on the page.
21. Save the revised document again with the same name and then submit it in the format specified by your instructor.
22. Save the SC_WD_5_VetTechResume file in the web page format (not as a single file web page) using the file name, SC_WD_5_VetTechResume. In the Save As dialog box, change the page title to Vet Tech Resume.
23. If necessary, change the view to Web Layout. (Notice that the watermark does not appear in Web Layout view.) Above the email address in the resume, on a separate line, enter the text www.cengage.com as the web address. Format the web address in the document as a hyperlink so that when a user clicks the web address, the associated webpage is displayed in the browser window.
24. Add a page color of your choice to the document. (Hint: Use the Design tab.) Add a pattern fill effect of your choice to the page color. (Hint: Click the Page Color button (Design tab | Page Background group) and then click Fill Effects on the Page Color menu.)
25. Apply a text highlight color of your choice to at least five words in the resume.

26. If requested by your instructor, insert a hyperlink to another resume document you created in this module or elsewhere and change the ScreenTip to read: Click for another sample resume.
27. Save the revised document again with the same name and then submit it in the format specified by your instructor.
28. Test the webpage by double-clicking its file name in File Explorer. Test the web address link on the webpage.
29. Copy the entire resume table. Paste the table with source formatting in a new Word document window. Click the Paste Options button and point the various paste options to see how they change the look of the pasted table. Close the Word window without saving the document.
30. Why would you add a pattern fill effect to a background?

Expand Your World

Create a solution that uses cloud or web technologies by learning and investigating on your own from general guidance.

Sharing a Resume Online and Creating a Calendar

Notes:

- You will use OneDrive and a job search website account, which you can create at no cost, to complete this assignment. If you do not have these accounts and do not want to create them, read Steps 9 through 12 in this assignment without performing the instructions.
- To complete this assignment, you will be required to use the Data Files. Please contact your instructor for information about accessing the Data Files.

Instructions: You are a business graduate with an accounting degree from Maple Leaf College. You will make some final edits to your resume and then will share it with potential employers. You will save it on your OneDrive account, invite others to view it, get a sharing link, send it via email, and post it on a job search website (Figure 5–87). You also will use a calendar template to help organize your upcoming appointments and important dates.

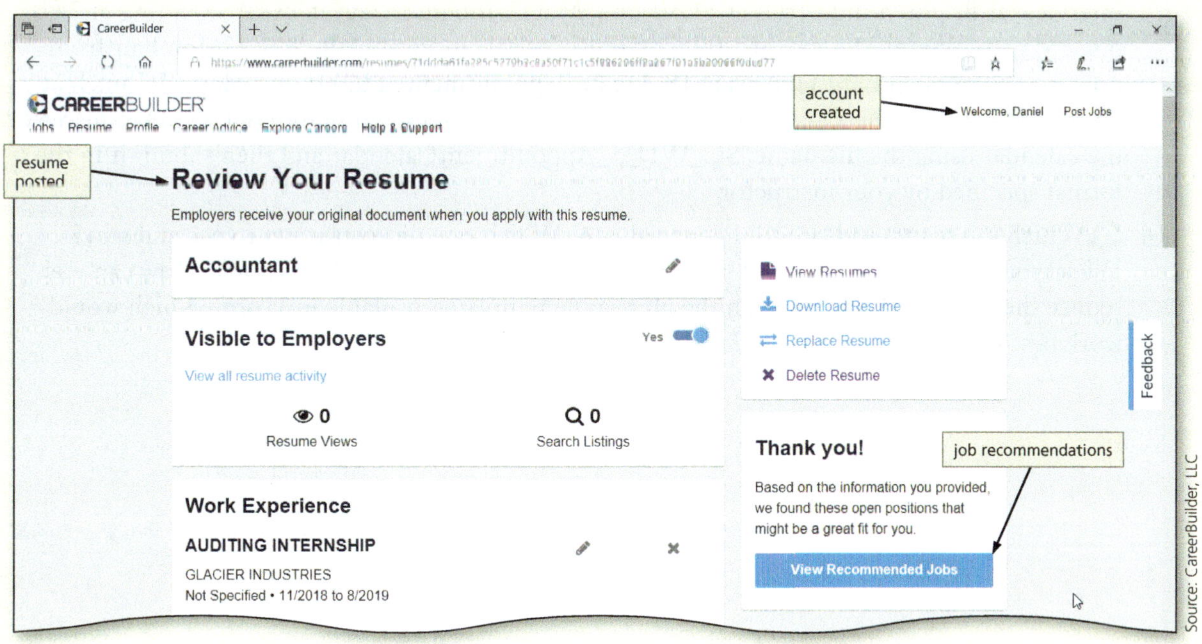

Figure 5–87

Continued >

Expand Your World *continued*

Perform the following tasks:

1. Start Word. Open the document, SC_WD_5-3.docx, which is located in the Data Files.
2. Click File on the ribbon and then click Save As and save the document using the new file name, SC_WD_5_AccountantResume.
3. If requested by your instructor, change the name at the top of the resume to your name.
4. Set custom margins to .75-inch top, bottom, left, and right so that the entire resume fits on a single page.
5. Reveal formatting of a heading in the resume. Notice that the headings use the Accent 1 color. Close the Reveal Formatting pane.
6. Create a custom theme color so that Accent 1 is a color different from 'Brown, Accent 1'. Save the custom theme with the name Accountant Resume Headings.
7. If requested by your instructor, save the current theme settings as the default.
8. Save the revised document again with the same name and then submit it in the format specified by your instructor.
9. Save the SC_WD_5_AccountantResume resume on your OneDrive account so that you can share it.
10. Using the Share button in Word, invite at least one of your classmates to view your resume document. If requested, include your instructor in the invitation.
11. In Word, get a sharing link for the resume. Send the sharing link in an email message to at least one of your classmates. Submit the link in the format requested by your instructor.
12. Export the resume to a PDF file. Search for the text, post resume online, using a search engine. Visit several of the job search websites and determine on which one you would like to post a resume. If requested, create an account or profile, fill in the requested information, and then upload the PDF format of the resume (shown in Figure 5–87). Submit the posting in the format requested by your instructor. Delete the posted resume from the job search website.
13. Browse through Word's calendar templates, download an appropriate calendar template, and then enter the following appointments in the calendar for the month of May: May 4–Job interview at Brighten Industries at 11:30 a.m., May 7–Job interview at TG Accounting at 2:00 p.m., May 8–Alumni Meeting at 1:00 p.m. in Room 103 in Pace Hall, May 12–Job Fair from noon to 4:00 p.m. in Bard Hall, May 18–Dentist appointment at 9:00 a.m., May 20–Lunch at noon with Dr. Chambers at Riverside Café, May 28–Eye doctor appointment at 1:00 p.m. Save the calendar using the file name, SC_WD_5_AppointmentCalendar and then submit it in the format specified by your instructor.
14. Which job search websites did you evaluate? Which one did you select to use and why? What would cause the file size of your resume to be too large to upload (post)? How can you reduce the file size? Look through the all resume templates available in Word. Which would work best for your resume? Why?

In the Lab

Design and implement a solution using creative thinking and problem-solving skills.

Create a Resume for a Graduating Criminal Justice Student

Problem: You are graduating with a degree in criminal justice from Marigold College. Because you soon will be seeking employment as an investigator with a law enforcement agency, you use a template to create a resume for your job search.

Part 1: Browse through Word's resume templates and select one you can use to create the resume. Use the concepts and techniques presented in this module to create and format the resume. The resume should contain the following content:

Name: Leo Moretti (if requested by your instructor, use your name).

Address: 2091 Willow Lane, Apt. 34, Bowling Green, KY, 42102 (if requested by your instructor, use your address).

Phone: 270-555-0177 (if requested by your instructor, use your phone number).

Email: leo@cengage.net (if requested by your instructor, use your email address).

Objective: To obtain a full time investigator position with a local or state law enforcement agency.

Education: B.A. Criminal Justice from Marigold College in May 2020. GPA 3.85/4.0. Awards received: Dean's List, every semester; Outstanding Student Award, May 2019; Criminal Justice Journal, 1st Place, cross-cultural perspectives article. Areas of concentration: Criminal law, International justice systems, Research methods, Victims' rights. A.A. Legal Studies from Hammond Community College in May 2018. GPA 3.80/4.00.

Experience: Teachers' Assistant at Marigold College from January 2019-Present.

Research trends in course topics, grade student assignments, guide students with projects, manage student communications, present lectures when instructors are off campus.

Memberships: Criminal Justice Club, Marigold College, Phi Delta Gamma National Honor Society; Student Government Association, Marigold College.

Community Service: Certified Victim Advocate at Bowling Green Community Services from October 2018-Present. Certified Victim Advocate Duties: Volunteer eight hours a week at the call center; Offer emotional support and provide information on victims' legal rights and the criminal justice process.

When you are finished with the resume, be sure to check the spelling and grammar. Save it in a form suitable for sharing using the file name, SC_WD_5_InvestigatorResume. Also save the resume as a webpage and format the webpage appropriately. Submit your assignment documents and answers to the Part 2 critical thinking questions in the format specified by your instructor.

Part 2: You made several decisions while creating the resume in this assignment: which template to use, where to position elements, how to format resume elements, in which format to save the document for sharing, and how to format the webpage elements. What was the rationale behind each of these decisions?

6 Using Mail Merge

Objectives

After completing this module, you will be able to:

- Explain the merge process
- Use the Mail Merge wizard and the Mailings tab on the ribbon
- Use a letter template as the main document for a mail merge
- Create and edit a recipient list in a data source
- Insert merge fields in a main document
- Use an IF field in a main document
- Merge form letters
- Select recipients to merge
- Sort a recipient list
- Address and print mailing labels and envelopes
- Change page orientation
- Merge all data records to a directory
- Convert text to a table

Introduction

People are more likely to open and read a personalized letter than a letter addressed as Dear Sir, Dear Madam, or To Whom It May Concern. Creating individual personalized letters, though, can be a time-consuming task. Thus, Word provides the capability of creating a form letter, which is an easy way to generate mass mailings of personalized letters. The basic content of a group of form letters is similar. Items such as name and address, however, vary from one letter to the next. With Word, you easily can address and print mailing labels or envelopes for the form letters.

Project: Form Letters, Mailing Labels, and a Directory

Both businesses and individuals regularly use form letters to communicate with groups of people via the postal service or email. Types of form letter correspondence include announcements of sales to customers, notices of benefits to employees, and job application letters to potential employers.

The project in this module follows generally accepted guidelines for writing form letters and uses Word to create the form letters shown in Figure 6–1. The form letters inform potential employers that you met at a job fair of your interest in a job opening at their organization. Each form letter states the potential employer's name and address, available job position, and whether the organization sells therapeutic medicine or medical devices.

To generate form letters, such as the ones shown in Figure 6–1, you create a main document for the form letter (Figure 6–1a), create or specify a data source, which contains a recipient list (Figure 6–1b), and then **merge**, or combine, the main document with the recipient list in the data source to generate a series of individual letters (Figure 6–1c). In Figure 6–1a, the main document represents the portion of the form letter that is repeated from one merged letter to the next. In Figure 6–1b, the recipient list in the data source contains the organization's contact person, name, address, available position, and type of product sold for various potential employers. To personalize each letter, you merge the potential employer data in the recipient list in the data source with the main document for the form letter, which generates or prints an individual letter for each potential employer listed in the recipient list in the data source.

Word provides two methods of merging documents: the Mail Merge wizard and the Mailings tab on the ribbon. The Mail Merge wizard, which uses the Mail Merge pane, is a step-by-step progression that guides you through the merging process. The Mailings tab provides buttons and boxes you use to merge documents. This module illustrates both techniques.

In this module, you will learn how to create the form letters shown in Figure 6–1. You will perform the following general tasks as you progress through this module:

1. Identify the main document for the form letters.
2. Create the recipient list for a data source.
3. Compose the main document for the form letters.
4. Merge the recipient list in the data source with the main document.
5. Address mailing labels.
6. Merge all recipients in a data source to a directory.

To Start Word and Specify Settings

If you are using a computer to step through the project in this module and you want your screens to match the figures in this book, you should change your screen's resolution to 1366 × 768. The following steps start Word, display formatting marks, change the zoom to page width, and verify ruler and Mouse mode settings.

1. Start Word and create a blank document in the Word window. If necessary, maximize the Word window.
2. If the Print Layout button on the status bar is not selected, click it so that your screen is in Print Layout view.
3. If the 'Show/Hide ¶' button (Home tab | Paragraph group) is not selected already, click it to display formatting marks on the screen.
4. To display the page the same width as the document window, if necessary, click the Page Width button (View tab | Zoom group).
5. Verify that the Ruler check box (View tab | Show group) is not selected. (If it is selected, click it to remove the check mark because you do not want the rulers to appear on the screen.)

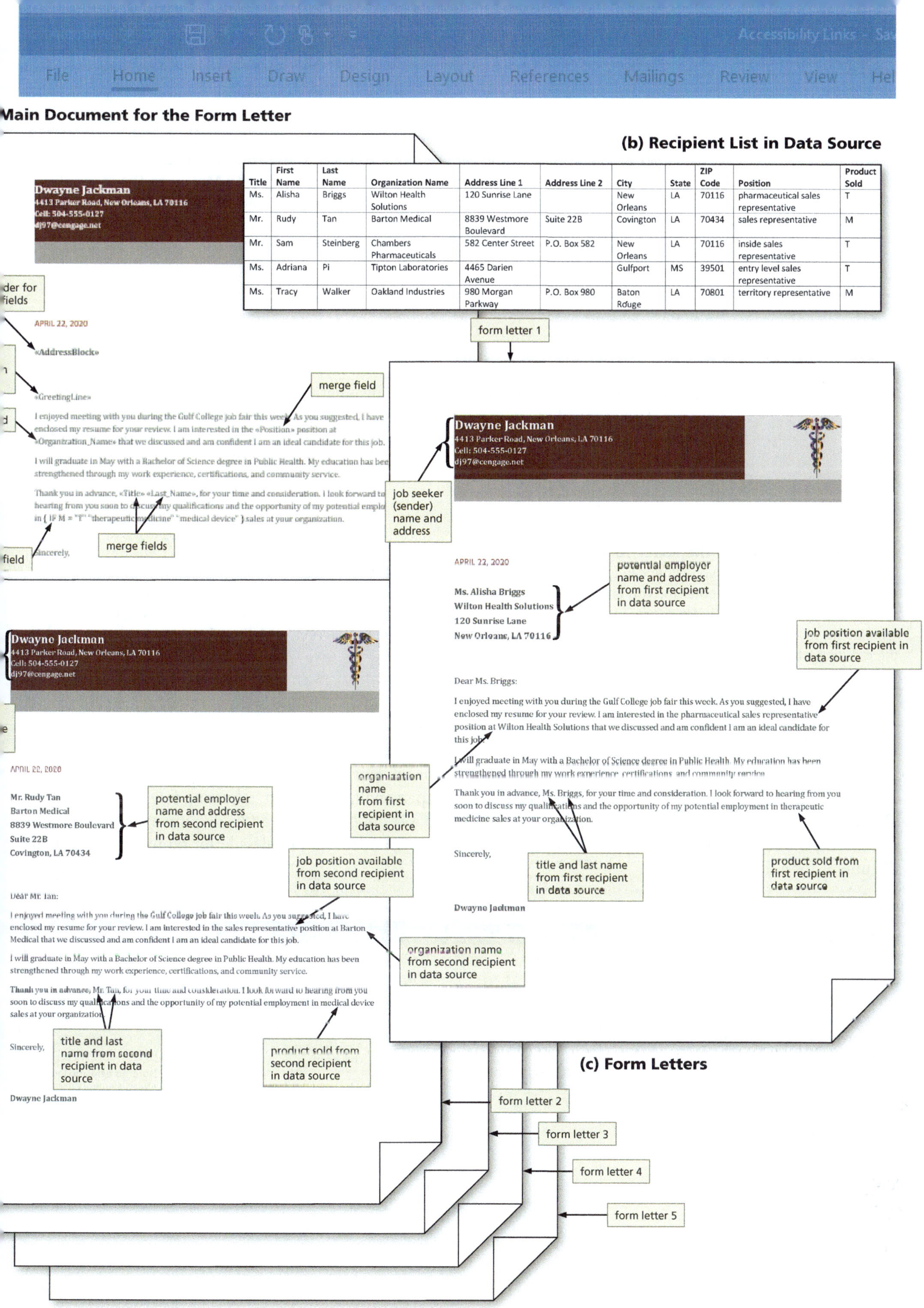

Title	First Name	Last Name	Organization Name	Address Line 1	Address Line 2	City	State	ZIP Code	Position	Product Sold
Ms.	Alisha	Briggs	Wilton Health Solutions	120 Sunrise Lane		New Orleans	LA	70116	pharmaceutical sales representative	T
Mr.	Rudy	Tan	Barton Medical	8839 Westmore Boulevard	Suite 22B	Covington	LA	70434	sales representative	M
Mr.	Sam	Steinberg	Chambers Pharmaceuticals	582 Center Street	P.O. Box 582	New Orleans	LA	70116	inside sales representative	T
Ms.	Adriana	Pi	Tipton Laboratories	4465 Darien Avenue		Gulfport	MS	39501	entry level sales representative	T
Ms.	Tracy	Walker	Oakland Industries	980 Morgan Parkway	P.O. Box 980	Baton Rouge	LA	70801	territory representative	M

Figure 6–1

BTW
Touch Mode Differences
The Microsoft 365 and Windows interfaces may vary if you are using Touch mode. For this reason, you might notice that the function or appearance of your touch screen differs slightly from this module's presentation.

6 If you are using a mouse and you want your screens to match the figures in the book, verify that you are using Mouse mode by clicking the Touch/Mouse Mode button on the Quick Access Toolbar and then, if necessary, clicking Mouse on the menu. (If your Quick Access Toolbar does not display the Touch/Mouse Mode button, click the 'Customize Quick Access Toolbar' button on the Quick Access Toolbar and then click Touch/Mouse Mode on the menu to add the button to the Quick Access Toolbar.)

Identifying the Main Document for Form Letters

The first step in the mail merge process is to identify the type of document you are creating for the main document. Typical installations of Word support five types of main documents: letters, email messages, envelopes, labels, and a directory. In this section of the module, you create letters as the main document. Later in this module, you will specify labels and a directory as the main document.

Consider This

How should you create the letter for the main document?
When creating form letters, you either can type the letter for the main document from scratch in a blank document window or use a letter template. If you enter the contents of the main document from scratch, you can compose it according to the block, modified block, or semi-block letter style, formatted appropriately with business letter spacing. Alternatively, you can use a letter template to save time because Word prepares a letter with text and/or formatting common to all letters. Then, you customize the resulting letter by selecting and replacing prewritten text.

To Start the Mail Merge Wizard

This module uses a template for the main document for the form letter, where you select predefined content controls and placeholder text and replace them with personalized content, adjusting formats as necessary. **Why?** You can use the same or similar style that you use with a resume so that the two documents complement one another. The following steps use the Mail Merge wizard to identify the Timeless letter template as the main document for a form letter.

1

- Click Mailings on the ribbon to display the Mailings tab.
- Click the 'Start Mail Merge' button (Mailings tab | Start Mail Merge group) to display the Start Mail Merge menu (Figure 6–2).

Q&A **What is the function of the E-mail Messages command?**
Instead of sending individual letters, you can send individual email messages using email addresses in the recipient list in the data source or using a Microsoft Outlook Contacts list as the data source.

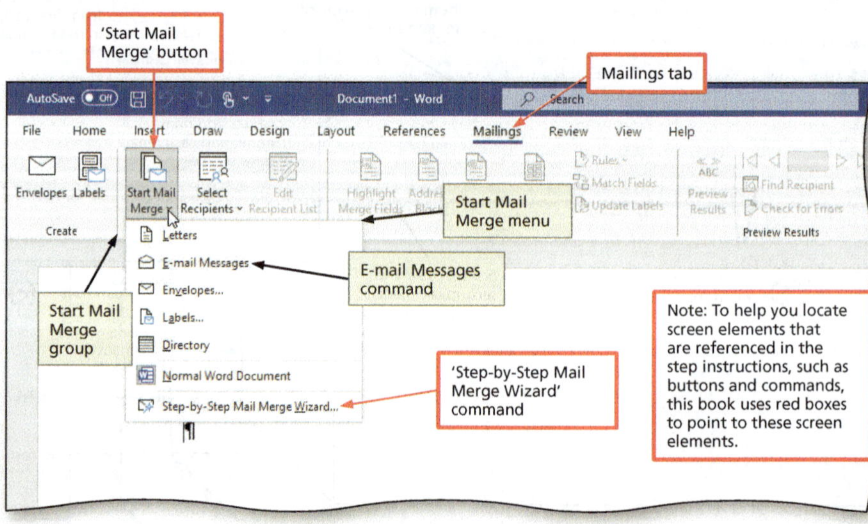

Figure 6–2

2

- Click 'Step-by-Step Mail Merge Wizard' on the Start Mail Merge menu to display Step 1 of the Mail Merge wizard in the Mail Merge pane (Figure 6–3).

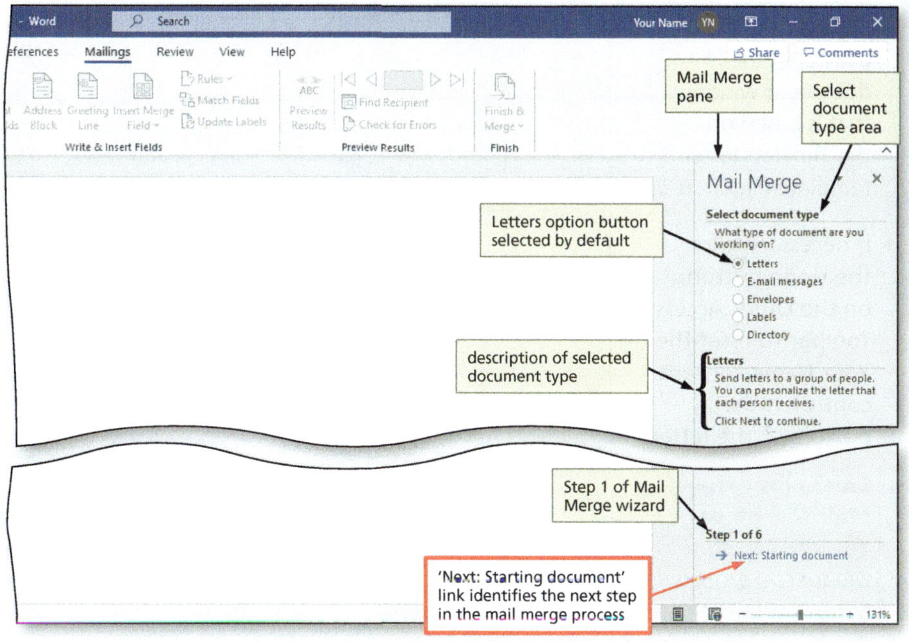

Figure 6–3

3

- Ensure that Letters is selected in the Select document type area and then click the 'Next: Starting document' link at the bottom of the Mail Merge pane to display Step 2 of the Mail Merge wizard, which requests you select a starting document.
- Click 'Start from a template' in the Select starting document area and then click the Select template link to display the Select Template dialog box.
- Click the Letters tab (Select Template dialog box) to display the Letters sheet and then click Timeless letter, which shows a preview of the selected template in the Preview area (Figure 6–4).

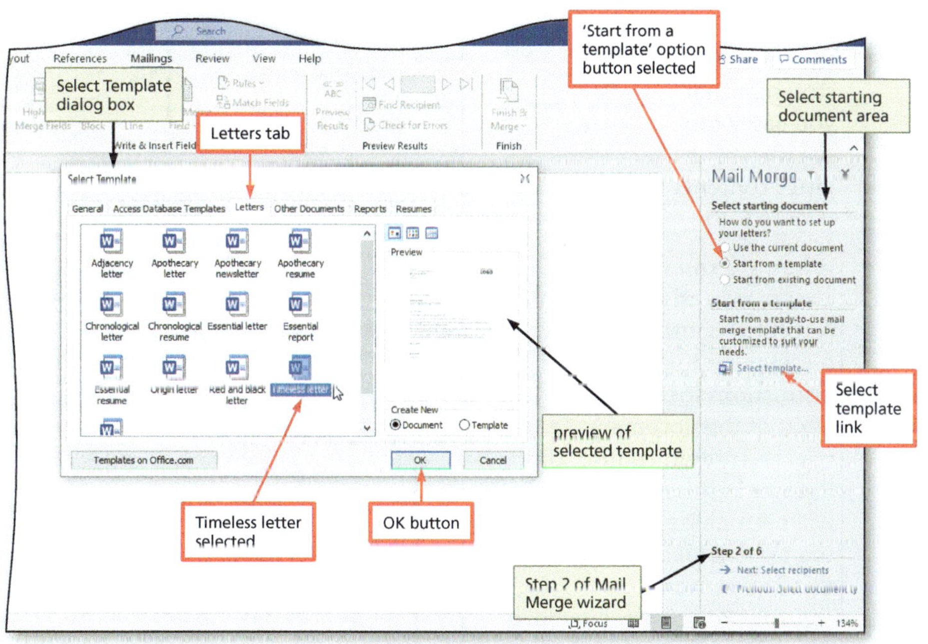

Figure 6–4

Experiment

- Click various Letter templates in the Letters sheet and watch the preview change in the right pane of the dialog box. When you are finished experimenting, click the Timeless letter template to select it.

Q&A

What if I cannot locate the Timeless letter template?

Click the Cancel button to close the dialog box, click the 'Start from existing document' option button in the Mail Merge pane to display options for opening a document in the pane, click the Open button that appears in the Mail Merge pane to display the Open dialog box, navigate to the location of the Support_WD_6_TimelessLetterTemplate.docx, click the file to select it, click the Open button (Open dialog box) to open the selected file, and then skip the remainder of these steps.

4

- Click OK to display a letter in the document window that is based on the Timeless letter template (Figure 6–5).
- If necessary, click the Undo button on the Quick Access Toolbar to reset the Your Name content control at the bottom of the letter.

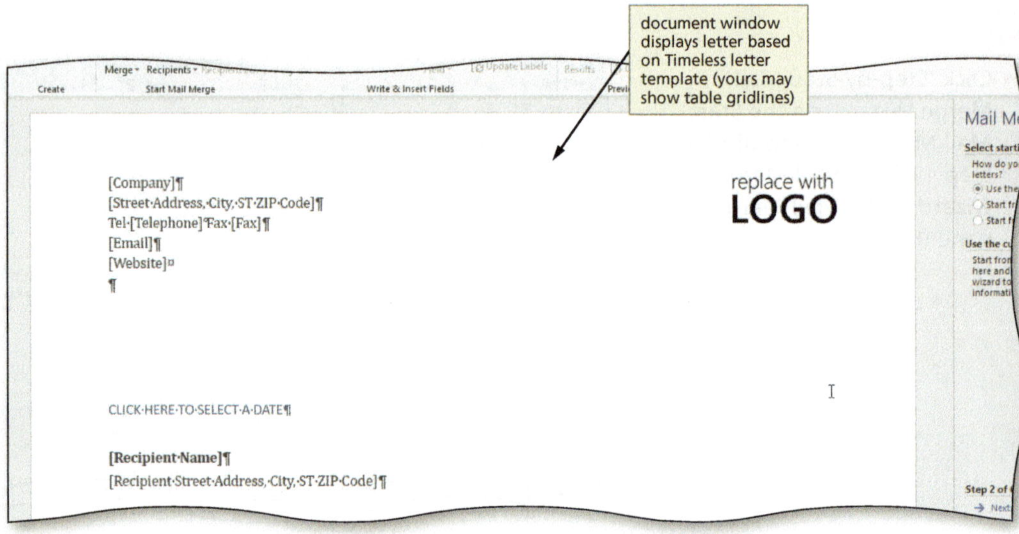

Figure 6–5

Q&A **Can I close the Mail Merge pane?**
Yes, you can close the Mail Merge pane at any time by clicking its Close button. When you want to continue with the merge process, you repeat these steps and Word will resume the merge process at the correct step in the Mail Merge wizard.

5

- Print the document shown on the screen so that you easily can see the entire letter contents (Figure 6–6).

Q&A **What are the content controls in the document?**
A content control contains placeholder text and instructions for filling in areas of the document. To select a content control, click it. Later in this module, you will personalize the placeholder text and content controls. You also will remove the content controls as you are finished adding text to them.

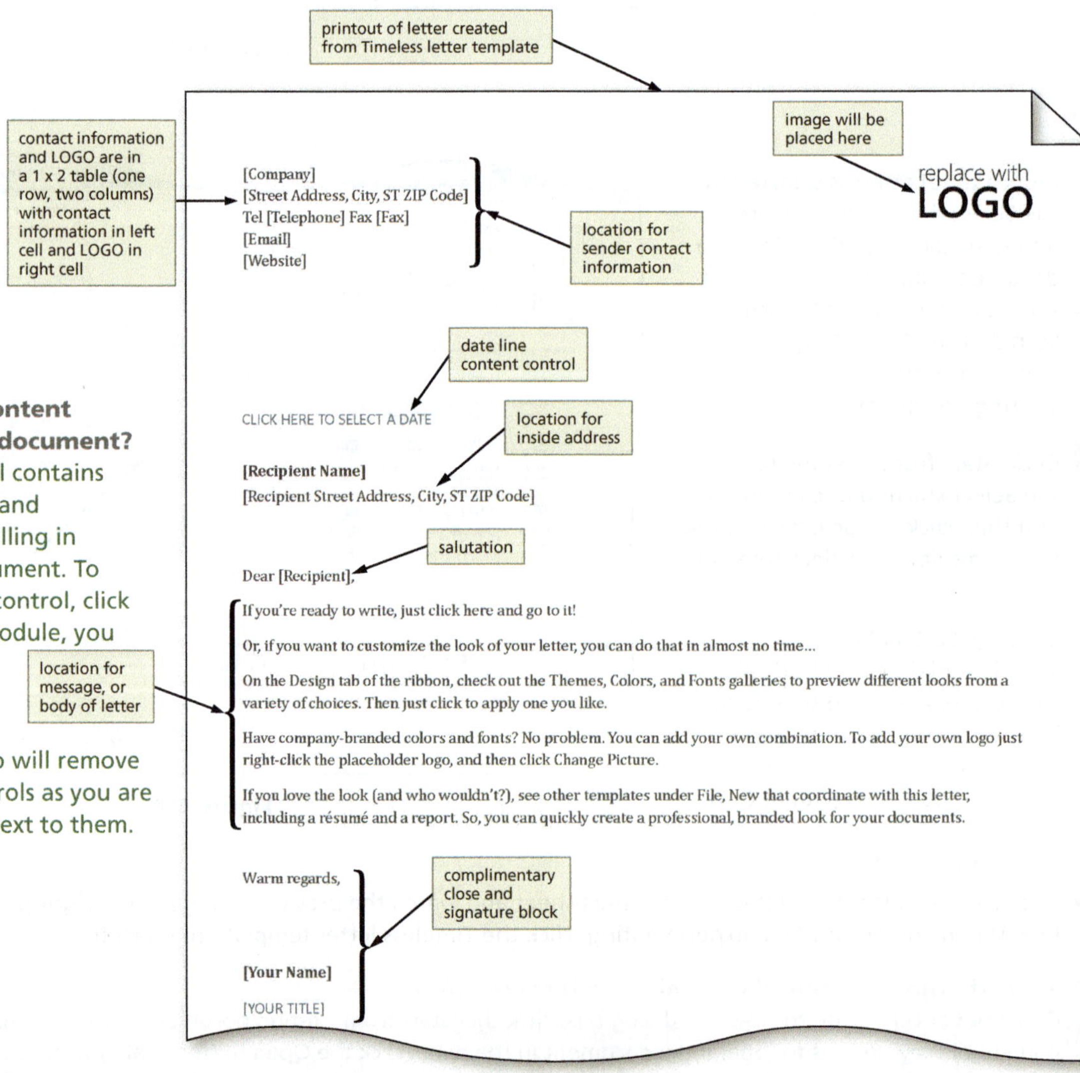

Figure 6–6

Other Ways

1. Open Backstage view, click New, type `letters` in 'Search for online templates' box, click Start searching button, click desired letter template, click Create button

To Change Theme Colors

Word provides document themes, which contain a variety of color schemes and other effects. This cover letter uses the Orange Red theme colors to match the theme colors used in the associated resume. The following steps change the theme colors.

1. Click Design on the ribbon to display the Design tab.
2. Click the Colors button (Design tab | Document Formatting group) to display the Colors gallery.
3. Scroll to and then click Orange Red in the Colors gallery to change the theme colors to the selected theme.

To Enter and Format the Sender Information

The next step is to enter the sender's contact information at the top of the letter. You will use the [Company] placeholder text for the sender's name. You will delete the [Fax] and [Website] placeholder text because this sender does not have a fax or website. Then, you will change the font size of the text. The following steps enter and format the sender information.

1. Select the placeholder text, [Company], and then type **Dwayne Jackman** as the sender name.
2. Select the placeholder text, [Street Address, City, ST ZIP Code], and then type **4413 Parker Road, New Orleans, LA 70116** as the sender's address.
3. Select the text, Tel, and then type **Cell:** as the label. Select the placeholder text, [Telephone], and then type **504-555-0127** as the sender's cell phone number.
4. Delete the Fax label and [Fax] placeholder text.
5. Select the placeholder text, [Email], and then type **dj97@cengage.net** as the sender's email address. (If Word automatically capitalizes characters in the email address, change the capital letters to lowercase letters.)
6. Delete the [Website] placeholder text.
7. Increase the font size of the name to 14 point, and decrease the font size of the street address, cell phone, and email address to 9 point.
8. Select the name and all contact information. Bold the text (shown in Figure 6–7).

To Change a Picture and Format It

The current picture in the letter contains the text, replace with LOGO, which is a placeholder for a picture. The following steps change a picture.

1. Right-click the picture to be changed (in this case, the picture placeholder with the text, replace with LOGO) to display a shortcut menu and then point to Change Picture on the shortcut menu (Figure 6–7).

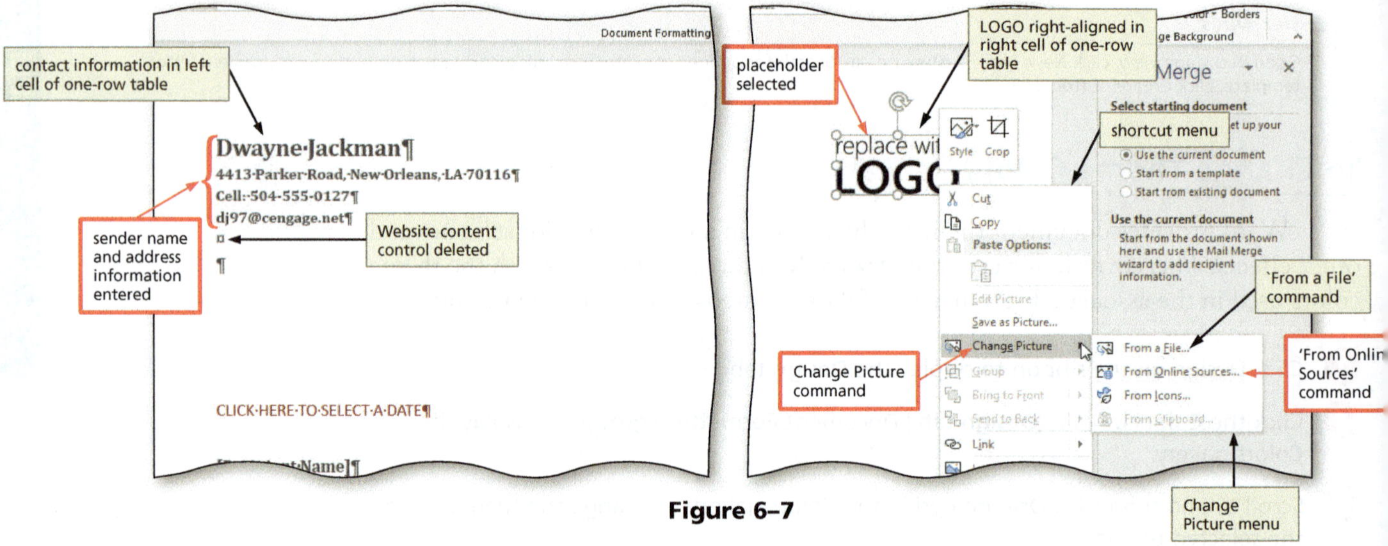

Figure 6–7

2. Click 'From Online Sources' on the Change Picture submenu to display the Online Pictures dialog box.

> **Q&A** **Can I use the Change Picture button (Picture Format tab | Adjust group) instead of the shortcut menu to display the Online Pictures dialog box?**
> Yes.

3. Type **caduceus** in the Search box (Online Pictures dialog box) and then press ENTER to display a list of images that matches the entered search text.

4. Scroll through the list of images to locate the one shown in Figure 6–8 (or a similar image), click the image to select it, and then click the Insert button (Online Pictures dialog box) to download the image, close the dialog box, and replace the selected placeholder with the new picture file (shown in Figure 6–8).

> **Q&A** **What if I cannot locate the same image?**
> Click Cancel and then repeat Step 1 above, click 'From a File' on the Change Picture submenu to display the Insert Picture dialog box, navigate to the Support_WD_6_Caduceus.png file in the Data Files (Insert Picture dialog box), and then click the Insert button to replace the selected placeholder with the new picture file.

5. Use the Shape Height and Shape Width boxes (Picture Format tab | Size group) to change the picture height to approximately .92" and width to .74". (Note: You might need to remove the check mark from the 'Lock aspect ratio' check box by clicking the Size Dialog Box Launcher (Picture Format tab | Size group) in order to size the image exactly.)

To Shade Cells and a Shape

In the letter in this module, the left and right cells of the table containing the contact information and picture are shaded different colors. These two cells are contained in a rectangular shape, which extends below these two cells. By shading the cells in the table and the rectangular shape each a separate color, you create a letterhead with three different colors. The following steps shade table cells and a shape.

1. Position the insertion point in the contact information (upper-left cell of table). Display the Layout tab and then, if necessary, click the View Gridlines button (Layout tab | Table group) to show table gridlines.

> **Q&A** **Why show table gridlines?**
> With table gridlines showing, the cells are easier to see.

2. Display the Table Design tab. With the insertion point in the left cell, click the Shading arrow (Table Design tab | Table Styles group) and then click 'Dark Red, Accent 2, Darker 25%' (sixth color, fifth row) to shade the current cell with the selected color.

3. Select the contact information in the left cell and change its font color to 'White, Background 1' (first color, first row).

4. Position the insertion point in the cell with the picture, click the Shading arrow (Table Design tab | Table Styles group) and then click 'Gray, Accent 5, Lighter 60%' (ninth color, third row) to shade the current cell with the selected color.

5. Position the insertion point on the paragraph mark below the shaded cell to select the rectangle drawing object. Display the Shape Format tab. Click the Shape Fill arrow (Shape Format tab | Shape Styles group) to display the Shape Fill gallery (Figure 6–8) and then click 'Gray, Text 2, Lighter 40%' (fourth color, fourth row) to shade the selected shape with the selected color.

6. Position the insertion point in the left cell. Hide table gridlines.

BTW

The Ribbon and Screen Resolution

Word may change how the groups and buttons within the groups appear on the ribbon, depending on the screen resolution of your computer. Thus, your ribbon may look different from the ones in this book if you are using a screen resolution other than 1366 × 768.

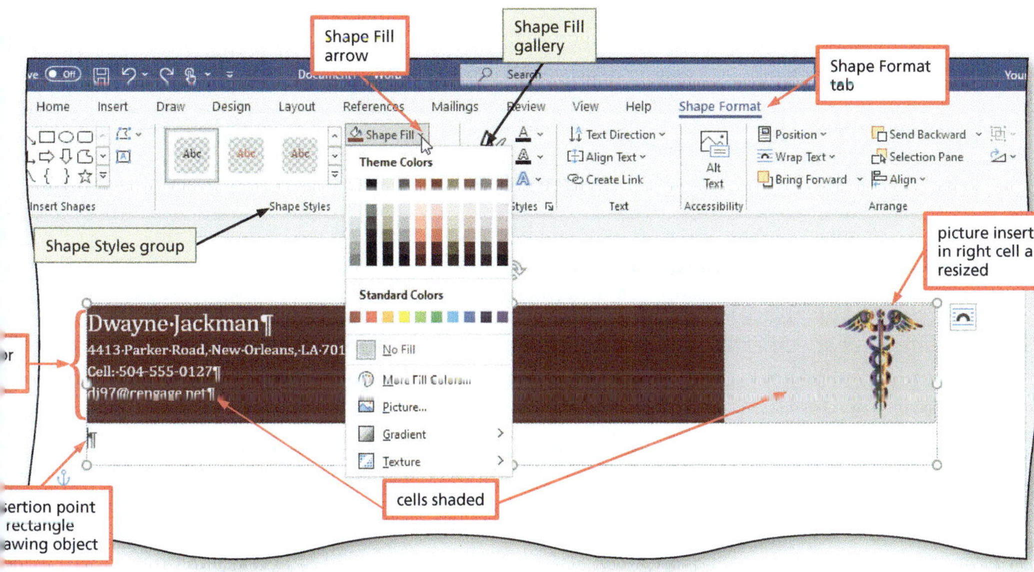

Figure 6–8

To Change Margin Settings

The Timeless letter template uses 1.9-inch top and .75-inch bottom, left, and right margins. You want the form letter to use 1-inch top and bottom margins and 1.25-inch left and right margins. The following steps change the margin settings.

1. Click the Date content control to deselect the drawing object.

2. Display the Layout tab. Click the Margins button (Layout tab | Page Setup group) to display the Margins gallery and then click Custom Margins at the bottom of the gallery to display the Page Setup dialog box.

3. Change the values in the Top, Bottom, Left, and Right boxes (Page Setup dialog box) to 1", 1", 1.25", and 1.25", respectively (Figure 6–9).

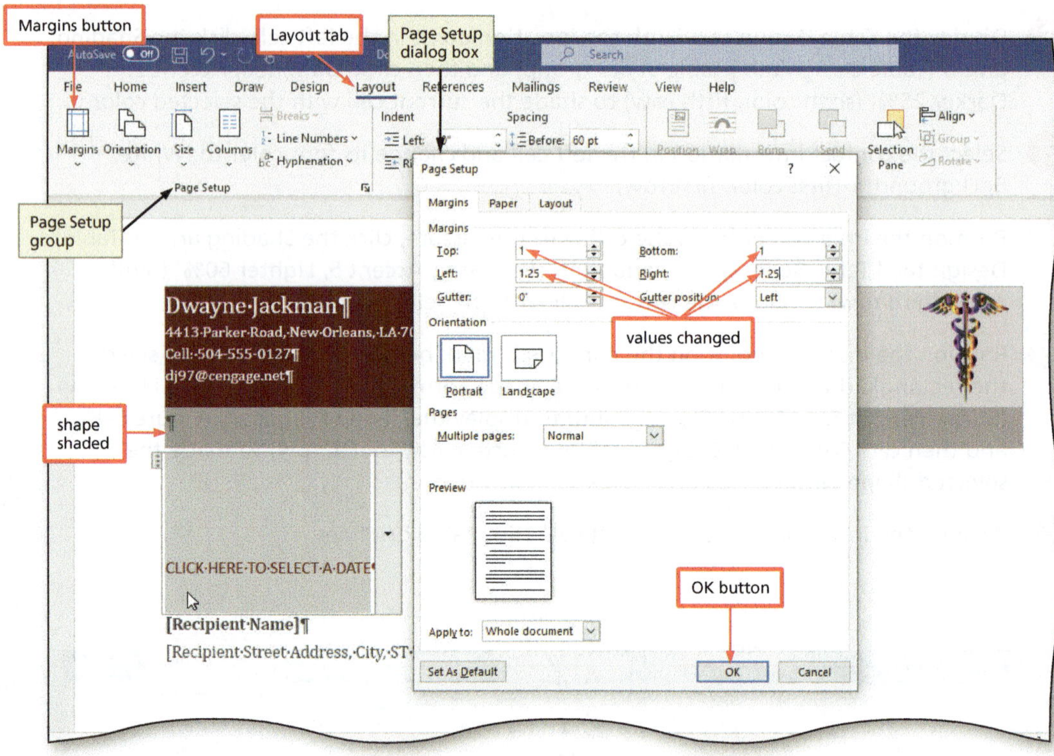

Figure 6–9

4 Click OK to change the margin values.

Q&A **Why is the top margin unchanged?**
The template specifies that the rectangle shape be positioned a certain distance from the top of the page, regardless of margin settings. The next steps change the position of the shape.

To Specify the Position of a Graphic

The next step is to change the distance between the shape and the top of the page. **Why?** You want a one-inch space above the shape. The following steps specify the position of a graphic.

1

- Click the rectangle shape to select it.
- Click the Layout Options button attached to the shape to display the Layout Options gallery (Figure 6–10).

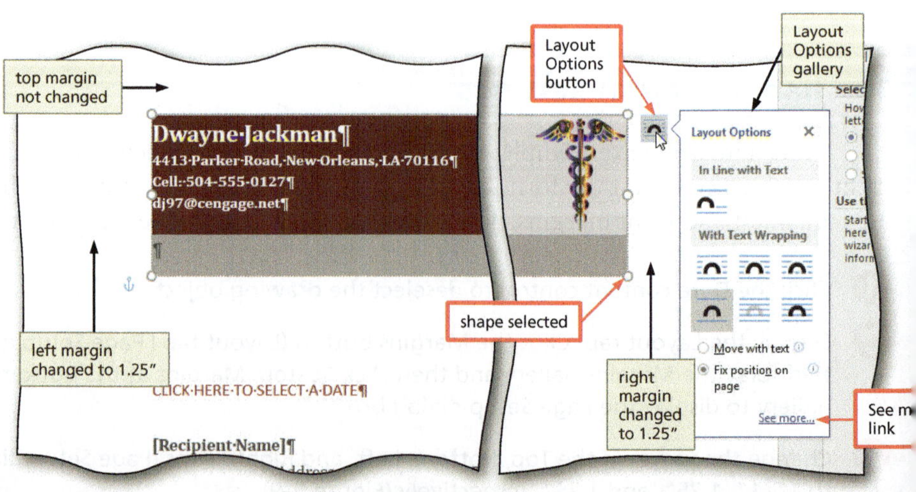

Figure 6–10

2

- Click the See more link (Layout Options gallery) to display the Position tab in the Layout dialog box.
- Click Absolute position in the Vertical area (Layout dialog box), select the value in the Absolute position box, and then type 1 to specify the distance in inches from the top of the page.
- If necessary, click the below arrow and then select Page (Figure 6–11).

Q&A **What is the difference between the specifications in the Horizontal and Vertical areas?**
Horizontal settings specify the graphic's position left to right on the page, whereas vertical settings specify the graphic's position top to bottom on the page.

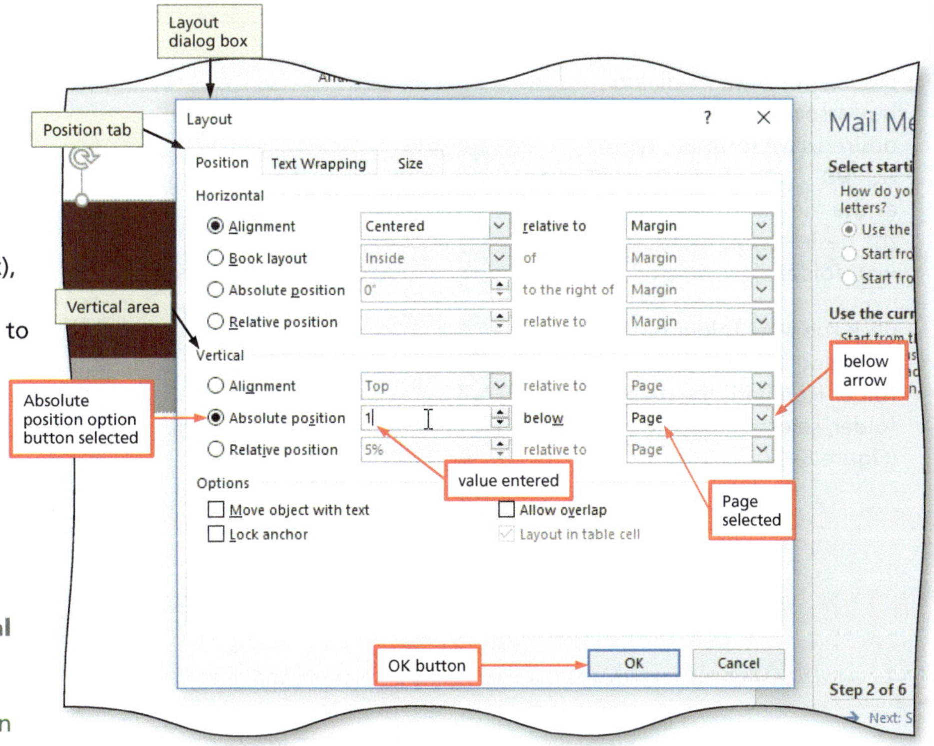

Figure 6–11

3

- Click OK to change the position of the selected graphic (Figure 6–12).

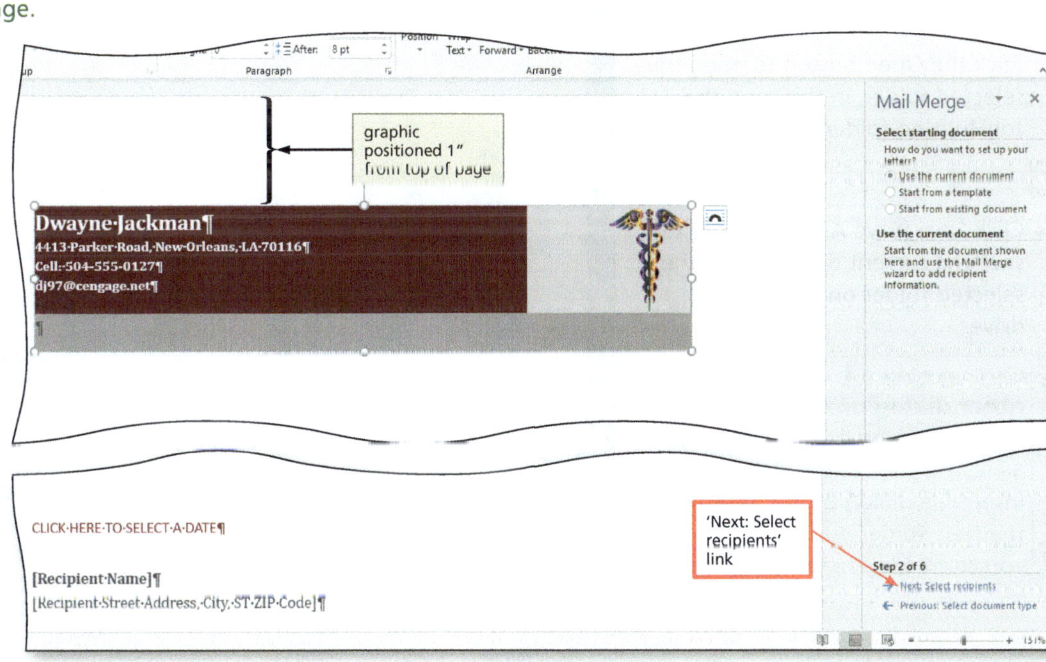

Figure 6–12

To Create a Folder while Saving

You have performed several tasks while creating this project and, thus, should save it. The following steps assume you already have created folders for storing files, for example, a CIS 101 folder (for your class) that contains a Word folder and module folders. You want to save this and all other documents created in this module in a folder called JobHunting folder. The following steps create a folder during the process of saving a document. **Why?** This folder does not exist, so you must create it. Rather than creating the folder in Windows, you can create folders in Word.

1

- Display the Save As dialog box associated with your desired save location, type **SC_WD_6_JackmanCoverLetter** as the file name, and navigate to the desired save location for the new folder.
- Click the New folder button (Save As dialog box) to display a new folder icon with the name, New folder, selected in the dialog box (Figure 6–13).

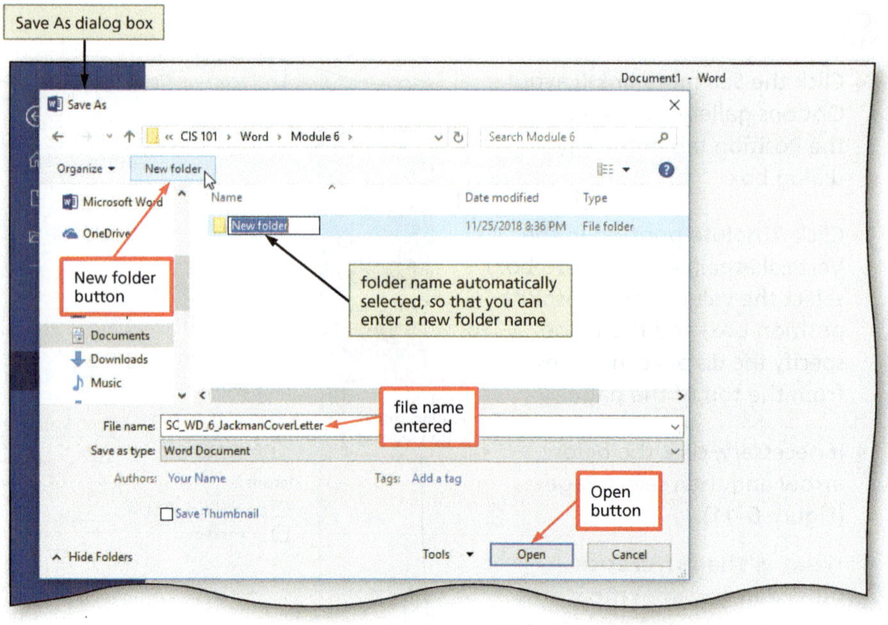

Figure 6–13

2

- Type **JobHunting** as the new folder name and then press ENTER to create the new folder.
- Click the Open button to open the selected folder, in this case, the JobHunting folder (Figure 6–14).

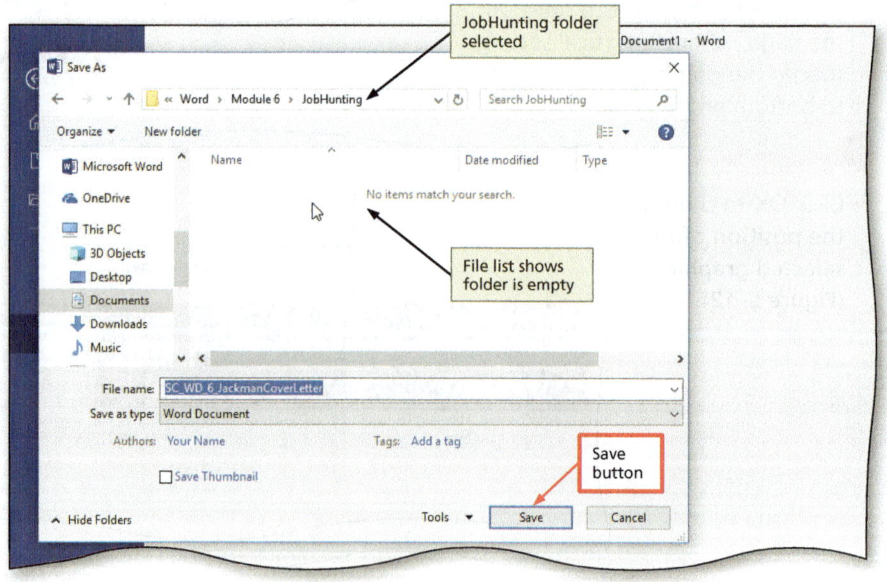

Figure 6–14

3

- Click Save (Save As dialog box) to save the current document in the selected folder on the selected drive.

Q&A

Can I create a folder in any other dialog box?

Yes. Any dialog box that displays a File list, such as the Open and Insert File dialog boxes, also has the New folder button, allowing you to create a new folder in Word instead of using Windows for this task.

Creating a Data Source

The **data source** is a file that contains the variable, or changing, values from one merged document to the next. A data source can be an Access database table, an Outlook contacts list, or an Excel worksheet. If the necessary and properly organized data already exists in one of these Microsoft 365 programs, you can instruct Word to use the existing file as the data source for the mail merge. Otherwise, you can create a new data source using one of these programs.

As shown in Figure 6–15, a data source often is shown as a table that consists of a series of rows and columns. Each row is called a **record.** The first row of a data source is called the **header record** because it identifies the name of each column. Each row below the header row is called a data record. A **data record** contains the complete set of related text for each recipient in the data source; the collection of data records is referred to as the recipient list. The data source for the project in this module contains five data records (recipients). In this project, each data record (recipient) identifies a different potential employer. Thus, five form letters will be generated from the recipient list in this data source.

Each column in the data source is called a **data field**, which represents a group of similar data. Each data field must be identified uniquely with a name, called a **field name**. For example, Position is the name of the data field (column) that contains the available job position. In this module, the data source contains 11 data fields with the following field names: Title, First Name, Last Name, Organization Name, Address Line 1, Address Line 2, City, State, ZIP Code, Position, and Product Sold.

BTW

Fields and Records

Field and record are terms that originate from the software development field. Do not be intimidated by these terms. A field is simply a column in a table, and a record is a row. Rather than using the term, field, some software developers identify a column of data as a variable or an attribute. All three terms (field, variable, and attribute) have the same meaning.

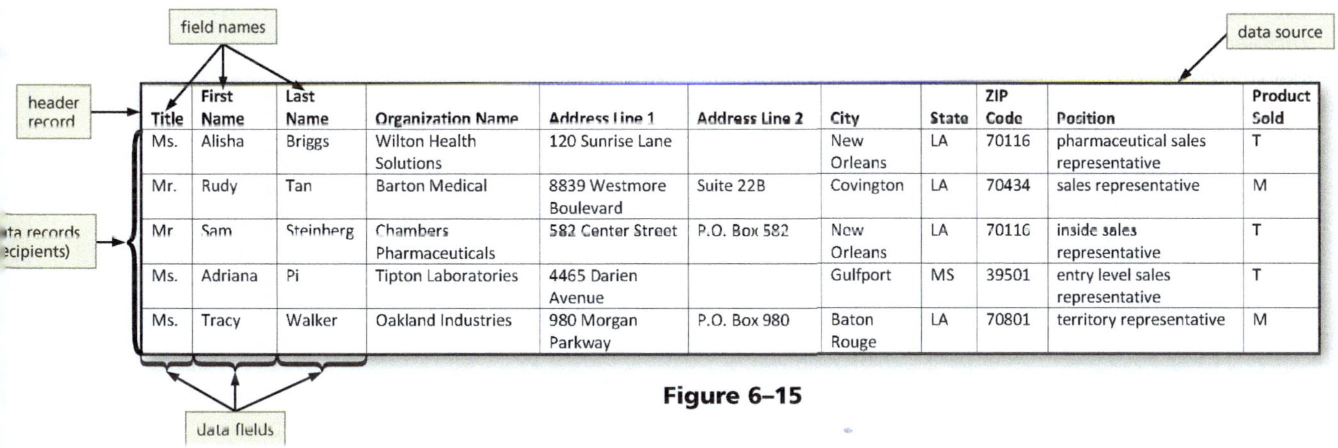

Title	First Name	Last Name	Organization Name	Address Line 1	Address Line 2	City	State	ZIP Code	Position	Product Sold
Ms.	Alisha	Briggs	Wilton Health Solutions	120 Sunrise Lane		New Orleans	LA	70116	pharmaceutical sales representative	T
Mr.	Rudy	Tan	Barton Medical	8839 Westmore Boulevard	Suite 22B	Covington	LA	70434	sales representative	M
Mr.	Sam	Steinberg	Chambers Pharmaceuticals	582 Center Street	P.O. Box 582	New Orleans	LA	70116	inside sales representative	T
Ms.	Adriana	Pi	Tipton Laboratories	4465 Darien Avenue		Gulfport	MS	39501	entry level sales representative	T
Ms.	Tracy	Walker	Oakland Industries	980 Morgan Parkway	P.O. Box 980	Baton Rouge	LA	70801	territory representative	M

Figure 6–15

Consider This

What guidelines should you follow when creating a data source?

When you create a data source, you will need to determine the fields it should contain. That is, you will need to identify the data that will vary from one merged document to the next. Following are a few important points about fields:

- For each field, you may be required to create a field name. Because data sources often contain the same fields, some programs create a list of commonly used field names that you may use.
- Field names must be unique; that is, no two field names may be the same.
- Fields may be listed in any order in the data source. That is, the order of fields has no effect on the order in which they will print in the main document.
- Organize fields so that they are flexible. For example, separate the name into individual fields: title, first name, and last name. This arrangement allows you to print a person's title, first name, and last name (e.g., Ms. Alisha Briggs) in the inside address but only the title and last name in the salutation (Dear Ms. Briggs).

To Type a New Recipient List for a Data Source

Word provides a list of 13 commonly used field names. This project uses 9 of the 13 field names supplied by Word: Title, First Name, Last Name, Company Name, Address Line 1, Address Line 2, City, State, and ZIP Code. This project does not use the other four field names supplied by Word: Country or Region, Home Phone, Work Phone, and E-mail Address. Thus, you will delete these four field names. Then, you will change the Company Name field name to Organization Name. **Why?** The term, organization, better describes the potential employers in this project. You also will add two new field names (Position and Product Sold) to the data source. **Why?** You want to reference the available position, as well as the product sold, in the form letter. The next steps type a new recipient list for a data source for a mail merge.

1

- Click the 'Next: Select recipients' link at the bottom of the Mail Merge pane (shown in Figure 6–12) to display Step 3 of the Mail Merge wizard, which requests you select recipients.
- Click 'Type a new list' in the Select recipients area, which displays the Type a new list area.
- Click the Create link to display the New Address List dialog box (Figure 6–16).

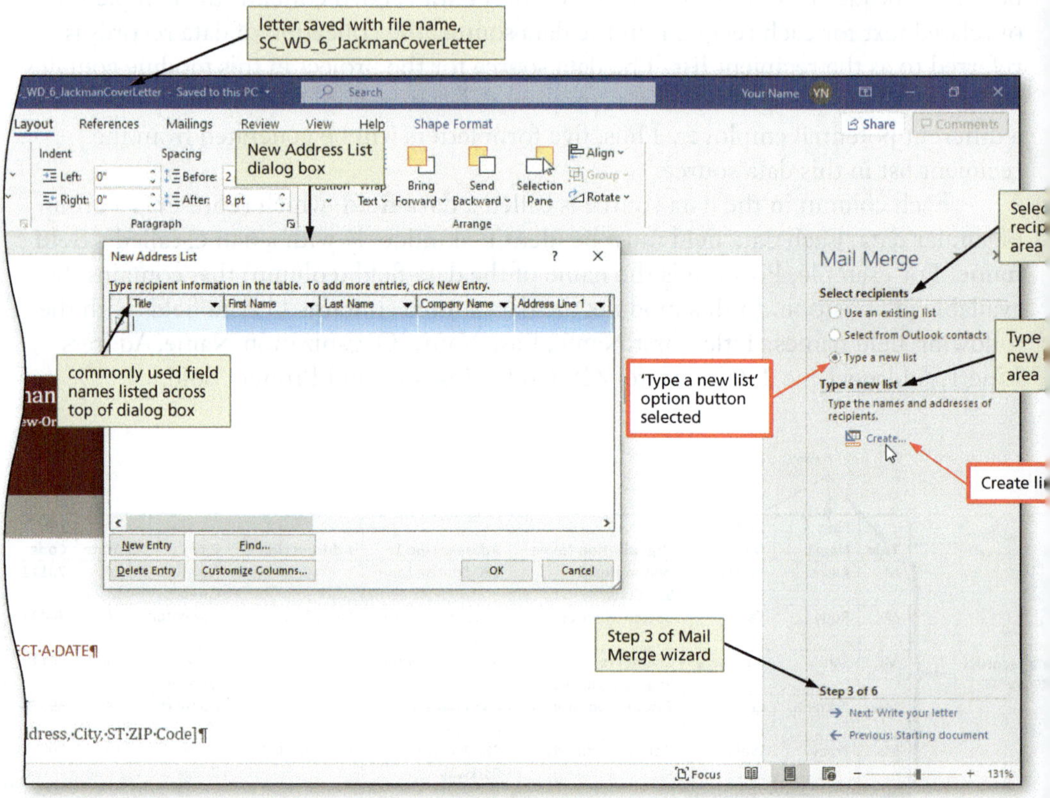

Figure 6–16

Q&A **When would I use the other two option buttons in the Select recipients area?**
If a data source already was created, you would use the first option: Use an existing list. If you wanted to use your Outlook contacts list as the data source, you would choose the second option.

2

- Click the Customize Columns button (New Address List dialog box) to display the Customize Address List dialog box (Figure 6–17).

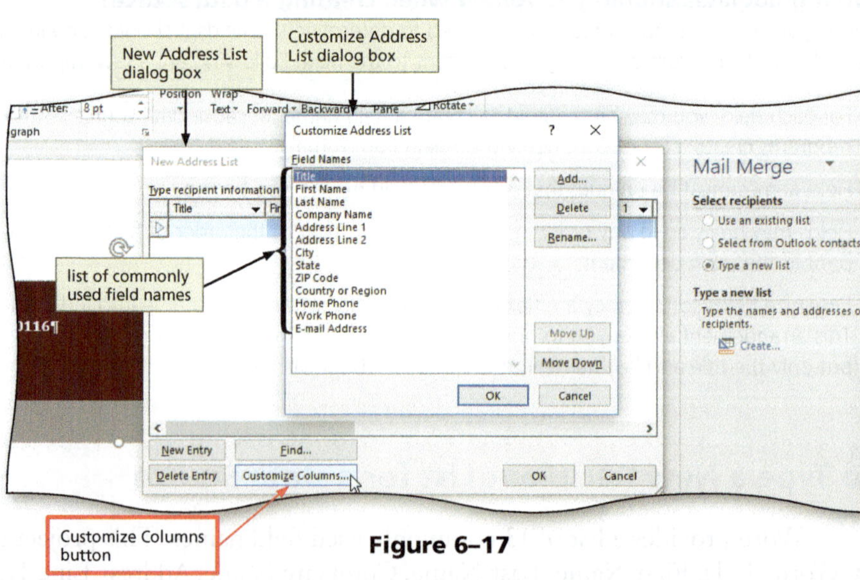

Figure 6–17

3

- Click 'Country or Region' in the Field Names list (Customize Address List dialog box) to select the field to be deleted and then click the Delete button to display a dialog box asking if you are sure you want to delete the selected field (Figure 6–18).

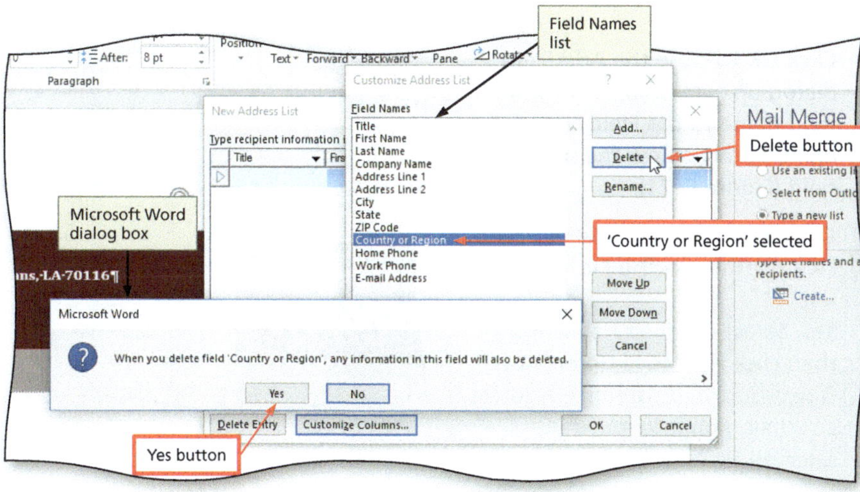

Figure 6–18

4

- Click Yes (Microsoft Word dialog box) to delete the field.
- Click Home Phone in the Field Names list to select the field. Click the Delete button (Customize Address List dialog box) and then click Yes (Microsoft Word dialog box) to delete the field.
- Use this same procedure to delete the Work Phone and E-mail Address fields.

5

- Click Company Name in the Field Names list to select the field to be renamed.
- Click the Rename button to display the Rename Field dialog box.
- Type `Organization Name` in the To text box (Rename Field dialog box) (Figure 6–19).

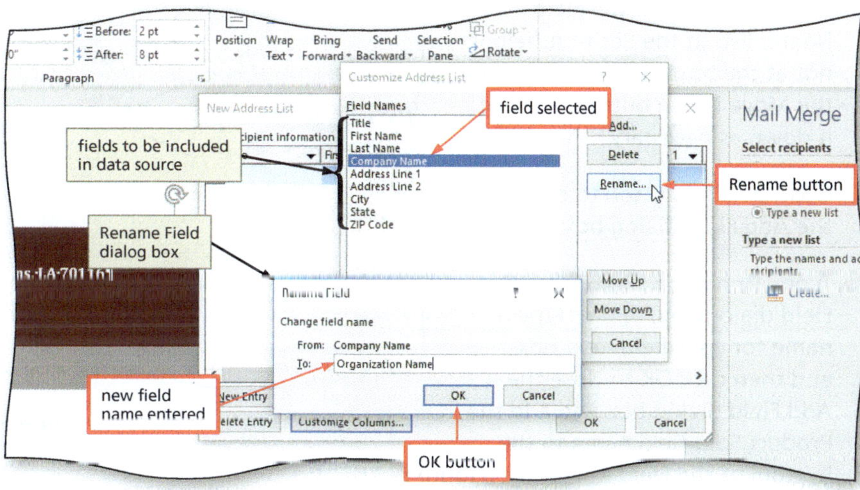

Figure 6–19

6

- Click OK to close the Rename Field dialog box and rename the selected field.

7

- Click the Add button to display the Add Field dialog box.
- Type `Position` in the 'Type a name for your field' text box (Add Field dialog box) (Figure 6–20).

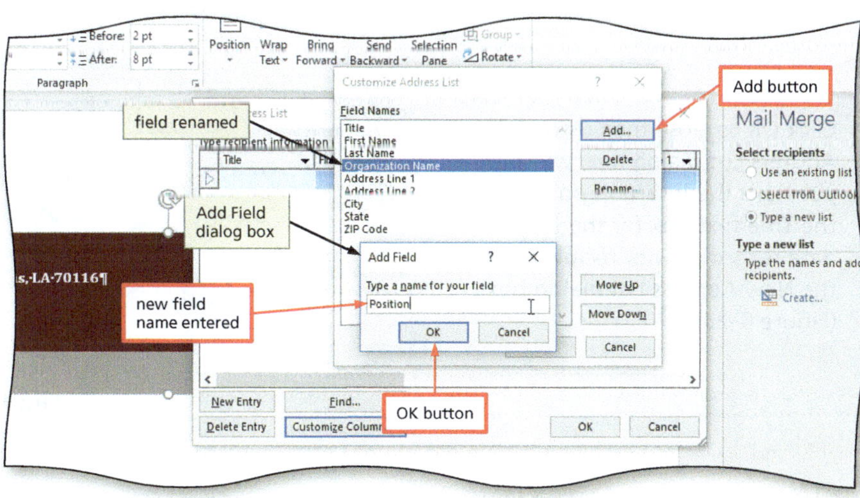

Figure 6–20

8

- Click OK to close the Add Field dialog box and add the Position field name to the Field Names list immediately below the selected field (Figure 6–21).

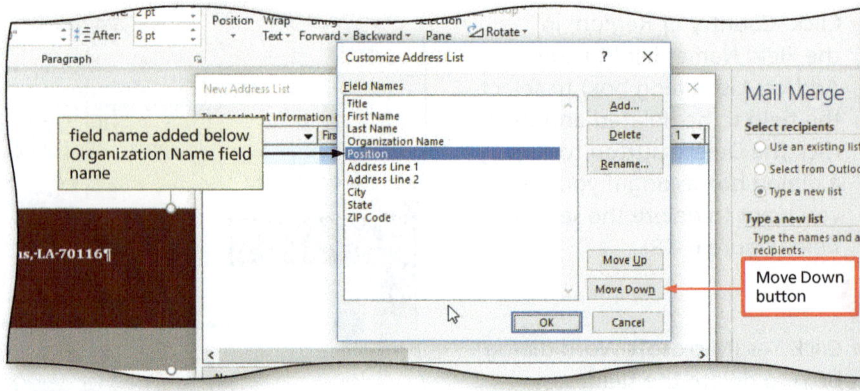

Figure 6–21

Q&A **Can I change the order of the field names in the Field Names list?**
Yes. Select the field name and then click the Move Up or Move Down button (Customize Address List dialog box) to move the selected field in the direction of the button name.

9

- With the Position field selected, click the Move Down button five times to position the selected field at the end of the Field Names list. (If the Position field is not at the bottom of the list, click the Move Down button to move it down as necessary.)
- Click the Add button to display the Add Field dialog box.
- Type **`Product Sold`** (Add Field dialog box) in the 'Type a name for your field' text box and then click OK to close the Add Field dialog box and add the Product Sold field name to the bottom of the Field Names list (Figure 6–22).

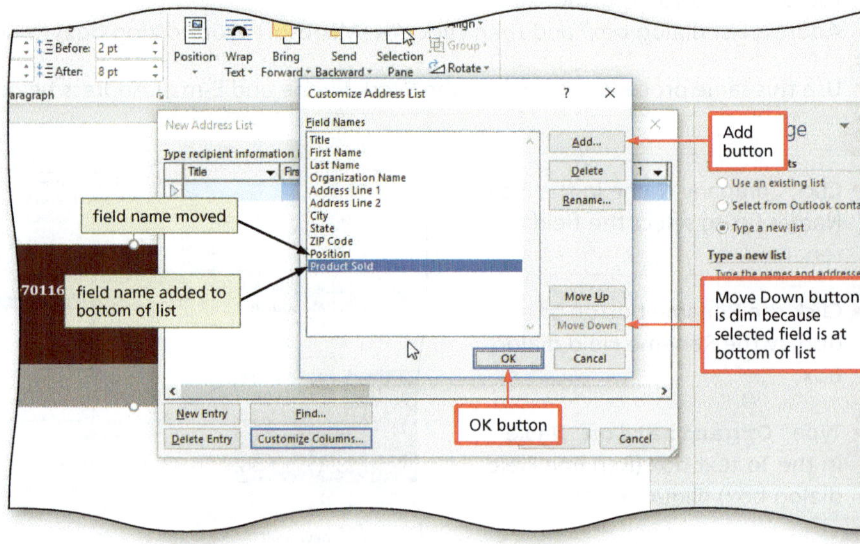

Figure 6–22

Q&A **Could I add more field names to the list?**
Yes. You would click the Add button for each field name you want to add.

10

- Click OK to close the Customize Address List dialog box, which positions the insertion point in the Title text box for the first data record (row or recipient) in the New Address List dialog box (Figure 6–23).

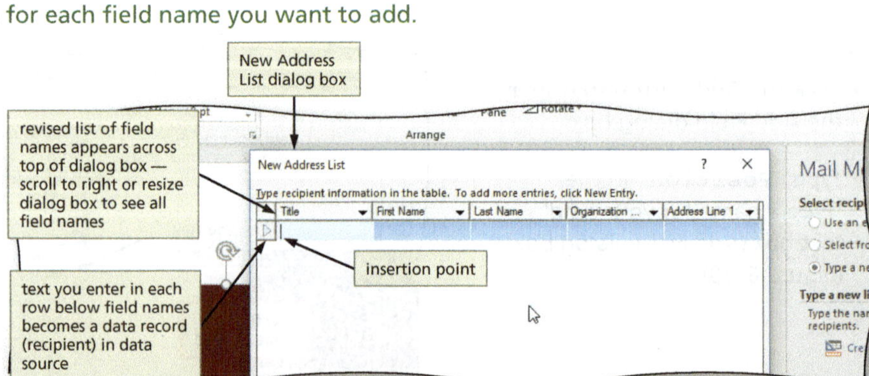

Figure 6–23

11

- Type **Ms.** and then press TAB to enter the title for the first data record.
- Type **Alisha** and then press TAB to enter the first name.
- Type **Briggs** and then press TAB to enter the last name.
- Type **Wilton Health Solutions** and then press TAB to enter the organization name.
- Type **120 Sunrise Lane** to enter the first address line (Figure 6–24).

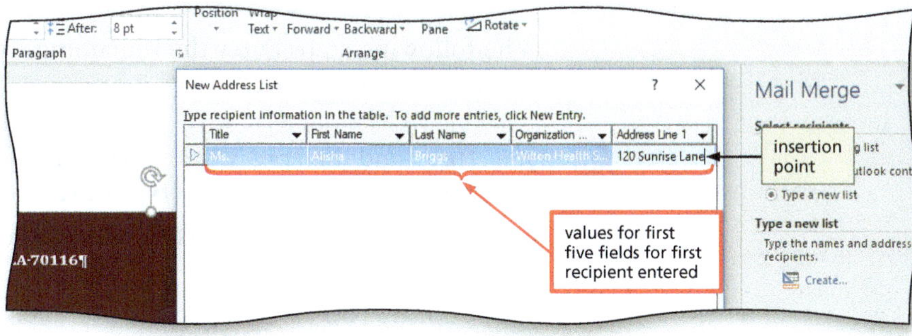

Figure 6–24

Q&A **What if I notice an error in an entry?**
Click the entry and then correct the error as you would in the document window.

What happened to the rest of the Organization Name entry?
It is stored in the field, but you cannot see the entire entry because it is longer than the display area.

12

- Press TAB twice to leave the second address line empty.
- Type **New Orleans** and then press TAB to enter the city.
- Type **LA** and then press TAB to enter the state code.
- Type **70116** and then press TAB to enter the ZIP code.
- Type **pharmaceutical sales representative** and then press TAB to enter the position.

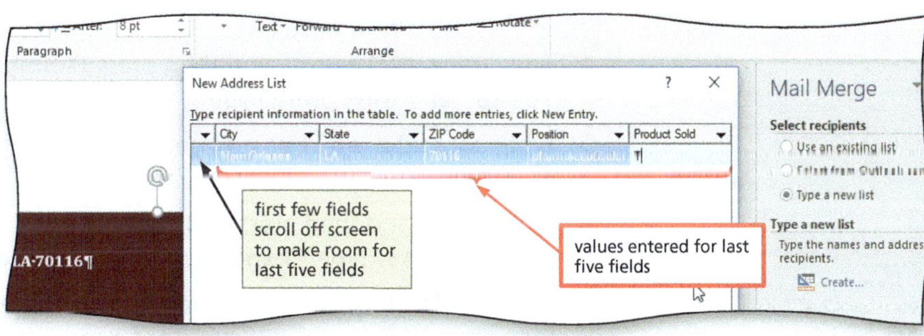

Figure 6–25

- Type **T** to enter the code for the product sold (Figure 6–25).

Q&A **What does the T mean in the product sold?**
You decide to enter T for therapeutic medicine and M for medical devices to minimize the amount of redundant typing for these records.

13

- Press TAB to add a new blank record and position the insertion point in the Title field of the new record (Figure 6–26).

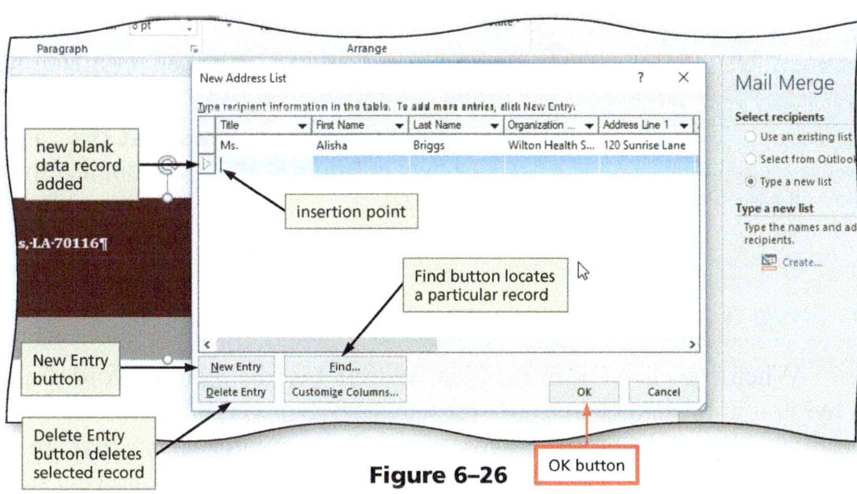

Figure 6–26

Other Ways

1. Click Select Recipients button (Mailings tab | Start Mail Merge group)

To Enter More Recipients

The following steps enter the remaining four data records (recipients) in the New Address List dialog box.

1. Type **Mr.** and then press TAB. Type **Rudy** and then press TAB. Type **Tan** and then press TAB. Type **Barton Medical** and then press TAB.
2. Type **8839 Westmore Boulevard** and then press TAB. Type **Suite 22B** and then press TAB.
3. Type **Covington** and then press TAB. Type **LA** and then press TAB. Type **70434** and then press TAB.
4. Type **sales representative** and then press TAB. Type **M** and then press TAB.

Q&A **Instead of pressing TAB, can I click the New Entry button at the end of one row to add a new blank record?**
Yes. Clicking the New Entry button at the end of a row has the same effect as pressing TAB.

5. Type **Mr.** and then press TAB. Type **Sam** and then press TAB. Type **Steinberg** and then press TAB. Type **Chambers Pharmaceuticals** and then press TAB.
6. Type **582 Center Street** and then press TAB. Type **P.O. Box 582** and then press TAB.
7. Type **New Orleans** and then press TAB. Type **LA** and then press TAB. Type **70116** and then press TAB.
8. Type **inside sales representative** and then press TAB. Type **T** and then press TAB.
9. Type **Ms.** and then press TAB. Type **Adriana** and then press TAB. Type **Pi** and then press TAB. Type **Tipton Laboratories** and then press TAB.
10. Type **4465 Darien Avenue** and then press TAB twice. Type **Gulfport** and then press TAB. Type **MS** and then press TAB. Type **39501** and then press TAB.
11. Type **entry level sales representative** and then press TAB. Type **T** and then press TAB.
12. Type **Ms.** and then press TAB. Type **Tracy** and then press TAB. Type **Walker** and then press TAB. Type **Oakland Industries** and then press TAB.
13. Type **980 Morgan Parkway** and then press TAB. Type **P.O. Box 980** and then press TAB.
14. Type **Baton Rouge** and then press TAB. Type **LA** and then press TAB. Type **70801** and then press TAB.
15. Type **territory representative** and then press TAB. Type **M** and then click OK (shown in Figure 6–26), which displays the Save Address List dialog box (shown in Figure 6–27).

BTW

Saving Data Sources
Word, by default, saves a data source in the My Data Sources folder on your computer or mobile device's default storage location. Likewise, when you open a data source, Word initially looks in the My Data Sources folder for the file. Because the data source files you create in Word are saved as Microsoft Access database file types, you can open and view these files in Access if you are familiar with Microsoft Access.

To Save a Data Source when Prompted by Word

When you click OK in the New Address List dialog box, Word displays the Save Address List dialog box. **Why?** You immediately save the data source so that you do not lose any entered information. By default, the save location is the My Data Sources folder on your computer's hard drive. In this module, you save the data source in the JobHunting folder created earlier in this module. The following steps save the data source.

1

- Type **SC_WD_6_JackmanProspectiveEmployers** in the File name box (Save Address List dialog box) as the name for the data source. Do not press ENTER after typing the file name because you do not want to close the dialog box at this time.
- Navigate to the desired save location for the data source (for example, the JobHunting folder) (Figure 6–27).

Q&A **What is a Microsoft Office Address Lists file type?**
It is a Microsoft Access database file. If you are familiar with Microsoft Access, you can open the SC_WD_6_JackmanProspectiveEmployers file in Access. You do not have to be familiar with Access or have Access installed on your computer, however, to continue with this mail merge process. Word stores a data source as an Access table simply because it is an efficient method of storing a data source.

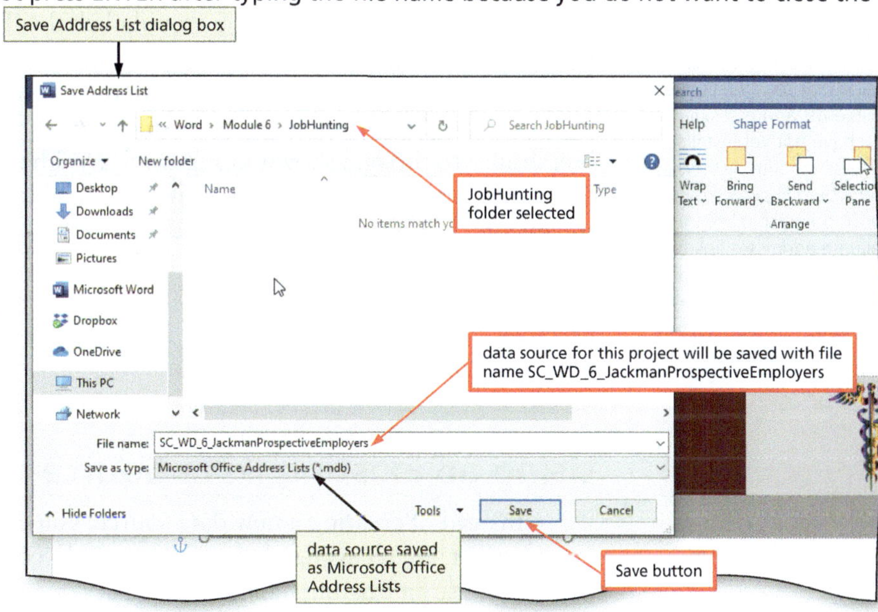

Figure 6–27

2

- Click Save (Save Address List dialog box) to save the data source in the selected folder using the entered file name and then display the Mail Merge Recipients dialog box (Figure 6–28).

Q&A **What if the fields in my Mail Merge Recipients list are in a different order?**
The order of fields in the Mail Merge Recipients list has no effect on the mail merge process. If Word rearranges the order, you can leave them in the revised order.

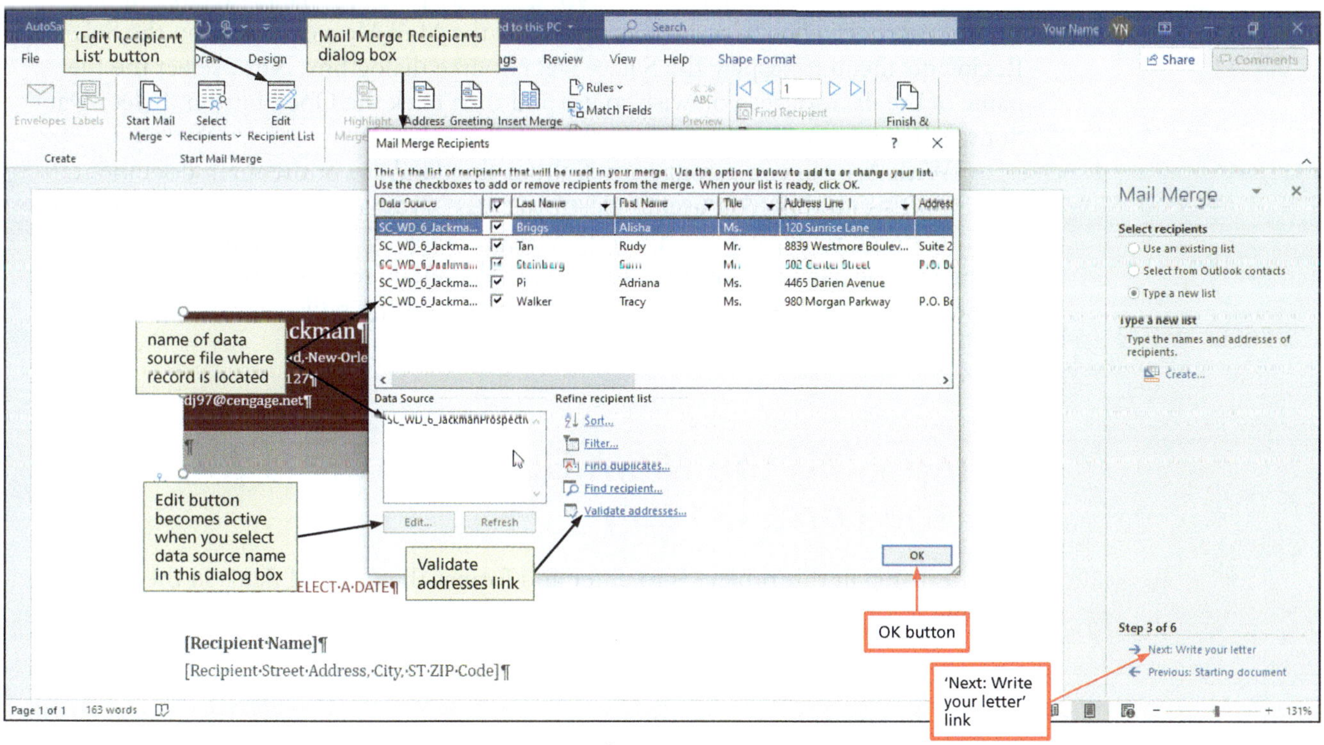

Figure 6–28

3

- Click OK to close the Mail Merge Recipients dialog box.

BTW
Validating Addresses
If you have installed address validation software, you can click the Validate addresses link (shown in Figure 6–28) in the Mail Merge Recipients dialog box to validate your recipients' addresses. If you have not yet installed address validation software and would like information about doing so, click the Validate addresses link in the Mail Merge Recipients dialog box and then click Yes in the Microsoft Word dialog box to display a related Microsoft webpage.

Editing Data Records (Recipients) in the Data Source

All of the data records (recipients) have been entered in the data source and saved with the file name, SC_WD_6_JackmanProspectiveEmployers. To add or edit recipients in the data source, you would click the 'Edit Recipient List' button (Mailings tab | Start Mail Merge group) to display the Mail Merge Recipients dialog box (shown in Figure 6–28). Click the data source name in the Data Source list and then click the Edit button (Mail Merge Recipients dialog box) to display the data records in a dialog box similar to the one shown in Figure 6–26. Then, add or edit records as described in the previous steps. If you want to edit a particular record and the list of data records (recipients) is long, you can click the Find button to locate an item, such as a last name, quickly in the list.

To delete a record, select it using the same procedure described in the previous paragraph. Then, click the Delete Entry button in the dialog box (shown in Figure 6–26).

Using an Existing Data Source

Instead of creating a new data source, you can use an existing Microsoft Outlook Contacts list, an Access database table, or an Excel table as a data source in a mail merge. To use an existing data source, select the appropriate option in the Select recipients area in the Mail Merge pane or click the Select Recipients button (Mailings tab | Start Mail Merge group) and then click the desired option on the Select Recipients menu.

For a Microsoft Outlook Contacts list, click 'Select from Outlook contacts' in the Mail Merge pane or 'Choose from Outlook Contacts' on the Select Recipients menu to display the Select Contacts dialog box. Next, select the contact folder you wish to import (Select Contacts dialog box) and then click OK.

For other existing data source types, such as an Access database table or an Excel worksheet, click 'Use an existing list' in the Mail Merge pane or on the Select Recipients menu to display the Select Data Source dialog box. Next, select the file name of the data source you wish to use and then click the Open button (Select Data Source dialog box).

With Access, you can use any field in the database in the main document. (Later in this module you use an existing Access database table as the data source.) For the merge to work correctly with an Excel table, you must ensure data is arranged properly and that the table is the only element in the file. The first row of the table should contain unique field names, and the table cannot contain any blank rows.

Composing the Main Document for the Form Letters

The next step in this project is to enter and format the text and fields in the main document for the form letters (shown in Figure 6–1a at the beginning of this module).

A **main document** contains the constant, or unchanging, text, punctuation, spaces, and graphics, as well as references to the data in the data source. You will follow these steps to compose the main document for the form letter.

1. Enter the date.
2. Enter the address block.
3. Enter the greeting line (salutation).
4. Enter text and insert a merge field.
5. Enter additional text and merge fields.
6. Insert an IF field.
7. Enter the remainder of the letter.
8. Merge the letters.

Consider This

What guidelines should you follow when composing the main document for a form letter?

The finished main document letter should look like a symmetrically framed picture with evenly spaced margins, all balanced below an attractive letterhead or return address. The content of the main document for the form letter should contain proper grammar, correct spelling, logically constructed sentences, flowing paragraphs, and sound ideas; it also should reference the data in the data source properly.

Be sure the main document for the form letter includes all essential business letter elements. All business letters should contain a date line, inside address, message, and signature block. Many business letters contain additional items, such as a special mailing notation(s), an attention line, a salutation, a subject line, a complimentary close, reference initials, and an enclosure notation. When finished, proofread your letter carefully.

To Display the Next Step in the Mail Merge Wizard

The following step displays the next step in the Mail Merge wizard, which is to write the letter.

1. Click the 'Next: Write your letter' link at the bottom of the Mail Merge pane (shown in Figure 6–28) to display Step 4 of the Mail Merge wizard in the Mail Merge pane (shown in Figure 6–29).

To Enter the Date from a Content Control

The next step is to enter the date in the letter. **Why?** All business letters should contain a date, which usually is positioned below the letterhead or return address. You can click the date content control and type the correct date, or you can click the arrow and select the date from a calendar. The following steps use the calendar to select the date.

1

- Click the Date content control to select it and then click its arrow to display a calendar.
- Scroll through the calendar months until the desired month appears, April 2020, in this case (Figure 6–29).

2

- Click 22 in the calendar to display the selected month, day, and year in the date line of the form letter (shown in Figure 6–30).
- Click outside the content control to deselect it.
- Right-click the date to display a shortcut menu and then click 'Remove Content Control' on the shortcut menu so that your text (the selected date) remains but the content control is deleted.

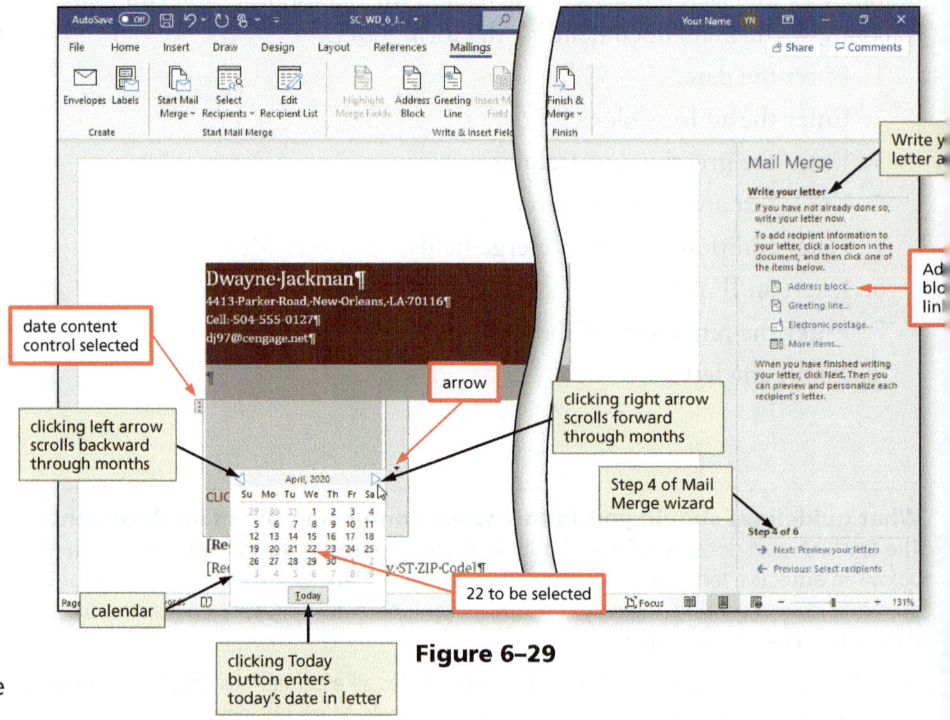

Figure 6–29

Q&A **Why delete the content control?**
You no longer need the content control because you already selected the date.

Other Ways

1. Type date in Date content control
2. Click 'Insert Date & Time' button (Insert tab | Text group)

Merge Fields

In this form letter, the inside address appears below the date line, and the salutation is placed below the inside address. The contents of the inside address and salutation are located in the data source. To link the data source to the main document, you insert the field names from the data source in the main document.

In the main document, field names linked to the data source are called **merge fields** because they merge, or combine, the main document with the contents of the data source; that is, merge fields indicate where the data from each data record (recipient) should be inserted when you perform a mail merge. When a merge field is inserted in the main document, Word surrounds the field name with **merge field characters**, which are chevrons (« ») that mark the beginning and ending of a merge field. Merge field characters are not on the keyboard; therefore, you cannot type them directly in the document. Word automatically displays them when a merge field is inserted in the main document.

Most letters contain an address and salutation. For this reason, Word provides an AddressBlock merge field and a GreetingLine merge field. The **AddressBlock merge field** contains several fields related to an address: Title, First Name, Middle Name, Last Name, Suffix, Company, Street Address 1, Street Address 2, City, State, and ZIP Code. When Word uses the AddressBlock merge field, it automatically looks for any fields in the associated data source that are related to an address and then formats the address block properly when you merge the data source with the main document. For example, if your inside address does not use a middle name, suffix, or company, Word omits these items from the inside address and adjusts the spacing so that the address prints correctly.

To Insert the AddressBlock Merge Field

The default format for the AddressBlock merge field is the first name and last name on one line, followed by the street address on the next line, and then the city, state, and postal code on the next line. In this letter, you want the potential employer's title (i.e., Ms.) to appear to the left of the first name. **Why?** You want to address the potential employers formally. You also want the organization name to appear above the street address, if it does not already. The following steps insert the AddressBlock merge field in this format.

1

- Delete the content control that contains placeholder text for the recipient's address and then press DELETE to delete the blank paragraph.
- Delete the [Recipient Name] placeholder text but leave the paragraph mark; position the insertion point to the left of the paragraph mark because you will insert the AddressBlock merge field in that location.
- Click the Address block link in the Mail Merge pane (shown in Figure 6–29) to display the Insert Address Block dialog box.
- Scroll through the list of recipient name formats (Insert Address Block dialog box) and then click the format 'Mr. Joshua Randall Jr.' in this list, because that format places the title to the left of the first name and last name.

Experiment

- Click various recipient name formats and watch the preview change in the dialog box. When finished experimenting, click 'Mr. Joshua Randall Jr.' for the format.

Q&A

Why is the 'Insert company name' check box dimmed?

The data source does not have a match to the Company Name in the AddressBlock merge field so this check box will be dimmed. Recall that earlier in this project the Company Name field was renamed as Organization Name, which causes the fields to be unmatched. The next step shows how to match the fields. If the Organization Name already appears in your AddressBlock merge field, proceed to Step 4.

- Click the Match Fields button (Insert Address Block dialog box) to display the Match Fields dialog box (Figure 6–30).

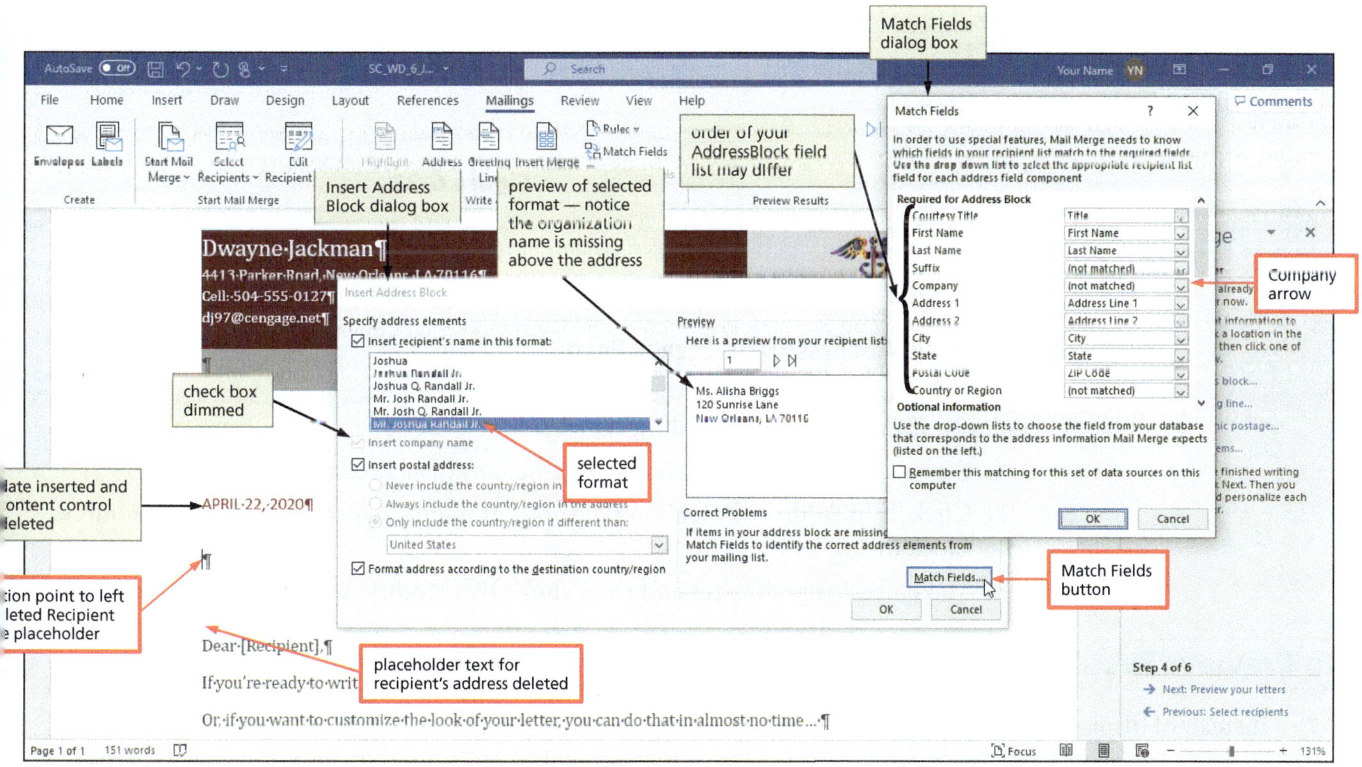

Figure 6–30

2

- Click the Company arrow (Match Fields dialog box) to display a list of fields in the data source and then click Organization Name to place that selected field as the match field (Figure 6–31).

3

- Click OK (Match Fields dialog box) to close the dialog box, and notice the 'Insert company name' check box no longer is dimmed (Insert Address Block dialog box) because the Company field now has a matched field in the data source.

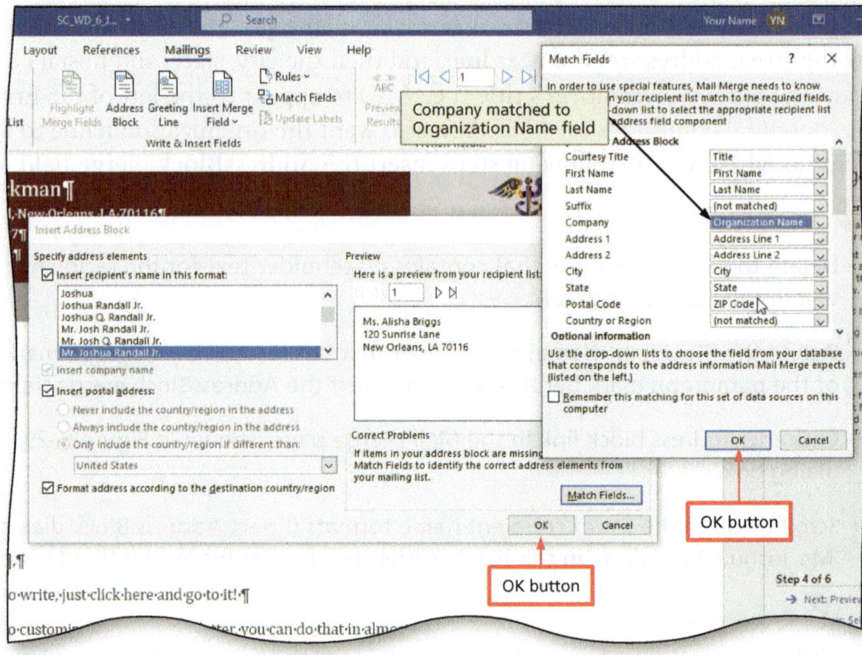

Figure 6–31

4

- Click OK (Insert Address Block dialog box) to insert the AddressBlock merge field at the location of the insertion point (Figure 6–32).

Figure 6–32

Other Ways

1. Click Address Block button (Mailings tab | Write & Insert Fields group), select options (Insert Greeting Line dialog box), click OK

To Edit the AddressBlock Merge Field

If you wanted to change the format of or match fields in the AddressBlock merge field, you would perform the following steps.

1. Right-click the AddressBlock merge field to display a shortcut menu.
2. Click 'Edit Address Block' on the shortcut menu to display the Modify Address Block dialog box.
3. Make necessary changes and then click OK (Modify Address Block dialog box).

To Preview Results in the Main Document

Instead of displaying merge fields, you can display merged data. **Why?** One way to see how fields, such as the AddressBlock fields, will look in the merged letter, is to preview results. The following step previews results.

1

- Click the Preview Results button (Mailings tab | Preview Results group) to display the values in the current data record, instead of the merge fields.
- Scroll up, if necessary, to view the address fields (Figure 6–33).

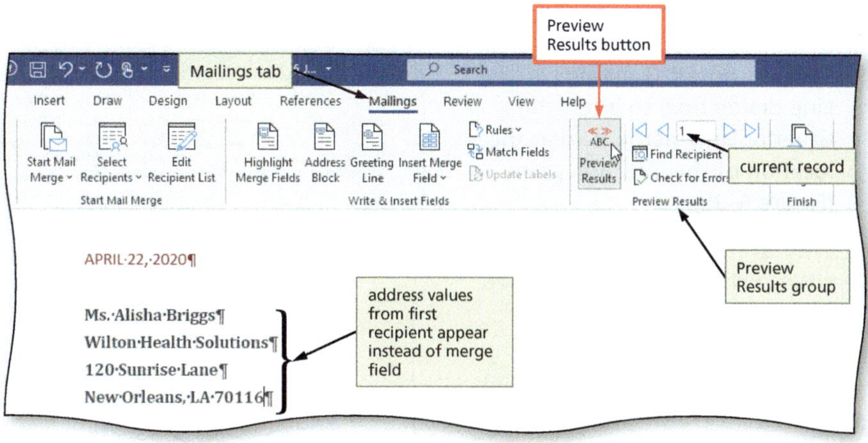

Figure 6–33

Q&A

How can I tell which record is showing?
The current record number is displayed in the Preview Results group.

Why is the spacing in my address different from Figure 6–33?
You may have inserted the AddressBlock field on the line in the template that contained the recipient's address, instead of the line that contained the recipient's name. To fix the address spacing, select the entire address and then change the spacing before and after to 2 pt (Layout tab | Paragraph group).

To Insert the GreetingLine Merge Field

The **GreetingLine merge field** contains text and fields related to a salutation. The default greeting for the salutation is in the format, Dear Alisha, followed by a comma. In this letter, you want the salutation to be followed by a colon. **Why?** Business letters use a more formal salutation (Dear Ms. Briggs:) in the cover letter. The following steps insert the GreetingLine merge field.

1

- Delete the word, Dear, the [Recipient] placeholder text, and the comma in the salutation but leave the paragraph mark; position the insertion point to the left of the paragraph mark because you will insert the GreetingLine merge field in that location.
- Click the Greeting line link in the Mail Merge pane to display the Insert Greeting Line dialog box.
- If necessary, click the middle arrow in the Greeting line format area (Insert Greeting Line dialog box); scroll to and then click the format, Mr. Randall, in this list because you want the title followed by the last name format.
- If necessary, click the rightmost arrow in the Greeting line format area and then click the colon (:) in the list (Figure 6–34).

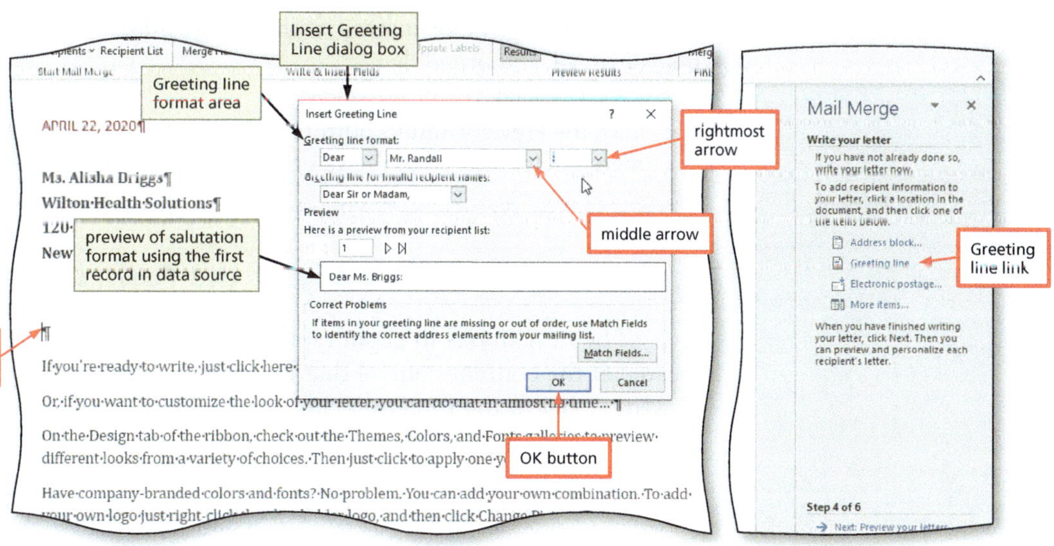

Figure 6–34

2

- Click OK (Insert Greeting Line dialog box) to insert the GreetingLine merge field at the location of the insertion point (Figure 6–35).

Q&A **Why are the values for the title and last name displayed instead of the merge field names?**
With the Preview Results button (Mailings tab | Preview Results group) still selected, the field values are displayed instead of the field names.

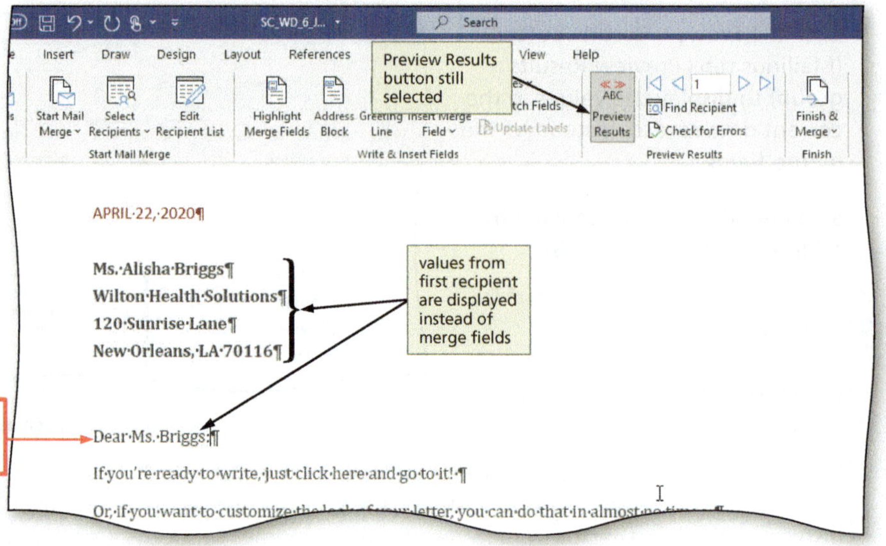

Figure 6–35

Other Ways

1. Click Greeting Line button (Mailings tab | Write & Insert Fields group), select options (Insert Greeting Line dialog box), click OK

To Edit the GreetingLine Merge Field

If you wanted to change the format of or match fields in the GreetingLine merge field, you would perform the following steps.

1. Right-click the GreetingLine merge field to display a shortcut menu.
2. Click 'Edit Greeting Line' on the shortcut menu to display the Modify Greeting Line dialog box.
3. Make the necessary changes and then click OK (Modify Greeting Line dialog box).

To View Merge Fields in the Main Document

Because you will be entering merge fields in the document next, you wish to display the merge fields instead of the merged data. The following step views merge fields instead of merged data.

1 Click the Preview Results button (Mailings tab | Preview Results group) to display the merge fields instead of the values in the current data record (shown in Figure 6–36).

To Begin Typing the Body of the Form Letter

The next step is to begin typing the message, or body of the letter, which is located at the content control that begins with the placeholder text, If you're ready to write..., below the GreetingLine merge field. The following steps begin typing the letter at the location of the content control.

1 Click the body of the letter to select the content control (Figure 6–36).

2 With the content control selected, type `I enjoyed meeting with you during the Gulf College job fair this week. As you suggested, I have enclosed my resume for your review. I am interested in the` and then press SPACEBAR (shown in Figure 6–37).

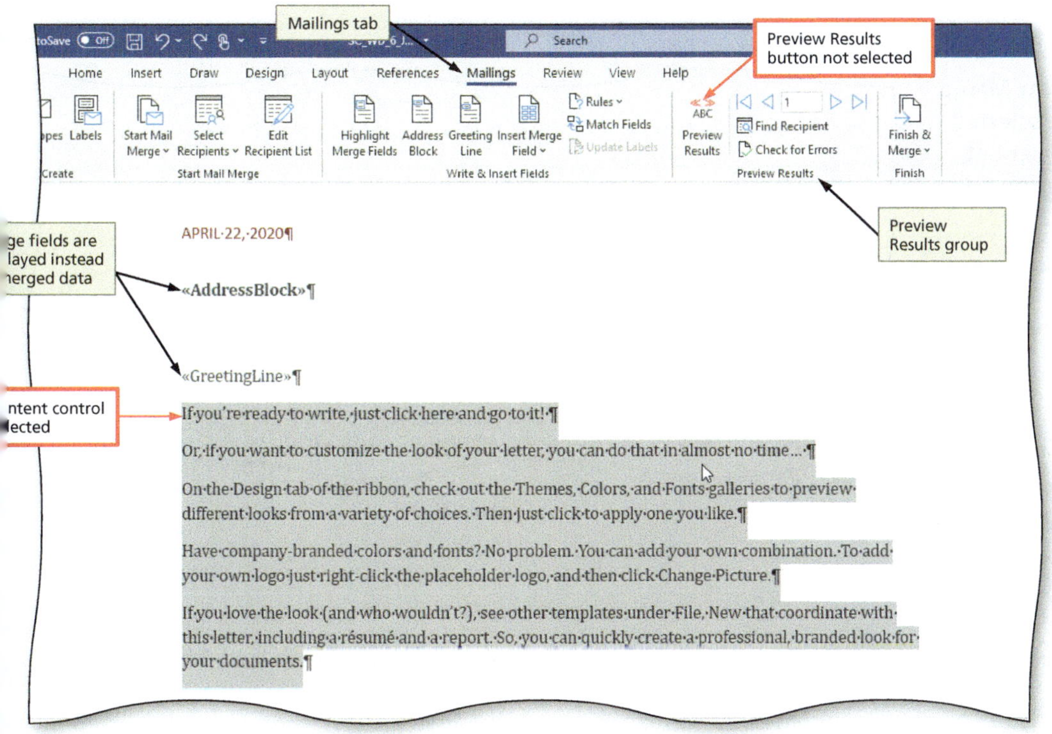

Figure 6–36

BTW

'Insert Merge Field' Button

If you click the 'Insert Merge Field' button instead of the 'Insert Merge Field' arrow (Figure 6–37), Word displays the Insert Merge Field dialog box instead of the Insert Merge Field menu. To insert fields from the dialog box, click the field name and then click the Insert button. The dialog box remains open so that you can insert multiple fields, if necessary. When you have finished inserting fields, click Close in the dialog box.

To Insert a Merge Field in the Main Document

The next step is to insert the Position merge field into the main document. **Why?** The first sentence in the first paragraph of the letter identifies the advertised job position, which is a merge field. To instruct Word to use data fields from the data source, you insert merge fields in the main document for the form letter. The following steps insert a merge field at the location of the insertion point.

1

- Click the 'Insert Merge Field' arrow (Mailings tab | Write & Insert Fields group) to display the Insert Merge Field menu (Figure 6–37).

Q&A

What if I accidentally click the 'Insert Merge Field' button instead of the arrow?
Click Cancel in the Insert Merge Field dialog box and repeat Step 1.

Why is the underscore character in some of the field names?
Word places an underscore character in place of the space in merge fields.

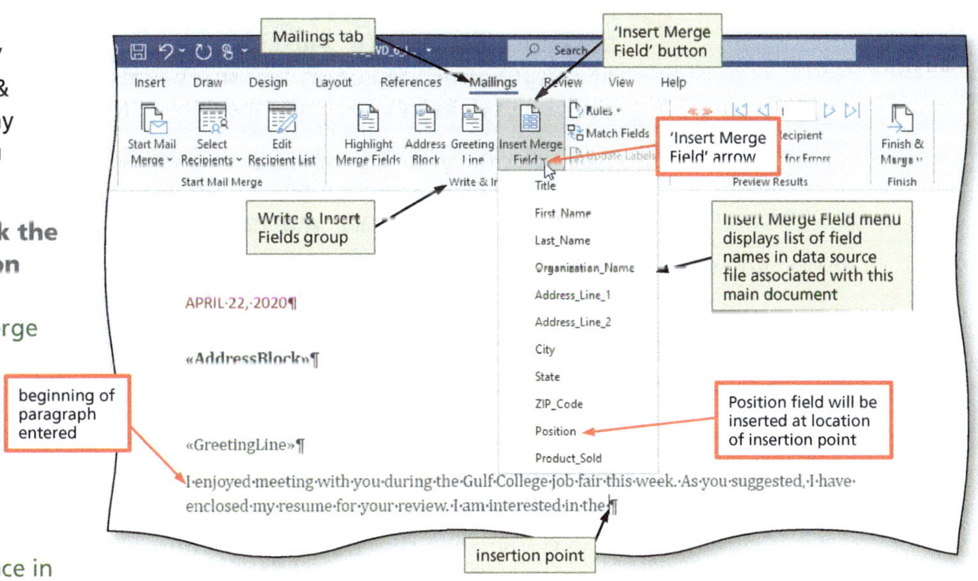

Figure 6–37

2

- Click Position on the Insert Merge Field menu to insert the selected merge field in the document at the location of the insertion point (Figure 6–38).

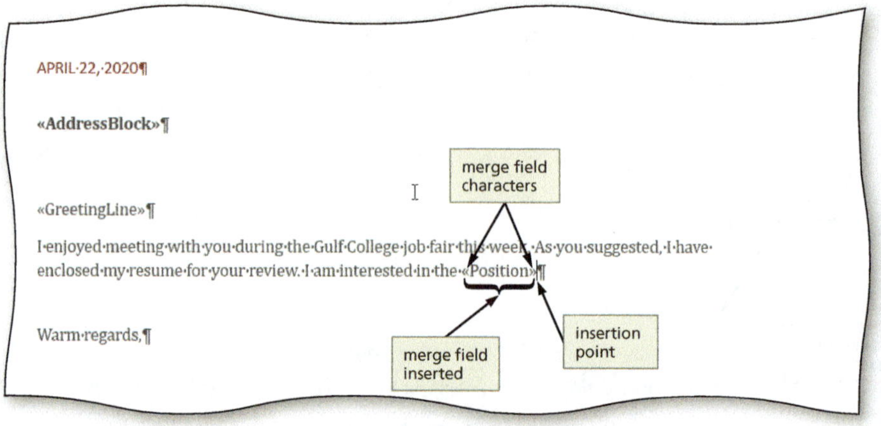

Figure 6–38

Q&A **Will the word, Position, and the chevron characters print when I merge the form letters?**
No. When you merge the data source with the main document, the value in the Position field (e.g., pharmaceutical sales representative) will print at the location of the merge field, Position.

Other Ways

1. Click 'Insert Merge Field' button (Mailings tab | Write & Insert fields group), click desired field (Insert Merge Field dialog box), click Insert button, click Close

BTW
Merge Fields
When you insert merge fields in a document, the displayed fields may be surrounded by braces instead of chevrons, and extra instructions may appear between the braces. If this occurs, then field codes have been turned on. To turn off field codes so that they are not displayed, press ALT+F9.

To Enter More Text and Merge Fields in the Main Document

The following steps enter more text and merge fields into the form letter.

1. With the insertion point at the location shown in Figure 6–38, press SPACEBAR, type **position at** and then press SPACEBAR again.
2. Click the 'Insert Merge Field' arrow (Mailings tab | Write & Insert Fields group) and then click Organization_Name on the Insert Merge Field menu to insert the selected merge field in the document. Press SPACEBAR. Type **that we discussed and am confident I am an ideal candidate for this job.**
3. Press ENTER. Type **I will graduate in May with a Bachelor of Science degree in Public Health. My education has been strengthened through my work experience, certifications, and community service.** and then press ENTER.
4. Type **Thank you in advance,** and then press SPACEBAR. Insert the Title merge field, press SPACEBAR, and then insert the Last Name merge field. Type **, for your time and consideration. I look forward to hearing from you soon to discuss my qualifications and the opportunity of my potential employment in** and then press SPACEBAR (shown in Figure 6–39).

IF Fields

In addition to merge fields, you can insert Word fields that are designed specifically for a mail merge. An **IF field** is an example of a Word field used during a mail merge that tests whether a condition is true. One form of the IF field is called an **If...Then:** If a condition is true, then perform an action. For example, if Mary owns a house, then send her information about homeowner's insurance. Another form of the IF field is called an **If...Then...Else**, where Word chooses between two options, depending on the contents of a particular field. If a condition is true, Word then performs an action; otherwise (else) Word performs a different action. For example, if John has an email address, then send him an email message; else send him the message via the postal service.

In this project, the form letter checks the product sold and displays text associated with the product sold. If the product sold is T, then the form letter should print the text, therapeutic medicine; else if the product sold is M, then the form letter should print the text, medical device. Thus, you will use an If...Then...Else: IF the Product_Sold is equal to T, then insert therapeutic medicine; else insert medical device.

The phrase that appears after the word If is called a rule, or condition. A **condition** consists of an expression, followed by a comparison operator, followed by a final expression.

BTW

IF Fields

The phrase, IF field, originates from computer programming. Do not be intimidated by the terminology. An IF field simply specifies a decision. Some software developers refer to it as an IF statement. Complex IF statements include one or more nested IF fields. A nested IF field is a second IF field inside the true or false text of the first IF field.

Expression The expression in a condition can be a merge field, a number, a series of characters, or a mathematical formula. Word surrounds a series of characters with quotation marks ("). To indicate an empty, or null, expression, Word places two quotation marks together ("").

Comparison Operator The comparison operator in a condition must be one of six characters: = (equal to or matches the text), <> (not equal to or does not match text), < (less than), <= (less than or equal to), > (greater than), or >= (greater than or equal to).

If the result of a condition is true, then Word evaluates the **true text**. If the result of the condition is false, Word evaluates the **false text** if it exists. In this project, the first expression in the condition is a merge field (Product_Sold); the comparison operator is equal to (=); and the second expression is the text "T". The true text is "therapeutic medicine". The false text is "medical device". The complete IF field is as follows:

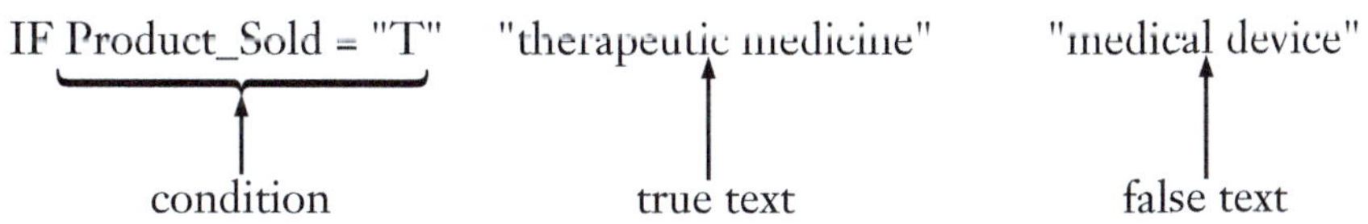

To Insert an IF Field in the Main Document

The next step is to insert an IF field in the main document. **Why?** You want to print the product sold in the letter. The following steps insert this IF field in the form letter: If the Product_Sold is equal to T, then insert therapeutic medicine, else insert medical device.

1

- With the insertion point positioned as shown in Figure 6–39, click the Rules button (Mailings tab | Write & Insert Fields group) to display the Rules menu (Figure 6–39).

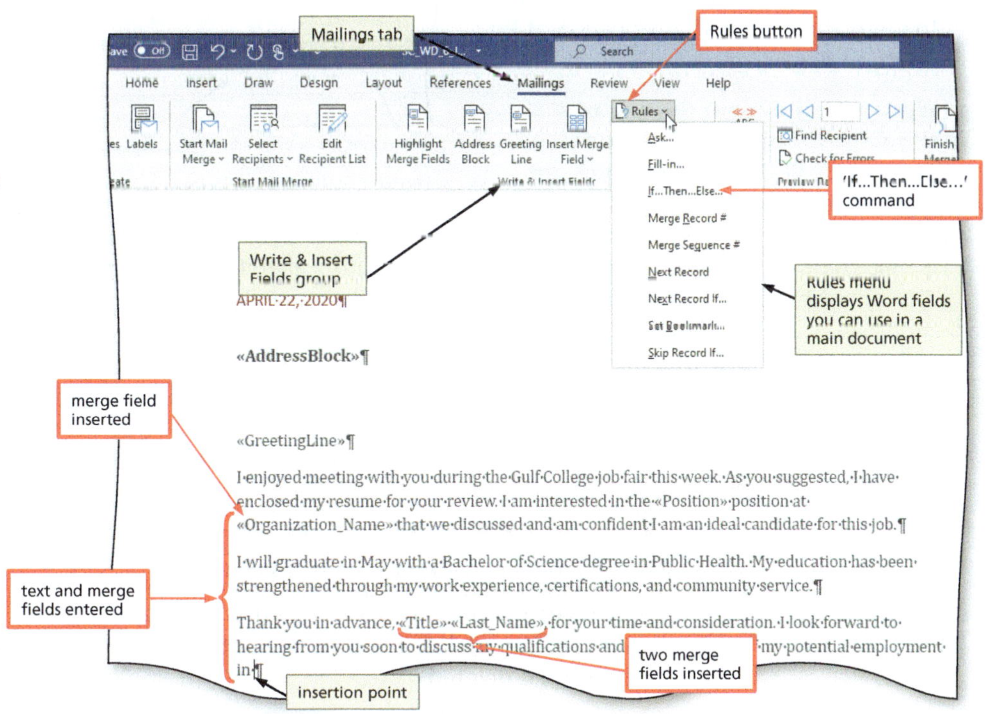

Figure 6–39

2

- Click 'If...Then...Else...' on the Rules menu to display the Insert Word Field: IF dialog box, which is where you enter the components of the IF field (Figure 6–40).

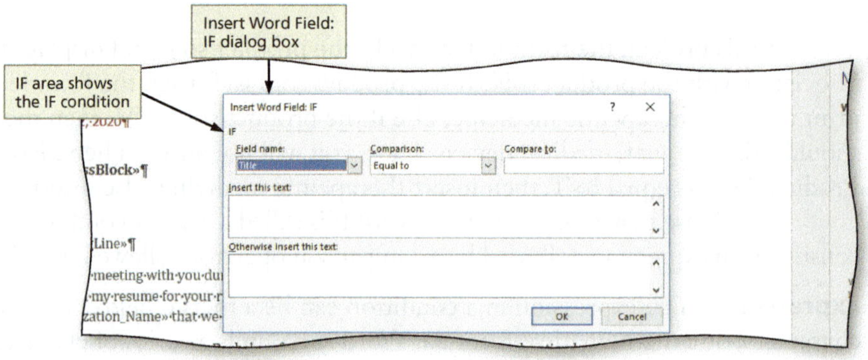

Figure 6–40

3

- Click the Field name arrow (Insert Word Field: IF dialog box) to display the list of fields in the data source.
- Scroll through the list of fields in the Field name list and then click Product_Sold to select the field.
- Position the insertion point in the Compare to text box and then type `T` as the comparison text.
- Press TAB and then type `therapeutic medicine` as the true text.
- Press TAB and then type `medical device` as the false text (Figure 6–41).

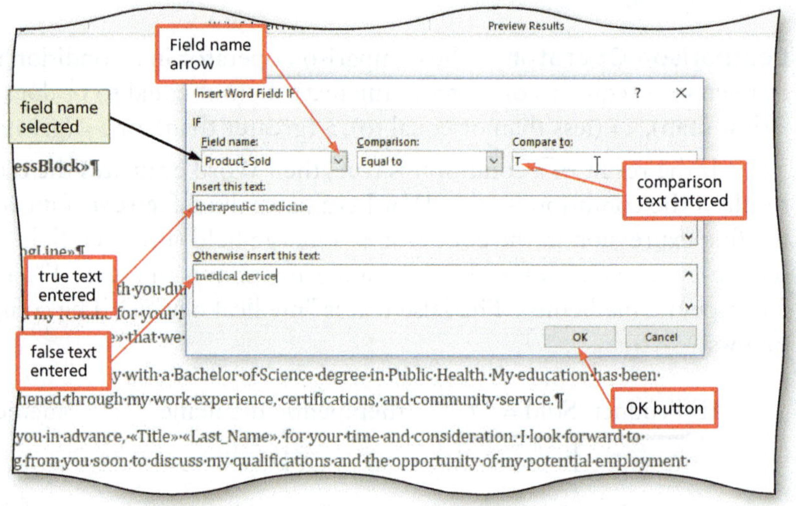

Figure 6–41

Q&A **Does the capitalization matter in the comparison text?**
Yes. The text, T, is different from the text, t, in a comparison. Be sure to enter the text exactly as you entered it in the data source.

4

- Click OK (Insert Word Field: IF dialog box) to insert the IF field at the location of the insertion point (Figure 6–42).

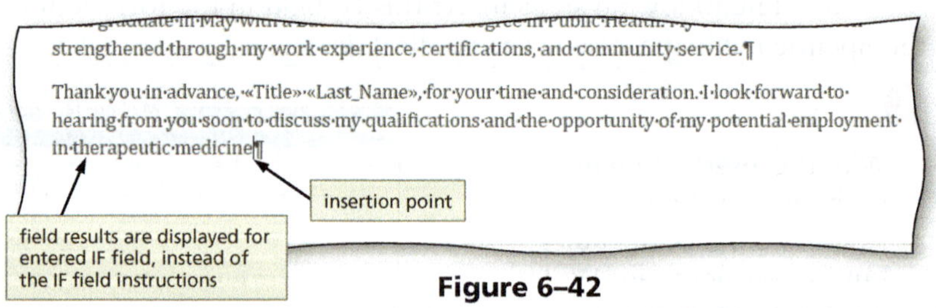

Figure 6–42

Q&A **Why does the main document display the text, therapeutic medicine, instead of the IF field instructions?**
The text, therapeutic medicine, is displayed because the first record in the data source has a product sold equal to T. Word, by default, evaluates the IF field using the current record and displays the results, called the **field results**, in the main document instead of displaying the IF field instructions. Later in the module, you will view the IF field instructions.

To Enter the Remaining Text in the Main Document

The following steps enter the remainder of the text into the form letter.

1. Press SPACEBAR. Type `sales at your organization.`
2. Change the closing to the word, Sincerely.
3. Change the placeholder text in the Your Name content control to Dwayne Jackman. If necessary, delete the content control so that the name remains but the content control is deleted.
4. Delete the Your Title content control and the paragraph mark that follows it (Figure 6–43).

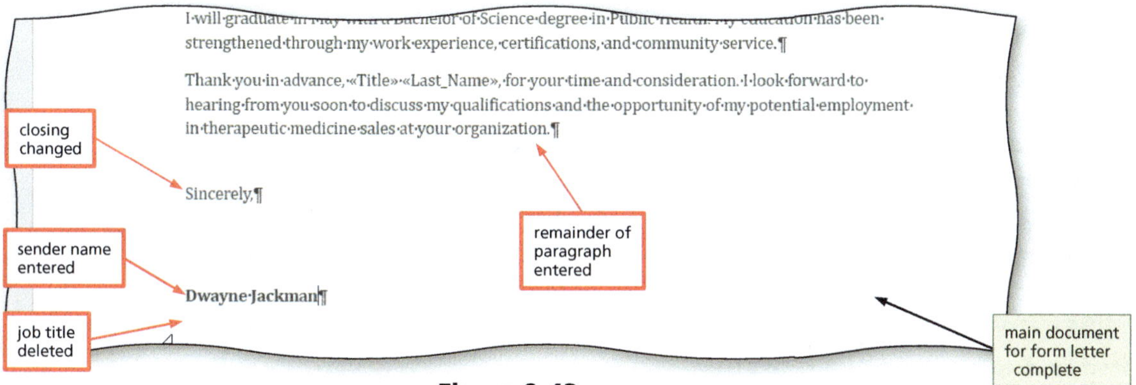

Figure 6–43

5 Make any additional adjustments to spacing, formats, etc., so that your main document looks like Figure 6–1 shown at the beginning of this module.

To Highlight Merge Fields

If you wanted to highlight all the merge fields in a document so that you could identify them quickly, you would perform the following steps.

1. Click the 'Highlight Merge Fields' button (Mailings tab | Write & Insert Fields group) to highlight the merge fields in the document.
2. When finished viewing merge fields, click the 'Highlight Merge Fields' button (Mailings tab | Write & Insert Fields group) again to remove the highlight from the merge fields in the document.

BTW

Word Fields
In addition to the IF field, Word provides other fields that may be used in form letters. For example, the ASK and FILLIN fields prompt the user to enter data for each record in the data source. The SKIP RECORD IF field instructs the mail merge not to generate a form letter for a data record if a specific condition is met.

To Toggle Field Codes

The instructions in the IF field are not displayed in the document; instead, the field results are displayed for the current record (shown in Figure 6–42). The instructions of an IF field are called **field codes**, and the default for Word is for field codes not to be displayed. Thus, field codes do not print or show on the screen unless you turn them on. You use one procedure to show field codes on the screen and a different procedure to print them on a hard copy.

The following steps show a field code on the screen. **Why?** You might want to turn on a field code to verify its accuracy or to modify it. Field codes tend to clutter the screen. Thus, most Word users turn them off after viewing them.

1

- If necessary, scroll to display the last paragraph of the letter in the document window.
- Right-click the field results showing the text, therapeutic medicine, to display a shortcut menu (Figure 6–44).

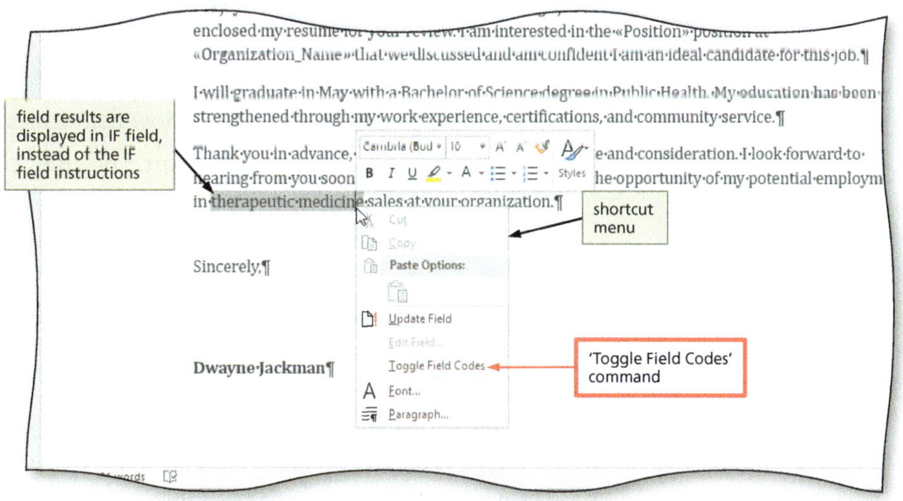

Figure 6–44

2

- Click 'Toggle Field Codes' on the shortcut menu to display the field codes instead of the field results for the IF field (Figure 6–45).

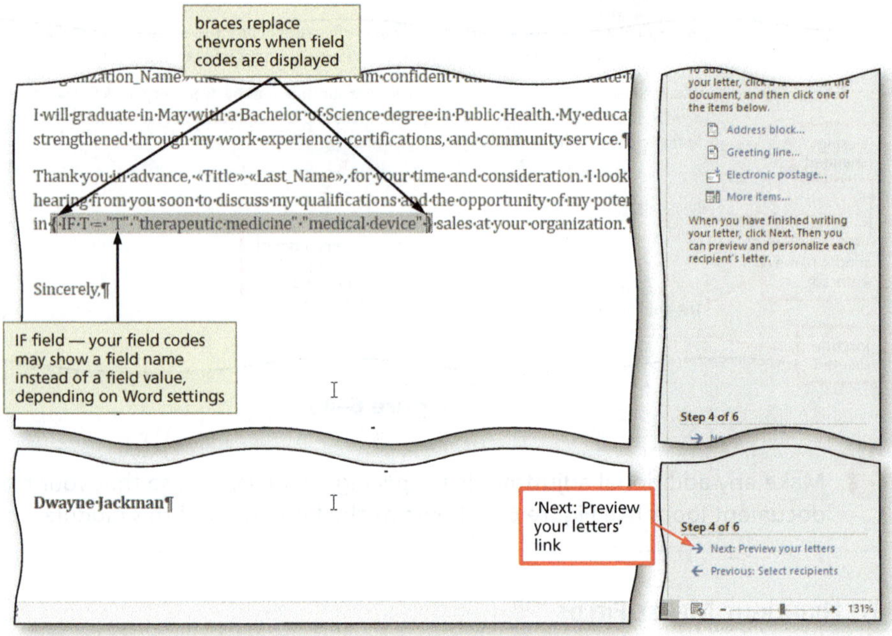

Figure 6–45

Q&A

Will displaying field codes affect the merged documents?
No. Displaying field codes has no effect on the merge process.

What if I wanted to display all field codes in a document?
You would press ALT+F9. Then, to hide all the field codes, press ALT+F9 again.

Why does the IF field turn gray?
Word, by default, shades a field in gray when the field is selected. The shading displays on the screen to help you identify fields; the shading does not print on a hard copy.

- sam Save the main document for the form letter again on the same storage location with the same file name.

Other Ways

1. With insertion point in field, press SHIFT+F9

BTW

Locking Fields
If you wanted to lock a field so that its field results cannot be changed, click the field and then press CTRL+F11. To subsequently unlock a field so that it may be updated, click the field and then press CTRL+SHIFT+F11.

To Print Field Codes in the Main Document

When you merge or print a document, Word automatically converts field codes that show on the screen to field results. You may want to print the field codes version of the form letter, however, so that you have a hard copy of the field codes for future reference. When you print field codes, you must remember to turn off the field codes option so that merged documents print field results instead of field codes. If you wanted to print the field codes in the main document, you would perform the following steps.

1. Open Backstage view and then click Options to display the Word Options dialog box.
2. Click Advanced in the left pane (Word Options dialog box) to display advanced options in the right pane and then scroll to the Print area in the right pane of the dialog box.
3. Place a check mark in the 'Print field codes instead of their values' check box.
4. Click OK to instruct Word to show field codes when the document prints.
5. Open Backstage view, click Print, and then click the Print button to print the document with all field codes showing.
6. Open Backstage view and then click Options to display the Word Options dialog box.
7. Click Advanced in the left pane (Word Options dialog box) to display advanced options in the right pane and then scroll to the Print area in the right pane of the dialog box.
8. Remove the check mark from the 'Print field codes instead of their values' check box.
9. Click OK to instruct Word to show field results the next time you print the document.

Opening a Main Document

You open a main document the same as you open any other Word document (i.e., clicking Open in Backstage view). If Word displays a dialog box indicating it will run an SQL command, click Yes (Figure 6–46).

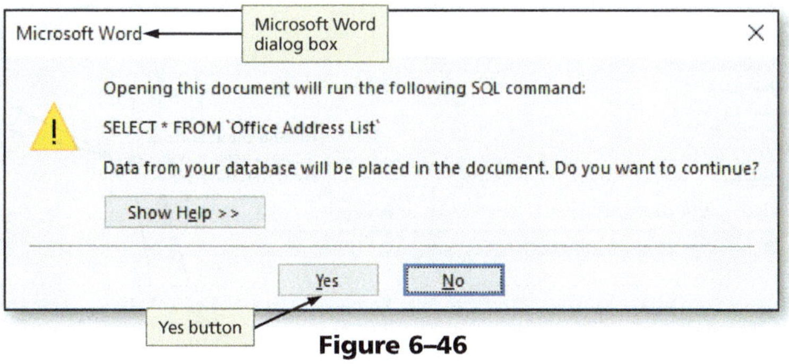

Figure 6–46

When you open a main document, Word attempts to open the associated data source file, too. If the data source is not in exactly the same location (i.e., drive and folder) as when it originally was saved, Word may display a dialog box indicating that it could not find the data source (Figure 6–47). When this occurs, click the 'Find Data Source' button to display the Open Data Source dialog box, which allows you to locate the data source file. (Word may display several messages or dialog boxes requiring you to click an OK (or similar) button until the one shown in Figure 6–47 appears.)

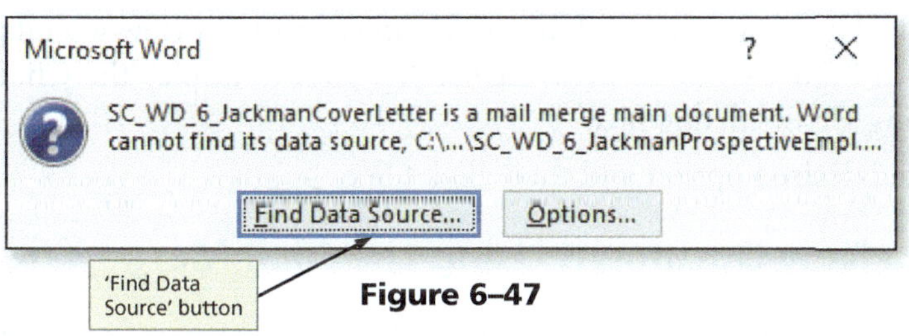

Figure 6–47

BTW

Data Source and Main Document Files

When you open a main document, if Word cannot locate the associated data source file or it does not display a dialog box with the 'Find Data Source' button, then the data source may not be associated with the main document. To associate the data source with the main document, click the Select Recipients button (Mailings tab | Start Mail Merge group), click 'Use an Existing List' on the Select Recipients menu, and then locate the data source file. When you save the main document, Word will associate the data source with the main document.

Break Point: If you want to take a break, this is a good place to do so. You can exit Word now. To resume later, start Word, open the file called SC_WD_6_JackmanCoverLetter.docx, and continue following the steps from this location forward.

Merging the Recipient List in the Data Source with the Main Document to Generate Form Letters

The next step in this project is to merge the recipient list in the data source with the main document to generate the form letters (shown in Figure 6–1c at the beginning of this module). **Merging** is the process of combining the contents of a data source with a main document.

You can merge the form letters to a new document, which you can edit, or merge them directly to a printer. You also have the option of merging all data in a data source or merging just a portion of it. The following sections discuss various ways to merge.

To Preview a Mail Merge Using the Mail Merge Wizard

Earlier in this module, you previewed the data in the letters using a button on the ribbon. The following step uses the Mail Merge wizard to preview the letters. **Why?** The next wizard step previews the letters so that you can verify the content is accurate before performing the merge.

1

- Click the 'Next: Preview your letters' link at the bottom of the Mail Merge pane (shown in Figure 6–45) to display Step 5 of the Mail Merge wizard in the Mail Merge pane (Figure 6–48).

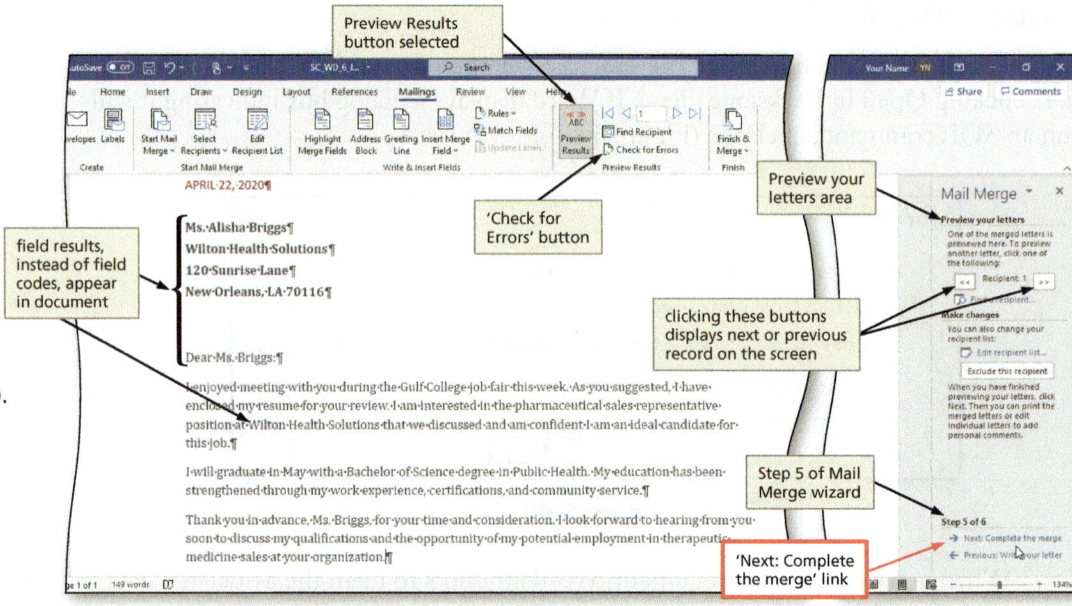

Figure 6–48

To Check for Errors

Before merging documents, you can instruct Word to check for errors that might occur during the merge process. If you wanted to check for errors, you would perform the following steps.

1. Click the 'Check for Errors' button (Mailings tab | Preview Results group) (shown in Figure 6–48) or press ALT+SHIFT+K to display the Checking and Reporting Errors dialog box.
2. Select the desired option and then click OK.

To Merge the Form Letters to a New Document Using the Mail Merge Wizard

With the data source and main document for the form letter complete, the next step is to merge them to generate the individual form letters. You can merge the letters to the printer or to a new document. **Why?** If you merge the documents to a new document, you can save the merged documents in a file and then print them later, review the merged documents for accuracy and edit them as needed, or you can add personal messages to individual merged letters. The following steps merge the form letters to a new document.

1

- Click the 'Next: Complete the merge' link at the bottom of the Mail Merge pane (shown in Figure 6–48) to display Step 6 of the Mail Merge wizard in the Mail Merge pane.
- Click the 'Edit individual letters' link in the Mail Merge pane to display the Merge to New Document dialog box (Figure 6–49).

Q&A **What if I wanted to print the merged letters immediately instead of reviewing them first in a new document window?**
You would click the Print link instead of the 'Edit individual letters' link.

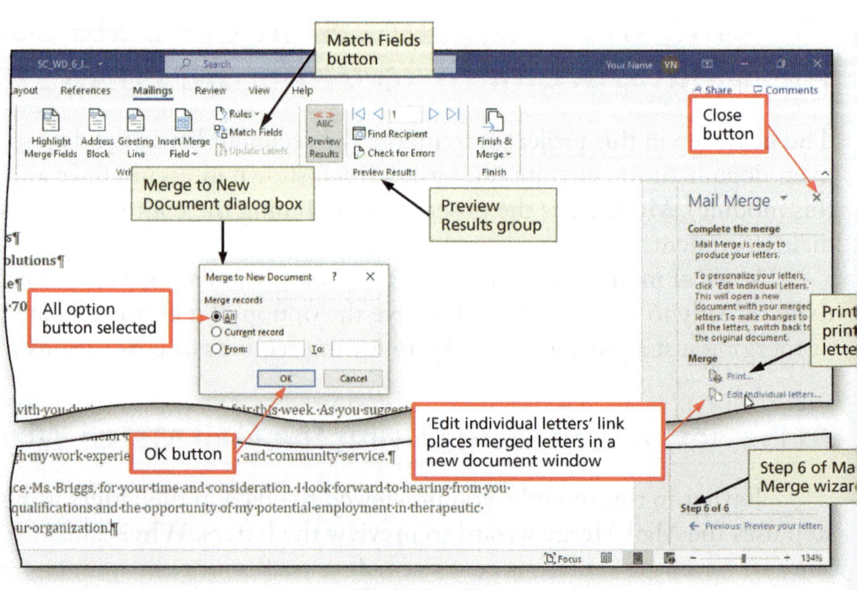

Figure 6–49

2

- If necessary, click All (Merge to New Document dialog box) so that all records in the data source are merged.

Q&A **Do I have to merge all records?**
No. Through this dialog box, you can merge the current record or a range of record numbers.

- Click OK to merge the letters to a new document, in this case, five individual letters — one for each potential employer in the recipient list in the data source. (If Word displays a dialog box containing a message about locked fields, click OK.)

3

- Display the View tab and then click the Multiple Pages button (View tab | Zoom group) so that you can see miniature versions of all five letters in the document window at once (Figure 6–50).

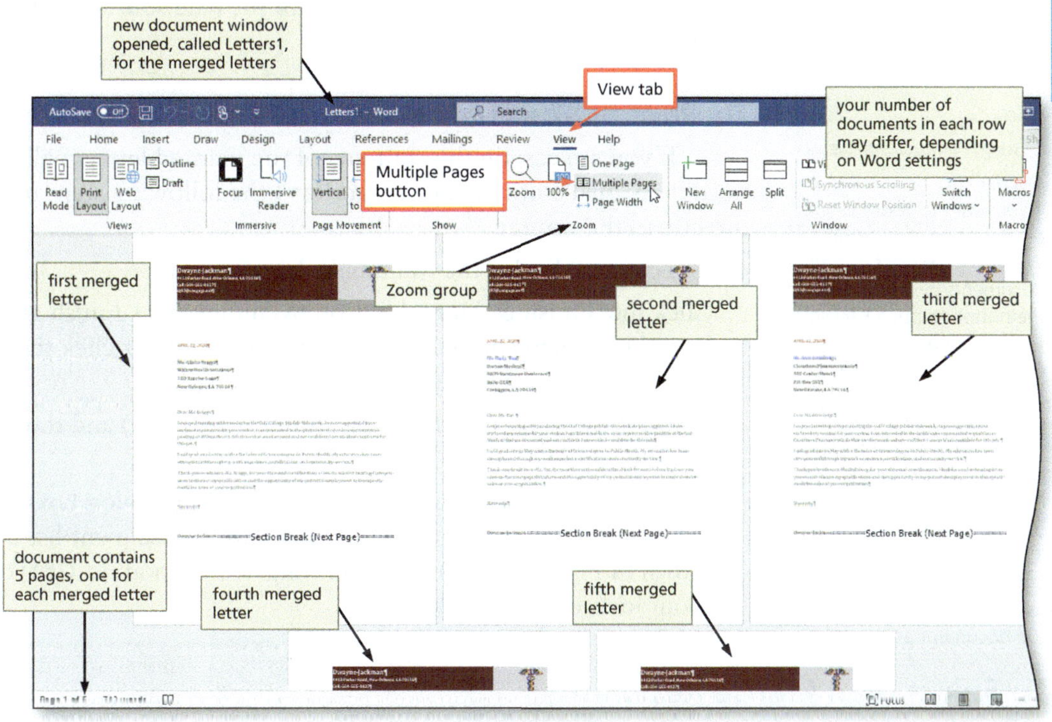

Figure 6–50

4

- Change the zoom back to page width.

Experiment

- Scroll through the merged documents so that you can read all five letters.

Q&A **Why does my screen show an extra blank page at the end?**
You might have a blank record in the recipient list in the data source, or the spacing may cause an overflow to a blank page.

Can I edit the merged letters?
Yes, you can edit the letters as you edit any other Word document. Always proofread the merged letters for accuracy before distributing them.

- **sam** Save the merged letters in the JobHunting folder on your hard drive, OneDrive, or other storage location using the file name, SC_WD_6_JackmanMergedCoverLetters. If requested by your instructor, print the merged letters. Close the document window containing the merged letters.

Q&A **Do I have to save the document containing the merged letters?**
No. You can close the document without saving it.

- Click the Close button on the Mail Merge pane title bar (shown in Figure 6–49) because you are finished with the Mail Merge wizard.

- If necessary, click the Preview Results button to show field codes instead of merged data.

Other Ways

1. Click 'Finish & Merge' button (Mailings tab | Finish group), click 'Edit Individual Documents'

Correcting Merge Field Errors in Merged Documents

If the wrong field results appear, Word may be mapping the fields incorrectly. To view fields, click the Match Fields button (Mailings tab | Write & Insert Fields group) (shown in Figure 6–49). Then, review the fields in the list. For example, Last Name should map to the Last Name field in the data source. If it does not, click the arrow to change the name of the data source field.

If the fields are mapped incorrectly, the data in the data source may be incorrect. For a discussion about editing records in the data source, refer to that section earlier in this module.

BTW
Conserving Ink and Toner
If you want to conserve ink or toner, you can instruct Word to print draft quality documents by clicking File on the ribbon to open Backstage view, clicking Options in Backstage view to display the Word Options dialog box, clicking Advanced in the left pane (Word Options dialog box), scrolling to the Print area in the right pane, placing a check mark in the 'Use draft quality' check box, and then clicking OK. Then, use Backstage view to print the document as usual.

To Merge the Form Letters to a Printer

If you are certain the contents of the merged letters will be correct and do not need individual editing, you can perform the following steps to merge the form letters directly to the printer.

1. If necessary, display the Mailings tab.
2. Click the 'Finish & Merge' button (Mailings tab | Finish group) and then click Print Documents on the Finish & Merge menu, or click the Print link (Mail Merge pane), to display the Merge to Printer dialog box.
3. If necessary, click All (Merge to Printer dialog box) and then click OK to display the Print dialog box.
4. Select desired printer settings. Click OK (Print dialog box) to print five separate letters, one for each potential employer in the recipient list in the data source, as shown in Figure 6–1c at the beginning of this module. (If Word displays a message about locked fields, click OK.)

To Select Mail Merge Recipients

Instead of merging all of the data records (recipients) in the data source, you can choose which data records to merge, based on a condition you specify. The dialog box in Figure 6–49 allows you to specify by record number which data records to merge. Often, though, you want to merge based on the contents of a specific field. The following steps select data records (recipients) for a merge. **Why?** You want to merge just those potential employers who sell medical devices.

1

- Click the 'Edit Recipient List' button (Mailings tab | Start Mail Merge group) to display the Mail Merge Recipients dialog box (Figure 6–51).

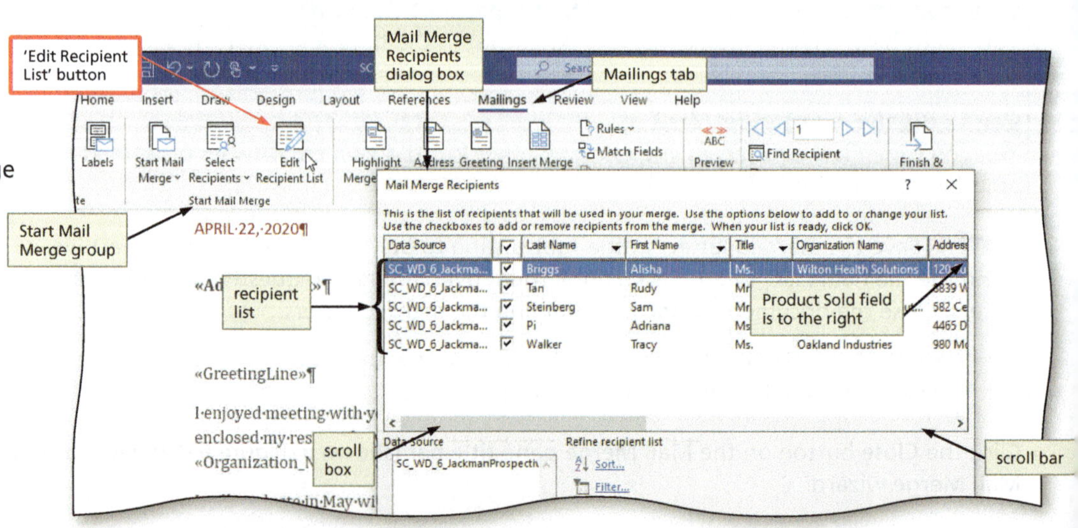

Figure 6–51

2

- Drag the scroll box to the right edge of the scroll bar (Mail Merge Recipients dialog box) so that the Product Sold field appears in the dialog box.
- Click the arrow to the right of the field name, Product Sold, to display sort and filter criteria for the selected field (Figure 6–52).

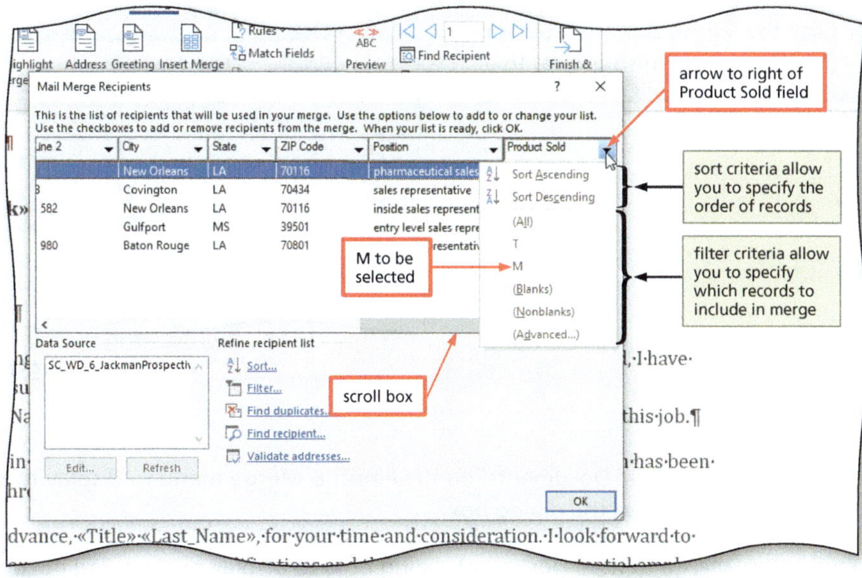

Figure 6–52

Q&A

What are the filter criteria in the parentheses?

The (All) option clears any previously set filter criteria. The (Blanks) option selects records that contain blanks in that field, and the (Nonblanks) option selects records that do not contain blanks in that field. The (Advanced) option displays the Filter and Sort dialog box, which allows you to perform more advanced record selection operations.

3

- Click M to reduce the number of data records displayed (Mail Merge Recipients dialog box) to two, because two potential employers sell medical devices (Figure 6–53).

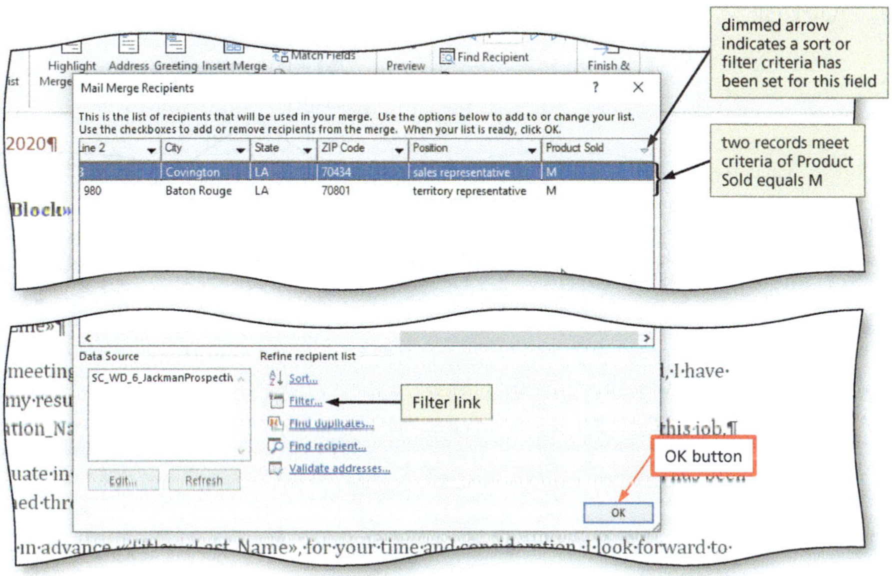

Figure 6–53

Q&A

What happened to the other three records that did not meet the criteria?

They still are part of the data source; they just are not appearing in the Mail Merge Recipients dialog box. When you clear the filter, all records will reappear.

4

- Click OK to close the Mail Merge Recipients dialog box.

Other Ways

1. Click Filter link (Mail Merge Recipients dialog box), click Filter Records tab (Sort and Filter dialog box), enter filter criteria, click OK

To Merge the Form Letters to a New Document Using the Ribbon

The next step is to merge the selected records. To do this, you follow the same steps described earlier. The difference is that Word will merge only those records that meet the criteria specified, that is, just those with a product sold equal to M (for medical device). **Why?** Word will merge only those data records that meet the specified filter criteria. The following steps merge the filtered data records (recipients) to a new document using the ribbon.

1

- Click the 'Finish & Merge' button (Mailings tab | Finish group) to display the Finish & Merge menu (Figure 6–54).

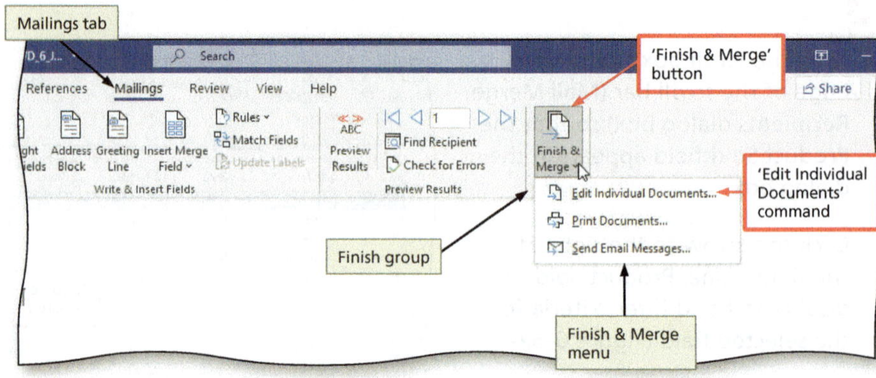

Figure 6–54

2

- Click 'Edit Individual Documents' on the Finish & Merge menu to display the Merge to New Document dialog box. If necessary, click All in the dialog box.
- Click OK (Merge to New Document dialog box) to display the merged documents in a new document window.

3

- Change the zoom so that both documents, one for each potential employer whose product sold field equals M, appear in the document window at the same time (Figure 6–55). (If Word displays a message about locked fields, click OK.)

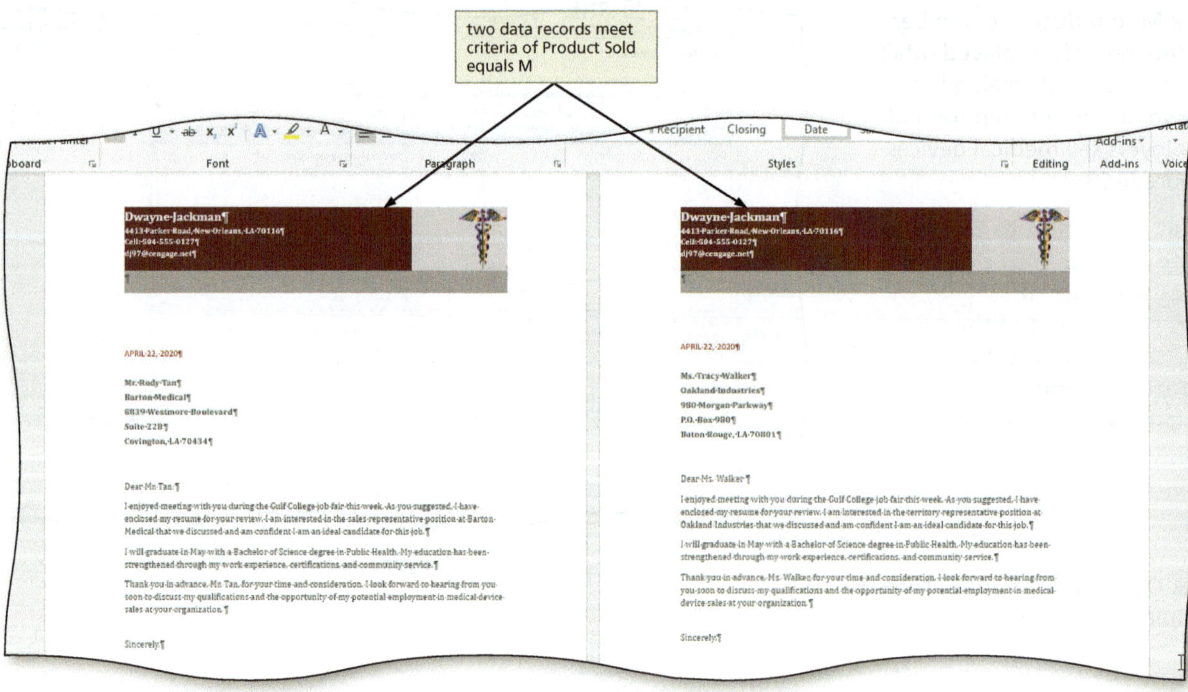

Figure 6–55

4

- Close the window. Do not save the merged documents.

To Remove a Merge Condition

The next step is to remove the merge condition. **Why?** You do not want future merges be restricted to potential employers with a product sold equal to M. The following steps remove a merge condition.

1

- Click the 'Edit Recipient List' button (Mailings tab | Start Mail Merge group) to display the Mail Merge Recipients dialog box.

2

- Click the Filter link (Mail Merge Recipients dialog box) to display the Filter and Sort dialog box.
- If necessary, click the Filter Records tab to display the Filter Records sheet (Figure 6–56).

Q&A **Can I specify a merge condition in this dialog box instead of using the box arrow in the Mail Merge Recipients dialog box?**
Yes.

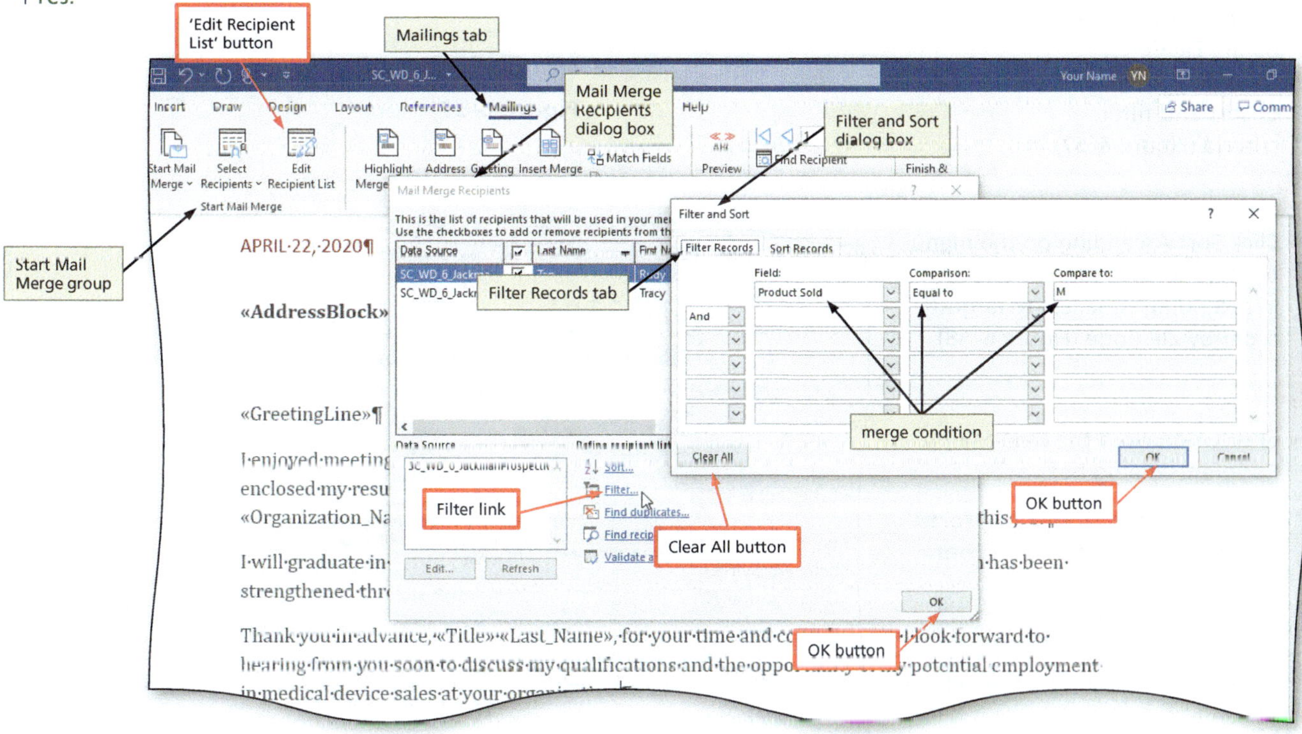

Figure 6–56

3

- Click the Clear All button (Filter and Sort dialog box) to remove the merge condition from the dialog box.
- Click OK in each of the two open dialog boxes to close the dialog boxes.

To Sort a Recipient List

The following steps sort the data records (recipient list) by ZIP code. **Why?** You may want the form letters printed in a certain order. For example, if you mail the form letters using the U.S. Postal Service's bulk rate mailing service, the post office requires that you sort and group the form letters by ZIP code.

1

- Click the 'Edit Recipient List' button (Mailings tab | Start Mail Merge group) to display the Mail Merge Recipients dialog box.
- Scroll to the right until the ZIP Code field shows in the dialog box.
- Click the arrow to the right of the field name, ZIP Code, to display a menu of sort and filter criteria (Figure 6–57).

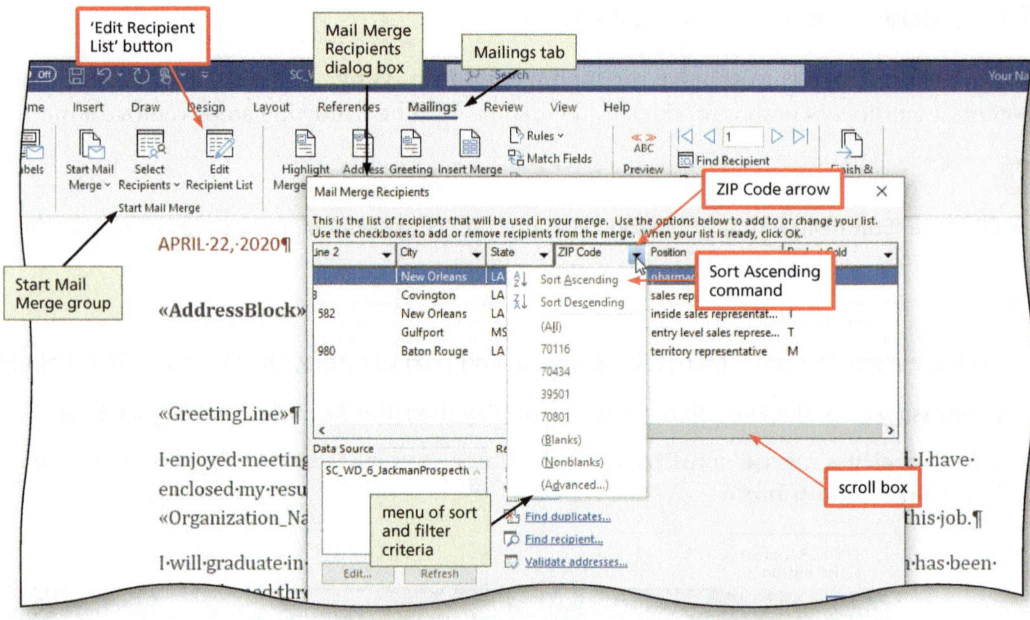

Figure 6–57

2

- Click Sort Ascending on the menu to sort the data source records in ascending (smallest to largest) order by ZIP Code (Figure 6–58).

3

- Click OK to close the Mail Merge Recipients dialog box.

Q&A **In what order would the form letters print if I merged them again now?**
Word would merge them in ZIP code order; that is, the record with ZIP code 39501 would appear first, and the record with ZIP code 70801 would appear last.

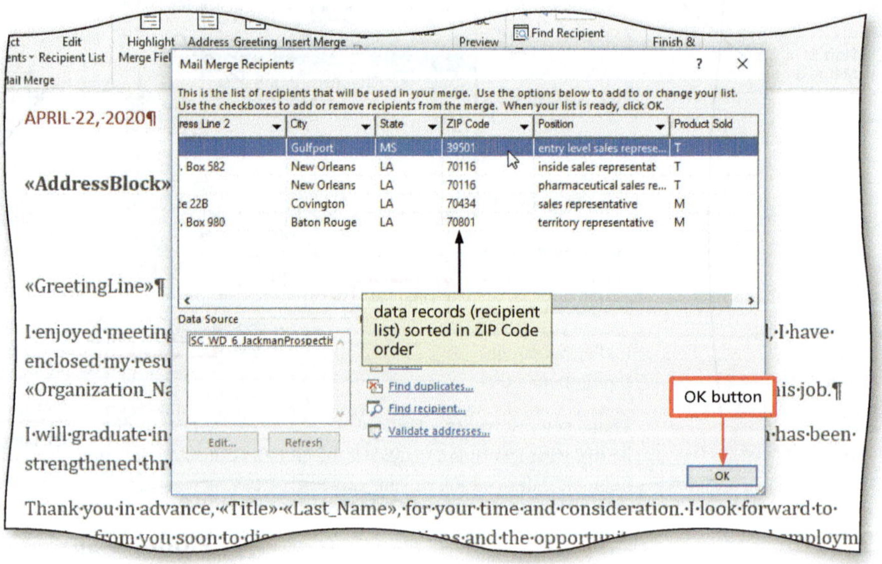

Figure 6–58

Other Ways

1. Click Sort link (Mail Merge Recipients dialog box), enter sort criteria (Sort and Filter dialog box), click OK

To Find Mail Merge Recipients

Why? If you wanted to find a particular data record in the recipient list in the data source and display that recipient's data in the main document on the screen, you can search for a field value. The following steps find Tan, which is a last name in the recipient list in the data source, and display that recipient's values in the form letter currently displaying on the screen.

1

- If necessary, click the Preview Results button (Mailings tab | Preview Results group) to show field results instead of merged fields on the screen.
- Click the Find Recipient button (Mailings tab | Preview Results group) to display the Find Entry dialog box.
- Type `Tan` in the Find text box (Find Entry dialog box) as the search text.
- Click the Find Next button to display the record containing the entered text (Figure 6–59).

2

- Click Cancel (Find Entry dialog box) to close the dialog box.

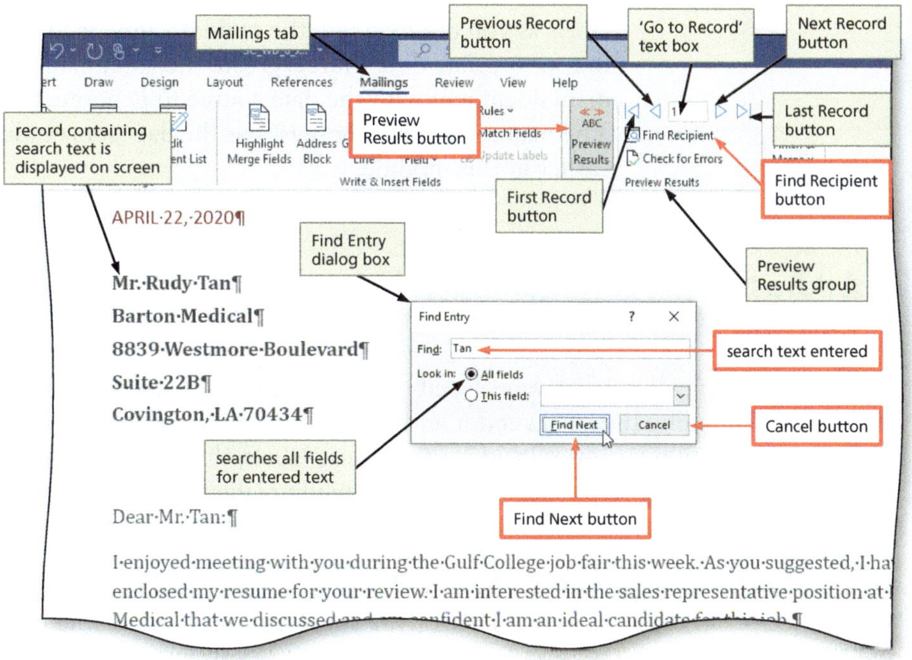

Figure 6–59

- Close the open document. If a Microsoft Word dialog box is displayed, click Save to save the changes.

Displaying Mail Merge Recipients in the Main Document

When you are viewing merged data in the main document (shown in Figure 6–59) — that is, the Preview Results button (Mailings tab | Preview Results group) is selected — you can click buttons and boxes in the Preview Results group on the Mailings tab to display different results and values. For example, click the Last Record button to display the values from the last record in the data source, the First Record button to display the values in record one, the Next Record button to display the values in the next consecutive record number, or the Previous Record button to display the values from the previous record number. You also can display a specific record by clicking the 'Go to Record' text box, typing the record number you would like to be displayed in the main document, and then pressing ENTER.

BTW
Closing Main Document Files
Word always asks if you want to save changes when you close a main document, even if you just saved the document. If you are sure that no additional changes were made to the document, click Don't Save; otherwise, click Save — just to be safe.

Addressing Mailing Labels and Envelopes

Now that you have merged and printed the form letters, the next step is to print addresses on mailing labels to be affixed to envelopes for the form letters. The mailing labels will use the same data source as the form letter, SC_WD_6_JackmanProspectiveEmployers. The format and content of the mailing labels will be exactly the same as the inside address in the main document for the form letter. That is, the first line will contain the title and first name followed by the last name. The second line will contain the organization name, and so on. Thus, you will use the AddressBlock merge field in the mailing labels.

You follow the same basic steps to create the main document for the mailing labels as you did to create the main document for the form letters. That is, determine the appropriate data source, create the label main document, and then merge the main document with the data source to generate the mailing labels and envelopes. The major difference here is that the data source already exists because you created it earlier in this module.

To Address and Print Mailing Labels Using an Existing Data Source

To address mailing labels, you specify the type of labels you intend to use. Word will request the label information, including the label vendor and product number. You can obtain this information from the box of labels. For illustration purposes in addressing these labels, the label vendor is Avery and the product number is J8158. The following steps address and print mailing labels using an existing data source. **Why?** You already created the data source earlier in this module, so you will use that data source.

Note: If your printer does not have the capability of printing mailing labels, read these steps without performing them. If you are in a laboratory environment, ask your instructor if you should perform these steps or read them without performing them.

1

- Open Backstage view. Click New in Backstage view to display the New screen. Click the Blank document thumbnail to open a new blank document window.
- If necessary, change the zoom to page width.
- Display the Mailings tab. Click the 'Start Mail Merge' button (Mailings tab | Start Mail Merge group) and then click 'Step-by-Step Mail Merge Wizard' on the Start Mail Merge menu to display Step 1 of the Mail Merge wizard in the Mail Merge pane.
- Click Labels in the Select document type area to specify labels as the main document type (Figure 6–60).

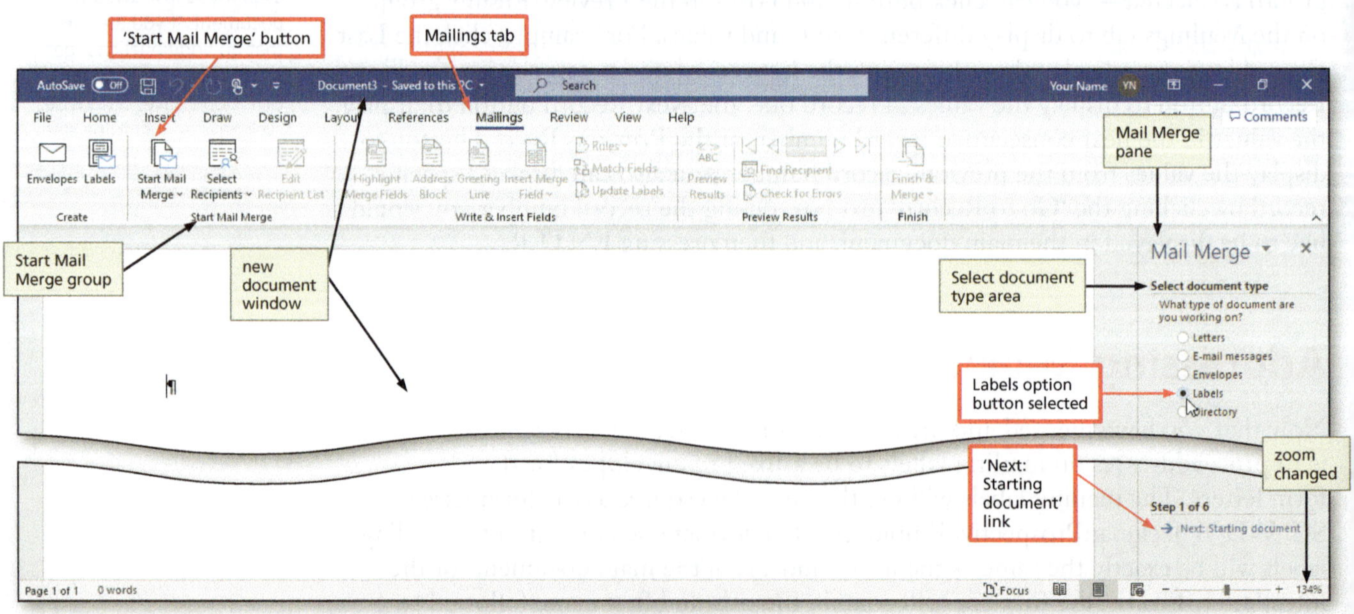

Figure 6–60

2

- Click the 'Next: Starting document' link at the bottom of the Mail Merge pane to display Step 2 of the Mail Merge wizard.
- In the Mail Merge pane, click the Label options link to display the Label Options dialog box.
- Select the label vendor and product number (in this case, Avery A4/A5 and J8158), as shown in Figure 6–61.

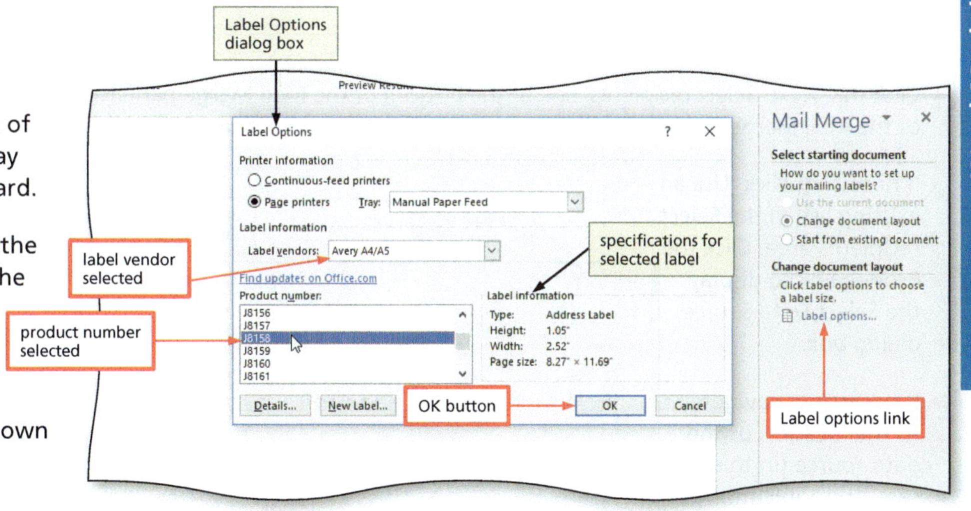

Figure 6–61

3

- Click OK (Label Options dialog box) to display the selected label layout as the main document (Figure 6–62).
- If gridlines are not displayed, click the View Gridlines button (Layout tab | Table group) to show gridlines.

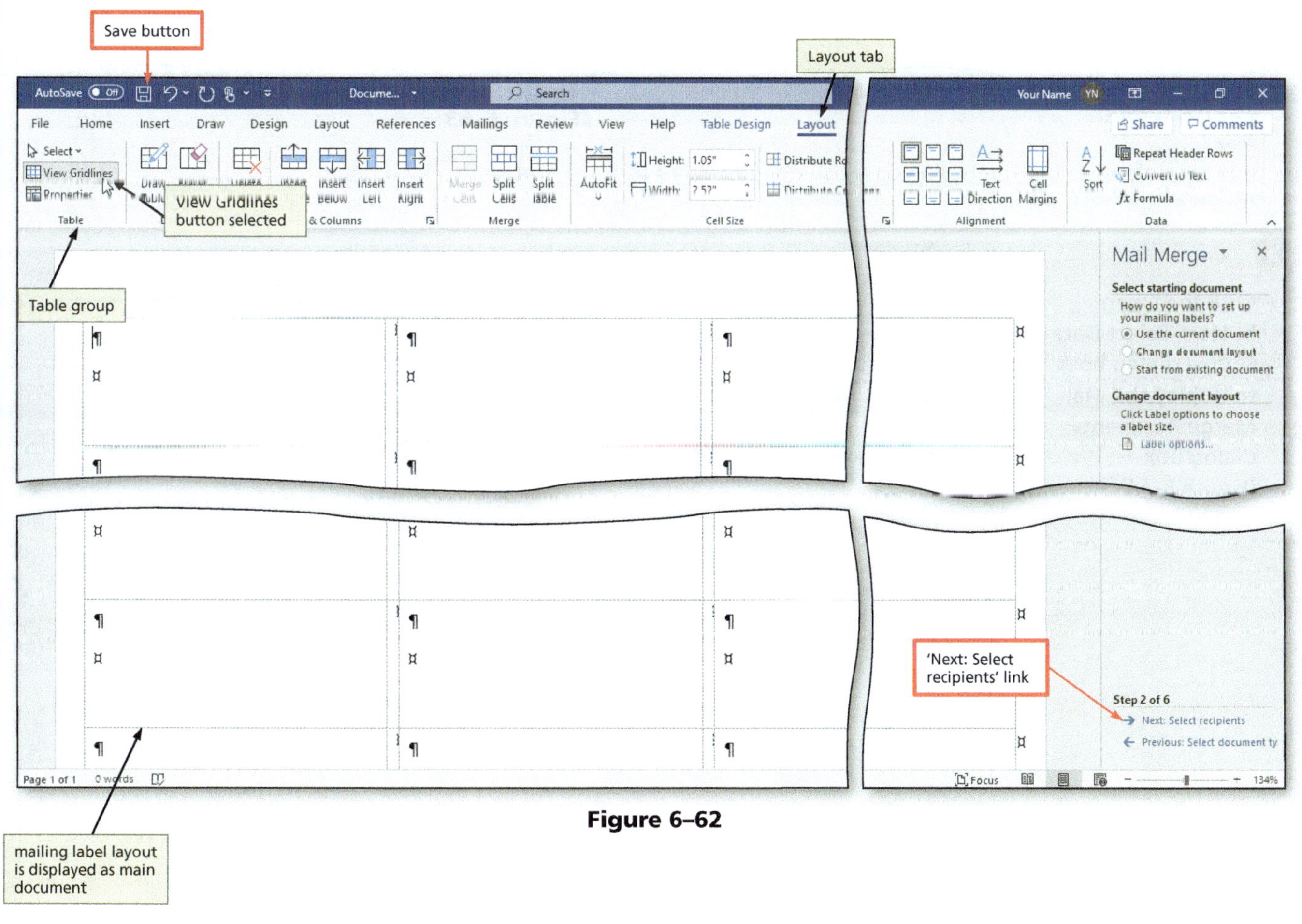

Figure 6–62

4

- Click the 'Next: Select recipients' link at the bottom of the Mail Merge pane to display Step 3 of the Mail Merge wizard, which allows you to select the data source.
- If necessary, click 'Use an existing list' in the Select recipients area. Click the Browse link to display the Select Data Source dialog box.
- If necessary, navigate to the location of the data source (in this case, the JobHunting folder).
- Click the file name, SC_WD_6_JackmanProspectiveEmployers, to select the data source you created earlier in the module (Figure 6–63).

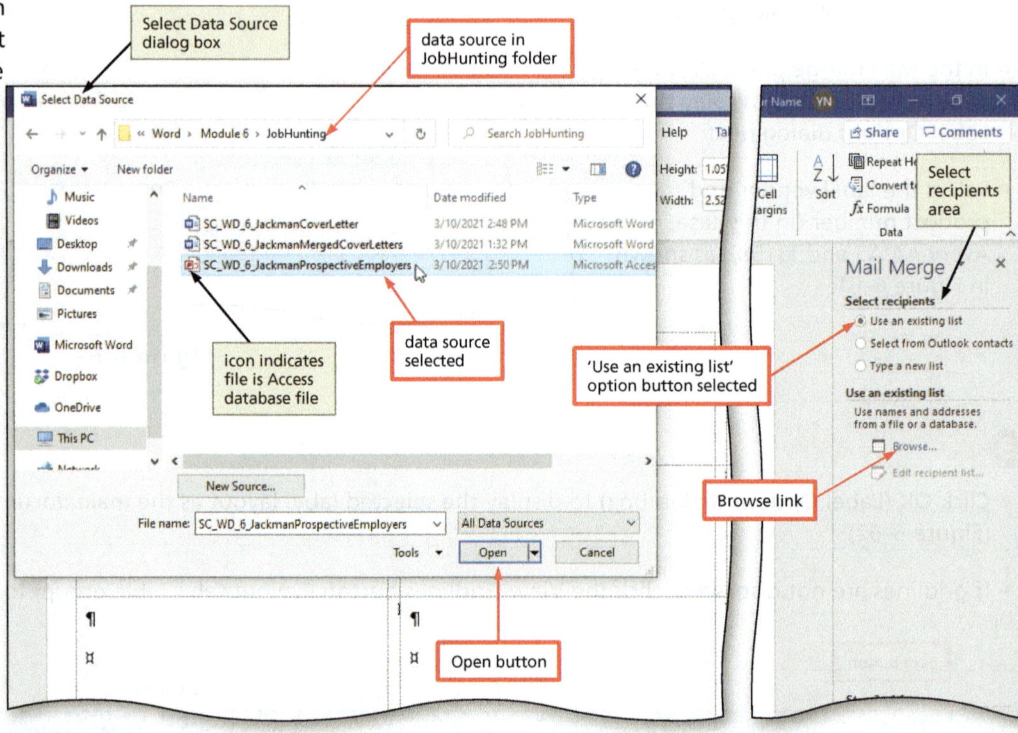

Figure 6–63

Q&A **What is the folder initially displayed in the Select Data Source dialog box?**
It is the default folder for storing data source files. Word looks in that folder, by default, for an existing data source.

5

- Click the Open button (Select Data Source dialog box) to display the Mail Merge Recipients dialog box (Figure 6–64).

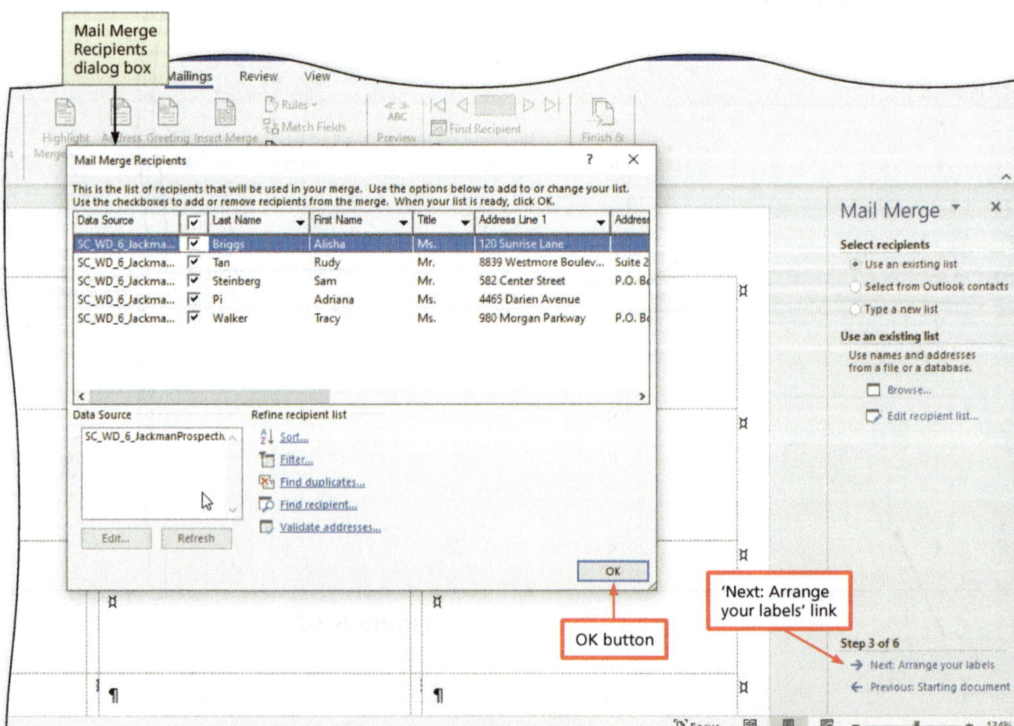

Figure 6–64

6

- Click OK (Mail Merge Recipients dialog box) to close the dialog box and insert the Next Record field in each label after the first.
- At the bottom of the Mail Merge pane, click the 'Next: Arrange your labels' link to display Step 4 of the Mail Merge wizard in the Mail Merge pane.
- In the Mail Merge pane, click the Address block link to display the Insert Address Block dialog box (Figure 6–65).

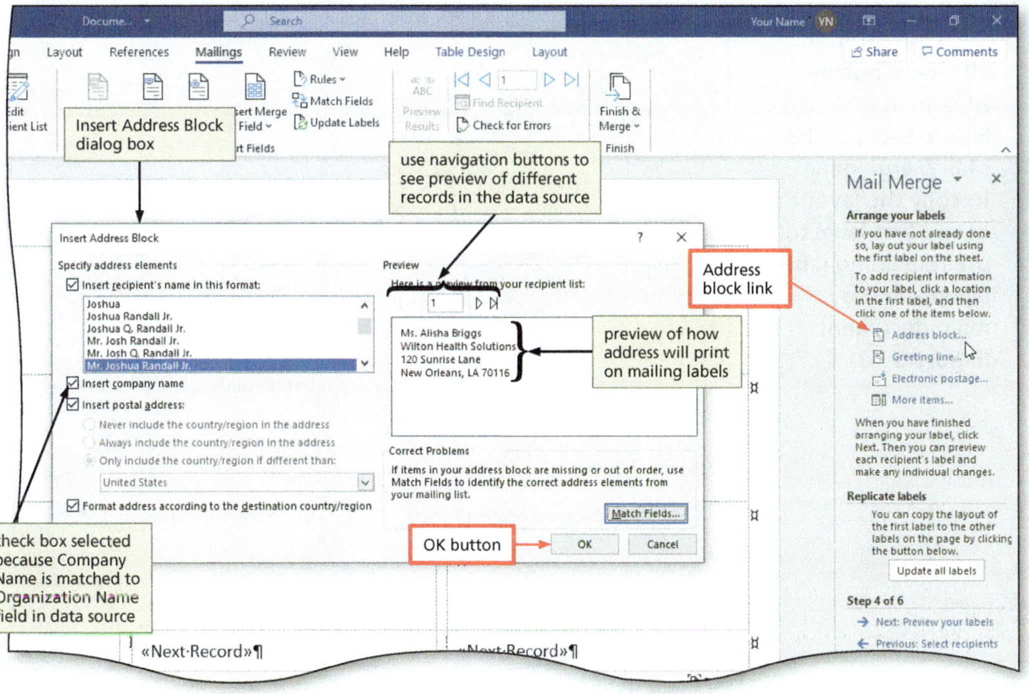

Figure 6–65

- If necessary, match the company name to the Organization Name field by clicking the Match Fields button (Insert Address Block dialog box), clicking the Company box arrow (Match Fields dialog box), clicking Organization Name in the list, and then clicking OK (Match Fields dialog box).

7

- Click OK to close the dialog box and insert the AddressBlock merge field in the first label of the main document (Figure 6–66).

Q&A

Do I have to use the AddressBlock merge field?

No. You can click the Insert Merge Field button (Mailings tab | Write & Insert Fields group) and then select the preferred fields for the mailing labels, organizing the fields as desired.

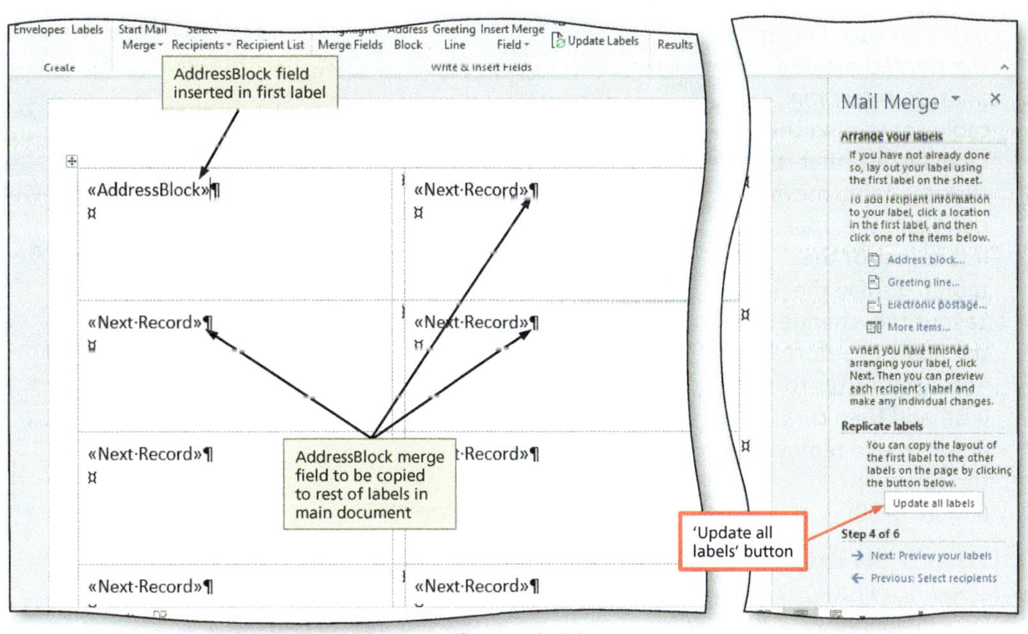

Figure 6–66

8

- Click the 'Update all labels' button (shown in Figure 6–66) in the Mail Merge pane to copy the layout of the first label to the remaining label layouts in the main document (Figure 6–67).

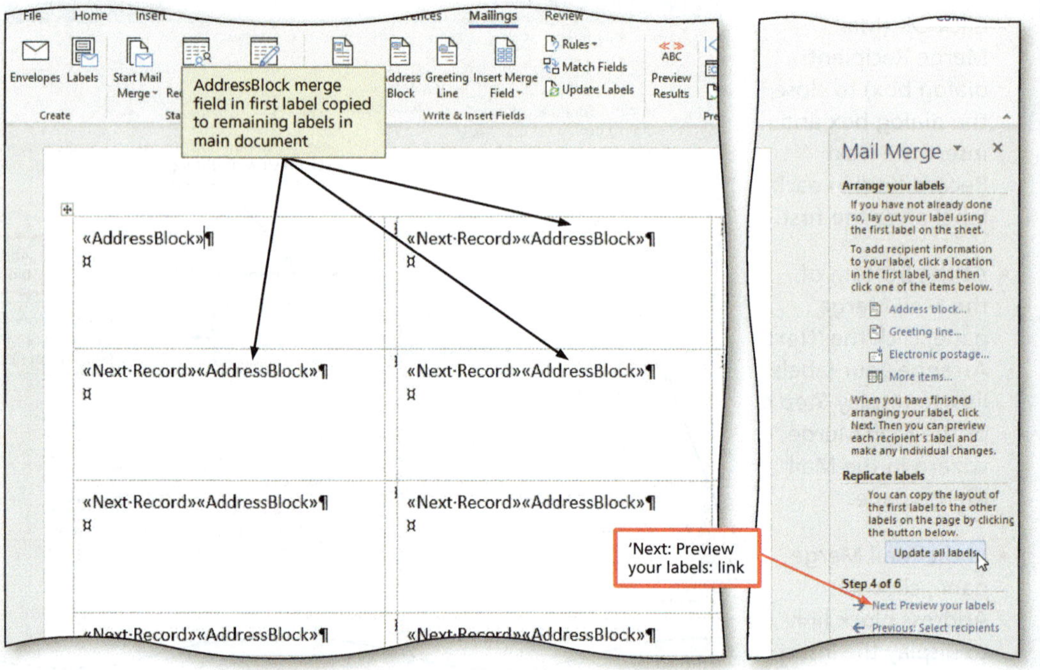

Figure 6–67

9

- Click the 'Next: Preview your labels' link at the bottom of the Mail Merge pane to display Step 5 of the Mail Merge wizard, which shows a preview of the mailing labels in the document window.

- Because you do not want a blank space between each line in the printed mailing address, select the table containing the label layout (that is, click the table move handle in the upper-left corner of the table), display the Layout tab, change the Spacing Before and After boxes to 0 pt, and then click anywhere to remove the selection (Figure 6–68).

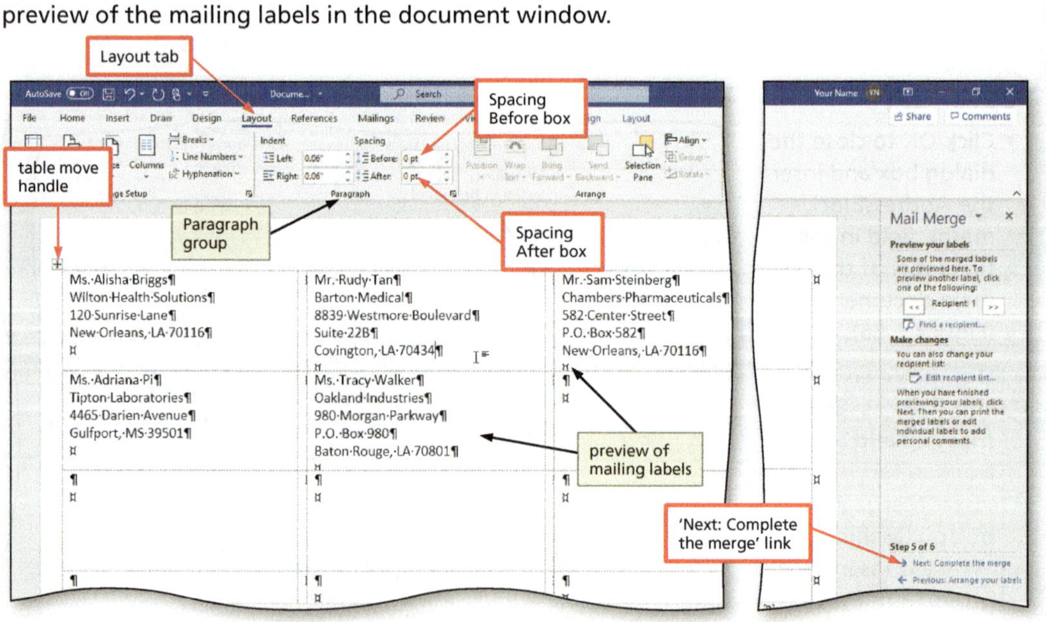

Figure 6–68

Q&A **What if the spacing does not change?**
Drag through the labels and try changing the Spacing Before and After boxes to 0 again.

10

- Click the 'Next: Complete the merge' link at the bottom of the Mail Merge pane to display Step 6 of the Mail Merge wizard.
- Click the 'Edit individual labels' link to display the Merge to New Document dialog box.
- If necessary, click All (Merge to New Document dialog box) so that all records in the data source will be included in the merge (Figure 6–69).

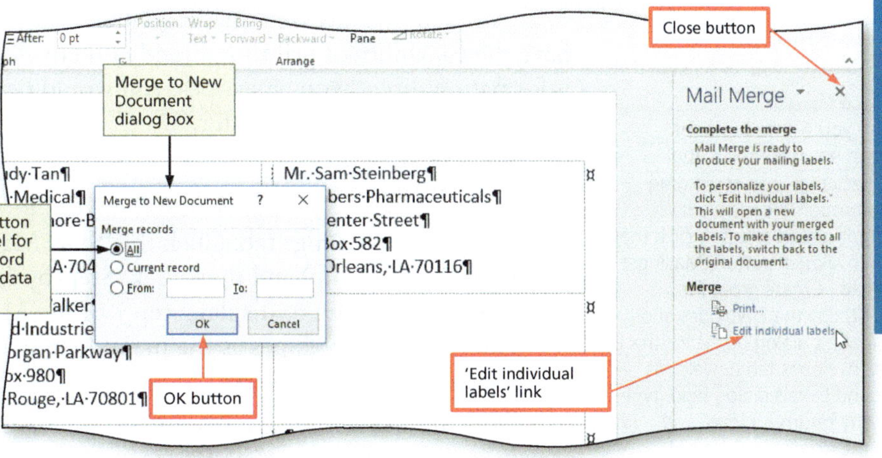

Figure 6–69

11

- Click OK (Merge to New Document dialog box) to merge the mailing labels to a new document.
- If necessary, insert a sheet of blank mailing labels in the printer.
- Save the merged mailing labels in the JobHunting folder on your hard drive, OneDrive, or other storage location using the file name, SC_WD_6_Jackman MergedMailingLabels. If requested by your instructor, print the merged labels (Figure 6–70).

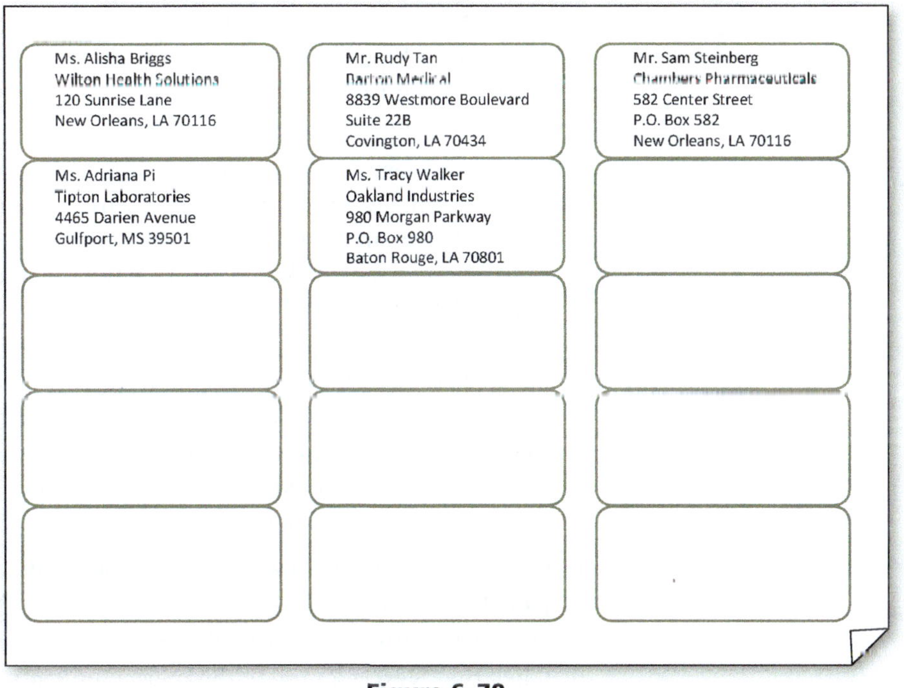

Figure 6–70

12

- Close the document window containing the merged labels.
- Click the Close button at the right edge of the Mail Merge pane.
- Display the Mailings tab. Click the Preview Results button to show field codes instead of merged data on the labels.
- Save the mailing label main document in the JobHunting folder on your hard drive, OneDrive, or other storage location using the file name, SC_WD_6_JackmanMailingLabelLayout.
- Close the mailing label main document.

Consider This

How should you position addresses on an envelope?

An envelope should contain the sender's full name and address in the upper-left corner of the envelope. It also should contain the addressee's full name and address, positioned approximately in the vertical and horizontal center of the envelope. The address can be printed directly on the envelope or on a mailing label that is affixed to the envelope.

BTW

Create Envelopes and Mailing Labels for a Single Recipient

If you wanted to print an envelope for a single recipient, you could drag through the recipient's address to select it, click the Envelopes button (Mailings tab | Create group) to display the Envelopes and Labels dialog box, click the Envelopes tab (Envelopes and Labels dialog box), type the return address, and then click the Print button. To print a mailing label for a single recipient, click the Labels button (Mailings tab | Create group) to display the Envelopes and Labels dialog box, type the address in the Delivery address box, if necessary, and then click the Print button. To print the same address on all labels on the page, select the 'Full page of the same label' option button in the Print area.

To Address and Print Envelopes

Instead of addressing mailing labels to affix to envelopes, your printer may have the capability of printing directly on envelopes. If you wanted to print address information directly on envelopes, you would perform the following steps to merge the envelopes directly to the printer.

1. Open Backstage view. Click New in Backstage view to display the New screen. Click the Blank document thumbnail to open a new blank document window.
2. Display the Mailings tab. Click the 'Start Mail Merge' button (Mailings tab | Start Mail Merge group) and then click 'Step-by-Step Mail Merge Wizard' on the Start Mail Merge menu to display Step 1 of the Mail Merge wizard in the Mail Merge pane. Specify envelopes as the main document type by clicking Envelopes in the Select document type area.
3. Click the 'Next: Starting document' link at the bottom of the Mail Merge pane to display Step 2 of the Mail Merge wizard. In the Mail Merge pane, click the Envelope Options link to display the Envelope Options dialog box.
4. Select the envelope size and then click OK (Envelope Options dialog box), which displays the selected envelope layout as the main document.
5. If your envelope does not have a preprinted return address, position the insertion point in the upper-left corner of the envelope layout and then type a return address.
6. Click the 'Next: Select recipients' link at the bottom of the Mail Merge pane to display Step 3 of the Mail Merge wizard, which allows you to select the data source. Select an existing data source or create a new one. At the bottom of the Mail Merge pane, click the 'Next: Arrange your envelope' link to display Step 4 of the Mail Merge wizard in the Mail Merge pane.
7. Position the insertion point in the middle of the envelope. In the Mail Merge pane, click the Address block link to display the Insert Address Block dialog box. Select desired settings and then click OK to close the dialog box and insert the AddressBlock merge field in the envelope layout of the main document. If necessary, match fields so that the Company is matched to the Organization_Name field.
8. Click the 'Next: Preview your envelopes' link at the bottom of the Mail Merge pane to display Step 5 of the Mail Merge wizard, which shows a preview of an envelope in the document window.
9. Click the 'Next: Complete the merge' link at the bottom of the Mail Merge pane to display Step 6 of the Mail Merge wizard. In the Mail Merge pane, click the Print link to display the Merge to Printer dialog box. If necessary, click All (Merge to Printer dialog box) so that all records in the data source will be included in the merge.
10. If necessary, insert blank envelopes in the printer. Click OK to display the Print dialog box. Click OK (Print dialog box) to print the addresses on the envelopes. Close the Mail Merge pane.

Merging All Data Records to a Directory

You may want to print the data records (recipient list) in the data source. Recall that the data source is saved as a Microsoft Access database table. Thus, you cannot open the data source in Word. To view the data source, you click the 'Edit Recipient List' button

(Mailings tab | Start Mail Merge group), which displays the Mail Merge Recipients dialog box. This dialog box, however, does not have a Print button.

One way to print the contents of the data source is to merge all data records in the data source into a single document, called a directory. A **directory** is a listing of data records (recipients) from the data source. A directory does not merge each data record to a separate document; instead, a directory lists all records together in a single document. When you merge to a directory, the default organization of a directory places each record one after the next, similar to the look of entries in a telephone book.

To create a directory, follow the same process as for the form letters. That is, determine the appropriate data source, create the directory main document, and then merge the main document with the data source to create the directory.

The directory in this module is more organized with the rows and columns divided and field names placed above each column (shown in Figure 6–83). To accomplish this look, the following steps are required:

1. Change the page orientation from portrait to landscape, so that each record fits on a single row.
2. Create a directory layout, placing a separating character between each merge field.
3. Merge the directory to a new document, which creates a list of all data records (recipients) in the data source.
4. Convert the directory to a table, using the separator character as the identifier for each new column.
5. Format the table containing the directory.
6. Sort the table by organization name within city, so that it is easy to locate a particular record.

To Change Page Orientation

When a document is in **portrait orientation**, the short edge of the paper is the top of the document, and the document is taller than it is wide. You can instruct Word to lay out a document in **landscape orientation**, so that the long edge of the paper is the top of the document, and the document is wider than it is tall. The following steps change the orientation of the document from portrait to landscape. **Why?** You want an entire record to fit on a single line in the directory.

1

- sam If necessary, create a new blank document in the Word window and change the zoom to page width.
- Display the Layout tab.
- Click the Orientation button (Layout tab | Page Setup group) to display the Orientation gallery (Figure 6–71).

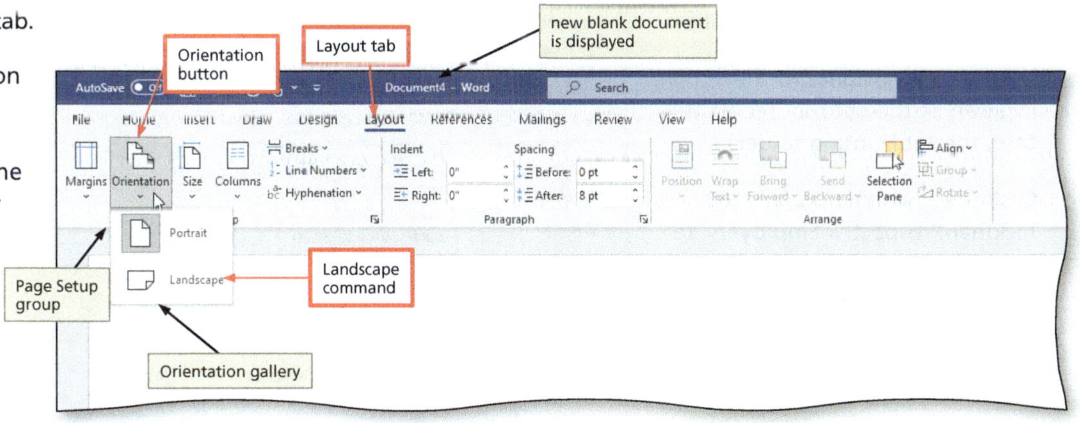

Figure 6–71

2

- Click Landscape in the Orientation gallery to change the page orientation to landscape.
- If necessary, change the zoom to page width again so that both the left and right edges of the page are visible in the document window.

To Merge to a Directory

The next steps merge the data records (recipients) in the data source to a directory. **Why?** You would like a listing of all data records (recipients) in the data source. For illustration purposes, the following steps use the buttons on the Mailings tab rather than using the Mail Merge wizard to merge to a directory.

1

- Display the Mailings tab.
- Click the 'Start Mail Merge' button (Mailings tab | Start Mail Merge group) to display the Start Mail Merge menu (Figure 6–72).

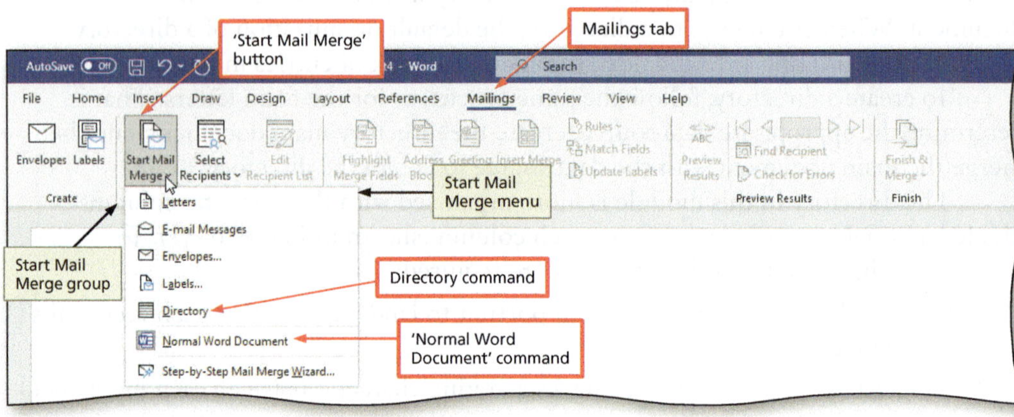

Figure 6–72

2

- Click Directory on the Start Mail Merge menu to select the main document type.

3

- Click the Select Recipients button (Mailings tab | Start Mail Merge group) to display the Select Recipients menu (Figure 6–73).

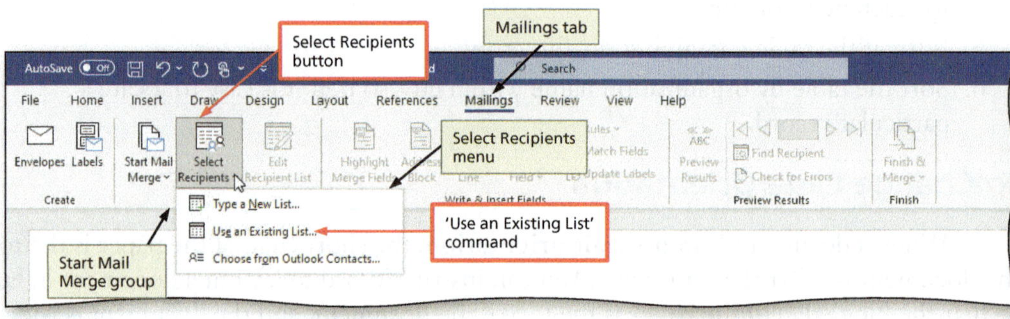

Figure 6–73

4

- Click 'Use an Existing List' on the Select Recipients menu to display the Select Data Source dialog box.
- If necessary, navigate to the location of the data source (in this case, the JobHunting folder).
- Click the file name, SC_WD_6_JackmanProspectiveEmployers, to select the data source you created earlier in the module (Figure 6–74).

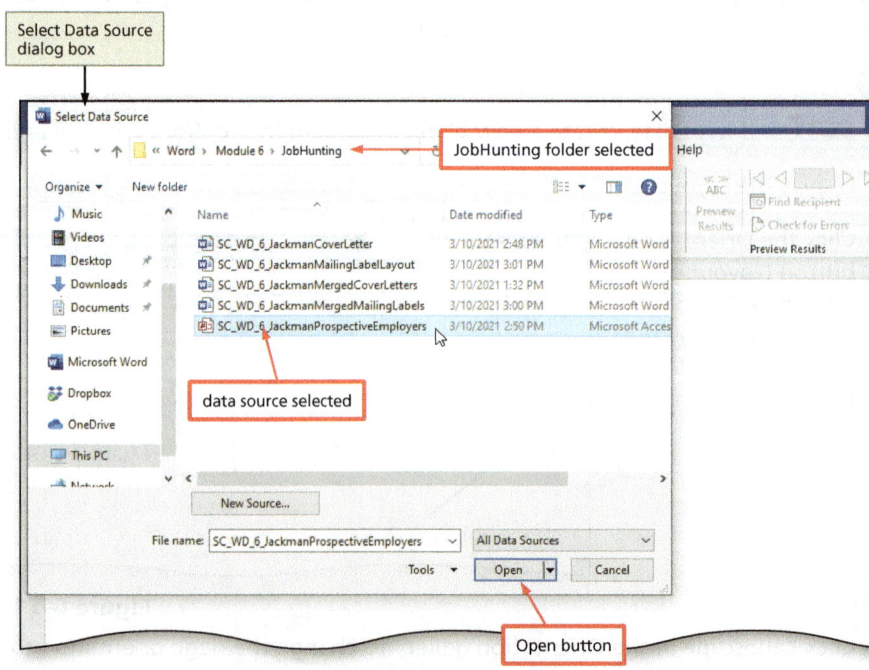

Figure 6–74

5

- Click the Open button (Select Data Source dialog box) to associate the selected data source with the current main document.

6

- Click the 'Insert Merge Field' arrow (Mailings tab | Write & Insert Fields group) to display the Insert Merge Field menu (Figure 6–75).

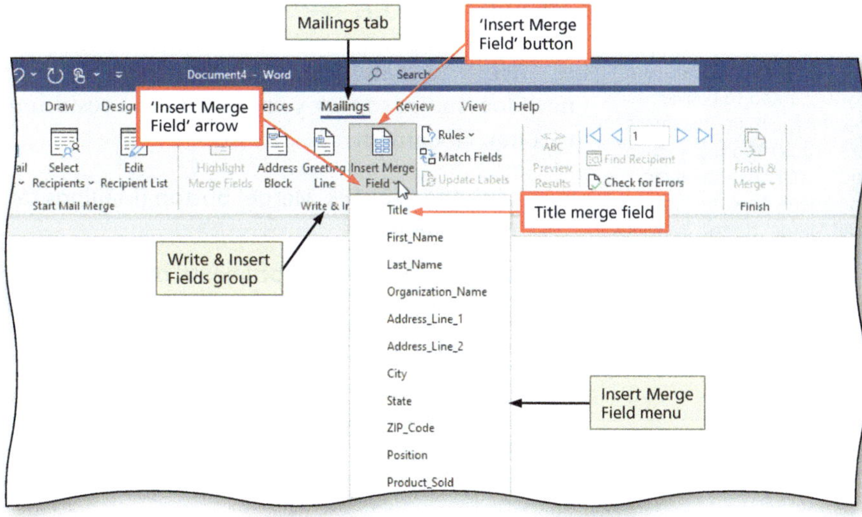

Figure 6–75

7

- Click Title on the Insert Merge Field menu to insert the selected merge field in the document.
- Press the COMMA (,) key to place a comma after the inserted merge field.

Q&A **Why insert a comma after the merge field?**
In the next steps, you will convert the entered merge fields to a table format with the records in rows and the fields in columns. To do this, Word divides the columns based on a character separating each field. In this case, you use the comma to separate the merge fields.

8

- Repeat Steps 6 and 7 for the First_Name, Last_Name, Organization_Name, Address_Line_1, Address_Line_2, City, State, and ZIP_Code fields on the Insert Merge Field menu, so that these fields in the data source appear in the main document separated by a comma, except do not type a comma after the last field (ZIP_Code).

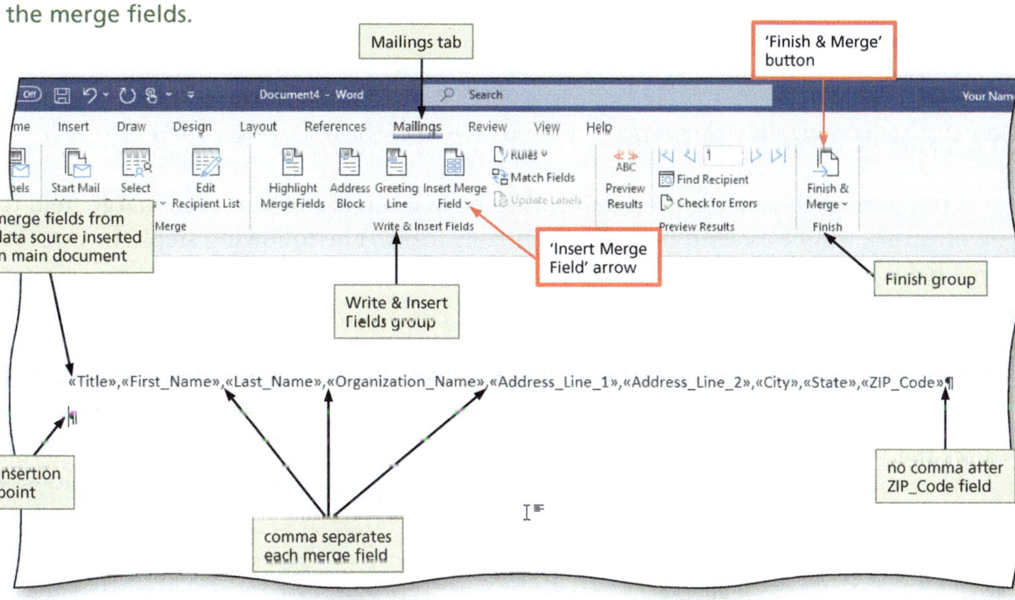

Figure 6–76

- Press ENTER (Figure 6–76).

Q&A **Why press ENTER after entering the merge fields names?**
This will place the first field in each data record at the beginning of a new line.

Why are the Position and Product_Sold fields not included in the directory?
You just want the directory listing to show the contact information for each potential employer.

9

- **sam** Save the directory main document in the JobHunting folder on your hard drive, OneDrive, or other storage location using the file name, SC_WD_6_JackmanPotentialEmployerDirectoryLayout.

BTW

Converting Main Document Files

If you wanted to convert a mail merge main document to a regular Word document, you would open the main document, click the 'Start Mail Merge' button (Mailings tab | Start Mail Merge group), and then click 'Normal Word Document' on the Start Mail Merge menu (shown in Figure 6–72).

To Merge to a New Document

The next step is to merge the data source and the directory main document to a new document, so that you can edit the resulting document. The following steps merge to a new document.

1. Click the 'Finish & Merge' button (Mailings tab | Finish group) to display the Finish & Merge menu.
2. Click 'Edit Individual Documents' on the Finish & Merge menu to display the Merge to New Document dialog box.
3. If necessary, click All (Merge to New Document dialog box).
4. Click OK to merge the data records to a directory in a new document window (Figure 6–77).

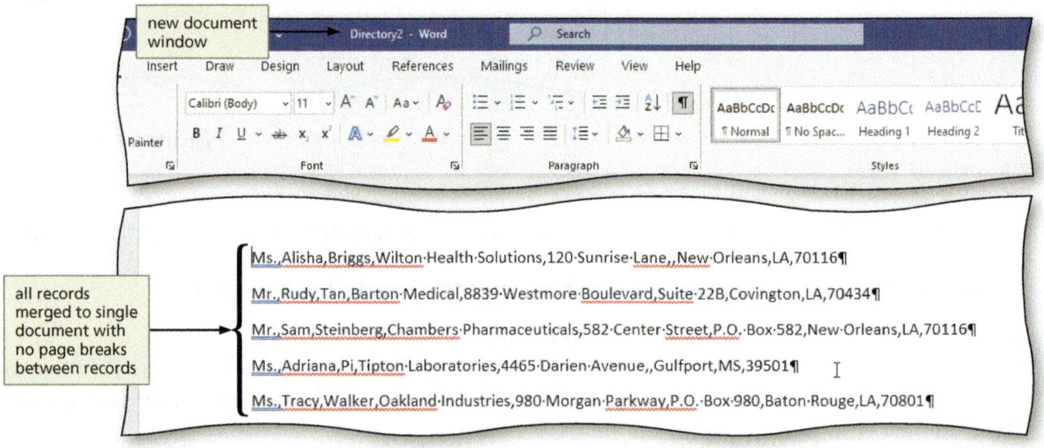

Figure 6–77

To Convert Text to a Table

You want each data record (recipient) to be in a single row and each merge field to be in a column. **Why?** The directory will be easier to read if it is in table form. The following steps convert the text containing the merge fields to a table.

1

- Press CTRL+A to select the entire document, because you want all document contents to be converted to a table.
- Display the Insert tab.
- Click the Table button (Insert tab | Tables group) to display the Table gallery (Figure 6–78).

Q&A

Can I convert a section of a document to a table?

Yes, simply select the characters, lines, or paragraphs to be converted before displaying the Convert Text to Table dialog box.

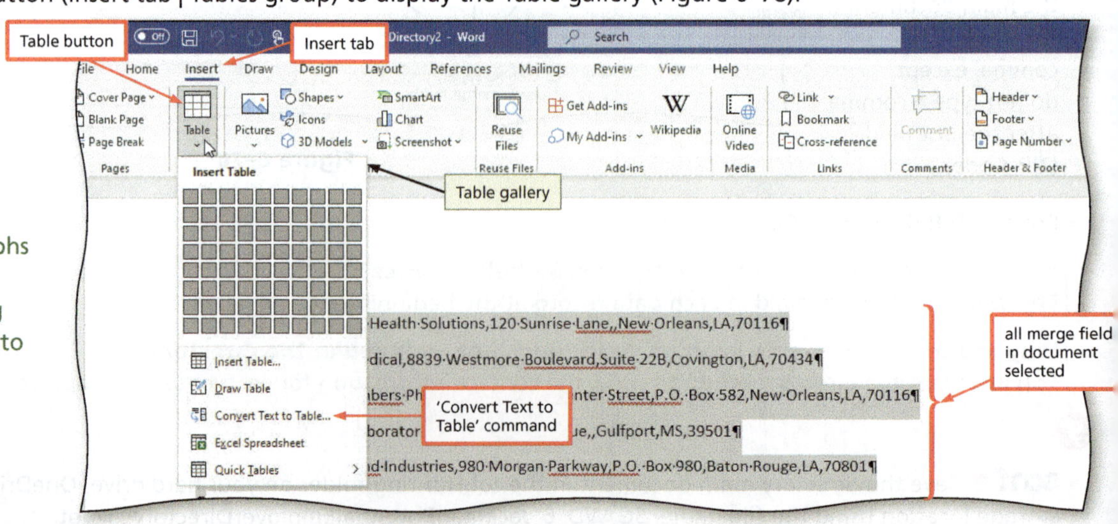

Figure 6–78

2

- Click 'Convert Text to Table' in the Table gallery to display the Convert Text to Table dialog box.
- If necessary, type 9 in the 'Number of columns' box (Convert Text to Table dialog box) to specify the number of columns for the resulting table.
- Click 'AutoFit to window', which instructs Word to fit the table and its contents to the width of the window.
- If necessary, click Commas to specify the character that separates the merge fields in the document (Figure 6–79).

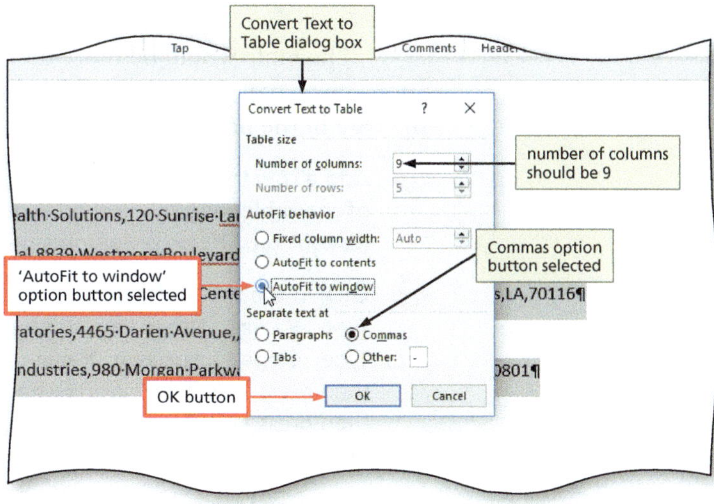

Figure 6–79

3

- Click OK to convert the selected text to a table and then, if necessary, click to remove the selection from the table (Figure 6–80).

Q&A **Can I format the table?**
Yes. You can use any of the commands on the Table Design and Layout tabs to change the look of the table.

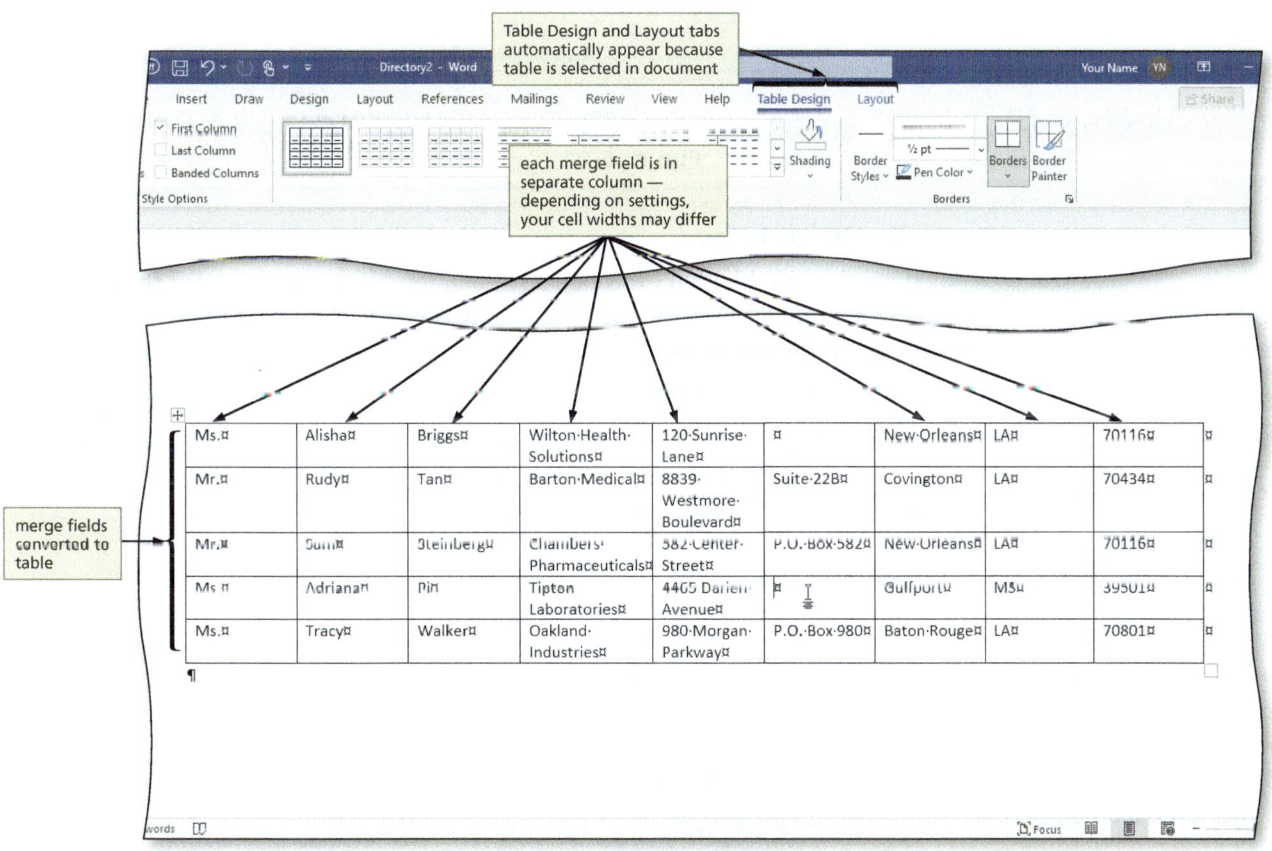

Ms.	Alisha	Briggs	Wilton Health Solutions	120 Sunrise Lane		New Orleans	LA	70116
Mr.	Rudy	Tan	Barton Medical	8839 Westmore Boulevard	Suite 22B	Covington	LA	70434
Mr.	Sam	Steinberg	Chambers Pharmaceuticals	582 Center Street	P.O. Box 582	New Orleans	LA	70116
Ms.	Adriana	Pi	Tipton Laboratories	4465 Darien Avenue		Gulfport	MS	39501
Ms.	Tracy	Walker	Oakland Industries	980 Morgan Parkway	P.O. Box 980	Baton Rouge	LA	70801

Figure 6–80

To Modify and Format a Table

The table would be more descriptive if the field names were displayed in a row above the actual data. The following steps add a row to the top of a table and format the data in the new row.

1. Add a row to the top of the table by positioning the insertion point in the first row of the table, displaying the Layout tab, and then clicking the Insert Above button (Layout tab | Rows & Columns group).
2. Click in the first (leftmost) cell of the new row. Type **`Title`** and then press TAB. Type **`First Name`** and then press TAB. Type **`Last Name`** and then press TAB. Type **`Organization Name`** and then press TAB. Type **`Address Line 1`** and then press TAB. Type **`Address Line 2`** and then press TAB. Type **`City`** and then press TAB. Type **`State`** and then press TAB. Type **`ZIP Code`** as the last entry in the row.
3. Bold the contents of the first row.
4. Use the AutoFit Contents command on the ribbon or the shortcut menu to make all columns as wide as their contents. If necessary, adjust individual column widths so that the table looks like Figure 6–81.
5. Center the table between the margins (Figure 6–81).

header row added and bold

Title	**First Name**	**Last Name**	**Organization Name**	**Address Line 1**	**Address Line 2**	**City**	**State**	**ZIP Code**
Ms.	Alisha	Briggs	Wilton Health Solutions	120 Sunrise Lane		New Orleans	LA	70116
Mr.	Rudy	Tan	Barton Medical	8839 Westmore Boulevard	Suite 22B	Covington	LA	70434
Mr.	Sam	Steinberg	Chambers Pharmaceuticals	582 Center Street	P.O. Box 582	New Orleans	LA	70116
Ms.	Adriana	Pi	Tipton Laboratories	4465 Darien Avenue		Gulfport	MS	39501
Ms.	Tracy	Walker	Oakland Industries	980 Morgan Parkway	P.O. Box 980	Baton Rouge	LA	70801

Figure 6–81

To Repeat Header Rows

If you had a table that exceeded a page in length and you wanted the header row (the first row) to appear at the top of the table on each continued page, you would perform the following steps.

1. Position the insertion point in the header row.
2. Click the 'Repeat Header Rows' button (Layout tab | Data group) (shown in Figure 6–82) to repeat the row containing the insertion point at the top of every page on which the table continues.

To Sort a Table by Multiple Columns

The next step is to sort the table. **Why?** In this project, the table records are displayed by organization name within city. The following steps sort a table by multiple columns.

1

- With the table selected or the insertion point in the table, click the Sort button (Layout tab | Data group) to display the Sort dialog box.
- Click the Sort by arrow (Sort dialog box); scroll to and then click City in the list.
- Click the first Then by arrow and then click Organization Name in the list.
- If necessary, click Header row so that the first row remains in its current location when the table is sorted (Figure 6–82).

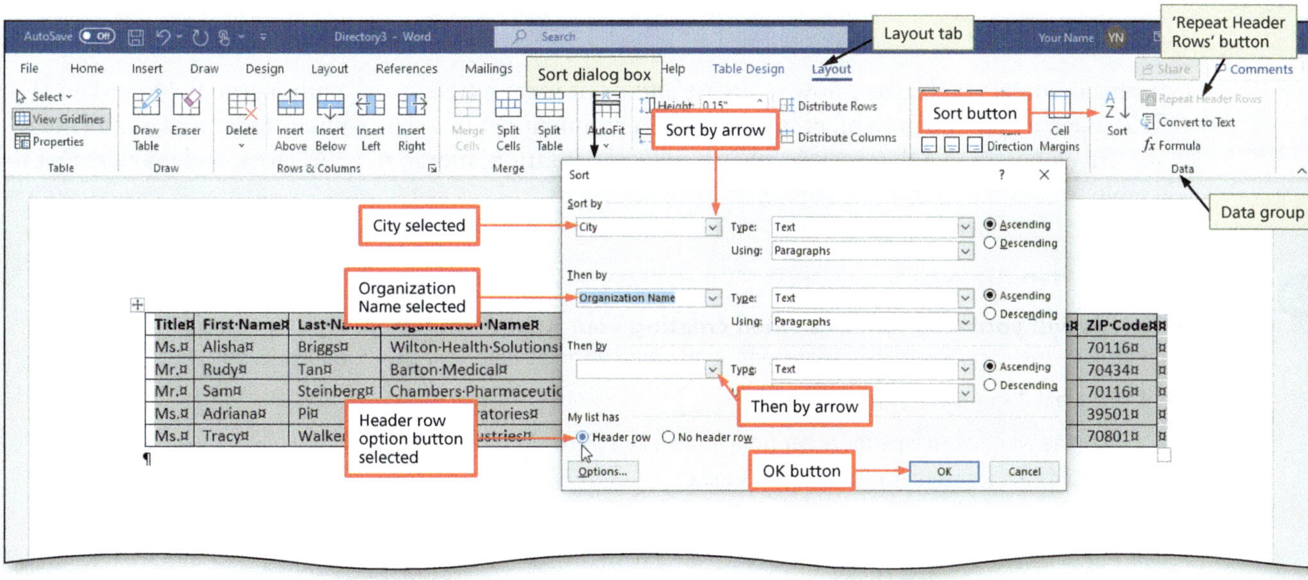

Figure 6–82

2

- Click OK to sort the records in the table in ascending Organization Name order within ascending City order (Figure 6–83).
- If necessary, click to deselect the table.
- **sam** Save the merged directory in the JobHunting folder on your hard drive, OneDrive, or other storage location using the file name, SC_WD_6_JackmanMergedPotentialEmployerDirectory.
- If requested by your instructor, print the merged directory.

Q&A **If Microsoft Access is installed on my computer, can I use that to print the data source?**
As an alternative to merging to a directory and printing the results, if you are familiar with Microsoft Access and it is installed on your computer, you can open and print the data source in Access.

- Close all open files, if necessary, and then exit Word.

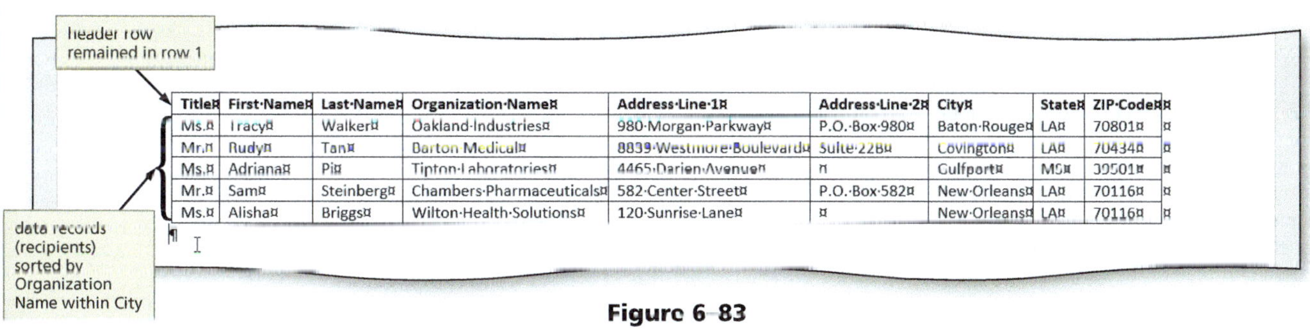

Figure 6–83

BTW
Distributing a Document
Instead of printing and distributing a hard copy of a document, you can distribute the document electronically. Options include sending the document via email; posting it on cloud storage (such as OneDrive) and sharing the file with others; posting it on social media, a blog, or other website; and sharing a link associated with an online location of the document. You also can create and share a PDF or XPS image of the document, so that users can view the file in Adobe Reader or XPS Viewer instead of in Word.

Summary

In this module, you learned how to create and print form letters, work with merge fields and an IF field, open a main document, create and edit a recipient list in a data source, address mailing labels and envelopes from a data source, change page orientation, merge to a directory, and convert text to a table.

Consider This: Plan Ahead

What decisions will you need to make when creating your next form letter?

Use these guidelines as you complete the assignments in this module and create your own form letters outside of this class.

1. Identify the main document for the form letter.
   a) Determine whether to type the letter from scratch in a blank document window or use a letter template.
2. Create or specify the recipient list for the data source.
   a) Determine if the data exists already in an Access database table, an Outlook contacts list, or an Excel worksheet.
   b) If you cannot use an existing data source, create a new one using appropriate field names.
3. Compose the main document for the form letter.
   a) Ensure the letter contains all essential business letter elements and is visually appealing.
   b) Be sure the letter contains proper grammar, correct spelling, logically constructed sentences, flowing paragraphs, and sound ideas.
   c) Properly reference the data in the data source.
4. Merge the main document with the data source to create the form letters.
   a) Determine the destination for the merge (i.e., a new document, the printer, etc.).
   b) Determine which data records to merge (all of them or a portion of them).
5. Determine whether to generate mailing labels or envelopes.
   a) Create or specify the data source.
   b) Ensure the mailing label or envelope contains all necessary information.
6. Create a directory of the data source.
   a) Create or specify the data source.
   b) If necessary, format the directory appropriately.

BTW

Printing Document Properties

To print document properties, click File on the ribbon to open Backstage view, click Print in Backstage view to display the Print screen, click the first button in the Settings area to display a list of options specifying what you can print, click Document Info in the list to specify you want to print the document properties instead of the actual document, and then click the Print button in the Print screen to print the document properties on the currently selected printer.

Apply Your Knowledge

Reinforce the skills and apply the concepts you learned in this module.

Editing, Printing, and Merging a Form Letter and Recipients in a Data Source

Note: To complete this assignment, you will be required to use the Data Files. Please contact your instructor for information about accessing the Data Files.

Instructions: Using a file manager, such as File Explorer in Windows, copy the file Support_WD_6_PrincetonOpticalPatientList in the Data Files to the location where you will save your documents in this assignment and then rename the copied file to SC_WD_6_PrincetonOpticalPatientList.

Start Word and create a new blank document. You will use this data source in the Mail Merge wizard to work with a main document for the form letters created by an optical assistant at Princeton Optical that reaches out to customers about eye examinations (Figure 6–84). You will enter a date using the date content control, insert the AddressBlock and GreetingLine merge fields, insert additional merge fields, print the form letter, edit the recipients in the data source, and merge the form letters.

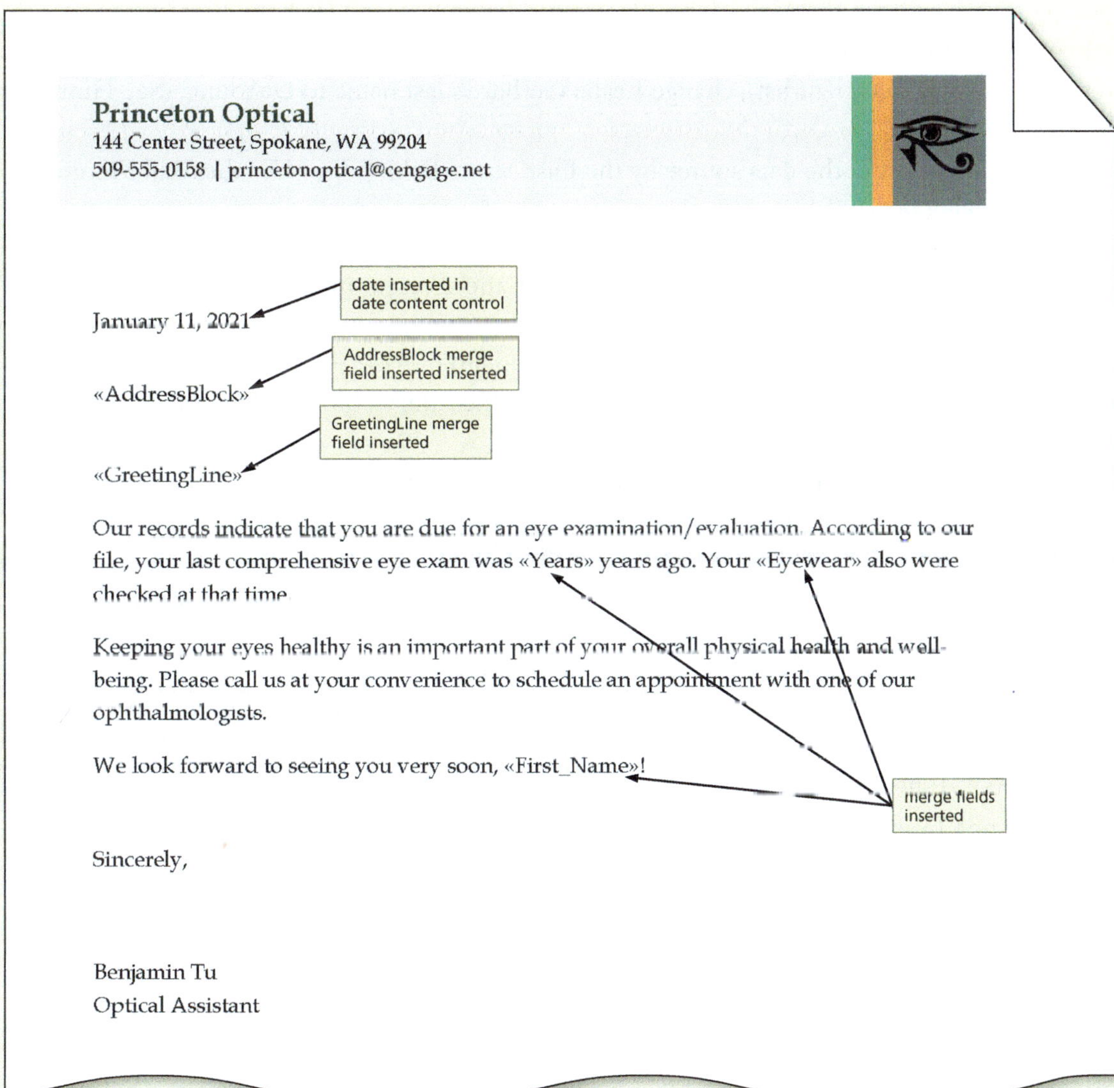

Princeton Optical
144 Center Street, Spokane, WA 99204
509-555-0158 | princetonoptical@cengage.net

January 11, 2021

«AddressBlock»

«GreetingLine»

Our records indicate that you are due for an eye examination/evaluation. According to our file, your last comprehensive eye exam was «Years» years ago. Your «Eyewear» also were checked at that time.

Keeping your eyes healthy is an important part of your overall physical health and well-being. Please call us at your convenience to schedule an appointment with one of our ophthalmologists.

We look forward to seeing you very soon, «First_Name»!

Sincerely,

Benjamin Tu
Optical Assistant

Figure 6–84

Continued >

Apply Your Knowledge *continued*

Perform the following tasks:

1. Start the Mail Merge wizard.
2. In Step 1 of the Mail Merge wizard, select Letters as the document type.
3. In Step 2 of the Mail Merge wizard, select 'Start from an existing document' as the starting document and then use the Open button in the Mail Merge pane to open the file called SC_WD_6-1.docx, which is located in the Data Files.
4. Save the document using SC_WD_6_PrincetonOpticalFormLetter as the file name.
5. In Step 3 of the Mail Merge wizard, select 'Use an existing list' and then use the Browse link to open the data source called SC_WD_6_PrincetonOpticalPatientList (the file you copied from the Data Files at the beginning of this assignment, which contains the patient recipient list). When the Mail Merge Recipients dialog box appears, click OK to close the dialog box.
6. If requested by your instructor, add a record to the data source that contains your personal information and uses two in the Years merge field and contacts in the Eyewear field. (Hint: Use the 'Edit recipient list' link in the Mail Merge pane or the 'Edit Recipient List' button (Mailings tab | Write & Insert Fields) to display the Mail Merge Recipients dialog box, click the data source name in the Mail Merge Recipients dialog box, and click the Edit button to display the Edit Data Source dialog box.)
7. In the data source (recipient list), change Leslie Gerhard's last name to DeYoung. (See Hint in Step 6 above.)
8. Sort the recipient list in the data source by the Last Name field. (Hint: Use the Mail Merge Recipients dialog box.)
9. Use the date content control to enter January 11, 2021 as the date. Right-click the date content control and then click 'Remove Content Control' on the shortcut menu to convert the content control to regular text.
10. Delete the text that reads InsertAddressBlockMergeFieldHere (do not delete the paragraph mark). Using Step 4 of the Mail Merge wizard, insert the AddressBlock field at the location of the deleted text in the letter.
11. Delete the text that reads InsertGreetingLineMergeFieldHere (do not delete the paragraph mark). Using Step 4 of the Mail Merge wizard, insert the GreetingLine merge field so that the salutation appears in the format, Dear Mr. Randall followed by a colon.
12. Edit the GreetingLine merge field so that the salutation appears in the format Dear Josh followed by a comma. (Hint: Right-click the GreetingLine field.)
13. Delete the text InsertYearsMergeFieldHere. At the location of the deleted text, use the Mail Merge wizard to insert the Years merge field by clicking the More items link in the Mail Merge pane, clicking Years (Insert Merge Field dialog box), clicking the Insert button, and then closing the dialog box. If necessary, press SPACEBAR after the Years merge field in the form letter.
14. Delete the text InsertEyewearMergeFieldHere. At the location of the deleted text, insert the Eyewear merge field by clicking the Insert Merge Field arrow (Mailings tab | Write & Insert Fields group) and then clicking Eyewear in the Insert Merge Field list. If necessary, press SPACEBAR after the Eyewear merge field in the form letter.
15. Delete the text InsertFirstNameMergeFieldHere and then press SPACEBAR. (If necessary, adjust spacing so that one space appears before the inserted merge field.) At the location of the deleted text, insert the First Name merge field.
16. Highlight the merge fields in the document. How many were highlighted? Remove the highlight from the merge fields.

17. In Step 5 of the Mail Merge wizard, preview the mail merge. Use the navigation buttons in the Mail Merge pane to view merged data from various data records in the recipient list in the data source. Click the Preview Results button (Mailings tab | Preview Results group) to view merge fields (turn off the preview results). Click the Preview Results button (Mailings tab | Preview Results group) again to view merged data again. Use the navigation buttons in the Preview Results group in the Mailings tab to display merged data from various records in the data source. What is the last name shown in the first record? The third record? The fifth record?
18. Use the 'Find a recipient' link in the Mail Merge pane in Step 5 of the Mail Merge wizard or the Find Recipient button (Mailings tab | Preview Results group) to find the name, Roberto. In what city does Roberto live?
19. Print the main document for the form letter (shown in Figure 6–84). If requested by your instructor, save the main document as a PDF.
20. Save the main document for the form letter again.
21. In Step 6 of the Mail Merge wizard, merge the form letters to a new document using the 'Edit individual letters' link. Save the new document with the file name, SC_WD_6_PrincetonOpticalMergedLetters. Close the merged letters document.
22. If requested by your instructor, merge the form letters directly to the printer using the Print link in Step 6 of the Mail Merge wizard.
23. Close the Mail Merge pane.
24. Submit the saved documents in the format specified by your instructor.
25. Answer the questions posed in #16, #17, and #18. If you did not want to use the AddressBlock and GreetingLine fields, how would you enter the address and salutation so that the letters printed the correct fields from each record?

Extend Your Knowledge

Extend the skills you learned in this module and experiment with new skills. You may need to use Help to complete the assignment.

Working with an IF Field and a Fill-In Field, and Merging Using Email and Access

Note: To complete this assignment, you will be required to use the Data Files. Please contact your instructor for information about accessing the Data Files.

Instructions: Using your file manager, such as File Explorer in Windows, copy the file Support_WD_6_ScenicHorizonsTravelCustomerList in the Data Files to the location where you will save your documents in this assignment and then rename the copied file to SC_WD_6_ScenicHorizonsTravelCustomerList.

Start Word. Open the document, SC_WD_6-2.docx, which is located in the Data Files. When you open the main document, if Word displays a dialog box about an SQL command, click the Yes button. When Word prompts for the name of the data source, navigate to and open the file you just copied named SC_WD_6_ScenicHorizonsTravelCustomerList. (If Word does not prompt for the data source name, change the data source to SC_WD_6_ScenicHorizonsTravelCustomerList.)

The Word document is a main document for a form letter from a travel agent with Scenic Horizons Travel confirming cruise bookings (Figure 6–85). You will modify the letter, insert and modify an IF field, insert a Fill-in field, print field codes, create envelopes for records in the data source, use an Access database file as a data source, and merge to email addresses.

Continued >

Extend Your Knowledge *continued*

Perform the following tasks:

1. Use Help to learn about mail merge, IF fields, Fill-in fields, and merging to email addresses.
2. Click File on the ribbon and then click Save As and save the document using the new file name, SC_WD_6_ScenicHorizonsTravelFormLetter.
3. Change the top and bottom margins to 1 inch and the left and right margins to 1.25 inches. Specify the position of the drawing image that contains the company information to 1 inch from the top of the page.
4. Position the insertion point to the left of the word, cabin, in the second sentence of the letter. At this location, insert an IF field that tests the value in the Cabin Type field. If the value in the Cabin Type field is a W, then the word, windows, should be displayed; otherwise, the word, balconies, should be displayed. If necessary, add a space after the inserted field in the document. View merged data and scroll through the data records to be sure the IF field works as intended.
5. When viewing merged data, you notice that the text to be displayed in the IF Field should be singular instead of plural. Edit the IF field so that the text displayed is window and balcony (instead of windows and balconies). (Hint: Use the 'Toggle Field Codes' command on the shortcut menu (right-click the IF field code in the document window) and edit the IF field directly in the document.)
6. Above the AddressBlock merge field (shown in Figure 6–85), insert a Fill-in field that asks this question: On what date will you be mailing these letters? Select the Ask once check box so that the question is asked only once, instead of for each letter. When merging the letters, use a date in March of 2021. What is the purpose of the Fill-in field?
7. Add a field to the data source called Cruise Type. Enter a value into this field for each data record in the recipient list, i.e., Alaskan, Caribbean, etc.
8. In the third sentence in the first paragraph and also the first sentence in the last paragraph, insert the new field called Cruise Type immediately to the left of the word, cruise. If necessary, add a space after the inserted field in the document.
9. If requested by your instructor, add a record to the data source that contains your personal information along with a cabin type of window and a cruise type of your choice.
10. Merge the letters to a new document. Save the merged letters using the file name, SC_WD_6_ScenicHorizonsTravelMergedLetters.
11. Print the main document for the form letter. If requested by your instructor, save the main document as a PDF.
12. Print the form letter with field codes showing; that is, print it with the 'Print field codes instead of their values' check box selected in the Word Options dialog box. Be sure to deselect this check box after printing the field codes version of the letter. How does this printout differ from the one printed in #11?
13. Filter the recipient list to show only those customers with window cabins. How many are there? Clear the filter.
14. Submit the main document and merged letters in the format specified by your instructor.
15. If your instructor requests, create envelopes for each letter in the data source using the Mail Merge wizard. Submit the merged envelopes in the format specified by your instructor.
16. If your instructor requests, create mailing labels for each letter in the data source using the Mail Merge wizard. While creating the mailing label main document, be sure to click the 'Update all labels' button so that all recipients appear on the mailing labels. Submit the merged mailing labels document in the format specified by your instructor.

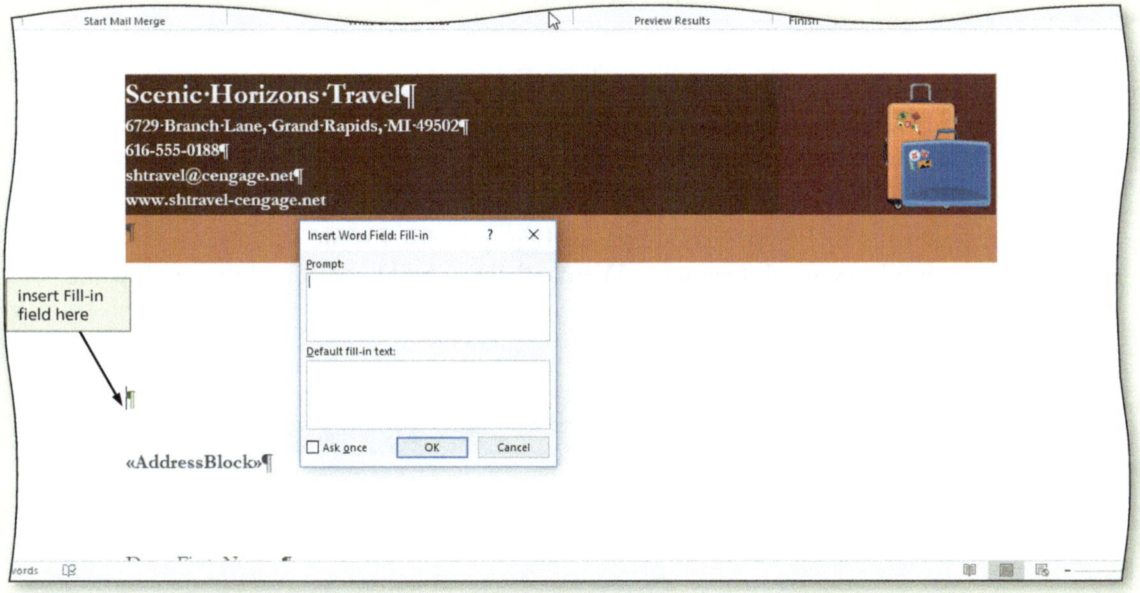

Figure 6–85

17. If your instructor requests, create a single mailing label for Bethany Ames because the envelope jammed when you were printing envelopes. (Hint: Use the Labels button (Mailings tab | Create group).)
18. If Access is installed on your computer or mobile device, and if you are familiar with Access and your instructor requests it, open the data source included with the assignment in Access and then print it from within Access.
19. If your instructor requests, display your personal record on the screen and merge the form letter to an email message, specifying that only the current record receives the message. Submit the merged email message in the format specified by your instructor.
20. Answer the questions posed in #6, #12, and #13. If you choose to merge to email addresses, what is the purpose of the various email formats?

Expand Your World

Create a solution that uses cloud or web technologies by learning and investigating on your own from general guidance.

Exploring Add-Ins for Microsoft 365 Apps

Instructions: You regularly use apps on your phone and tablet to look up a variety of information. In Microsoft 365 apps, you can use add-ins, which essentially are apps that work with Word (and the other Microsoft 365 apps). You would like to investigate some of the add-ins available for Word to determine which ones would be helpful for you to use.

Note: You will be required to use your Microsoft account to complete this assignment. If you do not have a Microsoft account and do not want to create one, read this assignment without performing the instructions.

Perform the following tasks:

1. Use Help to learn about add-ins. If necessary, sign in to your Windows account.
2. Start Word and create a new blank document. If you are not signed in already, sign in to your Microsoft Account in Word.

Continued >

Expand Your World *continued*

3. Click the Get Add-ins button (Insert tab | Add-ins group) to display the Office Add-ins dialog box. Click the STORE tab (Office Add-ins dialog box) to visit the online Office Store. (Note that if your Insert tab does not have a Get Add-ins button, search through Help for the location of the button in your version of Word that enables you to work with add-ins.)
4. Scroll through add-ins in the various categories (Figure 6–86). Locate a free add-in that you feel would be helpful to you while you use Word, click the Add button, and then follow the instructions to add the add-in to Word.

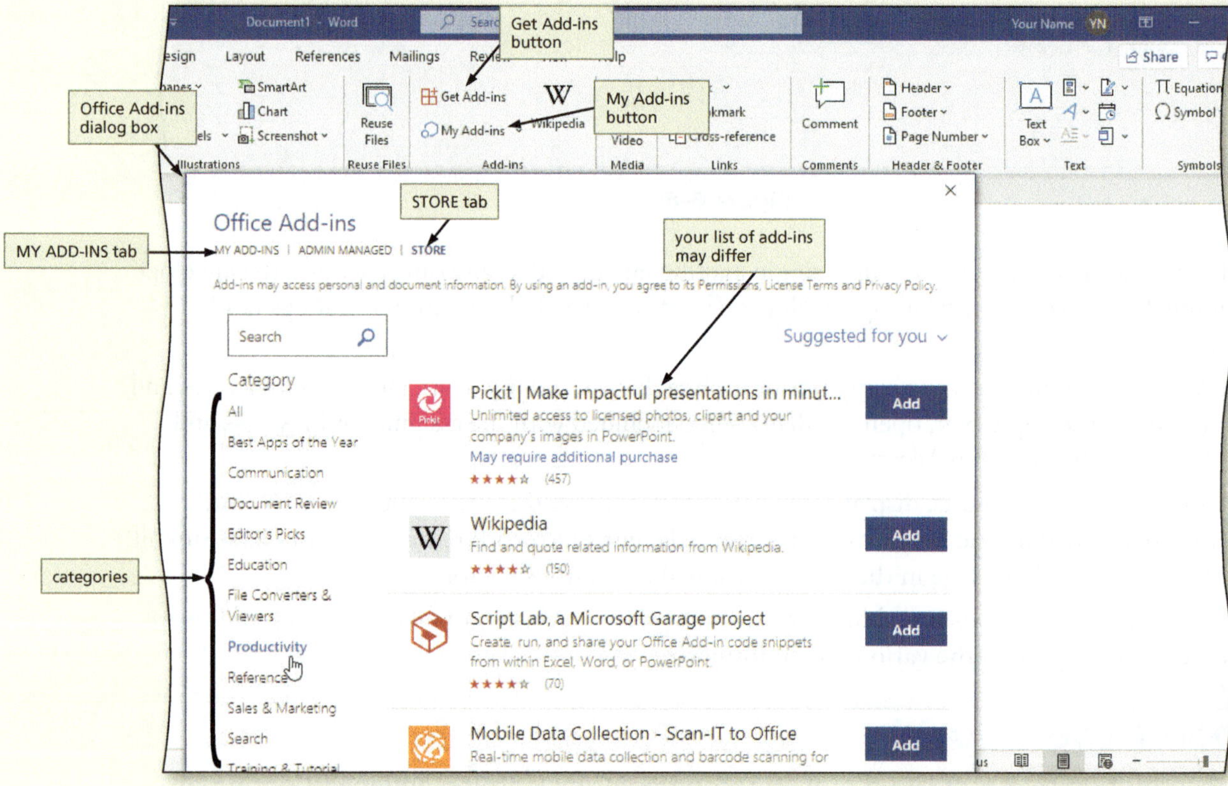

Figure 6–86

5. In Word, click the Get Add-ins button (Insert tab | Add-ins group) again to display the Office Add-ins dialog box. Click the MY ADD-INS tab to display the list of your add-ins, click the add-in you added, and click the Add button to use the add-in.
6. Practice using the add-in. Does the add-in work as you intended? Would you recommend the add-in to others? If you rated this add-in, what would your rating be? Why?
7. In Word, click the My Add-ins button (Insert tab | Add-ins group) to display the MY ADD-INS tab in the Office Add-ins dialog box. Click the 'Manage My Add-ins' link in the upper-right corner of the Office Add-ins dialog box to open the My Office and Sharepoint add-ins window in a browser and display available add-ins. Note that if you want to cancel a paid subscription to an add-in, you would do it in this window. Close the My Office and Sharepoint add-ins window.

8. To see add-ins included with Microsoft 365, open Backstage view, click Options to display the Word Options dialog box, and click Add-ins in the left pane (Word Options dialog box). To manage an add-in, select the desired add-in type in the Manage list at the bottom of the Word Options dialog box and then click the Go button.
9. In Word, click the My Add-ins button (Insert tab | Add-ins group) and then click 'See My Add-ins' at the bottom of the Get Add-ins list to display the MY ADD-INS tab in the Office Add-ins dialog box. Right-click the add-in you added in this assignment, click Remove on the shortcut menu, and then click the Remove button in the dialog box to remove the add-in from your Word app.
10. Which add-ins, if any, were already on your computer or mobile device? Which add-in did you download and why? Answer the questions in #6.

In the Lab

Design and implement a solution using creative thinking and problem-solving skills.

Use Mail Merge to Create Cover Letters for a Graduating Criminal Justice Student

Problem: You are graduating with a degree in criminal justice from Marigold College. You decide to create a cover letter for your resume as a form letter that you will send to potential employers. You will use the Mail Merge wizard to create the form letters and the recipient list for the data source. Place all files created in this assignment in a folder called Investigator Jobs; create the folder from within Word when saving.

Part 1: Use a letter template of your choice or design the letter from scratch for the main document for the form letter. Save the main document for the form letter with the file name, SC_WD_6_InvestigatorCoverLetter. Type a new data source using the data shown in Table 6-1. Delete the field names not used and add one field name: Position. Rename the Company_Name field to Organization_Name. If requested by your instructor, add a record to the data source that contains your personal information. (Be sure to match the Company Name to the Organization_Name field so that the organization name appears in the AddressBlock field.) Save the data source with the file name, SC_WD_6_InvestigatorProspectiveEmployers.

Table 6-1

Title	First Name	Last Name	Organization Name	Address Line 1	Address Line 2	City	State	ZIP Code	Position
Detective	Kristina	Stein	Warren County	293 Bailey Lane	Room 281	Bowling Green	KY	42102	associate investigator
Mr.	Jordan	Green	Granger Investigative Services	221 Second Street		Paducah	KY	42003	investigator
Sergeant	Adelbert	Martinez	Lexington Police Department	443 Cedar Lane	P.O. Box 443	Lexington	KY	40505	field investigator
Ms.	Cam	Lin	City of Middlesboro	101 Main Street	P.O. Box 101	Middlesboro	KY	40965	detective
Ms.	Michelle	Cole	Armour Investigations	32 Chamber Road	Unit 20C	Mount Sterling	KY	40353	investigator

Continued >

In the Labs *continued*

Use this information in the cover letter:

Name: Leo Moretti (if requested by your instructor, use your name).

Address: 2091 Willow Lane, Apt. 34, Bowling Green, KY, 42102 (if requested by your instructor, use your address).

Phone: 270-555-0177 (if requested by your instructor, use your phone number).

Email: leo@cengage.net (if requested by your instructor, use your email address).

First paragraph in body of letter, inserting a merge field as indicated: I will graduate from Marigold College in May with a Bachelor of Arts degree in Criminal Justice. My education, experience, and community service make me an ideal candidate for the InsertPositionMergeFieldHere position.

Second paragraph in body of letter: As shown on the accompanying resume, my background matches the job requirements posted through the Career Development Office at Marigold College. My coursework and experience have prepared me for law enforcement fieldwork.

Third paragraph in body of letter, inserting merge fields as indicated: Thank you in advance, InsertTitleMergeFieldHere InsertLastNameMergeFieldHere, for your time and consideration. I look forward to hearing from you soon to discuss the opportunity for my potential employment at InsertOrganizationNameMergeFieldHere.

In the main document, include the AddressBlock and GreetingLine merge fields. Use the concepts and techniques presented in this module to create and format this form letter. Be sure to check the spelling and grammar of the finished documents. Use the 'Check for Errors' button (Mailings tab | Preview Results group) to check if the main document contains merge errors and fix any errors identified. If requested by your instructor, save the main document as a PDF. Merge all records to a new document. Save the merged letters in a file called SC_WD_6_InvestigatorMergedCoverLetters.

In a new document window, create a directory of the recipient list in the data source. Begin by specifying the main document type as a directory. Change the page layout to landscape orientation. Change the margins to narrow. Insert all merge fields in the document, separating each with a comma. Save the directory layout with the file name, SC_WD_6_InvestigatorProspectiveEmployersDirectoryLayout. Merge the directory layout to a new document window. Convert the list of fields to a Word table (the table will have 10 columns). Add a row to the top of the table and insert field names in the empty cells. Format the table appropriately. Sort the table in the directory listing by the Last Name field. Save the merged directory with the file name, SC_WD_6_InvestigatorProspectiveEmployersMergedDirectoryListing.

Submit your assignment documents and answers to the Part 2 critical thinking questions in the format specified by your instructor.

Part 2: You made several decisions while creating the form letter, data source, and directory in this assignment: whether to use a template or create the letter from scratch, layout of letter elements, how to format elements, how to set up the data source, and how to format the directory. What was the rationale behind each of these decisions?

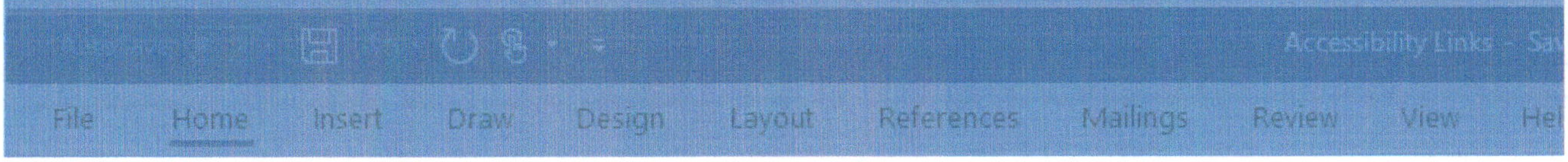

7 Creating a Newsletter

Objectives

After completing this module, you will be able to:

- Work with WordArt
- Set custom tab stops
- Crop a graphic
- Rotate a graphic
- Format a document in multiple columns
- Justify a paragraph
- Hyphenate a document
- Format a character as a drop cap
- Insert a column break
- Insert and format a text box
- Copy and paste using a split window
- Balance columns
- Modify and format a SmartArt graphic
- Copy and paste using the Office Clipboard
- Add an art page border

Introduction

Professional-looking documents, such as newsletters and brochures, often are created using desktop publishing software. With desktop publishing software, you can divide a document in multiple columns, wrap text around diagrams and other graphical images, change fonts and font sizes, add color and lines, and so on, to create an attention-grabbing document. Desktop publishing software, such as Microsoft Publisher, Adobe InDesign, or QuarkXpress, enables you to open an existing word processing document and enhance it through formatting tools not provided in your word processing app. Word, however, provides many of the formatting features that you would find in a desktop publishing app. Thus, you can use Word to create eye-catching newsletters and brochures.

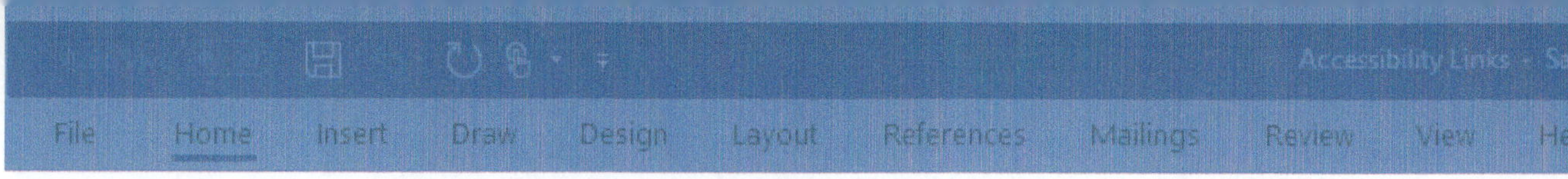

Project: Newsletter

A newsletter is a publication geared for a specific audience that is created on a recurring basis, such as weekly, monthly, or quarterly. The audience may be subscribers, employees, customers, patrons, students, etc.

The project in this module uses Word to produce the two-page newsletter shown in Figure 7–1. The newsletter is a monthly publication called Tech Tips that is written by the campus Tech Club for students and staff. Each issue of Tech Tips contains a feature article and announcements. This month's feature article discusses how to avoid malware infections. The feature article spans the first two columns of the first page of the newsletter and then continues on the second page. The announcements, which are located in the third column of the first page, inform readers about an upcoming webinar and discounts and announce the topic of the next issue's feature article.

The Tech Tips newsletter in this module incorporates the desktop publishing features of Word. The body of each page of the newsletter is divided in three columns. A variety of fonts, font sizes, and colors add visual appeal to the document. The first page has text wrapped around a pull-quote, and the second page has text wrapped around a graphic. Horizontal and vertical lines separate distinct areas of the newsletter, including a page border around the perimeter of each page.

The project in this module involves several steps requiring you to drag and drop. If you drag to the wrong location, you may want to cancel an action. Remember that you always can click the Undo button on the Quick Access Toolbar or press CTRL+Z to cancel your most recent action.

In this module, you will learn how to create the newsletter shown in Figure 7–1. You will perform the following general tasks as you progress through this module:

1. Create the nameplate for the first page of the newsletter.
2. Format the first page of the body of the newsletter.
3. Create a pull-quote on the first page of the newsletter.
4. Create the nameplate for the second page of the newsletter.
5. Format the second page of the body of the newsletter.
6. Add a page border to the newsletter.

Desktop Publishing Terminology

As you create professional-looking newsletters and brochures, you should be familiar with several desktop publishing terms. Figure 7–1 identifies these terms:

- A **nameplate**, or **banner**, is the portion of a newsletter that contains the title of the newsletter and usually an issue information line.
- The **issue information line** identifies the specific publication.
- A **ruling line**, usually identified by its direction as a **horizontal rule** or **vertical rule**, is a line that separates areas of the newsletter.
- A **subhead** is a heading within the body of the newsletter that is subordinate to a higher level heading.
- A **pull-quote** is a text box that contains a quote or excerpt from the document that is pulled, or copied, from the text of the document and given graphical emphasis when it is placed elsewhere in the document.

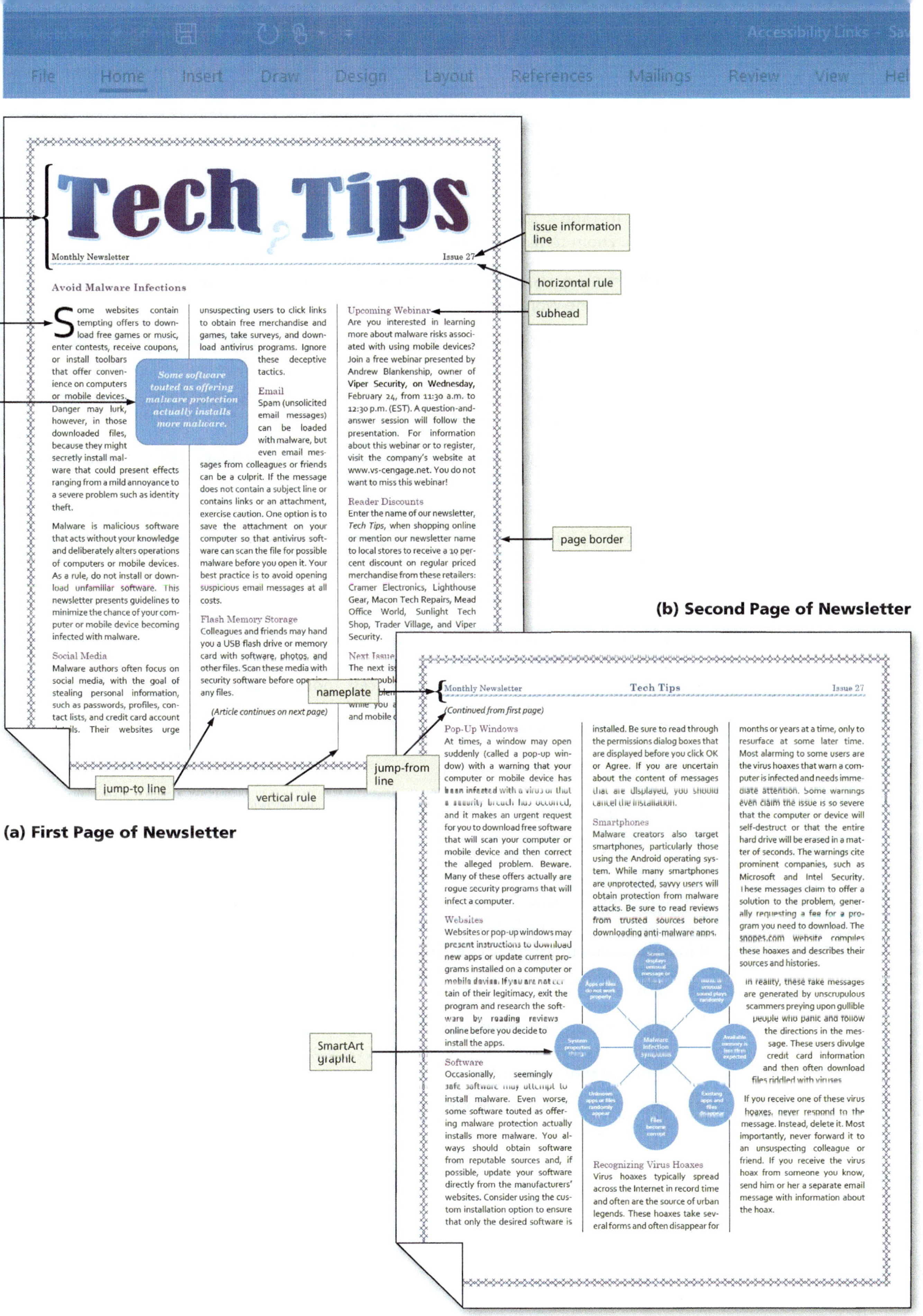
Accessibility Links - Sa
File
Home
Insert
Draw
Design
Layout
References
Mailings
Review
View
Hel
Tech Tips
Monthly Newsletter
Issue 27
Avoid Malware Infections
Some websites contain tempting offers to download free games or music, enter contests, receive coupons, or install toolbars that offer convenience on computers or mobile devices. Danger may lurk, however, in those downloaded files, because they might secretly install malware that could present effects ranging from a mild annoyance to a severe problem such as identity theft.
Malware is malicious software that acts without your knowledge and deliberately alters operations of computers or mobile devices. As a rule, do not install or download unfamiliar software. This newsletter presents guidelines to minimize the chance of your computer or mobile device becoming infected with malware.
Social Media
Malware authors often focus on social media, with the goal of stealing personal information, such as passwords, profiles, contact lists, and credit card account ils. Their websites urge
unsuspecting users to click links to obtain free merchandise and games, take surveys, and download antivirus programs. Ignore these deceptive tactics.
Some software touted as offering malware protection actually installs more malware.
Email
Spam (unsolicited email messages) can be loaded with malware, but even email messages from colleagues or friends can be a culprit. If the message does not contain a subject line or contains links or an attachment, exercise caution. One option is to save the attachment on your computer so that antivirus software can scan the file for possible malware before you open it. Your best practice is to avoid opening suspicious email messages at all costs.
Flash Memory Storage
Colleagues and friends may hand you a USB flash drive or memory card with software, photos, and other files. Scan these media with security software before op
any files.
(Article continues on next page)
Upcoming Webinar
Are you interested in learning more about malware risks associated with using mobile devices? Join a free webinar presented by Andrew Blankenship, owner of Viper Security, on Wednesday, February 24, from 11:30 a.m. to 12:30 p.m. (EST). A question-and-answer session will follow the presentation. For information about this webinar or to register, visit the company's website at www.vs-cengage.net. You do not want to miss this webinar!
Reader Discounts
Enter the name of our newsletter, Tech Tips, when shopping online or mention our newsletter name to local stores to receive a 10 percent discount on regular priced merchandise from these retailers: Cramer Electronics, Lighthouse Gear, Macon Tech Repairs, Mead Office World, Sunlight Tech Shop, Trader Village, and Viper Security.
Next Issue
The next is
while you a
and mobile
issue information line
horizontal rule
subhead
page border
nameplate
jump-from line
jump-to line
vertical rule
SmartArt graphic
(a) First Page of Newsletter
(b) Second Page of Newsletter
Monthly Newsletter
Tech Tips
Issue 27
(Continued from first page)
Pop-Up Windows
At times, a window may open suddenly (called a pop-up window) with a warning that your computer or mobile device has been infected with a virus or that a security breach has occurred, and it makes an urgent request for you to download free software that will scan your computer or mobile device and then correct the alleged problem. Beware. Many of these offers actually are rogue security programs that will infect a computer.
Websites
Websites or pop-up windows may present instructions to download new apps or update current programs installed on a computer or mobile device. If you are not certain of their legitimacy, exit the program and research the software by reading reviews online before you decide to install the apps.
Software
Occasionally, seemingly safe software may attempt to install malware. Even worse, some software touted as offering malware protection actually installs more malware. You always should obtain software from reputable sources and, if possible, update your software directly from the manufacturers' websites. Consider using the custom installation option to ensure that only the desired software is
installed. Be sure to read through the permissions dialog boxes that are displayed before you click OK or Agree. If you are uncertain about the content of messages that are displayed, you should cancel the installation.
Smartphones
Malware creators also target smartphones, particularly those using the Android operating system. While many smartphones are unprotected, savvy users will obtain protection from malware attacks. Be sure to read reviews from trusted sources before downloading anti-malware apps.
Malware Infection Symptoms
Apps or files do not work properly
Unknown apps or files randomly appear
Files become corrupt
Existing apps and files disappear
Available memory is less than expected
unusual sound plays randomly
Recognizing Virus Hoaxes
Virus hoaxes typically spread across the Internet in record time and often are the source of urban legends. These hoaxes take several forms and often disappear for
months or years at a time, only to resurface at some later time. Most alarming to some users are the virus hoaxes that warn a computer is infected and needs immediate attention. Some warnings even claim the issue is so severe that the computer or device will self-destruct or that the entire hard drive will be erased in a matter of seconds. The warnings cite prominent companies, such as Microsoft and Intel Security. These messages claim to offer a solution to the problem, generally requesting a fee for a program you need to download. The snopes.com website compiles these hoaxes and describes their sources and histories.
In reality, these fake messages are generated by unscrupulous scammers preying upon gullible people who panic and follow the directions in the message. These users divulge credit card information and then often download files riddled with viruses.
If you receive one of these virus hoaxes, never respond to the message. Instead, delete it. Most importantly, never forward it to an unsuspecting colleague or friend. If you receive the virus hoax from someone you know, send him or her a separate email message with information about the hoax.

Figure 7–1

To Start Word and Specify Settings

If you are using a computer to step through the project in this module and you want your screens to match the figures in this book, you should change your screen's resolution to 1366 × 768. The following steps start Word, display formatting marks, change the zoom to page width, and verify ruler and Mouse mode settings.

1. sam Start Word and create a blank document in the Word window. If necessary, maximize the Word window.
2. If the Print Layout button on the status bar is not selected, click it so that your screen is in Print Layout view.
3. If the 'Show/Hide ¶' button (Home tab | Paragraph group) is not selected already, click it to display formatting marks on the screen.
4. To display the page the same width as the document window, if necessary, click the Page Width button (View tab | Zoom group).
5. Verify that the Ruler check box (View tab | Show group) is not selected. (If it is selected, click it to remove the check mark because you do not want the rulers to appear on the screen.)
6. If you are using a mouse and you want your screens to match the figures in the book, verify that you are using Mouse mode by clicking the Touch/Mouse Mode button on the Quick Access Toolbar and then, if necessary, clicking Mouse on the menu. (If your Quick Access Toolbar does not display the Touch/Mouse Mode button, click the 'Customize Quick Access Toolbar' button on the Quick Access Toolbar and then click Touch/Mouse Mode on the menu to add the button to the Quick Access Toolbar.)

To Change Spacing above and below Paragraphs and Adjust Margins

Word is preset to use standard 8.5-by-11-inch paper, with 1-inch top, bottom, left, and right margins. For the newsletter in this module, all margins (left, right, top, and bottom) are .75 inches, which is not a predefined setting in the Margins gallery. Thus, the following steps set custom margins.

1. Display the Layout tab.
2. Click the Margins button (Layout tab | Page Setup group) to display the Margins gallery and then click Custom Margins at the bottom of the Margins gallery to display the Page Setup dialog box.
3. Change each value in the Top, Bottom, Left, and Right boxes (Page Setup dialog box) to .75 (Figure 7–2).
4. Click OK to change the margin values.

BTW

Touch Mode Differences

The Office and Windows interfaces may vary if you are using Touch mode. For this reason, you might notice that the function or appearance of your touch screen differs slightly from this module's presentation.

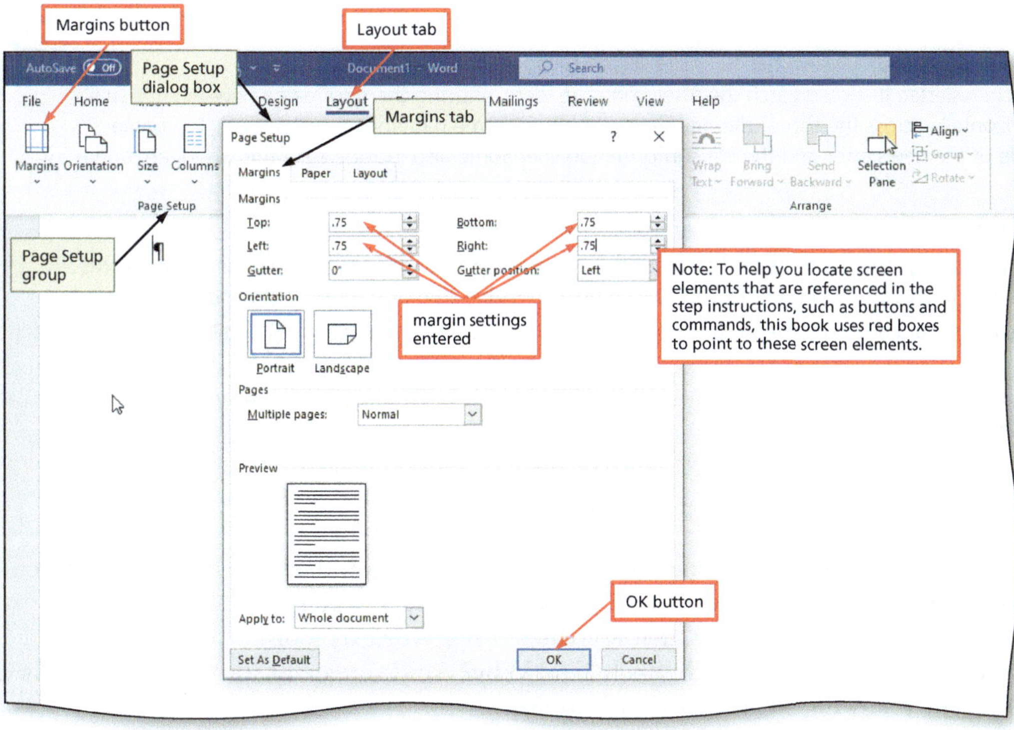

Figure 7–2

BTW

The Ribbon and Screen Resolution

Word may change how the groups and buttons within the groups appear on the ribbon, depending on the screen resolution of your computer. Thus, your ribbon may look different from the ones in this book if you are using a screen resolution other than 1366 × 768.

To Change Theme Colors and Fonts

The newsletter in this module uses the Office theme with the Violet II color scheme and a customized set of fonts. The following steps change the theme colors and fonts.

1. Display the Design tab.
2. Click the Colors button (Design tab | Document Formatting group) and then click Violet II in the Colors gallery to change the document colors.
3. Click the Fonts button (Design tab | Document Formatting group) and then click Customize Fonts in the Fonts gallery to display the Create New Theme Fonts dialog box.
4. Select Century Schoolbook as the Heading font and then select Corbel as the Body font (Create New Theme Fonts dialog box).
5. Type `Newsletter` in the Name text box to name the custom font and then click Save (Create New Theme Fonts dialog box).

Creating the Nameplate

The nameplate on the first page of this newsletter consists of the information above the multiple columns (shown in Figure 7–1a at the beginning of this module). In this project, the nameplate includes the newsletter title, Tech Tips, an image of a question mark, and the issue information line.

The following sections use the steps outlined below to create the nameplate for the first page of the newsletter in this module.

1. Enter and format the newsletter title using WordArt.
2. Set custom tab stops for the issue information line.
3. Enter text in the issue information line.
4. Add a horizontal rule below the issue information line.
5. Insert and format the image.

Consider This

How should you design a nameplate?

A nameplate visually identifies a newsletter. It should catch the attention of readers, enticing them to read a newsletter. Usually, the nameplate is positioned horizontally across the top of the newsletter, although some nameplates are vertical. The nameplate typically consists of the title of the newsletter and the issue information line. Some also include a subtitle, a slogan, and a graphical image or logo.

Guidelines for the newsletter title and other elements in the nameplate are as follows:

- Compose a title that is short, yet conveys the contents of the newsletter. In the newsletter title, eliminate unnecessary words such as these: the, newsletter. Use a decorative font in as large a font size as possible so that the title stands out on the page.
- Other elements on the nameplate should not compete in size with the title. Use colors that complement the title. Select easy-to-read fonts.
- Arrange the elements of the nameplate so that it does not have a cluttered appearance. If necessary, use ruling lines to visually separate areas of the nameplate.

To Convert Text to WordArt

A drawing object is a graphic, such as a shape, that you create using Word. Another type of drawing object, called **WordArt**, enables you to create decorative text in a text box or other shape with special effects, such as shadowed, rotated, stretched, skewed, and wavy effects, that is created using WordArt tools.

This project uses WordArt for the newsletter title, Tech Tips. **Why?** A title created with WordArt is likely to draw the reader's attention. The following steps convert text to WordArt.

1

- Type `Tech Tips` on the first line of the document and then select the entered text.
- Display the Insert tab.
- Click the WordArt button (Insert tab | Text group) to display the WordArt gallery (Figure 7–3).

Q&A Once I select a WordArt style, can I customize its appearance?
Yes. The next steps customize the WordArt style selected here.

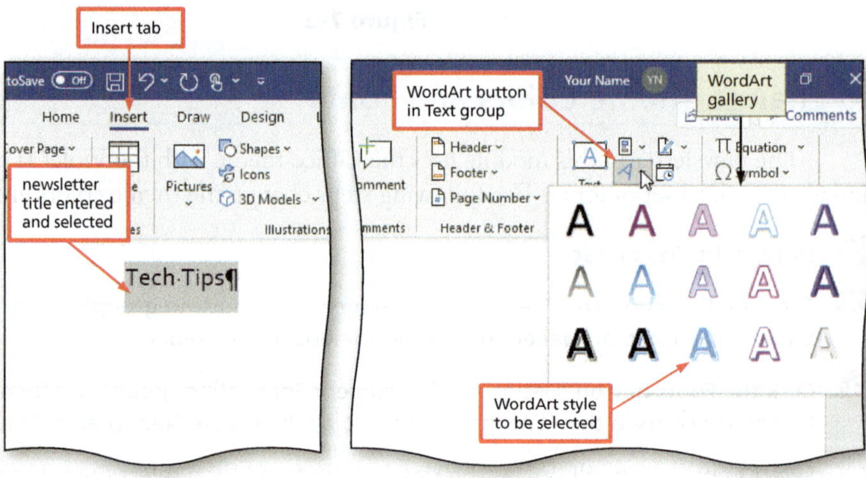

Figure 7–3

2

- Click 'Fill: Blue, Accent color 5; Outline: White, Background color 1; Hard Shadow: Blue, Accent color 5' in the WordArt gallery (third WordArt style in last row) to insert a drawing object in the document that is formatted according to the selected WordArt style, which contains the selected text, Tech Tips (Figure 7–4).

Q&A What if I do not select text before selecting a WordArt style?
The WordArt drawing object will contain the placeholder text, Your text here, which you can replace with your desired text.

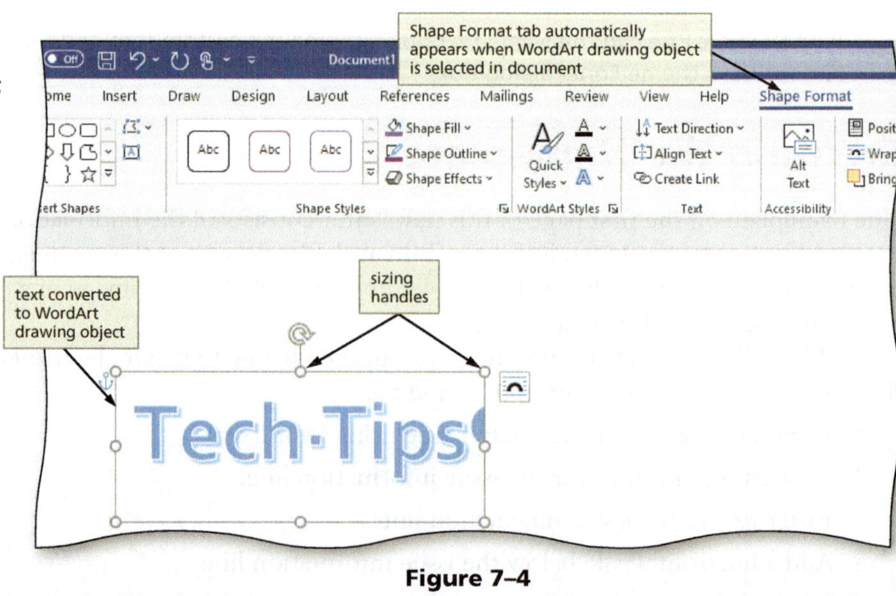

Figure 7–4

To Resize WordArt

You resize WordArt the same way you resize any other graphic. That is, you can drag its sizing handles or enter values in the Shape Height and Shape Width boxes. The next steps resize the WordArt drawing object.

1. With the WordArt drawing object selected, if necessary, display the Shape Format tab.
2. Change the value in the Shape Height box (Shape Format tab | Size group) to 1.44 and the value in the Shape Width box (Shape Format tab | Size group) to 7 (Figure 7–5). (Note that you may need to press ENTER after typing 7 in the Shape Width box for the change to take effect.)

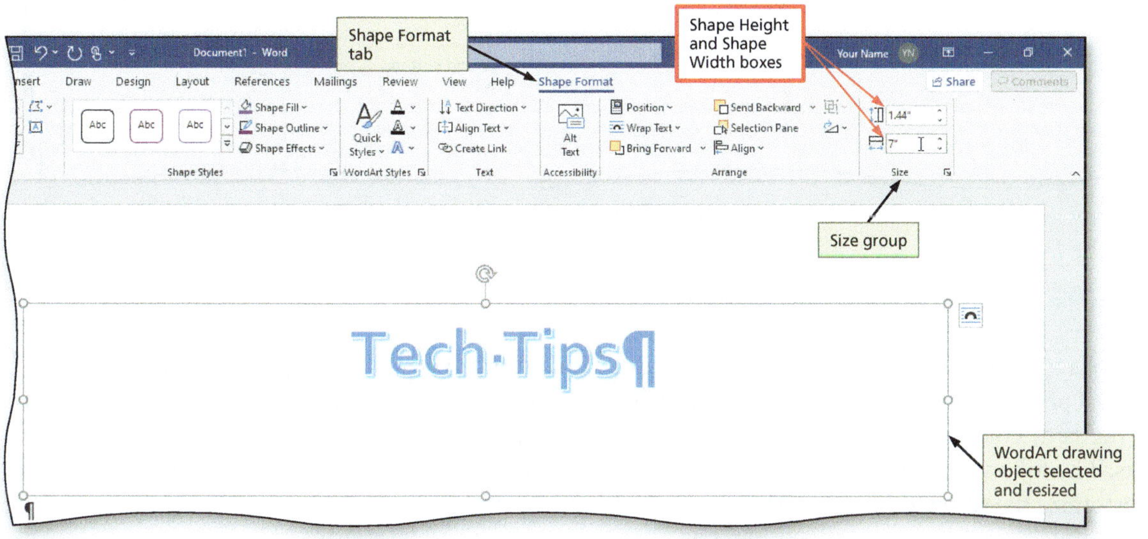

Figure 7–5

To Change the Font and Font Size of WordArt Text

You change the font and font size of WordArt text the same way you change the font and font size of any other text. That is, you select the text and then change its font and font size. The following steps change the font and font size of WordArt text.

1. Select the WordArt text, in this case, Tech Tips.
2. Change the font of the selected text to Bernard MT Condensed (or a similar font).
3. Change the font size of the selected text to 72 point (shown in Figure 7–6).

To Change an Object's Text Wrapping

When you insert a drawing object in a Word document, the default text wrapping is Square, which means text will wrap around the object in the shape of a square. Because you want the nameplate above the rest of the newsletter, you change the text wrapping for the drawing object to Top and Bottom. The following steps change a drawing object's text wrapping.

1. With the WordArt drawing object selected, click the Layout Options button that is attached to the WordArt drawing object to display the Layout Options gallery.

BTW

Deleting WordArt

If you want to delete a WordArt drawing object, right-click it and then click Cut on the shortcut menu, or select the WordArt drawing object and then click the Cut button (Home tab | Clipboard group).

2. Click 'Top and Bottom' in the Layout Options gallery so that the WordArt drawing object will not cover the document text (Figure 7–6).

3. Close the Layout Options gallery.

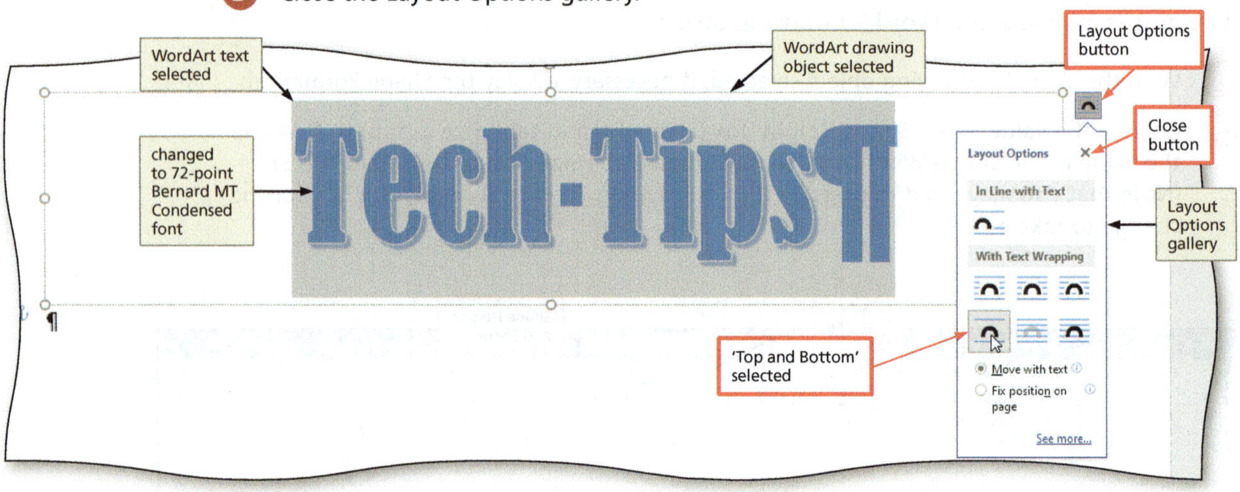

Figure 7–6

To Change the Text Fill Color of WordArt

The next step is to change the color of the WordArt text so that it displays a blue and plum gradient fill color. **Gradient** is a gradual progression of colors and shades, usually from one color to another color or from one shade to another shade of the same color. Word includes several built-in gradient fill colors, or you can customize one for use in drawing objects. The following steps change the fill color of the WordArt drawing object to a built-in gradient fill color and then customize the selected fill color. **Why?** Using a gradient fill color will add interest to the title.

1.
- With the WordArt drawing object selected, click the Text Fill arrow (Shape Format tab | WordArt Styles group) to display the Text Fill gallery.

Q&A The Text Fill gallery did not appear. Why not?
Be sure you click the Text Fill arrow, which is to the right of the Text Fill button. If you mistakenly click the Text Fill button, Word places a default fill in the selected WordArt instead of displaying the Text Fill gallery.

2.
- Point to Gradient in the Text Fill gallery to display the Gradient gallery (Figure 7–7).

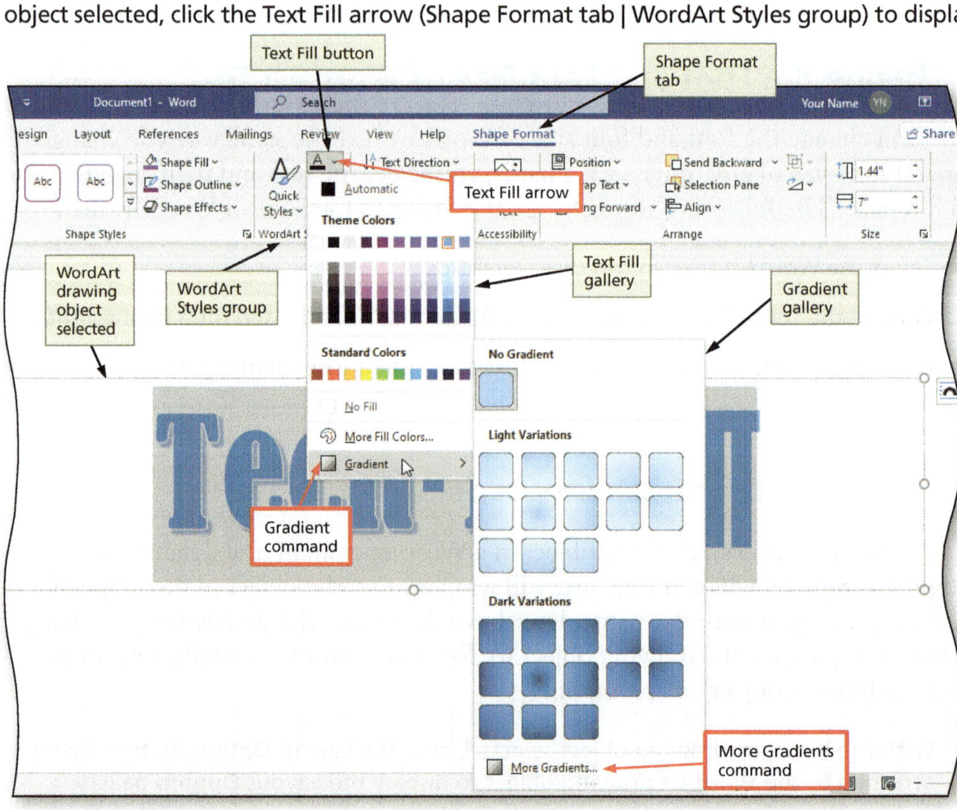

Figure 7–7

3

- Click More Gradients in the Gradient gallery to open the Format Shape pane. If necessary, click the Text Options tab in the Format Shape pane and then, if necessary, click the 'Text Fill & Outline' button. If necessary, expand the Text Fill section.
- Click Gradient fill in the Text Fill section to display options related to gradient colors in the pane (Figure 7–8).

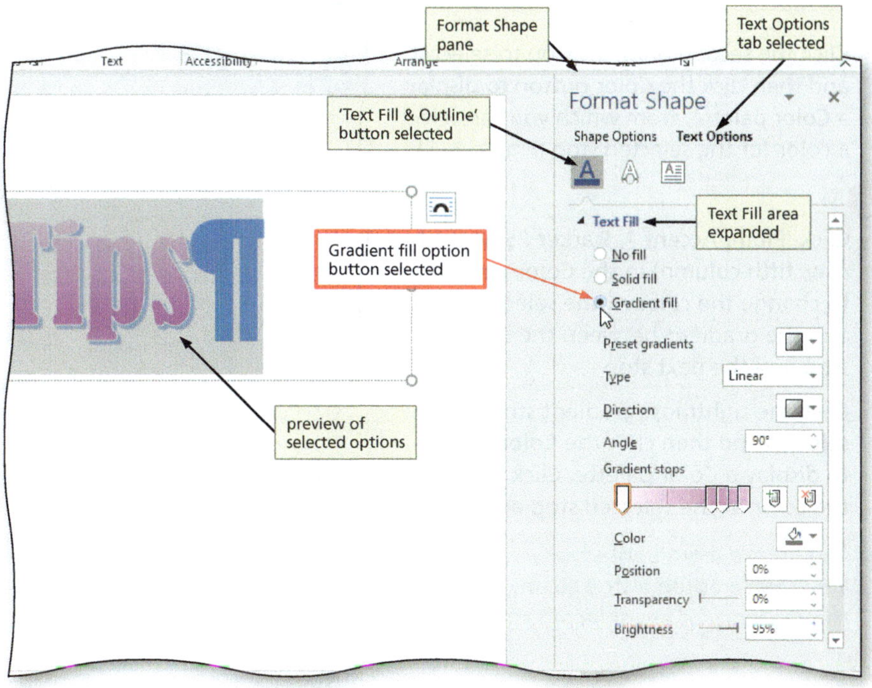

Figure 7–8

4

- Click the Preset gradients button in the Format Shape pane to display a palette of built-in gradient fill colors (Figure 7–9).

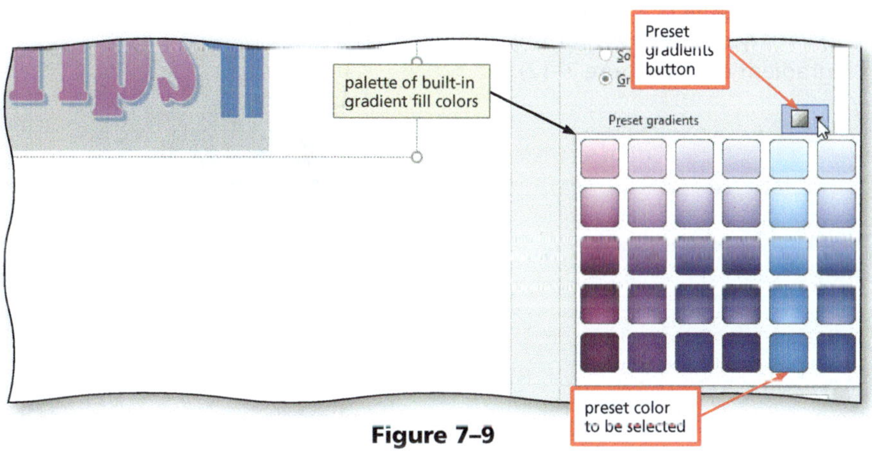

Figure 7–9

5

- Click 'Radial Gradient - Accent 5' (bottom row, fifth column) in the Preset gradients palette to select the built-in gradient color, which shows a preview in the Gradient stops area (Figure 7–10).

Q&A What is a gradient stop?
A gradient stop is the location where two colors blend. You can change the color of a stop so that Word changes the color of the blend. You also can add or delete stops, with a minimum of two stops and a maximum of ten stops per gradient fill color.

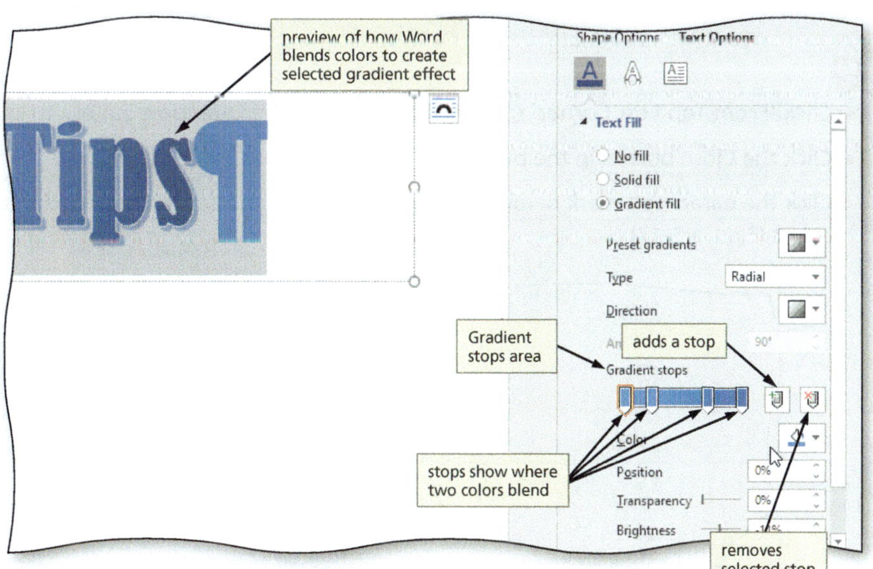

Figure 7–10

6

- Click the second gradient stop to select it and then click the Color button to display a Color palette, from which you can select a color for the selected stop (Figure 7–11).

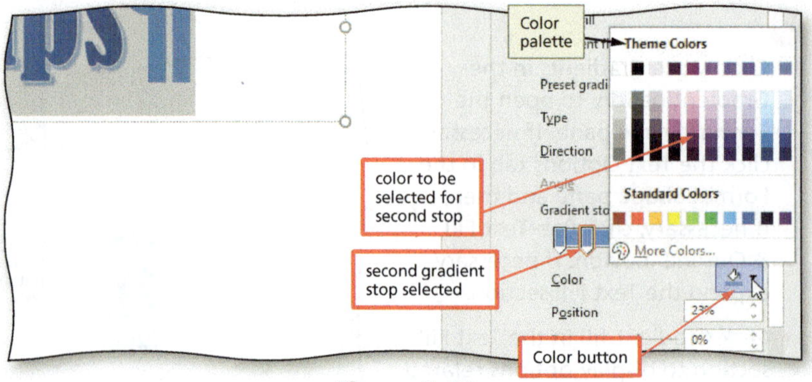

Figure 7–11

7

- Click 'Plum, Accent 1, Darker 25%' (fifth row, fifth column) in the Color palette to change the color of the selected stop and the gradient between the selected stop and the next stop.
- Click the rightmost gradient stop to select it and then click the Color button to display a Color palette. Click 'Plum, Accent 1, Darker 25%' (fifth row, fifth column) in the Color palette to change the color of the selected stop and the gradient between the selected stop and the previous stop.

Q&A Can I move a gradient stop?
Yes. You can drag a stop to any location along the color bar. You also can adjust the position, brightness, and transparency of any selected stop.

8

- Click the Direction button to display a gallery that shows a variety of directions for the gradient colors (Figure 7–12).

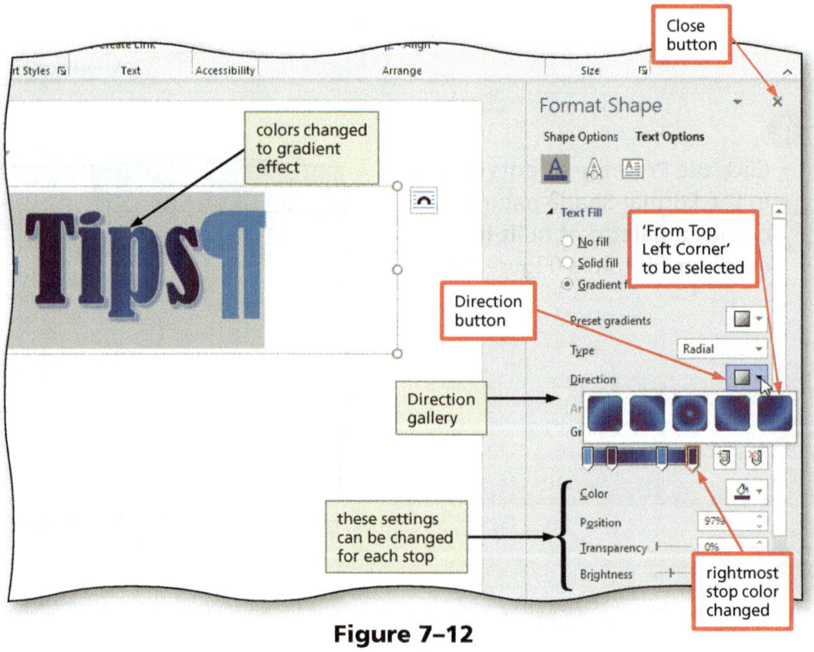

Figure 7–12

9

- Click 'From Top Left Corner' (rightmost option) in the Direction gallery to specify the direction to blend the colors.
- Click the Close button in the pane.
- Click the paragraph mark below the WordArt drawing object to deselect the text so that you can see its gradient fill colors (Figure 7–13).

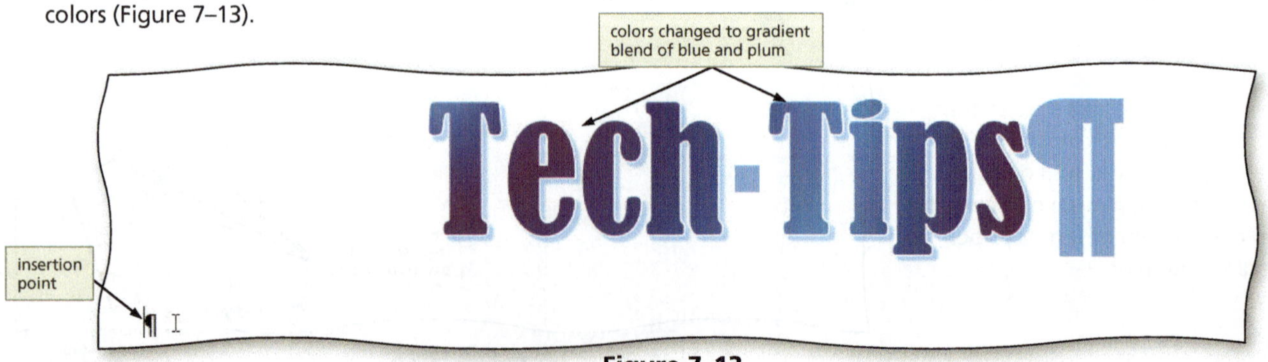

Figure 7–13

To Change the WordArt Shape Using the Transform Effect

Word provides a variety of shapes to make your WordArt more interesting. The following steps change the WordArt shape using the Transform effect. **Why?** The WordArt in this newsletter has a wavy appearance.

1

- Click the WordArt drawing object to select it.
- If necessary, display the Shape Format tab.
- Click the Text Effects button (Shape Format tab | WordArt Styles group) to display the Text Effects gallery.
- Point to Transform in the Text Effects gallery to display the Transform gallery.
- Point to 'Double Wave: Up-Down' (fourth effect, fifth row in Warp area) in the Transform gallery to display a Live Preview of the selected transform effect applied to the selected drawing object (Figure 7–14).

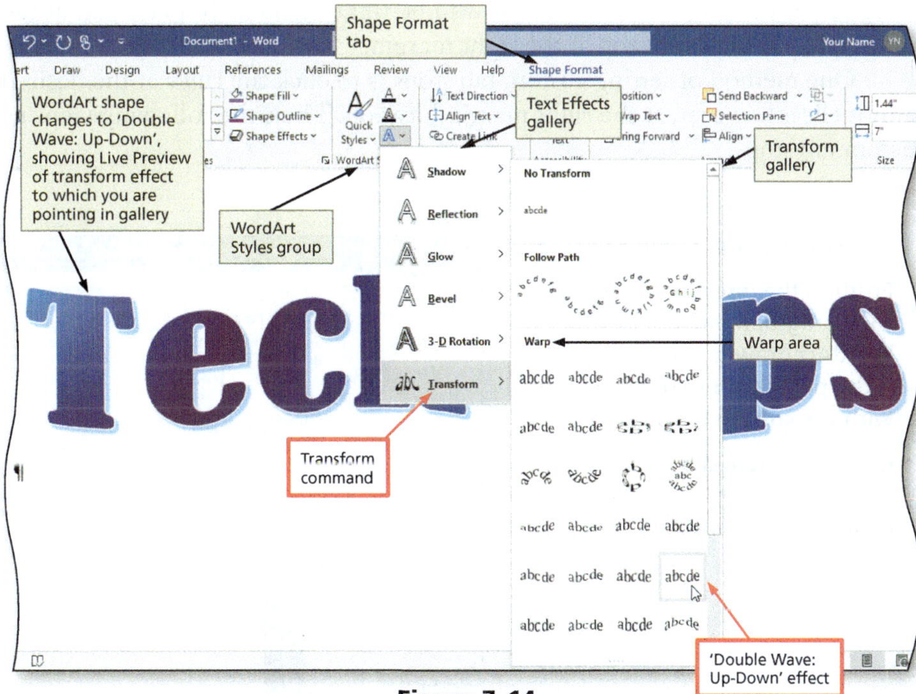

Figure 7–14

Experiment

- Point to various text effects in the Transform gallery and watch the selected drawing object conform to that transform effect.

2

- Click 'Double Wave: Up-Down' in the Transform gallery to change the shape of the WordArt drawing object.

To Apply a Glow Effect to WordArt

If you wanted to apply a glow effect to WordArt, you would perform the following steps:

1. Select the WordArt drawing object.
2. Click the Text Effects button (Shape Format tab | WordArt Styles group) to display the Text Effects gallery.
3. Point to Glow in the Text Effects gallery and then click the desired glow effect in the Glow gallery.

To Apply a Shadow Effect to WordArt

If you wanted to apply a shadow effect to WordArt, you would perform the following steps:

1. Select the WordArt drawing object.
2. Click the Text Effects button (Shape Format tab | WordArt Styles group) to display the Text Effects gallery.
3. Point to Shadow in the Text Effects gallery and then click the desired shadow effect in the Shadow gallery.

To Set Custom Tab Stops Using the Tabs Dialog Box

The issue information line in this newsletter contains the text, Monthly Newsletter, at the left margin and the issue number at the right margin (shown in Figure 7–1a at the beginning of this module). In Word, a paragraph cannot be both left-aligned and right-aligned. **Why?** If you click the Align Right button (Home tab | Paragraph group), for example, all text will be right-aligned. To place text at the right margin of a left-aligned paragraph, you set a tab stop at the right margin.

One method of setting custom tab stops is to click the ruler at the desired location of the tab stop. You cannot click, however, at the right margin location. Thus, the following steps use the Tabs dialog box to set a custom tab stop.

1

- If necessary, display the Home tab.
- Position the insertion point on the paragraph mark below the WordArt drawing object, which is the paragraph to be formatted with the custom tab stops.
- Click the Paragraph Dialog Box Launcher to display the Paragraph dialog box (Figure 7–15).

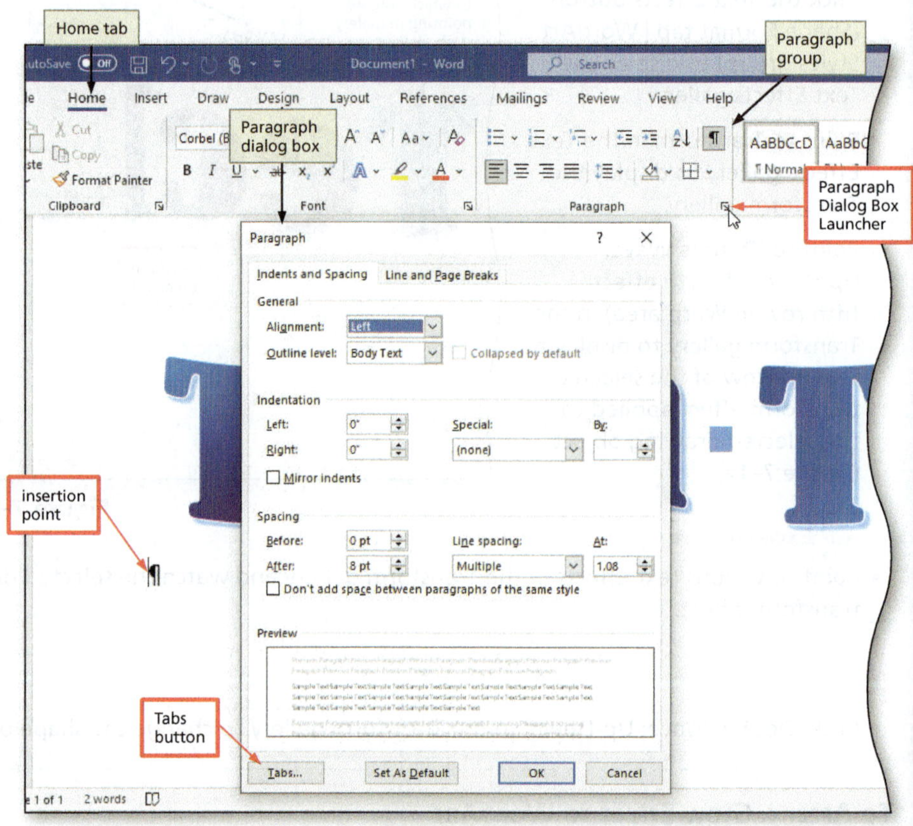

Figure 7–15

2

- Click the Tabs button (Paragraph dialog box) to display the Tabs dialog box.
- Type 7 in the 'Tab stop position' text box (Tabs dialog box).
- Click Right in the Alignment area to specify alignment for text at the tab stop (Figure 7–16).

3

- Click the Set button (Tabs dialog box) to set a right-aligned custom tab stop at the specified position.
- Click OK to set the defined tab stops.

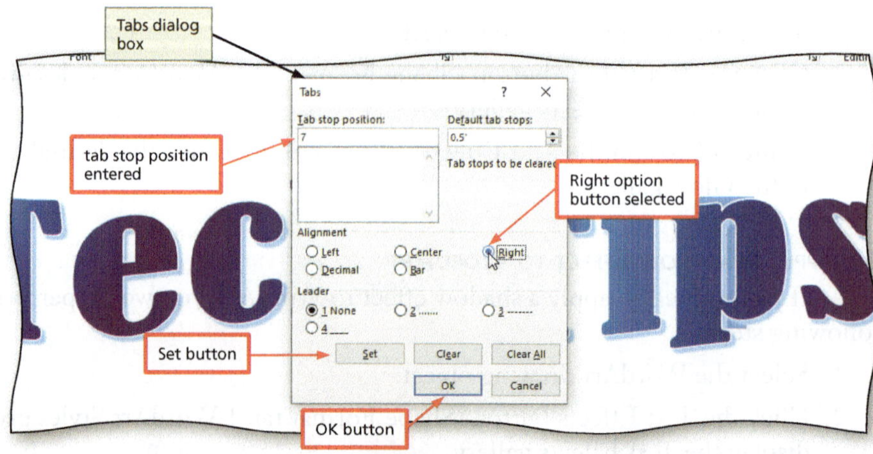

Figure 7–16

Other Ways

1. Click desired tab stop on ruler
2. Right-click paragraph (or, if using touch, tap 'Show Context Menu' button on Mini toolbar), click Paragraph on shortcut menu, click Tabs button (Paragraph dialog box), enter desired settings, click OK

To Enter Text

The following steps enter the issue information line text.

1 With the insertion point on the paragraph below the WordArt, change the font to Century Schoolbook (or a similar font) and the font size to 10 point.

2 Type `Monthly Newsletter` on line 2 of the newsletter.

3 Press TAB and then type `Issue 27` to complete the issue information line (Figure 7–17).

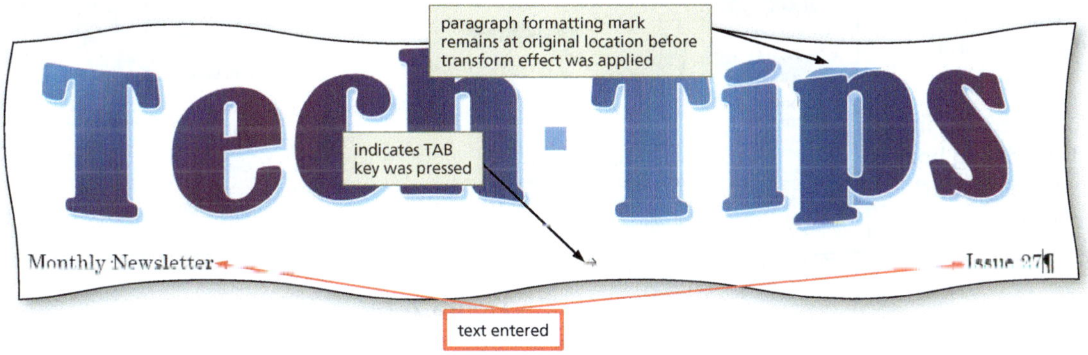

Figure 7–17

Q&A Why is the paragraph formatting mark in the middle of the newsletter title?
The formatting marks remain at the original location of the text before you applied the transform effect.

To Border One Edge of a Paragraph

In Word, you use borders to create ruling lines. Word can place borders on any edge of a paragraph; that is, Word can place a border on the top, bottom, left, and right edges of a paragraph.

One method of bordering paragraphs is by clicking the desired border in the Borders gallery. If you want to specify a particular border, for example, one with color, you use the Borders and Shading dialog box. The following steps use the Borders and Shading dialog box to place a border below a paragraph. **Why?** In this newsletter, the issue information line has a 3-point diagonally striped blue border below it.

1

- Click the Borders arrow (Home tab | Paragraph group) to display the Borders gallery (Figure 7–18).

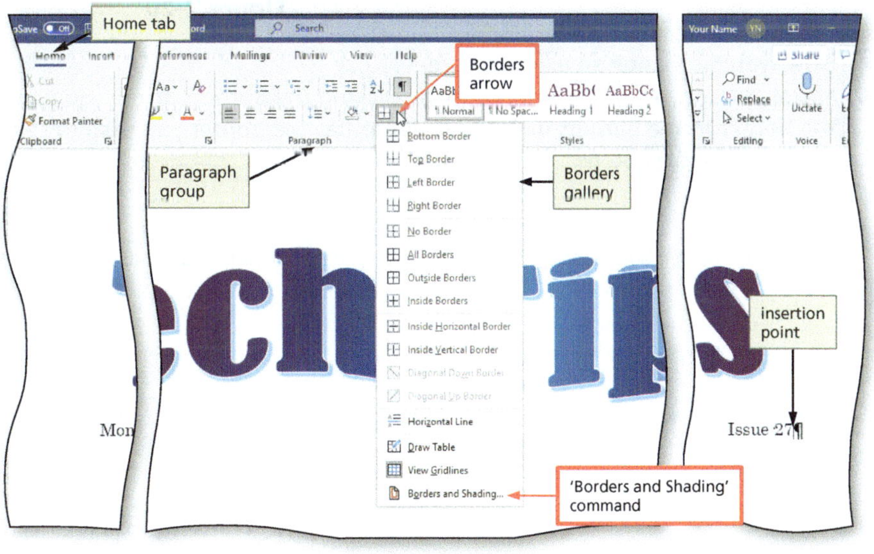

Figure 7–18

2

- Click 'Borders and Shading' in the Borders gallery to display the Borders and Shading dialog box.
- Click Custom in the Setting area (Borders and Shading dialog box) because you are setting just a bottom border.
- Scroll through the Style list and click the style shown in Figure 7–19, which is a diagonally striped line for the border.
- Click the Color button and then click 'Blue Accent 5, Darker 50%' (ninth column, bottom row) in the Color gallery.
- Click the Bottom Border button in the Preview area of the dialog box to show a preview of the selected border style (Figure 7–19).

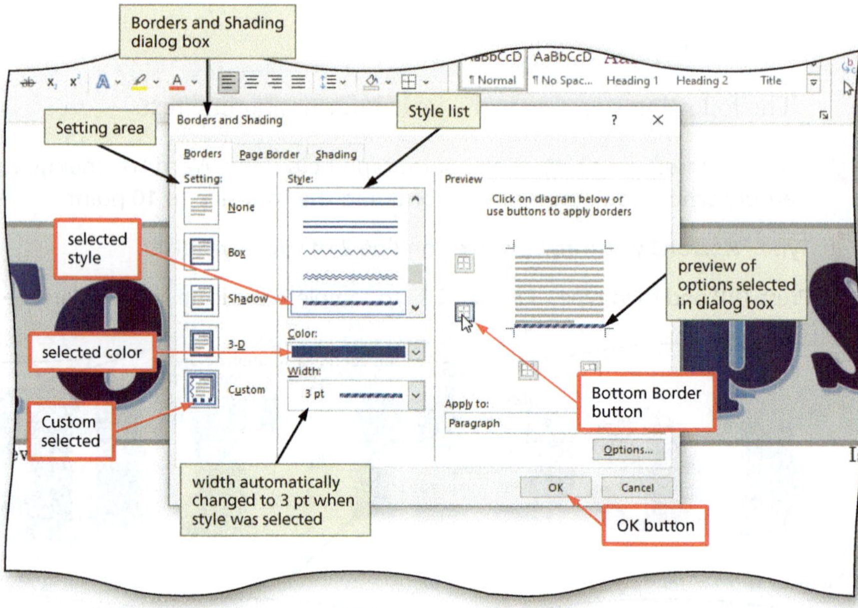

Figure 7–19

Q&A | What is the purpose of the buttons in the Preview area?
They are toggles that display and remove the top, bottom, left, and right borders from the diagram in the Preview area.

3

- Click OK to place the defined border on the paragraph containing the insertion point (Figure 7–20).

Figure 7–20

Q&A | How would I change an existing border?
You first remove the existing border by clicking the Borders arrow (Home tab | Paragraph group) and then clicking the border in the Borders gallery that identifies the border you wish to remove. Then, add a new border as described in these steps.

Other Ways

1. Click Page Borders button (Design tab | Page Background group), click Borders tab (Borders and Shading dialog box), select desired border, click OK

To Insert a Picture

The next steps insert an image of question marks in the nameplate.

1. Display the Insert tab.
2. Click the Pictures button (Insert tab | Illustrations group) and then click Online Pictures to display the Online Pictures dialog box.

3 Type `question marks` in the Search box (Online Pictures dialog box) to specify the search text and then press ENTER to display a list of images that match the entered search text.

4 Scroll through the list of images to locate the one shown in Figure 7–21 (or a similar image), click the image to select it, and then click the Insert button (Online Pictures dialog box) to download and insert the selected image at the location of the insertion point in the document.

Q&A

What if I cannot locate the same image as in Figure 7–21?
Click Cancel (Online Pictures dialog box) to close the dialog box, click the Pictures button (Insert tab | Illustrations group), click This Device to display the Insert Picture dialog box, navigate to and select the Support_WD_7_QuestionMarks.png file in the Data Files, and then click the Insert button (Insert Picture dialog box) to insert the picture.

What if my inserted image is not in the same location as in Figure 7–21?
The image may be in a different location, depending on the position of the insertion point when you inserted the image. In a later section, you will move the image to a different location.

To Change the Color of a Graphic

The following steps change the color of the graphic (the question marks) to a shade of blue.

1 With the graphic still selected, click the Color button (Picture Format tab | Adjust group) to display the Color gallery (Figure 7–21).

2 Click 'Blue, Accent color 5 Light' (sixth color, third row) in the Recolor area in the Color gallery to change the color of the selected graphic.

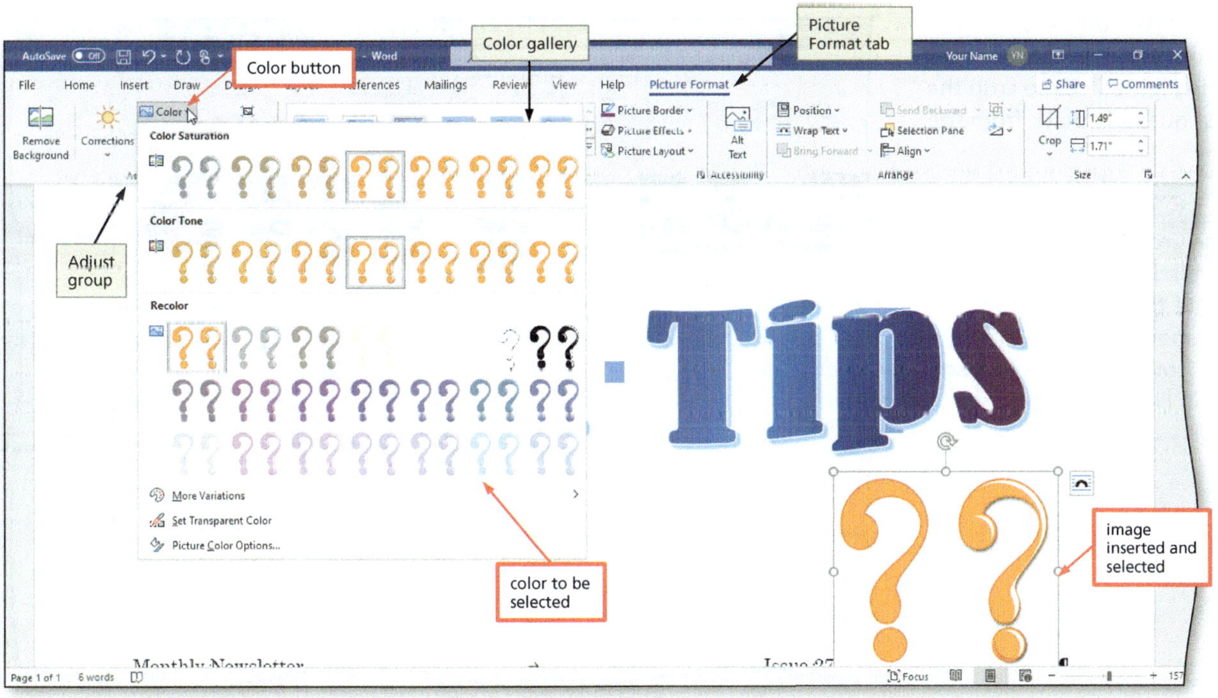

Figure 7–21

To Crop a Graphic

The next step is to format the image just inserted. You would like to remove the matte question mark on the left from the image. **Why?** You want just one question mark to appear in the newsletter. Word allows you to **crop**, or trim away part of, a graphic. The following steps crop a graphic.

1

- With the graphic selected, click the Crop button (Picture Format tab | Size group), which places cropping handles on the image in the document.

Q&A What if I mistakenly click the Crop arrow?
Click the Crop button.

- Position the pointer on the left-middle cropping handle so that it looks like a sideways letter T (Figure 7–22).

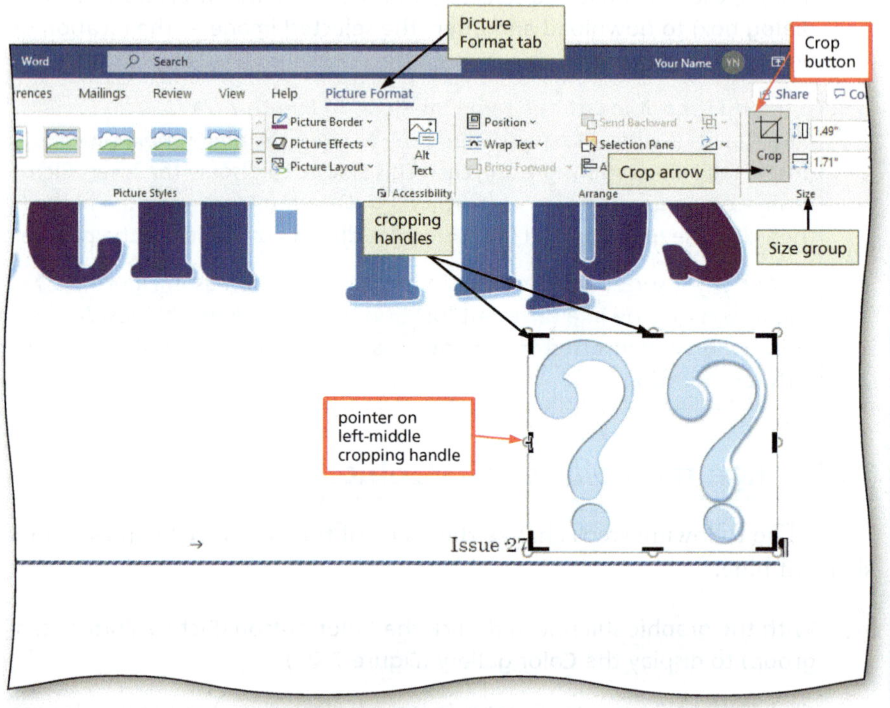

Figure 7–22

2

- Drag the left-middle cropping handle inward to the location shown in Figure 7–23 to crop the leftmost question mark from the image.

3

- Click the Crop button (Picture Format tab | Size group) to deactivate the cropping tool, which removes the cropping handles from the selected image (shown in Figure 7–24).

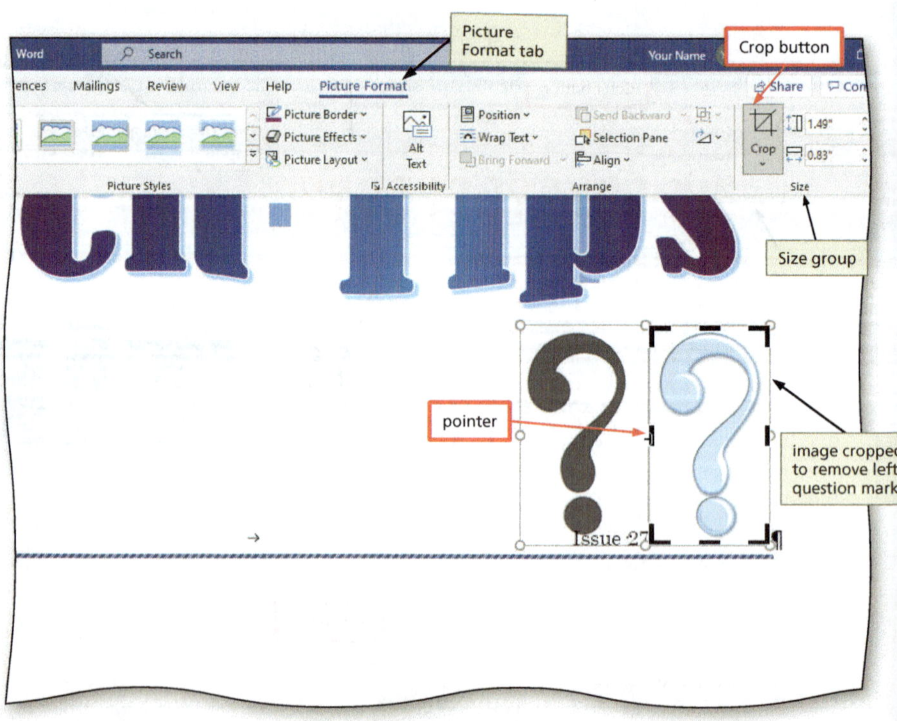

Figure 7–23

Other Ways

1. Right-click graphic, click Crop button on Mini toolbar, drag cropping handles, click Crop button (Picture Format tab | Size group)

To Change an Object's Text Wrapping and Size

When you insert an object (image) in a Word document, the default text wrapping is In Line with Text, which means the object is part of the current paragraph. Because you want the question mark image behind the newsletter title, you change the text wrapping for the image to Behind Text. The next steps change a drawing object's text wrapping and also change its size.

1. With the question mark graphic selected, click the Layout Options button attached to the graphic to display the Layout Options gallery.
2. Click Behind Text in the Layout Options gallery so that the image is positioned behind text in the document.
3. Close the Layout Options gallery.
4. Change the values in the Shape Height and Shape Width boxes (Picture Format tab | Size group) to .65" and .43", respectively. If you are not able to resize the graphic exactly, click the Size Dialog Box Launcher (Picture Format tab | Size group), remove the check mark from the 'Lock aspect ratio' check box, and then try again.

To Move a Graphic

The clip art image needs to be moved up so that the bottom of the question mark is between the words, Tech Tips, in the newsletter title. The following step moves a graphic.

1. Drag the graphic to the location shown in Figure 7–24.

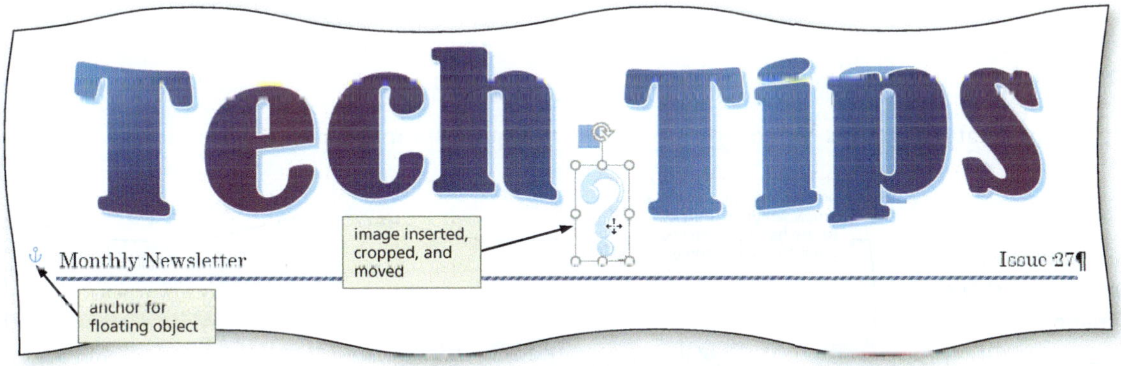

Figure 7–24

To Specify or Change the Absolute Position for a Floating Graphic

If you wanted to move a floating graphic and specify its absolute position, you would perform the following steps.

1. Select the graphic to be moved.
2. Click the Layout Options button attached to the graphic to display the Layout Options gallery.
3. Click the See more link (Layout Options gallery) to display the Position tab in the Layout dialog box.
4. Click Absolute position in the Vertical area (Layout dialog box), select the value in the Absolute position box, and then type the desired value to specify the distance in inches from the top of the page.
5. If necessary, click the below arrow and then select Page.
6. Click OK to change the position of the selected graphic to the specified position.

BTW

Anchors on Floating Objects

If you want to move an anchor on a floating object that is locked, you can unlock the anchor by selecting the object, clicking the Layout Options button attached to the object, clicking the See more link in the Layout Options gallery to display the Layout dialog box, clicking the Position tab, removing the check mark from the Lock anchor check box, and then clicking OK.

To Use the Selection Pane

The next step is to rotate the question mark image, but because it is positioned behind the text, it may be difficult to select it. The following step opens the Selection pane. **Why?** The Selection pane enables you easily to select items on the screen that are layered behind other objects.

1

- If necessary, click in the graphic object to display the Picture Format tab.
- Click the Selection Pane button (Picture Format tab | Arrange group) to open the Selection pane (Figure 7–25).

Experiment

- Click Text Box 1 in the Selection pane to select the WordArt drawing object. Click Picture 2 in the Selection pane to select the question mark image.

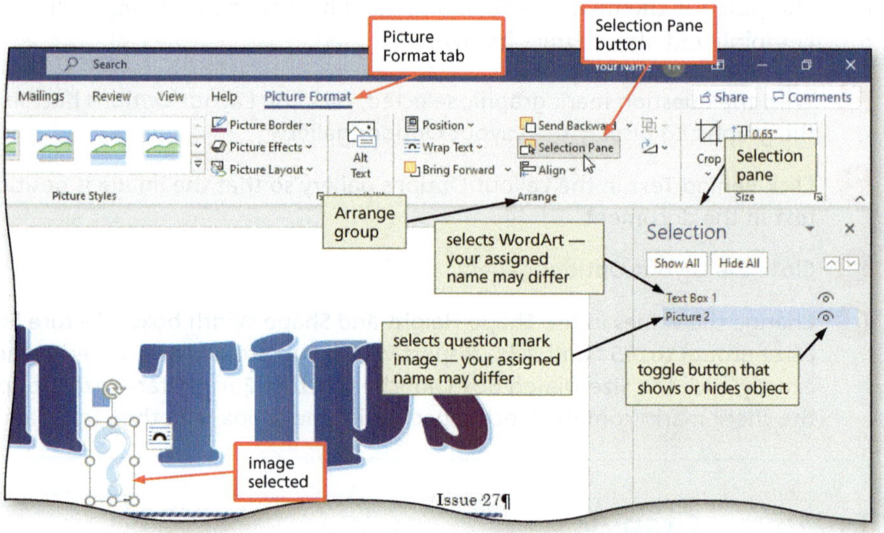

Figure 7–25

Q&A What are the displayed names in the Selection pane?

Word assigns names to each object in the document. The names displayed on your screen may differ.

Other Ways

1. Click in WordArt object, click Selection Pane button (Shape Format tab | Arrange group)

To Rotate a Graphic

The following steps rotate a graphic. **Why?** You would like the question mark image angled to the right a bit.

1

- If necessary, click Picture 2 in the Selection pane to select the question mark image.
- Position the pointer on the graphic's rotate handle (Figure 7–26).

Figure 7–26

2

- Drag the rotate handle clockwise to rotate the graphic slightly as shown in Figure 7–27. (You may need to rotate the graphic a few times to position it in the desired location.)

Figure 7–27

Q&A

Can I drag the rotate handle in any direction?
You can drag the rotate handle clockwise or counterclockwise.

What if I am using a touch screen?
Because the rotate handle is not available on a touch screen, you enter the degree of rotation in the Size dialog box. Tap the Rotate Objects button (Picture Format tab | Arrange group) to display the Rotate Objects menu, tap 'More Rotation Options' on the Rotate Objects menu to display the Size sheet in the Layout dialog box, change the Rotation value to 16, and then tap OK.

3

- Click the Close button in the Selection pane to close the pane.
- Click somewhere in the issue information line to deselect the graphic.
- Save the title page on your hard drive, OneDrive, or other storage location using the file name, SC_WD_7_TechTipsNewsletter.

Other Ways

1. Click Rotate Objects button (Picture Format tab | Arrange group), click 'More Rotation Options' on Rotate Objects menu, enter rotation value in Rotation box (Layout dialog box), click OK
2. Right-click object, click 'Size and Position' on shortcut menu, enter rotation value in Rotation box (Layout dialog box), click OK
3. Click Size Dialog Box Launcher (Picture Format tab | Size group), enter rotation value in Rotation box (Layout dialog box), click OK

Break Point: If you want to take a break, this is a good place to do so. You can exit Word now. To resume later, start Word, open the file called SC_WD_7_TechTipsNewsletter.docx, and continue following the steps from this location forward.

Formatting the First Page of the Body of the Newsletter

The next step is to format the first page of the body of the newsletter. The body of the newsletter in this module is divided in three columns (shown in Figure 7–1a at the beginning of this module). The first two columns contain the feature article, and the third column contains announcements. The characters in the paragraphs are aligned on both the right and left edges — similar to newspaper columns. The first letter in the first paragraph is much larger than the rest of the characters in the paragraph. A vertical rule separates the columns. The steps in the following sections format the first page of the body of the newsletter using these desktop publishing features.

Consider This

What guidelines should you follow when creating the body of a newsletter?

While content and subject matter of newsletters may vary, the procedures used to create newsletters are similar:

- **Write the body copy.** Newsletters should contain articles of interest and relevance to readers. Some share information, while others promote a product or service. Use active voice in body copy, which is more engaging than passive voice. Proofread the body copy to be sure it is error free. Check all facts for accuracy.
- **Organize body copy in columns.** Most newsletters arrange body copy in columns. The body copy in columns, often called **snaking columns** or newspaper-style columns, flows from the bottom of one column to the top of the next column.
- **Format the body copy.** Begin the feature article on the first page of the newsletter. If the article spans multiple pages, use a continuation line, called a jump or jump line, to guide the reader to the remainder of the article. The message at the end of the article on the first page of the newsletter is called a **jump-to line**, and a **jump-from line** marks the beginning of the continuation, which is usually on a subsequent page.
- **Maintain consistency.** Be consistent with placement of body copy elements in newsletter editions. If the newsletter contains announcements, for example, position them in the same location in each edition so that readers easily can find them.
- **Maximize white space.** Allow plenty of space between lines, paragraphs, and columns. Tightly packed text is difficult to read. Separate the text adequately from graphics, borders, and headings.

- **Incorporate color.** Use colors that complement those in the nameplate. Be careful not to overuse color. Restrict color below the nameplate to drop caps, subheads, graphics, and ruling lines. If you do not have a color printer, still change the colors because the colors will print in shades of black and gray, which add variety to the newsletter.
- **Select and format subheads.** Develop subheads with as few words as possible. Readers should be able to identify content of the next topic by glancing at a subhead. Subheads should be emphasized in the newsletter but should not compete with text in the nameplate. Use a larger, bold, or otherwise contrasting font for subheads so that they stand apart from the body copy. Use this same format for all subheads for consistency. Leave a space above subheads to visually separate their content from the previous topic. Be consistent with spacing above and below subheads throughout the newsletter.
- **Divide sections with vertical rules.** Use vertical rules to guide the reader through the newsletter.
- **Enhance the document with visuals.** Add energy to the newsletter and emphasis to important points with graphics, pull-quotes, and other visuals, such as drop caps to mark beginning of an article. Use these elements sparingly, however, so that the newsletter does not have a crowded appearance. Fewer, large visuals are more effective than several smaller ones. If you use a graphic that you did not create, be sure to obtain permission to use it in the newsletter and give necessary credit to the creator of the graphic.

To Clear Formatting

The next step is to enter the title of the feature article below the horizontal rule. To do this, position the insertion point at the end of the issue information line (after the 7 in Issue 27) and then press ENTER. Recall that the issue information line has a bottom border. When you press ENTER in a bordered paragraph, Word carries forward any borders to the next paragraph. Thus, after you press ENTER, you should clear formatting to format the new paragraph as the Normal style. The following steps clear formatting.

1. Click at the end of line 2 (the issue information line) so that the insertion point is immediately after the 7 in Issue 27. Press ENTER to advance the insertion point to the next line, which also moves the border down one line.
2. If necessary, display the Home tab. Click the 'Clear All Formatting' button (Home tab | Font group) to apply the Normal style to the location of the insertion point, which in this case moves the new paragraph below the border on the issue information line.

To Format Text as a Heading Style, Modify a Heading Style, and Adjust Spacing before and after the Paragraph

Below the bottom border in the nameplate is the title of the feature article, Avoid Malware Infections. The following steps apply the Heading 1 style to this paragraph, modify the style, and adjust the paragraph spacing.

1. If necessary, display formatting marks.
2. With the insertion point on the paragraph mark below the border, click Heading 1 (Home tab | Styles group) to apply the Heading 1 style to the paragraph containing the insertion point.
3. Decrease the font size to 12 point. Bold the paragraph. Update the Heading 1 style to reflect these changes.
4. Type **`Avoid Malware Infections`** as the title of the feature article.
5. Display the Layout tab. Change the Spacing Before box to 18 pt and the Spacing After box to 12 pt (Figure 7–28).

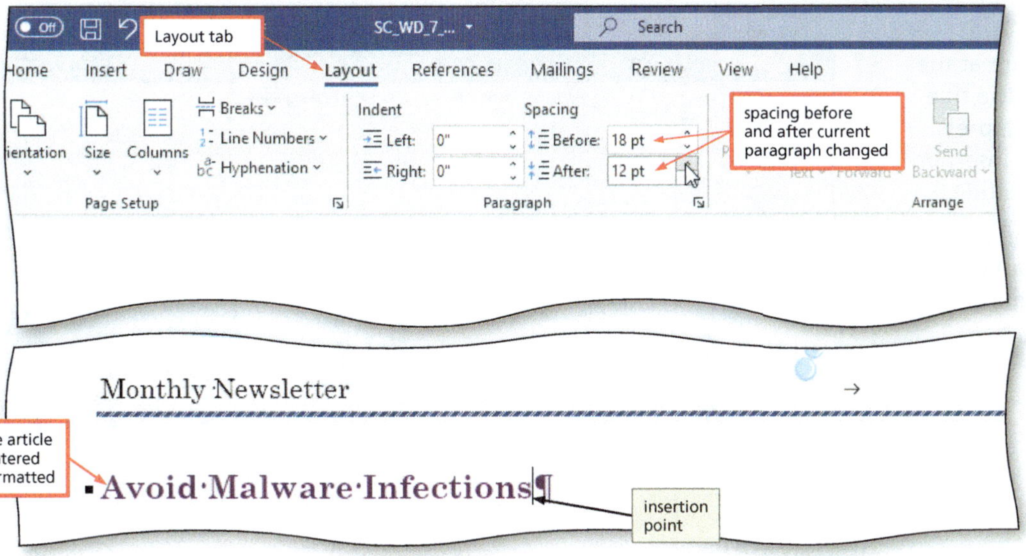

Figure 7–28

Columns

When you begin a document in Word, it has one column. You can divide a portion of a document or the entire document in multiple columns. Within each column, you can type, modify, or format text.

To divide a portion of a document in multiple columns, you use section breaks. Word requires that a new section be created each time you alter the number of columns in a document. Thus, if a document has a nameplate (one column) followed by an article of three columns followed by an article of two columns, the document would be divided in three separate sections.

Consider This

How should you organize the body copy in columns?

Be consistent from page to page with the number of columns. Narrow columns generally are easier to read than wide ones. Columns, however, can be too narrow. A two- or three-column layout generally is appealing and offers a flexible design. Try to have between five and fifteen words per line. To do this, you may need to adjust the column width, the font size, or the leading (line spacing). Font size of text in columns should be no larger than 12 point but not so small that readers must strain to read the text.

Sections

All Word documents have at least one section. A Word document can be divided into any number of sections. During the course of creating a document, you create a new **section** if you need to change the top margin, bottom margin, page alignment, paper size, page orientation, page number position, columns, or contents or position of headers, footers, or footnotes in just a portion of the document.

BTW

Section Numbers

If you want to display the current section number on the status bar, right-click the status bar to display the Customize Status Bar menu and then click Section on the Customize Status Bar menu. The section number appears at the left edge of the status bar. To remove the section number from the status bar, perform the same steps.

To Insert a Continuous Section Break

The next step is to insert a continuous section break below the nameplate. **Why?** In this module, the nameplate is one column and the body of the newsletter is three columns. The term, continuous, means the new section should be on the same page as the previous section, which, in this case, means that the three columns of body copy will be positioned directly below the nameplate on the first page of the newsletter. The following steps insert a continuous section break.

1

- With the insertion point at the end of the feature article title (shown in Figure 7–28), press ENTER to position the insertion point below the article title.
- Click the Breaks button (Layout tab | Page Setup group) to display the Breaks gallery (Figure 7–29).

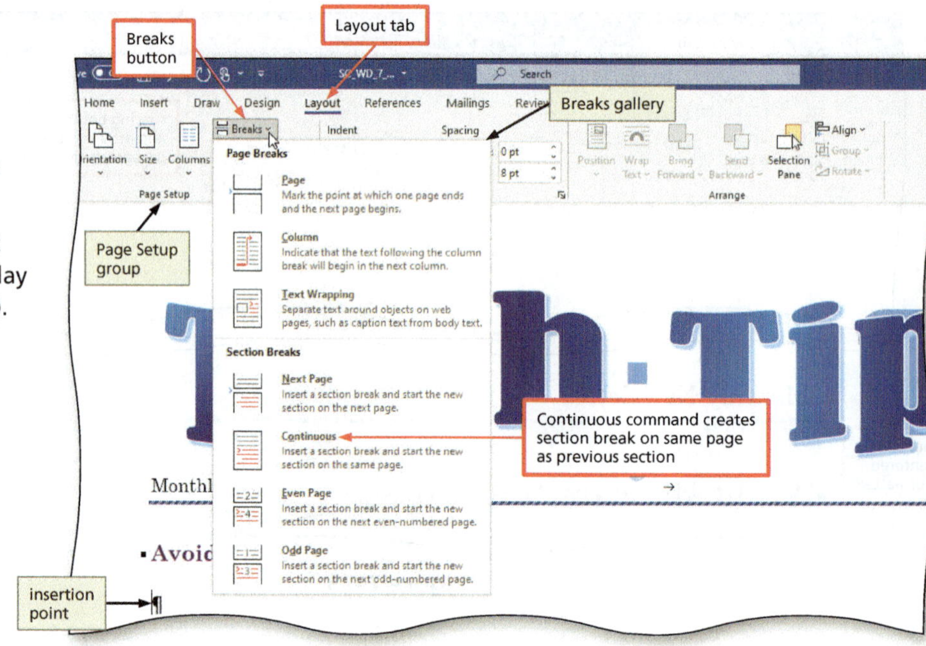

Figure 7–29

2

- Click Continuous in the Breaks gallery to insert a continuous section break above the insertion point (Figure 7–30).

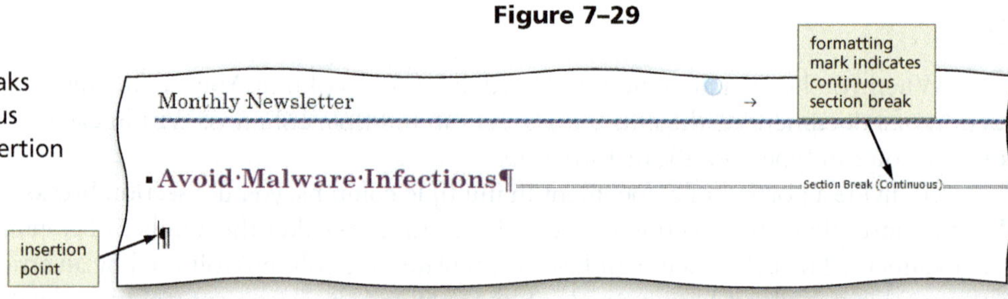

Figure 7–30

To Format Text in Columns

The document now has two sections. The nameplate is in the first section, and the insertion point is in the second section. The second section should be formatted to three columns. **Why?** The feature article and announcements appear in three columns that snake across the page. Thus, the following steps format the second section in the document as three columns.

1

- Click the Columns button (Layout tab | Page Setup group) to display the Columns gallery (Figure 7–31).

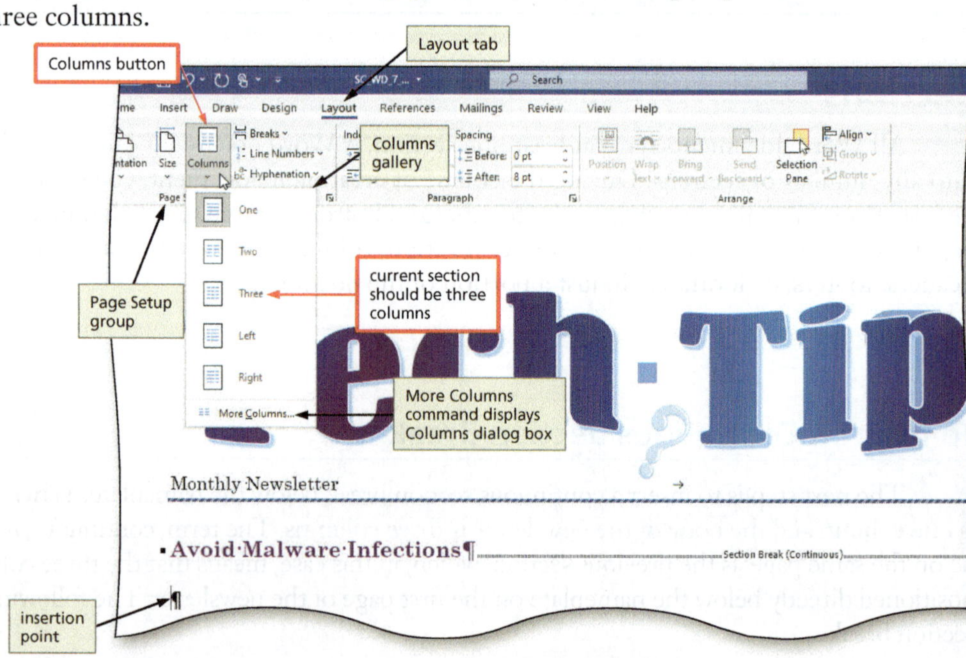

Figure 7–31

2

- Click Three in the Columns gallery to divide the section containing the insertion point in three evenly sized and spaced columns.
- Display the View tab and then, if necessary, click the Ruler check box so that the rulers appear on the screen (Figure 7–32).

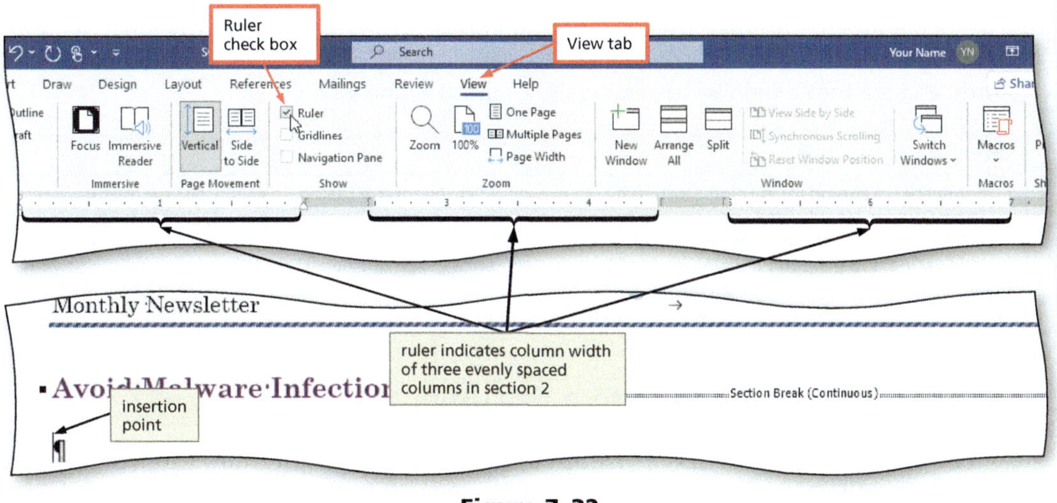

Figure 7–32

Q&A

Why display the rulers?
You want to see the column widths on the ruler.

What if I want columns of different widths?
You would click More Columns in the Columns gallery (shown in Figure 7–31), which displays the Columns dialog box. In this dialog box, you can specify varying column widths and spacing.

To Justify a Paragraph

The following step enters the first paragraph of the feature article using justified alignment. **Why?** The text in the paragraphs of the body of the newsletter is ***justified***, which means that the left and right margins are aligned, like the edges of newspaper columns.

1

- Display the Home tab.
- Click the Justify button (Home tab | Paragraph group) so that Word aligns both the left and right margins of typed text.
- Type the first paragraph of the feature article (Figure 7–33): `Some websites contain tempting offers to download free games or music, enter contests, receive coupons, or install toolbars that offer convenience on computers or mobile devices. Danger may lurk, however, in those downloaded files, because they might secretly install malware that could present effects ranging from a mild annoyance to a severe problem such as identity theft.` and then press ENTER.

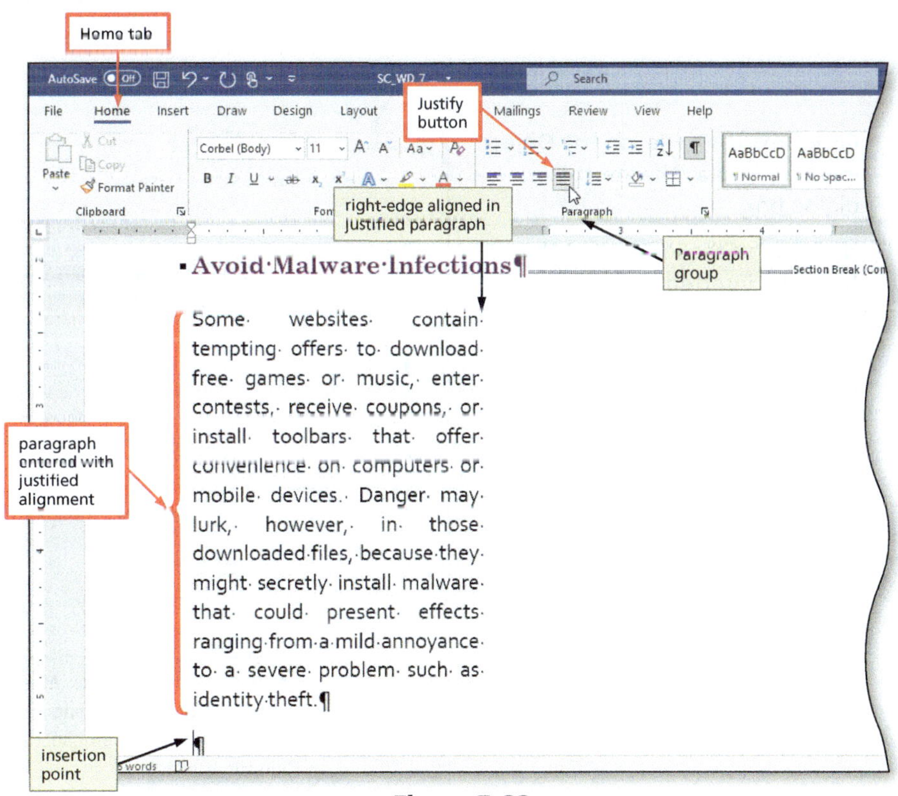

Figure 7–33

Q&A Why do some words have extra space between them?

When a paragraph is formatted to justified alignment, Word places extra space between words so that the left and right edges of the paragraph are aligned. To remedy big gaps, sometimes called rivers, you can add or rearrange words, change the column width, change the font size, and so on.

Other Ways

1. Right-click paragraph (or, if using touch, tap 'Show Context Menu' button on Mini toolbar), click Paragraph on shortcut menu, click 'Indents and Spacing' tab (Paragraph dialog box), click Alignment arrow, click Justified, click OK
2. Click Paragraph Dialog Box Launcher (Home tab or Layout tab | Paragraph group), click Indents and Spacing tab (Paragraph dialog box), click Alignment arrow, click Justified, click OK
3. Press CTRL+J

To Insert Text from a File into a Document

The next step is to insert a file named Support_WD_7_AvoidMalwareInfectionsArticle.docx in the newsletter. **Why?** To save you time typing, the rest of the feature article is located in the Data Files. Please contact your instructor for information about accessing the Data Files. The following steps insert the Support_WD_7_AvoidMalwareInfectionsArticle.docx file in a column of the newsletter.

1

- Display the Insert tab.
- With the insertion point positioned in the left column as shown in Figure 7–33, click the Object arrow (Insert tab | Text group) to display the Object menu (Figure 7–34).

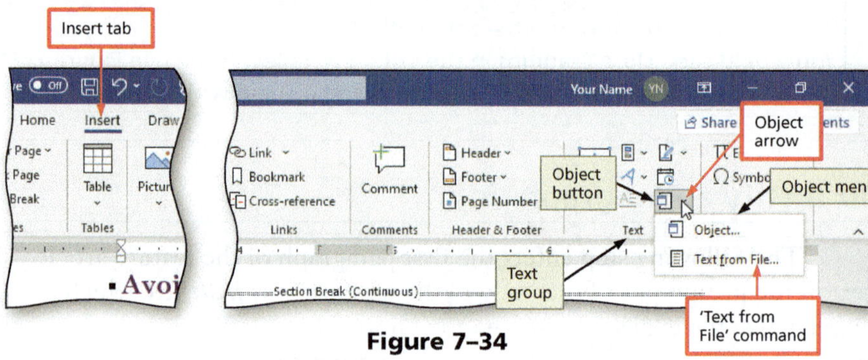

Figure 7–34

2

- Click 'Text from File' on the Object menu to display the Insert File dialog box.
- Navigate to the location of the file to be inserted.
- Click the file named Support_WD_7_AvoidMalware InfectionsArticle.docx to select the file (Figure 7–35).

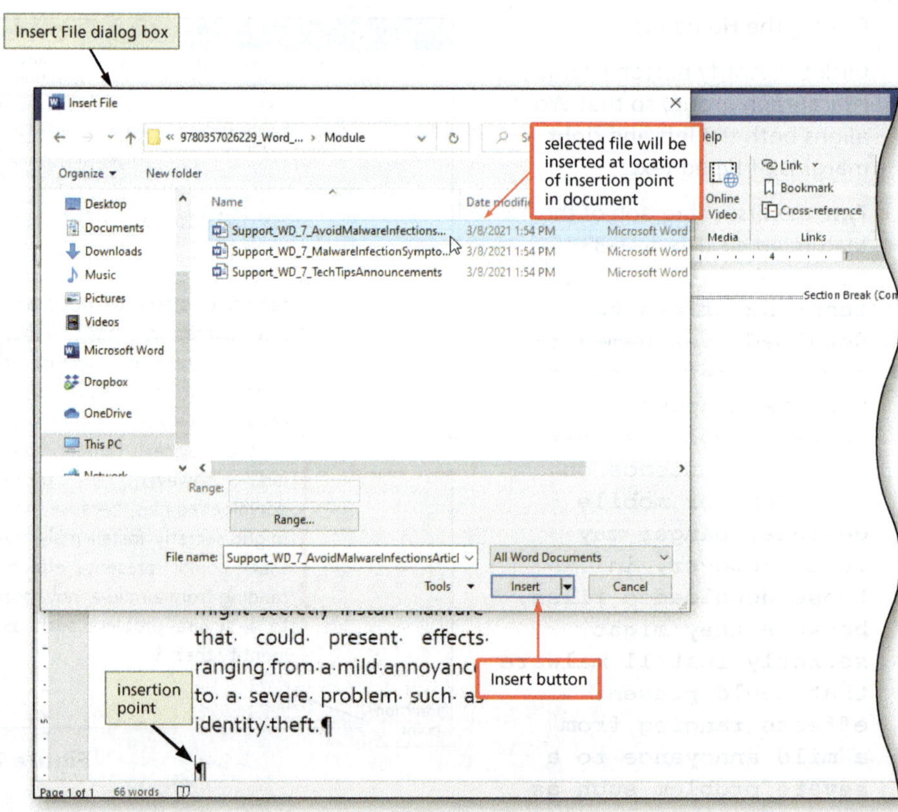

Figure 7–35

3

- Click the Insert button (Insert File dialog box) to insert the file, Support_WD_7_AvoidMalwareInfectionsArticle.docx, in the current document at the location of the insertion point.
- So that you can see the entire inserted article, display multiple pages on the screen by clicking the Multiple Pages button (View tab | Zoom group) (Figure 7–36).

4

- When you are finished viewing the document, change the zoom to page width so that the newsletter content is larger on the screen and then scroll to the top of the first page.

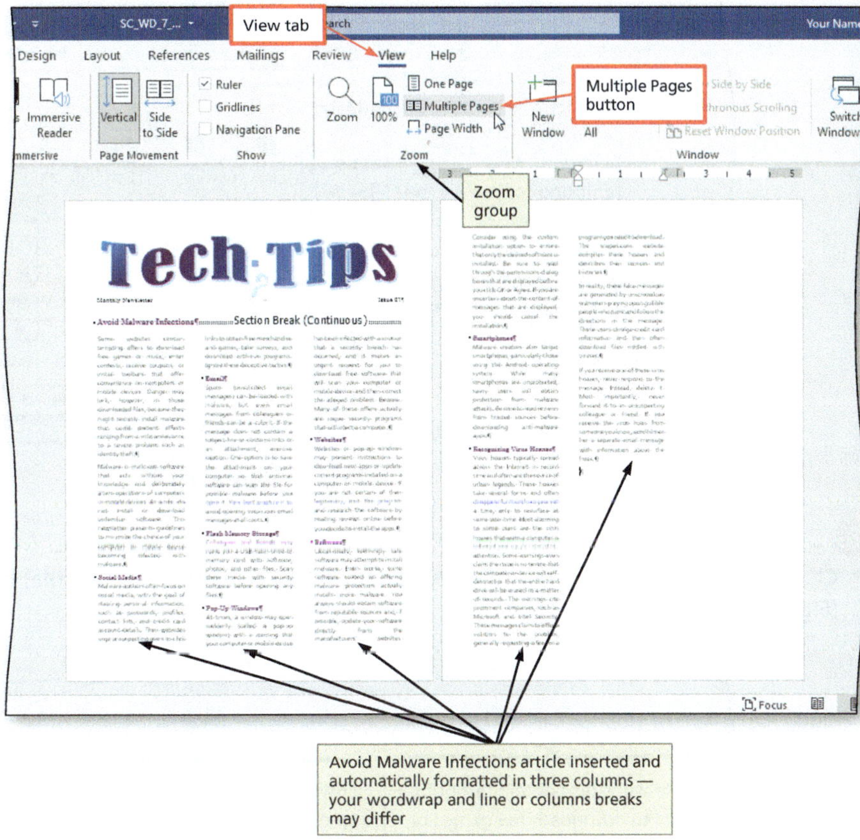

Figure 7–36

To Adjust the Width of Columns and Place a Vertical Line between Columns

The columns in the newsletter currently contain many rivers. **Why?** The justified alignment in the narrow column width often causes large gaps between words. To eliminate some of the rivers, you increase the size of the columns slightly in this newsletter. In newsletters, you often see a vertical rule (line) separating columns. Through the Columns dialog box, you can change column width and add vertical lines. The following steps increase column widths and add vertical lines between columns.

1

- Position the insertion point somewhere in the feature article text.
- Display the Layout tab.
- Click the Columns button (Layout tab | Page Setup group) to display the Columns gallery (shown in Figure 7–31).

2

- Click More Columns in the Columns gallery to display the Columns dialog box.
- If necessary, in the Width and spacing area (Columns dialog box), click the Width up arrow until the Width box reads 2.1".

Q&A How would I make the columns different widths?
You would remove the check mark from the 'Equal column width' check box and then set the individual column widths in the dialog box.

- Place a check mark in the Line between check box to select the check box (Figure 7–37).

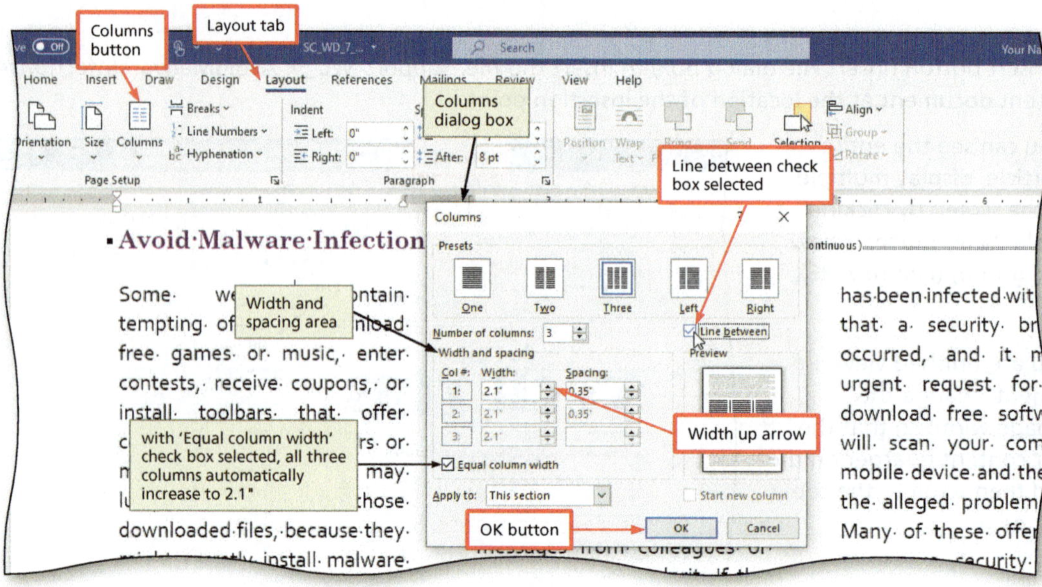

Figure 7–37

3

- Click OK to make the columns slightly wider and place a line (vertical rule) between each column in the document (Figure 7–38).

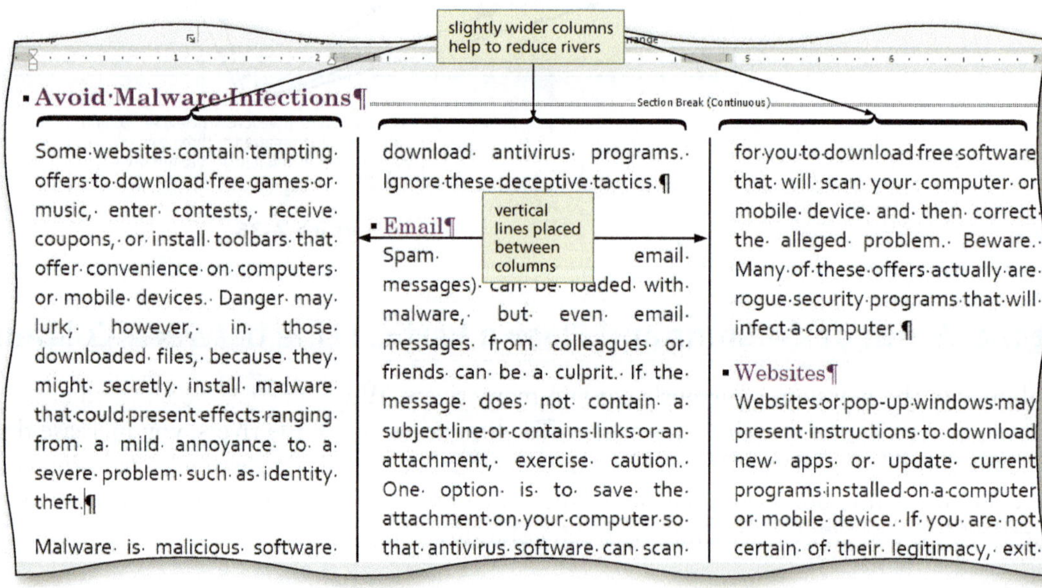

Figure 7–38

Other Ways

1. Double-click shaded space between columns on ruler, enter settings (Columns dialog box), click OK
2. To adjust column widths, drag column boundaries on ruler
3. To insert single rule, click Borders arrow (Home tab | Paragraph group)

To Hyphenate a Document

The following steps turn on the hyphenation feature. **Why?** To further eliminate some of the rivers in the columns of the newsletter, you turn on Word's hyphenation feature so that words with multiple syllables are hyphenated at the end of lines instead of wrapped in their entirety to the next line.

1

- Click the Hyphenation button (Layout tab | Page Setup group) to display the Hyphenation gallery (Figure 7–39).

Q&A What is the difference between Automatic and Manual hyphenation?

Automatic hyphenation places hyphens wherever words can break at a syllable in the document. With manual hyphenation, Word displays a dialog box for each word it could hyphenate, enabling you to accept or reject the proposed hyphenation.

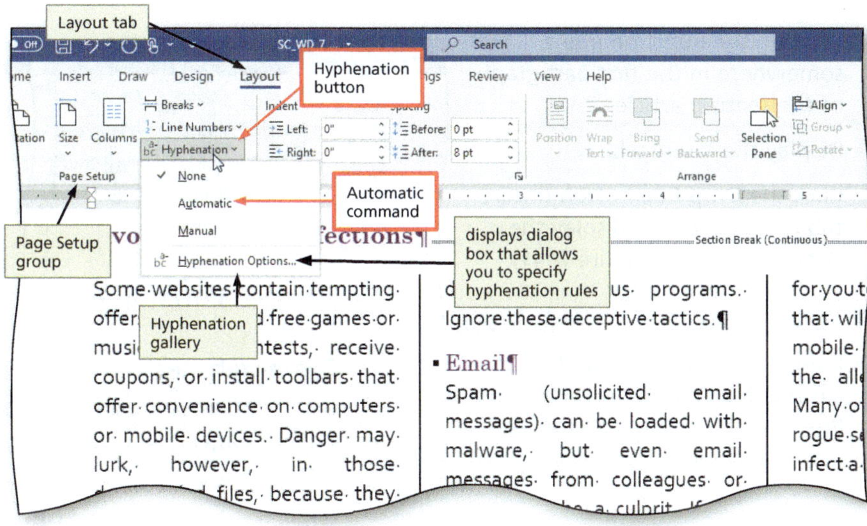

Figure 7–39

2

- Click Automatic in the Hyphenation gallery to hyphenate the document (Figure 7–40).

Q&A What if I do not want a particular word hyphenated?

You can reword text, and Word will redo the hyphenation automatically.

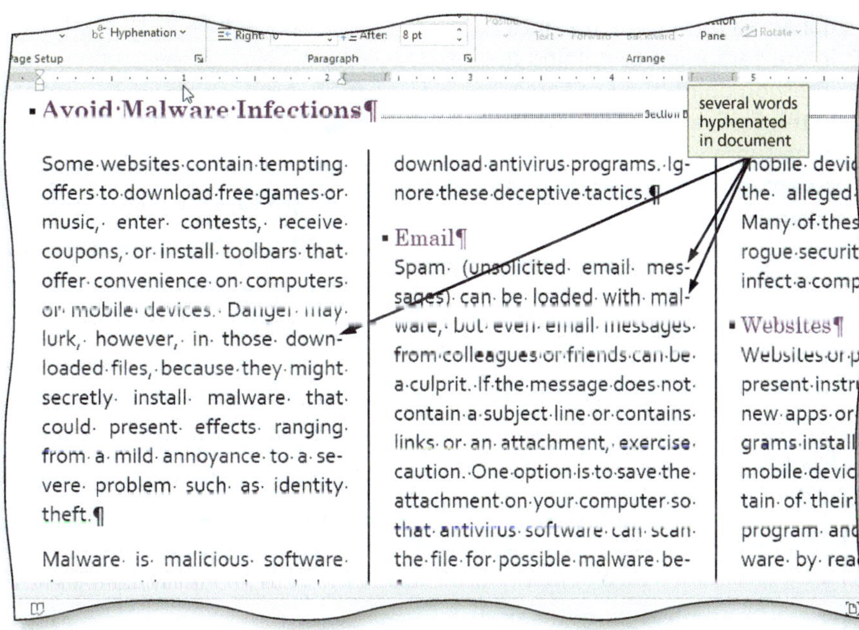

Figure 7–40

To Format a Character as a Drop Cap

The first character in the feature article in this newsletter — that is, the capital letter S — is formatted as a drop cap. **Why?** To add interest to an article, you often see a **drop cap,** which is a decorative, large, initial capital letter that extends below the other letters in the line. In Word, the drop cap can sink into the first few lines of text, or it can extend into the left margin, which often is called a stick-up cap. In this newsletter, the paragraph text wraps around the drop cap.

The following steps create a drop cap in the first paragraph of the feature article in the newsletter.

1

- Position the insertion point somewhere in the first paragraph of the feature article.
- Display the Insert tab.
- Click the Drop Cap button (Insert tab | Text group) to display the Drop Cap gallery (Figure 7–41).

Experiment

- Point to various commands in the Drop Cap gallery to see a Live Preview of the drop cap formats in the document.

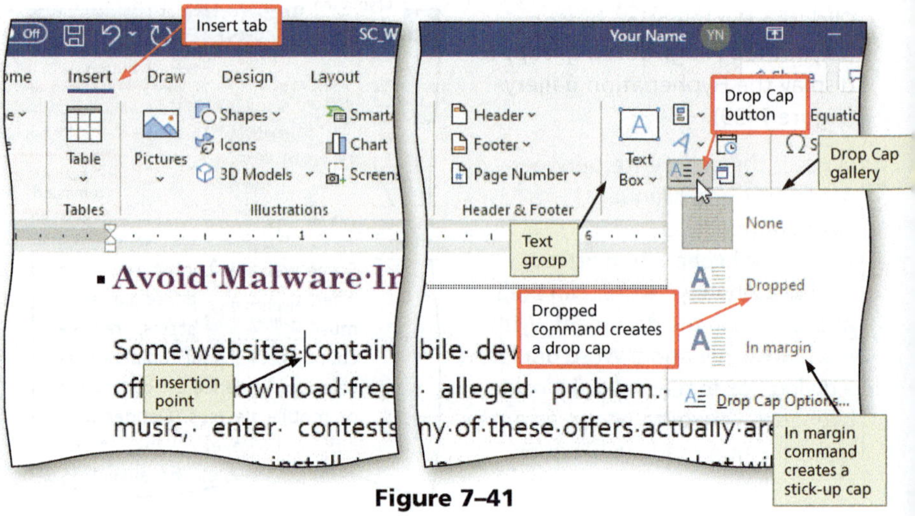

Figure 7–41

2

- Click Dropped in the Drop Cap gallery to format the first letter in the paragraph containing the insertion point (the S in Some, in this case) as a drop cap and wrap subsequent text in the paragraph around the drop cap (Figure 7–42).

Q&A What is the outline around the drop cap in the document?
When you format a letter as a drop cap, Word places a frame around it. A **frame** is a container for text that allows you to position the text anywhere on the page. Word formats a frame for the drop cap so that text wraps around it. The frame also contains a paragraph mark nonprinting character to the right of the drop cap, which may or may not be visible on your screen.

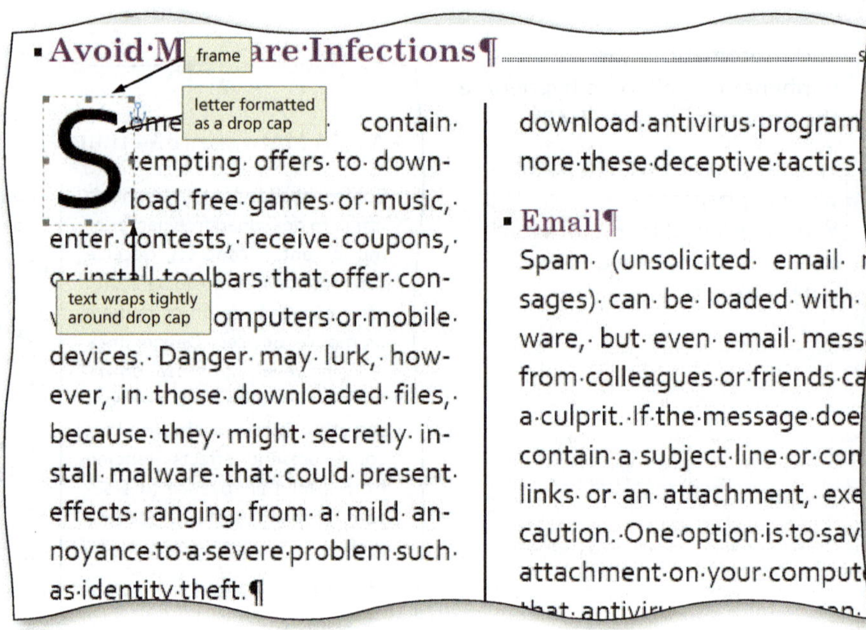

Figure 7–42

To Format the Drop Cap

The following step changes the font color of the drop cap.

1 With the drop cap selected, display the Home tab and then change the font color of the drop cap to 'Blue, Accent 5, Darker 50%' (ninth color, sixth row) in Font Color gallery (shown in Figure 7–1a at the beginning of this module).

Q&A What if my frame no longer is displayed?
Click the drop cap to select it. Then, click the selection rectangle to display the frame.

To Insert a Next Page Section Break

The third column on the first page of the newsletter is not a continuation of the feature article. **Why not?** The third column, instead, contains several reader announcements. The feature article continues on the second page of the newsletter (shown in Figure 7–1b at the beginning of this module). Thus, you must insert a next page section break, which is a section break that also contains a page break, at the bottom of the second column so that the remainder of the feature article moves to the second page. The following steps insert a next page section break in the second column.

1

- Position the insertion point at the location for the section break, in this case, to the left of the P in the Pop-Up Windows heading.
- Display the Layout tab.
- Click the Breaks button (Layout tab | Page Setup group) to display the Breaks gallery (Figure 7–43).

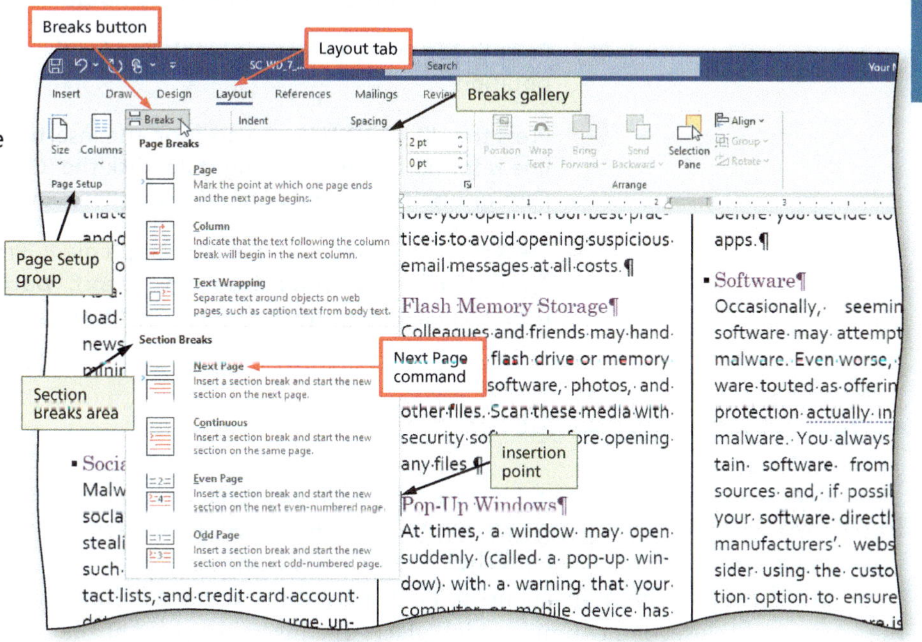

Figure 7–43

2

- In the Section Breaks area in the gallery, click Next Page to insert a next page section break, which positions the insertion point on the next page.
- If necessary, scroll to the bottom of the first page so that you can see the moved text (Figure 7–44).

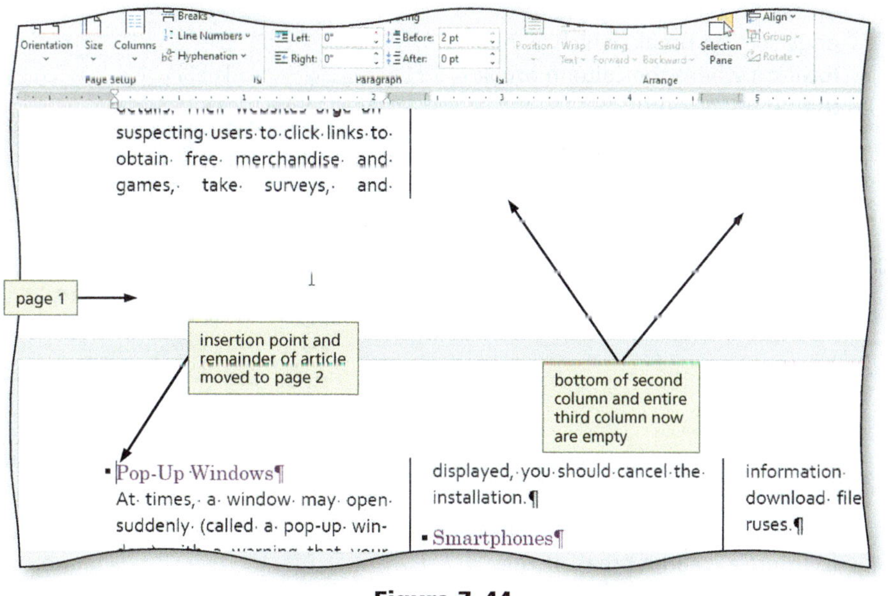

Figure 7–44

To Enter Text

The next step is to insert a jump-to line at the end of the second column, informing the reader where to look for the rest of the feature article. The following steps insert a jump-to line at the end of the text in the second column on the first page of the newsletter.

1. Scroll to display the end of the text in the second column of the first page of the newsletter and then position the insertion point to the left of the paragraph mark that is to the left of the section break notation.
2. Press ENTER twice to insert a blank line for the jump-to text above the section break notation.
3. Press the UP ARROW key to position the insertion point on the blank line. If the blank line is formatted in a heading style, click the 'Clear All Formatting' button (Home tab | Font group) so that the entered text follows the Normal style.
4. Press CTRL+R to right align the paragraph mark. Press CTRL+I to turn on the italic format. Type **`(Article continues on next page)`** as the jump-to text and then press CTRL+I again to turn off the italic format.

To Insert a Column Break

In the Tech Tips newsletters, for consistency, the reader announcements always begin at the top of the third column. If you insert the file containing the announcements at the current location of the insertion point, however, they will begin at the bottom of the second column. **Why?** The insertion point currently is at the bottom of the second column.

For the reader announcements to be displayed in the third column, you insert a **column break** at the bottom of the second column, which places the insertion point at the top of the next column. Thus, the following steps insert a column break at the bottom of the second column.

1

- Position the insertion point to the left of the paragraph mark on the line containing the next page section break, which is the location where the column break should be inserted.
- If necessary, display the Layout tab.
- Click the Breaks button (Layout tab | Page Setup group) to display the Breaks gallery (Figure 7–45).

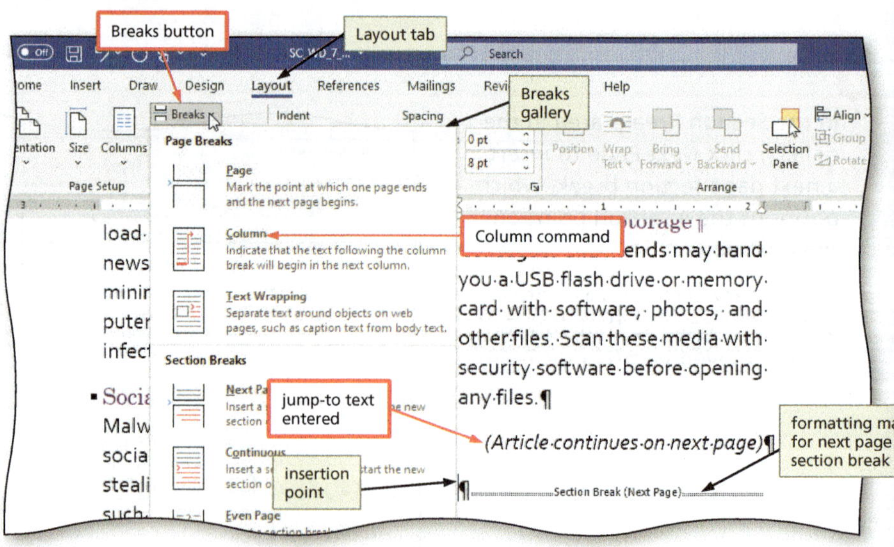

Figure 7–45

2

- Click Column in the Breaks gallery to insert a column break at the location of the insertion point and move the insertion point to the top of the next column (Figure 7–46).

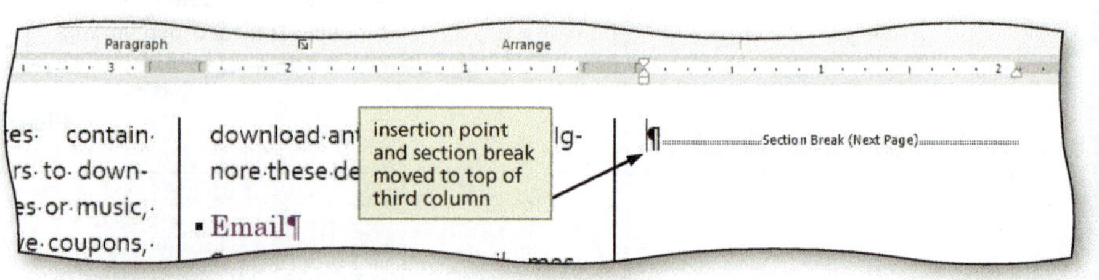

Figure 7–46

Q&A What if I wanted to remove a column break?
You would double-click it to select it and then click the Cut button (Home tab | Clipboard group) or press DELETE.

Other Ways

1. Press CTRL+SHIFT+ENTER

To Insert Text from a File in to a Document

So that you do not have to enter the entire third column of announcements in the newsletter, the next step in the project is to insert the file named Support_WD_7_TechTipsAnnouncements.docx in the third column of the newsletter. This file contains the three announcements: the first about an upcoming webinar, the second about reader discounts, and the third about the topic of the next newsletter issue.

The Support_WD_7_TechTipsAnnouncements.docx file is located in the Data Files. Please contact your instructor for information about accessing the Data Files. The following steps insert a file in a column of the newsletter.

1. With the insertion point at the top of the third column, display the Insert tab.
2. Click the Object arrow (Insert tab | Text group) to display the Object menu and then click 'Text from File' on the Object menu to display the Insert File dialog box.
3. Navigate to the location of the file to be inserted (in this case, the Data Files folder).
4. Click Support_WD_7_TechTipsAnnouncements.docx to select the file.
5. Click the Insert button (Insert File dialog box) to insert the file, Support_WD_7_TechTipsAnnouncements.docx, in the document at the location of the insertion point.

   Q&A What if text from the announcements column spills onto the second page of the newsletter?
   You will format text in the announcements column so that all of its text fits in the third column of the first page.

6. Press SHIFT+F5 to return the insertion point to the last editing location, in this case, the top of the third column on the first page of the newsletter (Figure 7–47).
7. Save the newsletter again on the same storage location with the same file name.

BTW

Inserting Documents
When you insert a Word document in another Word document, the entire inserted document is placed at the location of the insertion point. If the insertion point is positioned in the middle of the open document when you insert another Word document, the open document continues after the last character of the inserted document; therefore, pay close attention to where the insertion point is positioned before inserting a document.

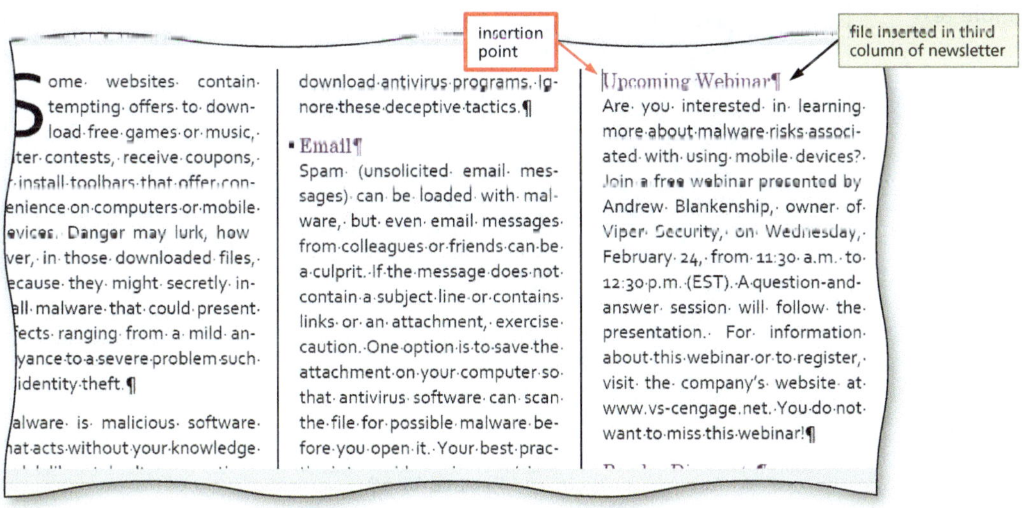

Figure 7–47

Creating a Pull-Quote

A pull-quote is text pulled, or copied, from the text of the document and given graphical emphasis so that it stands apart and commands the reader's attention. The newsletter in this project copies text from the first page of the newsletter and places it in a pull-quote, also on the first page between the first and second columns (shown in Figure 7–1a at the beginning of this module).

Consider This

What guidelines should you follow when using pull-quotes?

Because of their bold emphasis, pull-quotes should be used sparingly in a newsletter. Pull-quotes are useful for breaking the monotony of long columns of text. Typically, quotation marks are used only if you are quoting someone directly. If you use quotation marks, use curly (or smart) quotation marks instead of straight quotation marks.

To create the pull-quote in this newsletter, follow this general procedure:

1. Create a **text box**, which is an object that contains text and that allows you to position the text anywhere on the page.
2. Copy the text from the existing document to the Office Clipboard and then paste the text from the Office Clipboard to the text box.
3. Resize and format the text box.
4. Move the text box to the desired location.

To Insert a Preformatted Text Box

The first step in creating the pull-quote is to insert a text box. A text box is like a frame; the difference is that a text box has more graphical formatting options than does a frame. The following steps insert a built-in text box. **Why?** Word provides a variety of built-in text boxes, saving you the time of formatting the text box.

1

- Click the Text Box button (Insert tab | Text group) to display the Text Box gallery.

Experiment

- Scroll through the Text Box gallery to see the variety of available text box styles.
- Scroll to display Simple Quote in the Text Box gallery (Figure 7–48).

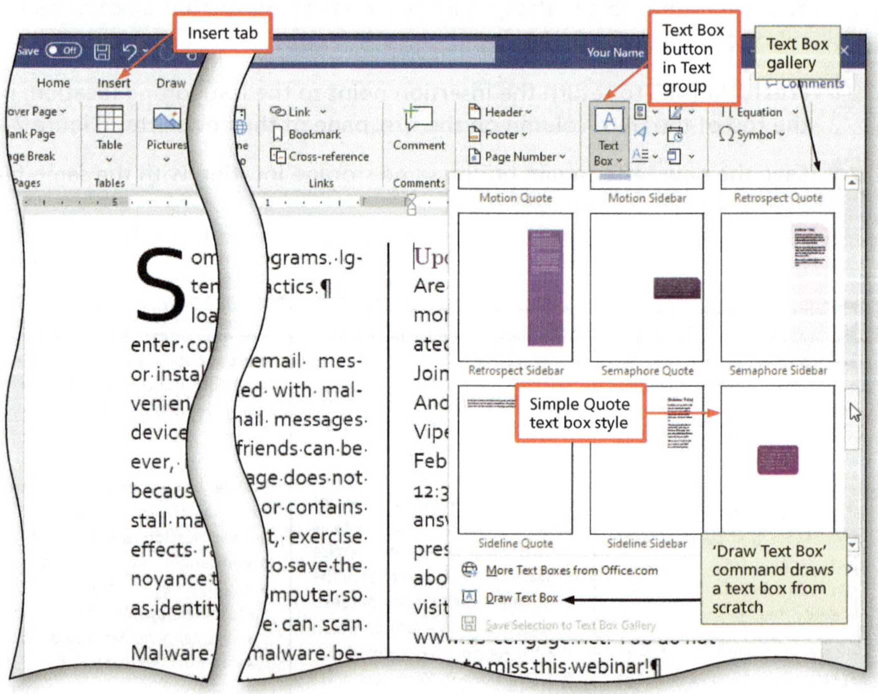

Figure 7–48

2

- Click Simple Quote in the Text Box gallery to insert that style of text box in the document.
- If necessary, drag the text box to the approximate location shown in Figure 7–49.

Q&A Does my text box need to be in the exact same location as in Figure 7–49?
No. You will move the text box later.

The layout of the first page is not correct because of the text box. What do I do?
You will enter text in the text box and then position it in the correct location. At that time, the layout of the first page will be fixed.

What if I did not want to insert a preformatted text box?
You would click 'Draw Text Box' at the bottom of the Text Box gallery (shown in Figure 7–48) and then draw the text box from scratch.

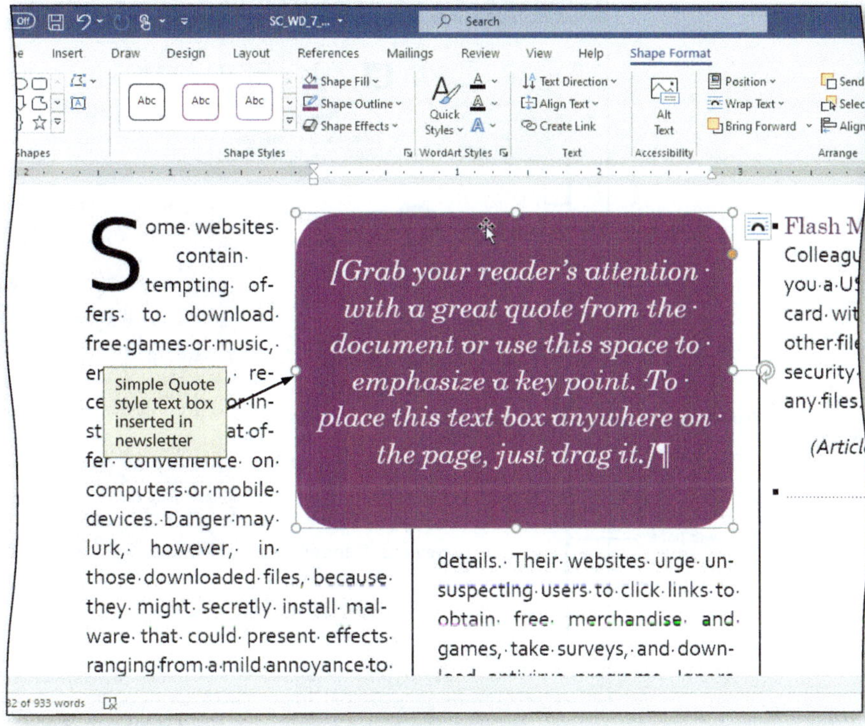

Figure 7–49

Other Ways

1. Click Quick Parts button (Insert tab | Text group), click 'Building Blocks Organizer' on Quick Parts menu, select desired text box name in Building blocks list, click Insert button

To Split the Word Window

The text that you will copy for the pull-quote is in the middle of the first page on the newsletter and the pull-quote (text box) is near the top of the first page of the newsletter. Thus, the next step is to copy the pull-quote text from the middle of the first page and then paste it in the pull-quote at the top of the first page. You would like to view the pull-quote and the text to be copied on the screen at the same time. **Why?** Viewing both simultaneously will simplify the copying and pasting process.

Word allows you to split the window in two separate panes, each containing the current document and having its own scroll bar. This enables you to scroll to and view two different portions of the same document at the same time. The following step splits the Word window.

1

- Display the View tab.
- Click the Split button (View tab | Window group) to divide the document window in two separate panes — both the upper and lower panes display the current document (Figure 7–50).

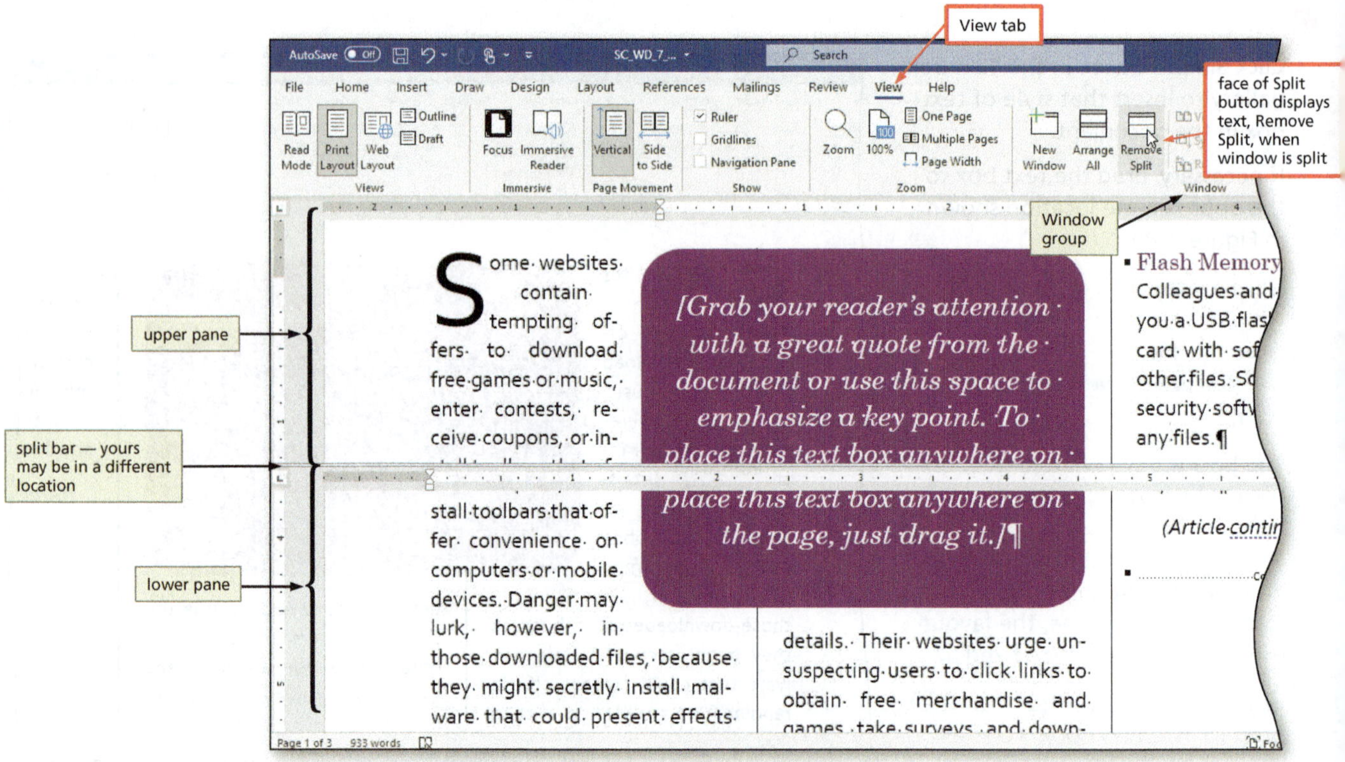

Figure 7–50

Other Ways

1. Press ALT+CTRL+S

To Arrange All Open Word Documents on the Screen

If you have multiple Word documents open and want to view all of them at the same time on the screen, you can instruct Word to arrange all the open documents on the screen from top to bottom. If you wanted to arrange all open Word documents on the same screen, you would perform the following steps.

1. Click the Arrange All button (View tab | Window group) to display each open Word document on the screen.
2. To make one of the arranged documents fill the entire screen again, maximize the window by clicking its Maximize button or double-clicking its title bar.

To Copy and Paste Using Split Windows

The following steps copy text from the middle of the first page of the newsletter to the Clipboard (the source) and then paste the text into the text box (the destination) at the top of the newsletter. **Why?** The item being copied is called the **source.** The location to which you are pasting is called the **destination.**

1

- In the upper pane, scroll so that all placeholder text in the text box is visible, as shown in Figure 7–51.
- In the lower pane, scroll to page 3 to display the text to be copied, as shown in Figure 7–51, and then select the text to be copied: some software touted as offering malware protection actually installs more malware.
- Display the Home tab.

- Click the Copy button (Home tab | Clipboard group) to copy the selected text to the Clipboard (Figure 7–51).

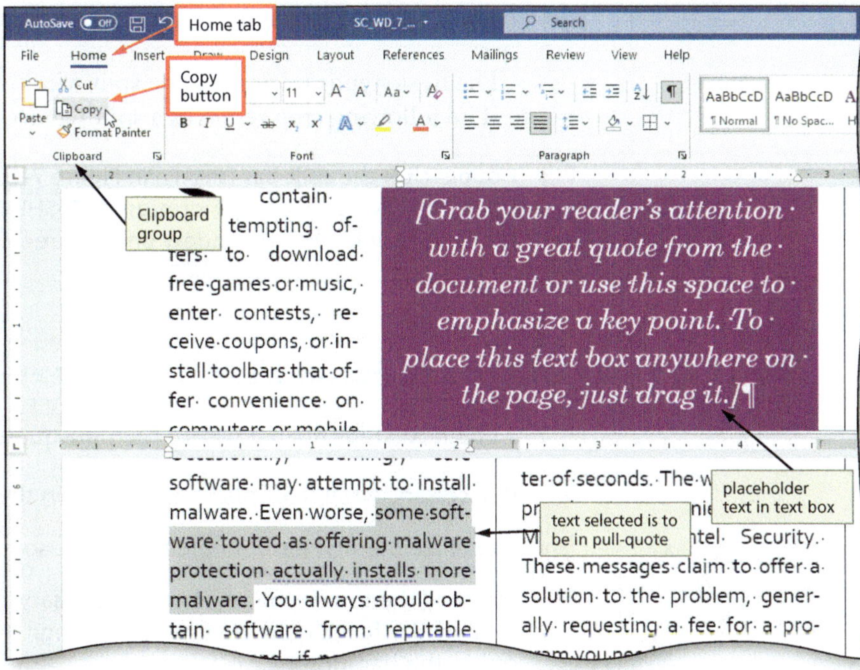

Figure 7–51

2

- In the upper pane, if necessary, scroll to display the text in the text box. Click the text in the text box to select it.
- Click the Paste arrow (Home tab | Clipboard group) to display the Paste menu (Figure 7–52).

Q&A What if I click the Paste button by mistake?
Click the Paste Options button to the right of the pasted text in the text box to display the Paste Options menu.

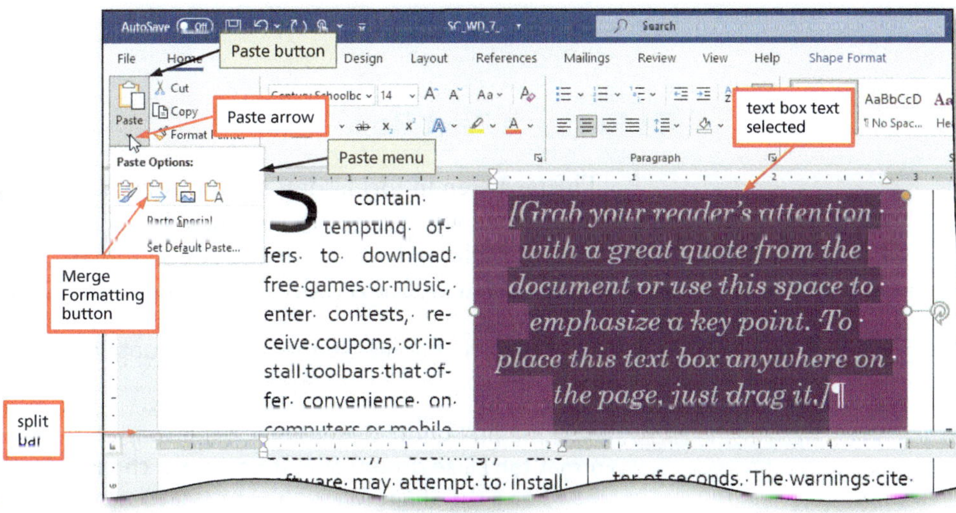

Figure 7–52

3

- Click the Merge Formatting button on the Paste menu to paste the copied text into the text box (shown in Figure 7–53).

Q&A Why select the Merge Formatting button on the Paste menu?
You want the pasted text to use the formats that were in the text box (the destination) instead of the formats of the copied text (the source).

Other Ways

1. Click copy on shortcut menu (or, if using touch, tap Copy on Mini toolbar), right-click where item is to be pasted, click 'Keep Source Formatting' in Paste Options area on shortcut menu (or, if using touch, tap Paste on Mini toolbar)
2. Select text to copy, press CTRL+C; select destination for pasted text, press CTRL+V

To Remove a Split Window

The next step is to remove the split window so that you can position the pull-quote. The following step removes a split window.

1. Double-click the split bar (shown in Figure 7–52), or click the Remove Split button (View tab | Window group), or press ALT+SHIFT+C to remove the split window and return to a single Word window on the screen.

To Edit and Format Text in the Text Box

The next steps format text in the pull-quote.

1. If necessary, scroll to display the text box in the document window.
2. Capitalize the first letter in the pull-quote so it reads: Some.
3. Select all the text in the text box, if necessary, change its font to Century Schoolbook (or a similar font), bold the text, and change its font size to 11 point. If necessary, center this paragraph.
4. Click in the text box to deselect the text, but leave the text box selected (shown in Figure 7–53).

To Resize a Text Box

The next step in formatting the pull-quote is to resize the text box. You resize a text box the same way as any other object. That is, you drag its sizing handles or enter values in the height and width boxes through the Size button (Shape Format tab | Size group). The following steps resize the text box and insert line break characters.

1. Drag the sizing handles so that the pull-quote looks about the same size as Figure 7–53.
2. Verify the pull-quote dimensions in the Shape Height and Shape Width boxes (Shape Format tab | Size group) and, if necessary, change the value in the Shape Height box to 1.85 and the Shape Width box to 1.4. (Note that depending on your printer and other settings that the text wrapping in your newsletter may not match the figure.)

Q&A What if some of the words in the text box are hyphenated?
Insert line break characters to eliminate any hyphenated words in the text box; that is, position the insertion point to the left of the first letter in the hyphenated word and then press SHIFT+ENTER to insert a line break character, which places the entire word on the next line and removes the hyphen.

BTW
Rotating Text Box Text
To rotate text in a text box, select the text box, click the Text Direction button (Shape Format tab | Text group), and then click the desired direction on the Text Direction menu.

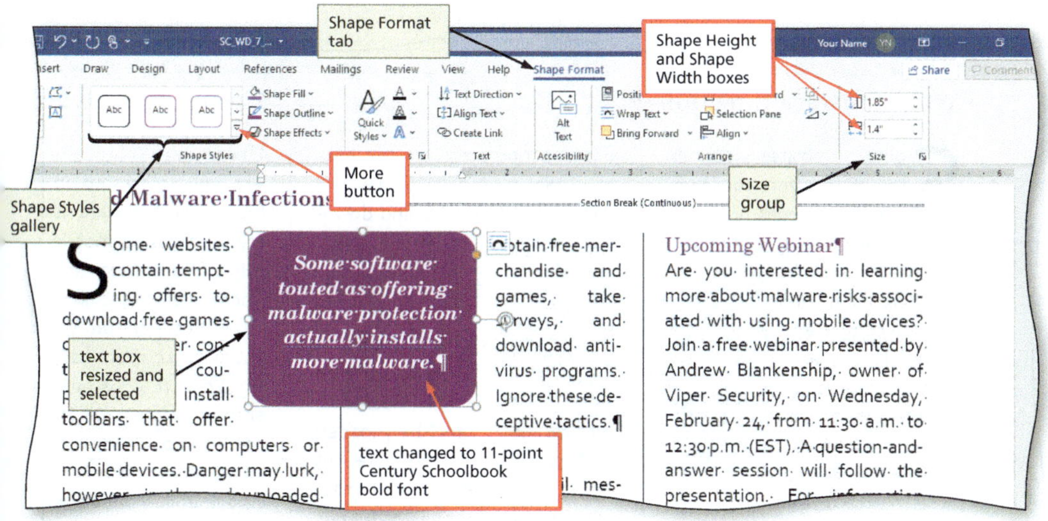

Figure 7–53

To Apply a Shape Style to a Text Box

The next step in formatting the pull-quote is to apply a shape style to the text box to coordinate its colors with the rest of the newsletter. The following steps apply a shape style to a text box.

1. With the text box still selected, click the More button (shown in Figure 7–53) in the Shape Styles gallery (Shape Format tab | Shape Styles group) to expand the gallery.
2. Point to 'Colored Fill - Blue, Accent 5' (sixth style, second row) in the Shape Styles gallery to display a Live Preview of that style applied to the text box (Figure 7–54).
3. Click 'Colored Fill - Blue, Accent 5' in the Shape Styles gallery to apply the selected style to the shape.

BTW

Text Box Styles
Like other drawing objects or pictures, text boxes can be formatted or have styles applied. You can change the fill in a text box by clicking the Shape Fill button or arrow (Shape Format tab | Shape Styles group), add an outline to a text box by clicking the Shape Outline button or arrow (Shape Format tab | Shape Styles group), and apply an effect, such as shadow or 3-D effects, by clicking the Shape Effects button (Shape Format tab | Shape Styles group).

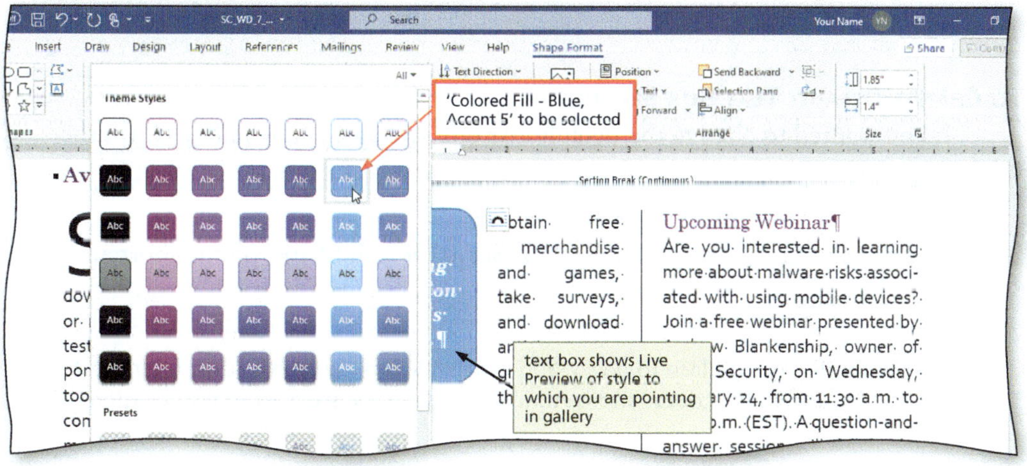

Figure 7–54

To Position a Text Box

The following steps move the text box to the desired location in the newsletter.

1. With the text box still selected, drag the text box to its new location (Figure 7–55). You may need to drag and/or resize the text box a couple of times so that it looks similar to this figure.

BTW

Moving Text Boxes

To move a text box using the keyboard, select the text box and then press the arrow keys on the keyboard. For example, each time you press the DOWN ARROW key, the selected text box moves down one space incrementally.

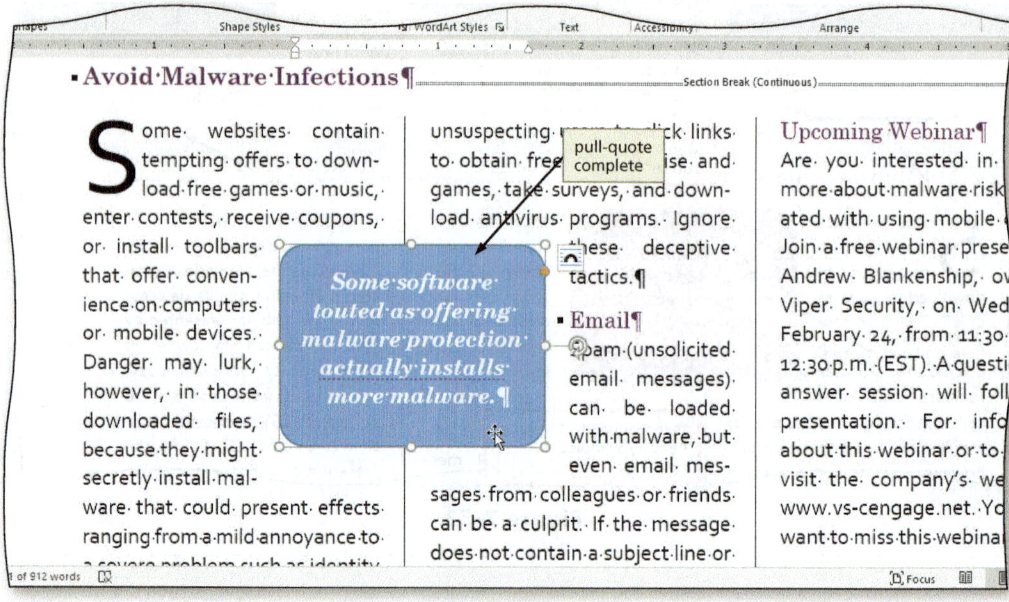

Figure 7–55

2 Click outside the text box to remove the selection.

Q&A Why does my text wrap differently around the text box?
Differences in wordwrap often relate to the printer used by your computer. Thus, your document may wordwrap around the text box differently.

3 If the jump-to line, which is supposed to appear at the bottom of the second column (shown in Figure 7–56), moved to the top of the third column, position the insertion point in the article title (Avoid Malware Infections) and decrease the spacing before and after (Layout tab) until the jump-to line moves back to the bottom of the second column.

4 Save the newsletter again on the same storage location with the same file name.

To Change Default Text Box Settings

If you wanted to change the default text box settings, you would perform the following steps.

1. Insert a text box and format it as desired.
2. Right-click the text box and then click 'Set as Default Shape' on the shortcut menu.

Break Point: If you want to take a break, this is a good place to do so. You can exit Word now. To resume later, start Word, open the file called SC_WD_7_TechTipsNewsletter.docx, and continue following the steps from this location forward.

Formatting the Second Page of the Newsletter

The second page of the newsletter (shown in Figure 7–1b at the beginning of this module) continues the feature article that began in the first two columns on the first page. The nameplate on the second page is less elaborate than the one on the first page of the newsletter. In addition to the text in the feature article, page two contains a graphic. The following sections format the second page of the newsletter in this project.

Consider This

How do you create a nameplate for inner pages of a newsletter?

The top of the inner pages of a newsletter may or may not have a nameplate. If you choose to create one for your inner pages, it should not be the same as, or compete with, the one on the first page. Inner page nameplates usually contain only a portion of the nameplate from the first page of a newsletter.

To Change Column Formatting

The document currently is formatted in three columns. The nameplate at the top of the second page, however, should be in a single column. **Why?** The nameplate should span across the top of the three columns below it. The next step, then, is to change the number of columns at the top of the second page from three to one.

As discussed earlier in this project, Word requires a new section each time you change the number of columns in a document. Thus, you first must insert a continuous section break and then format the section to one column so that the nameplate can be entered on the second page of the newsletter. The following steps insert a continuous section break and then change the column format.

1

- If you have a blank page between the first and second pages of the newsletter, position the insertion point to the left of the paragraph mark at the end of the third column on the first page of the newsletter and then press DELETE as many times as necessary to delete the blank line causing the overflow.
- Position the insertion point at the upper-left corner of the second page of the newsletter (to the left of P in Pop-Up).
- Display the Layout tab.
- Click the Breaks button (Layout tab | Page Setup group) to display the Breaks gallery (Figure 7–56).

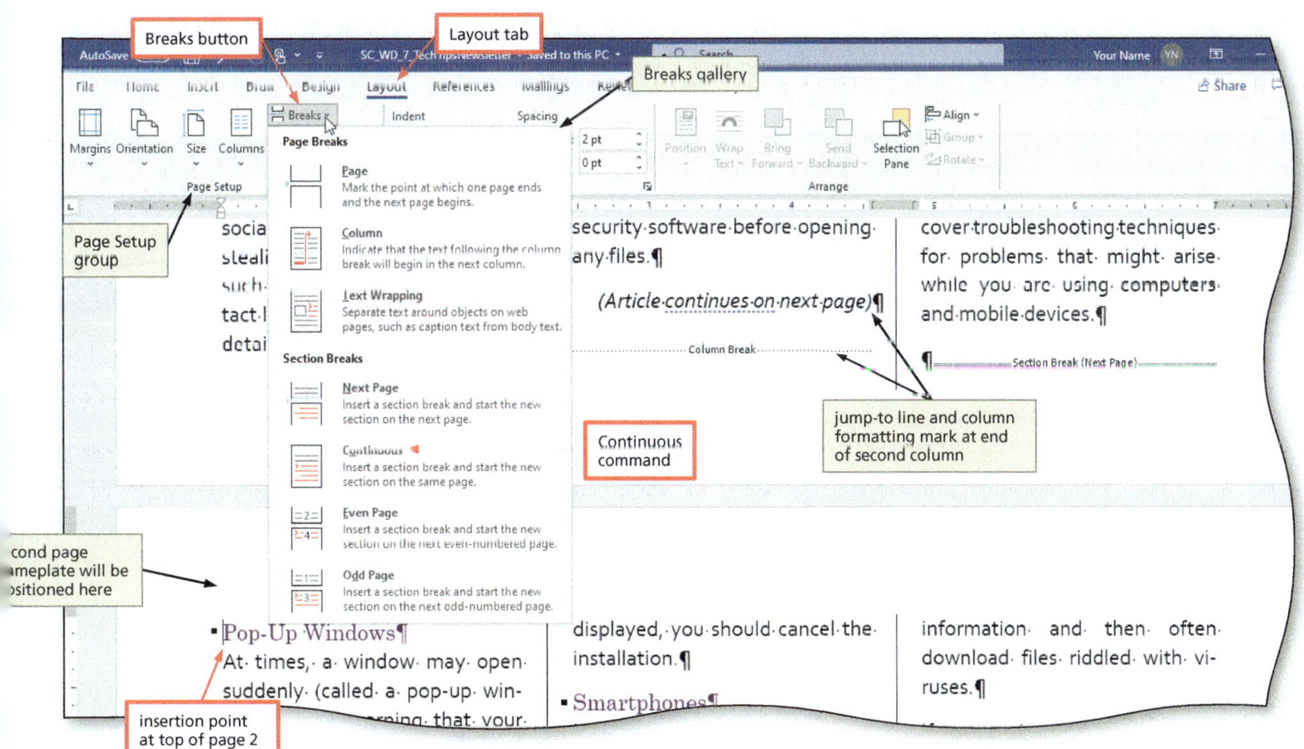

Figure 7–56

2

- Click Continuous in the Breaks gallery to insert a continuous section break above the insertion point.
- Press the UP ARROW key to position the insertion point to the left of the continuous section break just inserted.
- Click the Columns button (Layout tab | Page Setup group) to display the Columns gallery (Figure 7–57).

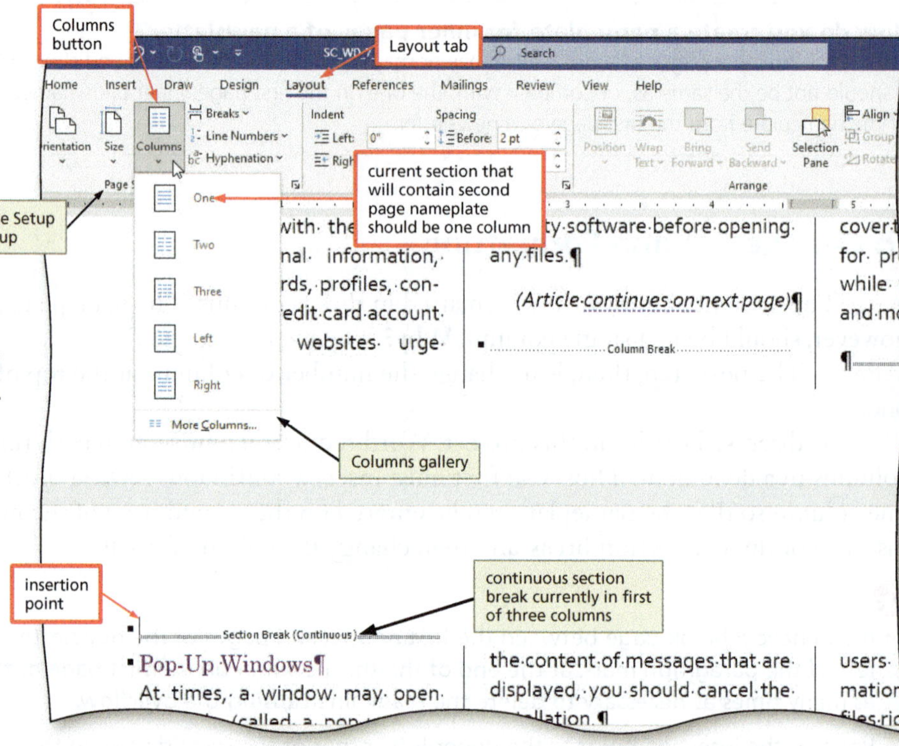

Figure 7–57

3

- Click One in the Columns gallery to format the current section to one column, which now is ready for the second page nameplate.
- If necessary, scroll to display the bottom of the first page and the top of the second page, so that you can see the varying columns in the newsletter (Figure 7–58).

Q&A Can I change the column format of existing text?

Yes. If you already have typed text and would like it to be formatted in a different number of columns, select the text, click the Columns button (Layout tab | Page Setup group), and then click the number of columns desired in the Columns gallery. Word automatically creates a new section for the newly formatted columns.

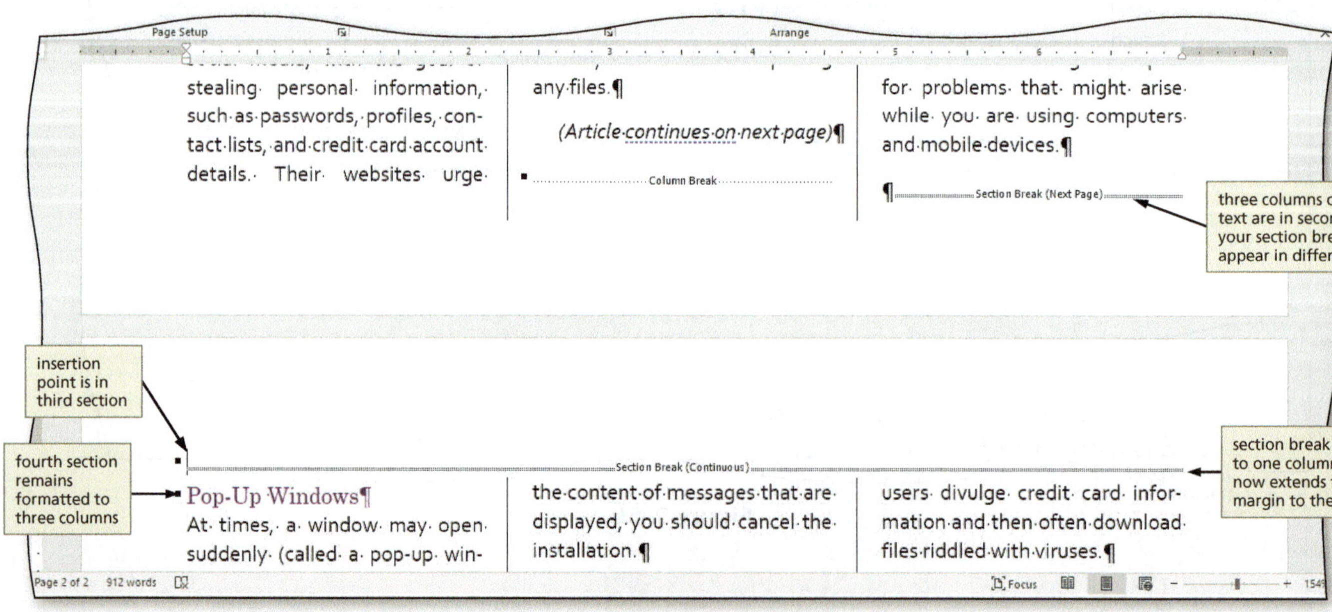

Figure 7–58

To Set Custom Tab Stops Using the Tabs Dialog Box

The nameplate on the second page of the newsletter contains the text, Monthly Newsletter, at the left margin, the newsletter title in the center, and the issue number at the right margin (shown in Figure 7–1b at the beginning of this module). To properly align the text in the center and at the right margin, you will set custom tab stops at these locations. The following steps set custom tab stops.

1. Press ENTER twice and then position the insertion point on the first line of the second page of the newsletter, which is the paragraph to be formatted with the custom tab stops.
2. Display the Home tab and then click the 'Clear All Formatting' button (Home tab | Font group) to apply the Normal style to the first line on the second page of the newsletter.
3. Click the Paragraph Dialog Box Launcher (Home tab | Paragraph group) to display the Paragraph dialog box and then click the Tabs button (Paragraph dialog box) to display the Tabs dialog box.
4. Type 3.5 in the Tab stop position text box (Tabs dialog box), click Center in the Alignment area to specify the tab stop alignment, and then click the Set button to set the custom tab stop.
5. Type 7 in the Tab stop position text box (Tabs dialog box), click Right in the Alignment area to specify the tab stop alignment, and then click the Set button to set the custom tab stop (Figure 7–59).
6. Click OK to set custom tab stops using the specified alignments.

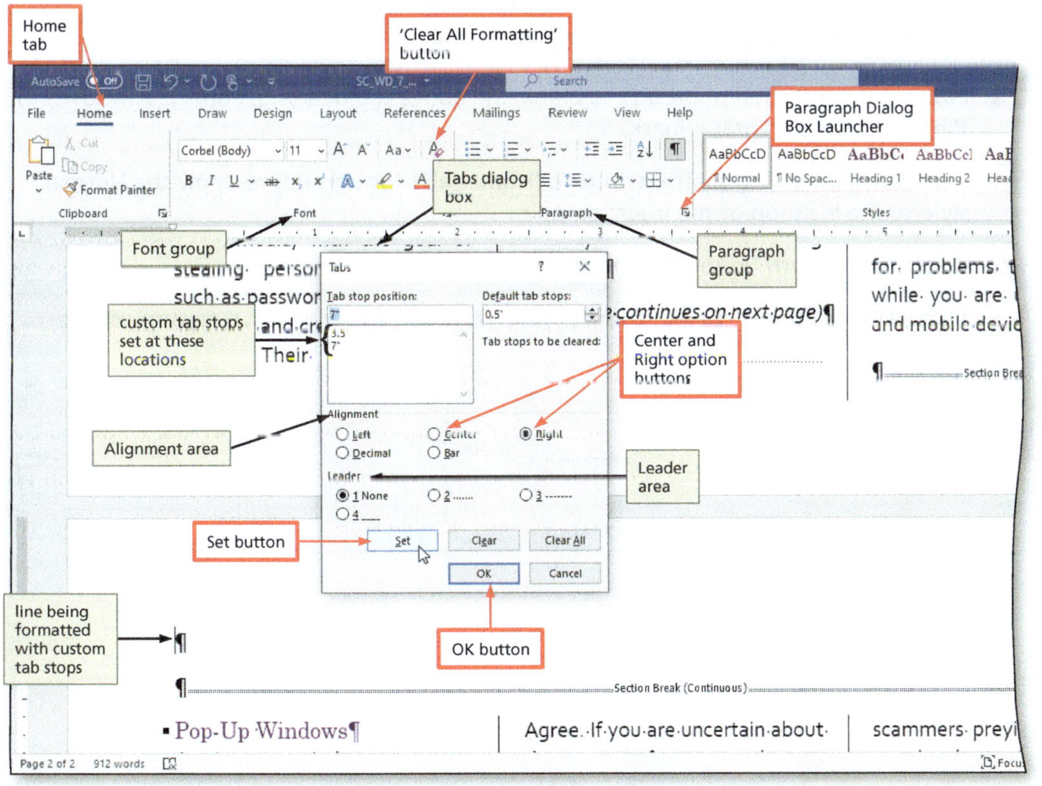

Figure 7–59

BTW

Sections

To see the formatting associated with a section, double-click the section break notation, or click the Page Setup Dialog Box Launcher (Layout tab | Page Setup group) to display the Page Setup dialog box. You can change margin settings and page orientation for a section in the Margins sheet. To change paper sizes for a section, click the Paper tab (Page Setup dialog box). The Layout tab (Page Setup dialog box) allows you to change header and footer specifications and vertical alignment for the section. To add a border to a section, click the Borders button in the Layout sheet.

BTW

Leader Characters

Leader characters, such as a series of dots, often are used in a table of contents to precede page numbers. Four types of leader characters, which Word places in the space occupied by a tab character, are available in the Leader area of the Tabs dialog box (shown in Figure 7–59).

To Format and Enter Text and Add a Border

The following steps enter the newsletter title at the top of the second page in the third section.

1. With the insertion point on the first line of the second page of the newsletter, click the Font Color arrow and then change the font color of the current text to 'Blue, Accent 5, Darker 50%' (ninth column, bottom row). Change the font to Century Schoolbook (or a similar font), the font size to 10 point, and type **`Monthly Newsletter`** at the left margin.
2. Press TAB to advance the insertion point to the centered tab stop. Increase the font size to 12 point and then click the Bold button (Home tab | Font group) to bold the text. Type **`Tech Tips`** at the centered tab stop.
3. Press TAB to advance the insertion point to the right-aligned tab stop. Reduce the font size to 10 point and then click the Bold button (Home tab | Font group) to turn off the bold format. Type **`Issue 27`** at the right-aligned tab stop.
4. Click the Borders button (Home tab | Paragraph group) to add a bottom border (shown in Figure 7–60).

Q&A Why is the border formatted already?
When you define a custom border, Word uses that custom border the next time you click the Borders button in the Borders gallery.

To Enter Text

The second page of the feature article on the second page of this newsletter begins with a jump-from line (the continued message) immediately below the nameplate. The next steps enter the jump-from line.

1. Position the insertion point on the blank line above the heading, Pop-Up Windows, to the left of the paragraph mark.
2. Click the 'Clear All Formatting' button (Home tab | Font group) to apply the Normal style to the location of the insertion point.
3. Press CTRL+I to turn on the italic format.
4. Type **`(Continued from first page)`** and then press CTRL+I to turn off the italic format (Figure 7–60).

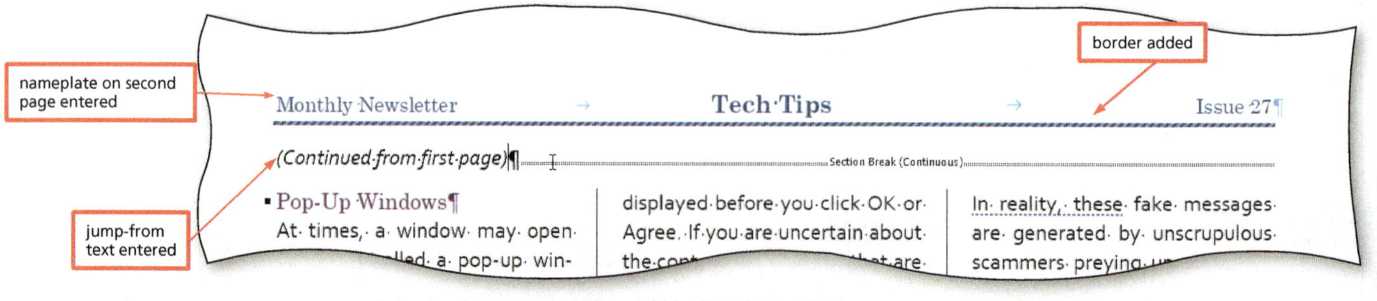

Figure 7–60

To Balance Columns

Currently, the text on the second page of the newsletter completely fills up the first and second columns and almost fills the third column. The text in the three columns should consume the same amount of vertical space. **Why?** Typically, the text in columns of a newsletter is balanced. To balance columns, you insert a continuous section break at the end of the text. The following steps balance columns.

1

- Scroll to the bottom of the text in the third column on the second page of the newsletter and then position the insertion point at the end of the text.
- If an extra paragraph mark is below the last line of text, press DELETE to remove the extra paragraph mark.
- Display the Layout tab.
- Click the Breaks button (Layout tab | Page Setup group) to display the Breaks gallery (Figure 7–61).

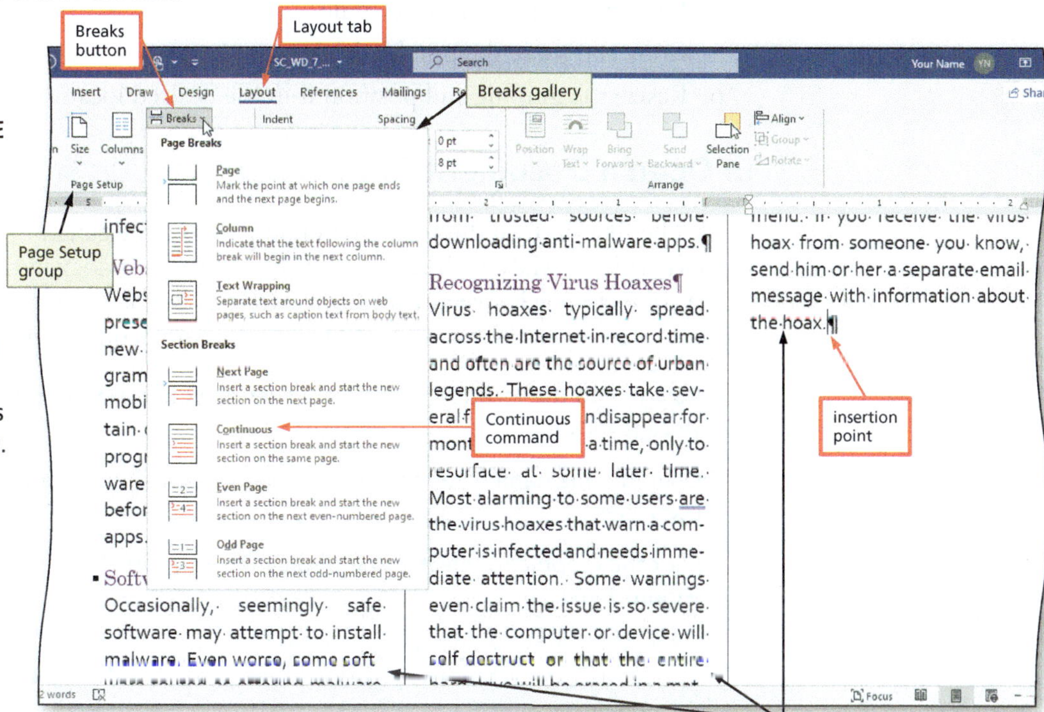

Figure 7–61

2

- Click Continuous in the Breaks gallery to insert a continuous section break, which balances the columns on the second page of the newsletter (Figure 7–62).
- Save the newsletter again on the same storage location with the same file name.

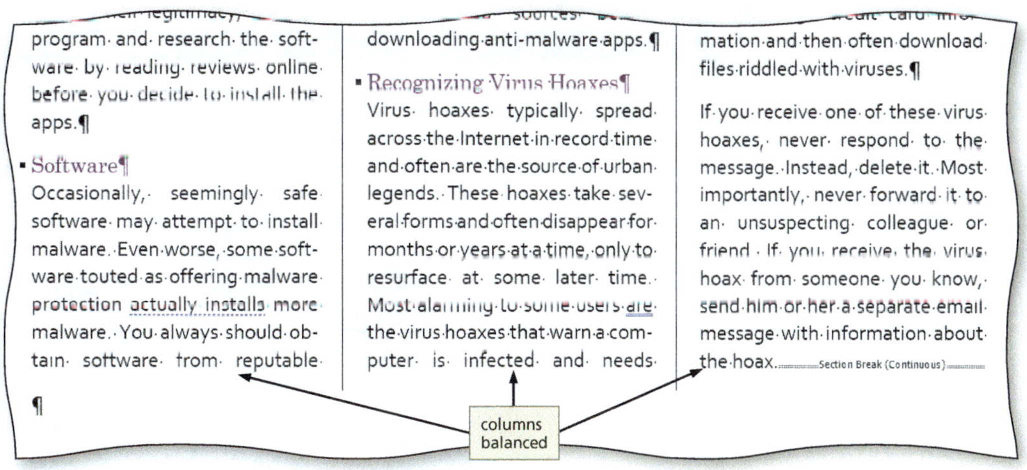

Figure 7–62

Modifying and Formatting a SmartArt Graphic

Microsoft Office includes SmartArt graphics, which are visual representations of ideas. Many different types of SmartArt graphics are available, allowing you to choose one that illustrates your message best.

In this newsletter, a SmartArt graphic is positioned on the second page, toward the bottom of the second column. Because the columns are small in the newsletter, it is best to work with a SmartArt graphic in a separate document window so that you easily can see all of its components. When finished editing the graphic, you can copy and paste it in the newsletter. You will follow these steps for the SmartArt graphic in this newsletter:

1. Open the document that contains the SmartArt graphic for the newsletter.
2. Modify the layout of the graphic.
3. Add a shape and text to the graphic.
4. Format a shape and the graphic.
5. Copy and paste the graphic in the newsletter.
6. Resize the graphic and position it in the desired location.

To Open a Document from Word

The first draft of the SmartArt graphic is in a file called Support_WD_7_MalwareInfectionSymptomsDiagram.docx in the Data Files. Please contact your instructor for information about accessing the Data Files. The following steps open the Support_WD_7_MalwareInfectionSymptomsDiagram.docx file.

1. Navigate to the location of the Data Files on your hard drive, OneDrive, or other storage location.
2. Open the file named Support_WD_7_MalwareInfectionSymptomsDiagram.docx in the Data Files.
3. Click the graphic to select it and display the SmartArt Design and Format tabs (Figure 7–63).

Q&A Is the *Tech Tips* Newsletter file still open?
Yes. Leave it open because you will copy the modified diagram to the second page of the newsletter.

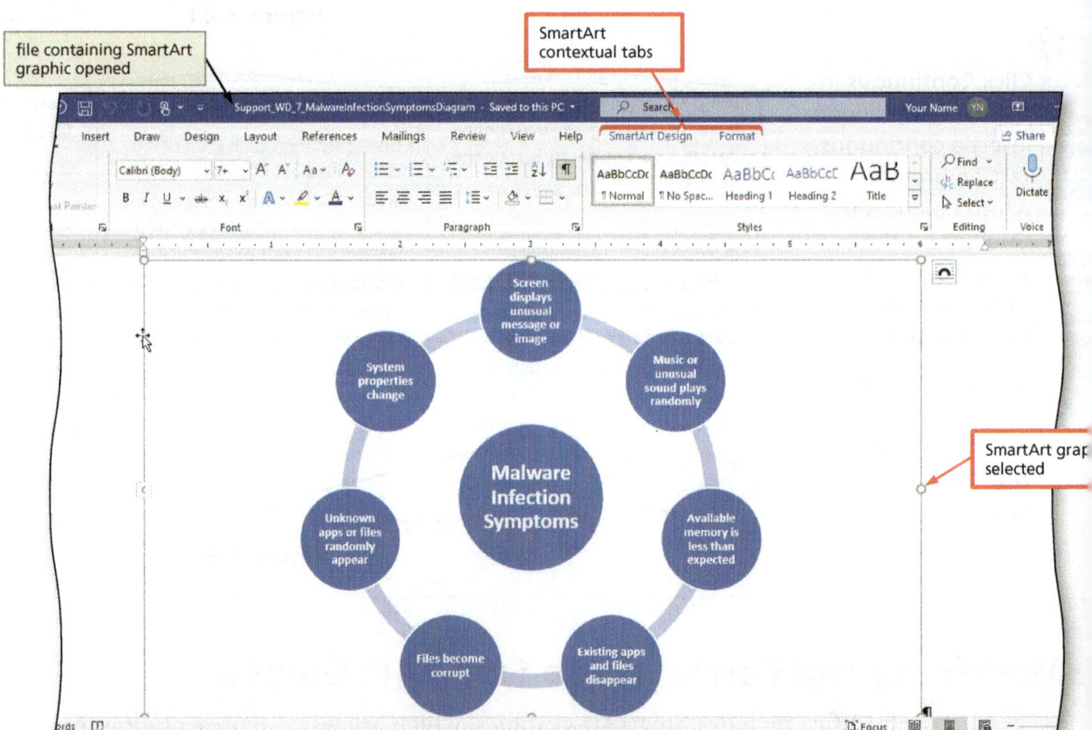

Figure 7–63

To Change the Layout of a SmartArt Graphic

The following step changes the layout of an existing SmartArt graphic. **Why?** The SmartArt graphic currently uses the Radial Cycle layout, and this newsletter uses the Basic Radial layout.

1

- If necessary, display the SmartArt Design tab.
- Scroll through the layouts in the Layouts gallery until Basic Radial appears, if necessary, and then click Basic Radial to change the layout of the SmartArt graphic (Figure 7–64).

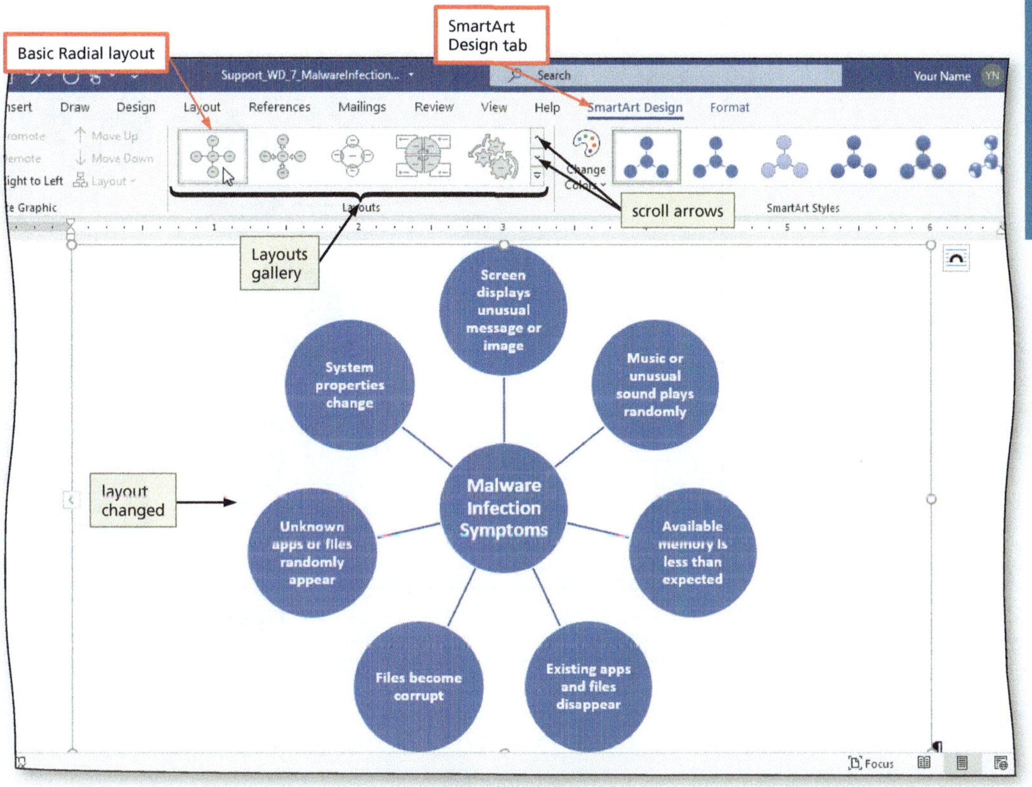

Figure 7–64

Other Ways

1. Right-click the selected graphic, click Layout button on Mini toolbar and select desired layout, or click Change Layout on shortcut menu, select desired layout, click OK

To Add a Shape to a SmartArt Graphic

The current SmartArt graphic has seven perimeter shapes. This newsletter has an eighth shape. The following step adds a shape to a SmartArt graphic.

1 With the diagram selected, click the Add Shape button (SmartArt Design tab | Create Graphic group) to add a shape to the SmartArt graphic (Figure 7–65).

Q&A

Why did my screen display a menu instead of adding a shape?
You clicked the Add Shape arrow instead of the Add Shape button. Clicking the Add Shape button adds the shape automatically; clicking the Add Shape arrow displays a menu allowing you to specify the location of the shape.

How do I delete a shape?
Select the shape by clicking it and then press DELETE, or right-click the shape and then click Cut on the Mini toolbar or shortcut menu.

How do I decrease the size of a SmartArt shape?
You drag the sizing handles or enter the desired value in the Height box (Format tab | Size group). You also can select the shape and then click the Smaller button (Format tab | Shapes group) to decrease the size of the selected shape. (Similarly, you can select the Larger button to increase the size of the selected shape.)

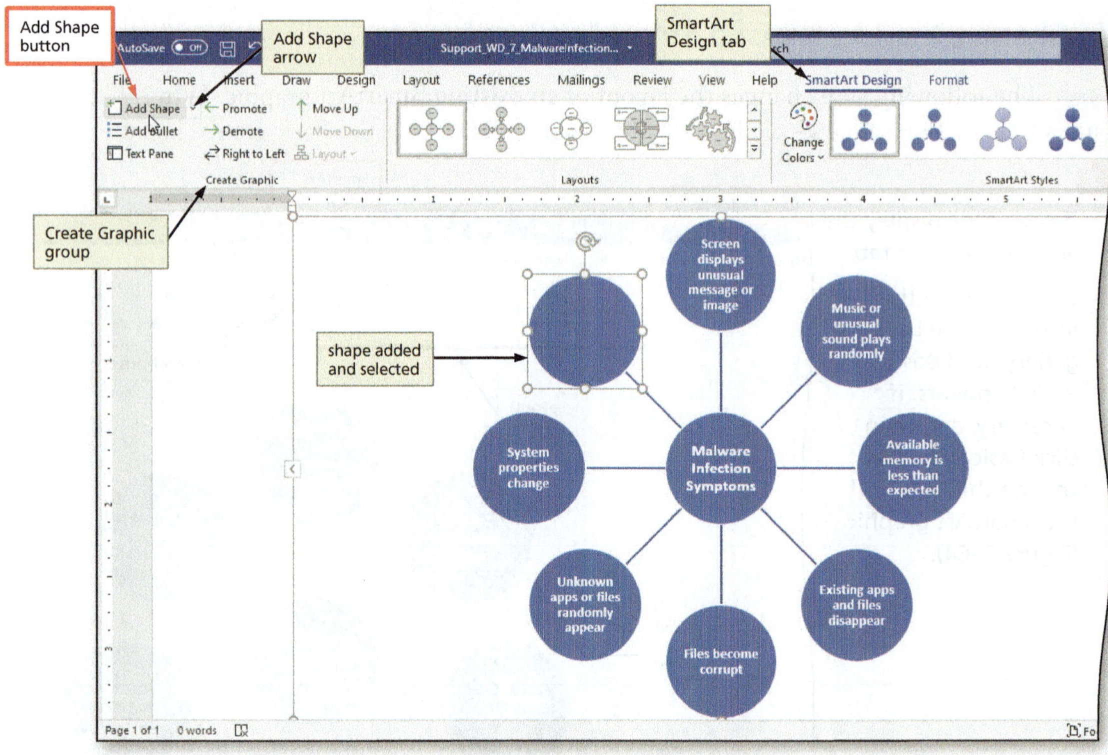

Figure 7–65

To Use the Text Pane to Add Text to a SmartArt Graphic

One way to add text to a SmartArt graphic is to add it directly to the shapes in a SmartArt graphic. In this project, however, you add text to a SmartArt graphic by entering the text through the Text Pane. **Why?** Some users prefer to enter text in the Text Pane instead of in the shape. The following steps use the Text Pane to add text to a shape.

1

- Click the Text Pane control, which is on the left side of the SmartArt graphic, to open the Text Pane to the left of the SmartArt graphic.

2

- In the Text Pane, if necessary, position the insertion point to the right of the bullet that has no text to its right.
- Type **`Apps or files do not work properly`** as the text for the shape (Figure 7–66).

3

- Click the Close button in the Text Pane to close the Text Pane.

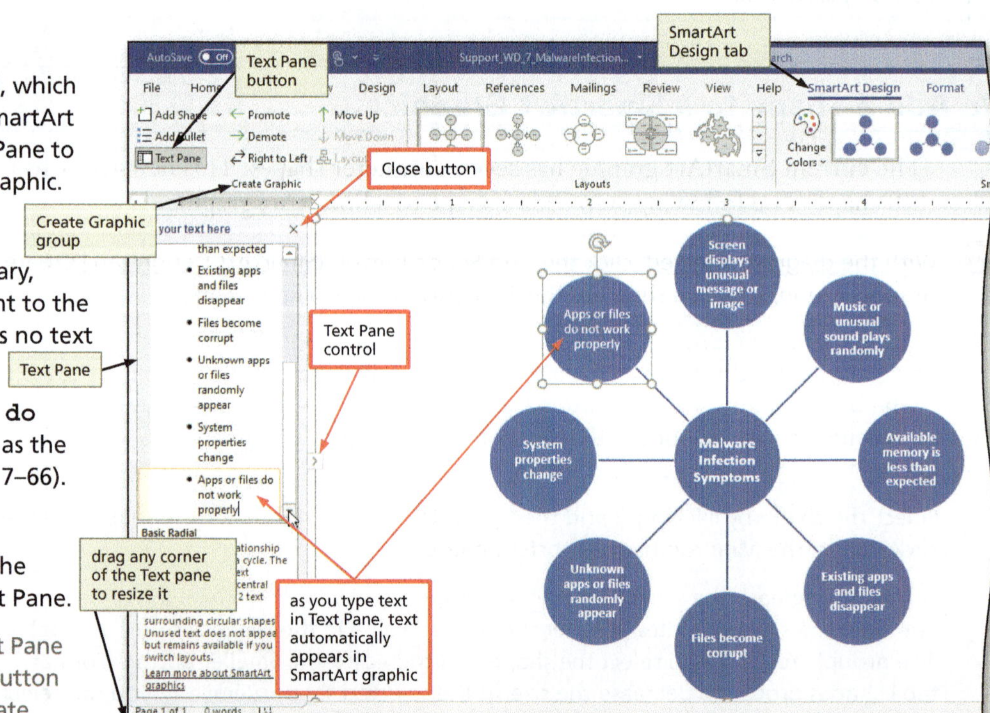

Figure 7–66

Q&A Can I instead close the Text Pane by clicking the Text Pane button (SmartArt Design tab | Create Graphic group)?
Yes.

Other Ways

1. Click Text Pane button (SmartArt Design tab | Create Graphic group)

To Format SmartArt Graphic Text

To format text in an entire SmartArt graphic, select the graphic and then apply the format. The following steps bold the text in the SmartArt graphic.

1. If necessary, click the shape just added to select it.
2. Display the Home tab. Click the Bold button (Home tab | Font group) to bold the text in the SmartArt graphic (shown in Figure 7–67).
3. Save the file containing the SmartArt graphic with a new file name on your hard drive, OneDrive, or other storage location using SC_WD_7_MalwareInfectionSymptomsDiagramModified as the file name.

BTW

Demoting Text Pane Text

Instead of pressing TAB in the Text Pane, you could click the Demote button (SmartArt Design tab | Create Graphic group) to increase (or move to the right) the indent for a bulleted item. You also can click the Promote button (SmartArt Design tab | Create Graphic group) to decrease (or move to the left) the indent for a bulleted item.

To Change a SmartArt Shape

If you wanted to change a SmartArt shape, you would perform the following steps.

1. Right-click the shape, point to Change Shape on the shortcut menu, and then select the desired shape in the Change Shape gallery.

or

1. Select the shape.
2. Click the Change Shape button (Format tab | Shapes group) and then select the desired shape in the Change Shape gallery.

To Add a Picture to a SmartArt Shape

If you wanted to add a picture to a SmartArt shape, you would perform the following steps.

1. Select the shape.
2. Click the Shape Fill arrow (Format tab | Shapes group) and then click Picture in the Shape Fill gallery to display the Insert Pictures dialog box.
3. Click 'From a File' to locate a picture on your storage media or click Online Pictures to search for a picture online. After locating the desired picture, click the Insert button in the appropriate dialog box to add the selected picture to the selected shape.

Copying and Pasting

The next step is to copy the SmartArt graphic from this document window and then paste it in the newsletter. To copy from one document and paste into another, you can use the Office Clipboard. Through the Office Clipboard, you can copy multiple items from any Office document and then paste them into the same or another Office document by following these general guidelines:

1. Items are copied from a **source document**. If the source document is not the active document, display it in the document window.
2. Open the Office Clipboard pane and then copy items from the source document to the Office Clipboard.

3. Items are copied to a **destination document**. If the destination document is not the active document, display the destination document in the document window.
4. Paste items from the Office Clipboard to the destination document.

To Copy a SmartArt Graphic Using the Office Clipboard

The following step copies the SmartArt graphic to the Office Clipboard. **Why?** Sometimes you want to copy multiple items to the Office Clipboard through the Clipboard pane and then paste them later.

1

- Click the Clipboard Dialog Box Launcher (Home tab | Clipboard group) to open the Clipboard pane.
- If the Office Clipboard in the Clipboard pane is not empty, click the Clear All button in the Clipboard pane.
- Select the SmartArt graphic in the document window and then click the Copy button (Home tab | Clipboard group) to copy the selected text to the Clipboard (Figure 7–67).

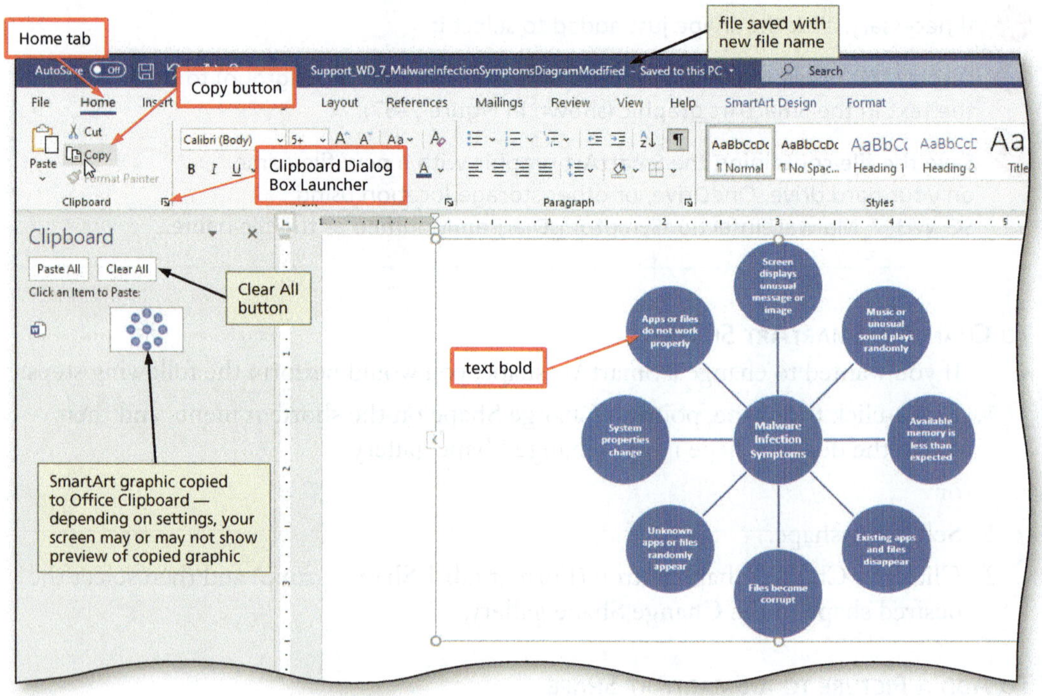

Figure 7–67

Other Ways

1. With Clipboard pane open, right-click selected item, click Copy on shortcut menu
2. With Clipboard pane open and item to copy selected, press CTRL+C

To Switch from One Open Document Window to Another

The following steps switch from the open SC_WD_7_MalwareInfectionSymptomsDiagramModified.docx document (the source document) to the open SC_WD_7_TechTipsNewsletter.docx document (the destination document). **Why?** You want to paste the copied diagram into the newsletter document.

1

- Point to the Word app button on the taskbar to display a Live Preview of the open documents or window titles of the open documents, depending on your computer's configuration (Figure 7–68).

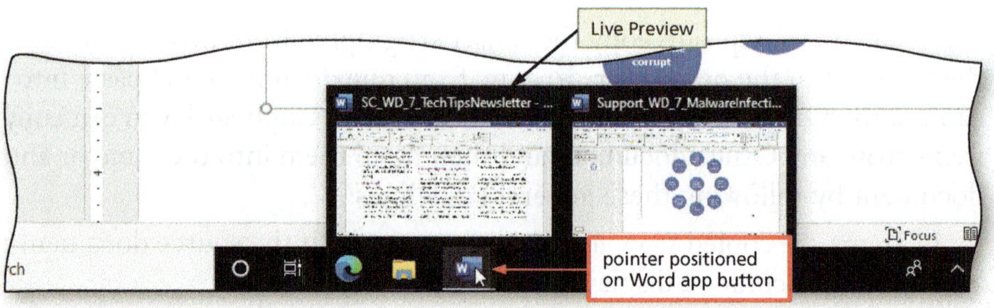

Figure 7–68

2

- Click the Live Preview of SC_WD_7_TechTipsNewsletter.docx on the Windows taskbar to display the selected document in the document window (shown in Figure 7–69).

Other Ways

1. Click Switch Windows button (View tab | Window group), click document name
2. Press ALT+TAB

To Paste from the Office Clipboard

The following steps paste from the Office Clipboard. **Why?** You want to paste the copied SmartArt graphic into the destination document, in this case, the newsletter document.

1

- Position the insertion point at the end of the Smartphones paragraph in the second column on the second page of the newsletter.
- If the Clipboard pane is not open on the screen, display the Home tab and then click the Clipboard Dialog Box Launcher (Home tab | Clipboard group) to open the Clipboard pane.
- Click the SmartArt graphic entry in the Office Clipboard to paste it in the document at the location of the insertion point (Figure 7–69).

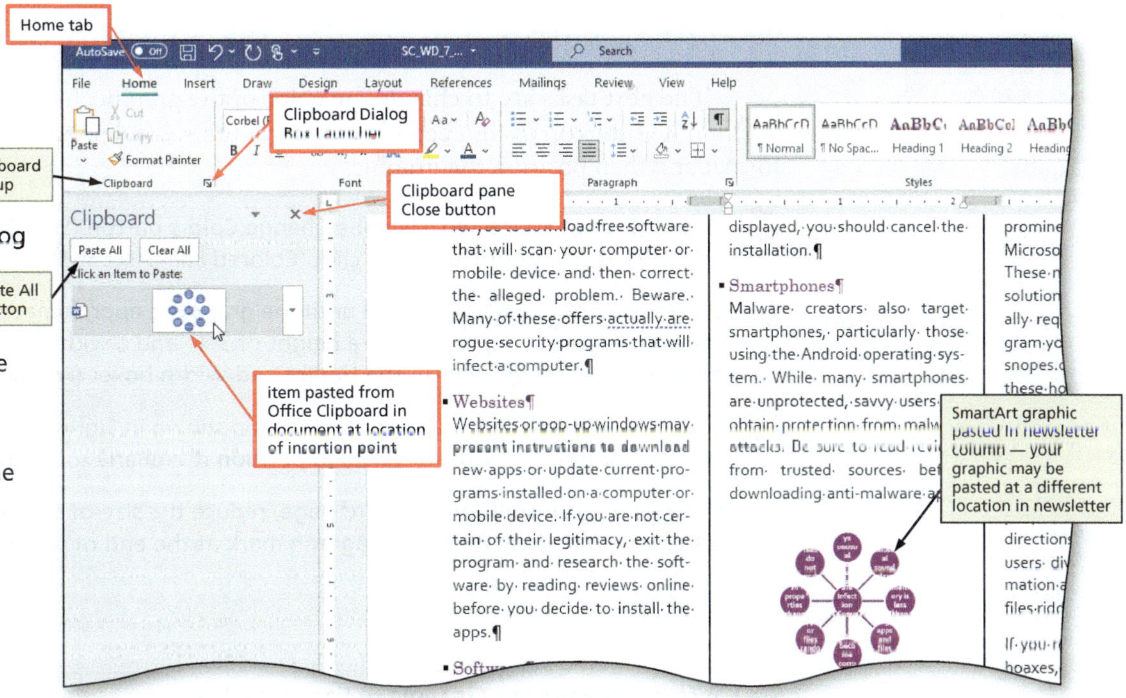

Figure 7–69

Q&A

What if my pasted graphic is in a different location?
The location of your graphic may differ. You will move the graphic in the next steps.

Does the destination document have to be a different document?
No. The source and destination documents can be the same document.

What is the function of the Paste All button?
If you have multiple items on the Office Clipboard, it pastes all items in a row, without any characters between them, at the location of the insertion point or selection.

2

- Click the Close button in the Clipboard pane.

Other Ways

1. With Clipboard pane open, right-click selected item, click Paste on shortcut menu
2. With Clipboard pane open, press CTRL+V

BTW
Clipboard Pane and Icon
You can control when the Clipboard pane opens on the Word screen and the Office Clipboard icon appears in the notification area on the taskbar. To do this, first open the Clipboard pane by clicking the Clipboard Dialog Box Launcher on the Home tab. Next, click the Options button at the bottom of the Clipboard pane and then click the desired option on the menu. For example, if you want to be able to open the Clipboard pane by clicking the Office Clipboard icon on the Windows taskbar, click 'Show Office Clipboard Icon on Taskbar' on the Options menu.

To Format a Graphic as Floating

The text in the newsletter should wrap tightly around the graphic; that is, the text should conform to the graphic's shape. Thus, the next step is to change the graphic from inline to floating with a wrapping style of tight. The following steps format the graphic as floating with tight wrapping.

1. Click the SmartArt graphic to select it.
2. With the SmartArt graphic selected, click the Layout Options button that is attached to the graphic to display the Layout Options gallery.
3. Click Tight in the Layout Options gallery to change the graphic from inline to floating with tight wrapping.
4. Close the Layout Options gallery.

To Format, Resize, and Position the SmartArt Graphic

The next tasks are to change the color of the graphic, increase its size, and then position it at the top of the second column on the second page. The following steps format and then position the graphic.

1. With the graphic selected, click the Change Colors button (SmartArt Design tab | SmartArt Styles group) and then click 'Colored Fill - Accent 5'.
2. Drag the sizing handles outward until the graphic is approximately the same size as shown in Figure 7–70, which has a height of 3.4" and a width of 4.33". (Verify the dimensions of the graphic in the Height and Width boxes (Format tab | Size group)).
3. Drag the edge of the graphic to the location shown in Figure 7–70. You may have to drag the graphic a couple of times to position it similarly to the figure.
4. If the newsletter spills onto a third page, reduce the size of the SmartArt graphic. You may need to delete an extra paragraph mark at the end of the document, as well.

To Layer the SmartArt Graphic in Front of Text

In Word, you can layer objects on top of or behind other objects. If you wanted to layer the SmartArt graphic on top of all text, you would perform the following steps.

1. Click the SmartArt graphic to select it. Click the Bring Forward arrow (Format tab | Arrange group) to display the Bring Forward menu.
2. Click 'Bring in Front of Text' on the Bring Forward menu to position the selected object on top of all text.

To Edit Wrap Points in an Object

In Word, you can change how text wraps around an object, called editing wrap points. The following steps edit the wrap points in the SmartArt diagram near the middle of the second page of the newsletter. **Why?** You want to ensure that text starts on a complete line below the bottom of the graphic.

1

- If necessary, click the SmartArt graphic to select it and then click the Format tab. If necessary, display the Arrange group (Format tab). Click the Wrap Text button (Format tab | Arrange group) to display the Wrap Text menu (Figure 7–70). (If your Format tab contains a Wrap Text button, click the button.)

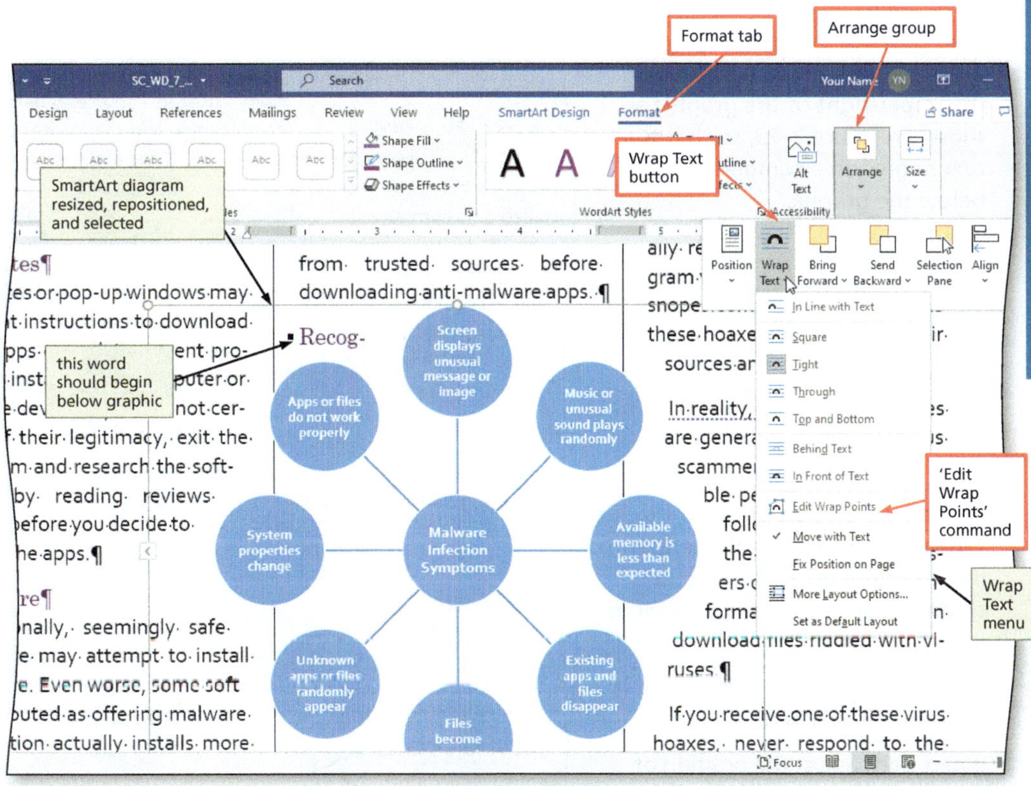

Figure 7–70

2

- Click 'Edit Wrap Points' on the Wrap Text menu to display wrap points around the graphic.
- Click the black wrap point to the upper-left of the top shape in the diagram, as shown in Figure 7–71, so that the pointer changes to a four-headed dot.

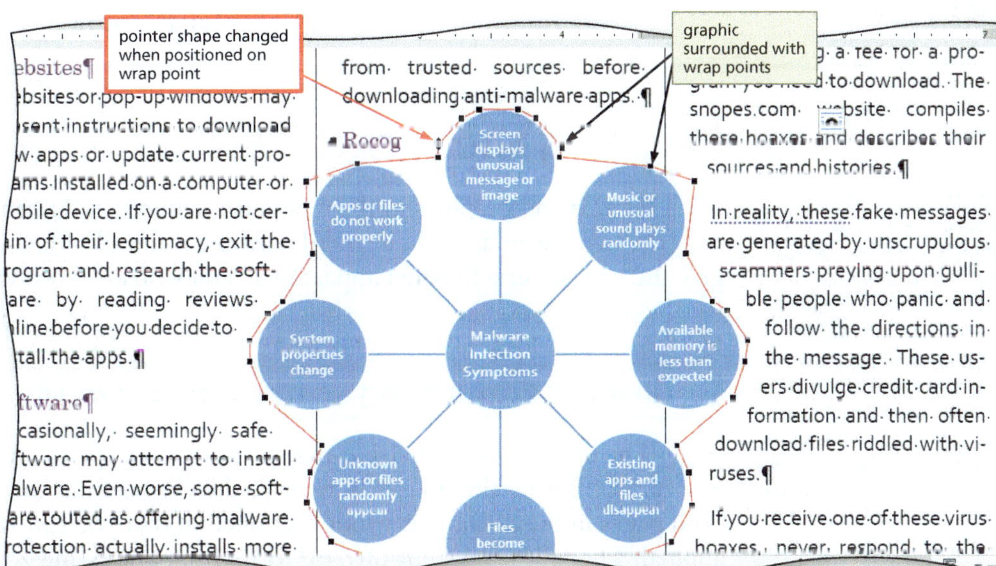

Figure 7–71

3

- Drag the black wrap point to the upper-left of the graphic as shown in Figure 7–72, so that the text (the first part of the word, Recognizing, in this case) will appear on a complete line below the shape.

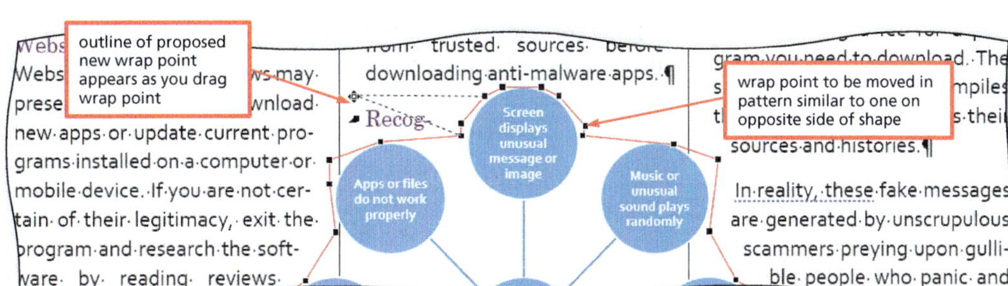

Figure 7–72

4

- Drag the black wrap point to the upper-right of the graphic as shown in Figure 7–73, so that the text begins on a complete line below the graphic.

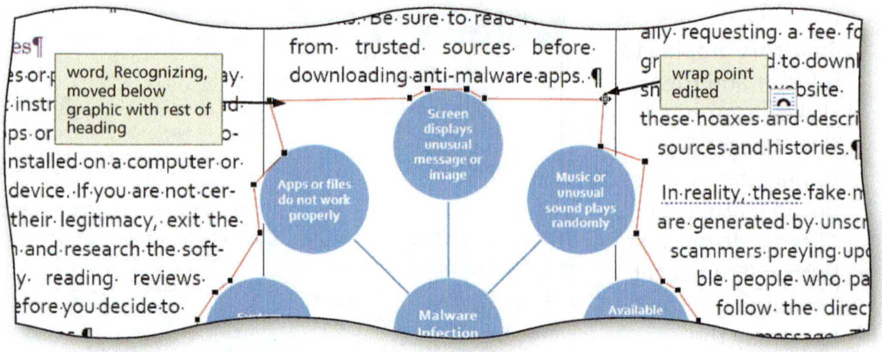

Figure 7–73

5

- Repeat the process at the bottom of the SmartArt graphic, as shown in Figure 7–74. (Note that due to printer drivers and other settings, your document may wrap differently than Figure 7–74).
- Click outside the graphic so that it no longer is selected.
- If necessary, adjust the position of the SmartArt graphic so that text wraps close to that shown in Figure 7–1 at the beginning of this module.

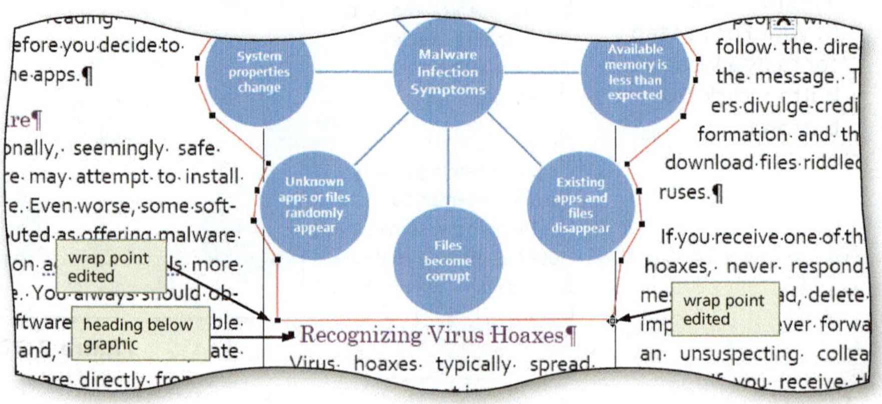

Figure 7–74

BTW
Space around Graphics
The space between a graphic and the text, which sometimes is called the run-around, should be at least 1/8" and should be the same for all graphics in a document. Adjust the run-around of a selected floating graphic by doing the following: click the Wrap Text button (Format tab | Arrange group), click 'More Layout Options' on the Wrap Text menu, click the Position tab (Layout dialog box), adjust the values in the Horizontal and Vertical boxes, and then click OK.

Finishing the Newsletter

With the text and graphics in the newsletter entered and formatted, the next step is to view the newsletter as a whole and determine if it looks finished in its current state. To give the newsletter a finished appearance, you will add a border to its edges.

To Turn Off Formatting Marks and Zoom Multiple Pages

The last step in formatting the newsletter is to place a border around its edges. You turn off formatting marks to remove the clutter from the screen, and you place both pages in the document window at once so that you can see all the page borders applied. The following steps turn off formatting marks and zoom multiple pages.

1. If necessary, display the Home tab and then turn off formatting marks.
2. Display the View tab and then display multiple pages on the screen. You may need to increase the zoom slightly so that the borders in the nameplates appear.

To Add an Art Page Border

The following steps add a page border around the pages of the newsletter. **Why?** This newsletter has a purple art border around the perimeter of each page.

1

- Display the Design tab.
- Click the Page Borders button (Design tab | Page Background group) to display the Borders and Shading dialog box. If necessary, click the Page Border tab.

Q&A What if I cannot select the Page Borders button because it is dimmed?
Click somewhere in the newsletter to make the newsletter the active document and then repeat Step 1.

2

- Click Box in the Setting area (Borders and Shading dialog box) to specify a border on all four sides of the page.
- Click the Art arrow, scroll to and then click the art border shown in Figure 7–75.
- Click the Color arrow and then click 'Purple, Accent 4, Darker 50%' (bottom row, eighth column) on the palette (Figure 7–75).

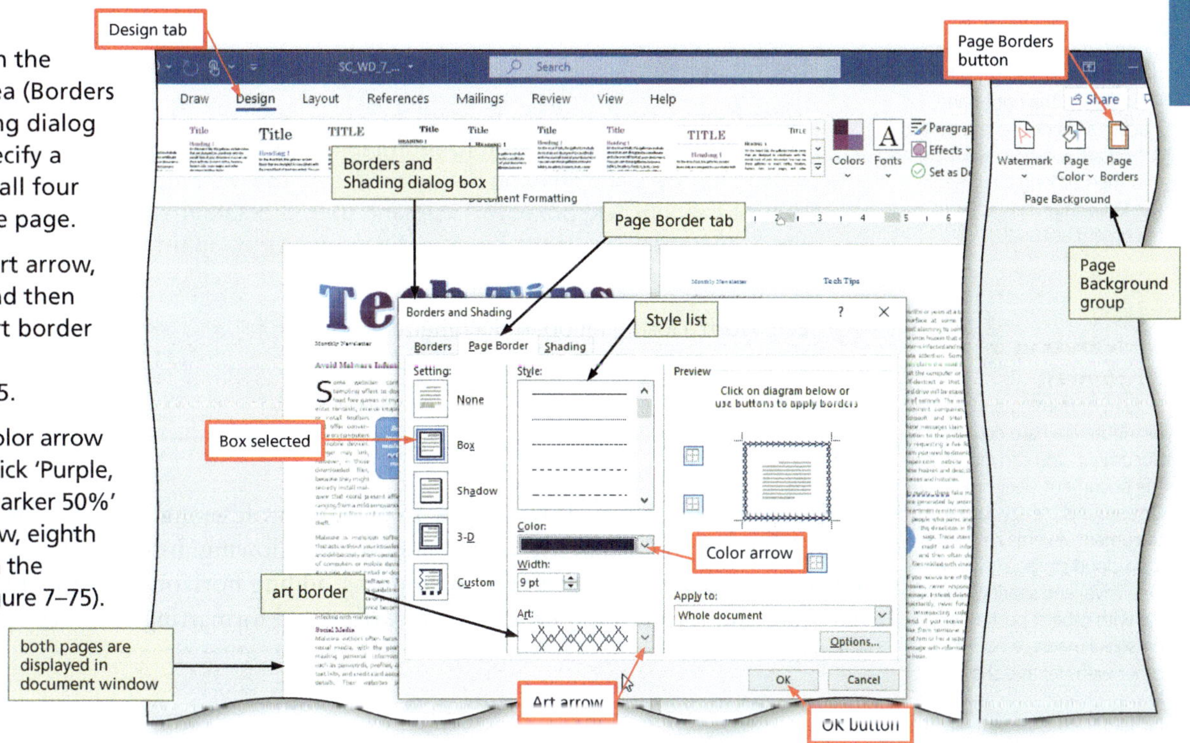

Figure 7–75

3

- Click OK to place the defined border on each page of the newsletter (Figure 7–76). (Note that depending on resolution, zoom, and other settings, the border in the document window may look different from how it appears on the printed document.)

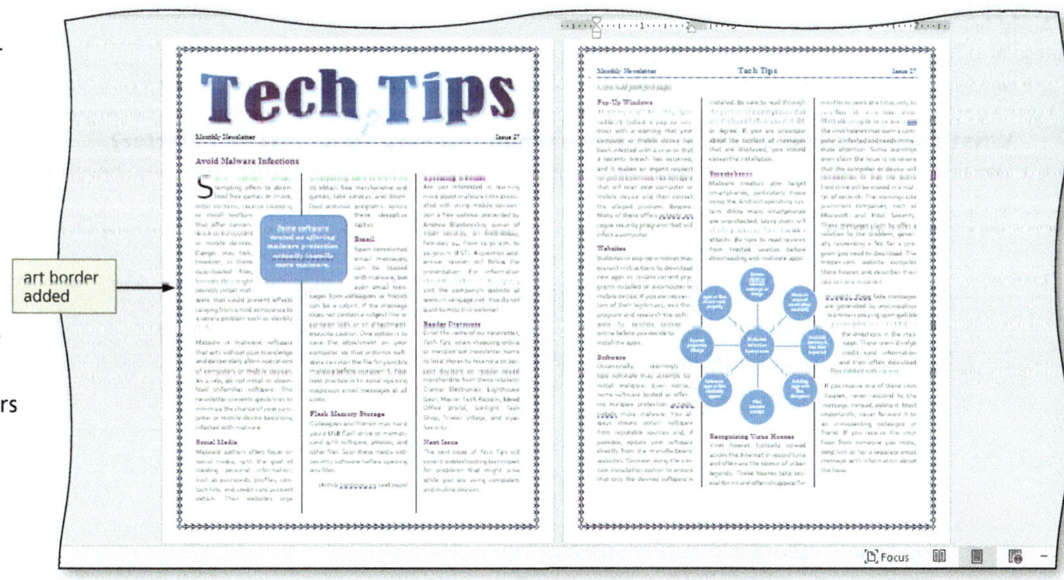

Figure 7–76

To Save and Print the Newsletter and then Exit Word

The newsletter now is complete. You should save the document, print it, and then exit Word.

1. **sam** Save the newsletter again on the same storage location with the same file name.
2. If desired, print the newsletter (shown in Figure 7–1 at the beginning of this module).

Q&A What if an error message appears about margins?
Depending on the printer you are using, you may need to set the margins differently for this project.

What if one or more of the borders do not print?
Click the Page Borders button (Design tab | Page Background group), click the Options button (Borders and Shading dialog box), click the Measure from arrow and click Text, change the four text boxes to 15 pt, and then click OK in each dialog box. Try printing the document again. If the borders still do not print, adjust the text boxes in the dialog box to a number smaller than 15 pt.

3. Exit Word, closing all open documents.

BTW
Conserving Ink and Toner
If you want to conserve ink or toner, you can instruct Word to print draft quality documents by clicking File on the ribbon to open Backstage view, clicking Options in Backstage view to display the Word Options dialog box, clicking Advanced in the left pane (Word Options dialog box), scrolling to the Print area in the right pane, placing a check mark in the 'Use draft quality' check box, and then clicking OK. Then, use Backstage view to print the document as usual.

BTW
Distributing a Document
Instead of printing and distributing a hard copy of a document, you can distribute the document electronically. Options include sending the document via email; posting it on cloud storage (such as OneDrive) and sharing the file with others; posting it on social media, a blog, or other website; and sharing a link associated with an online location of the document. You also can create and share a PDF or XPS image of the document, so that users can view the file in Adobe Reader or XPS Viewer instead of in Word.

Summary

In this module, you have learned how to create a professional-looking newsletter using Word's desktop publishing features, such as the following: inserting and modifying WordArt, organizing a document in columns, adding horizontal and vertical rules, inserting and formatting pull-quotes, inserting and formatting graphics, and adding an art page border.

Consider This: Plan Ahead

What decisions will you need to make when creating your next newsletter?

Use these guidelines as you complete the assignments in this module and create your own newsletters outside of this class.

1. Create the nameplate.
    a) Determine the location of the nameplate.
    b) Determine content, formats, and arrangement of text and graphics.
    c) If appropriate, use ruling lines.
2. Determine content for the body of the newsletter.
    a) Write the body copy.
    b) Organize the body copy in columns.
    c) Format the body copy and subheads.
    d) Incorporate color.
    e) Divide sections with vertical rules.
    f) Enhance with visuals.
3. Bind and distribute the newsletter.
    a) Determine if newsletters should be printed, posted on bulletin boards, sent as an email message, or posted on websites.
    b) For multipage newsletters that will be printed, determine the appropriate method of binding the pages.
    c) For online newsletters, select a format that most users will be able to open.

Apply Your Knowledge

Reinforce the skills and apply the concepts you learned in this module.

Working with Desktop Publishing Elements of a Newsletter

Note: To complete this assignment, you will be required to use the Data Files. Please contact your instructor for information about accessing the Data Files.

Instructions: Start Word. Open the document, SC_WD_7-1.docx, which is located in the Data Files. The document contains a newsletter, written by the public relations coordinator at Caruso Bank, that will be sent via email to customers and also placed on lobby tables at the bank. You are to modify the newsletter so that it appears as shown in Figure 7–77.

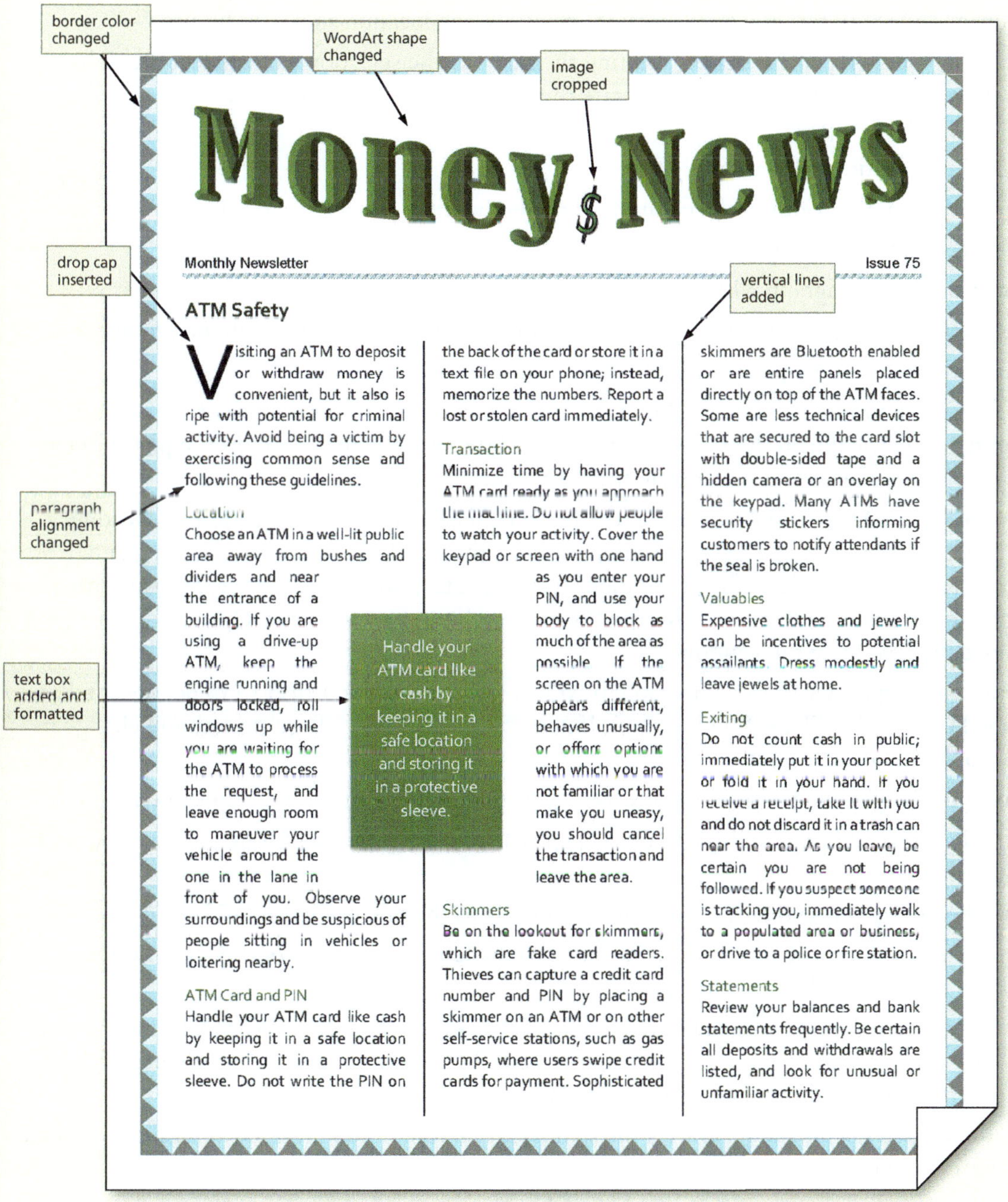

Figure 7–77

Continued >

Apply Your Knowledge *continued*

Perform the following tasks:

1. Click File on the ribbon and then click Save As and save the document using the new file name, SC_WD_7_MoneyNews.
2. Resize the WordArt shape to a height and width of 1.44" and 7", respectively. (Hint: Select the WordArt shape and then use the Shape Format tab.)
3. Change the text fill color of the WordArt text to Green, Accent 4. (Hint: Select the WordArt text and then use the Text Fill arrow (Shape Format tab | WordArt Styles group).)
4. Change the WordArt shape to Chevron: Down using the Transform Effect.
5. Crop the image of the dollar signs so that only the rightmost dollar sign shows. Change the height and width of the cropped image to 0.6" and 0.19", respectively. Change the wrapping of the image to behind text and then move the image to the location shown in Figure 7–77.
6. Open the Selection pane. Practice selecting the items in the selection pane. Select the dollar sign image using the Selection pane. Rotate the image clockwise as shown in Figure 7–77. Close the Selection pane.
7. Turn off automatic hyphenation.
8. Change the column width of the columns in the body of the newsletter to 2.1".
9. Add a vertical line between each column.
10. Format the first paragraph with a drop cap.
11. Change the alignment of the paragraph containing the drop cap from left-aligned to justified.
12. Change the color of the page border to 'Light Turquoise, Background 2'.
13. Insert a Whisp Quote preformatted text box into the newsletter near the top of the second column. Select the line in the lower-right corner of the text box that contains the placeholder text for citing a source and then delete the entire line.
14. Split the screen. Display the text box in the top screen and the ATM Card and PIN heading in the bottom screen. Copy the first sentence below the ATM Card and PIN heading and then paste the sentence into the placeholder text in the text box in the top screen using the destination theme. (Hint: Use the Merge Formatting button on the Paste Options menu.) Remove the split from the window.
15. Change the shape style of the pull-quote (text box text) to 'Intense Effect - Green, Accent 4' (Shape Format tab | Shape Styles group). If necessary, select the pull-quote text and change its color to White, Background 1.
16. Change the height and width of the text box (pull-quote) to 2.2 and 1.43, respectively.
17. Verify that the text in the pull-quote (text box text) is 12-point Corbel (Body). Center the text in the text box.
18. Move the pull-quote so that it is positioned similarly to the one in Figure 7–77.
19. If requested by your instructor, add your name to the left of the text, Monthly Newsletter, in the issue information line.
20. If the newsletter flows to two pages, reduce the size of elements such as WordArt or pull-quote, or adjust spacing above or below paragraphs so that the newsletter fits on a single page. Make any other necessary adjustments to the newsletter.
21. Save the revised document again with the same name and then submit it in the format specified by your instructor.
22. How many sections are in this newsletter? How many columns are in each section? If you wanted to add a second page to this newsletter, what type of section break would appear at the end of the first page?

Extend Your Knowledge

Extend the skills you learned in this module and experiment with new skills. You may need to use Help to complete the assignment.

Modifying and Enhancing a Newsletter

Note: To complete this assignment, you will be required to use the Data Files. Please contact your instructor for information about accessing the Data Files.

Instructions: Start Word. Open the document, SC_WD_7-2.docx, which is located in the Data Files. The document contains a draft of a newsletter, written by a human relations associate at Freedom Insurance, that will be distributed to all company employees. You will add and format WordArt, clear tabs, insert leader characters, add and format a drop cap, adjust the hyphenation rules, modify and format a SmartArt graphic, draw and format a text box, and move the page border closer to the text.

Perform the following tasks:

1. Use Help to learn more about WordArt options, hyphenation, tabs, SmartArt graphics, and art borders.
2. Click File on the ribbon and then click Save As and save the document using the new file name, SC_WD_7_WorkplaceChatter.
3. Convert the text, Workplace Chatter, in the nameplate to WordArt using a WordArt style of your choice. Change the text wrapping of the WordArt shape to 'Top and Bottom'. Resize the WordArt to approximately 1.44" × 7".
4. Change the WordArt shape using a transform effect of your choice, a glow effect of your choice, and a shadow effect of your choice.
5. Change the color of the WordArt text outline. Change the color of the WordArt text fill.
6. Add a shape fill color to the text box surrounding the WordArt.
7. Clear the tabs in the issue information line in the nameplate. Use the Tabs dialog box to insert a right-aligned tab stop at the 7" mark. Fill the tab space with a leader character of your choice.
8. Add a border of your choice below the issue information line.
9. Select the chomping head picture to the right of the News and Events heading. What object is attached to the picture's anchor? Unlock the anchor so that the anchor moves with the floating object. (Hint: Click the Layout Options button attached to the picture and then click the See more link in the Layout Options gallery.)
10. Move the chomping head picture up to the right of the News and Events heading by dragging it to an approximate location. Specify an absolute position of 1.75" to the right of the column and 2.5" below the top margin for the floating picture. (Hint: Click the Layout Options button and then click the See more link in the Layout Options gallery.)
11. Add a drop cap to the first paragraph in the body of the newsletter. Change the number of lines to drop from three to four. Change the distance from the text to 0.1".
12. Apply automatic hyphenation to the document. Change the hyphenation rules to limit consecutive hyphens to two.
13. Save the document again using the same file name. Keep the document open for the next step.
14. Open the document, SC_WD_7-3.docx, which is located in the Data Files. This document contains a SmartArt graphic.
15. Click File on the ribbon and then click Save As and save the document using the new file name, SC_WD_7_UpcomingActivitiesDiagram.

Continued >

Extend Your Knowledge *continued*

16. Decrease the size of the May shape so it is the same size as the April shape. (Hint: Use the Smaller button (Format tab | Shapes group).)
17. Change the layout of the SmartArt graphic to Hierarchy List.
18. Open the SmartArt Text Pane. Use the Text Pane to add the text, First Quarter Reports Due, to the empty shape in the SmartArt graphic. Close the SmartArt Text Pane.
19. Add a shape below the New Technology Training shape. Add the text, Branch Performance Evaluations, in the added shape.
20. Add the picture called Support_WD_7_RainDropsPattern.png to the April shape, and add the picture called Support_WD_7_FlowersPattern.png to the May shape (Figure 7–78). These pictures are located in the Data Files. (Hint: Use the Shape Fill arrow (Format tab | Shape Styles group).) Change the font color of the text, April and May, to a color of your choice. If necessary, bold the text, April and May.

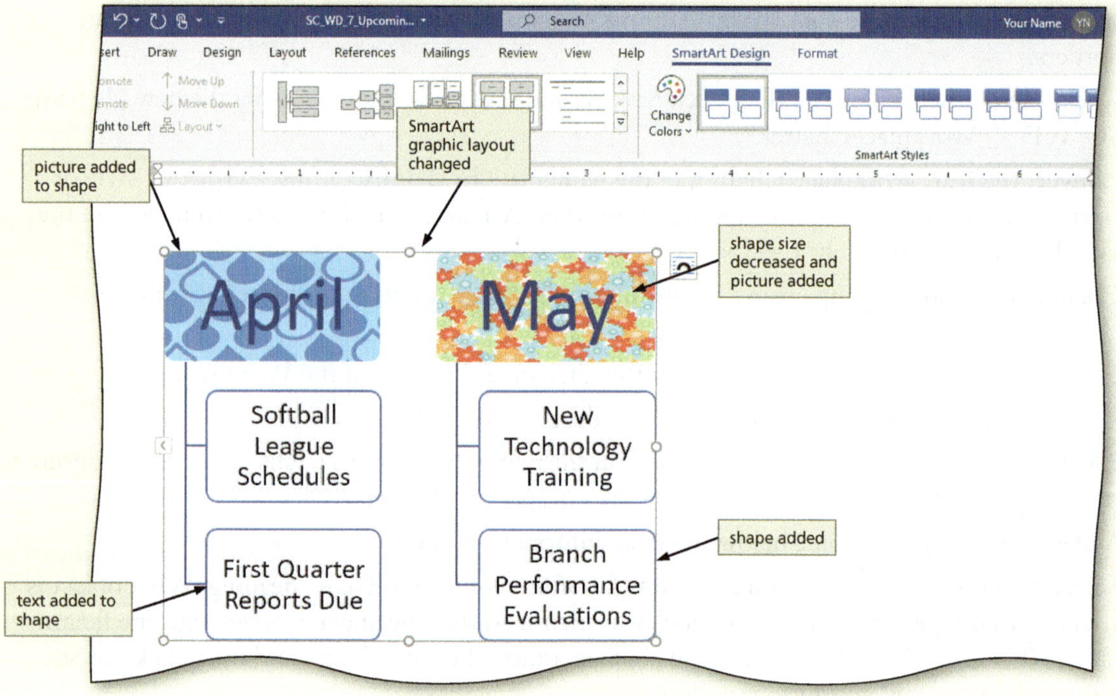

Figure 7–78

21. Change the shape of the April and May shapes to a shape of your choice. (Hint: Use the Change Shape button (Format tab | Shape Styles group).)
22. Save the document again using the same file name. Keep the document open for the next step.
23. Open the Clipboard pane. Clear all items from the Clipboard pane. Copy the SmartArt graphic to the Clipboard. Switch document windows so that the SC_WD_7_WorkplaceChatter.docx is displayed on the screen. Paste the SmartArt graphic from the Clipboard pane to the third column in the newsletter below the Upcoming Activities heading.
24. Change the text wrapping of the SmartArt graphic in the third column of the newsletter to 'Top and Bottom'. If necessary, change the height and width of the SmartArt graphic in the third column of the newsletter to 1.9" and 2", respectively. Change the layering of the SmartArt graphic so that it is in front of text.

25. Change the style of the SmartArt graphic in the newsletter to a style of your choice. Change the color of the SmartArt graphic in the newsletter to a color of your choice.
26. Draw a text box in the newsletter. Enter the text, New employees have joined our team, and spring sports are gearing up, in the text box. Change the wrapping of the text box to Square. Format and position the text box appropriately. If requested by your instructor, change the default text box setting to the settings of this new text box.
27. If the newsletter flows to two pages, reduce the size of elements, such as WordArt or the text box or the graphic, or adjust spacing above or below paragraphs so that the newsletter fits on a single page. Make any other necessary adjustments to the newsletter.
28. Add an art page border of your choice to the newsletter. Change the page border so that the border is closer to the text.
29. If requested by your instructor, add your name to the left of the text, Monthly Newsletter, in the issue information line.
30. Save the newsletter with the same file name.
31. Copy the text box to the Clipboard. Create a new blank document. Practice using the Paste All button in the Clipboard to paste all its contents to the new document. Close the document without saving it. Close the Clipboard pane.
32. Arrange both Word documents (the newsletter and diagram) on the screen. Scroll through both open windows. Close the document containing the diagram.
33. Submit the revised newsletter and diagram files in the format specified by your instructor.
34. Answer the question posed in #9. When you use hyphenation to divide words at the end of a line, what are the accepted guidelines for dividing the words? (Hint: Use a search engine to search the text, end of line hyphenation.)

Expand Your World

Create a solution that uses cloud or web technologies by learning and investigating on your own from general guidance.

Inserting Online Videos

Note: To complete this assignment, you will be required to use the Data Files. Please contact your instructor for information about accessing the Data Files.

Instructions: Start Word. Open the document, SC_WD_7-4.docx, which is located in the Data Files. The document contains a SmartArt diagram outlining the steps involved when a customer purchases from an online retailer. This diagram, which was designed by a marketing associate at the online retailer Kramer's, eventually will be incorporated in a newsletter for distribution to all online customers. You will add online videos above each step in the process for customers to view as they read the newsletter.

Perform the following tasks:

1. Use Help to learn about inserting online videos, noting their terms of use and privacy policies.
2. Click File on the ribbon and then click Save As and save the document using the new file name, SC_WD_7_CustomerPurchasingDiagram.
3. Change the position of the SmartArt diagram to 'Position in Top Center with Square Text Wrapping'. (Hint: Use the Format tab.)

Continued >

Expand Your World *continued*

4. Start a browser and go to one of the video websites that Word supports: vimeo.com, youtube.com, or slideshare.net.
5. In the search box on the video website, type **`how to tell if a website is secure`** and then press ENTER to display a list of videos that match your search criteria.
6. Select a video and then copy the URL of the video webpage from the Address bar of your browser.
7. In Word, display the Insert tab and then click the Online Video button (Insert tab | Media group) to display the Insert a video dialog box (Figure 7–79).

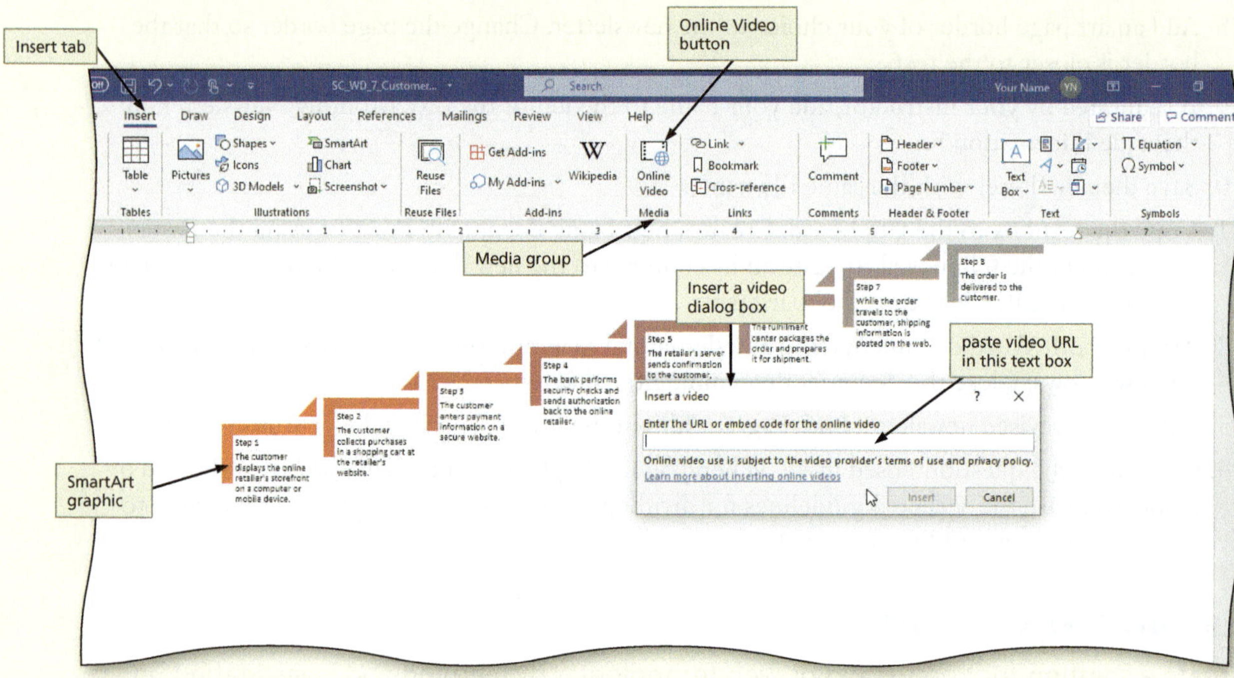

Figure 7–79

8. Paste the URL into the text box and then click Insert (Insert a video dialog box).
9. Change the wrapping of the video in the document to 'In Front of Text'. Resize the video in the document to approximately 0.4" × 0.53". Move the video in the document so that it is above Step 3 in the SmartArt diagram.
10. Repeat Steps 4 through 8 for each of the other steps in the SmartArt diagram, locating an online video appropriate to the content of the step.
11. Test each video by clicking it in the Word document to be sure it works as intended.
12. Save the document with the same file name. Export it to a PDF using the file name, SC_WD_7_CustomerPurchasingDiagram.
13. Access the SC_WD_7_CustomerPurchasingDiagram.pdf file through File Explorer. Test the videos in the PDF.
14. Submit the documents in the format specified by your instructor.
15. What options are available while you are watching a video from Word? What are some of the sources for the videos in the dialog box? Which videos did you insert in the form, and why? How do you play the videos inserted on the form?

In the Lab

Design and implement a solution using creative thinking and problem-solving skills.

Create a Newsletter for a Village Community

Note: To complete this assignment, you will be required to use the Data Files. Please contact your instructor for information about accessing the Data Files.

Problem: As the community relations coordinator for Oakwood Village, you have been assigned the task of creating a newsletter called Oakwood Bulletin, which will be distributed to all community members.

Part 1: The feature article in Issue 54 of the Oakwood Bulletin newsletter covers a community renovation project in the first two columns. The rightmost column of the newsletter contains community announcements. The text for the feature article and announcements is in the Data Files. The newsletter should contain a SmartArt graphic and a pull-quote (text box). Enhance the newsletter with a drop cap, WordArt, color, ruling lines, and a page border. Be sure to use appropriate desktop publishing elements, including a nameplate, columns of text, balanced columns, and a variety of font sizes, font colors, and shading. Use the concepts and techniques presented in this module to create and format the newsletter. While creating the newsletter, be sure to do the following:

1. Change all margins as necessary.
2. Create a nameplate that contains the newsletter title and an issue information line. Insert WordArt for the newsletter title. Format the WordArt as desired. Insert an appropriate picture or other image in the nameplate.
3. Below the nameplate, enter the title of the feature article.
4. Insert a continuous section break below the feature article title.
5. Format section 2 of the newsletter to three columns.
6. Insert the file called Support_WD_7_CommunityRenovationProjectArticle.docx in section 2 below the feature article title. (This article should span the first two columns of the newsletter.)
7. Insert a column break at the end of the feature article in the second column.
8. Insert the file called Support_WD_7_OakwoodBulletinAnnouncements.docx in the third column of the newsletter.
9. Insert a continuous section break at the end of the text in the third column to balance all columns in the newsletter.
10. Insert a text box for a pull-quote using text of your choice from the newsletter. Format and position the text box appropriately.
11. Insert a SmartArt graphic using text of your choice into the newsletter. Format and position the SmartArt graphic appropriately. Layer the SmartArt graphic in front of text, if necessary. Edit wrap points in the SmartArt graphic, if necessary.
12. Format the newsletter with a drop cap and appropriate font sizes, fonts, colors, and shading.
13. Add an appropriate page border to the newsletter.
14. Be sure to check spelling and grammar of the finished newsletter.

When you are finished with the newsletter, save it with the file name, SC_WD_7_OakwoodBulletin. Submit your assignment and answers to the Part 2 critical thinking questions in the format specified by your instructor.

Continued >

In the Lab *continued*

Part 2: You made several decisions while creating the newsletter in this assignment: how to organize and format the nameplate (location, content, formats, arrangement of text and graphics, ruling lines, etc.), how to organize and format the pull-quote (text box), how to organize and format the SmartArt graphic, and how to organize and format the body copy (columns, formats, headings and subheads, color, vertical rules, etc.). What was the rationale behind each of these decisions? When you proofread the document, what further revisions did you make and why?

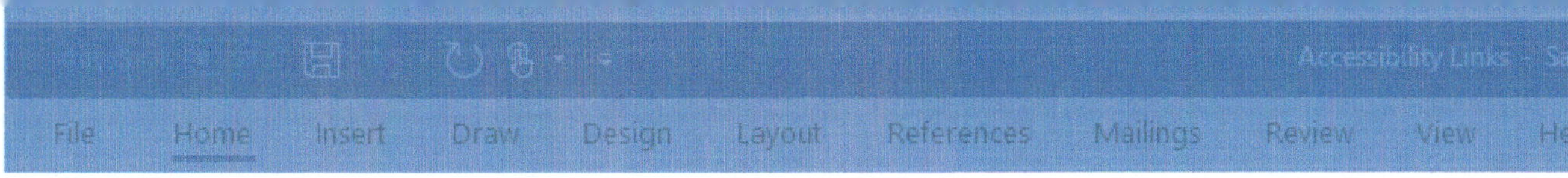

8 Using Collaboration, Integration, and Charts

Objectives

After completing this module, you will be able to:

- Track changes
- Review tracked changes
- Compare documents
- Combine documents
- Link an Excel worksheet to a Word document
- Break a link
- Create a chart in Word
- Format a Word chart
- View and scroll through side-by-side documents
- Create a new document for a blog post
- Insert a quick table
- Publish a blog post

Introduction

Word provides the capability for users to work with other users, or **collaborate**, on a document. For example, you can show edits made to a document so that others can review the edits. You also can merge edits from multiple users or compare two documents to determine the differences between them.

From Word, you can interact with other programs and incorporate the data and objects from those programs in a Word document. For example, you can link an Excel worksheet in a Word document or publish a blog post from Word. You also can use the charting features of Microsoft 365 in Word.

Project: Memo with Chart

A memo is an informal document that businesses use to correspond with others. Memos often are internal to an organization, for example, to employees or coworkers.

The project in this module uses Word to produce the memo shown in Figure 8–1. First, you open an existing document that contains the memo and the Word table. Next, you edit the document, showing the changes so that other users can review the changes. The changes appear on the screen with options that allow the author of the document to accept or reject the changes. Then, you chart the Word table using charting features available in several Microsoft 365 applications. In this module, you also learn how to link an Excel worksheet to a Word document and create a document for a blog post.

File Home Insert Draw Design Layout References Mailings Review View Hel

memo

Landmark Designs

To: Customer Service Associates

From: Shannon Popovich

Date: August 11, 2021

Subject: Available Home Designs

We have increased the number of home plans in our database by 30 percent! The table and chart below show the number of plans now available in several architectural styles, with the last column identifying the number of plans exclusive to Landmark Designs. Please familiarize yourself with all our new plans and let me know if you have any questions.

Word table

Home Plan Breakdown

Home Plan Style	Total Plans	Exclusive Plans
Colonial	1,229	98
Contemporary	3,270	214
European	3,118	323
Ranch	4,003	537
Tudor	4,326	509
Victorian	2,575	135

chart created from Word table

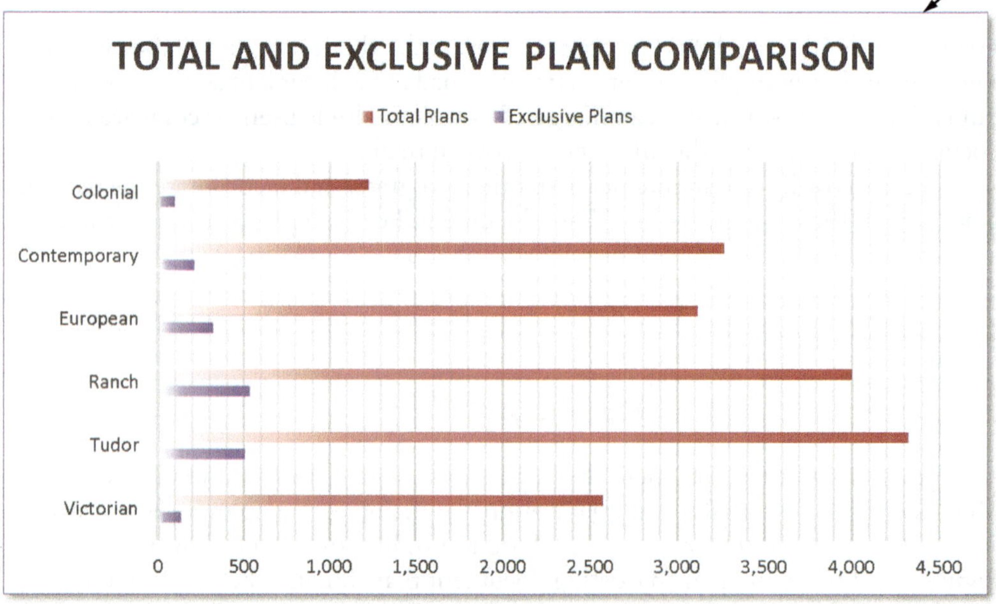

Figure 8–1

You will perform the following general tasks as you progress through this module:

1. Track changes in the memo with the table.
2. Review the tracked changes.
3. Link an Excel worksheet to a Word document.
4. Chart a Word table using Word's chart contextual tabs.
5. Create and publish a blog post.

To Start Word and Specify Settings

If you are using a computer to step through the project in this module and you want your screens to match the figures in this book, you should change your screen's resolution to 1366 × 768. The following steps start Word, display formatting marks, change the zoom to 100%, and verify ruler and Mouse mode settings.

1. Start Word and create a blank document in the Word window. If necessary, maximize the Word window.
2. If the Print Layout button on the status bar is not selected, click it so that your screen is in Print Layout view.
3. If the 'Show/Hide ¶' button (Home tab | Paragraph group) is not selected already, click it to display formatting marks on the screen (shown in Figure 8–2).
4. To display the page the same width as the document window, if necessary, click the Page Width button (View tab | Zoom group).
5. Verify that the Ruler check box (View tab | Show group) is not selected. (If it is selected, click it to remove the check mark because you do not want the rulers to appear on the screen.)
6. If you are using a mouse and you want your screens to match the figures in the book, verify that you are using Mouse mode by clicking the Touch/Mouse Mode button on the Quick Access Toolbar and then, if necessary, clicking Mouse on the menu. (If your Quick Access Toolbar does not display the Touch/Mouse Mode button, click the 'Customize Quick Access Toolbar' button on the Quick Access Toolbar and then click Touch/Mouse Mode on the menu to add the button to the Quick Access Toolbar.)

Reviewing a Document

Word provides many tools that allow users to collaborate on a document. One set of collaboration tools within Word allows you to track changes in a document and review the changes. That is, one computer user can create a document and another user(s) can make changes in the same document. Those changes then appear on the screen with options that allow the originator (author) to accept or reject the changes. With another collaboration tool, you can compare and/or merge two or more documents to determine the differences between them.

To illustrate Word's collaboration tools, this section follows these general steps:

1. Open a document to be reviewed.
2. Track changes in the document.
3. Accept and reject the tracked changes. For illustration purposes, you assume the role of originator (author) of the document in this step.
4. Compare the reviewed document to the original to view the differences.
5. Combine the original document with the reviewed document and with another reviewer's suggestions.

BTW

The Ribbon and Screen Resolution

Word may change how the groups and buttons within the groups appear on the ribbon, depending on the screen resolution of your computer. Thus, your ribbon may look different from the ones in this book if you are using a screen resolution other than 1366 × 768.

To Open a Document and Save It with a New File Name

Assume your coworker has created a draft of a memo and is sending it to you for review. The file, called SC_WD_8-1.docx, is located in the Data Files. Please contact your instructor for information about accessing the Data Files. To preserve the original memo, you save the open document with a new file name. The following steps save an open document with a new file name.

If your instructor wants you to submit your work as a SAM Project for automatic grading, you must download the Data Files from the assignment launch page.

1. Navigate to the location of the Data Files on your hard drive, OneDrive, or other storage location.
2. sam Open the file SC_WD_8-1.docx.
3. Navigate to the desired save location on your hard drive, OneDrive, or other storage location.
4. Save the file just opened on your hard drive, OneDrive, or other storage location using SC_WD_8_LandmarkDesignsMemo_withTrackedChanges as the file name (Figure 8–2).
5. To display the page the same width as the document window, click the Page Width button (View tab | Zoom group).

BTW

Document Inspector

If you wanted to ensure that all revisions were removed from a document, you could use the document inspector. Open Backstage view, display the Info screen, click the 'Check for Issues' button, and then click Inspect Document. Place a check mark in the 'Comments, Revisions, and Versions' check box and then click the Inspect button (Document Inspector dialog box). If any revisions are located, click the Remove All button.

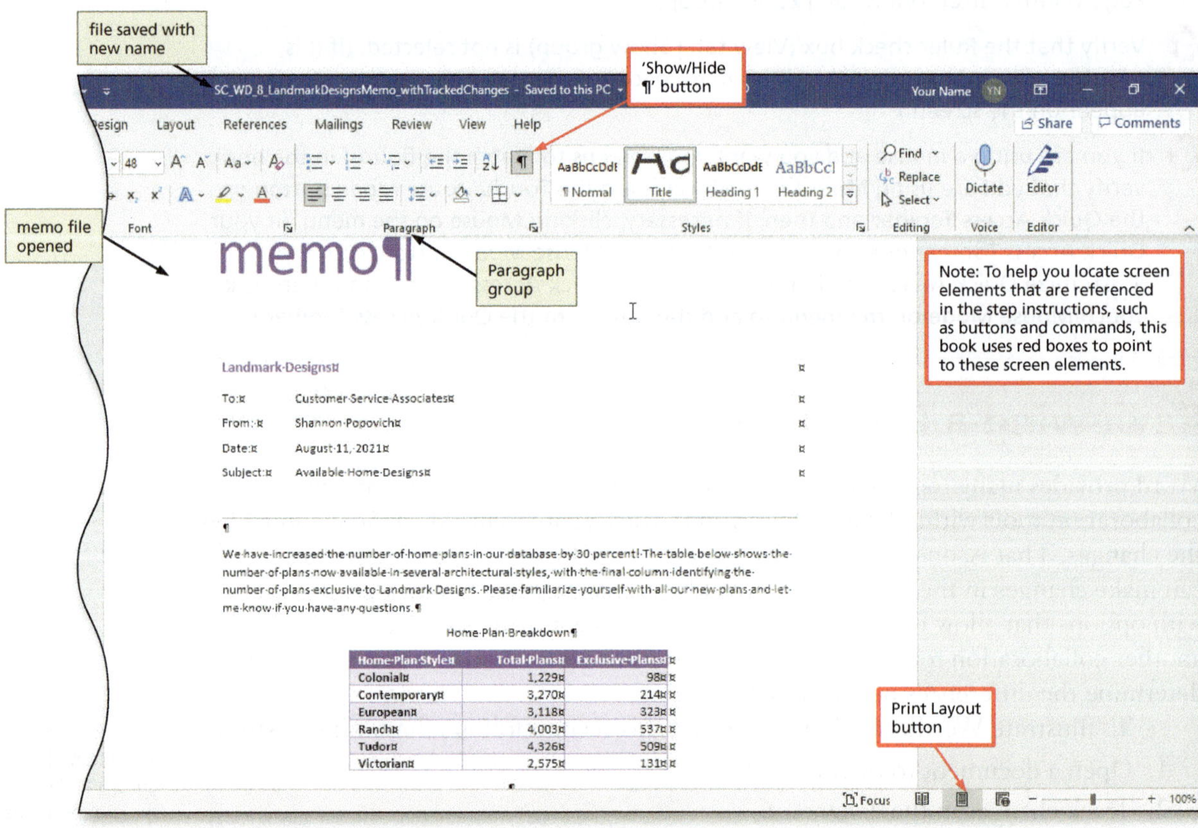

Figure 8–2

To Customize the Status Bar

You can customize the items that appear on the status bar. The status bar presents information about a document, the progress of current tasks, the status of certain commands and keys, and controls for viewing. Some indicators and buttons appear and disappear as you type text or perform certain commands. Others remain on the status bar at all times.

The following steps customize the status bar to show the Track Changes indicator. **Why?** The Track Changes indicator does not appear by default on the status bar.

1

- If the status bar does not show a desired item (in this case, the Track Changes indicator), right-click anywhere on the status bar to display the Customize Status Bar menu.

2

- Click the item on the Customize Status Bar menu that you want to show (in this case, Track Changes) to place a check mark beside the item, which also immediately may show as an indicator on the status bar (Figure 8–3).

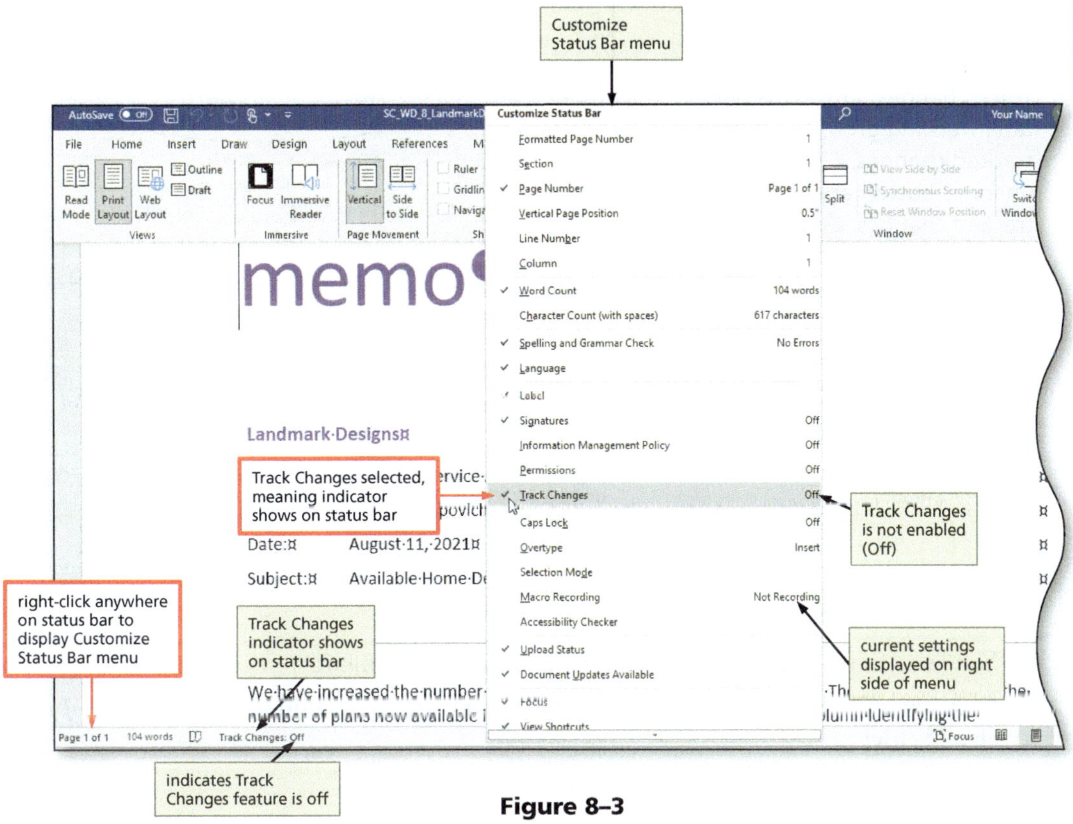

Figure 8–3

Q&A **Can I show or hide any of the items listed on the Customize Status Bar menu?**
Yes, click the item to display or remove its check mark.

3

- Click anywhere outside of the Customize Status Bar menu or press ESC to remove the menu from the screen.

To Enable Tracked Changes

When you edit a document that has the track changes feature enabled, Word uses annotations to mark all text or graphics that you insert, delete, or modify and refers to the revisions as **markups** or **revision marks**. An author can identify the changes a reviewer (user) has made by looking at the markups in a document. The author also has the ability to accept or reject any change that a reviewer has made to a document.

The following step enables tracked changes. **Why?** To track changes in a document, you must enable (turn on) the track changes feature.

1

- If the Track Changes indicator on the status bar shows that the track changes feature is off, click the Track Changes indicator on the status bar to enable the track changes feature.

Experiment

- Display the Review tab. Click the Track Changes button (Review tab | Tracking group) to disable tracked changes. Click the Track Changes button again to enable tracked changes. Click the Track Changes indicator on the status bar to disable tracked changes. Click the Track Changes indicator on the status bar again to enable tracked changes (Figure 8–4).

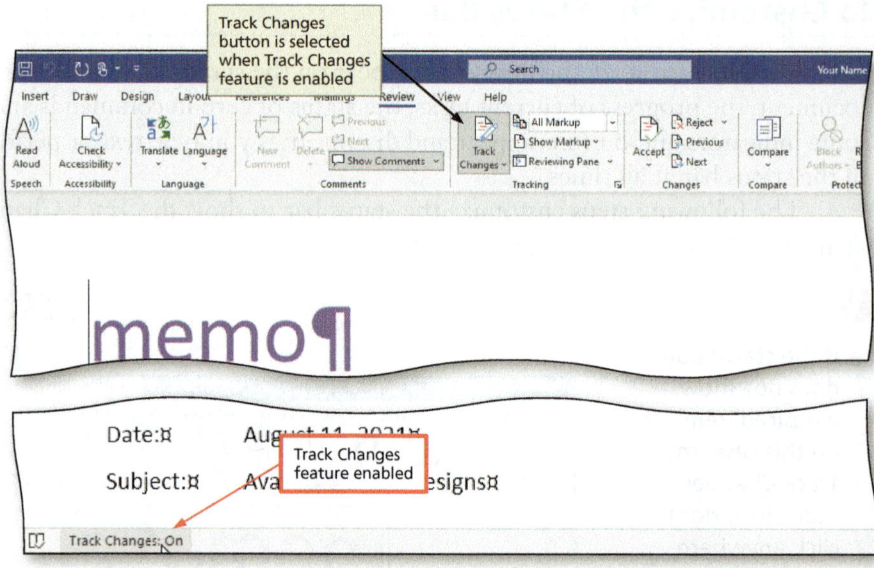

Figure 8–4

Other Ways

1. Click Track Changes button (Review tab | Tracking group)
2. Click Track Changes arrow (Review tab | Tracking group), click Track Changes
3. Press CTRL+SHIFT+E

To Track Changes

You have four suggested changes for the current document:

1. Insert the words, and chart, after the word, table, in the second sentence so that it reads: The table and chart below …
2. Delete the letter, s, at the end of the word, shows.
3. Insert the word, unique, before the word, plans, in the second sentence so that it reads: ... the number of unique plans exclusive to Landmark Designs.
4. Change the word, final, to the word, last, in the second sentence so that it reads: ... with the last column identifying....

The following steps track these changes as you enter them in the document. **Why?** You want edits you make to the document to show so that others can review the edits.

1

- Position the insertion point immediately to the left of the word, below, in the second sentence of the memo to position the insertion point at the location for the tracked change (Figure 8–5).

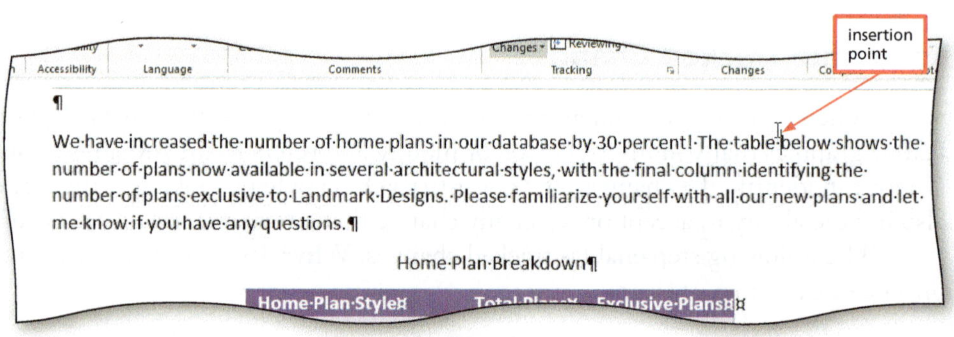

Figure 8–5

2

- Type **and chart** and then press SPACEBAR to insert the typed text as a tracked change (Figure 8–6).

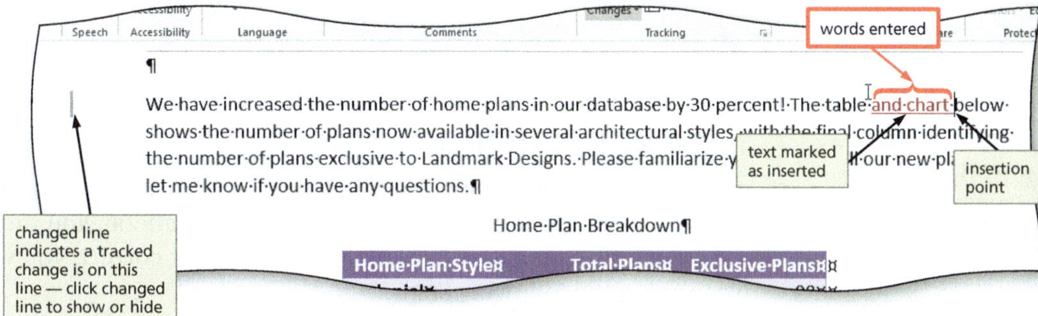

Figure 8–6

Q&A

Why is the inserted text in color and underlined?
When the track changes feature is enabled, Word marks (signals) all text inserts by underlining them and changing their color, and marks all deletions by striking through them and changing their color.

What is the vertical bar in the margin?
The bar is called a changed line, which indicates a tracked change is on the line to the right of the bar.

3

- In the same sentence, delete the s at the end of the word, shows (so that it reads, show), to mark the letter for deletion (Figure 8–7).

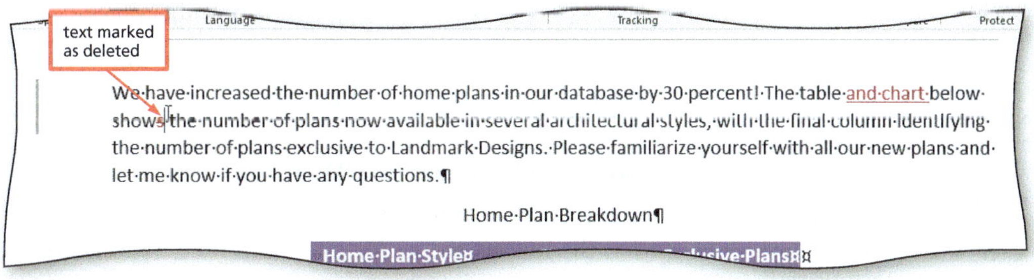

Figure 8–7

4

- In the same sentence on the next line, position the insertion point immediately to the left of the word, plans. Type **unique** and then press SPACEBAR to insert the typed text as a tracked change (Figure 8–8).

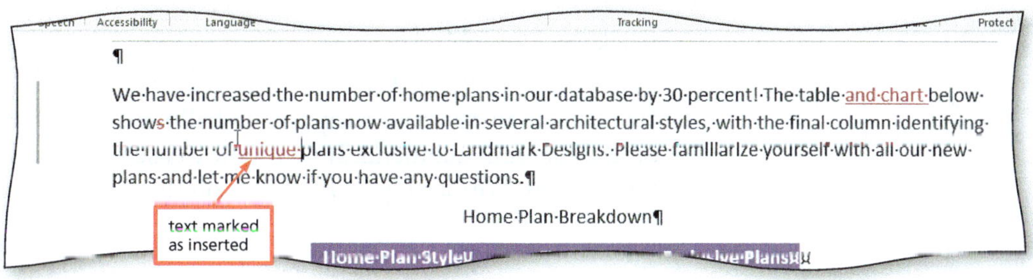

Figure 8–8

5

- In the same sentence, double-click the word, final, to select it.
- Type **last** as the replacement text, which tracks a deletion and an insertion change (Figure 8–9).

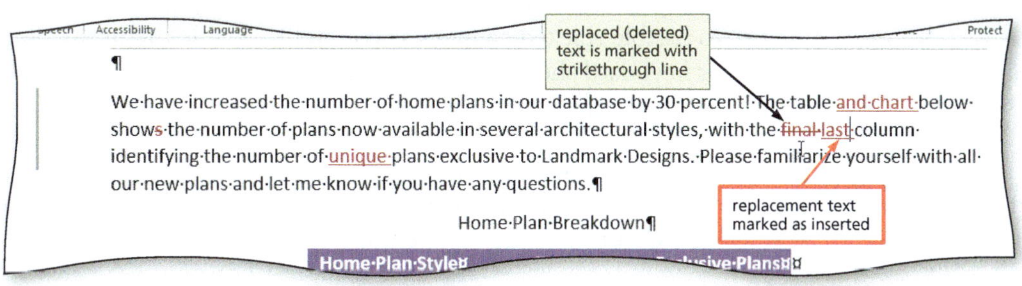

Figure 8–9

Q&A **Can I see the name of the person who tracked a change?**
You can point to a tracked change in the document window; Word then will display a ScreenTip that identifies the reviewer's name and the type of change made by that reviewer.

BTW
Limiting Authors
If you wanted to restrict formatting or editing, you would click the Restrict Editing button (Review tab | Protect group) or open Backstage view, display the Info screen, click the Protect Document button, and then click Restrict Editing to open the Restrict Editing pane. To restrict formatting, select the 'Limit formatting to a selection of styles' check box, click the Settings link, select the styles to allow and disallow (Formatting Restrictions dialog box), and then click OK. To restrict editing, select the 'Allow only this type of editing in the document' check box, click the box arrow, and then select the desired editing restriction. To restrict formatting or editing to certain authors, select part of the document and select the users who are allowed to edit the selected areas and then click the 'Yes, Start Enforcing Protection' button. To block authors from making changes to selected text, click the Block Authors button (Review tab | Protect group) and then select the authors to block in the list.

BTW
Lock Tracking
If you wanted to require a password to turn off tracked changes (lock tracking), you would click the Track Changes arrow (Review tab | Tracking group), click Lock Tracking on the Track Changes menu, enter the password in each text box, and then click OK (Lock Tracking dialog box). If you do not enter a password, Word will turn off tracked changes but will not require a password to unlock tracking. To turn off tracked changes (unlock tracking), follow the same procedure, entering the password when prompted, if necessary.

To Change the User Name

Word uses predefined settings for the reviewer's initials and/or name that appears in the document window, the comment balloon, and the Reviewing pane. If the reviewer's name (user name) or initials are not correct, you would change them by performing the following steps.

1a. Click the Tracking Dialog Box Launcher (Review tab | Tracking group) to display the Track Changes Options dialog box. Click the 'Change User Name' button (Track Changes Options dialog box) to display the Word Options dialog box.

or

1b. Open Backstage view and then click Options to display the Word Options dialog box. If necessary, click General in the left pane.

2. Enter the correct name in the User name text box (Word Options dialog box), and enter the correct initials in the Initials text box.

3. Click OK to change the reviewer information. If necessary, click OK in the Track Changes Options dialog box.

To Change How Markups Are Displayed

The tracked changes entered in the previous steps appeared inline, which means that the inserts are underlined and the deletions are shown as strikethroughs. The default Word setting displays comments and formatting changes in balloons in a markup area to the right of the document and all other changes inline. If you wanted to change how markups (and comments) are displayed, you would perform the following steps.

1. Click the Show Markup button (Review tab | Tracking group) to display the Show Markup menu and then point to Balloons on the Show Markup menu.
2. If you want all revisions to appear in balloons, click 'Show Revisions in Balloons' on the Balloons submenu. If you want to use the default Word setting, click 'Show Only Formatting in Balloons' on the Balloons submenu.

To Disable Tracked Changes

When you have finished tracking changes, you should disable (turn off) the track changes feature so that Word stops marking your revisions. You follow the same steps to disable tracked changes as you did to enable them; that is, the indicator or button or keyboard shortcut functions as a toggle, turning the track changes feature on or off each time the command is issued. The following step disables tracked changes.

1. To turn the track changes feature off, click the Track Changes indicator on the status bar, or click the Track Changes button (Review tab | Tracking group), or press CTRL+SHIFT+E (Figure 8–10).

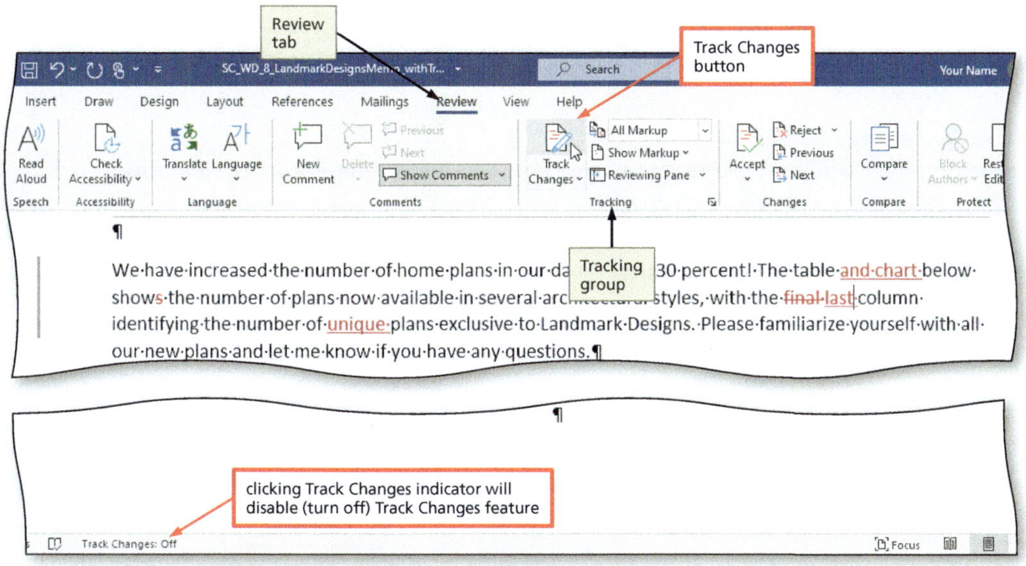

Figure 8–10

To Use the Reviewing Pane or the Markup Area

Word provides a Reviewing pane that can be opened and then displayed either at the left edge (vertically) or the bottom (horizontally) of the screen. **Why?** As an alternative to reading through tracked changes in the document window or in balloons in the markup area, some users prefer to view tracked changes in the Reviewing pane. The following steps open the Reviewing pane.

1

- Click the Reviewing Pane arrow (Review tab | Tracking group) to display the Reviewing Pane menu (Figure 8–11).

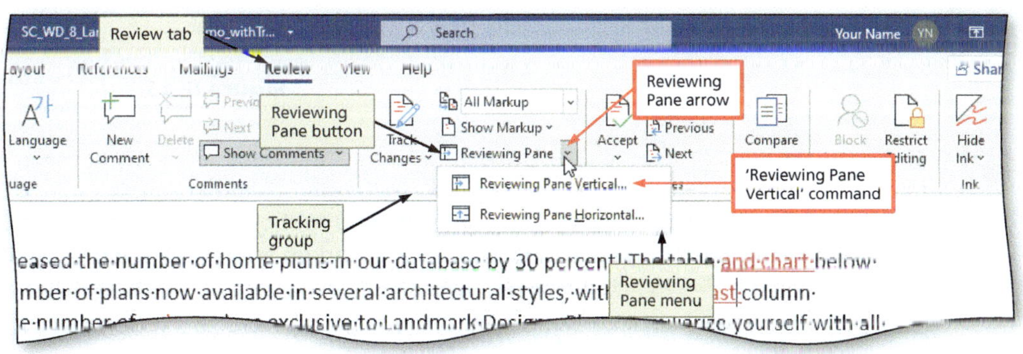

Figure 8–11

2

- Click 'Reviewing Pane Vertical' on the Reviewing Pane menu to open the Reviewing pane on the left side of the Word window (Figure 8–12).

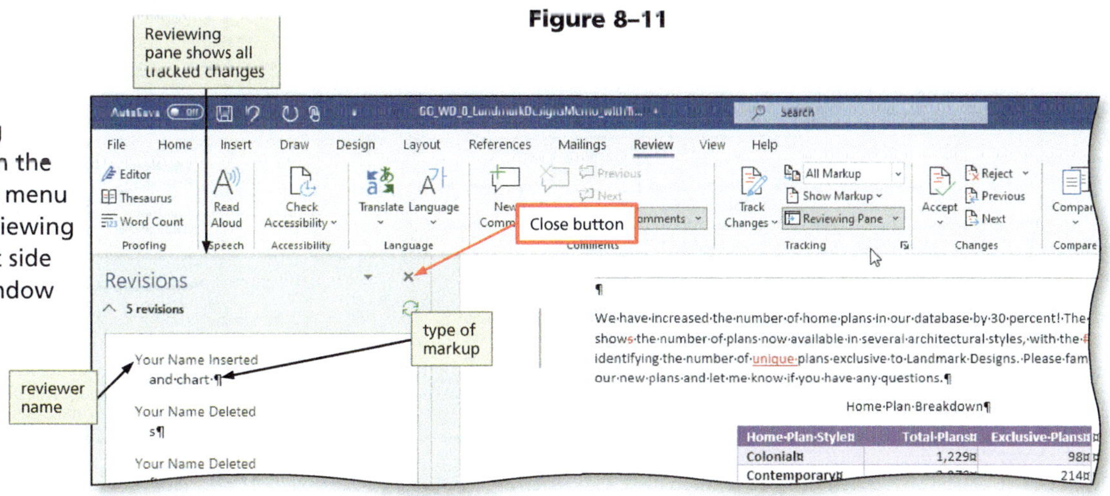

Figure 8–12

Q&A **What if I click the Reviewing Pane button instead of the arrow?**
Word opens the Reviewing pane in its most recent location, that is, either vertically on the left side of the screen or horizontally on the bottom of the screen.

Can I edit revisions in the Reviewing pane?
Yes. Simply click in the Reviewing pane and edit the text the same way you edit in the document window.

3

- Click the Close button in the Reviewing pane to close the pane.

Q&A **Can I also click the Reviewing Pane button on the ribbon to close the pane?**
Yes.

4

- Click the Show Markup button (Review tab | Tracking group) to display the Show Markup menu.
- Point to Balloons on the Show Markup menu to display the Balloons submenu (Figure 8–13).

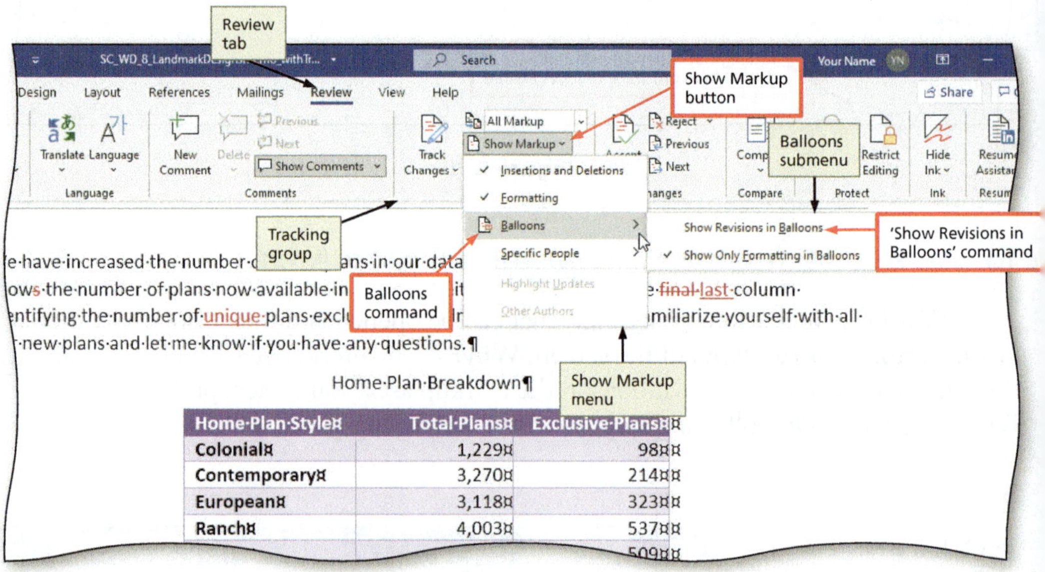

Figure 8–13

5

- Click 'Show Revisions in Balloons' on the Balloons submenu to show the markup area in the Word window (Figure 8–14). If necessary, change the zoom so that the markup area is displayed in the Word window.

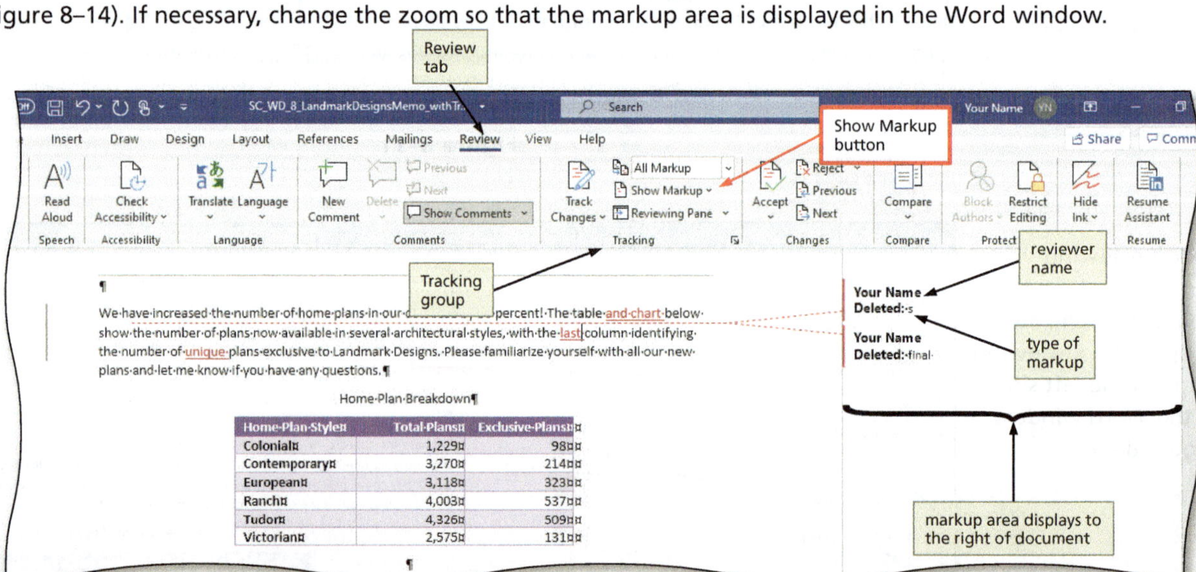

Figure 8–14

6

- Click the Show Markup button (Review tab | Tracking group) to display the Show Markup menu.
- Point to Balloons on the Show Markup menu to display the Balloons submenu and then click 'Show Only Formatting in Balloons' on the Balloons submenu to remove the markup area from the Word window and place all markups except formatting inline.
- If necessary, change the zoom to page width.

To Display Tracked Changes as Simple Markup

Word provides a Simple Markup option instead of the All Markup option for viewing tracked changes and comments. **Why?** Some users feel the All Markup option clutters the screen and prefer the cleaner look of the Simple Markup option. The following steps display tracked changes using the Simple Markup option.

1

- Click the 'Display for Review' arrow (Review tab | Tracking group) to display the Display for Review menu (Figure 8–15).

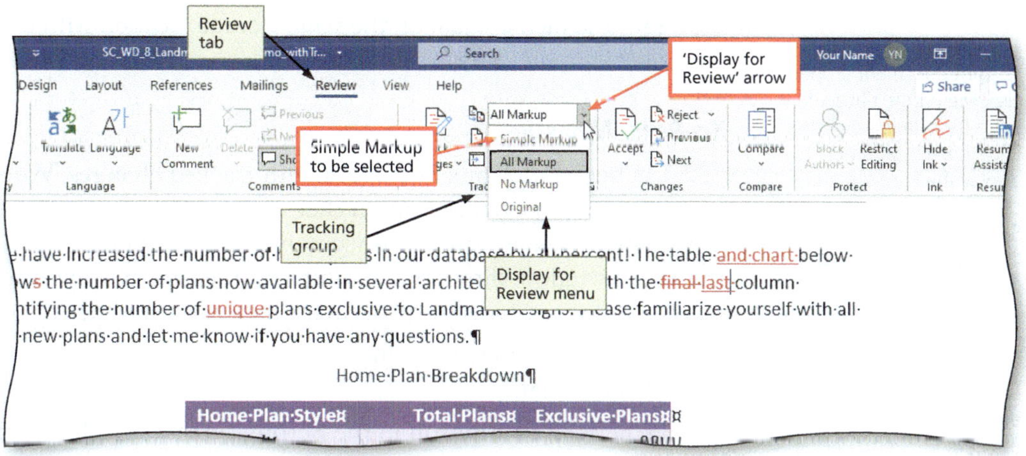

Figure 8–15

2

- Click Simple Markup on the Display for Review menu to show a simple markup instead of all markups in the document window (Figure 8–16).

Experiment

- Click the changed line to display the tracked changes and switch back to displaying All Markup. Click the changed line again to hide the tracked changes and switch to Simple Markup.

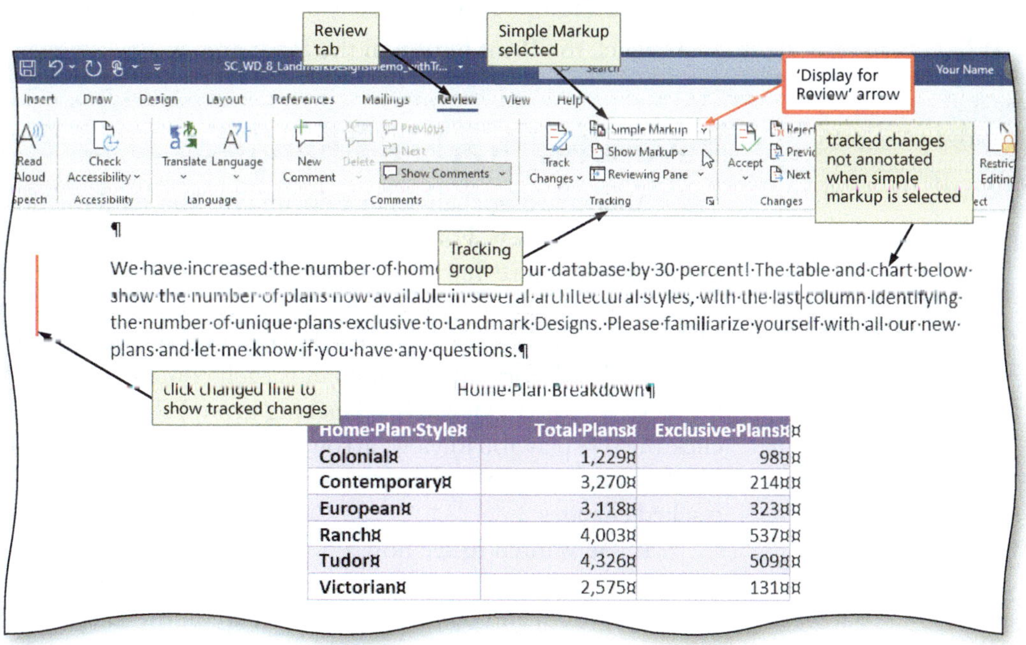

Figure 8–16

To Show All Markup

You prefer to show all markup where tracked changes are annotated in the document window. The following steps show all markup.

1. Click the 'Display for Review' arrow (Review tab | Tracking group) (shown in Figure 8–16) and then click All Markup on the Display for Review menu to instruct Word to display the document with all proposed edits shown as markup (shown in Figure 8–17).

Q&A **What are the other Display for Review options?**
If you click the 'Display for Review' arrow, several options appear. Simple Markup means Word incorporates proposed changes in the document and places a changed line near the margin of the line containing the proposed change. All Markup means that all proposed changes are highlighted. No Markup shows the proposed edits as part of the final document, instead of as markup. Original shows the document before changes.

2. Save the memo again on the same storage location with the same file name.

BTW
Printing Document Properties
To print document properties, click File on the ribbon to open Backstage view, click Print in Backstage view to display the Print screen, click the first button in the Settings area to display a list of options specifying what you can print, click Document Info in the list to specify you want to print the document properties instead of the actual document, and then click the Print button in the Print screen to print the document properties on the currently selected printer.

BTW
Inserting Document Properties
If you wanted to insert document properties into a document, you would click the Quick Parts button (Insert tab | Text group) to display the Quick Parts menu, point to Document Property on the Quick Parts menu, and then click the property you want to insert on the Document Property menu. If you wanted to insert document properties into a header or footer, you would display the Header & Footer tab, click the Document Info button (Header & Footer tab | Insert group), click the document property to insert or point to Document Property on the Document Info menu and then click the document property to insert.

To Print Markups

When you print a document with tracked changes, Word chooses the zoom percentage and page orientation that will best show the comments on the printed document. You can print the document with its markups, which looks similar to how the Word window shows the markups on the screen, or you can print just the list of the markups. If you wanted to print markups, you would perform the following steps.

1. Open Backstage view and then click Print in Backstage view to display the Print screen.
2. Click the first button in the Settings area to display a list of options specifying what you can print. To print the document with the markups, if necessary, place a check mark to the left of Print Markup. To print just the markups (without printing the document), click 'List of Markup' in the Document Info area.
3. Click the Print button in the Print area in Backstage view.

Reviewing Tracked Changes

After tracking changes in a document, you send the document to the originator for his or her review. For demonstration purposes in this module, you assume the role of originator and review the tracked changes in the document.

To do this, be sure the markups are displayed on the screen. Click the Show Markup button (Review tab | Tracking group) and verify that the 'Insertions and Deletions' and Formatting commands each contain a check mark. Ensure the 'Display for Review' box (Review tab | Tracking group) shows All Markup; if it does not, click the 'Display for Review' arrow (Review tab | Tracking group) and then click All Markup on the Display for Review menu. This option shows the final document with tracked changes.

If you wanted to see how a document would look if you accepted all the changes, without actually accepting them, click the 'Display for Review' arrow (Review tab | Tracking group) and then click No Markup on the Display for Review menu. If you print this view of the document, it will print how the document will look if you accept all the changes. If you wanted to see how the document looked before any changes were made, click the 'Display for Review' arrow (Review tab | Tracking group) and then click Original on the Display for Review menu. When you have finished reviewing the various options, if necessary, click the 'Display for Review' arrow (Review tab | Tracking group) and then click All Markup on the Display for Review menu.

To Review Tracked Changes

The next step is to review the tracked changes in the marked-up document using the Review tab. **Why?** You could scroll through the document and point to each markup to read it, but you might overlook one or more changes using this technique. A more efficient method is to use the Review tab to review the changes one at a time, deciding whether to accept, modify, or delete each change. The following steps review the changes in the document.

1

- Position the insertion point at the beginning of the document, so that Word begins the review of tracked changes from the top of the document.
- Click the Next button (Review tab | Changes group), which causes Word to locate and select the first markup in the document (in this case, the inserted words, and chart) (Figure 8–17).

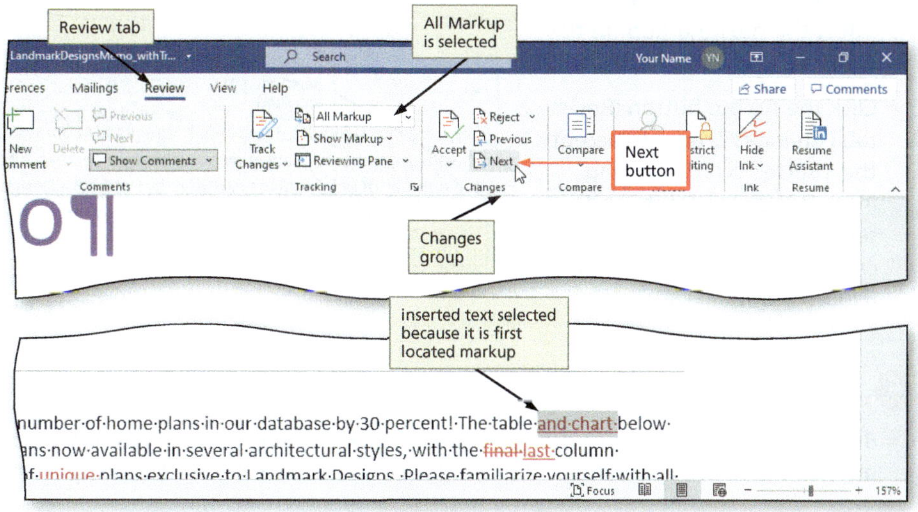

Figure 8–17

Q&A **What if my document also had contained comments?**
When you click the Next button (Review tab | Changes group), Word locates only the next tracked change. To display the next comment, click the Next button in the Comments group.

2

- Because you agree with this change, click the Accept button (Review tab | Changes group) to accept the insertion of the words, and chart, and instruct Word to locate and select the next markup (in this case, the deleted letter, s) (Figure 8–18).

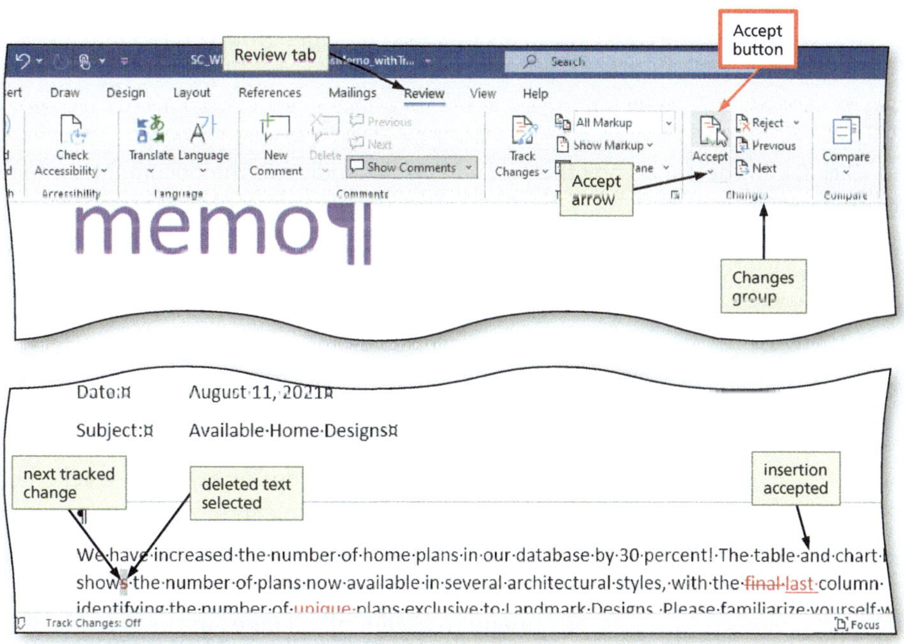

Figure 8–18

Q&A **What if I accidentally click the Accept arrow (Review tab | Changes group)?**
Click 'Accept and Move to Next' on the Accept menu.

What if I wanted to accept the change but not search for the next tracked change?
You would click the Accept arrow and then click 'Accept This Change' on the Accept menu.

3

- Click the Accept button (Review tab | Changes group) to accept the deleted letter, s, and instruct Word to locate and select the next markup (in this case, the deleted word, final).
- Click the Accept button (Review tab | Changes group) to accept the deleted word, final, and instruct Word to locate and select the next markup (in this case, the inserted word, last).
- Click the Accept button (Review tab | Changes group) to accept the inserted word, last, and instruct Word to locate and select the next markup (in this case, the inserted word, unique) (Figure 8–19).

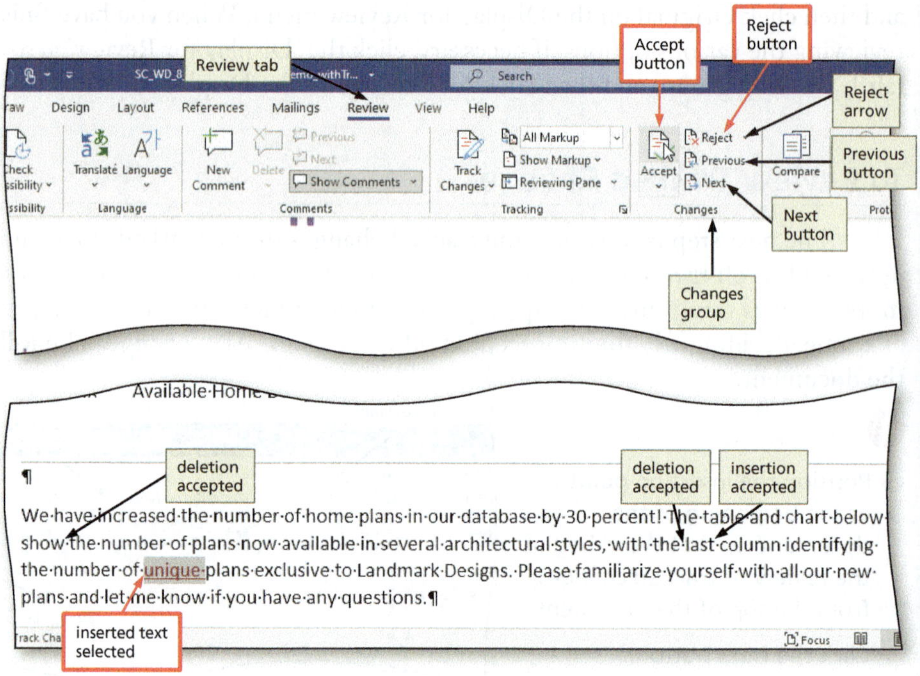

Figure 8–19

4

- Because you do not agree with this change, click the Reject button (Review tab | Changes group) to reject the marked insertion, and instruct Word to locate and select the next markup if one exists.

Q&A

What if I accidentally click the Reject arrow (Review tab | Changes group)?
Click 'Reject and Move to Next' on the Reject menu.

What if I wanted to reject the change but not search for the next tracked change?
You would click the Reject arrow (Review tab | Changes group) and then click Reject Change on the Reject menu.

What if I did not want to accept or reject a change but wanted to locate the next tracked change?
You would click the Next button (Review tab | Changes group) to locate the next tracked change. Likewise, to locate the previous tracked change, you would click the Previous button (Review tab | Changes group).

5

- Click OK in the dialog box that appears, which indicates the document contains no more comments or tracked changes.
- sam Save the reviewed file on your hard drive, OneDrive, or other storage location using SC_WD_8_LandmarkDesignsMemo_Reviewed as the file name.

Other Ways

1. Right-click tracked change (or, if using touch, tap 'Show Context Menu' button on Mini toolbar), click desired command on shortcut menu

To Accept or Reject All Tracked Changes

If you wanted to accept or reject all tracked changes in a document at once, you would perform the following step.

1. To accept all tracked changes, click the Accept arrow (Review tab | Changes group) to display the Accept menu and then click 'Accept All Changes' on the menu to accept all changes in the document and continue tracking changes or click 'Accept All Changes and Stop Tracking' to accept all changes in the document and stop tracking changes.

   or

1. To reject all tracked changes, click the Reject arrow (Review tab | Changes group) to display the Reject menu and then click 'Reject All Changes' on the menu to reject all changes in the document and continue tracking changes or click 'Reject All Changes and Stop Tracking' to reject all changes in the document and stop tracking changes.

Changing Tracking Options

If you wanted to change the color and markings reviewers use for tracked changes or change how balloons are displayed, use the Advanced Track Changes Options dialog box (Figure 8–20). To display the Advanced Track Changes Options dialog box, click the Tracking Dialog Box Launcher (Review tab | Tracking group) and then click the Advanced Options button (Track Changes Options dialog box).

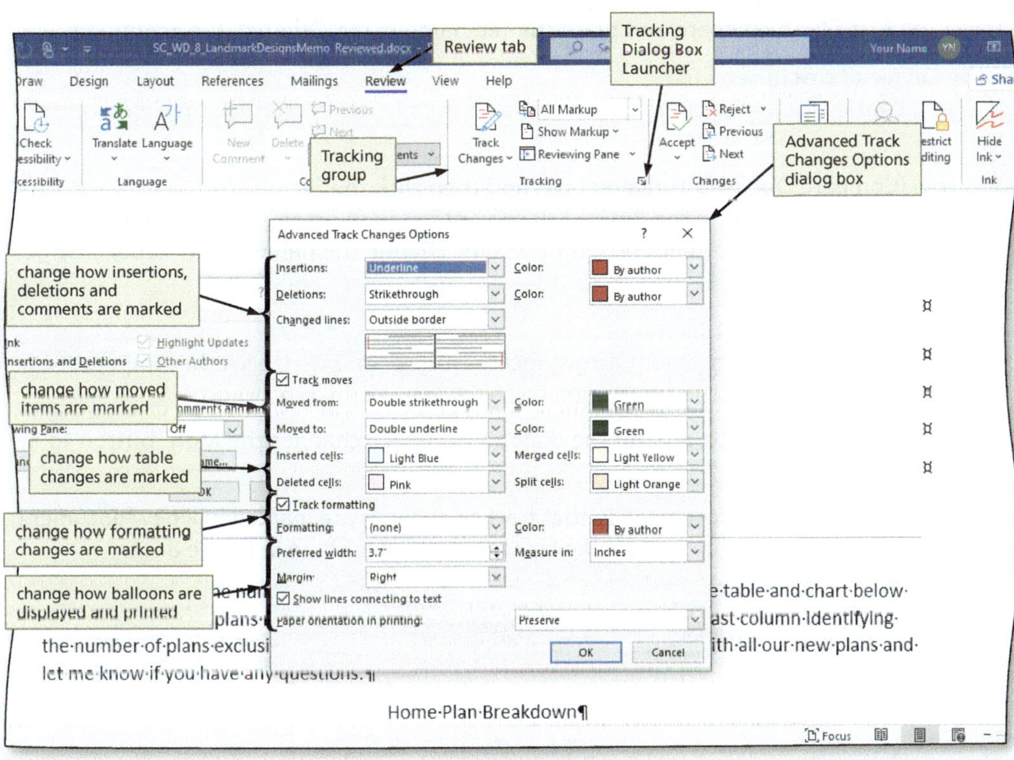

Figure 8–20

BTW

Compare and Merge

If you wanted to compare two documents and merge the changes into an existing document instead of into a new document, you would click the Original document option button (Compare Documents dialog box) to merge into the original document or click the Revised document option button (Compare Documents dialog box) to merge into the revised document (shown in Figure 8–22), and then click OK.

To Compare Documents

With Word, you can compare two documents to each other. **Why?** Comparing documents allows you easily to identify any differences between two files because Word displays the differences between the documents as tracked changes for your review. By comparing files, you can verify that two separate files have the same or different content. If no tracked changes are found, then the two documents are identical.

Assume you want to compare the original SC_WD_8-1.docx document with the SC_WD_8_LandmarkDesignsMemo_Reviewed.docx document so that you can identify the changes made to the document. The following steps compare two documents.

1

- If necessary, display the Review tab.
- Click the Compare button (Review tab | Compare group) to display the Compare menu (Figure 8–21).

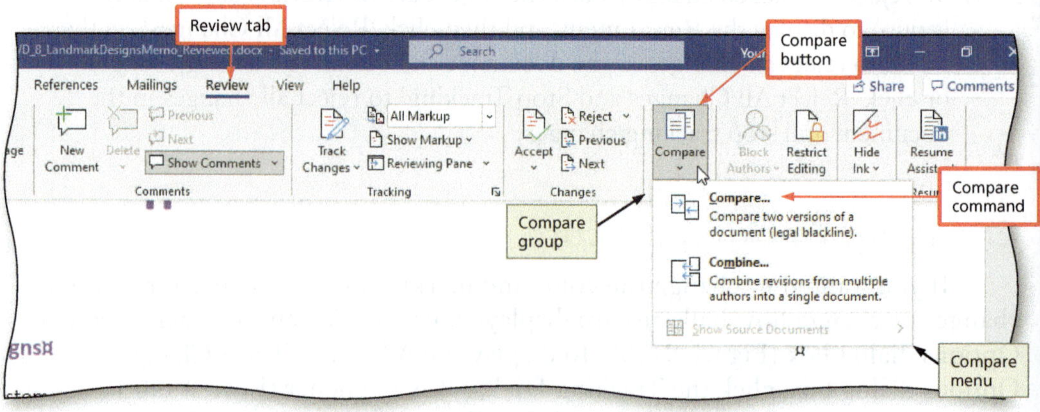

Figure 8–21

2

- Click Compare on the Compare menu to display the Compare Documents dialog box.
- Click the Original document arrow (Compare Documents dialog box) and then click the file, SC_WD_8-1.docx, in the Original document list to select the first file to compare and place the file name in the Original document box.

Q&A **What if the file is not in the Original document list?**
Click the Open button to the right of the Original document arrow, locate the file, and then click the Open button (Open dialog box).

- Click the Revised document arrow (Compare Documents dialog box) and then click the file, SC_WD_8_LandmarkDesignsMemo_Reviewed.docx, in the Revised document list to select the second file to compare and place the file name in the Revised document box. If necessary, change the name in the 'Label changes with' box to your name.

Q&A **What if the file is not in the Revised document list?**
Click the Open button to the right of the Revised document arrow, locate the file, and then click the Open button (Open dialog box).

- If a More button appears in the dialog box, click it to expand the dialog box, which changes the More button to a Less button.
- If necessary, in the Show changes in area, click New document so that tracked changes are marked in a new document. Ensure that all your settings in the expanded dialog box (below the Less button) match those in Figure 8–22.

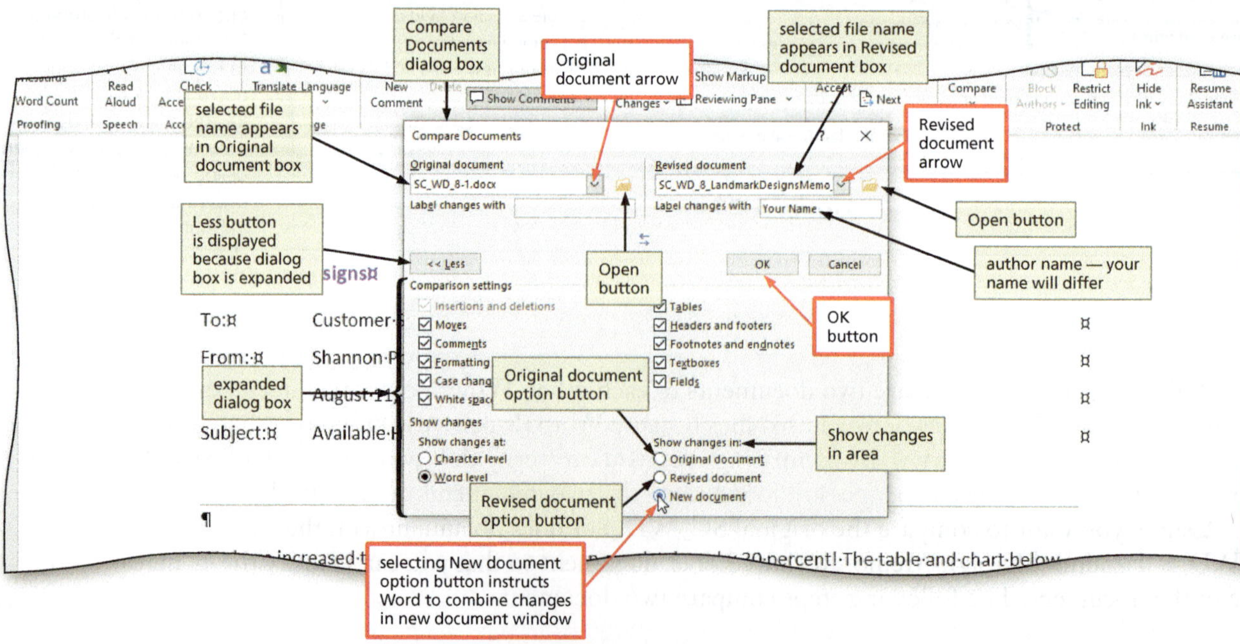

Figure 8–22

3

- Click OK to open a new document window and display the differences between the two documents as tracked changes in a new document window; if the Reviewing pane opens on the screen, click its Close button. Note that, depending on settings, your compare results may differ from Figure 8–23; for example, your screen already may show source documents, which is covered in Step 4.

4

- Click the Compare button (Review tab | Compare group) to display the Compare menu and then point to 'Show Source Documents' on the Compare menu (Figure 8–23).

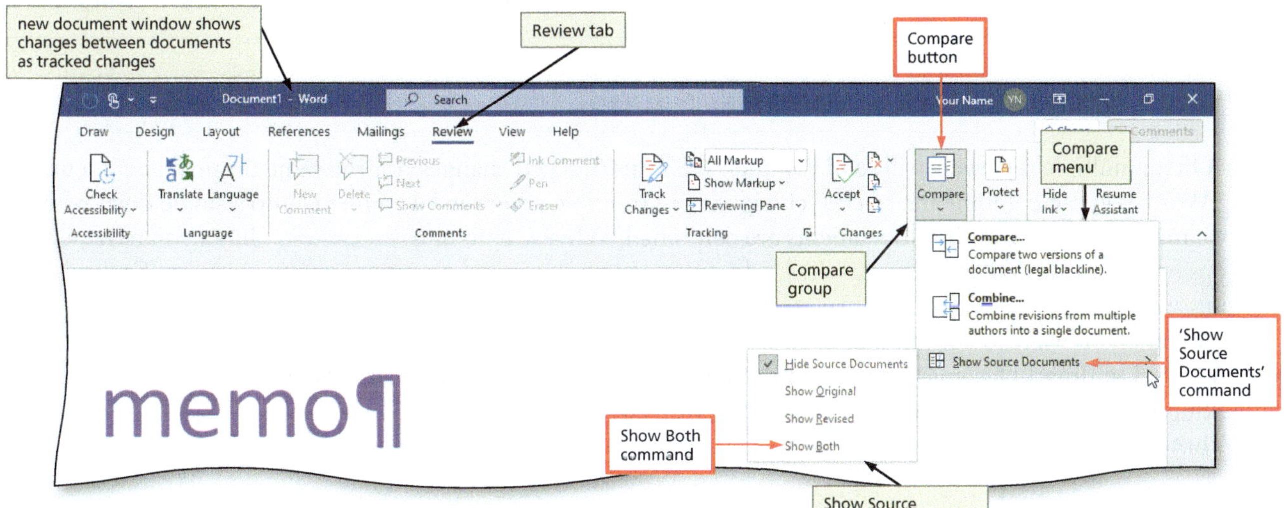

Figure 8–23

5

- Click Show Both on the Show Source Documents submenu so that the original and source documents appear on the screen with the compared document; if the Reviewing pane opens on the screen, click its Close button (Figure 8–24). Note that, depending on settings, your compare results may differ from Figure 8–24.

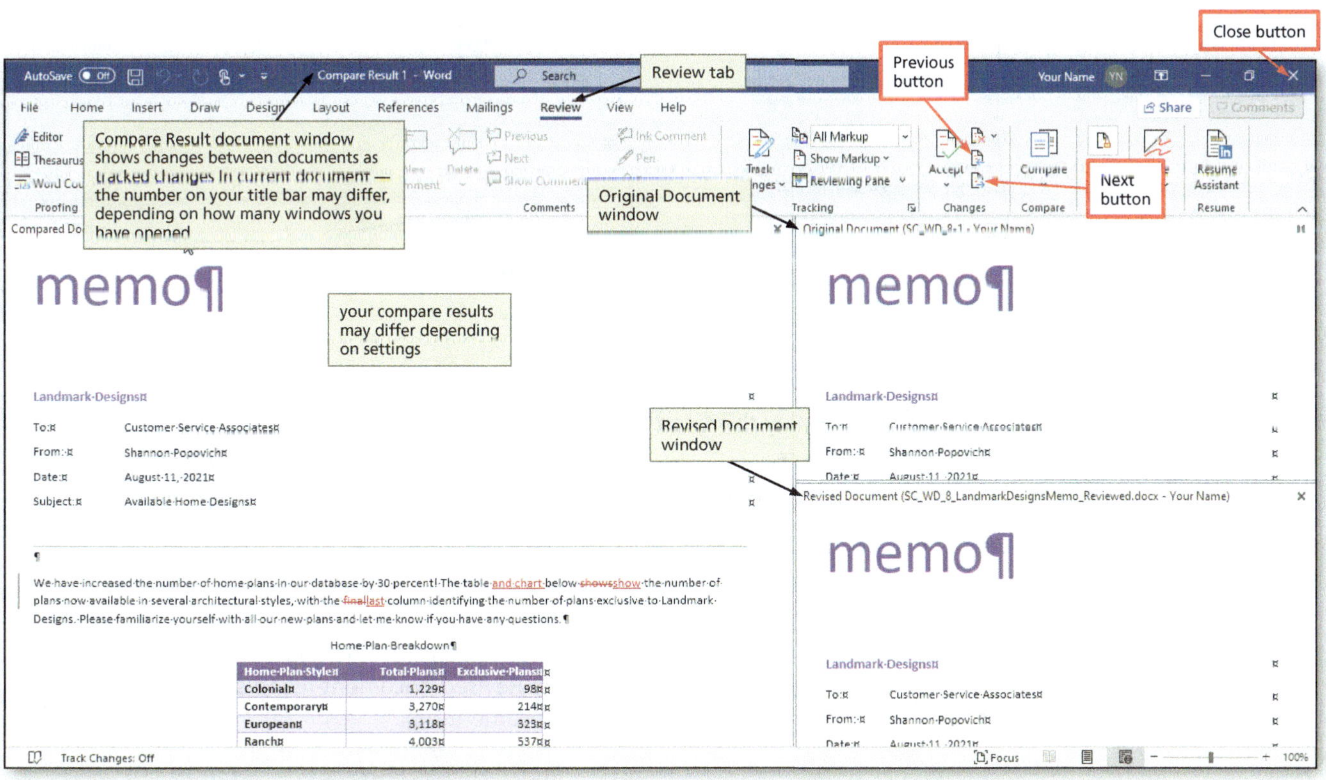

Figure 8–24

Experiment

- Click the Next button (Review tab | Changes group) to display the first tracked change in the compared document. Continue clicking the Next or Previous buttons. You can accept or reject changes in the compared document using the same steps described earlier in the module.
- Scroll through the windows and watch them scroll synchronously.

6

- When you have finished comparing the documents, click the Close button in the document window (shown in Figure 8–24) and then click the Don't Save button when Word asks if you want to save the compare results.

To Combine Revisions from Multiple Authors

Often, multiple reviewers will send you their markups (tracked changes) for the same original document. Using Word, you can combine the tracked changes from multiple reviewers' documents into a single document, two documents at a time, until all documents are combined. **Why?** Combining documents allows you to review all markups from a single document, from which you can accept and reject changes and read comments. Each reviewer's markups are shaded in a different color to help you visually differentiate among multiple reviewers' markups.

Assume you want to combine the original SC_WD_8-1.docx document with the SC_WD_8_LandmarkDesignsMemo_withTrackedChanges.docx document and also with a document called Support_WD_8_LandmarkDesignsMemo_ReviewedByJPerez.docx. The following steps combine these three documents, two at a time.

1

- Click the Compare button (Review tab | Compare group) to display the Compare menu (Figure 8–25).

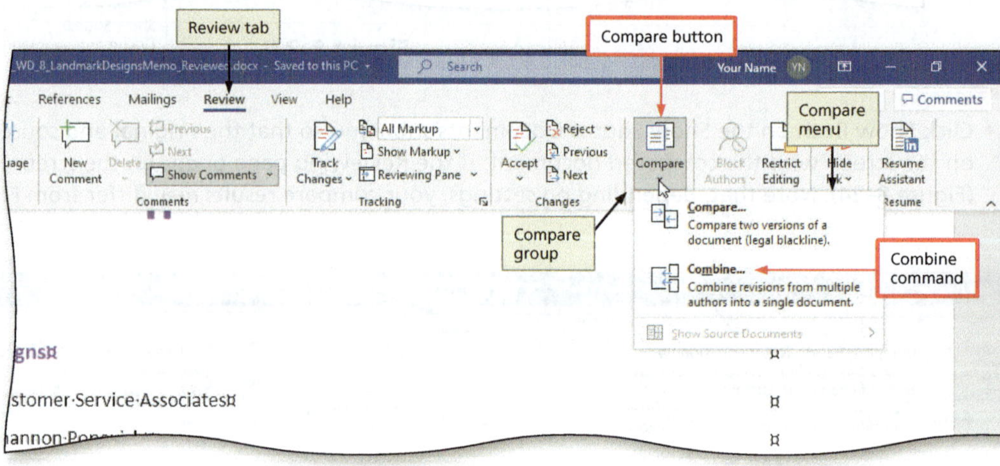

Figure 8–25

2

- Click Combine on the Compare menu to display the Combine Documents dialog box.
- Click the Original document arrow (Combine Documents dialog box) and then click the file, SC_WD_8-1.docx, in the Original document list to select the first file to combine and place the file name in the Original document box.

Q&A **What if the file is not in the Original document list?**
Click the Open button to the right of the Original document arrow, locate the file, and then click the Open button (Open dialog box).

- Click the Revised document arrow (Combine Documents dialog box) and then click the file, SC_WD_8_LandmarkDesignsMemo_withTrackedChanges.docx, in the Revised document list to select the second file to combine and place the file name in the Revised document box.

Q&A

What if the file is not in the Revised document list?

Click the Open button to the right of the Revised document arrow, locate the file, and then click the Open button (Open dialog box).

- If a More button appears in the dialog box, click it to expand the dialog box, which changes the More button to a Less button.
- In the Show changes in area, if necessary, click Original document so that tracked changes are marked in the original document (SC_WD_8-1.docx). Ensure that all your settings in the expanded dialog box (below the Less button) match those in Figure 8–26.

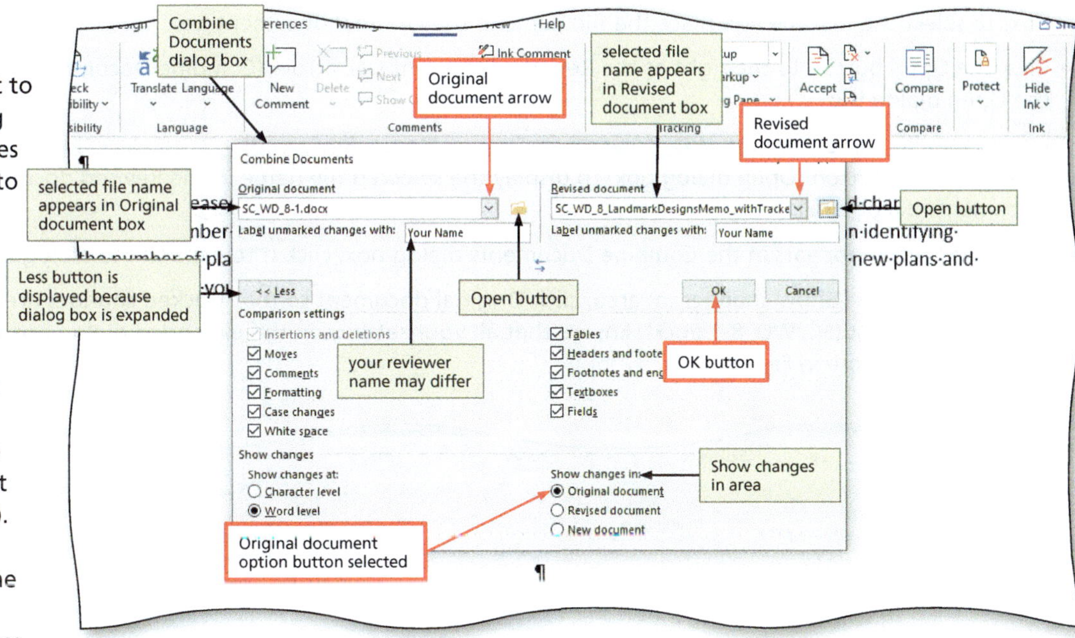

Figure 8–26

3

- Click OK to combine SC_WD_8-1.docx with SC_WD_8_LandmarkDesignsMemo_withTrackedChanges.docx and display the differences between the two documents as tracked changes in the original document (Figure 8–27).

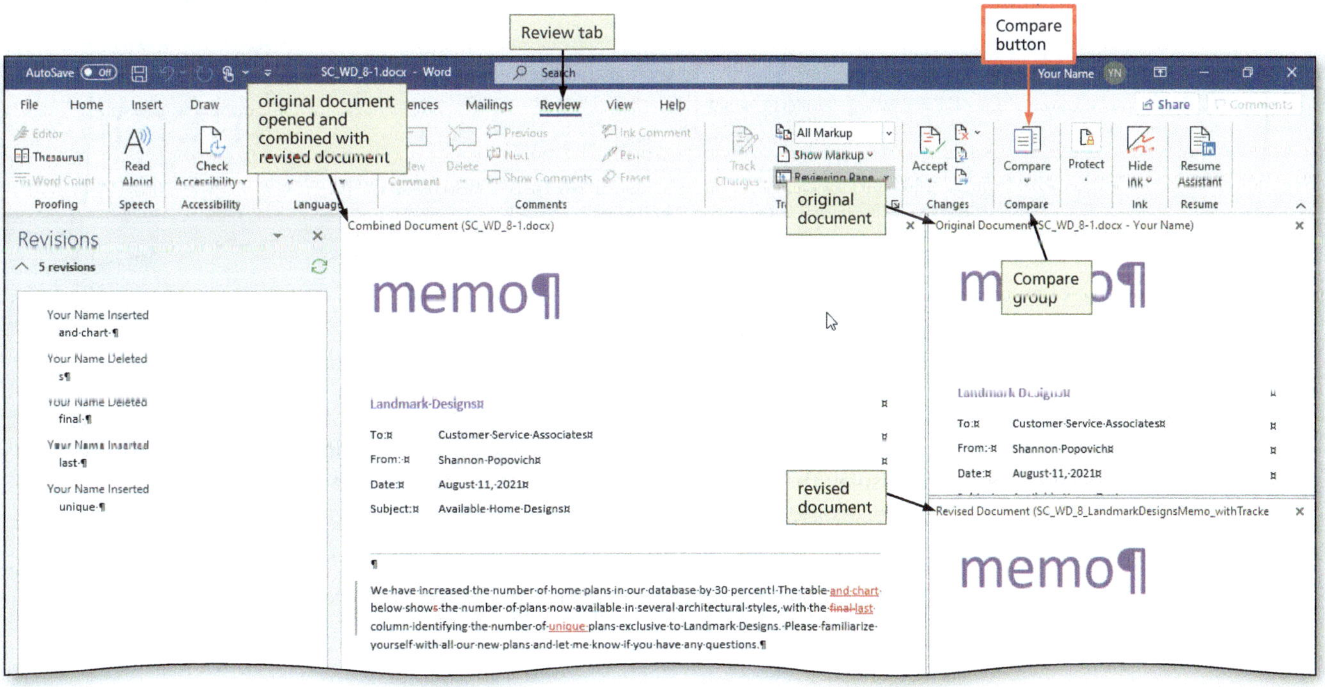

Figure 8–27

- Click the Compare button again (Review tab | Compare group) and then click Combine on the Compare menu to display the Combine Documents dialog box.
- Locate and display the file name, SC_WD_8-1.docx, in the Original document text box (Combine Documents dialog box) to select the first file and place the file name in the Original document box.
- Click the Open button to the right of the Revised document box arrow (Combine Documents dialog box) to display the Open dialog box.
- Locate the file name, Support_WD_8_LandmarkDesignsMemo_ReviewedByJPerez.docx, in the Data Files and then click the Open button (Open dialog box) to display the selected file name in the Revised document box (Combine Documents dialog box).
- If a More button appears in the Combine Documents dialog box, click it to expand the dialog box.
- If necessary, in the 'Show changes in' area, click Original document so that tracked changes are marked in the original document (SC_WD_8-1.docx). Ensure that all your settings in the expanded dialog box (below the Less button) match those in Figure 8–28.

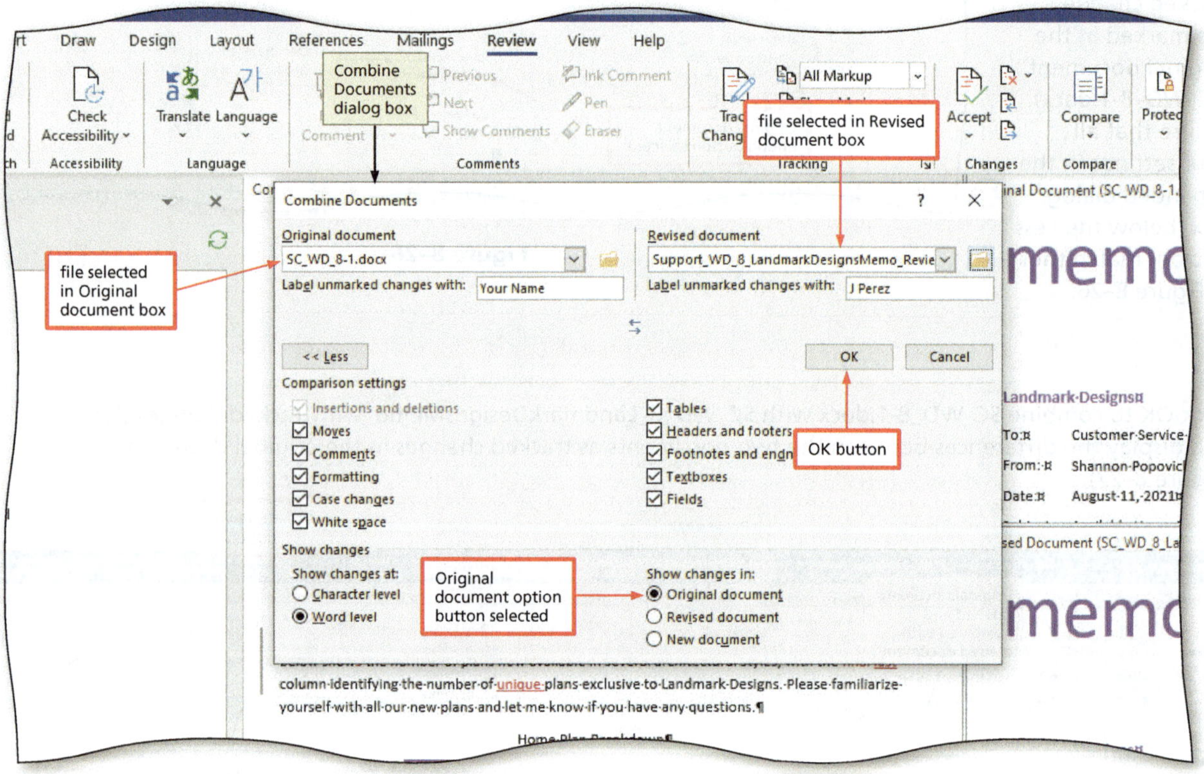

Figure 8–28

4

- Click OK to combine the Support_WD_8_LandmarkDesignsMemo_ReviewedByJPerez.docx document with the currently combined document and display the differences among the three documents as tracked changes in the original document (Figure 8–29). If necessary, scroll to see the table in the memo.

Q&A **What if my screen does not display the original and source documents?**
Click the Compare button (Review tab | Compare group) to display the Compare menu, point to 'Show Source Documents' on the Compare menu, and then click Show Both on the Show Source Documents submenu.

Experiment

- Click the Next button (Review tab | Changes group) to display the first tracked change in the combined document. Continue clicking the Next or Previous buttons. You can accept or reject changes in the combined document using the same steps described earlier in the module.

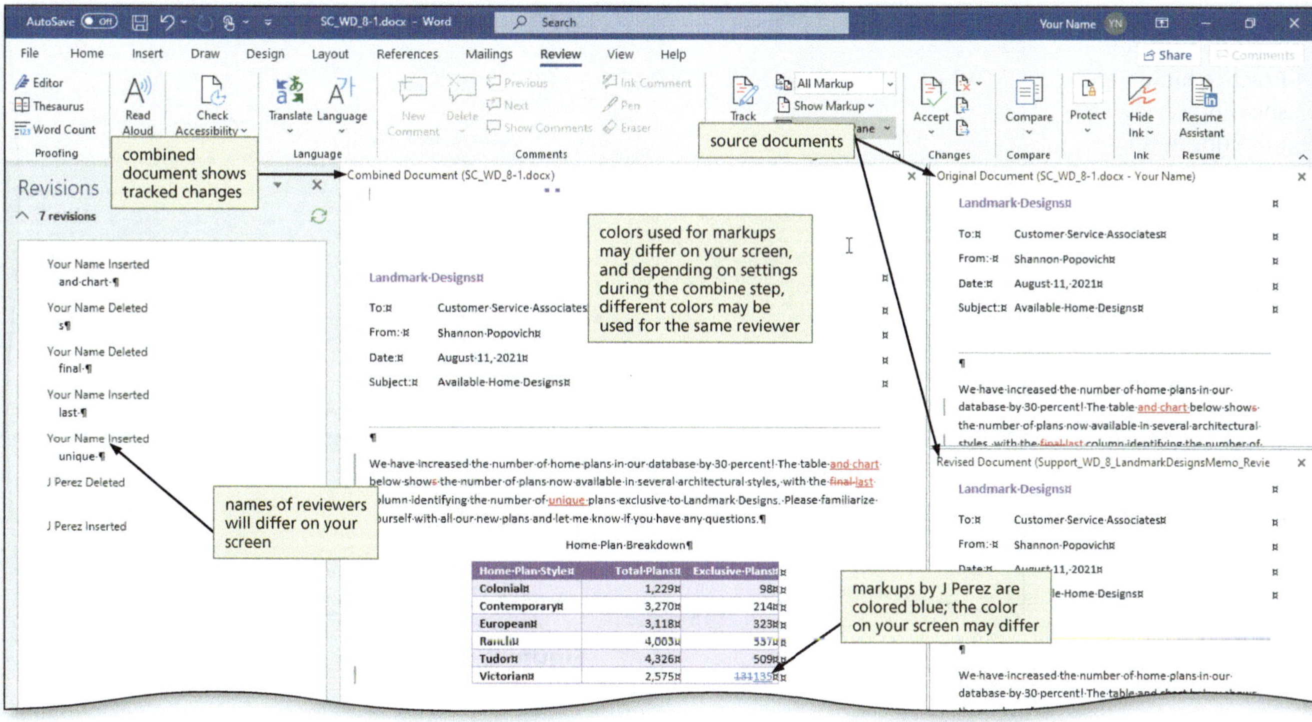

Figure 8–29

To Show Tracked Changes and Comments by a Single Reviewer

Why? Instead of looking through a document for a particular reviewer's markups, you can show markups by reviewer. The following steps show the markups by the reviewer named J Perez.

1

- Click the Show Markup button (Review tab | Tracking group) to display the Show Markup menu and then point to Specific People on the Show Markup menu to display the Specific People submenu (Figure 8–30).

Q&A **What if my Specific People submenu differs?**
Your submenu may have additional, different, or duplicate reviewer names or colors, depending on your Word settings.

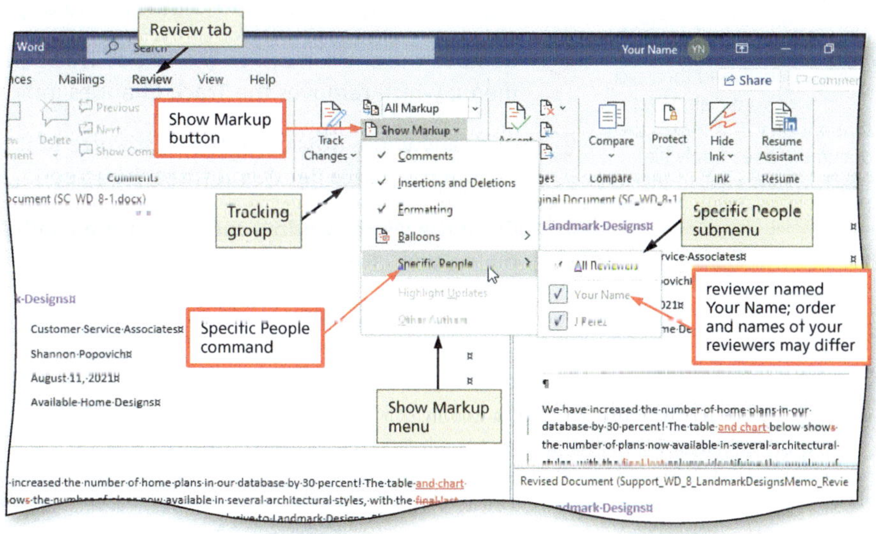

Figure 8–30

2

- Click Your Name on the Specific People submenu to hide the selected reviewer's markups and leave other markups on the screen (Figure 8–31).

Q&A **Are the Your Name reviewer markups deleted?**
No. They are hidden from view.

Experiment

- Practice hiding and showing reviewer markups in this document.

3

- Redisplay all reviewer comments by clicking the Show Markup button (Review tab | Tracking group), pointing to Specific People, and then clicking All Reviewers on the Specific People submenu.

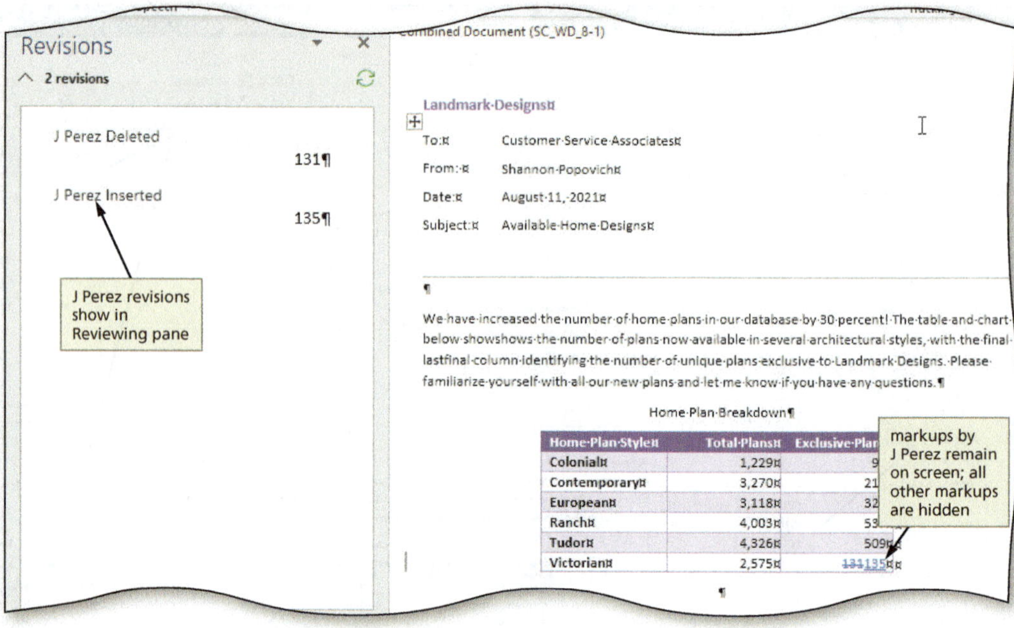

Figure 8–31

BTW

Mark as Final

If you wanted to mark a document as final so that users could not make further edits to it, you would perform these steps. Open Backstage view, display the Info screen, click the Protect Document button, click 'Mark as Final', and then click OK in the Word dialog box that appears. This makes the document a read-only file, which prevents any further edits.

To Customize the Status Bar and Close the Document

You are finished working with tracked changes in this module. The following steps remove the Track Changes indicator from the status bar and close the combined document without saving it.

1. Right-click anywhere on the status bar to display the Customize Status Bar menu.
2. Remove the check mark to the left of Track Changes on the Customize Status Bar menu, which removes the Track Changes indicator from the status bar.
3. Click anywhere outside of the Customize Status Bar menu, or press ESC, to remove the Customize Status Bar menu from the screen.
4. Close the Word window containing the combined document. When Word displays the dialog box, click the Don't Save button.
5. Close any other open Word documents.

Break Point: If you want to take a break, this is a good place to do so. You can exit Word now. To resume later, start Word and continue following the steps from this location forward.

BTW

Linking to External Content

If you wanted to link to external document content, you would click the Object button (Insert tab | Text group), click the Create from File tab (Object dialog box), locate the external file, place a check mark in the 'Link to file' check box, and then click OK.

Linking an Excel Worksheet to a Word Document

With Microsoft Office, you can copy part or all of a document created in one Office program to a document created in another Office program. The item being copied, or exchanged between another document or program, is called the **object**. For example, you could copy an Excel worksheet (the object) that is located in an Excel workbook (the source file) to a Word document (the destination file). That is, an object is copied from a source to a destination.

You can use one of three techniques to exchange objects from one program to another: copy and paste, embed, or link.

- **Copy and paste:** When you copy an object and then paste it, the object becomes part of the destination document. You edit a pasted object using editing features of the destination program. For example, when you select an Excel worksheet in an Excel workbook, click the Copy button (Home tab | Clipboard group) in Excel, and then click the Paste button (Home tab | Clipboard group) in Word, the Excel worksheet becomes a Word table.
- **Embed:** When you embed an object, like a pasted object, it becomes part of the destination document. The difference between an embedded object and a pasted object is that you edit the contents of an embedded object using the editing features of the source program. The embedded object, however, contains static data; that is, any changes made to the object in the source program are not reflected in the destination document. If you embed an Excel worksheet in a Word document, the Excel worksheet remains as an Excel worksheet in the Word document. When you edit the Excel worksheet from within the Word document, you will use Excel editing features.
- **Link:** A linked object, by contrast, does not become a part of the destination document even though it appears to be a part of it. Rather, a connection is established between the source and destination documents so that when you open the destination document, the linked object appears as part of it. When you edit a linked object, the source program runs and opens the source document that contains the linked object. For example, when you edit a linked worksheet, Excel runs and displays the Excel workbook that contains the worksheet; you then edit the worksheet in Excel. Unlike an embedded object, if you open the Excel workbook that contains the Excel worksheet and then edit the Excel worksheet, the linked object will be updated in the Word document, too.

BTW

Linked Objects

When you open a document that contains linked objects, Word displays a dialog box asking if you want to update the Word document with data from the linked file. Click Yes only if you are certain the linked file is from a trusted source; that is, you should be confident that the source file does not contain a virus or other potentially harmful program before you instruct Word to link the source file to the destination document.

Consider This

How do you determine which method to use: copy/paste, embed, or link?

- If you simply want to use the object's data and have no desire to use the object in the source program, then copy and paste the object.
- If you want to use the object in the source program but you want the object's data to remain static if it changes in the source file, then embed the object.
- If you want to ensure that the most current version of the object appears in the destination file, then link the object. If the source file is large, such as a video clip or a sound clip, link the object to keep the size of the destination file smaller.

The steps in this section show how to link an Excel worksheet (the object), which is located in an Excel workbook (the source file), to a Word document (the destination file). The Word document is similar to the same memo used in the previous section, except that it does not contain the table. To link the worksheet to the memo, you will follow these general steps:

1. Start Excel and open the Excel workbook that contains the object (worksheet) you want to link to the Word document.
2. Select the object (worksheet) in Excel and then copy the selected object to the Clipboard.
3. Switch to Word and then link the copied object to the Word document.

Note: The steps in this section assume you have Microsoft Excel 365 installed on your computer. If you do not have Excel 365, read the steps in this section without performing them.

To Open a Word Document, Start Excel, and Open an Excel Workbook

The first step in this section is to open the memo that is to contain the link to the Excel worksheet object. The memo file, named SC_WD_8-2.docx, is located in the Data Files. The Excel worksheet to be linked to the memo is in an Excel workbook called Support_WD_8_HomePlanBreakdown_inExcel.xlsx, which also is located in the Data Files. Please contact your instructor for information about accessing the Data Files. The following steps open a Word document, start Excel, and open an Excel workbook. (Do not exit Word or close the open Word document during these steps.)

1. In Word, open the file called SC_WD_8-2.docx located in the Data Files (Figure 8–32).
2. Start Excel and open a blank workbook.
3. In Excel, open the file called Support_WD_8_HomePlanBreakdown_inExcel.xlsx in the Data Files.

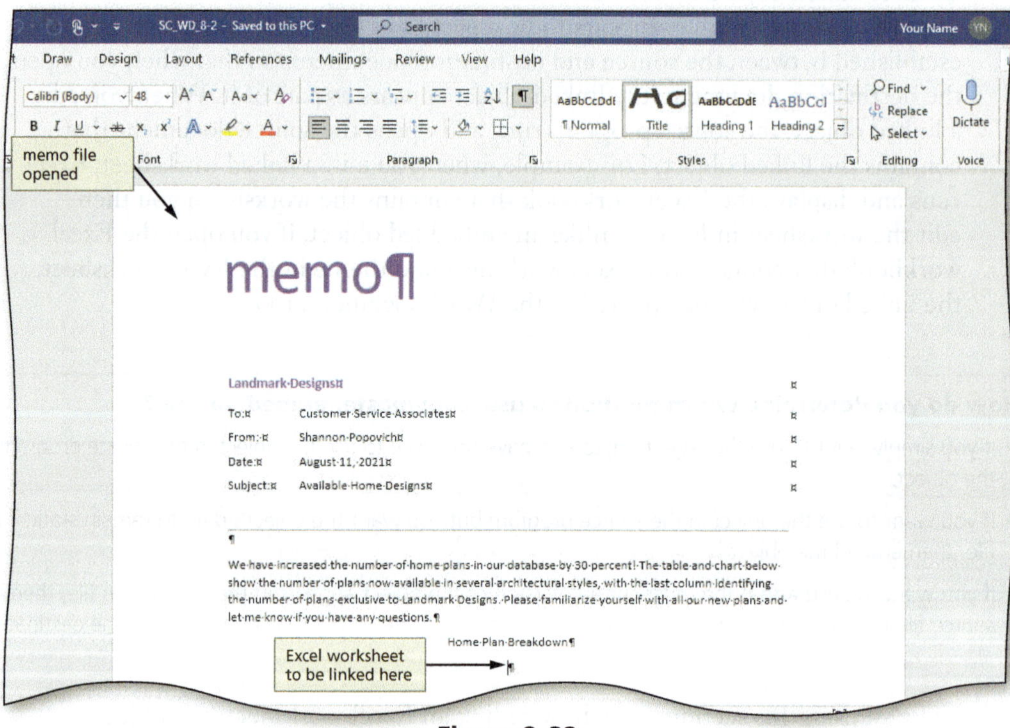

Figure 8–32

BTW

Opening Word Documents with Links

When you open a document that contains a linked object, Word attempts to locate the source file associated with the link. If Word cannot find the source file, open Backstage view, display the Info screen, then click 'Edit Links to Files' in the Related Documents area at the bottom of the right pane to display the Links dialog box. Next, select the appropriate source file in the list (Links dialog box), click the Change Source button, locate the source file, and then click OK.

Excel Basics

The Excel window contains a rectangular grid that consists of columns and rows. A column letter above the grid identifies each column. A row number on the left side of the grid identifies each row. The intersection of each column and row is a cell. A cell is referred to by its unique address, which is the coordinates of the intersection of a column and a row. To identify a cell, specify the column letter first, followed by the row number. For example, cell reference A1 refers to the cell located at the intersection of column A and row 1 (Figure 8–33).

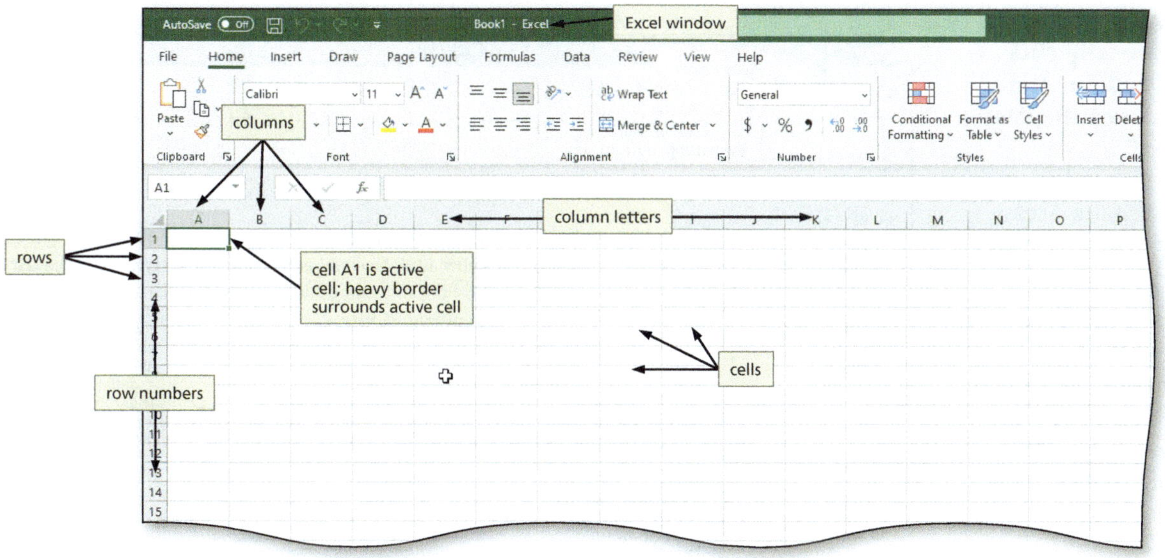

Figure 8–33

To Link an Excel Worksheet to a Word Document

The following steps link an Excel worksheet to a Word document. **Why?** You want to copy the Excel worksheet to the Clipboard and then link the Excel worksheet to the Word document.

1

- In the Excel window, drag through the cells in the range A1 through C7 to select them.
- In the Excel window, click the Copy button (Home tab | Clipboard group) to copy the selected cells to the Clipboard (Figure 8–34).

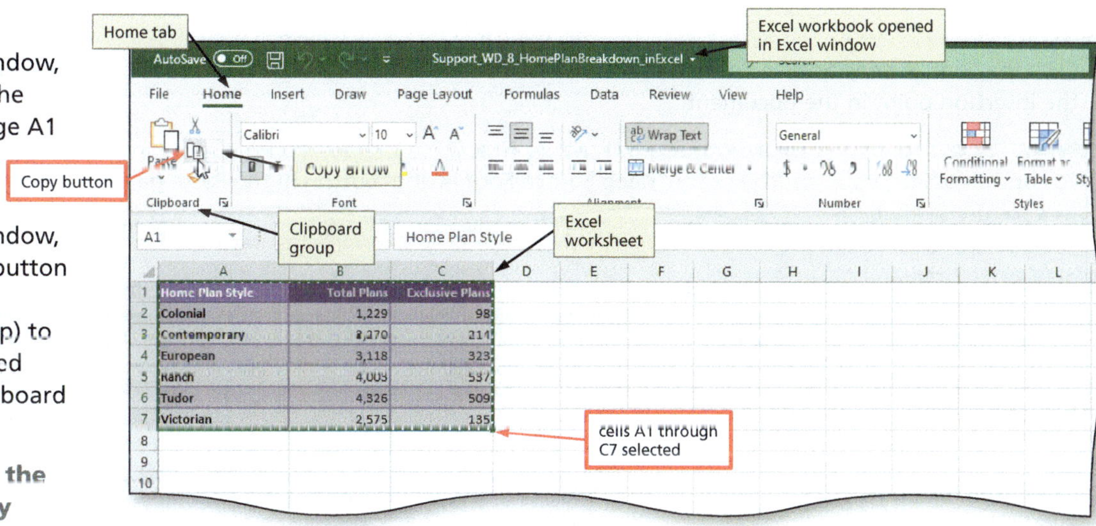

Figure 8–34

Q&A

What if I click the Copy arrow by mistake?
Click Copy on the Copy menu.

What is the dotted line around the selected cells?
Excel surrounds copied cells with a moving marquee to help you visually identify the copied cells.

2

- Click the Word app button on the taskbar to switch to Word and display the open document in the Word window.
- Position the insertion point on the paragraph mark below the table title.
- In Word, click the Paste arrow (Home tab | Clipboard group) to display the Paste gallery.

Q&A **What if I accidentally click the Paste button instead of the Paste arrow?**
Click the Undo button on the Quick Access Toolbar and then click the Paste arrow.

- Point to the 'Link & Keep Source Formatting' button in the Paste gallery to display a Live Preview of that paste option (Figure 8–35).

Experiment

- Point to the various buttons in the Paste gallery to display a Live Preview of each paste option.

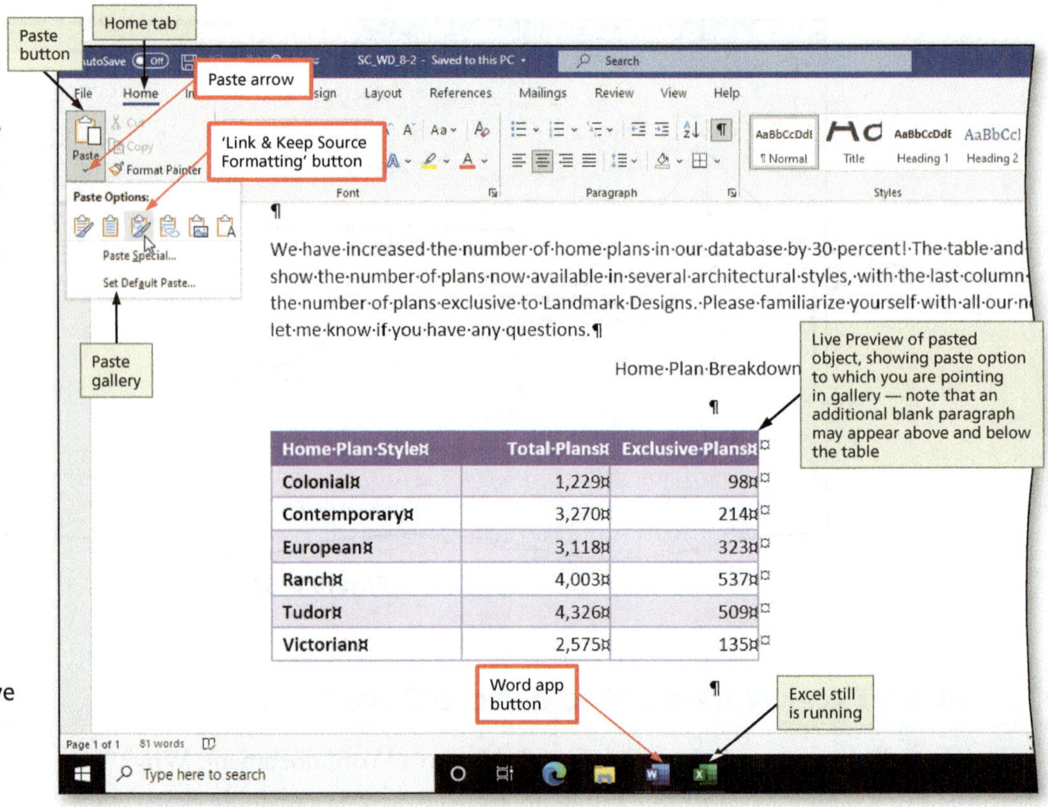

Figure 8–35

3

- Click the 'Link & Keep Source Formatting' button in the Paste gallery to paste and link the object at the location of the insertion point in the document.

Q&A **What if I wanted to copy an object instead of link it?**
To copy an object, you would click the 'Keep Source Formatting' button in the Paste gallery. To convert the object to a picture so that you can use tools on Word's Picture Format tab to format it, you would click the Picture button in the Paste gallery.

- Select and then center the linked Excel table using the same technique you use to select and center a Word table.
- Click outside the table to deselect it (Figure 8–36).

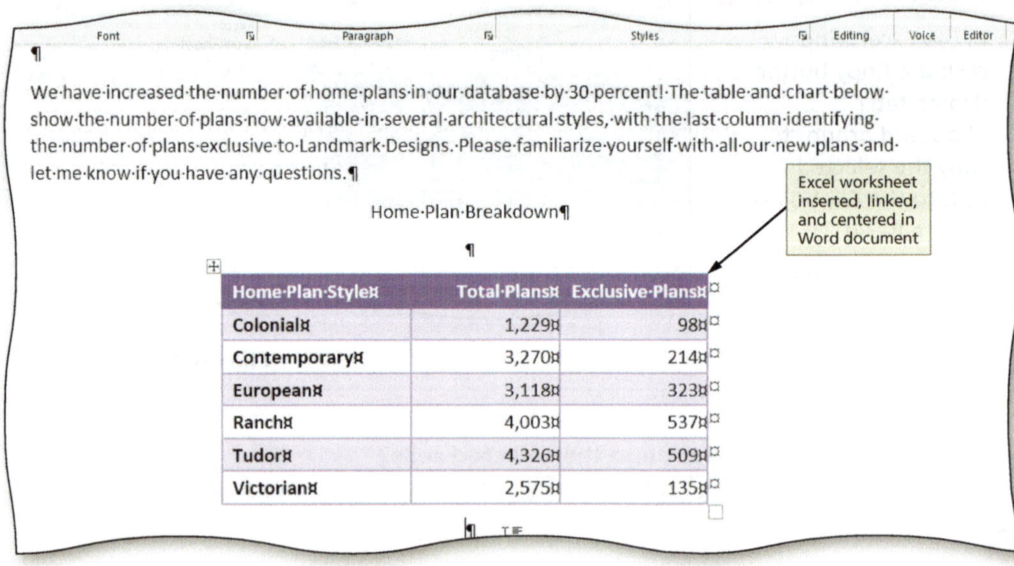

Figure 8–36

Q&A **What if I wanted to delete the linked worksheet?**
You would select the linked worksheet and then press DELETE.

Other Ways

1. Click Paste arrow (Home tab | Clipboard group), click Paste Special, click Paste link (Paste Special dialog box), click 'Microsoft Excel Worksheet Object' in As list, click OK
2. To link an entire source file, click Object button (Insert tab | Text group), click Create from File tab (Object dialog box), locate file, click 'Link to file' check box, click OK

To Embed an Excel Worksheet in a Word Document

If you wanted to embed an Excel worksheet in a Word document, instead of link it, you would perform the following steps.

1. Start Excel.
2. In Excel, select the worksheet cells to embed. Click the Copy button (Home tab | Clipboard group) to copy the selected cells to the Clipboard.
3. Switch to Word. In Word, click the Paste arrow (Home tab | Clipboard group) to display the Paste gallery and then click Paste Special in the Paste gallery to display the Paste Special dialog box.
4. Select the Paste option button (Paste Special dialog box), which indicates the object will be embedded.
5. Select 'Microsoft Excel Worksheet Object' as the type of object to embed.
6. Click OK to embed the contents of the Clipboard in the Word document at the location of the insertion point.

To Edit a Linked Object

At a later time, you may find it necessary to change the data in the Excel worksheet. Any changes you make to the Excel worksheet while in Excel will be reflected in the Excel worksheet in the Word document because the objects are linked to the Word document. If you wanted to edit a linked object, such as an Excel worksheet, you would perform these steps.

1. In the Word document, right-click the linked Excel worksheet, point to 'Linked Worksheet Object' on the shortcut menu, and then click Edit Link on the Linked Worksheet Object submenu to start Excel and open the source file that contains the linked worksheet.
2. In Excel, make changes to the Excel worksheet.
3. Click the Save button on the Quick Access Toolbar to save the changes.
4. Exit Excel.
5. If necessary, redisplay the Word window.
6. If necessary, to update the worksheet with the edited Excel data, click the Excel worksheet in the Word document and then press F9, or right-click the linked object and then click Update Link on the shortcut menu to update the linked object with the revisions made to the source file.

BTW

Editing Embedded Objects

If you wanted to edit an embedded object in the Word document, you would double-click the object to display the source program's interface in the destination program. For example, double-clicking an embedded Excel worksheet in a Word document displays the Excel ribbon in the Word window. To redisplay the Word ribbon in the Word window, double-click outside of the embedded object.

To Break a Link

Why? You can convert a linked or embedded object to a Word object by breaking the link. That is, you break the connection between the source file and the destination file. When you break a linked object, such as an Excel worksheet, the linked object becomes a Word object, a Word table in this case. The following steps break the link to the Excel worksheet.

1

- Right-click the linked object (the linked Excel worksheet, in this case) to display a shortcut menu.
- Point to 'Linked Worksheet Object' on the shortcut menu to display the Linked Worksheet Object submenu (Figure 8–37).

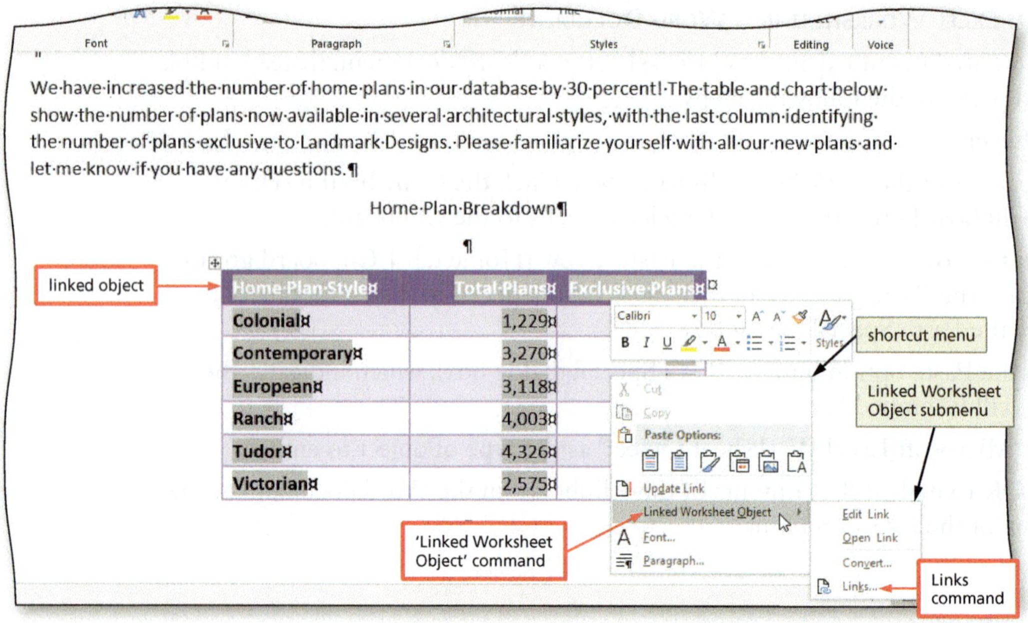

Figure 8–37

2

- Click Links on the Linked Worksheet Object submenu to display the Links dialog box.
- If necessary, click the source file listed in the dialog box to select it (Links dialog box).
- Click the Break Link button, which displays a dialog box asking if you are sure you want to break the selected links (Figure 8–38).

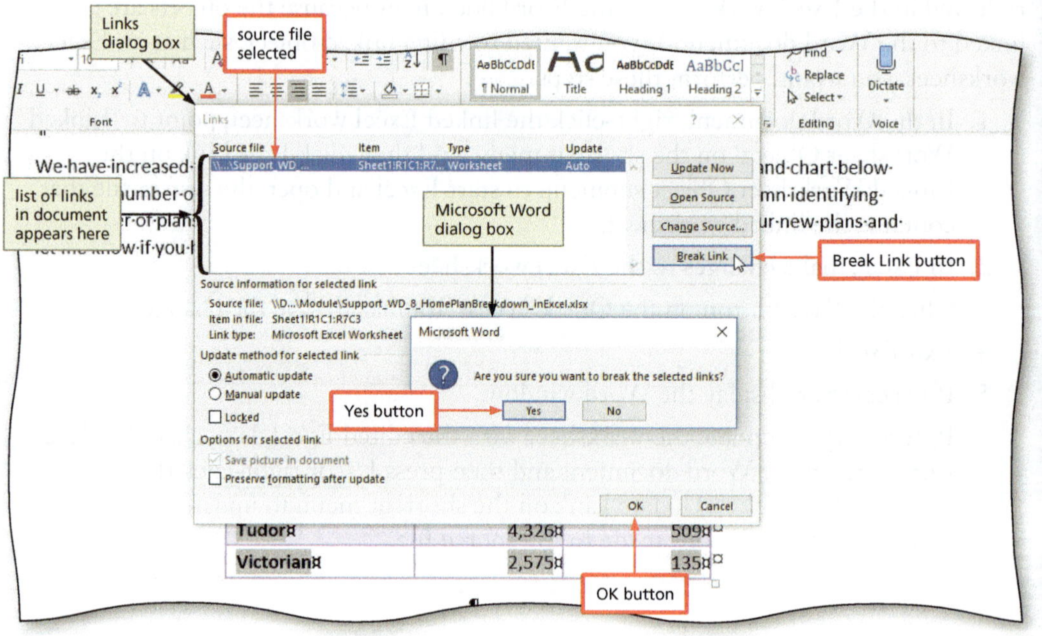

Figure 8–38

3

- Click Yes in the dialog box to remove the source file from the list (break the link).

Q&A **How can I verify the link is broken?**
Right-click the table in the Word document to display a shortcut menu. If the shortcut menu does not contain a 'Linked Worksheet Object' command, a link does not exist for the object. Or, when you double-click the table, Excel should not open an associated workbook.

- Close the Word document without saving it.
- Exit Excel without saving changes to the workbook.

Other Ways

1. Select link, press CTRL+SHIFT+F9

Consider This

Why would you break a link?

If you share a Word document that contains a linked object, such as an Excel worksheet, users will be asked by Word if they want to update the links when they open the Word document. If users are unfamiliar with links, they will not know how to answer the question. Further, if they do not have the source program, such as Excel, they may not be able to open the Word document. When sharing documents, it is recommended you convert links to a regular Word object; that is, break the link.

Charting a Word Table

Several Office applications, including Word, enable you to create charts from data. In the following pages, you will insert and format a chart of the Home Plan Breakdown Word table using the chart contextual tabs in Word. You will follow these general steps to insert and then format the chart:

1. Create a chart of the table.
2. Remove a data series from the chart.
3. Apply a chart style to the chart.
4. Change the colors of the chart.
5. Add a chart element.
6. Edit a chart element.
7. Format chart elements.
8. Add an outline to the chart.

To Open and Save a Document

The next step is to open the Home Plan Breakdown Memo file that contains the final wording so that you can create a chart of its Word table. This file, called SC_WD_8-3.docx, is located in the Data Files. Please contact your instructor for information about accessing the Data Files. The following steps open a document and then save it with a new file name.

1 sam Navigate to the Data Files and then open the file called SC_WD_8-3.docx.

2 Save the memo on your hard drive, OneDrive, or other storage location using SC_WD_8_LandmarkDesignsMemo_withTableandClusteredChart as the file name.

BTW

Touch Mode Differences

The Office and Windows interfaces may vary if you are using Touch mode. For this reason, you might notice that the function or appearance of your touch screen differs slightly from this module's presentation.

To Insert a Chart

The following steps insert a default chart and then copy the data to be charted from the Word table in the Word document to a chart spreadsheet. **Why?** To chart a table, you fill in or copy the data into a chart spreadsheet that automatically opens after you insert the chart.

1

- Position the insertion point on the centered paragraph mark below the table because the chart will be inserted at the location of the insertion point.
- Display the Insert tab.
- Click the Chart button (Insert tab | Illustrations group) to display the Insert Chart dialog box.
- Click Bar in the left pane (Insert Chart dialog box) to display the available types of bar charts in the right pane.

Experiment

- Click the various types of charts in the left pane and watch the subtypes appear in the right pane. When finished experimenting, click Bar in the left pane.

- If necessary, click Clustered Bar in the right pane to select the chart type (Figure 8–39).

Experiment

- Click the various types of bar charts in the right pane and watch the graphic change in the right pane. When finished experimenting, click Clustered Bar in the right pane.

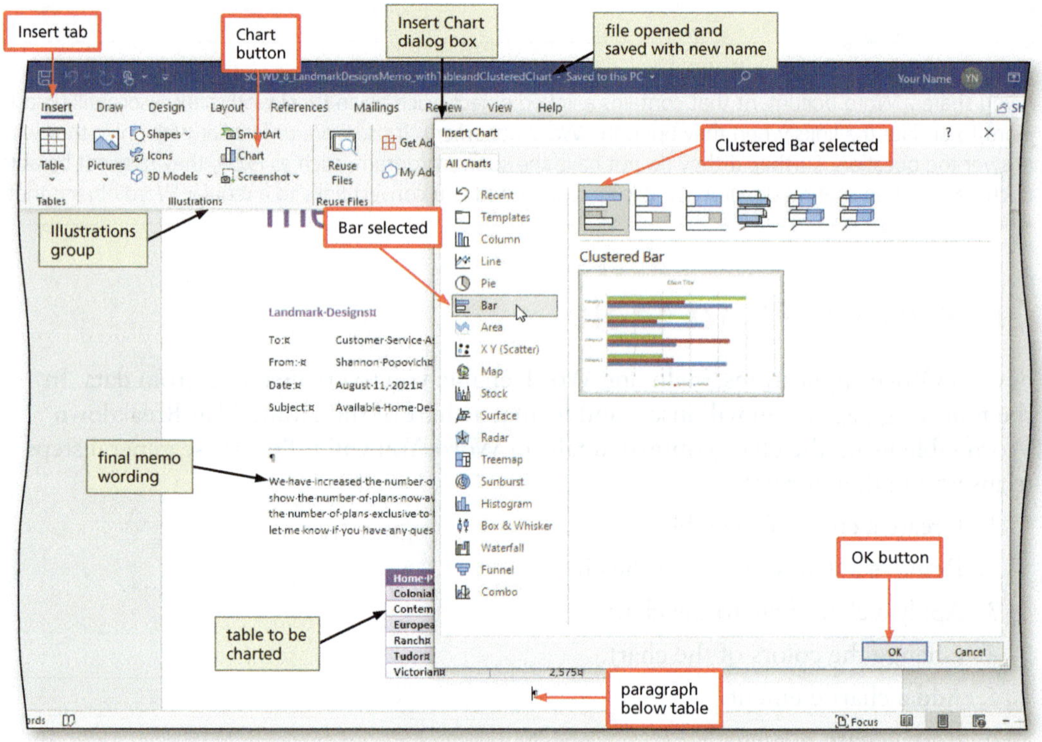

Figure 8–39

2

- Click OK so that Word creates a default clustered bar chart in the Word document at the location of the insertion point (Figure 8–40). If necessary, click the chart to select it.

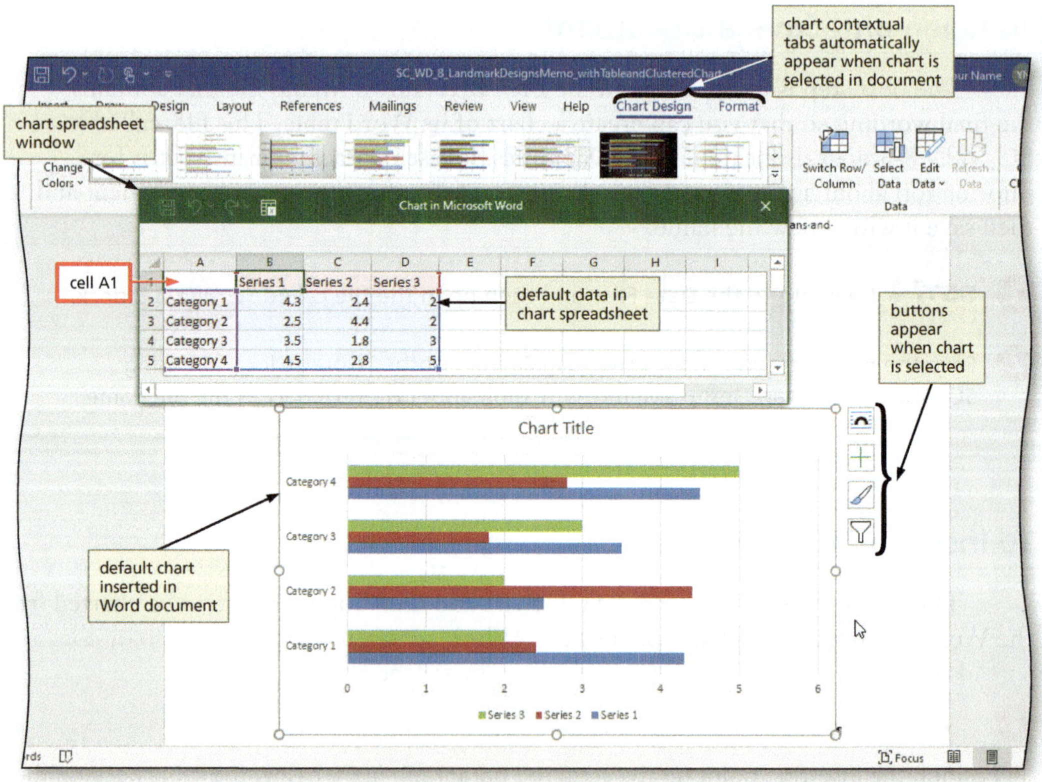

Figure 8–40

Q&A

What are the requirements for the format of a table that can be charted?

The chart spreadsheet window shows the layout for the selected chart type. In this case, the categories are in the rows and the series are in the columns. Notice the categories appear in the chart in reverse order.

3

- In the Word document, if necessary, select the table to be charted. (If necessary, drag the chart spreadsheet window or scroll in the document window so that the table is visible.)
- Click the Copy button (Home tab | Clipboard group) to copy the selected table to the Clipboard (Figure 8–41).

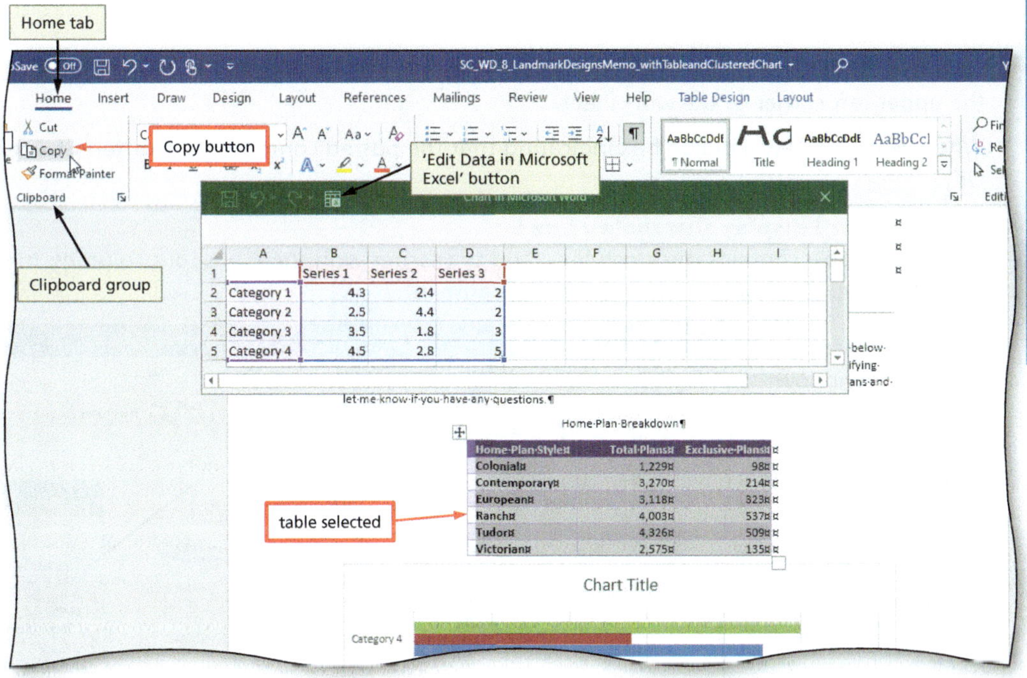

Figure 8–41

Q&A **Instead of copying table data to the chart spreadsheet, could I type the data directly into the spreadsheet?**

Yes. If the chart spreadsheet window does not appear, click the Edit Data arrow (Chart Design tab | Data group) and then click Edit Data on the menu. You also can click the 'Edit Data in Microsoft Excel' button to use Excel to enter the data (if Excel is installed on your computer), or click the Edit Data arrow (Chart Design tab | Data group) and then click 'Edit Data in Excel' on the Edit Data menu. You edit (modify) existing data and add new data in rows and columns the same way you would in an Excel worksheet.

4

- In the chart spreadsheet window, click the Select All button (upper-left corner of worksheet) to select the entire worksheet.
- Right-click the selected worksheet to display a Mini toolbar or shortcut menu (Figure 8–42).

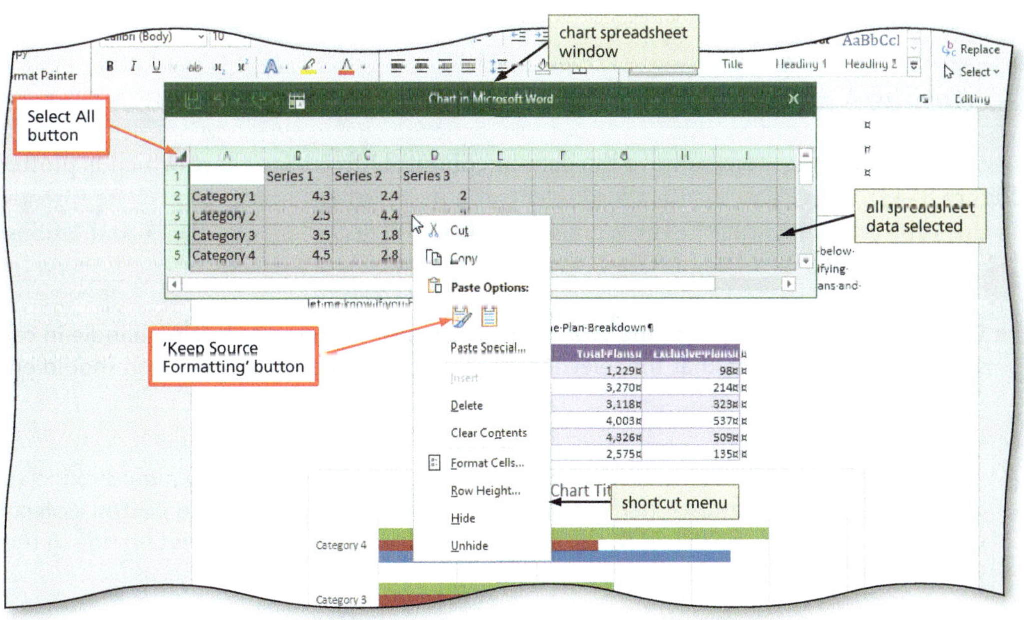

Figure 8–42

5

- Click the 'Keep Source Formatting' button on the shortcut menu to paste the contents of the Clipboard starting in the upper-left corner of the worksheet.
- When Word displays a dialog box indicating that the pasted contents are a different size from the selection, click OK.

Q&A

Why did Word display this dialog box?
The source table contains three columns, and the target worksheet has four columns. In the next section, you will delete the fourth column from the chart spreadsheet.

- Resize the chart worksheet window by dragging its window edges and move it by dragging its title bar so the worksheet window appears as shown in Figure 8–43. Notice that the chart in the Word window automatically changes to reflect the new data in the chart worksheet (Figure 8–43).

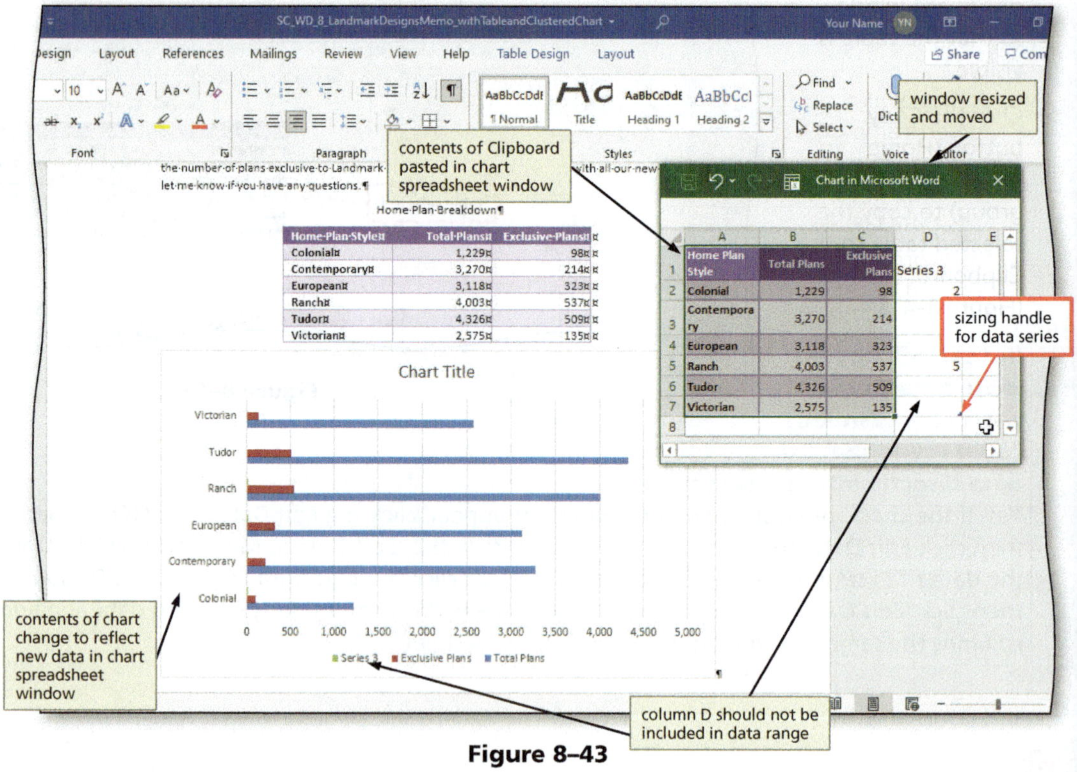

Figure 8–43

To Remove a Data Series from the Chart

The following steps remove the data in column D from the chart, which is plotted as Series 3 (shown in Figure 8–43). **Why?** By default, Word selects the first four columns in the chart spreadsheet window. The chart in this project covers only the three columns: Home Plan Style, Total Plans, and Exclusive Plans.

1

- Ensure the chart is selected in the Word document and then drag the sizing handle in cell D7 of the chart spreadsheet leftward so that the selection ends at cell C7; that is, the selection should encompass cells A1 through C7 (Figure 8–44).

Q&A

How would I add a data series?
Add a column of data to the chart spreadsheet. Drag the sizing handle outward to include the series, or you could click the Select Data button (Chart Design tab | Data group), click the Add button (Select Data Source dialog box), click the Select Range button (Edit Series dialog box), drag through the data range in the worksheet, and then click OK.

How would I add or remove data categories?
Follow the same steps to add or remove data series, except work with spreadsheet rows instead of columns.

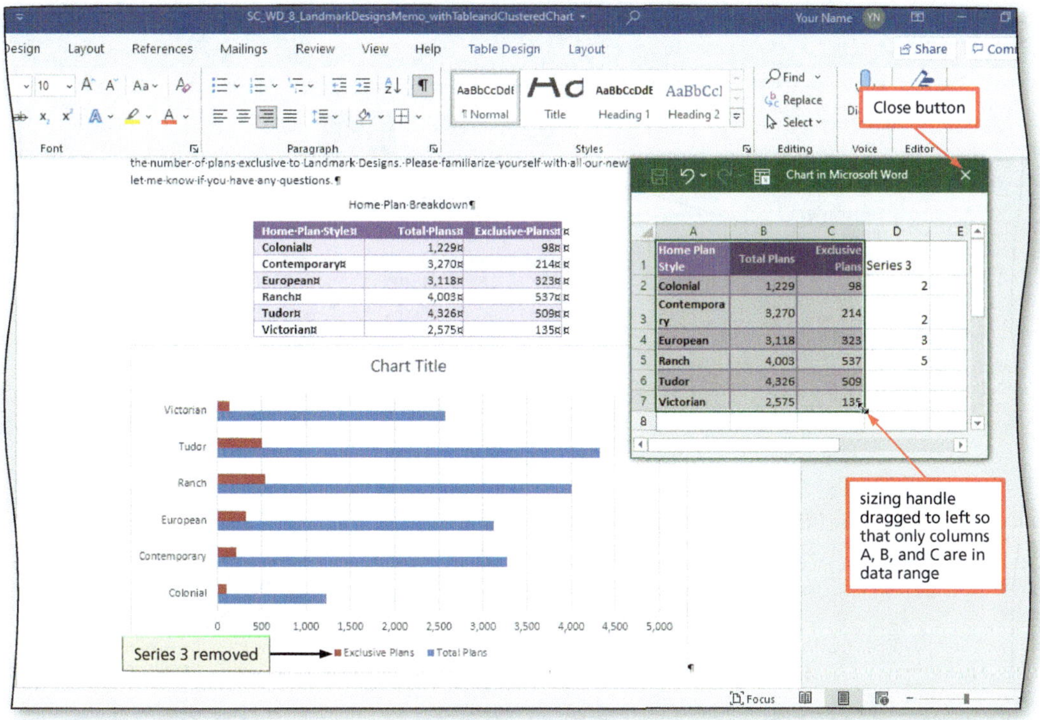

Figure 8–44

2

- Close the chart spreadsheet window by clicking its Close button.

Q&A

How would I copy an existing chart and paste it with source formatting?
To copy the chart, you would select it and then click the Copy button (Home tab | Clipboard group), or right-click the chart and then click Copy on the shortcut menu, or press CTRL+C. To paste the chart with source formatting, you would position the insertion point at the desired paste location, click the Paste arrow (Home tab | Clipboard group) or right-click the chart, and click the 'Keep Source Formatting' button on the Paste menu or shortcut menu.

Other Ways

1. Click Select Data button (Chart Design tab | Data group), click series to remove (Select Data Source dialog box), click Remove button, click OK

To Apply a Chart Style

The next step is to apply a chart style to the chart. **Why?** Word provides a Chart Styles gallery, allowing you to change the chart's format to a more visually appealing style. The following steps apply a chart style to a chart.

1

- If necessary, click the chart to select it.
- Display the Chart Design tab.
- Point to Style 8 in the Chart Styles gallery (Chart Design tab | Chart Styles group) to display a Live Preview of that style applied to the graphic in the document (Figure 8–45).

Experiment

- Point to various styles in the Chart Styles gallery and watch the style of the chart change in the document window.

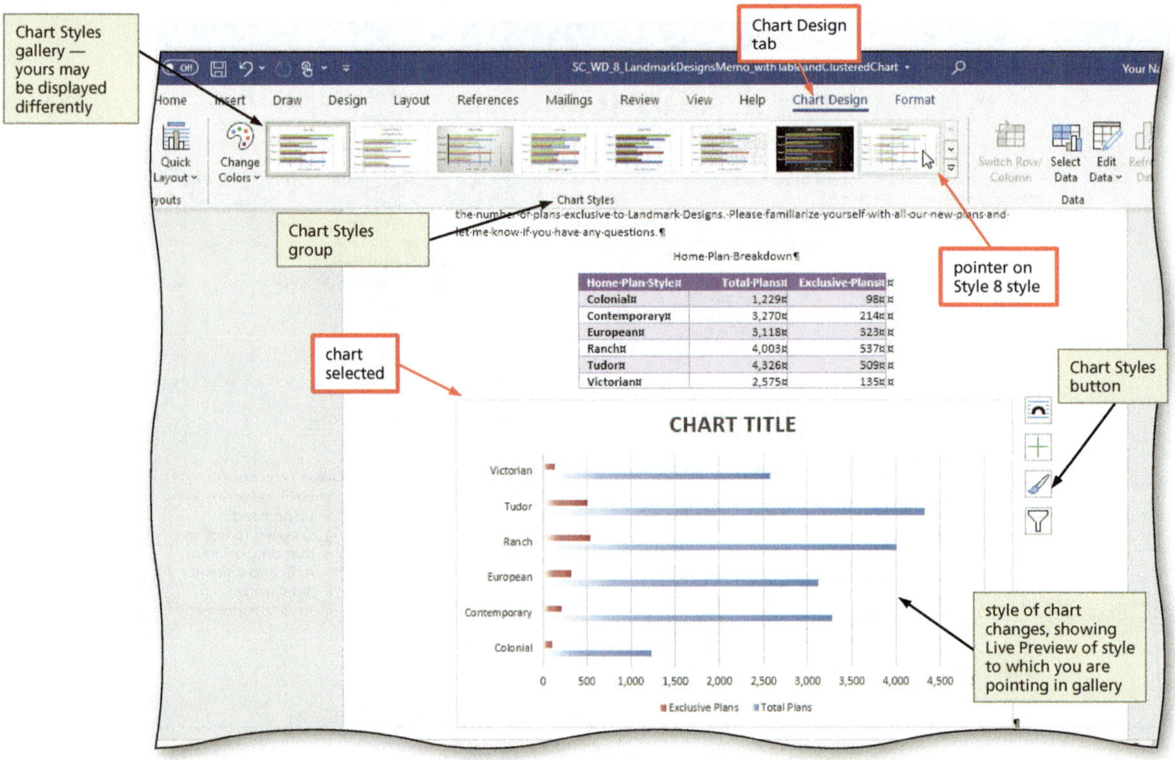

Figure 8–45

2

- Click Style 8 in the Chart Styles gallery (Chart Design tab | Chart Styles group) to apply the selected style to the chart.

Other Ways

1. Click Chart Styles button attached to chart, click Style tab, click desired style

To Change Colors of a Chart

The following steps change the colors of the chart. **Why?** Word provides a predefined variety of colors for charts. You select one that best matches the colors already used in the letter.

1

- With the chart selected, click the Change Colors button (Chart Design tab | Chart Styles group) to display the Change Colors gallery.

Q&A **What if the chart is not selected?**
Click the chart to select it.

- Point to 'Colorful Palette 3' in the Change Colors gallery to display a Live Preview of the selected color applied to the chart in the document (Figure 8–46).

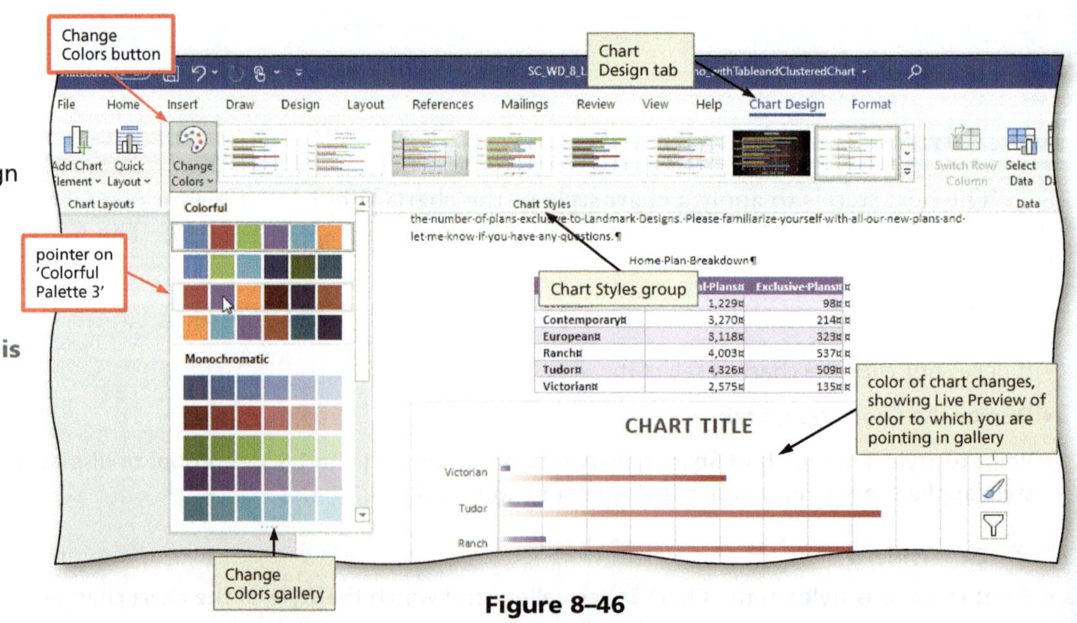

Figure 8–46

Experiment

- Point to various colors in the Change Colors gallery and watch the colors of the chart change in the document window.

2

- Click 'Colorful Palette 3' in the Change Colors gallery to apply the selected color to the chart.

Other Ways

1. Click Chart Styles button attached to chart, click Color tab, click desired style

To Add a Chart Element

The following steps add minor vertical gridlines to the chart. **Why?** You want to add more vertical lines to the chart so that it is easier to see the dollar values associated with each bar length.

1

- With the chart selected, click the 'Add Chart Element' button (Chart Design tab | Chart Layouts group) to display the Add Chart Element gallery and then point to Gridlines to display the Gridlines submenu (Figure 8–47).

Experiment

- Point to various elements in the Add Chart Element gallery so that you can see the other types of elements you can add to a chart. When finished, point to Gridlines.

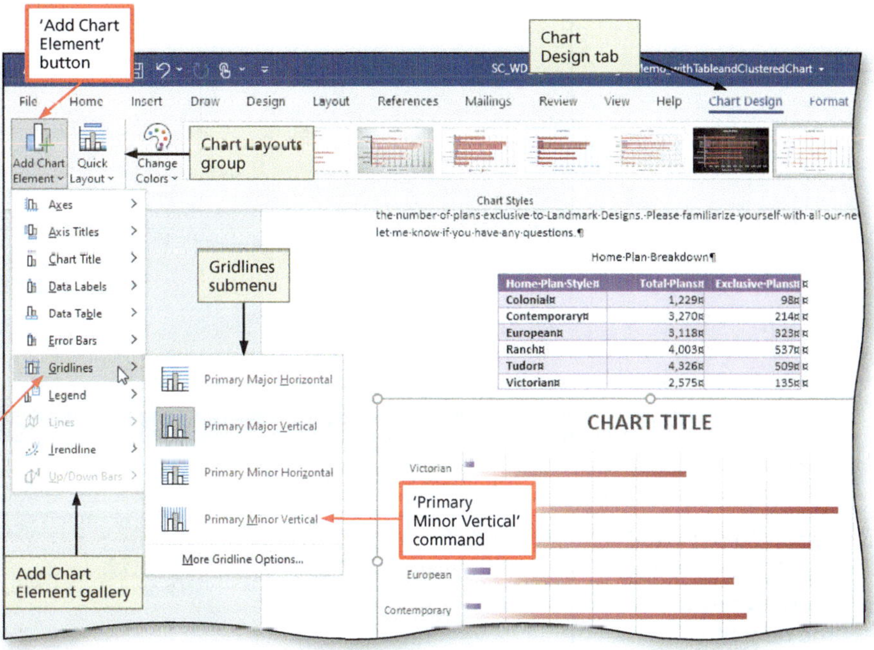

Figure 8–47

2

- Click 'Primary Minor Vertical' on the Gridline submenu to add vertical minor gridlines to the chart (Figure 8–48).

Q&A

How would I add data labels to a chart?

Click the 'Add Chart Element' button (Chart Design tab | Chart Layouts group), point to Data Labels, and then click the desired location for the data labels.

How would I remove a chart element?

Select the chart element and then press DELETE.

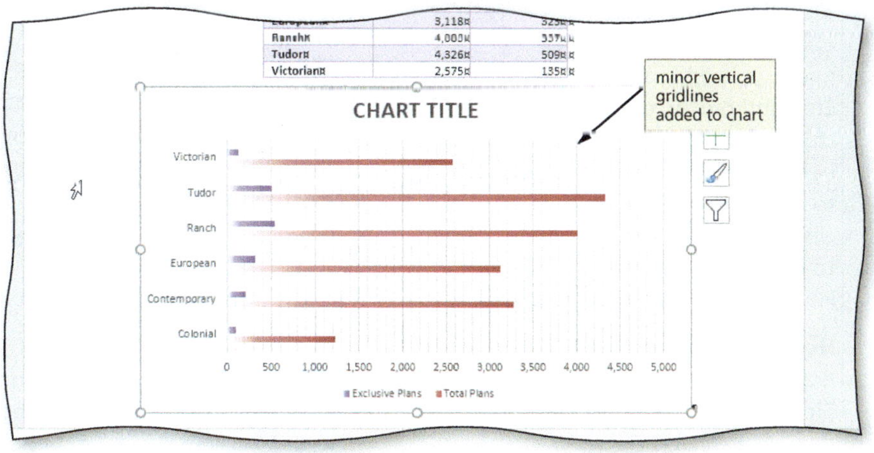

Figure 8–48

To Select a Chart Element and Edit It

The following steps change the chart title. **Why?** You want to change the title from the default to a more meaningful name.

1

- Display the Format tab.
- With the chart selected, click the Chart Elements arrow (Format tab | Current Selection group) to display the Chart Elements list (Figure 8–49).

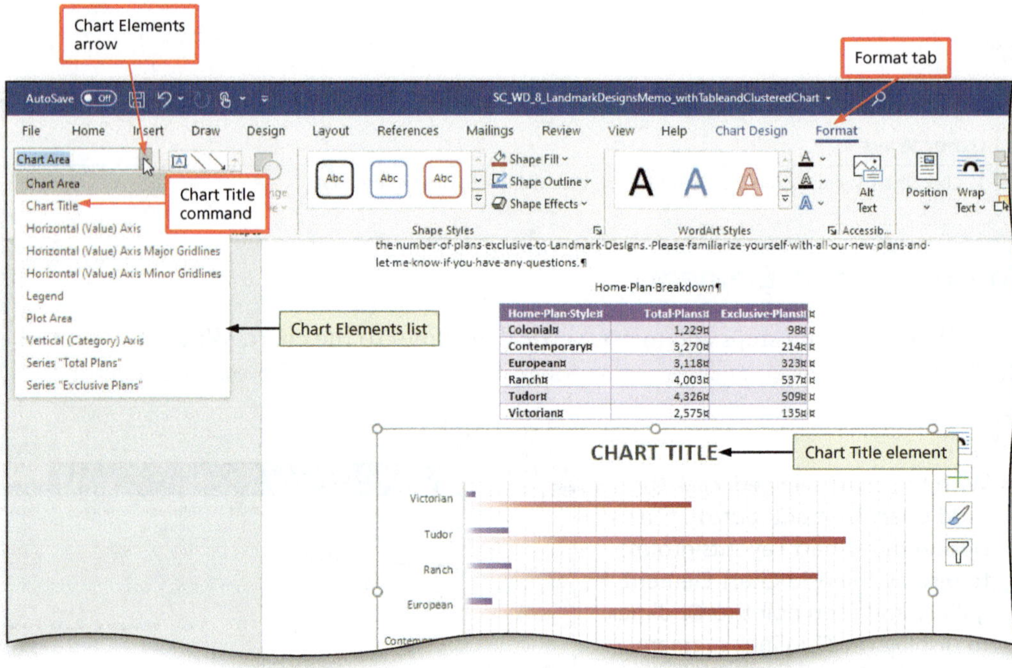

Figure 8–49

2

- Click Chart Title in the Chart Elements list to select the chart's title.
- Type **Total and Exclusive Plan Comparison** as the new title (Figure 8–50).

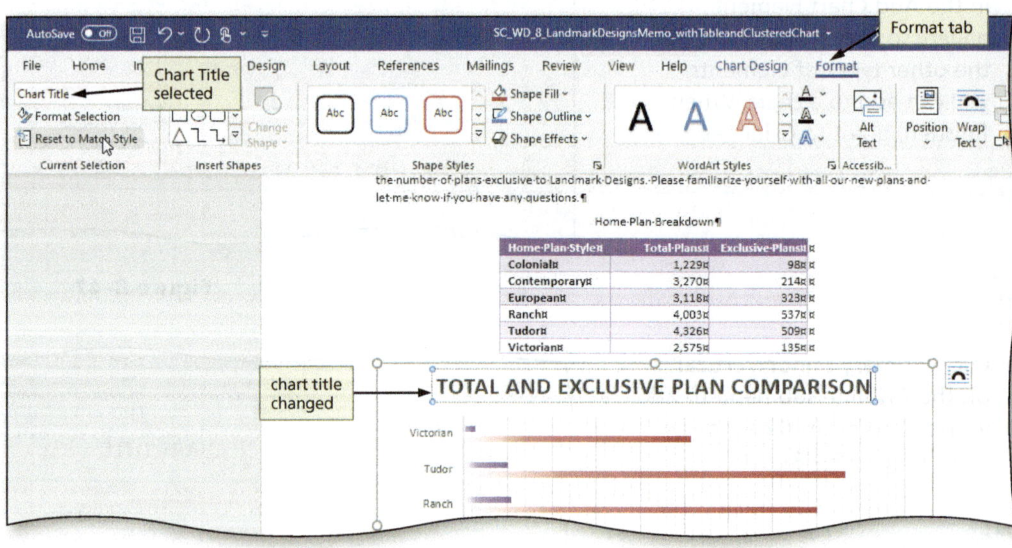

Figure 8–50

Q&A

How would I add an axis title to the chart?
Click the 'Add Chart Element' button (Chart Design tab | Chart Layouts group), point to Axis Titles, and then click the desired axis to be titled (Primary Horizontal or Primary Vertical). Click the default axis title added to the chart and then edit it as desired.

How would I add an axis to a chart?
If a chart did not already contain an axis when you created it, you could add one by clicking the 'Add Chart Element' button (Chart Design tab | Chart Layouts group), point to Axis, and then click the desired axis.

Other Ways

1. Click chart element in chart to select element

To Format Chart Elements

Currently, the category names on the vertical axis are in reverse order of the row labels in the table; that is, category names are in alphabetical order from bottom to top and the row labels in the table are in alphabetical order from top to bottom. The following steps format axis elements. **Why?** You want the categories to display in the same order as the table, the maximum value on the horizontal axis to be 4,500 instead of 5,000, and the legend to appear at the top of the chart.

1

- If necessary, select the chart by clicking it.
- With the chart selected, click the Chart Elements arrow (Format tab | Current Selection group) to display the Chart Elements list and then click 'Vertical (Category) Axis'.
- Click the Chart Elements button attached to the right of the chart to display the Chart Elements gallery.
- Point to and then click the Axes arrow in the Chart Elements gallery to display the Axes fly-out menu (Figure 8–51).

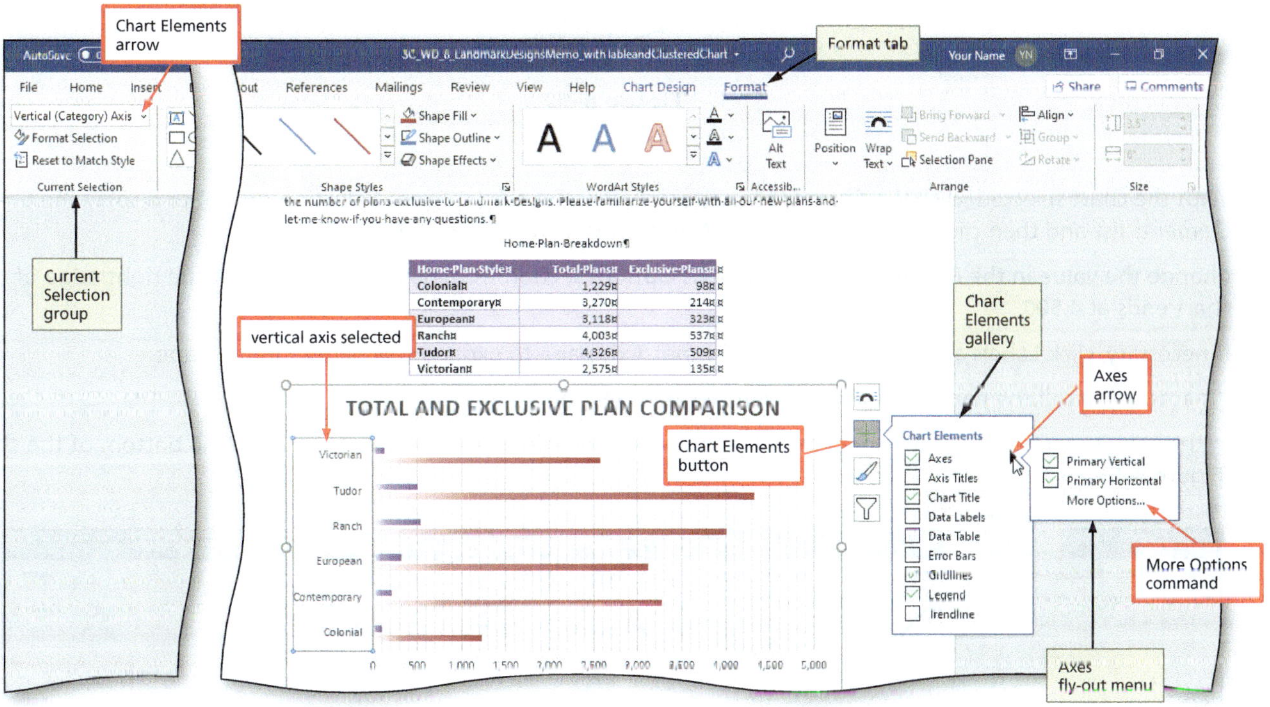

Figure 8–51

2

- Click More Options on the Axes fly-out menu to open the Format Axis pane.
- If necessary, click the Chart Elements arrow (Format tab | Current Selection group) to display the Chart Elements list and then click 'Vertical (Category) Axis' to select the vertical axis.
- If necessary, click Axis Options in the Format Axis pane to expand the section.
- Place a check mark in the 'Categories in reverse order' check box in the Format Axis pane so that the order of the categories in the chart matches the order of the categories in the table (Figure 8–52).

Q&A **Why did the horizontal axis move from the bottom of the chart to the top?**
When you reverse the categories, the horizontal axis automatically moves from the bottom of the chart to the top of the chart. Notice that the series names below the chart also are reversed.

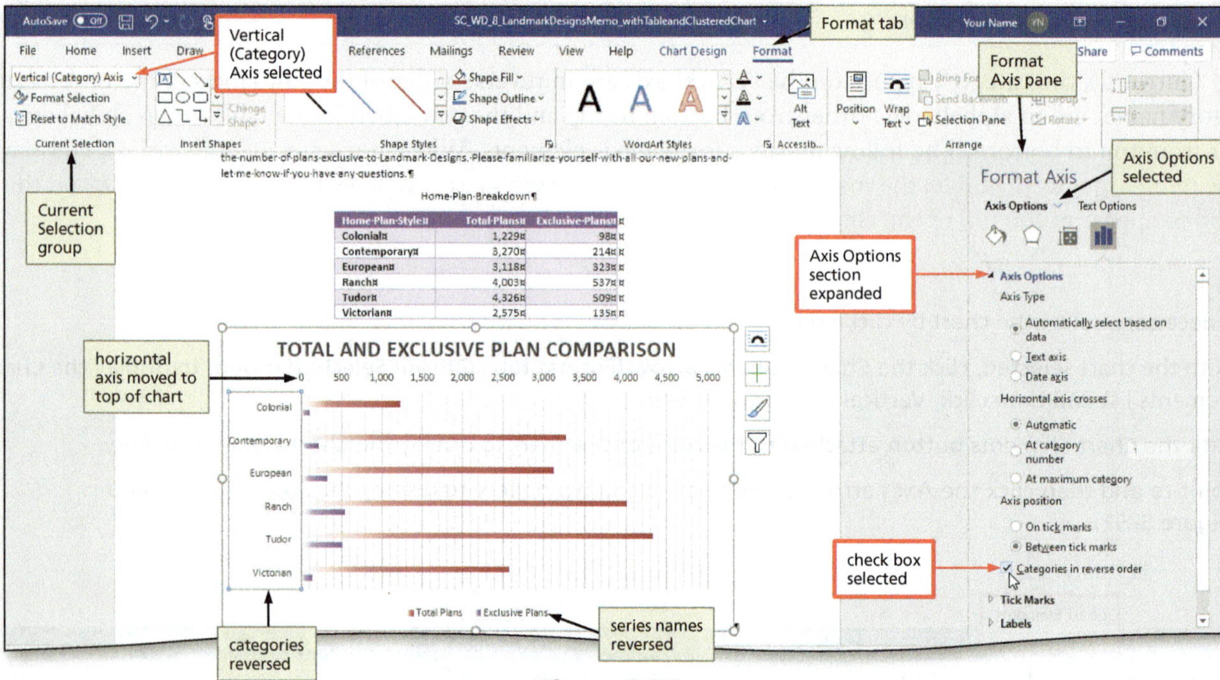

Figure 8–52

3

- With the chart selected, click the Chart Elements arrow (Format tab | Current Selection group) to display the Chart Elements list and then click 'Horizontal (Value) Axis' to select the horizontal axis.
- Change the value in the Maximum box in the Axis Options section from 5000 to 4500 so that the right edge of the chart ends at 4,500.
- If necessary, click Labels at the bottom of the Format Axis pane to expand this section in the pane.
- If necessary, scroll the pane to display the entire Labels section.
- In the Labels section, click the Label Position arrow and then click High to move the axis to the bottom of the chart (Figure 8–53).

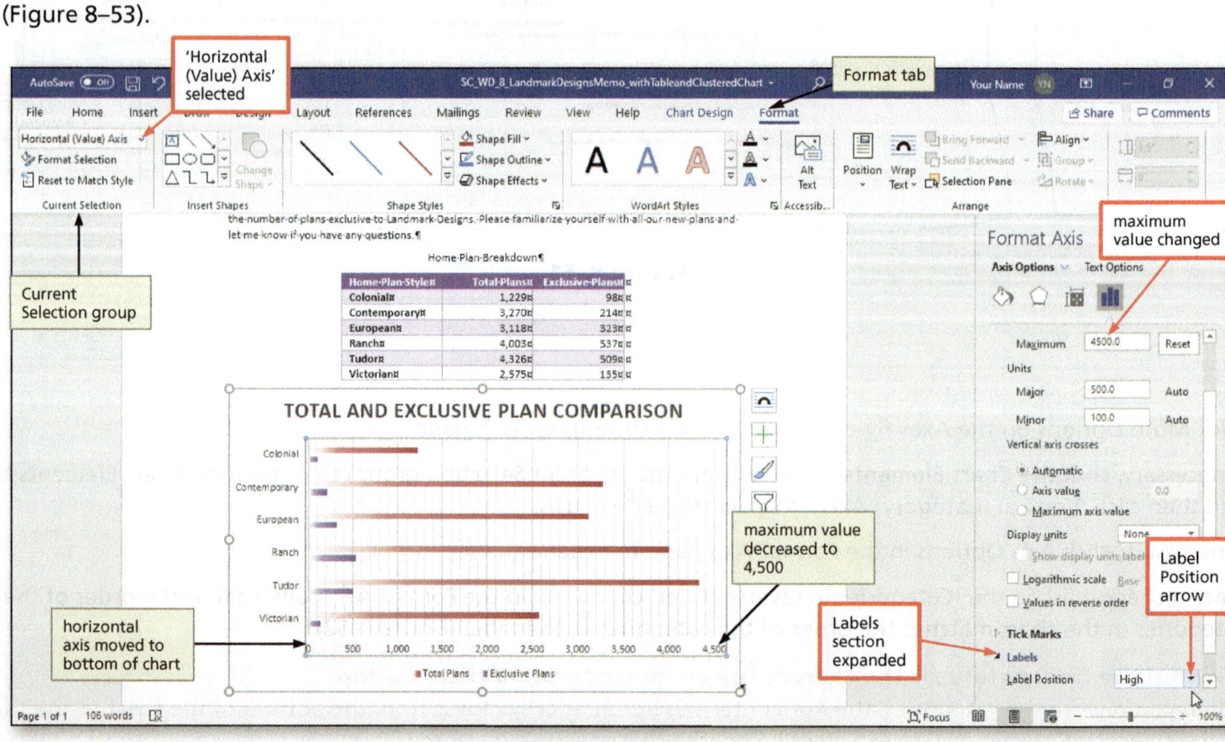

Figure 8–53

Experiment

- Click Number at the bottom of the Format Axis pane to expand this section and review the various number formats you can apply.

4

- With the chart selected, click the Chart Elements arrow (Format tab | Current Selection group) to display the Chart Elements list and then click Legend.

Q&A **What happened to the Format Axis pane?**
It now is the Format Legend pane. The pane title and options change, depending on the element you are using or formatting.

- If necessary, click Legend Options to expand the section in the Format Legend pane.
- Click Top to select the option button and move the legend to the top of the chart (Figure 8–54).

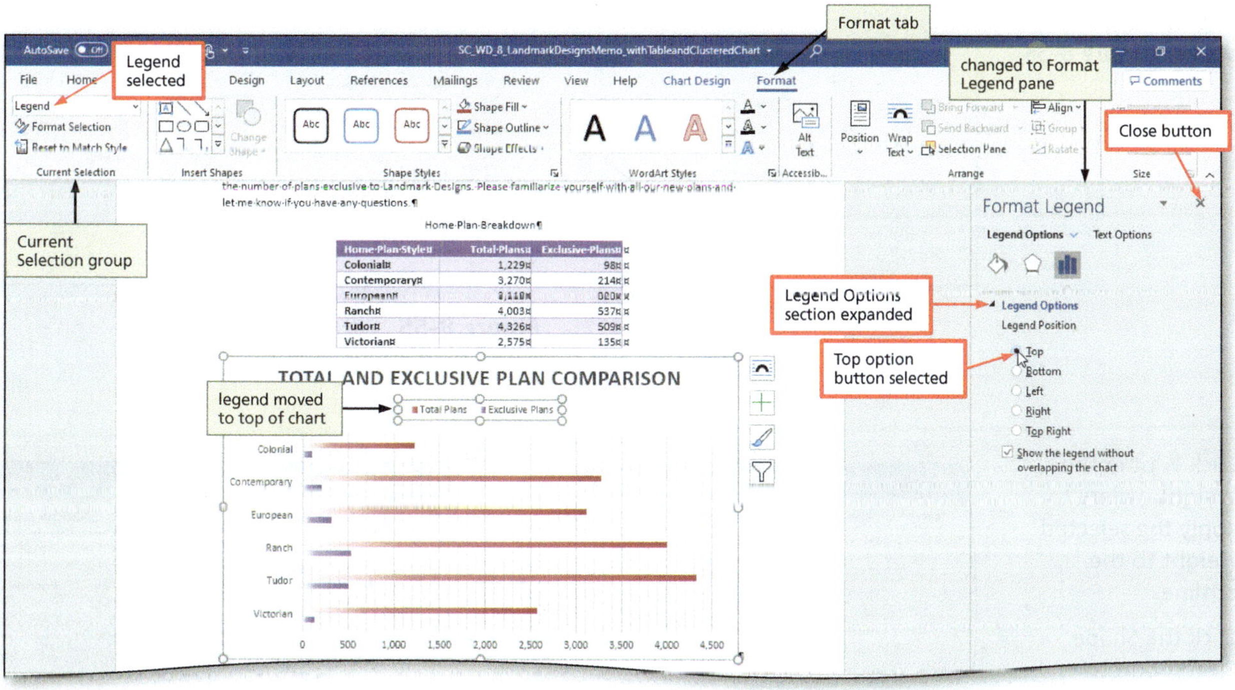

Figure 8–54

5

- Close the Format Legend pane by clicking its Close button.

Q&A **How would I add a legend to a chart?**
Click the 'Add Chart Element' button (Chart Design tab | Chart Layouts group), point to Legend, and then click the desired location for the legend.

To Add an Outline to a Chart

The following steps add an outline to the chart with a shadow. **Why?** You want a border surrounding the chart.

1

- With the chart selected, click the Chart Elements arrow (Format tab | Current Selection group) to display the Chart Elements list and then, if necessary, click Chart Area to select the chart area.
- Click the Shape Outline arrow (Format tab | Shape Styles group) to display the Shape Outline gallery.

2

- Click 'Purple, Accent 4' (eighth color, first row) in the Shape Outline gallery to change the outline color.
- Click the Shape Outline arrow (Format tab | Shape Styles group) again and then point to Weight in the Shape Outline gallery to display the Weight gallery (Figure 8–55).

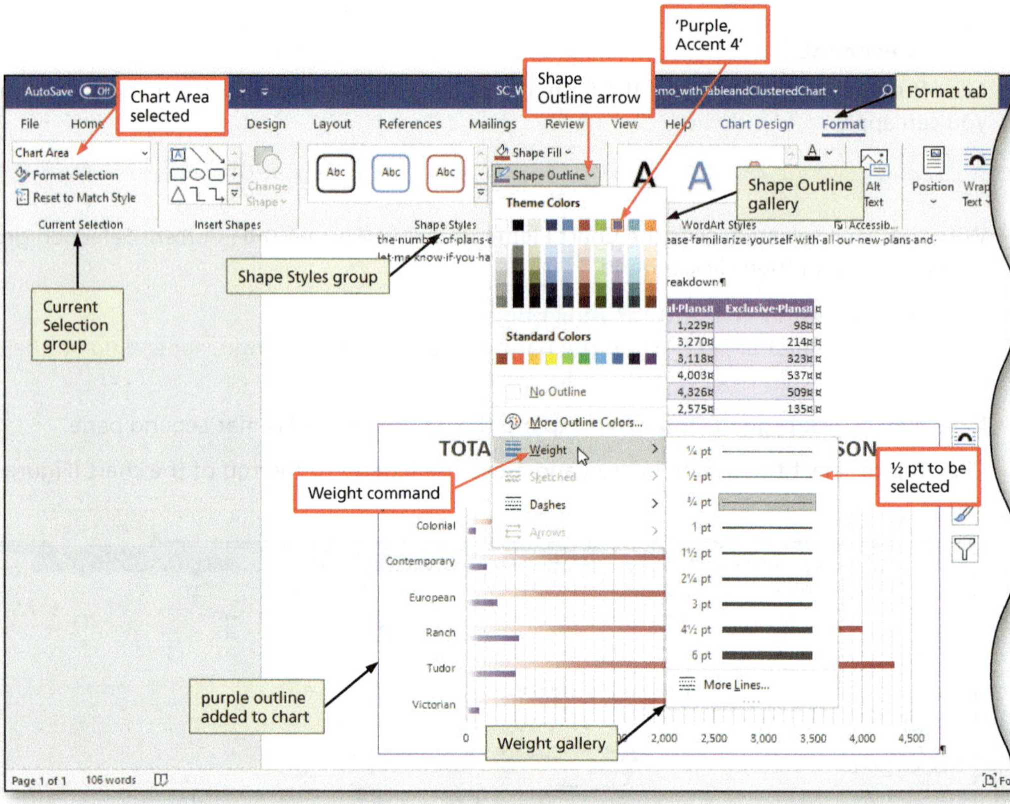

Figure 8–55

3

- Click ½ pt in the Weight gallery to apply the selected weight to the outline.
- Click the Shape Effects button (Format tab | Shape Styles group) and then point to Shadow in the Shape Effects gallery to display the Shadow gallery (Figure 8–56).

4

- Click 'Offset: Bottom Right' in the Shadow gallery to apply the selected shadow to the outline.
- Save the modified memo in the same storage location using the same file name.

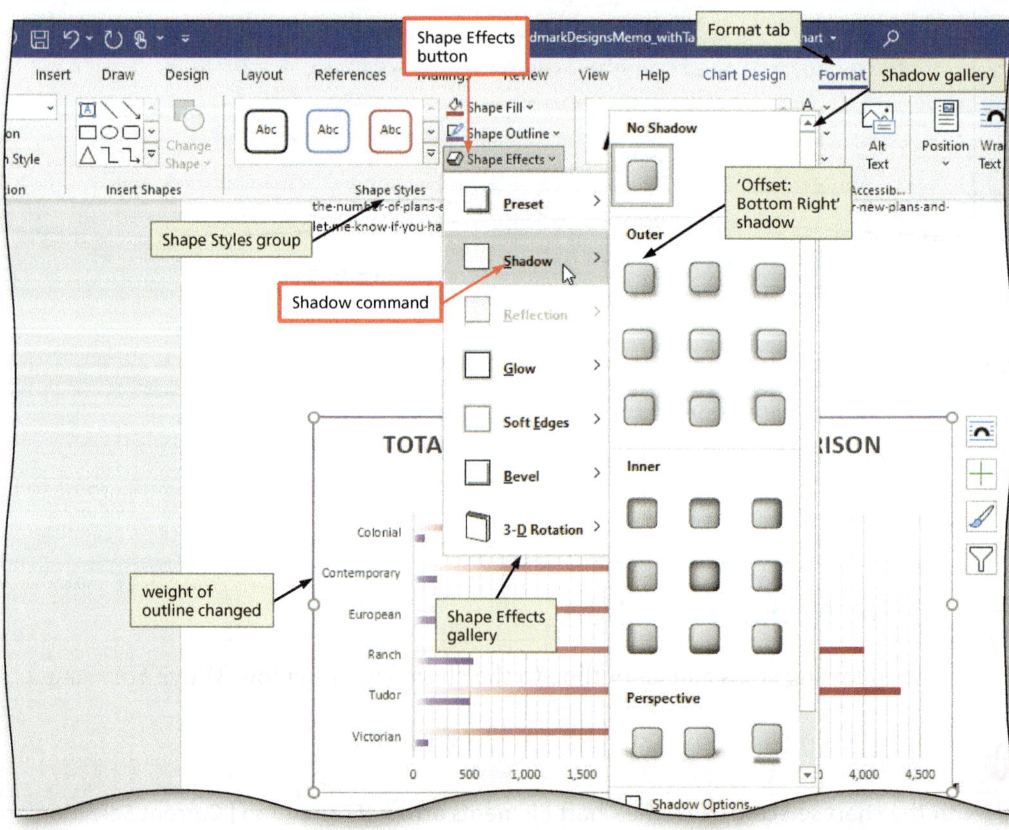

Figure 8–56

To Change a Chart Type

The following steps change the chart type. **Why?** After reviewing the document, you would like to see how the chart looks as a 3-D clustered bar chart.

1

- Display the Chart Design tab.
- Click the 'Change Chart Type' button (Chart Design tab | Type group) to display the Change Chart Type dialog box.
- Click Column in the left pane to change the chart to a column chart.
- Click '3-D Clustered Column' in the right pane (Change Chart Type dialog box) in the right pane to change the chart type (Figure 8–57).

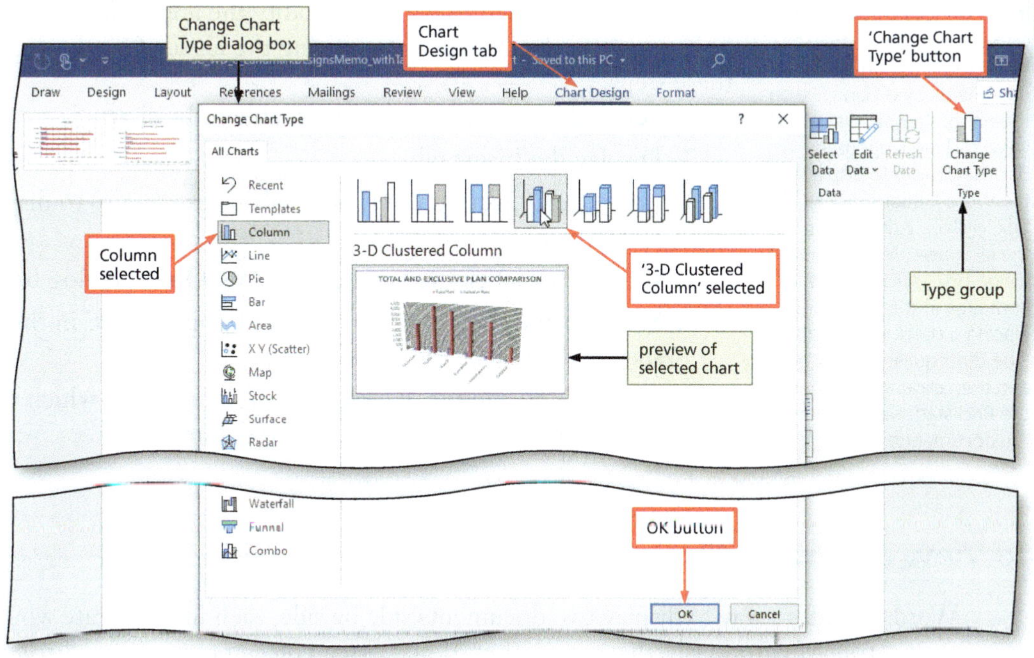

Figure 8–57

Experiment

- Point to the chart preview in the dialog box to see in more detail how the chart will look in the document.

2

- Click OK to change the chart type (Figure 8–58).
- Click outside the chart to deselect it.
- **sam** Save the revised memo on your hard drive, OneDrive, or other storage location using the file name, SC_WD_8_LandmarkDesignsMemo_withTableand3-DColumnChart.

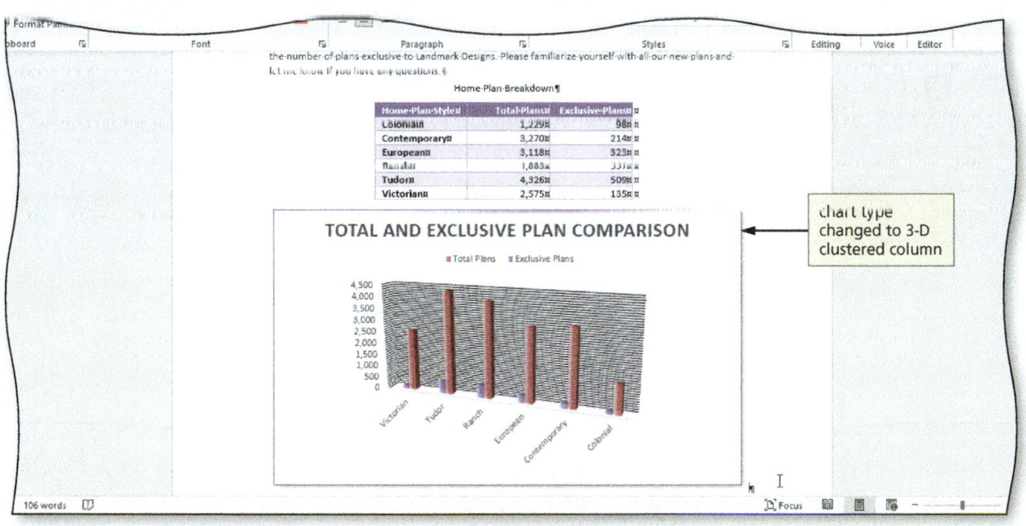

Figure 8–58

To Chart a Word Table Using Microsoft Graph

In previous versions of Word, you charted Word tables using an embedded program called Microsoft Graph, or simply Graph. When working with the chart, Graph has its own menus and commands because it is a program embedded in Word. Using Graph commands, you can modify the appearance of the chart after you create it. If you wanted to create a chart using the legacy Graph program, you would perform these steps.

1. Select the rows and columns or table to be charted.
2. Display the Insert tab.
3. Click the Object button (Insert tab | Text group) to display the Object dialog box.
4. If necessary, click the Create New tab (Object dialog box).
5. Scroll to and then select 'Microsoft Graph Chart' in the Object type list to specify the object being inserted.
6. Click OK to run the Microsoft Graph program, which creates a chart of the selected table or selected rows and columns.

BTW

Conserving Ink and Toner

If you want to conserve ink or toner, you can instruct Word to print draft quality documents by clicking File on the ribbon to open Backstage view, clicking Options in Backstage view to display the Word Options dialog box, clicking Advanced in the left pane (Word Options dialog box), scrolling to the Print area in the right pane, placing a check mark in the 'Use draft quality' check box, and then clicking OK. Then, use Backstage view to print the document as usual.

To View and Scroll through Documents Side by Side

Word provides a way to display two documents side by side, each in a separate window. By default, the two documents scroll synchronously, that is, together. If necessary, you can turn off synchronous scrolling so that you can scroll through each document individually. The following steps display documents side by side. **Why?** You would like to see how the document with the clustered chart looks alongside the document with the 3-D clustered column chart.

1

- Position the insertion point at the top of the document because you want to begin viewing side by side from the top of the documents.
- Open the file called SC_WD_8_LandmarkDesignsMemo_withTableandClusteredChart.docx so that both documents are open in Word.
- Display the View tab (Figure 8–59).

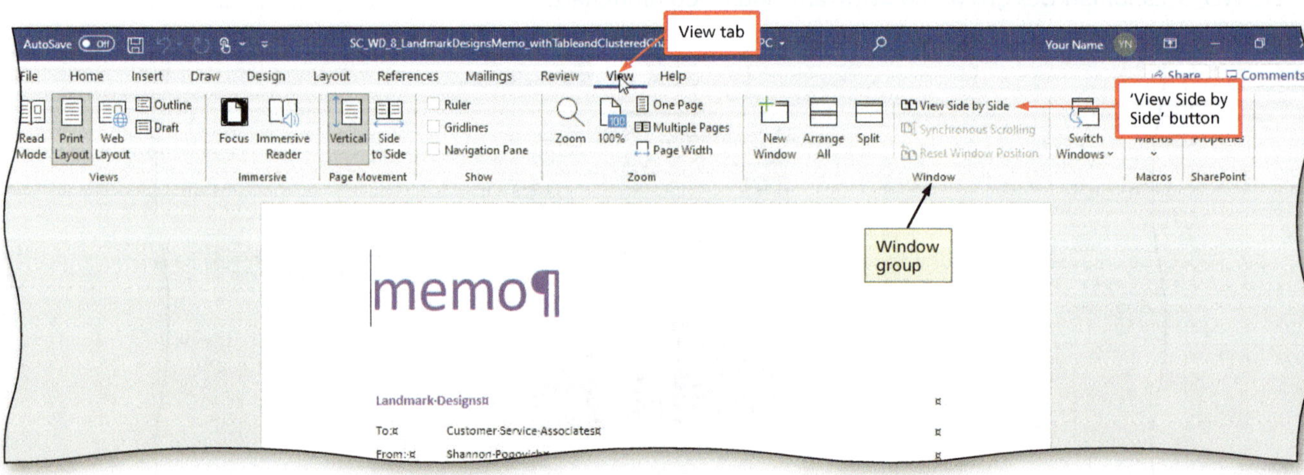

Figure 8–59

2

- Click the 'View Side by Side' button (View tab | Window group) to display each open window side by side (Figure 8–60).

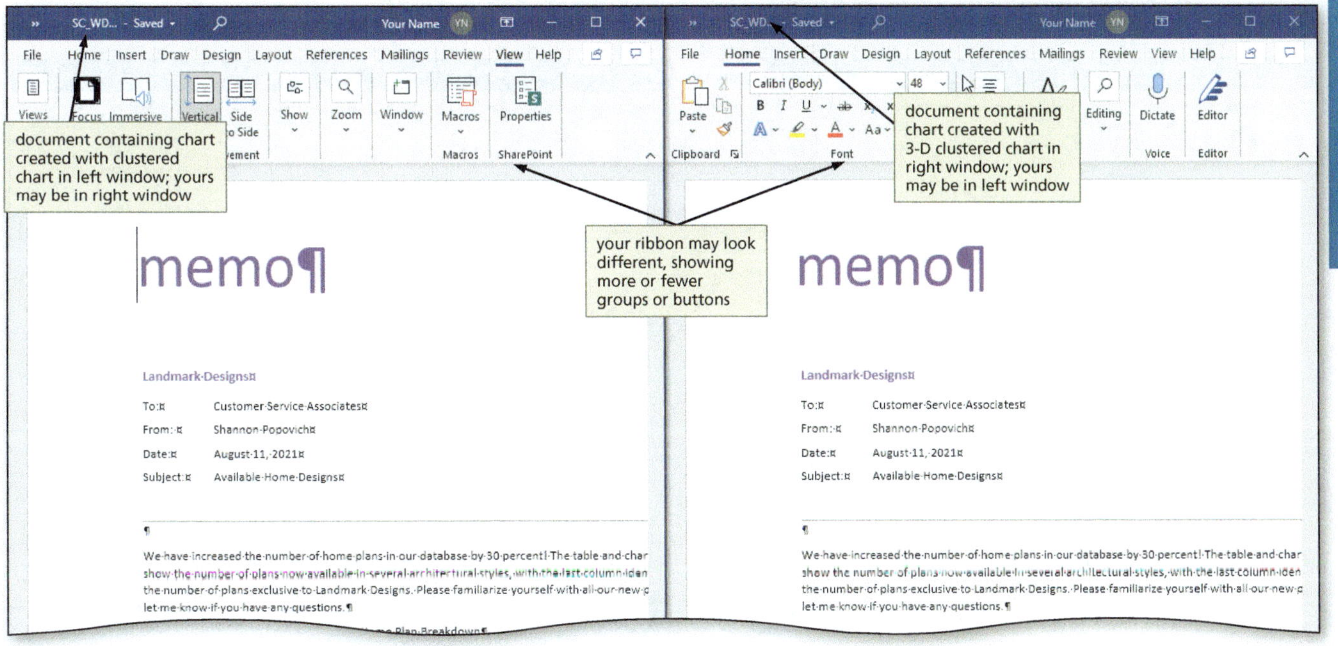

Figure 8–60

3

- If necessary, adjust the zoom to fit the memo contents in each window.
- Scroll to the bottom of one of the windows and notice how both windows (documents) scroll together (Figure 8–61).

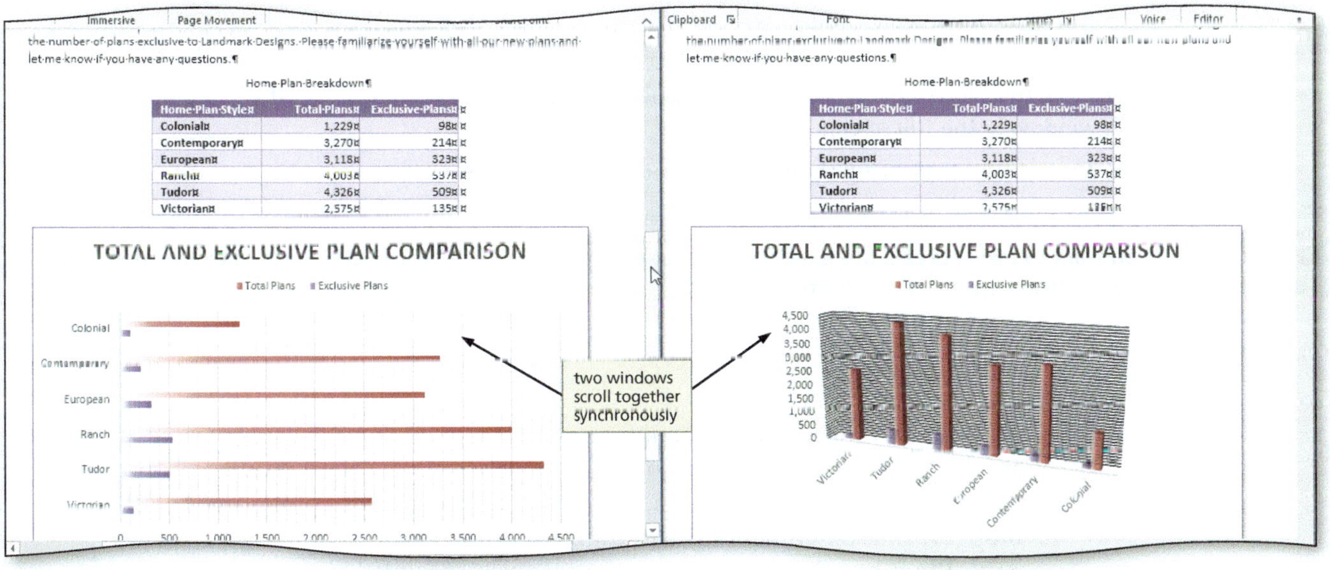

Figure 8–61

Q&A **Can I scroll through one window separately from the other?**
By default, synchronous scrolling is active when you display windows side by side. If you want to scroll separately through the windows, simply turn off synchronous scrolling.

4

- If necessary, display the View tab (in either window). (Note that because the ribbons are smaller, you may need to click the Window group button first so that the Synchronous Scrolling button is visible.)
- Click the Synchronous Scrolling button (View tab | Window group) to turn off synchronous scrolling.

5

- Scroll to the top of the window on the right and notice that the window on the left does not scroll because you turned off synchronous scrolling (Figure 8–62).

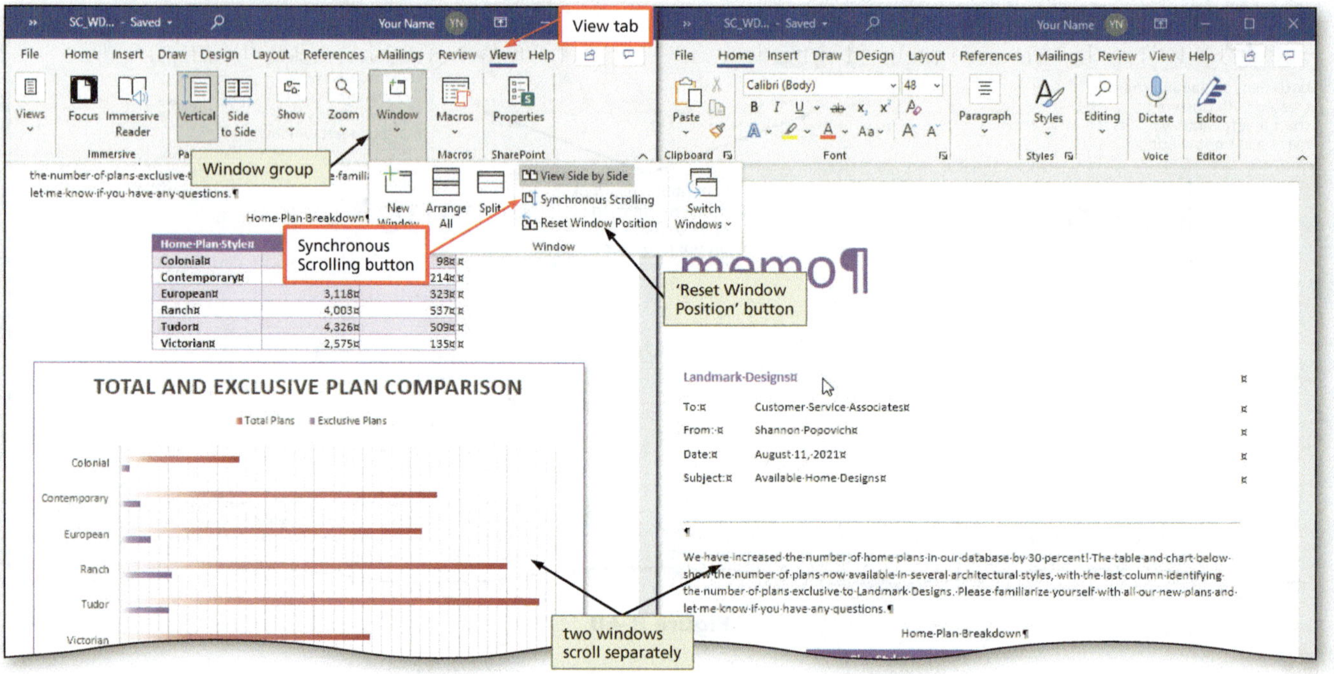

Figure 8–62

Q&A **What is the purpose of the 'Reset Window Position' button?**
It repositions the side-by-side windows so that each consumes the same amount of screen space.

6

- In either window, click the 'View Side by Side' button (View tab | Window group) to turn off side-by-side viewing and display each window in the full screen.
- Close each open Word document, saving them if prompted.

Break Point: If you want to take a break, this is a good place to do so. You can exit Word now. To resume later, start Word and continue following the steps from this location forward.

Creating a Blog Post

A **blog**, short for **weblog**, is an informal website consisting of date- or time-stamped articles, or **posts**, in a diary or journal format, usually listed in reverse chronological order. Blogs reflect the interests, opinions, and personalities of the author, called the **blogger**, and sometimes of the website visitors as well.

Blogs have become an important means of worldwide communications. Businesses create blogs to communicate with employees, customers, and vendors. Teachers create blogs to collaborate with other teachers and students, and home users create blogs to share aspects of their personal life with family, friends, and others.

This section of the module creates a blog post and then publishes it to a registered blog account at WordPress, which is a blogging service on the web. The blog relays current events for the employees of Landmark Designs. This specific blog post is a communication about the upcoming events.

Consider This

What should you consider when creating and posting on a blog?

When creating a blog post, you should follow these general guidelines:

1. **Create a blog account on the web.** Many websites exist that allow users to set up a blog free or for a fee. Blogging services that work with Word 365 include SharePoint blog, Telligent Community, TypePad, and WordPress. For illustration purposes in this module, a free blog account was created at WordPress.com.
2. **Register your blog account in Word.** Before you can use Word to publish a blog post, you must register your blog account in Word. This step establishes a connection between Word and your blog account. The first time you create a new blog post, Word will ask if you want to register a blog account. You can click the Register Later button if you want to learn how to create a blog post without registering a blog account.
3. **Create a blog post.** Use Word to enter the text and any graphics in your blog post. Some blogging services accept graphics directly from a Word blog post. Others require that you use a picture hosting service to store pictures you use in a blog post.
4. **Publish a blog post.** When you publish a blog post, the blog post in the Word document is copied to your account at the blogging service. Once the post is published, it appears at the top of the blog webpage. You may need to click the Refresh button in the browser window to display the new post.

To Register a Blog Account

Once you set up a blog account with a blog provider, you must register it in Word so that you can publish your Word post on the blog account. If you wanted to register a blog account, with WordPress for example, you would perform the following steps.

1. Click the Manage Accounts button (Blog Post tab | Blog group) to display the Blog Accounts dialog box.
2. Click the New button (Blog Accounts dialog box) to display the New Blog Account dialog box.
3. Click the Blog arrow (New Blog Account dialog box) to display a list of blog providers and then select your provider in the list.
4. Click the Next button to display the New [Provider] Account dialog box (i.e., a New WordPress Account dialog box would appear if you selected WordPress as the provider).
5. In the Blog Post URL text box, replace the <Enter your blog URL here> text with the web address for your blog account. (Note that your dialog box may differ, depending on the provider you select.)

Q&A **What Is a URL?**
A URL (Uniform Resource Locator), often called a web address, is the unique address for a webpage. For example, the web address for a WordPress blog account might be smith.wordpress.com; in that case, the complete blog post URL would read as http://smith.wordpress.com/xhlrpc.php in the text box.

6. In the Enter account information area, enter the user name and password you use to access your blog account.

Q&A **Should I click the Remember Password check box?**
If you do not select this check box, Word will prompt you for a password each time you publish to the blog account.

7. If your blog provider does not allow pictures to be stored, click the Picture Options button, select the correct option for storing your posted pictures, and then click OK (Picture Options dialog box).
8. Click OK to register the blog account.
9. When Word displays a dialog box indicating the account registration was successful, click OK.

To Create a Blank Document for a Blog Post

The following steps create a new blank Word document for a blog post. **Why?** Word provides a blog post template you can use to create a blank blog post document.

1

- Open Backstage view.
- Click New in Backstage view to display the New screen.
- Click the Blog post thumbnail to select the template and display it in a preview window (Figure 8–63).

Q&A **What should I do if the Blog post thumbnail is not listed on the New screen?**
Click the 'Search for online templates' box, type `blog post`, and then press ENTER.

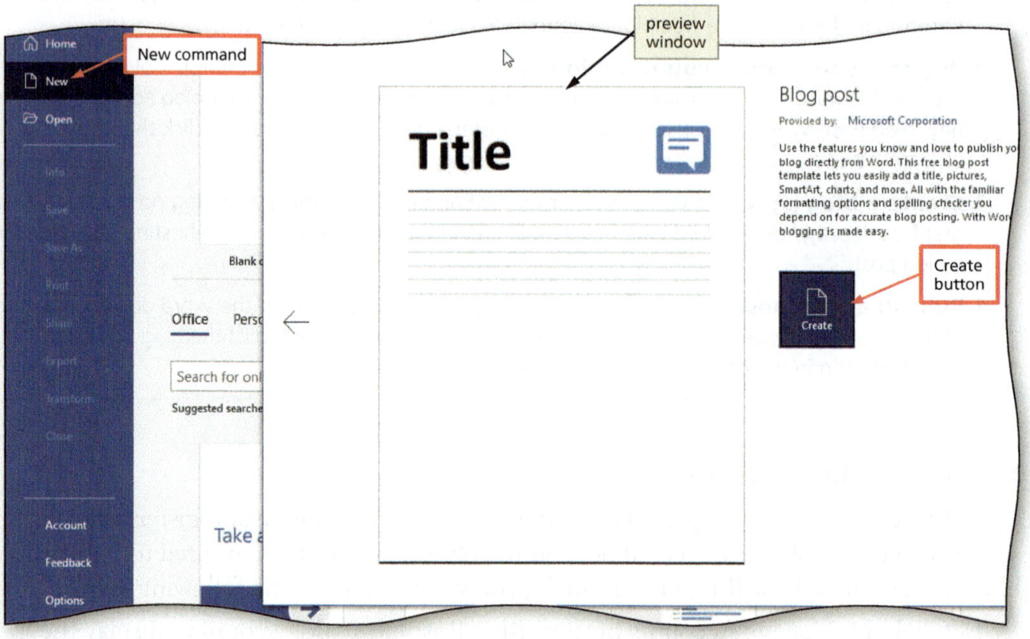

Figure 8–63

2

- Click the Create button in the preview window to create a new document based on the selected template (Figure 8–64). If necessary, adjust the zoom so that the text is readable on the screen.

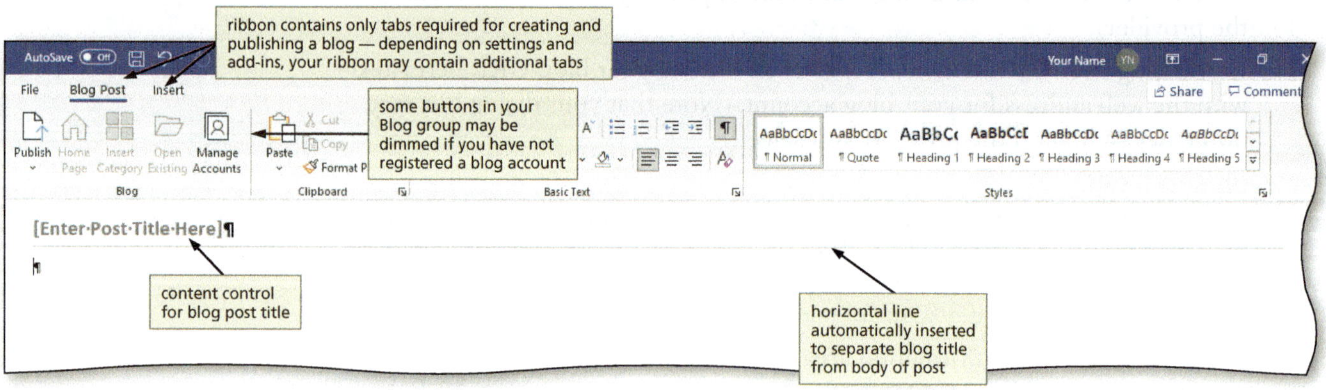

Figure 8–64

Q&A **What if a Register a Blog Account dialog box appears?**
Click the Register Later button to skip the registration process at this time. Or, if you have a blog account, you can click the Register Now button and follow the instructions to register your account.

Why did the ribbon change?
When creating a blog post, the ribbon in Word changes to display only the tabs required to create and publish a blog post.

To Enter Text

The next step is to enter the blog post title and text in the blog post. The following steps enter text in the blog post.

1 Click the 'Enter Post Title Here' content control and then type **`Appreciation Events`** as the blog title.

2 Position the insertion point below the horizontal line and then type these two lines of text, pressing ENTER at end of each sentence (Figure 8–65):

`Thank you to everyone for helping our organization realize an increase in revenue during the second quarter!`

`See the following calendar for key dates, including appreciation events!`

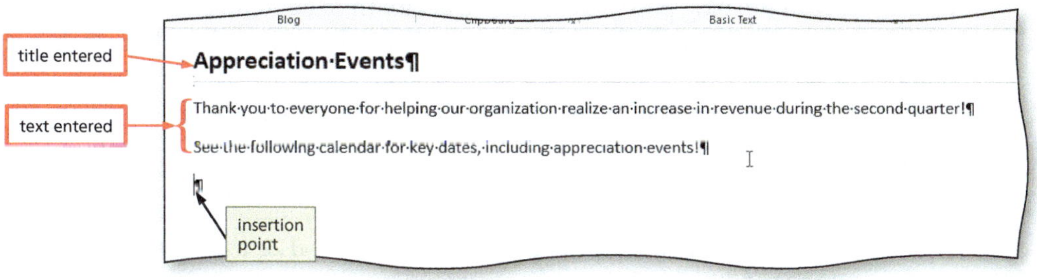

Figure 8–65

Q&A **Can I format text in the blog post?**
Yes, you can use the Basic Text and other groups on the ribbon to format the post.

To Insert a Quick Table

Word provides several quick tables, which are preformatted table styles that you can customize. Calendar formats are one type of quick table. The following steps insert a calendar in the blog. **Why?** You will post the upcoming key dates in the calendar.

1

- Display the Insert tab.
- With the insertion point positioned as shown in Figure 8–65, click the Table button (Insert tab | Tables group) to display the Table gallery.
- Point to Quick Tables in the Table gallery to display the Quick Tables gallery (Figure 8–66).

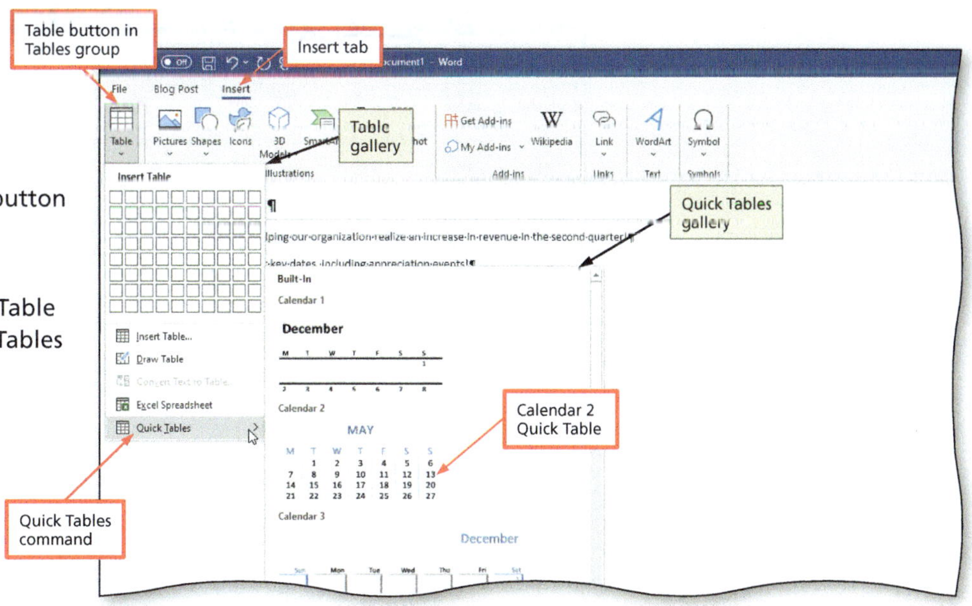

Figure 8–66

2

- Click Calendar 2 in the Quick Tables gallery to insert the selected Quick Table in the document at the location of the insertion point (Figure 8–67).

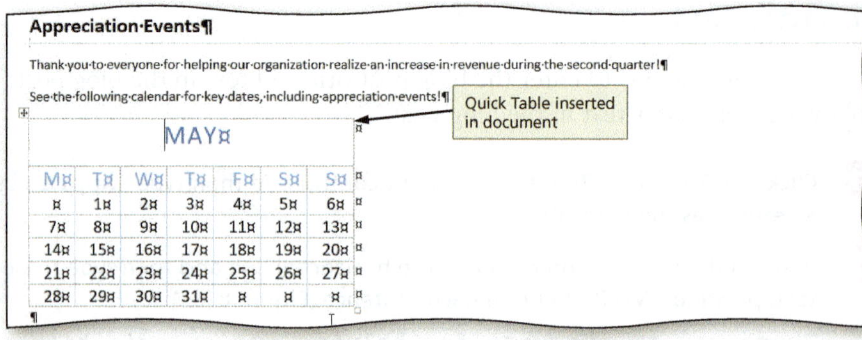

Figure 8–67

To Edit and Format a Table

The calendar in the blog post should show the month of September with a first day of the month starting on Wednesday. The following steps edit the table and apply a quick style.

1. Change the month in the first cell of the table from May to September.
2. Edit the contents of the cells in the table so that the first day of the month starts on a Wednesday and the 30 (the last day of the month) is on a Thursday.
3. Enter the text in the appropriate cells for September 1, 7, 16, and 22, as shown in Figure 8–68.
4. If necessary, display the Table Design tab.
5. Remove the check mark from the First Column check box (Table Design tab | Table Style Options group) because you do not want the first column in the table formatted differently.
6. Apply the 'Grid Table 1 Light - Accent 6' table style to the table.
7. If necessary, left-align the heading and resize the table column widths to 1".
8. Make any other necessary adjustments so that the table appears as shown in Figure 8–68.
9. Save the blog on your hard drive, OneDrive, or other storage location using SC_WD_8_LandmarkDesignsBlog as the file name.

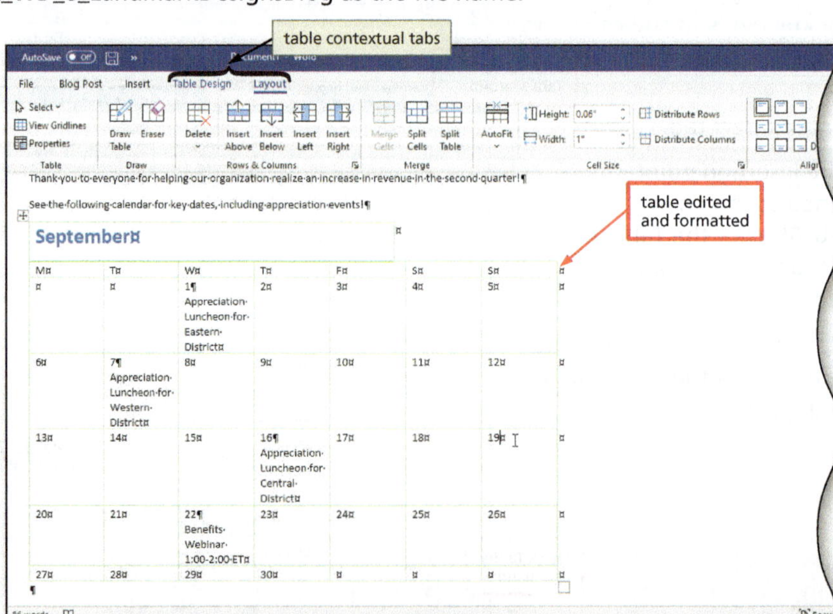

Figure 8–68

Note: If you have not registered a blog account, read the next series of steps without performing them.

To Publish a Blog Post

The following step publishes the blog post. **Why?** Publishing the blog post places the post at the top of the webpage associated with this blog account.

1

- Display the Blog Post tab.
- Click the Publish button (Blog Post tab | Blog group), which causes Word to display a brief message that it is contacting the blog provider and then display a message on the screen that the post was published (Figure 8–69).

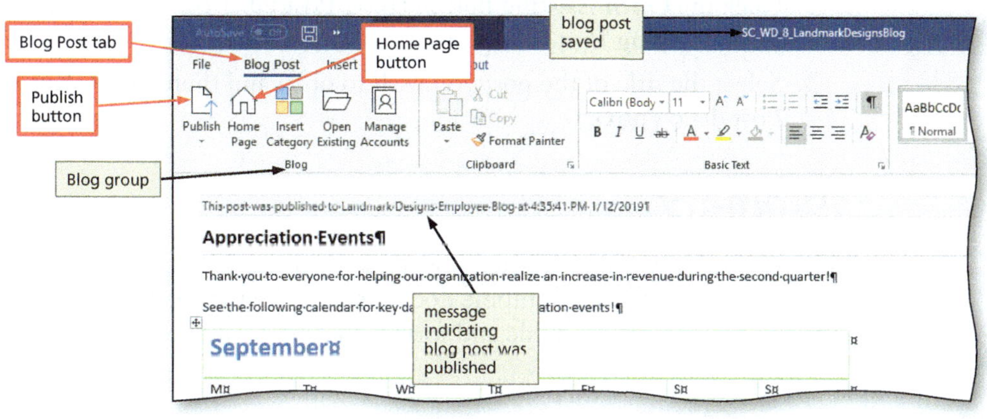

Figure 8–69

To Display a Blog Webpage in a Browser Window

The following steps display the current blog account's webpage in a browser window. **Why?** You can view a blog account associated with Word if you want to verify a post was successful.

1

- Click the Home Page button (Blog Post tab | Blog group) (shown in Figure 8–69), which starts the default browser (Microsoft Edge, in this case) and displays the webpage associated with the registered blog account in the browser window. You may need to click the Refresh button in your browser window to display the most current webpage contents (Figure 8–70).

Figure 8–70

Q&A **What if the wrong webpage is displayed?**
You may have multiple blog accounts registered with Word. To select a different blog account registered with Word, switch back to Word, click the Manage Accounts button (Blog Post tab | Blog group), click the desired account (Blog Accounts dialog box), and then click the Close button. Then, repeat Step 1.

2

- Exit both the browser and Word.

BTW
Deleting Blog Posts
If you want to delete a blog post from your blog account, sign in to your blog account and then follow the instructions from your blog provider to delete a post from your blog.

To Open an Existing Blog Post

If you wanted to open an existing blog post to modify or view it in Word, you would perform the following steps.

1. Click the Open Existing button (Blog Post tab | Blog group) to display the Open Existing Post dialog box.
2. Select the title of the post you wish to open and then click OK (Open Existing Post dialog box).

Summary

In this module, you have learned how to track changes, review tracked changes, compare documents and combine documents, link or embed an Excel worksheet to a Word document, chart a table and format the chart, and create and publish a blog post.

Consider This: Plan Ahead

What decisions will you need to make when creating documents to share or publish?
Use these guidelines as you complete the assignments in this module and create your own shared documents outside of this class.

1. If sharing documents, be certain received files and copied objects are virus free.
   a) Do not open files created by others until you are certain they do not contain a virus or other malicious program (malware).
   b) Use an antivirus program to verify that any files you use are free of viruses and other potentially harmful programs.
2. If necessary, determine how to copy an object.
   a) Your intended use of the Word document will help determine the best method for copying the object: copy and paste, embed, or link.
3. Enhance a document with appropriate visuals.
   a) Use visuals to add interest, clarify ideas, and illustrate points. Visuals include tables, charts, and graphical images (i.e., pictures).
4. If desired, post communications on a blog.

BTW
Distributing a Document
Instead of printing and distributing a hard copy of a document, you can distribute the document electronically. Options include sending the document via email; posting it on cloud storage (such as OneDrive) and sharing the file with others; posting it on social media, a blog, or other website; and sharing a link associated with an online location of the document. You also can create and share a PDF or XPS image of the document, so that users can view the file in Adobe Reader or XPS Viewer instead of in Word.

Apply Your Knowledge

Reinforce the skills and apply the concepts you learned in this module.

Collaborating with Tracked Changes and Other Tools

Note: To complete this assignment, you will be required to use the Data Files. Please contact your instructor for information about accessing the Data Files.

Instructions: Start Word. Open the document, SC_WD_8-4.docx, which is located in the Data Files. Written by the public relations coordinator at Galewood Financial, the document contains tips to prevent identity theft. You are to review the document before it is finalized for customers.

Perform the following tasks:

1. Click File on the ribbon and then click Save As and save the document using the new file name, SC_WD_8_IdentityTheft_Reviewed.
2. If necessary, customize the status bar so that it displays the Track Changes indicator.
3. Enable (turn on) tracked changes.
4. If requested by your instructor, change the user name and initials so that your name and initials are displayed in the tracked changes.
5. Open the Reviewing pane. How many tracked changes are in the document? Close the Reviewing pane.
6. If necessary, change the 'Display for Review' box (Review tab | Tracking group) to Simple Markup and then notice how the screen appears. Change it to No Markup and then Original and notice the how the screen appears. Change it to All Markup for the remainder of this exercise.
7. Click the Show Markup button (Review tab | Tracking group) and be sure these types of markup are selected so that they show when tracking changes: Insertions and Deletions, and Formatting.
8. Show revisions in balloons. (Hint: Use the Show Markup button (Review tab | Tracking group).) Show only formatting in balloons.
9. With the insertion point at the top of the document, use the Next button (Review tab | Changes group) to go to the first tracked change in the document. Use the same button to go to the next tracked change. Use the Previous button (Review tab | Changes group) to go to the previous tracked change.
10. Keep the tracked changes currently in the document. Track the changes shown in Figure 8–71 as additional tracked changes in the document. What color are the two markups that were in the original document? What color are the additional markups that you tracked in this step?

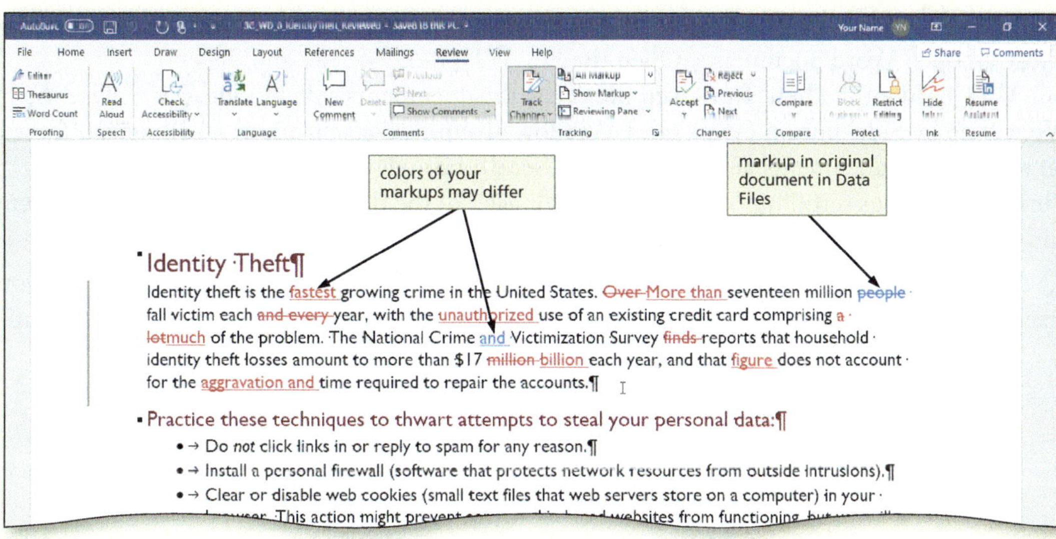

Figure 8–71

Continued >

Apply Your Knowledge *continued*

11. Save the reviewed document with the tracked changes again with the same name and then submit it in the format specified by your instructor.
12. Lock tracked changes in the document — do not enter a password in the dialog box. (Hint: Use the Track Changes button (Review tab | Tracking group).) What happens to the Track Changes button when you lock tracked changes? Unlock tracked changes.
13. Print the document with tracked changes.
14. Click File on the ribbon and then click Save As and save the document using the new file name, SC_WD_8_IdentityTheft_Final.
15. Show only your tracked changes in the document. Show all users' tracked changes in the document.
16. Hide tracked insertions and deletions. (Hint: Click the Show Markup button (Review tab | Tracking group).) Show tracked insertions and deletions.
17. Reject the tracked change in the document that deleted the word, people.
18. Reject the tracked change in the document that inserted the word, and.
19. Accept the tracked change in the document that inserted the word, fastest.
20. Accept the tracked change in the document that deleted the word, finds.
21. Accept all the remaining tracked changes in the document.
22. Disable (turn off) tracked changes. Remove the Track Changes indicator from the status bar.
23. If requested by your instructor, add your name in the header of the document as a document property. (Hint: Use the Document Info button (Header & Footer tab | Insert group).)
24. Save the final document again with the same name and then submit it in the format specified by your instructor. Close the document.
25. Compare the SC_WD_8-4.docx file (original document) with the SC_WD_8_IdentityTheft_Final file (revised document) into a new document. In the Compare Result window, hide source documents. (Hint: Click the Compare button (Review tab | Compare group).) In the Compare Result window, show both source documents. Save the compare result with the file name SC_WD_8_IdentityTheft_Compared and then submit it in the format specified by your instructor. Close the document.
26. Combine the SC_WD_8-4.docx file (original document) with the SC_WD_8_IdentityTheft_Final file (revised document) into a new document. Save the compare result with the file name SC_WD_8_IdentityTheft_Combined and then submit it in the format specified by your instructor. Close the document.
27. Close all open Word documents. Open the SC_WD_8-4.docx file and the SC_WD_8_IdentityTheft_Reviewed file. View the documents side by side. (Hint: Use the 'View Side by Side' button (View tab | Window group).) If synchronous scrolling is off, turn it on to scroll the documents at the same time. Scroll through each of the documents. Turn synchronous scrolling off. Scroll through each of the documents. Close both documents and exit Word.
28. Answer the questions posed in #5, #10, and #12. How would you change the color of your tracked changes? How would you determine if two documents contained the same content?

Extend Your Knowledge

Extend the skills you learned in this module and experiment with new skills. You may need to use Help to complete the assignment.

Working with Charts

Note: To complete this assignment, you will be required to use the Data Files. Please contact your instructor for information about accessing the Data Files.

Instructions: Start Word. Open the document, SC_WD_8-5.docx, which is located in the Data Files. The document is a memo draft, written to the district superintendent at Cherry Hill Schools from the office manager about elementary school enrollment. You are to chart the Word table in the memo using Word's charting tools. You also create another similar memo using an Excel table.

Perform the following tasks:

1. Use Help to learn more about charts in Word, linking objects, and embedding objects.
2. Click File on the ribbon and then click Save As and save the document using the new file name, SC_WD_8_SchoolEnrollmentsMemo.
3. Insert a Line with Markers chart on the centered paragraph below the table. In the document window, select the bottom five rows in the table (do not copy the table title row) and then copy the selected rows. In the chart spreadsheet window, select the entire worksheet and then paste the contents with source formatting.
4. Resize the chart spreadsheet window to display all its data. Remove the Series 3 data series from the chart spreadsheet window by dragging the sizing handle.
5. Resize the column headings in the chart spreadsheet window by dragging their borders. Close the chart spreadsheet window.
6. Remove the primary horizontal axis chart element from the chart by using the 'Add Chart Element' button (Chart Design tab | Chart Layouts group). Use the same procedure to add the horizontal axis back to the chart.
7. Remove the legend chart element from the chart by using the 'Add Chart Element' button (Chart Design tab | Chart Layouts group). Use the same procedure to add the legend back to bottom of the chart.
8. Select the vertical (value) axis chart element. (Hint: Use the Current Selection group in the Format tab.) Click the Format Selection button to open the Format Axis pane. Change the value in the Minimum box in the Axis Options section to 250 and the value in the Maximum box to 550.
9. Add data labels to the chart so they appear above each point (Figure 8–72). (Hint: Use the 'Add Chart Element' button (Chart Design tab | Chart Layouts group).)
10. Change the value of the Elwood Elementary current enrollment from 443 to 453 using the Edit Data button (Chart Design tab | Data group). (Note that the change may not occur immediately in the chart.) Change the value in the table in the Word document also.
11. Change the chart style to a style of your choice. (Hint: Use the Chart Design tab.)
12. Change the colors of the chart to colors of your choice.
13. Change the position of the chart legend to a location of your choice. (Hint: Use the 'Add Chart Element' button (Chart Design tab | Chart Layouts group).)
14. Remove the chart title from the chart by using the 'Add Chart Element' button (Chart Design tab | Chart Layouts group). Use the same procedure to add the chart title back to the chart. Select the chart title and enter appropriate text as the chart title.

Continued >

Extend Your Knowledge *continued*

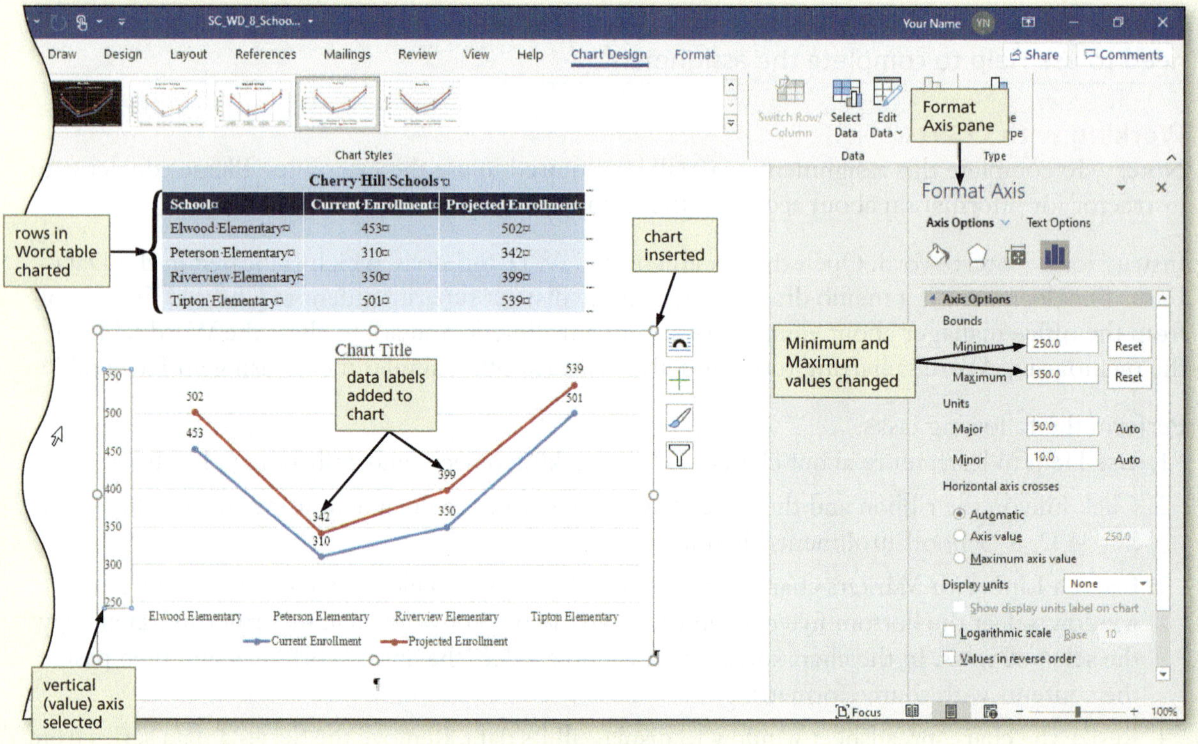

Figure 8–72

15. Add a vertical axis title with the text, Number of Students. (Hint: Use the 'Add Chart Element' button (Chart Design tab | Chart Layouts group).) Remove the outline from around the vertical axis title using the Shape Outline button (Format tab | Shape Styles group).
16. Add an outline of your choice to border the chart.
17. Save the document again with the same name and then submit it in the format specified by your instructor.
18. Copy the chart. Create a new document window and then paste the chart using source formatting (and embed the workbook).
19. Change the chart type to a bar chart.
20. Use the chart spreadsheet window to add this row of data to the chart: Westside Elementary, 401 for current enrollment, and 439 for projected enrollment. Be sure to drag the sizing handle to include the newly added row of data.
21. Select the vertical axis and then open the Format Axis pane. Select the 'Categories in reverse order' check box.
22. Remove the horizontal axis title. Remove the horizontal axis chart element.
23. Make any additional changes you feel appropriate for the chart.
24. Save the revised chart document using the file name, SC_WD_8_SchoolEnrollmentsBarChart. Submit the document in the format specified by your instructor.
25. If you have Excel and your instructor requests, perform the following steps:
    a. Open the document, SC_WD_8-6.docx, which is located in the Data Files. Click File on the ribbon and then click Save As and save the document using the new file name, SC_WD_8_SchoolEnrollmentsMemo_withExcelTable.
    b. Start Excel and open the workbook, SC_WD_8-7.xlsx, which is located in the Data Files. In Excel, copy the table (the cells in the range A1 through C5). Click File on the ribbon and then click Save As and save the workbook using the new file name, SC_WD_8_SchoolEnrollmentsTable.

c. In Word, on the blank line below the paragraph, insert the copied object (Excel table) by using the 'Keep Source Formatting' button on the Paste menu. Change one of the enrollment values and notice that you edit the inserted object as you edit any other Word element. Delete the copied table.

d. In Word, on the blank line below the paragraph, embed the copied object (Excel table) by clicking Paste Special on the Paste menu, clicking 'Microsoft Excel Worksheet Object' (Paste Special dialog box), and then clicking OK. Try changing one of the enrollment values. Notice that you cannot because the Excel table is embedded. Double-click the embedded table to open an Excel window in the Word window. Change one of the enrollment values in the embedded Excel window. Click outside the embedded Excel window to close it and notice the value changes in the embedded table. Delete the embedded table.

e. In Excel, copy the table (the cells in the range A1 through C5) again. In Word, on the blank line below the paragraph, link the copied object (Excel table) by using the 'Link & Keep Source Formatting' button on the Paste menu.

   i. In Excel, change the Elwood Elementary current enrollment from 443 to 453. Save the modified workbook in Excel. In Word, right-click the linked Excel table and then click Update Link on the shortcut menu to update the linked Excel object in Word.

   ii. Center the linked table. Copy the linked table.

   iii. Insert a chart of your choice of the linked table. Format the chart appropriately.

   iv. In Excel, change the Tipton Elementary projected enrollment from 539 to 545. Save the modified workbook in Excel. In Word, right click the linked Excel table and then click Update Link on the shortcut menu to update the linked Excel object in Word.

   v. Edit the chart data using the Edit Data button (Chart Design tab | Data group) and then change the Tipton Elementary projected enrollment from 539 to 545 in the chart spreadsheet window.

   vi. Break the link between the Excel table in the Word document and the Excel worksheet in the Excel workbook. If necessary, center the table in the Word document and change the font color of the header row to Black.

   vii. Save the document again with the same name and then submit it in the format specified by your instructor. Exit Word and Excel, closing any open documents.

26. Which chart color and styles did you use in this assignment? Why?

Expand Your World

Create a solution that uses cloud or web technologies by learning and investigating on your own from general guidance.

Creating a Blog Account Using a Blogger Service

Instructions: As a data analyst at Bradford Communications, you have been asked to create a blog account so that blog posts can be used to communicate with managers and staff. You research a variety of blogging services and select one for use.

Note: You will use a blog account, many of which you can create at no cost, to complete this assignment. If you do not want to create a blog account, perform the first step and then read the remaining steps in this assignment without performing them.

Perform the following tasks:

1. In Word, create the blog post shown in Figure 8–73. Insert a Quick Table using the tabular list option. Delete two rows from the table. Edit the data and format the table as shown in the figure. Save the blog file using the file name, SC_WD_8_InternetSubscriberBlog.

Continued >

Expand Your World *continued*

2. Start a browser. Research these blogging services: SharePoint blog, Telligent Community, TypePad, and WordPress.
3. Navigate to the blogger service with which you want to set up an account and then follow the instructions to set up an account.
4. Set up your blog in the blogger service.
5. In Word, register your blog account (refer to the section in this module titled To Register a Blog Account).
6. In Word, publish your blog post to your account.
7. Which blogger service did you select and why? Would you recommend this blogger service? Why or why not?

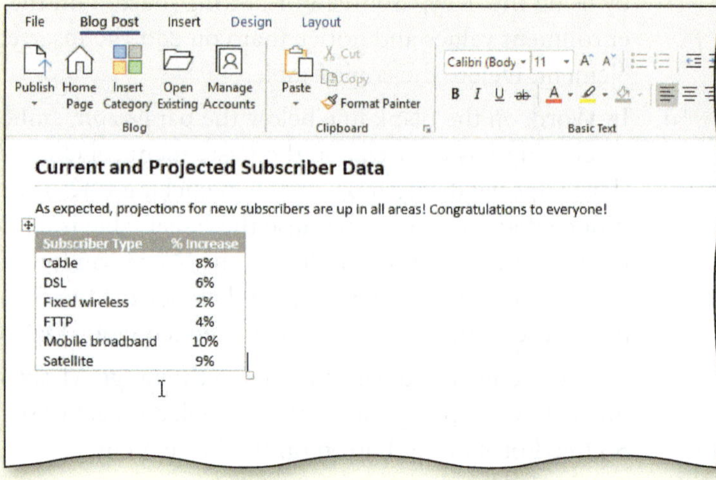

Figure 8–73

In the Lab

Design and implement a solution using creative thinking and problem-solving skills.

Create a Sales Summary Memo with a Table and Chart for an Office Supply Retailer

Problem: As an accounting associate director of Sunlight Office Supplies, you have been asked to create a memo to sales managers showing the second quarter sales figures by category. The memo should contain a table and chart.

Part 1: You are to create a memo to sales managers with a subject of Second Quarter Sales. Use today's date.

The wording for the text in the memo is as follows: Second quarter sales figures have been compiled. The table and chart below show sales by category for the second quarter.

The data for the table is as follows:

- technology: April $125,217, May $113,268, June $114,839
- paper: April $23,546, May $14,687, June $19,983
- office supplies: April $22,658, May $23,821, June $22,034
- breakroom supplies: April $9,302, May $8,843, June $8,001

Create a chart of all table data.

Use the concepts and techniques presented in this module to create and format the memo and its text, table, and chart. Be sure to check the spelling and grammar of the finished memo. When you are finished with the memo, save it with the file name, SC_WD_8_SalesMemo. Submit your assignment and answers to the Part 2 critical thinking questions in the format specified by your instructor.

Part 2: You made several decisions while creating the memo in this assignment: whether to use a memo template or create a memo from scratch, and how to organize and format the memo, table, and chart (fonts, font sizes, colors, shading, styles, etc.). What was the rationale behind each of these decisions? When you proofread the document, what further revisions did you make and why?

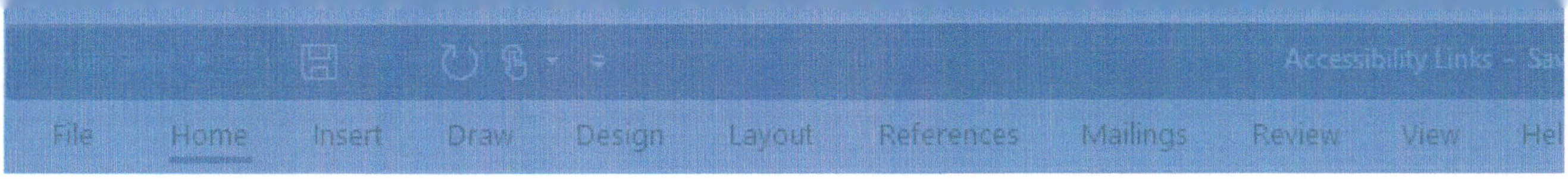

9 Creating a Reference Document

Objectives

After completing this module, you will be able to:

- Insert a screenshot
- Add and modify a caption
- Insert a cross-reference
- Insert and link text boxes
- Compress pictures
- Work in Outline view
- Work with a master document and subdocuments
- Insert a symbol
- Insert and modify a table of contents
- Use the Navigation Pane
- Insert and update a table of figures
- Insert, modify, and update an index
- Specify different odd and even page footers
- Insert bookmarks

Introduction

During the course of your academic studies and professional activities, you may find it necessary to compose a document that is many pages or even hundreds of pages in length. When composing a long document, you must ensure that the document is organized so that a reader easily can locate material in that document. Sometimes a document of this nature is called a reference document.

Project: Reference Document

A **reference document** is any multipage document organized so that users easily can locate material and navigate through the document. Examples of reference documents include user guides, term papers, pamphlets, manuals, proposals, and plans.

The project in this module uses Word to produce the reference document shown in Figure 9–1. This reference document, titled *Using Word*, is a multipage guide

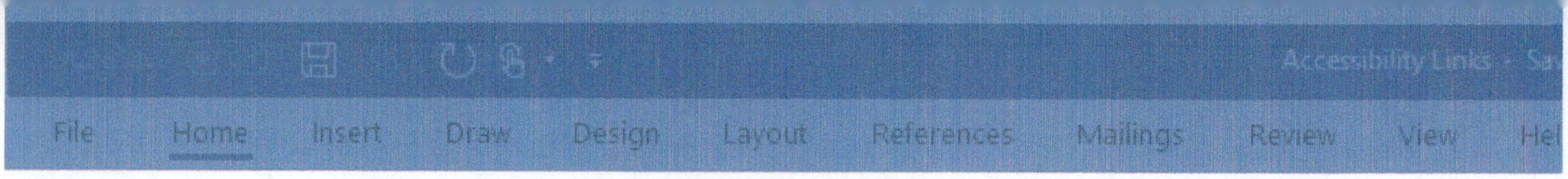

that is distributed by the Information Resource Center at Wilmington College to students and staff. Notice that the inner margin between facing pages has extra space to allow duplicated copies of the document to be bound (i.e., stapled or fastened in some manner) — without the binding covering the words.

The *Using Word* reference document begins with a cover page designed to encourage the target audience to open the document and read it. Next is the copyright page, followed by the table of contents. The document then describes how to insert four types of images in a Word document: online image, picture from a file, shape, and screenshot. The end of this reference document has a table of figures and an index to assist readers in locating information contained within the document. A miniature version of the *Using Word* reference document is shown in Figure 9–1.

The section of the *Using Word* reference document that is titled Inserting Images in Word Documents is a document that you create from a draft. The draft of this document is located in the Data Files. Please contact your instructor for information about accessing the Data Files. After editing content in the draft document, you will incorporate a final version in the reference document.

You will perform the following general tasks as you progress through this module:

1. Modify a draft of a document.
2. Create a master document with a subdocument for the reference document.
3. Organize the reference document.

To Start Word and Specify Settings

If you are using a computer to step through the project in this module and you want your screens to match the figures in this book, you should change your screen's resolution to 1366 × 768. The following steps start Word and verify ruler and Mouse mode settings.

1. Start Word and create a blank document in the Word window. If necessary, maximize the Word window.
2. If the Print Layout button on the status bar is not selected, click it so that your screen is in Print Layout view.
3. Verify that the Ruler check box (View tab | Show group) is not selected. (If it is selected, click it to remove the check mark because you do not want the rulers to appear on the screen.)
4. If you are using a mouse and you want your screens to match the figures in the book, verify that you are using Mouse mode by clicking the Touch/Mouse Mode button on the Quick Access Toolbar and then, if necessary, clicking Mouse on the menu. (If your Quick Access Toolbar does not display the Touch/Mouse Mode button, click the 'Customize Quick Access Toolbar' button on the Quick Access Toolbar and then click Touch/Mouse Mode on the menu to add the button to the Quick Access Toolbar.)

BTW
Touch Mode Differences
The Office and Windows interfaces may vary if you are using Touch mode. For this reason, you might notice that the function or appearance of your touch screen differs slightly from this module's presentation.

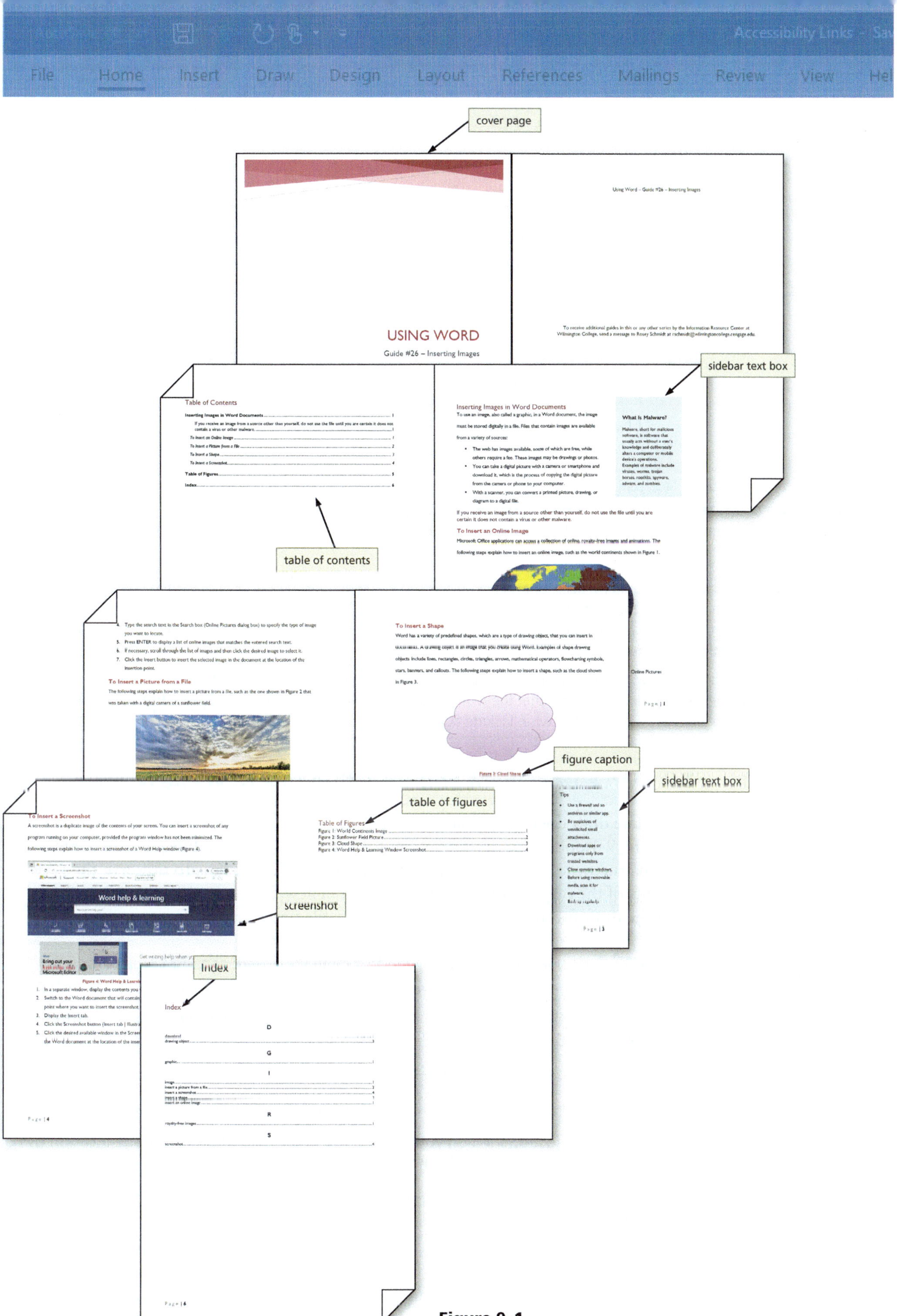

File
Home
Insert
Draw
Design
Layout
References
Mailings
Review
View
cover page
USING WORD
Guide #26 – Inserting Images
sidebar text box
table of contents
figure caption
sidebar text box
table of figures
screenshot
Index

Figure 9–1

Preparing a Document to Be Included in a Reference Document

You will make several modifications to the draft document:

1. Insert a screenshot.
2. Insert captions for the figures (images) in the document.
3. Insert references to the figures in the text.
4. Mark an index entry.
5. Insert text boxes that contain information about malware.
6. Compress the pictures.

The following pages outline these changes.

Consider This

How should you prepare a document to be included in a longer document?

Ensure that reference elements in a document, such as captions and index entries, are formatted properly and entered consistently.

- **Captions:** A **caption** is text that identifies, titles, or explains an accompanying graphic, figure, or photo. If the figure, for example, is identified with a number, the caption may include the word, Figure, along with the figure number (i.e., Figure 1). In the caption, separate the figure number from the text of the figure by a space or punctuation mark, such as a period or colon (i.e., Figure 1: World Continents Image).
- **Index Entries:** If your document will include an index, read through the document and mark any terms or headings that you want to appear in the index. Include any term that the reader may want to locate quickly. Omit figures from index entries if the document will have a table of figures; otherwise, include figures in the index if appropriate.

To Open a Document and Save It with a New File Name

The draft document that you will insert in the reference document is named SC_WD_9-1.docx. The draft document is located in the Data Files. Please contact your instructor for information about accessing the Data Files. To preserve the contents of the original draft, you save it with a new file name. The following steps open the draft file and then save it with a new file name.

BTW

Protected View

To keep your computer safe from potentially dangerous files, Word may automatically open certain files in Protected view, which is a restricted mode. To see the Protected view settings, click File on the ribbon to open Backstage view, click Options to display the Word Options dialog box, click Trust Center in the left pane (Word Options dialog box), click the 'Trust Center Settings' button in the right pane to display the Trust Center dialog box, and then click Protected View in the left pane to show the current Protected view settings.

1. sam If your instructor wants you to submit your work as a SAM Project for automatic grading, you must download the Data Files from the assignment launch page.
2. Navigate to the location of the Data Files on your hard drive, OneDrive, or other storage location.
3. Open the file named SC_WD_9-1.docx.
4. Navigate to the desired save location on your hard drive, OneDrive, or other storage location.
5. Save the file just opened on your hard drive, OneDrive, or other storage location using SC_WD_9_InsertingImages as the file name.
6. If the 'Show/Hide ¶' button (Home tab | Paragraph group) is selected, click it to hide formatting marks.

Q&A **What if some formatting marks still appear after I click the 'Show/Hide ¶' button?**

Open Backstage view, click Options to display the Word Options dialog box, click Display in the left pane (Word Options dialog box), remove the check mark from the Hidden text check box, and then click OK.

7 Display the View tab and then click the Multiple Pages button (View tab | Zoom group) to display multiple pages in the document window; if necessary, use the Zoom slider to adjust the zoom so that all four pages are visible in the document window at once (Figure 9–2).

Note: To help you locate screen elements that are referenced in the step instructions, such as buttons and commands, this book uses red boxes to point to these screen elements.

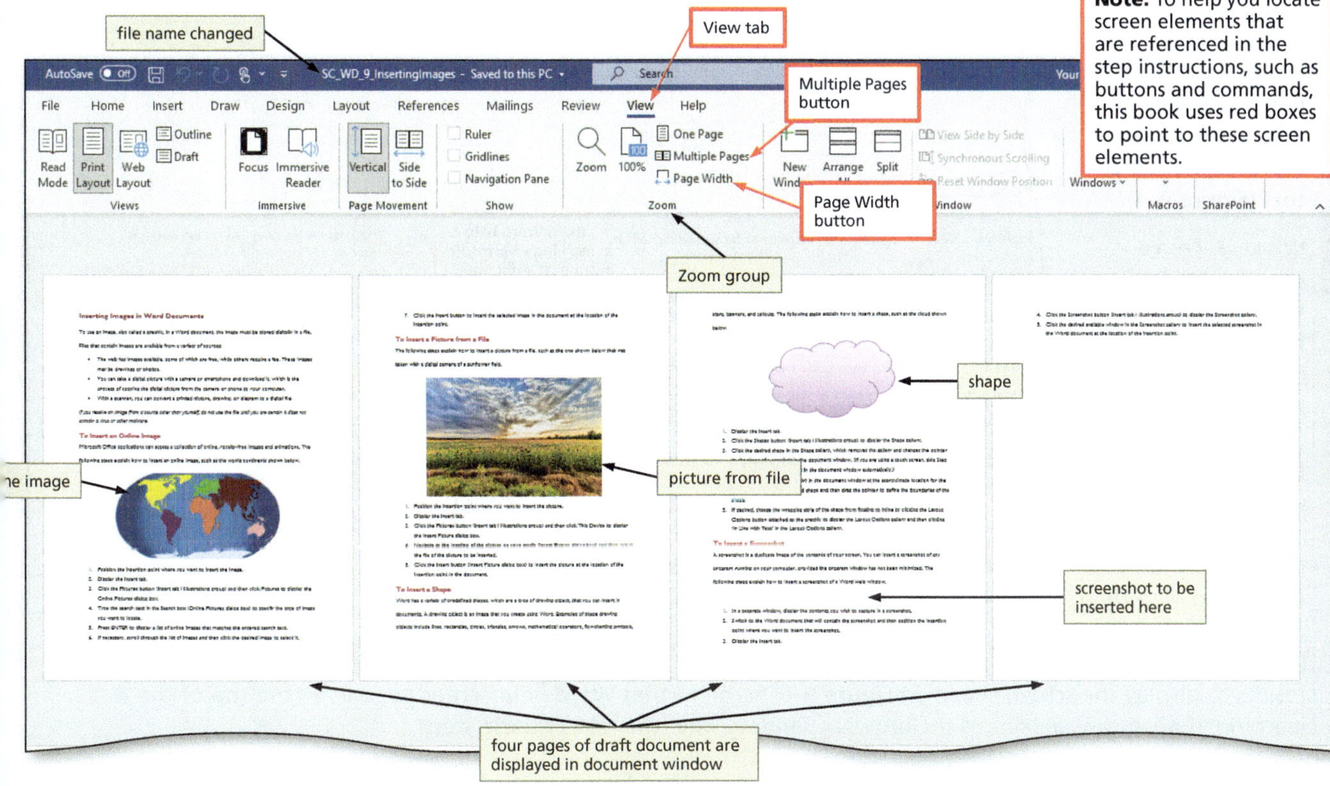

Figure 9–2

8 When you have finished viewing the document, click the Page Width button (View tab | Zoom group) to display the document as wide as possible in the document window.

To Insert a Screenshot

A **screenshot** is a duplicate image of the contents of your computer or mobile device's screen or active window. The current document is missing a screenshot of a Word help center window. To insert a screenshot, you first must display the screen for which you want a screenshot in a window on your computer or mobile device. **Why?** From within Word, you can insert a screenshot of any app running on your computer, provided the app has not been minimized. You then can resize or position the inserted screenshot as you do any other Word object. The following steps insert a screenshot in a document.

1

- Type **Word help & learning** in the Search box to display search results (Figure 9–3).

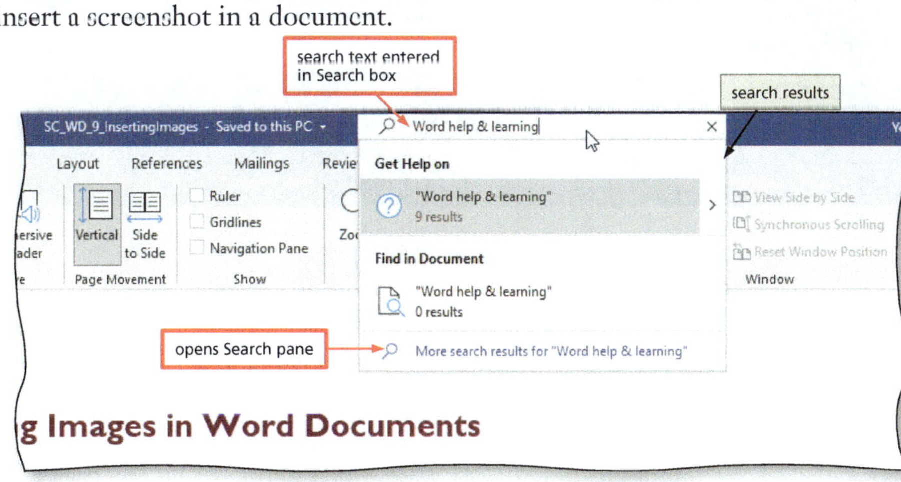

Figure 9–3

2

- Click 'More search results for "Word help & learning"' in the search results to open the Search pane with links to information that matches the search text (Figure 9–4).

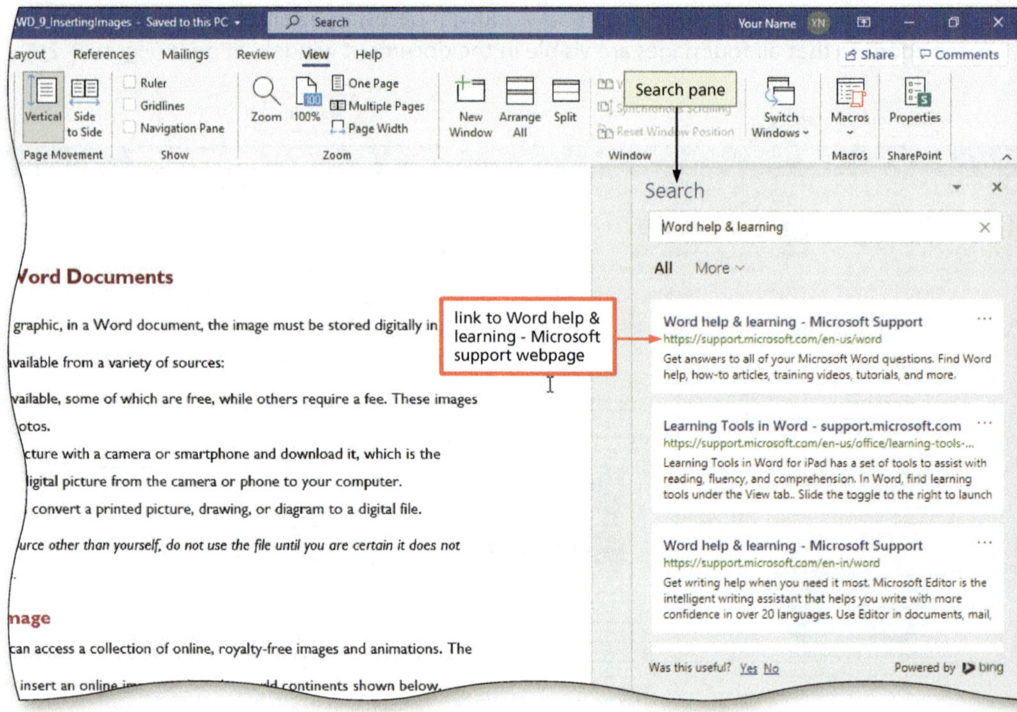

Figure 9–4

Q&A **What if 'More search results for "Word help & learning"' does not appear in my search results?**
Press ESC to close the search results. Open a browser window, search for the text, Word help & learning, and then click the appropriate link in the search results to display the screen shown in Figure 9–5. Scroll so that Word help center appears at the top of the & learning; if necessary, maximize the browser window. Skip the rest of these steps.

3

- Click the link to 'Word help & learning - Microsoft Support' in the Search pane to open a browser window with the associated webpage displayed and then scroll so that Word help & learning appears at the top of the screen; if necessary, maximize the browser window (Figure 9–5).

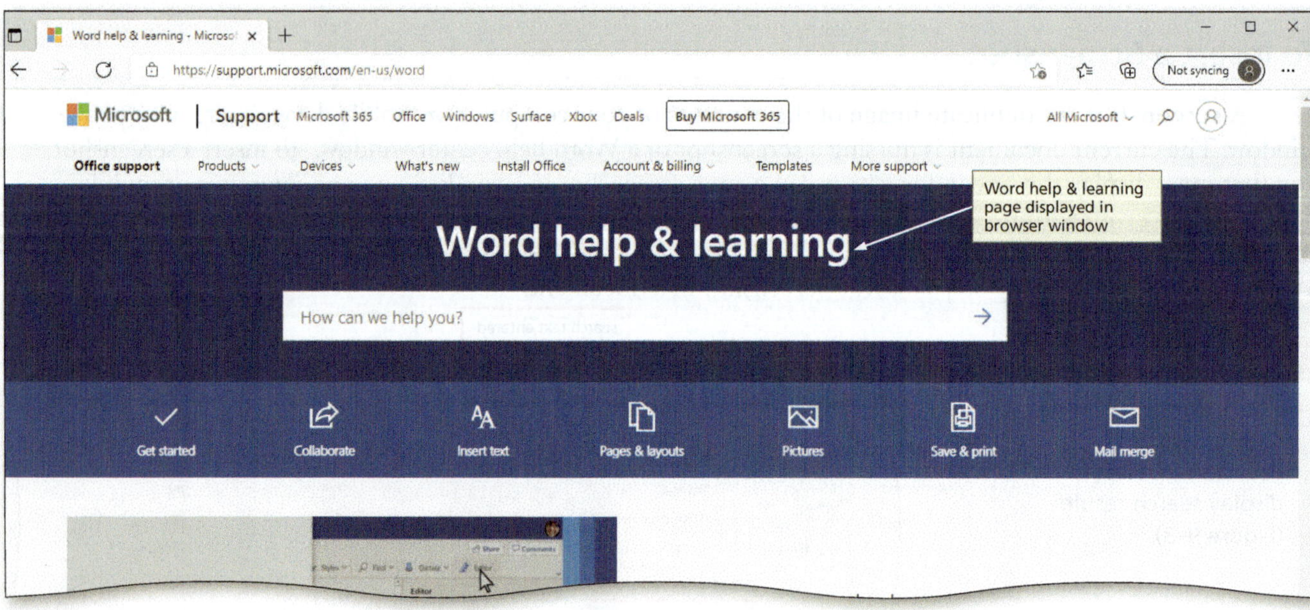

Figure 9–5

Q&A **What if I do not have access to the Internet or the correct webpage does not appear?**
The screenshot is located in the Data Files. You can click the Pictures button (Insert tab | Illustrations group), navigate to the file called Support_WD_9_WordHelpWindow.tif in the Data Files, and then click the Insert button (Insert Picture dialog box). Close the Search pane and then skip the rest of these steps.

4

- Leave the browser window open, switch to the Word window, close the Search pane, and position the insertion point in the document where the screenshot should be inserted (in this case, on the centered blank line above the numbered list in the To Insert a Screenshot section at the bottom of the document).
- Display the Insert tab.
- Click the Screenshot button (Insert tab | Illustrations group) to display the Screenshot gallery (Figure 9–6).

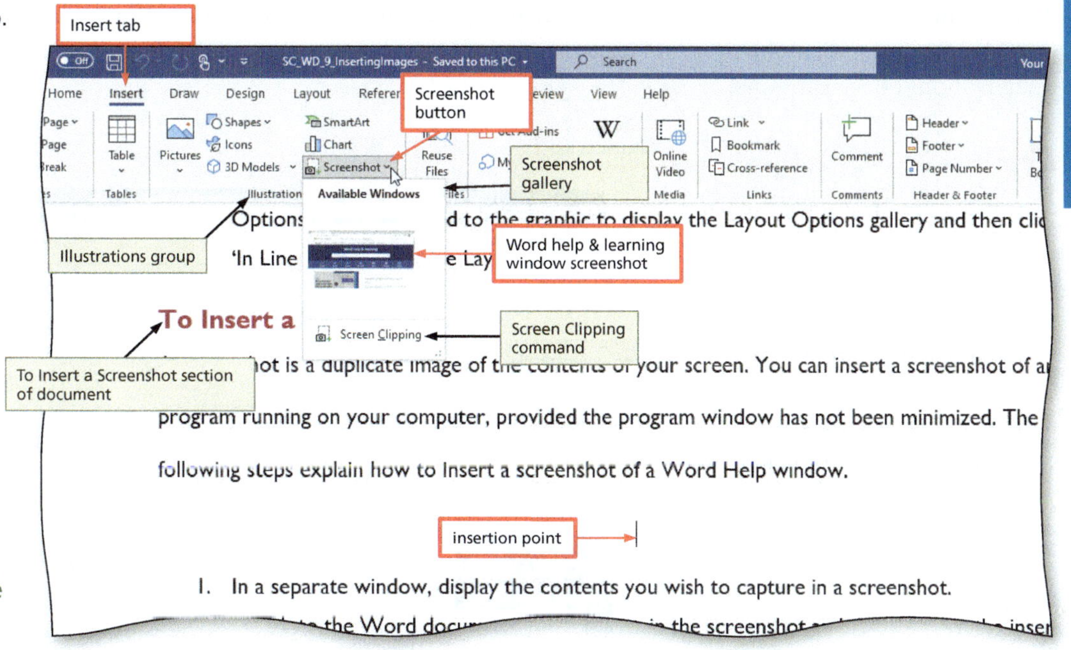

Figure 9–6

Q&A **What is a screen clipping?**
A screen clipping is a section of a window. When you select Screen Clipping in the Screenshot gallery, the window turns opaque so that you can drag through the part of the window to be included in the document.

Why does my Screenshot gallery show more windows?
You have additional programs running on your desktop, and their windows are not minimized.

5

- Click the Word help & learning window screenshot in the Screenshot gallery to insert the selected screenshot in the Word document at the location of the insertion point. (If a dialog box appears about hyperlinking the screenshot, click No.)
- Verify that the values in the Shape Height and Shape Width boxes (Picture Format tab | Size group) are approximately 3.5" tall by 6.5" wide (Figure 9–7).

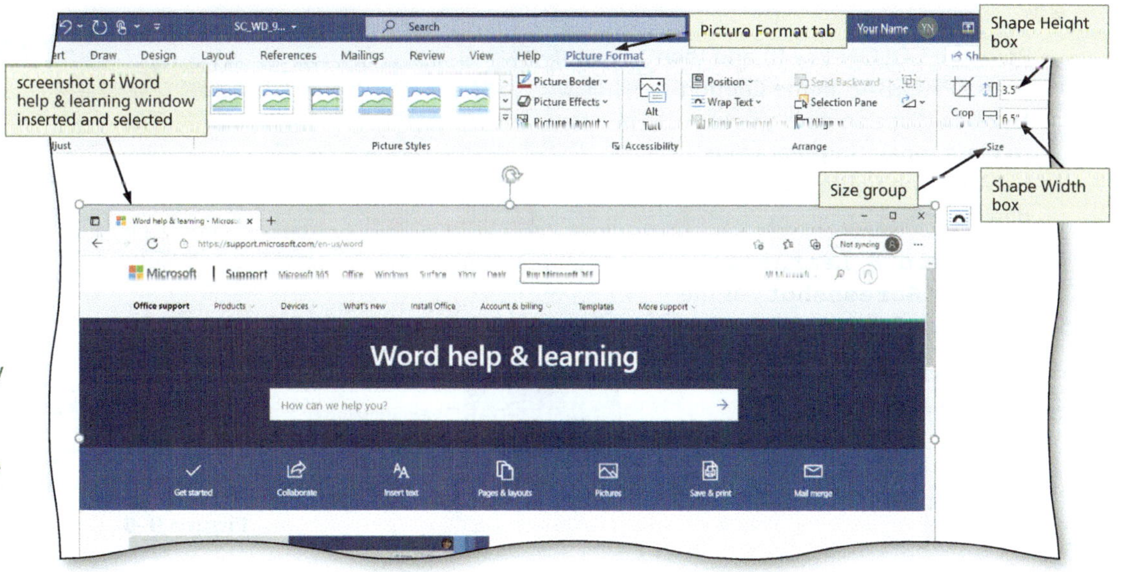

Figure 9–7

Q&A **Why can I not set the exact measurements shown above?**
You may need to click the Size Dialog Box Launcher (Picture Format tab | Size group) to display the Size sheet in the Layout dialog box and then remove the checkmark from the 'Lock aspect ratio' check box.

Why did the screenshot appear on a new page?
The screenshot is too tall to fit at the bottom of page 3.

To Insert a Caption

In Word, you can insert a caption for an equation, a figure, and a table. If you move, delete, or insert captions in a document, Word renumbers remaining captions in the document automatically. In this reference document, the captions contain the word, Figure, followed by the figure number, a colon, and a figure description. The following steps insert a caption for an image, specifically, the screenshot. **Why?** The current document contains four images: an image from an online source, a picture from a file, a shape, and a screenshot. All of these images should have captions.

1

- If the screenshot is not selected already, click it to select the image on which you want a caption.
- Display the References tab.
- Click the Insert Caption button (References tab | Captions group) to display the Caption dialog box with a figure number automatically assigned to the selected image (Figure 9–8).

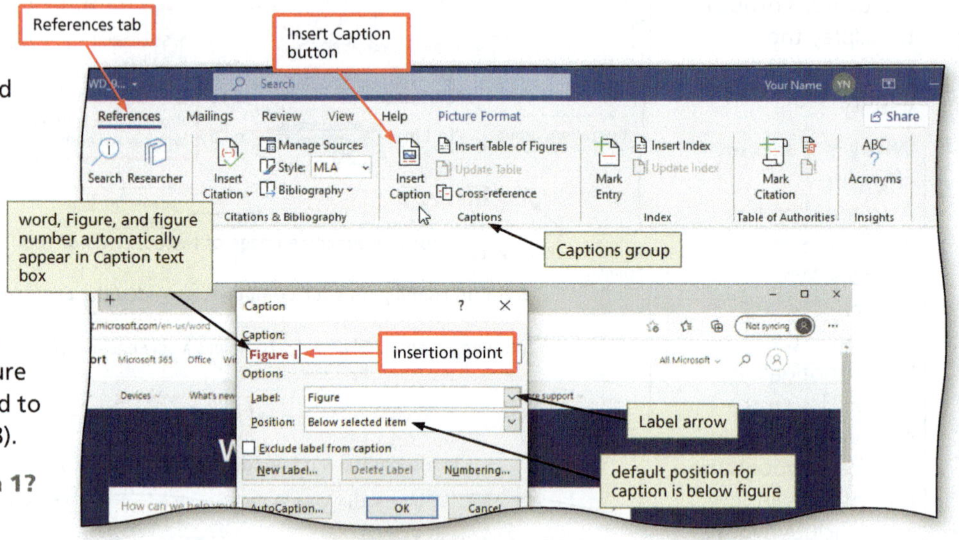

Figure 9–8

Q&A

Why is the figure number a 1?
No other captions have been assigned in this document yet. When you insert a new caption, or move or delete items containing captions, Word automatically updates caption numbers throughout the document.

What if the Caption text box has the label Table or Equation instead of Figure?
Click the Label arrow (Caption dialog box) and then click Figure in the Label list.

2

- Press the COLON key (:) and then press SPACEBAR in the Caption text box (Caption dialog box) to place separating characters between the figure number and description.
- Type `Help & Learning Window Screenshot` as the figure description (Figure 9–9).

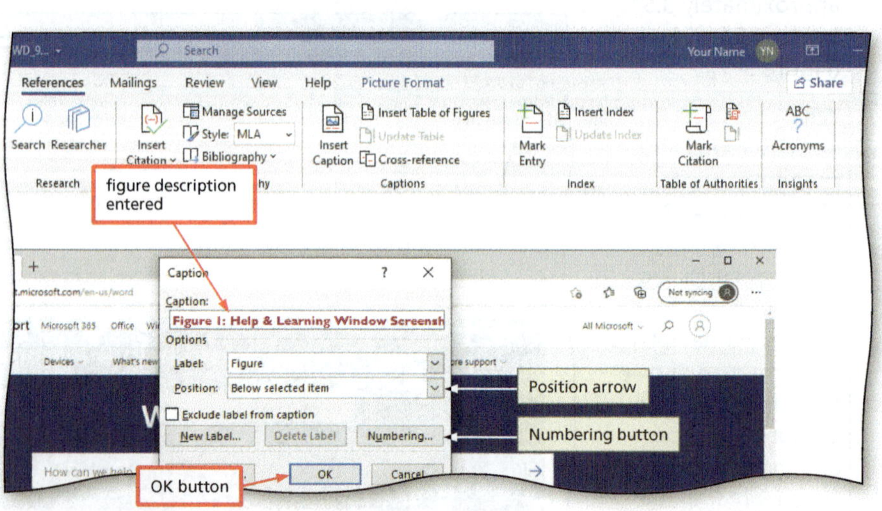

Figure 9–9

Q&A

Can I change the format of the caption number?
Yes, click the Numbering button (Caption dialog box), adjust the format as desired, and then click OK.

3

- Click OK to insert the caption below the selected image.
- If necessary, scroll to display the caption in the document window (Figure 9–10).

Q&A **How do I change the position of a caption?**
Click the Position arrow (Caption dialog box) and then select the desired position of the caption.

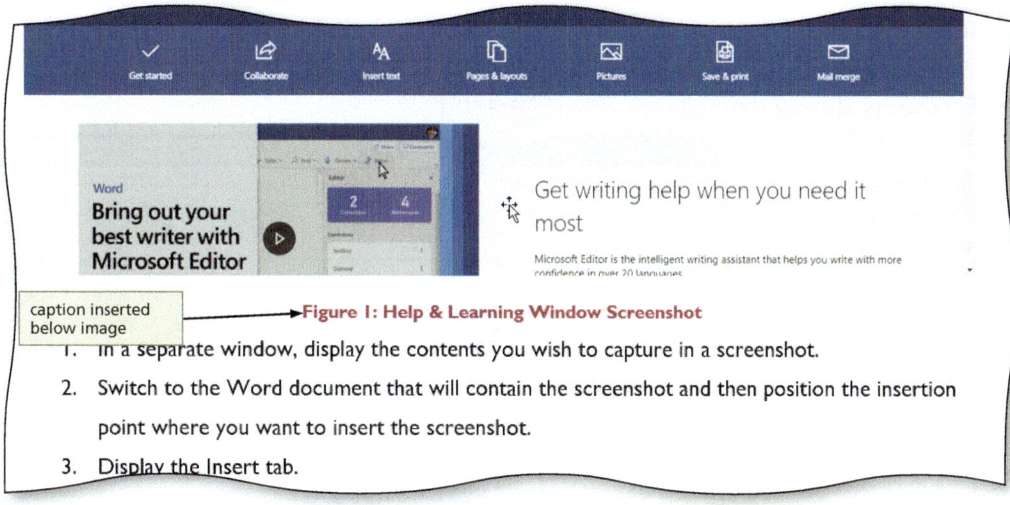

Figure 9–10

Caption Numbers

Each caption number contains a field. A **field** is code that serves as a placeholder for data that can change in a document. Examples of fields include page numbers, merge fields, IF fields, the current date, and caption numbers. You update caption numbers using the same technique used to update any other field. That is, to update all caption numbers, select the entire document and then press F9, or right-click the field and then click Update Field on the shortcut menu. When you print a document, Word updates the caption numbers automatically, regardless of whether the document window displays the updated caption numbers.

BTW
Captions
If a caption appears with extra characters inside curly braces ({}), Word is displaying field codes instead of field results. Press ALT+F9 to display captions correctly as field results. If Word prints fields codes for captions, click File on the ribbon to open Backstage view, click Options in Backstage view to display the Word Options dialog box, click Advanced in the left pane (Word Options dialog box), scroll to the Print section in the right pane, remove the check mark from the 'Print field codes instead of their values' check box, click OK, and then print the document again.

To Hide White Space

White space is the space displayed in the margins at the top and bottom of pages (including any headers and footers) and also space between pages. To make it easier to see the text in this document as you scroll through it, the following step hides white space.

1 Position the pointer in the document window in the space between the pages or below the last page in the document and then double-click when the pointer changes to a 'Hide White Space' button to hide white space.

To Insert a Cross-Reference

The next step in this project is to insert a reference to the new figure. **Why?** In reference documents, the text should reference each figure specifically and, if appropriate, explain the contents of the figure.

Because figures may be inserted, deleted, or moved, you may not know the actual figure number in the final document. For this reason, Word provides a method of inserting a **cross-reference**, which is text that electronically refers the reader to another part of the document, such as a heading, caption, or footnote. You can click a cross-reference to move directly to that specific location in the document. By inserting a cross-reference to the caption, the text that mentions the figure will be updated whenever the caption to the figure is updated. The following steps insert a cross-reference.

1

- At the end of the last sentence below the To Insert a Screenshot heading, position the insertion point to the left of the period, press SPACEBAR, and then press the LEFT PARENTHESIS [( ] key.
- If necessary, display the References tab.
- Click the Cross-reference button (References tab | Captions group) to display the Cross-reference dialog box (Figure 9–11).

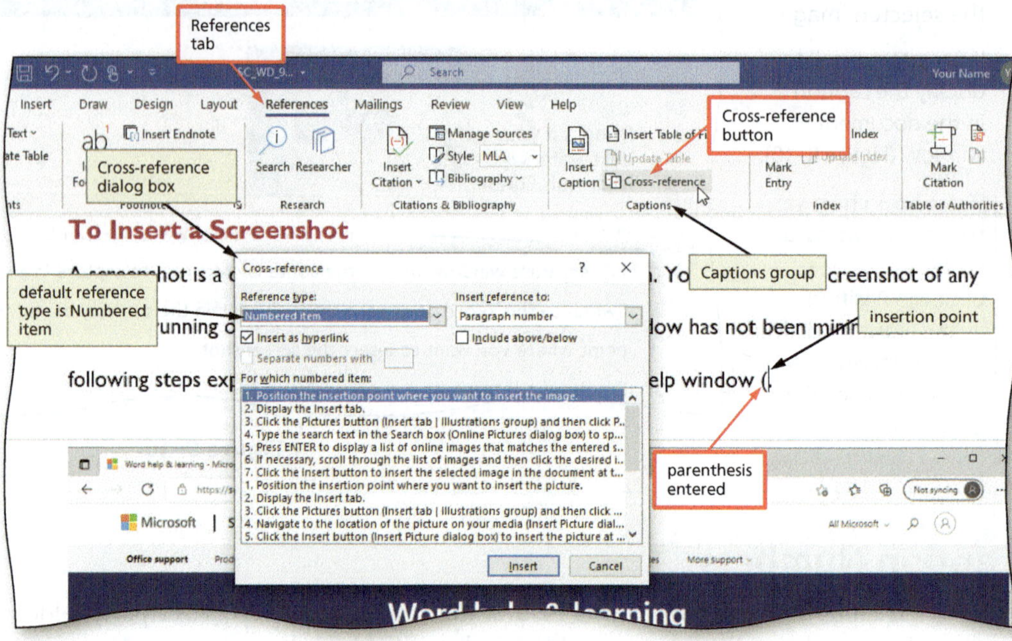

Figure 9–11

2

- Click the Reference type arrow (Cross-reference dialog box) to display the Reference type list; scroll to and then click Figure, which displays a list of figures from the document in the For which caption list (which, at this point, is only one figure).
- If necessary, click 'Figure 1: Help & Learning Window Screenshot' in the For which caption list to select the caption to reference.
- Click the 'Insert reference to' arrow and then click 'Only label and number' to instruct Word that the cross-reference in the document should list just the label, Figure, followed by the figure number (Figure 9–12).

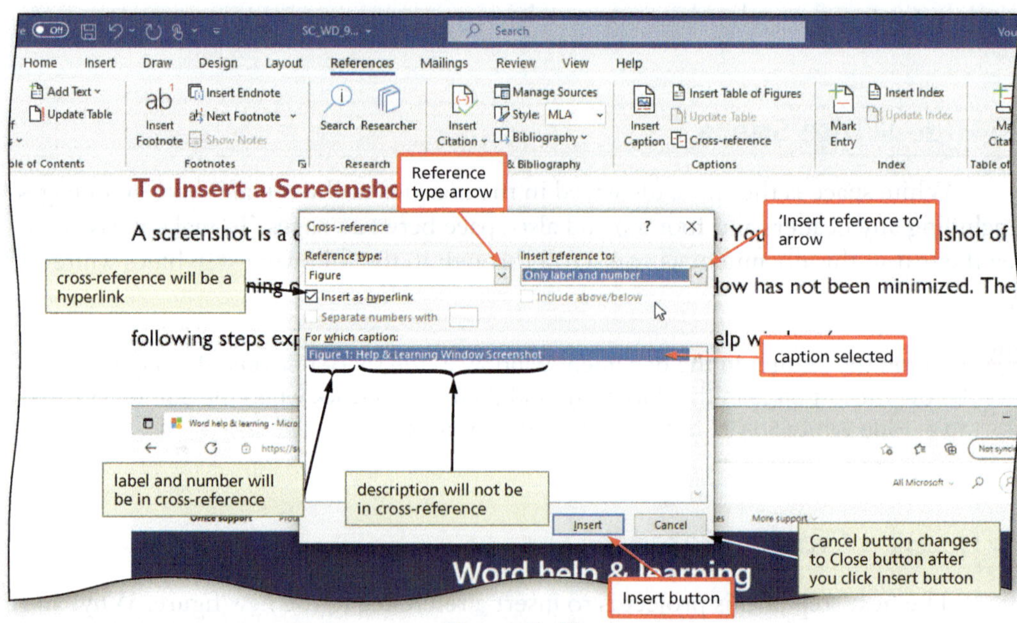

Figure 9–12

3

- Click the Insert button to insert the cross-reference in the document at the location of the insertion point.

Q&A

What if my cross-reference is shaded in gray?
The cross-reference is a field. Depending on your Word settings, fields may appear shaded in gray to help you identify them on the screen.

4

- Click the Close button (Cross-reference dialog box).
- Press the RIGHT PARENTHESIS [ )] key to close off the cross-reference (Figure 9–13).

Q&A **How do I update a cross-reference if a caption is added, deleted, or moved?**
In many cases, Word automatically updates a cross-reference in a document if the item to which it refers changes. To update a cross-reference manually, select the cross-reference and then press F9, or right-click the cross-reference and then click Update Field on the shortcut menu.

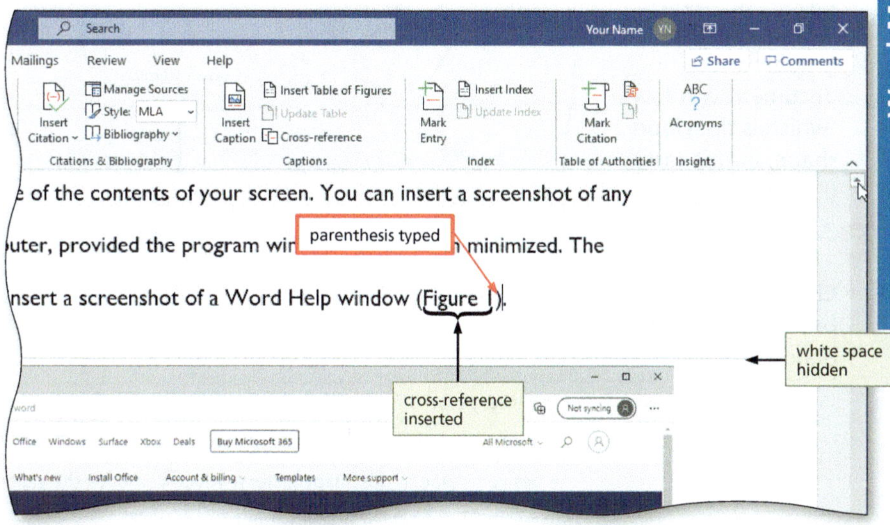

Figure 9–13

Other Ways

1. Click Cross-reference button (Insert tab | Links group)

To Go to an Object

Often, you would like to bring a certain page, image, or other part of a document into view in the document window. Although you could scroll through the document to find a desired page, image, or part of the document, Word enables you to go to a specific location via the Go To sheet in the Find and Replace dialog box.

The following steps go to an image. **Why?** The next step in this module is to add a caption to another image, which is a type of graphic, in the document, so you want to display the image in the document window.

1

- Display the Home tab.
- Click the Find arrow (Home tab | Editing group) to display the Find menu (Figure 9–14).

2

- Click Go To on the Find menu to display the Go To sheet in the Find and Replace dialog box.
- Scroll through the Go to what list and then click Graphic to select it.

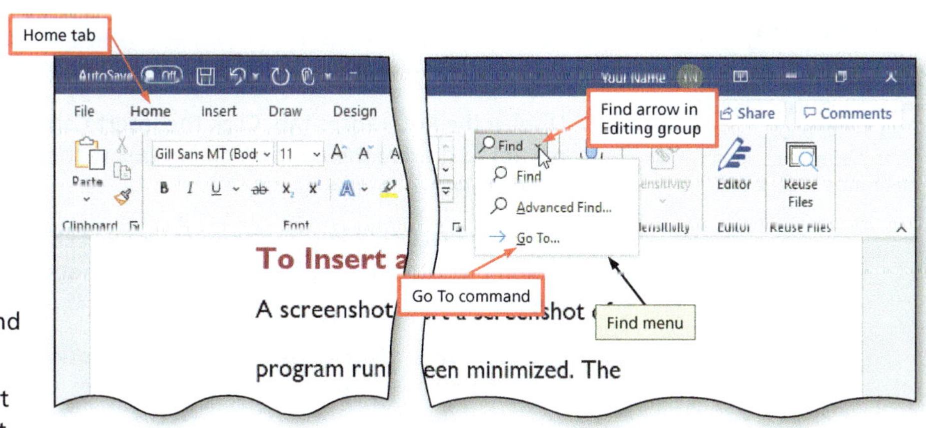

Figure 9–14

- Click the Previous button to display the previous graphic in the document window (which is the cloud shape, in this case) (Figure 9–15).

3

- Click the Close button to close the dialog box.

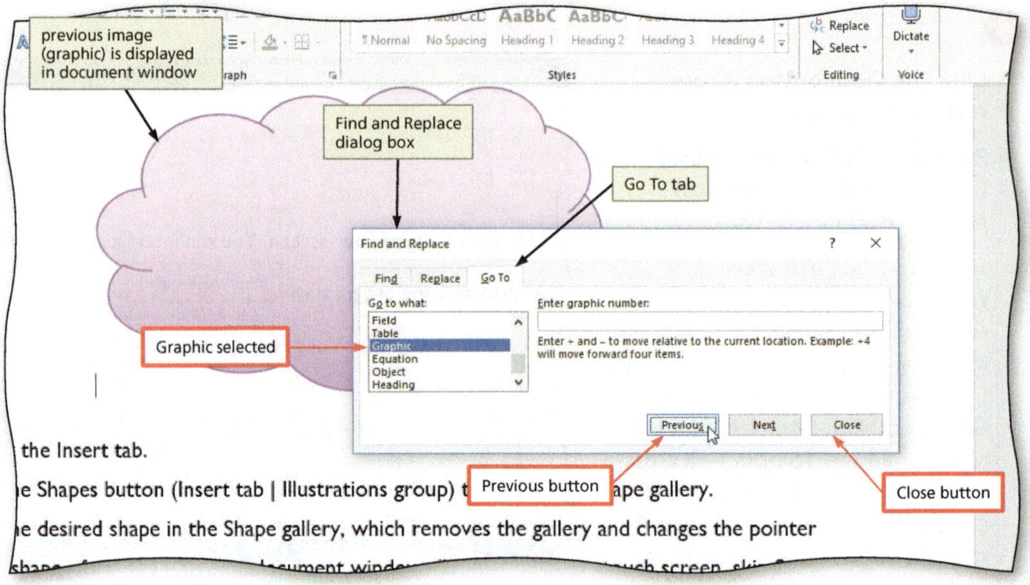

Figure 9–15

Q&A

What if I wanted go to the next section or other location in a document?

You can go to any location listed in the Go to what list, including a page, section, line, bookmark, comment, footnote, endnote, field, table, graphic, equation, object, or heading. To go to a section, for example, you would select section in the Go to what list and then click the Next button in the Go To sheet (Find and Replace dialog box). You also can go to the next section header or footer using the Next button (Header & Footer tab | Header & Footer group).

Other Ways

1. Press CTRL+G

BTW

The Ribbon and Screen Resolution

Word may change how the groups and buttons within the groups appear on the ribbon, depending on the screen resolution of your computer. Thus, your ribbon may look different from the ones in this book if you are using a screen resolution other than 1366 × 768.

To Insert Captions and Cross-References

The previous steps inserted a caption for the screenshot image and then inserted a cross-reference to that caption. The following steps insert captions for the remaining three images in the document (that is, the cloud shape, the picture, and the online image).

1. Click the cloud shape to select the image for which you want to insert a caption.

2. Display the References tab. Click the Insert Caption button (References tab | Captions group) to display the Caption dialog box with a figure number automatically assigned to the selected image.

3. Press the COLON (:) key and then press SPACEBAR in the Caption text box (Caption dialog box) to place separating characters between the figure number and description.

4. Type `Cloud Shape` as the figure description and then click OK to insert the caption below the selected image.

5. At the end of the last sentence above the cloud image, change the word, below, to the word, in, and then press SPACEBAR.

6. Click the Cross-reference button (Insert or References tab | Links or Captions group) to display the Cross-reference dialog box, if necessary, click 'Figure 1: Cloud Shape' in the For which caption list to select the caption to reference, click the Insert button (Cross-reference dialog box) to insert the cross-reference at the location of the insertion point, and then click the Close button in the Cross-reference dialog box.

Q&A

Why did I not need to change the settings for the reference type and reference to in the dialog box?

Word retains the previous settings in the dialog box.

7. Display the Home tab. Click the Find arrow (Home tab | Editing group) to display the Find menu and then click Go To on the Find menu or press CTRL+G to display the Go To sheet in the Find and Replace dialog box. With Graphic selected in the Go to what list, click the Previous button to display the previous image in the document window (which is the sunflower field picture in this case). Click the Close button to close the dialog box.

8. Repeat Steps 1 through 7 to insert the caption, Sunflower Field Picture, for the picture of the sunflower field and the caption, World Continents Image, for the image of the world continents. Also add a cross-reference to the sentence above each image, replacing the word, below, with the word, in, as shown in Figure 9–16.

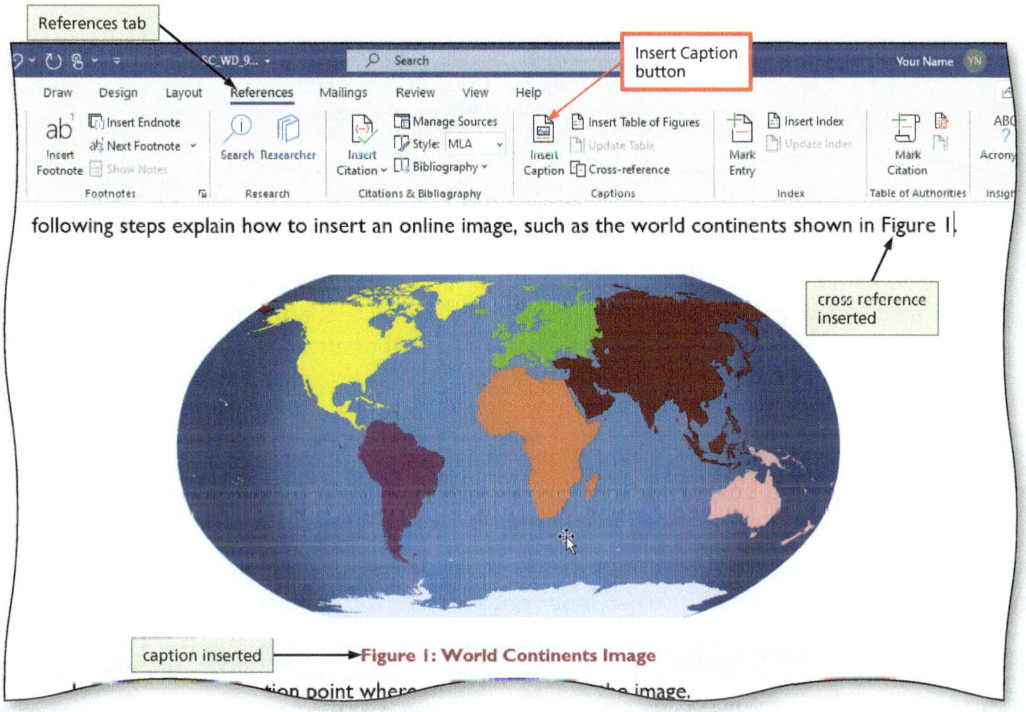

Figure 9–16

BTW

Link to Graphic

If you wanted to link a graphic in a document to a webpage, you would click the Link button (Insert tab | Links group), click 'Existing File or Web Page' in the Link to bar, enter the web address in the Address box (Insert Hyperlink dialog box), and then click OK. To display the webpage associated with the graphic, CTRL+click the graphic.

To Mark an Index Entry

The last page of the reference document in this project is an index, which lists important terms discussed in the document along with each term's corresponding page number. For Word to generate the index, you first must mark any text you wish to appear in the index. **Why?** When you mark an index entry, Word creates a field that it uses to build the index. Index entry fields are hidden and are displayed on the screen only when you show formatting marks, that is, when the 'Show/Hide ¶' button (Home tab | Paragraph group) is selected.

In this document, you want the words, drawing object, in the second sentence below the To Insert a Shape heading to be marked as an index entry. The following steps mark an index entry.

1

- Select the text you wish to appear in the index (the words, drawing object, in the To Insert a Shape section of the document in this case).
- Click the Mark Entry button (References tab | Index group) to display the Mark Index Entry dialog box with the selected text entered in the Main entry text box (Figure 9–17).

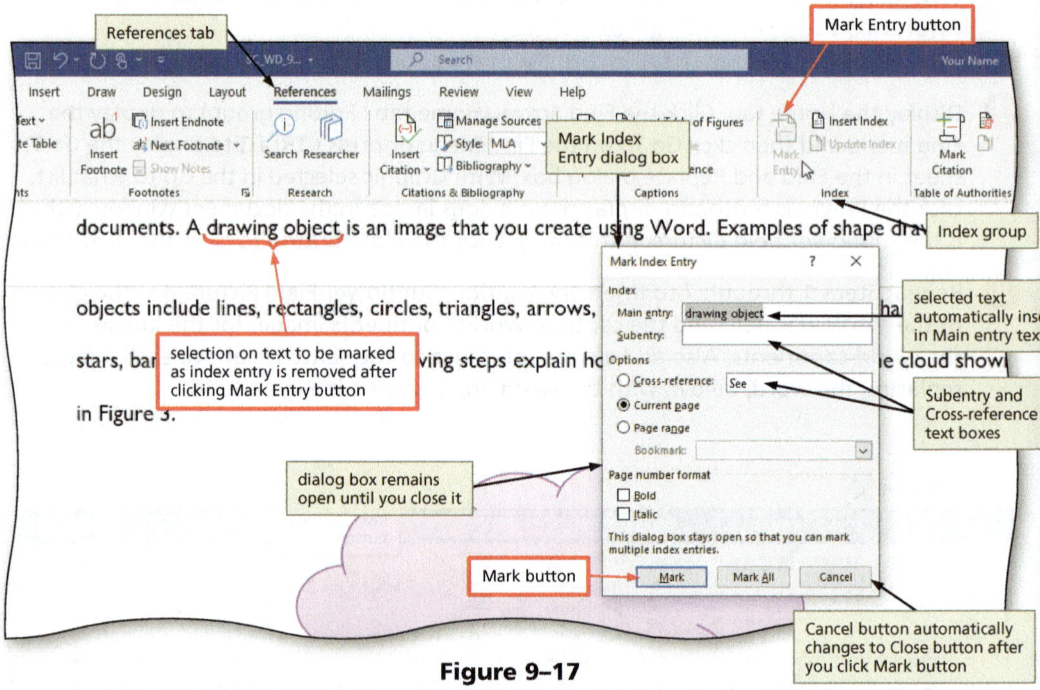

Figure 9–17

Q&A **How would I enter a second-level index entry?**
Enter the second-level text in the Subentry text box. If you wanted a third-level index entry, you would place a colon after the second-level in the Subentry text box and then enter the third-level text after the colon. You also can enter a cross-reference to another index entry by entering the text for the other entry in the Cross-reference text box after the text, *See*.

2

- Click the Mark button (Mark Index Entry dialog box) to mark the selected text in the document as an index entry.

Q&A **Why do formatting marks now appear on the screen?**
When you mark an index entry, Word automatically shows formatting marks (if they are not showing already) so that you can see the index entry field. Notice that the marked index entry begins with the letters, XE.

- Click the Close button in the Mark Index Entry dialog box to close the dialog box; scroll up, if necessary, to display the To Insert a Shape heading (Figure 9–18).

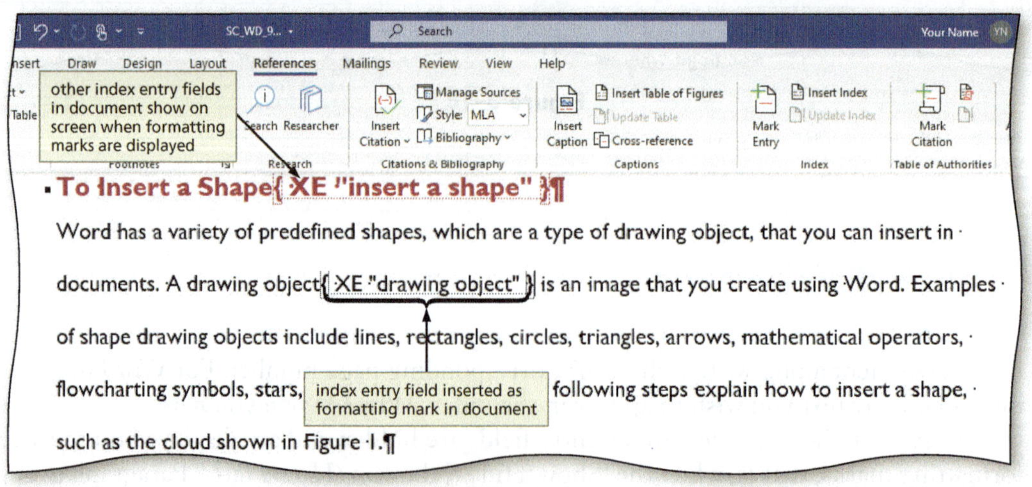

Figure 9–18

Q&A **How could I see all index entries marked in a document?**
With formatting marks displaying, you could scroll through the document, scanning for all occurrences of XE, or you could use the Navigation Pane (that is, place a check mark in the Navigation Pane check box (View tab | Show group)) to find all occurrences of XE.

Other Ways

1. Select text, press ALT+SHIFT+X

To Mark Multiple Index Entries

Word leaves the Mark Index Entry dialog box open until you close it, which allows you to mark multiple index entries without having to reopen the dialog box repeatedly. To mark multiple index entries, you would perform the following steps.

1. With the Mark Index Entry dialog box displayed, click in the document window; scroll to and then select the next index entry.
2. If necessary, click the Main entry text box (Mark Index Entry dialog box) to display the selected text in the Main entry text box.
3. Click the Mark button.
4. Repeat Steps 1 through 3 for all entries. When finished, click the Close button in the Mark Index Entry dialog box.

BTW

Index Entries
Index entries may include a switch, which is a backslash followed by a letter inserted after the field text. Switches include \b to apply bold formatting to the entry's page number, \f to define an entry type, \i to make the entry's page number italic, \r to insert a range of page numbers, \t to insert specified text in place of a page number, and \y to specify that the subsequent text defines the pronunciation for the index entry. A colon in an index entry precedes a subentry keyword in the index.

To Hide Formatting Marks

To remove the clutter of index entry fields from the document, you should hide formatting marks. The following step hides formatting marks.

1 Display the Home tab. If the 'Show/Hide ¶' button (Home tab | Paragraph group) is selected, click it to hide formatting marks.

Q&A **What if the index entries still appear after clicking the 'Show/Hide ¶' button?**
Open Backstage view, click Options to display the Word Options dialog box, click Display in the left pane (Word Options dialog box), remove the check mark from the Hidden text check box, and then click OK.

To Show White Space

For the remainder of creating this project, you would like to see headers, footers, and margins. Thus, you should show white space. The following step shows white space.

1 Position the pointer in the document window on a page break notation and then double-click when the pointer changes to a 'Show White Space' button to show white space.

To Insert a Sidebar Text Box

A **sidebar text box** is a text box that is positioned adjacent to the body of a document, running across the top or bottom of a page or along the right or left edge of a page, and contains auxiliary information. The following steps insert a built-in sidebar text box. **Why?** Sidebar text boxes take up less space on the page than text boxes positioned in the middle of the page.

1

- Be sure the insertion point is near the top of page 1 of the document, as shown in Figure 9–19.

Q&A **Does the insertion point need to be at the top of the page?**
The insertion point should be close to where you want to insert the text box.

- Display the Insert tab.

- Click the Text Box button (Insert tab | Text group) to display the Text Box gallery.

Experiment

- Scroll through the Text Box gallery to see the variety of available text box styles.
- Scroll to display Grid Sidebar in the Text Box gallery (Figure 9–19).

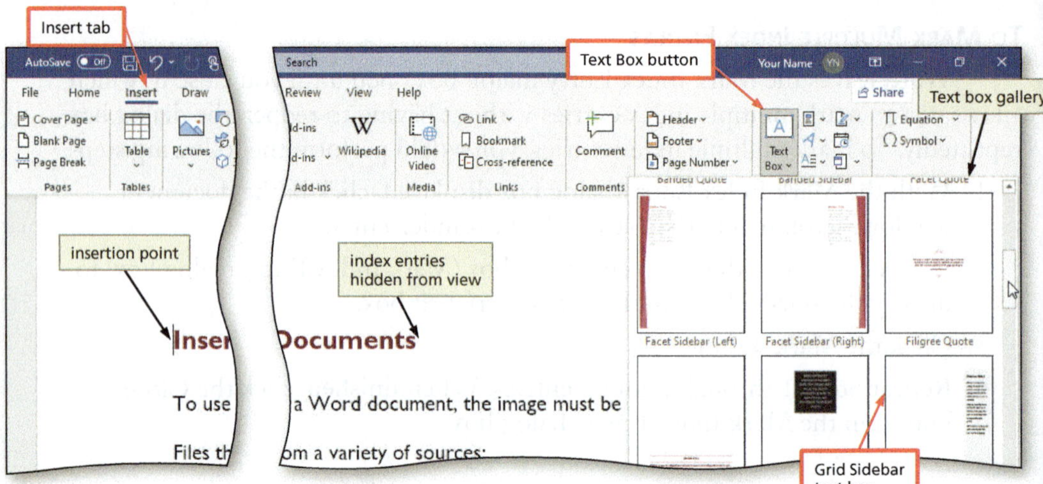

Figure 9–19

2

- Click Grid Sidebar in the Text Box gallery to insert that text box style in the document (Figure 9–20).

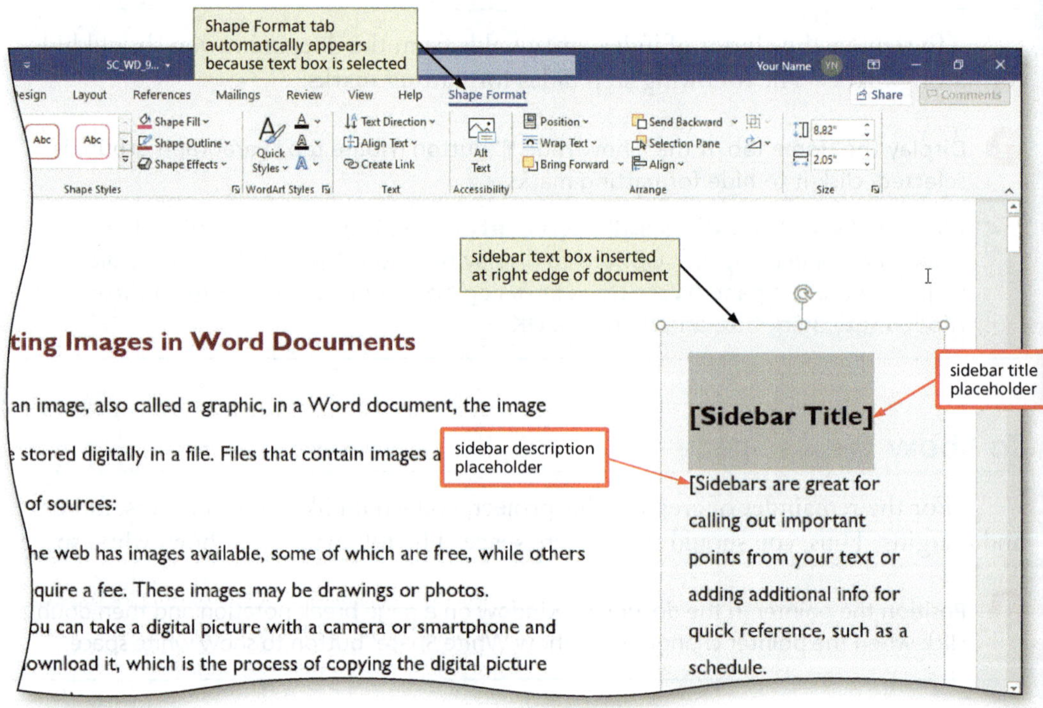

Figure 9–20

Other Ways

1. Click 'Explore Quick Parts' button (Insert tab | Text group), click 'Building Blocks Organizer' on Explore Quick Parts menu, select desired text box name in Building blocks list, click Insert button

To Enter and Format Text in the Sidebar Text Box

The next step is to enter the text in the sidebar text box. The following steps enter text in the text box.

1. If necessary, click the sidebar title placeholder in the text box to select it.
2. Type `What Is Malware?` and then change the font size of the entered text to 12 point.
3. Click the sidebar description placeholder and then type the following paragraph: **Malware, short for malicious software, is software that usually acts without a user's knowledge and deliberately alters a computer or mobile device's operations. Examples of malware**

include viruses, worms, trojan horses, rootkits, spyware, adware, and zombies. Change the font size of the entered text to 10 point.

4. Press ENTER. Change the font size to 12 point. Type **Malware Protection Tips** and then press ENTER.

5. Change the font size to 10 point. Click the Bullets button (Home tab | Paragraph group) to bullet the list. Click the Decrease Indent button (Home tab | Paragraph group) to move the bullet symbol left one-half inch. Type **Use a firewall and an antivirus or similar app.** and then press ENTER.

6. Type **Be suspicious of unsolicited email attachments.** and then press ENTER.

7. Type **Download apps or programs only from trusted websites.** and then press ENTER.

8. Type **Close spyware windows.** and then press ENTER.

9. Type **Before using removable media, scan it for malware.** and then press ENTER.

10. Type **Back up regularly.** to enter the last line.

11. Change the line spacing of the paragraphs entered in Steps 3 and 4 to 1.15 using the Line and Paragraph Spacing button (Home tab | Paragraph group).

12. Select the text box by clicking its edge and then change its fill color to Blue-Gray, Accent 6, Lighter 40% by using the Shape Fill arrow (Shape Format tab | Shape Styles group).

13. Click the One Page button (View tab | Zoom group) so that you can see all of the entered text at once (Figure 9–21).

14. Change the zoom to page width.

BTW

Building Blocks
Many of the objects that you can insert through the Building Blocks gallery are available as built-in objects in galleries on the ribbon. Some examples are cover pages in the Cover Page gallery (Insert tab | Pages group), equations in the Equation gallery (Insert tab | Symbols group), footers in the Footer gallery (Insert tab | Header & Footer group), headers in the Header gallery (Insert tab | Header & Footer group), page numbers in the Page Number gallery (Insert tab | Header & Footer group), text boxes in the Text Box gallery (Insert tab | Text group), and watermarks in the Watermark gallery (Design tab | Page Background group).

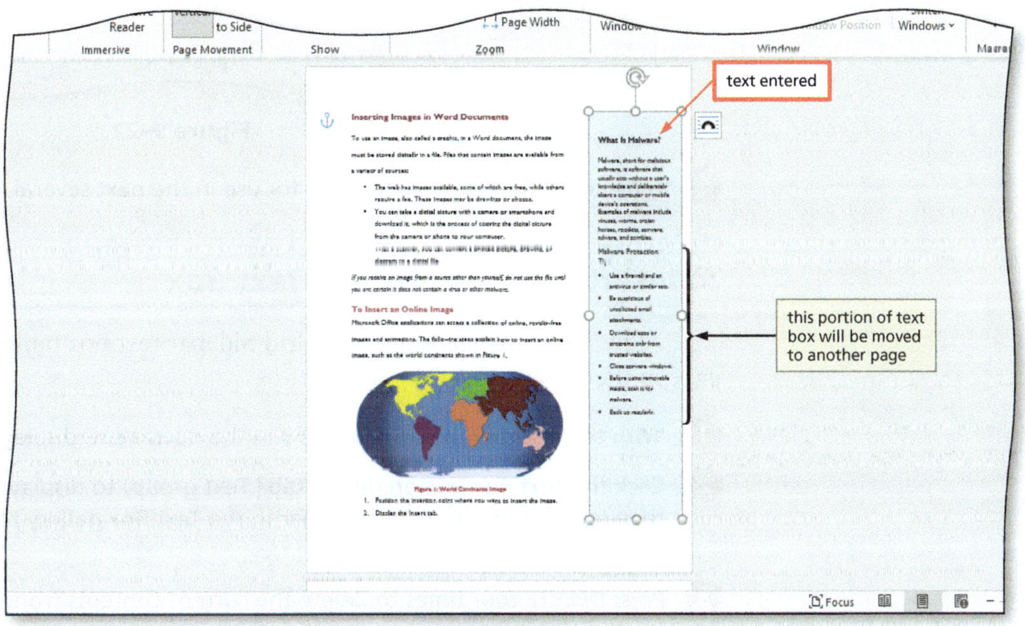

Figure 9–21

To Use the Navigation Pane to Go to a Page

Instead of one long text box, this project splits the text box across the edge of two pages, specifically, the first and third pages of this document. The following steps use the Navigation Pane to display page 3 in the document window so that you can insert another text box on that page.

1. If necessary, display the View tab. Place a check mark in the Navigation Pane check box (View tab | Show group) to open the Navigation Pane at the left edge of the Word window. If desired, drag the edge of the Navigation Pane to widen or narrow the pane so that it looks like Figure 9–22.

BTW
Deleting Building Blocks
To delete an existing building block, click the 'Explore Quick Parts' button (Insert tab | Text group) to display the Explore Quick Parts menu, click 'Building Blocks Organizer' on the Explore Quick Parts menu to display the Building Blocks Organizer dialog box, select the building block to delete (Building Blocks Organizer dialog box), click the Delete button, click Yes in the dialog box that appears, and then close the Building Blocks Organizer dialog box.

2. Click the Pages tab in the Navigation Pane to display thumbnail images of the pages in the document.
3. Scroll to and then click the thumbnail of the third page in the Navigation Pane to display the top of the selected page in the top of the document window (Figure 9–22).

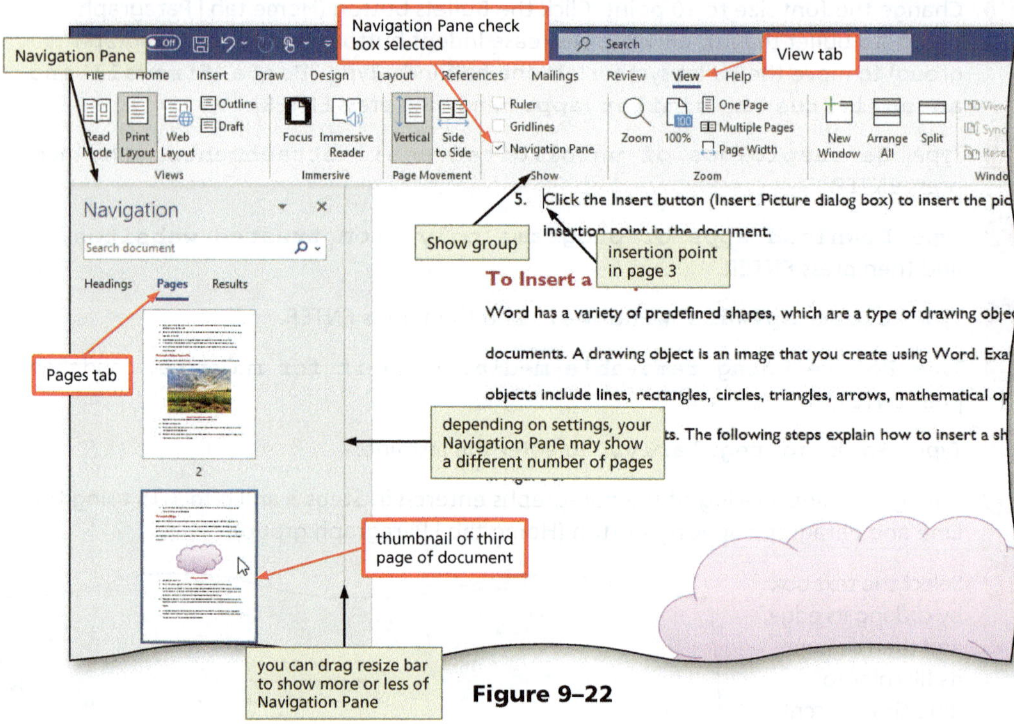

Figure 9–22

4. Leave the Navigation Pane open for use in the next several steps.

To Insert Another Sidebar Text Box

The following steps insert a Grid Sidebar text box building block on the third page in the document.

1. With the insertion point on page 3 in the document, display the Insert tab.
2. Click the Text Box button (Insert tab | Text group) to display the Text Box gallery and then locate and select Grid Sidebar in the Text Box gallery to insert that text box style in the document.
3. Press DELETE four times to delete the current contents from the text box (Figure 9–23).

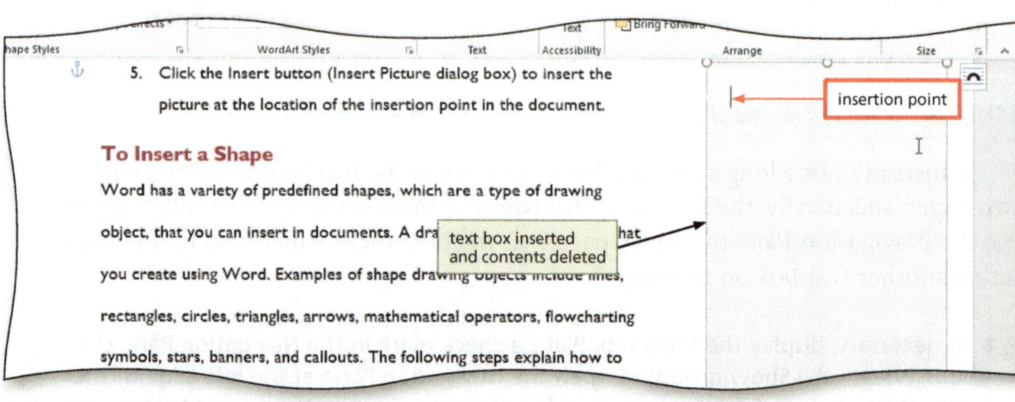

Figure 9–23

To Link Text Boxes

Word allows you to link two separate text boxes. **Why?** You can flow text from one text box into the other. To link text boxes, the second text box must be empty, which is why you deleted the contents of the text box in the previous steps. The following steps link text boxes.

1

- Click the thumbnail of the first page in the Navigation Pane to display the top of the selected page in the document window.
- Click an edge of the text box on the first page to select it.
- If necessary, display the Shape Format tab.
- Click the Create Link button (Shape Format tab | Text group), which changes the pointer to the shape of a pitcher.
- Move the pointer in the document window to see its new shape (Figure 9–24).

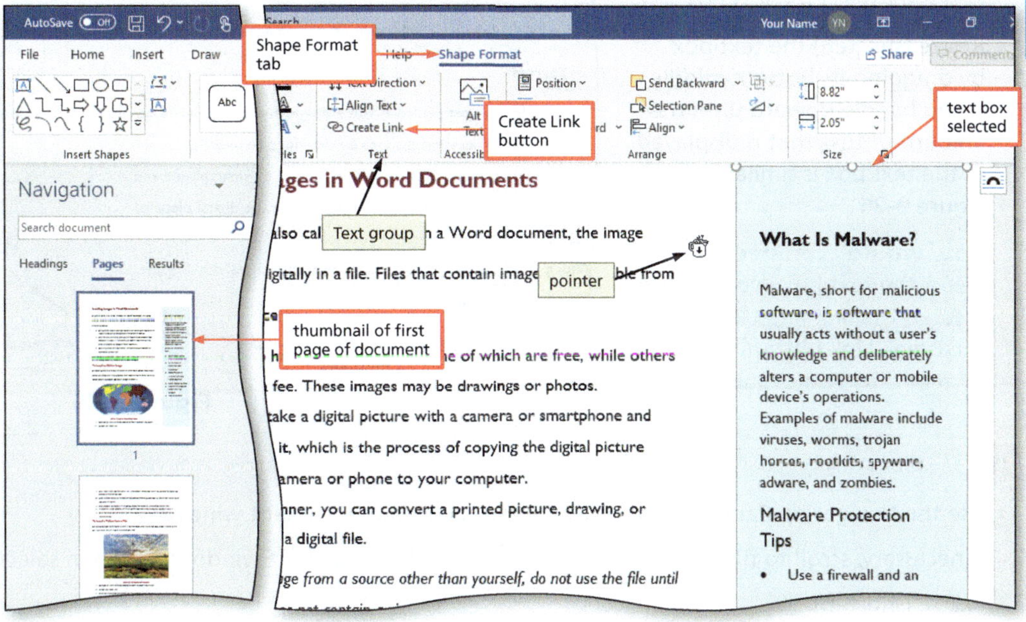

Figure 9–24

2

- Scroll through the document to display the second text box, which is located on the third page, in the document window.

Q&A **Can I use the Navigation Pane to go to the second text box?**
No. If you click in the Navigation Pane, the link process will stop and the pointer will return to its default shape.

- Position the pointer in the empty text box, so that the pointer shape changes to a pouring pitcher (Figure 9–25).

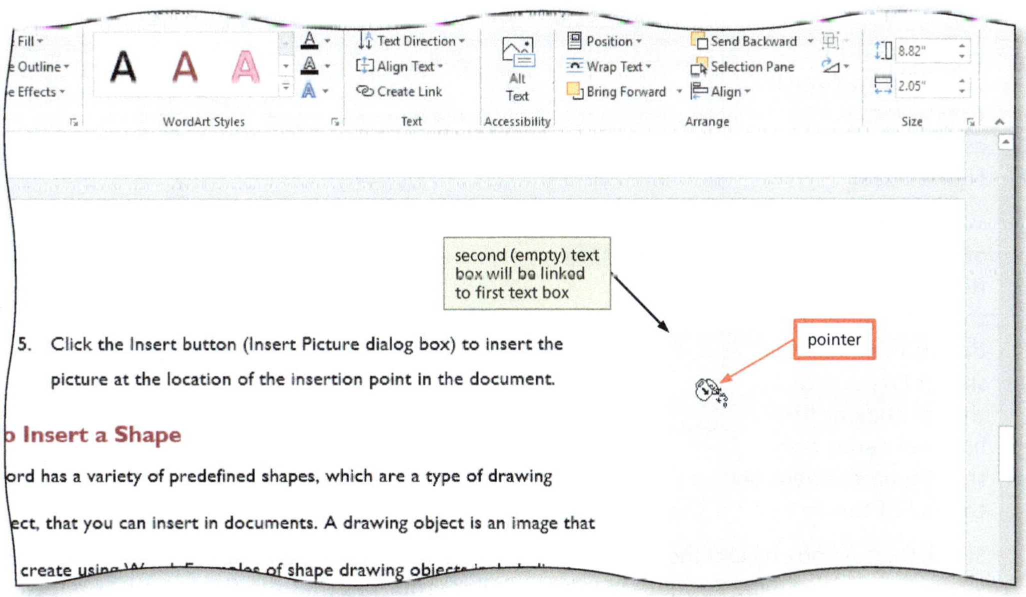

Figure 9–25

3

- Click the empty text box to link it to the first text box (or, if using a touch screen, you will need to use a stylus to tap the empty text box).
- Scroll to display the first text box in the document window and then, if necessary, select the text box.
- Resize (shorten) the text box by dragging its bottom-middle sizing handle upward until the amount of text that is displayed in the text box is similar to Figure 9–26.

Q&A **How would I remove a link?** Select the text box in which you created the link and then click the Break Link button (Shape Format tab | Text group).

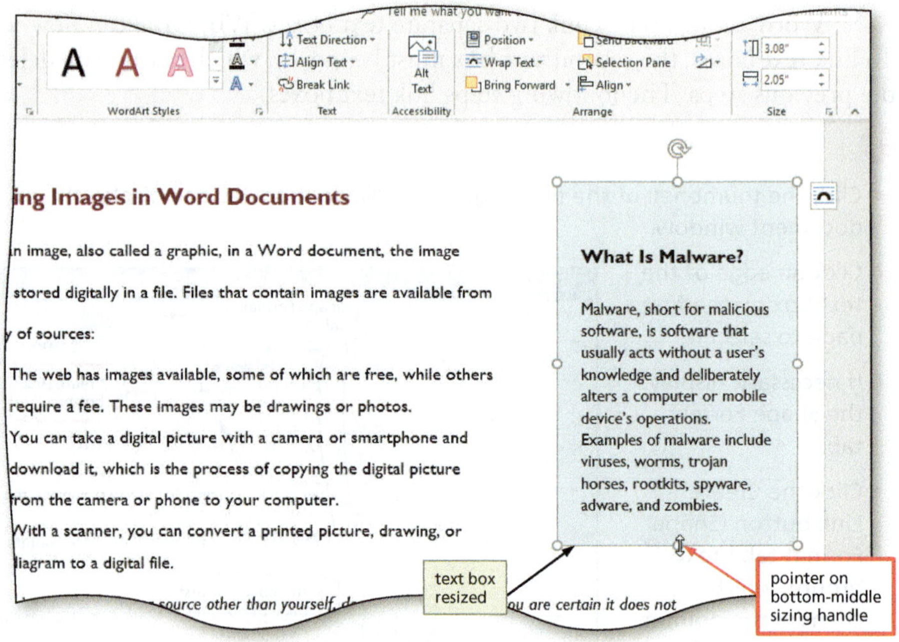

Figure 9–26

4

- Use the Navigation Pane to display the third page in the document window.
- If necessary, scroll to display the second text box in the document window and then select the text box.
- Resize (shorten) the text box by dragging its bottom-middle sizing handle upward until the amount of text that is displayed in the text box is similar to Figure 9–27.
- Drag the entire text box downward to position it as shown in Figure 9–27.
- Verify that all of Step #5 in the document fits on the third page. If it does not, adjust the size or location of the text box or the line and paragraph spacing on the page so that all of the To Insert a Shape text fits on the third page.

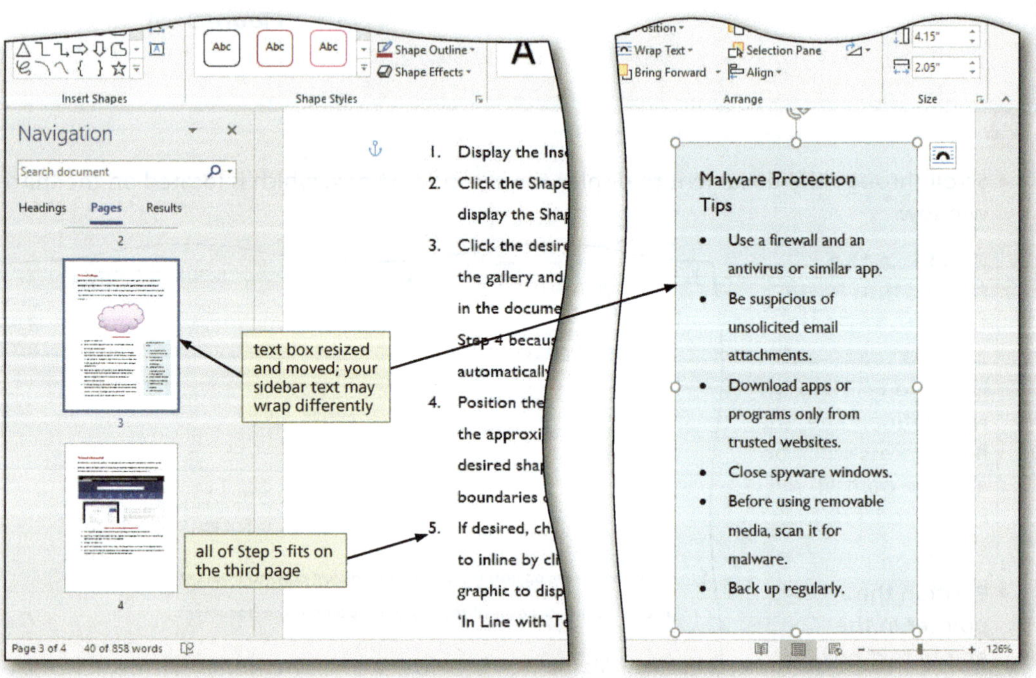

Figure 9–27

- Select the text box by clicking its edge and then change its fill color to Blue-Gray, Accent 6, Lighter 40% by using the Shape Fill arrow (Shape Format tab | Shape Styles group) so that the final text box appears as shown in Figure 9–27.
- If necessary, insert a page break to the left of the To Insert a Shape heading so that the heading begins at the top of the third page.

To Compress Pictures

If you plan to use email to send a Word document that contains pictures or other images or post it for downloading, you may want to reduce its file size to speed up file transmission time. **Why?** Pictures and other images in Word documents can increase the size of these files. In Word, you can compress pictures, which reduces the size of the Word document. Compressing the pictures in Word does not cause any loss in their original quality. The following steps compress pictures in a document.

1

- Click a picture in the document to select it, such as the sunflower field, and then display the Picture Format tab.
- Click the Compress Pictures button (Picture Format tab | Adjust group) to display the Compress Pictures dialog box.
- If the 'Apply only to this picture' check box (Compress Pictures dialog box) contains a check mark, remove the check mark so that all pictures in the document are compressed.
- If necessary, click 'Print (220 ppi): excellent quality on most printers and screens' in the Resolution area to specify how images should be compressed (Figure 9–28).

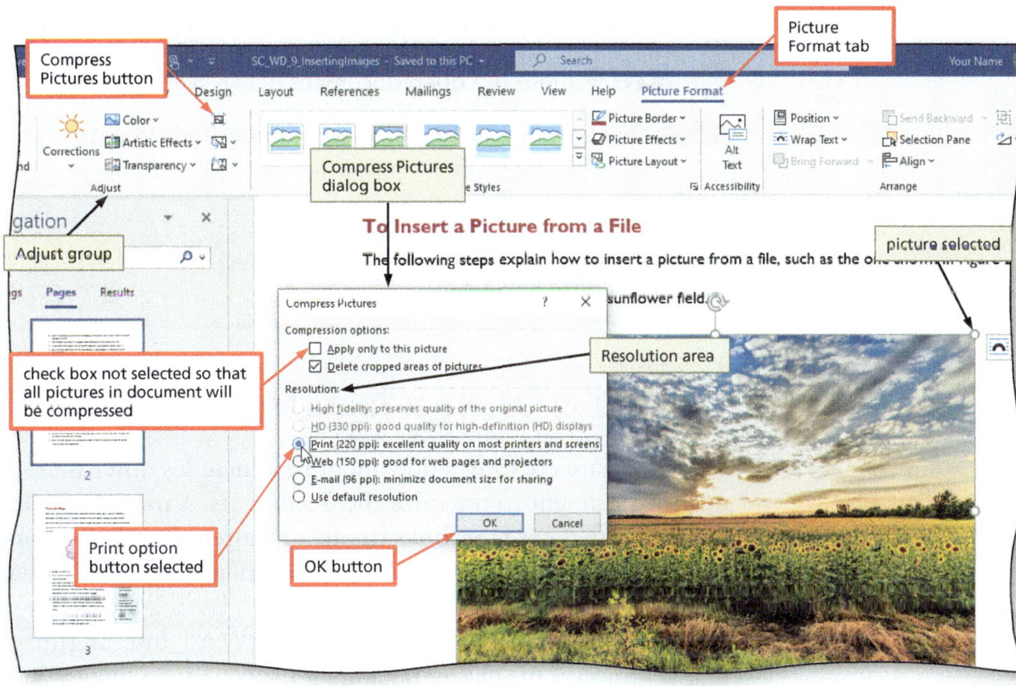

Figure 9–28

2

- Click OK to compress all pictures in the document.

Q&A **Can I compress a single picture?**
Yes. Select the picture and then place a check mark in the 'Apply only to this picture' check box (Compress Pictures dialog box).

Other Ways

1. Click the Tools button in Save As dialog box, click Compress Pictures on Tools menu, select options (Compress Pictures dialog box), click OK

To Save Pictures in Other Formats

You can save any image in a document as a picture file for use in other documents or apps. If you wanted to save an image in a Word document, you would perform the following steps.

1. Right-click the image to display a shortcut menu.
2. Click 'Save as Picture' on the shortcut menu to display the Save As Picture dialog box.
3. Navigate to the location you want to save the image.

BTW

Compressing Pictures
Selecting a lower ppi (pixels per inch) in the Resolution area (Compress Picture dialog box) creates a smaller document file but also lowers the quality of the images.

4. Click the 'Save as type' arrow (Save As Picture dialog box) and then select the image type for the saved image.
5. Click the Save button (Save As Picture dialog box) to save the image in the specified location using the specified image type.

To Close Open Panes, Documents, and Windows

The following steps close the open Word document and the browser window.

1. If necessary, update the cross references and then close the Navigation Pane.
2. Save the document again on the same storage location with the same file name.
3. sam Close the open document (leave Word running).
4. If necessary, display the browser window and close it.

Break Point: If you want to take a break, this is a good place to do so. You can exit Word now. To resume later, start Word and continue following the steps from this location forward.

Working with a Master Document

BTW

Master Documents

Master documents can be used when multiple people prepare different sections of a document or when a document contains separate elements, such as the modules in a book. If multiple people in a network need to work on the same document simultaneously, each person can work on a section (subdocument); all subdocuments can be stored together collectively in a master document on the network server.

When you are creating a document that includes other files, you may want to create a master document to organize the documents. A **master document** is simply a document that contains links to one or more other documents, each of which is called a **subdocument**. In addition to subdocuments, a master document can contain its own text and images.

The master file is SC_WD_9_UsingWord_InsertingImages_MasterDocument.docx in this project. This master document file contains a link to one subdocument: SC_WD_9_InsertingImages.docx. The master document also contains other items: a cover page, a copyright page, a table of contents, a table of figures, and an index. The following sections create this master document and insert the necessary elements in the document to create the finished SC_WD_9_UsingWord_InsertingImages_MasterDocument.docx.

To Change the Document Theme

The first step in creating this master document is to change its document theme to Gallery. The following steps change the document theme.

1. sam If necessary, start Word and create a new blank document.
2. Click Design on the ribbon to display the Design tab.
3. Click the Themes button (Design tab | Document Formatting group) to display the Themes gallery.
4. Click Gallery in the Themes gallery to change the document theme to the selected theme.

Outlines

To create a master document, Word must be in Outline view. You then enter the headings of the document as an outline using Word's built-in heading styles. In an outline, the major heading is displayed at the left margin with each subordinate, or lower-level, heading indented. In Word, the built-in Heading 1 style is displayed at the left margin in Outline view. Heading 2 style is indented below Heading 1 style, Heading 3 style is indented further, and so on. (Outline view works similarly to multilevel lists.)

You do not want to use a built-in heading style for the paragraphs of text within the document, because when you create a table of contents, Word places all lines formatted using the built-in heading styles in the table of contents. Thus, the text below each heading is formatted using the Body Text style.

Each heading should print at the top of a new page. Because you might want to format the pages within a heading differently from those pages in other headings, you insert next page section breaks between each heading.

To Switch to Outline View

The following steps switch to Outline view. **Why?** To create a master document, Word must be in Outline view.

1

- Display the View tab (Figure 9–29).

2

- Click the Outline button (View tab | Views group), which displays the Outlining tab on the ribbon and switches to Outline view.

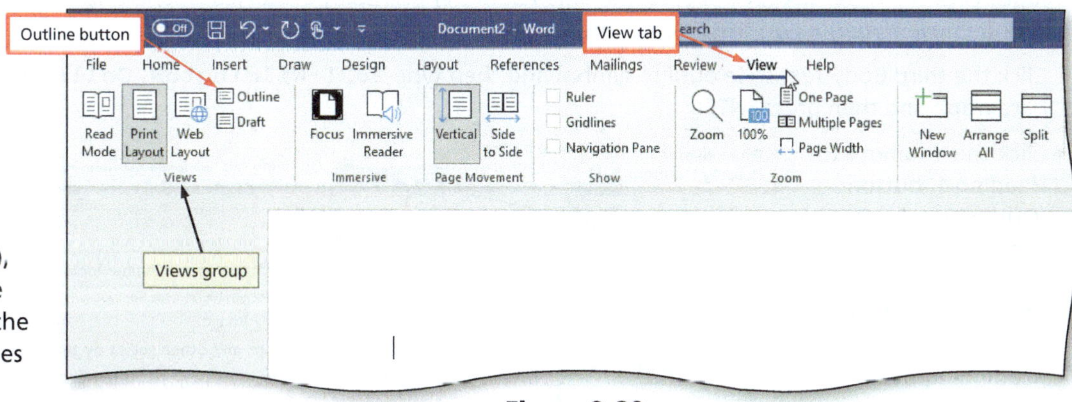

Figure 9–29

- Be sure the 'Show Text Formatting' check box is selected and the 'Show First Line Only' check box is not selected (Outlining tab | Outline Tools group) (Figure 9–30).

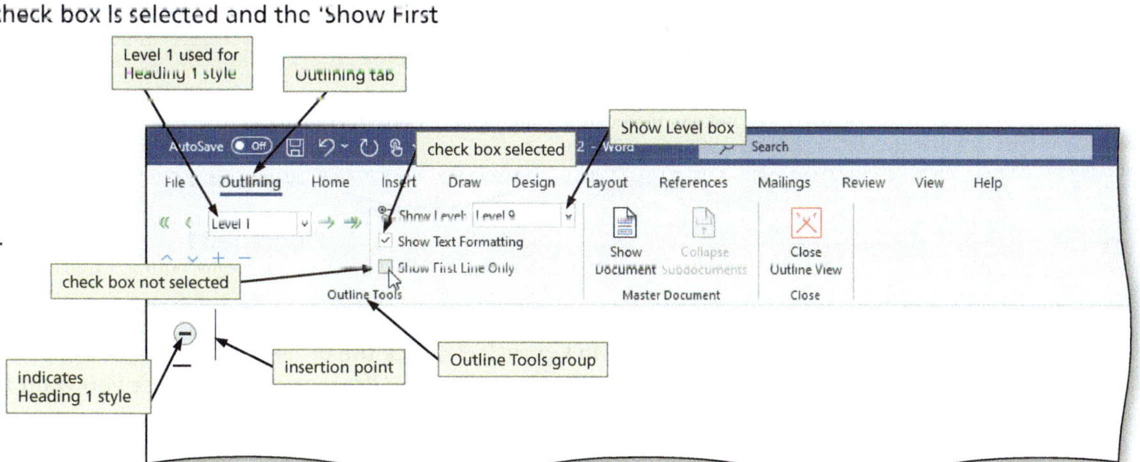

Figure 9–30

Q&A

Can I specify the number of levels (headings) that will be displayed in the outline?

Yes, click the Show Level box (Outlining tab | Outline Tools group) and then select the desired level. The selected level and all higher levels will appear in the outline. To show all levels, select All Levels.

To Enter Text in Outline View

The SC_WD_9_UsingWord_InsertingImages_MasterDocument.docx document contains these three major headings: Inserting Images in Word Documents, Table of Figures, and Index. The heading, Inserting Images in Word Documents, is not entered in the outline. **Why not?** It is part of the subdocument inserted in the master document.

The first page of the outline (the copyright page) does not contain a heading; instead it contains three paragraphs of body text, which you enter directly in the outline. The Inserting Images in Word Documents content is inserted from the subdocument. You will instruct Word to create the content for the Table of Figures and Index later in this module. The following steps create an outline that contains headings and body text to be used in the master document.

1

- Click the 'Demote to Body Text' button (Outlining tab | Outline Tools group), so that you can enter the paragraphs of text for the copyright page.
- Type `Using Word - Guide #26 - Inserting Images` as the first paragraph in the outline and then press ENTER.
- Type `To receive additional guides in this or any other series by the Information Resource Center at Wilmington College, send a message to Rosey Schmidt at rschmidt@wilmingtoncollege.cengage.edu.` as the second paragraph in the outline and then press ENTER.

Q&A **Why is only my first line of text in the paragraph displayed?**
Remove the check mark from the 'Show First Line Only' check box (Outlining tab | Outline Tools group).

- Right-click the hyperlink (in this case, the email address) to display a shortcut menu and then click Remove Hyperlink on the shortcut menu.
- Click the third Body Text style outline symbol and then type `2021 Wilmington College` as the third paragraph and then press ENTER.
- Click the 'Promote to Heading 1' button (Outlining tab | Outline Tools group) because you are finished entering body text and will enter the remaining headings in the outline next (Figure 9–31).

Q&A **Could I press SHIFT+TAB instead of clicking the 'Promote to Heading 1' button?**
Yes.

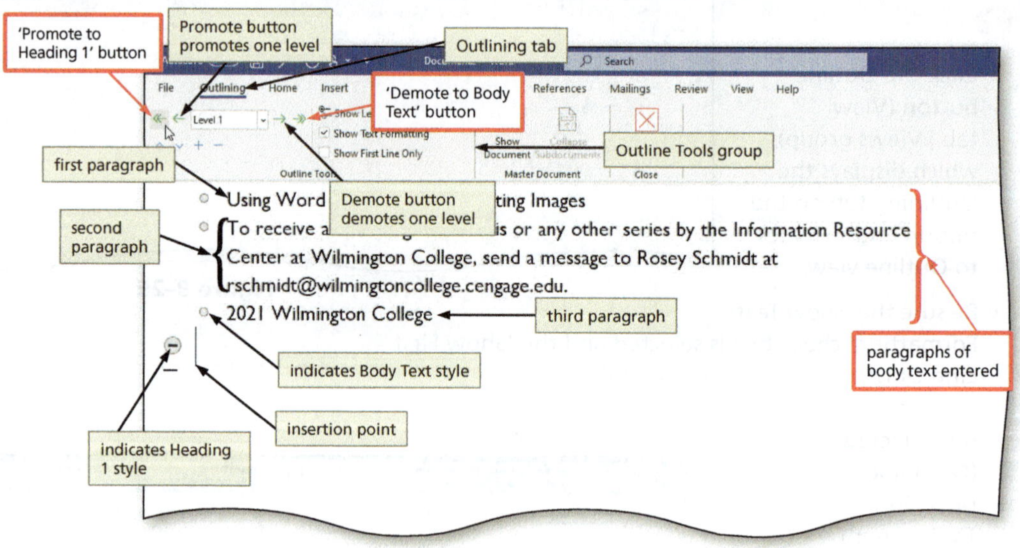

Figure 9–31

2

- Display the Layout tab.
- With the insertion point positioned as shown in Figure 9–31, click the Breaks button (Layout tab | Page Setup group) and then click Next Page in the Section Breaks area in the Breaks gallery because you want to enter a next page section break before the next heading.

3

- Type `Table of Figures` and then press ENTER.
- Repeat Step 2.

4

- Type **Index** as the last entry (Figure 9–32).

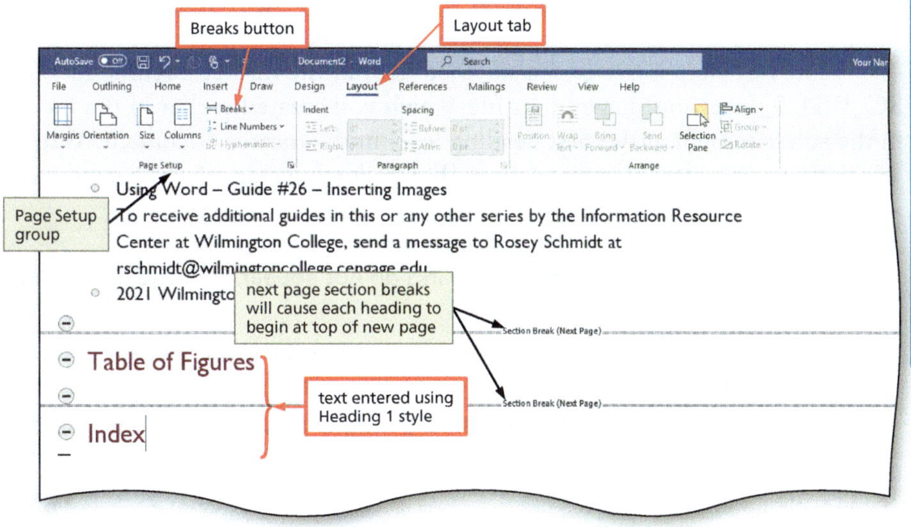

Figure 9–32

To Show Only the First Line of Each Paragraph in Outline View

Users often instruct Word to display just the first line of each paragraph of body text. **Why?** When only the first line of each paragraph is displayed, the outline often is more readable. The following step displays only the first line of body text paragraphs.

1

- Display the Outlining tab.
- Place a check mark in the 'Show First Line Only' check box (Outlining tab | Outline Tools group), so that Word displays only the first line of each paragraph (Figure 9–33).

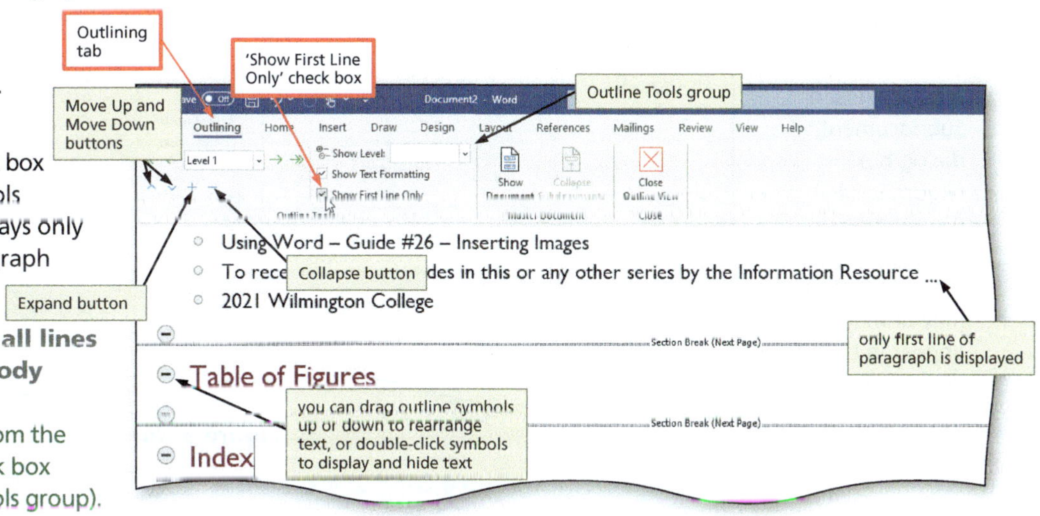

Figure 9–33

Q&A

How would I redisplay all lines of the paragraphs of body text?
Remove the check mark from the 'Show First Line Only' check box (Outlining tab | Outline Tools group).

Why do the outline symbols contain a minus sign?
The minus sign means the outline level does not have any subordinate levels. If an outline symbol contains a plus sign, it means the outline level has subordinate levels. If you double-click an outline symbol that contains a plus sign, the section under the heading will expand (show) if it is collapsed (hidden) and will collapse if it is expanded. Or with the insertion point in the heading, you can click the Expand and Collapse buttons (Outlining tab | Outline Tools group).

How do I move headings in Outline view?
You can drag the outline symbols up or down to rearrange headings. You also can position the insertion point in a heading and then click the Move Up or Move Down button (Outlining tab | Outline Tools group) to move a heading up or down, respectively.

- Save this master document on your hard drive, OneDrive, or other storage location using the file name, SC_WD_9_UsingWord_InsertingImages_MasterDocument.

Other Ways

1. Press CTRL+SHIFT+L

To Insert a Subdocument in a Master Document

The next step is to insert a subdocument in the master document. The subdocument to be inserted is the SC_WD_9_InsertingImages.docx file, which you created earlier in the module. Word places the first line of text in the subdocument at the first heading level in the master document. **Why?** The first line in the subdocument was defined using the Heading 1 style. The following steps insert a subdocument in a master document.

1

- Display the Home tab. If formatting marks do not appear, click the 'Show/Hide ¶' button (Home tab | Paragraph group) to display formatting marks.
- Position the insertion point where you want to insert the subdocument (on the section break above the Table of Figures heading).
- Display the Outlining tab. Click the Show Document button (Outlining tab | Master Document group) so that all commands in the Master Document group appear.
- Click the Insert button (Outlining tab | Master Document group) to display the Insert Subdocument dialog box.
- Locate and select the SC_WD_9_InsertingImages.docx file (Insert Subdocument dialog box) (Figure 9–34). (Depending on settings, the file extension of .docx may or may not appear in the dialog box.)

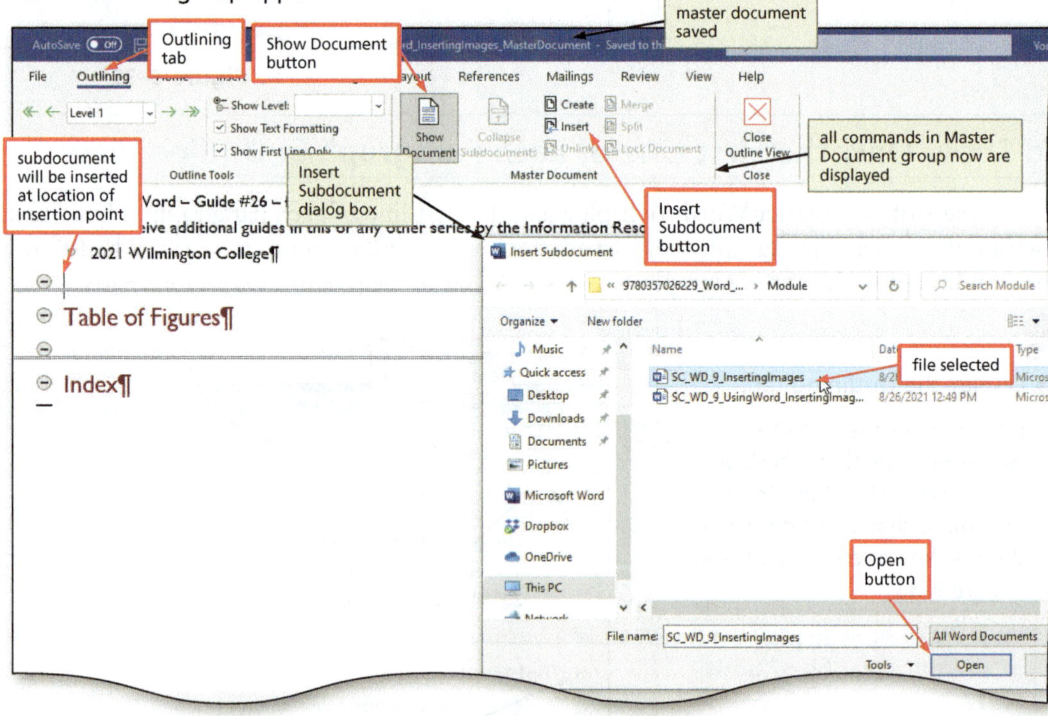

Figure 9–34

2

- Click the Open button (Insert Subdocument dialog box) to insert the selected file as a subdocument.
- If Word displays a dialog box about styles, click the 'No to All' button.
- Press CTRL+HOME to position the insertion point at the top of the document (Figure 9–35).

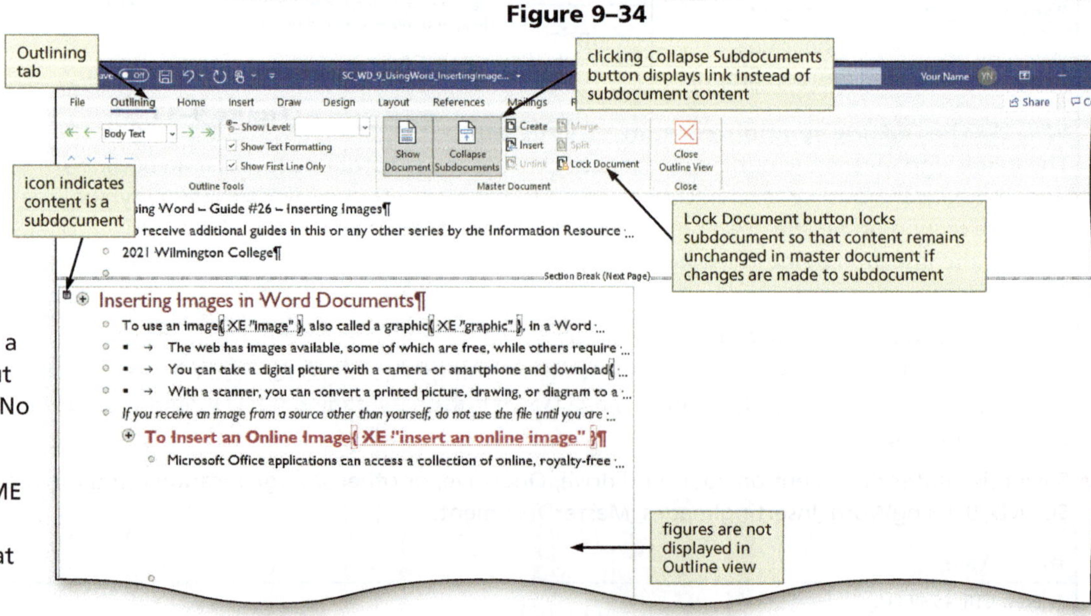

Figure 9–35

Master Documents and Subdocuments

When you open the master document, the subdocuments initially are collapsed; that is, they are displayed as hyperlinks (Figure 9–36). To work with the contents of a master document after you open it, switch to Outline view and then expand the subdocuments by clicking the Expand Subdocuments button (Outlining tab | Master Document group).

You can open a subdocument in a separate document window and modify it. To open a collapsed subdocument, click the hyperlink. To open an expanded subdocument, double-click the subdocument icon to the left of the document heading (shown in Figure 9–36).

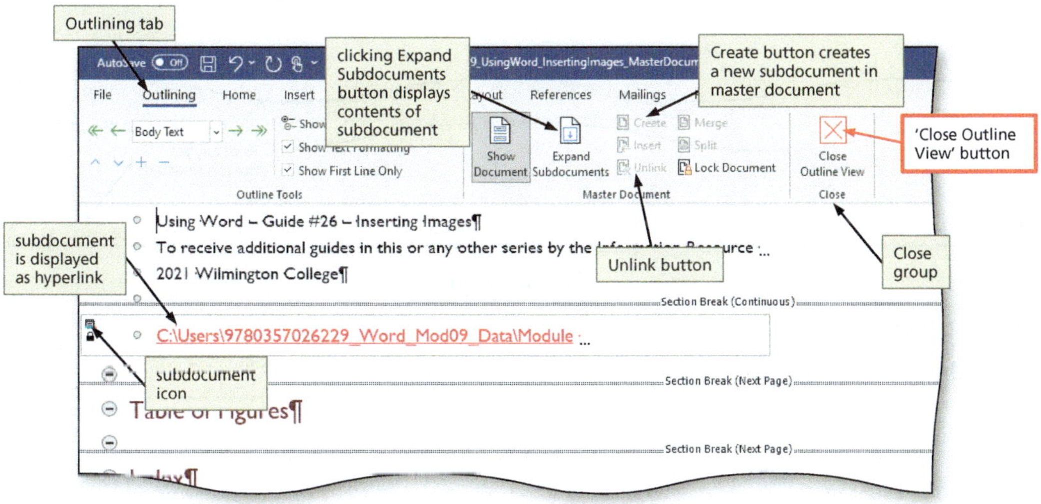

Figure 9–36

If, for some reason, you wanted to remove a subdocument from a master document, you would expand the subdocuments, click the subdocument icon to the left of the subdocument's first heading, and then press DELETE. Although Word removes the subdocument from the master document, the subdocument file remains on the storage media.

Occasionally, you may want to convert a subdocument to part of the master document — breaking the connection between the text in the master document and the subdocument. To do this, expand the subdocuments, click the subdocument icon, and then click the Unlink button (Outlining tab | Master Document group).

BTW

Locked Subdocuments

If a lock icon is displayed next to a subdocument's name, then the master document is collapsed, the subdocument is open in another Word window, or the subdocument has been locked using the Lock Document button (Outlining tab | Master Document group) (shown in Figure 9–35). If the master document is collapsed, simply click the Expand Subdocuments button (Outlining tab | Master Document group). If the subdocument is open in another Word window, close it. If the subdocument has been locked, you will be able to display the contents of the subdocument but will not be able to modify it. To unlock the subdocument, click the Lock Document button (Outlining tab | Master Document group).

To Hide Formatting Marks

To remove the clutter of index entry fields from the document, you should hide formatting marks. The following step hides formatting marks.

1. Display the Home tab. If the 'Show/Hide ¶' button (Home tab | Paragraph group) is selected, click it to hide formatting marks.

To Close Outline View

The following step closes Outline view. **Why?** You are finished organizing the master document.

1

- Display the Outlining tab.
- Click the 'Close Outline View' button (shown in Figure 9–36) (Outlining tab | Close group) to redisplay the document in Print Layout view, which selects the Print Layout button on the status bar.

- If necessary, press CTRL+HOME to display the top of the document (Figure 9–37).

Experiment

- Scroll through the document to familiarize yourself with the sections. When finished, display the top of the document in the document window.
- Note that the document should contain seven pages. If it contains any extra blank pages, delete the blank pages.

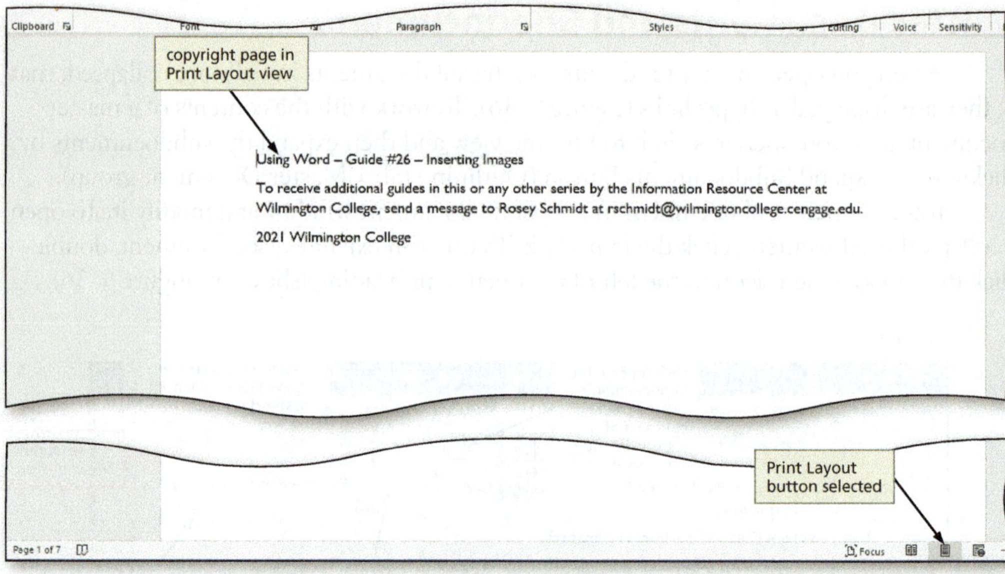

Figure 9–37

- Save the document again on the same storage location with the same file name.

Organizing a Reference Document

Reference documents are organized and formatted so that users easily can navigate through and read the document. The reference document in this module includes the following elements: a copyright page, a cover page, a table of contents, a table of figures, an index, odd and even page footers, and a gutter margin. This section illustrates the tasks required to include these elements.

Consider This

What elements are common to reference documents?

Reference documents often include a cover page, a table of contents, a table of figures or list of tables (if one exists), and an index.

- **Cover Page.** A cover page (sometimes called a title page) should contain, at a minimum, the title of the document. Some also contain the author, a subtitle, an edition or volume number, and the date written.
- **Table of Contents.** The table of contents should list the title (heading) of each chapter or section and the starting page number of the chapter or section. You may use a leader character, such as a dot or hyphen, to fill the space between the heading and the page number. Sections preceding the table of contents are not listed in it — list only material that follows the table of contents.
- **Table of Figures or List of Tables.** If you have multiple figures or tables in a document, consider identifying all of them in a table of figures or a list of tables. The format of the table of figures or list of tables should match the table of contents.
- **Index.** The index usually is set in two columns or one column. The index can contain any item a reader might want to look up, such as a heading or a key term. If the document does not have a table of figures or list of tables, also include figures and tables in the index.

To Insert a Cover Page

Word has many predefined cover page formats that you can use for the cover page in a document. The following steps insert a cover page.

1. Display the Insert tab.

2. Click the Cover Page button (Insert tab | Pages group) to display the Cover Page gallery.

Q&A **Does it matter where I position the insertion point before inserting a cover page?**
No. By default, Word inserts the cover page as the first page in a document.

3. Click Facet in the Cover Page gallery to insert the selected cover page as the first page in the current document.

4. Display the View tab. Click the One Page button (View tab | Zoom group) to display the entire cover page in the document window (Figure 9–38).

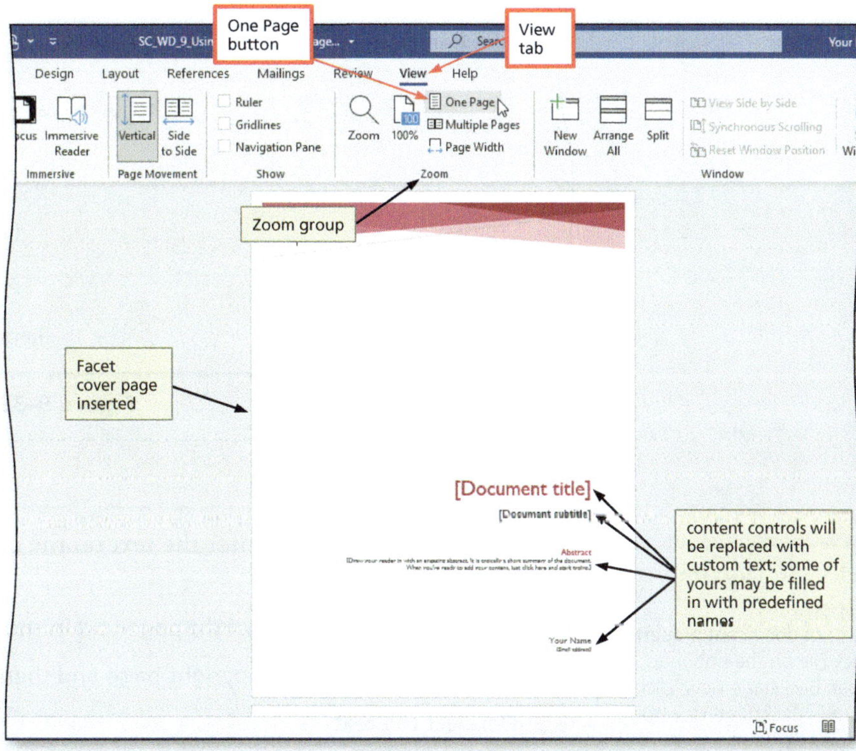

Figure 9–38

To Enter Text in Content Controls

The next step is to select content controls on the cover page and replace their instructions or text with the cover page information. Keep in mind that the content controls present suggested text. Depending on settings on your computer or mobile device, some content controls already may contain customized text, which you will change. You can enter any appropriate text in any content control. The following steps enter cover page text on the cover page.

1. Change the zoom back to page width.

2. Click the [Document title] content control and then type `Using Word` as the title.

3. Click the [Document subtitle] content control and then type `Guide #26 - Inserting Images` as the subtitle.

4. Click the content control that begins with the instruction, [Draw your reader in with an engaging abstract...] and then type `A series of guides designed to strengthen your Word skills` to complete the abstract text.

5. Select the text in the author content control and then type `Information Resources Center` as the name (Figure 9–39).

Q&A **Why is my author content control filled in?**
Depending on settings, your content control already may display an author name.

6. Delete the [Email address] content control.

BTW

Advanced Paragraph Options

A widow occurs when the last line of a paragraph appears by itself at the top of a page, and an orphan occurs when the first line of a paragraph appears by itself at the bottom of a page. To prevent widows and orphans, click the Paragraph Dialog Box Launcher (Home tab | Paragraph group), click the Line and Page Breaks tab (Paragraph dialog box), place a check mark in the 'Widow/Orphan control' check box, and then click OK. Similarly, you can select the 'Keep with next' check box to keep selected paragraphs together, the 'Keep lines together' check box to keep selected lines together, and the 'Page break before' check box to insert a page break before the selected paragraph.

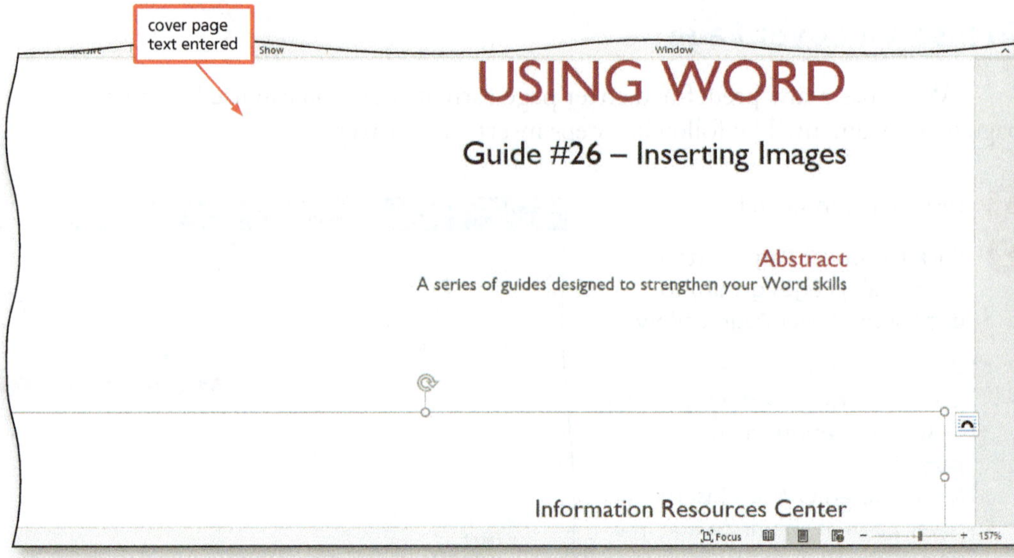

Figure 9–39

To Center Text

The next step is to center the text on the copyright page. The following steps center text.

1. Scroll to display the copyright page text in the document window.
2. Select the text on the copyright page and then center it.
3. Deselect the text.

BTW
Printing Document Properties
To print document properties, click File on the ribbon to open Backstage view, click Print in Backstage view to display the Print screen, click the first button in the Settings area to display a list of options specifying what you can print, click Document Info in the list to specify you want to print the document properties instead of the actual document, and then click the Print button in the Print screen to print the document properties on the currently selected printer.

To Insert a Continuous Section Break and Change the Margins in the Section

The margins on the copyright page are wider than the rest of the document. To change margins for a page, the page must be in a separate section. The next steps insert a continuous section break and then change the margins.

1. Position the insertion point at the location for the section break, in this case, to the left of U in Using on the copyright page.
2. Display the Layout tab. Click the Breaks button (Layout tab | Page Setup group) to display the Breaks gallery.
3. Click Continuous in the Breaks gallery to insert a continuous section break to the left of the insertion point.
4. Click the Margins button (Layout tab | Page Setup group) to display the Margins gallery and then click Wide in the Margins gallery to change the margins on the copyright page to the selected settings (Figure 9–40).

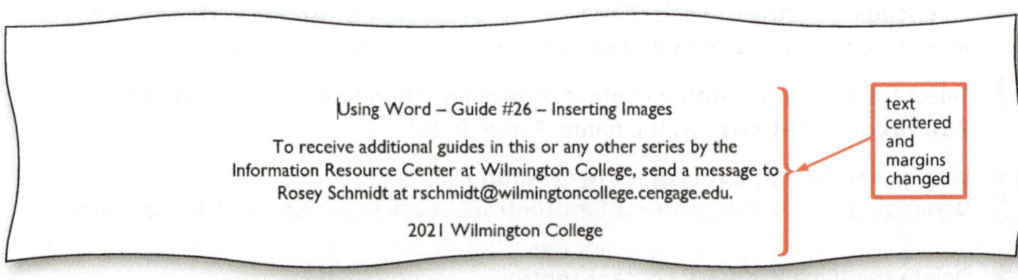

Figure 9–40

To Insert a Symbol from the Symbol Dialog Box

Word provides a method of inserting dots and other symbols, such as letters in the Greek alphabet and mathematical characters, that are not on the keyboard or in the Symbol gallery. The following steps insert a copyright symbol in the document. **Why?** You want the copyright symbol to the left of the copyright year.

1

- If necessary, position the insertion point at the location where the symbol should be inserted (in this case, to the left of the copyright year).
- Display the Insert tab.
- Click the Symbol button (Insert tab | Symbols group) to display the Symbol gallery (Figure 9–41).

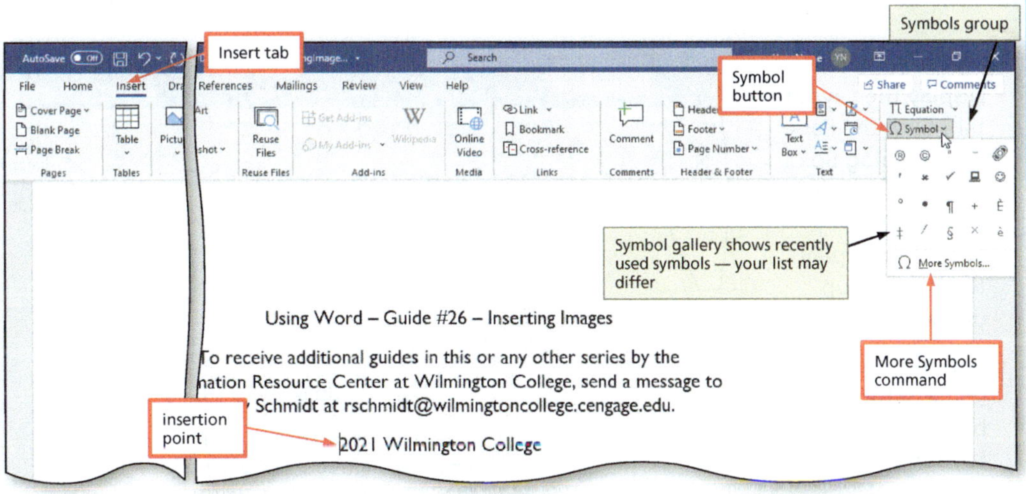

Figure 9–41

Q&A **What if the symbol I want to insert already appears in the Symbol gallery?**
You can click any symbol shown in the Symbol gallery to insert it in the document.

2

- Click More Symbols in the Symbol gallery to display the Symbol dialog box.
- If the font in the Font box is not (normal text), click the Font arrow (Symbol dialog box) and then scroll to and click (normal text) to select this font.
- If the subset in the Subset box is not Latin-1 Supplement, click the Subset arrow and then scroll and click Latin-1 Supplement to select this subset.
- In the list of symbols, if necessary, scroll to the copyright symbol shown in Figure 9–42 and then click the symbol to select it.
- Click the Insert button (Symbol dialog box) to place the selected symbol in the document to the left of the insertion point (Figure 9–42).

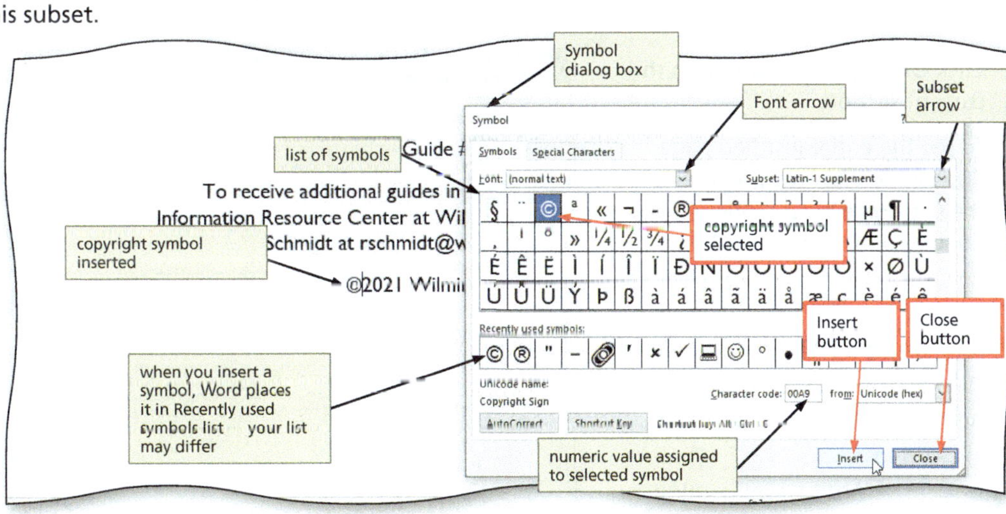

Figure 9–42

Q&A **Why is the Symbol dialog box still open?**
The Symbol dialog box remains open because often you will need to insert the same or additional symbols elsewhere in the document.

3

- Click the Close button (Symbol dialog box) to close the dialog box.
- Press SPACEBAR to insert a space between the copyright symbol and the year.

To Adjust Vertical Alignment on a Page

You can instruct Word to center the contents of a page vertically using one of two options: place an equal amount of space above and below the text on the page, or evenly space each paragraph between the top and bottom margins. The following steps vertically center text on a page. **Why?** The copyright page in this project evenly spaces each paragraph on a page between the top and bottom margins, which is called justified vertical alignment.

1

- Display the Layout tab. Click the Page Setup Dialog Box Launcher (Layout tab | Page Setup group) to display the Page Setup dialog box.
- Click the Layout tab (Page Setup dialog box) to display the Layout sheet.
- Click the Vertical alignment arrow and then click Justified (Figure 9–43).

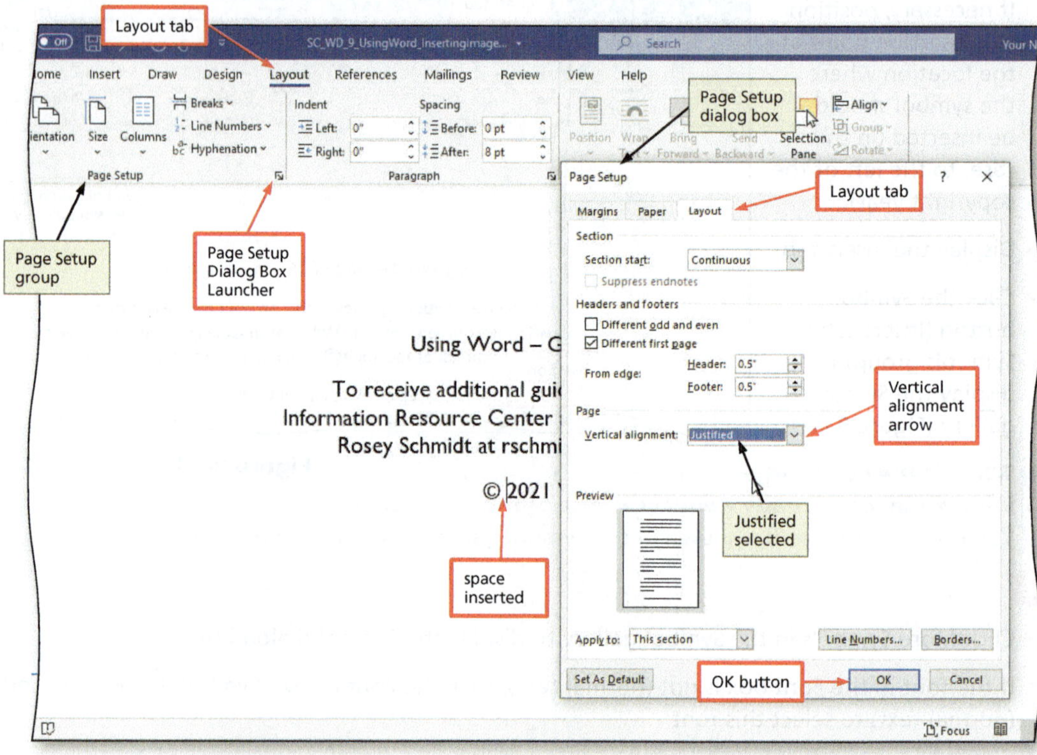

Figure 9–43

2

- Click OK to justify the text in the current section.
- To see the entire justified page, display the View tab and then click the One Page button (View tab | Zoom group) (Figure 9–44).

3

- Change the zoom back to page width.

Q&A **What are the other vertical alignments?**
Top, the default, aligns contents starting at the top margin on the page. Center places all contents centered vertically on the page, and Bottom places contents at the bottom of the page.

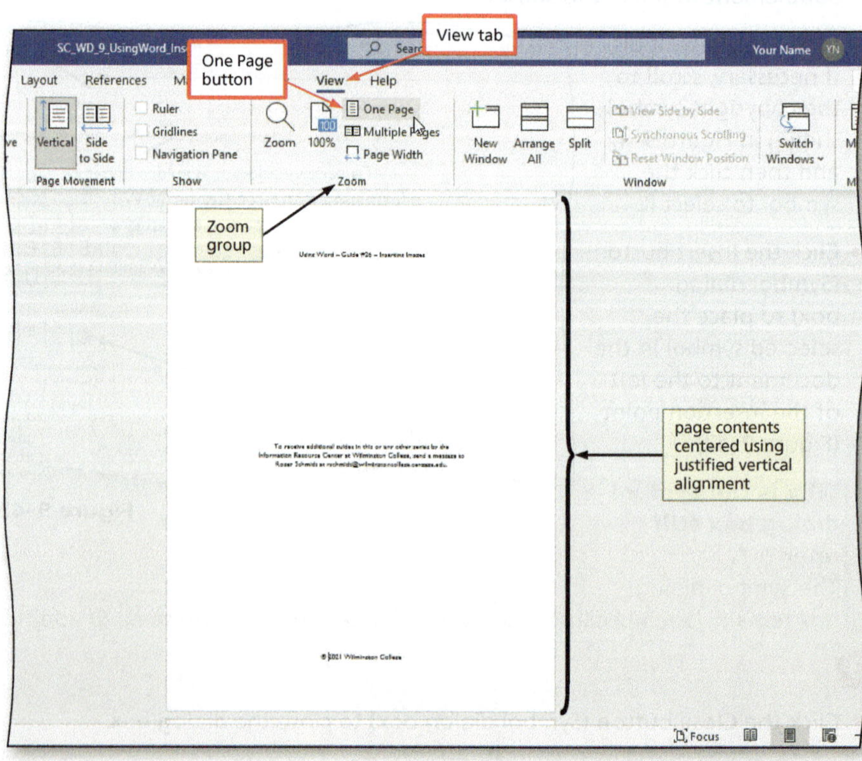

Figure 9–44

To Insert a Blank Page

The following step inserts a blank page. **Why?** In the reference document in this module, the table of contents is on a page after the copyright page.

1

- Position the insertion point to the left of the word, Inserting, on the first page of the subdocument (as shown in Figure 9–45). (Note that with the insertion point in this location, this blank page that will contain the table of contents may be housed in the subdocument instead of the master document.)
- Display the Insert tab.

Q&A **Why are several of the buttons, including the Blank Page button, dimmed on the ribbon?**
Your subdocument either is open in another window or is locked. If the subdocument is open in another window, close it. If it is locked, switch to Outline view and then click the Lock Document button (Outlining tab | Master Document group) to unlock it.

- Click the Blank Page button (Insert tab | Pages group) to insert a blank page at the location of the insertion point.
- If necessary, scroll to display the blank page in the document window (Figure 9–45).

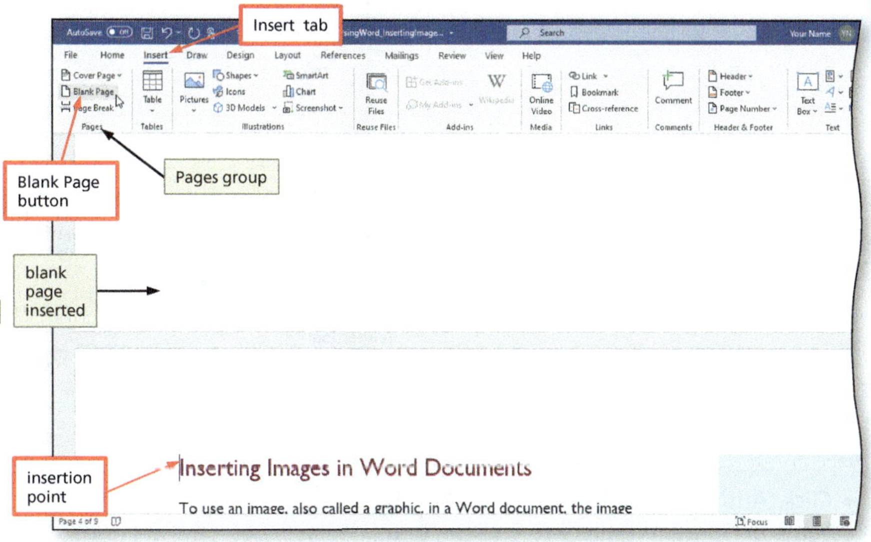

Figure 9–45

To Insert a Table of Contents

A table of contents lists all headings in a document and their associated page numbers. When you use Word's built-in heading styles (for example, Heading 1, Heading 2, and so on), you can instruct Word to insert a table of contents using these headings. In the reference document in this module, the heading of each section uses the Heading 1 style, and subheadings use the Heading 2 style.

The following steps use a predefined building block to insert a table of contents. **Why?** Using Word's predefined table of contents formats can be more efficient than creating a table of contents from scratch.

1

- Position the insertion point at the top of the blank page 3, which is the location for the table of contents. (If necessary, show formatting marks so that you easily can see the paragraph mark at the top of the page.)
- Ensure that formatting marks do not show.

Q&A **Why should I hide formatting marks?**
Formatting marks, especially those for index entries, sometimes can cause wrapping to occur on the screen that will be different from how the printed document will wrap. These differences could cause a heading to move to the next page. To ensure that the page references in the table of contents reflect the printed pages, be sure that formatting marks are hidden when you insert a table of contents.

- Display the References tab.

- Click the 'Table of Contents' button (References tab | Table of Contents group) to display the Table of Contents gallery (Figure 9–46).

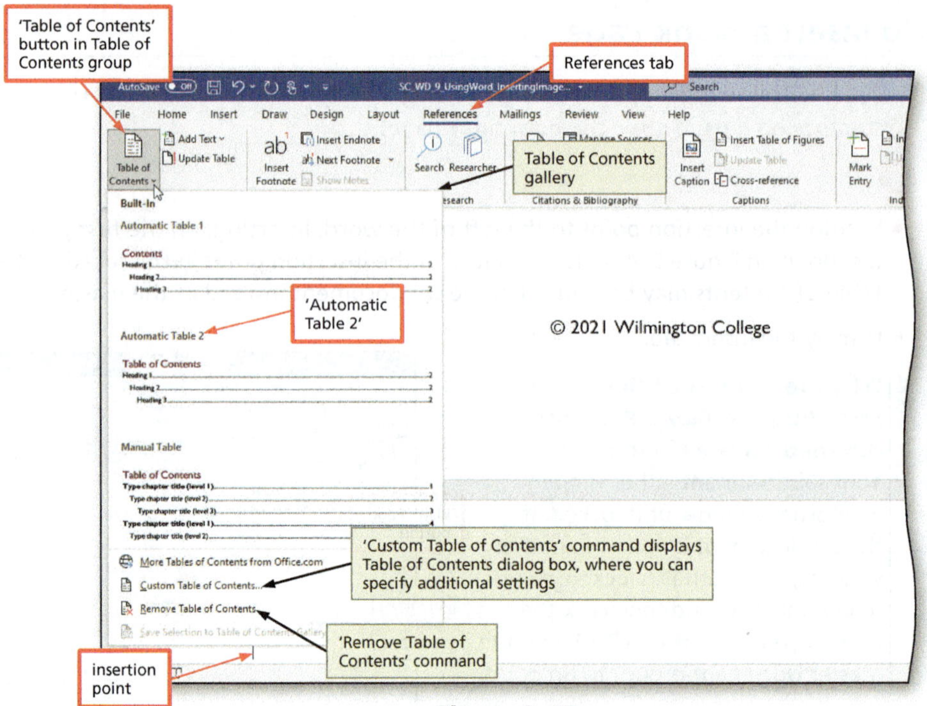

Figure 9–46

2

- Click 'Automatic Table 2' in the Table of Contents gallery to insert the table of contents at the location of the insertion point (Figure 9–47). If necessary, scroll to see the table of contents.

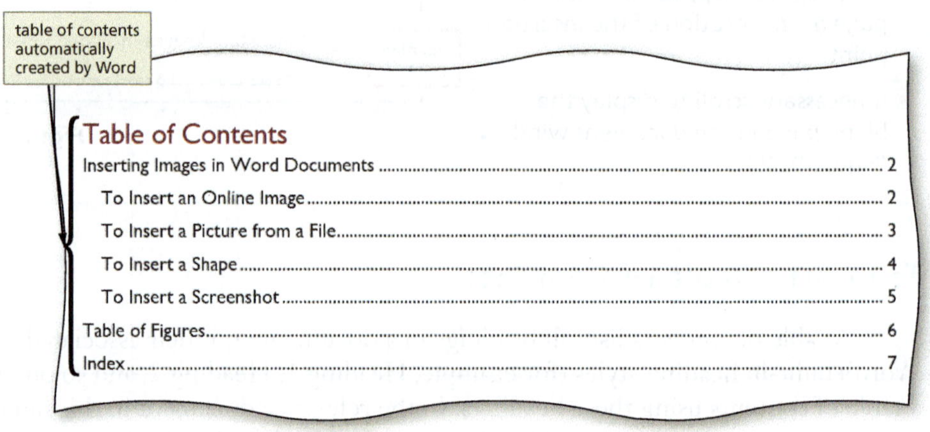

Figure 9–47

Q&A

How would I delete a table of contents?

You would click the 'Table of Contents' button (References tab | Table of Contents group) and then click 'Remove Table of Contents' in the Table of Contents gallery (shown in Figure 9-46).

Other Ways

1. Click 'Table of Contents' button (References tab | Table of Contents group), click 'Custom Table of Contents', select table of contents options (Table of Contents dialog box), click OK
2. Click 'Explore Quick Parts' button (Insert tab | Text group), click 'Building Blocks Organizer', select desired table of contents building block (Building Blocks Organizer dialog box), click Insert button, click Close

To Insert a Continuous Section Break and Change the Starting Page Number in a Section

The table of contents should not be the starting page number; instead, the subdocument should be the starting page number in the document. To change the starting page number, the page must be in a separate section. The following steps insert a continuous section break and then change the starting page number for the table of contents.

1. Position the insertion point at the location for the section break, in this case, to the left of I in Inserting Images in Word Documents on page 4 of the document.
2. Display the Layout tab. Click the Breaks button (Layout tab | Page Setup group) to display the Breaks gallery.
3. Click Continuous in the Breaks gallery to insert a continuous section break to the left of the insertion point.
4. Position the insertion point in the table of contents.
5. Display the Insert tab. Click the Page Number button (Insert tab | Header & Footer group) to display the Page Number menu and then click 'Format Page Numbers' on the Page Number menu to display the Page Number Format dialog box.
6. Click the Start at down arrow (Page Number Format dialog box) until 0 is displayed in the Start at box (Figure 9–48).
7. Click OK to change the starting page for the current section.

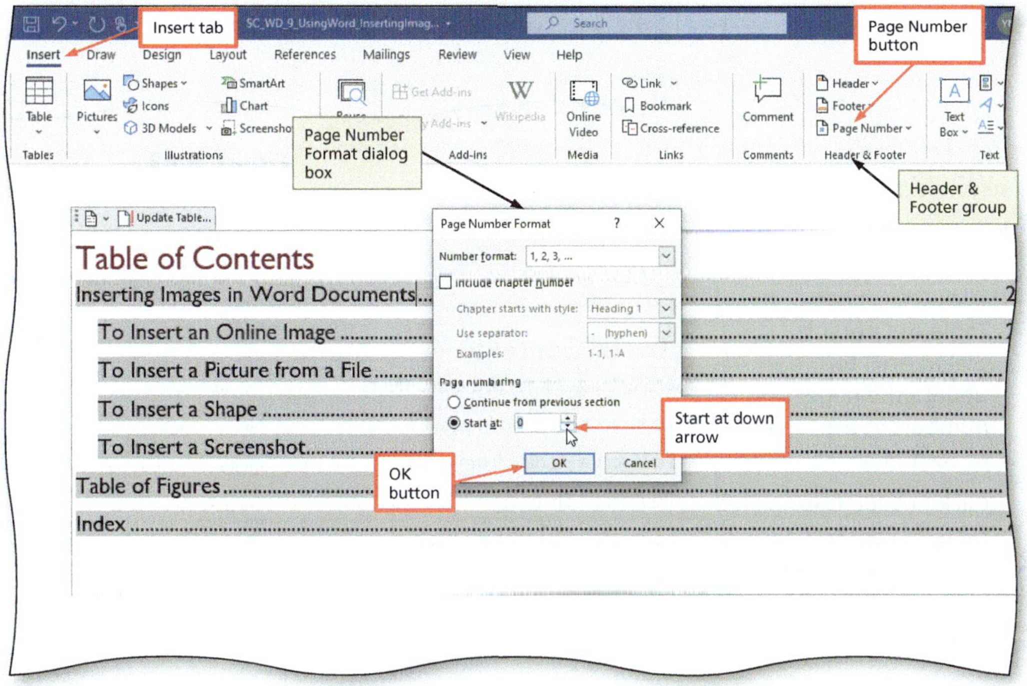

Figure 9–48

To Update Page Numbers in a Table of Contents

When you change a document, you should update the associated table of contents. The following steps update the page numbers in the table of contents. **Why?** The starting page number change will affect the page numbers in the table of contents.

1

- If necessary, click the table of contents to select it.

Q&A **Why does the ScreenTip say 'CTRL+Click to follow link'?**
Each entry in the table of contents is a link. If you hold down CTRL while clicking an entry in the table of contents, Word will display the associated heading in the document window.

2

- Click the Update Table button that is attached to the table of contents to display the Update Table of Contents dialog box.

- Ensure the 'Update page numbers only' option button is selected because you want to update only the page numbers in the table of contents (Figure 9–49).

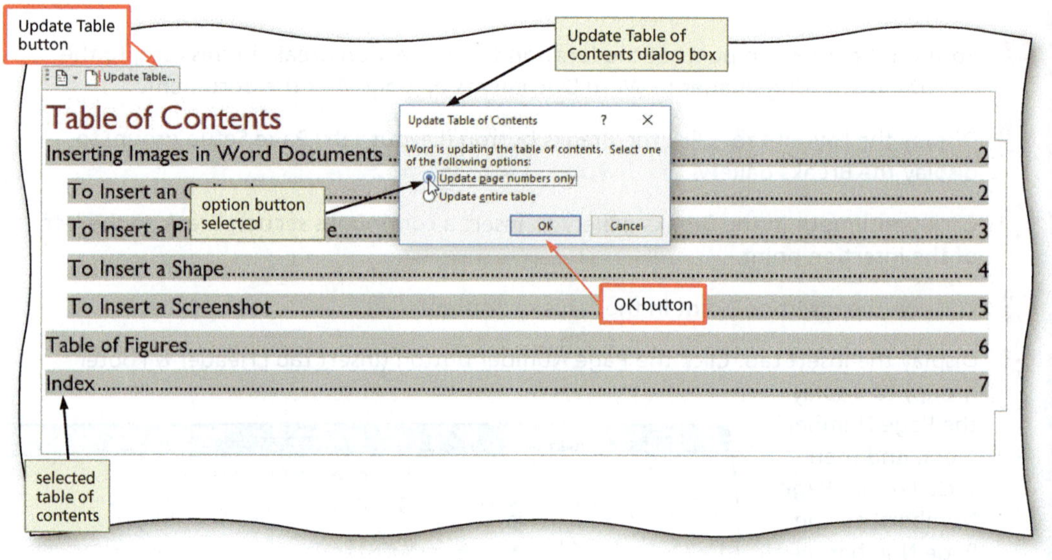

Figure 9–49

3

- Click OK (Update Table of Contents dialog box) to update the page numbers in the table of contents.
- Click outside the table of contents to remove the selection from the table (Figure 9–50).

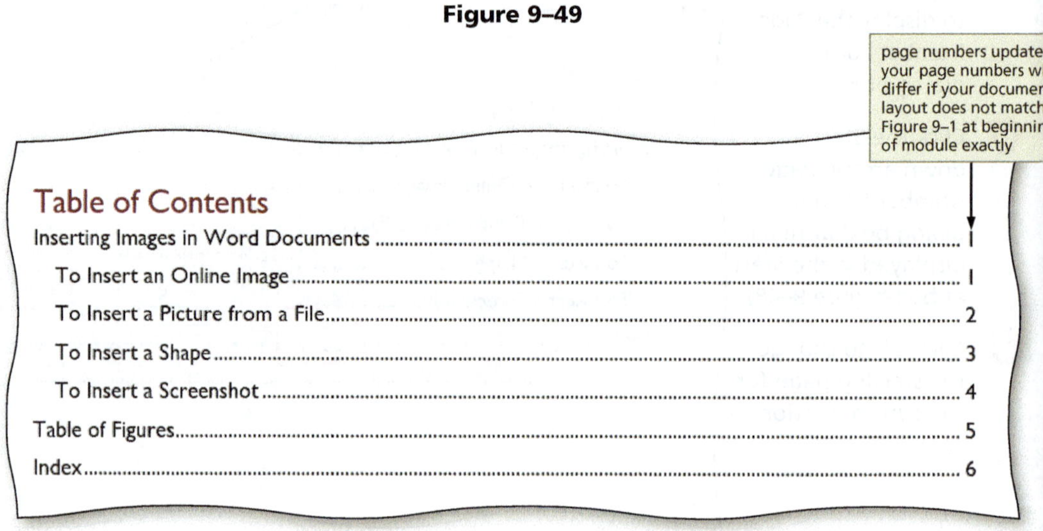

Figure 9–50

Other Ways

1. Select table, click Update Table button (References tab | Table of Contents group)
2. Select table, press F9

To Find a Format

The subdocument contains a sentence of text formatted as italic. To find this text in the document, you could scroll through the document until it is displayed on the screen. A more efficient way is to find the italic format using the Find and Replace dialog box. The following steps find a format. **Why?** You want to add the text to the table of contents.

1

- If necessary, display the Home tab.
- Click the Find arrow (Home tab | Editing group) to display the Find menu (Figure 9–51).

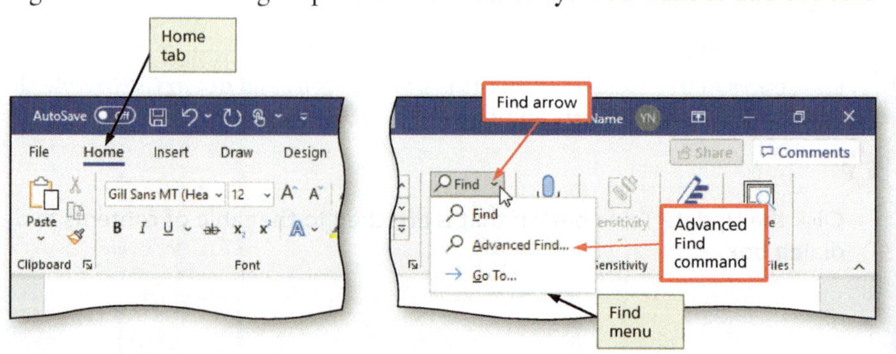

Figure 9–51

2

- Click Advanced Find on the Find menu to display the Find and Replace dialog box.
- If Word displays a More button in the Find and Replace dialog box, click it so that it changes to a Less button and expands the dialog box.
- Click the Format button (Find and Replace dialog box) to display the Format menu (Figure 9–52).

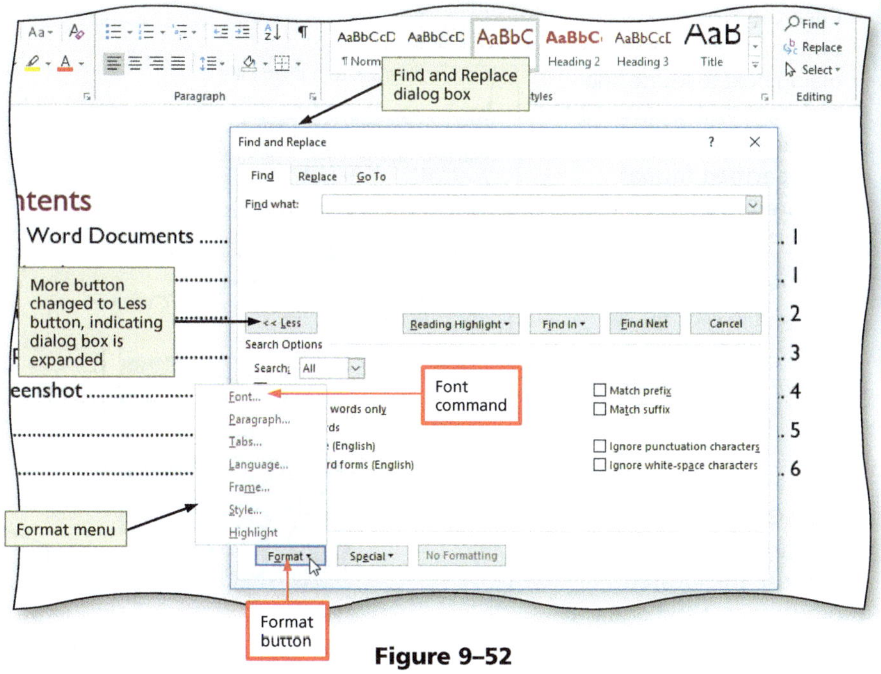

Figure 9–52

3

- Click Font on the Format menu to display the Find Font dialog box. If necessary, click the Font tab (Find Font dialog box) to display the Font sheet.
- Click Italic in the Font style list because that is the format you want to find (Figure 9–53).

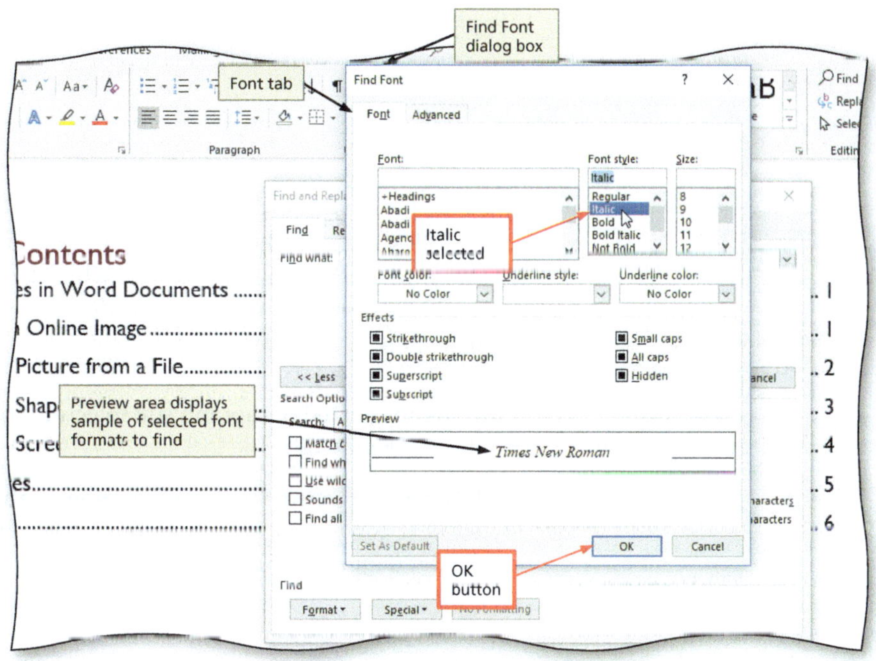

Figure 9–53

4

- Click OK to close the Find Font dialog box.
- Be sure no text is in the Find what text box (or click the Find what arrow and then click [Formatting Only]).
- Be sure all check boxes in the Search Options area are cleared.

- Click the Find Next button (Find and Replace dialog box) to locate and highlight in the document the first occurrence of the specified format (Figure 9–54).

Q&A **How do I remove a find format?**
You would click the No Formatting button in the Find and Replace dialog box.

5

- Click Cancel (Find and Replace dialog box) because the located occurrence is the one you wanted to find.

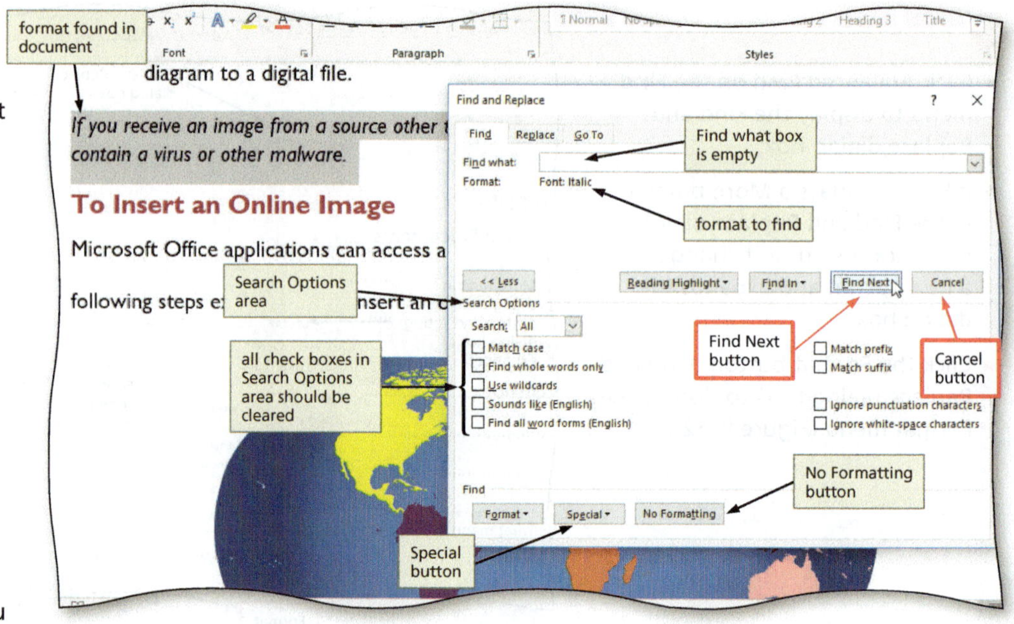

Figure 9–54

Q&A **Can I search for (find) special characters, such as page breaks?**
Yes. To find special characters, you would click the Special button in the Find and Replace dialog box.

Other Ways

1. Press CTRL+F

BTW

Find and Replace

The expanded Find and Replace dialog box allows you to specify how Word locates search text. For example, selecting the Match case check box instructs Word to find the text exactly as you typed it, and selecting the 'Find whole words only' check box instructs Word to ignore text that contains the search text (i.e., the word, then, contains the word, the). If you select the Use wildcards check box, you can use wildcard characters in a search. For example, with this check box selected, the search text of *ing would search for all words that end with the characters, ing.

To Format Text as a Heading

The following steps format a paragraph of text as a Heading 3 style. Occasionally, you may want to add a paragraph of text, which normally is not formatted using a heading style, to a table of contents. One way to add the text to the table of contents is to format it as a heading style.

1 With the formatted paragraph still selected (shown in Figure 9–54), if necessary, display the Home tab.

2 Click Heading 3 in the Styles gallery (Home tab | Styles group) to apply the selected style to the current paragraph in the document. Click outside the paragraph to deselect it (Figure 9–55).

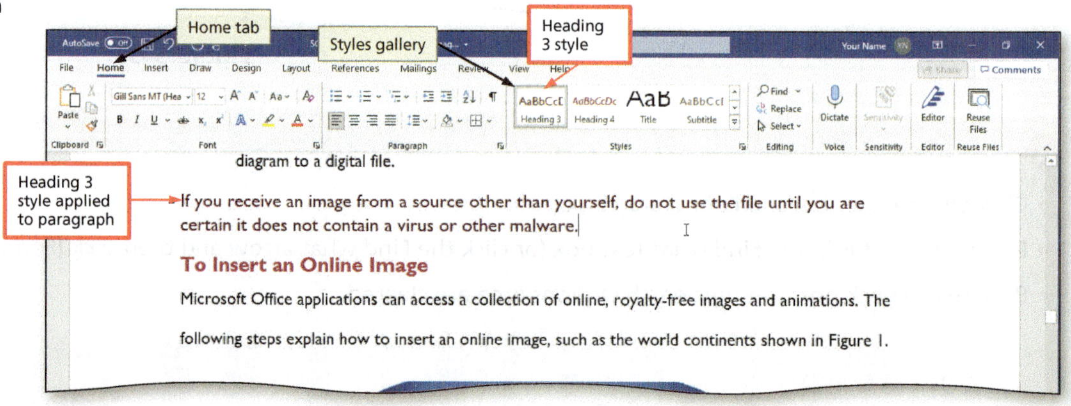

Figure 9–55

To Retain Formatting when Adding Text to the Table of Contents

If you wanted to retain formatting of text when adding it to the table of contents, you would perform the following steps.

1. Position the insertion point in the paragraph of text that you want to add to the table of contents.
2. Click the Add Text button (References tab | Table of Contents group) to display the Add Text menu.
3. Click the desired level on the Add Text menu, which adds the format of the selected style to the selected paragraph and adds the paragraph of text to the table of contents.

BTW

Table of Contents Styles

If you wanted to change the level associated with each style used in a table of contents, click the Options button in the Table of Contents dialog box (shown in Figure 9–59), enter the desired level number in the text box beside the appropriate heading or other styled item, and then click OK. To change the formatting associated with a style, click the Modify button in the Table of Contents dialog box.

To Update the Entire Table of Contents

The following steps update the entire table of contents. **Why?** The text changed to the Heading 3 style should appear in the table of contents.

1

- Display the table of contents in the document window.
- Click the table of contents to select it.
- Click the Update Table button that is attached to the table of contents to display the Update Table of Contents dialog box.
- Click the 'Update entire table' option button (Update Table of Contents dialog box) because you want to update the entire table of contents (Figure 9–56).

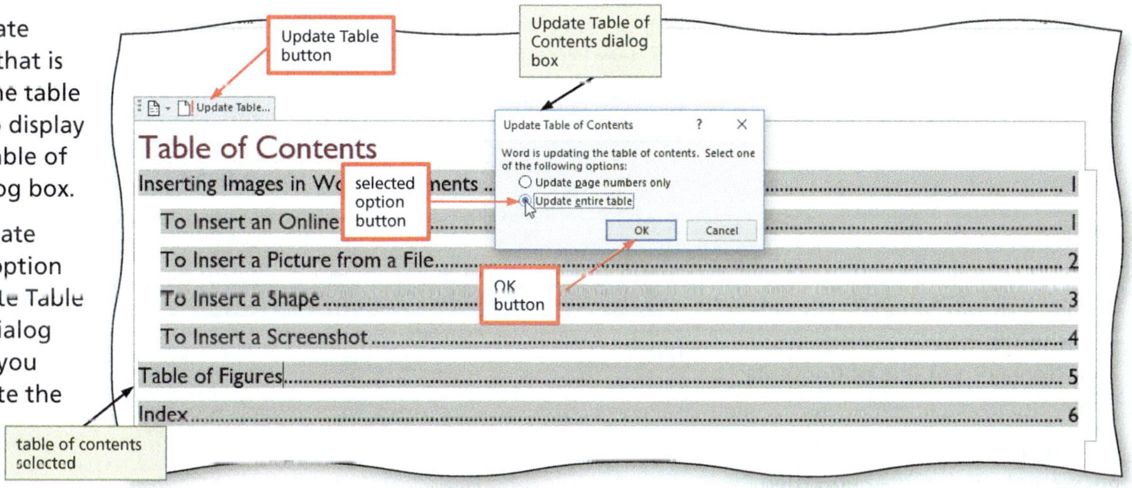

Figure 9–56

2

- Click OK (Update Table of Contents dialog box) to update the entire table of contents (Figure 9–57).

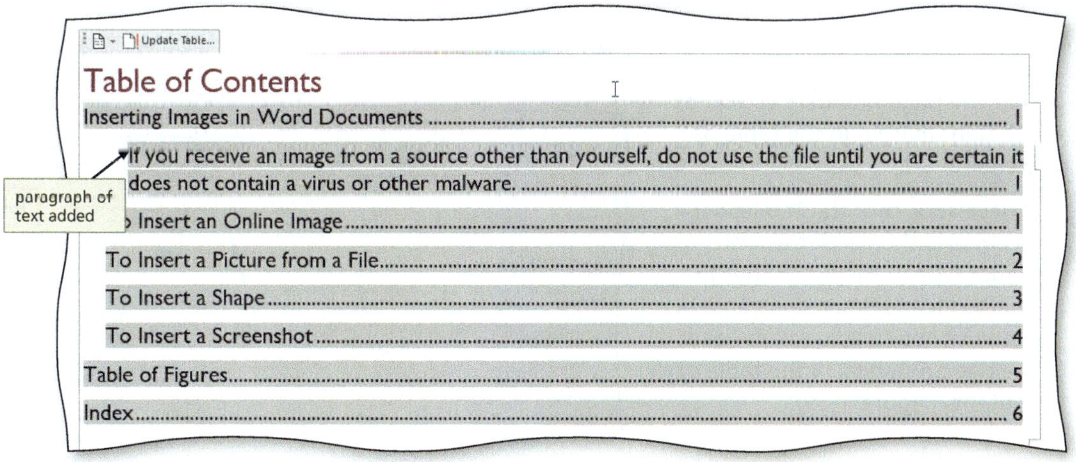

Figure 9–57

Other Ways

1. Select table, click Update Table button (References tab | Table of Contents group)
2. Select table, press F9

To Change the Format of a Table of Contents

You can change the format of the table of contents to any of the predefined table of contents styles or to custom settings. The following steps change the table of contents format. **Why?** In this table of contents, you specify the format, page number alignment, and tab leader character.

1

- Display the References tab.
- Click the 'Table of Contents' button (References tab | Table of Contents group) to display the Table of Contents gallery (Figure 9–58).

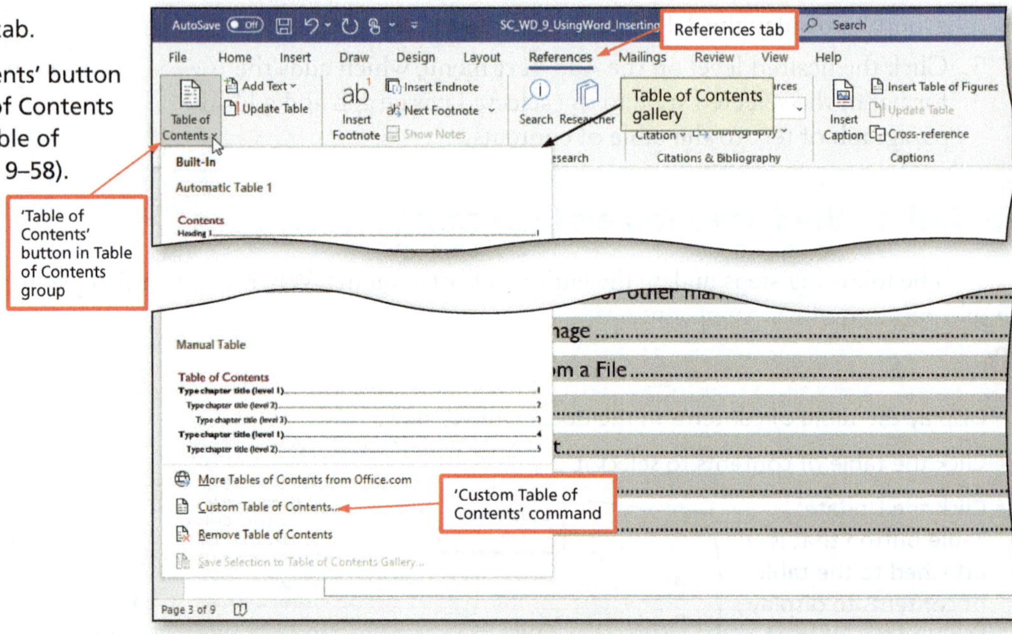

Figure 9–58

2

- Click 'Custom Table of Contents' in the Table of Contents gallery to display the Table of Contents dialog box.
- Click the Formats arrow (Table of Contents dialog box) and then click Simple to change the format style for the table of contents.
- Place a check mark in the 'Right align page numbers' check box so that the page numbers appear at the right margin in the table of contents.
- If necessary, click the Tab leader arrow and then click the first leader type in the list so that the selected leader characters appear between the heading name and the page numbers in the table of contents (Figure 9–59).

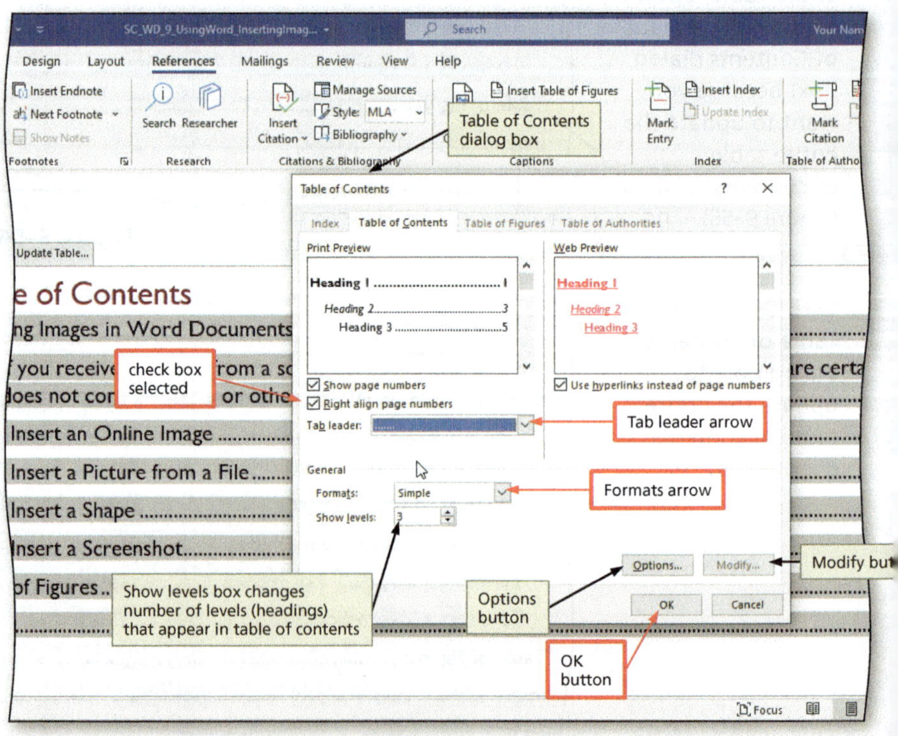

Figure 9–59

3

- Click OK to modify the table of contents according to the specified settings. When Word displays a dialog box asking if you want to replace the selected table of contents, click OK (Figure 9–60).

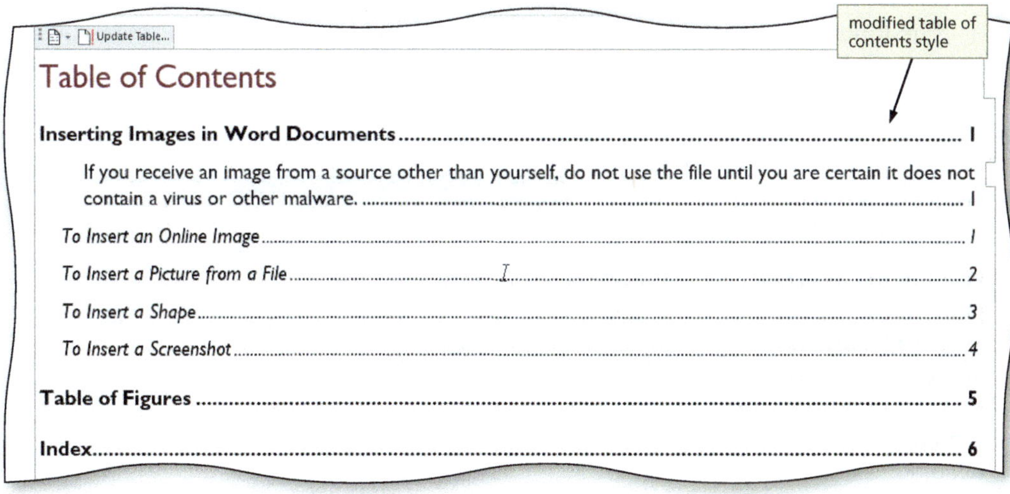

Figure 9–60

To Use the Navigation Pane to Go to a Heading in a Document

When you use Word's built-in heading styles in a document, you can use the Navigation Pane to go to headings in a document quickly. **Why?** When you click a heading in the Navigation Pane, Word displays the page associated with that heading in the document window. The following step uses the Navigation Pane to display an associated heading in the document window.

1

- Display the View tab. Place a check mark in the Navigation Pane check box (View tab | Show group) to open the Navigation Pane at the left edge of the Word window.
- If necessary, click the Headings tab in the Navigation Pane to display the text that is formatted using Heading styles.
- Click the 'Table of Figures' heading in the Navigation Pane to display the top of the selected page in the top of the document window (Figure 9–61).

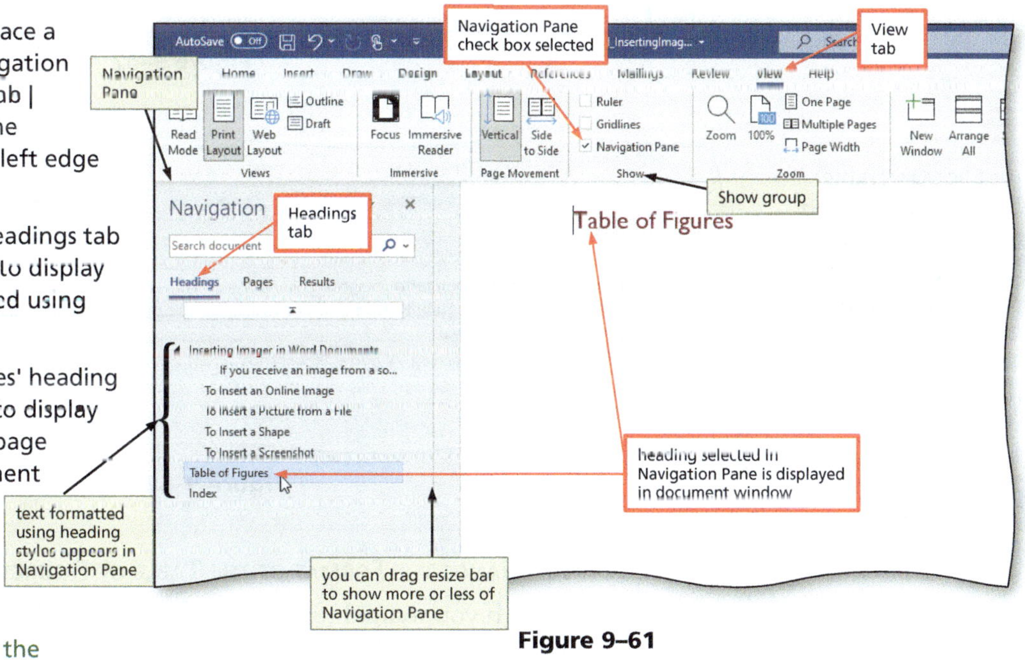

Figure 9–61

Q&A **What if all of the headings are not displayed?**
Right-click a heading in the Navigation Pane and then click Expand All on the shortcut menu to ensure that all headings are displayed. (Note that you can click Collapse All on the shortcut menu to collapse all headings in the Navigation Pane.) If a heading still is not displayed, verify that the heading is formatted with a heading style. To display or hide subheadings below a heading in the Navigation Pane, click the triangle to the left of the heading. If a heading is too wide for the Navigation Pane, you can point to the heading to display a ScreenTip that shows the complete title.

To Insert a Table of Figures

The following steps insert a table of figures. **Why?** At the end of the reference document is a table of figures, which lists all figures and their corresponding page numbers. Word generates this table of figures from the captions in the document.

1

- Ensure that formatting marks are not displayed.
- Position the insertion point at the end of the Table of Figures heading and then press ENTER, so that the insertion point is on the line below the heading.
- Display the References tab.
- Click the 'Insert Table of Figures' button (References tab | Captions group) to display the Table of Figures dialog box.
- Be sure that all settings in your dialog box match those in Figure 9–62.

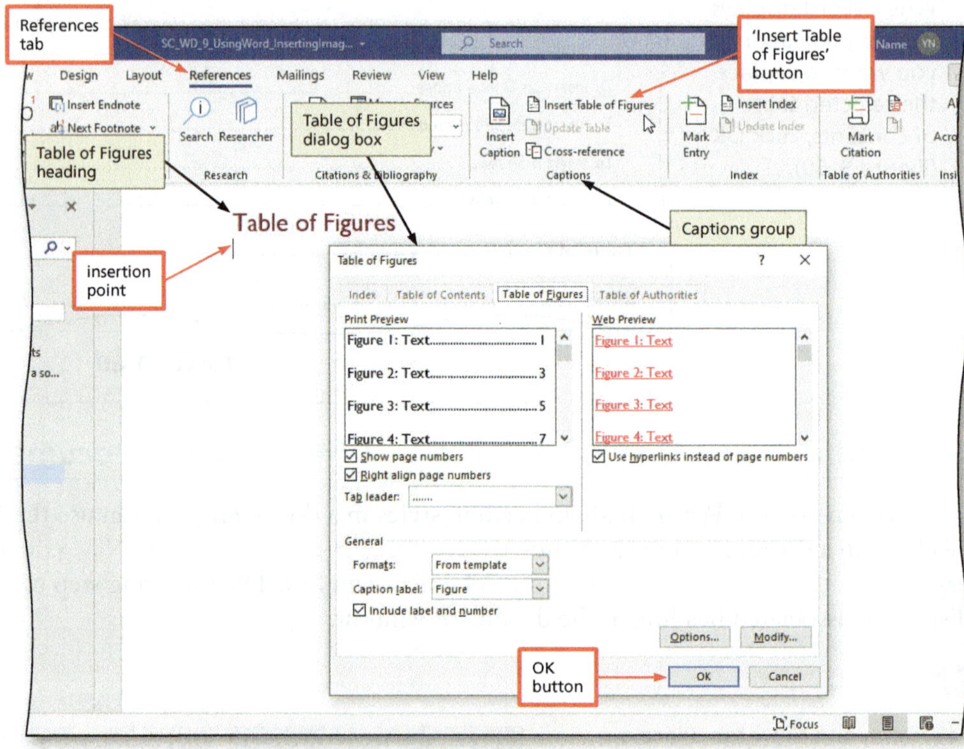

Figure 9–62

2

- Click OK (Table of Figures dialog box) to insert a table of figures at the location of the insertion point (Figure 9–63).

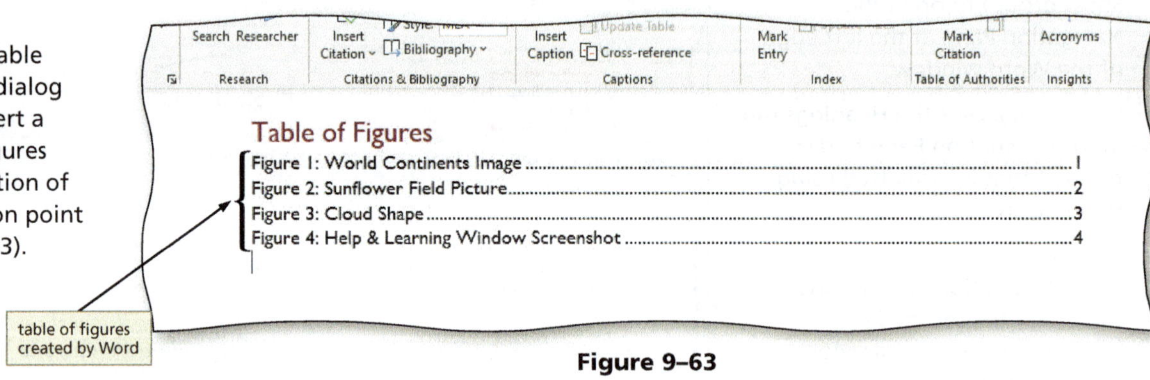

Figure 9–63

BTW

Replace Formats

You can click the Replace tab (Find and Replace dialog box) to find and replace formats. Enter the format to find in the Find what text box and then follow the same steps to enter the format to replace or the format to remove (i.e., Not Bold in the Font style list) in the Replace with text box. Next, click the Replace or Replace All button to replace the next occurrence of the format or all occurrences of the format in the document.

To Change the Format of the Table of Figures

If you wanted to change the format of the table of figures, you would perform the following steps.

1. Click the table of figures to select it.
2. Click the 'Insert Table of Figures' button (References tab | Captions group) to display the Table of Figures dialog box.
3. Change settings in the dialog box as desired.
4. Click OK (Table of Figures dialog box) to apply the changed settings.
5. Click OK when Word asks if you want to replace the selected table of figures.

To Edit a Caption and Update the Table of Figures

The following steps change the Figure 4 caption and then update the table of figures. **Why?** When you modify captions in a document or move illustrations to a different location in the document, you will have to update the table of figures.

1

- Click the heading, To Insert a Screenshot, in the Navigation Pane to display the selected heading in the document window. (If this heading is not at the top of page 7, insert a page break to position the heading at the top of a new page.)
- Insert the text, Word, in the Figure 4 caption so that it reads: Word Help & Learning Window Screenshot (Figure 9–64).

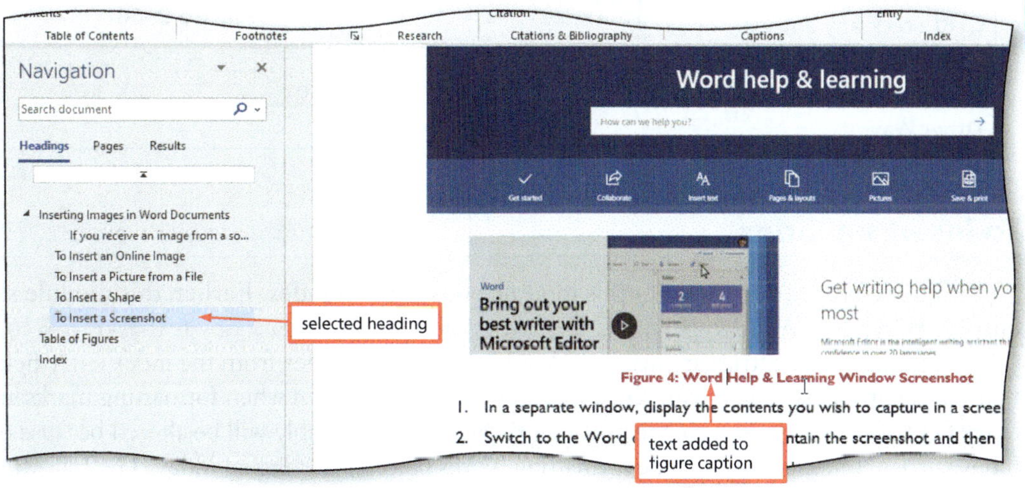

Figure 9–64

2

- Click the heading, Table of Figures, in the Navigation Pane to display the Table of Figures heading in the document window.
- Click the table of figures to select it.
- Click the Update Table button (References tab | Captions group) to display the Update Table of Figures dialog box.
- Click 'Update entire table' (Update Table of Figures dialog box), so that Word updates the contents of the entire table of figures instead of updating only the page numbers (Figure 9–65).

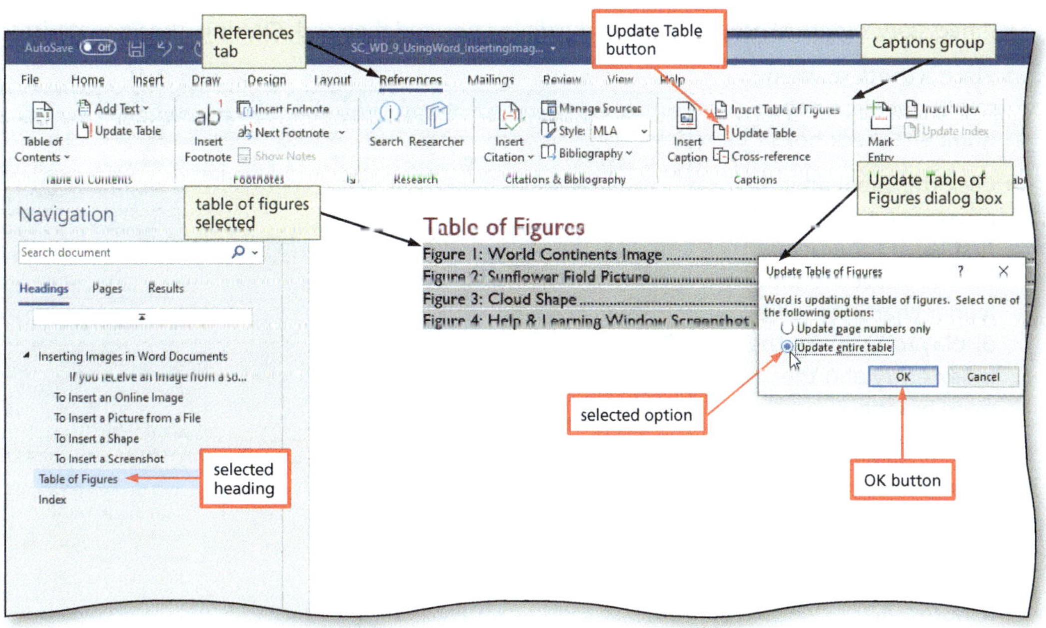

Figure 9–65

3

- Click OK to update the table of figures and then click outside the table to deselect it (Figure 9–66).

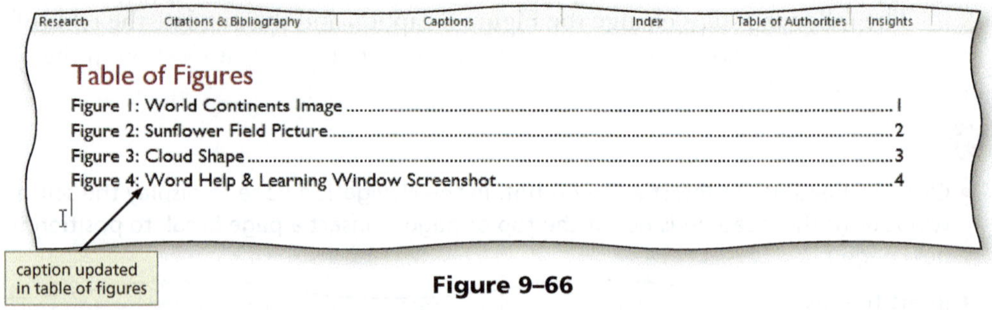

Figure 9–66

Q&A **Are the entries in the table of figures links?**
Yes. As with the table of contents, you can CTRL+click any entry in the table of figures and Word will display the associated figure in the document window.

Other Ways

1. Select table of figures, press F9

To Insert an Index

The reference document in this module ends with an index. Earlier, this module showed how to mark index entries. **Why?** For Word to generate the index, you first must mark any text you wish to appear in the index.

Once all index entries are marked, Word can insert the index from the index entry fields in the document. Recall that index entry fields begin with XE, which appears on the screen when formatting marks are displayed. When index entry fields show on the screen, the document's pagination probably will be altered because of the extra text in the index entries. Thus, be sure to hide formatting marks before inserting an index. The following steps insert an index.

1

- Click the heading, Index, in the Navigation Pane to display the Index heading in the document window.
- Click to the right of the Index heading and then press ENTER, so that the insertion point is on the line below the heading.
- Ensure that formatting marks are not displayed.
- Click the Insert Index button (References tab | Index group) to display the Index dialog box.
- If necessary, click the Formats arrow in the dialog box and then click Classic in the Formats list to change the index format.
- Place a check mark in the 'Right align page numbers' check box.
- Click the Tab leader arrow and then click the first leader character in the list to specify the leader character to be displayed between the index entry and the page number.
- Click the Columns down arrow until the number of columns is 1 to change the number of columns in the index (Figure 9–67).

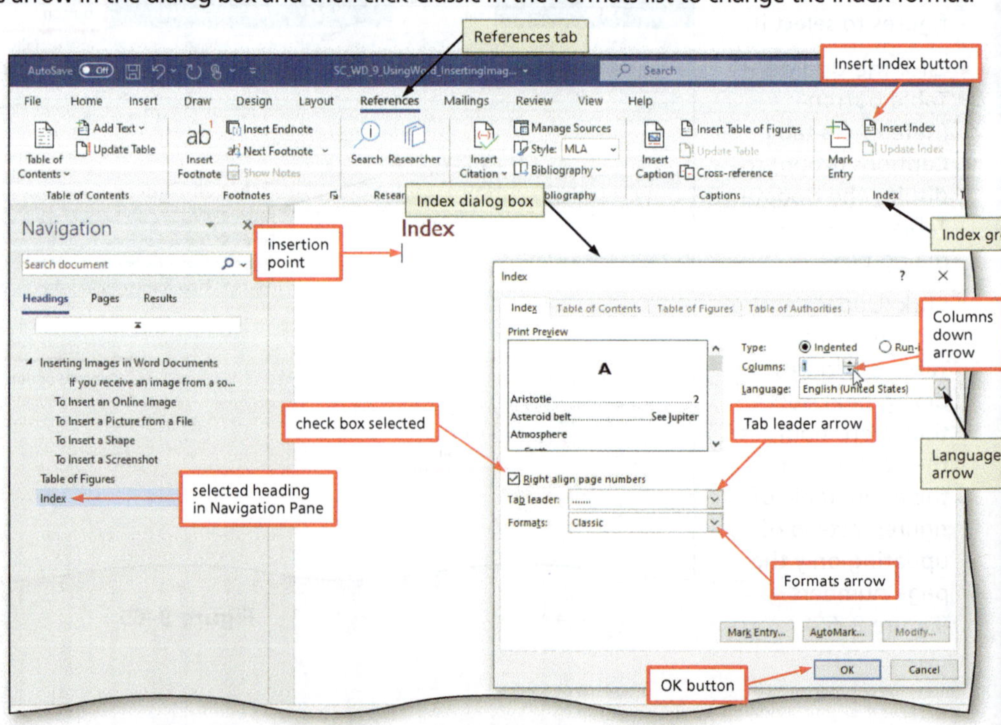

Figure 9–67

2

- Click OK (Index dialog box) to insert an index at the location of the insertion point (Figure 9–68).

Q&A **How would I change the language used in the index?**
If multiple languages are installed, click the Language arrow (shown in Figure 9–67) (Index dialog box) and then click the desired language.

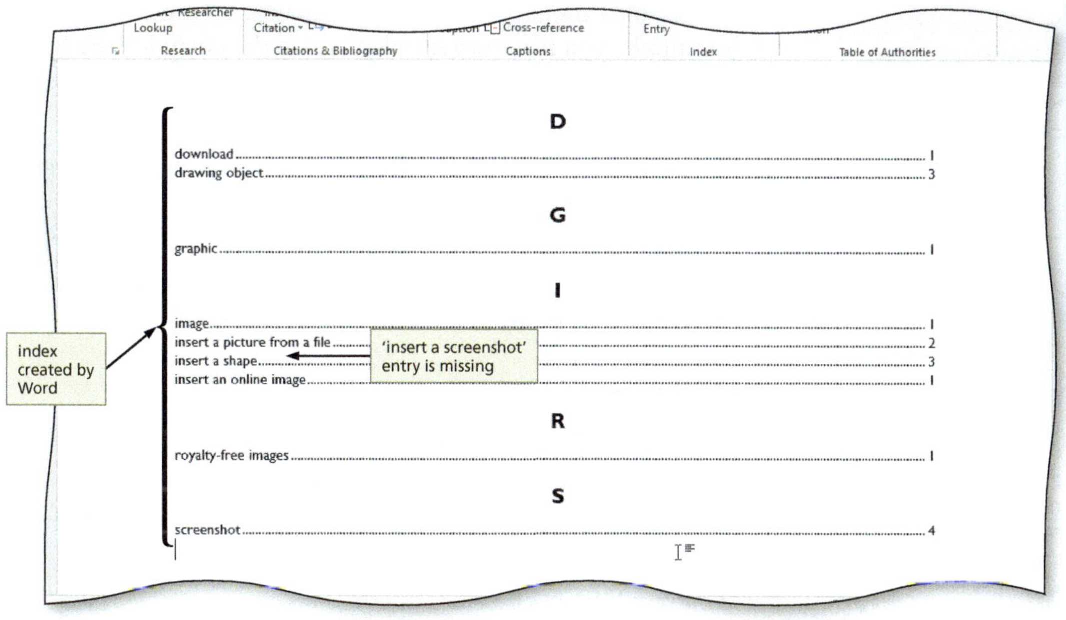

Figure 9–68

To Mark Another Index Entry

Notice in Figure 9–68 that the 'insert a screenshot' index entry is missing. The following steps mark an index entry in the Insert a Screenshot section.

1. Click the heading, To Insert a Screenshot, in the Navigation Pane to display the selected heading in the document window.
2. Select the words, Insert a Screenshot, in the heading.
3. Click the Mark Entry button (References tab | Index group) to display the Mark Index Entry dialog box.
4. Type `insert a screenshot` in the Main entry text box (Mark Index Entry dialog box) so that the entry is all lowercase (Figure 9–69).
5. Click the Mark button to mark the entry.
6. Close the dialog box.
7. Hide formatting marks.

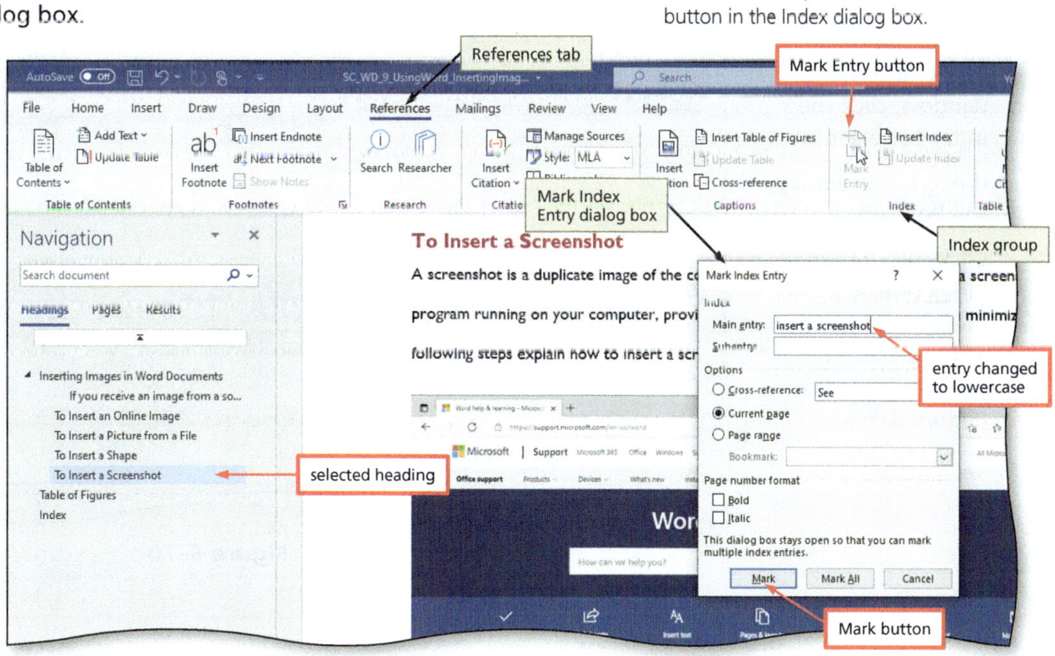

Figure 9–69

BTW
Index Files
Instead of marking index entries in a document, you can create a concordance file that contains all index entries you wish to mark. A concordance file contains two columns: the first column identifies the text in the document you want Word to mark as an index entry, and the second column lists the index entries to be generated from the text in the first column. To mark entries in the concordance file, click the AutoMark button in the Index dialog box.

BTW
Navigation Pane
You can drag any heading in the Navigation Pane to reorganize document content. For example, you could drag the To Insert a Screenshot heading upward in the Navigation Pane so that its content appears earlier in the document. You also can promote a heading by right-clicking the heading and then clicking Promote on the shortcut menu. Likewise, you can demote a heading by right-clicking the heading and then clicking Demote on the shortcut menu. To delete a heading and all its contents, right-click the heading and then click Delete on the shortcut menu. If you wanted to print all content in a heading, you would right-click the heading and then click 'Print Heading and Content' on the shortcut menu.

To Edit an Index Entry

At some time, you may want to change an index entry after you have marked it. For example, you may forget to lowercase the entry for the headings. If you wanted to change an index entry, you would perform the following steps.

1. Display formatting marks.
2. Locate the XE field for the index entry you wish to change (i.e., { XE "Insert a Screenshot" }).
3. Change the text inside the quotation marks (i.e., { XE "insert a screenshot" }).
4. Update the index as described in the steps in the upcoming steps titled To Update an Index.

To Delete an Index Entry

If you wanted to delete an index entry, you would perform the following steps.

1. Display formatting marks.
2. Select the XE field for the index entry you wish to delete (i.e., { XE "insert a screenshot" }).
3. Press DELETE.
4. Update the index as described in the steps in the next set of steps.

To Update an Index

The following step updates an index. **Why?** After marking a new index entry, you must update the index.

1

- Click the heading, Index, in the Navigation Pane to display the selected heading in the document window.
- In the document window, click the index to select it.
- If necessary, display the References tab.
- Click the Update Index button (References tab | Index group) to update the index (Figure 9–70).

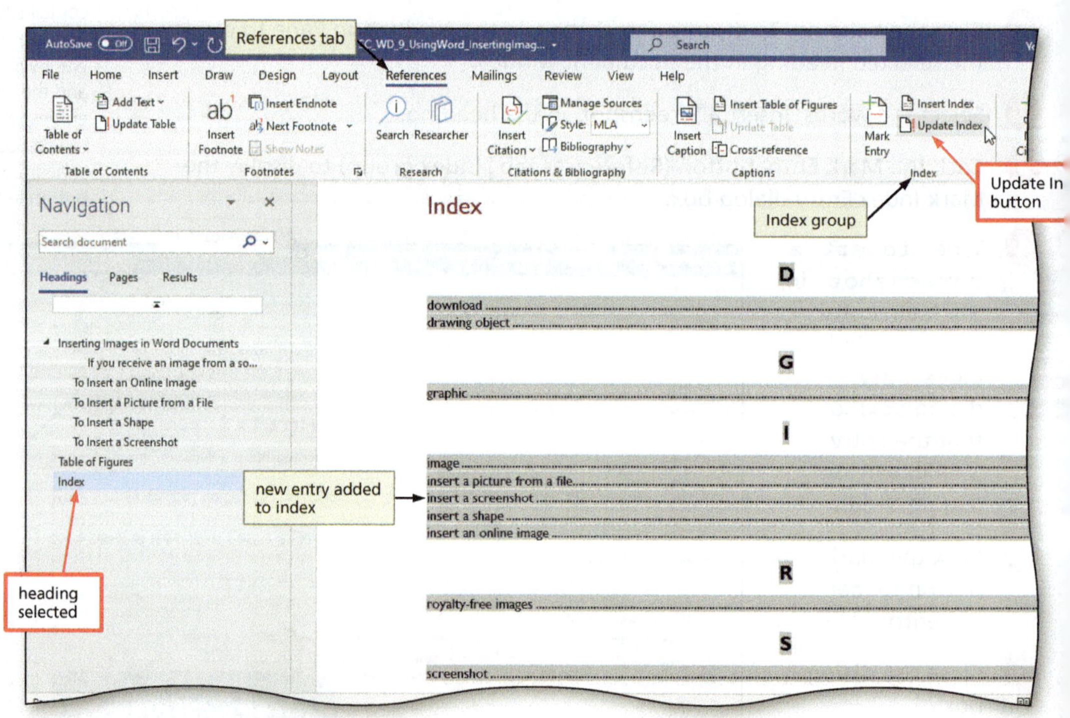

Figure 9–70

Other Ways

1. Select index, press F9

To Change the Format of the Index

If you wanted to change the format of the index, you would perform the following steps.

1. Click the index to select it.
2. Click the Insert Index button (References tab | Index group) to display the Index dialog box.
3. Change settings in the dialog box as desired. If you want to modify the style used for the index, click the Modify button.
4. Click OK (Index dialog box) to apply the changed settings.
5. Click OK when Word asks if you want to replace the selected index.

BTW

Field Codes

If your index, table of contents, or table of figures displays odd characters inside curly braces ({}), then Word is displaying field codes instead of field results. Press ALT+F9 to display the index or table correctly.

To Delete an Entire Index

If you wanted to delete an index, you would perform the following steps.

1. Click the index to select it.
2. Press SHIFT+F9 to display field codes.
3. Drag through the entire field code, including the braces, and then press DELETE.

Table of Authorities

In addition to inserting an index, table of figures, and table of contents, you can use Word to insert a table of authorities. Legal documents often include a **table of authorities** to list references to cases, rules, statutes, etc., along with the page number(s) on which the references appear. To create a table of authorities, you mark the citations first and then insert the table of authorities.

The procedures for marking citations, editing citations, inserting the table of authorities, changing the format of the table of authorities, and updating the table of authorities are the same as those for indexes. The only difference is that you use the buttons in the Table of Authorities group on the References tab instead of the buttons in the Index group.

To Mark a Citation

If you wanted to mark a citation, creating a citation entry, you would perform the following steps.

1. Select the long, full citation that you wish to appear in the table of authorities (for example, State v. Smith 220 J.3d 167 (UT, 1997)).
2. Click the Mark Citation button (References tab | Table of Authorities group) or press ALT+SHIFT+I to display the Mark Citation dialog box.
3. If necessary, click the Category arrow (Mark Citation dialog box) and then select a new category type.
4. If desired, enter a short version of the citation in the Short citation text box.
5. Click the Mark button to mark the selected text in the document as a citation.

Q&A **Why do formatting marks now appear on the screen?**

When you mark a citation, Word automatically shows formatting marks (if they are not showing already) so that you can see the citation field. The citation entry begins with the letters, TA.

BTW

Inserting Endnotes

To insert an endnote, click the Insert Endnote button (Reference tab | Footnotes group), which places a separator line and the endnote text at the end of the document. Enter desired endnote text to the right of the note reference mark below the separator line.

BTW
Advanced Layout Options
You can adjust Word's advanced layout options by clicking File on the ribbon to open Backstage view, clicking Options in Backstage view to display the Word Options dialog box, clicking Advanced in the left pane (Word Options dialog box), scrolling to the Layout options for area in the right pane, placing a check mark in the desired settings, and then clicking OK.

6. Click the Close button in the Mark Citation dialog box.

Q&A
How could I see all marked citation entries in a document?
With formatting marks displaying, you could scroll through the document, scanning for all occurrences of TA, or you could use the Navigation Pane (that is, place a check mark in the Navigation Pane check box (View tab | Show group)) to find all occurrences of TA.

To Mark Multiple Citations

Word leaves the Mark Citation dialog box open until you close it, which allows you to mark multiple citations without having to redisplay the dialog box repeatedly. To mark multiple citations, you would perform the following steps.

1. With the Mark Citation dialog box displayed, click in the document window; scroll to and then select the next citation.
2. If necessary, click the Selected text text box (Mark Citation dialog box) to display the selected text in the Selected text text box.
3. Click the Mark button.
4. Repeat Steps 1 through 3 for all citations you wish to mark. When finished, click the Close button in the dialog box.

To Edit a Citation Entry

At some time, you may want to change a citation entry after you have marked it. For example, you may need to change the case of a letter. If you wanted to change a citation entry, you would perform the following steps.

1. Display formatting marks.
2. Locate the TA field for the citation entry you wish to change.
3. Change the text inside the quotation marks.
4. Update the table of authorities as described in the steps at the end of this section.

To Delete a Citation Entry

If you wanted to delete a citation entry, you would perform the following steps.

1. Display formatting marks.
2. Select the TA field for the citation entry you wish to delete.
3. Press DELETE, or click the Cut button (Home tab | Clipboard group), or right-click the field and then click Cut on the Mini toolbar or shortcut menu.
4. Update the table of authorities as described in the steps at the end of this section.

To Insert a Table of Authorities

Once all citations are marked, Word can build a table of authorities from the citation entries in the document. Recall that citation entries begin with TA, and they appear on the screen when formatting marks are displayed. When citation entries show on the screen, the document's pagination probably will be altered because of the extra text in the citation entries. Thus, be sure to hide formatting marks before inserting a table of authorities. To insert a table of authorities, you would perform the following steps.

BTW
Line Numbers
If you wanted to insert line numbers in a document, click the Line Numbers button (Layout tab | Page Setup group) and then click the desired line number setting on the Line Numbers menu.

1. Position the insertion point at the location for the table of authorities.
2. Ensure that formatting marks are not displayed.
3. Click the 'Insert Table of Authorities' button (References tab | Table of Authorities group) to display the Table of Authorities dialog box.

4. If necessary, select the category to appear in the table of authorities by clicking the desired option in the Category list, or leave the default selection of All so that all categories will be displayed in the table of authorities.
5. If necessary, click the Formats arrow (Table of Authorities dialog box) and then select the desired format for the table of authorities.
6. If necessary, click the Tab leader arrow and then select the desired leader character in the list to specify the leader character to be displayed between the marked citation and the page number.
7. If you wish to display the word, passim, instead of page numbers for citations with more than four page references, select the Use passim check box.

Q&A **What does the word, passim, mean?**
Here and there.

8. Click OK (Table of Authorities dialog box) to create a table of authorities using the specified settings at the location of the insertion point.

BTW
Different First Page Header or Footer
If you wanted only the first page of a document to have a different header or footer, you could place a check mark in the 'Different First Page' check box (Header & Footer tab | Options group). Doing so instructs Word to create a first page header or first page footer that can contain content that differs from the rest of the headers or footers.

To Update a Table of Authorities

If you add, delete, or modify citation entries, you must update the table of authorities to display the new or modified citation entries. If you wanted to update a table of authorities, you would perform the following steps.

1. In the document window, click the table of authorities to select it.
2. Click the Update Table button (References tab | Table of Authorities group) or press F9 to update the table of authorities.

To Change the Format of the Table of Authorities

If you wanted to change the format of the table of authorities, you would perform the following steps.

1. Click the table of authorities to select it.
2. Click the 'Insert Table of Authorities' button (References tab | Table of Authorities group) to display the Table of Authorities dialog box.
3. Change settings in the dialog box as desired. To change the style of headings, alignment, etc., click the Formats arrow and then click From template; next, click the Modify button to display the Style dialog box, make necessary changes, and then click OK (Style dialog box).
4. Click OK (Table of Authorities dialog box) to apply the changed settings.
5. Click OK when Word asks if you want to replace the selected category of the table of authorities.

To Delete a Table of Authorities

If you wanted to delete a table of authorities, you would perform the following steps.

1. Click the table of authorities to select it.
2. Press SHIFT+F9 to display field codes.
3. Drag through the entire field code, including the braces, and then press DELETE, or click the Cut button (Home tab | Clipboard group), or right-click the field and then click Cut on the Mini toolbar or shortcut menu.

BTW
Inserting Equations
To insert a built-in equation in a document, click the Equation arrow (Insert tab | Symbols group) and then select the desired equation to insert the equation in an equation editor in the document. To enter your own equation, click the Equation button (Insert tab | Symbols group) or click the Equation arrow and then click 'Insert New Equation' on the Equation menu to insert the equation editor in the document. Use buttons and boxes on the Equation tab to enter and format the equation in the equation editor box.

To Specify Different Odd and Even Page Footers Using a Footer Building Block

The *Using Word* document is designed so that it can be duplicated back-to-back. That is, the document prints on nine separate pages. When it is duplicated, however, pages are printed on opposite sides of the same sheet of paper. **Why?** Back-to-back duplicating saves resources because it enables the nine-page document to use only five sheets of paper.

In many books and documents that have facing pages, the page number is always on the same side of the page — often on the outside edge. In Word, you accomplish this task by specifying one type of header or footer for even-numbered pages and another type of header or footer for odd-numbered pages. The following steps specify alternating footers beginning on the fourth page of the document (the beginning of the subdocument).

1

- If necessary, hide formatting marks.
- Use the Navigation Pane to display the page with the heading, Inserting Images in Word Documents.
- Display the Insert tab.
- Click the Footer button (Insert tab | Header & Footer group) and then click Edit Footer to display the footer area.
- Be sure the 'Link to Previous' button (Header & Footer tab | Navigation group) is not selected.

Q&A **What is the purpose of the 'Link to Previous' button?**
If you want to continue using the same header or footer from a previous section, you would select the 'Link to Previous' button. If you want to create a different header or footer from the previous section, you would ensure the 'Link to Previous' button is not selected.

- Place a check mark in the 'Different Odd & Even Pages' check box (Header & Footer tab | Options group), so that you can enter a different footer for odd and even pages.
- Delete any text that appears in the section 3 footer.
- If necessary, click the Next button (Header & Footer tab | Navigation group) to display the desired footer page (in this case, the Odd Page Footer -Section 4-).

2

- Click the 'Insert Alignment Tab' button (Header & Footer tab | Position group) to display the Alignment Tab dialog box so that you can set the position of the footer.
- Click Right (Alignment Tab dialog box) because you want to place a right-aligned tab stop in the footer (Figure 9–71).

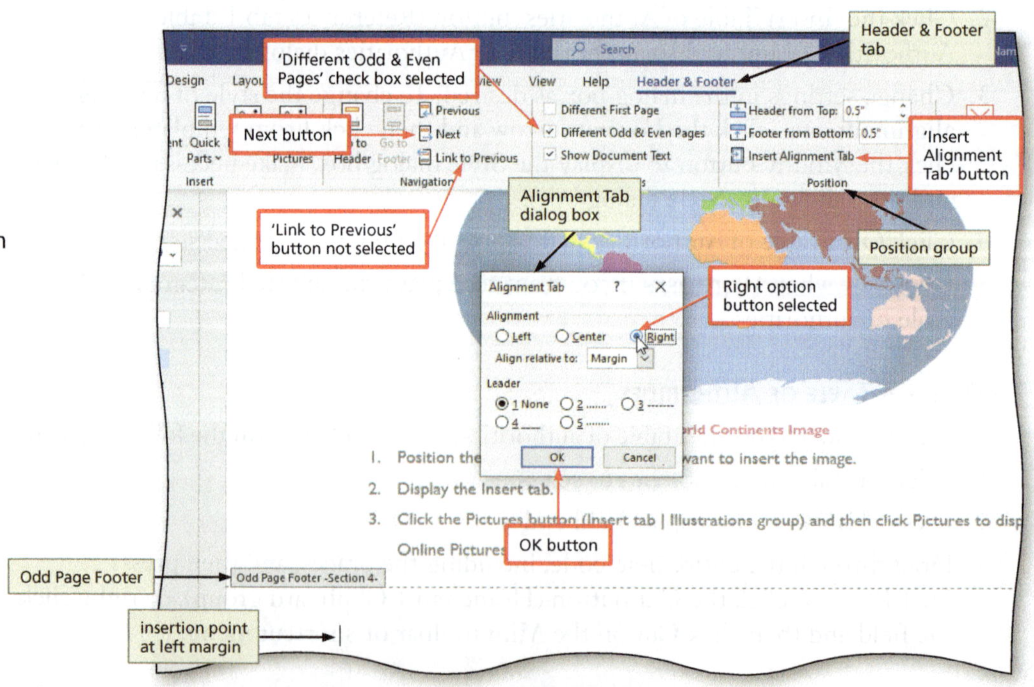

Figure 9–71

3

- Click OK to align the paragraph and insertion point in the footer at the right margin.
- Click the Page Number button (Header & Footer tab | Header & Footer group) to display the Page Number gallery.
- Point to Current Position in the Page Number gallery to display the Current Position gallery (Figure 9–72).

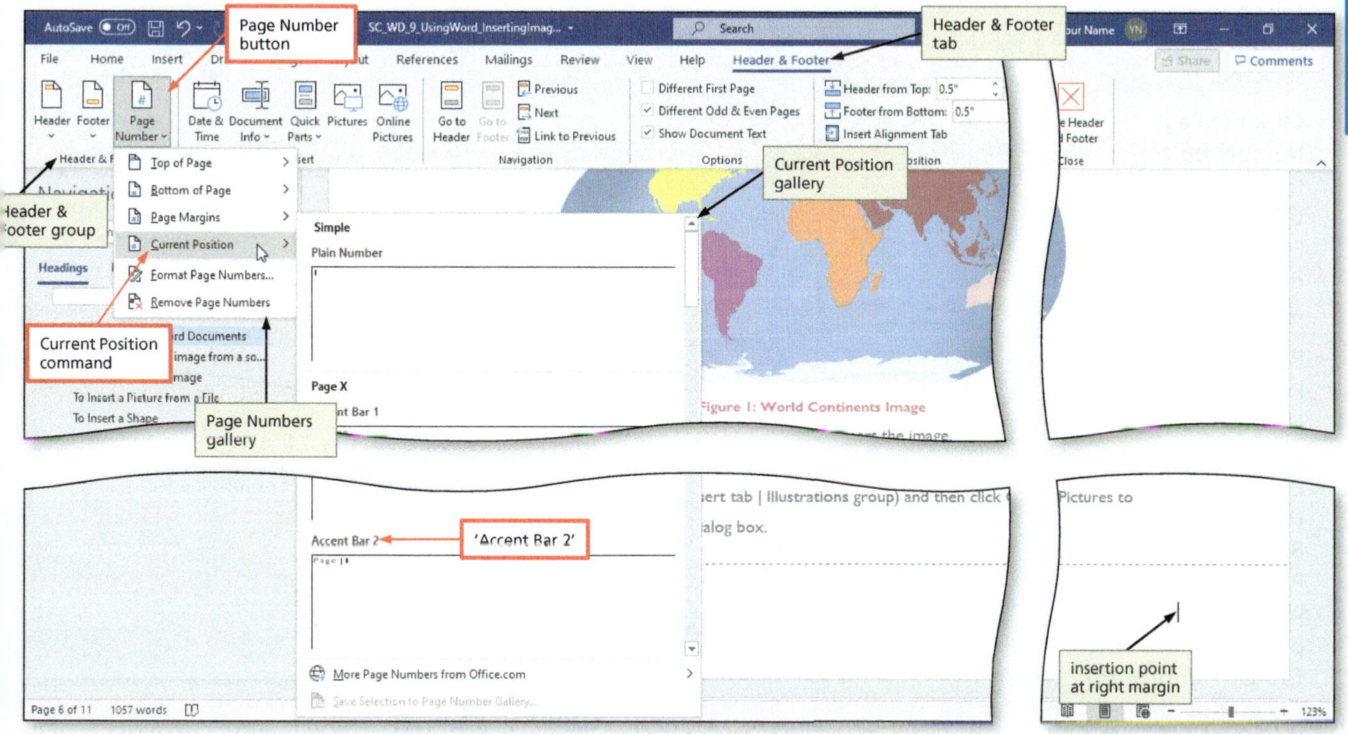

Figure 9–72

4

- Click 'Accent Bar 2' in the Current Position gallery to insert the selected page number in the footer (Figure 9–73).

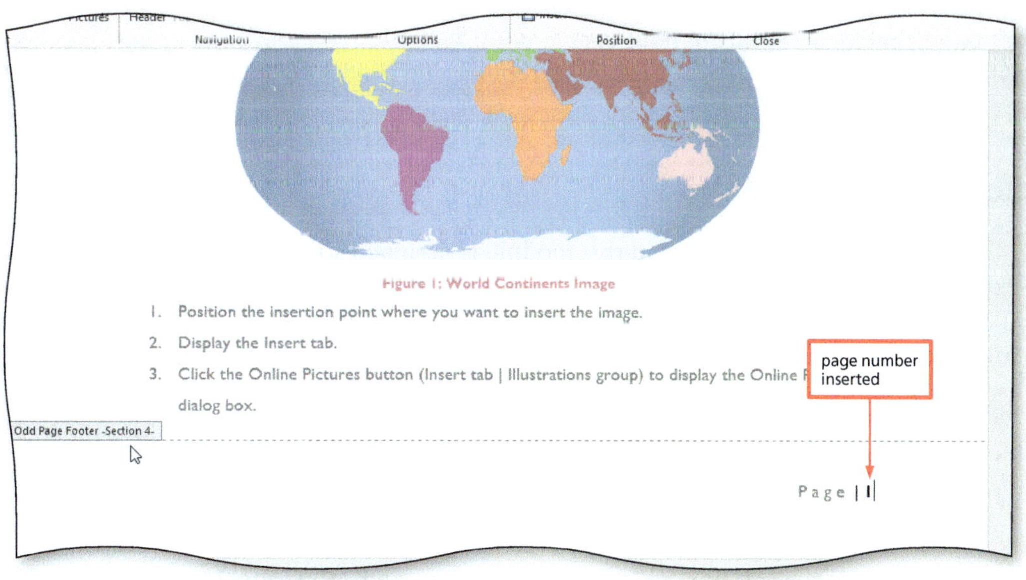

Figure 9–73

5

- Click the Next button (Header & Footer tab | Navigation group) to display the next footer, in this case, Even Page Footer -Section 4-.
- Be sure the 'Link to Previous' button (Header & Footer tab | Navigation group) is not selected.
- Click the Page Number button (Header & Footer tab | Header & Footer group) to display the Page Number gallery.
- Point to Current Position in the Page Number gallery to display the Current Position gallery and then click 'Accent Bar 2' in the Current Position gallery to insert the selected page number in the footer (Figure 9–74).

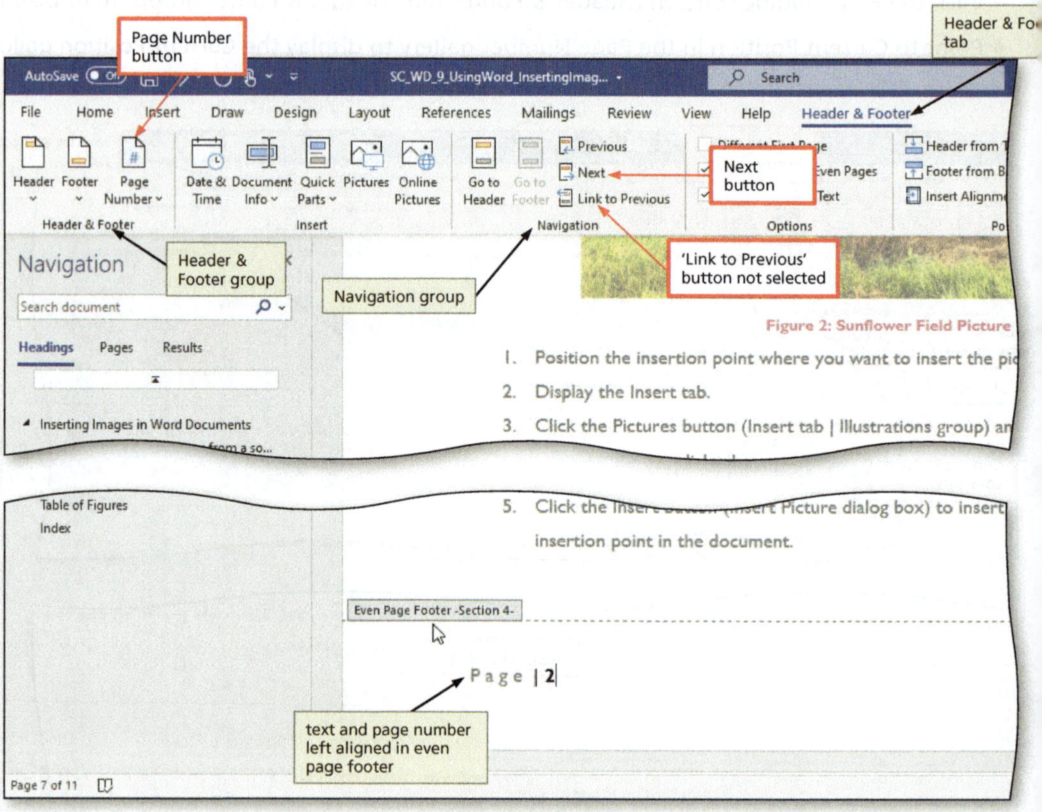

Figure 9–74

- If necessary, fix any incorrect page numbers in the document by positioning the insertion point on the page, clicking the Page Number button (Insert tab | Header & Footer group), clicking the 'Format Page Numbers' command on the Format Page Numbers menu, entering the desired page number in the Start at box, and then clicking OK.
- Close headers and footers.

Q&A **Can I specify alternating headers?**
Yes. Follow the same basic procedure, except insert a header building block or header text.

To Set a Gutter Margin

The reference document in this module is designed so that the inner margin between facing pages has extra space. **Why?** Extra space on facing pages allows printed versions of the documents to be bound (such as stapled) — without the binding covering the words. This extra space in the inner margin is called the **gutter margin.** The following steps set a three-quarter-inch left and right margin and a one-half-inch gutter margin.

1

- Display the Layout tab.
- Click the Margins button (Layout tab | Page Setup group) and then click Custom Margins in the Margins gallery to display the Page Setup dialog box.
- Type `.75` in the Left box, `.75` in the Right box, and `.5` in the Gutter box (Page Setup dialog box).
- Click the Apply to arrow and then click Whole document (Figure 9–75).

2

- Click OK (Page Setup dialog box) to set the new margins for the entire document.

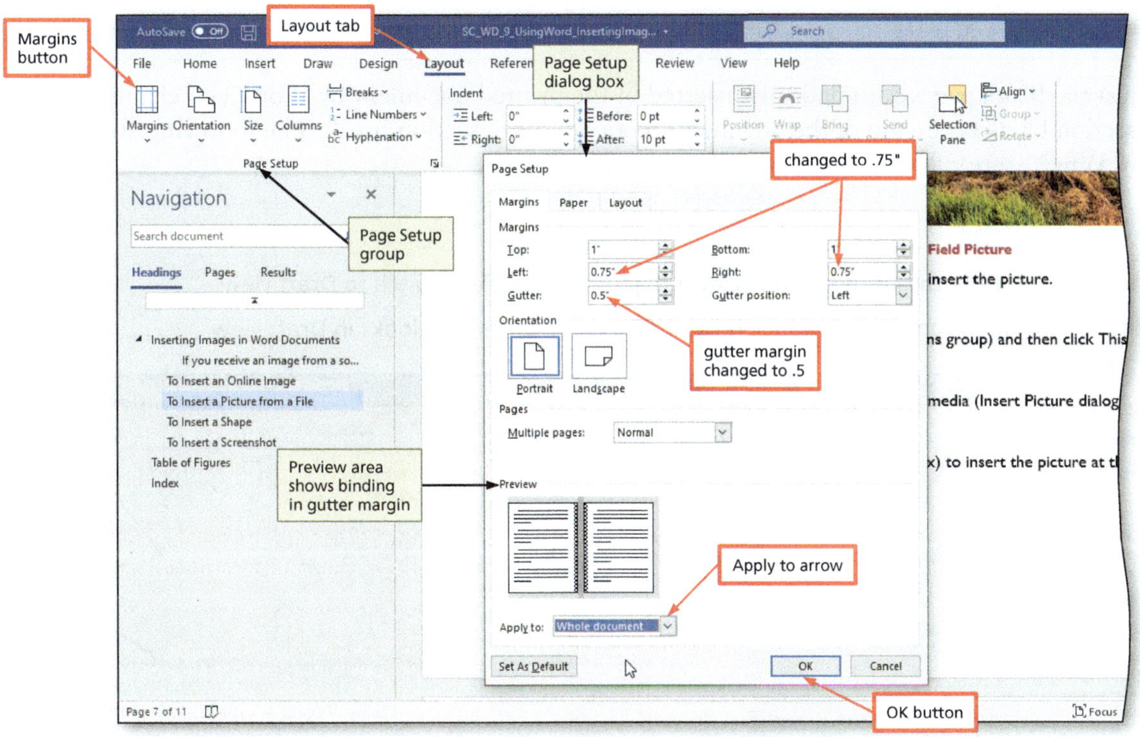

Figure 9–75

To Check the Layout of the Printed Pages

To view the layout of all the pages in the document, the following steps display all the pages as they will print.

1. Open Backstage view.
2. Click Print to display all pages of the document in the right pane, as shown in Figure 9–76. (If all pages are not displayed, change the Zoom level to 10%.)

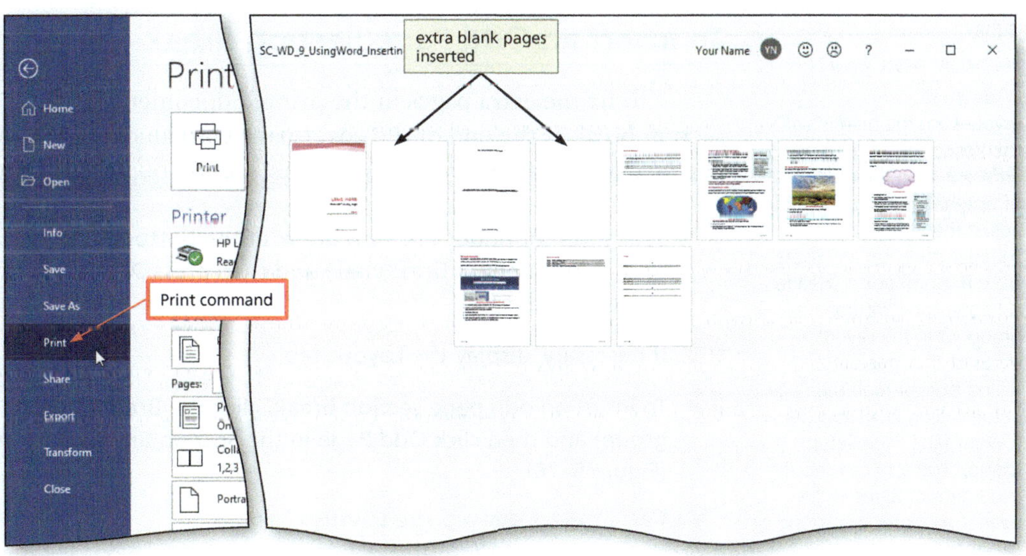

Figure 9–76

Q&A **Why do blank pages appear in the middle of the document?**
When you insert even and odd headers or footers, Word may add pages to fill the gaps.

3. Close Backstage view.

To Switch to Draft View

To adjust the blank pages automatically inserted in the printed document by Word, you change the continuous section break at the top of the document to an odd page section break. The following step switches to Draft view. **Why?** Section breaks are easy to see in Draft view.

1

- Display the View tab. Click the Draft button (View tab | Views group) to switch to Draft view.
- Scroll to the top of the document and notice how different the document looks in Draft view (Figure 9–77).

Q&A **What happened to the images, footers, and other items?**
They do not appear in Draft view because Draft view is designed to make editing text in a document easier.

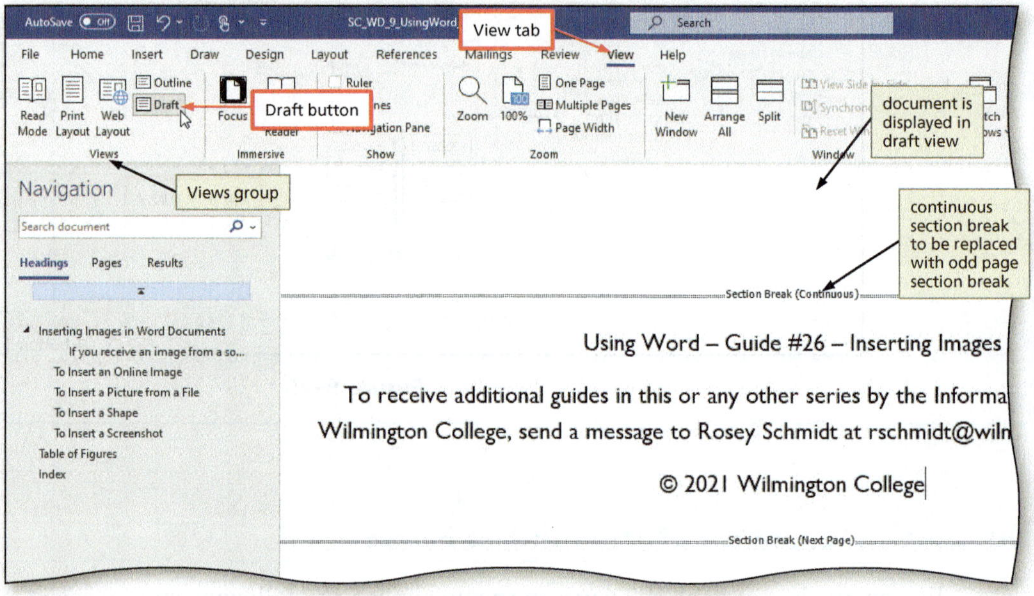

Figure 9–77

BTW
Header and Footer Margins
If you want the margins of the header or footer to be different from the default of one-half inch, you would adjust the margin in the 'Header from Top' or 'Footer from Bottom' boxes (Header & Footer tab | Position group) or in the Layout sheet of the Page Setup dialog box through the Page Setup Dialog Box Launcher (Layout tab | Page Setup group). You also can specify alignment of items in the header or footer by clicking the 'Insert Alignment Tab' button (Header & Footer tab | Position group) and then clicking the desired alignment in the Alignment Tab dialog box.

To Insert an Odd Page Section Break

To fix the extra pages in the printed document, you will replace the continuous section break at the end of the cover page with an odd page section break. With an odd page section break, Word starts the next section on an odd page instead of an even page.

1. Select the continuous section break at the bottom of the cover page (or top of the document in Draft view) and then press DELETE to delete the selected section break.
2. If necessary, display the Layout tab.
3. To insert an odd page section break, click the Breaks button (Layout tab | Page Setup group) and then click Odd Page in the Section Breaks area in the Breaks gallery (Figure 9–78).

   Q&A **Can I insert even page section breaks?**
   Yes. To instruct Word to start the next section on an even page, click Even Page in the Breaks gallery.

4. Click the Print Layout button on the status bar to switch to Print Layout view.

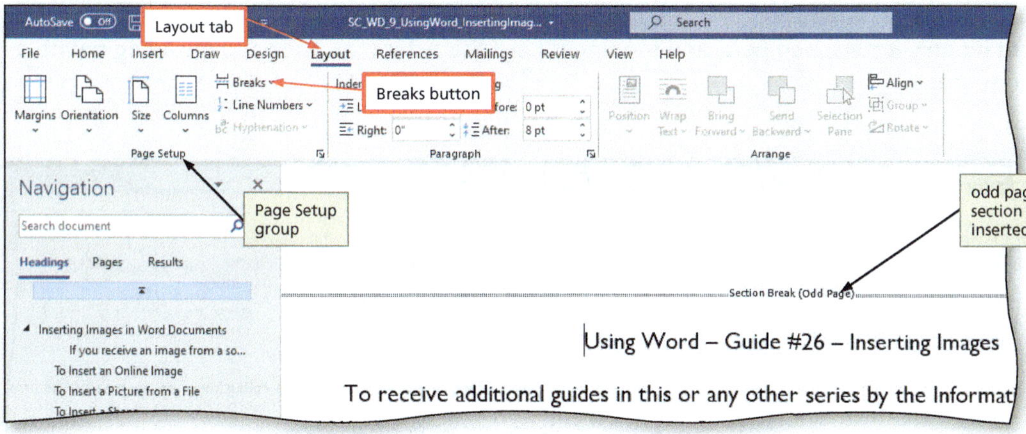

Figure 9–78

To Insert a Bookmark

A **bookmark** is a physical location in a document that you name so that you can reference it later. The following steps insert bookmarks. **Why?** Bookmarks assist users in navigating through a document online. For example, you could bookmark the headings in the document, so that users easily could jump to these areas of the document.

1

- Use the Navigation Pane to display the To Insert an Online Image heading in the document window and then select the heading in the document.
- Display the Insert tab and then, if necessary, display the Links group (Figure 9–79).

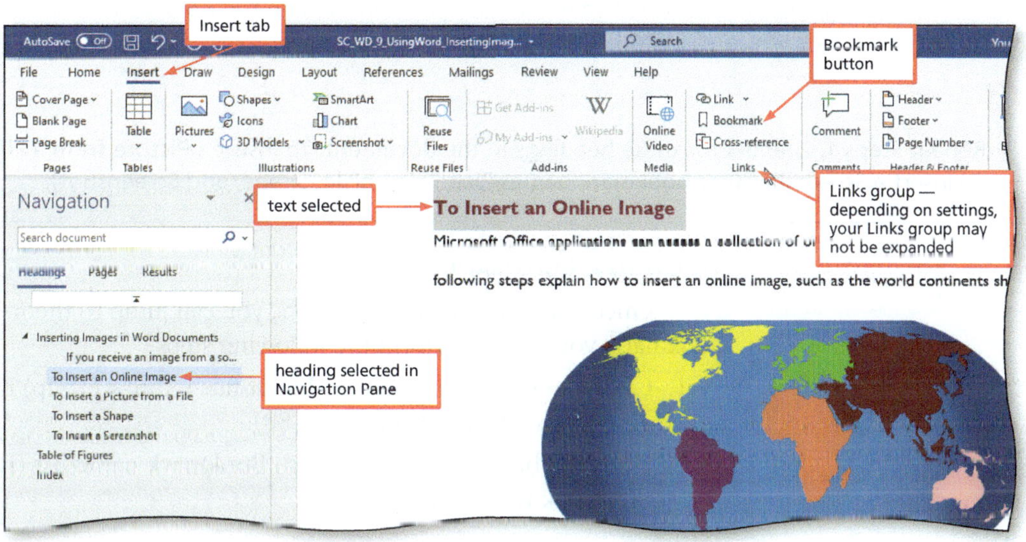

Figure 9–79

2

- Click the Bookmark button (Insert tab | Links group) to display the Bookmark dialog box.
- Type `OnlineImage` in the Bookmark name text box (Figure 9–80).

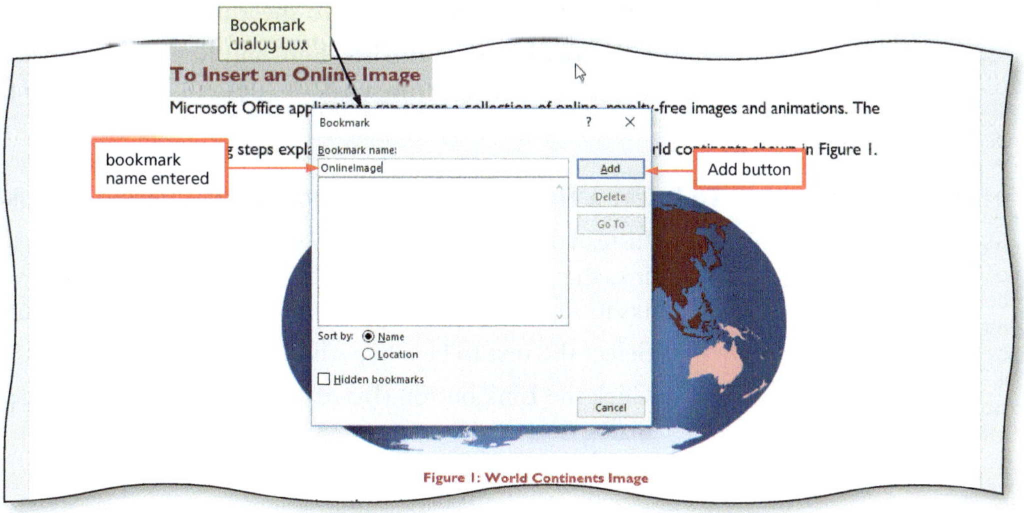

Figure 9–80

Q&A **What are the rules for bookmark names?**
Bookmark names can contain only letters, numbers, and the underscore character (_). They also must begin with a letter and cannot contain spaces.

3

- Click the Add button (Bookmark dialog box) to add the bookmark name to the list of existing bookmarks in the document; click anywhere to remove the selection (Figure 9–81).

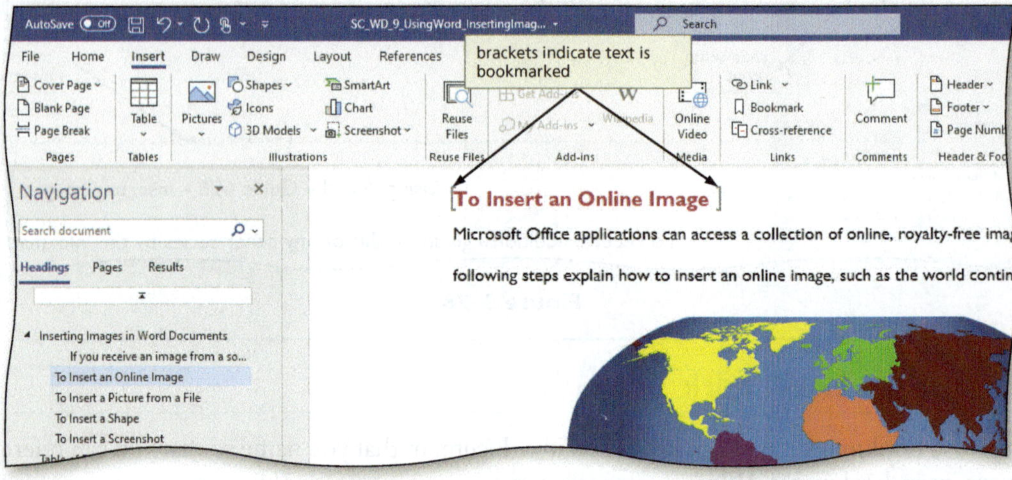

Figure 9–81

Q&A **What if my screen does not show the brackets around the bookmark?**
Click File on the ribbon to open Backstage view, click Options to display the Word Options dialog box, click Advanced in the left pane (Word Options dialog box), scroll to the Show document content area in the right pane, place a check mark in the Show bookmarks check box, and then click OK

4

- Repeat Steps 1, 2, and 3 for these headings in the document: To Insert a Picture from a File, To Insert a Shape, and To Insert a Screenshot (use bookmark names PictureFromFile, Shape, and Screenshot).

To Go to a Bookmark

Once you have added bookmarks, you can jump to them. If you wanted to go to a bookmark, you would perform the following steps.

1. Click the Bookmark button (Insert tab | Links group) to display the Bookmark dialog box (shown in Figure 9–80).
2. Click the bookmark name in the Bookmark name list (Bookmark dialog box) and then click the Go To button.

or

1. Press F5 to display the Go To sheet in the Find and Replace dialog box.
2. Click Bookmark in the list (Find and Replace dialog box), click the 'Enter bookmark name' arrow, click the desired bookmark in the list, and then click the Go To button.

BTW
Hyperlink to Bookmark
If you wanted to insert a hyperlink to a bookmark in a document, click the Cross-reference button (Insert tab | Links group), select Bookmark in the Reference type list (Cross-reference dialog box), select the desired bookmark in the For which bookmark list, be sure the 'Insert as hyperlink' check box is selected, and then click OK. To display the bookmark associated with the link, CTRL+click the link.

To Insert a Hyperlink to a Location in the Current Document

Instead of or in addition to bookmarks in online documents, you can insert hyperlinks that link one part of a document to another. If you wanted to insert a hyperlink that links to a heading or bookmark in the document, you would follow these steps.

1. Select the text to be a hyperlink.
2. Click the Link button (Insert tab | Links group) to display the Insert Hyperlink dialog box.

3. In the Link to bar (Insert Hyperlink dialog box), click 'Place in This Document', so that Word displays all the headings and bookmarks in the document.
4. Click the heading or bookmark to which you want to link.
5. Click OK.

To Save and Print a Document and Then Exit Word

The reference document for this project now is complete. The following steps save and print the document and then exit Word.

1. sam Save the document again as a Word (.docx) file on the same storage location with the same file name.
2. If requested by your instructor, print the finished document (shown in Figure 9–1 at the beginning of this module).
3. If requested by your instructor, save the document as a PDF file and submit the PDF in the format requested by your instructor.
4. If requested by your instructor, unlink the subdocument so that it is converted to be part of the master document by clicking the Outline button (View tab | Views group) to switch to Outline view, clicking the Show Document button (Outlining tab | Master Document group) to show all buttons in the Master Document group, click somewhere in the subdocument, and then click the Unlink button (Outlining tab | Master Document group) to break the connection between the text in the master document and the subdocument so that all content is in a single file. Click File on the ribbon, click Save As, save the unlinked document using SC_WD_9_UsingWord_InsertingImages_UnlinkedDocument as the Word file name, and then submit the unlinked Word document in the format requested by your instructor.
5. Exit Word.

BTW

Conserving Ink and Toner

If you want to conserve ink or toner, you can instruct Word to print draft quality documents by clicking File on the ribbon to open Backstage view, clicking Options in Backstage view to display the Word Options dialog box, clicking Advanced in the left pane (Word Options dialog box), scrolling to the Print area in the right pane, placing a check mark in the 'Use draft quality' check box, and then clicking OK. Then, use Backstage view to print the document as usual.

BTW

Distributing a Document

Instead of printing and distributing a hard copy of a document, you can distribute the document electronically. Options include sending the document via email; posting it on cloud storage (such as OneDrive) and sharing the file with others; posting it on social media, a blog, or other website; and sharing a link associated with an online location of the document. You also can create and share a PDF or XPS image of the document, so that users can view the file in Adobe Reader or XPS Viewer instead of in Word.

Summary

In this module, you learned how to insert a screenshot, insert captions, insert cross-references, insert a sidebar text box, link text boxes, compress pictures, use Outline view, work with master documents and subdocuments, and insert a table of contents, a table of figures, and an index.

Consider This: Plan Ahead

What decisions will you need to make when creating reference documents?

Use these guidelines as you complete the assignments in this module and create your own reference documents outside of this class.

1. Prepare a document to be included in a longer document.
   a) If a document contains multiple images (figures), each figure should have a caption and be referenced from within the text.
   b) All terms in the document that should be included in the index should be marked as an index entry.
2. Include elements common to a reference document, such as a cover page, a table of contents, and an index.
   a) The cover page entices passersby to take a copy of the document.
   b) A table of contents at the beginning of the document and an index at the end helps a reader locate topics within the document.
   c) If a document contains several images, you also should include a table of figures.
3. Prepare the document for distribution, including page numbers, gutter margins for binding, bookmarks, and hyperlinks as appropriate.

Apply Your Knowledge

Reinforce the skills and apply the concepts you learned in this module.

Working with Outline View

Note: To complete this assignment, you will be required to use the Data Files. Please contact your instructor for information about accessing the Data Files.

Instructions: Start Word. Open the document, SC_WD_9-2.docx, which is located in the Data Files. Written by the school administration office manager at Washington Elementary, the document is an outline for a reference document that, when complete, will be distributed to faculty and staff. You are to modify the outline. The final outline is shown in Figure 9–82.

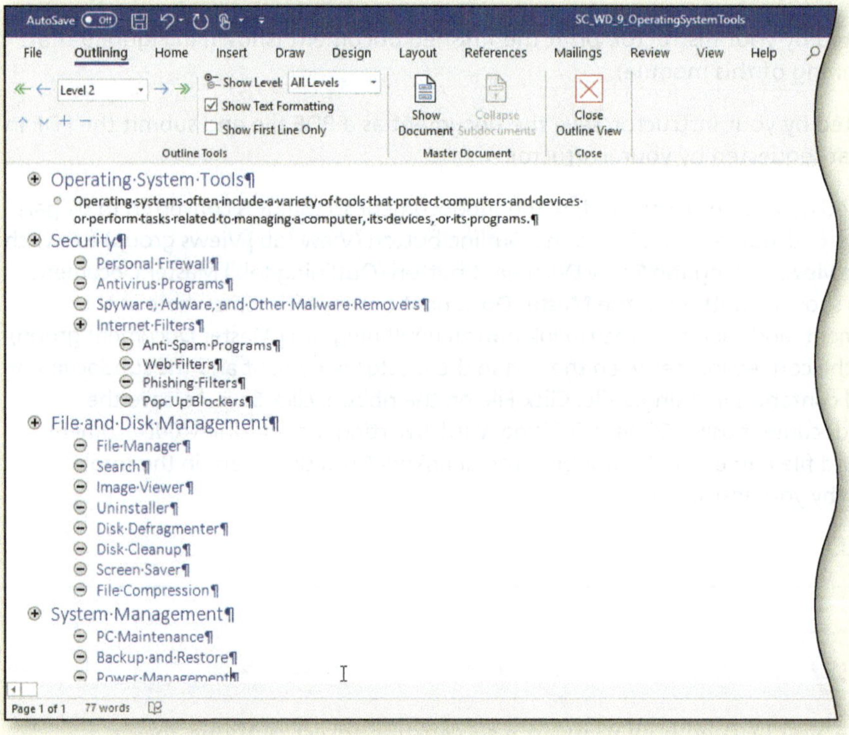

Figure 9–82

Perform the following tasks:

1. Click File on the ribbon and then click Save As and save the document using the new file name, SC_WD_9_OperatingSystemTools.
2. If necessary, switch to Outline view.
3. In the File and Disk Management section, move the Screen Saver heading down three lines so that it is immediately above the File Compression heading.
4. Promote the Security heading so that it is Level 1 instead of Level 2.
5. Demote the Power Management heading so that it is Level 2 instead of Level 1.
6. Demote the Anti-Spam Programs heading so that it is Level 3 instead of Level 2.
7. Move the File and Disk Management heading and all of its subheadings up so that they appear immediately above the System Management heading. (Hint: When you move a heading, all of its subheadings move with it.)

8. Practice collapsing and expanding headings in Outline view by collapsing the Security heading and then expanding the heading.
9. Change the word, Recover, in the System Management section to the word, Restore, so that heading reads: Backup and Restore.
10. Immediately below the Personal Firewall heading, insert a Level 2 heading with the text, Antivirus Programs.
11. Delete the duplicate Image Viewer heading in the File and Disk Management section.
12. Remove the check mark from the 'Show Text Formatting' check box (Outlining tab | Outline Tools group). Place the check mark in the check box again. What is the purpose of this check box?
13. Ensure that the 'Show First Line Only' check box (Outlining tab | Outline Tools group) does not contain a check mark.
14. Add a blank line below the Operating System Tools heading. Demote the heading to body text. Enter this sentence as the body text, including the punctuation: Operating systems often include a variety of tools that protect computers and devices or perform tasks related to managing a computer, its devices, or its programs.
15. If requested by your instructor, add your name after the sentence entered in the previous step.
16. Place a check mark in the 'Show First Line Only' check box (Outlining tab | Outline Tools group). Remove the check mark from the check box again. What is the purpose of this check box?
17. Close Outline View. How does the document differ when displayed in Print Layout view?
18. Use the View tab to open the Navigation Pane.
19. Practice collapsing and expanding headings in the Navigation Pane by collapsing the Security heading and then expanding the heading.
20. Use the Navigation Pane to go to the System Management heading. Go to the Security heading. If necessary, expand the Security heading. Go to the Web Filters heading.
21. If necessary, expand the Web Filters heading. Using the Navigation Pane, promote the Phishing Filters heading so that it is the same level as the Web Filters heading.
22. Using the Navigation Pane, demote the Pop-Up Blockers heading so that it is the same level as the Web Filters heading.
23. Close the Navigation Pane.
24. Switch to Outline view.
25. Use the Show Level arrow (Outlining tab | Outline Tools group) to show only Level 1 headings. Show up to Level 2 headings. Show up to Level 3 headings. Lastly, show all levels.
26. Save the document again with the same name and then submit it in the format specified by your instructor. Close the document.
27. Answer the questions posed in #12, #16, and #17. What are two different ways to expand and collapse items in an outline, to move items up and down an outline, and to demote and promote items in an outline?

Extend Your Knowledge

Extend the skills you learned in this module and experiment with new skills. You may need to use Help to complete the assignment.

Creating a Reference Document with a Cover Page, a Table of Contents, and an Index

Note: To complete this assignment, you will be required to use the Data Files. Please contact your instructor for information about accessing the Data Files.

Continued >>

Extend Your Knowledge *continued*

Instructions: Start Word. Open the draft document, SC_WD_9-3.docx, which is located in the Data Files. The draft discusses backup procedures and a disaster recovery plan, written by the information security specialist at Donner Outpatient Center. You are to insert a cover page, a table of contents, headers and footers, and an index.

Perform the following tasks:

1. Use Help to expand your knowledge about a cover page, a table of contents, headers and footers, marking index entries, and an index.
2. Click File on the ribbon and then click Save As and save the document using the new file name, SC_WD_9_DisasterRecovery.
3. Insert the Banded style cover page. Use the following information on the cover page: title – Disaster Recovery; author – Information Security Center; company name – Donner Outpatient Center; company address – 104 Whitaker Avenue, Cedar Hills, UT 84062.
4. If requested by your instructor, use your name as the author instead of Information Security Center.
5. Insert a blank page between the cover page and the Backup Procedures heading.
6. Insert a table of contents on the blank page using the Automatic Table 1 style.
7. Mark the following terms in the document as index entries: backup, backup program, full backup, differential backup, incremental backup, selective backup, continuous data protection, Cloud backup services, disaster recovery plan, hot site, failover, and cold site. Lowercase the first letter in the index entry for the words, Cloud, so that the entire entry appears in lowercase letters in the index.
8. Mark the following items in the document as index entries that have the subentry of the text, in a disaster recovery plan (Figure 9–83): emergency plan, backup plan, recovery plan, and test plan.

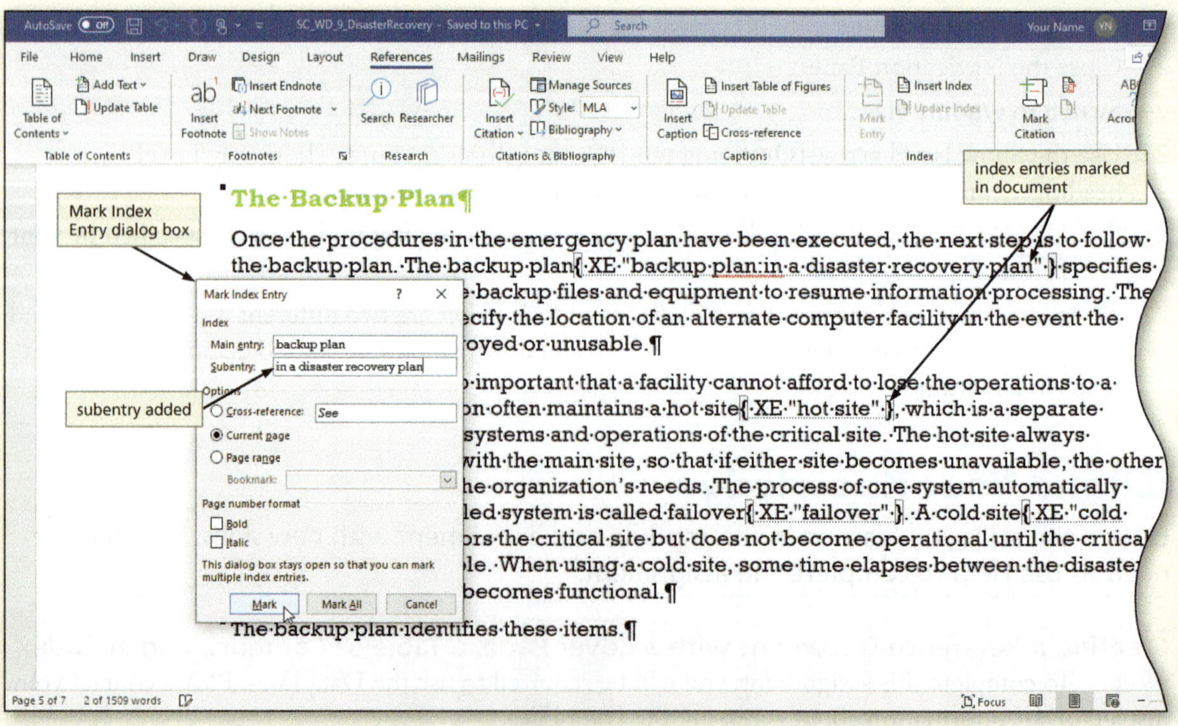

Figure 9–83

9. On a separate page at the end of the document, insert the word, Index, formatted in the Heading 1 style and then insert an index for the document. Remember to hide formatting marks prior to building the index. Use the From template format using one column, with right-aligned page numbers and leader characters of your choice.
10. Update the table of contents so that it includes the index.
11. Mark another term of your choice in the document as an index entry. Update the index so that it includes this term.
12. Change the format of the table of contents to a format of your choice. (Hint: Select the table of contents, click the 'Table of Contents' button (References tab | Table of Contents group), click 'Custom Table of Contents' on the menu, and then select the desired format in the dialog box.) In the Table of Contents dialog box, remove the check mark from the 'Right align page numbers' check box and then see how the table of contents looks in the document.
13. Redisplay the Table of Contents dialog box and then place a check mark in the 'Right align page numbers' check box. Select a tab leader character of your choice for the table of contents.
14. Find the bold italic format in the document and replace it with just an italic format. (Hint: Use the Replace dialog box and find the Bold Italic format and replace with the Not Bold format.)
15. Specify to prevent widows and orphans in the document, if necessary. (Hint: Use the Paragraph Dialog Box Launcher and select options in the Line and Page Breaks sheet.)
16. Select each of the numbered lists and the lead-in sentence above them, and then specify to keep with next and keep lines together so that the paragraph lines stay together. (Hint: Use the Paragraph Dialog Box Launcher and select options in the Line and Page Breaks sheet.)
17. Specify that the paragraph containing the Disaster Recovery Plan heading should have a page break before it. (Hint: Use the Paragraph Dialog Box Launcher and select options in the Line and Page Breaks sheet.)
18. Insert a continuous section break to the left of the B in the Backup Procedures heading.
19. Format the page number on page with the Backup Procedures heading to begin on page 1. (Hint: Use the Page Number button (Insert tab | Header & Footer group).)
20. On the page that begins with the Backup Procedures heading, insert a footer by clicking the Footer button (Insert tab | Header & Footer group) and then clicking Edit Footer. Be sure the 'Different First Page' check box (Header & Footer tab | Options group) is not selected. Select the 'Different Odd & Even Pages' check box (Header & Footer tab | Options group). Be sure the 'Link to Previous' button (Header & Footer tab | Navigation group) is not selected. Use the 'Insert Alignment Tab' button (Header & Footer tab | Position group) to set right alignment for the position of the odd page footer. Use the Page Number button (Header & Footer tab | Header & Footer group) to insert the Accent Bar 2 page number style at the current position. If necessary, set the starting page number to 1 on the page containing the Backup Procedures heading
21. Click the Next button (Header & Footer tab | Navigation group) to go to the next section footer. Insert the Accent Bar 2 page number style at the left margin for the even page footer. The cover page and table of contents should not have a page number (you may need to delete the footer contents on these pages).
22. Update the page numbers in the table of contents.
23. Insert a bookmark for the Backup Procedures and Disaster Recovery Plan headings in the document.
24. Practice going to each bookmark created in the previous step.
25. If requested by your instructor, set gutter margins as follows: From the page with the Backup Procedures heading forward, set the left and right margins to .75" and set a gutter margin

Continued >

Extend Your Knowledge *continued*

of .5" (be sure to position the insertion point to the left of the B in Backup Procedures and select 'This point forward' in the dialog box). Open Backstage view and then click Print to display the Print screen so that you can see if extra pages were inserted due to the gutter margin. Close Backstage view.

26. If you performed the previous step, you may need to fix extra pages in the document by switching to Draft view, deleting the continuous section break, and then inserting an even page section break or an odd page section break using the Breaks button (Layout tab | Page Setup group). Practice inserting one, check the pages in the Print screen in Backstage view, undo the insert or delete odd or even section break and then insert the other. When finished, switch to Print Layout view. If necessary, reinsert page numbers in the even or odd footers (be sure the Link to Previous button is not selected).
27. On a blank line below the index, use the Cross-reference button (Insert tab | Links group) to insert a cross-reference to one of the bookmarks as a hyperlink. Then, practice going to the link by CTRL+clicking the link. Delete the inserted cross-reference.
28. On the same blank line, use the Link button (Insert tab | Links group) to insert a hyperlink to a place in the document of your choice. After inserting the link, practice going to the link by CTRL+clicking the link. Delete the inserted link.
29. Position the insertion point on the Backup Procedures heading. Use the Line Numbers button (Layout tab | Page Setup group) to display continuous line numbers. Scroll through the document to see how line numbers are applied. Remove the line numbers from the document.
30. Save the document again and then submit it in the format specified by your instructor.
31. If required by your instructor or if you would like to practice with citations and a table of authorities, open the draft document again, SC_WD_9-3.docx, which is located in the Data Files. Add this text to the end of the last paragraph: State v. Carstens J.3d 169 (UT, 2021). Select the text just added and then mark the citation using the Mark Citation button (References tab | Table of Authorities group). Insert a new page at the end of the document and then insert a table of authorities on the blank page. At the end of another paragraph in the document, type this text: Barnes v. Wilson 212 F.4d 228 (FL, 2021). Update the table of authorities. Close the document without saving.
32. If you wanted the index entries to appear in bold in the index but remain not bold in the document, what steps would you take to accomplish this?

Expand Your World

Create a solution that uses cloud or web technologies by learning and investigating on your own from general guidance.

Inserting Equations, Symbols, Screenshots, and Screen Clippings, and Using an Online Photo Editor

Instructions: As an assistant to the business manager at IT Training Solutions, you have been asked to insert sample mathematical symbols and equations in a Word document, take a screenshot of the screen, and then use an online photo editor to enhance the screenshot. Be creative — the screen shown in Figure 9–84 is only a sample solution. Your document should look different.

Perform the following tasks:

1. Start Word and create a blank document. Change the margins to Narrow. Enter the title, Mathematical Symbols and Equations in Word. Format the entered title appropriately at the top of the page.
2. On a line below the title, insert a mathematical symbol of your choice using the Symbol dialog box. (Hint: Click the Subset arrow in the Symbol dialog box and then click Mathematical Operators.) Select the entered mathematical symbol and then place it in a text box by clicking the Text Box button (Insert tab | Text group) and then clicking 'Draw Text Box'. Insert three more mathematical operators using this procedure. Position, resize, and format the text boxes as desired.
3. Insert a text box in the document. Delete any text in the text box and insert a built-in equation of your choice using the Equation arrow (Insert tab | Symbols group). Select the equation and format and position it as desired.
4. Insert another text box in the document and delete any text in the text box. So that you can type an equation in the text box, click the Equation button (Insert tab | Symbols group) or click the Equation arrow and then click 'Insert New Equation'. Use the Equation tab to insert an equation of your choice in the equation editor box. Select the equation and format and position it as desired. The title and all text boxes should fit in the document window (Figure 9–84).

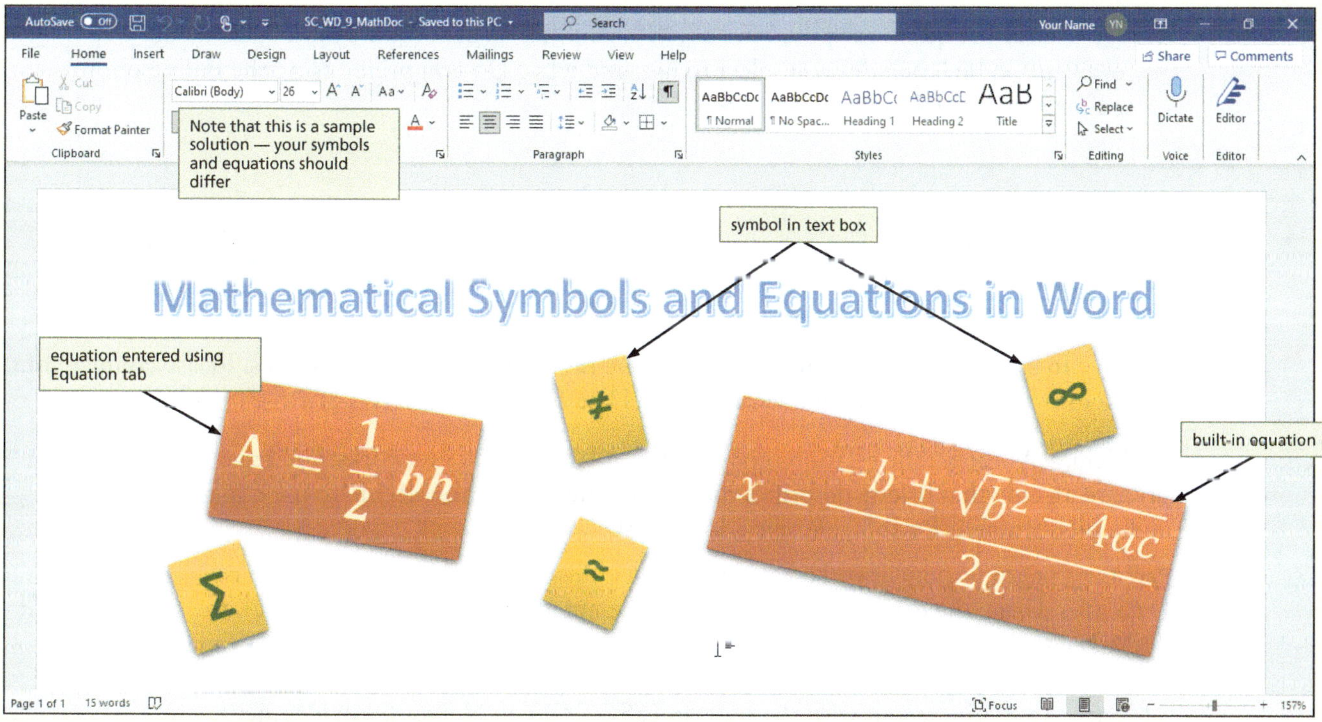

Figure 9–84

5. Save the document with the file name, SC_WD_9_MathDoc.
6. From Word, create a blank document so that you have two separate Word windows open. Enter the text, Screenshot, at the top of the blank document. Then, insert a screenshot of the window containing the SC_WD_9_MathDoc file. Center the screenshot.
7. On a blank line below the inserted screenshot, enter the text, Screen clipping. Then, insert a screen clipping of just the mathematical symbols and equations. Center the screen clipping.

Continued >

Expand Your World *continued*

8. Save the document with the screenshot and screen clipping with the file name, SC_WD_9_MathDocScreens.
9. Save the Word screenshot as a JPEG file with the name, SC_WD_9_MathScreenshot. (Hint: Right-click the image and then click 'Save as Picture' on the submenu.)
10. Save the screen clipping as a JPEG file with the file name, SC_WD_9_MathScreenClipping.
11. Locate the saved JPEG files and then double-click them. In what program did they open?
12. Submit the documents in the format specified by your instructor.
13. Start a browser. Search for the text, online photo editor, using a search engine. Visit several of the online photo editors and determine which you would like to use to edit an image. Navigate to the desired online photo editor.
14. In the photo editor, open the SC_WD_9_MathScreenClipping image that you created in Step 10. Use the photo editor to enhance the image. Apply at least five enhancements. Which enhancements did you apply?
15. If requested by your instructor, add your name as a text element to the photo.
16. Save the revised image with the file name, SC_WD_9_MathScreenClippingEnhanced. In what format did the online photo editor save the file? Submit the image in the format specified by your instructor.
17. Answer the questions posed in #11, #14, and #16. Which online photo editors did you evaluate? Which one did you select to use, and why? Do you prefer using the online photo editor or Word to enhance images?

In the Lab

Design and implement a solution using creative thinking and problem-solving skills.

Using a Master and Subdocument for a Reference Document

Note: To complete this assignment, you will be required to use the Data Files. Please contact your instructor for information about accessing the Data Files.

Problem: As the public relations coordinator at Cloud Link Networks, you have been asked to prepare a guide that briefly describes the types of networks. You decide to use a master document and a subdocument for this reference document.

Part 1: The subdocument you created is in a file called SC_WD_9-4.docx, which is located in the Data Files. Using the concepts and techniques presented in this module, along with the source content in the Data Files, create and format the master document with the subdocument. While creating the documents, be sure to do the following:

1. Save the subdocument with the file name, SC_WD_9_NetworkSubdocument.
2. In the subdocument, mark at least 10 terms as index entries.
3. Insert the following six images in the Data Files in appropriate locations in the subdocument:
   - Support_WD_9_Networks.jpg
   - Support_WD_9_ClientServerNetwork.jpg
   - Support_WD_9_PeerToPeerNetwork.jpg
   - Support_WD_9_RingNetwork.jpg
   - Support_WD_9_StarNetwork.jpg
   - Support_WD_9_BusNetwork.jpg

4. Insert appropriate captions for each of the six images.
5. Insert a cross-reference to each of the captions.
6. Compress one of the images and then compress all of the images.
7. Insert a sidebar text box that contains text about networks you use at home or school. Insert another blank text box in the document. Link the two text boxes and then save the file.
8. Create a master document in a new document window in Outline view. Insert appropriate headings for a Table of Figures and an Index. Insert the subdocument file that is called SC_WD_9_NetworkSubdocument in the appropriate location. Be sure to insert a next page section break between each line in the master document in Outline view. Save the master document with the file name, SC_WD_9_NetworkReferenceDocument. Switch to Print Layout view.
9. Insert an appropriate cover page.
10. Insert a table of contents, a table of figures, and an index.
11. Modify one of the figure captions and the update the table of figures.
12. Format the document with a footer that contains a page number. Practice using the 'Link to Previous' button (Header & Footer tab | Navigation group) to continue the footer from a previous section and then create a footer that is different from the previous section.
13. Format the document with a header that is different from the first page.
14. Practice going to the next and previous sections in the document.
15. If requested by your instructor, insert an endnote that contains your name in the document.
16. Be sure to check the spelling and grammar of the finished documents.
17. When you are finished with the master document and subdocuments, save them again and then also save the file as a PDF with the file name, SC_WD_9_NetworkReferenceDocument. Submit your documents and answers to the Part 2 critical thinking questions in the format specified by your instructor.
18. Close all documents and then reopen the master document. In Outline view, expand the document. Collapse the subdocument. Show the subdocument.
19. Practice locking and unlocking a subdocument.
20. Unlink the subdocument. Close the document without saving changes.

Part 2: You made several decisions while creating the reference document in this assignment: which terms to mark as index entries, what text to use for captions, and how to organize and format the subdocument and master document (table of contents, table of figures, index, etc.). What was the rationale behind each of these decisions? When you proofread the document, what further revisions did you make and why?

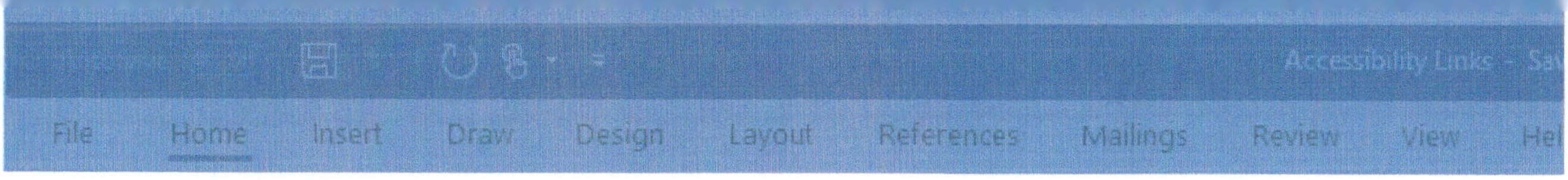

10 Creating an Online Form

Objectives

After completing this module, you will be able to:

- Save a document as a template
- Change paper size
- Add page color
- Insert and format an icon graphic
- Use a table to control layout
- Show the Developer tab
- Insert plain text, drop-down list, check box, rich text, combo box, and date picker content controls
- Edit placeholder text
- Change properties of content controls
- Insert and format a rectangle shape
- Restrict editing to filling in a form
- Open a new document based on a template
- Fill in a form

Introduction

During your personal and professional life, you undoubtedly have filled in countless forms. Whether a federal tax form, a time card, a job application, an order, a deposit slip, a request, or a survey, a form is designed to collect information. In the past, forms were printed; that is, you received the form on a piece of paper, filled it in with a pen or pencil, and then returned it manually. An **online form** contains labels and corresponding blank areas in which a user electronically enters the requested information. You use a computer or mobile device to access, fill in, and then return an online form. In Word, you easily can create an online form for electronic distribution; you also can fill in that same form using Word.

Project: Online Form

Today, businesses and individuals are concerned with using resources efficiently. To minimize paper waste, protect the environment, enhance office efficiency, and improve access to data, many businesses have moved toward a paperless office. Thus, online forms have replaced many paper forms. You access online forms on a website, on a company's intranet, or from your inbox if you receive the form via email.

The project in this module uses Word to produce the online form shown in Figure 10–1. Meal Time Express is a meal service company that provides an online form for potential customers to complete if they are interested in obtaining more

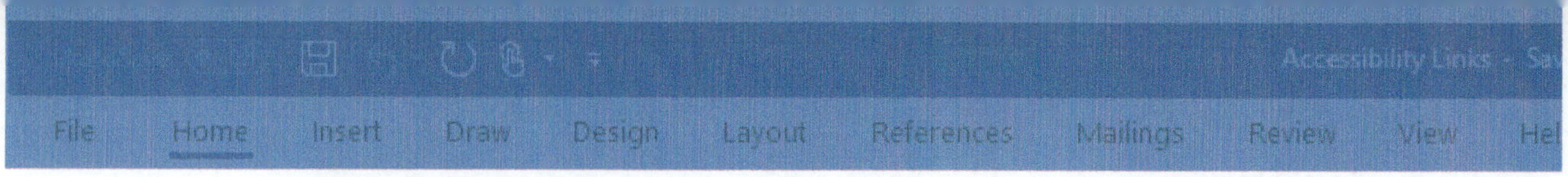
File
Home
Insert
Draw
Design
Layout
References
Mailings
Review
View

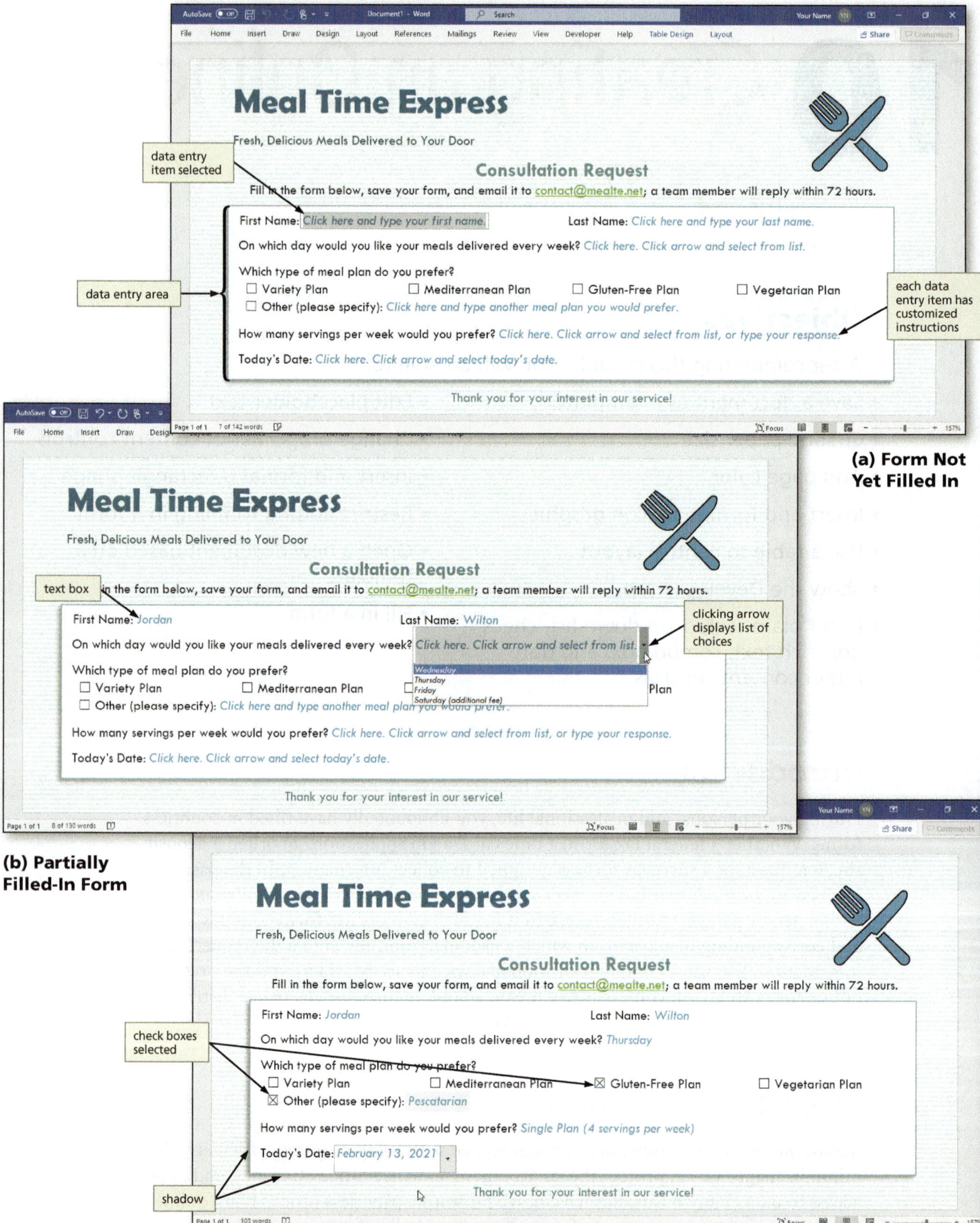
data entry item selected
data entry area
each data entry item has customized instructions
Meal Time Express
Fresh, Delicious Meals Delivered to Your Door
Consultation Request
Fill in the form below, save your form, and email it to contact@mealte.net; a team member will reply within 72 hours.
First Name: Click here and type your first name.
Last Name: Click here and type your last name.
On which day would you like your meals delivered every week? Click here. Click arrow and select from list.
Which type of meal plan do you prefer?
Variety Plan
Mediterranean Plan
Gluten-Free Plan
Vegetarian Plan
Other (please specify): Click here and type another meal plan you would prefer.
How many servings per week would you prefer? Click here. Click arrow and select from list, or type your response.
Today's Date: Click here. Click arrow and select today's date.
Thank you for your interest in our service!
(a) Form Not Yet Filled In
text box
clicking arrow displays list of choices
First Name: Jordan
Last Name: Wilton
Wednesday
Thursday
Friday
Saturday (additional fee)
(b) Partially Filled-In Form
check boxes selected
shadow
On which day would you like your meals delivered every week? Thursday
Other (please specify): Pescatarian
How many servings per week would you prefer? Single Plan (4 servings per week)
Today's Date: February 13, 2021
(c) Filled-In Form

Figure 10–1

information from a company team member. Designed by the communications specialist at Meal Time Express, the form is available on the company's website, where a potential customer can download it, enter the requested information, save it, and then send it back using the email address on the form.

Figure 10–1a shows how the form is displayed on a user's screen initially, Figure 10–1b shows the form partially filled in by one user, and Figure 10–1c shows how this user filled in the entire form.

The data entry area of the form contains three text boxes (named First Name, Last Name, and Other Meal Plan Type), one drop-down list box (named Delivery Day), five check boxes (named Variety Plan, Mediterranean Plan, Gluten-Free Plan, Vegetarian Plan, and Other Meal Plan Type), a combination text box/drop-down list box (named Servings per Week), and a date picker (named Today's Date).

The form is designed so that it fits completely within a Word window that is set at a page width zoom and has the ribbon collapsed, which reduces the chance a user will have to scroll the window while filling in the form. The data entry area of the form is enclosed by a rectangle that has a shadow on its left and bottom edges.

You will perform the following general tasks as you progress through this module:

1. Save a document as a template.
2. Set form formats for the template.
3. Enter text, graphics, and content controls in the form.
4. Protect the form.
5. Use the form.

To Start Word and Specify Settings

If you are using a computer to step through the project in this module and you want your screens to match the figures in this book, you should change your screen's resolution to 1366 × 768. The following steps start Word, display formatting marks, change the zoom to page width, ensure rulers are not displayed, and verify ruler and Mouse mode settings.

1. Start Word and create a blank document in the Word window. If necessary, maximize the Word window.
2. If the Print Layout button on the status bar is not selected, click it so that your screen is in Print Layout view.
3. If the 'Show/Hide ¶' button (Home tab | Paragraph group) is not selected already, click it to display formatting marks on the screen.
4. To display the page the same width as the document window, if necessary, click the Page Width button (View tab | Zoom group).
5. If the rulers are displayed on the screen, click the Ruler check box (View tab | Show group) to remove the rulers from the Word window.
6. If you are using a mouse and you want your screens to match the figures in the book, verify that you are using Mouse mode by clicking the Touch/Mouse Mode button on the Quick Access Toolbar and then, if necessary, clicking Mouse on the menu. (If your Quick Access Toolbar does not display the Touch/Mouse Mode button, click the 'Customize Quick Access Toolbar' button on the Quick Access Toolbar and then click Touch/Mouse Mode on the menu to add the button to the Quick Access Toolbar.)

Saving a Document as a Template

A **template** is a file with a theme applied and that may contain formatted placeholder text, headers and footers, and graphics, some of which you replace with your own information. Every Word document you create is based on a template. When you select the Blank document thumbnail on the Word start screen or in the New screen of Backstage view, Word creates a document based on the Normal template. Word also provides other templates for more specific types of documents, such as memos, letters, and resumes. Creating a document based on these templates can improve your productivity because Word has defined much of the document's appearance for you.

In this module, you create an online form. If you create and save an online form as a Word document, users will be required to open that Word document to display the form on the screen. Next, they will fill in the form. Then, to preserve the content of the original form, they will have to save the form with a new file name. If they accidentally click the Save button on the Quick Access Toolbar during the process of filling in the form, Word will replace the original blank form with a filled-in form.

If you create and save the online form as a template instead, users will open a new document window that is based on that template. This displays the form on the screen as a brand new Word document; that is, the document does not have a file name. Thus, the user fills in the form and then clicks the Save button on the Quick Access Toolbar to save the filled-in form. By creating a Word template for the form, instead of a Word document, the original template for the form remains intact when the user clicks the Save button.

BTW
Saving Templates
When you save a template that contains building blocks, the building blocks are available to all users who access the template.

To Save a Document as a Template

The following steps save a new blank document as a template. **Why?** The template will be used to create the online form shown in Figure 10–1.

1

- With a new blank document in the Word window, open Backstage view and then click Export in the left pane of Backstage view to display the Export screen.
- Click 'Change File Type' in the Export screen to display information in the right pane about various file types that can be opened in Word.
- Click Template in the right pane to specify the file type for the current document (Figure 10–2).

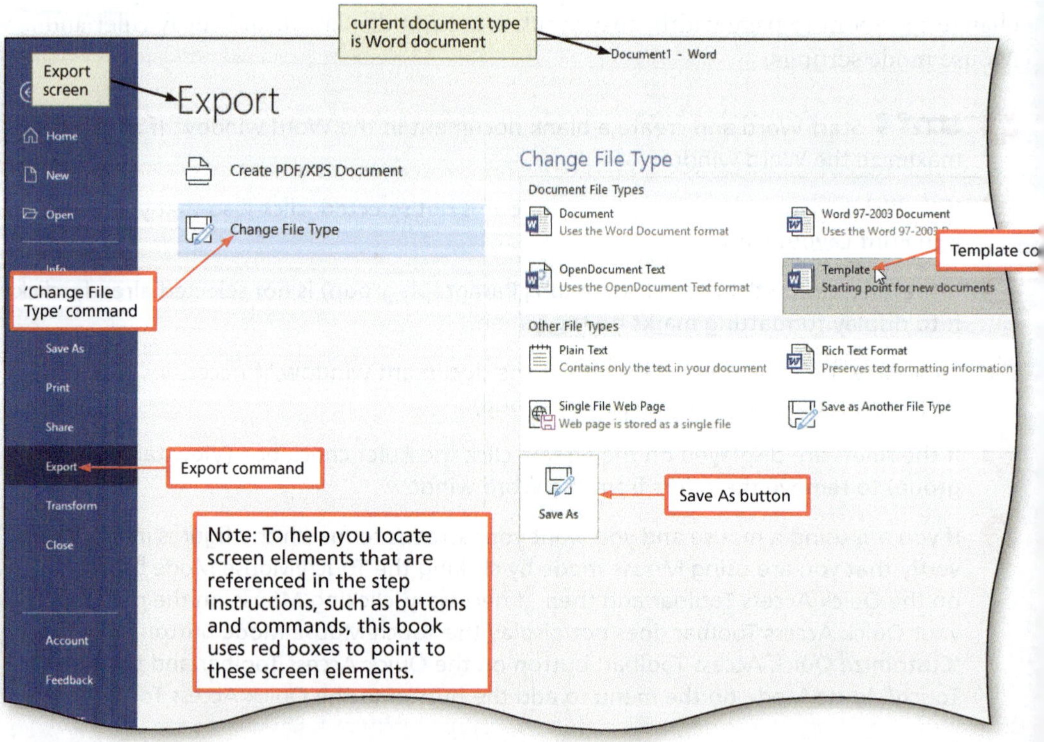

Figure 10–2

2

- Click the Save As button to display the Save As dialog box with the file type automatically changed to Word Template.

Q&A **How does Word differentiate between a saved Word template and a saved Word document?** Files typically have a file name and a file extension. The file extension identifies the file type. The source program often assigns a file type to a file. A Word document has an extension of .docx, whereas a Word template has an extension of .dotx. Thus, a file named JulyReport.docx is a Word document, and a file named JulyReport.dotx is a Word template.

- In the File name box, type **SC_WD_10_MealTimeExpressForm** to change the file name and then navigate to the desired save location (Figure 10–3).

Q&A **Why is my save location the Custom Office Templates folder?** The default save location for your templates may be the Custom Office Templates folder. If you are using a home computer, you can save your template in that folder. If you are using a public computer, you should change the save location to your local storage location.

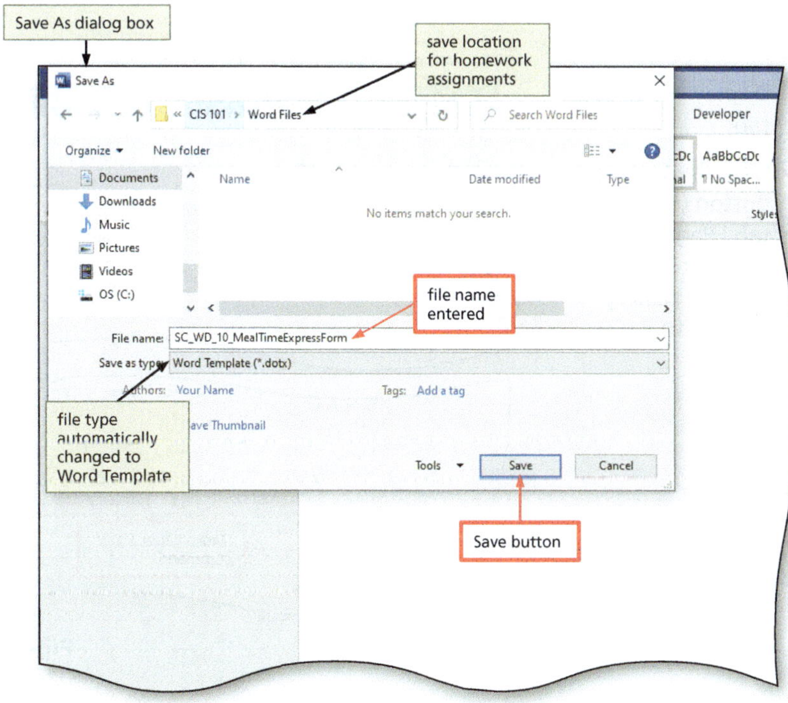

Figure 10–3

3

- Click Save (Save As dialog box) to save the document as a Word template with the entered file name in the specified location.

Other Ways

1. Press F12, change document type to Word Template
2. Open Backstage view, click Save As, change document type to Word Template

Changing Document Settings

To enhance the look of the form, you change several default settings in Word:

1. Display the page as wide as possible in the document window to maximize the amount of space for text and graphics on the form, called page width zoom.
2. Change the size of the paper so that it fits completely within the document window.
3. Adjust the margins so that as much text as possible will fit in the document.
4. Change the theme colors to the Blue Green color set and the theme fonts to the Tw Cen MT font set.
5. Add a teal page color with a pattern.

The first item was completed earlier in the module. The following sections make the remaining changes to the document.

BTW

The Ribbon and Screen Resolution

Word may change how the groups and buttons within the groups appear on the ribbon, depending on the screen resolution of your computer. Thus, your ribbon may look different from the ones in this book if you are using a screen resolution other than 1366 × 768.

To Change Paper Size

For the online form in this module, all edges of the page appear in the document window. Currently, only the top, left, and right edges are displayed in the document window. The following steps change paper size. **Why?** To display all edges of the document in the document window in the current resolution, change the height of the paper from 11 inches to 4 inches.

1

- Display the Layout tab.
- Click the Size button (Layout tab | Page Setup group) to display the Size gallery (Figure 10–4).

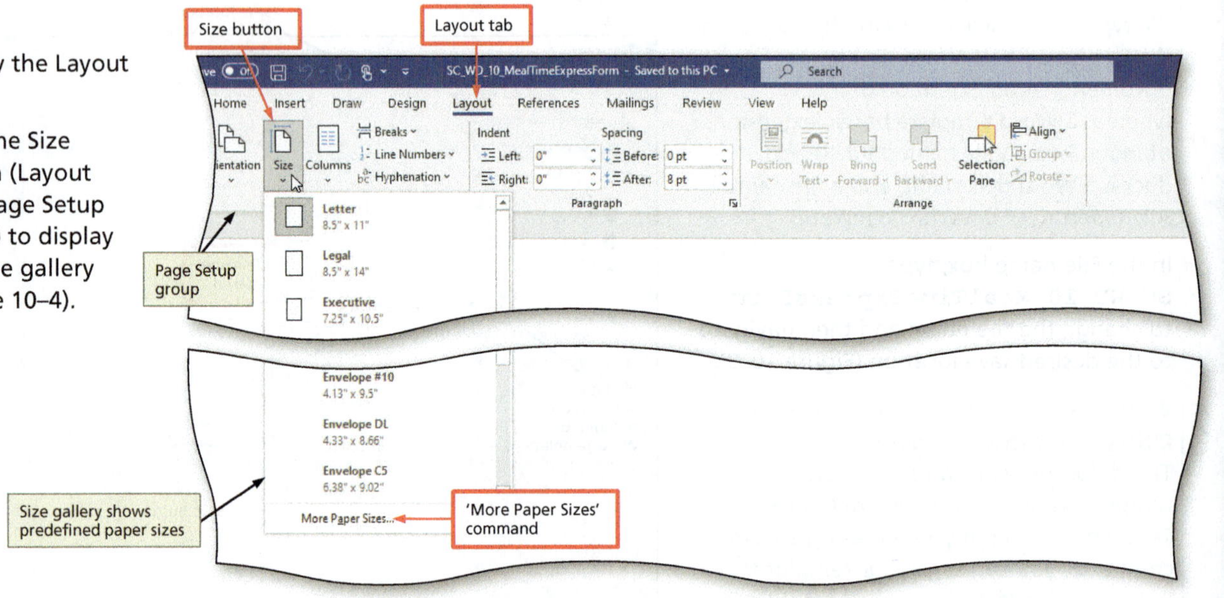

Figure 10–4

2

- Click 'More Paper Sizes' in the Size gallery to display the Paper sheet in the Page Setup dialog box.
- In the Height box (Page Setup dialog box), type **4** as the new height (Figure 10–5).

3

- Click OK to change the paper size to the entered measurements, which, in this case, are 8.5 inches wide by 4 inches tall.

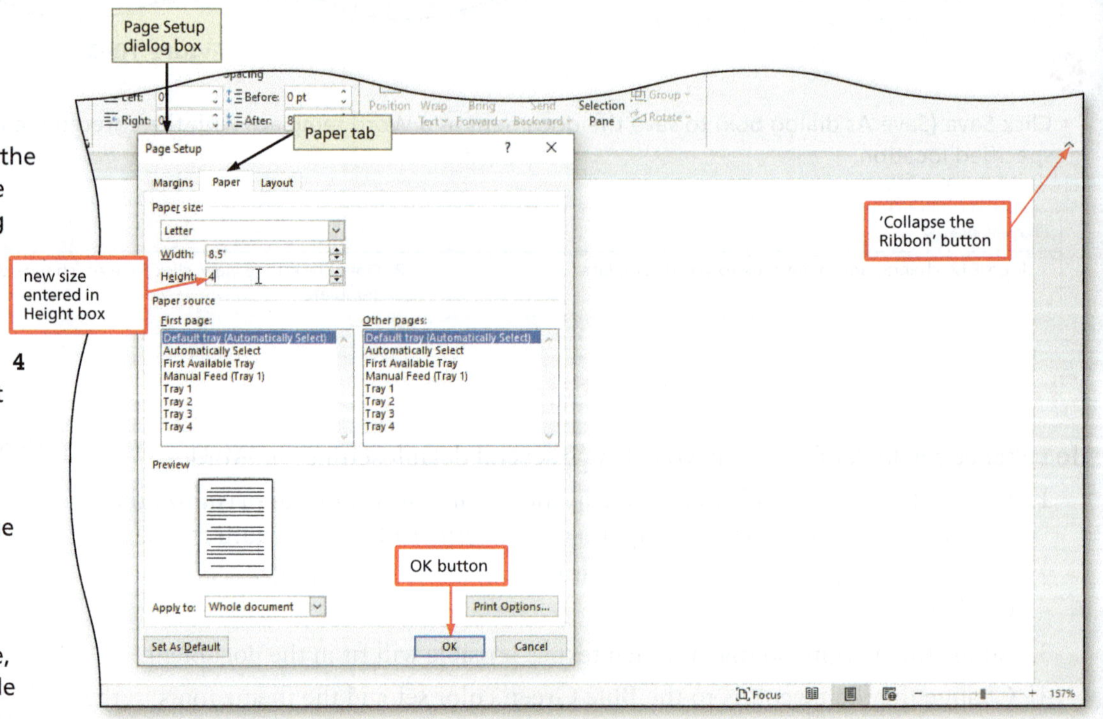

Figure 10–5

To Collapse the Ribbon

To display more of a document or other item in the Word window, you can collapse the ribbon, which hides the groups on the ribbon and displays only the main tabs. For the online form to fit entirely in the Word window, you collapse the ribbon. The following step collapses the ribbon so that you can see how the form fits in the document window.

1. Click the 'Collapse the Ribbon' button on the ribbon (shown in Figure 10–5) to collapse the ribbon (Figure 10–6).

Q&A

What happened to the 'Collapse the Ribbon' button?
The 'Pin the ribbon' button replaces the 'Collapse the Ribbon' button when the ribbon is collapsed. You will see the 'Pin the ribbon' button only when you expand a ribbon by clicking a tab.

What if the height of my document does not match the figure?
You may need to show white space. To do this, position the pointer above the top of the page below the ribbon and then double-click when the pointer changes to a 'Show White Space' button (or, if using touch, double-tap below the page). Or, your screen resolution may be different; if so, you may need to adjust the page height or width values.

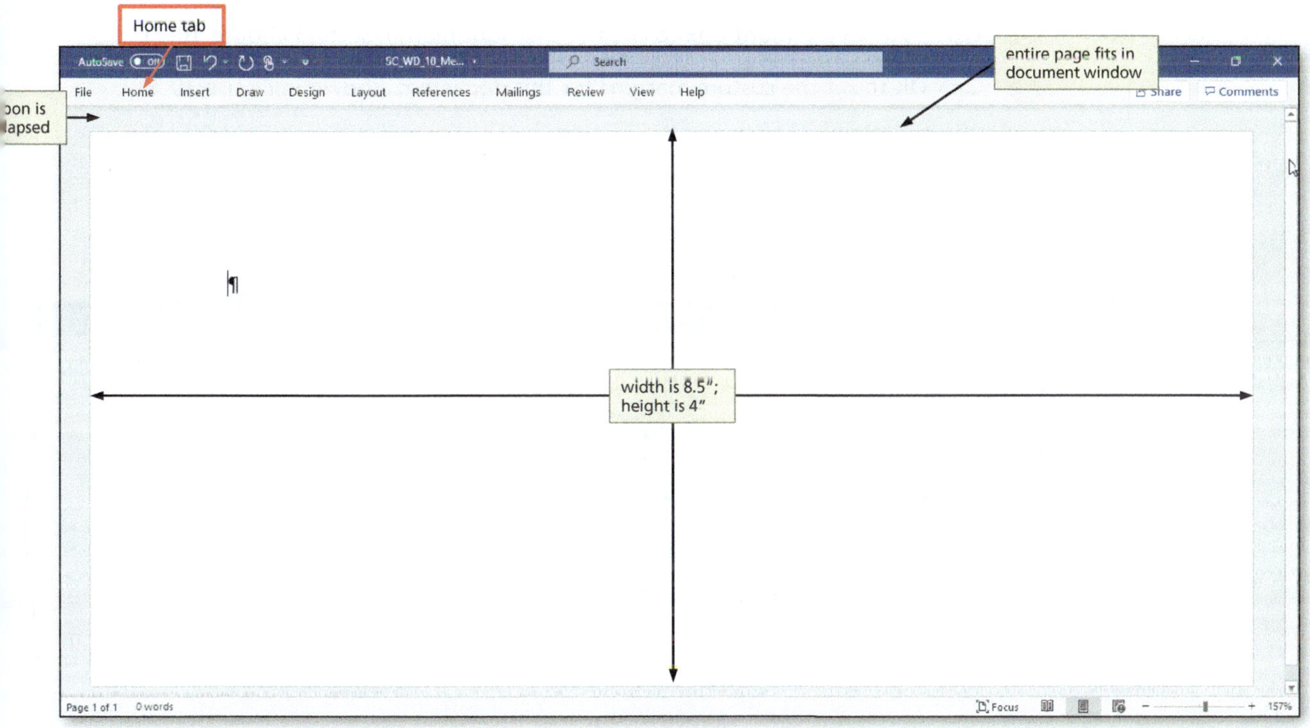

Figure 10–6

To Expand the Ribbon

After you verify that the entire form will fit in the document window, you should expand the ribbon so that you can see the groups while creating the online form. The following steps expand the ribbon.

1. Click Home on the collapsed ribbon to expand the Home tab.
2. Click the 'Pin the ribbon' button on the expanded Home tab to restore the ribbon.

Q&A

Can I also double-click Home (or any other tab) on the collapsed ribbon to expand the ribbon?
Yes.

BTW

Touch Mode Differences

The Office and Windows interfaces may vary if you are using Touch mode. For this reason, you might notice that the function or appearance of your touch screen differs slightly from this module's presentation.

To Set Custom Margins

Recall that Word is preset to use 1-inch top, bottom, left, and right margins. To maximize the space for the contents of the form, this module sets the left and right margins to .5 inches, the top margin to .25 inches, and the bottom margin to 0 inches. The following steps set custom margins.

1. Display the Layout tab. Click the Margins button (Layout tab | Page Setup group) to display the Margins gallery.
2. Click Custom Margins in the Margins gallery to display the Margins sheet in the Page Setup dialog box.
3. Type `.25` in the Top box (Page Setup dialog box) to change the top margin setting.
4. Type `0` (zero) in the Bottom box to change the bottom margin setting.

Q&A

Why set the bottom margin to zero?

This allows you to place form contents at the bottom of the page, if necessary.

5. Type `.5` in the Left box to change the left margin setting.
6. Type `.5` in the Right box to change the right margin setting (Figure 10–7).
7. Click OK to set the custom margins for this document (shown in Figure 10–8).

Q&A

What if Word displays a dialog box indicating margins are outside the printable area?

Click the Ignore button because this is an online form that is not intended for printing.

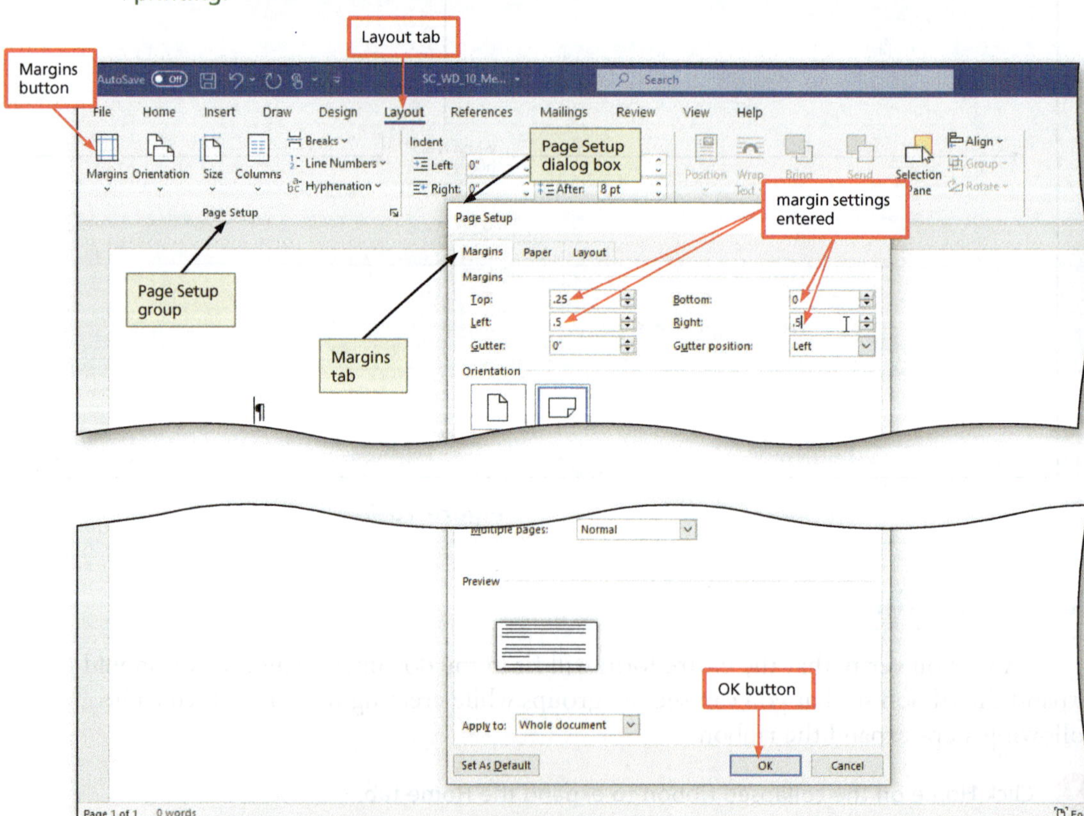

Figure 10–7

To Change the Theme Colors and Theme Fonts

The following steps change the document theme colors to Blue Green and the theme fonts to Tw Cen MT.

1. Display the Design tab. Click the Colors button (Design tab | Document Formatting group) and then click Blue Green in the Colors gallery to change the theme colors.
2. Click the Fonts button (Design tab | Document Formatting group) and then scroll through the Fonts gallery to display the Tw Cen MT font set (Figure 10–8).
3. Click 'Tw Cen MT' in the Fonts gallery to change the font set.
4. If necessary, change the font size to 11 point.

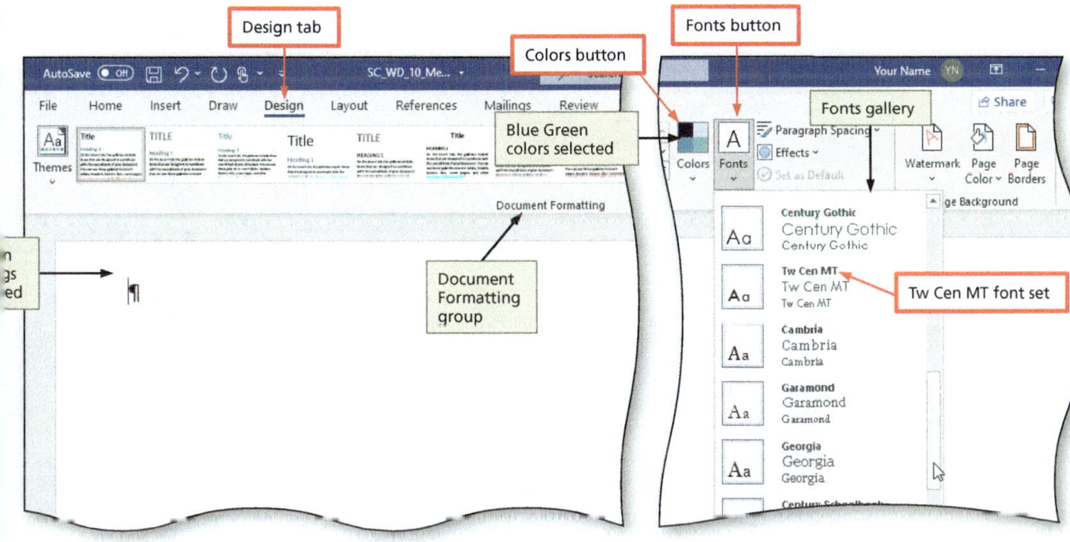

Figure 10–8

To Add a Page Color

The following steps add a page color. **Why?** This online form uses a shade of teal for the page color (background color) so that the form is more visually appealing.

1.
- Display the Design tab. Click the Page Color button (Design tab | Page Background group) to display the Page Color gallery.
- Point to 'Teal, Accent 3, Lighter 40%' (seventh color in the fourth row) in the Page Color gallery to display a Live Preview of the selected background color (Figure 10–9).

Experiment

- Point to various colors in the Page Color gallery and watch the page color change in the document window.

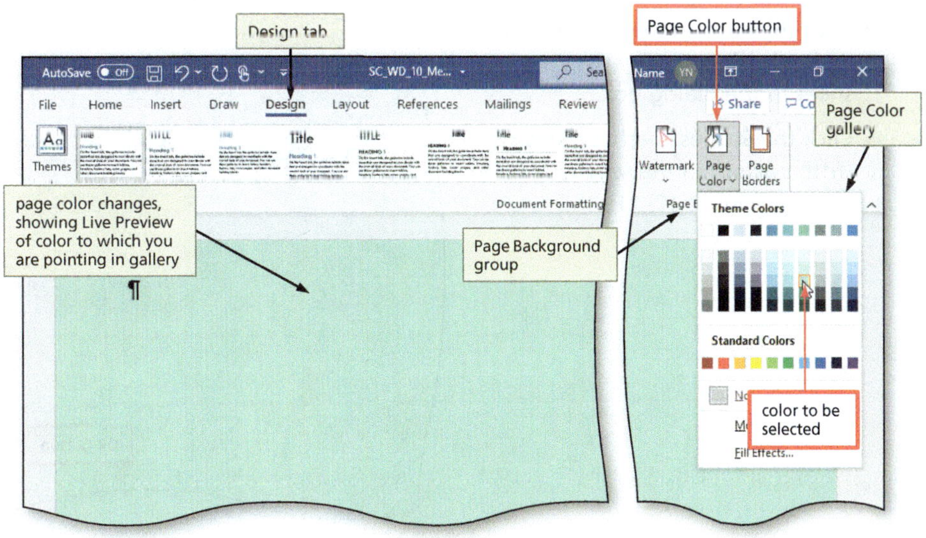

Figure 10–9

2

- Click 'Teal, Accent 3, Lighter 40%' to change the page color to the selected color.

Q&A **Do page colors print?**
When you change the page color, it appears only on the screen. Changing the page color does not affect a printed document.

To Apply a Pattern Fill Effect to a Page Color

When you changed the page color in the previous steps, Word placed a solid color on the screen. The following steps add a pattern to the page color. **Why?** For this online form, the solid background color is a little too bold. To soften the color, you can add a pattern to it.

1

- Click the Page Color button (Design tab | Page Background group) to display the Page Color gallery (Figure 10–10).

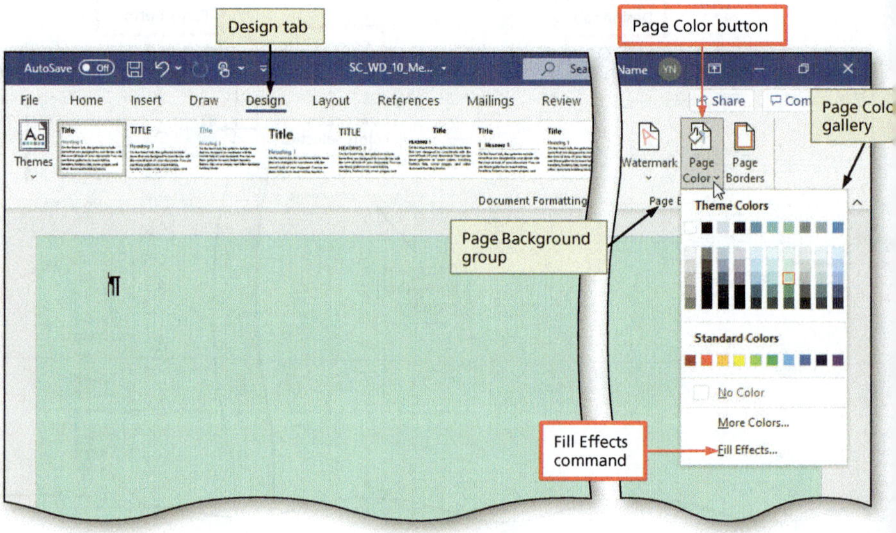

Figure 10–10

2

- Click Fill Effects in the Page Color gallery to display the Fill Effects dialog box.
- Click the Pattern tab (Fill Effects dialog box) to display the Pattern sheet in the dialog box.
- Click the Stripes: Slashes pattern (fifth pattern in the second row) to select it (Figure 10–11).

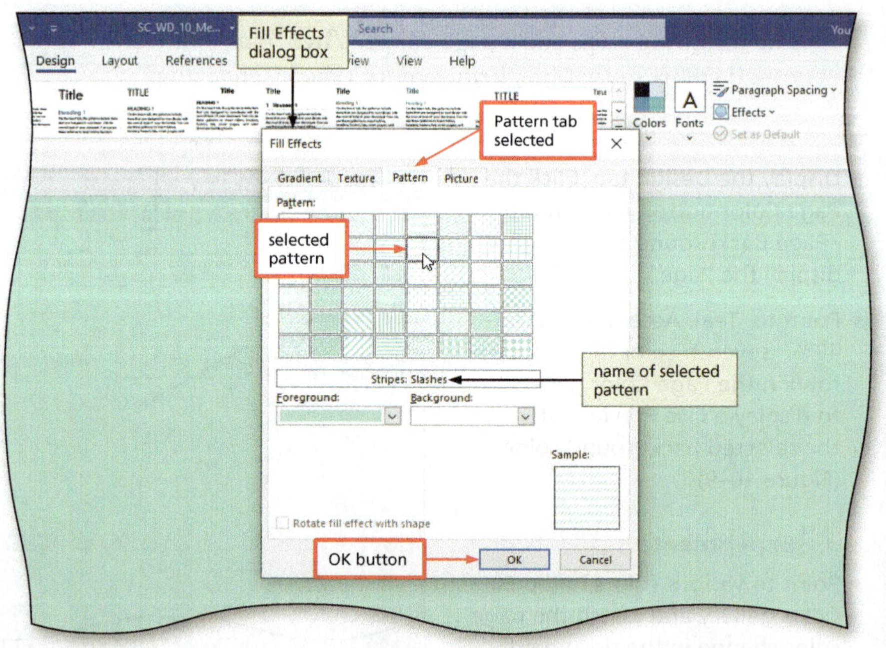

Figure 10–11

3

- Click OK to add the selected pattern to the current page color (Figure 10–12).

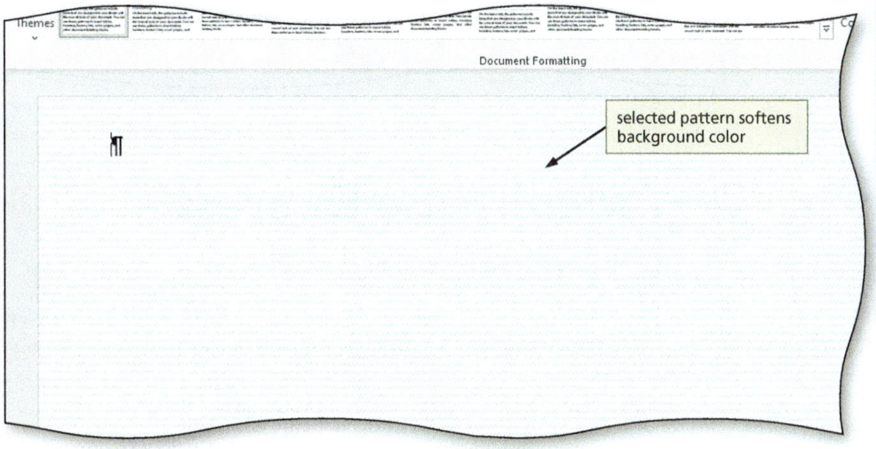

Figure 10–12

Enter Content in the Online Form

The next step in creating the online form in this module is to enter the text, graphics, and content controls in the document. The following sections describe this process.

BTW

Highlighting Text

You can highlight text in online documents. If you click the 'Text Highlight Color' button (Home tab | Font group) without first selecting any text, the highlighter remains active until you turn it off. This allows you to continue selecting text that you want to be highlighted. To deactivate the highlighter, click the 'Text Highlight Color' button (Home tab | Font group) again, click the 'Text Highlight Color' arrow (Home tab | Font group), and then click Stop Highlighting on the Text Highlight Color menu, or press ESC.

To Enter and Format Text

The following steps enter the text at the top of the online form.

1. Type `Meal Time Express` and then press ENTER.
2. Type `Fresh, Delicious Meals Delivered to Your Door` and then press ENTER.
3. Type `Consultation Request` and then press ENTER.
4. Type `Fill in the form below, save your form, and email it to contact@mealte.net; a team member will reply within 72 hours.` and then press ENTER.

Q&A **Why did the email address change color?**
In this document theme, the color for a hyperlink is a shade of green. When you pressed ENTER, Word automatically formatted the hyperlink in this color.

5. Format the characters on the first line to 28-point Berlin Sans FB Demi font with the color of Aqua, Accent 1, Darker 25%. (Ensure that the spacing after this paragraph is 8 point.)
6. Format the characters on the second line to the color of Blue-Gray, Accent 5, Darker 50%. (Ensure that the spacing after this paragraph is 8 point.)
7. Format the characters on the third line to 16-point bold font with the color of Blue-Gray, Accent 5, Darker 25% and center the text on the line. Remove space before and after this paragraph (spacing before and after should be 0 point).
8. Center the text on the fourth line and increase the spacing after this line to 12 point.
9. Be sure that the font size of text entered on the second and fourth lines is 11 point.

10 Position the insertion point on the blank line below the text (Figure 10–13). (Ensure that the font size is 11 point at the location of the insertion point.)

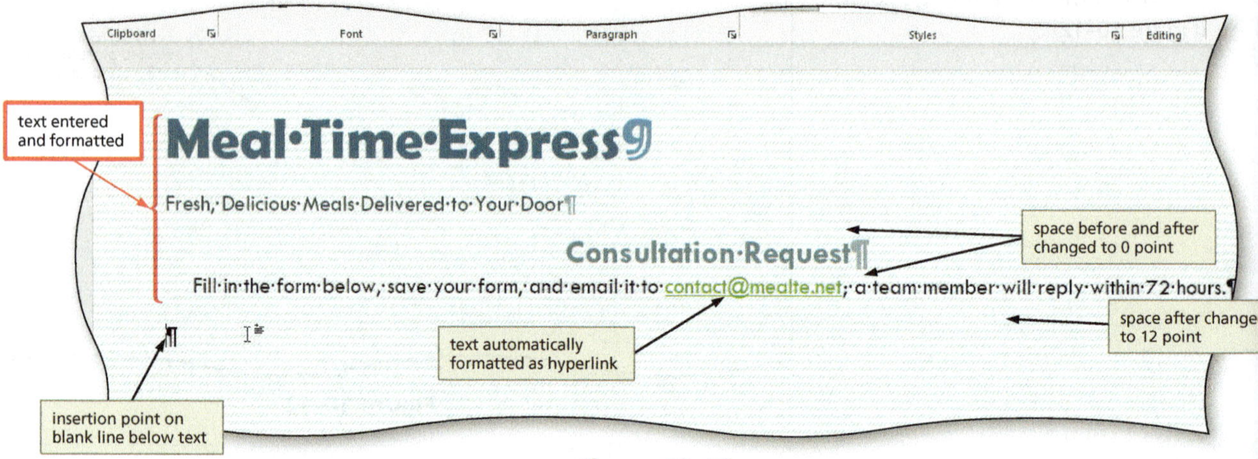

Figure 10–13

To Insert an Icon

Word includes a library of icons that you can insert in documents. The following steps insert an icon that shows an image of a fork and knife in the document. **Why?** You want an image in the form to give it visual appeal.

1

- Display the Insert tab.
- Click the Icons button (Insert tab | Illustrations group) to display the Insert Icons dialog box.
- Scroll through the category list near the top of the window, if necessary, click the 'Food And Drinks' link , if necessary scroll through the list of Food and Drinks icons, and then click the fork and knife icon to select the icon (Figure 10–14).

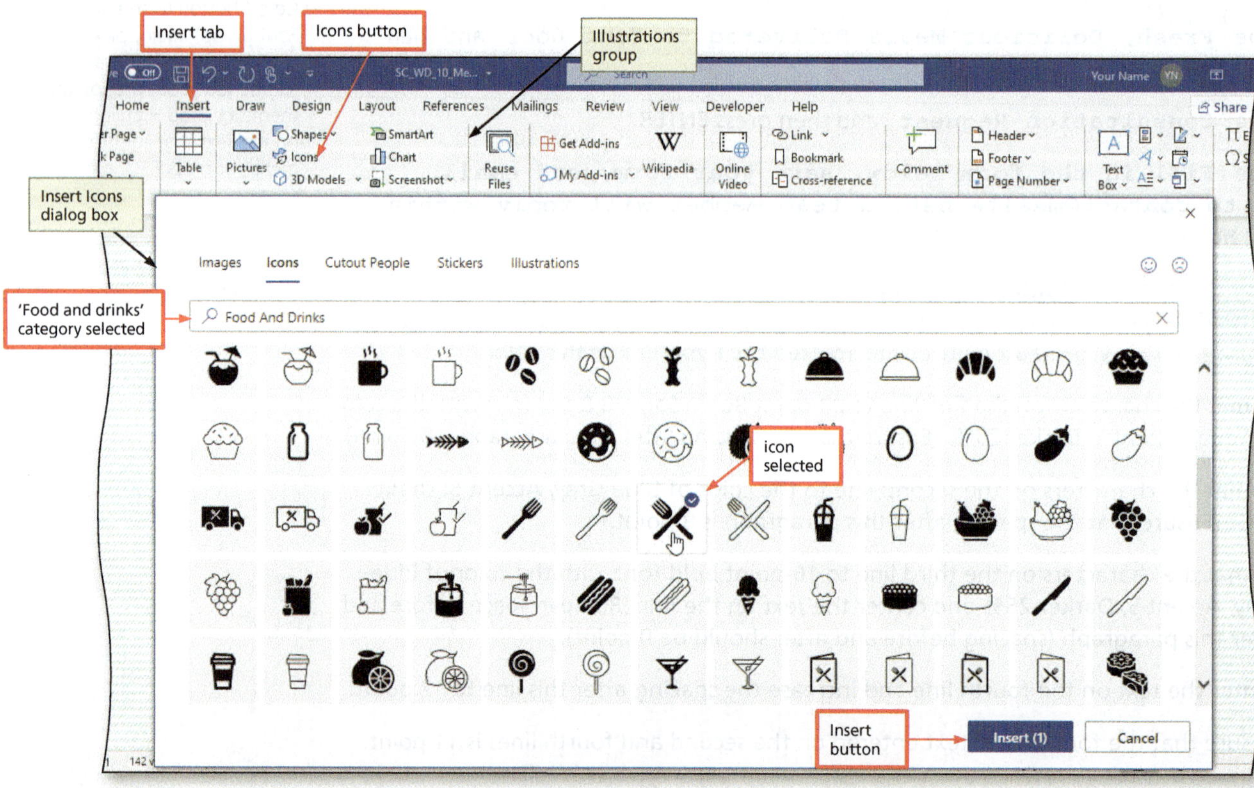

Figure 10–14

Q&A

What if my dialog box does not contain the same category or icon?
Select any appropriate icon in the dialog box.

What if the Icons button is not available in my version of Word?
A similar image is located in the Data Files. You can click the Pictures button (Insert tab | Illustrations group), click This Device, navigate to the file called Support_WD_10_Fork_and_Spoon.png in the Data Files, and then click the Insert button (Insert Picture dialog box) to insert the image. Change the height of the inserted image to 1", change the width to .73", and skip Step 2. Note that your image will look similar to, but not exactly like, the figures in this module.

Can I select multiple icons at once in the open dialog box?
Yes, all selected icons will be inserted in the document.

2

- Click the Insert button (Insert Icons dialog box) to place the selected icon in the document to the left of the insertion point (Figure 10–15).
- If necessary, use the Height and Width boxes (Graphics Format tab | Size group) to change these values to 1".

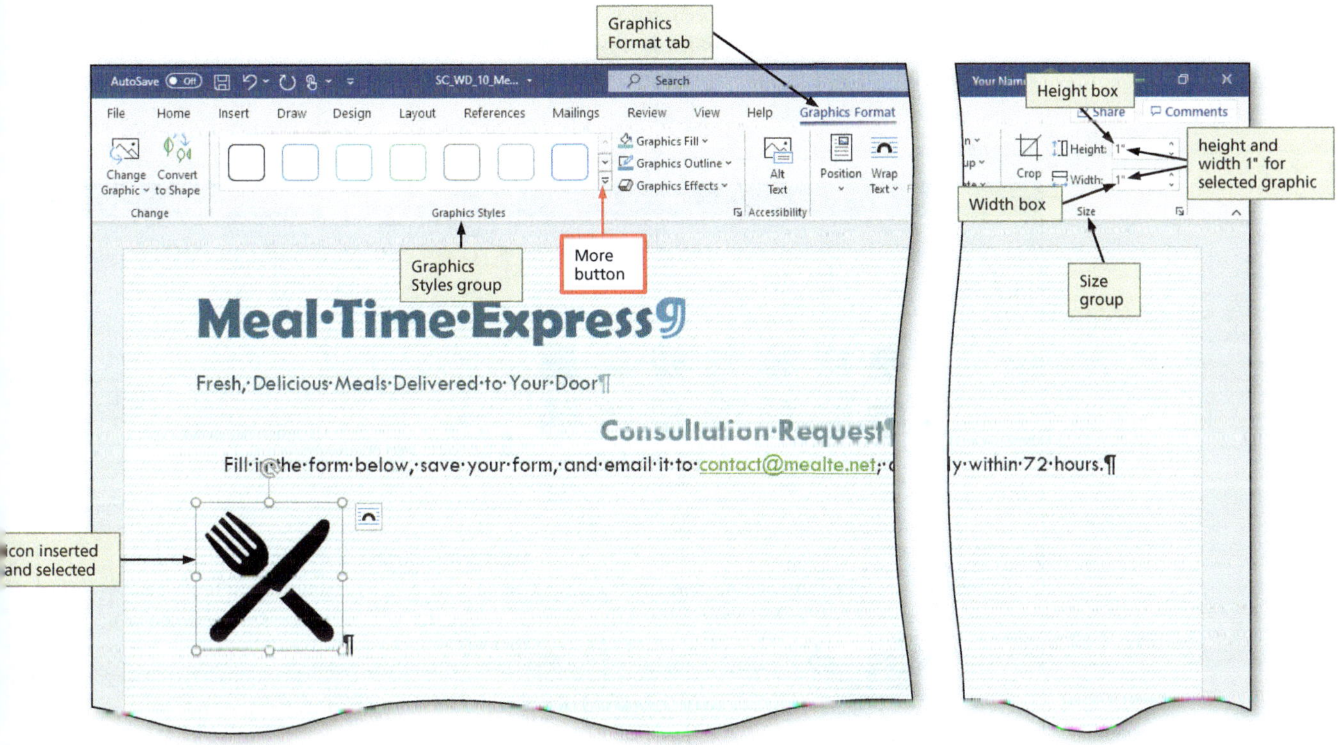

Figure 10–15

Q&A

What if my icon is inserted in a location different from Figure 10–15?
You will move the icon in a later step.

To Apply a Graphics Style

Word provides a variety of predefined styles you can apply to graphics. The following steps apply a graphics style to the selected icon.

1. With the icon still selected, click the More button (Graphics Format tab | Graphics Styles group) (shown in Figure 10–15) to display the Graphics Styles gallery.

2. Point to 'Colored Fill - Accent 1, Dark 1 Outline' in the Graphics Styles gallery to display a Live Preview of the selected graphics style applied to the icon in the document window (Figure 10–16).

Experiment

- If you are using a mouse, point to various styles in the Graphics Styles gallery and watch the graphics style change in the document window.

3. Click 'Colored Fill - Accent 1, Dark 1 Outline' in the Graphics Styles gallery to apply the selected graphics style to the selected icon.

Q&A **What if my version of Word did not have the Icons button and I inserted a picture from the Data Files instead?**
Click the Color button (Picture Format tab | Adjust group) to display the Color gallery and then click 'Aqua, Accent color 1, Light' in the Recolor area to change the color. Note that your image will look similar to, but not exactly like, the figures in this module.

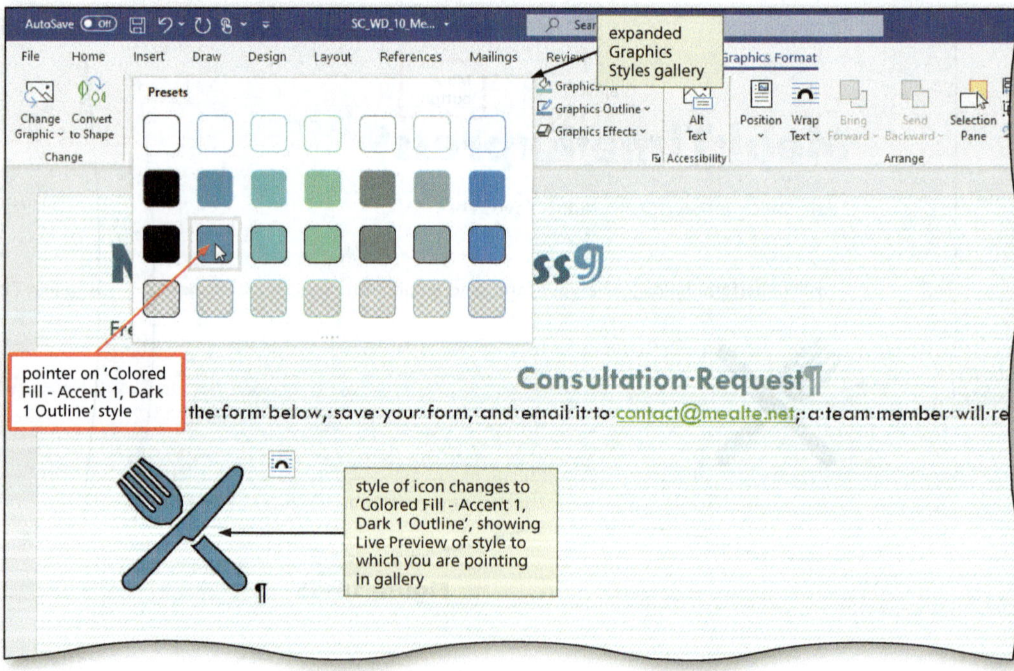

Figure 10–16

To Format a Graphic's Text Wrapping

Word inserted the fork and knife icon as an inline graphic, that is, as part of the current paragraph. In this online form, the graphic should be positioned to the right of the company name (shown in Figure 10–1 at the beginning of this module).

Thus, the graphic should be a floating graphic instead of an inline graphic. The text in the online form should not wrap around the graphic. Thus, the graphic should float in front of the text. The following steps change the graphic's text wrapping to In Front of Text.

1. With the graphic selected, click the Layout Options button attached to the graphic to display the Layout Options gallery (Figure 10–17).
2. Click 'In Front of Text' in the Layout Options gallery to change the graphic from inline to floating with the selected wrapping style.
3. Click the Close button in the Layout Options gallery to close the gallery.

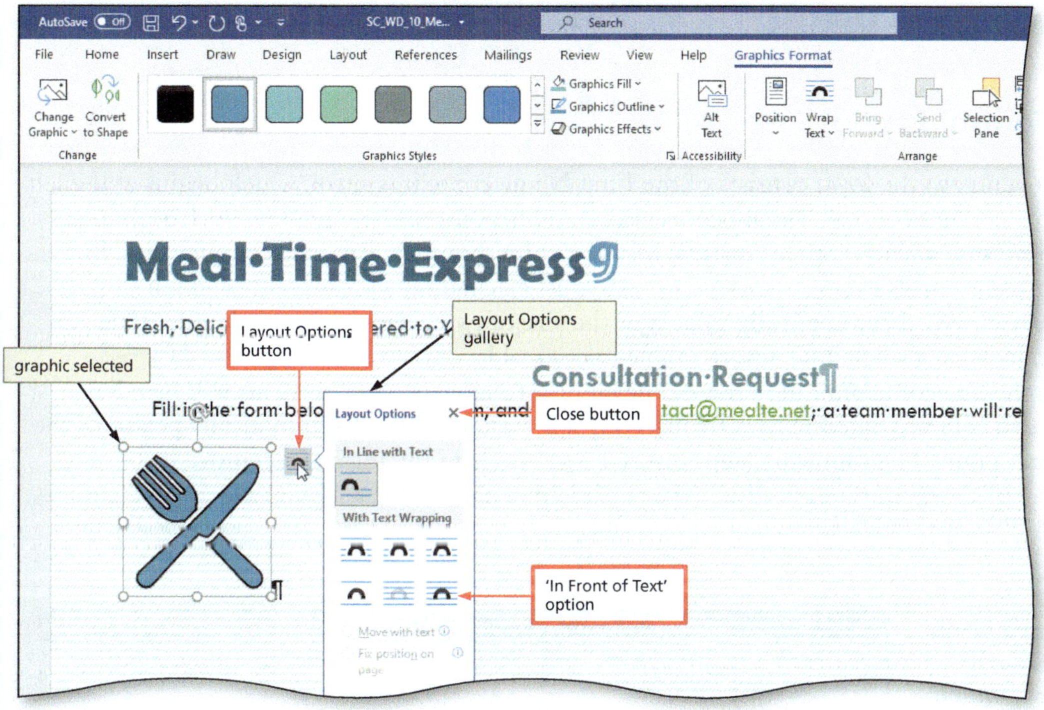

Figure 10–17

BTW
Ordering Graphics
If you have multiple graphics displaying on the screen and would like them to overlap, you can change their stacking order by using the Bring Forward and Send Backward arrows (Picture Format tab | Arrange group). The 'Bring to Front' command on the Bring Forward menu displays the selected object at the top of the stack, and the 'Send to Back' command on the Send Backward menu displays the selected object at the bottom of the stack. The Bring Forward and Send Backward commands each move the graphic forward or backward one layer in the stack. These commands also are available through the shortcut menu that is displayed when you right click a graphic.

To Move a Graphic

The final step associated with the graphic is to move it so that it is positioned on the right side of the online form. The following steps move a graphic.

1. If necessary, scroll to display the top of the form in the document window.
2. Drag the graphic to the location shown in Figure 10–18.

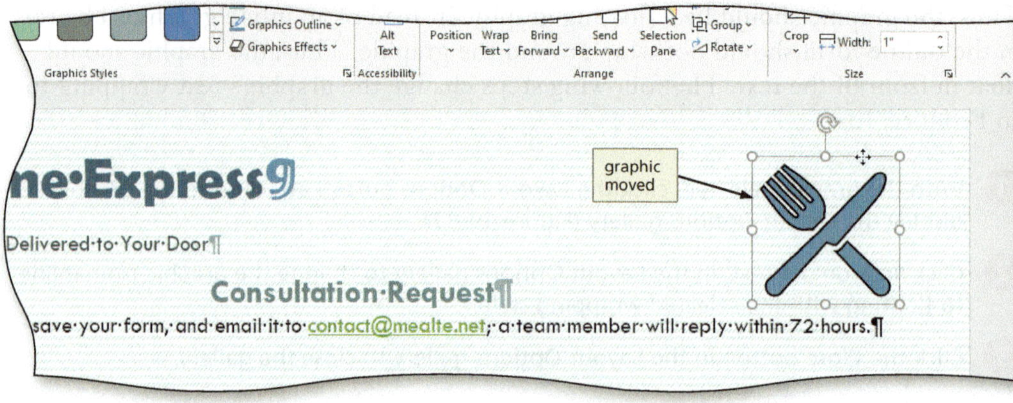

Figure 10–18

To Use a Table to Control Layout

The first line of data entry in the form consists of the First Name content control, which begins at the left margin, and the Last Name content control, which begins at the center point of the same line. At first glance, you might decide to set a tab stop at each content control location. This, however, can be a complex task. For example, to place two content controls evenly across a row, you must calculate the location of each tab stop. If you insert a 2 × 1 table instead, Word automatically calculates the size of two evenly spaced columns. Thus, to enter multiple content controls on a single line, insert a table to control layout.

In this online form, the line containing the First Name and Last Name content controls will be a 2 × 1 table, that is, a table with two columns and one row. By inserting a 2 × 1 table, Word automatically positions the second column at the center point. The following steps insert a 2 × 1 table in the form and remove its border. **Why?** When you insert a table, Word automatically surrounds it with a border. Because you are using the tables solely to control layout, you do not want the table borders visible.

1

- Position the insertion point where the table should be inserted, in this case, on the blank paragraph mark below the text on the form.
- Display the Insert tab. Click the Table button (Insert tab | Tables group) to display the Table gallery (Figure 10–19).

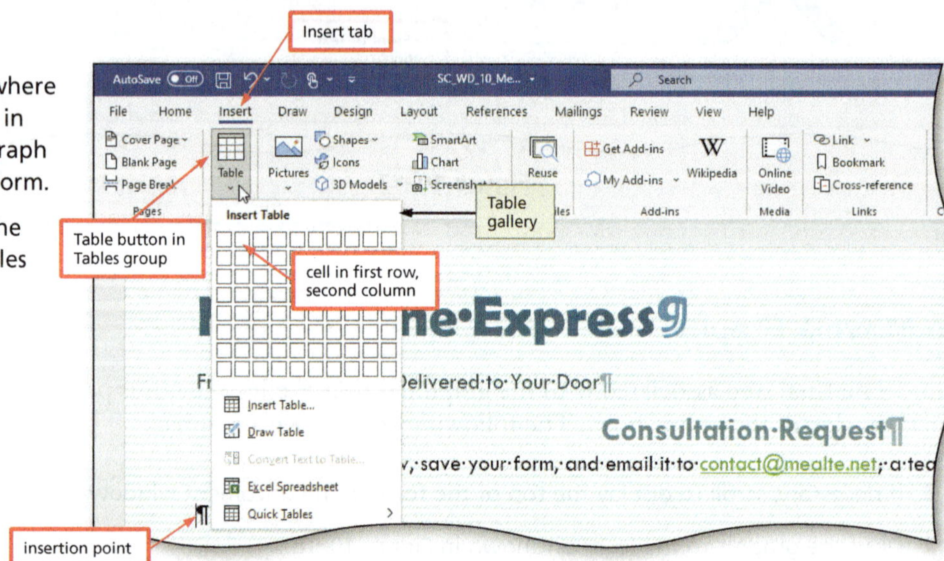

Figure 10–19

2

- Click the cell in the first row and second column of the grid to insert an empty 2 × 1 table at the location of the insertion point.
- Select the table.

Q&A **How do I select a table?**
Point somewhere in the table and then click the table move handle that appears in the upper-left corner of the table (or, if using touch, tap the Select button (Layout tab | Table group) and then tap Select Table on the Select menu).

- If necessary, display the Table Design tab.
- Click the Borders arrow (Table Design tab | Borders group) to display the Borders gallery (Figure 10–20).

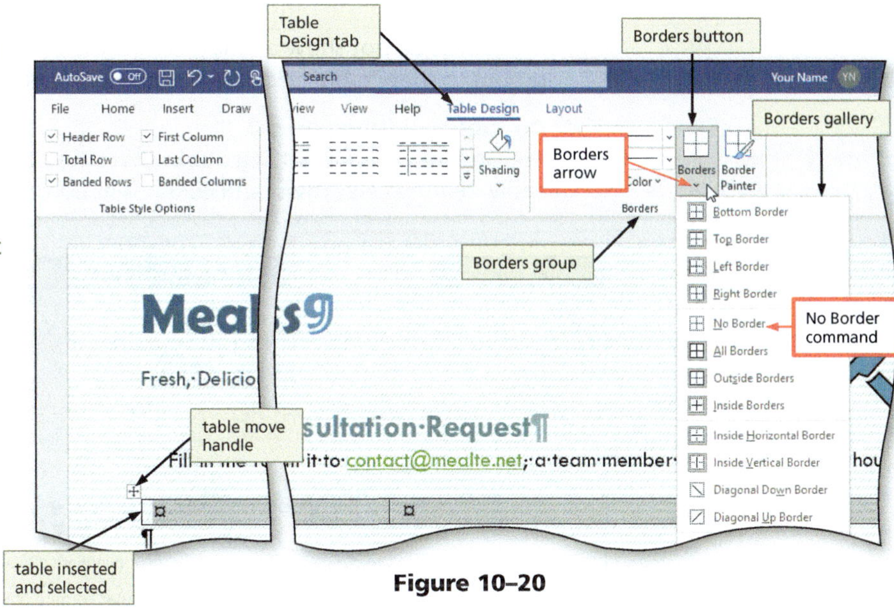

Figure 10–20

3

- Click No Border in the Borders gallery to remove the borders from the table.

4

- Click the first cell of the table to remove the selection (Figure 10–21).

Q&A **My screen does not display the end-of-cell marks. Why not?**
Display formatting marks by clicking the 'Show/Hide ¶' button (Home tab | Paragraph group).

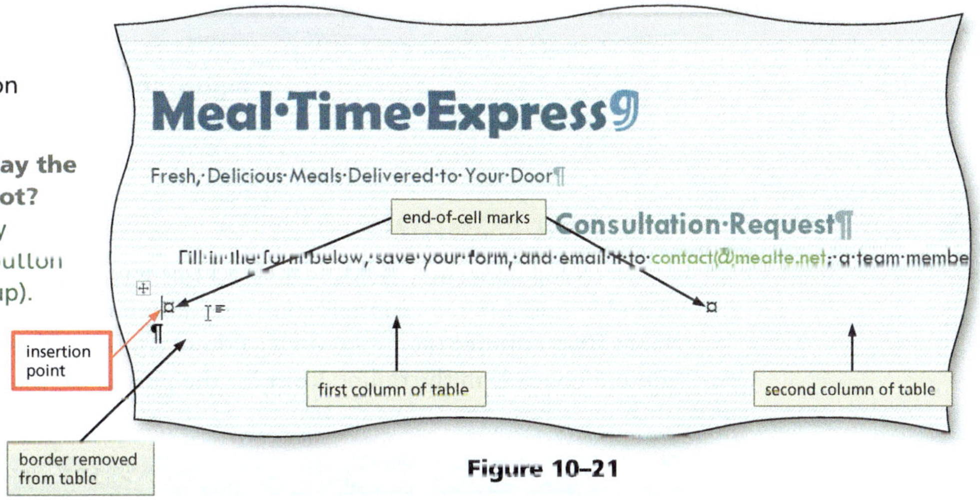

Figure 10–21

Other Ways

1. Click Table button (Insert tab | Tables group), click Insert Table in Table gallery, enter number of columns and rows (Insert Table dialog box), click OK

To Show Table Gridlines

When you remove the borders from a table, you no longer can see the individual cells in the table. To help identify the location of cells, you can display **gridlines**, which are nonprinting lines that show cell boundaries in a table. The following steps show gridlines.

1 If necessary, position the insertion point in a table cell.

2 Display the Layout tab.

3 If gridlines do not show already, click the View Gridlines button (Layout tab | Table group) to show table gridlines on the screen (Figure 10–22).

Q&A

Do table gridlines print?
No. Gridlines are formatting marks that show only on the screen. Gridlines help users easily identify cells, rows, and columns in borderless tables.

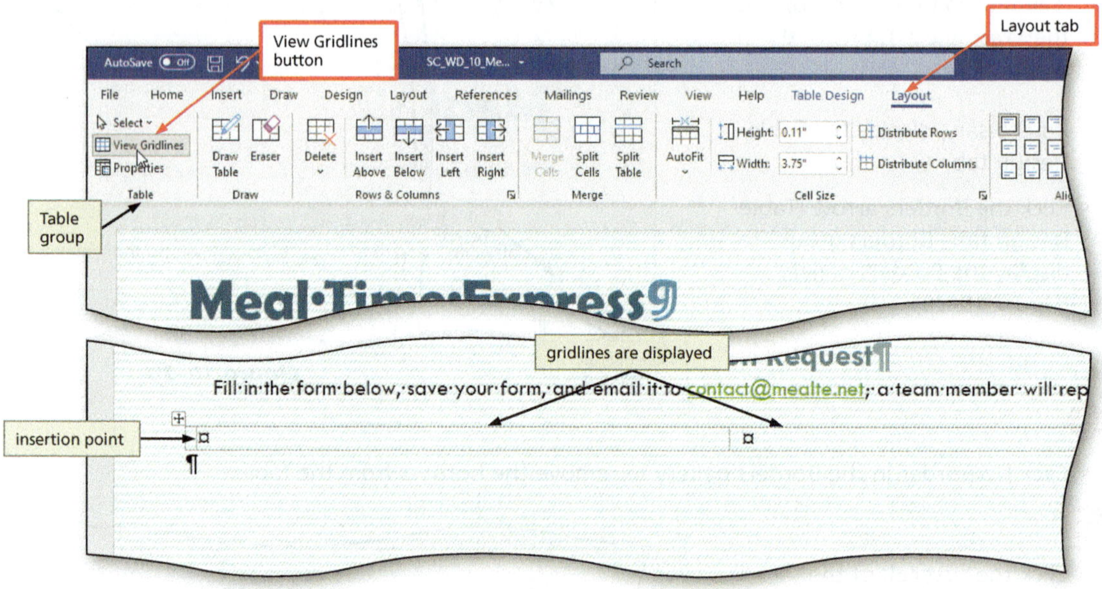

Figure 10–22

Content Controls

To add data entry fields in a Word form, you insert content controls. Word includes nine different content controls you can insert in your online forms. Table 10–1 outlines the use of each of these controls. The following sections insert content controls in the online form for the project in this module.

Table 10–1 Content Controls

Type	Icon	Use
Building Block Gallery		User selects a built-in building block from the gallery.
Check Box		User selects or deselects a check box.
Combo Box		User types text entry or selects one item from a list of choices.
Date Picker		User interacts with a calendar to select a date or types a date in the placeholder.
Drop-Down List		User selects one item from a list of choices.
Picture		User inserts a drawing, a shape, a picture, image, or a SmartArt graphic.
Plain Text	Aa	User enters text, which may not be formatted.
Repeating Section		Users can instruct Word to create a duplicate of the content control.
Rich Text	Aa	User enters text and, if desired, may format the entered text.

Consider This

How do you determine the correct content control to use for each data entry field?

For each data entry field, decide which content control best maps to the type of data the field will contain. The field specifications for the fields in this module's online form are listed below:

- The First Name, Last Name, and Other Meal Plan Types data entry fields will contain text. The first two will be plain text content controls and the last will be a rich text content control.
- The Delivery Day data entry field must contain one of these four values: Wednesday, Thursday, Friday, Saturday (additional fee). This field will be a drop-down list content control.
- The Variety Plan, Mediterranean Plan, Gluten-Free Plan, Vegetarian Plan, and Other Meal Plan Type data entry fields will be check boxes that the user can select or deselect.
- The Servings per Week data entry field can contain one of these three values: Single Plan, Double Plan, and Family Plan. In addition, users should be able to enter their own value in this data entry field if none of these three values is applicable. A combo box content control will be used for this field.
- The Today's Date data entry field should contain only a valid date value. Thus, this field will be a date picker content control.

To Show the Developer Tab

To create a form in Word, you use buttons on the Developer tab. The following steps show the Developer tab on the ribbon. **Why?** Because it allows you to perform more advanced tasks not required by everyday Word users, the Developer tab does not appear on the ribbon by default.

1

- Open Backstage view and, if necessary, scroll to display the Options command (Figure 10–23).

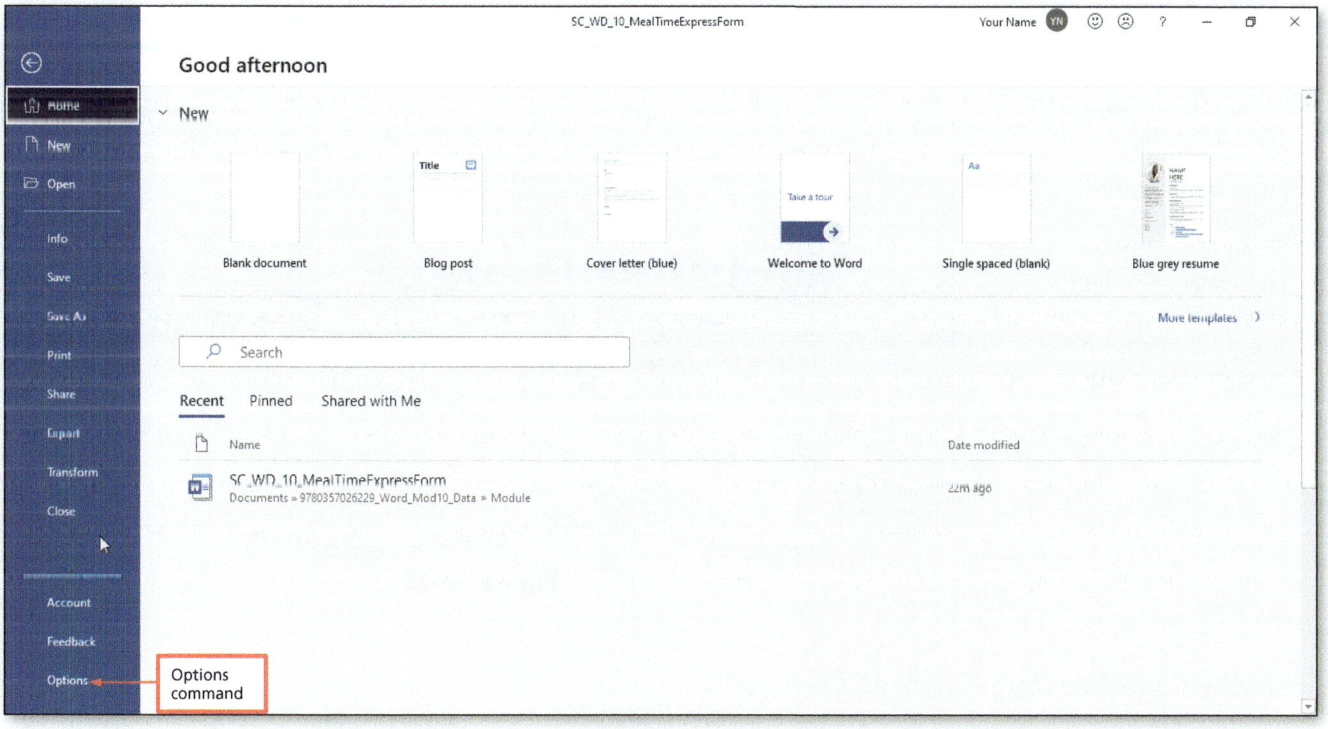

Figure 10–23

2

- Click Options in the left pane of Backstage view to display the Word Options dialog box.
- Click Customize Ribbon in the left pane (Word Options dialog box) to display associated options in the right pane.
- Place a check mark in the Developer check box in the Main Tabs list (Figure 10–24).

Q&A **What are the plus symbols to the left of each tab name?**
Clicking the plus symbol expands to show the groups.

Can I show or hide any tab in this list?
Yes. Place a check mark in the check box to show the tab, or remove the check mark to hide the tab.

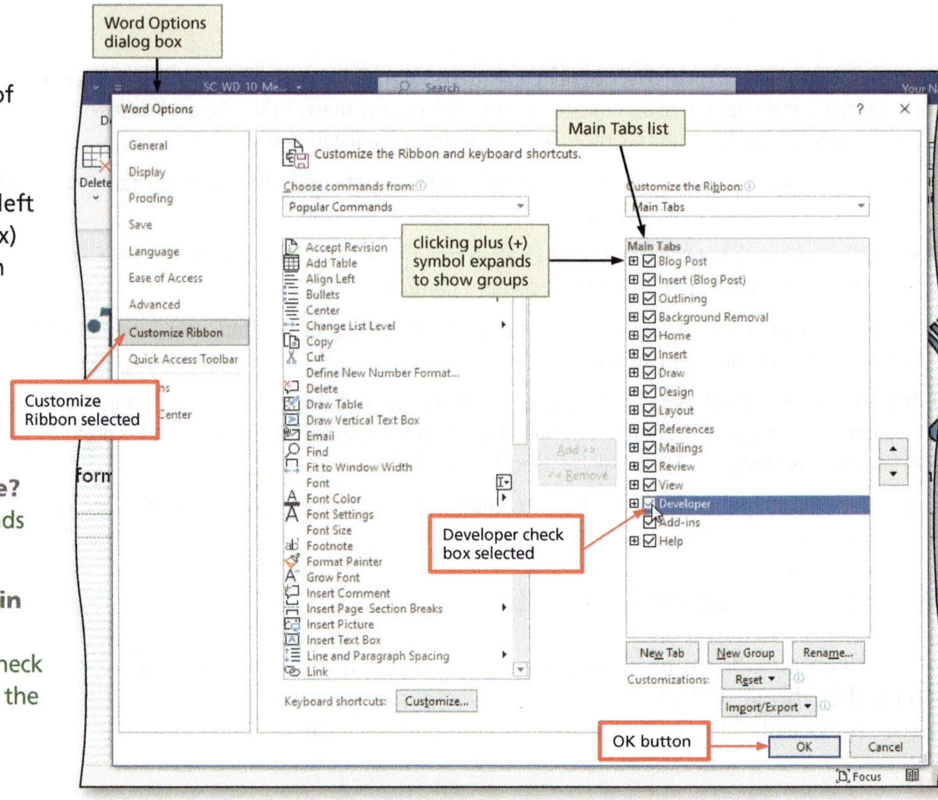

Figure 10–24

3

- Click OK to show the Developer tab on the ribbon (Figure 10–25).

Q&A **How do I remove the Developer tab from the ribbon?**
Follow these same steps, except remove the check mark from the Developer check box (Word Options dialog box).

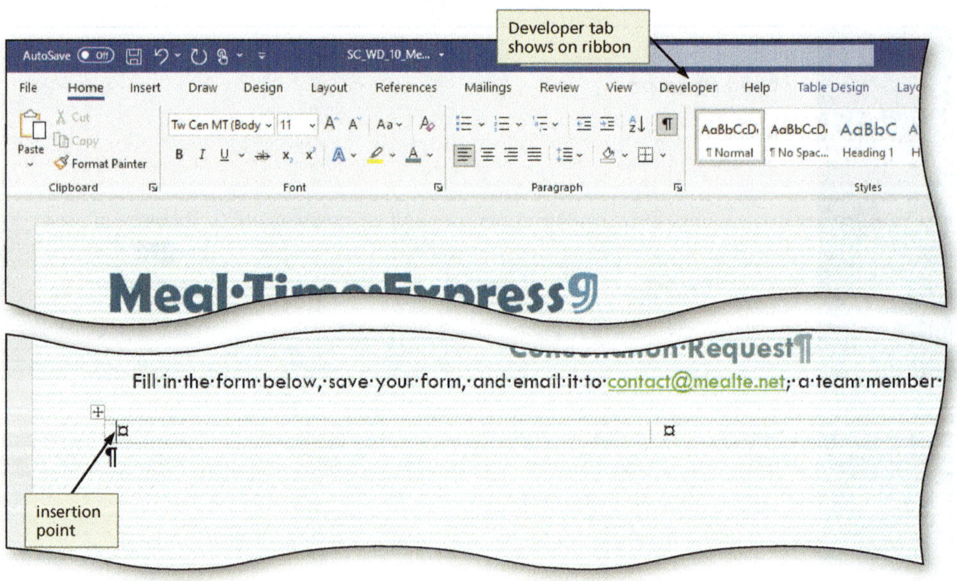

Figure 10–25

To Insert a Plain Text Content Control

The first item that a user enters in the Consultation Request is the user's first name. Because the first name entry contains text that the user should not format, this online form uses a plain text content control for the First Name data entry field. The following steps enter the label, First Name:, followed by a plain text content control. **Why?** The label, First Name:, is displayed to the left of the plain text content control. To improve readability, a colon or some other character often separates a label from the content control.

1

- With the insertion point in the first cell of the table as shown in Figure 10–25, type `First Name:` as the label for the content control.
- Press SPACEBAR (Figure 10–26).

Figure 10–26

2

- Display the Developer tab.
- Click the 'Plain Text Content Control' button (Developer tab | Controls group) to insert a plain text content control at the location of the insertion point (Figure 10–27).

Q&A **Is the plain text content control similar to the content controls that I have used in templates installed with Word, such as in the letter, memo, and resume templates?**
Yes. The content controls you insert through the Developer tab have the same functionality as the content controls in the templates installed with Word.

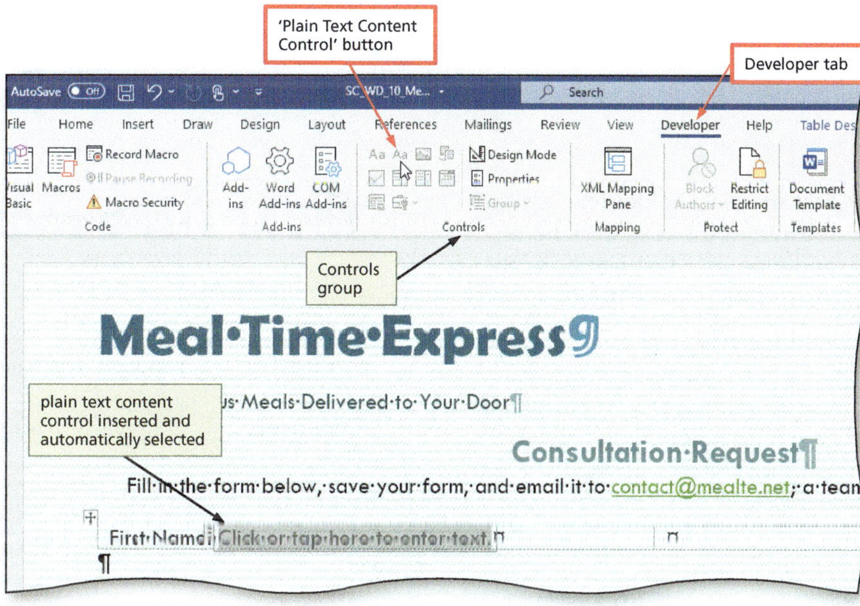

Figure 10–27

To Use Design Mode to Edit Placeholder Text

A content control displays **placeholder text**, which is default text that indicates where text can be typed in documents. The default placeholder text for a plain text content control is the instruction, Click or tap here to enter text. The following steps edit the placeholder text for the plain text content control just entered. **Why?** You can change the wording in the placeholder text so that it is more instructional or applicable to the current form.

1

- With the plain text content control selected (shown in Figure 10–27), click the Design Mode button (Developer tab | Controls group) to turn on Design mode, which displays tags at the beginning and ending of the placeholder text (Figure 10–28).

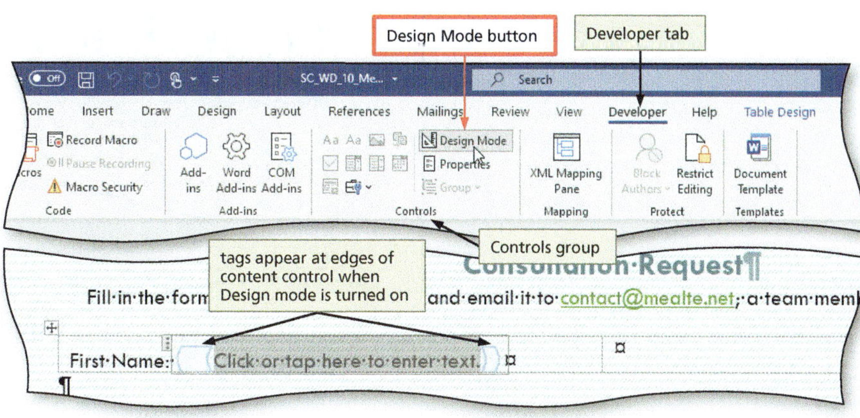

Figure 10–28

2

- Even if it already is selected, drag through the placeholder text, Click or tap here to enter text., because you want to edit the instruction (Figure 10–29).

Figure 10–29

3

- Edit the placeholder text so that it contains the text, Click here and type your first name., as the instruction (Figure 10–30).

Q&A **What if the placeholder text wraps to the next line?**
Because of the tags at each edge of the placeholder text, the entered text may wrap in the table cell. Once you turn off Design mode, the placeholder text should fit on a single line. If it does not, you can adjust the font size of the placeholder text to fit.

Figure 10–30

4

- Click the Design Mode button (Developer tab | Controls group) to turn off Design mode (Figure 10–31).

Q&A **What if I notice an error in the placeholder text?**
Follow these steps again to turn on Design mode, correct the error, and then turn off Design mode.

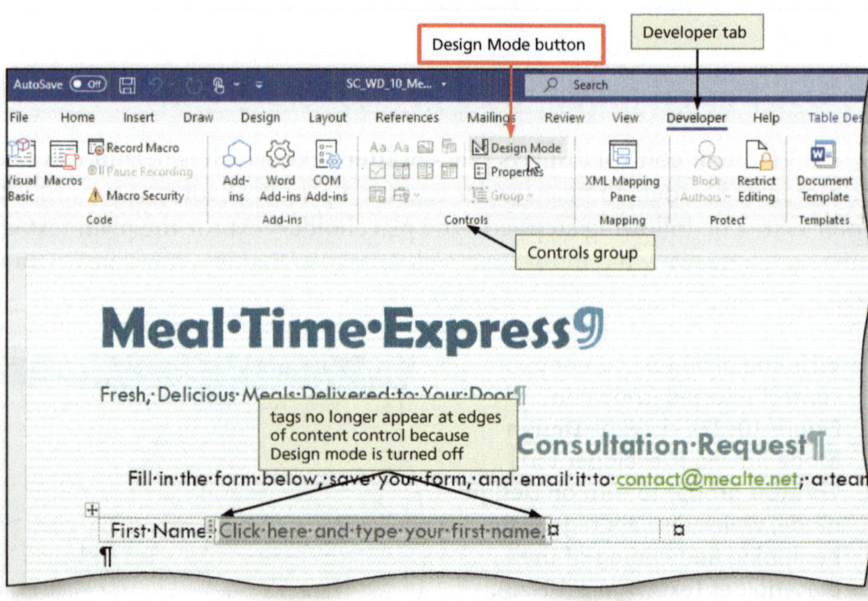

Figure 10–31

To Change the Properties of a Plain Text Content Control

You can change a variety of properties to customize content controls. The following steps change the properties of a plain text content control. **Why?** In this form, you assign a tag name to a content control for later identification. You also apply a style to the content control to define how text will look as a user types data or makes selections, and you lock the content control so that a user cannot delete the content control during the data entry process.

1

- With the content control selected, click the Properties button (Developer tab | Controls group) to display the Content Control Properties dialog box (Figure 10–32).

Q&A **How do I know the content control is selected?**
A selected content control is surrounded by an outline. Its placeholder text also may be shaded.

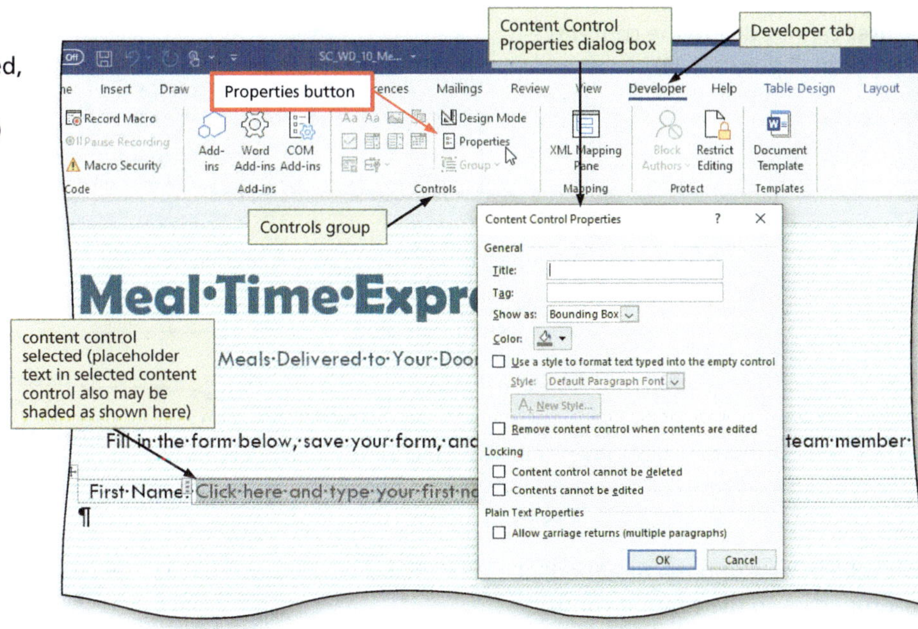

Figure 10–32

2

- Type **First Name** in the Tag text box (Content Control Properties dialog box).
- Place a check mark in the 'Use a style to format text typed into the empty control' check box so that the Style box becomes active.
- Click the Style arrow to display the Style list (Figure 10–33).

Q&A **Why leave the Title text box empty?**
When you click a content control in a preexisting Word template, the content control may display an identifier in its top-left corner. For templates that you create, you can instruct Word to display this identifier, called the Title, by changing the properties of the content control. In this form, you do not want the identifier to appear.

What is a bounding box?
A bounding box is a rectangle that surrounds the content control on the form. You can show content controls with a bounding box, with tags, or with no visible markings.

What if the Intense Emphasis style is not displayed in the Style list?
Close the Content Control Properties dialog box. Click the Styles Dialog Box Launcher to open the Styles pane, click the Options button in the Styles pane to display the Style Pane Options dialog box, click the 'Select styles to show' arrow and then click All Styles (Style Pane Options dialog box), click OK to close the dialog box, and then close the Styles pane. Repeat Steps 1 and 2 above.

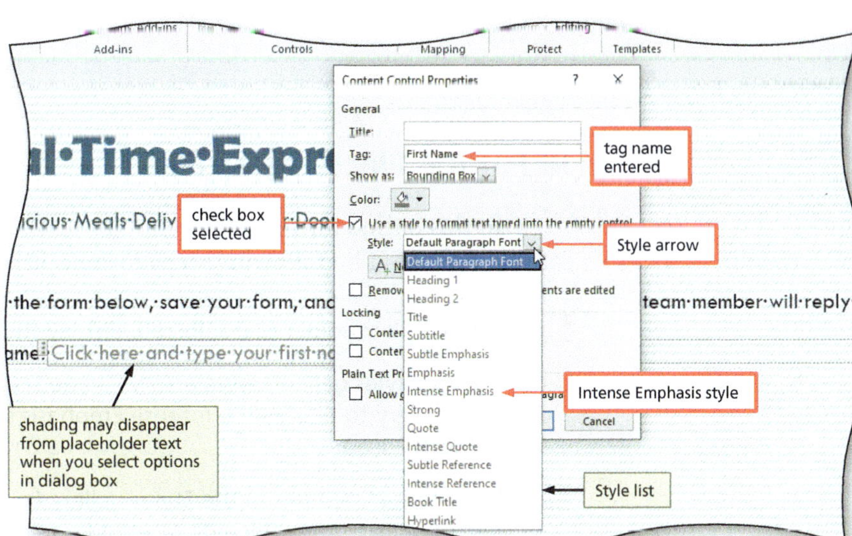

Figure 10–33

3

- Click Intense Emphasis to select the style for the content control.
- Place a check mark in the 'Content control cannot be deleted' check box so that the user cannot delete the content control (Figure 10–34).

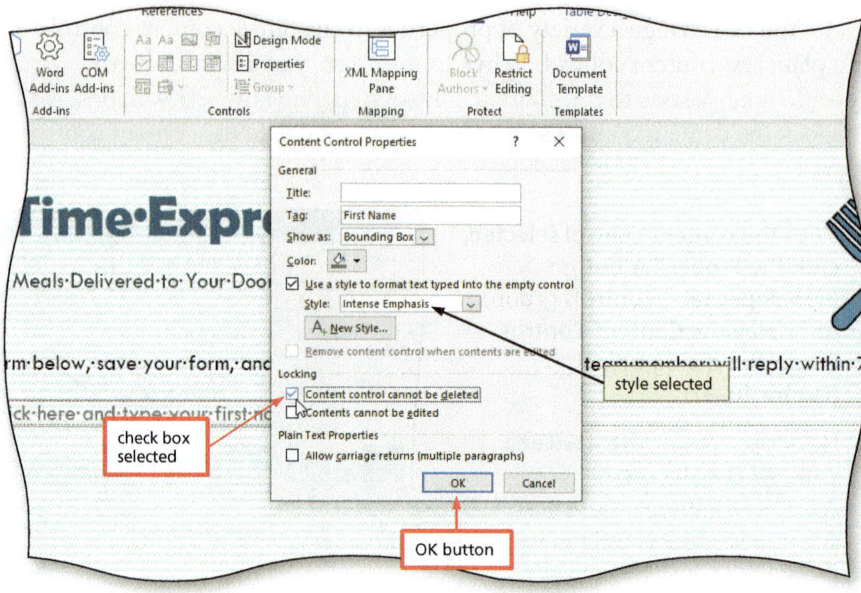

Figure 10–34

4

- Click OK to assign the modified properties to the content control (Figure 10–35).

Q&A

Why is the placeholder text not formatted to the selected style, Intense Emphasis, in this case?
When you apply a style to a content control, as described in these steps, the style is applied to the text the user types during the data entry process. To change the appearance of the placeholder text, apply a style using the Home tab as described in the next steps.

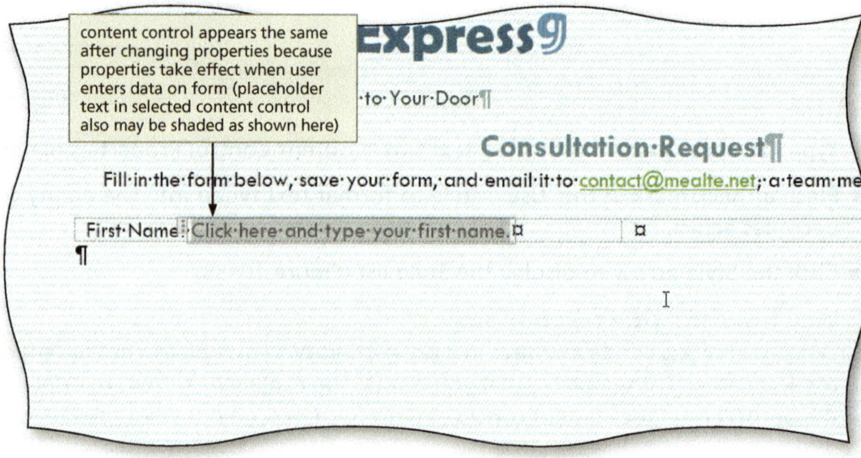

Figure 10–35

To Format Placeholder Text

In this online form, the placeholder text has the same style applied to it as the content control. The following steps format placeholder text.

1. With the placeholder text selected, display the Home tab.
2. Click the Styles gallery down arrow (Home tab | Styles group) to scroll through the Styles gallery to display the Intense Emphasis style or click the More button (Home tab | Styles group).
3. Click Intense Emphasis in the Styles gallery (even if it is selected already) to apply the selected style to the selected placeholder text (Figure 10–36).

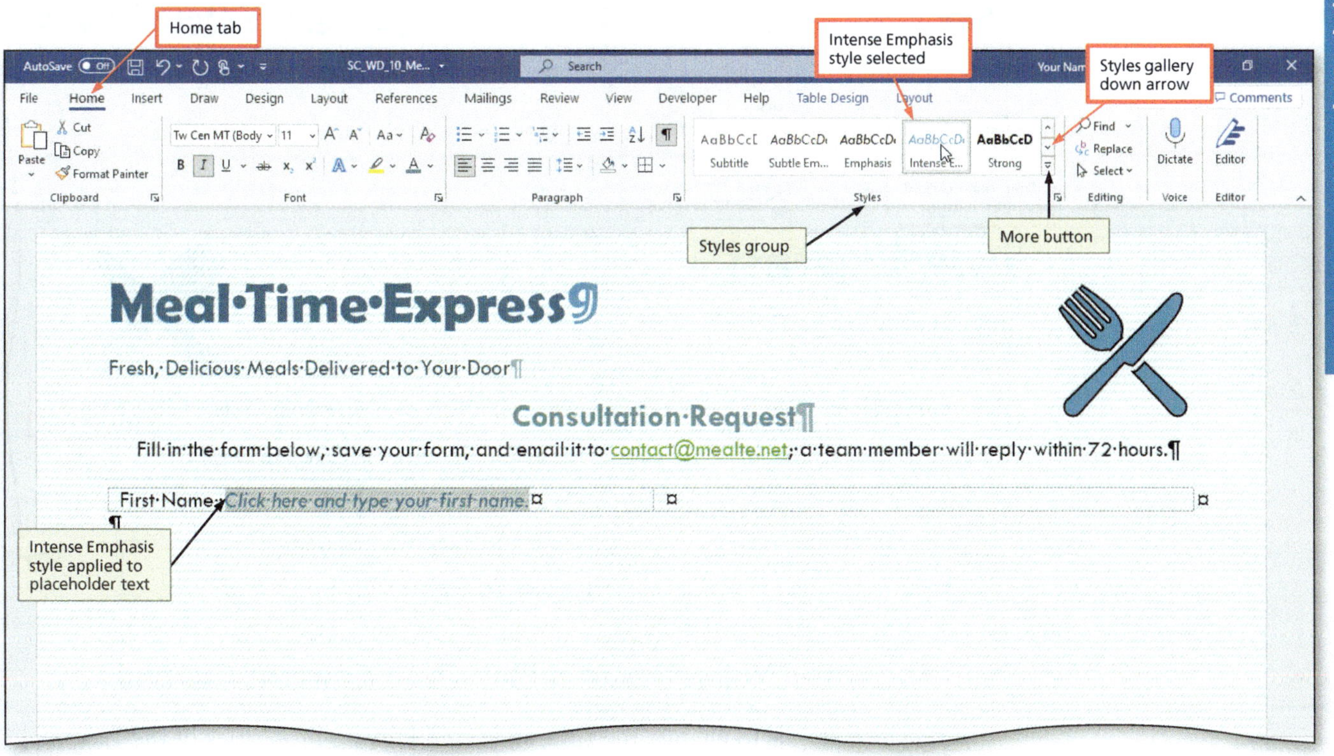

Figure 10–36

To Insert Another Plain Text Content Control and Use Design Mode to Edit Its Placeholder Text

The second item that a user enters in the Consultation Request is the user's last name. The steps for entering the last name content control are similar to those for the first name, because the last name also is a plain text content control. The following steps enter the label, Last Name:, and then insert a plain text content control and edit its placeholder text.

BTW
Deleting Content Controls
To delete a content control, in Design Mode, right-click it and then click 'Remove Content Control' on the shortcut menu.

1. Position the insertion point in the second cell (column) in the table.
2. With the insertion point in the second cell of the table, type `Last Name:` as the label for the content control and then press SPACEBAR.
3. Display the Developer tab. Click the 'Plain Text Content Control' button (Developer tab | Controls group) to insert a plain text content control at the location of the insertion point.
4. With the plain text content control selected, click the Design Mode button (Developer tab | Controls group) to turn on Design mode (Figure 10–37).
5. Select the placeholder text to be changed.
6. Edit the placeholder text so that it contains the text, Click here and type your last name., as the instruction.
7. Click the Design Mode button (Developer tab | Controls group) to turn off Design mode.

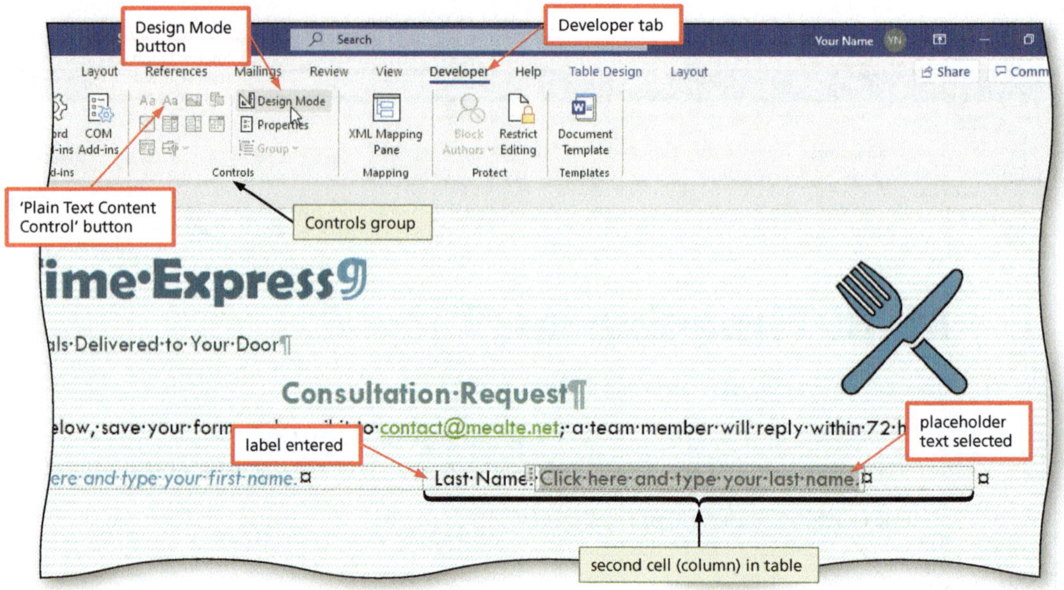

Figure 10–37

To Change the Properties of a Plain Text Content Control

The next step is to change the title, style, and locking properties of the Last Name content control, just as you did for the First Name content control. The following steps change properties of a plain text content control.

1. With the content control selected, click the Properties button (Developer tab | Controls group) to display the Content Control Properties dialog box.
2. Type `Last Name` in the Tag text box (Content Control Properties dialog box).
3. Place a check mark in the 'Use a style to format text typed into the empty control' check box to activate the Style box.
4. Click the Style arrow and then select Intense Emphasis in the list to specify the style for the content control.
5. Place a check mark in the 'Content control cannot be deleted' check box (Figure 10–38).
6. Click OK to assign the properties to the content control.

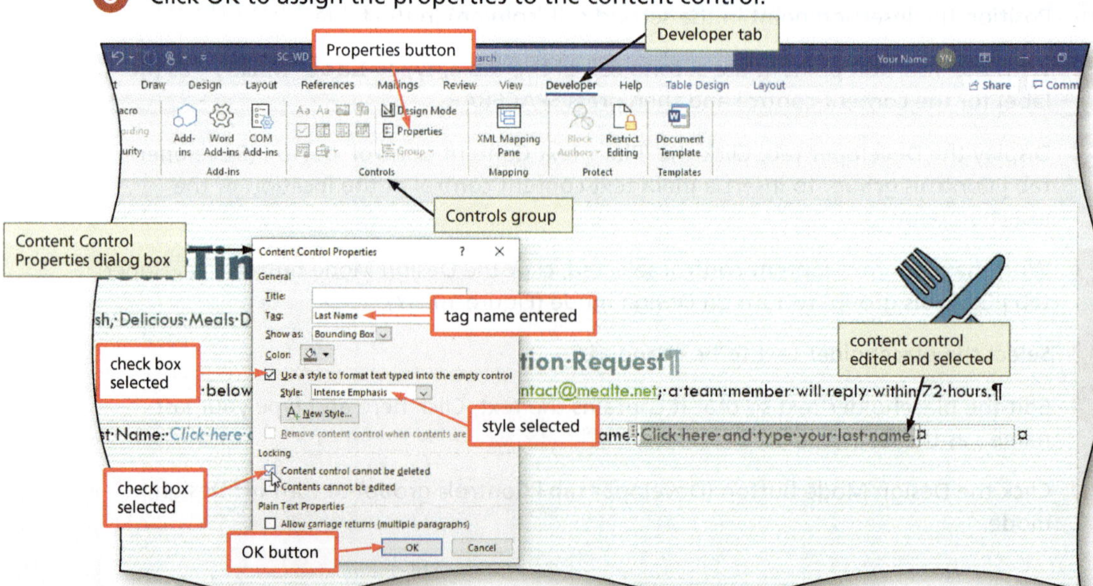

Figure 10–38

To Format Placeholder Text

As with the placeholder text for the first name, the placeholder text for the last name should use the Intense Emphasis style. The following steps format placeholder text.

1. With the last name placeholder text selected, display the Home tab.
2. Locate and select the Intense Emphasis style in the Styles gallery (Home tab | Styles group) to apply the selected style to the selected placeholder text.

To Increase Space before a Paragraph

The next step in creating this online form is to increase space before a paragraph so that the space below the table is consistent with the space between other elements on the form. The following steps increase space before a paragraph.

1. Position the insertion point on the blank line below the table.
2. Display the Layout tab.
3. Change the value in the Spacing Before box (Layout tab | Paragraph group) to 8 pt to increase the space between the table and the paragraph (shown in Figure 10–39). (Ensure that the spacing after this paragraph also is 8 point.) (Note that you may need to type the value in the box instead of using the arrow keys.)

To Insert a Drop-Down List Content Control

In the online form in this module, the user selects from one of these four choices for the Delivery Day content control: Wednesday, Thursday, Friday, or Saturday (additional fee). The following steps insert a drop-down list content control. **Why?** To present a set of choices to a user in the form of a drop-down list, from which the user selects one, insert a drop-down list content control. To view the set of choices, the user clicks the arrow at the right edge of the content control.

1

- With the insertion point positioned on the blank paragraph mark below the First Name content control, using either the ruler or the Layout tab, change the left indent to 0.06" so that the entered text aligns with the text immediately above it (that is, the F in First).
- Type **On which day would you like your meals delivered every week?** and then press SPACEBAR.

2

- Display the Developer tab.
- Click the 'Drop-Down List Content Control' button (Developer tab | Controls group) to insert a drop-down list content control at the location of the insertion point (Figure 10–39).

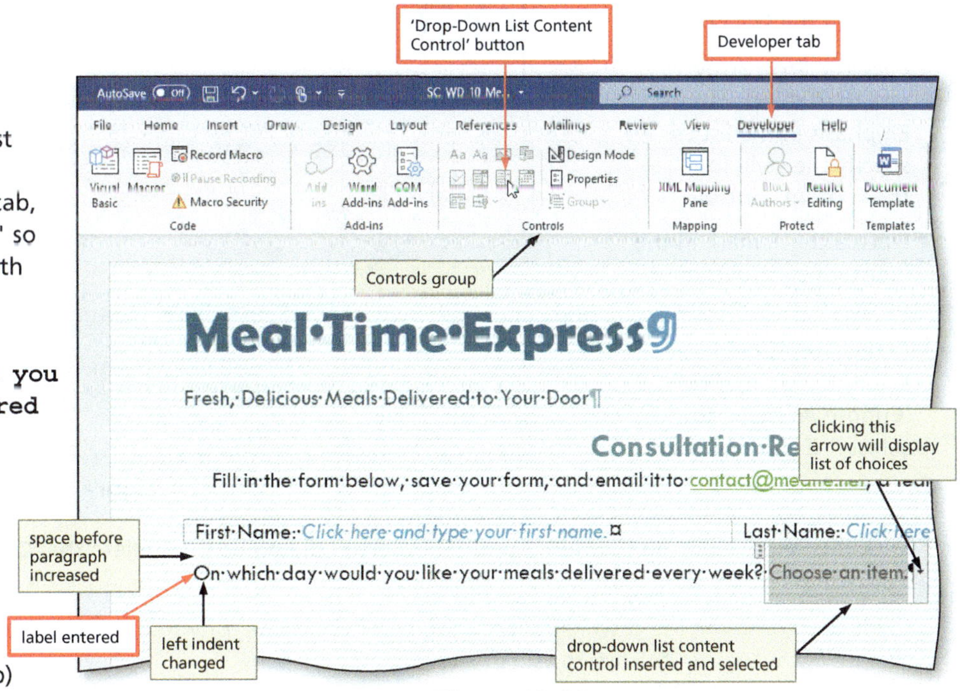

Figure 10–39

To Use Design Mode to Edit Placeholder Text

The following steps edit the placeholder text for the drop-down list content control.

1. With the drop-down list content control selected, click the Design Mode button (Developer tab | Controls group) to turn on Design mode.
2. Edit the placeholder text so that it contains this instruction, which contains two separate sentences: Click here. Click arrow and select from list.
3. Click the Design Mode button (Developer tab | Controls group) to turn off Design mode.

To Change the Properties of a Drop-Down List Content Control

The following steps change the properties of a drop-down list content control. **Why?** In addition to identifying a tag, selecting a style, and locking the drop-down list content control, you can specify the choices that will be displayed when a user clicks the arrow to the right of the content control.

1

- With the drop-down list content control selected, click the Properties button (Developer tab | Controls group) to display the Content Control Properties dialog box.
- Type `Delivery Day` in the Tag text box (Content Control Properties dialog box).
- Place a check mark in the 'Use a style to format text typed into the empty control' check box to activate the Style box.
- Click the Style arrow and then select Intense Emphasis in the list to specify the style for the content control.
- Place a check mark in the 'Content control cannot be deleted' check box.
- In the Drop-Down List Properties area, click 'Choose an item.' to select it (Figure 10–40).

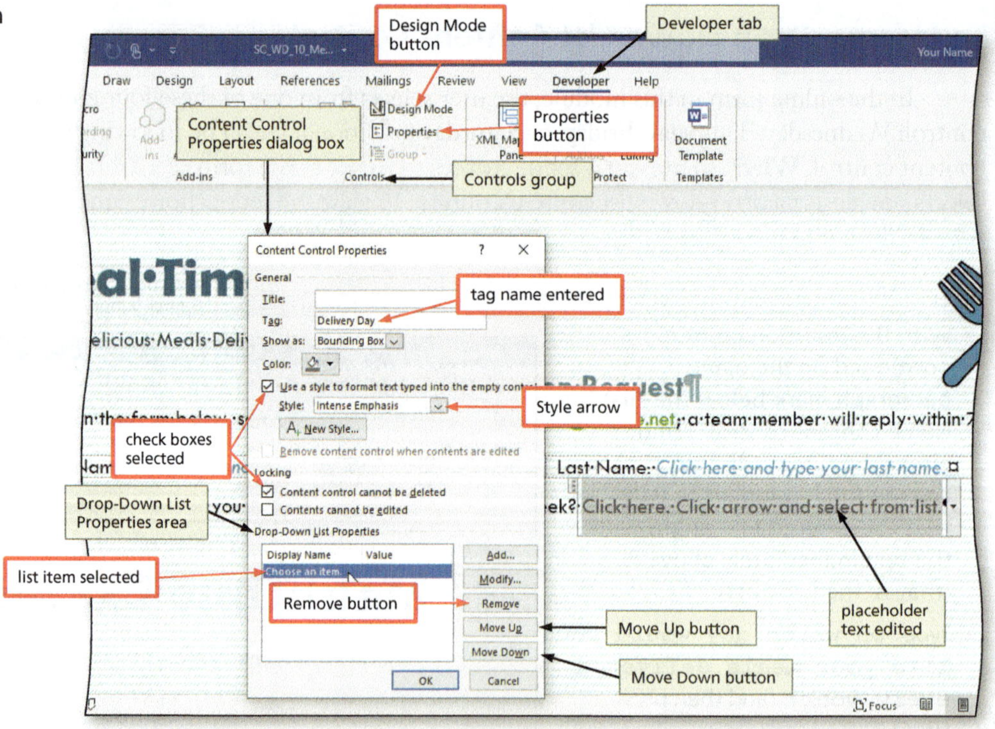

Figure 10–40

2

- Click the Remove button (Content Control Properties dialog box) to delete the 'Choose an item.' entry.

Q&A

Why delete the 'Choose an item.' entry?
If you leave it in the list, it will appear as the first item in the list when the user clicks the content control arrow. You do not want it in the list, so you delete it.

Can I delete any entry in a drop-down list using the Remove button?
Yes, select the entry in this dialog box and then click the Remove button. You also can rearrange the order of entries in a list by selecting the entry and then clicking the Move Up or Move Down buttons.

3

- Click the Add button to display the Add Choice dialog box.
- Type `Wednesday` in the Display Name text box (Add Choice dialog box), and notice that Word automatically enters the same text in the Value text box (Figure 10–41).

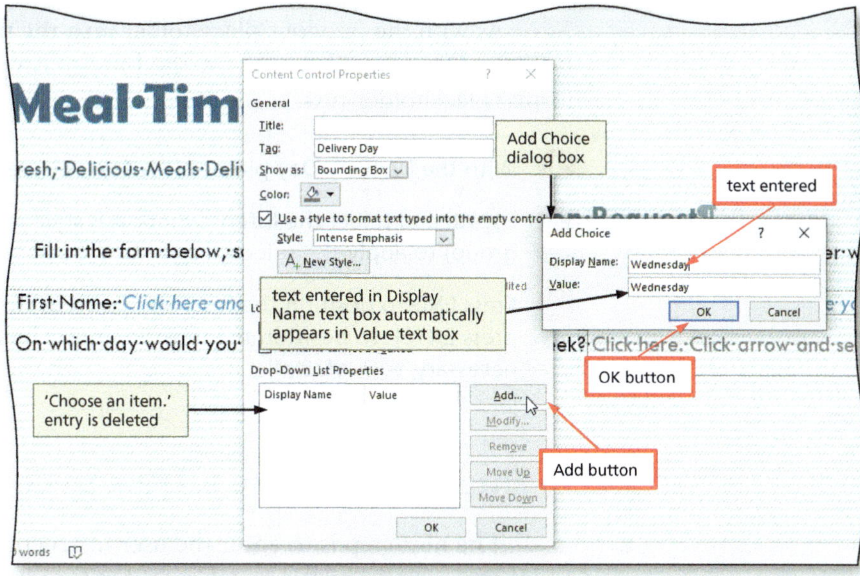

Figure 10–41

Q&A **What is the difference between a display name and a value?**
Often, they are the same, which is why when you type the display name, Word automatically enters the same text in the Value text box. Sometimes, however, you may want to store a shorter or different value. If the display name is long, entering shorter values makes it easier for separate programs to analyze and interpret entered data.

4

- Click OK (Add Choice dialog box) to add the entered display name and value to the list of choices in the Drop-Down List Properties area (Content Control Properties dialog box).

5

- Click the Add button to display the Add Choice dialog box.
- Type `Thursday` in the Display Name text box.
- Click OK to add the entry to the list.
- Click the Add button to display the Add Choice dialog box.
- Type `Friday` in the Display Name text box.
- Click OK to add the entry to the list.
- Click the Add button to display the Add Choice dialog box.
- Type `Saturday (additional fee)` in the Display Name text box.
- Click OK to add the entry to the list (Figure 10–42).

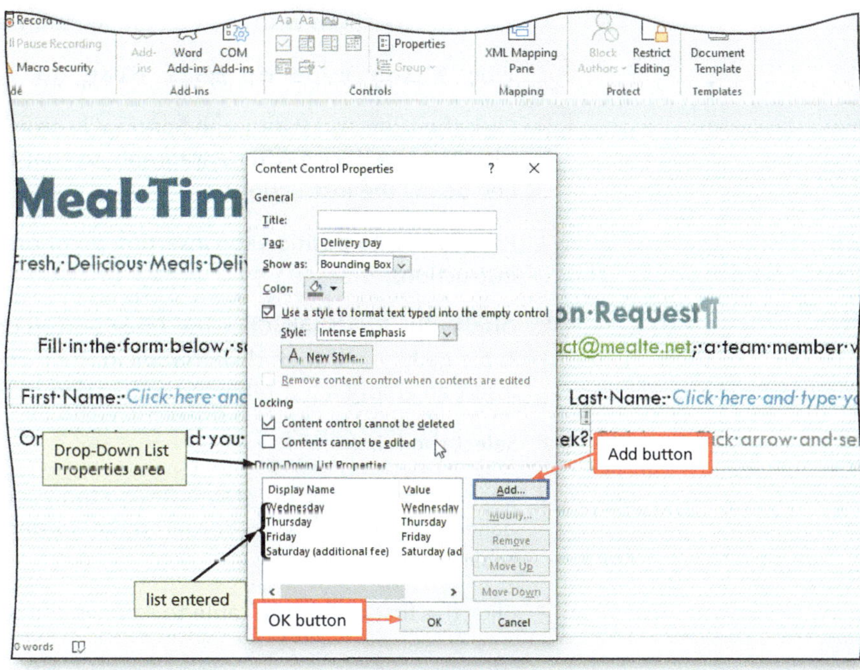

Figure 10–42

6

- Click OK (Content Control Properties dialog box) to change the content control properties.

Q&A **What if I want to change an entry in the drop-down list?**
You would select the drop-down list content control, click the Properties button (Developer tab | Controls group) to display the Content Control Properties dialog box, select the entry to change, click the Modify button, adjust the entry, and then click OK.

To Format Placeholder Text

As with the previous placeholder text, the placeholder text for the content Delivery Day control should use the Intense Emphasis style. The following steps format placeholder text.

1. With the Delivery Day placeholder text selected, display the Home tab.
2. Locate and select the Intense Emphasis style in the Styles gallery (Home tab | Styles group) to apply the selected style to the selected placeholder text.
3. Press END to position the insertion point at the end of the current line and then press ENTER to position the insertion point below the Delivery Day content control. If necessary, turn off italics.

To Enter Text and Use a Table to Control Layout

The next step is to enter the user instructions for the check box content controls and insert a 4 × 1 borderless table so that four evenly spaced check boxes can be displayed horizontally below the check box instructions. The following steps enter text and insert a borderless table.

1. With the insertion point positioned on the paragraph below the Delivery Day content control, click Normal in the Styles gallery (Home tab | Styles group) to format the current paragraph to the Normal style.
2. Using either the ruler or the Layout tab, change the left indent to 0.06" so that the entered text aligns with the text immediately above it (that is, the O in On).
3. Type `Which type of meal plan do you prefer?` as the instruction.
4. Click the 'Line and Paragraph Spacing' button (Home tab | Paragraph group) and then click 'Remove Space After Paragraph' so that the check boxes will appear one physical line below the instructions.
5. Press ENTER to position the insertion point on the line below the check box instructions.
6. Display the Insert tab. Click the Table button (Insert tab | Tables group) to display the Table gallery and then click the cell in the first row and fourth column of the grid to insert an empty 4 × 1 table at the location of the insertion point.
7. Select the table.
8. Click the Borders arrow (Table Design tab | Borders group) to display the Borders gallery and then click No Border in the Borders gallery to remove the borders from the table.
9. Click the first cell of the table to remove the selection (shown in Figure 10–43).

BTW
Break Header or Footer Link
If you do not want the header or footer in a section to be copied to the previous section, you would deselect the 'Link to Previous' button (Header & Footer tab | Navigation group).

To Insert a Check Box Content Control

The following step inserts the first check box content control. **Why?** In the online form in this module, the user can select up to five check boxes: Variety Plan, Mediterranean Plan, Gluten-Free Plan, Vegetarian Plan, and Other.

1

- Position the insertion point at the location for the check box content control, in this case, the leftmost cell in the 4 × 1 table.
- Display the Developer tab.
- Click the 'Check Box Content Control' button (Developer tab | Controls group) to insert a check box content control at the location of the insertion point (Figure 10–43).

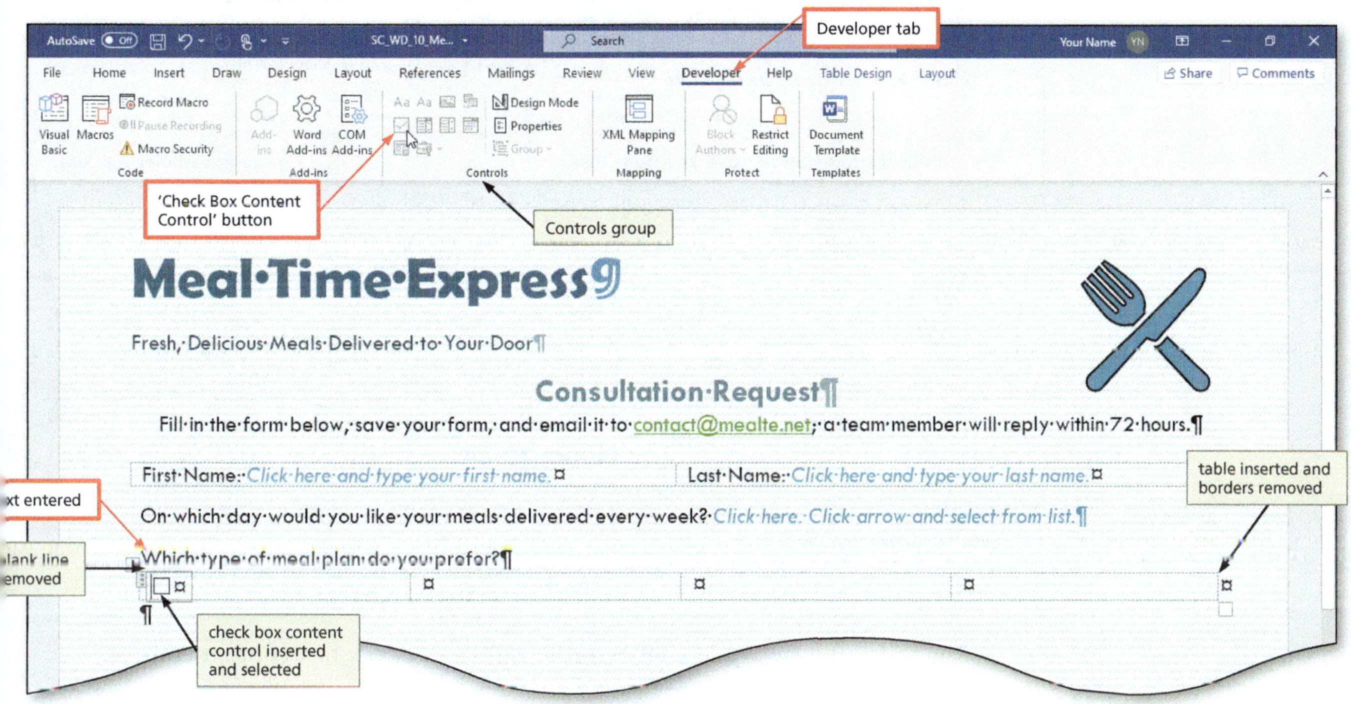

Figure 10–43

To Change the Properties of a Check Box Content Control

The next step is to change the title and locking properties of the content control. The following steps change properties of a check box content control.

1 With the content control selected, click the Properties button (Developer tab | Controls group) to display the Content Control Properties dialog box.

2 Type `Variety Plan` in the Tag text box (Content Control Properties dialog box).

3 Click the Show as arrow and then select None in the list, because you do not want a border surrounding the check box content control.

4. Place a check mark in the 'Content control cannot be deleted' check box (Figure 10–44).
5. Click OK to assign the properties to the selected content control.

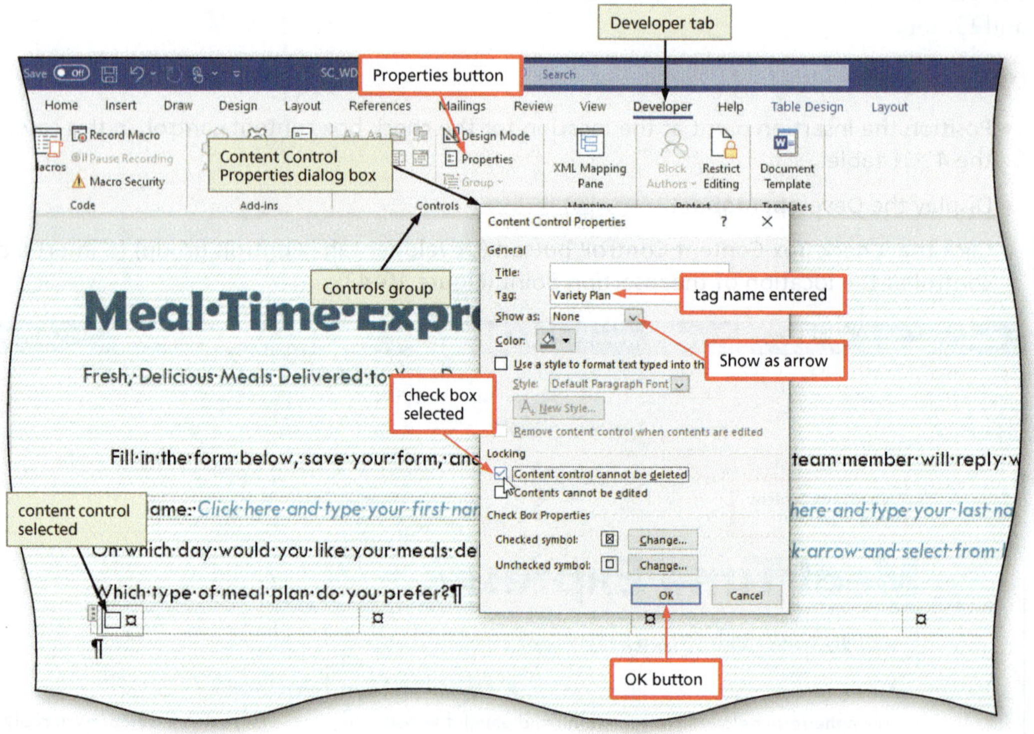

Figure 10–44

To Add a Label to a Check Box Content Control

The following steps add a label to the right of a check box content control.

1. With content control selected, press END twice to position the insertion point after the inserted check box content control.
2. Press SPACEBAR and then type `Variety Plan` as the check box label (Figure 10–45).

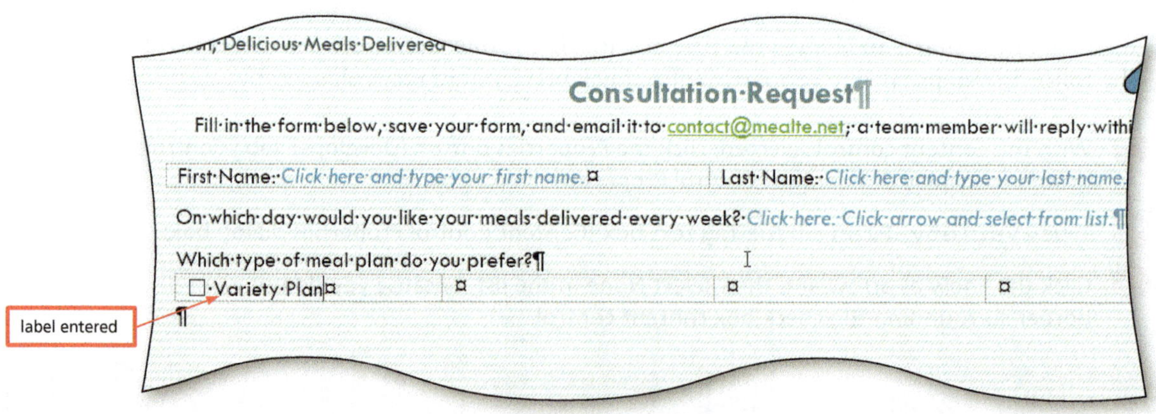

Figure 10–45

To Insert Additional Check Box Content Controls

The following steps insert the remaining check box content controls and their labels.

1. Press TAB to position the insertion point in the next cell, which is the location for the next check box content control.
2. Click the 'Check Box Content Control' button (Developer tab | Controls group) to insert a check box content control at the location of the insertion point.
3. With the content control selected, click the Properties button (Developer tab | Controls group) to display the Content Control Properties dialog box.
4. Type **`Mediterranean Plan`** in the Tag text box (Content Control Properties dialog box).
5. Click the Show as arrow and then select None in the list, because you do not want a border surrounding the check box content control.
6. Place a check mark in the 'Content control cannot be deleted' check box and then click OK to assign the properties to the selected content control.
7. With content control selected, press END twice to position the insertion point after the inserted check box content control.
8. Press SPACEBAR and then type **`Mediterranean Plan`** as the check box label.
9. Repeat Steps 1 through 8 for the Gluten-Free Plan and Vegetarian Plan check box content controls.
10. Position the insertion point on the blank line below the 4 × 1 table and then repeat Steps 2 through 8 for the Other Meal Plan Type check box content control, which has the label, Other (please specify):, followed by SPACEBAR. If necessary, using either the ruler or the Layout tab, change the left indent so that the check box above is aligned with the check box below (Figure 10–46).

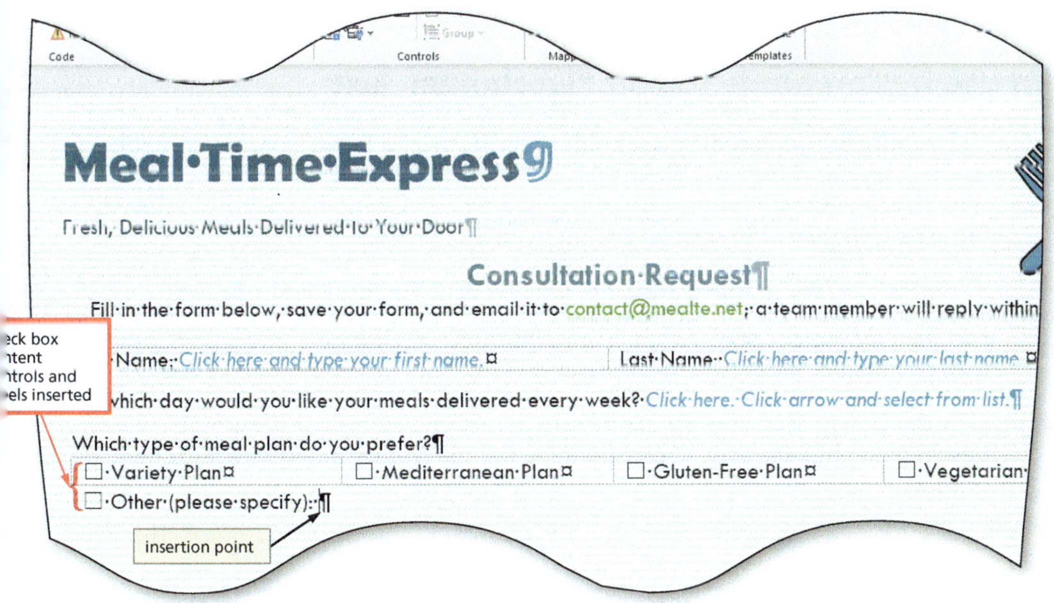

Figure 10–46

To Insert a Rich Text Content Control

The next step is to insert the content control that enables users to type in any other type of meal plan they prefer. The difference between a plain text and rich text content control is that the users can format text as they enter it in the rich text content control. The following step inserts a rich text content control. **Why?** Because you want to allow users to format the text they enter in the Other Meal Plan Type content control, you use the rich text content control.

1

- If necessary, position the insertion point at the location for the rich text content control (shown in Figure 10–46).
- If necessary, display the Developer tab.
- Click the 'Rich Text Content Control' button (Developer tab | Controls group) to insert a rich text content control at the location of the insertion point (Figure 10–47).

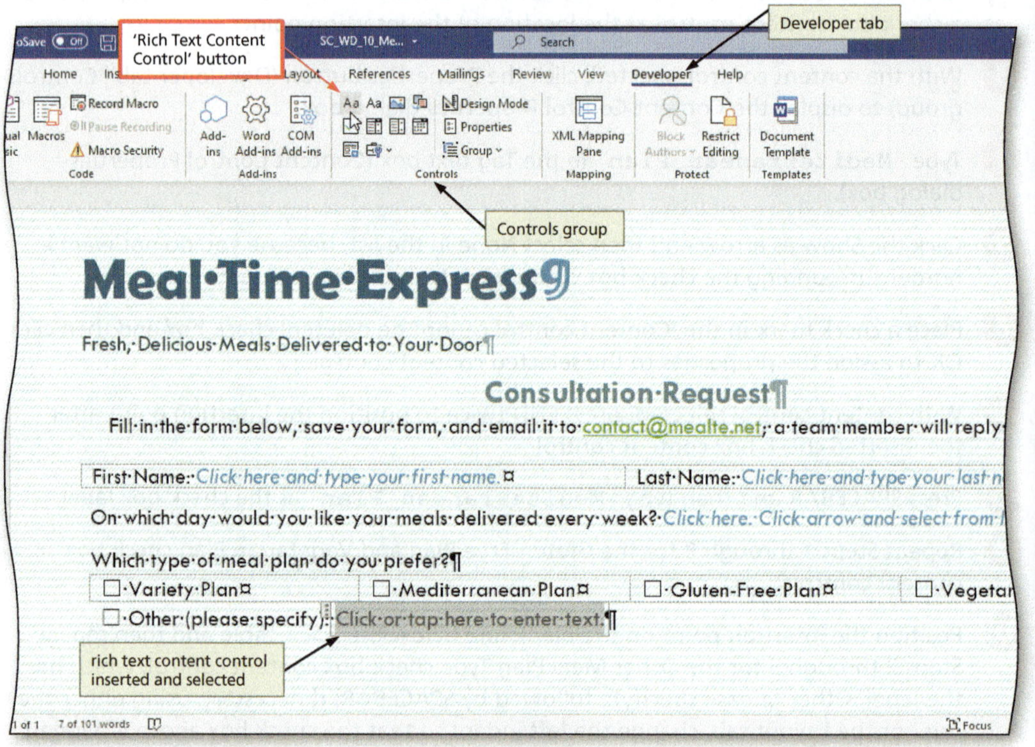

Figure 10–47

To Use Design Mode to Edit Placeholder Text

The following steps edit placeholder text for the rich text content control.

1. With the rich text content control selected, click the Design Mode button (Developer tab | Controls group) to turn on Design mode.
2. If necessary, scroll to display the content control in the document window.
3. Edit the placeholder text so that it contains the text, Click here and type another meal plan you would prefer., as the instruction.
4. Click the Design Mode button (Developer tab | Controls group) to turn off Design mode. If necessary, scroll to display the top of the form in the document window.

To Change the Properties of a Rich Text Content Control

In the online form in this module, you change the same three properties for the rich text content control as for the plain text content control. That is, you enter a tag name, specify the style, and lock the content control. The following steps change the properties of the rich text content control.

1. With the content control selected, click the Properties button (Developer tab | Controls group) to display the Content Control Properties dialog box.

2. Type `Other Meal Plan Type` in the Tag text box (Content Control Properties dialog box).

3. Place a check mark in the 'Use a style to format text typed into the empty control' check box to activate the Style box.

4. Click the Style arrow and then select Intense Emphasis in the list to specify the style for the content control.

5. Place a check mark in the 'Content control cannot be deleted' check box (Figure 10–48).

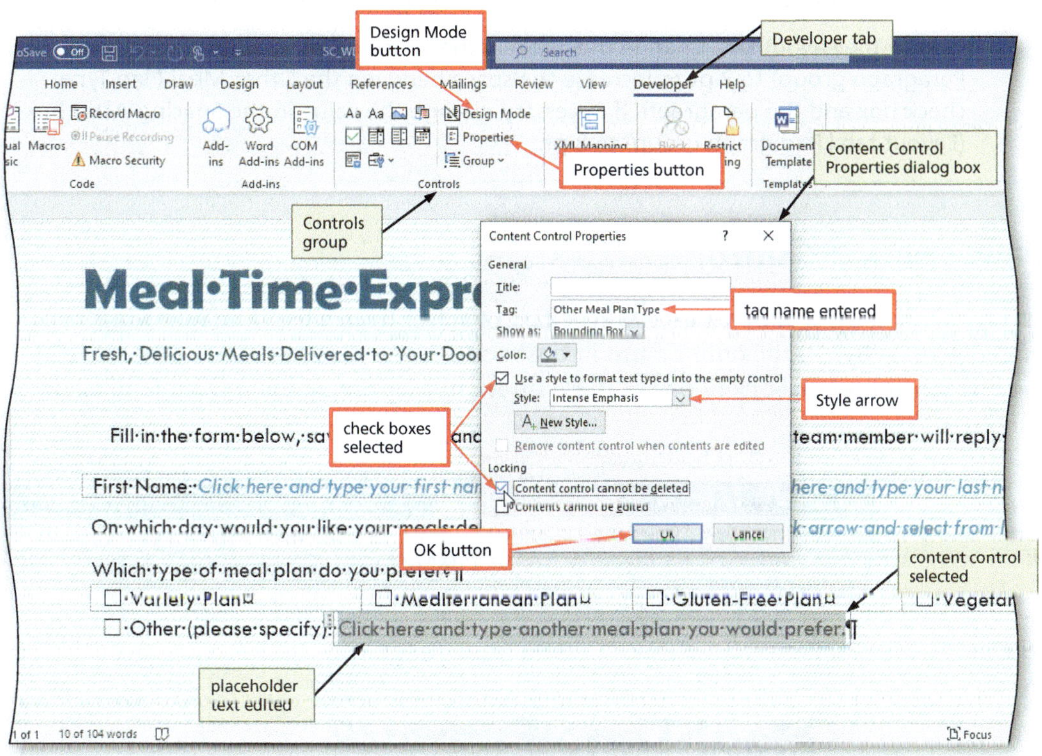

Figure 10–48

6. Click OK to assign the properties to the content control.

To Format Placeholder Text and Add Space before a Paragraph

The placeholder text for the Other Meal Plan Type text entry should use the Intense Emphasis style, and the space below the check boxes should be consistent with the space between other elements on the form. The next steps format placeholder text and increase space before a paragraph.

1. With the Other Meal Plan Type placeholder text selected, display the Home tab.
2. Locate and select the Intense Emphasis style in the Styles gallery (Home tab | Styles group) to apply the selected style to the selected placeholder text.
3. Press END to position the insertion point on the paragraph mark after the Other Meal Plan Type content control and then press ENTER to position the insertion point below the Other Meal Plan Type content control.
4. If necessary, display the Home tab. With the insertion point positioned on the paragraph below the Other Meal Plan Type content control, click Normal in the Styles gallery (Home tab | Styles group) to format the current paragraph to the Normal style.
5. Using either the ruler or the Layout tab, change the left indent to 0.06" so that the entered text aligns with the text two lines above it (that is, the W in Which).
6. Display the Layout tab. Change the value in the Spacing Before box (Layout tab | Paragraph group) to 8 pt to increase the space between the Other Meal Plan Type check box and the paragraph. If necessary, change the value in the Spacing After box (Layout tab | Paragraph group) to 8 pt.

To Insert a Combo Box Content Control

In Word, a combo box content control allows a user to type text or select from a list. The following steps insert a combo box content control. **Why?** In the online form in this module, users can type their own entry in the Servings Per Week content control or select from one of these three choices: Single Plan, Double Plan, or Family Plan.

1

- With the insertion point positioned on the blank paragraph mark, type **How many servings per week would you prefer?** and then press SPACEBAR.

2

- Display the Developer tab.
- Click the 'Combo Box Content Control' button (Developer tab | Controls group) to insert a combo box content control at the location of the insertion point (Figure 10–49).

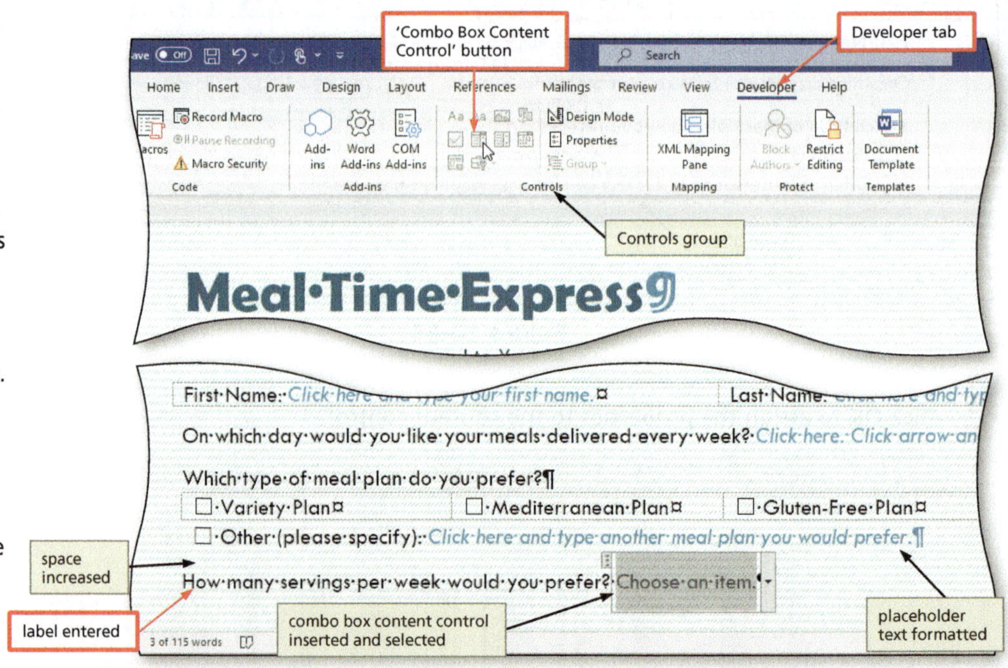

Figure 10–49

To Use Design Mode to Edit Placeholder Text

The following steps edit the placeholder text for the combo box content control.

1. With the combo box content control selected, click the Design Mode button (Developer tab | Controls group) to turn on Design mode.

2. If necessary, scroll to page 2 to display the combo box content control.

Q&A

What if the content control moves to another page?
Because Design mode displays tags, the content controls and placeholder text are not displayed in their proper positions on the screen. When you turn off Design mode, the content controls will return to their original locations and the extra page should disappear.

3. Edit the placeholder text so that it contains this instruction, which contains two sentences (Figure 10–50): Click here. Click arrow and select from list, or type your response.

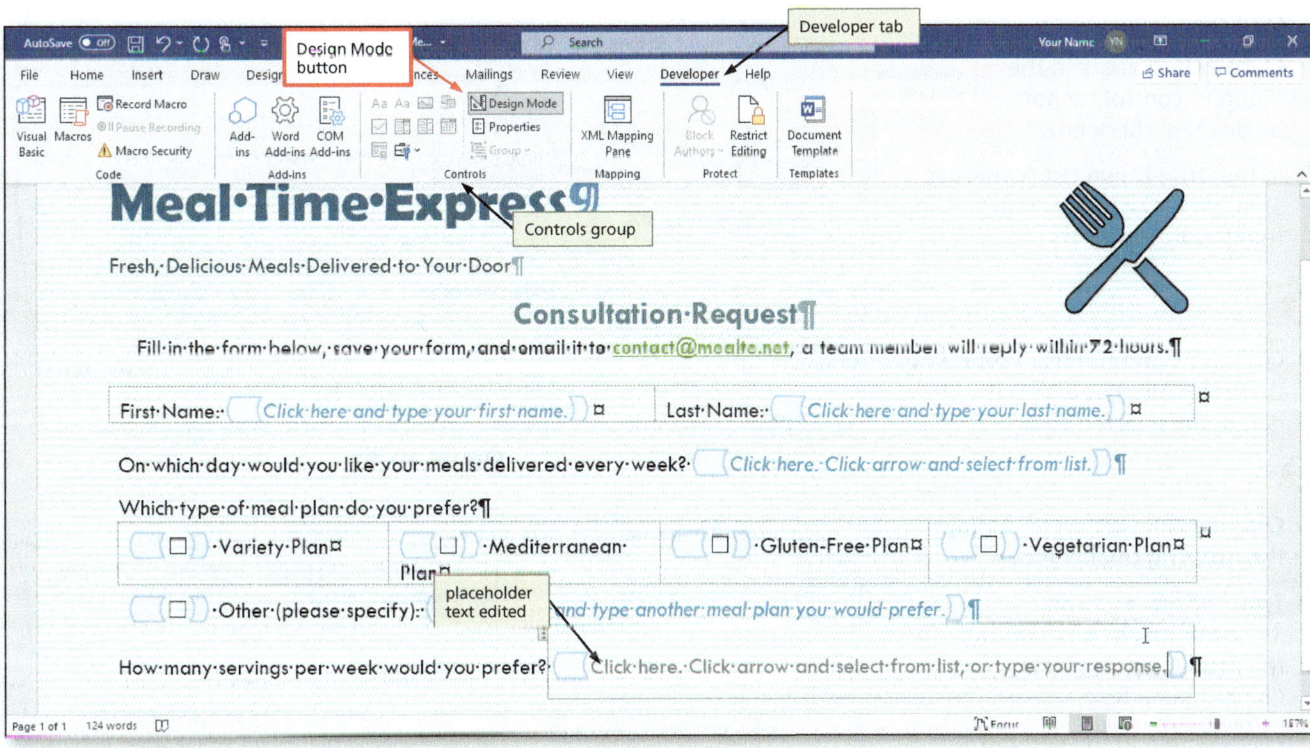

Figure 10–50

4. Click the Design Mode button (Developer tab | Controls group) to turn off Design mode.

To Change the Properties of a Combo Box Content Control

You follow similar steps to enter the list for a combo box content control as you do for the drop-down list content control. The following steps change the properties of a combo box content control. **Why?** You enter the tag name, specify the style for typed text, and enter the choices for the drop-down list.

1

- With the content control selected, click the Properties button (Developer tab | Controls group) to display the Content Control Properties dialog box.
- Type **`Servings per Week`** in the Tag text box (Content Control Properties dialog box).
- Place a check mark in the 'Use a style to format text typed into the empty control' check box to activate the Style box.
- Click the Style arrow and then select Intense Emphasis in the list to specify the style for the content control.
- Place a check mark in the 'Content control cannot be deleted' check box.
- In the Drop-Down List Properties area, click 'Choose an item.' to select it (Figure 10–51).

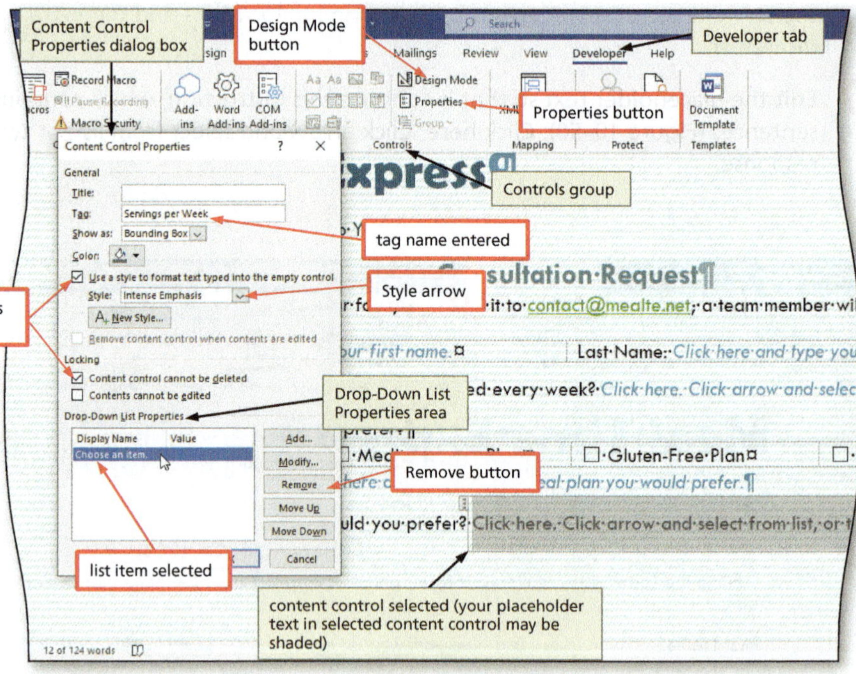

Figure 10–51

2

- Click the Remove button (Content Control Properties dialog box) to delete the selected entry.

3

- Click the Add button to display the Add Choice dialog box.
- Type **`Single Plan (4 servings per week)`** in the Display Name text box (Add Choice dialog box).
- Click OK to add the entered display name to the list of choices in the Drop-Down List Properties area (Content Control Properties dialog box).
- Click the Add button and add **`Double Plan (8 servings per week)`** to the list.
- Click the Add button and add **`Family Plan (16 servings per week)`** to the list (Figure 10–52).

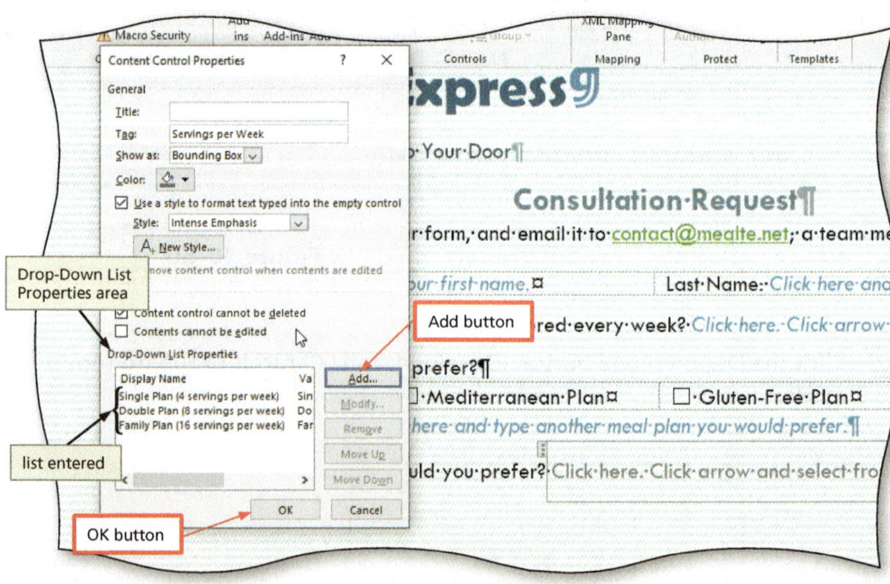

Figure 10–52

4

- Click OK (Content Control Properties dialog box) to change the content control properties.

Q&A **How do I make adjustments to entries in the list?**
Follow the same procedures as you use to make adjustments to entries in a drop-down list content control.

To Format Placeholder Text

As with the previous placeholder text, the placeholder text for the Servings per Week should use the Intense Emphasis style. The following steps format placeholder text.

1. With the Servings per Week placeholder text selected, display the Home tab.
2. Locate and select the Intense Emphasis style in the Styles gallery (Home tab | Styles group) to apply the selected style to the selected placeholder text.
3. Press END to position the insertion point at the end of the current line and then press ENTER to position the insertion point below the Servings per Week content control.
4. Click Normal in the Styles list (Home tab | Styles group) to format the current paragraph to the Normal style.
5. Using either the ruler or the Layout tab, change the left indent to 0.06" so that the entered text aligns with the text above it (that is, the H in How).

To Insert a Date Picker Content Control

To assist users with entering dates, Word provides a date picker content control, which displays a calendar when the user clicks the arrow to the right of the content control. Users also can enter a date directly in the content control without using the calendar. The following steps enter the label, Today's Date:, and a date picker content control. **Why?** The last item that users enter in the Consultation Request is today's date.

1

- With the insertion point below the Servings per Week content control, type `Today's Date:` as the label for the content control and then press SPACEBAR.

2

- Display the Developer tab.
- Click the 'Date Picker Content Control' button (Developer tab | Controls group) to insert a date picker content control at the location of the insertion point (Figure 10–53).

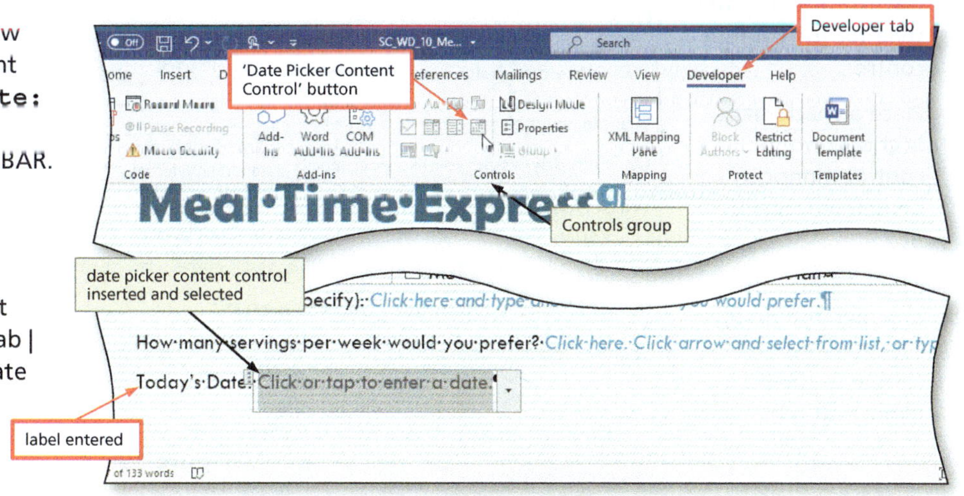

Figure 10–53

To Use Design Mode to Edit Placeholder Text

The following steps edit the placeholder text for the date picker content control.

1. With the date picker content control selected, click the Design Mode button (Developer tab | Controls group) to turn on Design mode.
2. If necessary, scroll to display the date picker content control.
3. Edit the placeholder text so that it contains this instruction, which contains two sentences: Click here. Click arrow and select today's date.
4. Click the Design Mode button (Developer tab | Controls group) to turn off Design mode.
5. If necessary, scroll to display the top of the form in the document window.

To Change the Properties of a Date Picker Content Control

The following steps change the properties of a date picker content control. **Why?** In addition to identifying a tag name for a date picker content control, specifying a style, and locking the control, you will specify how the date will be displayed when the user selects it from the calendar.

1

- With the content control selected, click the Properties button (Developer tab | Controls group) to display the Content Control Properties dialog box.
- Type **`Today's Date`** in the Tag text box.
- Place a check mark in the 'Use a style to format text typed into the empty control' check box to activate the Style box.
- Click the Style arrow and then select Intense Emphasis in the list to specify the style for the content control.
- Place a check mark in the 'Content control cannot be deleted' check box.
- In the Display the date like this area, click the desired format in the list (Figure 10–54).

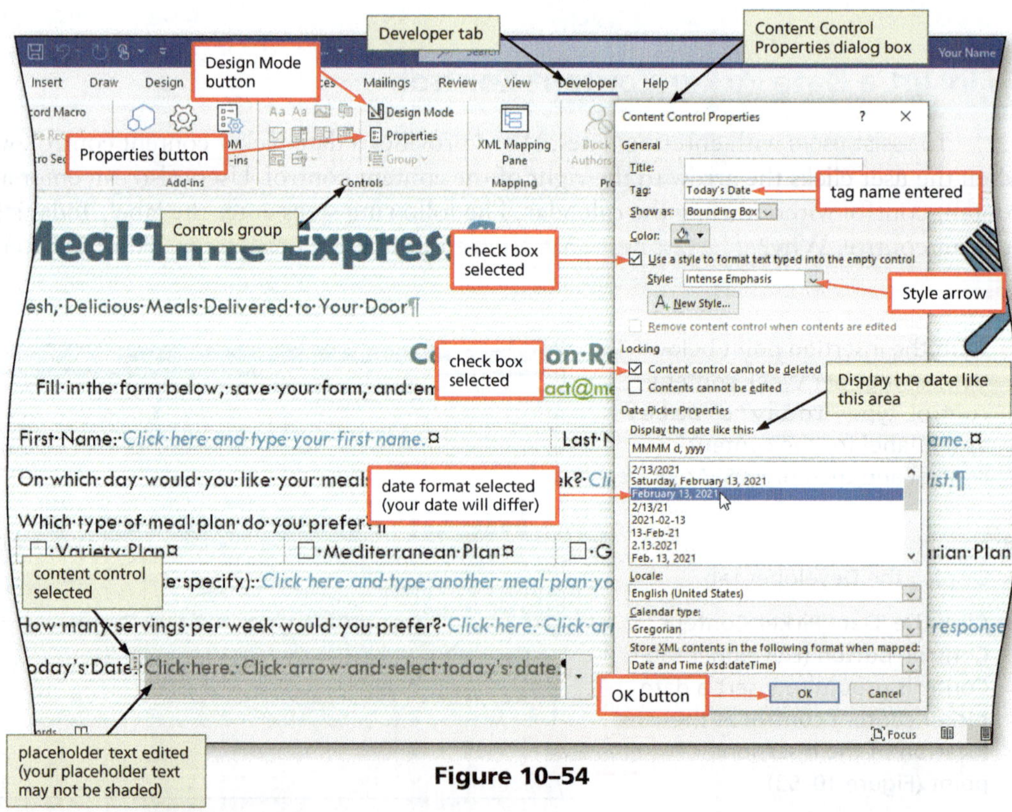

Figure 10–54

2

- Click OK to change the content control properties.

To Format Placeholder Text

As with the previous placeholder text, the placeholder text for today's date should use the Intense Emphasis style. The following steps format placeholder text.

1. With the today's date placeholder text selected, display the Home tab.
2. Locate and select the Intense Emphasis style in the Styles gallery (Home tab | Styles group) to apply the selected style to the selected placeholder text.
3. Press END to position the insertion point at the end of the current line and then press ENTER to position the insertion point below the Today's Date content control.
4. Click Normal in the Styles gallery (Home tab | Styles group) to format the current paragraph to the Normal style.

To Enter and Format Text

The following steps enter and format the line of text at the bottom of the online form.

1. Be sure the insertion point is on the line below the Today's Date content control.
2. Center the paragraph mark.
3. Format the text to be typed with the color of Blue-Gray, Accent 5, Darker 25%.
4. Type **`Thank you for your interest in our service!`**
5. Change the space before the paragraph to 18 point (Figure 10–55). If necessary, change the space after the paragraph to 8 point.
6. If the text flows to a second page, reduce spacing before paragraphs in the form so that all lines fit on a single page.

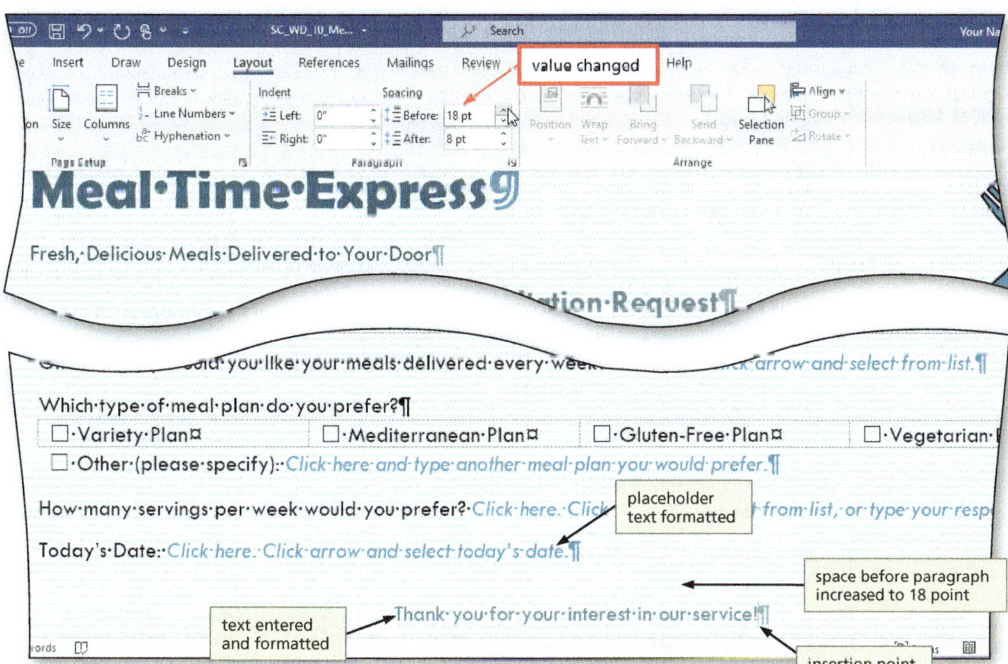

Figure 10–55

BTW

Other Content Controls

To insert a picture content control in a document or template, click the 'Picture Content Control' button (Developer tab | Controls group). When the user clicks the picture content control, the Insert Pictures dialog box is displayed, enabling the user to locate the desired picture. To insert a repeating section content control, select the table or paragraph that you want to repeat and then click the 'Repeating Section Content Control' button (Developer tab | Controls group) to create a duplicate of the selected content in the document or template. To insert a building block gallery content control, select the 'Building Block Gallery Content Control' button (Developer tab | Controls group); then click the Properties button (Developer tab | Controls group) and select the desired gallery to be displayed in the Document Building Block Properties area (Content Control Properties dialog box). When you click the 'Explore Quick Parts' button attached to the top of the building block gallery content control in the document, the selected gallery appears.

To Hide Gridlines and Formatting Marks

Because you are finished with the tables in this form and will not enter any additional tables, you will hide the gridlines. You also are finished with entering and formatting text on the screen. To make the form easier to view, you hide the formatting marks, which can clutter the screen. The following steps hide gridlines and formatting marks.

1. If necessary, position the insertion point in a table cell.
2. Display the Layout tab. If gridlines are showing, click the View Gridlines button (Layout tab | Table group) to hide table gridlines.
3. Display the Home tab. If the 'Show/Hide ¶' button (Home tab | Paragraph group) is selected, click it to remove formatting marks from the screen.
4. Save the template again on the same storage location with the same file name.

Break Point: If you want to take a break, this is a good place to do so. You can exit Word now. To resume later, start Word, open the file called SC_WD_10_MealTimeExpressForm.dotx, and continue following the steps from this location forward.

To Draw a Rectangle

The next step is to emphasize the data entry area of the form. The data entry area includes all the content controls in which a user enters data. The following steps draw a rectangle around the data entry area, and subsequent steps format the rectangle. **Why?** To call attention to the data entry area of the form, this module places a rectangle around the data entry area, changes the style of the rectangle, and then adds a shadow to the rectangle.

1

- Position the insertion point on the last line in the document (shown in Figure 10–55).
- Display the Insert tab.
- Click the Shapes button (Insert tab | Illustrations group) to display the Shapes gallery (Figure 10–56).

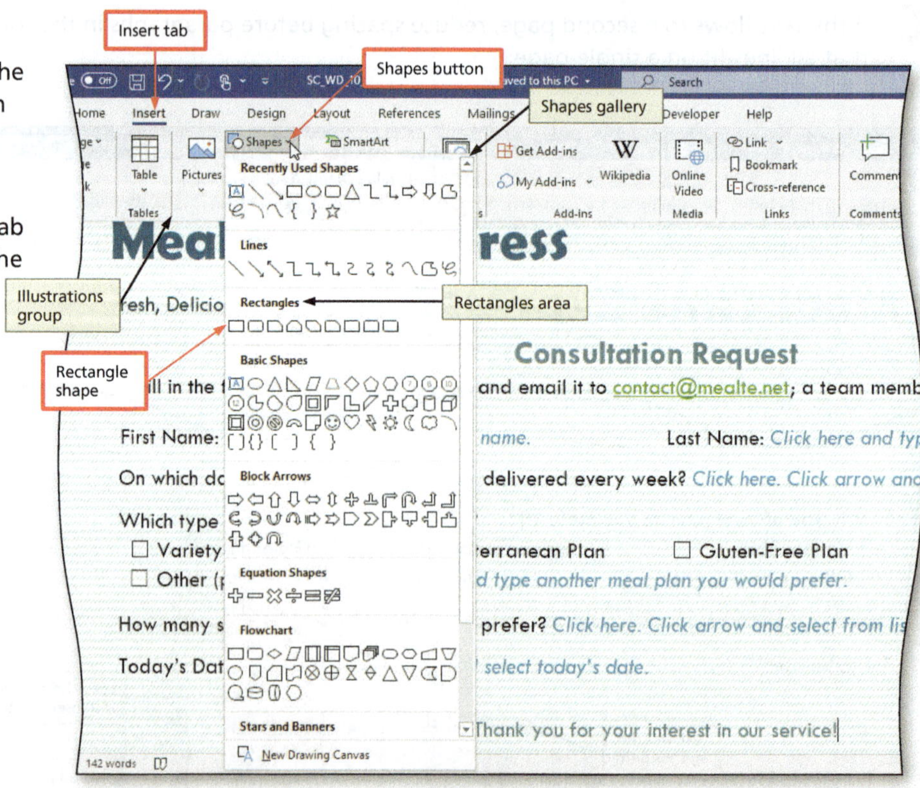

Figure 10–56

2

- Click the Rectangle shape in the Rectangles area of the Shapes gallery, which removes the gallery and changes the pointer to the shape of a crosshair in the document window.

Q&A **What if I am using a touch screen?**
Proceed to Step 5 because the shape is inserted in the document window after you tap the rectangle shape in the Shapes gallery.

- Position the pointer (a crosshair) in the approximate location for the upper-left corner of the desired shape (Figure 10–57).

Figure 10–57

3

- Drag the pointer downward and rightward to form a rectangle around the data entry area, as shown in Figure 10–58.

Figure 10–58

4

- Release the mouse button to draw the rectangle shape on top of the data entry area (Figure 10–59).

Q&A **What happened to all the text in the data entry area?**
When you draw a shape in a document, Word initially places the shape in front of, or on top of, any text in the same area. You can change the stacking order of the shape so that it is displayed behind the text. Thus, the next steps move the shape behind the text.

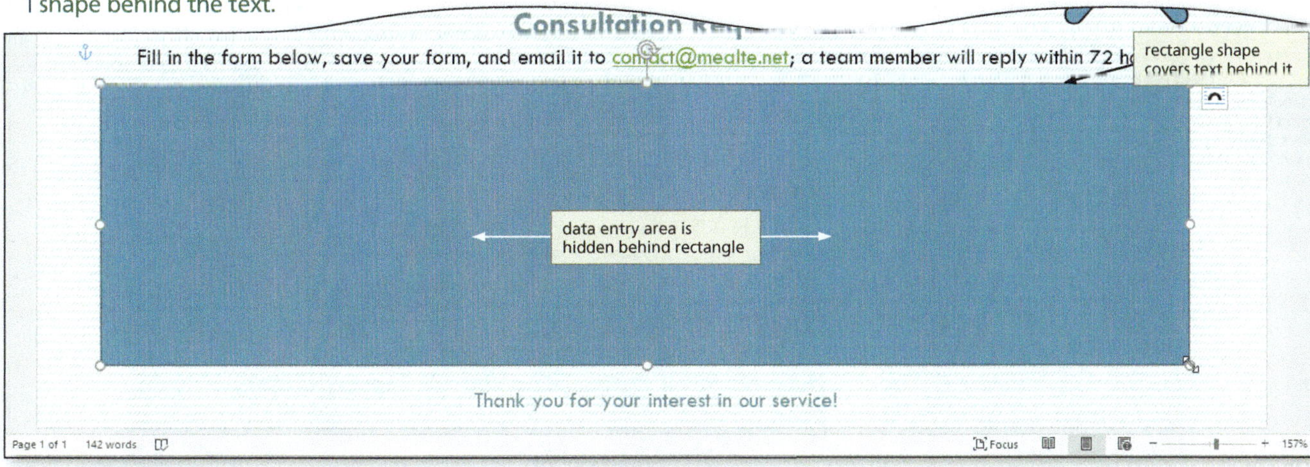

Figure 10–59

5

- If necessary, change the values in the Shape Height and Shape Width boxes (Shape Format tab | Size group) to 1.95" and 7.58" (shown in Figure 10–62).

To Send a Graphic behind Text

The following steps send a graphic behind text. **Why?** You want the rectangle shape graphic to be positioned behind the data entry area text, so that you can see the text in the data entry area along with the shape.

1

- If necessary, display the Shape Format tab.
- With the rectangle shape selected, click the Layout Options button attached to the graphic to display the Layout Options gallery (Figure 10–60).

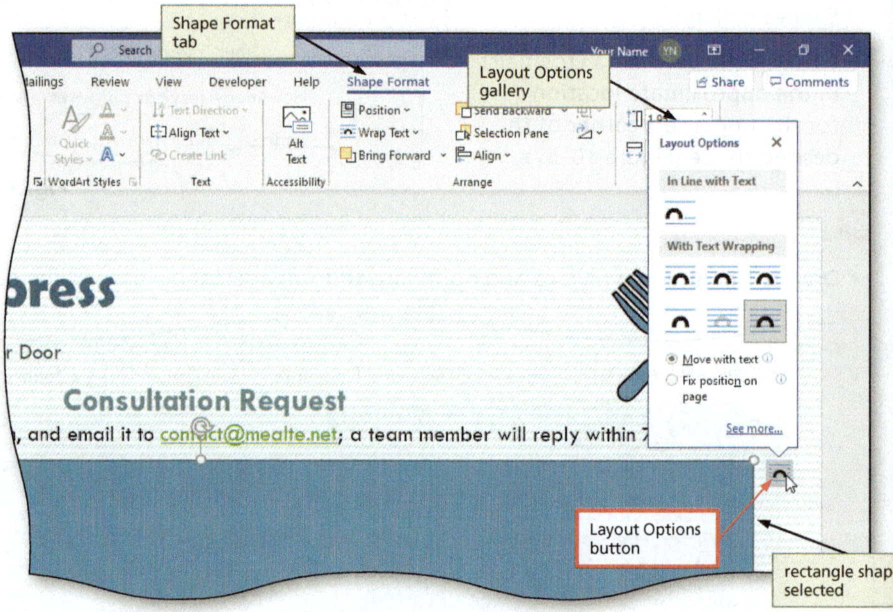

Figure 10–60

2

- Click Behind Text in the Layout Options gallery to position the rectangle shape behind the text (Figure 10–61).

Q&A **What if I want a shape to cover text?**
You would click 'In Front of Text' in the Layout Options gallery.

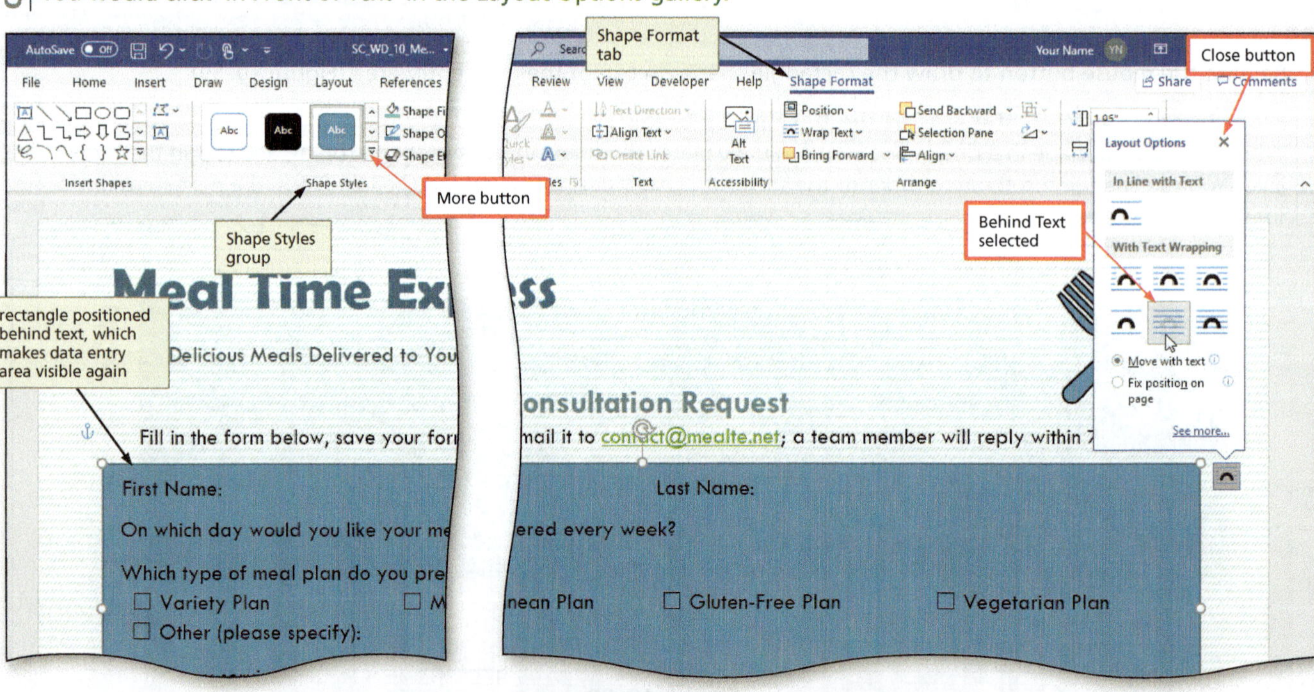

Figure 10–61

3

- Click the Close button in the Layout Options gallery to close the gallery.

Other Ways

1. Click Wrap Text button (Shape Format tab | Arrange group), click desired option
2. Right-click object (or, if using touch, tap 'Show Context Menu' button on Mini toolbar), point to Wrap Text on shortcut menu, click desired option

To Apply a Shape Style with an Outline

The next step is to apply a shape style to the rectangle, so that the text in the data entry area is easier to read. The following steps apply a style to the rectangle shape.

1 With the shape still selected, click the More button in the Shape Styles gallery (Shape Format tab | Shape Styles group) (shown in Figure 10–61) to expand the Shape Styles gallery.

2 Point to 'Colored Outline - Blue-Gray, Accent 5' in the Shape Styles gallery (sixth effect in first row) to display a Live Preview of that style applied to the rectangle shape in the form (Figure 10–62).

3 Click 'Colored Outline - Blue-Gray, Accent 5' in the Shape Styles gallery to apply the selected style to the selected shape.

BTW

Formatting Shapes

Like other drawing objects or pictures, shapes can be formatted or have styles applied. You can change the fill in a shape by clicking the Shape Fill arrow (Shape Format tab | Shape Styles group), add an outline or border to a shape by clicking the Shape Outline arrow (Shape Format tab | Shape Styles group), and apply an effect (such as shadow or 3-D effects) by clicking the Shape Effects arrow (Shape Format tab | Shape Styles group).

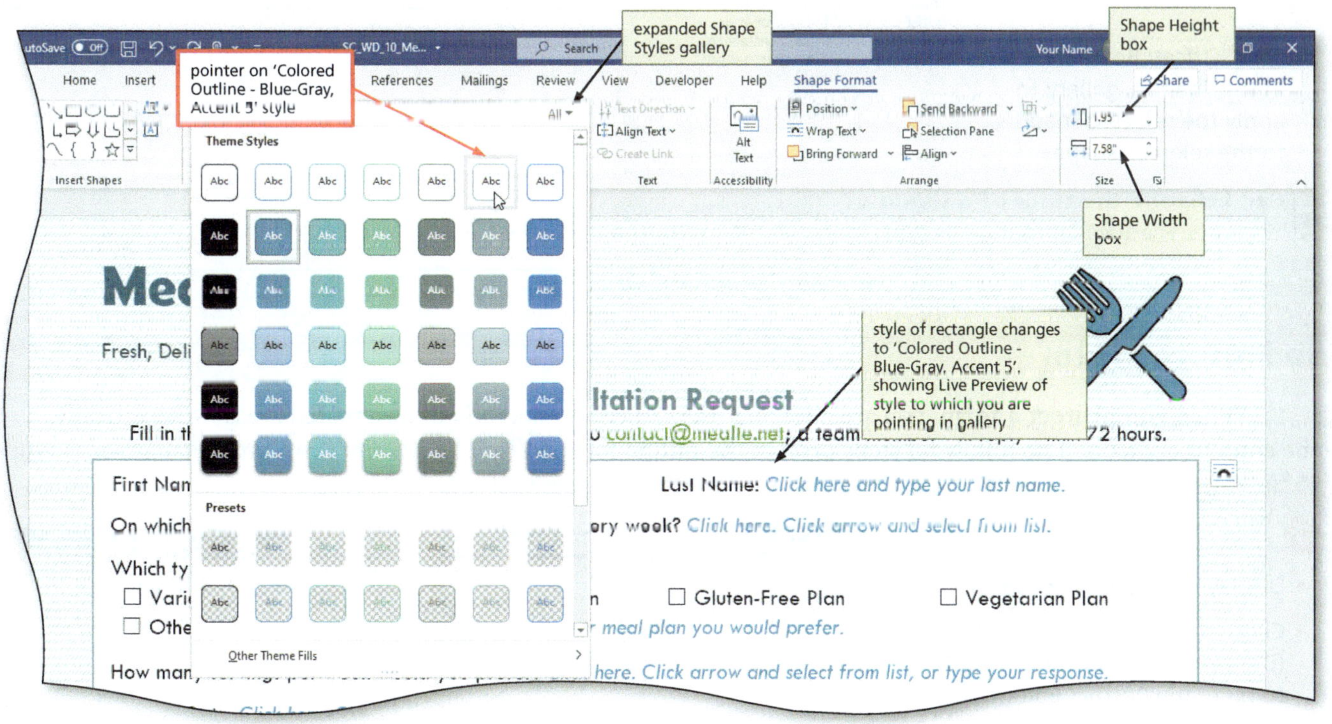

Figure 10–62

To Add a Shadow to a Shape

The following steps add a shadow to the rectangle shape. **Why?** To further offset the data entry area of the form, this online form has a shadow on the outside bottom and left edges of the rectangle shape.

1

- With the shape still selected, click the Shape Effects button (Shape Format tab | Shape Styles group) to display the Shape Effects menu.

2

- Point to Shadow on the Shape Effects menu to display the Shadow gallery.
- Point to 'Offset: Bottom Left' in the Outer area in the Shadow gallery to display a Live Preview of that shadow effect applied to the selected shape in the document (Figure 10–63).

Experiment

- Point to various shadows in the Shadow gallery and watch the shadow on the selected shape change.

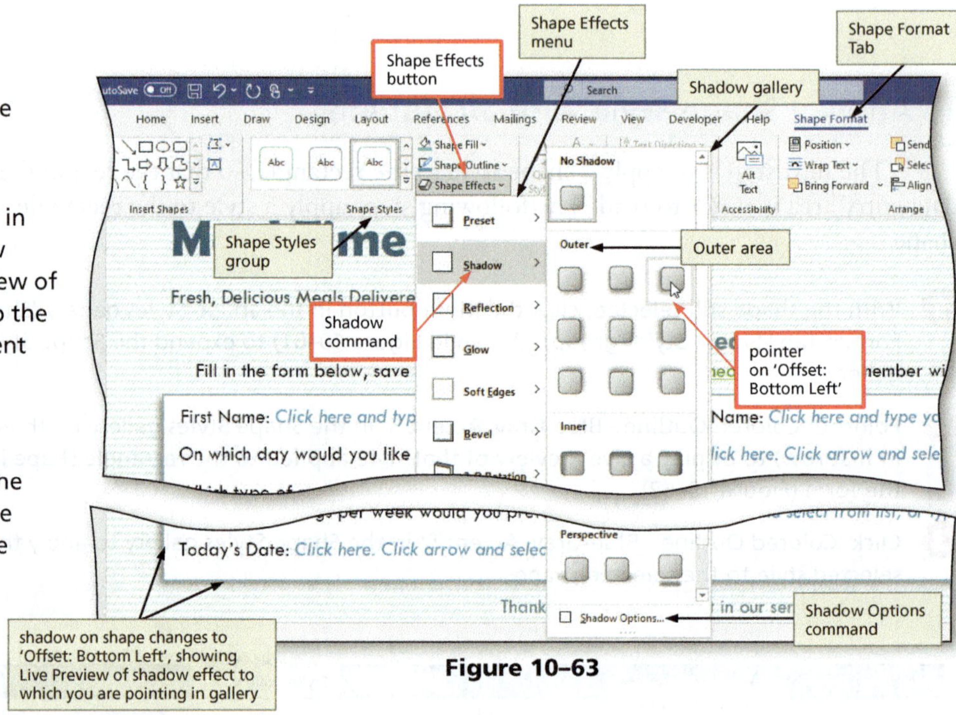

Figure 10–63

3

- Click 'Offset: Bottom Left' in the Shadow gallery to apply the selected shadow to the selected shape.

Q&A **Can I change the color of a shadow?**
Yes. Click Shadow Options (shown in Figure 10–63) in the Shadow gallery.

To Protect a Form

When you **protect a form**, you are allowing users to enter data only in designated areas — specifically, the content controls. The following steps protect the online form. **Why?** To prevent unwanted changes and edits to the form, it is crucial that you protect a form before making it available to users.

1

- Display the Developer tab.
- Click the Restrict Editing button (Developer tab | Protect group) to open the Restrict Editing pane (Figure 10–64).

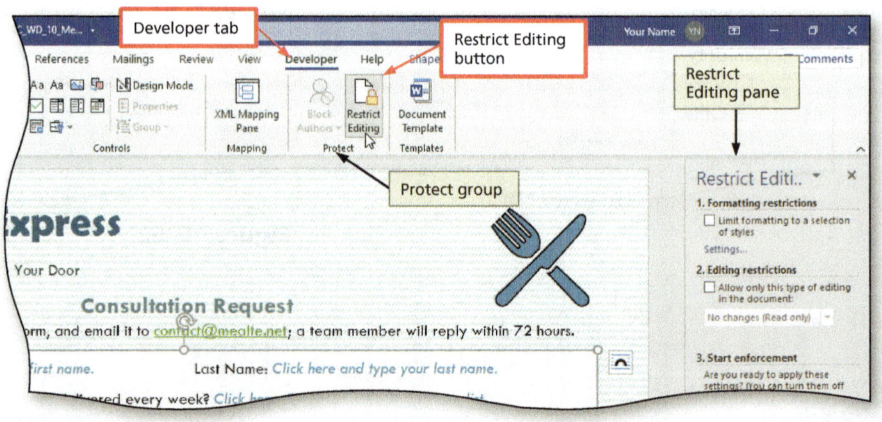

Figure 10–64

2

- In the Editing restrictions area, place a check mark in the 'Allow only this type of editing in the document' check box and then click its arrow to display a list of the types of allowed restrictions (Figure 10–65).

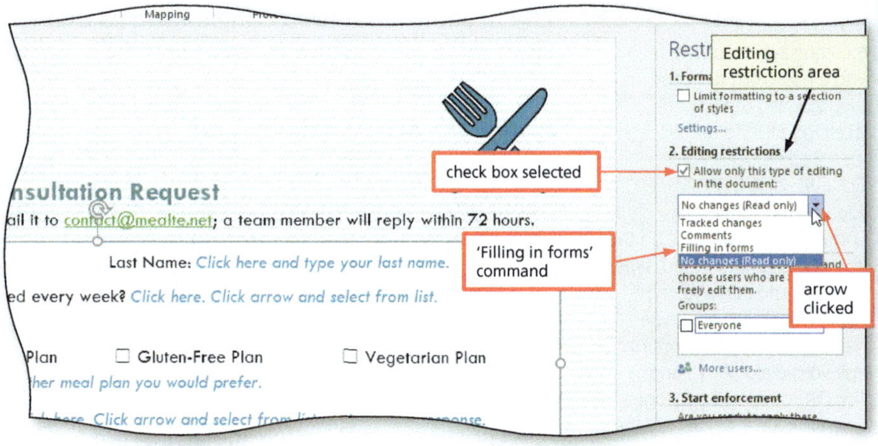

Figure 10–65

3

- Click 'Filling in forms' in the list to instruct Word that the only editing allowed in this document is to the content controls.
- In the Start enforcement area, click the 'Yes, Start Enforcing Protection' button, which displays the Start Enforcing Protection dialog box (Figure 10–66).

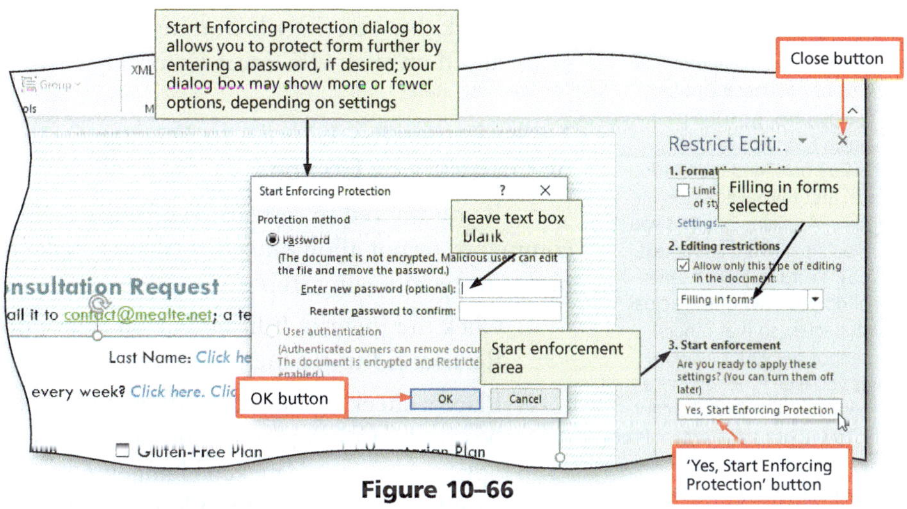

Figure 10–66

4

- Click OK (Start Enforcing Protection dialog box) to protect the document without a password.

Q&A **What if I enter a password?**
If you enter a password, only a user who knows the password will be able to unprotect the document.

- Close the Restrict Editing pane to show the protected form (Figure 10–67).

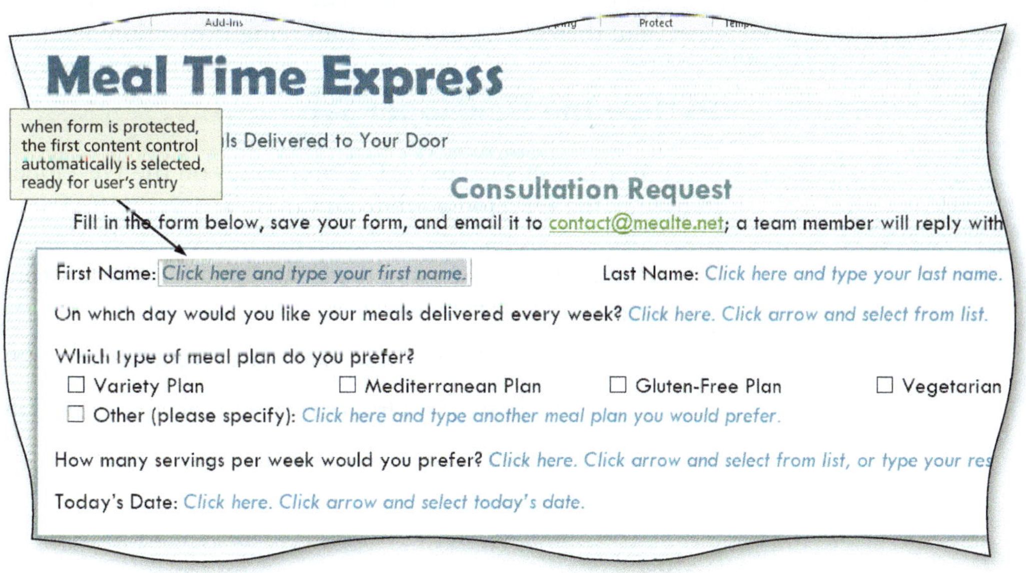

Figure 10–67

Other Ways

1. Open Backstage view, click Info, click Protect Document button, click Restrict Editing on Protect Document menu

BTW
Password-Protecting Documents
You can save documents with a password to keep unauthorized users from accessing files. To do this, open Backstage view, click Info, click the Protect Document button, click 'Encrypt with Password' on the Protect Document menu, type the password in the Encrypt Document dialog box, type the password again (Confirm Password dialog box), and click OK; or open Backstage view, click Save As, display the Save As dialog box, click the Tools button (Save As dialog box), click General Options on the Tools menu, type the password in the appropriate text box (General Options dialog box), type the password again (Confirm Password dialog box), and then click OK and the Save button (Save As dialog box). As you type a password in the text box, Word displays a series of dots instead of the actual characters so that others cannot see your password as you type it. To remove a password from a document, follow these steps except leave the password text box blank.

Be sure to keep the password confidential. Choose a password that is easy to remember and that no one can guess. Do not use any part of your first or last name, Social Security number, birthday, and so on. Use a password that is at least six characters long, and if possible, use a mixture of numbers and letters.

Protecting Documents

In addition to protecting a form so that it only can be filled in, Word provides several other options in the Restrict Editing pane.

To Set Formatting Restrictions

If you wanted to restrict users from making certain types of formatting changes to a document, you would perform the following steps.

1. Click the Restrict Editing button (Developer tab | Protect group) to open the Restrict Editing pane.
2. Place a check mark in the 'Limit formatting to a selection of styles' check box in the Formatting restrictions area.
3. Click the Settings link and then select the types of formatting you want to allow (Formatting Restrictions dialog box).
4. Click OK.
5. Click the 'Yes, Start Enforcing Protection' button, enter a password if desired, and then click OK (Start Enforcing Protection dialog box).

To Set Editing Restrictions to Tracked Changes or Comments or No Edits

If you wanted to restrict users' edits to allow only tracked changes, allow only comments, or not allow any edits (that is, make the document read only), you would perform the following steps.

1. Click the Restrict Editing button (Developer tab | Protect group) to open the Restrict Editing pane.
2. Place a check mark in the 'Allow only this type of editing in the document' check box in the Editing restrictions area, click the arrow, and then click the desired option — that is, Tracked changes, Comments, or No changes (Read only) — to specify the types of edits allowed in the document.
3. Click the 'Yes, Start Enforcing Protection' button, enter a password if desired, and then click OK (Start Enforcing Protection dialog box).

To Hide the Developer Tab

You are finished using the commands on the Developer tab. Thus, the following steps hide the Developer tab from the ribbon.

1. Open Backstage view and then click Options in the left pane of Backstage view to display the Word Options dialog box.
2. Click Customize Ribbon in the left pane (Word Options dialog box).
3. Remove the check mark from the Developer check box in the Main Tabs list.
4. Click OK to hide the Developer tab from the ribbon.

BTW
Setting Exceptions to Editing Restrictions
You can use the Restrict Editing pane to allow editing in just certain areas of the document, a procedure referred to as adding users excepted from restrictions. To do this, place a check mark in the 'Allow only this type of editing in the document' check box and then change the associated text box to 'No changes (Read only)', which instructs Word to prevent any editing to the document. Next, select the placeholder text for which you want to waive user restrictions and place a check mark in the Everyone check box in the Exceptions (optional) area to instruct Word that the selected item can be edited — the rest of the form will be read only.

To Hide the Ruler, Collapse the Ribbon, Save the Template, and Exit Word

If the ruler is displayed on the screen, you want to hide it. You also want to collapse the ribbon so that when you test the form in the next steps, the ribbon is collapsed. Finally, the online form template for this project now is complete, so you can save the template again and exit Word. The following steps perform these tasks.

1. If the ruler is displayed on the screen, remove the check mark from the Ruler check box (View tab | Show group).
2. Click the 'Collapse the Ribbon' button on the ribbon (shown in Figure 10–5 earlier in this module) to collapse the ribbon.
3. Save the template again on the same storage location with the same file name.
4. sam Exit Word.

BTW

Protected Documents

If you open an existing form that has been protected, Word will not allow you to modify the form's appearance until you unprotect it. To unprotect a form (or any protected document), open the Restrict Editing pane by clicking the Restrict Editing button (Developer tab | Protect group) or open Backstage view, display the Info screen, click the Protect Document button, and click Restrict Editing on the Protect Document menu. Then, click the Stop Protection button in the Restrict Editing pane and close the pane. If this unencrypted document has been protected with a password, you will be asked to enter the password when you attempt to unprotect the document.

Working with an Online Form

When you create a template, you use the Open command in Backstage view to open the template so that you can modify it. After you have created a template, you then can make it available to users. Users do not open templates with the Open command in Word. Instead, a user creates a new Word document that is *based* on the template, which means the title bar displays the default file name, Document1 (or a similar name) rather than the template name. When Word creates a new document that is based on a template, the document window contains any text and formatting associated with the template. If a user accesses a letter template, for example, Word displays the contents of a basic letter in a new document window.

To Use File Explorer to Create a New Document That Is Based on a Template

When you save a template on storage media, as instructed earlier in this module, a user can create a new document that is based on the template through File Explorer. **Why?** This allows the user to work with a new document instead of risking the chance of altering the original template. The following steps create a new Word document that is based on the SC_WD_10_MealTimeExpressForm.dotx template.

1.
- Click the File Explorer button on the Windows taskbar to open a File Explorer window.
- Navigate to the location of the saved template (Figure 10–68).

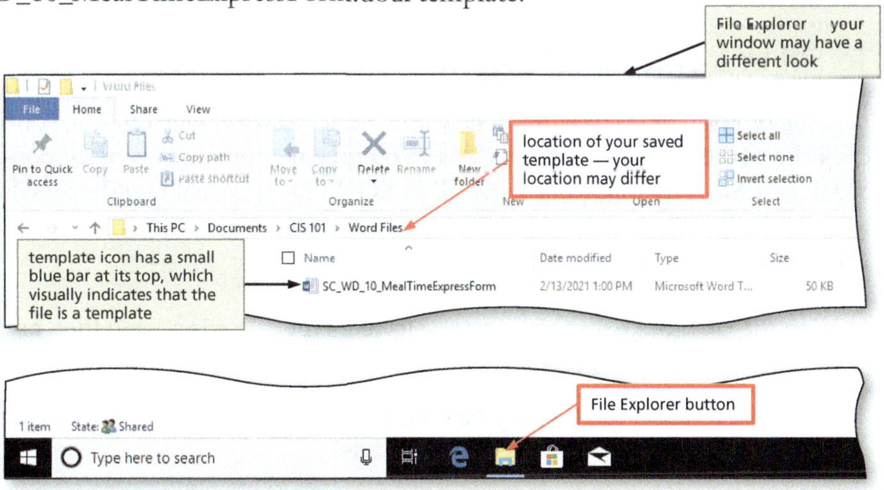

Figure 10–68

2

- Double-click the SC_WD_10_MealTimeExpressForm.dotx file in the File Explorer window, which starts Word and creates a new document that is based on the contents of the selected template (Figure 10–69).

Q&A

Why did my background page color disappear?
If the background page color does not appear, open Backstage view, click Options to display the Word Options dialog box, click Advanced in the left pane (Word Options dialog box), scroll to the Show document content section, place a check mark in the 'Show background colors and images in Print Layout view' check box, and then click OK.

Why does my ribbon show only three tabs: File, Tools, and View?
Your screen is in Read mode. Click the View tab and then click Edit Document to switch to Print Layout view.

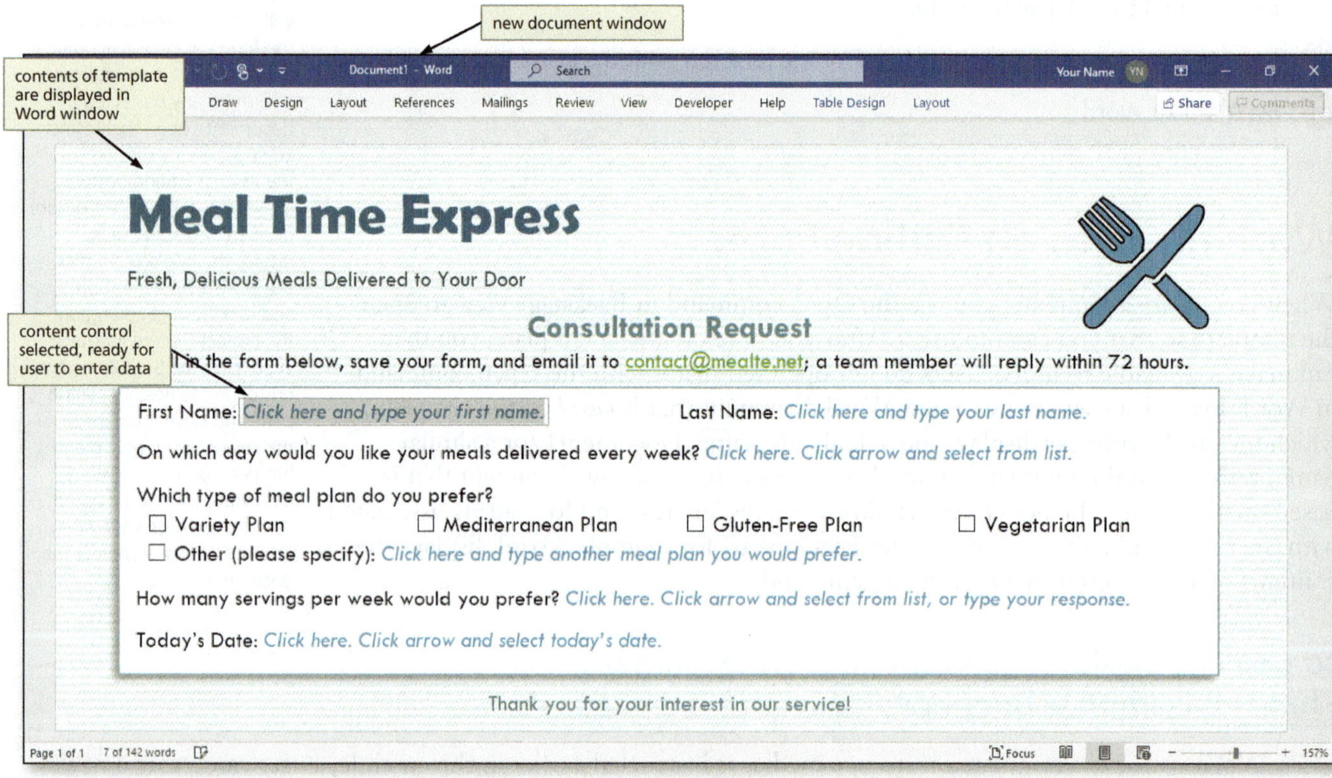

Figure 10–69

To Fill In a Form and Save It

The next step is to enter data in the form. To advance from one content control to the next, a user can click the content control or press TAB. To move to a previous content control, a user can click it or press SHIFT+TAB. The following steps fill in SC_WD_10_MealTimeExpressForm. **Why?** You want to test the form to be sure it works as you intended.

1

- With the First Name content control selected, type `Jordan` and then press TAB.
- Type `Wilton` in the Last Name content control.
- Press TAB to select the Delivery Day content control and then click its arrow to display the list of choices (shown in Figure 10–1b at the beginning of this module).
- Click Thursday in the list.

- Click the Gluten-Free Plan and Other Meal Plan Type check boxes to select them.
- Type **Pescatarian** in the Other Meal Plan Type content control.
- Click the Servings per Week content control and then click its arrow to display the list of choices (Figure 10–70).

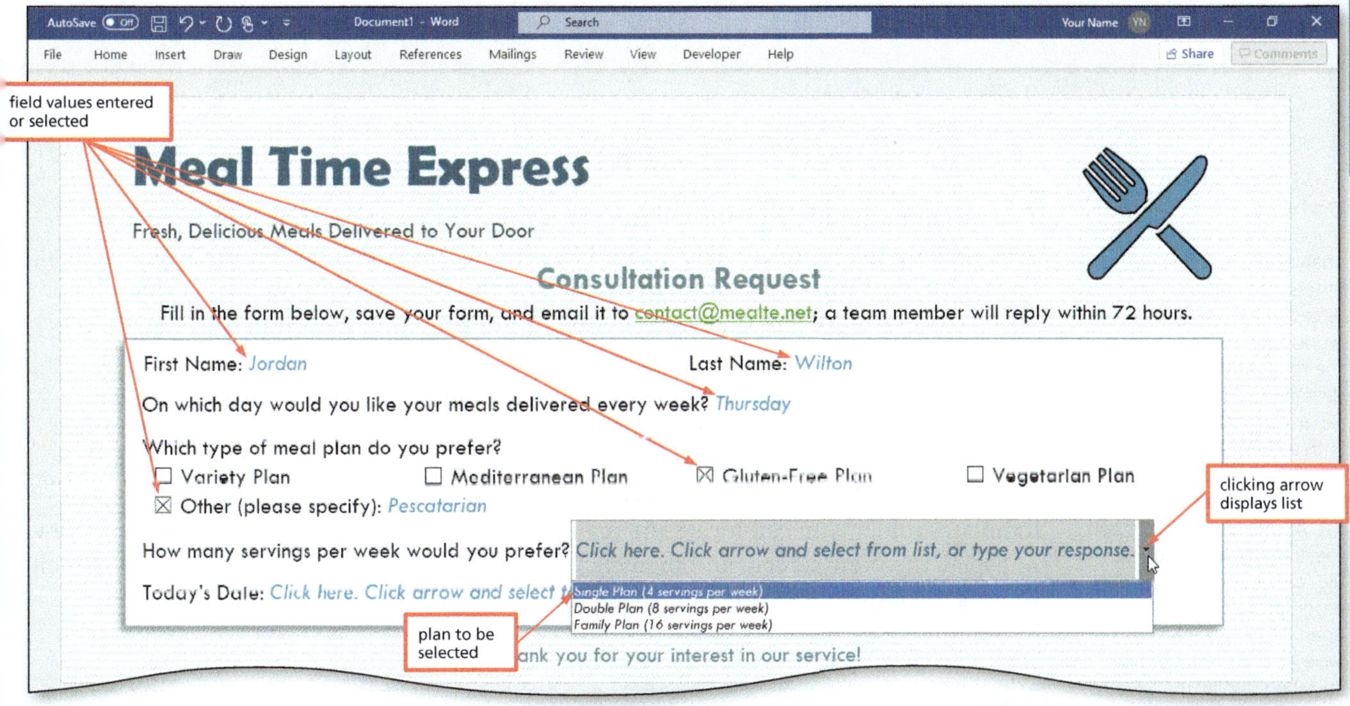

Figure 10–70

2

- Select Single Plan (4 servings per week) in the list.
- Click the Today's Date content control and then click its arrow to display a calendar (Figure 10–71).

3

- Click February 13, 2021 in the calendar to complete the data entry (shown in Figure 10–1c at the beginning of this module).

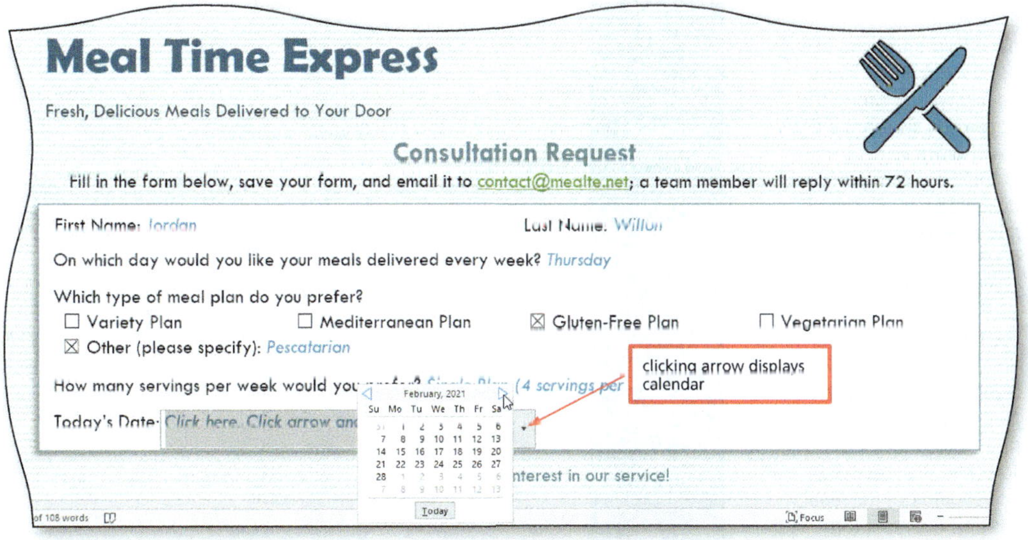

Figure 10–71

4

- Save the file on your storage location with the file name, SC_WD_10_WiltonConsultationRequest. If Word asks if you want to also save changes to the document template, click No.

Q&A

Can I print the form?

You can print the document as you print any other document. Keep in mind, however, that the colors used were designed for viewing online. Thus, different color schemes would have been selected if the form had been designed for a printout.

- Exit Word. (If Word asks if you want to save the modified styles, click the Don't Save button.)
- If the File Explorer window still is open, close it.

BTW

Linking a Form to a Database

If you want to use or analyze the data that a user enters into a form in an Access database or an Excel worksheet, you could save the form data in a comma-delimited text file. This file separates each data item with a comma and places quotation marks around text data items. Then, you can use Access or Excel to import the comma-delimited text file for use in the respective program. To save form data, open Backstage view, click Save As in Backstage view, and then display the Save As dialog box. Click the Tools button (Save As dialog box) and then click Save Options on the Tools menu to display the Word Options dialog box. Click Advanced in the left pane (Word Options dialog box), scroll to the Preserve fidelity when sharing this document area in the right pane, place a check mark in the 'Save form data as delimited text file' check box, and then click OK. Next, be sure the file type is Plain Text (Save As dialog box) and then click the Save button to save the file as a comma-delimited text file. You can import the resulting comma-delimited file in an Access database or an Excel worksheet. To convert successfully, you should use the legacy controls (i.e., text form field, check box form field, etc.), which are available through the Legacy Tools button (Developer tab | Controls group).

Working with Templates

If you want to modify a protected template, open it by clicking Open in Backstage view, clicking the template name, and then clicking the Open button in the dialog box. Then, you must **unprotect a form** by clicking the Restrict Editing button (Developer tab | Protect group) and then clicking the Stop Protection button in the Restrict Editing pane.

When you created the template in this module, you saved it on your local storage location. In environments other than an academic setting, you would not save the template on your own storage location; instead, you would save the file in the Custom Office Templates folder. When you save a template in the Custom Office Templates folder, you can locate the template by opening Backstage view, clicking New to display the New screen, and then clicking the Personal tab in the New screen, which displays the template in the New screen (Figure 10–72).

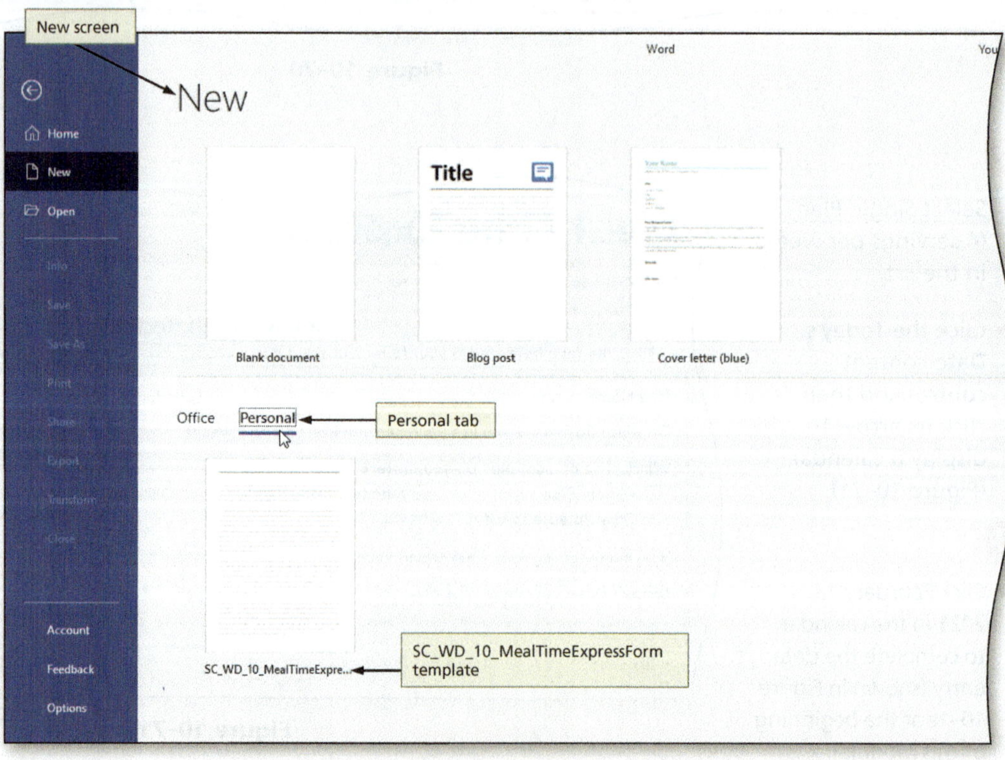

Figure 10–72

Summary

In this module, you learned how to create an online form. Topics covered included saving a document as a template, changing paper size, using a table to control layout, showing the Developer tab, inserting and formatting content controls, editing placeholder text, changing properties of content controls, and protecting a form.

Consider This: Plan Ahead

What decisions will you need to make when creating online forms?

Use these guidelines as you complete the assignments in this module and create your own online forms outside of this class.

1. Design the form.
   a) To minimize the time spent creating a form while using a computer or mobile device, consider sketching the form on a piece of paper first.
   b) Design a well-thought-out draft of the form — being sure to include all essential form elements, including the form's title, text and graphics, data entry fields, and data entry instructions.
2. For each data entry field, determine its field type and/or list of possible values that it can contain.
3. Save the form as a template, instead of as a Word document, to simplify the data entry process for users of the form.
4. Create a functional and visually appealing form.
   a) Use colors that complement one another.
   b) Draw the user's attention to important sections.
   c) Arrange data entry fields in logical groups on the form and in an order that users would expect.
   d) Data entry instructions should be succinct and easy to understand.
   e) Ensure that users can enter and edit data only in designated areas of the form.
5. Determine how the form data will be analyzed.
   a) If the data entered in the form will be analyzed by a program outside of Word, create the data entry fields so that the entries are stored in separate fields that can be shared with other programs.
6. Test the form, ensuring it works as you intended.
   a) Fill in the form as if you are a user.
   b) Ask others to fill in the form to be sure it is organized in a logical manner and is easy to understand and complete.
   c) If any errors or weaknesses in the form are identified, correct them and test the form again.
7. Publish or distribute the form.
   a) Not only does an online form reduce the need for paper, it saves the time spent making copies of the form and distributing it.
   b) When the form is complete, post it on social media, the web, or your company's intranet, or email it to targeted recipients.

Apply Your Knowledge

Reinforce the skills and apply the concepts you learned in this module.

Working with an Online Form

Note: To complete this assignment, you will be required to use the Data Files. Please contact your instructor for information about accessing the Data Files.

Instructions: Start Word. Open the template, SC_WD_10-1.dotx, which is located in the Data Files. The template is a draft of an online survey created by Carter's Recycling Service, a new recycling facility, that will be emailed to community members by the community relations coordinator at the New Town Village Hall requesting feedback on potential upcoming village services. You are to modify the template. The final template is shown in Figure 10–73.

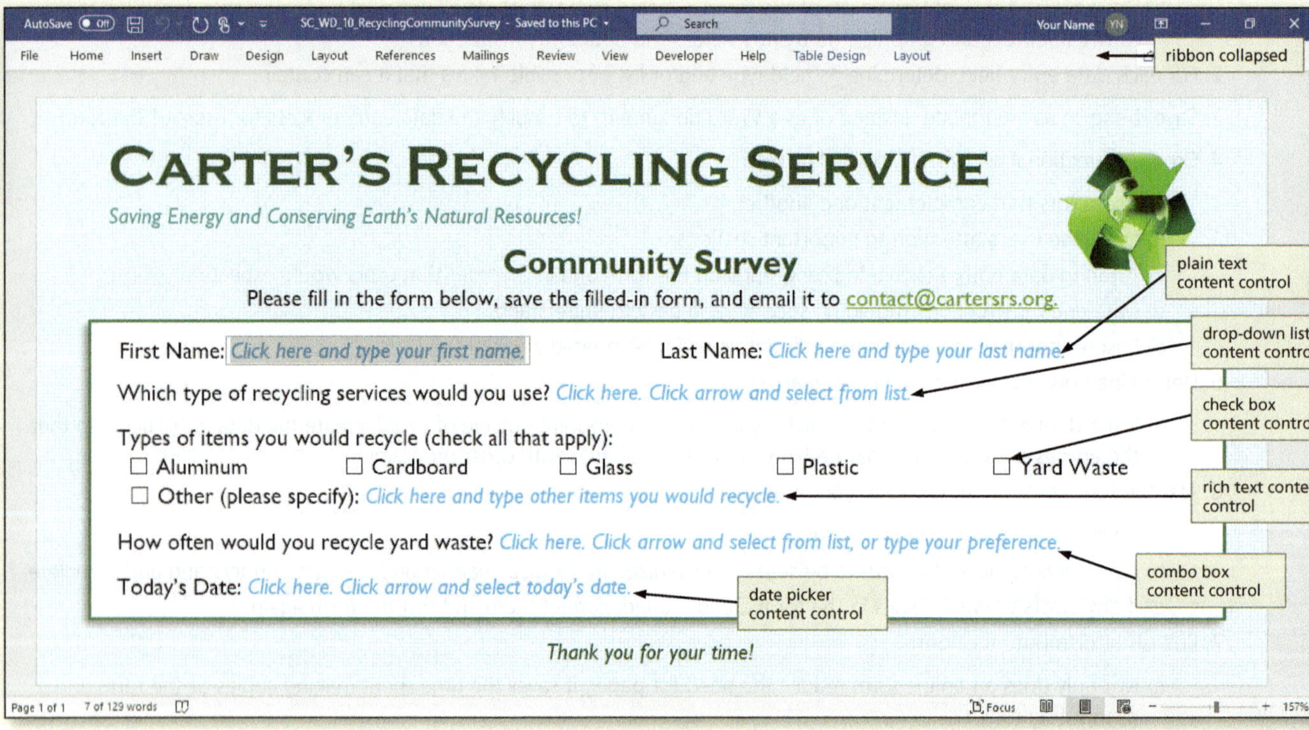

Figure 10–73

Perform the following tasks:

1. Click File on the ribbon and then click Save As and save the document using the new file name, SC_WD_10_RecyclingCommunitySurvey.
2. Add the page color Turquoise, Accent 1, Lighter 80% to the template. Apply the Small grid pattern fill effect to the template. (Hint: Use the Page Color button (Design tab | Page Background group).)
3. Remove the table border from each of the two tables in the form. (Hint: One at a time, select each table using the Select button (Layout tab | Table group) and then use the Borders arrow (Table Design tab | Borders group).)
4. If necessary, use the View Gridlines button (Layout tab | Table group) to show table gridlines.
5. If necessary, show the Developer tab on the ribbon.

6. In the 2 × 1 table in the data entry area, in the cell to the right of the First Name content control, enter the text, Last Name:, followed by a space as the label and then use the Developer tab to insert a plain text content control in the cell after the label.
7. Select the inserted plain text content control and then turn on Design mode. Edit the placeholder text so that it reads: Click here and type your last name. Turn off Design mode.
8. Change the properties of the plain text content control as follows: enter Last Name as the tag, select the 'Use a style to format text typed into the empty control' check box, select the Intense Emphasis style for the text to be typed in the content control, and select the 'Content control cannot be deleted' check box.
9. Use the Styles group in the Home tab to format the placeholder text in the plain text content control to the Intense Emphasis style.
10. In the data entry area, to the right of the type of recycling services question, insert a drop-down list content control.
11. Select the inserted drop-down list content control and then turn on Design mode. Edit the placeholder text so that it contains two sentences that read: Click here. Click arrow and select from list. When you have finished editing the placeholder text, turn off Design mode.
12. Change the properties of the drop-down list content control as follows: enter Recycling Services as the tag, select the 'Use a style to format text typed into the empty control' check box, select the Intense Emphasis style for the text to be typed in the content control, select the 'Content control cannot be deleted' check box, and set these four choices for the list: Fee-Based Curbside Recycling, Free Drop-Off Locations, Both, Neither (be sure to delete the default choice of Choose an item.).
13. Use the Styles group on the Home tab to format the placeholder text in the drop-down list content control to the Intense Emphasis style.
14. In the 5 × 1 table in the data entry area, in the cell to the right of the Glass content control, insert a check box content control.
15. Change the properties of the check box content control as follows: enter Plastic as the tag, select the Show as box and then select None, and select the 'Content control cannot be deleted' check box.
16. One blank space to the right of the inserted check box content control, enter Plastic as the label.
17. In the 5 × 1 table in the data entry area, in the cell to the right of the Plastic content control, insert a check box content control.
18. Change the properties of the check box content control as follows: enter Yard Waste as the tag, select the Show as box and then select None, and select the 'Content control cannot be deleted' check box.
19. One space to the right of the inserted check box content control, enter the text, Yard Waste, as the label.
20. In the data entry area, to the right of the Other (please specify): check box, insert a rich text content control.
21. Select the inserted rich text content control and then turn on Design mode. Edit the placeholder text so that it reads: Click here and type other items you would recycle. Turn off Design mode.
22. Change the properties of the rich text content control as follows: enter Other Recycle Items as the tag, select the 'Use a style to format text typed into the empty control' check box, select the Intense Emphasis style for the text to be typed in the content control, and select the 'Content control cannot be deleted' check box.

Continued ›

Apply Your Knowledge *continued*

23. Use the Styles group on the Home tab to format the placeholder text in the rich text content control to the Intense Emphasis style.
24. In the data entry area, to the right of the frequency of recycling yard waste question, insert a combo box content control.
25. Select the inserted combo box content control and then turn on Design mode. Edit the placeholder text so it contains two sentences that read: Click here. Click arrow and select from list, or type your preference. When you have finishing editing the placeholder text, turn off Design mode.
26. Change the properties of the combo box content control as follows: enter Yard Waste Frequency as the tag, select the 'Use a style to format text typed into the empty control' check box, select the Intense Emphasis style for the text to be typed in the content control, select the 'Content control cannot be deleted' check box, and set these four choices for the list: Twice a year, Four times a year, Monthly, Never. (Be sure to delete the default choice of Choose an item.)
27. Use the Styles group in the Home tab to format the placeholder text in the combo box content control to the Intense Emphasis style.
28. At the bottom of the data entry area, to the right of the Today's Date: label, insert a Date Picker content control.
29. Select the inserted date picker content control and then turn on Design mode. Edit the placeholder text so that it contains two sentences that read: Click here. Click arrow and select today's date. When you have finished editing the placeholder text, turn off Design mode.
30. Change the properties of the date picker content control as follows: enter Today's Date as the tag, select the 'Use a style to format text typed into the empty control' check box, select the Intense Emphasis style for the text to be typed in the content control, select the 'Content control cannot be deleted' check box, and select the date in this format: February 13, 2021.
31. Use the Styles group on the Home tab to format the placeholder text in the date picker content control to the Intense Emphasis style.
32. If table gridlines show, hide them. (Hint: Position the insertion point in one of the two tables in the form and the use the View Gridlines button (Layout tab | Table group).)
33. Collapse the ribbon. If necessary, adjust spacing above and below paragraphs as necessary so that all contents fit on a single screen with the ribbon collapsed.
34. Use the Restrict Editing pane to set editing restrictions to filling in forms and then start enforcing protection (do not use a password). Close the Restrict Editing pane.
35. Save the form again with the same file name and then submit it in the format specified by your instructor. Close the template and exit Word.
36. Open a File Explorer window. Locate the SC_WD_10_RecyclingCommunitySurvey.dotx template you just created and then double-click the template in File Explorer to create a new document based on the template.
37. When Word displays a new document based on the template, if necessary, collapse the ribbon, hide formatting marks, and change the zoom to page width. Your screen should look like Figure 10–73 and display Document1 (or a similar name) on the title bar instead of the file name.
38. Test your form as follows:
    a. With the First Name content control selected, enter your first name.
    b. Press TAB and then enter your last name in the last name content control.
    c. Click the Recycling Services content control, click its arrow, and then click Both in the list.

d. Click the Cardboard, Glass, and Plastic check boxes to select them.

e. Click the Other check box. If necessary, click the Other text box and then enter Steel in the text box.

f. Click the Recycle Yard Waste Frequency content control to select it, click its arrow, press ESC because none of these choices answers the question, and enter the text, Every other month, as the response.

g. Click the Today's Date content control, click the arrow to display a calendar, and then select today's date in the calendar.

h. Close the form without saving it. (If any content controls do not work as intended, use Word to open the SC_WD_10_RecyclingCommunitySurvey.dotx template, unprotect the template, modify it as appropriate, protect the template again, save it, and then retest it as described in this step.)

39. If the recycling service wanted the community member's middle name on the same line as the first and last names, how would you evenly space the three items across the line?

Extend Your Knowledge

Extend the skills you learned in this module and experiment with new skills. You may need to use Help to complete the assignment.

Working with Icons, Picture Content Controls, Passwords, and More

Note: To complete this assignment, you will be required to use the Data Files. Please contact your instructor for information about accessing the Data Files.

Instructions: Start Word. Open the template, SC_WD_10-2.dotx, which is located in the Data Files. This template is a draft of an online freshman orientation feedback form, written by the campus life coordinator at Harper View College.

You will unprotect the form, insert and format icons, group images, insert a picture content control in a text box, practice inserting repeating section and building block gallery content controls, change a shape's shadow color, customize theme colors, and protect a document (form, in this case) with passwords.

Perform the following tasks:

1. Use Help to review and expand your knowledge about these topics: unprotecting documents, picture content controls, text boxes, grouping objects, shadows, shape fill effects, changing theme colors, and protecting forms with passwords.
2. Click File on the ribbon, click Save As, and then save the template using the new file name, SC_WD_10_FreshmanOrientationForm.
3. Unprotect the document. (Hint: Use the Developer tab on the ribbon or the Info screen in Backstage view.)
4. Change the paper size to a width of 8.5 inches and a height of 4 inches.
5. Insert two appropriate icons of your choice in the template. (Hint: Use the Icons button (Insert tab | Illustrations group). If your version of Word does not include the Icons button, insert two appropriate images using the Online Picture button or insert the images that are called Support_WD_10_Backpack.png and Support_WD_10_Books.png from the Data Files.)
6. Change the wrapping of each of the inserted images to In Front of Text. For only one of the images, change the color, fill, outline, effects, or style to options of your choice. Move the two images on the page so that they overlap each other. Select the image on the top and send it

Continued >

Extend Your Knowledge *continued*

backward. (Hint: Right-click the image and then use commands on the submenu or use buttons in the Arrange group on the ribbon.) Select the image on the bottom and bring it forward. Select the image on top and send it to the back. Select the image on the bottom and bring it to the front.

7. For the image you have not yet formatted, change its color, fill, outline, effects, or style to options of your choice.
8. Move one image on one side of the college name and the other image on the other side. Resize the images as appropriate.
9. Group the two images at the top of the form together. Move the grouped graphics. Return them to their original location.
10. Select the college name and then use the 'Text Effects and Typography' button (Home tab | Font group) to add a reflection of your choice to the college name. Adjust spacing above and below paragraphs as necessary so that the entire form fits on a single page.
11. Change the Orientation Start Date content control to a format other than M/d/yyyy (i.e., 2/16/2021).
12. Insert a simple text box into the empty space on the right side of the data entry area by clicking the Text Box button (Insert tab | Text group) and then clicking 'Simple Text Box' in the Text Box gallery. Change the wrapping of the inserted text box to In Front of Text. Resize the text box so that it fits completely in the data entry area. Remove space after the paragraph. Delete the placeholder in the text box.
13. In the text box, type the label, Student Photo:, and then resize the text as necessary. Below the label, insert a picture content control in the text box. Resize the picture content control so that it fits in the text box and then center both the picture and label in the text box (Figure 10–74). Remove the border from the text box.

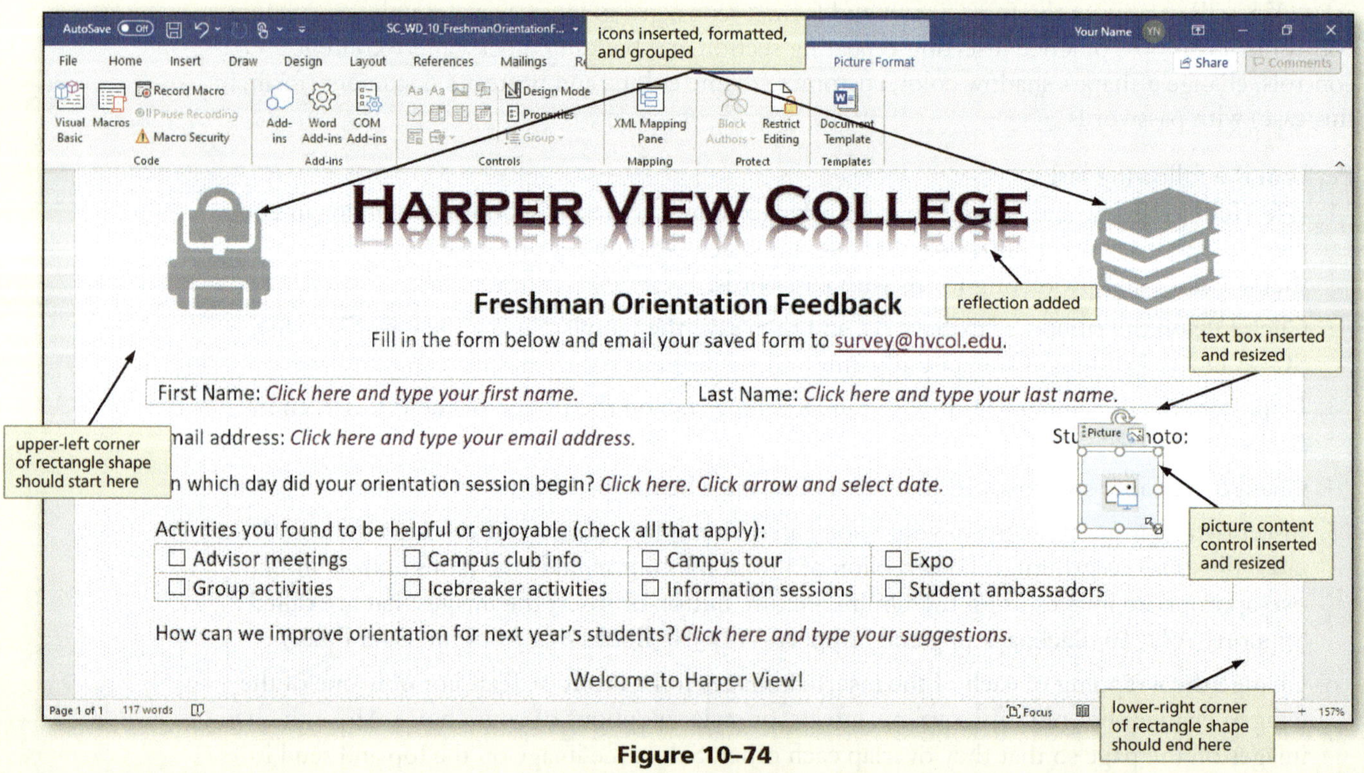

Figure 10–74

14. Select one of the tables in the data entry area. Insert a repeating section content control. Click the insert control (the plus sign) at the far-right edge of the table with the repeating section content control. What happens when you click the insert control? Click the Undo button on the Quick Access Toolbar to undo the added duplicate table row. Click the Undo button again to undo the insert of the repeating section content control or delete the content control manually.
15. Click to the right of the last line on the template. Insert a building block gallery content control. Click the Properties button (Developer tab | Controls group) to display the Content Control Properties dialog box. Change the value in the Gallery box in the Document Building Block Properties area to Equations and then click OK. In the template, click the 'Explore Quick Parts' button attached to the top of the building block gallery content control. What is displayed when you click this button? Delete the building block gallery content control by right-clicking it and then clicking 'Remove Content Control' on the shortcut menu.
16. Hide table gridlines, if they are showing.
17. Add a page color of your choice to the template. Apply a pattern fill effect of your choice to the page color background.
18. Insert a rectangle shape around the data entry area (starting in the upper-left corner by the First Name label and ending in the lower-right corner to the right of the Orientation Suggestions rich text content control).
19. Send the rectangle shape backward, which sends the shape back one layer. Send the rectangle shape behind text. Note that in this case, these two commands yield the same result.
20. Change the shape fill in the rectangle shape to a color of your choice. Change the shape outline on the rectangle shape to a color or style of your choice. If necessary, change the font color or style of text in the data entry area so that it is readable on the background color.
21. Add a shadow to the rectangle and then change the color of the shadow on the rectangle to a color other than the default.
22. Customize the theme colors for the hyperlink to a color of your choice (Hint: Use the Customize Colors command in Colors gallery (Design tab | Document Formatting group).) Save the modified theme colors.
23. Make any necessary formatting changes to the form.
24. If requested by your instructor, change the email address above the data entry area to your email address.
25. Restrict formatting in the document using the 'Limit formatting to a selection of styles' check box. Click the Settings link (Restrict Editing pane) and then select document formatting restrictions. Remove the formatting restrictions just set in the form.
26. Restrict editing in the document to tracked changes. Change the restrict editing selection to comments. Finally, restrict editing to filling in the form and protect the unencrypted form using the word, fun, as the password in the Start Enforcing Protection dialog box. What is the purpose of this password?
27. If requested by your instructor, use the Info screen in Backstage view to encrypt the document with a password. Use the word, fun, as the password. (Hint: You will need to use the Restrict Editing pane to remove the password added in the previous step before you can complete this step.) What is the purpose of this password? (Note that to delete the password, you would remove the password in the Password text box in the Encrypt Document dialog box.)
28. Save the form again with the same name and then submit it in the format specified by your instructor. Close the template and exit Word.

Continued >

Extend Your Knowledge *continued*

29. Test the form using your own data for the responses. When filling in the form, use your own photo for the student photo or the use the picture called Support_WD_10_FaceShot in the Data Files for the picture content control. If required by your instructor, save the filled-in form and then submit it in the format specified by your instructor.
30. If your document had multiple pages with headers and footers and did not want the same headers or footers to appear on different pages, what button would you click to break the link between the sections?
31. Answer the questions posed in #14, #15, #26, #27, and #30. What is the advantage of grouping graphics? Besides changing the color of the shadow, what other shadow settings can you adjust?

Expand Your World

Create a solution that uses cloud or web technologies by learning and investigating on your own from general guidance.

Using Microsoft Forms to Create an Online Survey

Instructions: You will use Microsoft Forms, which is part of Office 365, to prepare an online form. As a marketing coordinator at Harkin Realtors, you will create an online client survey. Figure 10–75 shows a portion of the survey. You will enter the questions Microsoft Forms and then use its tools to enter settings for the responses.

Perform the following tasks:

1. Start a browser. Search for the text, Microsoft Forms, using a search engine. Visit websites to learn about Microsoft Forms. Navigate to the Microsoft Forms website. You will need to sign in to your OneDrive account.
2. Create a new form using Microsoft Forms. Use SC_WD_10_HarkinRealtors.docx as the file name.
3. Enter the text, Client Survey, as the description.
4. Click the Add new button. Select Text as the type of question. Enter the text, Who was your agent?, in the text box. Make this question required.
5. Click the Add new button. Select Rating as the type of question. Enter the text, How would you rate your agent (with five stars being the highest rating)?, in the text box. Make this question required.
6. Click the Add new button. Select Choice as the type of question. Enter the text, Which type of real estate did you purchase or sell through our agency?, in the text box. Enter these three options: Single-family home, Condominium, Land. Add an 'Other' option. Make this question required.
7. Click the Add new button. Select Date as the type of question. Enter the text, On what date was your closing held?, in the text box. Make this question required.
8. Add an appropriate theme to the form.
9. Preview the form on a computer (Figure 10–75). (Hint: Adjust the zoom in the browser window to see more of the form in the window at once.) If requested by your instructor, take a screenshot of the preview and submit the screenshot in the format requested by your instructor. Save the screenshot with the file name, SC_WD_10_HarkinRealtors.

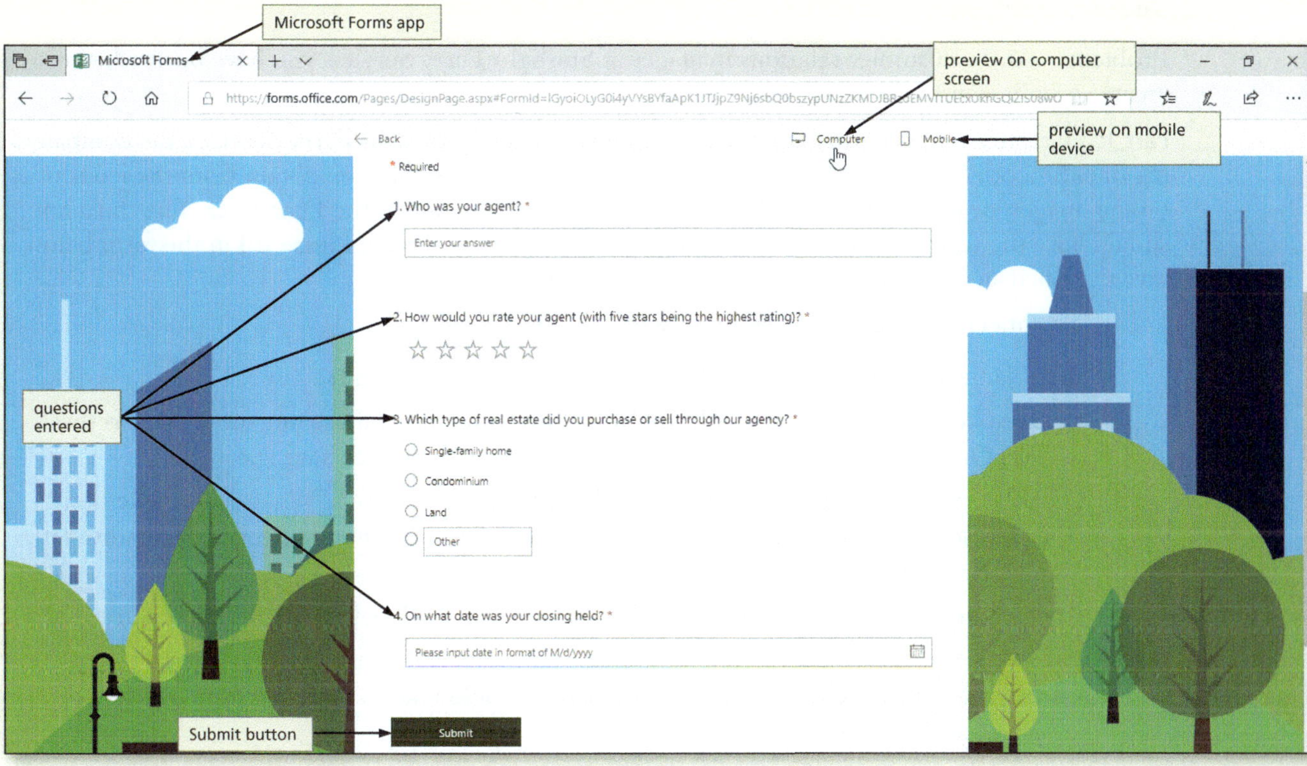

Figure 10–75

10. Preview the form on a mobile device. Click the Back button to return to the form design screen.
11. Click the 'More form settings' button in the upper-right corner of the screen, click Settings on the menu, and review the additional form settings options.
12. Click the Send button and review the sharing and sending options.
13. If requested by your instructor, copy the form link and email it to your instructor.
14. If requested by your instructor, click the 'Get a link to duplicate' button (or a similar button), copy this link, and email it to your instructor.
15. Copy the form link. Open a new browser tab and paste the link into the browser address bar. Fill in the form in the new browser window using responses of your choice and then click the Submit button.
16. Redisplay your form window and then click the Responses tab to see how Microsoft Forms tabulates results.
17. Close the Microsoft Forms window. If necessary, sign out of your OneDrive account.
18. What is Microsoft Forms? Do you prefer using Microsoft Forms or the Word desktop app to create online forms? Why?

In the Lab

Design and implement a solution using creative thinking and problem-solving skills.

Create an Online Form for a Ferry Service

Note: To complete this assignment, you may be required to use the Data Files. Please contact your instructor for information about accessing the Data Files.

Continued >

In the Lab *continued*

Problem: As the customer relations manager at Starlight Ferry Service, you have been asked to create an online customer satisfaction survey.

Part 1: Create a template that contains the company name (Starlight Ferry Service), the company's tag line (Smooth Sailing Every Day!), and an appropriate image that you obtain from the icons or online images, or use the Support_WD_10_FerryBoat.png image in the Data Files. The third line should have the text, Satisfaction Survey. The fourth line should read: Please fill in the form below, save the filled-in form, and then email it to survey@starlightfs.org.

The data entry area should contain the following:

- First Name and Last Name are plain text content controls within a table.
- A combo box content control with the label, How often do you use our services?, has these choices: Once or twice a year, Monthly, Weekly, More than once a week.
- The following instruction should appear above these check boxes: What do you like best about our services (check all that apply)?; the check boxes are Food selection, Friendly staff, Price, Cleanliness, and Other (please specify).
- A rich text content control after the Other (please specify) label allows customers to enter their own response.
- A drop-down list content control with the label, Would you recommend Starlight Ferry Service?, has these choices: Yes, No, Maybe.
- A date picker content control with the label, What date did you last use our service?

On the line below the data entry area, include the text: Thank you for your time!

Use the concepts and techniques presented in this module to create and format the online form. Use meaningful placeholder text for all content controls. (For example, the placeholder text for the First Name plain text content control could be as follows: Click here and type your first name.) Apply a style to the placeholder text. Assign names, styles, and locking to each content control (so that the content controls cannot be deleted). Draw a rectangle around the data entry area of the form and format the rectangle appropriately. Add a page color. Be sure to change the page size and margins, and adjust spacing as necessary above and below paragraphs, so that the entire form fits in the document window.

When you are finished creating the form, protect it so that editing is restricted to filling in the form and then save it as a template with the file name, SC_WD_10_StarlightSatisfactionSurvey. Test the form and make any necessary corrections. Submit the form in the format specified by your instructor.

Part 2: You made several decisions while creating the online form in this assignment: placeholder text to use and how to organize and format the online form (fonts, font sizes, styles, colors, etc.). What was the rationale behind each of these decisions? When you proofread and tested the online form, what further revisions did you make, and why? How would you recommend publishing or distributing this online form?

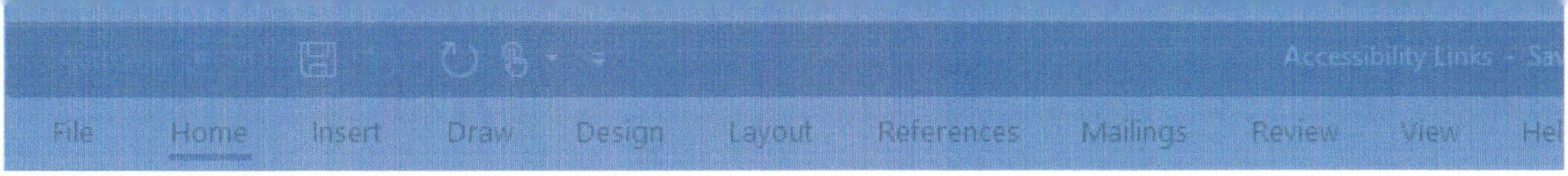

11 Enhancing an Online Form and Using Macros

Objectives

After completing this module, you will be able to:

- Unprotect a document
- Specify macro settings
- Convert a table to text
- Insert and edit a field
- Create a character style
- Apply and modify fill effects
- Change a shape
- Remove a background from a graphic
- Apply an artistic effect to a graphic
- Insert and format a text box
- Group objects
- Record and execute a macro
- Customize the Quick Access Toolbar
- Edit a macro's VBA code
- Work with 3-D models

Introduction

Word provides many tools that allow you to improve the appearance, functionality, and security of your documents. This module discusses tools used to perform the following tasks:

- Modify text and content controls.
- Enhance with color, shapes, effects, and graphics.
- Automate a series of tasks with a macro.

Project: Online Form Revised

This module uses Word to improve the visual appearance of and add macros to the online form created in Module 10, producing the online form shown in Figure 11–1a. This project begins with the Meal Time Express Consultation Request online form created in Module 10 and then enhances it and improves its functionality. Thus, if you created the online form template in Module 10, you will use that file in this module. If you did not create the online form template in Module 10, see your instructor for a copy.

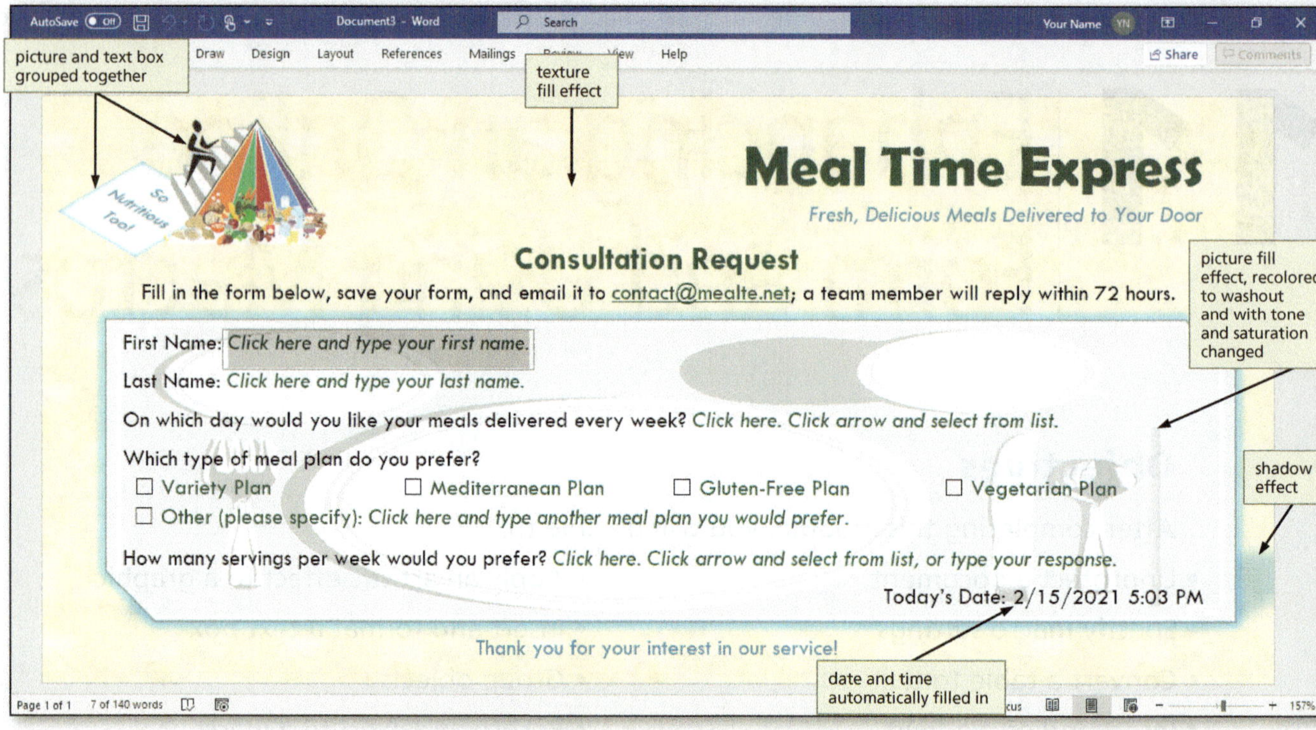

(a) Modified and Enhanced Online Form

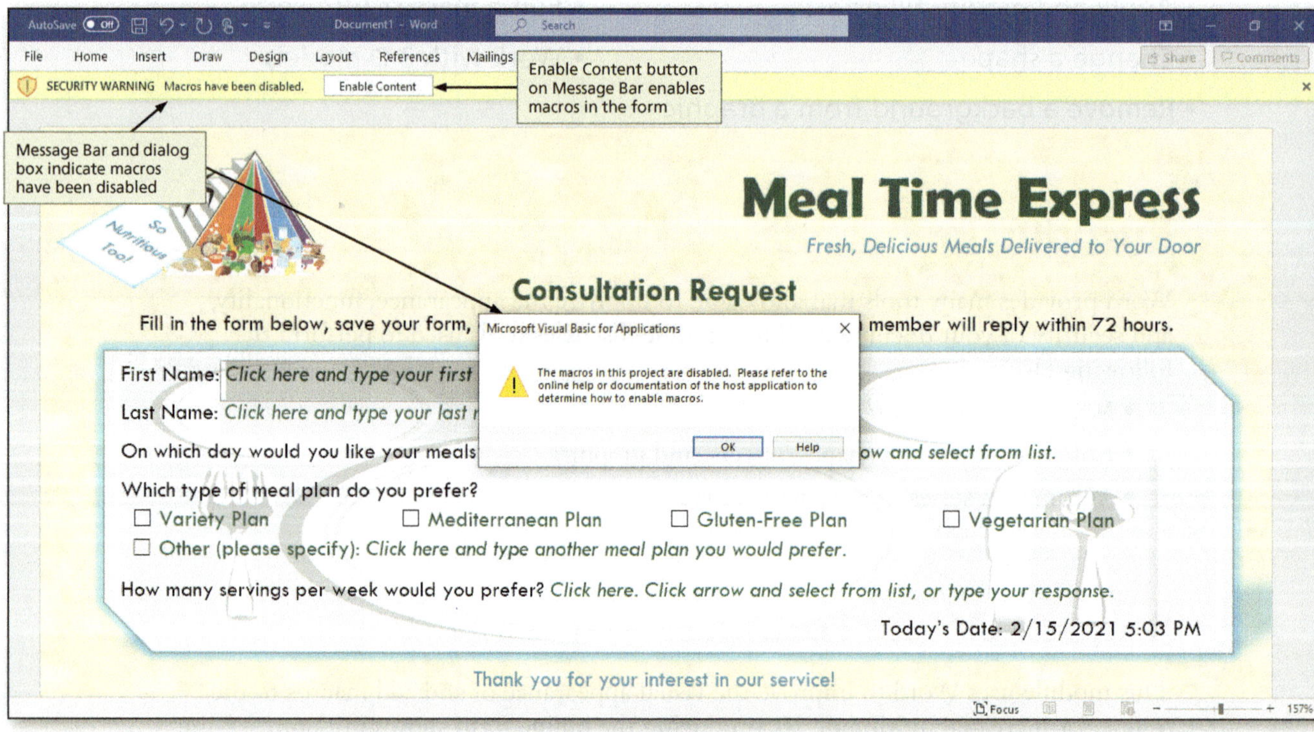

(b) Macros in Online Form Generate Security Warning

Figure 11–1

This project modifies the fonts and font colors of the text in the Meal Time Express Consultation Request online form and enhances the contents of the form to include a texture fill effect, a picture fill effect, and a text box and picture grouped together. The date in the form automatically displays the computer or mobile device's system date, instead of requiring the user to enter the date.

This form also includes macros to automate tasks. A **macro** is a named set of instructions, written in the Visual Basic programming language, that performs tasks automatically in a specified order. One macro allows the user to hide formatting marks and the ruler by pressing a keyboard shortcut (sometimes called a shortcut key) or clicking a button on the Quick Access Toolbar. Another macro specifies how the form is displayed initially on a user's Word screen. As shown in Figure 11–1b, when a document contains macros, Word may generate a security warning. If you are sure the macros are from a trusted source and free of viruses, then enable the content. Otherwise, do not enable the content, which protects your computer from potentially harmful viruses or other malicious software.

You will perform the following general tasks as you progress through this module:

1. Save a document as a macro-enabled template.
2. Modify the text and form content controls.
3. Enhance the form's visual appeal.
4. Create macros to automate tasks in the form.
5. Insert and format a 3-D model.

To Start Word and Specify Settings

If you are using a computer to step through the project in this module and you want your screens to match the figures in this book, you should change your screen's resolution to 1366 × 768. The following steps start Word, hide formatting marks, ensure rulers are not displayed, change the zoom to page width, and verify ruler and Mouse mode settings.

1. Start Word and create a blank document in the Word window. If necessary, maximize the Word window.
2. If the Print Layout button on the status bar is not selected, click it so that your screen is in Print Layout view.
3. If the 'Show/Hide ¶' button (Home tab | Paragraph group) is selected, click it to hide formatting marks because you will not use them in this project.
4. If the rulers are displayed on the screen, click the Ruler check box (View tab | Show group) to remove the rulers from the Word window because you will not use the rulers in this project.
5. If the edges of the page do not extend to the edge of the document window, display the View tab and then click the Page Width button (View tab | Zoom group).
6. If you are using a mouse and you want your screens to match the figures in the book, verify that you are using Mouse mode by clicking the Touch/Mouse Mode button on the Quick Access Toolbar and then, if necessary, clicking Mouse on the menu. (If your Quick Access Toolbar does not display the Touch/Mouse Mode button, click the 'Customize Quick Access Toolbar' button on the Quick Access Toolbar and then click Touch/Mouse Mode on the menu to add the button to the Quick Access Toolbar.)

BTW
The Ribbon and Screen Resolution
Word may change how the groups and buttons within the groups appear on the ribbon, depending on the screen resolution of your computer. Thus, your ribbon may look different from the ones in this book if you are using a screen resolution other than 1366 × 768.

To Save a Macro-Enabled Template

The project in this module contains macros. Thus, the first step in this module is to open the Meal Time Express Consultation Request template created in Module 10 and then save the template as a macro-enabled template. **Why?** To provide added security to templates, a basic Word template cannot store macros. Word instead provides a specific type of template, called a **macro-enabled template**, in which you can store macros.

1

- sam Open the template named SC_WD_10_MealTimeExpressForm.dotx that you created in Module 10. If you did not create the online form template in Module 10, see your instructor for a copy.

2

- Open Backstage view, click Save As to display the Save As screen, display the Save As dialog box, and navigate to the desired save location.
- Type **`SC_WD_11_MealTimeExpressFormModified`** in the File name text box (Save As dialog box) to change the file name.
- Click the 'Save as type' arrow to display the list of available file types and then click 'Word Macro-Enabled Template (*.dotm)' in the list to change the file type (Figure 11–2). (Before proceeding, verify that your file type changed to Word Macro-Enabled Template.)

3

- Click the Save button (Save As dialog box) to save the file using the entered file name as a macro-enabled template.

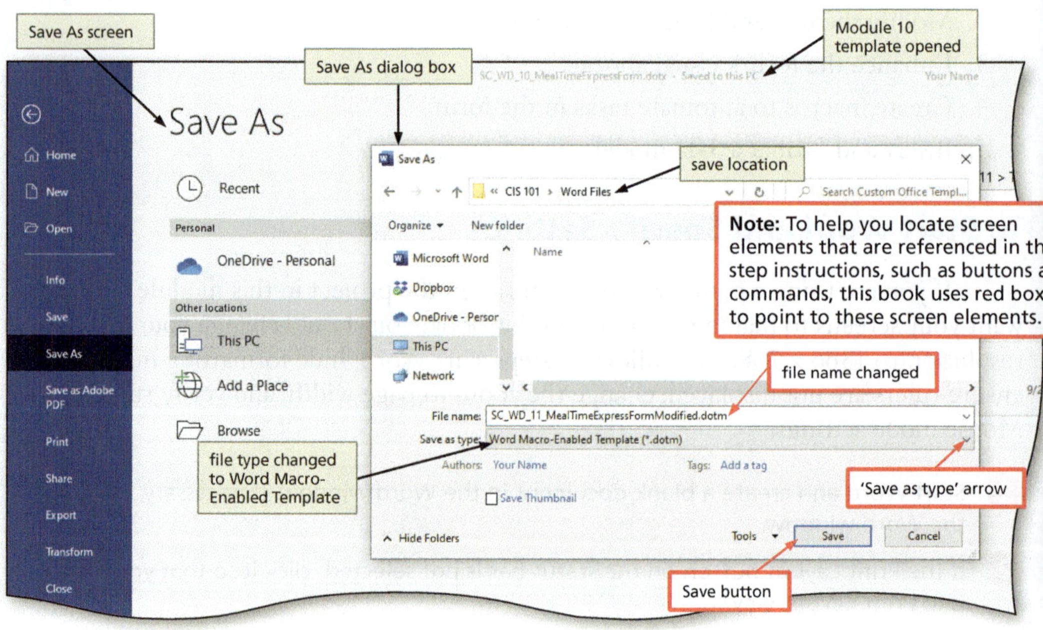

Figure 11–2

Q&A **How does Word differentiate between a Word template and a Word macro-enabled template?** A Word template has an extension of .dotx, whereas a Word macro-enabled template has an extension of .dotm. Also, the icon for a macro-enabled template contains an exclamation point.

BTW
Macro-Enabled Documents
The previous set of steps showed how to create a macro-enabled template. If you wanted to create a macro-enabled document, you would click the 'Save as type' arrow (Save As dialog box), click 'Word Macro-Enabled Document', and then click the Save button.

To Show the Developer Tab

Many of the tasks you will perform in this module use commands on the Developer tab. Thus, the following steps show the Developer tab on the ribbon.

1. Open Backstage view and then click Options in the left pane of Backstage view to display the Word Options dialog box.
2. Click Customize Ribbon in the left pane (Word Options dialog box) to display associated options in the right pane.
3. If it is not selected already, place a check mark in the Developer check box in the Main Tabs list.
4. Click OK to show the Developer tab on the ribbon.

To Unprotect a Document

The SC_WD_11_MealTimeExpressFormModified.dotm template is protected. In a protected form, users enter data only in designated areas, specifically, the content controls. The following steps unprotect a document. **Why?** Before this form can be modified, it must be unprotected. Later in this project, after you have completed the modifications, you will protect it again.

1

- Display the Developer tab.
- Click the Restrict Editing button (Developer tab | Protect group) to open the Restrict Editing pane (Figure 11–3).

2

- Click the Stop Protection button in the Restrict Editing pane to unprotect the form.
- Click the Close button in the Restrict Editing pane to close the pane.

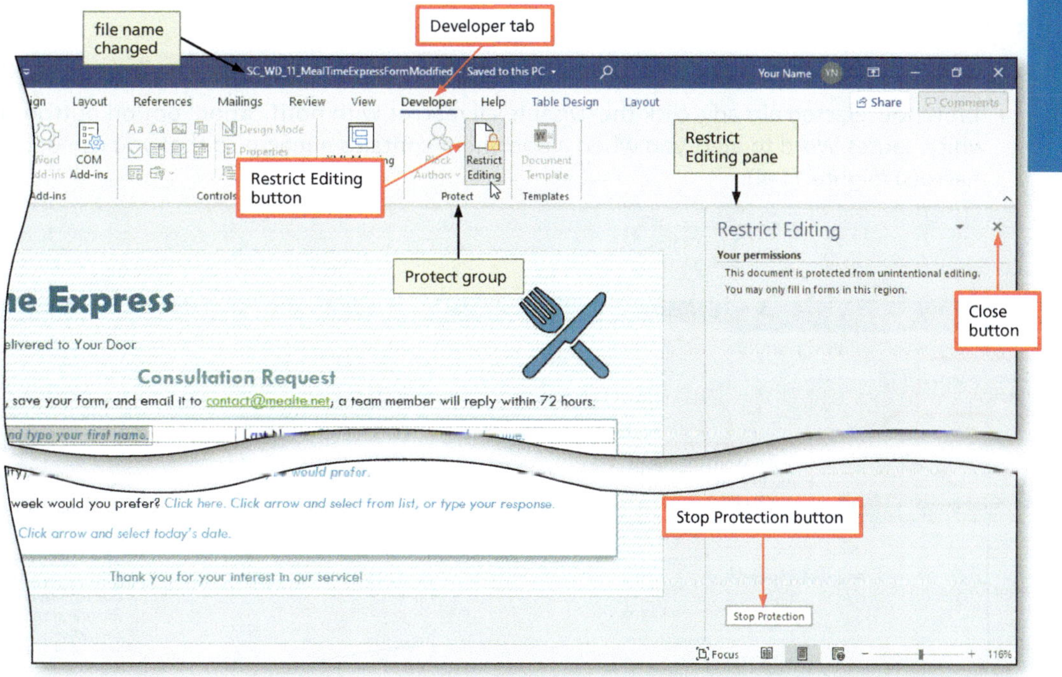

Figure 11–3

Other Ways

1. Click File on ribbon, if necessary, click Info in Backstage view, click Protect Document button, click Restrict Editing on Protect Document menu, click Stop Protection button in Restrict Editing pane

Consider This

How do you protect a computer from macro viruses?

A **computer virus** is a type of malicious software, or malware, which is a potentially damaging computer program that affects, or infects, a computer or mobile device negatively by altering the way the computer or mobile device works, usually without the user's knowledge or permission. Millions of known viruses and other malicious programs exist. The increased use of networks, the Internet, and email has accelerated the spread of computer viruses and other malicious programs.

- To combat these threats, most computer users run an **antivirus program** that locates viruses and other malware and destroys the malicious programs before they infect a computer or mobile device. Macros are known carriers of viruses and other malware. For this reason, you can specify a macro setting in Word to reduce the chance your computer or mobile device will be infected with a macro virus. These macro settings allow you to enable or disable macros. An **enabled macro** is a macro that Word (or any other Office application) will execute, and a **disabled macro** is a macro that is unavailable to Word (or any other program).
- As shown in Figure 11–1b at the beginning of this module, you can instruct Word to display a security warning on a Message Bar if it opens a document that contains a macro(s). If you are confident of the source (author) of the document and macros, enable the macros. If you are uncertain about the reliability of the source of the document and macros, then do not enable the macros.

To Specify Macro Settings in Word

Why? When you open the online form in this module, you want the macros enabled. At the same time, your computer or mobile device should be protected from potentially harmful macros. Thus, you will specify a macro setting that allows you to enable macros each time you open this module's online form or any document that contains a macro from an unknown source. The following steps specify macro settings.

1

- Click the Macro Security button (Developer tab | Code group) to display the Trust Center dialog box.
- If it is not selected already, click the 'Disable all macros with notification' option button (Trust Center dialog box), which causes Word to alert you when a document contains a macro so that you can decide whether to enable the macro(s) (Figure 11–4).

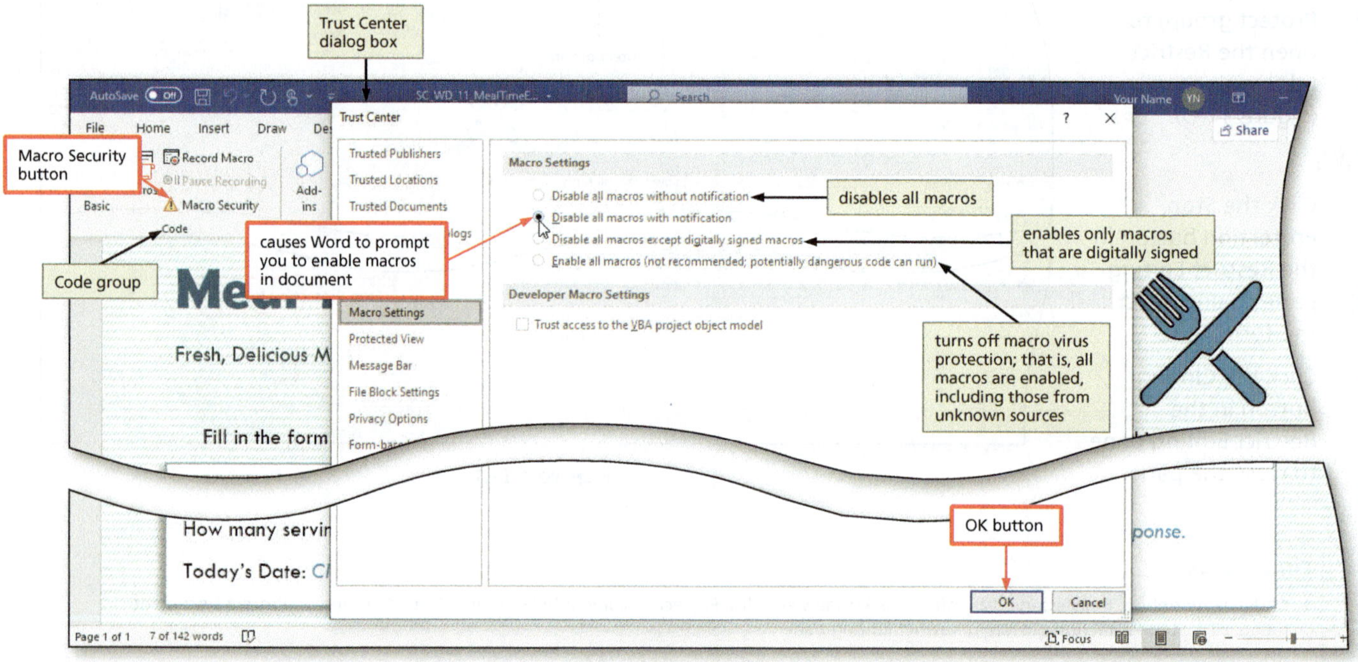

Figure 11–4

2

- Click OK to close the dialog box.

Other Ways

1. Click File on ribbon, click Options in Backstage view, click Trust Center in left pane (Word Options dialog box), click 'Trust Center Settings' button in right pane, if necessary, click Macro Settings in left pane (Trust Center dialog box), select desired setting, click OK in each dialog box

Modifying Text and Form Content Controls

The form created in Module 10 is enhanced in this module by performing these steps:

1. Delete the current image.
2. Change the fonts, colors, and alignments of the first four lines of text and the last line.
3. Convert the 2 × 1 table containing the First Name and Last Name content controls to text so that each of these content controls is on a separate line.
4. Delete the date picker content control and replace it with a date field.
5. Modify the color of the hyperlink and the check box labels.

The following pages apply these changes to the form.

To Delete a Graphic, Format Text, and Change Paragraph Alignment

The online form in this module contains a different image. It also has different formats for the company name, business tag line, form name, form instructions, date line, and thank you line. The following steps delete the image, format text, and change paragraph alignment.

1. Click the image of the fork and knife to select it and then press DELETE to delete the selected image.
2. Change the color of the first line of text, Meal Time Express, and the third line of text, Consultation Request, to 'Teal, Accent 3, Darker 50%' (seventh color in sixth row).
3. Change the color of the business tag line and the last line on the form, Thank you for your interest in our service!, to Aqua, Accent 1 (fifth color in first row).
4. Right-align the first and second lines of text (company name and business tag line).
5. Italicize the business tag line.
6. Right-align the line of text containing the Today's Date content control.
7. If necessary, widen the rectangle surrounding the data entry area to include the entire date placeholder (Figure 11–5).

BTW

Touch Mode Differences

The Office and Windows interfaces may vary if you are using Touch mode. For this reason, you might notice that the function or appearance of your touch screen differs slightly from this module's presentation.

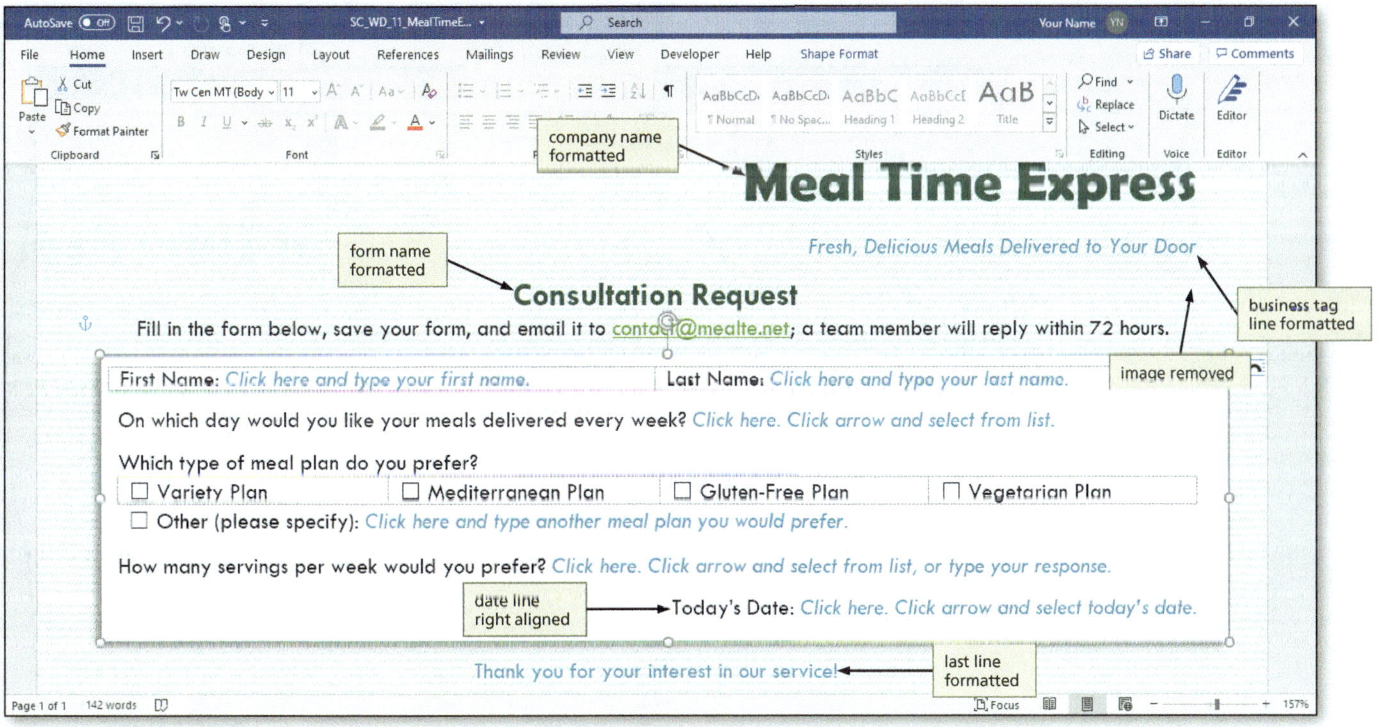

Figure 11–5

To Change the Properties of a Plain Text Content Control

In this online form, the First Name and Last Name content controls are on separate lines. In Module 10, you selected the 'Content control cannot be deleted' check box in the Content Control Properties dialog box so that users could not delete the content control accidentally while filling in the form. With this check box selected, however, you cannot move a content control from one location to another on the form. Thus, the following steps change the locking properties of the First Name and Last Name content controls so that you can rearrange them.

1. Display the Developer tab.
2. Click the First Name content control to select it.
3. Click the Properties button (Developer tab | Controls group) to display the Content Control Properties dialog box.
4. Remove the check mark from the 'Content control cannot be deleted' check box (Content Control Properties dialog box) (Figure 11–6).
5. Click OK to assign the modified properties to the content control.
6. Click the Last Name content control to select it and then click the Properties button (Developer tab | Controls group) to display the Content Control Properties dialog box.
7. Remove the check mark from the 'Content control cannot be deleted' check box (Content Control Properties dialog box) and then click OK to assign the modified properties to the content control.

BTW
Saving and Resetting Themes
If you have changed the theme colors or theme fonts and want to save this combination for future use, save it as a new theme by clicking the Themes button (Design tab | Document Formatting group), clicking 'Save Current Theme' in the Themes gallery, entering a theme name in the File name box (Save Current Theme dialog box), and then clicking Save. If you want to reset the theme template to the default, you would click the Themes button (Design tab | Document Formatting group) and then click 'Reset to Theme from Template' in the Themes gallery.

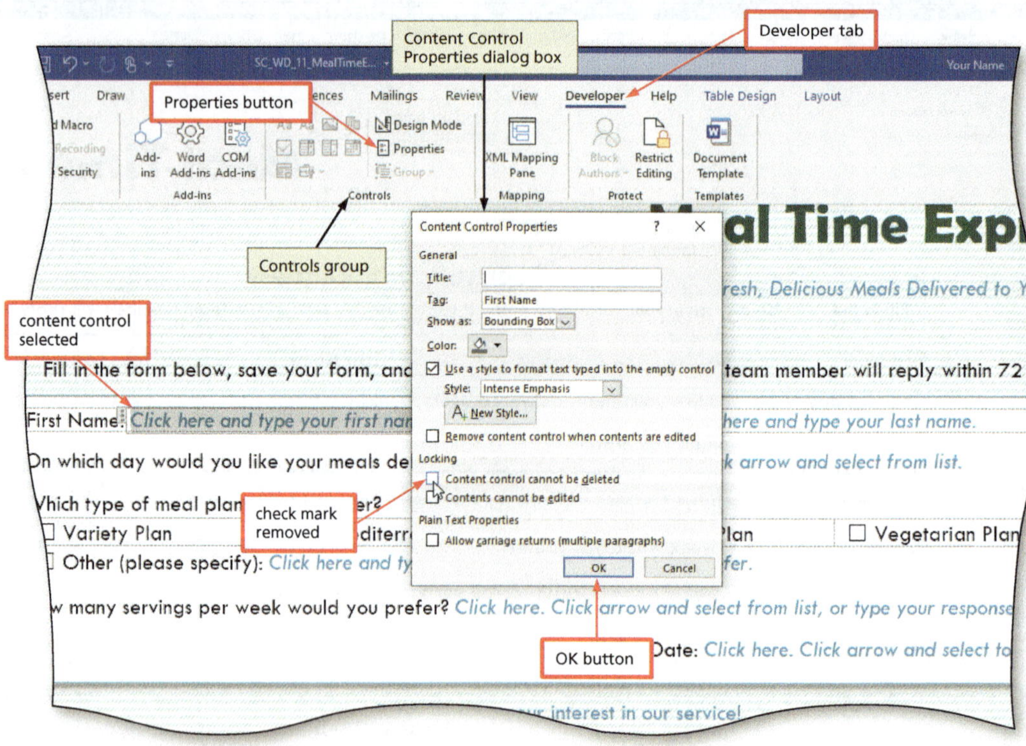

Figure 11–6

To Convert a Table to Text

The First Name and Last Name content controls currently are in a 2 × 1 table. The following steps convert the table to regular text, placing a paragraph break at the location of the second column. **Why?** In this online form, these content controls are on separate lines, one below the other. That is, they are not in a table.

1

- Position the insertion point somewhere in the table.
- Display the Layout tab.
- Click the 'Convert to Text' button (Layout tab | Data group) to display the Convert Table To Text dialog box.
- Click Paragraph marks (Convert Table To Text dialog box), which will place a paragraph mark at the location of each new column in the table (Figure 11–7).

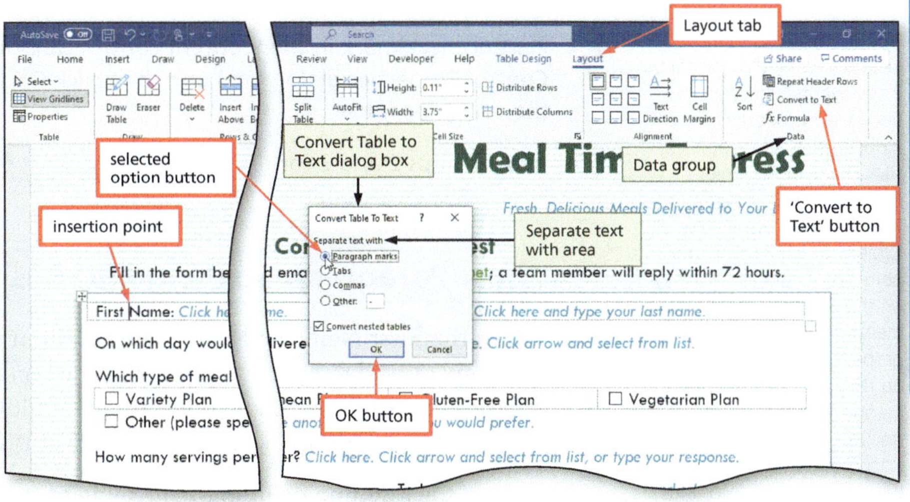

Figure 11–7

2

- Click OK to convert the table to text, separating each column with the specified character, a paragraph mark in this case.

Q&A **Why did the Last Name content control move below the First Name content control?**
The Separate text with area (Convert Table To Text dialog box) controls how the table is converted to text. The Paragraph marks setting converts each column in the table to a line of text below the previous line. The Tabs setting places a tab character where each column was located, and the Commas setting places a comma where each column was located.

3

- With the First Name and Last Name lines selected, using either the ruler or the Layout tab, change the left indent to 0.06" so that the text aligns with the text immediately below it (that is, the O in On), as shown in Figure 11–8.

4

- Click anywhere to remove the selection from the text.

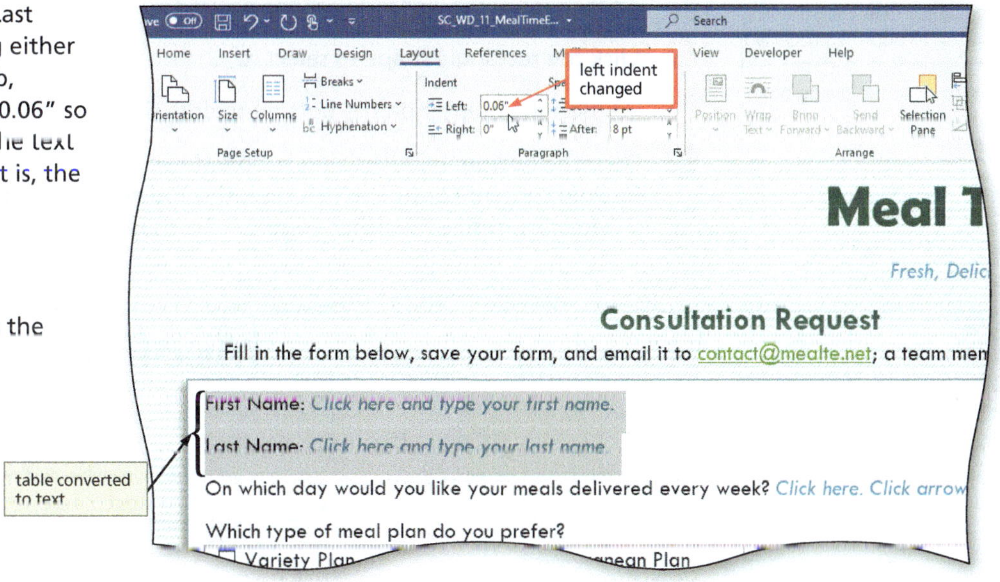

Figure 11–8

To Change the Properties of a Plain Text Content Control

You are finished moving the First Name and Last Name content controls. The following steps reset the locking properties of these content controls.

1 Display the Developer tab.

2 Click the First Name content control to select it and then click the Properties button (Developer tab | Controls group) to display the Content Control Properties dialog box.

BTW
Document Properties
If you wanted to insert document properties in a document, you would click the 'Explore Quick Parts' button (Insert tab | Text group) to display the Explore Quick Parts menu, point to Document Property on the Explore Quick Parts menu, and then click the property you want to insert on the Document Property menu. To create a custom document property for a document, open Backstage view, if necessary, click Info to display the Info screen, click the Properties button in the far right pane to display the Properties menu, click Advanced Properties on the Properties menu to display the Document Properties dialog box, click the Custom tab (Document Properties dialog box) to display the Custom sheet, enter the name of the new property in the Name text box, select its type and enter its value in the dialog box, click the Add button to add the property to the document, and then click OK to close the dialog box.

3. Place a check mark in the 'Content control cannot be deleted' check box (Content Control Properties dialog box) and then click OK to assign the modified properties to the content control.
4. Repeat Steps 2 and 3 for the Last Name content control.

To Adjust Paragraph Spacing and Resize the Rectangle Shape

With the First Name and Last Name content controls on separate lines, the thank you line moved to a second page, and the rectangle outline in the data entry area now is too short to accommodate the text. The following steps adjust paragraph spacing and extend the rectangle shape downward so that it surrounds the entire data entry area.

1. Position the insertion point in the first line of text on the form (the company name) and then adjust the spacing after to 0 pt (Layout tab | Paragraph group).
2. Position the insertion point in the second line of text on the form (the business tag line) and then adjust the spacing after to 6 pt (Layout tab | Paragraph group).
3. Adjust the spacing after to 6 pt for the First Name and Last Name lines.
4. Adjust the spacing before and after to 6 pt for the line that begins, On which day would you like..., and the line that begins, How many servings per week...
5. Adjust the spacing before to 12 pt for the thank you line.
6. Scroll to display the entire form in the document window. If necessary, reduce spacing after other paragraphs so that the entire form fits in a single document window.
7. Click the rectangle shape to select it.
8. Position the pointer on the bottom-middle sizing handle of the rectangle shape.
9. Drag the bottom-middle sizing handle downward so that the shape includes the bottom content control, in this case, the Today's Date content control (Figure 11–9). If necessary, resize the other edges of the shape to fit the text.

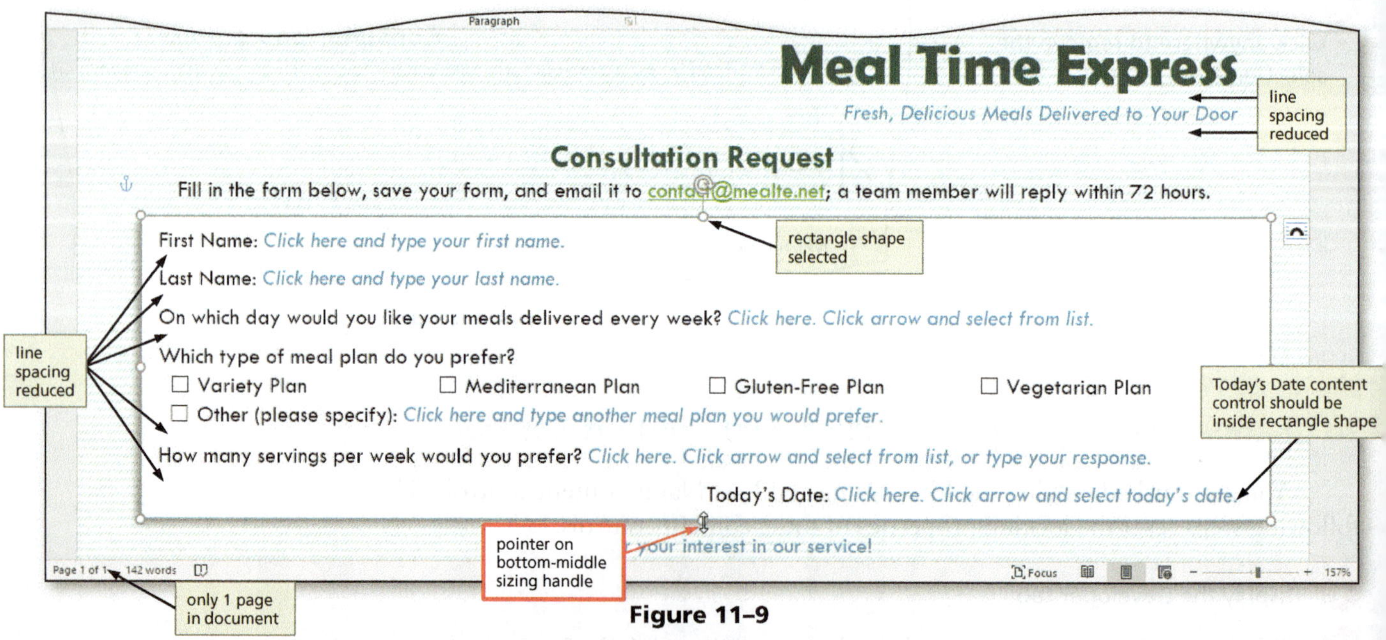

Figure 11–9

To Change the Properties of a Date Picker Content Control

In this online form, instead of the user entering the current date, the computer or mobile device's system date will be filled in automatically by Word. Thus, the Today's Date content control is not needed and can be deleted. To delete the content control, you first will need to remove the check mark from the 'Content control cannot be deleted' check box in the Content Control Properties dialog box. The following steps change the locking properties of the Today's Date content control and then delete the content control.

1. Display the Developer tab.
2. Click the Today's Date content control to select it.
3. Click the Properties button (Developer tab | Controls group) to display the Content Control Properties dialog box.
4. Remove the check mark from the 'Content control cannot be deleted' check box (Content Control Properties dialog box) (Figure 11–10).

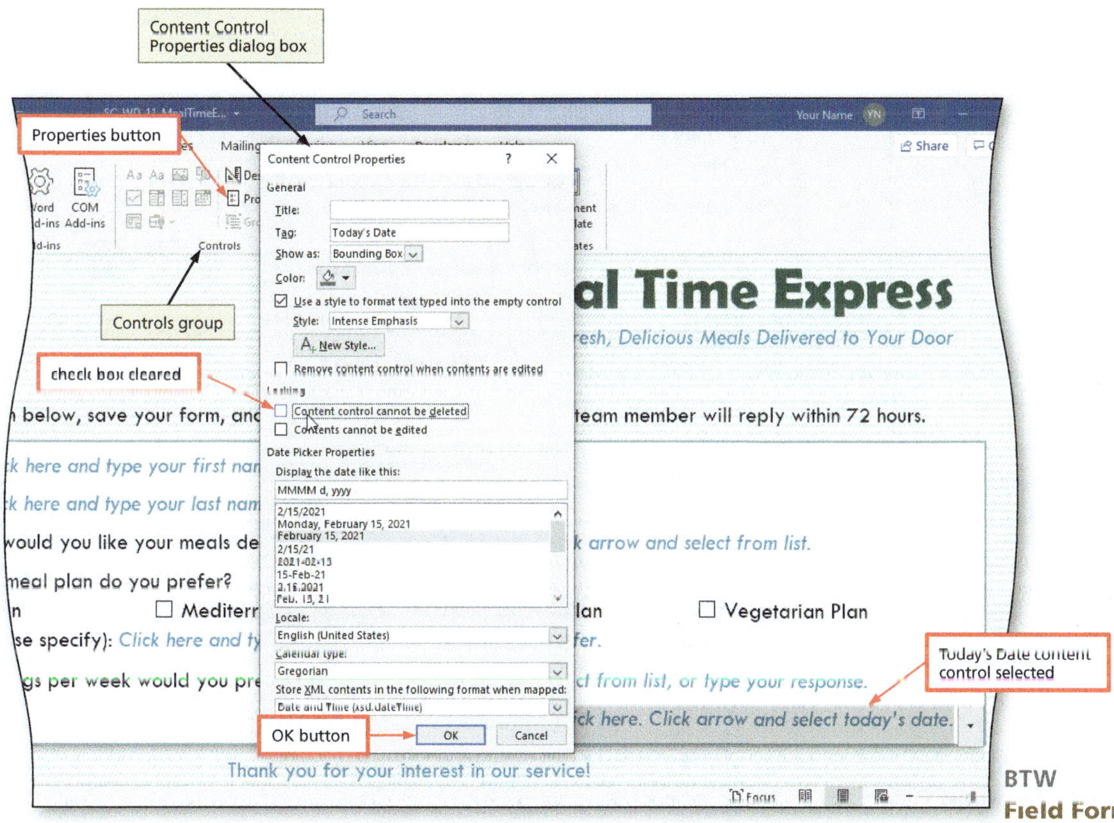

Figure 11–10

5. Click OK to assign the modified properties to the content control.
6. Right-click the Today's Date content control to display a shortcut menu and then click 'Remove Content Control' on the shortcut menu to delete the selected content control.

BTW

Field Formats

If you wanted to create custom field formats, you would click the Field Codes button (Field dialog box) (shown in Figure 11–15) to display advanced field properties in the right pane in the dialog box, click the Options button to display the Field Options dialog box, select the format to apply in the Formatting list, click the 'Add to Field' button, and then click OK in each open dialog box.

To Insert a Date Field

The following steps insert the date and time as a field in the form at the location of the insertion point. **Why?** The current date and time is a field so that the form automatically displays the current date and time. Recall that a field is a set of codes that instructs Word to perform a certain action.

1

- Display the Insert tab.
- With the insertion point positioned as shown in Figure 11–11, which is the location for the date and time, click the 'Explore Quick Parts' button (Insert tab | Text group) to display the Explore Quick Parts menu.

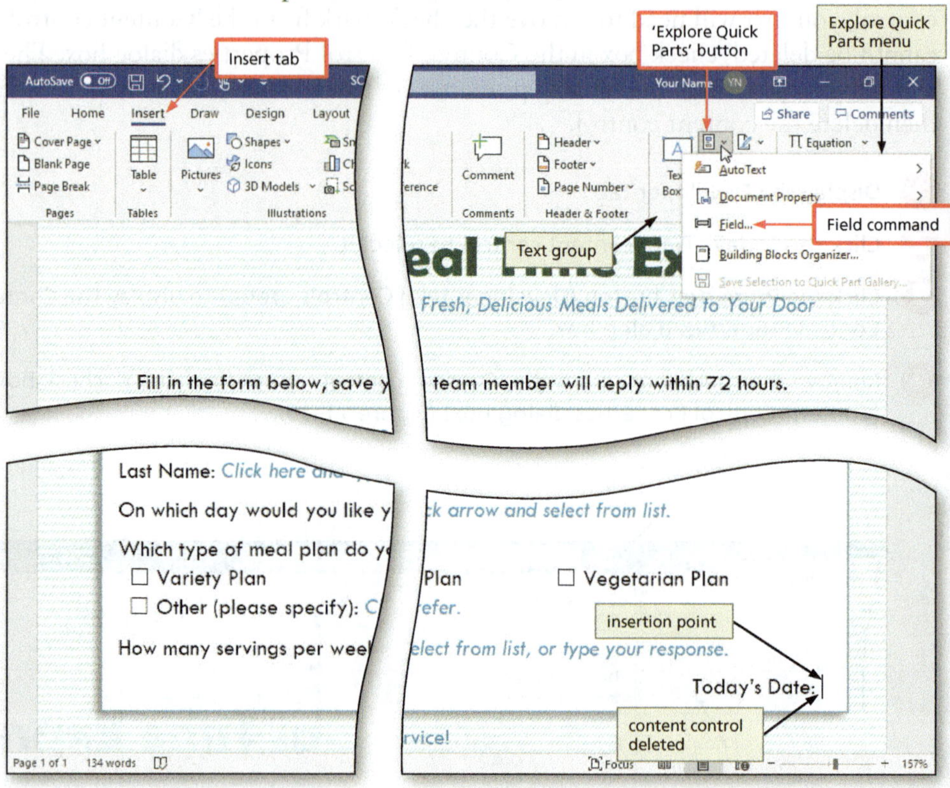

Figure 11–11

2

- Click Field on the Explore Quick Parts menu to display the Field dialog box.
- Scroll through the Field names list (Field dialog box) and then click Date, which displays the Date formats list in the Field properties area.
- Click the date in the format of 2/15/2021 1:58:56 PM in the Date formats list to select a date format — your date and time will differ (Figure 11–12).

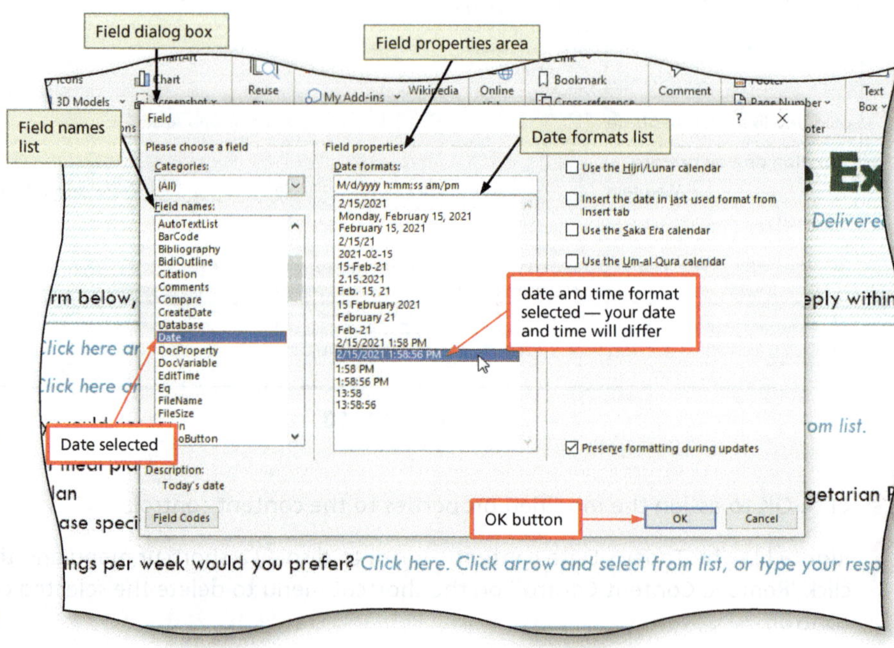

Figure 11–12

Q&A **What controls the date that appears?**
Your current computer or mobile device date appears in this dialog box. The format for the selected date shows in the Date formats box. In this case, the format for the selected date is M/d/yyyy h:mm:ss am/pm, which displays the date as month/day/year hours:minutes:seconds AM/PM.

3

- Click OK to insert the current date and time that automatically will be filled in at the location of the insertion point (Figure 11–13).

Q&A **How do I delete a field?**
Select it and then press DELETE or click the Cut button (Home tab | Clipboard group), or right-click the field and then click Cut on the shortcut menu or Mini toolbar.

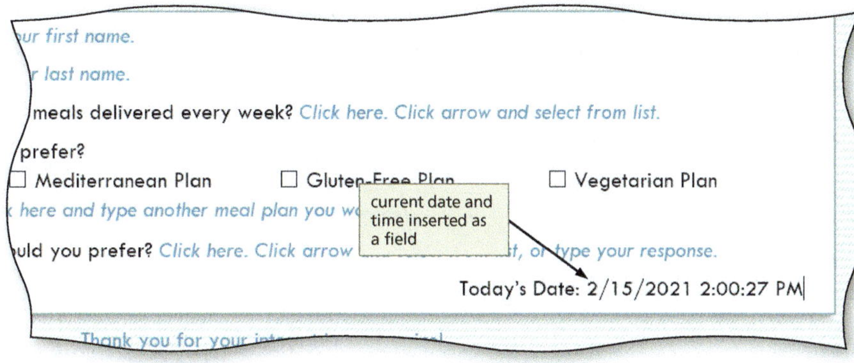

Figure 11–13

Other Ways

1. Click 'Insert Date and Time' button (Insert tab | Text group), select date format (Date and Time dialog box), place check mark in Update automatically check box, click OK

To Edit a Field

The following steps edit the field. **Why?** After you see the date and time in the form, you decide not to include the seconds in the time. That is, you want just the hours and minutes to be displayed.

1

- Right-click the date field to display a shortcut menu (Figure 11–14).

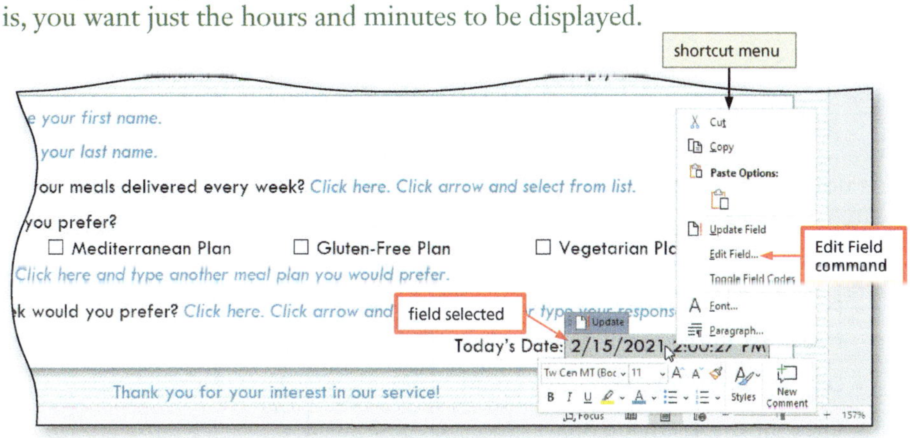

Figure 11–14

2

- Click Edit Field on the shortcut menu to display the Field dialog box.
- If necessary, scroll through the Field names list (Field dialog box) and then click Date to display the Date formats list in the Field properties area.
- Select the desired date format, in this case 2/15/2021 2:02 PM (Figure 11–15).

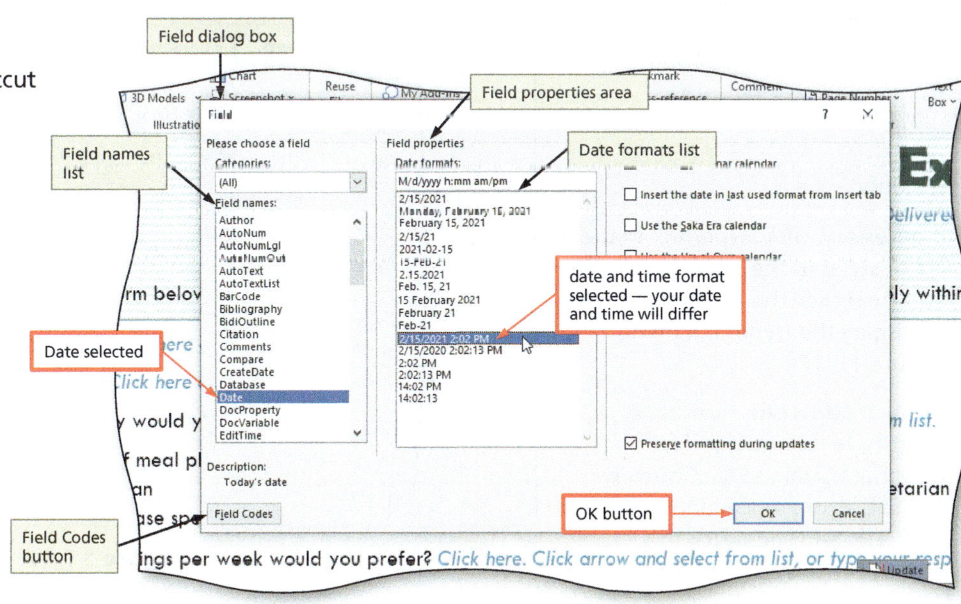

Figure 11–15

3

- Click OK to insert the edited field at the location of the insertion point (Figure 11–16).

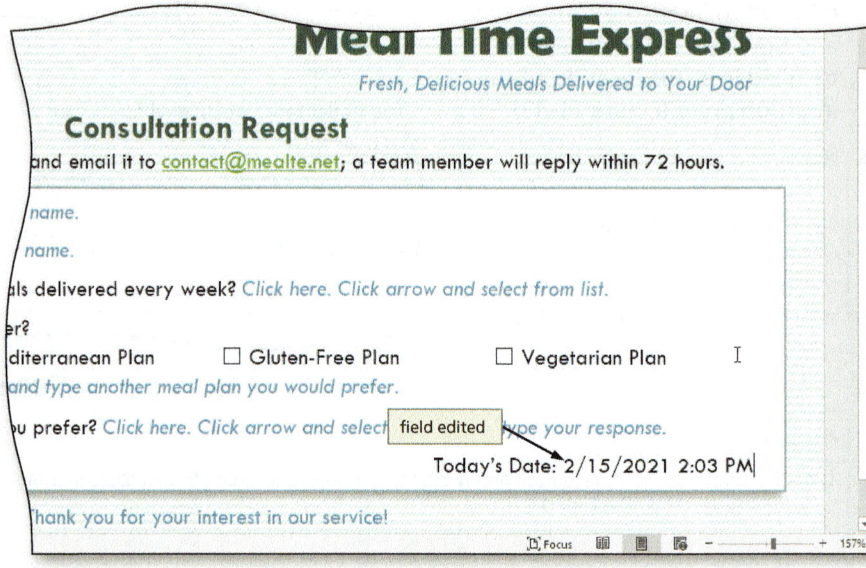

Figure 11–16

To Modify a Style Using the Styles Pane

In this online form, the hyperlink should be the same color as the company name so that the hyperlink is noticeable. The following steps modify a style using the Styles pane. **Why?** The Hyperlink style is not in the Styles gallery. To modify a style that is not in the Styles gallery, you can use the Styles pane.

1

- Position the insertion point in the hyperlink in the form.
- Display the Home tab.
- Click the Styles Dialog Box Launcher (Home tab | Styles group) to open the Styles pane.

Q&A **What if the Styles pane is floating in the window?**
Double-click its title bar to lock it to the right edge of the document window.

- If necessary, click Hyperlink in the list of styles in the pane to select it and then click the Hyperlink arrow to display the Hyperlink menu (Figure 11–17).

Q&A **What if the style I want to modify is not in the list?**
Click the Manage Styles button at the bottom of the pane, locate the style, and then click the Modify button in the dialog box.

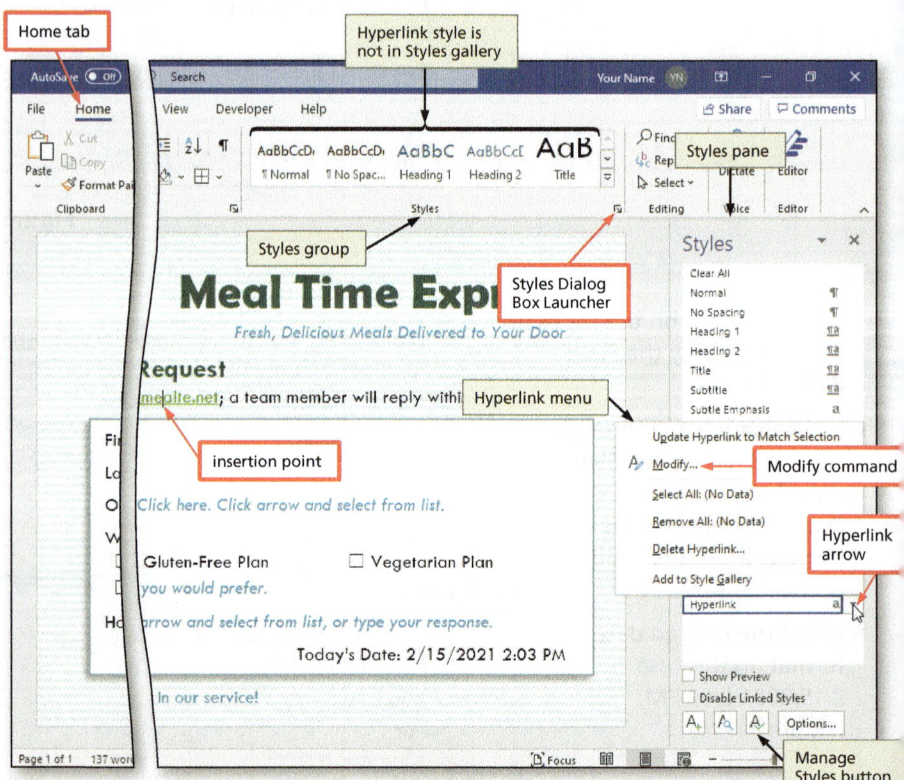

Figure 11–17

2

- Click Modify on the Hyperlink menu to display the Modify Style dialog box.
- Click the Font Color arrow (Modify Style dialog box) to display the Font Color gallery (Figure 11–18).

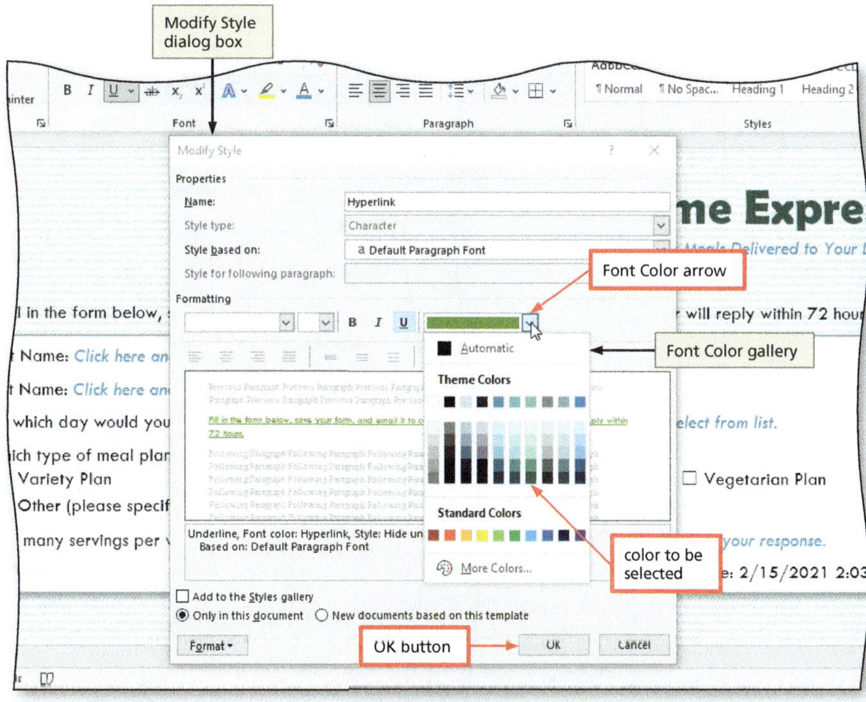

Figure 11–18

3

- Click 'Teal, Accent 3, Darker 50%' (seventh color in sixth row) as the new hyperlink color.
- Click OK to close the dialog box. Close the Styles pane (Figure 11–19).

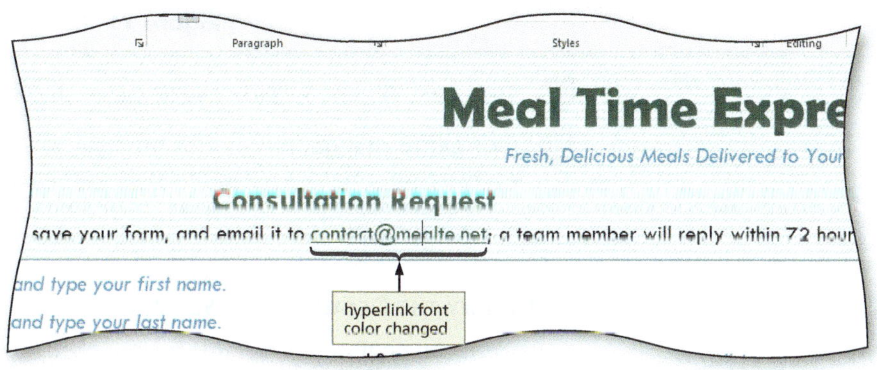

Figure 11–19

To Modify a Style

In this online form, the placeholder text is to be the same color as the company name. Currently, the placeholder text is formatted using the Intense Emphasis style, which uses a shade of aqua as the font color. Thus, the following steps modify the color of the Intense Emphasis style to a shade of orange.

1 Scroll through the Styles gallery (Home tab | Styles group) to locate the Intense Emphasis style.

2 Right-click Intense Emphasis in the Styles gallery to display a shortcut menu and then click Modify on the shortcut menu to display the Modify Style dialog box.

3 Click the Font Color arrow (Modify Style dialog box) to display the Font Color gallery (Figure 11–20).

BTW

Hidden Styles and Text

Some styles are hidden, which means they do not appear in the Styles pane. You can display all styles, including hidden styles, by clicking the Manage Styles button in the Styles pane (Figure 11–17), which displays the Manage Styles dialog box. Click the Edit tab, if necessary, and then locate the style name in the Select a style to edit list. To format text as hidden, select the text, click the Font Dialog Box Launcher (Home tab | Font group) to display the Font dialog box, select the Hidden check box in the Effects area, and then click OK (Font dialog box). To see hidden text on the screen, show formatting marks. Hidden text does not print.

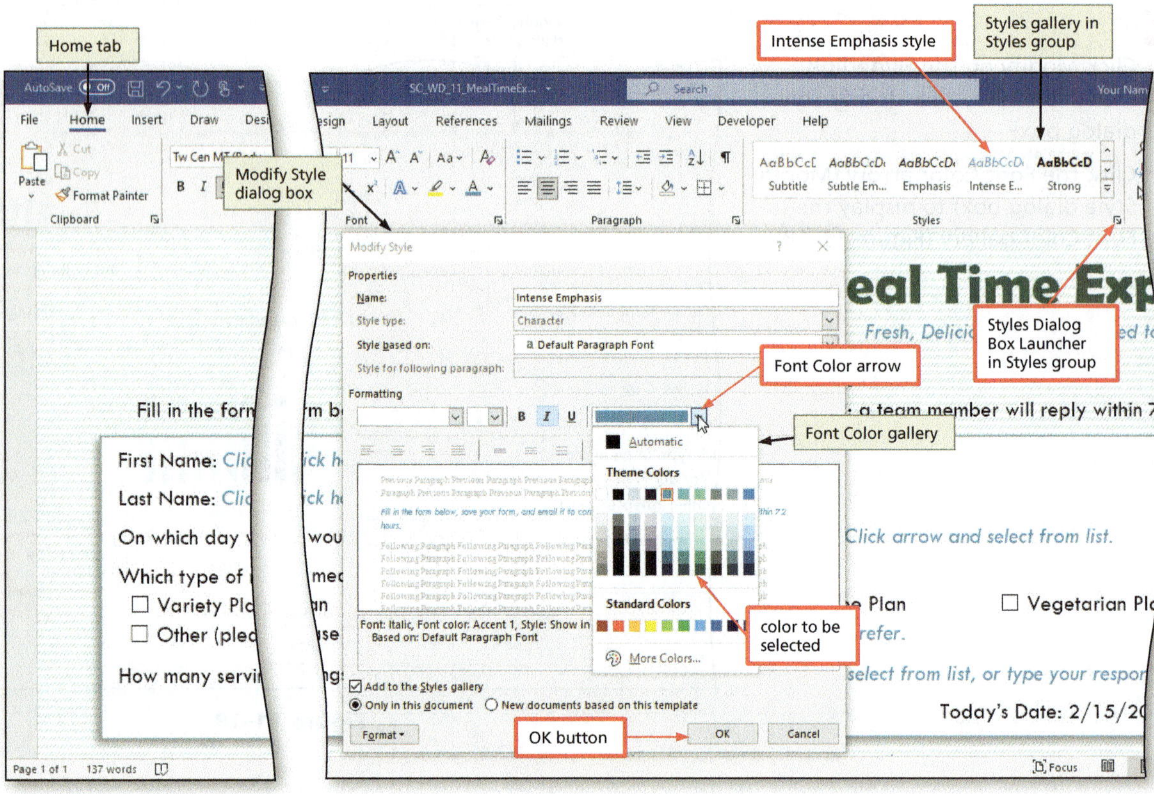

Figure 11–20

4. Click 'Teal, Accent 3, Darker 50%' (seventh color in sixth row) as the new color.
5. Click OK to change the color of the style, which automatically changes the color of every item formatted using this style in the document.

BTW

Assign a Shortcut Key to a Style

If you wanted to assign a shortcut key to a style, you would right-click the style name in the Styles gallery (Home tab | Styles group) or open the Styles pane and then click the style arrow, click Modify Style on the menu to display the Modify Style dialog box, click the Format button (Modify Style dialog box), click Shortcut key on the Format menu to display the Customize Keyboard dialog box, press the desired shortcut key(s) (Customize Keyboard dialog box), click the Assign button to assign the shortcut key to the style, click the Close button to close the Customize Keyboard dialog box, and then click OK to close the Modify Style dialog box.

To Modify the Default Font Settings

You can change the default font so that the current document and all future documents use the new font settings. That is, if you exit Word, restart the computer or mobile device, and start Word again, documents you create will use the new default font. If you wanted to change the default font from 11-point Calibri to another font, font style, font size, font color, and/or font effects, you would perform the following steps.

1. Click the Font Dialog Box Launcher (Home tab | Font group) to display the Font dialog box.
2. Make desired changes to the font settings in the Font dialog box.
3. Click the 'Set As Default' button to change the default settings to those specified in Step 2.
4. When the Microsoft Word dialog box is displayed, select the desired option button and then click OK.

To Reset the Default Font Settings

To change the font settings back to the default, you would follow the steps in the previous section, using the default font settings when performing Step 2. If you do not remember the default settings, you would perform the following steps to restore the original Normal style settings.

1. Exit Word.
2. Use File Explorer to locate the Normal.dotm file (be sure that hidden files and folders are displayed and include system and hidden files in your search), which is the file that contains default font and other settings.
3. Rename the Normal.dotm file to oldnormal.dotm file so that the Normal.dotm file no longer exists.
4. Start Word, which will recreate a Normal.dotm file using the original default settings.

BTW

Advanced Character Attributes

If you wanted to set advanced character attributes, you would click the Font Dialog Box Launcher (Home tab | Font group) to display the Font dialog box, click the Advanced tab (Font dialog box) to display the Advanced sheet, select the desired Character Spacing or OpenType Features settings, and then click OK.

To Create a Character Style

In this online form, the check box labels are to be the same color as the placeholder text. The following steps create a character style called Check Box Labels. **Why?** Although you could select each of the check box labels and then format them, a more efficient technique is to create a character style. If you decide to modify the formats of the check box labels at a later time, you simply change the formats assigned to the style to automatically change all characters in the document based on that style.

1

- Position the insertion point in one of the check box labels.
- Click the Styles Dialog Box Launcher (Home tab | Styles group) (shown in Figure 11–20) to open the Styles pane.
- Click the Manage Styles button in the Styles pane to display the Manage Styles dialog box (Figure 11–21).

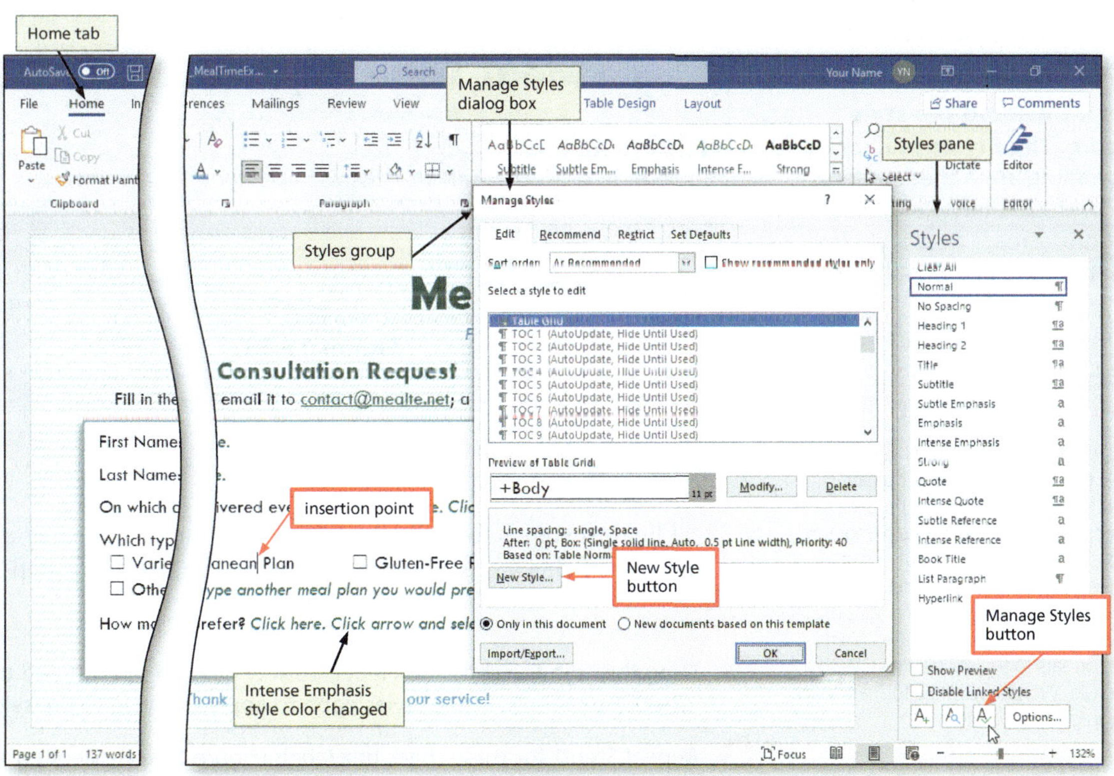

Figure 11–21

2

- Click the New Style button (Manage Styles dialog box) to display the Create New Style from Formatting dialog box.
- Type `Check Box Labels` in the Name text box (Create New Style from Formatting dialog box) as the name of the new style.
- Click the Style type arrow and then click Character so that the new style does not contain any paragraph formats.
- Click the Font Color arrow to display the Font Color gallery and then click 'Teal, Accent 3, Darker 50%' (seventh color in sixth row) as the new color (Figure 11–22).

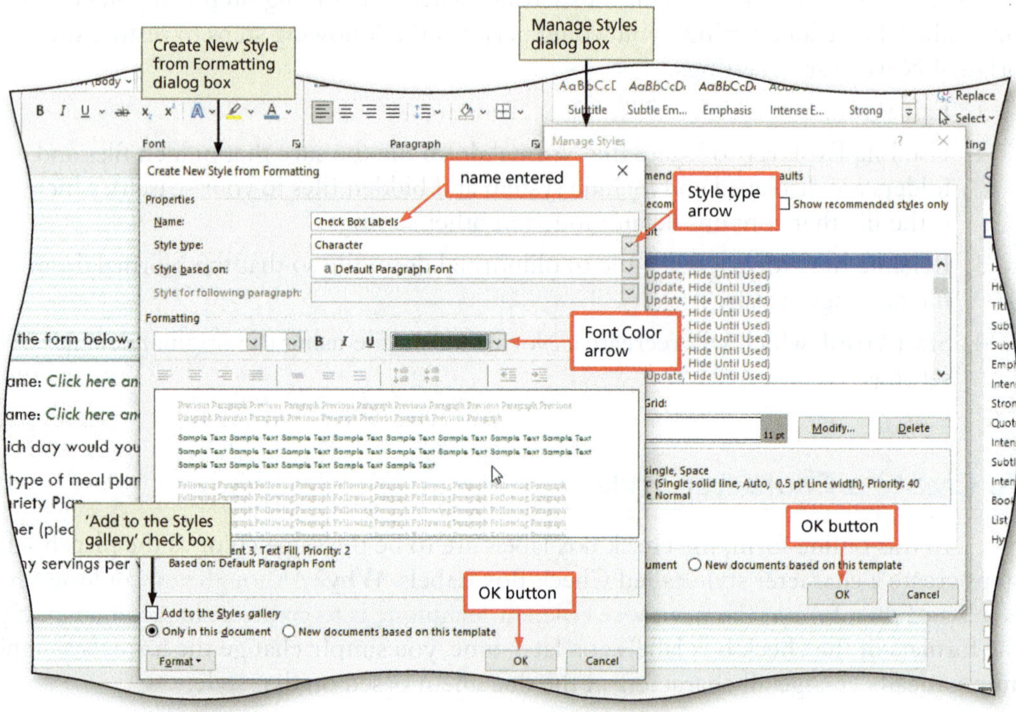

Figure 11–22

3

- Click OK in each open dialog box to create the new character style, Check Box Labels in this case, and insert the new style name in the Styles pane (Figure 11–23).

Q&A **What if I wanted the style added to the Styles gallery?** You would place a check mark in the 'Add to the Styles gallery' check box (Create New Style from Formatting dialog box), shown in Figure 11–22.

Figure 11–23

BTW

Character vs. Paragraph Styles

In the Styles pane, character styles display a lowercase letter a to the right of the style name, and paragraph styles show a paragraph mark. If a style has character and paragraph settings, then both a lowercase letter a and the paragraph mark are displayed to the right of the style name. With a character style, Word applies the formats to the selected text. With a paragraph style, Word applies the formats to the entire paragraph.

To Apply a Style

The next step is to apply the Check Box Labels style just created to the first row of check box labels in the form. The following steps apply a style.

1. Drag through the check box label, Variety Plan, to select it and then click 'Check Box Labels' in the Styles pane to apply the style to the selected text.
2. Repeat Step 1 for these check box labels (Figure 11–24): Mediterranean Plan, Gluten-Free Plan, Vegetarian Plan, and Other (please specify):.

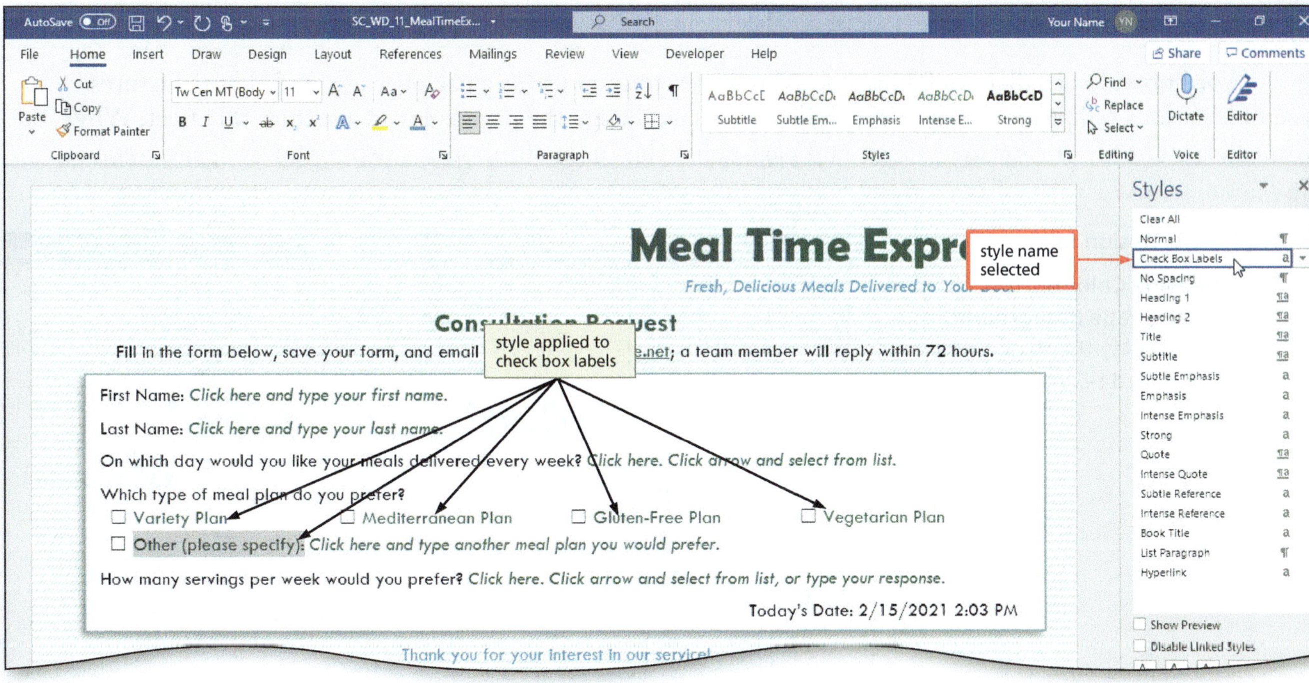

Figure 11–24

Q&A

Do I have to drag through one word labels to apply a style?

No. You simply can position the insertion point in the word before clicking the desired style to apply.

3. Close the Styles pane.
4. If necessary, click anywhere to remove the selection from the check box label.
5. Save the template again on the same storage location with the same file name.

BTW

Saving Templates

When you save a template that contains building blocks, the building blocks are available to all users who access the template.

Break Point: If you want to take a break, this is a good place to do so. You can exit Word now. To resume later, start Word, open the file called SC_WD_11_MealTimeExpressFormModified.dotm, and continue following the steps from this location forward.

Enhancing with Color, Shapes, Effects, and Graphics

You will enhance the form created in Module 10 by performing these steps:

1. Apply a texture fill effect for the page color.
2. Change the appearance of the shape.
3. Change the color of a shadow on the shape.
4. Fill a shape with a picture.
5. Insert a picture, remove its background, and apply an artistic effect.
6. Insert and format a text box.
7. Group the picture and the text box together.

The following pages apply these changes to the form.

To Use a Fill Effect for the Page Color

Word provides a gallery of 24 predefined textures you can use as a page background. These textures resemble various wallpaper patterns. The following steps change the page color to a texture fill effect. **Why?** Instead of a simple color for the background page color, this online form uses a texture for the page color.

1

- Display the Design tab.
- Click the Page Color button (Design tab | Page Background group) to display the Page Color gallery (Figure 11–25).

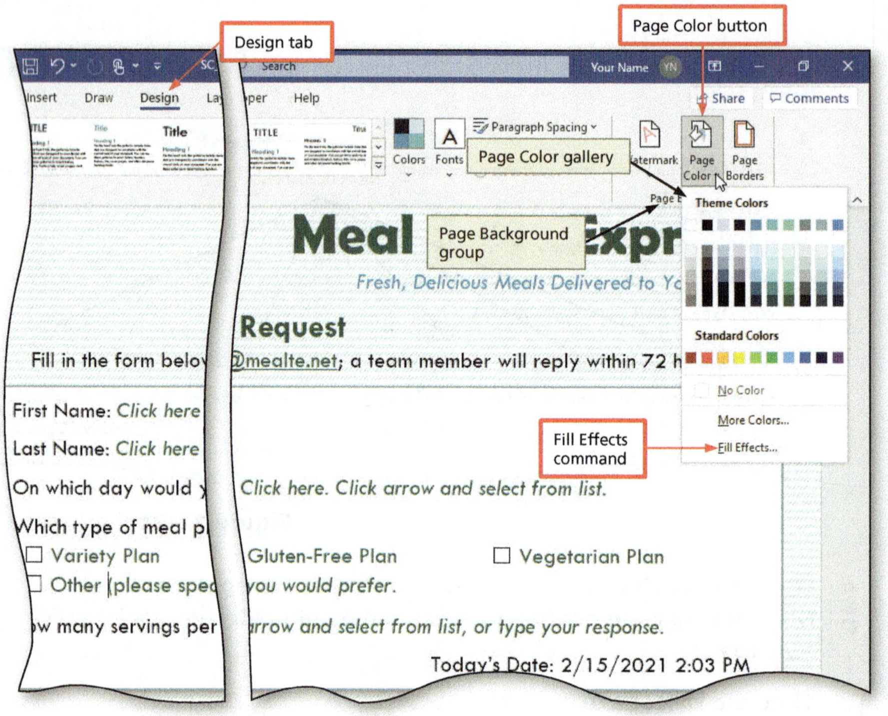

Figure 11–25

2

- Click Fill Effects in the Page Color gallery to display the Fill Effects dialog box.
- Click the Texture tab (Fill Effects dialog box) to display the Texture sheet.
- Scroll to, if necessary, and then click the Parchment texture in the Texture gallery to select the texture (Figure 11–26).

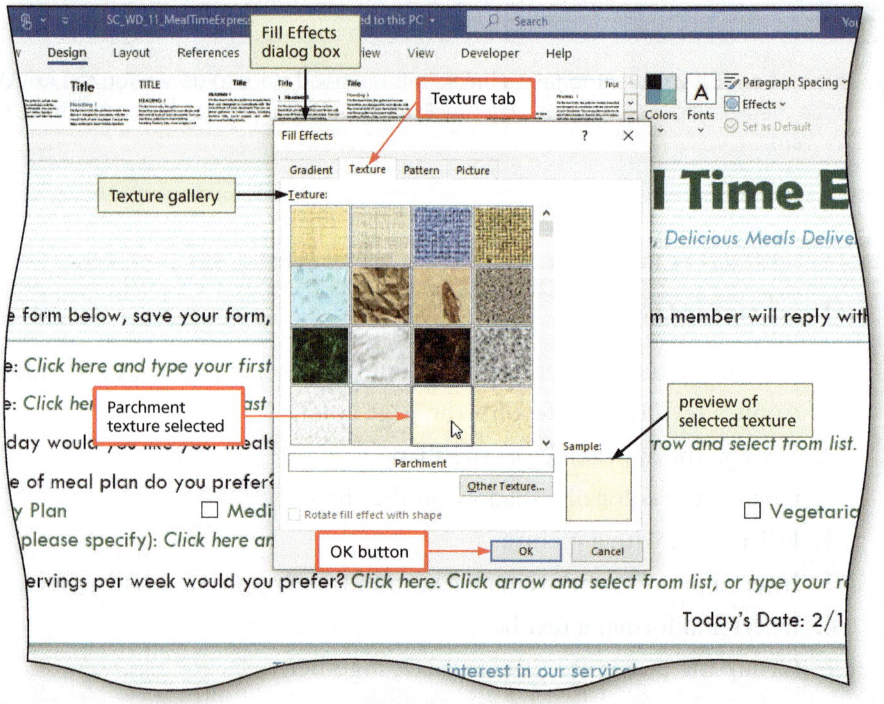

Figure 11–26

3

- Click OK to apply the selected texture as the page color in the document (Figure 11–27).

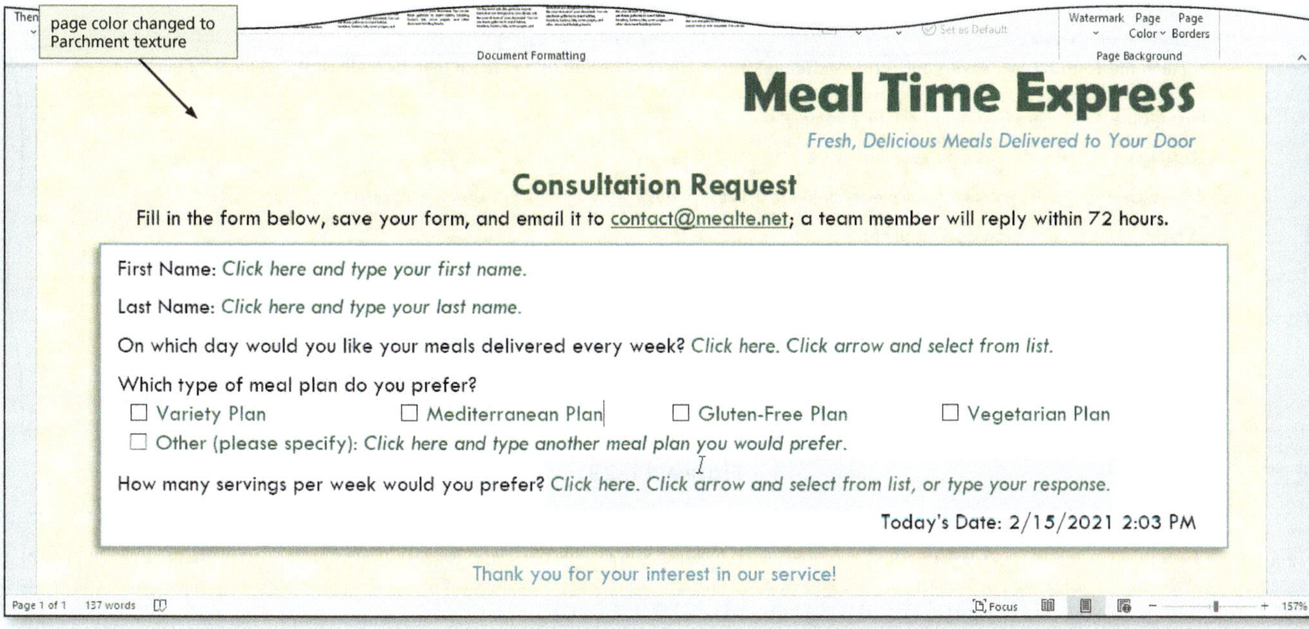

Figure 11–27

Q&A

How would I remove a texture page color?
You would click the Page Color button (Design tab | Page Background group) and then click No Color in the Page Color gallery.

To Change a Shape

The following steps change a shape. **Why?** This online form uses a variation of the standard rectangle shape.

1

- Click the rectangle shape to select it.
- Display the Shape Format tab.
- Click the Edit Shape button (Shape Format tab | Insert Shapes group) to display the Edit Shape menu.
- Point to Change Shape on the Edit Shape menu to display the Change Shape gallery (Figure 11–28).

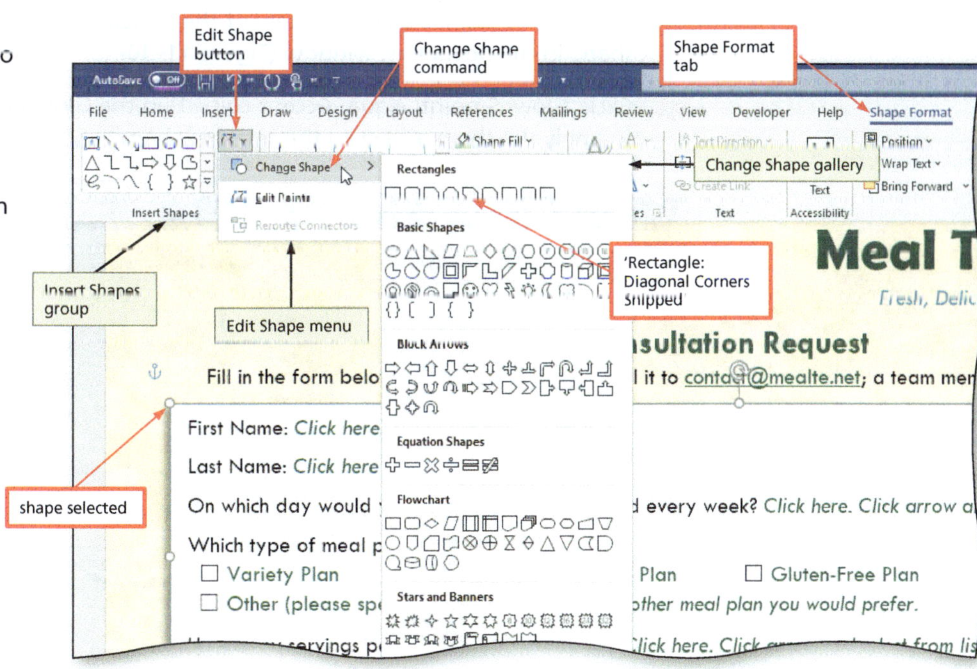

Figure 11–28

2

- Click 'Rectangle: Diagonal Corners Snipped' in the Rectangles area in the Change Shape gallery to change the selected shape (Figure 11–29).

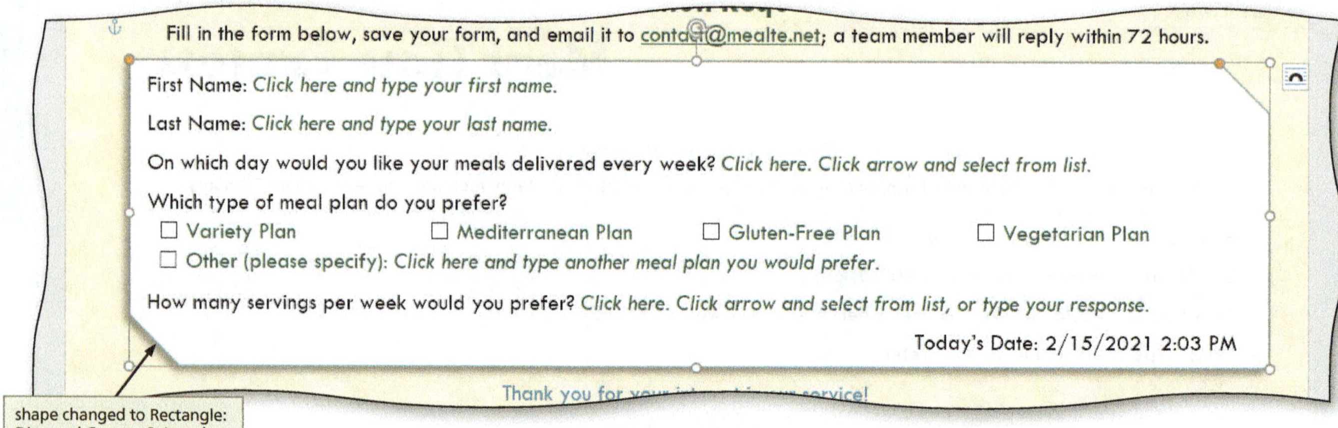

Figure 11–29

To Apply a Glow Shape Effect

The next step is to apply a glow effect to the rectangle shape. You can apply the same effects to shapes as to pictures. That is, you can apply shadows, reflections, glows, soft edges, bevels, and 3-D rotations to pictures and shapes. The following steps apply a shape effect.

1. With the rectangle shape selected, click the Shape Effects button (Shape Format tab | Shape Styles group) to display the Shape Effects menu.
2. Point to Glow on the Shape Effects menu to display the Glow gallery.
3. Point to 'Glow: 5 point; Aqua, Accent color 1' in the Glow Variations area (first glow in first row) to display a Live Preview of the selected glow effect applied to the selected shape in the document window (Figure 11–30).
4. Click 'Glow: 5 point; Aqua, Accent color 1' in the Glow gallery (first glow in first row) to apply the shape effect to the selected shape.

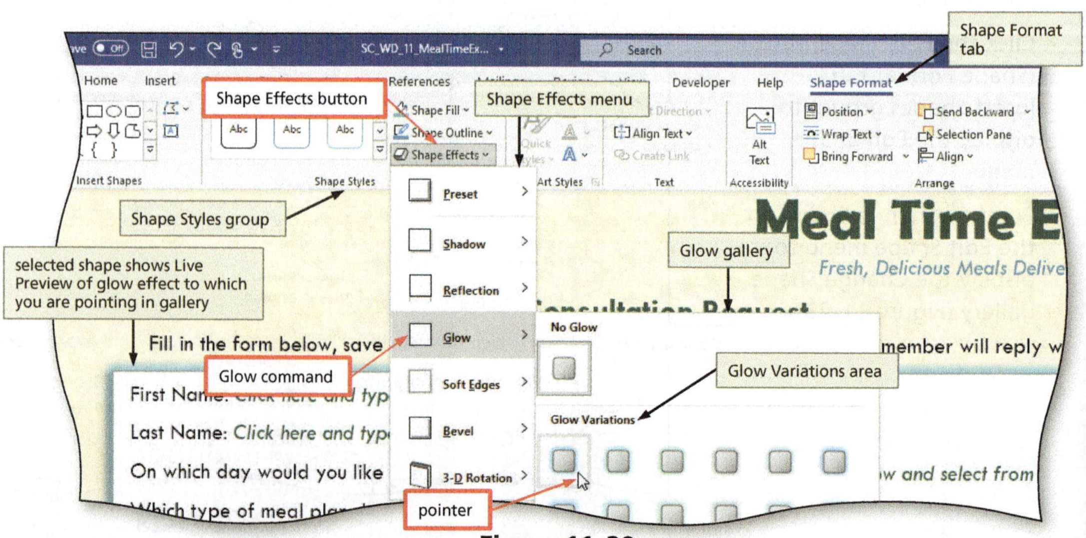

Figure 11–30

To Apply a Shadow Shape Effect

The following steps apply a shadow effect and change its color. **Why?** The rectangle in this online form has a shadow with a similar color to the placeholder text.

1

- With the rectangle shape still selected, click the Shape Effects button (Shape Format tab | Shape Styles group) again to display the Shape Effects menu.
- Point to Shadow on the Shape Effects menu to display the Shadow gallery.
- Point to 'Perspective: Upper Right' in the Perspective area at the bottom of the Shadow gallery to display a Live Preview of that shadow applied to the shape in the document (Figure 11–31).

Experiment

- Point to various shadows in the Shadow gallery and watch the shadow on the selected shape change.

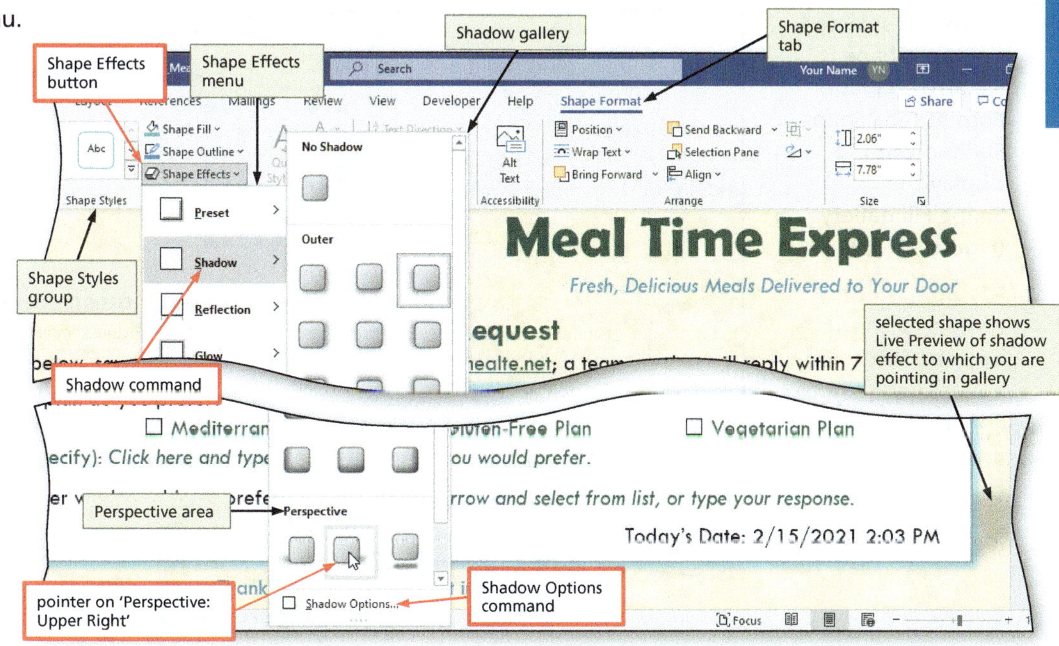

Figure 11–31

2

- Click 'Perspective: Upper Right' in the Shadow gallery to apply the selected shadow to the selected shape.
- Click the Shape Effects button (Shape Format tab | Shape Styles group) again to display the Shape Effects menu.
- Point to Shadow in the Shape Effects menu to display the Shadow gallery.
- Click Shadow Options in the Shadow gallery to open the Format Shape pane.
- Click the Shadow Color button (Format Shape pane) and then click 'Aqua, Accent 1' (fifth color in first row) in the Shadow Color gallery to change the shadow color.
- Click the Transparency down arrow as many times as necessary until the Transparency box displays 60% to change the amount of transparency in the shadow (Figure 11–32).

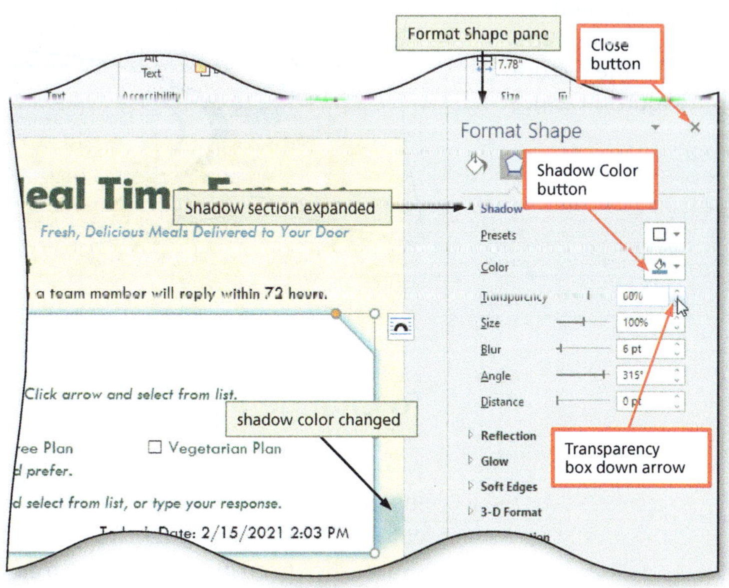

Figure 11–32

3

- Click the Close button to close the Format Shape pane.

To Fill a Shape with a Picture

The following steps fill a shape with a picture. **Why?** The rectangle in this online form contains a picture of a table setting. The picture, called Support_WD_11_TableSetting.png, is located on the Data Files. Please contact your instructor for information about accessing the Data Files.

1

- With the rectangle shape still selected, click the Shape Fill arrow (Shape Format tab | Shape Styles group) to display the Shape Fill gallery (Figure 11–33).

Q&A **My Shape Fill gallery did not appear. Why not?** You clicked the Shape Fill button instead of the Shape Fill arrow. Repeat Step 1.

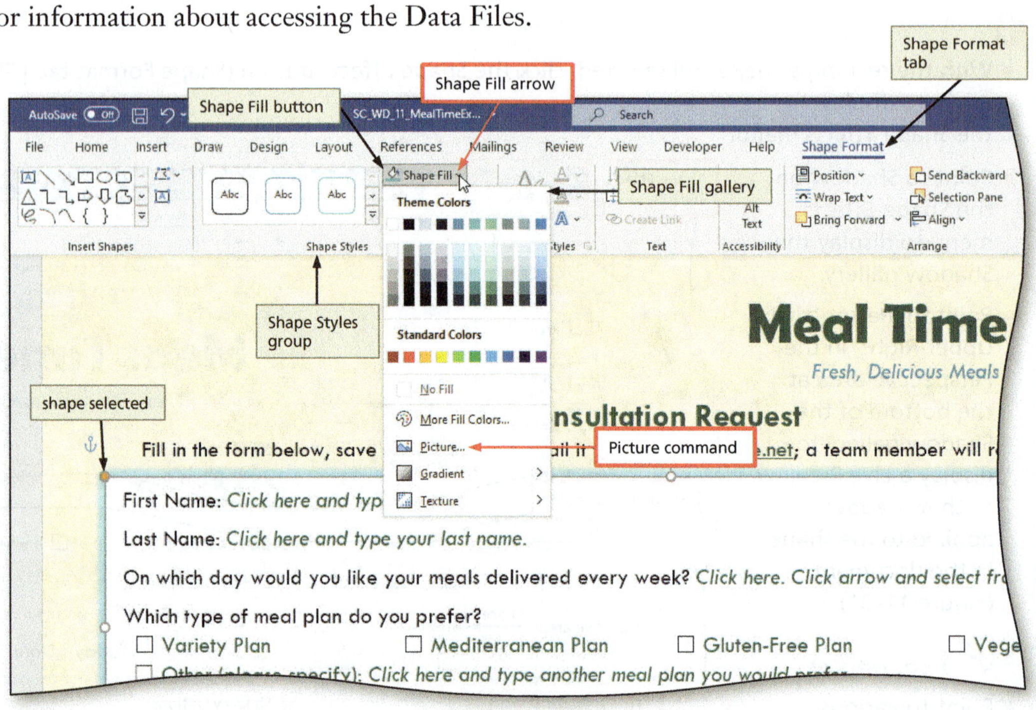

Figure 11–33

2

- Click Picture in the Shape Fill gallery to display the Insert Pictures dialog box.
- Click the 'From a File' button (Insert Pictures dialog box) to display the Insert Picture dialog box. Locate and then select the file called Support_WD_11_TableSetting.png (Insert Picture dialog box).
- Click the Insert button (Insert Picture dialog box) to fill the rectangle shape with the picture (Figure 11–34).

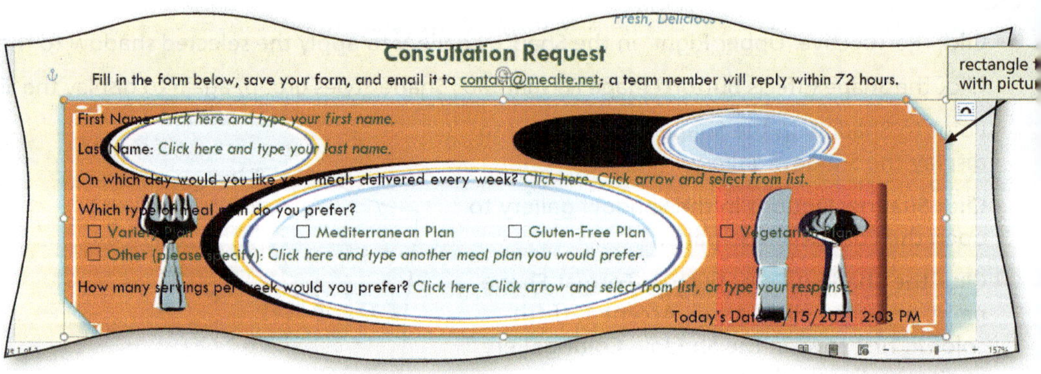

Figure 11–34

To Change the Color of a Picture

The text in the rectangle shape is difficult to read because the picture just inserted is too dark. You can experiment with adjusting the brightness, contrast, and color of a picture so that the text is readable. In this project, the color is changed to the washout setting and the saturation and tone are changed so that the text is easier to read. The following steps change the color, tone, and saturation of the picture.

1. Display the Picture Format tab.
2. With the rectangle shape still selected, click the Color button (Picture Format tab | Adjust group) to display the Color gallery.
3. Click Washout in the Recolor area in the Color gallery to apply the selected color to the selected picture.
4. Click the Color button again (Picture Format tab | Adjust group) and then click Temperature: 11200K in the Color Tone area in the Color gallery to apply the selected temperature to the selected picture.
5. Click the Color button again (Picture Format tab | Adjust group) and then point to Saturation: 0% in the Color Saturation area to display a Live Preview of the selected saturation applied to the selected picture (Figure 11–35).
6. Click Saturation: 0% in the Color gallery to apply the selected saturation to the selected picture.

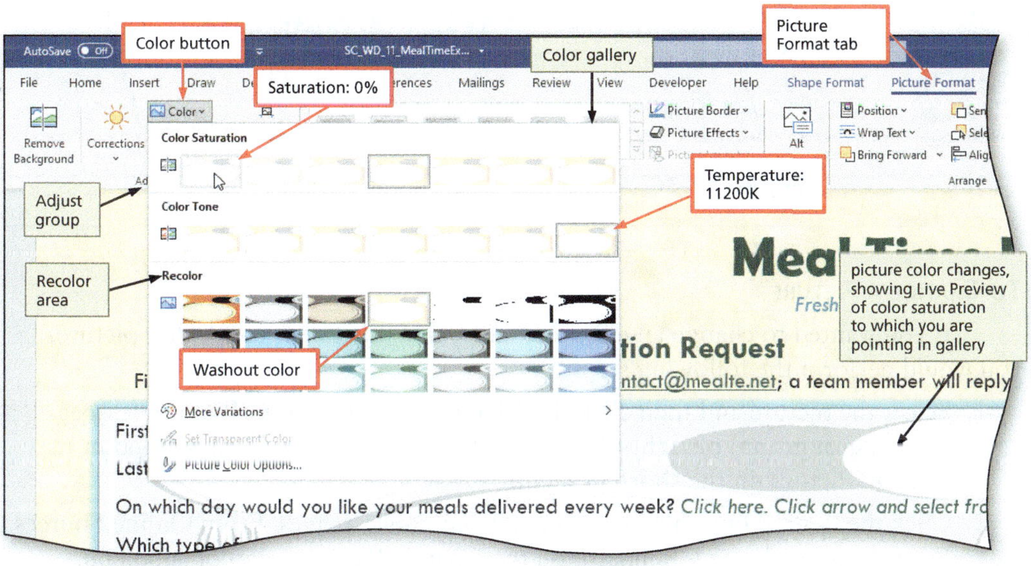

Figure 11–35

To Insert, Change Wrapping Style, and Resize a Picture

The top of the online form in this module contains a picture of a food pyramid. The picture, called Support_WD_11_FoodPyramid.png, is located in the Data Files. Please contact your instructor for information about accessing the Data Files.

You will change the wrapping style of the inserted picture so that it can be positioned in front of the text. Because the graphic's original size is too large, you also will resize it. The following steps insert a picture, change its wrapping style, and resize it.

1. Position the insertion point in a location near where the picture will be inserted, in this case, near the top of the online form.
2. Display the Insert tab. Click the Pictures button (Insert tab | Illustrations group) and then click This Device to display the Insert Picture dialog box.
3. Locate and then click the file called Support_WD_11_FoodPyramid.png (Insert Picture dialog box) to select the file.

BTW

Drawing Canvas

Some users prefer inserting graphics on a drawing canvas, which is a rectangular boundary between a shape and the rest of the document; it also is a container that helps you resize and arrange shapes on the page. To insert a drawing canvas, click the Shapes button (Insert tab | Illustrations group) and then click 'New Drawing Canvas' in the Shapes gallery. You can use the Shape Format tab to insert objects in the drawing canvas or format the appearance of the drawing canvas.

4. Click the Insert button to insert the picture at the location of the insertion point.
5. With the picture selected, click the Wrap Text button (Picture Format tab | Arrange group) and then click 'In Front of Text' so that the graphic can be positioned on top of text.
6. Change the value in the Shape Height box (Picture Format tab | Size group) to 1.01" and the value in the Shape Width box (Picture Format tab | Size group) to 1.31".
7. If necessary, scroll to display the online form in the document window (Figure 11–36).

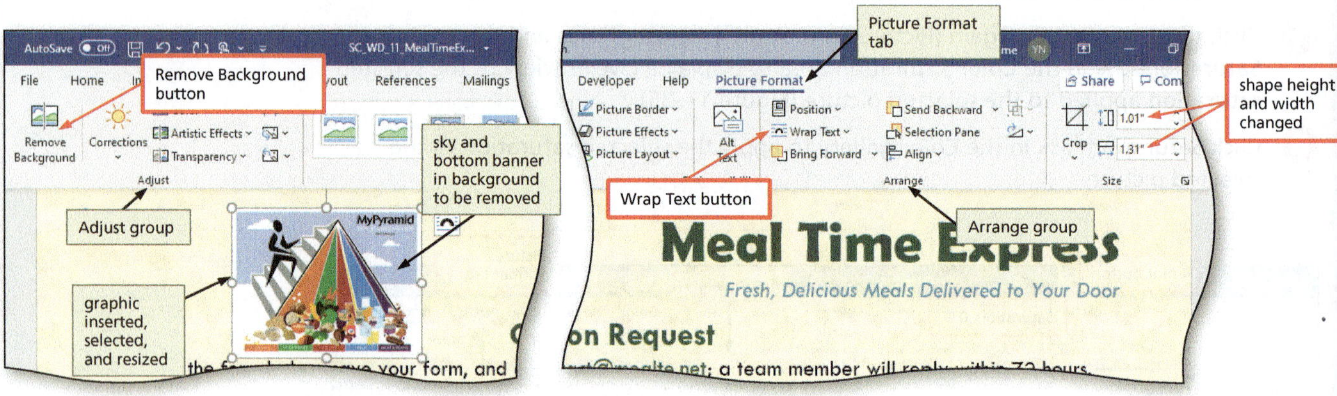

Figure 11–36

To Change a Picture

If you wanted to change an existing picture in a document to another picture, you would perform the following steps.

1. Select the picture and then click the Change Picture button (Picture Format tab | Adjust group) or right-click the picture to be changed and then point to Change Picture on the shortcut menu.
2. Click the desired option (From a File, From Stock Images, From Online Sources, From Icons, or From Clipboard) on the Change Picture menu or submenu.
3. Locate the desired replacement picture and then click OK.

To Remove a Background

In Word, you can remove a background from a picture. The following steps remove a background. **Why?** You remove the sky and bottom banner in the background from the picture of the food pyramid.

1

- With the food pyramid picture selected, click the Remove Background button (Picture Format tab | Adjust group) (shown in Figure 11–36), to display the Background Removal tab and show the proposed area to be deleted in purple (Figure 11–37).

Q&A **What is the Background Removal tab?**
You can draw around areas to keep or areas to remove by clicking the respective buttons on the Background Removal tab. If you mistakenly mark too much, use the 'Mark Areas to Remove' button. When finished marking, click the Keep Changes button, or to start over, click the 'Discard All Changes' button.

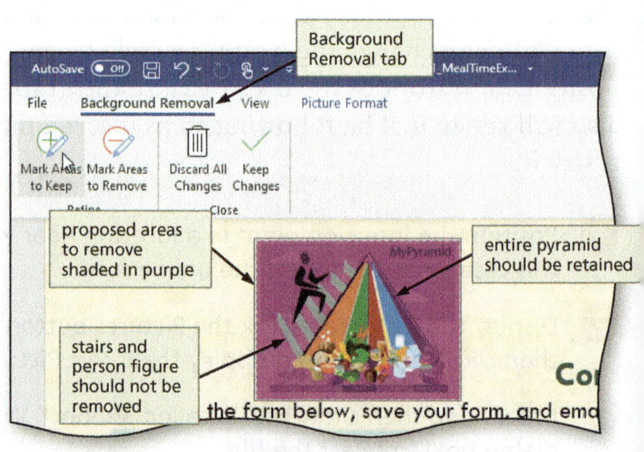

Figure 11–37

2

- Click the 'Mark Areas to Keep' button (Background Removal tab | Refine group) and then use the pointer to drag over areas that should remain in the image. If necessary, click the 'Mark Areas to Remove' button (Background Removal tab | Refine group) and use the pointer to drag over areas that should be deleted from the image. Your resulting areas to keep and delete should look similar to Figure 11–38.

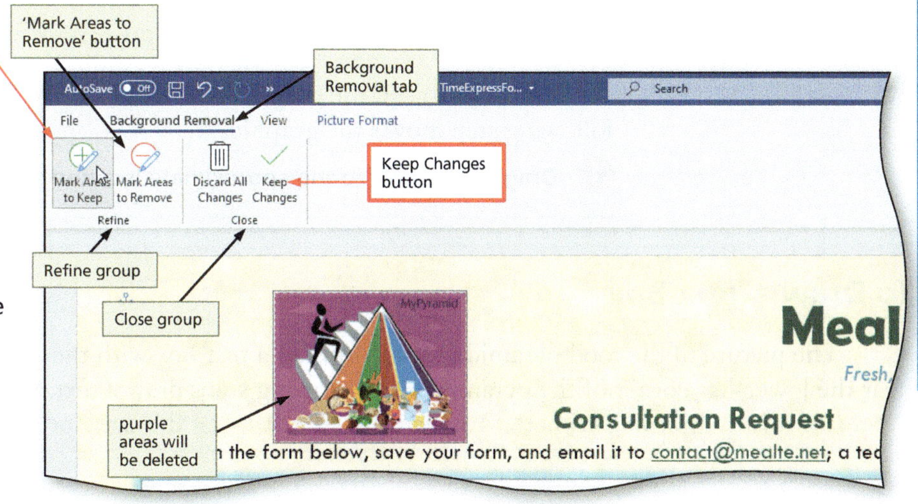

Figure 11–38

Q&A **How can you tell from the image which areas will be removed?**
The areas in purple will be removed from the image.

3

- Click the Keep Changes button (Background Removal tab | Close group) to remove the area shaded purple and to close the Background Removal tab (Figure 11–39).

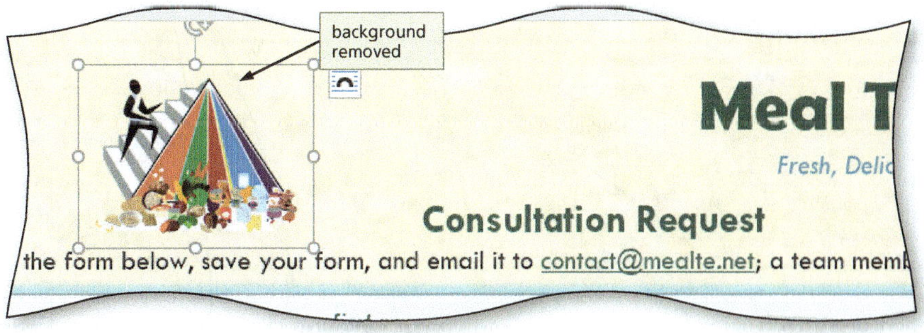

Figure 11–39

To Apply an Artistic Effect

Word provides several different artistic effects, such as blur, line drawing, and paint brush, that alter the appearance of a picture. The following steps apply an artistic effect to the picture. **Why?** You want to soften the look of the picture a bit.

1

- With the picture still selected, click the Artistic Effects button (Picture Format tab | Adjust group) to display the Artistic Effects gallery (Figure 11–40).

2

- Click Crisscross Etching (third effect in the fourth row) in the Artistic Effects gallery to apply the selected effect to the selected picture.

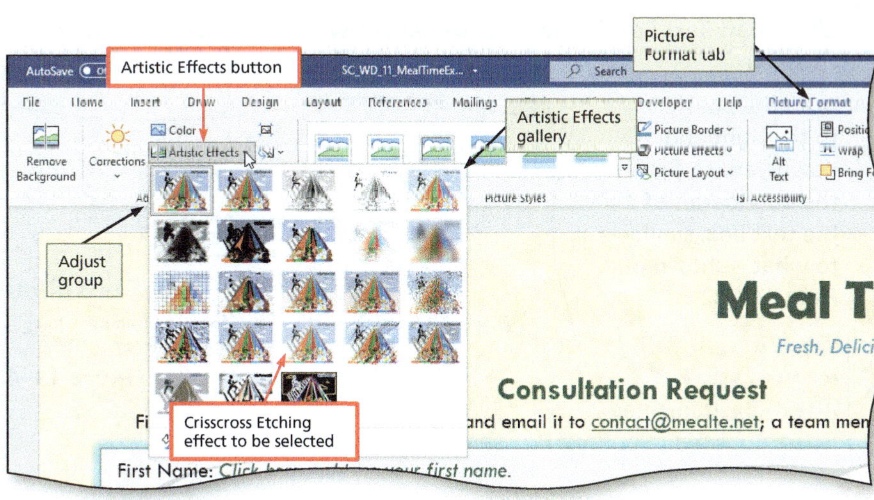

Figure 11–40

To Move the Graphic

In this project, the graphic is to be positioned on the left edge of the form. The following step moves the graphic.

1 Drag the graphic to the approximate location shown in Figure 11–41.

To Draw a Text Box

The picture of the food pyramid in this form has a text box with the words, So Nutritious Too!, positioned near the lower-left corner of the pyramid. The following steps draw a text box. **Why?** The first step in creating the text box is to draw its perimeter. You draw a text box using the same procedure as you do to draw a shape.

1

- Position the insertion point somewhere in the top of the online form.
- Display the Insert tab.
- Click the Text Box button (Insert tab | Text group) to display the Text Box gallery (Figure 11–41).

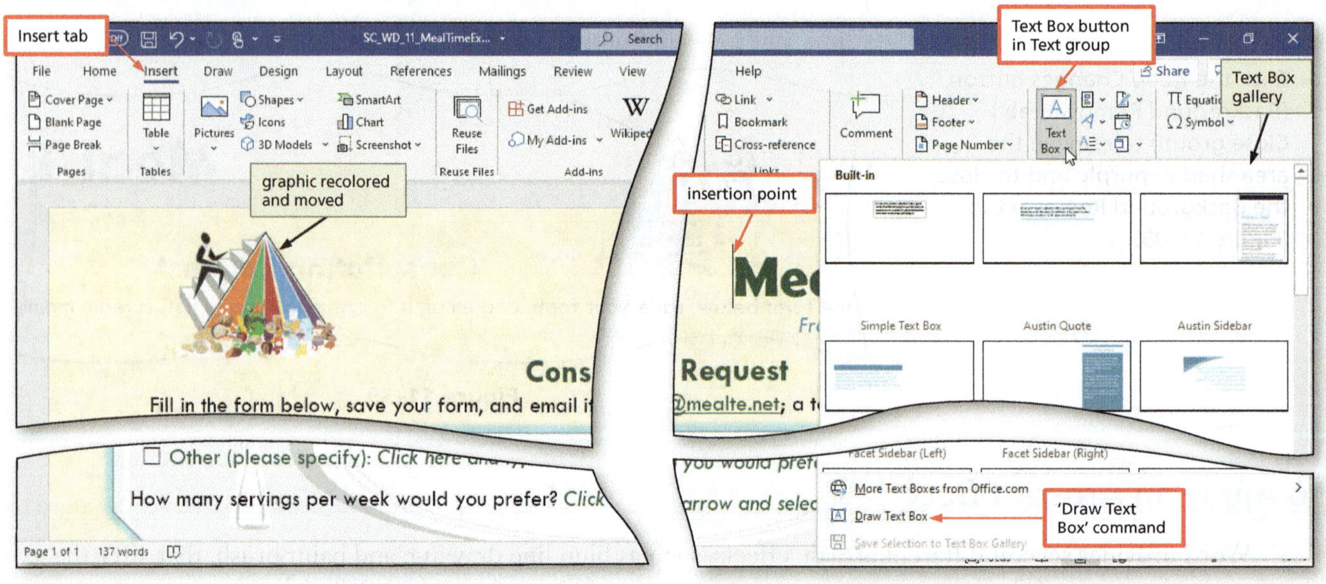

Figure 11–41

2

- Click 'Draw Text Box' in the Text Box gallery, which removes the gallery and changes the shape of the pointer to a crosshair.
- Drag the pointer to the right and downward to form the boundaries of the text box, similar to what is shown in Figure 11–42.

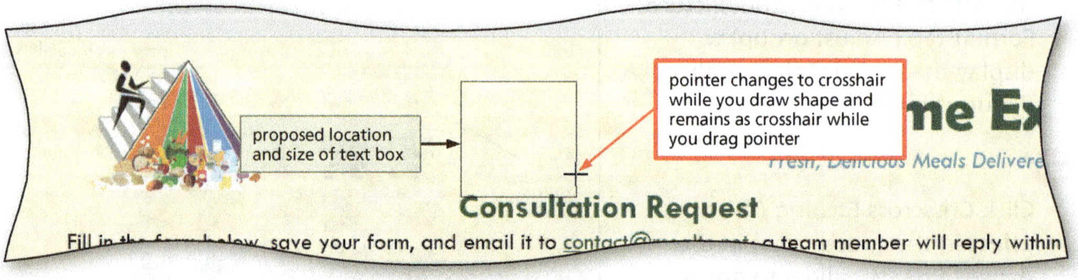

Figure 11–42

Q&A **What if I am using a touch screen?**
A text box is inserted in the document window. Proceed to Step 4.

3

- Release the mouse button so that Word draws the text box according to your drawing in the document window.

4

- Verify your shape is the same approximate height and width as the one in this project by changing the values in the Shape Height and Shape Width boxes (Shape Format tab | Size group) to 0.76" and 0.83", respectively (Figure 11–43).

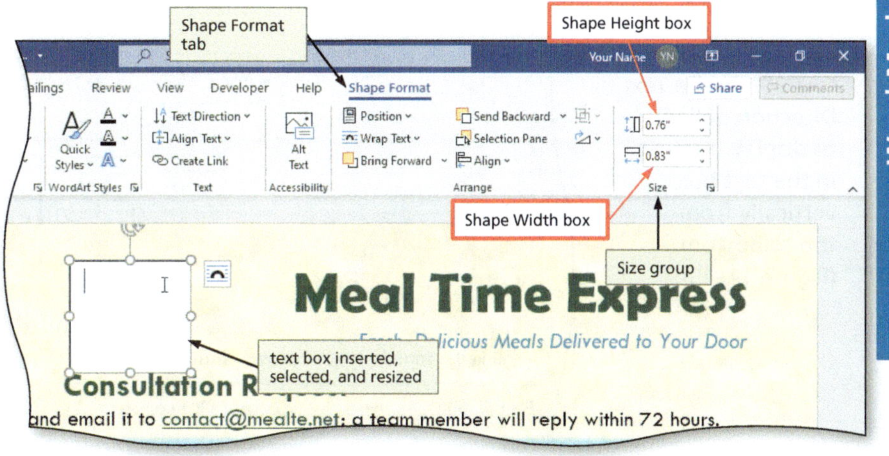

Figure 11–43

To Add Text to a Text Box and Format the Text

The next step is to add the phrase, So Nutritious Too!, centered in the text box using a text effect. You add text to a text box using the same procedure you do when adding text to a shape. The following steps add text to a text box.

1 Display the Home tab. With the text box selected, click the Center button (Home tab | Paragraph group) so that the text you enter is centered in the text box.

2 With the text box selected, click the 'Text Effects and Typography' button (Home tab | Font group) and then click 'Fill: Aqua, Accent color 1; Shadow' (second effect in first row) in the Text Effects and Typography gallery to specify the format for the text in the text box.

3 If your insertion point is not positioned in the text box (shape), right-click the shape to display a shortcut menu and the Mini toolbar and then click Edit Text on the shortcut menu or Mini toolbar to place an insertion point centered in the text box.

4 Type `So Nutritious Too!` as the text for the text box (shown in Figure 11–44). (If necessary, adjust the height of the text box to fit the text.)

To Change Text Direction in a Text Box

The following steps change text direction in a text box. **Why?** The direction of the text in the text box should be vertical instead of horizontal.

1

- Display the Shape Format tab.
- With the shape still selected, click the Text Direction button (Shape Format tab | Text group) to display the Text Direction gallery (Figure 11–44).

Q&A **What if my text box no longer is selected?**
Click the text box to select it.

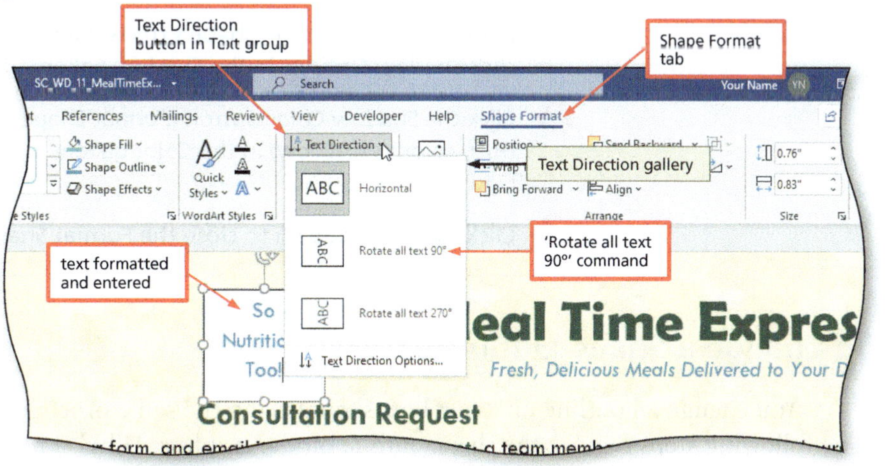

Figure 11–44

2

- Click 'Rotate all text 90°' in the Text Direction gallery to display the text in the text box vertically from top to bottom (Figure 11–45).

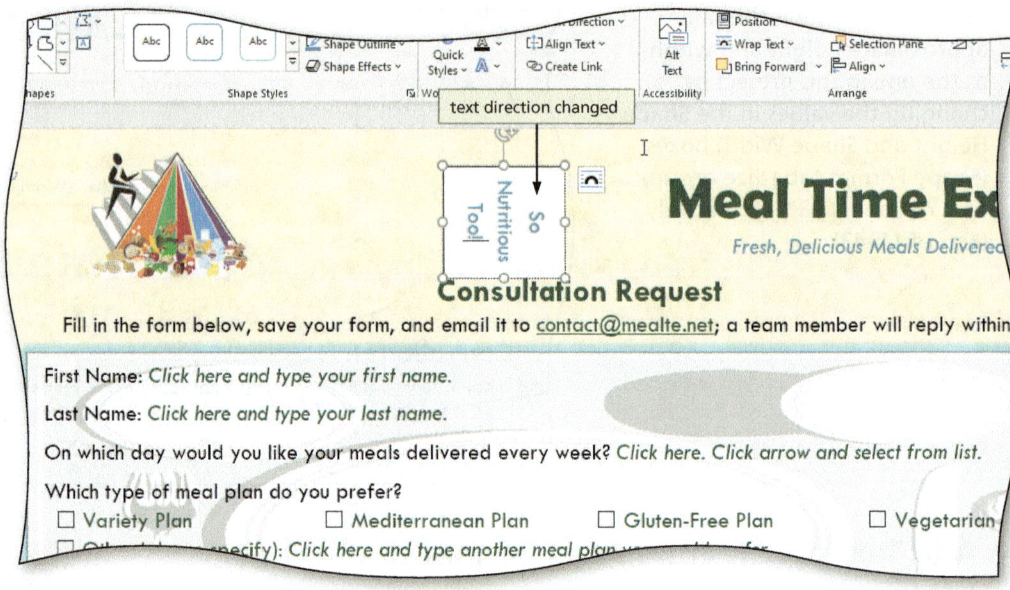

Figure 11–45

Other Ways

1. Right-click text box, click Format Shape on shortcut menu, click Text Options tab (Format Shape pane), click Layout & Properties button, expand Text Box section, click Text direction box, select desired direction, click Close button

To Apply a Shadow Shape Effect to a Text Box

The text box in this online form has an inside shadow that is in the same color as the business tag line. The following steps apply a shadow effect and change its color.

1. Move the text box to the right so that it is visible when you change the shadows and colors.
2. With the text box still selected, click the Shape Effects button (Shape Format tab | Shape Styles group) to display the Shape Effects menu.
3. Point to Shadow in the Shape Effects menu to display the Shadow gallery and then click Inside: Center in the Inner area of the Shadow gallery to apply the selected shadow to the selected shape.
4. Click the Shape Effects button (Shape Format tab | Shape Styles group) again to display the Shape Effects menu.
5. Point to Shadow in the Shape Effects menu to display the Shadow gallery and then click Shadow Options in the Shadow gallery to display the Format Shape pane.
6. Click the Shadow Color button (Format Shape pane) and then click 'Aqua, Accent 1' (fifth color in first row) in the Color gallery to change the shadow color (shown in Figure 11–46).
7. Click the Close button to close the Format Shape pane.

To Change a Shape Outline of a Text Box

You change an outline on a text box (shape) using the same procedure as you do with a picture. The following steps remove the shape outline on the text box. **Why?** The text box in this form has no outline.

1

- With the text box still selected, click the Shape Outline arrow (Shape Format tab | Shape Styles group) to display the Shape Outline gallery (Figure 11–46).

Q&A **The Shape Outline gallery did not display. Why not?**
You clicked the Shape Outline button instead of the Shape Outline arrow. Repeat Step 1.

Experiment

- Point to various colors in the Shape Outline gallery and watch the color of the outline on the text box change in the document.

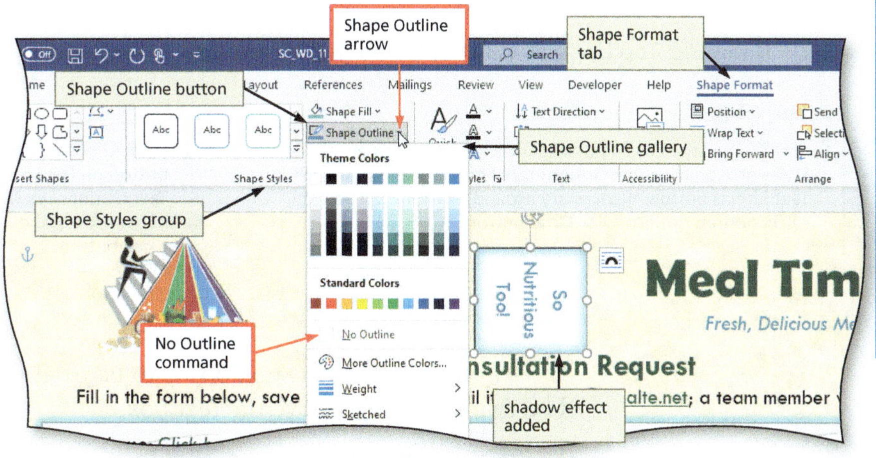

Figure 11–46

2

- Click No Outline in the Shape Outline gallery to remove the outline from the selected shape.

Other Ways

1. Click Shape Styles Dialog Box Launcher (Shape Format tab | Shape Styles group); expand Line section (Format Shape pane); click No line to remove line, or click Solid line, click Outline color button, and select desired color to change line color; click Close button
2. Right-click text box (or, if using touch, tap 'Show Context Menu' button on Mini toolbar), click Format Shape on shortcut menu, expand Line section (Format Shape pane), click No line to remove line, or click Solid line, click Outline color button, and select desired color to change line color; click Close button

To Apply a 3-D Effect to a Text Box

Word provides 3-D effects for shapes (such as text boxes) that are similar to those it provides for pictures. The following steps apply a 3-D rotation effect to a text box. **Why?** In this form, the text box is rotated using a 3-D rotation effect.

1

- Move the text box to the left so that you can see it when you change to a 3-D effect.
- With the text box selected, click the Shape Effects button (Shape Format tab | Shape Styles group) to display the Shape Effects gallery.
- Point to '3-D Rotation' in the Shape Effects gallery to display the 3-D Rotation gallery.
- Point to 'Isometric: Top Up' in the Parallel area (third rotation in first row) to display a Live Preview of the selected 3-D effect applied to the text box in the document window (Figure 11–47).

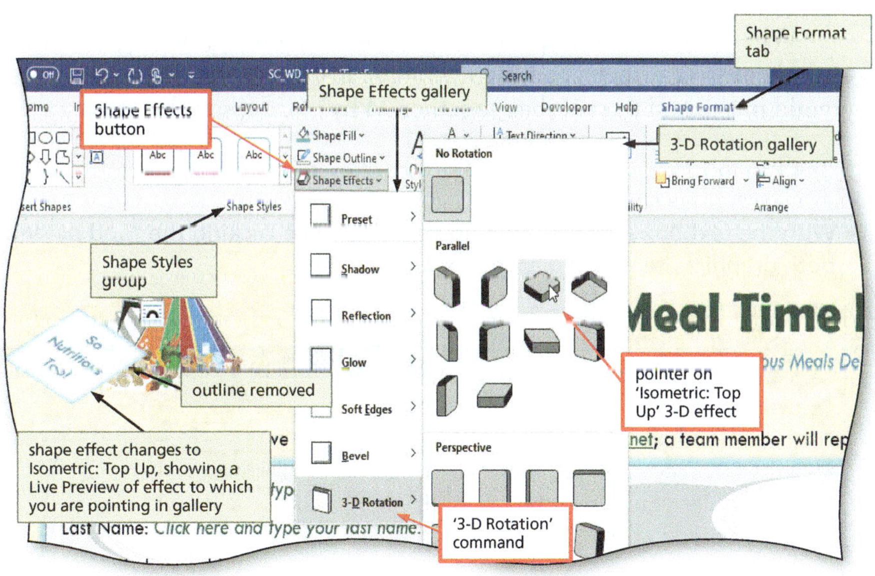

Figure 11–47

Experiment

- Point to various 3-D rotation effects in the 3-D Rotation gallery and watch the text box change in the document window.

2

- Click 'Isometric: Top Up' in the 3-D Rotation gallery to apply the selected 3-D effect.

Other Ways

1. Click Shape Styles Dialog Box Launcher (Shape Format tab | Shape Styles group), click Text Options tab (Format Shape pane), click Text Effects button, if necessary expand 3-D Rotation Section, select desired options, click Close button
2. Right-click text box (or, if using touch, tap 'Show Context Menu' button on Mini toolbar), click Format Shape on shortcut menu, click Text Options tab (Format Shape pane), click Text Effects button, if necessary expand 3-D Rotation Section, select desired options, click Close button

To Move the Text Box

In this project, the text box is to be positioned near the lower-left of the graphic. The following steps move the text box.

1 With the text box selected, click the Send Backward arrow (Shape Format tab | Arrange group) and then click 'Send to Back' on the Send Backward menu to send the text box behind the pyramid image.

2 Drag the text box to the location shown in Figure 11–48. (You may need to drag the text box a couple of times to position it as shown in the figure.)

Figure 11–48

To Group Objects

When you have multiple graphics, such as pictures, shapes, and text boxes, positioned on a page, you can group them so that they are a single graphic instead of separate graphics. The following steps group the food pyramid image and the text box together. **Why?** Grouping the graphics makes it easier to move them because they all move together as a single graphic.

1

- With the text box selected, hold down CTRL while clicking the food pyramid image (that is, CTRL+click), so that both graphics are selected at the same time.

Q&A **What if I had more than two graphics (i.e., pictures, shapes, text boxes, etc.) that I wanted to group?**
For each subsequent graphic to select, CTRL+click the graphic, which enables you to select multiple objects at the same time.

- Click the Group Objects button (Shape Format tab | Arrange group) to display the Group Objects menu (Figure 11–49).

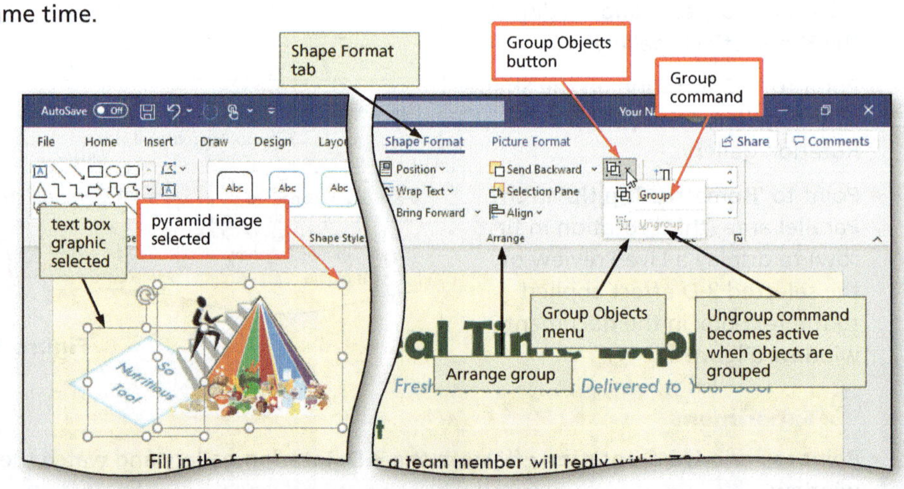

Figure 11–49

2

- Click Group on the Group Objects menu to group the selected objects into a single selected object (Figure 11–50).

Q&A **What if I wanted to ungroup grouped objects (i.e., pictures, shapes, text boxes, etc.)?**
Select the object to ungroup, click the Group Objects button (Shape Format tab | Arrange group), and then click Ungroup on the Group Objects menu.

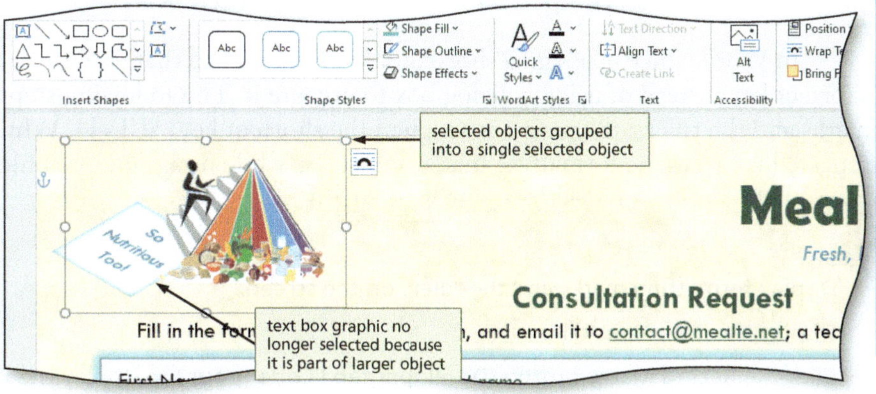

Figure 11–50

3

- Click outside of the graphic to position the insertion point in the document and deselect the graphic.
- Save the template again on the same storage location with the same file name.

Break Point: If you want to take a break, this is a good place to do so. You can exit Word now. To resume later, start Word, open the file called SC_WD_11_MealTimeExpressFormModified.dotm, and continue following the steps from this location forward.

Using a Macro to Automate a Task

A macro consists of a series of Word commands or instructions that are grouped together as a single command. This single command is a convenient way to automate a difficult or lengthy task. Macros often are used to simplify formatting or editing activities, to combine multiple commands into a single command, or to select an option in a dialog box using a shortcut key.

To create a macro, you can use the macro recorder or the Visual Basic Editor. With the macro recorder, Word generates the VBA instructions associated with the macro automatically as you perform actions in Word. If you wanted to write the VBA instructions yourself, you would use the Visual Basic Editor. This module uses the macro recorder to create a macro and the Visual Basic Editor to modify it.

The **macro recorder** creates a macro based on a series of actions you perform while the macro recorder is recording. The macro recorder is similar to a video camera: after you start the macro recorder, it records all actions you perform while working in a document and stops recording when you stop the macro recorder. To record a macro, you follow this sequence of steps:

1. Start the macro recorder and specify options about the macro.
2. Execute the actions you want recorded.
3. Stop the macro recorder.

After you record a macro, you can execute the macro, or play it, any time you want to perform the same set of actions.

BTW

Naming Macros

If you give a new macro the same name as an existing built-in command in Microsoft Word, the new macro's actions will replace the existing actions. Thus, you should be careful not to assign a macro a name reserved for automatic macros (see Table 11–1) or any Word commands. To view a list of built-in macros in Word, click the Macros button (View tab | Macros group) to display the Macros dialog box. Click the Macros in arrow and then click Word commands.

To Record a Macro and Assign It a Shortcut Key

In Word, you can assign a shortcut key to a macro so that you can execute the macro by pressing the shortcut key instead of using a dialog box to execute it. The following steps record a macro that hides formatting marks and the rulers; the macro is assigned the shortcut key, ALT+H. **Why?** Assume you find that you are repeatedly hiding the formatting marks and rulers while designing the online form. To simplify this task, the macro in this project hides these screen elements.

1

- Display formatting marks and the rulers on the screen.
- Display the Developer tab.
- Click the Record Macro button (Developer tab | Code group) to display the Record Macro dialog box.
- Type `HideScreenElements` in the Macro name text box (Record Macro dialog box).

Q&A **Do I have to name a macro?**
If you do not enter a name for the macro, Word assigns a default name. Macro names can be up to 255 characters in length and can contain only numbers, letters, and the underscore character. A macro name cannot contain spaces or other punctuation.

- Click the 'Store macro in' arrow and then click 'Documents Based On SC_WD_11_MealTimeExpressFormModified'. Note that, depending on settings, your file name also may show the extension .dotm at the end.

Q&A **What is the difference between storing a macro with the document template versus the Normal template?**
Macros saved in the Normal template are available to all future documents; macros saved with the document template are available only with a document based on the template.

- Before proceeding, verify that your Store macro in location is set to 'Documents Based On SC_WD_11_MealTimeExpressFormModified'.
- In the Description text box, type this sentence (Figure 11–51): `Hide formatting marks and the rulers.`

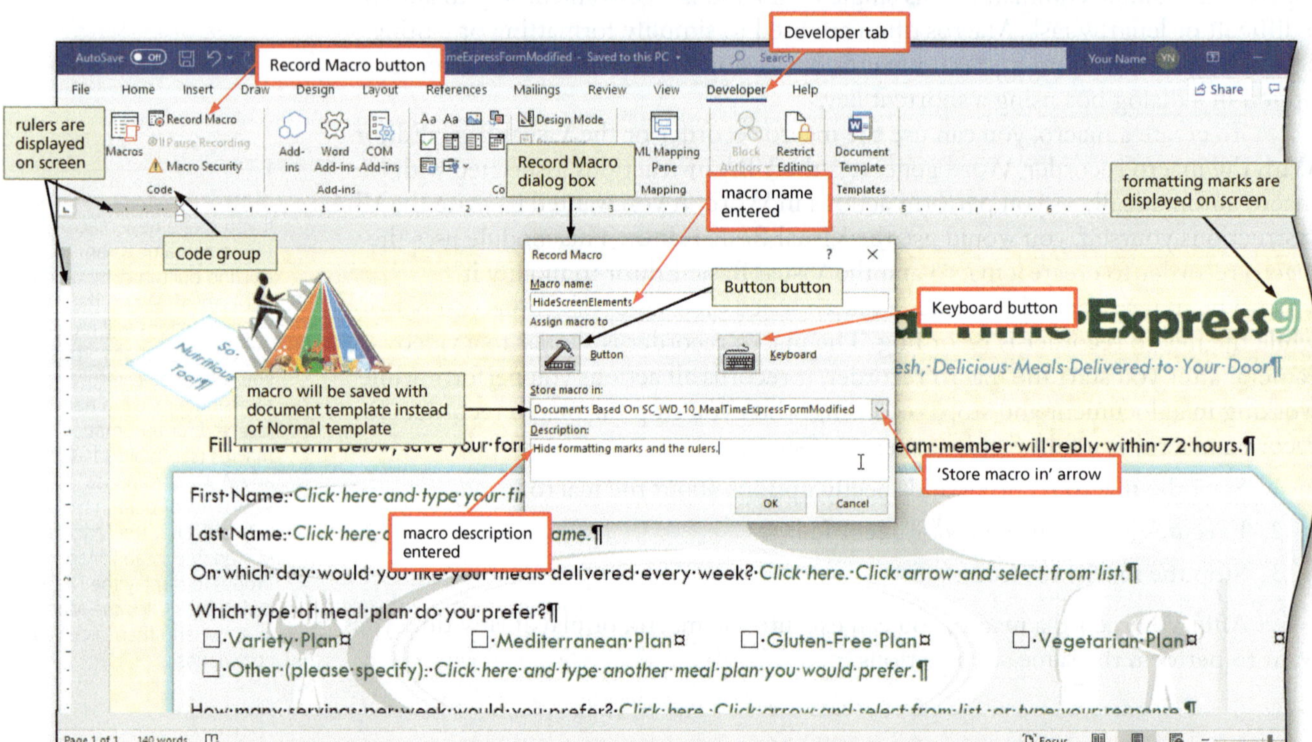

Figure 11–51

2

- Click the Keyboard button (shown in Figure 11–51) to display the Customize Keyboard dialog box.
- Press ALT+H to display the characters, ALT+H, in the 'Press new shortcut key' text box (Customize Keyboard dialog box) (Figure 11–52).

Q&A **Can I type the letters in the shortcut key (ALT+H) in the text box instead of pressing them?**
No. Although typing the letters places them in the text box, the shortcut key is valid only if you press the shortcut key combination itself.

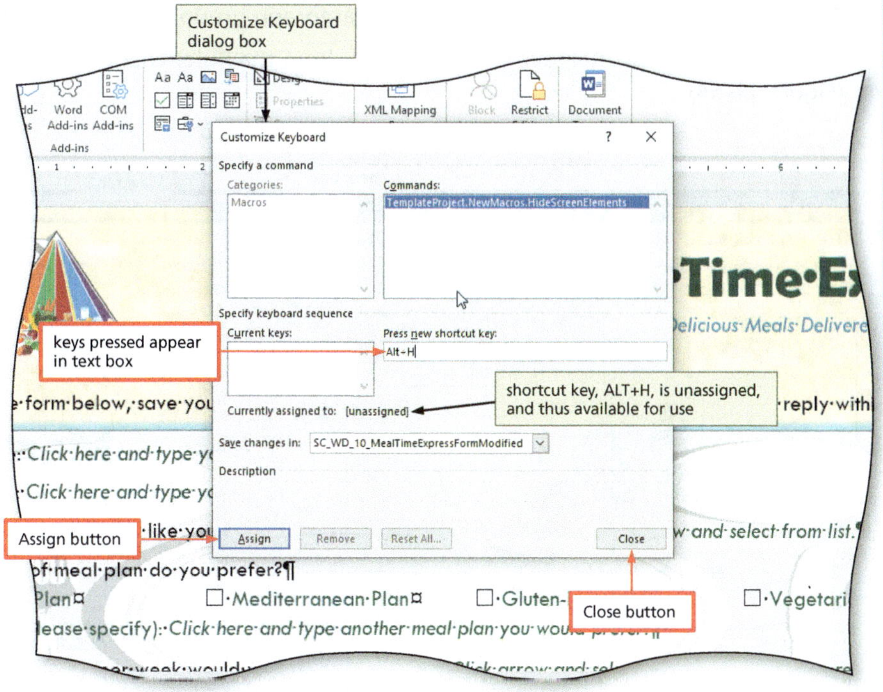

Figure 11–52

3

- Click the Assign button (Customize Keyboard dialog box) to assign the shortcut key, ALT+H, to the macro named HideScreenElements.
- Click the Close button (Customize Keyboard dialog box), which closes the dialog box, displays a Macro Recording button on the status bar, and starts the macro recorder (Figure 11–53).

Q&A **How do I record the macro?**
While the macro recorder is running, any action you perform in Word will be part of the macro until you stop or pause the macro.

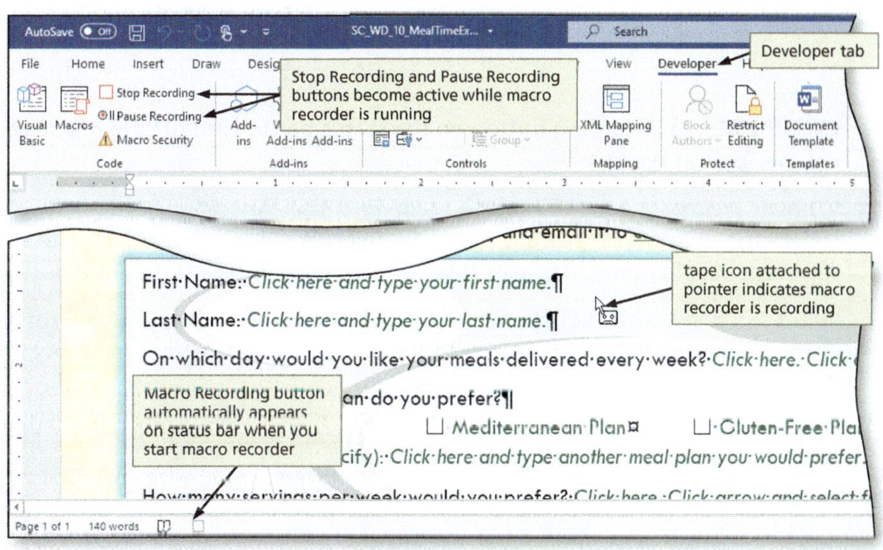

Figure 11–53

What is the purpose of the Pause Recording button (Developer tab | Code group)?
If, while recording a macro, you want to perform some actions that should not be part of the macro, click the Pause Recording button to suspend the macro recorder. The Pause Recording button changes to a Resume Recorder button that you click when you want to continue recording.

4

- Display the Home tab.

Q&A **What happened to the tape icon?**
While recording a macro, the tape icon might disappear from the pointer when the pointer is on a menu, on the ribbon, or in a dialog box.

- Click the 'Show/Hide ¶' button (Home tab | Paragraph group) to hide formatting marks.
- Display the View tab. Remove the check mark from the Ruler check box (View tab | Show group) to hide the rulers (Figure 11–54).

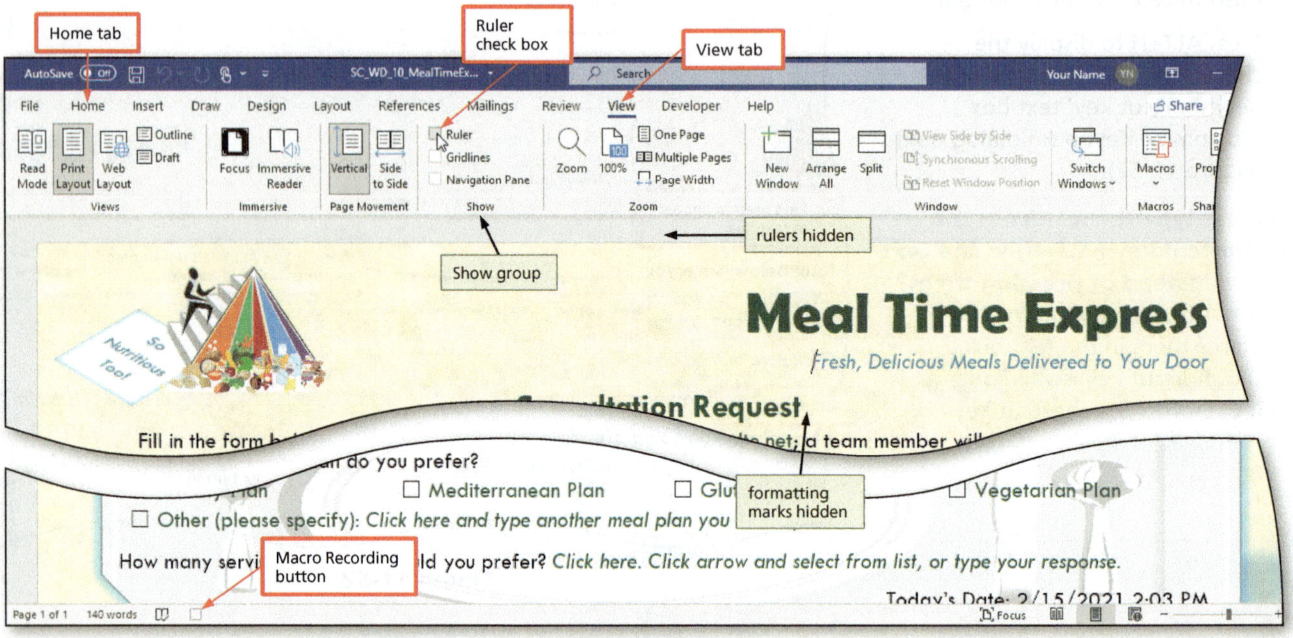

Figure 11–54

5

- Click the Macro Recording button on the status bar to turn off the macro recorder, that is, to stop recording actions you perform in Word.

Q&A

What if I made a mistake while recording the macro?
Delete the macro and record it again. To delete a macro, click the Macros button (Developer tab | Code group), select the macro name in the list (Macros dialog box), click the Delete button, and then click the Yes button.

What if I wanted to assign the macro to a button instead of a shortcut key?
You would click the Button button in the Record Macro dialog box (shown in Figure 11–51) and then follow Steps 4 and 5 in this section.

Other Ways

1. Click Macros arrow (View tab | Macros group), click Record Macro on Macros menu
2. Press ALT+F8, click Create button (Macros dialog box)

To Run a Macro

The next step is to execute, or run, the macro to ensure that it works. Recall that this macro hides formatting marks and the rulers, which means you must be sure the formatting marks and rulers are displayed on the screen before running the macro. Because you created a shortcut key for the macro in this project, the following steps show formatting marks and the rulers so that you can run the HideScreenElements macro using the shortcut key, ALT+H.

BTW

Running Macros
You can run a macro by clicking the Macros button (Developer tab | Code group or View tab | Macros group) or by pressing ALT+F8 to display the Macros dialog box, selecting the macro name in the list, and then clicking the Run button (Macros dialog box).

1. Display formatting marks on the screen.
2. Display rulers on the screen.
3. Press ALT+H, which causes Word to perform the instructions stored in the HideScreenElements macro, that is, to hide formatting marks and rulers.

To Add a Command and a Macro as Buttons on the Quick Access Toolbar

Word allows you to add buttons to and delete buttons from the Quick Access Toolbar. You also can assign a command, such as a macro, to a button on the Quick Access Toolbar. The following steps add an existing command to the Quick Access Toolbar and assign a macro to a new button on the Quick Access Toolbar. **Why?** This module shows how to add the New File command to the Quick Access Toolbar and also shows how to create a button for the HideScreenElements macro so that instead of pressing the shortcut keys, you can click the button to hide formatting marks and the rulers.

1

- Click the 'Customize Quick Access Toolbar' button on the Quick Access Toolbar to display the Customize Quick Access Toolbar menu (Figure 11–55).

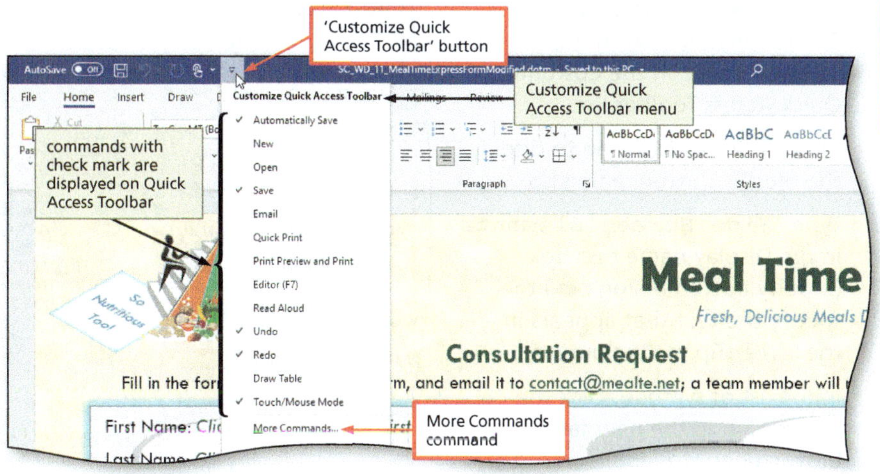

Figure 11–55

Q&A **What happens if I click the commands listed on the Customize Quick Access Toolbar menu?**
If the command does not have a check mark beside it and you click it, Word places the button associated with the command on the Quick Access Toolbar. If the command has a check mark beside it and you click (deselect) it, Word removes the command from the Quick Access Toolbar.

2

- Click More Commands on the Customize Quick Access Toolbar menu to display the Word Options dialog box with Quick Access Toolbar selected in the left pane.
- Scroll through the list of popular commands (Word Options dialog box) and then click New File to select the command.
- Click the Add button to add the selected command (New File, in this case) to the Customize Quick Access Toolbar list (Figure 11–56). Note that the built-in ScreenTip for the New File command is New Blank Document.

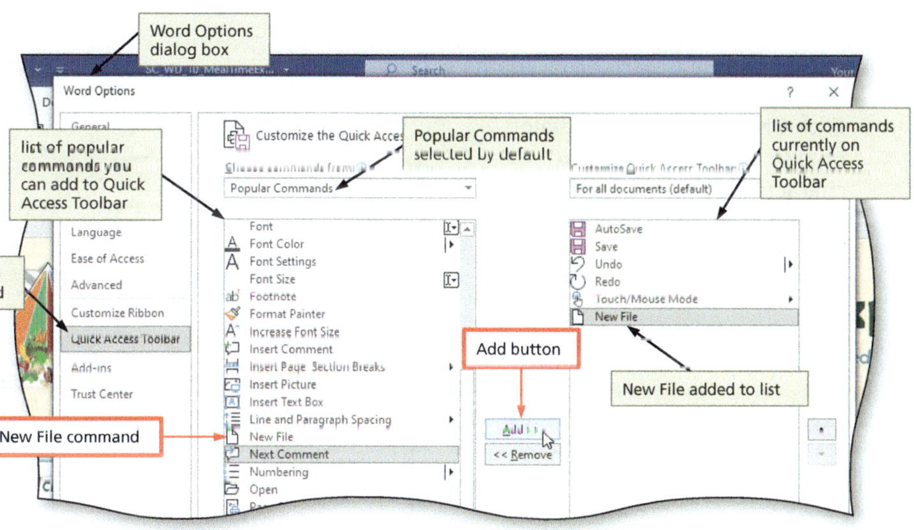

Figure 11–56

3

- Click the 'Choose commands from' arrow to display a list of categories of commands (Figure 11–57).

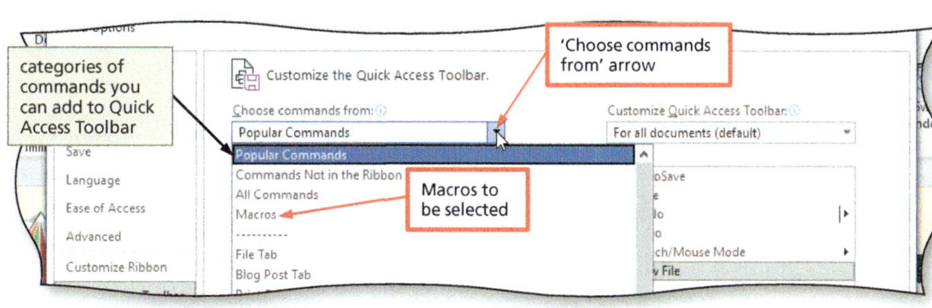

Figure 11–57

4

- Click Macros in the Choose commands from list to display the macro in this document.
- If necessary, click the macro to select it.
- Click the Add button (Word Options dialog box) to display the selected macro in the Customize Quick Access Toolbar list.
- Click the Modify button to display the Modify Button dialog box.
- Type **`Hide Screen Elements`** in the Display name text box (Modify Button dialog box) to specify the text that appears in the ScreenTip for the button.
- In the list of symbols, click the screen icon as the new face for the button (Figure 11–58).

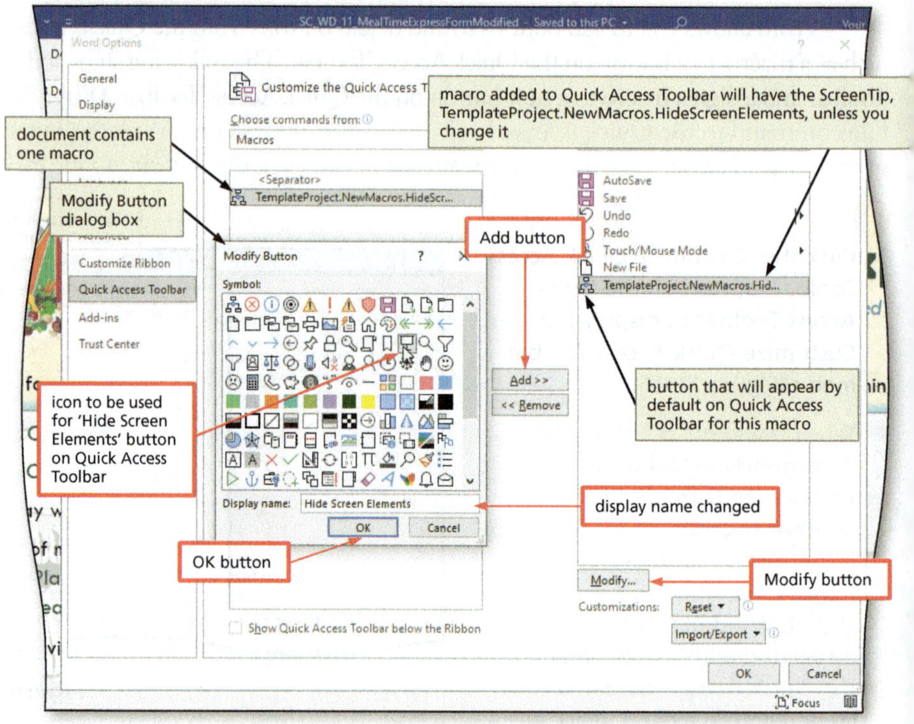

Figure 11–58

5

- Click OK (Modify Button dialog box) to change the button characteristics in the Customize Quick Access Toolbar list (Figure 11–59).

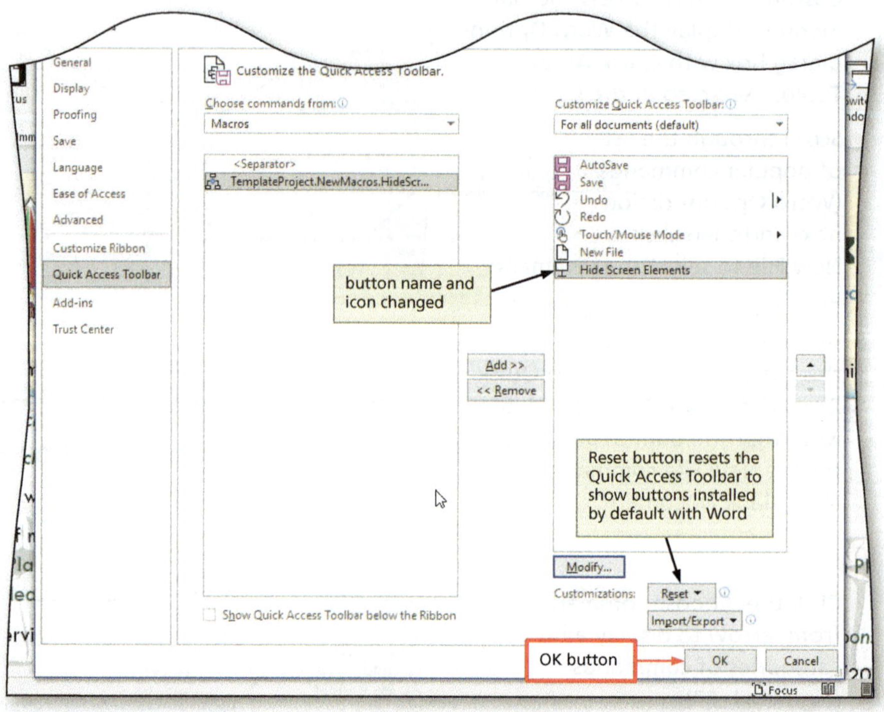

Figure 11–59

6

- Click OK (Word Options dialog box) to add the buttons to the Quick Access Toolbar (Figure 11–60).

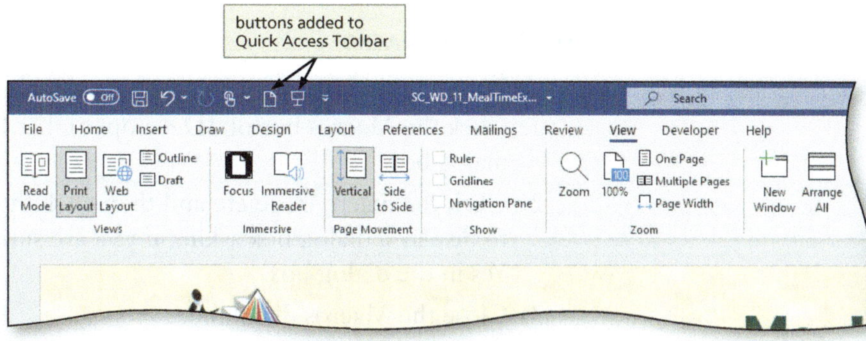

Figure 11–60

Other Ways

1. Right-click Quick Access Toolbar, click 'Customize Quick Access Toolbar' on shortcut menu

To Use the New Buttons on the Quick Access Toolbar

The next step is to test the new buttons on the Quick Access Toolbar, that is, the 'New Blank Document' button and the 'Hide Screen Elements' button, which will execute, or run, the macro that hides formatting marks and the rulers. The following steps use buttons on the Quick Access Toolbar.

1. Click the 'New Blank Document' button on the Quick Access Toolbar to display a new blank document window. Close the new blank document window.
2. Display formatting marks on the screen.
3. Display rulers on the screen.
4. Click the 'Hide Screen Elements' button on the Quick Access Toolbar, which causes Word to perform the instructions stored in the HideScreenElements macro, that is, to hide formatting marks and the rulers.

To Delete Buttons from the Quick Access Toolbar

The following steps delete the 'New Blank Document' button and the 'Hide Screen Elements' button from the Quick Access Toolbar. **Why?** If you no longer plan to use a button on the Quick Access Toolbar, you can delete it.

1

- Right-click the button to be deleted from the Quick Access Toolbar, in this case the 'Hide Screen Elements' button, to display a shortcut menu (Figure 11–61).

2

- Click 'Remove from Quick Access Toolbar' on the shortcut menu to remove the button from the Quick Access Toolbar.

3

- Repeat Steps 1 and 2 for the 'New Blank Document' button on the Quick Access Toolbar.

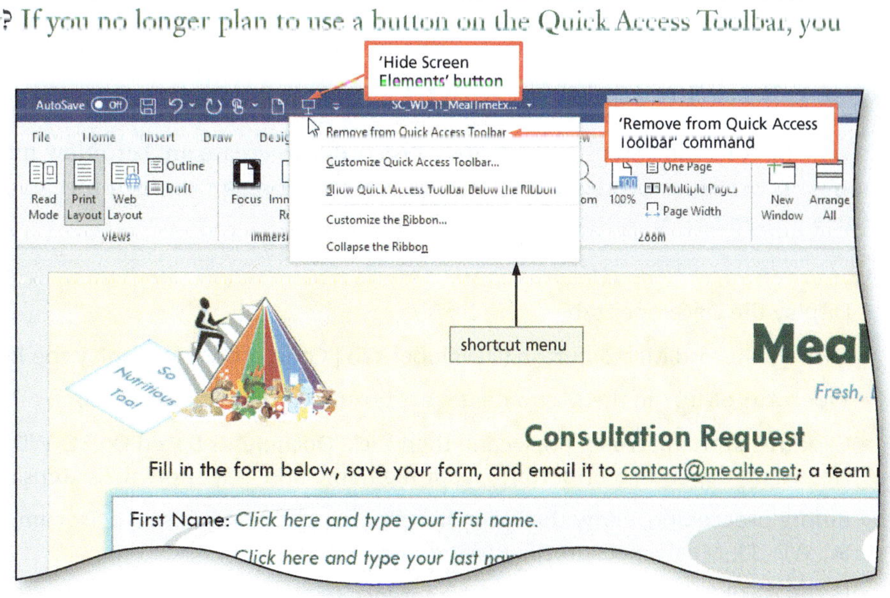

Figure 11–61

To Delete a Macro

If you wanted to delete a macro, you would perform the following steps.

1. Click the Macros button (Developer tab | Code group) to display the Macros dialog box.
2. Click the macro to delete and then click the Delete button (Macros dialog box) to display a dialog box asking if you are sure you want to delete the macro. Click Yes in the dialog box.
3. Close the Macros dialog box.

Automatic Macros

The previous section showed how to create a macro, assign it a unique name (HideScreenElements) and a shortcut key, and then add a button that executes the macro on the Quick Access Toolbar. This section creates an **automatic macro**, which is a macro that executes automatically when a certain event occurs. Word has five prenamed automatic macros. Table 11–1 lists the name and function of these automatic macros.

Table 11–1 Automatic Macros

Macro Name	Event That Causes Macro to Run
AutoClose	Closing a document that contains the macro
AutoExec	Starting Word
AutoExit	Exiting Word
AutoNew	Creating a new document based on a template that contains the macro
AutoOpen	Opening a document that contains the macro

BTW

Automatic Macros

A document can contain only one AutoClose macro, one AutoNew macro, and one AutoOpen macro. The AutoExec and AutoExit macros, however, are not stored with the document; instead, they must be stored in the Normal template. Thus, only one AutoExec macro and only one AutoExit macro can exist for all Word documents.

The automatic macro you choose depends on when you want certain actions to occur. In this module, when a user creates a new Word document that is based on the SC_WD_11_MealTimeExpressFormModified.dotm template, you want to be sure that the zoom is set to page width. Thus, the AutoNew automatic macro is used in this online form.

To Create an Automatic Macro

The following steps use the macro recorder to create an AutoNew macro. **Why?** The online form in this module is displayed properly when the zoom is set to page width. Thus, you will record the steps to zoom to page width in the AutoNew macro.

1

- Display the Developer tab.
- Click the Record Macro button (Developer tab | Code group) to display the Record Macro dialog box.
- Type `AutoNew` in the Macro name text box (Record Macro dialog box).
- Click the 'Store macro in' arrow and then click 'Documents Based On SC_WD_11_MealTimeExpressFormModified'. Note that, depending on settings, your file name also may show the extension .dotm at the end.
- Before proceeding, verify that your Store macro in location is set to 'Documents Based On SC_WD_11_MealTimeExpressFormModified'.
- In the Description text box, type this sentence (Figure 11–62): `Specifies how the form initially is displayed.`

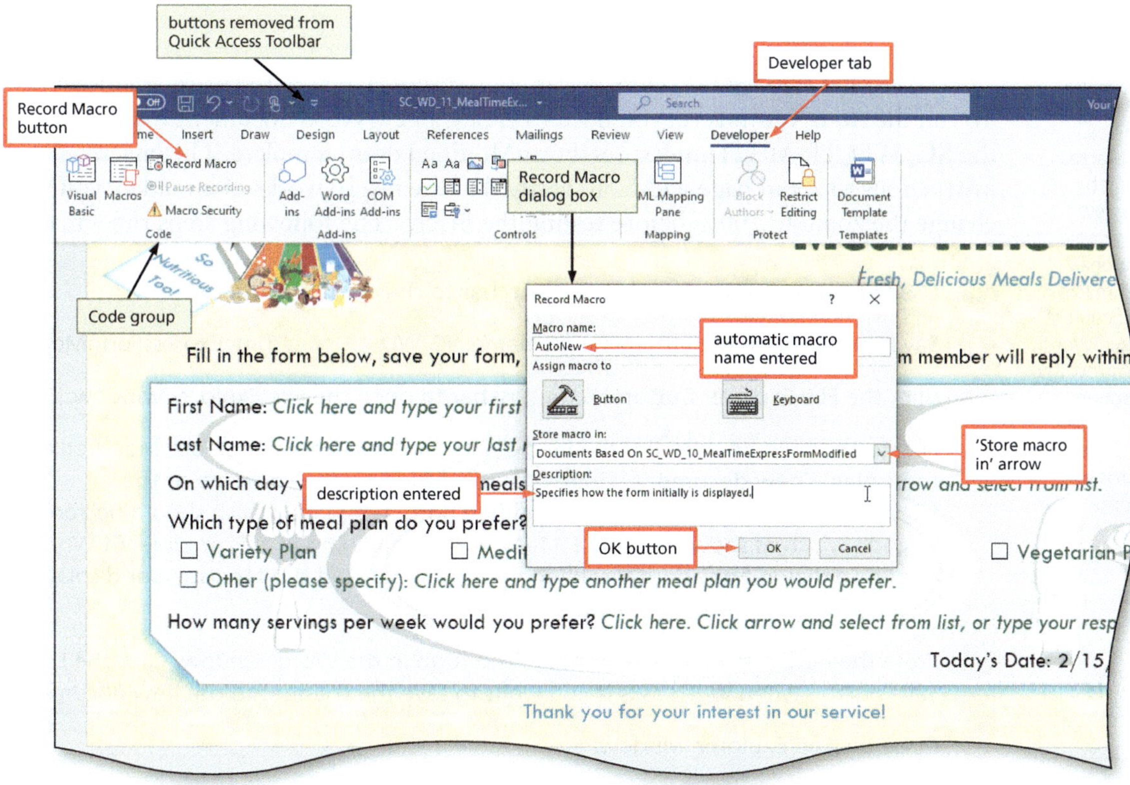

Figure 11–62

2

- Click OK to close the Record Macro dialog box and start the macro recorder.
- Display the View tab.
- Click the Page Width button (View tab | Zoom group) to zoom page width (Figure 11–63).

3

- Click the Macro Recording button on the status bar to turn off the macro recorder, that is, stop recording actions you perform in Word.

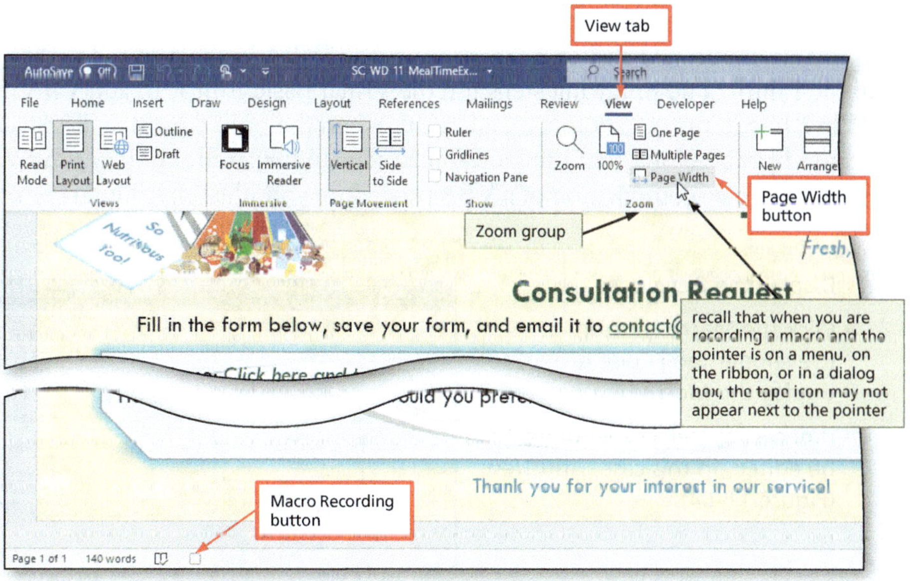

Figure 11–63

Q&A

How do I test an automatic macro?

Activate the event that causes the macro to execute. For example, the AutoNew macro runs whenever you create a new Word document that is based on the template.

BTW

Display Macros

If you wanted to display macros in a document, you would click the Macros button (View tab | Macros group or Developer tab | Code group) and review the list in the Macro name area (Macros dialog box). To restrict the list to macros saved in only this document or to see all macros in Word, click the Macros in arrow and select the desired option. You also can click the Organizer button (Macros dialog box) to see a list of macros in a document or in Word.

To Run the AutoNew Macro

The next step is to execute, or run, the AutoNew macro to ensure that it works. To run the AutoNew macro, you need to create a new Word document that is based on the SC_WD_11_MealTimeExpressFormModified.dotm template. This macro contains instructions to zoom page width. To verify that the macro works as intended, you will change the zoom to 100% before testing the macro. The following steps run a macro.

1. Use the Zoom Out button on the status bar to change the zoom to 100%.
2. Save the template with the same file name, SC_WD_11_MealTimeExpressFormModified.
3. Click the File Explorer button on the taskbar to open the File Explorer window.
4. Locate and then double-click the file SC_WD_11_MealTimeExpressFormModified.dotm to display a new document window that is based on the contents of the SC_WD_11_MealTimeExpressFormModified.dotm template, which should be zoomed to page width as shown in Figure 11–1a at the beginning of this module. (If Word displays a dialog box about disabling macros, click OK. If the Message Bar displays a security warning, click the Enable Content button.)
5. Close the new document that displays the form in the Word window. Click the Don't Save button when Word asks if you want to save the changes to the new document.
6. Close the File Explorer window.
7. Change the zoom back to page width.

To Edit a Macro's VBA Code

As mentioned earlier, a macro consists of VBA instructions. To edit a recorded macro, you use the Visual Basic Editor. The following steps use the Visual Basic Editor to add VBA instructions to the AutoNew macro. **Why?** In addition to zooming page width when the online form is displayed in a new document window, you would like to be sure that the Developer tab is hidden and the ribbon is collapsed. These steps are designed to show the basic composition of a VBA procedure and illustrate the power of VBA code statements.

1

- Display the Developer tab.
- Click the Macros button (Developer tab | Code group) to display the Macros dialog box.
- If necessary, select the macro to be edited, in this case, AutoNew (Figure 11–64).

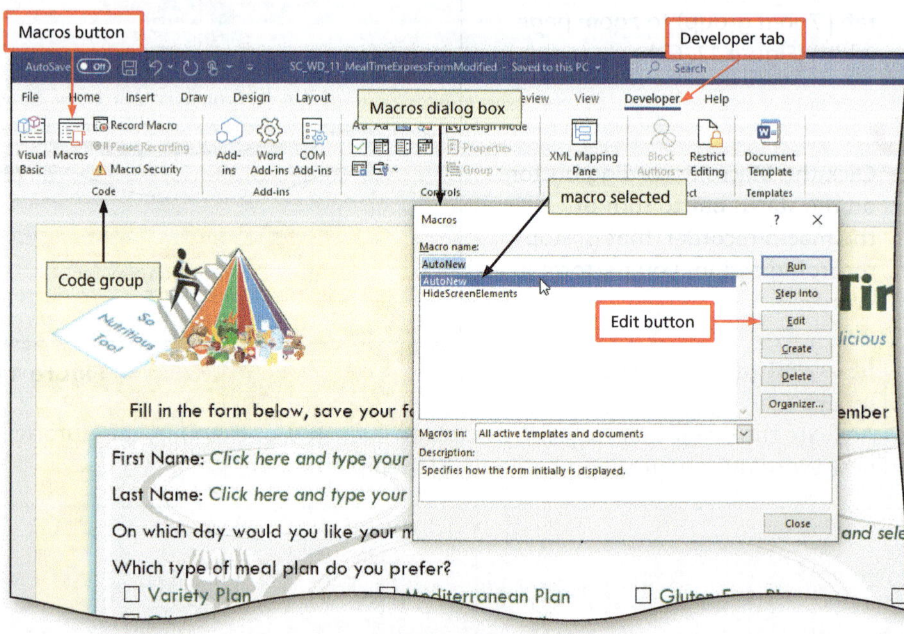

Figure 11–64

2

- Click the Edit button (Macros dialog box) to open the Visual Basic Editor window and display the VBA code for the AutoNew macro in the Code window — your screen may look different depending on previous Visual Basic Editor settings (Figure 11–65).

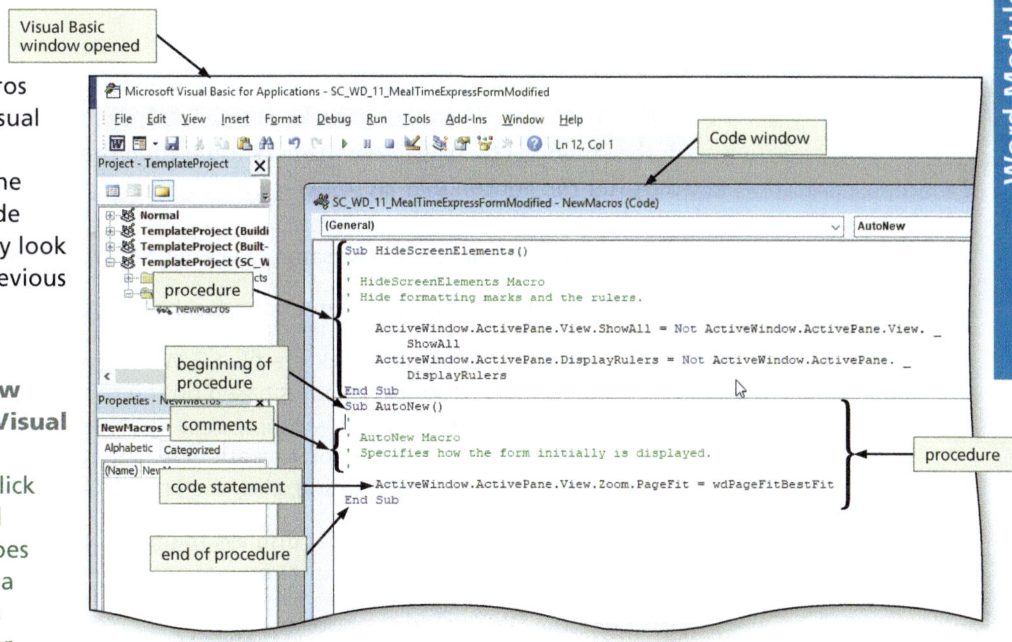

Figure 11–65

Q&A **What if the Code window does not appear in the Visual Basic Editor?**
In the Visual Basic Editor, click View on the menu bar and then click Code. If it still does not appear and you are in a network environment, this feature may be disabled for some users.

What are the lines of text (instructions) in the Code window?
The named set of instructions associated with a macro is called a **procedure**. It is this set of instructions — beginning with the word, Sub, and continuing sequentially to the line with the words, End Sub — that executes when you run the macro. The instructions within a procedure are called **code statements**.

3

- Position the insertion point at the end of the second-to-last line in the AutoNew macro (that is, after the text, wdPageFitBestFit) and then press ENTER to insert a blank line for a new code statement.
- On a single line aligned below the code statement on the previous line, type `Options.ShowDevTools = False` and then press ENTER, which enters the VBA code statement that hides the Developer tab.

Q&A **What are the lists that appear in the Visual Basic Editor as I enter code statements?**
The lists present valid statement elements to assist you with entering code statements. Because they are beyond the scope of this module, ignore them.

- On a single line aligned below the code statement on the previous line, type `If Application.CommandBars.Item("Ribbon").Height > 100 Then` and then press ENTER, which enters the beginning VBA if statement that determines whether to collapse the ribbon.
- On a single line, press TAB, type `ActiveWindow.ToggleRibbon` and then press ENTER, which enters the beginning VBA code statement that collapses the ribbon.
- On a single line, press SHIFT+TAB and then type `End If` to enter the ending VBA code statement that determines whether to collapse the ribbon (Figure 11–66).

4

- Click the Close button on the right edge of the Microsoft Visual Basic window title bar.

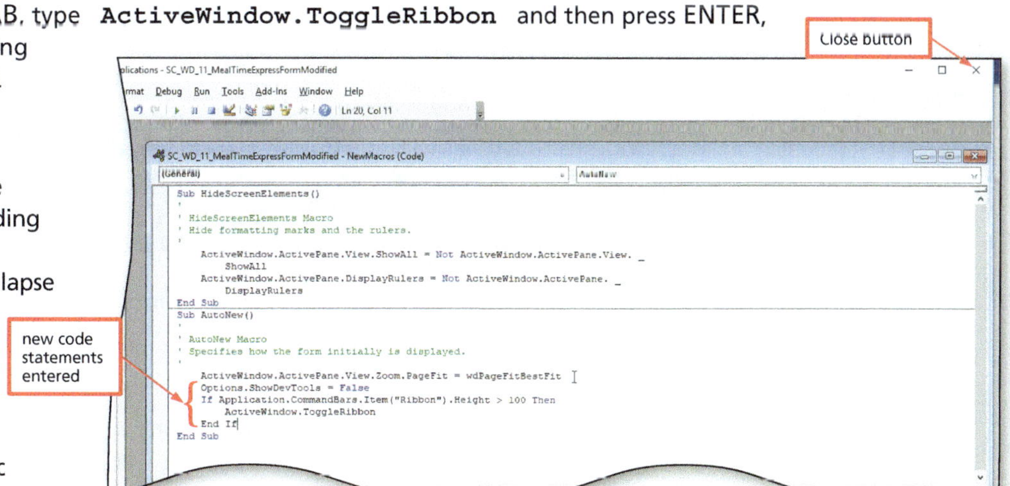

Figure 11–66

To Run the AutoNew Macro

The next step is to execute, or run, the AutoNew macro again to ensure that it works. To be sure the macro works as intended, ensure the Developer tab is displayed on the ribbon. The AutoNew macro should hide the Developer tab. The following steps run the automatic macro.

1. Save the template with the same file name, SC_WD_11_MealTimeExpressFormModified.
2. Click the File Explorer button on the taskbar to open the File Explorer window.
3. Locate and then double-click the file SC_WD_11_MealTimeExpressFormModified.dotm to open a new document that is based on the contents of the this template, which should be zoomed to page width, show a collapsed ribbon, and display no Developer tab. (If Word displays a dialog box about disabling macros, click OK. If the Message Bar displays a security warning, click the Enable Content button.)
4. Close the new document that displays the form in the Word window. Click the Don't Save button when Word asks if you want to save the changes to the new document.
5. Close the File Explorer window.

BTW

VBA

VBA includes many more statements than those presented in this module. You may need a background in programming if you plan to write VBA code instructions in macros you develop and if the VBA code instructions are beyond the scope of those instructions presented in this module. If you wanted to create a macro using VBA in the Visual Basic window, you would click the Macros button (View tab | Macros group or Developer tab | Code group), enter the macro name in the Macro name text box (Macros dialog box), select where you want the macro to be saved in the Macros in list, and click the Create button to open the Visual Basic window, where you can enter VBA code statements.

VBA

As shown in the previous steps, a VBA procedure begins with a Sub statement and ends with an End Sub statement. The Sub statement is followed by the name of the procedure, which is the macro name (AutoNew). The parentheses following the macro name in the Sub statement are required. They indicate that arguments can be passed from one procedure to another. Passing arguments is beyond the scope of this module, but the parentheses still are required. The End Sub statement signifies the end of the procedure and returns control to Word.

Comments often are added to a procedure to help you remember the purpose of the macro and its code statements at a later date. Comments begin with an apostrophe (') and appear in green in the Code window. The macro recorder, for example, placed four comment lines below the Sub statement. These comments display the name of the macro and its description, as entered in the Record Macro dialog box. Comments have no effect on the execution of a procedure; they simply provide information about the procedure, such as its name and description, to the developer of the macro.

For readability, code statement lines are indented four spaces. Table 11–2 explains the function of each element of a code statement.

Table 11–2 Elements of a Code Statement

Code Statement Element	Definition	Examples
Keyword	Recognized by Visual Basic as part of its programming language; keywords appear in blue in the Code window	Sub End Sub
Variable	An item whose value can be modified during program execution	ActiveWindow.ActivePane.View.Zoom.PageFit
Constant	An item whose value remains unchanged during program execution	False
Operator	A symbol that indicates a specific action	=

2

- Click 'Stock 3D Models' on the 3D Models menu to display the Online 3D Models dialog box with categories of online 3-D models displayed in the dialog box (Figure 11–68).

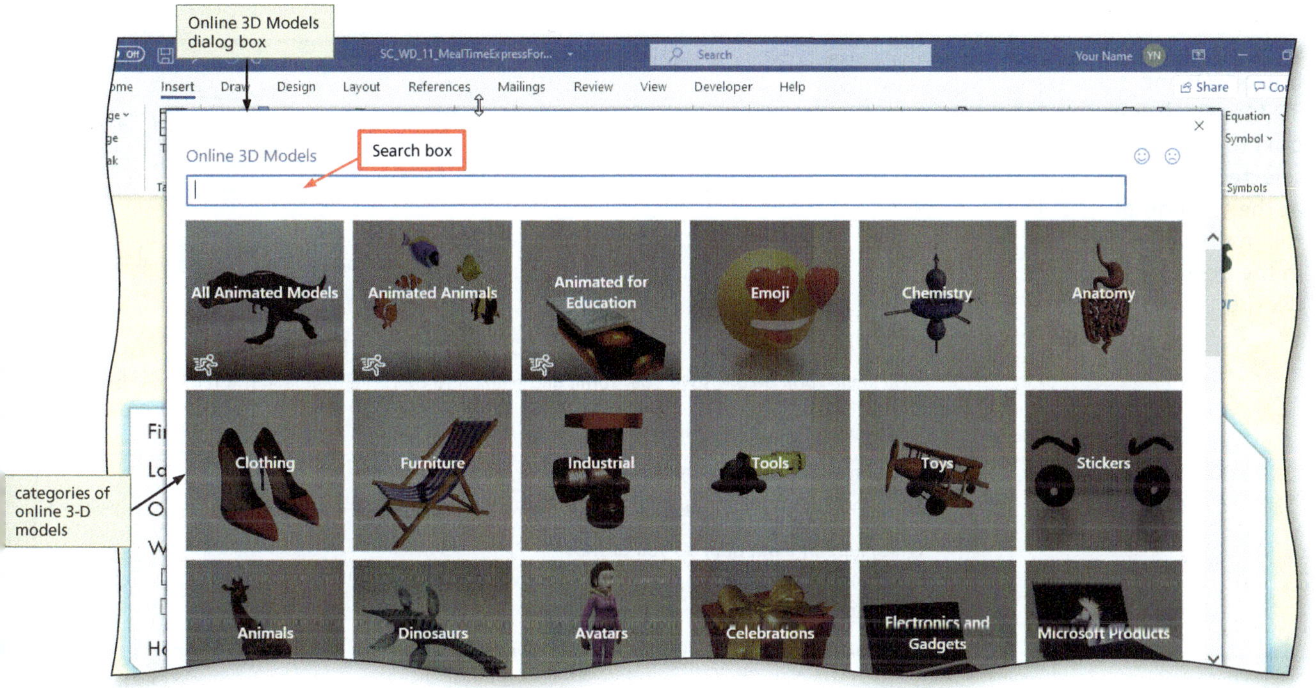

Figure 11–68

Q&A **Can I click the categories to see 3-D models?**
Yes, you can click categories or type search text in the Search box.

3

- Type **plate** in the Search box (Online 3D Models dialog box) to specify the search text.
- Press ENTER to display a list of online 3-D models that matches the entered search text.
- Scroll through the search results and then click the desired 3-D model to select it (Figure 11–69).

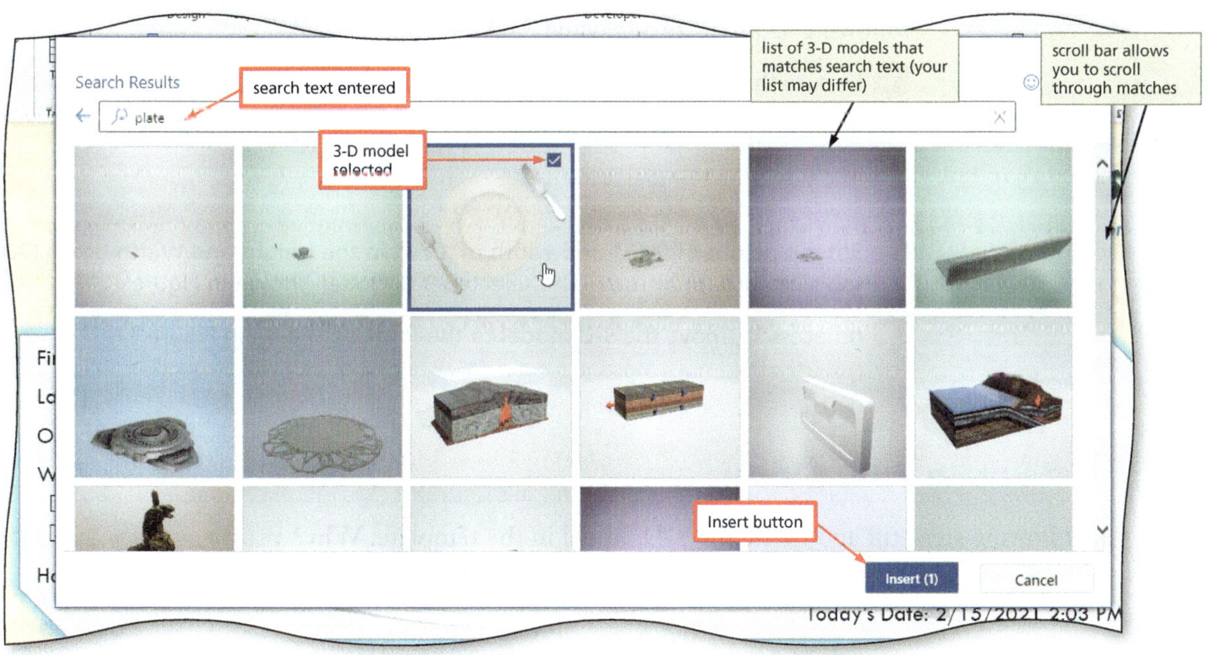

Figure 11–69

Q&A **What if I cannot locate the exact 3-D model selected in Figure 11–69?**
Select any 3-D model so that you can practice using 3-D models.

4

- Click the Insert button (Online 3D Models dialog box) to insert the selected 3-D model at the location of the insertion point in the document (Figure 11–70).

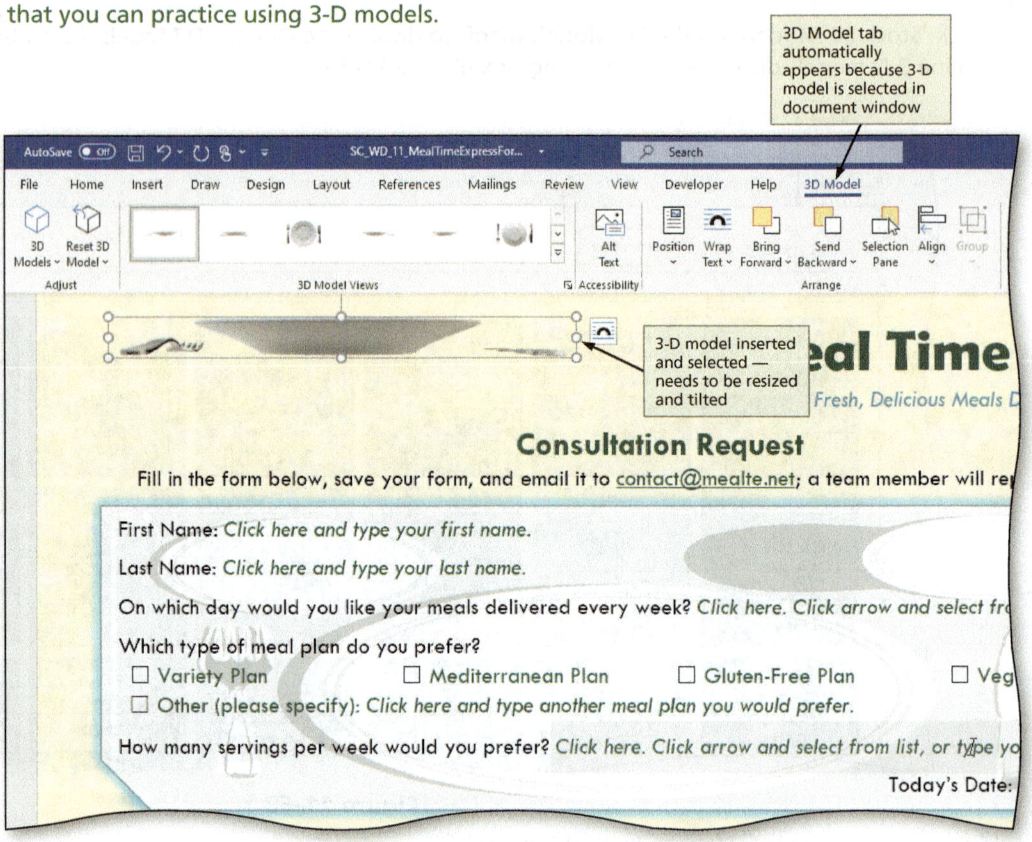

Figure 11–70

To Resize a 3-D Model

You resize a 3-D model the same way you resize any other graphic. You can drag its sizing handles that appear at the corner or middle locations of the selected 3-D model or use the Height and Width buttons (3D Model tab | Size group). The following steps resize a selected 3-D model.

1 Be sure the 3-D model still is selected.

Q&A **What if the object (3-D model) is not selected?**
To select a 3-D model, click it.

2 Enter a height of 0.15" and width of 1.74" in the Height and Width boxes (3D Model tab | Size group) to resize the selected 3-D model (shown in Figure 11–71).

3 If necessary, move the 3-D model to the location shown in Figure 11–71.

To Tilt and Rotate a 3-D Model

The following steps tilt and rotate the 3-D model in the template. **Why?** You want to show a different view of the table setting.

1

- Position the pointer on the 3-D model until the rotate pointer appears and then drag the 3-D model down and to the right in a clockwise motion so that the view resembles Figure 11–71.

Figure 11–71

2

- Continue to drag the 3-D control clockwise down and to the right so that the view resembles Figure 11–72.

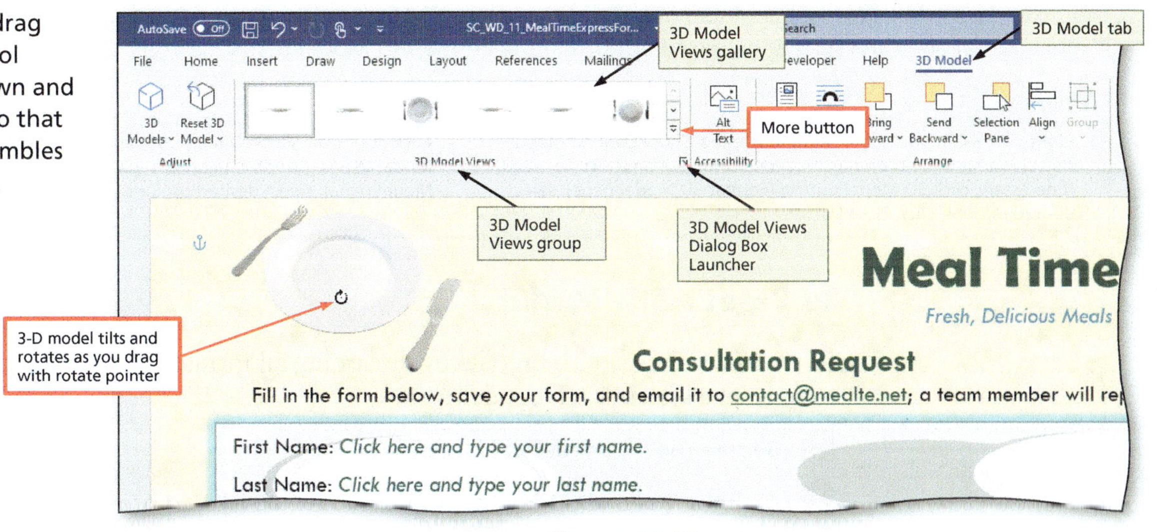

Figure 11–72

To Apply a 3-D Model View

Word provides more than 15 different views of 3-D models. **Why?** The 3-D model views enable you to select a tilted and rotated view of a 3-D model without dragging the 3-D control. The following steps apply a 3-D model view to the selected 3-D model.

1

- Ensure the 3-D model still is selected and that the 3D Model tab is displayed on the ribbon.

Q&A **What if the 3-D model is not selected?**
Click it to select it.

- Click the More button in the 3D Model Views gallery (3D Model tab | 3D Model Views group) (shown in Figure 11–72) to expand the gallery.

- Point to 'Above Front Left' in the 3D Model Views gallery to display a Live Preview of that view applied to the 3-D model in the template (Figure 11–73).

Experiment

- Point to various 3-D model views in the 3D Model Views gallery and watch the view of the 3-D model change in the document window.

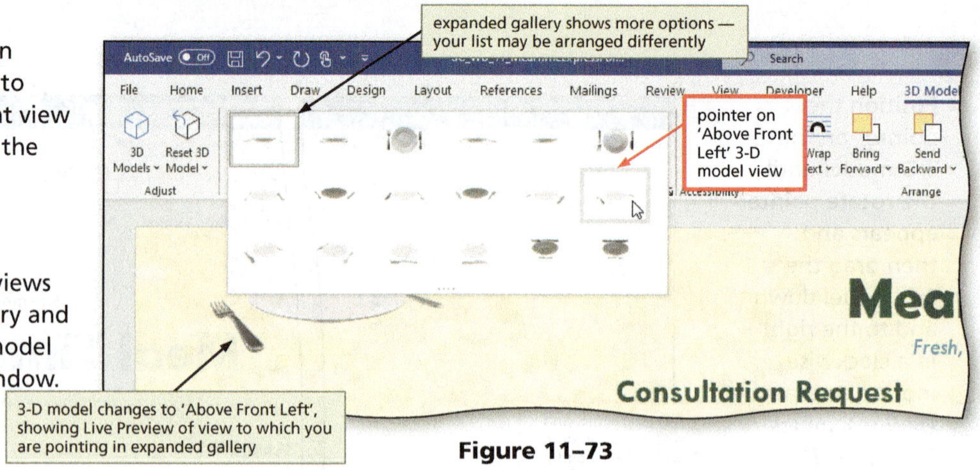

Figure 11–73

2

- Click 'Above Front Left' in the 3D Model Views gallery to apply the view to the selected 3-D model.

Q&A **What if I wanted to format the 3-D model further?**
You could open the Format 3D Model pane by clicking the 3D Model Views Dialog Box Launcher (shown in Figure 11-72) and then selecting desired options in the Format 3D Model pane.

Other Ways

1. Right-click 3-D model (or, if using touch, tap 'Show Context Menu' button on Mini toolbar), click 'Format 3D Model' on shortcut menu, if necessary, click 3D Model button (Format 3D Model pane), select desired options, click Close button
2. Click 3D Model Views Dialog Box Launcher (3D Model tab | 3D Model Views group), if necessary, click 3D Model button (Format 3D Model pane), select desired options, click Close button

To Reset a 3-D Model

You can reset a 3-D model by discarding all formatting changes. The following steps reset a selected 3-D model.

1. Be sure the 3-D model still is selected.
2. Click the 'Reset 3D Model' arrow (3D Model tab | Adjust group) to display the Reset 3D Model menu (Figure 11–74).
3. Click 'Reset 3D Model' on the Reset 3D Model menu to discard all formatting changes.
4. Click the Undo button (Quick Access Toolbar) to restore the 3-D model with your changes.

Q&A **What is the purpose of the 'Reset 3D Model and Size' command on the Reset 3D Model menu?**
In addition to discarding all formatting changes, it resets the size to the 3-D model's original size.

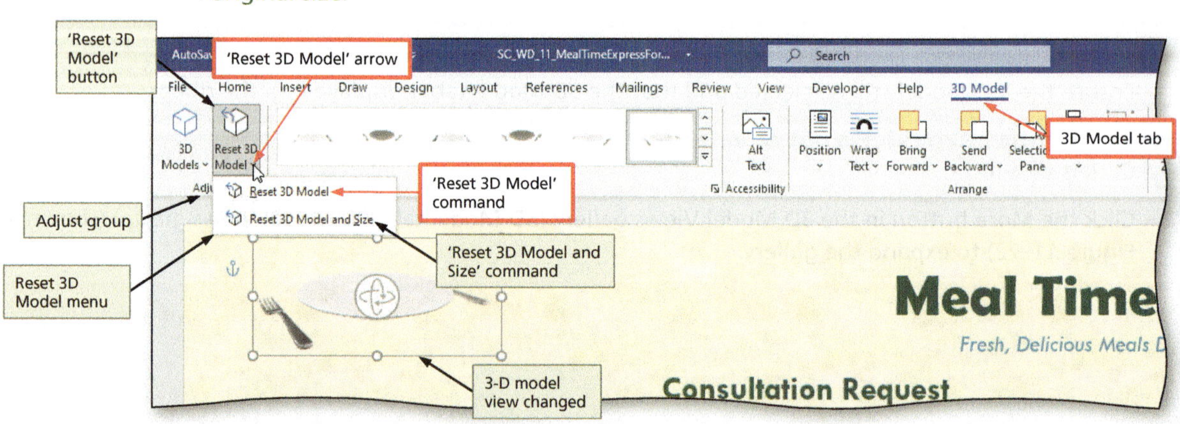

Figure 11–74

To Save the Template, Protect It, and Exit Word

You now are finished with the 3-D model in the online form and with this project. The following steps save the form again, protect it, and then exit Word.

1. Open Backstage view and then, if necessary, display the Info screen.
2. Click the Protect Document button to display the Protect Document menu.
3. Click Restrict Editing on the Protect Document menu to open the Restrict Editing pane.
4. In the Editing restrictions area, if necessary, place a check mark in the 'Allow only this type of editing in the document' check box, click its arrow, and then select 'Filling in forms' in the list.
5. Click the 'Yes, Start Enforcing Protection' button and then click OK (Start Enforcing Protection dialog box) to protect the document without a password.
6. Close the Restrict Editing pane.
7. Save the template again on the same storage location with the same file name.
8. Exit Word.

Supplementary Word Tasks

If you plan to take the certification exam, you should be familiar with the skills in the following sections.

Adding a Digital Signature to a Document

Some users attach a **digital signature** to a document to verify its authenticity. A digital signature is an electronic, encrypted, and secure stamp of authentication on a document. This signature confirms that the file originated from the signer (file creator) and that it has not been altered.

A digital signature references a digital certificate. A **digital certificate** is code attached to a file, macro project, email message, or other digital content that verifies the identity of the creator of the file. Many users who receive online forms enable the macros based on whether they are digitally signed by a developer on the user's list of trusted sources. You can obtain a digital certificate from a commercial certification authority or from your network administrator.

Once a digital signature is added, the document becomes a read-only document, which means that modifications cannot be made to it. Thus, you should create a digital signature only when the document is final. In Word, you can add two types of digital signatures to a document: (1) an invisible digital signature or (2) a signature line.

BTW

Removing Metadata

If you wanted to remove document metadata, such as personal information and comments, you would do the following with the document open in a document window: open Backstage view, if necessary, click Info in Backstage view to display the Info screen, click the 'Check for Issues' button in the Info screen to display the Check for Issues menu, click Inspect Document on the Check for Issues menu to display the Document Inspector dialog box, click the Inspect button (Document Inspector dialog box) to instruct Word to inspect the document, review the results (Document Inspector dialog box), and then click the Remove All button(s) for any item that you do not want to be saved with the document. When you have finished removing information, click the Close button to close the dialog box.

To Add an Invisible Digital Signature to a Document

An invisible digital signature does not appear as a tangible signature in the document. If the status bar displays a Signatures button, the document has an invisible digital signature. If you wanted to add an invisible digital signature to a document, you would perform the following steps.

1. Open Backstage view and then, if necessary, display the Info screen.
2. Click the Protect Document button to display the Protect Document menu and then click 'Add a Digital Signature' on the Protect Document menu to display the Sign dialog box. (If a dialog box appears indicating you need a digital ID,

BTW
Password-Protecting Documents
You can save documents with a password to keep unauthorized users from accessing files. To do this, open Backstage view, click Info, click the Protect Document button, click 'Encrypt with Password' on the Protect Document menu, type the password in the Encrypt Document dialog box, type the password again (Confirm Password dialog box), and click OK; or open Backstage view, click Save As, display the Save As dialog box, click the Tools button (Save As dialog box), click General Options on the Tools menu, type the password in the appropriate text box (General Options dialog box), type the password again (Confirm Password dialog box), and then click OK and the Save button (Save As dialog box). As you type a password in the text box, Word displays a series of dots instead of the actual characters so that others cannot see your password as you type it. To remove a password from a document, follow these steps except leave the password text box blank.

Be sure to keep the password confidential. Choose a password that is easy to remember and that no one can guess. Do not use any part of your first or last name, Social Security number, birthday, and so on. Use a password that is at least six characters long, and if possible, use a mixture of numbers and letters.

click the Yes button and then follow the on-screen instructions. If a dialog box about signature services appears, click OK.)

3. Type the purpose of the digital signature in the 'Purpose for signing this document' text box.
4. Click the Sign button to add the digital signature, show the Signatures button on the status bar, and display Marked as Final on a Message Bar.

Q&A
How can I view or remove the digital signatures in a document?
Open Backstage view, if necessary, display the Info screen, and then click the View Signatures button to open the Signatures pane. To remove a digital signature, click the arrow beside the signature name, click Remove Signature on the menu, and then click Yes in the dialog box.

To Add a Signature Line to a Document

A **digital signature line**, which resembles a printed signature placeholder, allows a recipient of the electronic file to type a signature, include an image of the signature, or write a signature using the ink feature on a mobile computer or device. Digital signature lines enable organizations to use paperless methods of obtaining signatures on official documents, such as contracts. If you wanted to add a digital signature line to a document, you would perform the following steps.

1. Position the insertion point at the location for the digital signature.
2. Display the Insert tab. Click the 'Add a Signature Line' button (Insert tab | Text group) to display the Signature Setup dialog box. (If a dialog box appears about signature services, click OK.)
3. Type the name of the person who should sign the document in the appropriate text box.
4. If available, type the signer's title and email address in the appropriate text boxes.
5. Place a check mark in the 'Allow the signer to add comments in the Sign dialog' check box so that the recipient can send a response back to you.
6. Click OK (Signature Setup dialog box) to insert a signature line in the document at the location of the insertion point.

Q&A
How does a recipient insert their digital signature?
When the recipient opens the document, a Message Bar appears that contains a View Signatures button. The recipient can click the View Signatures button to open the Signatures pane, click the requested signature arrow, and then click Sign on the menu (or double-click the signature line in the document) to display a dialog box that the recipient then completes.

Copying and Renaming Styles and Macros

If you have created a style or macro in one document or template, you can copy the style or a macro to another so that you can use it in a second document or template.

To Copy a Style from One Template or Document to Another

If you wanted to copy a style from one template or document to another, you would perform the following steps.

1. Open the document or template into which you want to copy the style.
2. If necessary, click the Styles Dialog Box Launcher (Home tab | Styles group) to open the Styles pane, click the Manage Styles button at the bottom of the Styles pane to display the Manage Styles dialog box, and then click the

Import/Export button (Manage Styles dialog box) to display Styles sheet in the Organizer dialog box. Or, click the Document Template button (Developer tab | Templates group) to display the Templates and Add-ins dialog box, click the Organizer button (Templates and Add-ins dialog box) to display the Organizer dialog box, and then, if necessary, click the Styles tab to display the Styles sheet in the dialog box. Notice that the left side of the dialog box displays the style names in the currently open document or template.

3. Click the Close File button (Organizer dialog box) to clear the right side of the dialog box.

Q&A **What happened to the Close File button?**
It changed to an Open File button.

4. Click the Open File button (Organizer dialog box) and then locate the file that contains the style you wish to copy. Notice that the styles in the located document or template appear on the right side of the dialog box.
5. On the right side of the dialog box, select the style you wish to copy and then click the Copy button to copy the selected style to the document or template on the left. You can continue to copy as many styles as necessary.
6. When finished copying styles, click the Close button to close the dialog box.

To Rename a Style

If you wanted to rename a style, you would perform the following steps.

1. Open the document or template that contains the style to rename.
2. If necessary, click the Styles Dialog Box Launcher (Home tab | Styles group) to open the Styles pane, click the Manage Styles button at the bottom of the Styles pane to display the Manage Styles dialog box, and then click the Import/Export button (Manage Styles dialog box) to display the Styles sheet in the Organizer dialog box. Or, click the Document Template button (Developer tab | Templates group) to display the Templates and Add-ins dialog box, click the Organizer button (Templates and Add-ins dialog box) to display the Organizer dialog box, and then, if necessary, click the Styles tab to display the Styles sheet in the dialog box. Notice that the left side of the dialog box displays the style names in the currently open document or template.
3. Select the style you wish to rename and then click the Rename button (Organizer dialog box) to display the Rename dialog box.
4. Type the new name of the style in the text box and then click OK (Rename dialog box).

Q&A **Can I delete styles too?**
Yes, click the Delete button (Organizer dialog box) to delete any selected styles.

5. When finished renaming styles, click the Close button (Organizer dialog box) to close the dialog box.

To Copy a Macro from One Template or Document to Another

If you wanted to copy a macro from one template or document to another, you would perform the following steps.

1. Open the document or template into which you want to copy the macro.
2. If necessary, click the Macros button (Developer tab | Code group or View tab | Macros group) to display the Macros dialog box and then click the Organizer button (Macros dialog box) to display Macro Project Items sheet in the Organizer dialog box. Or, click the Document Template button (Developer tab | Templates group) to display the Templates and Add-ins dialog box, click the Organizer button (Templates and Add-ins dialog box) to display the Organizer dialog box, and then, if necessary, click the Macro Project Items tab to

BTW

Fields

In addition to using content controls where users can enter data into a form, you can insert fields from the Fields dialog box so that Word will automatically fill in and display the field's value on the form. If you are working with a mail merge document instead of an online form and wanted to prompt users to fill in a field value, you could use the ASK or FILLIN fields in the main document for the form letter.

display the Macro Project Items sheet in the dialog box. Notice that the left side of the dialog box displays the macro names in the currently open document or template.

3. Click the Close File button (Organizer dialog box) to clear the right side of the dialog box.

Q&A **What happened to the Close File button?**
It changed to an Open File button.

4. Click the Open File button (Organizer dialog box) and then locate the file that contains the macro you wish to copy. Notice that the macros in the located document or template appear on the right side of the dialog box.
5. On the ride side of the dialog box, select the macro you wish to copy and then click the Copy button to copy the selected macro to the document or template on the left. You can continue to copy as many macros as necessary.
6. When finished copying macros, click the Close button (Organizer dialog box) to close the dialog box.

To Rename a Macro

If you wanted to rename a macro, you would perform the following steps.

1. Open the document that contains the macro to rename.
2. If necessary, click the Macros button (Developer tab | Code group or View tab | Macros group) to display the Macros dialog box and then click the Organizer button (Macros dialog box) to display Macro Project Items sheet in the Organizer dialog box. Or, click the Document Template button (Developer tab | Templates group) to display the Templates and Add-ins dialog box, click the Organizer button (Templates and Add-ins dialog box) to display the Organizer dialog box, and then, if necessary, click the Macro Project Items tab to display the Macro Project Items sheet in the dialog box. Notice that the left side of the dialog box displays the macro names in the currently open document or template.
3. Select the macro you wish to rename and then click the Rename button (Organizer dialog box) to display the Rename dialog box.
4. Type the new name of the macro in the text box and then click OK (Rename dialog box).

Q&A **Can I delete macros, too?**
Yes, click the Delete button (Organizer dialog box) to delete any selected macros.

5. When finished renaming macros, click the Close button to close the dialog box.

Preparing a Document for Internationalization

Word provides internationalization features you can use when creating documents and templates. Use of features should be determined based on the intended audience of the document or template. By default, Word uses formatting consistent with the country or region selected when installing Windows. In addition to inserting symbols, such as those for currency, and using date and time formats that are recognized internationally or in other countries, you can set the language used for proofing tools and other language preferences.

To Set the Language for Proofing Tools

If you wanted to change the language that Word uses to proof documents or templates, you would perform the following steps.

1. Click the Language button (Review tab | Language group) to display the Language menu.
2. Click 'Set Proofing Language' on the Language menu to display the Language dialog box. (If you want to set this language as the default, click the 'Set As Default' button.)
3. Select the desired language to use for proofing tools and then click OK.

To Set Language Preferences

If you wanted to change the language that Word uses for editing, display, Help, and ScreenTips, you would perform the following steps.

1. Click the Language button (Review tab | Language group) to display the Language menu and then click Language Preferences on the Language menu to display the language settings in the Word Options dialog box. Or, open Backstage view, click Options in the left pane to display the Word Options dialog box, and then click Language in the left pane (Word Options dialog box) to display the language settings.
2. Select preferences for the editing language, display language, and Help language, and then click OK.

Working with XML

You can convert an online form to the XML format so that the data in the form can be shared with other programs, such as Microsoft Access. XML is a popular format for structuring data, which allows the data to be reused and shared. **XML**, which stands for Extensible Markup Language, is a language used to mark up structured data so that it can be more easily shared between different computer programs. An **XML file** is a text file containing XML tags that identify field names and data. Each data item is called an **element**. Businesses often create standard XML file layouts and tags to describe commonly used types of data.

In Word, you can save a file in a default XML format, in which Word parses the document into individual components that can be used by other programs. Or, you can identify specific sections of the document as XML elements; the elements then can be used in other programs, such as Access. This feature may not be available in all versions of Word.

BTW

Opening Files

In addition to current and previous versions of Word documents and templates, XML and PDF files, and webpage files, you can open a variety of other types of documents through the Open dialog box, including rich text format, text files, OpenDocument text, and WordPerfect files. To open these documents, open Backstage view, click Open to display the Open screen, click the Browse button to display the Open dialog box, click the file type arrow (Open dialog box), click the desired file type to open, locate the file, and then click the Open button to open the file and display its contents in a Word window. Through the Save dialog box, you can save the open file in its native format or save it as a Word document or template.

To Save a Document in the Default XML Format

If you wanted to save a document in the XML format, you would perform the following steps.

1. Open the file to be saved in the XML format (for example, a form containing content controls).
2. Open Backstage view and then click Save As to display the Save As screen.
3. Navigate to the desired save location and then display the Save As dialog box.
4. Click the 'Save as type' arrow (Save As dialog box), click 'Word XML Document' in the list, and then click the Save button to save the template as an XML document.

Q&A

How can I identify an XML document?

XML documents typically have an .xml extension.

To Attach a Schema File

To identify sections of a document as XML elements, you first attach an XML schema to the document, usually one that contains content controls. An **XML schema** is a special type of XML file that describes the layout of elements in other XML files. Word users typically do not create XML schema files. Software developers or other technical personnel create an XML schema file and provide it to Word users. XML schema files, often simply called **schema files**, usually have an extension of .xsd. Once the schema is attached, you can use the 'XML Mapping Pane' button (Developer tab | Mapping group) to insert controls from the schema into the document. If you wanted to attach a schema file to a document, such as an online form, you would perform the following steps.

1. Open the file to which you wish to attach the schema, such as an online form that contains content controls.
2. Open Backstage view and then use the Save As command to save the file with a new file name, to preserve the contents of the original file.
3. Click the Document Template button (Developer tab | Templates group) to display the Templates and Add-ins dialog box.
4. Click the XML Schema tab (Templates and Add-ins dialog box) to display the XML Schema sheet and then click the Add Schema button to display the Add Schema dialog box.
5. Locate and select the schema file (Add Schema dialog box) and then click the Open button to display the Schema Settings dialog box.
6. Enter the URI and alias in the appropriate text boxes (Schema Settings dialog box) and then click OK to add the schema to the Schema Library and to add the namespace alias to the list of available schemas in the XML Schema sheet (Templates and Add-ins dialog box).

Q&A

What is a URI and an alias?

Word uses the term, URI, also called a **namespace**, to refer to the schema. Because these names are difficult to remember, you can define a namespace alias. In a setting outside of an academic environment, a computer administrator would provide you with the appropriate namespace entry.

7. If necessary, place a check mark in the desired schema's check box.
8. Click OK, which causes Word to attach the selected schema to the open document and open the XML Structure pane in the Word window.

To Delete a Schema from the Schema Library

To delete a schema from a document, you would remove the check mark from the schema name's check box in the XML Schema sheet in the Templates and Add-ins dialog box. If you wanted to delete a schema altogether from the Schema Library, you would do the following.

1. Click the Document Template button (Developer tab | Templates group) to display the Templates and Add-ins dialog box.
2. Click the XML Schema tab (Templates and Add-ins dialog box) to display the XML Schema sheet and then click the Schema Library button to display the Schema Library dialog box.
3. Click the schema you want to delete in the Select a schema list (Schema Library dialog box) and then click the Delete Schema button.
4. When Word displays the Schema Library dialog box asking if you are sure you want to delete the schema, click Yes.
5. Click OK (Schema Library dialog box) and then click the Cancel button (Templates and Add-ins dialog box).

Summary

In this module, you learned how to enhance the look of text and graphics, automate a series of tasks with a macro, and work with 3-D models. You also learned about several supplementary tasks that you should know if you plan to take the certification exam.

Consider This: Plan Ahead

What decisions will you need to make when creating macro-enabled and enhanced online forms?

Use these guidelines as you complete the assignments in this module and create your own online forms outside of this class.

1. Save the form to be modified as a macro-enabled template, if you plan to include macros in the template for the form.
2. Enhance the visual appeal of a form.
   a) Arrange data entry fields in logical groups on the form and in an order that users would expect.
   b) Draw the user's attention to important sections.
   c) Use colors and images that complement one another.
3. Add macros to automate tasks.
   a) Record macros, if possible.
   b) If you are familiar with computer programming, write VBA code to extend capabilities of recorded macros.
4. Determine how the form data will be analyzed.
   a) If the data entered in the form will be analyzed by a program outside of Word, create the data entry fields so that the entries are stored in a format that can be shared with other programs.

Apply Your Knowledge

Reinforce the skills and apply the concepts you learned in this module.

Working with Images, Shapes, and Fields

Note: To complete this assignment, you will be required to use the Data Files. Please contact your instructor for information about accessing the Data Files.

Instructions: Start Word. Open the template called SC_WD_10_RecyclingCommunitySurvey.dotx that you created in the Apply Your Knowledge Student Assignment in Module 10. If you did not complete the Apply Your Knowledge Student Assignment in Module 10, see your instructor for a copy. In this assignment, you enhance the Carter's Recycling Service online form created in Module 10 by changing colors and pictures, removing an image background, adding an artistic effect to an image, changing saturation and tone, grouping images, using a texture fill effect, changing a shape, inserting a date field, rotating text in a shape, and applying 3-D effects to a shape (Figure 11–75).

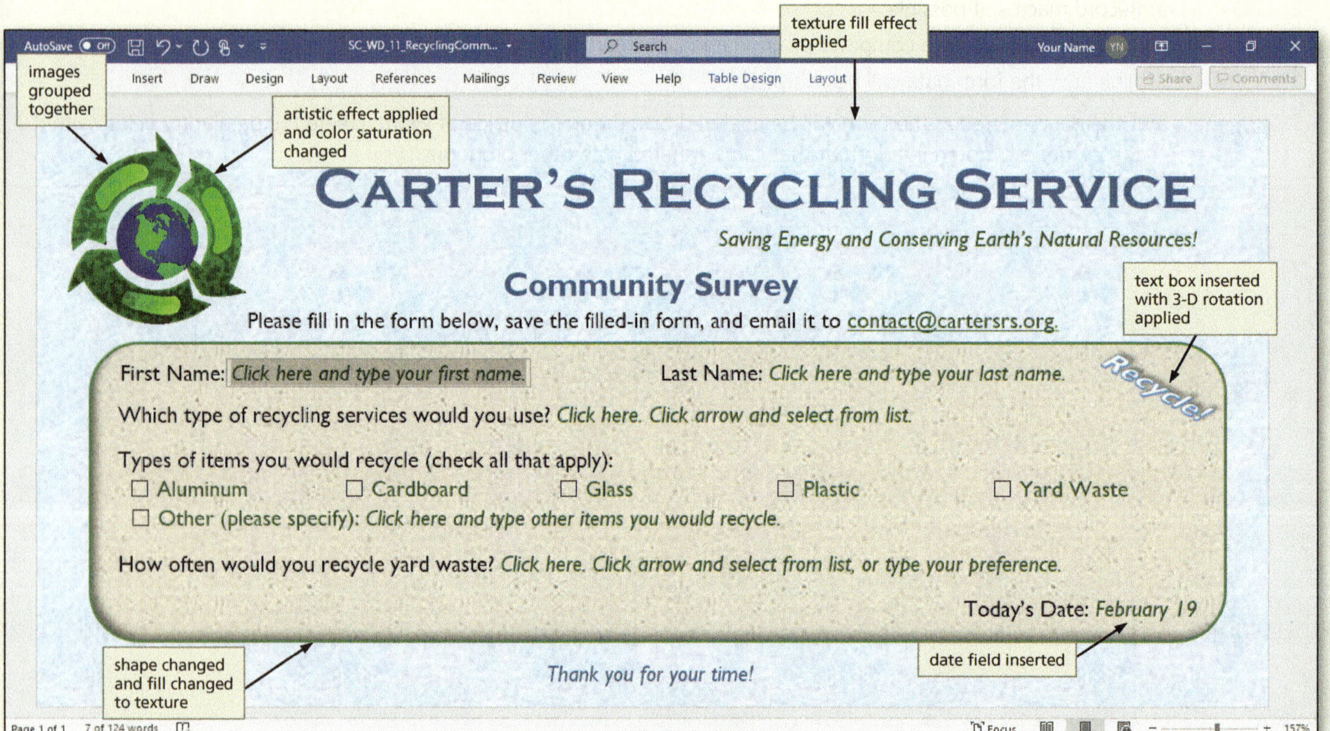

Figure 11–75

Perform the following tasks:

1. Click File on the ribbon, click Save As, and then save the template using the new file name, SC_WD_11_RecyclingCommunitySurveyModified.
2. Unprotect the template.
3. Change the font color of the title (Carter's Recycling Service), the third line (Community Survey), and the last line on the form (Thank you for your time!) to Blue, Accent 2, Darker 25%.
4. Change the font color of the tag line (Saving Energy and Conserving Earth's Natural Resources!) and the email address (contact@cartersrs.org) to Dark Green, Accent 5, Darker 25%.

5. Select the image in the upper-right corner and then open the Selection pane, which you may use throughout this assignment. Use the Layout Options button attached to the image or the Wrap Text button (Picture Format tab | Arrange group) to change the layout to In Front of Text.
6. Move the image in the upper-right corner of the form to the upper-left corner. Right-align the first two lines of text (the company name and the tag line).
7. Modify the Intense Emphasis style to use the color, Dark Green, Accent 5, Darker 25%.
8. Create a character style with the name Check Box Labels for all check boxes in the data entry area that uses an 11-point Gill Sans MT (Body) font and a color of Dark Green, Accent 5, Darker 25%. Apply the new character style to the check box labels in the form: Aluminum, Cardboard, Glass, Plastic, Yard Waste, Other (please specify):.
9. Change the image in the upper-left corner of the form with the earth image called Support_WD_11_WorldInHands.png, which is located in the Data Files. (Hint: Use the Change Picture button (Picture Format tab | Adjust group) and then click 'From a File' on the Change Picture menu, or right-click the image, point Change Picture on the shortcut menu, and then click 'From a File' on the Change Picture submenu.)
10. Use the Bring Forward arrow (Picture Format tab | Arrange group) to bring the selected image to the front (so that the earth image can be positioned in front of the recycle image later in this assignment).
11. Use the Remove Background button (Picture Format tab | Adjust group) to remove the background from the new image so that just the earth remains; that is, remove the hands from the image. Note that you may need to use the 'Mark Areas to Keep' button on the image of the earth.
12. Also in the upper-left corner of the form but in a separate location from the earth image, insert the recycle image called Support_WD_11_RecycleSymbol.png, which is located in the Data Files. Change the size of the inserted image to a height of 1.3" and a width of 1.23".
13. Use the Layout Options button attached to the recycle image or the Wrap Text button (Picture Format tab | Arrange group) to change the wrap style to In Front of Text. Use the Send Backward arrow (Picture Format tab | Arrange group) to send the selected image to the back (so that the earth image can be positioned in front of the recycle image).
14. First move the recycle image and then move the earth image to the center and on top of the recycle image as shown in Figure 11–75.
15. Apply the Watercolor Sponge artistic effect to the recycle symbol image and then change the color saturation of the same image (the recycle symbol) to 400% and the color tone to Temperature: 8800 K.
16. Group the recycle and earth images together. Ungroup the images. Regroup the images. If necessary, move the grouped images so that they appear as shown in Figure 11–75.
17. Change the page color to the Blue tissue paper texture fill effect.
18. Change the shape around the data entry area to Rectangle: Rounded Corners.
19. Change the fill of the rectangle shape to the Recycled paper texture fill effect.
20. Apply the 'Inside: Bottom Left' shadow effect to the rectangle shape.
21. Display the Developer tab. Change the properties of the date picker content control so that its contents can be deleted and then delete the content control. Use the 'Explore Quick Parts' button (Insert tab | Text group) to insert a date field after the Today's Date: label in the format month day (i.e., September 13), so that the date field is automatically filled in on the form.

Continued >

Apply Your Knowledge *continued*

Right-align the line containing the date. If necessary, change the format of the displayed date field to Intense Emphasis. Hide the Developer tab.

22. Draw a text box that is approximately 1.15" × 0.73" that contains the text, Recycle!, centered in the text box. Remove the outline from the text box (shape). Change the direction of text in the text box (shape) to Rotate all text 90°. Select the text and use the 'Text Effects and Typography' button (Home tab | Font group) to apply the effect called Fill: White, Outline: Blue, Accent color 2; Hard Shadow: Blue, Accent color 2. Increase the font size to 18 point. Select the text box and then apply the 3-D rotation shape effect called 'Isometric: Top Up' to the text box (shape). Then, apply the Offset: Right shadow shape effect to the text box. Remove the fill from the text box (shape). Move the text box to the upper-right corner of the data entry area as shown in Figure 11–75.
23. Select the text box, click the Send Backward arrow (Shape Format tab | Arrange group), and then click 'Send Behind Text' on the Send Backward menu to send the text box behind text. (Note this step is necessary so that you can group the rectangle and text box shapes together.) Select the rectangle shape and then the text box shape. With both shapes selected, group the two shapes together. Ungroup the shapes. Regroup the shapes. If necessary, close the Selection pane.
24. If requested by your instructor, change the email address on the form to your email address.
25. If necessary, adjust spacing above and below paragraphs so that all contents fit on a single screen.
26. Protect the form to restrict editing to filling in forms. Save the form again with the same file name and then submit it in the format specified by your instructor. Collapse the ribbon.
27. Access the template through File Explorer and test it using your own data for the responses. If necessary, make necessary corrections to the form.
28. What is the advantage of creating a style for the check box labels?

Extend Your Knowledge

Extend the skills you learned in this module and experiment with new skills. You may need to use Help to complete the assignment.

Enhancing a Form and Working with Macros

Note: To complete this assignment, you will be required to use the Data Files. Please contact your instructor for information about accessing the Data Files.

Instructions: Start Word. Open the template called SC_WD_10_FreshmanOrientationForm.dotx that you created in the Extend Your Knowledge Student Assignment in Module 10. If you did not complete the Extend Your Knowledge Student Assignment in Module 10, see your instructor for a sample solution file. In this assignment, you enhance the Harper View College online form created in Module 10 by changing colors and pictures, converting a table to text, and working with macros.

Perform the following tasks:

1. Click File on the ribbon and then click Save As and save the template as a macro-enabled template using the new file name, SC_WD_11_FreshmanOrientationFormModified.
2. Unprotect the password-protected template. Enter the password, fun, when prompted.
3. Select the grouped graphics at the top of the form and delete them.
4. Use the 'Text Effects and Typography' button (Home tab | Font group) to remove the reflection from the school name at the top of the form.

5. In the rectangle that surrounds the data entry area, use the Shape Fill arrow (Shape Format tab | Shape Styles group) to insert the picture called Support_WD_11_Books.png, which is located in the Data Files, in the rectangle shape. Change the color of the picture in the rectangle to Washout.
6. Convert the table to text for the 2 × 1 table containing the First Name: and Last Name: labels and associated First Name and Last Name content controls. (Hint: You will need to change the properties of the content controls so that their contents can be deleted before you can convert the table to text. When finished, reset the content controls so that their contents cannot be deleted.) Change the left indent to 0.06" on these two lines.
7. Delete the Student Photo content control and its text box shape.
8. If necessary, adjust spacing above and below paragraphs so that all contents fit on a single screen.
9. Adjust the size of the rectangle shape so that it covers all content controls in the data entry area.
10. Change the page background to a texture or color of your choice.
11. Change the font color of the school name (Harper View College) and the last line on the form (Welcome to Harper View!) to a color of your choice. If desired, change the color of other text on the form.
12. Customize macro security settings to the 'Disable all macros with notification' option.
13. Show formatting marks and the ruler on the screen. Record a macro that hides the formatting marks and the rulers. Name it HideScreenElements. Store it in Documents Based On SC_WD_11_FreshmanOrientationFormModified template (Figure 11–76). Assign it the shortcut key, ALT+H. Run the macro to test it.
14. Add a button to the Quick Access Toolbar for the macro created in Step 13. Test the button and then delete the button from the Quick Access Toolbar.

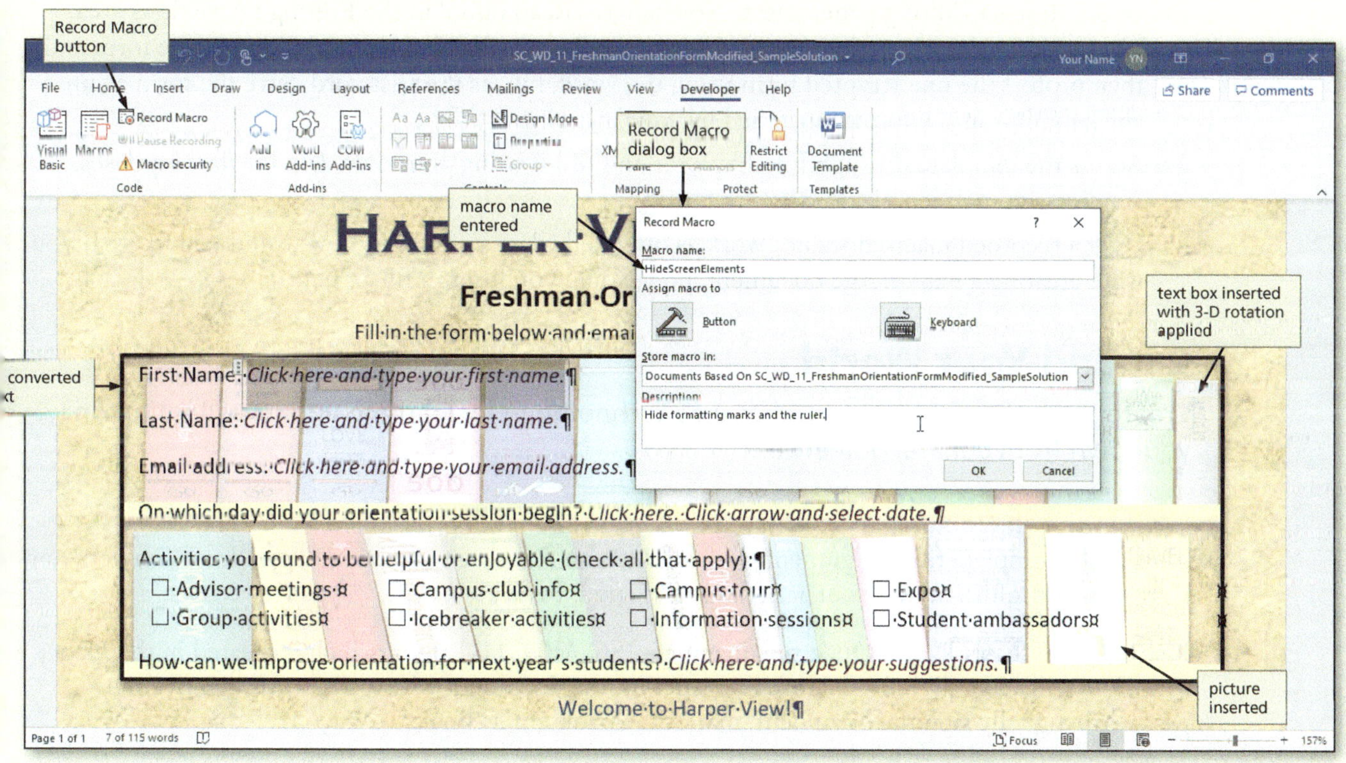

Figure 11–76

Continued >

Extend Your Knowledge *continued*

15. Create an automatic macro called AutoNew using the macro recorder. Store it in Documents Based On SC_WD_11_FreshmanOrientationFormModified template. The macro should change the view to page width. While recording the macro, pause the recording and then resume recording the macro.
16. Edit the AutoNew macro so that it also hides the Developer tab and the ribbon. (Hint: You will need to open the Visual Basic Editor window from the Macros dialog box to display the VBA code for the AutoNew macro and then enter the appropriate VBA code statements in the Visual Basic Editor.)
17. Display all macros.
18. If requested by your instructor, create a macro of your choice using the Visual Basic window.
19. If requested by your instructor, display the Organizer dialog box. Close the file on the right side and then open another template of your choice. Copy the Intense Emphasis style from the SC_WD_11_FreshmanOrientationFormModified file to the template you opened on the right side. Then, delete the Intense Emphasis style from the template on the right side. Copy the macros from the SC_WD_11_FreshmanOrientationFormModified file to the template on the right side. Then, delete the copied macros from the template on the right side. Close the Organizer dialog box.
20. If requested by your instructor, add a custom document property by opening Backstage view, clicking Info, clicking the Properties button in the right pane, clicking Advanced Properties, clicking the Custom tab, entering the text, My Name, in the Name text box, selecting Text in the Type box if necessary, typing your name as the value, clicking the Add button, and then clicking OK (Properties dialog box). Then, in the form, in place of the school name (Harper View), insert the custom field by clicking the 'Explore Quick Parts' button (Insert tab | Text group), clicking Field, selecting Document Information in the Categories area, clicking DocProperty in the Field names list, selecting My Name in the Property list, and then clicking OK.
21. In the Restrict Editing pane, select 'No changes (Read only)' in the Editing restrictions area. Next, change the protection on the form in the Restrict Editing pane to filling in the form and then protect the unencrypted form using the word, fun, as the password. Save the form again and submit it in the format specified by your instructor.
22. Access the template through File Explorer and test it using your own data for the responses. If necessary, make corrections to the form.
23. If a recorded macro does not work as intended when you test it, how would you fix it? If you were creating a mail merge document, how would you insert a fill-in field?

Expand Your World

Create a solution that uses cloud or web technologies by learning and investigating on your own from general guidance.

Working with Document Security and Digital IDs

Note: To complete this assignment, you will be required to use the Data Files. Please contact your instructor for information about accessing the Data Files.

Instructions: Start Word. Open the document, SC_WD_11-1.docx, which is located in the Data Files. You will add a digital signature line, encrypt the document with a password, remove the password, digitally sign the document, mark the document as final.

Perform the following tasks:

1. Use Help to review and expand your knowledge about these topics: signature lines, passwords, document encryption, marking the document as final, and digital IDs.
2. Click File on the ribbon, click Save As, and then save the document using the new file name, SC_WD_11_AddressChangeRequest.
3. Position the insertion point on the blank line at the end of the document and then click the 'Add a Signature Line' button (Insert tab | Text group) to display the Signature Setup dialog box. Fill in the information to add a signature line to the document. If requested by your instructor, use your personal information in the signature line; otherwise, use the recipient name and title.
4. Encrypt the document with the password, fun.
5. Save the document again on the same storage location with the same file name. Then, close the document and reopen it. Enter the password when prompted.
6. Click the View Signatures button on the Signatures Bar that appears in the document to open the Signatures pane. Close the Signatures pane.
7. Remove the password from the document. (Hint: To delete a password, follow the same steps as to add a password, except delete all content from the password text box so that it is blank.)
8. Double-click the digital signature to sign the document.
9. Click the Edit Anyway button on the Message Bar.
10. Select the signature line in the document and then use the Font dialog box to format the text as hidden. If formatting marks are showing, hide formatting marks so that the hidden text is not visible in the document. Show formatting marks, select the hidden signature line, and then use the Font dialog box to unhide the text.
11. Click the 'Add a Signature Line' arrow (Insert tab | Text group) and then click 'Add Signature Services' on the Protect Document menu, which starts a browser and opens an Office Help window with a list of services that issue digital IDs (Figure 11–77). (If Word displays a Get a Digital ID dialog box, click Yes.)

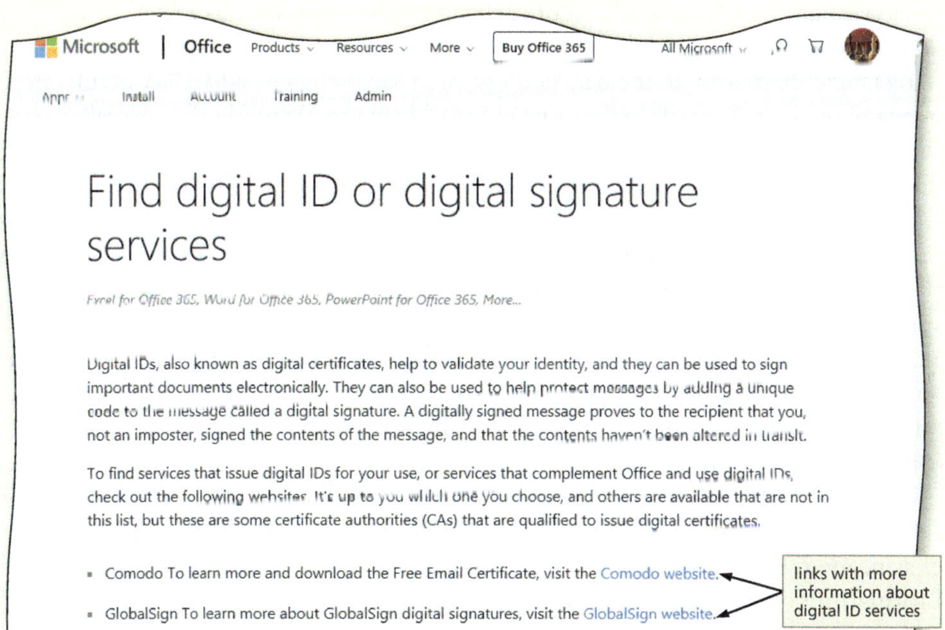

Figure 11–77

12. Click the link beside each service to learn more about each one.

Continued >

Expand Your World *continued*

13. Use a search engine to read reviews about these services and determine which digital ID service you would recommend. Close the browser window.
14. Use Backstage view to add a digital signature to the document.
15. If requested by your instructor, set the proofing language to English (United States).
16. Mark the document as final. (Hint: Use the Protect Document button in Backstage view.)
17. Submit the document in the format specified by your instructor.
18. Which digital ID services did you evaluate? When you read the reviews, were there other services not listed on the Office website? If so, what were their names? Which digital ID service would you recommend? Why? When you marked the document as final, what text appeared on the title bar? What text appeared in the Message Bar? What appeared on the status bar?

In the Lab

Design and implement a solution using creative thinking and problem-solving skills.

Modifying an Online Form for a Ferry Service

Problem: As customer relations manager at Starlight Ferry Service, you created the online customer satisfaction survey that was defined in the In the Lab Student Assignment in Module 10. Although you were pleased with the initial design, you believe the form can be improved by enhancing its appearance and adding macros to it.

Part 1: Open the template called SC_WD_10_StarlightSatisfactionSurvey.dotx that you created in the In the Lab Student Assignment in Module 10. If you did not complete the In the Lab Student Assignment in Module 10, see your instructor for a sample solution file. Click File on the ribbon and then click Save As and save the template as a macro-enabled template using the new file name, SC_WD_11_StarlightSatisfactionSurveyModified.

In this assignment, enhance the Starlight Ferry Service online form by changing the font and color of the service name, tag line, and form title; changing the page color to a texture; and changing the font and color of the last line. Apply an artistic effect to the image that you used on the form. Change the rectangle shape around the data entry area. In the rectangle, add a picture fill effect using the image of the ferry boat (if desired, one is available in the Data Files for use called Support_WD_11_FerryBoat.png) and recolor it as necessary. Change the color of the shadow in the rectangle. Draw a text box with the text, See you again soon!, and apply a 3-D effect to the text box.

Specify the appropriate macro security level. Record a macro that hides screen elements and then assign the macro to a button on the Quick Access Toolbar. Record another macro of your choice for a task you would like to automate. Add a button to the Quick Access Toolbar for any Word command not on the ribbon.

Use the concepts and techniques presented in this module to modify the online form. Be sure to save it as a macro-enabled template. Protect the form, test it, and submit it along with the answers to the Part 2 critical thinking questions in the format specified by your instructor.

If working with a 3-D model is required by your instructor, save the form using a new file name, SC_WD_11_StarlightSatisfactionSurveyModified_3-DModel. Delete the current image at the top of the form and the insert an appropriate 3-D model in its place. Resize and position the 3-D model as needed. Practice rotating and tilting the 3-D model. Format the 3-D model using additional formatting options of your choice. Protect the form, test it, and submit it in the format specified by your instructor.

Part 2: You made several decisions while creating the online form in this assignment: formats to use (i.e., fonts, font sizes, colors, styles, etc.), graphics to use, which task to automate, and which button to add to the Quick Access Toolbar. What was the rationale behind each of these decisions? When you proofread and tested the online form, what further revisions did you make, and why?

Index

Note: Page numbers in **bold** indicate key terms.

A

accessibility checker, WD 3-56
active tab, **WD 1-6**
Add Chart Element button, WD 8-35, WD 8-39
adding
  axis title to chart(s), WD 8-36
  chart element, WD 8-35
  command to Quick Access Toolbar, WD 11-37–11-39
  data series, WD 8-32
  digital signature, WD 11-51–11-52
  label to check box content control, WD 10-32
  outline to chart in Word table, WD 8-39–8-40
  page border, WD 1-59–1-60
  page color, WD 10-9–10-10
  paragraph border, WD 3-21–3-22, WD 3-41–3-42
  picture border, WD 3-16–3-17
  picture to SmartArt shape, WD 7-47
  row(s) to table, WD 4-37–4-38
  shadow to shape, WD 10-46
  shape to SmartArt graphic, WD 7-45–7-46
  style, to Style gallery, WD 11-18
  table border, WD 4-53–4-55
  text to shape, WD 3-10–3-11
additional check box content controls, inserting, WD 10-33
AddressBlock merge field, **WD 6-22**
  editing, WD 6-24
  inserting, WD 6-23–6-24
addresses
  positioning on an envelope, WD 6-47
  validating, WD 6-20
addressing
  envelopes, WD 6-41–6-48
  envelopes and mailing labels, WD 3-57–3-58
  mailing labels, WD 6-41–6-48
  mailing labels using an existing data source, WD 6-42–6-48
adjusting vertical alignment on a page, WD 9-32
Adobe Reader, **WD 5-34**
  viewing PDF file in, WD 5-34–5-36
advanced character attributes, WD 11-17
advanced layout options, WD 9-48
aligning/alignment
  changing paragraph, WD 11-7
  paragraphs, WD 1-27
alphabetical Works Cited page, WD 2-30–2-42
alternating headers, WD 9-52
alternative text, **WD 3-57**
  adding to graphics, WD 3-57
  adding to tables, WD 3-57
alt text. *See* alternative text
antivirus program, **WD 11-5**
APA (American Psychological Association) style, **WD 2-2**
applying
  graphics style, WD 10-13–10-14
  pattern fill effect to page color, WD 10-10–10-11
  shape style with an outline, WD 10-45
  style, WD 5-29
Arrange All button, WD 7-34
artistic effects, WD 11-27
art page border, WD 7-52–7-53
authors
  combining revisions from multiple, WD 8-18–8-22
  limiting, in track changes, WD 8-8
AutoComplete, WD 2-13
  feature, using, WD 5-19–5-20
AutoCorrect
  building blocks *vs.*, WD 5-21
  feature, WD 2-18
AutoCorrect dialog box, WD 2-20–2-21
  entering more text, WD 2-21
AutoCorrect Options button, **WD 2-18–2-19**
AutoFit, WD 4-50
AutoFit button, WD 4-31
AutoFit Contents, WD 4-31
AutoFormat As You Type feature, WD 3-38B
AutoFormat As You Type options, WD 1-42
automatically updated properties, **WD 1-61**
automatic hyphenation, WD 7-27
automatic macros, WD 11-40–11-44. *See also* macro(s)
  creating, WD 11-40–11-41
  defined, **WD 11-40**
  testing, WD 11-41
automatic page breaks, **WD 2-35–2-38**. *See also* soft page breaks
automatic spelling correction, WD 1-15
AutoNew macro, WD 11-42
  running, WD 11-44
AutoRecover, WD 5-46
AutoSave, WD 5-46
axis title, adding to chart(s), WD 8-36

B

background(s)
  page color, disappearing, WD 10-50
  removing, WD 11-26–11-27
  repagination, **WD 2-35**
Backstage view, **WD 1-21**, WD 11-45
  closing the current open document without exiting Word, WD 1-63
  conserving ink and toner, WD 2-53, WD 3-56
  saving a template, WD 3-12
banner, **WD 7-2**
bibliographical reference list, WD 2-40–2-42
bibliography, **WD 2-39**
bibliography field
  converting to regular text, WD 2-44
  updating, WD 2-43–2-44
bibliography field, updating, WD 2-43–2-44
blank page, inserting, WD 9-33
blog, **WD 8-44**
  creating, WD 8-44–8-50
  creating blank document for, WD 8-46
  defined, **WD 8-44**
  deleting, WD 8-50
  entering text, WD 8-47
  format text, WD 8-47
  guidelines, WD 8-45
  inserting table in, WD 8-47–8-48
  post, WD 8-49
  publishing, WD 8-49
  registering account, WD 8-45
  webpage displaying in browser window, WD 8-49–8-50
blog account, WD 8-45
blogger, **WD 8-44**
body copy, **WD 1-20**
  formatting, WD 7-19
  organizing, WD 7-19
  writing, WD 7-19
bold text, **WD 1-48**
bookmark(s)
  defined, **WD 9-55**
  hyperlink to, WD 9-56
  inserting, WD 9-55–9-57
bookmark names, WD 9-56
border, **WD 3-21**
  adding, WD 7-42, WD 7-52–7-53
  formatted, WD 7-42
Borders gallery, WD 7-14
bounding box, WD 10-23
browser, testing webpage in, WD 5-53–5-54
building block elements (Quick Parts)
  editing properties of, WD 5-34
  inserting, WD 5-32–5-34
building blocks
  vs. AutoCorrect, WD 5-21
  creating, WD 5-17–5-18
  defined, **WD 5-17**
  deleting, WD 9-18
  inserting, WD 5-20–5-21
  modifying, WD 5-18–5-19
Building Blocks Organizer, **WD 5-32**
Building Blocks Organizer dialog box, WD 9-18
bullet character, WD 4-20
  changing, to picture bullets, WD 4-26–4-28
  changing, to predefined bullet character, WD 4-28
bulleted list, **WD 1-40–1-41**, WD 3-38–3-39, WD 4-19–4-23
  changing bullet color, WD 4-20–4-21
  changing paragraph indent, WD 4-22–4-23
  inserting page break, WD 4-23
  selecting predefined character for, WD 4-20
bullets, WD 4-28
  removing from paragraph, WD 5-23
business letter(s), WD 3-1–3-3
  addressing and printing envelopes and mailing labels, WD 3-57–3-58
  common styles of, WD 3-25
  complimentary close, WD 3-25
  creating, WD 3-23–3-39
  creating letterhead, WD 3-4–3-23
  date line, WD 3-25
  entering more text and saving, WD 3-39
  entering the inside address and salutation, WD 3-28–3-29
  inserting tables, WD 3-29–3-35
  inside address, WD 3-25
  message, WD 3-25
  salutation, WD 3-25
  saving and printing, WD 3-56
  signature block, WD 3-25
  working with SmartArt graphics, WD 3-39–3-57
buttons
  deleting, from Quick Access Toolbar, WD 11-39
  new, on Quick Access Toolbar, WD 11-39

C

caption numbers, WD 9-9–9-22
closing open panes, documents, and windows, WD 9-22
compressing pictures, WD 9-21–9-22
entering and formatting text in sidebar text box, WD 9-16–9-17
going to an object, WD 9-11–9-12
hiding formatting marks, WD 9-15
hiding white space, WD 9-9
inserting another sidebar text box, WD 9-18
inserting captions and cross-references, WD 9-13
inserting cross-reference, WD 9-9–9-11
inserting sidebar text box, WD 9-15–9-16
linking text boxes, WD 9-19–9-20
marking index entry, WD 9-13–9-15
showing white space, WD 9-15
using the Navigation Pane to go to a page, WD 9-17–9-18
captions, WD 9-9
defined, **WD 9-4**
editing, WD 9-43–9-44
inserting, WD 9-8–9-9, WD 9-12–9-13
cell(s), **WD 3-29**
aligning data in, WD 4-34–4-35
entering text in, WD 4-45
merging, WD 4-51–4-52
shade, WD 6-8–6-9
spacing, WD 4-40
splitting, in table, WD 4-43–4-44
cell boundary, WD 4-44–4-45
Center button, WD 4-36
centering
paragraphs, WD 1-27, WD 1-28, WD 1-43, WD 1-51
text on the copyright page, WD 9-30
changing
bullet to predefined symbol, WD 5-27
document theme, WD 9-22
document theme and theme fonts, WD 10-9
format of table of authorities, WD 9-49
format of table of contents, WD 9-40–9-41
format of the index, WD 9-47
format of the table of figures, WD 9-42
margin settings, WD 6-9–6-10
object's text wrapping, WD 3-17
page orientation, WD 6-49
paper size, WD 10-6
picture, WD 11-26
picture and formatting it, WD 6-7–6-8
properties of check box content control, WD 10-31–10-32
properties of combo box content control, WD 10-38–10-39
properties of date picker content control, WD 10-40
properties of drop-down list content control, WD 10-28–10-30
properties of plain text content control, WD 10-23–10-24
properties of rich text content control, WD 10-35–10-36
shape, WD 11-21–11-22
theme colors, WD 5-6, WD 6-7
theme effects, WD 5-13
theme fonts, WD 5-8–5-9
changing document settings, WD 10-5–10-11
adding page color, WD 10-9–10-10
applying pattern fill effect to page color, WD 10-10–10-11
changing document theme and theme fonts, WD 10-9
changing paper size, WD 10-6
collapsing the ribbon, WD 10-7
expanding the ribbon, WD 10-7
setting custom margins, WD 10-8
character(s)
formatting, WD 1-23–1-50, **WD 1-24**, WD 4-7–4-9
keyboard shortcuts for formatting, WD 2-15
modifying spacing, WD 4-7–4-9
single *vs.* multiple, WD 1-28–1-41
widths, WD 1-12
character style
creating, WD 11-17–11-18
vs. paragraph style, WD 11-18
chart(s)
adding axis title to, WD 8-36
adding data labels to, WD 8-35
changing colors of, WD 8-34–8-35
inserting, WD 8-29–8-32
memo with, WD 8-1–8-3
removing data series from, WD 8-32–8-33
style, applying, WD 8-33–8-34
chart element
adding, WD 8-35
editing, WD 8-36
formatting, WD 8-37–8-39
selecting, WD 8-36
check box content control
adding label to, WD 10-32
changing properties of, WD 10-31–10-32
inserting, WD 10-31
checking
for errors, WD 6-34
layout of the printed pages, WD 9-53
chronological resume, WD 5-6
citation(s), WD 2-22–2-25
changing bibliography style, WD 2-22–2-23
editing, WD 2-32–2-33
entering more text, WD 2-25
inserting for new source, WD 2-23–2-25
inserting using an existing source, WD 2-46
moving, WD 2-47
citation entry
deleting, WD 9-48
editing, WD 9-48
citation placeholder
enter more text and inserting, WD 2-35
inserting, WD 2-27
citations
marking, WD 9-47–9-48
marking multiple, WD 9-48
clear formatting, **WD 3-22**
Clipboard pane, WD 7-50
Close File button, WD 11-53
closing
main document files, WD 6-41
opening panes, documents, and windows, WD 9-22
Outline view, WD 9-27–9-28
collaboration, WD 1-1
tools of Word, WD 8-3
'Collapse the Ribbon' button, WD 10-7
collapsing, ribbon, WD 10-7
color(s)
adding page, WD 10-9–10-10
changing, of shadow, WD 10-46
changing theme, WD 6-7
column(s), WD 7-21
adjusting width, WD 7-25–7-26
balancing, WD 7-43
boundary, WD 4-31
changing formatting of, WD 7-39–7-40
changing width, WD 4-30–4-32, WD 4-51
deleting, WD 4-46
of different widths, WD 7-23
distributing, WD 4-41–4-42
formatting text in, WD 7-22–7-23
inserting, WD 4-46
organizing body copy in, WD 7-21
placing vertical lines between, WD 7-25–7-26
sorting table by multiple, WD 6-54–6-55
table, resizing using AutoFit, WD 4-50
column break
defined, **WD 7-30**
inserting, WD 7-30–7-31
removing, WD 7-31
combo box content control
changing properties of, WD 10-38–10-39
inserting, WD 10-36–10-37
command, **WD 1-3**
comment(s), **WD 2-57**
deleting, WD 2-61–2-62
deleting all, WD 2-62–2-63
in document, WD 2-57–2-63
Document Inspector, using, WD 2-63
editing, in comment box, WD 2-60
going to, WD 2-59, WD 2-60
hide and show, WD 2-61
inserting, WD 2-57–2-58
inserting another, WD 2-58–2-59
locating by reviewer, WD 2-60
replying to, WD 2-60–2-61
resolving, WD 2-62
comment box, WD 2-60
comparison operator, WD 6-29
complimentary close, **WD 3-25**
composing, main document for form letters, WD 6-20–6-33
compressing pictures, WD 9-21–9-22
computer virus, **WD 11-5**
condition, **WD 6-29**
expression in, WD 6-29
conserving ink and toner, WD 9-57
Content Control Properties dialog box, WD 10-23
content controls, WD 6-6, WD 10-18–10-19. *See also* specific content controls
changing properties of Date picker, WD 11-11
changing properties of plain text, WD 11-8, WD 11-9–11-10
and cover page, WD 4-6–4-7
defined, **WD 4-6**
deleting, WD 6-22, WD 10-25
entering date from, WD 6-21–6-22
entering text in, WD 4-6–4-7, WD 5-9–5-10, WD 5-14, WD 5-21–5-26, WD 9-29–9-30
entering text in more, WD 5-10
inserting additional check box, WD 10-33
inserting check box, WD 10-31
inserting combo box, WD 10-36–10-37
inserting date picker, WD 10-39
inserting drop-down list, WD 10-27–10-28
moving to another page, WD 10-37
removing, WD 4-15–4-16
contextual tabs, **WD 1-7**
continuous section break, WD 7-21–7-22

contrast, **WD 3-16**
control layout
  entering text and using table to, WD 10-30
  using table to, WD 10-16–10-17
converting
  main document files, WD 6-52
  text to table, WD 6-52–6-53
copy and paste option
  copying an object, WD 8-26
  in Excel worksheet, WD 8-23
copying
  macros, WD 11-52–11-54
  SmartArt graphic, WD 7-47–7-52
  SmartArt graphic using Office Clipboard, WD 7-48
  styles, WD 11-52–11-54
  table row, WD 5-16–5-17
  text, **WD 1-66**
correcting merge field errors in merged documents, WD 6-36
cover page, **WD 4-4**, WD 9-28
  deleting, WD 4-6
  designing effective, WD 4-5
  entering text in content controls, WD 4-6–4-7
  formatting characters, WD 4-7–4-9
  inserting, WD 4-5–4-6, WD 9-29
  modifying character spacing, WD 4-7–4-9
  sales proposal, WD 4-4–4-9
Create Source dialog box, WD 2-23
creating
  automatic macros, WD 11-40–11-41
  blank document for blog post, WD 8-46
  blog, WD 8-44–8-50
  building block, WD 5-17–5-18
  business letters, WD 3-23–3-39
  character style, WD 11-17–11-18
  custom theme colors, WD 5-12–5-13
  custom theme fonts, WD 5-11–5-12
  data source, WD 6-12–6-20
  envelopes and mailing labels for single recipient, WD 6-48
  folder while saving, WD 6-11–6-12
  letterhead, WD 3-4–3-23
  new document from an online template, WD 5-3–5-6
  paragraph style, WD 5-28
Creative Commons, WD 3-13
cropping, graphic, WD 7-16
cross-references, **WD 9-9**
  inserting, WD 9-9–9-11, WD 9-12–9-13
custom dictionaries, WD 2-52–2-57
  setting the default, WD 2-52–2-53
  viewing or modifying entries in, WD 2-52
customization
  how Word opens email attachments, WD 5-46
  status bar, WD 8-5
custom margins, setting, WD 5-7, WD 10-8
Custom Office Templates folder, WD 10-5
custom tab stops, WD 7-12
  setting, using Tabs dialog box, WD 7-41
custom theme colors, creating, WD 5-12–5-13
custom theme fonts, creating, WD 5-11–5-12
cutting, text, WD 1-66, **WD 1-66**

D

data
  aligning, in cells, WD 4-34–4-35
  deleting table, WD 3-37
  entering in tables, WD 3-31–3-32
  entering more in tables, WD 3-32
database
  linking form to, WD 10-52
data field, **WD 6-13**
Data Files, WD 8-4, WD 8-24, WD 9-2
data labels adding, to chart(s), WD 8-35
data records, **WD 6-13**
  merging to directory, WD 6-48–6-55
data series
  adding, WD 8-32
  removing, from chart, WD 8-32–8-33
data sources
  addressing mailing labels using an existing, WD 6-42–6-48
  creating, WD 6-12–6-20
  defined, **WD 6-12**
  editing data records (recipients) in, WD 6-20
  entering more recipients, WD 6-18
  guidelines to follow when creating, WD 6-13
  printing mailing labels using an existing, WD 6-42–6-48
  saving, WD 6-18
  saving when prompted by Word, WD 6-18–6-19
  type new recipient list for, WD 6-13–6-17
  using an existing, WD 6-20
date field. *See also* field(s)
  deleting, WD 11-13
  inserting, WD 11-12–11-13
date line, **WD 3-25**
date picker content control, WD 11-11
  changing properties of, WD 10-40
  inserting, WD 10-39
decreasing indent of paragraph, WD 5-26–5-27
default save location, setting, WD 5-49
deleting
  blank paragraph, WD 4-42
  blog, WD 8-50
  building blocks, WD 9-18
  buttons from Quick Access Toolbar, WD 11-39
  citation entry, WD 9-48
  column(s), WD 4-46
  content controls, WD 10-25
  cover page, WD 4-6
  date field, WD 11-13
  entire index, WD 9-47
  footer(s), WD 4-17
  graphics, WD 11-7, WD 11-46
  header(s), WD 4-15
  index entry, WD 9-46
  linked worksheet, WD 8-26
  macros, WD 11-40, WD 11-54
  page break, WD 4-12
  paragraph, WD 5-17
  row, WD 5-17, WD 5-22
  schema, WD 11-56
  table cells, WD 4-46
  table of authorities, WD 9-49
designing
  cover page, WD 4-5
  nameplate, WD 7-6
desktop publishing terminology, WD 7-2
destination, **WD 7-34**
destination document, **WD 7-48**
Developer tab, WD 11-4
  hiding, WD 10-48
  showing, WD 10-19–10-20
Dialog Box Launcher, **WD 1-8**
dictionaries
  custom, WD 2-52–2-57
  main, WD 2-52–2-57
digital certificate, **WD 11-51**
digital signature
  adding, WD 11-51–11-52
  adding invisible, WD 11-51–11-52
  defined, **WD 11-51**
  line, **WD 11-52**
dimension of table, **WD 3-29**
directory, WD 6-1–6-4
  defined, **WD 6-49**
  merging all data records to, WD 6-48–6-55
  merging data records (recipients) to, WD 6-50–6-51
disabled macro, **WD 11-5**
Display for Review options, WD 8-12
displaying, next step in Mail Merge wizard, WD 6-21
distributing document(s), WD 6-55, WD 8-50, WD 9-57
document(s)
  additions, WD 1-64
  allowing no changes in, WD 11-45
  bold selected text and saving the letterhead, WD 3-12
  caption numbers, WD 9-9–9-22
  change the zoom to page width, WD 1-65
  changing settings, WD 10-5–10-11
  changing style set, WD 5-50–5-51
  checking document compatibility, WD 5-38–5-39
  checking spelling and grammar in, WD 1-16–1-18
  closing, WD 1-63
  closing the opening panes, documents, and windows, WD 9-22
  colors to choose when creating, WD 1-57
  comments in, WD 2-57–2-63
  comparing, WD 8-15–8-18
  compatibility, checking, WD 5-38–5-39
  compressing pictures, WD 9-21–9-22
  correcting errors and revising, WD 1-64–1-72
  correcting merge field errors in merged, WD 6-36
  creating blank, WD 1-3–1-5
  creating from an online template, WD 5-3–5-6
  creating webpage from, WD 5-46–5-54
  deletions, WD 1-64
  destination, WD 7-48
  distributing, WD 3-59, WD 4-57, WD 5-37, WD 6-55, WD 7-54, WD 8-50, WD 9-57
  enhancing accessibility of, WD 3-56–3-57
  entering and formatting text in sidebar text box, WD 9-16–9-17
  entering text in, WD 1-12–1-23
  exporting to XPS document, WD 5-37–5-38
  exporting Word document to PDF file and view PDF file in Adobe Reader, WD 5-34–5-36
  extra page in, WD 4-41
  file types, WD 5-40–5-41
  getting sharing link, WD 5-43–5-44
  going to an object, WD 9-11–9-12
  hiding formatting marks, WD 9-15
  hiding white space, WD 9-9
  highlighting text, WD 5-51–5-52
  inserting another sidebar text box, WD 9-18

document(s), *(Continued)*
inserting building block elements (Quick Part), WD 5-32–5-34
inserting caption, WD 9-8–9-9
inserting captions and cross-references, WD 9-12–9-13
inserting cross-reference, WD 9-9–9-11
inserting current date in, WD 3-27–3-28
inserting screenshot, WD 9-5–9-7
inserting sidebar text box, WD 9-15–9-16
inserting text in existing, WD 1-65–1-66
inspector, WD 8-4
for internationalization, WD 11-54–11-55
linking text boxes, WD 9-19–9-20
linking to external content, WD 8-22
marking as final, WD 8-22
marking index entry, WD 9-13–9-15
merging form letters using Mail Merge wizard, WD 6-34–6-35
modifications, WD 1-64
navigating, WD 1-20–1-21
opening, WD 1-64–1-65, WD 8-4, WD 8-29
opening document and saving with new file name, WD 9-4–9-5
opening PDF file from Word to edit it, WD 5-36–5-38
password-protecting, WD 10-48, WD 11-52
preparing to be included in reference document, WD 9-4–9-22
printing, WD 1-71–1-72
printing properties of, WD 6-56
printing specific pages in, WD 4-9–4-11
protected, WD 10-49
removing watermark, WD 5-44–5-45
reviewing, WD 8-3–8-22
saving, WD 2-53, WD 8-4, WD 8-29
saving, as a template, WD 10-4–10-5
saving as webpage, WD 5-47–5-49
saving for the first time, WD 1-21–1-23
saving with new file name, WD 3-24
saving Word 2019 document in an earlier Word format, WD 5-39–5-40
sections and section breaks, WD 3-40
sending, using email, WD 5-45–5-46
settings, changing, WD 2-4–2-8
sharing on OneDrive, WD 5-42–5-43
sharing with others, WD 5-31–5-46
showing white space, WD 9-15
testing webpage in browser, WD 5-53–5-54
types of changes made to, WD 1-64
unprotecting, WD 11-5
unsaved versions, WD 11-45
using Navigation Pane to go to a heading in, WD 9-41
using Navigation Pane to go to a page, WD 9-17–9-18
viewing side by side, WD 8-42–8-44
window, **WD 1-5**
and wordwrap, WD 4-10, WD 4-11
document properties, **WD 1-61**, WD 11-10
automatically updated properties, WD 1-61
changing, WD 1-61–1-62
inserting, WD 8-12
printing, WD 1-72, WD 8-12
standard properties, WD 1-61
document theme, **WD 1-25**
changing, WD 1-25–1-26, WD 9-22, WD 10-9
double-spaced paragraph, **WD 2-6**
downloading, **WD 1-50**
draft file
sales proposal, WD 4-2–4-4
saving with new file name, WD 4-2
Draft view switching, WD 9-54
drag and drop, **WD 1-69–1-70**
drawing
canvas, WD 11-25
object, **WD 3-5**
rectangle, WD 10-42–10-44
text box, WD 11-28–11-29
drop cap
defined, **WD 7-27**
formatting, WD 7-28
formatting character as, WD 7-27–7-28
outline around, WD 7-28
drop-down list content control
changing properties of, WD 10-28–10-29
inserting, WD 10-27

E

editing. *See also* formatting
AddressBlock merge field, WD 6-24
caption, WD 9-43–9-44
chart element, WD 8-36
citation entry, WD 9-48
citations, WD 2-32–2-33
comment in a comment box, WD 2-60
data records (recipients) in data source, WD 6-20
embedded objects, WD 8-27
field(s), WD 11-13–11-14
GreetingLine merge field, WD 6-26
hyperlink, WD 5-50
index entry, WD 9-46
linked objects, WD 8-27
lists, WD 4-19–4-29
sources, WD 2-30–2-32, WD 2-37
source using Source Manager dialog box, WD 2-43
table(s), WD 8-48
tables, WD 4-30–4-55
VBA code, WD 11-42–11-43
editing restrictions, setting exceptions to, WD 10-48
editing source using Source Manager dialog box, WD 2-43
editing wrap points
described, WD 7-50
in object, WD 7-50–7-52
element, **WD 11-55**
E-mail Messages command, WD 6-4
email, sending document using, WD 5-45–5-46
embedding
an object in Excel worksheet, WD 8-23
Excel worksheet in a Word document, WD 8-27
enabled macro, **WD 11-5**
endnotes, **WD 2-25**
changing location of, WD 2-33
entering more text, WD 2-34
inserting, WD 9-47
working with, WD 2-33–2-34
end-of-cell marks, WD 10-17
entering
date from content control, WD 6-21–6-22
and formatting text, WD 10-11–10-12
line break, WD 5-25
more text and merge fields in the main document, WD 6-28
remaining text in the main document, WD 6-30–6-31
sender information, WD 6-7
text, WD 3-20, WD 3-21, WD 3-40–3-41, WD 10-11–10-12
in content controls, WD 5-9–5-10, WD 5-14, WD 5-21–5-26, WD 9-29–9-30
in Outline view, WD 9-24–9-25
in the sidebar text box, WD 9-16–9-17
and using table to control layout, WD 10-30
envelopes
addressing, WD 6-41–6-48, WD 6-48
positioning on, WD 6-47
and printing, WD 3-57–3-58
and labels, WD 3-58
printing, WD 6-48
equations, inserting, WD 9-49
errors, checking for, WD 6-34
Excel
basics, WD 8-24–8-28
opening workbook in, WD 8-24
starting, WD 8-24
Excel worksheet
copy and paste option in, WD 8-23
embedding
an object, WD 8-23
in Word document, WD 8-27
linking from, WD 8-23
linking Word to, WD 8-22–8-29
exceptions, setting to editing restrictions, WD 10-48
expanding the ribbon, WD 10-7
exporting
Word document to PDF file and view PDF file in Adobe Reader, WD 5-34–5-36
Word document to XPS document, WD 5-37–5-38
expression, in condition, WD 6-29

F

false text, **WD 6-29**
field(s), WD 2-23, **WD 9-9**
codes, **WD 6-31**, WD 6-31–6-32, WD 9-47
described, WD 11-54
editing, WD 11-13–11-14
formats, WD 11-11
locking, WD 6-32
name, **WD 6-13**
file(s), **WD 1-21**
types, WD 5-40–5-41
file name, **WD 1-21**
opening document and saving it with new, WD 9-4–9-5
saving document with the same, WD 1-71
saving existing document with different, WD 1-49–1-50
saving existing document with the same, WD 1-62–1-63
files, opening, 11-55, WD
file type, WD 1-23
fill effect, and page color, WD 11-20–11-21
filtered web page format, WD 5-47
Find and Replace dialog box, WD 2-49–2-52, WD 9-38
finding, format, WD 9-36–9-38
finding mail merge recipients, WD 6-40–6-41

first-line indent paragraphs, **WD 2-16–2-18**
floating graphic, WD 7-17
floating objects, **WD 3-6**, WD 3-6–3-23
flyer. *See also* document(s)
body copy, WD 1-20
described, WD 1-2
entering more text, WD 1-19–1-20
formatted, WD 1-24
formatting suggestions in, WD 1-25
headline, WD 1-20
inserting blank line, WD 1-18–1-19
navigating a document, WD 1-20–1-23
with a picture, WD 1-2–1-3
positioning a picture on, WD 1-52
signature line, WD 1-20
text in, WD 1-20
unformatted, WD 1-24
folder, **WD 1-3**
creating, while saving, WD 6-11–6-12
organizing files, WD 1-49
folders, organizing files and, WD 2-25
font(s), **WD 1-24**
changing, WD 7-6
color, of selected text, WD 1-35
of selected text, WD 1-30–1-31
of WordArt, WD 7-7
sans serif, WD 1-25
serif, WD 1-25
Font dialog box, WD 4-19
font set, **WD 5-8**
font settings
modifying, WD 11-16
resetting default, WD 11-17
font size, **WD 1-24**
changing, of selected text, WD 1-29 –1-30, WD 1-35–1-36, WD 1-38
changing, of WordArt, WD 7-7
footer(s), **WD 2-8**, WD 4-9
deleting, WD 4-17
entering into a document, WD 2-9
inserting formatted, WD 4-16–4-18
Footer Building Block, specifying different odd and even page footers using, WD 9-50–9-52
Footer Link, WD 10-30
footnotes, **WD 2-25**, WD 2-25–2-27
changing location of, WD 2-33
entering more text, WD 2-34
inserting, WD 2-26
working with, WD 2-33–2-35
Footnote Text style, WD 2-28–2-33
editing citation, WD 2-32–2-33
editing source, WD 2-30–2-32
modifying style using shortcut menu, WD 2-28–2-30
form(s)
filling in and saving it, WD 10-50–10-52
linking to database, WD 10-52
printing, WD 10-52
protecting, WD 10-46–10-48
unprotecting, **WD 10-52**
Format Legend pane, WD 8-39
Format Painter button, using, WD 3-45–3-46
formats, **WD 1-23**
finding, WD 9-36–9-38
replacing, WD 9-42
formatted flyer, WD 1-24
formatting. *See also* editing
body copy, WD 7-19
changing columns, WD 7-39–7-40
character(s), WD 4-7–4-9
character as drop cap, WD 7-27–7-28
chart element, WD 8-37–8-39
clearing, WD 3-22–3-23, WD 3-43, WD 7-20
drop cap, WD 7-28
first page of the body of newsletter, WD 7-19–7-31
graphic's text wrapping, WD 10-14–10-15
lists, WD 4-19–4-29
marks, WD 7-52, WD 10-42
modifying page, WD 4-9–4-19
page numbers, WD 4-18–4-19
paragraphs, WD 7-13
border, WD 3-41–3-42
and characters, WD 1-23–1-50
picture, WD 1-50–1-57
placeholder text, WD 10-24–10-25, WD 10-30, WD 10-39, WD 10-41
and adding space before a paragraph, WD 10-36
requirements, for table(s), WD 8-30
retaining when adding text to table of contents, WD 9-39
revealing, WD 5-29
second page of newsletter, WD 7-38–7-52
sender information, WD 6-7
shapes, WD 10-45
single *vs.* multiple paragraphs and characters, WD 1-28–1-41
SmartArt graphic, WD 7-43–7-47
SmartArt graphic text, WD 7-47
subheads, WD 7-20
table(s), WD 8-48
tables, WD 4-30–4-55, WD 6-54
text, WD 3-20, WD 3-40–3-41, WD 7-20–7-21, WD 10-11–10-12, WD 11-7
in blog, WD 8-47
in columns, WD 7-22–7-23
as heading, WD 9-38–9-39
as hyperlink, WD 5-49–5-50
in the sidebar text box, WD 9-16–9-17
using Font dialog box, WD 4-19
using cut and paste to move table rows and paragraphs with source, WD 5-14–5-16
formatting marks, **WD 1-14**
displaying, WD 1-14
hiding, WD 9-15, WD 9-27
formatting, paragraphs with hanging indent, WD 2-42
form content controls
changing properties of, WD 11-8
modifying, WD 11-6–11-19
form letters, WD 6-1–6-4
beginning typing the body of, WD 6-26–6-27
composing main document for, WD 6-20–6-33
guidelines to follow when composing main document for, WD 6-21
identifying main document for, WD 6-4–6-12
merging recipient list in data source with main document to generate, WD 6-33–6-41
merging to new document using Mail Merge wizard, WD 6-34–6-35
merging to new document using the ribbon, WD 6-37–6-38
Formula box, WD 4-38
formula(s) inserting, in table, WD 4-38–4-39
frame, **WD 7-28**
functional resume, WD 5-6

G

gallery, **WD 1-7**
glow effect, and WordArt, WD 7-11
glow shape effect, applying, WD 11-22
gradient
defined, **WD 7-8**
stop, WD 7-9, WD 7-10
graphic(s). *See also* SmartArt graphic
behind text, sending, WD 10-44–10-45
color, in nameplate, WD 7-15
cropping, in nameplate, WD 7-16
deleting, WD 11-46
floating, WD 7-17
formatting, as floating, WD 7-50
formatting text wrapping of, WD 10-14–10-15
link to, WD 9-13
moving, WD 7-17, WD 10-15–10-16, WD 11-28
ordering, WD 10-15
rotating, WD 7-18–7-19
space around, WD 7-52
specifying position of, WD 6-10–6-11
GreetingLine merge field, **WD 6-25**
editing, WD 6-26
inserting, WD 6-25–6-26
gridlines, WD 4-42–4-43
defined, **WD 4-42**, **WD 10-17**
hiding, WD 4-53, WD 10-42
showing table, WD 10-17–10-18
viewing, WD 5-8
Group Objects menu, WD 11-32–11-33
groups, **WD 1-6**
gutter margin, **WD 9-52**
setting, WD 9-52–9-53

H

hanging indent, **WD 2-42**
formatting paragraphs with, WD 2-42
hard page break, **WD 2-39**. *See also* manual page break
hashtag (#) symbol, WD 4-39
header(s), **WD 2-8**, WD 4-9, WD 10-30
alternating, WD 9-52
closing, WD 2-12
creating, WD 2-8–2-12
deleting, WD 4-15
entering text in, WD 2-10
inserting, WD 2-9
inserting formatted, WD 4-14–4-15
record, **WD 6-13**
rows, repeating, WD 6-51
heading style, WD 4-12–4-13
formatting text as, WD 7-20–7-21, WD 9-38–9-39
modifying, WD 7-20–7-21
headline, **WD 1-20**
Headlines theme, WD 7-5
Help, WD 1-72–1-76
obtaining while working in Word, WD 1-75–1-76
pane, WD 1-74–1-75
hidden styles, WD 11-15
hidden text, WD 11-15
hiding
Developer tab, WD 10-48
formatting marks, WD 9-15, WD 9-27
gridlines, WD 10-42
white space, WD 9-9

highlighting
defined, **WD 5-51**
text, WD 5-51–5-52, WD 10-11
Home tab, **WD 1-6**
horizontal axis, chart, WD 8-37
horizontal rule, **WD 7-2**
horizontal ruler, **WD 2-16**
HTML (Hypertext Markup Language), **WD 5-46**
hyperlink(s), **WD 1-42**
to bookmark, WD 9-56
editing, WD 5-50
formatting text as, WD 5-49–5-50
inserting, WD 5-50
removing, WD 1-42–1-43
hyphenation, WD 7-26–7-27, WD 7-36
automatic, WD 7-27
manual, WD 7-27
hyphens, WD 3-39

I

icons
inserting, WD 10-11–10-13
multiple, WD 10-13
identifying, main document for form letters, WD 6-4–6-12
IF fields, **WD 6-28**, WD 6-28–6-29, WD 6-29
If...Then...Else field, **WD 6-28**
If...Then: field, **WD 6-28**
'Increase Font Size' button, WD 3-11
increasing, space before paragraph, WD 10-27
index, WD 9-28
changing format of, WD 9-47
deleting entire, WD 9-47
inserting, WD 9-44–9-45
updating, WD 9-46–9-47
index entries, WD 9-4
deleting, WD 9-46
editing, WD 9-46
marking, WD 9-13–9-15
marking another, WD 9-45–9-46
multiple, WD 9-15
second-level, WD 9-14
index files, WD 9-45
information, looking up, WD 2-54
Information Resource Center (Wilmington College), WD 9-2
ink, conserving, WD 1-71, WD 2-53, WD 3-56
ink, conserving, WD 8-42
inline objects, **WD 3-6–3-23**
Insert Control, **WD 3-35**
inserting
additional check box content controls, WD 10-33
AddressBlock merge field, WD 6-23–6-24
another sidebar text box, WD 9-18
blank page, WD 9-33
bookmark, WD 9-55–9-57
building block, WD 5-20–5-21
building block elements (Quick Part), WD 5-32–5-34
caption, WD 9-8–9-9
captions and cross-references, WD 9-12–9-13
chart, WD 8-29–8-32
check box content control, WD 10-31
column(s), WD 4-46
column break, WD 7-30–7-31
combo box content control, WD 10-36–10-37
continuous section break and change the starting page number in section, WD 9-34–9-35
continuous section break and changing margins in section, WD 9-30
cover page, WD 4-5–4-6, WD 9-29
cross-reference, WD 9-9–9-11
date field, WD 11-12–11-13
date picker content control, WD 10-39
3-D models, WD 11-46–11-48
document properties, WD 8-12
documents, WD 7-31
drop-down list content control, WD 10-27–10-28
endnotes, WD 9-47
equations, WD 9-49
formatted footer(s), WD 4-16–4-18
formatted header(s), WD 4-14–4-15
GreetingLine merge field, WD 6-25–6-26
hyperlinks, WD 5-50
hyperlink to location in current document, WD 9-56–9-57
icon, WD 10-12–10-13
IF field in the main document, WD 6-29–6-30
index, WD 9-44–9-45
in main document, WD 6-29–6-30
merge field in the main document, WD 6-27–6-28
next page section break, WD 7-29
odd page section break, WD 9-54–9-55
page break, WD 3-39–3-40
page break in bulleted list, WD 4-23
pictures, WD 11-25–11-26
plain text content control, WD 10-20–10-21
plain text content control and using design mode to edit placeholder text, WD 10-25–10-26
rich text content control, WD 10-34
row(s), WD 4-51–4-52
screenshot, WD 9-5–9-7
shape, WD 3-5–3-6
sidebar text box, WD 9-15–9-16
special characters, WD 3-21
subdocument in master document, WD 9-26
symbol from the Symbol dialog box, WD 9-31
symbol from the Symbol gallery, WD 3-20–3-21
table in blog, WD 8-47–8-48
table of authorities, WD 9-48–9-49
table of contents, WD 9-33–9-34
table of figures, WD 9-42
text from file in document, WD 7-24–7-25
text from file into document, WD 7-31
insertion point, **WD 1-5**
moving with keyboard, WD 1-20
Insert Merge Field button, WD 6-27, WD 6-45
insert mode, **WD 1-66**
inside address, **WD 3-25**
issue information line, **WD 7-2**
italic, **WD 1-46**
italicized text, WD 1-46

J

jump-from line, **WD 7-19**
jump-to line, **WD 7-19**, WD 7-30
justified paragraph, **WD 1-27**

K

'Keep Source Formatting' button, WD 8-26
keyboard key combinations. *See* keyboard shortcuts
keyboard shortcuts, **WD 2-15**
displaying the rulers, WD 2-16
for formatting, WD 2-15–2-20
for formatting characters, WD 2-15
for formatting paragraphs, WD 2-15
for formatting text, WD 2-15–2-20
formatting text using, WD 2-15–2-16
KeyTips, **WD 1-9**

L

labels
adding to check box content control, WD 10-32
envelopes and, WD 3-58
mailing, WD 3-57–3-58
printing, WD 3-57–3-58
landscape orientation, **WD 6-49**
language preferences in Word, WD 11-55
leader characters, WD 7-41
left-aligned paragraphs, **WD 1-25**
left paragraph indent, WD 4-13–4-14
letterhead
adding paragraph border, WD 3-21–3-22
adding picture border, WD 3-16–3-17
adding text to shape, WD 3-10–3-11
adjusting brightness and contrast of picture, WD 3-16
appearance of elements in, WD 3-4
applying shape effect, WD 3-10
applying shape style, WD 3-8–3-9
bold selected text and saving the letterhead document, WD 3-12
changing object's position, WD 3-7
changing object's text wrapping, WD 3-8, WD 3-17
changing shape outline, WD 3-9
changing the color of picture, WD 3-15
clear formatting, WD 3-22–3-23
contents of, WD 3-4
copying object, WD 3-18
creating, WD 3-4–3-23
defined, **WD 3-4**
entering text, WD 3-21
flipping object, WD 3-19–3-20
floating *vs.* inline objects, WD 3-6–3-23
formatting and entering text, WD 3-20
inserting online picture, WD 3-12–3-13
inserting shape, WD 3-5–3-6
inserting symbol from the Symbol gallery, WD 3-20–3-21
moving object, WD 3-18, WD 3-19
placement of elements in, WD 3-4
resizing picture to percent of original size, WD 3-14
using 'Increase Font Size' button, WD 3-11
using paste options to paste object, WD 3-18–3-19
limiting authors, track changes, WD 8-8
line(s)
inserting blank, WD 1-18–1-19
multiple, WD 1-37
selecting, WD 1-28–1-29
signature, WD 1-20

line break
  characters, WD 5-25
  defined, **WD 5-25**
  entering, WD 5-25
line numbers, WD 9-48
line spacing, **WD 2-6**
  adjusting, WD 2-6–2-8
  changing, WD 2-6–2-7
  removing space after paragraph, WD 2-7–2-8
link
  to graphic, WD 9-13
  removing, WD 9-20
linked objects, WD 8-23
  editing, WD 8-27
'Linked Worksheet Object' command, WD 8-28
linking form to database, WD 10-52
linking text boxes, WD 9-19–9-20
links/linking
  breaking, WD 8-27–8-29
  from Excel worksheet, WD 8-23
  opening word documents with, WD 8-24
  Word to Excel worksheet, WD 8-22–8-29
lists
  editing, WD 4-19–4-29
  formatting, WD 4-19–4-29
  making adjustments to entries in, WD 10-39
  of tables, WD 9-28
Live Preview, **WD 1-7**, WD 1-26
locked subdocuments, WD 9-27
lock tracking, WD 8-8

M

macro(s)
  added as button to Quick Access Toolbar, WD 11-37–11-39
  assigning shortcut key to, WD 11-34–11-36
  automatic, WD 11-40–11-44
  for automating tasks, WD 11-33–11-45
  copying and renaming, WD 11-53–11-54
  defined, **WD 11-3**
  deleting, WD 11-40, WD 11-54
  disabled, WD 11-5
  displaying, WD 11-42
  enabled, WD 11-5
  enabled template, WD 11-4
  naming, WD 11-33
  in online form, WD 11-2
  recording, WD 11-34–11-36
  running, WD 11-36
  setting in Word, WD 11-6
  VBA code editing, WD 11-42–11-43
  viruses, WD 11-5
macro-enabled template, **WD 11-4**
macro recorder, **WD 11-33**
mailing labels, WD 6-1–6-1
  addressing, WD 6-41–6-48
mail merge
  addressing mailing labels and envelopes, WD 6-41–6-48
  changing margin settings, WD 6-9–6-10
  changing picture and formatting it, WD 6-7–6-8
  changing theme colors, WD 6-7
  composing main document for form letters, WD 6-20–6-33
  creating data source, WD 6-12–6-20
  creating folder while saving, WD 6-11–6-12
  displaying recipients in main document, WD 6-41
  entering and formatting the sender information, WD 6-7
  finding recipients, WD 6-40–6-41
  identifying main document for form letters, WD 6-4–6-12
  merging all data records to directory, WD 6-48–6-55
  merging recipient list in data source with main document to generate form letters, WD 6-33–6-41
  previewing using Mail Merge wizard, WD 6-33–6-34
  removing merge condition, WD 6-39
  selecting recipients, WD 6-36–6-37
  shade cells and shape, WD 6-8–6-9
  sorting recipient list, WD 6-39–6-40
  specifying position of graphic, WD 6-10–6-11
  starting Mail Merge wizard, WD 6-4–6-7
  starting Word and specify settings, WD 6-2–6-4
Mail Merge pane, WD 6-6
Mail Merge Recipients dialog box, WD 6-20, WD 6-39
mail merge recipients, selecting, WD 6-36–6-37
Mail Merge wizard, WD 6-2
  displaying the next step in, WD 6-21
  merging form letters to new document using, WD 6-34–6-35
  previewing mail merge using, WD 6-33–6-34
  starting, WD 6-4–6-7
main document, **WD 6-21**
  beginning typing the body of form letter, WD 6-26–6-27
  composing for form letters, WD 6-20–6-33
  displaying next step in Mail Merge wizard, WD 6-21
  entering more text and merge fields in, WD 6-28
  entering remaining text in, WD 6-30–6-31
  entering the date from content control, WD 6-21–6-22
  identifying for form letters, WD 6-4–6-12
  IF fields, WD 6-28–6-29
  inserting AddressBlock merge field, WD 6-23–6-24
  inserting GreetingLine merge field, WD 6-25–6-26
  inserting IF field in, WD 6-29–6-30
  inserting merge field in, WD 6-27–6-28
  merging recipient list in data source to generate form letters, WD 6-33–6-41
  opening, WD 6-33
  previewing results in, WD 6-24–6-25
  printing field codes in, WD 6-32
  toggle field codes, WD 6-31–6-32
  viewing merge fields in, WD 6-26
manual hyphenation, WD 7-27
manual page break, **WD 2-39**. *See also* hard page break
margins
  adjusting, WD 1-11, WD 7-4–7-5
  header and footer, WD 9-54
  settings, changing, WD 6-9–6-10
'Mark as Final' button, WD 8-22
Mark Index Entry dialog box, WD 9-15
marking
  another index entry, WD 9-45–9-46
  index entry, WD 9-13–9-15
  multiple citations, WD 9-48
marks, formatting, WD 10-42
markups, **WD 8-5**. *See also* track changes
  changing, WD 8-8
  printing, WD 8-12
  using, WD 8-9–8-11
master documents
  changing the document theme, WD 9-22
  closing Outline view, WD 9-27–9-28
  defined, **WD 9-22**
  entering text in Outline view, WD 9-24–9-25
  hiding formatting marks, WD 9-27
  inserting subdocument in, WD 9-26
  outlines, WD 9-23–9-26
  showing only first line of each paragraph in Outline view, WD 9-25
  and subdocuments, WD 9-27–9-28
  switching to Outline view, WD 9-23
  working with, WD 9-22–9-28
maximized window, WD 1-5
memo
  with chart, WD 8-1–8-3
  contents, WD 8-43
  described, WD 8-1
  draft of, WD 8-4
menu, **WD 1-3**
merge, **WD 6-2**
merge fields, WD 6-22, **WD 6-22**
  AddressBlock, WD 6-23–6-24
  characters, **WD 6-22**
  correcting errors in merged documents, WD 6-36
  entering in the main document, WD 6-28
  GreetingLine, WD 6-25–6-26
  highlighting, WD 6-31
  inserting in main document, WD 6-27–6-28
  viewing in main document, WD 6-26
Merge Formatting button, WD 7-35
merging
  all data records to directory, WD 6-48–6-55
  cell(s), WD 4-51–4-52
  data records (recipients) to directory, WD 6-50–6-51
  data source and directory main document to new document, WD 6-52
  defined, **WD 6-33**
  form letters to new document using ribbon, WD 6-37–6-38
  form letters to new document using the Mail Merge wizard, WD 6-34–6-35
  form letters to printer, WD 6-36
  recipient list data source with main document to generate form letters, WD 6-33–6-41
  table cells, WD 4-47–4-48
message, **WD 3-25**
metadata, removing, WD 11-51
Microsoft Account Area, WD 1-9
Microsoft accountsign out of, WD 1-75–1-76
Microsoft graph, charting Word table using, WD 8-42
Microsoft updates, WD 1-24
Microsoft Word. *See* Word
Mini toolbar, **WD 1-9**
  turning off, WD 1-9
  using to format text, WD 1-43–1-45
MLA documentation style, **WD 2-2–2-4**
  date formats, WD 2-13
  modifying, WD 2-5–2-6

MLA (Modern Language Association of America) style. *See* MLA documentation style
modifying
building block, WD 5-18–5-19
character(s) spacing, WD 4-7–4-9
font settings, WD 11-16
form content controls, WD 11-6–11-19
heading style, WD 7-20–7-21
page formatting, WD 4-9–4-19
SmartArt graphic, WD 7-43–7-47
style, WD 11-15–11-17
using Styles Dialog Box, WD 5-30
using Styles pane, WD 11-14–11-15
table, WD 6-54
text, WD 11-6–11-19
Mouse mode, WD 1-8
moving, graphic, WD 10-15–10-16
multilevel list, WD 4-23–4-29, WD 4-19
changing bullet character to picture bullets, WD 4-26–4-28
defined, **WD 4-23**
sorting paragraphs, WD 4-29
multiple columns, sorting table by, WD 6-54–6-55
multiple icons in open dialog box, WD 10-13
multiple index entries, WD 9-15
multiple lines, selecting, WD 1-37
Multiple Pages button, WD 4-55
multiple pages, changing zoom to, WD 2-55–2-56

N

nameplate, **WD 7-2**
bordering one edge of paragraph, WD 7-13–7-14
changing font and font size of WordArt, WD 7-7
changing graphic color, WD 7-15
changing object's text wrapping, WD 7-7–7-8
changing object's text wrapping and size, WD 7-17
changing the Text Fill color of WordArt, WD 7-8–7-10
changing WordArt shape using Transform effect, WD 7-11
converting text to WordArt, WD 7-6
creating newsletter, WD 7-5–7-19
cropping graphic, WD 7-16
designing, WD 7-6
entering text, WD 7-13
for inner pages, WD 7-39
inserting picture, WD 7-14–7-15
moving graphic, WD 7-17
resizing WordArt, WD 7-7
rotating graphic, WD 7-18–7-19
setting custom tab stops using Tabs dialog box, WD 7-12–7-13
using Selection pane, WD 7-18
namespace, **WD 11-56**
naming macros, WD 11-33
Navigation Pane, WD 2-45, WD 9-46
opening, WD 2-45
using to go to a heading in document, WD 9-41
using to go to a page, WD 9-17–9-18
New Address List dialog box, WD 6-18
new document
merging data source to, WD 6-52
merging directory main document to, WD 6-52
newsletter
creating nameplate of, WD 7-5–7-19
creating pull-quote, WD 7-32–7-38
defined, WD 7-2
and desktop publishing terminology, WD 7-2–7-3
finishing, WD 7-52–7-54
formatting second page of, WD 7-38–7-52
formatting the first page of the body of, WD 7-19–7-31
guidelines for creating, WD 7-19–7-20
introduction, WD 7-1
printing, WD 7-54
project, WD 7-2–7-5
saving, WD 7-54
next page section break, WD 7-29
nonadjacent text, WD 1-47
nonbreaking spaces and hyphens, WD 3-39
Normal style, **WD 1-10, WD 2-5**
Normal template, WD 11-34
note reference mark, **WD 2-25**
note text, **WD 2-26**
numbered list, **WD 1-38**, WD 1-38–1-39, WD 5-27

O

object(s), WD 8-22
changing position, WD 3-7
changing text wrapping of, WD 7-7–7-8, WD 7-17
copying, WD 3-18
copying an, WD 8-26
editing wrap points in, WD 7-50–7-52
embedded, editing, WD 8-27
flipping, WD 3-19–3-20
floating *vs.* inline, WD 3-6–3-23
going to an, WD 9-11–9-12
grouping, WD 3-20
moving, WD 3-18, WD 3-19
size, changing, WD 7-17
using paste options to paste, WD 3-18–3-19
odd page section break, inserting, WD 9-54–9-55
Office Clipboard, **WD 1-66**
copying SmartArt graphic using, WD 7-48
icon, WD 7-50
pasting SmartArt graphic using, WD 7-49
OneDrive, WD 1-21
sharing document on, WD 5-42–5-43
Online 3D Models dialog box, WD 11-46
online form, **WD 10-1–10-53**
and Backstage view, WD 11-45
changing document settings, WD 10-5–10-11
defined, **WD 10-1**
enhancing, WD 11-6–11-19
enhancing with color, shapes, effects, and graphics, WD 11-19–11-33
entering content in, WD 10-11–10-49
macros in, WD 11-2
modified and enhanced, WD 11-2
revised, WD 11-1–11-6
saving document as template, WD 10-4–10-5
starting Word and specifying settings, WD 10-3
unprotecting document, WD 11-5
working with, WD 10-49–10-52
working with templates, WD 10-52
online form, entering content in, WD 10-11–10-49
adding label to check box content control, WD 10-32
adding shadow to shape, WD 10-46
applying graphics style, WD 10-13–10-14
applying shape style with outline, WD 10-45
changing properties of content controls, WD 10-23–10-24, WD 10-26, WD 10-28–10-30, WD 10-31–10-32, WD 10-35–10-36, WD 10-38–10-39, WD 10-40
drawing rectangle, WD 10-42–10-44
entering and formatting text, WD 10-11–10-12, WD 10-41
entering text and using table to control layout, WD 10-30
formatting graphic's text wrapping, WD 10-14–10-15
formatting placeholder text, WD 10-24–10-25, WD 10-27, WD 10-30, WD 10-39, WD 10-41
formatting placeholder text and adding space before paragraph, WD 10-36
hiding gridlines and formatting marks, WD 10-42
hiding ruler, collapse ribbon, saving template, and exit Word, WD 10-49
hiding the Developer tab, WD 10-48
increasing space before paragraph, WD 10-27
inserting additional check box content controls, WD 10-33
inserting an icon, WD 10-12–10-13
inserting content controls, WD 10-20–10-21, WD 10-27–10-28, WD 10-31, WD 10-36–10-37, WD 10-39
inserting plain text content control and using design mode to edit placeholder text, WD 10-25–10-26
inserting rich text content control, WD 10-34
moving graphic, WD 10-15–10-16
protecting form, WD 10-46–10-48
sending graphic behind text, WD 10-44–10-45
showing Developer tab, WD 10-19–10-20
showing table gridlines, WD 10-17–10-19
using design mode to edit placeholder text, WD 10-21–10-22, WD 10-28, WD 10-34, WD 10-37, WD 10-40
using table to control layout, WD 10-16–10-17
online picture, inserting, WD 3-12–3-13
Online Pictures dialog box, WD 6-8
opening
PDF file from Word to edit it, WD 5-36–5-38
document and saving with new file name, WD 9-4–9-5
main document, WD 6-33
ordering graphics, WD 10-15
organizing reference document, WD 9-28–9-57
Original document list, WD 8-16, WD 8-18
outlines, WD 9-23–9-26
applying shape style with, WD 10-45
outline to a chart, WD 8-39–8-40
Outline view
closing, WD 9-27–9-28
entering text in, WD 9-24–9-25
showing only the first line of each paragraph in, WD 9-25
switching to, WD 9-23

P

page(s)
  adjusting vertical alignment on, WD 9-32
  centering text on the copyright, WD 9-30
  checking the layout of printed, WD 9-53
  going to a, WD 2-45–2-46
  using the Navigation Pane to go to, WD 9-17–9-18
page break, WD 4-12
  automatic, WD 2-35
  in bulleted list, WD 4-23
  hard, WD 2-39
  inserting, WD 2-39, WD 3-39–3-40
  manual, WD 2-39
page color
  adding, WD 10-9–10-10
  applying pattern fill effect to, WD 10-10–10-11
  using fill effect for, WD 11-20–11-21
page contents, centering vertically, WD 5-31
page, enhancing, WD 1-57–1-64
page formatting
  applying heading styles, WD 4-12–4-13
  deleting page break, WD 4-12
  and Font dialog box, WD 4-19
  format page numbers, WD 4-18–4-19
  inserting formatted footer, WD 4-16–4-18
  inserting formatted header, WD 4-14–4-15
  left paragraph indent, WD 4-13–4-14
  modifying, WD 4-9–4-19
  printing specific pages, WD 4-9–4-11
  removing content controls, WD 4-15–4-16
page numbers, WD 4-10
  formatting, WD 4-18–4-19
  inserting, WD 2-10–2-11
  updating in table of contents, WD 9-35–9-36
page orientation, changing, WD 6-49
page section break, inserting an odd, WD 9-54–9-55
page width, changing zoom to, WD 1-13, WD 1-65
pane, **WD 1-8**
  closing open, WD 9-22
  Help, WD 1-74–1-75
paper size, changing, WD 10-6
paragraph(s)
  adjusting spacing, WD 7-20–7-21, WD 11-10
  aligning, WD 1-27
  applying preset text effect to selected text, WD 1-32–1-33
  bulleted list, WD 1-40–1-41
  centered, WD 1-27
  centering another, WD 1-28, WD 1-43
  changing alignment, WD 11-7
  changing case of selected text, WD 1-31–1-32
  changing font color of selected text, WD 1-35
  changing font of selected text, WD 1-30–1-31
  changing font size of selected text, WD 1-29–1-30, WD 1-35–1-36, WD 1-38
  changing spacing before and after, WD 1-60–1-61
  changing spacing of, WD 7-4–7-5
  changing zoom percentage, WD 1-36
  vs. character style, WD 11-18
  decreasing indent of, WD 5-26–5-27
  deleting, WD 5-17
  deleting blank, WD 4-42
  double-spaced, WD 2-6
  first-line indent, WD 2-16–2-18
  formatting, **WD 1-23**, WD 1-23–1-50, WD 7-13
    with a hanging indent, WD 2-42
  formatting placeholder text and adding space before, WD 10-36
  increasing space before, WD 10-27
  justifying, WD 7-23–7-24
  keyboard shortcuts for formatting, WD 2-15
  left-aligned, WD 1-25
  numbered list, WD 1-38–1-39
  removing bullets from, WD 5-23
  removing space after, WD 2-7–2-8
  right-aligned, WD 2-10
  selecting, WD 1-34
    line, WD 1-28–1-29
    multiple lines, WD 1-37
  shading, WD 1-33–1-34
  single *vs.* multiple, WD 1-28–1-41
  sorting, WD 4-29
  undo and redo an action, WD 1-40
paragraph border
  adding, WD 3-21–3-22, WD 3-41–3-42
  formatting, WD 3-41–3-42
paragraph indent, D 4-13–4-14
  changing, in bulleted list, WD 4-22–4-23
paragraph spacing, **WD 2-6**
  adjusting, WD 2-6–2-8
  removing space after a paragraph, WD 2-7–2-8
parenthetical references, **WD 2-2**
Password-Protecting Documents, WD 10-48
paste, **WD 1-66**
Paste All button, WD 7-49
Paste Option, WD 7-35
paste options menu, WD 1-68–1-69
pasting
  SmartArt graphic, WD 7-47–7-52
  SmartArt graphic from Office Clipboard, WD 7-49
  table row, WD 5-16–5-17
Pause Recording button, WD 11-35
PDF (Portable Document Format) file, **WD 5-34**
  exporting Word document to, WD 5-34–5-36
  opening from Word to edit, WD 5-36–5-38
  viewing in Adobe Reader, WD 5-34–5-36
picture(s). *See also* graphic(s)
  adding border to, WD 3-16–3-17
  adding to SmartArt shape, WD 7-47
  adjusting brightness and contrast of, WD 3-16
  applying effects, WD 1-56–1-57
  change the zoom to one page, WD 1-53
  changing, WD 6-7–6-8
  changing color of, WD 3-15
  compressing, WD 9-21–9-22
  formatting, WD 1-50–1-57, WD 6-7–6-8
  inserting, WD 1-50–1-57
    from a file, WD 1-51–1-52
    in nameplate, WD 7-14–7-15
    online, WD 3-12–3-13
  resizing
    an object proportionally, WD 1-53–1-55
    to percent of original size, WD 3-14
  saving in other formats, WD 9-21–9-22
picture border, adding, WD 3-16–3-17
picture bullets, WD 4-26–4-28
pictures
  changing color of, WD 11-24–11-25
  filling shape with, WD 11-24
  inserting, WD 11-25–11-26
  resizing, WD 11-25–11-26
  wrapping style of, WD 11-25–11-26
Picture Tools Background Removal tab, WD 11-26
'Pin the ribbon' button, WD 10-7
placeholder(s)
  citation, WD 2-27, WD 2-35
  text, WD 2-9
placeholder text, **WD 5-9**, **WD 10-21**
  error in, WD 10-22
  formatting, WD 10-24–10-25, WD 10-30, WD 10-39, WD 10-41
    and adding space before paragraph, WD 10-36
  inserting plain text content control and using design mode to edit, WD 10-25–10-26
  using design mode to edit, WD 10-21–10-22, WD 10-28, WD 10-34, WD 10-37, WD 10-40
plagiarize, defined, **WD 2-13**
plain text content controls
  changing properties of, WD 10-23–10-24, WD 11-8, WD 11-9–11-10
  inserting, WD 10-20–10-21
  selecting, WD-23
planning proposal, **WD 4-1**
pointer, **WD 1-5**, WD 1-6
points, **WD 1-25**
portrait orientation, **WD 6-49**
positioning
  SmartArt graphic, WD 7-50
  text box, WD 7-37–7-38
posts, WD 8-44
predefined bullet character, WD 4-28
preformatted text box, WD 7-32–7-33
Preview area buttons, WD 7-14
previewing
  mail merge using the Mail Merge wizard, WD 6-33–6-34
  results in the main document, WD 6-24–6-25
printed pages, checking the layout of, WD 9-53
printer, merging form letters to, WD 6-36
printing
  business letters, WD 3-56
  document and then exit Word, WD 9-57
  document properties, WD 6-56, WD 8-12, WD 9-30
  envelopes and mailing labels, WD 3-57–3-58
  field codes in main document, WD 6-32
  form, WD 10-52
  mailing labels using an existing data source, WD 6-42–6-48
  markups, WD 8-12
Print Layout view, **WD 1-5**, WD 1-71
print scaling, WD 4-11
proofing tools, WD 11-55
proofreading, **WD 2-42**
proposal
  planning, WD 4-1
  research, WD 4-1
  sales (*See* sales proposal)
protected documents, WD 10-49
Protected View, WD 9-4
protecting
  documents, WD 10-48
  form, **WD 10-46–10-48**

publishing
  blog, WD 8-49
  defined, **WD 5-54**
  webpage, WD 5-54
pull-quote, **WD 7-2**
  applying shape to text box, WD 7-37
  copy and paste using split Word window, WD 7-34–7-35
  creating, WD 7-32–7-38
  editing and formatting text, WD 7-36
  guidelines when using, WD 7-32
  inserting preformatted text box, WD 7-32–7-33
  positioning text box, WD 7-37–7-38
  removing split Word window, WD 7-36
  resizing text box, WD 7-36–7-37
  splitting Word window, WD 7-33–7-34

Q

Quick Access Toolbar, **WD 1-8–1-9**
  adding command to, WD 11-37–11-39
  adding macro as button to, WD 11-37–11-39
  customizing, WD 11-37
  using new buttons on, WD 11-39

R

readability statistics, WD 2-52
Read Mode, **WD 1-70**
Read mode color, WD 2-56–2-57
recipient list, sorting, WD 6-39–6-40
record(s)
  data, WD 6-13
  defined, **WD 6-13**
  header, WD 6-13
rectangle
  drawing, WD 10-42–10-44
  shape resizing, WD 11-10
Redo button, WD 1-40
reference document, WD 9-1–9-3
  creating, WD 9-1–9-57
  defined, **WD 9-1**
  elements common to, WD 9-28
  master document, working with, WD 9-22–9-28
  organizing, WD 9-28–9-57
  preparing document to be included in, WD 9-4–9-22
  starting Word and specifying settings, WD 9-2–9-3
reference document, organizing
  adjusting vertical alignment on a page, WD 9-32
  centering text on copyright page, WD 9-30
  changing format of table of contents, WD 9-40–9-41
  checking layout of printed pages, WD 9-53
  editing caption and updating table of figures, WD 9-43–9-44
  entering text in content controls, WD 9-29–9-30
  finding a format, WD 9-36–9-38
  formatting text as heading, WD 9-38–9-39
  inserting an index, WD 9-44–9-45
  inserting an odd page section break, WD 9-54–9-55
  inserting blank page, WD 9-33
  inserting bookmark, WD 9-55–9-57
  inserting continuous section break and change margins in section, WD 9-30
  inserting continuous section break and change the starting page number in section, WD 9-34–9-35
  inserting cover page, WD 9-29
  inserting symbol from the Symbol dialog box, WD 9-31
  inserting table of contents, WD 9-33–9-34
  inserting table of figures, WD 9-42
  marking another index entry, WD 9-45–9-46
  saving and printing document and then exit Word, WD 9-57
  setting gutter margin, WD 9-52–9-53
  specifying different odd and even page footers using footer building block, WD 9-50–9-52
  switching to Draft view, WD 9-54
  table of authorities, WD 9-47–9-49
  updating an index, WD 9-46–9-47
  updating entire table of contents, WD 9-39
  updating page numbers in table of contents, WD 9-35–9-36
  using Navigation Pane to go to heading in document, WD 9-41
Register a Blog Account dialog box, WD 8-46
Remember Password check box, WD 8-45
removing
  bullets from paragraph, WD 5-23
  merge condition, WD 6-39
renaming
  macros, WD 11-53–11-54
  styles, WD 11-52–11-53
replacing formats, WD 9-42
research paper, **WD 2-1**, WD 2-42–2-57
  alphabetical Works Cited page, WD 2-38–2-42
  AutoCorrect dialog box, WD 2-20–2-21
  automatic page breaks, WD 2-35–2-38
  citations, WD 2-22–2-25
  comments in document, WD 2-57–2-63
  creating bibliographical reference list, WD 2-40–2-42
  endnotes, WD 2-33–2-35
  footnotes, WD 2-25–2-27, WD 2-33–2-35
  Footnote Text style, WD 2-28–2-33
  keyboard shortcuts for formatting, WD 2-15–2-20
  proofreading, WD 2-42–2-57
  researcher and, WD 2-54–2-55
  revising, WD 2-42–2-57
  text of, WD 2-12–2-38
research paper text, WD 2-12–2-38
  AutoCorrect dialog box, WD 2-20–2-21
  automatic page breaks, WD 2-35–2-38
  citations, WD 2-22–2-25
  click and type, WD 2-14
  endnotes, WD 2-33–2-35
  entering name and course information, WD 2-13
  footnotes, WD 2-25–2-27, WD 2-33–2-35
  Footnote Text style, WD 2-28–2-33
  keyboard shortcuts for formatting, WD 2-15–2-20
  typing, WD 2-12–2-38
research proposal, **WD 4-1**
'Reset 3D Model and Size' command, WD 11-50
'Reset Window Position' button, WD 8-44
resizing, **WD 1-53**, WD 7-7
  an object proportionally, WD 1-53–1-55
  3-D models, WD 11-48
  pictures, WD 11-25–11-26
  picture to percent of original size, WD 3-14
  rectangle shape, WD 11-10
  SmartArt graphic, WD 3-55–3-56, WD 7-50
  table columns, WD 5-24
  WordArt, WD 7-7
resolution, WD 2-4
  changing a computer's, WD 1-3
resume, WD 5-1–5-3
  applying style, WD 5-29
  building blocks *vs.* AutoCorrect, WD 5-21
  center page contents vertically, WD 5-31
  changing bullet to predefined symbol, WD 5-27
  changing theme colors, WD 5-6
  changing theme fonts, WD 5-8–5-9
  chronological, WD 5-6
  copying and pasting table row, WD 5-16–5-17
  creating building block, WD 5-17–5-18
  creating custom theme colors, WD 5-12–5-13
  creating custom theme fonts, WD 5-11–5-12
  creating new document from an online template, WD 5-3–5-6
  creating paragraph style, WD 5-28
  decreasing indent of paragraph, WD 5-26–5-27
  defined, **WD 5-1**
  deleting row and paragraph, WD 5-17, WD 5-22
  entering line break, WD 5-25
  entering text in content controls, WD 5-9–5-10, WD 5-14, WD 5-21–5-26
  entering text in more content controls, WD 5-10
  functional, WD 5-6
  inserting building block, WD 5-20–5-21
  modifying building block, WD 5-18–5-19
  modifying style using Styles Dialog Box, WD 5-30
  removing bullets from paragraph, WD 5-23
  resizing table columns, WD 5-24
  resume template, WD 5-6
  revealing formatting, WD 5-29
  setting custom margins, WD 5-7
  start Word and specify settings, WD 5-3
  using AutoComplete feature, WD 5-19–5-20
  using cut and paste to move table rows and paragraphs with source formatting, WD 5-14–5-16
  using template to create, WD 5-3–5-31
  viewing gridlines, WD 5-8
Resume Assistant, WD 5-6
resume template, WD 5-6
Retrospect header design, WD 4-14
revealing formatting, WD 5-29
reviewer, track changes comments by single, WD 8-21–8-22
reviewing
  document(s), WD 8-3–8-22
  track changes, WD 8-12–8-15
Reviewing pane, WD 8-9–8-11
  editing revisions in, WD 8-10
Revised document list, WD 8-16, WD 8-19
revised online form, WD 11-1–11-6
revising, research paper, WD 2-42–2-57
revision marks, **WD 8-5**
Rewrite Suggestions feature, WD 2-42
ribbon, **WD 1-6–1-8**, WD 8-3, WD 8-46, WD 11-3
  collapsing, WD 10-7
  Developer tab, WD 11-4
  displaying different tab on, WD 1-10
  expanding, WD 10-7

- merging the form letters to a new document using, WD 6-37–6-38
- resolution, WD 10-5

ribbon resolution, WD 9-12
rich text content control
- changing properties of, WD 10-35–10-36
- inserting, WD 10-34

right-aligned paragraph, **WD 1-27**, WD 2-10
rotate handle, **WD 1-52**, WD 3-6
row(s)
- adding, to table, WD 4-37–4-38
- boundary, WD 4-31
- changing height of, WD 4-53
- deleting, WD 5-17, WD 5-22
- distribution, WD 4-45
- height, changing, WD 4-32–4-33
- inserting, WD 4-51–4-52
- selecting, WD 4-32, WD 5-14

ruler(s)
- displaying, WD 2-16
- horizontal, WD 2-16
- vertical, WD 2-16

ruler, displaying, WD 3-26
ruling line, **WD 7-2**

S

sales proposal
- body of, WD 4-11
- cover page, creating, WD 4-4–4-9
- defined, **WD 4-1**
- editing and formatting lists, WD 4-19–4-29
- editing and formatting tables, WD 4-30–4-55
- modifying page formatting, WD 4-9–4-19
- overview, WD 4-1–4-2

salutation, **WD 3-25**
sans serif fonts, **WD 1-25**
saved Word document, WD 10-5
saved Word template, WD 10-5
saving, **WD 1-21**
- creating folder while, WD 6-11–6-12
- customized themes, WD 5-13
- data sources, WD 6-18
- data source when prompted by Word, WD 6-18–6-19
- document(s), WD 8-4
- document and then exit Word, WD 9-57
- document as template, WD 10-4–10-5
- document for the first time, WD 1-21–1-23
- document in XML, WD 11-55
- document with new file name, WD 3-24
- document with same file name, WD 1-71
- existing document with different file name, WD 1-49–1-50
- existing document with same file name, WD 1-62–1-63
- pictures in other formats, WD 9-21–9-22
- template, WD 11-19
- templates, WD 10-4
- templates with new name, WD 11-45–11-46
- Word 365 document as different file type, WD 5-41
- Word document as webpage, WD 5-47–5-49
- Word 365 document in an earlier Word format, WD 5-39–5-40

schema, deleting, WD 11-56
schema files, **WD 11-56**
screen clipping, WD 9-7
screen resolution, WD 8-3, WD 9-12, WD 10-5, WD 11-3
screenshot
- defined, **WD 9-5**
- inserting, WD 9-5–9-7

ScreenTip, **WD 1-8**
scroll arrow, **WD 1-5**
scroll bars, **WD 1-5**
- using to scroll vertically with mouse, WD 1-21

scroll box, **WD 1-5**
scrolling, through documents side by side, WD 8-42–8-44
Search box, **WD 1-8**, WD 1-73–1-74
Search pane, WD 2-54
second-level index entry, WD 9-14
sections, **WD 7-21**, WD 7-41
- inserting continuous section break and change margins in, WD 9-30
- inserting continuous section break and change the starting page number in, WD 9-34–9-35
- numbers, WD 7-21

selecting mail merge recipients, WD 6-36–6-37
selection handle, **WD 1-39**
Selection pane, WD 7-18
selection rectangle, **WD 1-52**
sender information
- entering, WD 6-7
- formatting, WD 6-7

serif fonts, **WD 1-25**
setting custom margins, WD 10-8
shading, **WD 1-33–1-34**
- cells and shape, WD 6-8–6-9
- table cells, WD 4-52–4-53

Shading arrow, WD 4-52
shadow
- adding to shape, WD 10-46
- changing color of, WD 10-46

shadow effect, and WordArt, WD 7-11
shadow shape effect
- applying, WD 11-23
- applying to text box, WD 11-30

shape(s)
- adding picture SmartArt, WD 7-47
- adding shadow to, WD 10-46
- adding text to, WD 3-10–3-11
- adding, to SmartArt graphic, WD 7-45–7-46
- applying effect, WD 3-10
- changing, WD 11-21–11-22
- changing outline, WD 3-9
- changing SmartArt, WD 7-47
- deleting, WD 7-45
- filling with pictures, WD 11-24
- formatting, WD 10-45
- glow shape effect, WD 11-22
- inserting, WD 3-5–3-6
- resizing, WD 3-6
- shading, WD 6-8–6-9

Shape Outline gallery, WD 11-31
shape style, applying, WD 3-8–3-9
sharing
- document with others, WD 5-31–5-46
- link, WD 5-43–5-44

shortcut keys. *See also* keyboard shortcuts
- assigning to macros, WD 11-34–11-36
- assigning to style, WD 11-16

shortcut menu, **WD 1-9**, WD 2-28–2-30
showing
- Developer tab, WD 10-19–10-20
- table gridlines, WD 10-17–10-19

Show Source Documents, WD 8-20
sidebar text box, **WD 9-15**
- entering text in, WD 9-16–9-17
- formatting text in, WD 9-16–9-17
- inserting, WD 9-15–9-16
- inserting another, WD 9-18

signature block, **WD 3-25**
signature line, **WD 1-20**
Simple Markup, WD 2-57
Simple Markup option, WD 8-11
single file web page format, WD 5-47
size, changing object's, WD 7-17
sizing handles, **WD 1-52**
small caps
- defined, **WD 4-7**
- formatting characters in, WD 4-7–4-9

SmartArt graphics, **WD 3-46**, WD 3-46–3-56. *See also* graphic(s)
- adding alternative text to, WD 3-57
- adding and formatting paragraph border, WD 3-41–3-42
- adding shape to, WD 3-51–3-52, WD 7-45–7-46
- add more shapes and text to, WD 3-52–3-53
- add text to shapes in, WD 3-50–3-51
- applying SmartArt style, WD 3-55
- applying style and entering more text, WD 3-43–3-44
- business letters and, WD 3-39–3-57
- changing colors of, WD 3-54
- changing layout of, WD 7-45
- changing underline style, WD 3-44–3-45
- clear formatting, WD 3-43
- copying, WD 7-47–7-52
- decrease size of, WD 7-45
- deleting shapes from, WD 3-49–3-50
- entering and formatting text, WD 3-40–3-41
- formatting, WD 7-43–7-47, WD 7-50
- inserting, WD 3-47–3-48
- inserting page break, WD 3-39–3-40
- modifying, WD 7-43–7-47
- pasting, WD 7-47–7-52
- positioning, WD 7-50
- resetting, WD 3-55
- resizing, WD 3-55–3-56, WD 7-50
- text formatting, WD 7-47
- types, WD 3-46
- using Format Painter button, WD 3-45–3-46
- using Text Pane to add text to, WD 7-46
- working with, WD 3-39–3-57

SmartArt shape
- adding picture, WD 7-47
- changing, WD 7-47

soft page breaks, **WD 2-35**
Sort dialog box, WD 4-36–4-37
sorting, **WD 4-29**
- paragraphs, WD 4-29
- recipient list, WD 6-39–6-40
- table by multiple columns, WD 6-54–6-55

source(s), **WD 7-34**
- editing, WD 2-30–2-32, WD 2-37
- inserting citation using existing, WD 2-46

source document, **WD 7-47**
Source Manager dialog box, WD 2-43
space increasing, before paragraph, WD 10-27
spacing
- after punctuation, WD 2-21
- cell(s), WD 4-40
- between words, WD 7-24

special characters, inserting, WD 3-21
specifying different odd and even page footers using Footer Building Block, WD 9-50–9-52
specifying, position of graphic, WD 6-10–6-11

Index

spelling and grammar checks, WD 1-15–1-20, WD 2-50–2-52
inserting blank line, WD 1-18–1-19
spelling and grammar errors, entering more text with, WD 1-16
Spelling & Grammar button, WD 4-57
split Word window
copy and paste using, WD 7-34–7-35
removing, WD 7-36
spreadsheet, copying table data to, WD 8-31
standard properties, **WD 1-61**
status bar, **WD 1-5**
customization, WD 8-5
style, **WD 2-4–2-6**. *See also* Cell styles
adding, to Style gallery, WD 11-18
applying, WD 2-39–2-40, WD 3-24–3-26, WD 3-43–3-44, WD 5-29, WD 11-18–11-19
assigning shortcut key to, WD 11-16
copying and renaming, WD 11-52–11-53
formats, WD 2-28
hidden, WD 11-15
modifying, WD 2-5–2-6, WD 11-15–11-17
modifying, using Styles pane, WD 11-14–11-15
updating to match a selection, WD 2-8
style (picture), **WD 1-25**
applying, WD 1-55–1-56
styles dialog box, modifying style using, WD 5-30
style set, changing, WD 5-50–5-51
Styles pane, modifying style using, WD 11-14–11-15
subdocuments
closing Outline view, WD 9-27–9-28
defined, **WD 9-22**
hiding formatting marks, WD 9-27
inserting in master document, WD 9-26
locked, WD 9-27
Subentry text box, WD 9-14
subheads, **WD 7-2**
formatting, WD 7-20
selecting, WD 7-20
submenu, **WD 1-73**, WD 8-21–8-22
switching
to Draft view, WD 9-54
to Outline view, WD 9-23
symbol(s)
changing bullet to predefined, WD 5-27
inserting from Symbol gallery, WD 3-20–3-21
inserting from the Symbol dialog box, WD 9-31
Symbol dialog box, WD 9-31
inserting symbol from, WD 9-31
synonym, **WD 2-49**

T

tab, **WD 1-6**
active, WD 1-6
character, **WD 3-25**
contextual, WD 1-7
Home, WD 1-6
table(s), **WD 3-29–3-35**
adding alternative text to, WD 3-57
adding more text to, WD 3-37
adding rows, WD 4-37–4-38
aligning, WD 3-37
applying style, WD 3-32–3-34
border, adding, WD 4-53–4-55
centering, WD 4-35–4-36
columns, resizing using AutoFit, WD 4-50
contents, selecting, WD 3-35–3-37
converting text to, WD 6-52–6-53
converting to text, WD 11-8–11-9
deleting data in, WD 3-37–3-39
Draw Table feature, WD 3-35
editing, WD 4-30–4-55, WD 8-48
entering data in, WD 3-31–3-32
entering more data in, WD 3-32
formatting, WD 4-30–4-55, WD 6-54, WD 8-48
headings, WD 4-37
inserting columns in, WD 3-37
inserting empty, WD 3-30–3-31
inserting formula in, WD 4-38–4-39
inserting row in, WD 3-35–3-37
modifying, WD 6-54
move handle, WD 4-31, WD 4-35
moving, WD 3-35, WD 4-30
requirements for formatting, WD 8-30
resize handle, WD 4-31
resizing columns, WD 5-24
resizing columns and rows, WD 3-37
row, copying and pasting, WD 5-16–5-17
selecting, WD 10-17
selecting column, WD 3-34–3-35
selecting contents in, WD 3-35–3-37
sorting, WD 4-36–4-37
sorting by multiple columns, WD 6-54–6-55
style, applying, WD 4-33–4-34
using to control layout, WD 10-16–10-17
Word (*See* Word table)
table cells
change the direction of text in, WD 4-48–4-49
changing margins in, WD 4-41
deleting, WD 4-46
merging, WD 4-47–4-48
shading, WD 4-52–4-53
splitting, WD 4-43–4-44
table gridlines
print, WD 10-18
showing, WD 10-17–10-18
table of authorities, **WD 9-47**, WD 9-47–9-49
changing format of, WD 9-49
deleting, WD 9-49
deleting citation entry, WD 9-48
editing citation entry, WD 9-48
inserting, WD 9-48–9-49
marking citation, WD 9-47–9-48
marking multiple citations, WD 9-48
updating, WD 9-49
table of contents, WD 9-28
changing the format of, WD 9-40–9-41
inserting, WD 9-33–9-34
retain formatting when adding text to, WD 9-39
styles, WD 9-39
updating entire, WD 9-39
updating page numbers in, WD 9-35–9-36
table of figures, WD 9-28
changing the format of, WD 9-42
inserting, WD 9-42
updating, WD 9-43–9-44
Table Tools Design tab, WD 4-33
Tabs Dialog box, WD 3-25
Tabs dialog box, WD 3-25 WD 7-12, WD 7-41
tab stops, **WD 3-25**
setting custom, WD 3-26–3-27
types of alignment, WD 3-26
using to align text, WD 3-25–3-29
tag name, WD 2-27
tape icon, WD 11-35
template(s), **WD 10-4**
creating new document from online, WD 5-3–5-6
defined, **WD 5-1**
resume, WD 5-6
saving, WD 10-4, WD 11-19
saving document as, WD 10-4–10-5
saving with new name, WD 11-45–11-46
storing macro in document *vs.* Normal, WD 11-34
using File Explorer to create new document based on, WD 10-49–10-50
using to create resume, WD 5-3–5-31
Word *vs.* macro-enabled template, WD 11-4
working with, WD 10-52
text
adding to shape, WD 3-10–3-11
adding to text box, WD 11-29
applying preset text effect to selected, WD 1-32–1-33
applying style and entering more, WD 3-43–3-44
bold, WD 1-48
centered, WD 2-40
changing case of selected, WD 1-31–1-32
changing font color of selected, WD 1-35
changing font of selected, WD 1-30–1-31
changing font size of selected, WD 1-29–1-30, WD 1-35–1-36, WD 1-38
changing the direction in table cells, WD 4-48–4-49
changing zoom to page width, WD 1-13
in columns, formatting, WD 7-22–7-23
converting table to, WD 11-8–11-9
converting to table, WD 6-52–6-53
converting to WordArt, WD 7-6
copying and pasting, WD 1-67–1-68
in the data entry area, WD 10-43
deleting or cutting, WD 1-66–1-67
direction changing in text box, WD 11-29–11-30
displaying formatting marks, WD 1-14
entering, WD 3-20, WD 3-21, WD 3-40–3-41, WD 7-42
entering and formatting, WD 10-11–10-12
entering, in blog, WD 8-47
entering, in cell, WD 4-45
entering in content controls, WD 4-6–4-7, WD 5-9–5-10, WD 5-14, WD 5-21–5-26, WD 9-29–9-30
entering in document, WD 1-12–1-23
entering, in header, WD 2-10
entering, in more content controls, WD 5-10
entering in Outline view, WD 9-24–9-25
entering in sidebar text box, WD 9-16–9-17
entering in the main document, WD 6-28
entering more, WD 2-38
entering remaining in the main document, WD 6-30–6-31
false, WD 6-29
finding, WD 2-47–2-48
formatting, WD 3-20, WD 3-40–3-41, WD 7-20–7-21, WD 7-42, WD 11-7
in blog, WD 8-47
as heading, WD 9-38–9-39
as hyperlink, WD 5-49–5-50
in sidebar text box, WD 9-16–9-17
using Font dialog box, WD 4-19
hidden, WD 11-15
highlighting, WD 5-51–5-52, WD 10-11

inserting, from file in document, WD 7-24–7-25
inserting, in an existing document, WD 1-65–1-66
italicizing, WD 1-46
keyboard shortcuts for formatting, WD 2-15–2-20
modifying, WD 11-6–11-19
moving, WD 1-69–1-70
nonadjacent, WD 1-47
replacing, WD 2-48–2-49
selecting, WD 1-48–1-50
sending graphic behind, WD 10-44–10-45
techniques for selecting, WD 1-49
true, WD 6-29
typing, WD 1-12
underlined, WD 1-45–1-46
using Mini toolbar to format, WD 1-43–1-45
Wordwrap, WD 1-15

text box, **WD 7-32**
adding text to, WD 11-29
applying a 3-D effect to, WD 11-31–11-32
applying shape to, WD 7-37
changing Shape Outline of, WD 11-30–11-31
changing text direction in, WD 11-29–11-30
drawing, WD 11-28–11-29
editing and formatting text in, WD 7-36
inserting preformatted, WD 7-32–7-33
linking, WD 9-19–9-20
moving, WD 7-38, WD 11-32
positioning, WD 7-37–7-38
resizing, WD 7-36–7-37
shadow shape effect applying to, WD 11-30
styles, WD 7-37
text rotation, WD 7-36

Text Fill color, changing, WD 7-8–7-10
Text Fill gallery, WD 7-8
Text Pane
demoting, WD 7-47
using, to add text to SmartArt graphic, WD 7-46

text wrapping, WD 3-7
changing object's, WD 3-8, WD 3-17, WD 7-7–7-8, WD 7-17
formatting graphic's, WD 10-14–10-15

theme(s)
document, WD 1-25–1-26
saving and resetting, WD 11-8

theme colors, **WD 1-58**
changing, WD 1-58, WD 5-6, WD 7-5
Headlines theme, WD 7-5

theme effects, changing, WD 5-13
theme fonts, changing, WD 5-8–5-9, WD 10-9
thesaurus, **WD 2-49**
using, WD 2-49–2-50
thread, WD 2-58
3-D effect, applying to text box, WD 11-31–11-32
3-D models
applying, WD 11-49–11-50
deleting graphic, WD 11-46
inserting, WD 11-46–11-48
resetting, WD 11-50
resizing, WD 11-48
saving template and exiting Word, WD 11-51
saving template with new file name, WD 11-45–11-46
tilting and rotating, WD 11-48–11-49
working with, WD 11-45–11-51

Timeless letter template, WD 6-5
title page, WD 9-28
toner, conserving, WD 1-71, WD 2-53, WD 3-56, WD 8-42
Touch mode, WD 8-29, WD 11-7
touch mode differences, WD 3-3, WD 6-4, WD 9-2, WD 10-8
Touch/Mouse mode, WD 1-8
touch screen, WD 7-19
centering a table using, WD 4-35–4-36
changing column width using, WD 4-31, WD 4-51
moving cell boundary using, WD 4-45
rotating graphics using, WD 7-19
selecting table rows using, WD 5-14

track changes
accepting changes in, WD 8-13–8-15
and changing markups, WD 8-8
changing tracking options, WD 8-15–8-22
and changing user name, WD 8-8
disable, WD 8-8–8-9
displaying as simple markup, WD 8-11
enabling, WD 8-5–8-6
limiting authors, WD 8-8
markups, WD 8-5
rejecting changes in, WD 8-14–8-15
reviewing, WD 8-12–8-15
revision marks, WD 8-5
Track Changes indicator, WD 8-5
tracking, WD 8-6–8-8
vertical bar, WD 8-7

Track Changes Options dialog box, WD 15
true text, **WD 6-29**

U

underlined text, **WD 1-45–1-46**
Undo button, WD 1-40
unformatted flyer, WD 1-24
unprotecting form, **WD 10-52**
unsaved documents
deleting, WD 2-53
recovering, WD 2-53

updating
entire table of contents, WD 9-39
index, WD 9-46–9-47
page numbers in table of contents, WD 9-35–9-36
table of authorities, WD 9-49
table of figures, WD 9-43–9-44

URI, WD 11-56
URL (Uniform Resource Locator), WD 8-45
USB flash drive, WD 1-21
user name changing, and track changes, WD 8-8
using
design mode to edit placeholder text, WD 10-21–10-22, WD 10-28, WD 10-34, WD 10-37, WD 10-40
File Explorer to create new document based on template, WD 10-49–10-50
table to control layout, WD 10-16–10-17

Using Word 2019 reference document, WD 9-1–9-2

V

vertical alignments, WD 9-32
vertical rule, **WD 7-2**
vertical ruler, **WD 2-16**
View Gridlines button, WD 4-43
viewing, merge fields in main document, WD 6-26
virus, **WD 1-50**
Visual Basic Editor (VBA), WD 11-44–11-45
macros code editing, WD 11-42–11-43

W

watermark
creating, WD 4-55–4-57
defined, **WD 4-55**
removing, WD 5-44–5-45

weblog, **WD 8-44**
webpage
creating from document, WD 5-46–5-54
displaying in browser window, WD 8-50
format, WD 5-47
publishing, WD 5-54
saving Word document as, WD 5-47–5-49
testing in browser, WD 5-53–5-54

white space, WD 7-19
hiding, WD 2-35–2-36, WD 9-9
showing, WD 2-35–2-36, WD 9-15

windows, closing the opening, WD 9-22
Word. *See also* document(s)
adjusting margins, WD 7-4–7-5
AutoCorrect entry, WD 2-19–2-20
AutoCorrect feature, WD 2-18
AutoCorrect Options button, WD 2-18–2-19
Balloons submenu, WD 8-10
bordering one edge of paragraph, WD 7-13–7-14
changing spacing, WD 7-4–7-5
changing theme colors, WD 1-58, WD 7-5
checking spelling in, WD 4-57
collaboration tools, WD 8-3
columns, WD 7-21
correcting errors and revising document, WD 1-64–1-72
creating blank document, WD 1-3–1-5
creating webpage from, WD 5-46–5-54
cutting, copying, and pasting, WD 1-66–1-72
defined, **WD 1-1**
described, WD 1-1
displaying the Paste Options menu, WD 1-68–1-69
enabling track changes, WD 8-5–8-6
enhancing the page, WD 1-57–1-64
exiting, WD 1-76, WD 2-63, WD 4-57
exporting to PDF file, WD 5-34–5-36
exporting to XPS document, WD 5-37–5-38
filtered web page format, WD 5-47
formatting paragraphs and characters, WD 1-23–1-50
Help, WD 1-72–1-76, WD 2-20, WD 3-29
hiding the ruler, collapse the ribbon, save the template, and exit, WD 10-49
Icons button not available in, WD 10-13
inserting and formatting picture in, WD 1-50–1-57
linking Excel worksheet to, WD 8-22–8-29
macro settings in, WD 11-6
navigating document, WD 1-20–1-21
note text in, WD 2-26
obtaining Help while working in, WD 1-75–1-76
opening document in, WD 8-24
opening PDF file from, to edit it, WD 5-36–5-38
printing document and then exit, WD 9-57
printing the document, WD 4-57

Word. *See also* document(s), (*Continued*)
programs in, WD 8-1
protecting documents, WD 10-48
readability statistics, WD 2-52
Reviewing pane, WD 8-9–8-11
saving
data source when prompted by, WD 6-18–6-19
document, WD 4-57
document and then exit, WD 9-57
as webpage, WD 5-47–5-49
sections, WD 7-21
settings, WD 8-3
editing restrictions to tracked changes or comments or no edits, WD 10-48
formatting restrictions, WD 10-48
language preferences, WD 11-55
single file web page format, WD 5-47
spelling and grammar check, WD 1-15–1-20
starting, WD 8-3
and changing Word settings, WD 3-3
and specifying settings, WD 2-4, WD 6-2–6-4, WD 7-4, WD 9-2–9-3, WD 11-3
and using, WD 1-3–1-11
supplementary tasks, WD 11-51–11-56
switching to Print Layout view, WD 1-71
switching to Read Mode, WD 1-70
template *vs.* macro-enabled template, WD 11-4
theme color in, WD 1-58
web page format, WD 5-47
word(s)
counting, WD 2-34
selecting group of, WD 1-45
WordArt, **WD 7-6**. *See also* graphic(s)
applying glow effect to, WD 7-11
applying shadow effect to, WD 7-11
changing font and font size of, WD 7-7
changing shape, using Transform effect, WD 7-11
customizing, WD 7-6
deleting, WD 7-7
Word 365 document
saving as a different file type, WD 5-41
saving in an earlier Word format, WD 5-39–5-40
Word Options dialog box, WD 9-4, WD 9-56
Word table
adding chart element, WD 8-35
adding outline to chart, WD 8-39–8-40
applying chart style, WD 8-33–8-35
changing chart type, WD 8-41–8-42
charting, WD 8-29–8-44
using Microsoft graph, WD 8-42
formatting chart element, WD 8-37–8-39
inserting a chart, WD 8-29–8-32
opening and saving document, WD 8-29
removing data series from chart, WD 8-32–8-33
selecting and editing chart element, WD 8-36
Word window, WD 1-5–1-9
active tab, **WD 1-6**
contextual tabs, **WD 1-7**
copy and paste using split, WD 7-34–7-35
Dialog Box Launcher, **WD 1-8**
document window, **WD 1-5**
gallery, **WD 1-7**
group, **WD 1-6**
Home tab, **WD 1-6**
insertion point, **WD 1-5**
KeyTips, **WD 1-9**
Live Preview, **WD 1-7**
Microsoft Account Area, WD 1-9
Mini toolbar, **WD 1-9**
pane, **WD 1-8**
pointer, **WD 1-5**
Quick Access Toolbar, **WD 1-8**–1-9
removing split, WD 7-36
ribbon, **WD 1-6**–1-8
ScreenTip, **WD 1-8**
scroll arrow, **WD 1-5**
scroll bars, **WD 1-5**
scroll box, **WD 1-5**
Search box, **WD 1-8**
shortcut menu, **WD 1-9**
splitting, WD 7-33–7-34
status bar, **WD 1-5**
tab, **WD 1-6**
wordwrap, **WD 1-14**, WD 1-14–1-15, WD 4-10
text as you type, WD 1-15
working
with an online form, WD 10-49–10-52
with templates, WD 10-52
works cited page, **WD 2-4**
creating alphabetical, WD 2-38–2-42
wrapping style of pictures, WD 11-25–11-26
wrist injury, minimizing, WD 1-20

X

XML (Extensible Markup Language)
defined, **WD 11-55**
saving document in, WD 11-55
working with, WD 11-55–11-56
XML file, **WD 11-55**
XML schema, **WD 11-56**
XPS (XML Paper Specification) document
defined, **WD 5-37**
exporting Word document to, WD 5-37–5-38
XPS Viewer, WD 5-37–5-38

Z

zoom/zooming, WD 1-16
changing to one page, WD 1-53
changing to multiple pages, WD 2-55–2-56
changing to page width, WD 1-13
multiple pages, WD 7-52
percentage, changing, WD 1-36